ISBN 978-1-5280-3272-8
PIBN 10921587

Historic, archived document

Do not assume content reflects current
scientific knowledge, policies, or practices.

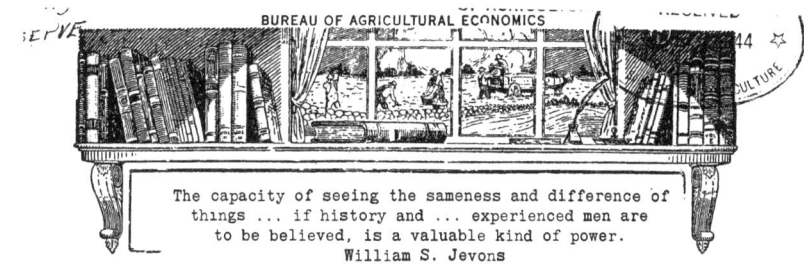

BUREAU OF AGRICULTURAL ECONOMICS

The capacity of seeing the sameness and difference of
things ... if history and ... experienced men are
to be believed, is a valuable kind of power.
William S. Jevons

Vol. 10   January 1936   No. 1

FEATURES IN THIS ISSUE

320759
AGRICULTURAL ECONOMICS LITERATURE

Vol. 10   January 1936   No. 1

AMERICAN RURAL FICTION, 1935* by Caroline B. Sherman

Workers who are interested in the farm and the farm family can scarcely afford to overlook our rural fiction. A member of a seminar in rural sociology in one of our largest universities has pointed out that Dickens' novels have long been regarded as important social studies, that Scott's work has always had significance for the historian, and that Knut Hamsun is everywhere recognized as a potent interpreter for Norway. American rural fiction is perhaps even more pointedly significant in that it is usually short and well directed.

So meaningful has it become during the last two or three decades that rural sociologists have recommended rural fiction as a valuable level of study, for as one of them has written, the novelist's methods and interpretive intuition set a standard of excellence from the standpoint of completeness of picturization that the social scientist may well strive to attain. The novelist's treatment necessarily has the advantage of bringing complex situations clearly into view and such writing may suggest important topics for study in a more objective way.

Recently an educator from a large university urged rural leaders to make more use of our best rural fiction because of its value in providing an understanding of human and family relationships. He declared that our best novelists gain a better hold on his teacher-students than do psychologists and sociologists because through their work a rich vicarious experience is possible. Here and there at leading institutions graduate students in sociology have turned to fiction for material on which to base their theses. One has analyzed English novels for their depiction of family life; another has analyzed American fiction for a similar purpose; another has studied modern rural fiction critically to ascertain its contribution to social analysis.

Changes in the economic phases of eras or areas and their impact and influence on the lives of individuals, families, and communities are proving to be fruitful and sometimes dramatic themes for rural fiction as witness even so late developments as the changing character of farm ownership in New England. We have long read in fiction of the movement West and the opening up of western homesteads. Only comparatively recently have we had searching fictional studies of their effect on New England, and later, on the various ways in which New England family life has met this challenge of the West.

The mere facts of economic changes and the tabulation of their results on the market place form only a partial record. The effect on the human families involved and on their daily life is really the significant thing and until that is recorded the economic and social story is but half told.

*Books cited in this review are not available in the Library System of the Department of Agriculture.

With this truth growing yearly more evident, a plan to include at least
an annual mention of some of our significant rural fiction in this journal
has crystallized. In fact, some of the farm life fiction of this year has
social and economic implications that could not well be ignored.

Selected List of Rural Fiction

Aldrich, Bess Streeter. Spring came on forever. 333PP. New York,
    Appleton-Century Co., 1935.
        A Nebraska homesteader's family carried through four generations.

Carroll, Gladys Hasty. A few foolish ones. 384pp. New York, The
    Macmillan Co., 1935.
        Sixty years of decline of activity in a Maine community tempered
    by the distinctive quality of spirit of fine Maine men and women.

Chase, Mary Ellen. Silas Crockett. 404pp. New York, The Macmillan Co.,
    1935.
        Social and economic changes during the lives of four generations
    of a Maine seafaring family.

Coffin, Robert P. Tristram. Red sky in the morning. 288pp. New York,
    The Macmillan Co., 1935.
        Maine backgrounds dominate this story of human disintegration.

Davis, Harold L. Honey in the horn. 380pp. Harper and Brothers, 1935.
        Zestful story of the pioneer period of Oregon, 1906-08, touching
    on sheep herding, hop-picking, wheat-ranching, horse trading and
    other pioneer Oregon industries.

Eastman, Elaine Goodale. Hundred maples. 285pp. Brattleboro,
    Vermont, Stephen Daye Press, 1935.
        A New England woman's enlightened contest with the hardships
    of farm life.

Field, Rachael Lyman. Time out of mind. 462pp. New York, The Mac-
    millan Co., 1935.
        Supremacy and decline of the shipbuilding industry of the Maine
    Coast and the effect on the disintegration of a leading family.

Glasgow, Ellen. Vein of iron. 46pp. New York, Harcourt, Brace & Co.,
    Inc., 1935.
        How a once-dominant family of the Great Valley of Virginia meets
    the changes and vicissitudes of the last two decades.

Green, Paul. This body the earth. 422pp. New York, Harper and
    Brothers, 1935.
        One poor white, among many "no-account" Southern tenants, who
    vainly craved actual ownership of land.

Kantor, MacKinlay. The voice of Bugle Ann. 128pp. New York, Coward-
McCann, Inc., 1935.
Coming of fences in the hound raising and training districts of the
Ozarks plays havoc with the native industry.

Lane, Rose Wilder. Old home town. 309pp. New York, Longmans, Green
and Co., 1935.
An evocation of the American spirit of the small town of yesteryear.

Lanham, Edwin. The wind blew west. 489pp. New York, Longmans, Green
and Co., 1935.
Authentic story of promotion and development of a community in
northern Texas.

Oskison, John M. Brothers three. 448pp. New York, The Macmillan Co.,
1935.
Development of a manorial estate on a Cherokee Allotment in
Oklahoma and its fortunes in modern days.

Rawlings, Marjorie Kinnan. Golden apples. 352pp. New York, Charles
Scribner's Sons, 1935.
Wild "hammock" country of Florida and its distinctive inhabitants
form the sinews of this story.

Roberts, Elizabeth Madox. He sent forth a raven. 255pp. New York,
The Viking Press, 1935.
A biblically-flavored and pastel-like treatment of many farm
economic problems of recent years in Kentucky.

Sandoz, Mari. Old Jules. 424pp. Boston, Little, Brown and Co., 1935.
This biography of a fighting homesteader of the Nebraska Sand-
hills is not unlike some of our biographical fiction.

Sykes, Hope Williams. Second hoeing. 309pp. New York, G. P. Putnam's
Sons, 1935.
Painful adjustment of stable patriarchal Russian families now in
our West to the dynamic American materialistic culture.

SIGNED REVIEWS

Douglass, P. F. The economic independence of Poland, a study in trade adjustments to political objectives. 134pp. Cincinnati, The Ruter press. 1934.
280.177 D74
"What realistically does a state created in post-war negotiations do to
build its future." The author raises this question and says the purpose
of this monograph is "to trace the development of Poland's economic life
and to study the adjustments of trade to political objectives." He force-
fully points out in his preface on "Politics and Economics" the economic
consequences and necessary adjustments after a great war in our modern society both from the standpoint of industries and of sovereignties: "In-

dustries, which have been producing for the political emergency which has
engulfed the society in which they function, must readjust their programs
to an altered situation... The Society of Nations awakens from its revelry
to find itself bound together by a new and particularly onerous bond - a
nexus of debtor-creditor relationships." This situation, of course, becomes still further complicated when many new sovereign states are created.
Hence, a great post-war problem arose, namely "How could these new states be
integrated into the world economy in such a way as to give them political
influence in the Society of Nations and insure their domestic prosperity."

In selecting Poland Dr. Douglass has chosen a seemingly very favored example for studying the development of a new political state. On the treaty
paper the case for the political and economic independence of that country
was made to look bright - the country and people had a long national tradition and a population sufficiently large to rank it among the larger powers
of Europe; important economic sections were also taken from the territory
of the defeated powers and a special outlet to the sea was formed. Though
the time which has elapsed since the new state was formed is not very long
as history goes and has also been characterized by many unusual difficulties,
both national and international, it is long enough to indicate several significant trends and provide much evidence for appraising the economic independence of Poland. This seems particularly true when it is remembered that
most of the new state had previously been united and had a long historical
unity and tradition.

The method of study used in this monograph of 184 pages is in large
part statistical: The story of Poland's agriculture, industry and especially
trade during recent years as told by figures. To a considerable extent it
also involves translation in that much of the factual data used and comments
made are either quoted or based upon material published in foreign languages,
especially German, also Polish and French. It is not possible, of course,
to make comparisons to any significant extent between Poland's post-war and
pre-war economic activities. The component parts, which make up Poland today, had been integral parts of three other countries for a century and a
quarter or more. Thus, it is necessary to continue the statistical picture
to post-war years and as the author admits, this period has many features
affecting statistical or year-to-year comparisons. The Polish-Russian
boundary was not definitely fixed until early 1921; then Poland went through
a period of monetary inflation so that "it was not until the period from
1927-1929", states Dr. Douglass, "that Polish domestic and foreign business
could develop unrestricted by extraordinary influences." Then came the depression which greatly restricted the foreign trade objectives that were
being attempted.

To the reviewer, this monograph seems to fall short of the objective
the author has in mind - it seems much more of an assembly of available
economic statistics than a critical examination of the question involved.
There are few factual conclusions to be found concerning the question
of trade adjustments to political objectives, though after reading the
economic philosophy expressed in the preface one feels that this study will
be a real contribution to this most interesting and timely problem.
Travel and first hand investigations in Poland provide one with some very
definite conclusions on this subject, however inadequate the statistical

series may be. As most of the material used and comments made appear to be based on foreign published sources and are very impersonal, the style does not make for easy reading. One is also struck by an apparent change in style between parts like the preface on "Politics and Economics" and the general factual presentation of the monograph. The latter and particularly the agricultural sections somehow tend to remind one of a university class room research or seminar study and provide rather difficult reading. The organization and presentation of the material, it seems, might have been very effectively improved.

As agriculture is, of course, a very important part of Poland's economy in fact, the most important, it deserves a very careful analysis. Though this has been recognized and attempted to some extent in the study, there is still much to be desired by the agricultural economist. Too much credence is given to statistics of a single year or short periods and also in many cases to reports released several years ago. The real features of the agricultural situation and trends and marketing factors in particular are discussed quite briefly for the most part. A fuller discussion, particularly of the marketing practices and possibilities of development, would have considerably strengthened, in the reviewer's opinion, not only the chapters on "Poland as an Agricultural State" and "Poland's Agricultural Exports" but would have afforded some very good evidence for appraising the progress of "trade adjustments to political objectives". Agricultural policy, in fact the whole question of government policy and aims, could also have been given a special treatment to advantage in such a study.

Though the monograph lacks much of what a technical worker may want, and though it is also somewhat statistical and heavily annotated (along with several quotations in French) for the average lay reader, it is a helpful contribution to the economic literature available in English on Poland. It brings together much other scattered and original source material and can be recommended for any one who wants an introduction to some of the problems involved in national trade re-organization and particularly to certain aspects of Poland's economic organization and life. As perhaps of special interest at this time, the reader's attention is invited to one of Dr. Douglass' observations regarding Poland's free access to the sea which involves the famous Polish Corridor question, namely "when the economic independence of Poland is studied as divorced from political programs, free access to the Baltic Sea seems to be of only limited and certainly not decisive importance." It also seems significant to note that the author says "the conviction is gaining ground in Poland that economic independence cannot be achieved by a self-imposed isolation from industrial countries and by building up an industry which produces at costs which make domestic products far more expensive than the same commodities imported. There seems to be a strengthening recognition of the fact that Poland's chief concern must be to play a determining part in the economic development of the industrial countries of north-western and central Europe by supplying them with agricultural products and raw materials." Whether this signifies economic independence or continued dependence may appear debatable. - Gordon P. Boals, Assistant Agricultural Attaché, Foreign Agricultural Service Division

hnson, E. R., Huebner, G. G. and Henry, A. K.   Transportation by water.
665pp. New York, London, D. Appleton-Century company, inc., 1935.
(Appleton's transportation series)   289.3 J632T
    References at end of most of the chapters.
    This general textbook on water transportation, foreign and domestic,
ocean and inland, is the result, for two of the authors at least, of many
years of work in this field. It provides a broad picture of the physical
nature of transportation operations. The technological development of
the industry is reviewed, briefly, but in a way which indicates why the
major improvements were improvements. The economy of centralizing the
market for dock labor is explained, although the problem of who shall
control the hiring halls - an issue in a recent Pacific Coast strike -
is not examined. The chapter on wharfage and storage also helps to give
a concrete idea of the difference between efficiency and inefficiency
in our department of operations. It hardly seems necessary, however,
to inform the reader that when cargo falls from a sling the results are
unfortunate (p.171) The rise of combinations is traced and the identity
and magnitude of the more important operators are indicated. The protean
character of business organization in ocean transport is made clear.
(The same enterprise may concurrently be a line operator, a tramp operator, a broker, a freight forwarder) The effect of changes in immigration
on passenger services and charges is traced. The numerous provisions of
law regulating and aiding marine transport are fully covered. On the
whole the book is the best introduction to the subject now available.
One important function of a textbook, however - that of introducing the
reader to the literature of the subject - is inadequately fulfilled.
The "references" are too few, consist too largely of titles of other textbooks, and include too little contemporary material.
    When the discussion verges on economic analysis it sometimes falters.
The definition of monopoly (p.357) ignores marginal theory. The fact
that less capital is involved in the organization of contract than of
common carriers, does not necessarily explain why their operating costs
should be lower. (p.127) The thought involved in saying that steamship
companies can "save the profit" (p.164) of contract stevedores by doing
their own stevedoring is confused. One wonders how the reduction of the
International Mercantile Marine Company's capital stock made the position
of the company "less unfavorable" (p.110), since capital stock is not a
liability on which interest or principal must be paid. It is not clear
why international regional competition is regarded as more intense than
domestic regional competition in their effects on ocean and rail rates
respectively (p.360).
    The treatment of rates lacks concreteness. Not one actual rate is
quoted. The reader obtains no idea of how the rates on any commodities
compare with their values - in other words, no idea of their economic
importance. The authors approve of conference control of ocean rates
and advocate government control of inland water rates. This position
they apparently base on the supposed advantages of stability of rates
and equality of treatment of different shippers. "Fluctuating rates
that result from unrestricted competition seriously interfere with
trade" (p.371) Fluctuations in rates undoubtedly make trade more spec-

ulative and injure some traders while benefiting others; but it has yet to be shown that they reduce the total volume of trade. On the other hand, such control of rates as the authors advocate or approve tends to be associated with inflexibility of rates in the presence of changes in price levels and/or general economic conditions. Thus, the conference-fixed rate on citrus fruit from Los Angeles to Liverpool was $1.00 in 1929 and 1934, although this amounted to 26 percent of the farm price in the former year and 56 percent in the latter. On the other hand, ocean rates on wheat, which have not been susceptible to conference control, have declined sharply during the depression. The authors think there is little likelihood that the transportation of the great staples of commerce, which are largely handled by tramps, will be monopolized (p.361) It is interesting to note that schemes of minimum rates on grain in tramps from North Atlantic and Argentine ports and in other trades have been in effect during recent months, and are reported to be successful.

Speaking of inland water transportation, the authors subscribe to the current opinion that there is a surplus of transportation facilities of all kinds in the United States, but seemingly take as their criterion depression conditions (p.546). They apparently sympathize with the idea of charging for the use of publicly improved waterways, but do not give recognition to the bearing of the principle of sunk costs on this question.

They favor a vigorous merchant marine policy for the United States, although they regard it as "certain" that the government itself should not own merchant vessels. Their advocacy apparently rests more largely on the belief that a strong national marine promotes our commerce than on considerations of national defense. The question is not examined from the point of view of comparative advantage or of our being a creditor nation. The problem of making sure that government aid really goes to promote American shipping and not to pay excessive allowances to subsidiaries or salaries is not specifically discussed. Without citing examples, the authors say that "flagrant discriminations" against American shippers in rates "have occurred at times" but concede that these are "exceptional" and believe they can be corrected by regulation (p.413)

The Bureau of Railway Economics, incidentally, is not a government agency (References, p. 564). - Thor Hultgren, Associate Agricultural Economist, Division of Statistical and Historical Research.

DESCRIPTIVE NOTES AND ABSTRACTS

Agricultural Adjustment Administration

Chamber of commerce of the United States of America. Agricultural department committee. Agricultural prices and production under the Adjustment administration. Committee report. 50pp. Washington, D. C., Chamber of commerce of the United States, 1935. 281.12 C353

Contents: The background of the Agricultural Adjustment Act; The Agricultural Adjustment Act, The cotton control program; the wheat control program; The hog control program; The corn control program; The cattle control program; The tobacco control program; Dairy products; Marketing agreements - General; and Conclusions.

Chamber of commerce of the United States of America. Agricultural department Agri-
cultural adjustment act; analytical statement of law with amendments.
October, 1935.   37pp. Washington, D. C., Agricultural department,
Chamber of commerce of the United States, 1935.   281.12 C35A

United States. United States of America, petitioner, v. William M. Butler
et al., receivers of Hoosac mills corporation. On writ of certiorari
to the United States circuit court of appeals for the first circuit.
Brief for the United States. 280pp. [Washington, U. S. Govt. print.
off., 1935] 281.372 Un33
      At head of title: No. 401. In the Supreme court of the United States.
   October term 1935.
      Bibliographical foot-notes.
      The Library of the U. S. Department of Agriculture has also a 100-
   page Appendix to the brief for the United States, which contains "Foreign
   laws limiting production of agricultural commodities", pp.79-100.

Agricultural Economics - Mexico

Partido nacional revolucionario.   Secretaría de acción agraria. Los problemas
   agrícolas de México... año 1, t. 1-2   2v. México, D. F., 1934.
   281.9 P25
      Sub-title: Anales de la economía agrícola mexicana.
      These two volumes contain articles by Mexican authorities on the agri-
   cultural economic situation in Mexico.
      Partial contents: v. 1 - Posibilidades de la ganadería mexicana, by José
   Figueroa. - pp. 19-42. (On livestock raising in Mexico and the possibilities
   of its development. The author calls for better livestock, improved feeding
   methods, and more sanitary control); El consumo de la carne en México, by
   Francisco Moguel. - pp. 65-126. (A study of meat consumption in Mexico,
   illustrated by tables and diagrams. One table shows meat production from
   1840 to 1932); La política de irrigación que más conviene a la agricultura
   mexicana, by Miguel A. Gleason. - pp. 127-147. (After a brief survey of
   tne work of irrigation in Mexico the author concludes that the irrigation
   policy best suited to actual conditions in Mexico would include the completion of large projects already started with the determination not to
   start any more, the complete settlement of the country already irrigated,
   and the instigation and development of small irrigation projects.);
   Formas para la fijación del salario mínimo, by Ramón Fernández y Fernández. -
   pp. 149-166. (Lists seven rules for establishing a minimum salary); La sit-
   uación forestal en México, by Camilo del Moral. - pp. 167-197. (A study
   of forestry conditions in Mexico); Estudio económico y jurídico sobre la
   propiedad forestal en México, by Salvador Guerrero. - pp. 199-215. (The
   author suggests a plan for the exploitation of Mexican forests in the interests of the State); La ley de colonización y el problema de la tierra en
   México, by Rafael L. Ocampo. - pp. 217-242. (A brief survey of the four
   characteristic epochs of land colonization in Mexico: The pre-Hispanic
   epoch; that which was originated by the law of August 18, 1824; that cre-

ated by the law of December 15, 1883; and the present period initiated by
the law of April 5, 1925. Emphasis is placed on the work accomplished
under the law of 1926 and suggestions are made for its future application);
La educación agrícola como fundamento de reorganización de nuestra economía
rural, by Bernardo Arrieta. - pp. 243-264. (Agricultural education as a
basis for the reorganization of Mexico's rural economy); Hay problema de
relocalización de la producción agrícola en México? by José Lazcano Romero. -
pp. 293-339. (The author decides that there is in Mexico a problem affecting agricultural production, and particularly that of cereals, which calls
for a policy of restriction of acreage and intensive production by modern
methods), El capital en la agricultura mexicana, by René Becerra. - pp. 341-
369. (Defines capital and studies its relation to the land in Mexico).
    v. 2. - La producción ejidal frente a la producción agrícola privada,
by Gilberto Fabila. - pp. 370-438. (The author studies the differences that
exist between communal and private agricultural production for the economic,
social, political, and juridical point of view. He sees in the communal
distribution of land a system which will change the national agricultural
production of Mexico. It implies the absorption of a large part of the
private property in the old agricultural zones or its relegation to different sections of the country. He sees in the communal land system the
only solution of Mexico's agrarian problem); Las tierras de labor en la
agricultura mexicana, by Adolfo Vargas Chiquini. - pp. 439-469. (A study
of cultivated land in Mexico); Desenvolvimiento agrícola en México, by
Gumaro García de la Cadena. - pp. 471-521. (A historical survey of the
development of agriculture in Mexico); La función económica del Servicio
Meteorologico en la agricultura, by Alfonso Contreras. - pp. 523-561. (The
economic function of the meteorological service in agriculture); El credito
agrícola como fundamento de la reorganización de la economía agrícola, by
Ernesto Martinez de Alba. - pp. 563-583. (The importance and the functions of agricultural credit as a state activity are discussed, based on
the experience of the Banco Nacional de Crédito Agrícola in handling its
daily problems); La fruticultura como una transformación racional de la
agricultura mexicana, by Carlos Noriega. - pp. 585-616. (The author sees
in fruit cultivation a rational means of placing private agriculture in
Mexico on a new economic plane); Formas en que los impuestos locales gravan
la agricultura, by Héctor Lazos. - pp. 617-667. (The burden of local taxation on agriculture and suggestions for its alleviation)

Agricultural Indebtedness - Rumania

Cristoveano, N. C.   Essai critique sur la politique roumaine en matière
    de dettes agricoles. 498pp. Paris, 1933.   284.2 C86
        Thèse - Univ. de Paris.
        Bibliography, pp. [483]-486.
        A study of agricultural indebtedness in Rumania, its causes, the
    most immediate of which is shown to be the lack of organization of
    agricultural credit, and the measures adopted by the Rumanian Govern-
    ment for its relief. The laws of April 19, 1932, October 26, 1932, and
    April 14, 1933 are discussed at length.

Saskatchewan. University. College of agriculture. Dept. of farm management.
Studies of farm indebtedness and financial progress of Saskatchewan
farmers. Report no. 3. Surveys made at Indian Head and Balcarres;
Grenfell and Wolseley; and Neudorf and Lemberg. 53 pp. Saskatoon,
Sask., 1935. (Saskatchewan. University. College of agriculture. Agricultural extension. Bulletin no. 68) 7 Sa76A no. 68
    "In these reports are shown some of the many important differences
found in Saskatchewan farm businesses. The districts of Indian Head
and Balcarres are in many respects quite unlike those adjoining in the
Grenfell and Wolseley, and Neudorf and Lemberg areas, but these differences are actually less marked than those noted in the investigations
of the previous year in the block of land included in the municipalities of Brokenshell, Wellington, and Scott.
    "Apart from the differences in general farm organization which
characterize these districts are the important variations between farms
of the same study. It has not been possible to give full consideration
to these individual deviations from the typical organization of the
district in these publications. The objective in this report has been
limited to a representation of the significant features of the survey
to provide a factual basis for an understanding of the present financial
situation of Saskatchewan farmers. As far as possible, a cross section
of the district has been portrayed. In all research in agricultural
economics there must be constant recognition of the fact that there
are many things which contribute to farm success or failure which do
not permit of satisfactory statistical analysis.
    "The reports of this series of regional studies of farm indebtedness
and financial progress have been prepared on a uniform plan to facilitate
comparison of important data in the different districts. This is the
third report to be published. A fourth will follow shortly, covering
the study made in 1934 in the agricultural areas adjacent to Humboldt."
-Observations.

Agricultural Labor - France

Pepault, André.   Le rôle de l'immigration agricole étrangère dans l'économie
    française.   232pp.   Paris, 1933.   282.2 P19
        Thèse - Univ. de Paris.
        Bibliography, pp. [228]-229.
        "In addition to an account of the regulation and the mechanism of the
    introduction of the foreign agricultural labour supply in France, this
    book contains an exhaustive study of the foreign working population em-
    ployed in agriculture in that country and of the occupational and social
    characteristics of immigrants of different nationalities. The author
    examines in turn the advantages and disadvantages of the immigration of
    seasonal workers, farmers (owners, tenant farmers or métayers), and per-
    manent wage earners. The work ends with a considered review of the dif-
    ferent aspects of the problem of the assimilation of immigrants." -
    International Labour Review, v. 30, no. 4, Oct. 1934, p. 571.

Poszwa, Louis. L'émigration polonaise agricole en France. 215pp. Paris, Gebethner & Wolff, 1930. 282.2 P84
   Bibliography, pp. 209-212.
   The author discusses the historical, economic, and political reasons for the emigration of Polish agricultural workers and for their immigration into France. He describes the methods by which this immigration is carried out and gives an account of the working, social, and religious conditions under which the immigrants live.

Agriculture - Puy-de-Dôme - France

Roux, Paul. Les populations rurales du Puy-de-Dôme. Monographies rédigées à l'occasion de l'enquête agricole de 1929, par Ph. Arbos..., Marc Dousse..., Lucien Gachon... Guy de Guerines..., Élie Lapayre... Jean Lhéritier. 439pp. Clermont-Ferrand, Impr. générale de Bussac, 1933. 281.174 R76
   A detailed account of the condition of agriculture and of living conditions of the rural population of Puy-de-Dôme in 1930. Attention is called to the fact that changes have taken place since then, due to the depression.

Australia

Pratt, Ambrose, ed. The national handbook of Australia's industries, edited by Ambrose Pratt, Edward Leeson sub-editor. Published with the commendation of the prime minister of the Commonwealth and the premiers of all the Australian states. 671pp. Melbourne, The Specialty press pty. ltd., 1934. 280.1992 P88
   "In this book will be found a comprehensive account of every industry now functioning in Australia that is competent to supply the needs of external consumers; together with a description of the processes of production; the methods employed to insure a high and standardised excellence in the quality of the products; the processes of transport that are available to convey the goods into the hands of overseas purchasers in a condition satisfactory to all concerned, and of the machinery of exchange which can be utilised to initiate and complete each individual commercial transaction that may be undertaken." - Introductory note signed by the Prime Minister of the Commonwealth of Australia.

Cooperation - Czechoslovakia - Rumania

Polin, Raymond and Charon, J. G. Les coopératives rurales et l'état en Tchecoslovaquie et en Roumanie. Préface de C. Bouglé. 164pp. Paris, F. Alcan, 1934. (Nouvelle bibliothèque économique) 280.2 P754
   At head of title: Travaux du Centre de documentation sociale.
   Bibliography, pp [95]-97, [161]
   Agricultural cooperation in Czechoslovakia is studied in its relation to the land and the distribution of property, to the farmer, and to the State. It is shown to be an entity at once autonomous and yet in close relation with the dominant party of the government, the agrarian party. The State has aided it to become a monopoly but it will find itself a State monopoly.
   In Rumania the agrarian reform is shown to have brought about such a

change in land tenure as to have necessitated a new cooperative policy.
The credit institution which was the type of cooperative par excellence
seems to have been replaced by a type with more fundamental economic
power and a more highly developed cooperative spirit. This type may be
called upon to form the basis of a directed economy made necessary by
the new subdivision of property. - A. M. Hannay.

Cooperation - Denmark

Pierre, prince of Greece. Les coopératives agricoles danoises et le marché
  extérieur. 181pp. Paris, Librairie du recueil Sirey, 1935. 280.2 P61
    Bibliography, pp. [177]-178.
    The author traces the origin of cooperation in Denmark to a time of
  critical importance in the economic history of the country when it appeared simultaneously with a profound transformation in agricultural production. During the second half of the nineteenth century changes in
  the conditions of Danish agricultural export made a radical change in production necessary. Emphasis was placed on the production and export of
  butter, bacon, and eggs, and, because of the peculiar characteristics of
  the economic and social life of Denmark, that would not have been possible except on a cooperative basis. The author points out that the rapid
  and powerful development of Danish agricultural cooperatives is due to
  their having made the change in agricultural production possible by
  adapting it to the requirements of the foreign market. In this they differ from similar organizations in other countries which have not a rôle
  as distinctly national as those of Denmark. The origin and development
  of the Danish agricultural cooperatives are studied as the movement spread
  to all branches of agricultural production and finally became the dominant
  factor in the progress and prosperity of the whole country. Finally,
  the author discusses the fate of the cooperatives during the depression
  which has threatened Denmark's production of animal products and thus
  compromised the prosperity and the very existence of those cooperatives.
  Three courses are suggested, if cooperation is not to be thrown overboard.
  They are increase of prices on the foreign market, decreased cost of production of products to be exported or loss of capital and adaptation of
  production on a more modest scale to the new conditions of the foreign
  market. The last solution seems most probable to the author who finds it
  difficult to believe that a nation, that has been able to make the humble
  egg one of its most important sources of wealth can be on the brink of
  shipwreck in the economic storms of today.--A. M. Hannay.

Trothe, C. D. von. Der direkte weg vom erzeuger zum verbraucher. Ziel und
  ergebnis der bestrebungen zur verminderung der handelsspanne und ordnung
  der marktbeziehungen bei der verteilung landwirtschaftlicher produkte.
  175pp. Berlin, Wien, Industrieverlag Spaeth & Linde, 1935. (Frankfurt
  am Main. Universität. Institut für genossenschaftswesen. Veröffentlichungen
  ...hft. 9) 280.29 F85 hft.9
    Bibliography, pp. [163]-175.
    This is a study of pre-war and post-war attempts to lower the cost
  of the distribution of agricultural products and to improve market conditions so as to insure fair prices by a direct cooperative association
  of producers and consumers.

Cooperative Purchasing of Farm Supplies

Lister, J. H.   Cooperative purchasing of farm supplies in Oregon - 1933.
     27pp. mimeogr. [Washington D. C., Aug. 1935]   (U. S. Farm credit administra-
     tion. Cooperative division. Miscellaneous report no. 3, Aug. 1935)
     166.3 M68 no.3
          "Research, service, and educational series."
          "In the spring of 1934, information was obtained from 31 cooperative
     associations in the State of Oregon, with reference to the purchase of
     farm supplies for their members during 1933. The following report is
     based upon this survey. It is not presented as a detailed technical
     analysis of cooperative activities in the purchase of farm supplies in
     Oregon, but as a general statement of the nature and extent of these
     activities and an indication of the possible advantages to patrons of
     cooperative purchasing associations." - Summary.

Cotton - Production Control

Rousse, T. A.   Government control of cotton production. 309pp. Austin,
     Tex., 1935. (The University of Texas bulletin no. 3538)   281,372 R76
     Bibliography, pp. [43]-46.
          This is a handbook for debaters giving suggestive briefs and quota-
     tions from authorities on both the affirmative and negative side of the
     question of cotton control.

Deserts on the March

Sears, P. B.   Deserts on the march.   231pp. Norman, University of Oklahoma
     press, 1935. 277.12 Sel
          The author traces the conquest of the American continent in relation
     to our natural resources and in the concluding chapter writes:
          "We have reviewed, without professional language, the verdict of
     science upon an impersonal matter - the unbalance between man and his
     surroundings. In the chapter just preceding we have suggested that the
     institution of private ownership deserves further trial, or perhaps
     better, a genuine trial, before it is discarded as a means to achieve
     that order which is essential to the welfare of the human race. But
     we must bear in mind that science, as such, affords us no sanctions.
     It may inform us with regard to any particular social or economic sys-
     tem, but it cannot make our decisions for us...
          "Surely it should be clear that the grassland and the forest must be
     restored and protected to an extent not yet dreamed of, not for reasons
     of sentiment, but because they represent sources of certain return under
     all conditions. And to the balance which they display must man look for
     his soundest lessons in the construction of his fields to be buffered
     against whatever may come.
          "Only with the works of his hands thus attuned to the compelling frame
     of soil and climate will destructive change take its proper place as a
     dim memory of the hideous thing which it is."

Cassady. Ralph, Jr., and Ostlund, H. J. The retail distribution structure
   of the small city, based on a study of the Waseca, Minnesota, retail
   plant and trade area. 107pp. Minneapolis, University of Minnesota
   Press. 1935. (Minnesota. University. Studies in economics and business,
   no. 12, Aug. 1935) 280.9 M663 no.12.
      "This study is one of a series undertaken by the University of
   Minnesota on the distribution of consumer goods. Throughout the
   series the objectives have been to depict the organization of society
   for marketing commodities, to measure as objectively as possible the
   costs of distribution, and to draw attention to the implications of some
   of the dynamic changes that are in progress." - Foreword.

Economic Geography - Asia.

Berasmark, D. R. Economic geography of Asia. 618pp. New York, Prentice-
   Hall, inc., 1935.   278.18 B45
      Bibliography at end of each chapter.
      Contains much material of agricultural interest.

Economic Lessons of 1929-1931

Unclaimed wealth utilization committee, Geneva. The economic lessons of 1929-
   1931; the first eleven bulletins of the Committee issued under the chairmanship of A. H. Abbati. With an introduction by Professor T. E. Gregory.
   94pp. London, P. S. King & son, ltd., 1932. 280 Unl 1st ser.
      Partial contents: The beliefs, objects and methods of the unclaimed
   wealth utilization committee; Insufficient buying and trade depression;
   The distinction between saving and investment; The dimensions of unclaimed wealth and of hoarded savings; When the order of the day is
   "Sauve qui Peut", General trade depression in the making; Budgetary
   policy in the present situation; and The outflow of gold from England.

Economics

Cassel, Gustav. On quantitative thinking in economics. 181pp. Oxford,
   Clarendon press, 1935. 280 C27Q
      In the introductory chapter the author writes:
      "In its knowledge of actual facts as well as of historical develop-
   ment economic science has made wonderful progress during the last generation. Theoretical exposition, however, has hardly kept pace with
   this progress, and the foundations of economic theory have been especially
   neglected.
      "Economics must essentially be a quantitative science dealing with
   quantities and their relations to one another and with conditions of
   equilibrium between forces that must be conceived quantitatively. A
   scientific study of economics, therefore, requires a certain acquaintance with the first principles of quantitative research. Most economists,
   however, have been brought up on other lines, and their equipment for
   quantitative thinking has often been defective. The result is that economic science has suffered at every stage of its growth from serious de-

fects in quantitative thinking. The present state of the science offers
clear evidence of this weakness.

"The mathematical form widely used nowadays in the discussion of economic problems is no guarantee of a deeper understanding of the quantitative nature of the problems. Authors may have acquired a certain
amount of technical knowledge of mathematical formulae and methods of
calculation and still have not acquired that strict training in quantitative thinking that would enable them to understand and critically judge
how such mathematical methods must be handled and how much economic reality
can be read into them. It has not even been generally realized that
mathematics is an instrument for handling measurable quantities, and that
the use of mathematics therefore always presupposes a measurability of
the quantities considered. In fact, a mathematical treatment of economics has no value, and may easily be quite misleading, if it is not
based on a thorough examination of the quantitative nature of the concepts introduced and on the adoption of definite measures for these quantities...

"I propose in this little volume to offer some critical and constructive remarks on quantitative thinking in economics. I do not pretend to
present a systematic treatment of the subject. This would be possible
only in a complete exposition of economic science. My Theory of Social
Economy is an endeavour - resolute in spite of all its unavoidable shortcomings - to build up economics as a quantitative science. In the following pages I hope to throw more light upon some of the main problems involved in this task. I shall have to give fresh emphasis to the quantitative nature both of concepts and of methods, and I shall have to insist,
more urgently than ever, upon the necessity of purging economic science
from a lot of vague notions, false reasonings, and untenable constructions,
which - in spite of all earlier criticism - still dominate and daily remind us of the low standard of quantitative thinking prevalent in our
science.

"Criticism of this kind has often been recognized as justified.
Nevertheless, economists have been reluctant to draw the ultimate conclusions and to reject uses of terms and presentations or problems and
'laws' which retain their position in economic science only by virtue
of sterile tradition. This vacillating is intolerable. Either the
criticism must be proved to be not justified, or - if that is not possible - a radical cleansing of economic science must be undertaken,
and efforts must be concentrated on the task of giving a more satisfactory quantitative foundation to economic theory."

The other chapters are: Production; Value and money; Income and its
use; Gradual approximation; Quantitative relations between product and
factors of production; The equilibrium theory of prices.

Economics - Canada

Canadian institute on economics and politics. Addresses and outlines of ad-
dresses given at the Canadian institute on economics and politics, Lake
Couchiching, Ontario, August 8 to 17, 1935. 60pp. mimeogr. [n.p.]
National council YMCAs, Canada [1935]   280.9 C163 1935
Partial contents: The philosophy of social conflict (An outline) by
George A. Coe; The foreign policies of the United States, by Quincy Wright;
The new deal down to date (an outline) by Bruce Bliven; Some historical

- 15 -

backgrounds of present Canadian-American relations, by Reginald G. Trotter; Principles of Canadian foreign policy, by Hon. Newton W. Rowell; The business man's contribution to the national recovery, by J. M. Macdonnell.

Family Budgets - India

Singh, Kartar, and Singh, Ajaib. Family budgets, 1933-34 of six tenant-cultivators in the Lyallpur district, being the second year's accounts of some cultivators on the Risalewala farm near Lyallpur. 43pp. [Lahore, "C & M. Gazette" ltd.] 1935. (India. Punjab. Board of economic inquiry. Publication no.44) 281.9 In2 no.44
    "The first of the 'Family Budgets of Tenant-Cultivators in the Lyallpur District,' was published in 1934, and this is the second publication of this series. This year's accounts have been worked out on the same lines as last year, except that the period covered by the last year's publication was from 1st November 1932 to 31st October 1933, while in this it is from 1st June 1933 to 31st May 1934. This change has been effected because it was considered desirable that the periods covered by these accounts and 'Farm Accounts in the Punjab' should be the same.
    "The present publication deals with six families of tenant-cultivators instead of only four as was done in the former one.

Farm Business

Horne, R. L. The farm business. 60pp. Chicago, Ill., The University of Chicago press [1935] 281.12 H78
    Bibliography, pp. 59-60.
    "This pamphlet is one of a series [of 'American Primers'] prepared under a grant from the General Education Board to the American Council on Education. The pamphlets are designed to meet, first of all, the needs of workers' and adult education groups for readable materials in the social sciences. The publication of the series represents an attempt to present, in a spirit of scientific inquiry but in non-technical language, a discussion of current issues in economics, politics and sociology.
    "The editor of the series is Dr. Percy W. Bidwell." - Introductory Statement.

Farm Income - Devon and Cornwall

Long, W. H. Financial results on certain Devon and Cornish farms for the year 1933/34. 12pp., mimeogr. Newton Abbot, Devon, 1935. (Seale-Hayne agricultural college, Newton Abbot, Devon. Dept. of economics. Farmers' report no. 10) 281.9 Sel no.10
    "There was a slight improvement in the returns of 1926/27 and 1927/28, but the best that can be said of these two years is that conditions were not quite as bad as in 1925/26.
    "The next two years show a real recovery, and the returns of the accounting farmers were at least L1 an acre better than the average of the 3 preceding years. The year 1928/29 was chiefly notable for the recovery in cattle and sheep. In 1929/30, although this improvement in

livestock was not maintained the effect of the Agricultural De-rating
Act and the fall in prices of feeding stuffs especially, and of other
expenses, was to leave a profit which even exceeded the profit of
1928/29.
    "Then followed two years of depression, the second of which returned
results which are unequalled in their severity throughout the period.
The next year, 1932/33 showed an improvement over its predecessor but
that is the best that can be said of it. No other year than 1931/32 was
as depressed as 1932/33. Weather conditions in these years were not
up to average and they must have played their part in intensifying the
depression. But the root cause of the trouble was the catastrophic
fall in world prices of food stuffs and raw materials. This was first
felt in 1929 and it has been largely responsible for the economic dis-
equilibrium that has overcome the greater part of the world during the
last four or five years.
    "It is when we come to the last year of this analysis 1933/34, that
the buoyancy that has characterised agriculture in its previous depressions once more becomes apparent. A century ago the lean times
that followed the Napoleonic Wars were succeeded by the Golden Age of
English Agriculture in the '60's, and the quietly prosperous years in
the first decade of this century served to soften, though they could not
eradicate, the memory of the 80's and '90's. The war period and the
slump that succeeded it is, let us hope, unique and therefore unsuitable for comparisons, but of the subsequent depressions evidence is contained in these pages of agriculture's resilience and of her success,
however modest, in overcoming misfortune.
    "This report contains a rather fuller account than usual of the gen-
eral returns from farming in the South West as shown by the accounts.
The extra space has been taken because this report is possibly the
last report that will be presented in the present form."

Farm Organizations

Hunt, R. L.   A history of farmer movements in the Southwest, 1873-1925. 192pp.
    [n.p., 1935?] 30.9 H91
        As the book was privately printed, information about purchasing it
    should be procured from the author who is Associate Professor of agri-
    cultural economics, Agricultural and Mechanical College of Texas, College
    Station, Texas.
        The author's preface reads in part as follows:
        "The attention that has been given to control of production and market-
    ing of agricultural products in recent years makes a study of the history
    of farmer movements and the evolution of ideas in regard to economic prob-
    lems of agriculture intensely interesting. If proper attention could
    be given to the activities, successes, and failures of past farmer or-
    ganizations, many pitfalls in the future could be avoided. Farmers
    should not have to learn by experience the same lessons over and over
    again. They should be able to profit by the experience of those who
    have gone before them and not make the same mistakes again. In the fol-
    lowing pages I have tried to record accurately the activities of four
    major farmer organizations in the Southwest. More attention has been given
    to Texas organizations simply because I have had greater opportunities

to make more extensive studies of farmer activities in this State. Furthermore, several of the successive farmer organizations that have spread over the United States during the past 65 years have had their origin in Texas. I have tried to give a better understanding of the background, origin and development of the organizations that have had their origin in Texas. No attempt has been made to trace the spread of the various organizations over the United States or to analyze their activities in all the states. That these organizations did in Texas was more or less typical of what was tried in other states."

The organizations included are the Texas State Grange, Farmer's Alliance in Texas, Farmers' Educational and Cooperative Union, and the Farm-Labor Union. Chapters are devoted to the cotton price control and cotton marketing plans of the Farmers' Union in Texas and the marketing of cotton and fruits and vegetables by the Farm-labor union.

Taber, L. J.   Address... before the National grange annual session. Sacramento, Calif., November 13, 1935. 28pp. [Springfield, Mass., 1935] Pam. Coll.

The extracts which follow have been taken from the introductory paragraphs:

"This Annual Session of the National Grange marks anew the continuing strength and power of rural organization. Every state touching the Pacific Ocean has made outstanding Grange growth. California leads the nation in the number of new Granges. Washington leads in net gain in membership, and Oregon stands in the forefront with a well-balanced program. Every state west of the Mississippi, but one, and more than three-fourths of the states of the nation, have a net gain in Grange membership during the year. We rejoice to find the star of the great state of Texas again floating in the National Grange flag. With the number of states represented, with our net gain in membership, and with our finances at the highest point since 1878, we find a positive and eloquent testimonial of the service of the Grange...

"Along with growth, size, and national development, comes the sobering responsibility that a truly national organization must take a national viewpoint on all problems. We cover every section of the nation. There is hardly a farm product grown that is not produced by some member of our organization. There is not a farm commodity or a rural problem that must not be faced by members of our fraternity: therefore, the Grange dare not take a narrow, partisan, or sectional viewpoint on any problem confronting rural life."

Food Investigations

Gt. Brit. Dept. of scientific and industrial research.   Index to the literature of food investigation, v. 6, no.2, Sept. 1934. Comp. by Agnes Elizabeth Glennie... assisted by Gwen Davies. 621pp.   London, H. M. Stationery off., 1935.   241.64 G792

This very useful index is arranged under the following sections: Meat; Pig-flesh, Poultry and game; Fish; Eggs; Dairy produce; Fats and oils, Fruit and vegetables; Grain, crops and seeds; Theory of canning; Theory of freezing and chilling; Bacteriology; Mycology; and Engineering.

Fruit - Argentina

Argentine fruit distributors ltd. S. A. Argentine fruit distributors, ltd.,
    1935. Consejos tecnicos, clasificacion, embalaje, venta. 63pp.
    [Buenos Aires, Printed by Mercatali brothers] 1935.   280.393 Ar3
        "This little book has been prepared with the idea of informing per-
    sons interested in the new Pio Negro fruit district in Southern Argentina,
    which is rapidly taking its place among the major apple and pear districts
    of the world." - Introduction.

Institute of Rural Economics

Institute of rural economics. Rutgers university. Viewpoints on economic
    and social issues and their relation to rural life, 1935. Lectures
    and discussions of the Institute of rural economics, Rutgers university.
    230pp. New Brunswick, N. J. [1935] 280.9 In79
        Contents: Economic planning of land in New Jersey (including The
    idea of economic planning for agriculture, by E. G. Nourse; The problem
    of soil erosion, by Linwood L. Lee; The wild land problem in New Jersey,
    by Charles P. Wilber; What rural life offers, by Lita Bane). - One
    year of the AAA (including Licensing agreements, by J. W. Tapp; The
    dairy side of the picture, by E. W. Gaumnitz; Reduction programs, by
    John D. Black; Mid-west farmers' reaction to the AAA, by P. E. Johnston).
    - One year of the NRA (including The consumer, by Robert S. Lynd; The
    farmer, by Allen G. Waller; The laborer, by Louis Marciante). - Money
    and banking (including Our present monetary situation, by Eugene E.
    Agger; The present banking situation, by B. Haggott Beckhart; One year
    of the Farm Credit Administration, by E. H. Thomson). - Social security -
    Relief (including Rural rehabilitation in New Jersey, by F. P. Gilbert). -
    Democracy and the economic crisis. - New Jersey agricultural problems
    (including Young people consider rural life; Commodity groups). - Programs.

International Organization of Agriculture.

Houillier, F.   L'Organisation internationale de l'agriculture, Les institu-
    tions agricoles internationales et l'action internationale en agricul-
    ture. Preface de m. Jules Gautier.   305pp.   Paris, Librarie technique
    et economique, 1935.   281 H81.
        Bibliography, pp. [279]-296.
        A historical survey of the origin, constitution and functions of the
    principal international agricultural institutions is followed by a dis-
    cussion of their activities along certain definite lines such as the
    struggle against plant and animal pests, protection against fraud, and
    the various international attempts to mitigate the effects of the world
    agricultural crisis, in general, and with reference to certain products,
    such as grain, sugar, wine, beer, fruits and vegetables, livestock and
    animal products, forestry products, textiles, and rubber.

Italy. Ministero dell'agricoltura e delle foreste. La legge sulla Bonifica
integrale nel quinto anno di applicazione. 463pp. Roma, Istituto
poligrafico dello stato, 1935. 282.9 Itl
This is the fifth report of the Italian undersecretary of State in
charge of land reclamation and improvement. It refers mainly to the
year 1933/34 and contains substantially the same type of material as
the three preceding reports for the years 1930 to 1933. It covers
the operations carried on during the year, the pertinent legislation,
the financial administrative and technical problems, and the activities
of the National Association of Consortia for Land Improvement and Irrigation, and of the National Secretariat of Mountainous Regions. The
appendices contain speeches by the Minister of Agriculture and Forests
and the Under-Secretary of State for Land Reclamation and Improvement,
laws, decrees, and circulars issued by the Minister of Agriculture and
the above-mentioned national organizations. The report is preceded by
the speech of Mussolini on the occasion of the inauguration of Littoria
as the ninety-third province of the kingdom.

Land Settlement - Austria

Österreichisches kuratorium für wirtschaftlichkeit. Arbeitsausschuss
"Innenkolonisation". Der aufbau des österreichischen siedlungswerkes.
Bericht des ÖKW-Arbeitsausschusses "Innenkolonisation". Hrsg. vom
Österreichischen kuratorium für wirtschaftlichkeit. 191pp. Wien, J.
Springer, 1933. (On cover: Österreichisches kuratorium für wirtschaftlichkeit. ÖKW-Veroffentlichung 14) 282.2 Os7
A study of the whole question of land settlement in Austria, its
economic and social importance, types of settlement, the procuring of
the land and its utilization, buildings, labor, and financial organization, the choice of settlers and their training, land settlement legislation, and some practical examples of land settlement activity. A summary
of legislative measures for the promotion of land settlement is given for
the following countries: Germany, Bulgaria, Denmark, Estonia, Italy, Yugoslavia, Poland, Rumania, Sweden, Czechoslovakia, and Hungary.

Land Settlement - England

Orwin, C. S. and Darke, W. F. Back to the land. 93 pp. London, P. S. King
& son ltd., 1935. 282.2 Or9
The authors' foreword reads as follows:
"It is natural, perhaps, at a time when unemployment in many of the
great industries of the country is so great and so persistent, that the
possibility of finding an outlet upon the land for many of the redundant
workers in urban and mining industries should be considered. On the
face of things, indeed, this should be something more than a possibility.
Responsible statesmen have drawn attention to the disproportion of industrial and rural workers in Britain by contrast with other great countries, and they and other social economists have commented upon the

persistence of the peasant farmer in all the older countries except our own.

"The facts cannot be refuted, but the interpretation of them commonly given is misleading. It ignores the economic evolution of Britain in the last 150 years, which eliminated so many of the peasant farmers. It takes no account of the dependence of this country on its export manufacturing trade, and on its carrying services. It overlooks the necessity imposed on non-industrialised countries for exporting agricultural produce. It forgets that a standard of living lower, and often far lower, than that which has been achieved by the rural workers in Britain is accepted in all the peasant-farming countries of the rest of the world.

"In the following pages, the authors have traced the history of attempts to re-settle the land in England, and they have indicated and discussed the limiting factors. It is no part of their purpose to discourage or discredit the provision of small holdings, but they are impressed with the danger of looking to land settlement as a means even of the smallest alleviation of industrial unemployment, and they feel that the advocacy which it has received calls for a reply."

Land Settlement - Germany

Arndt, Gotthard. Grundsätze der siedlungspolitik und siedlungsmethode
  Friedrichs des Grossen.   75pp. Breslau, 1934.   282.2 Ar6
    Inaug.-diss. - Leipzig.
    "Erscheint zugleich als hft. 52 der Schriften zur förderung der inneren kolonisation." - p. [2]
    Bibliography, pp. 72-74
    An account of the land settlement policy and methods of Frederick the Great.

Elshoff, Friedrich.   Zwei jahre vorstädtische kleinsiedlung; eine untersuchung über die wirtschaftliche lage u. das ergebnis der stadtrandsiedlung.
  68pp. Münster (Westf.), Wirtschafts- und sozialwissenschaftlicher verlag e.v., 1934. (Added t.-p.: Forschungsstelle für siedlungs- und wohnungswesen an der Universität Münster i.W. Materialiensammlung, hrsg. von... W. D. Preyer. bd. 11) 282.2 E17
    The author recalls the aim of suburban settlement as formulated by Dr. Saasen in the interests of the unemployed, the part-time workers, those whose incomes have depreciated, the recipients of social insurance money, the war victims, and even those who have full time jobs for the time being but who would be protected against the effect of this or future depressions.

    Details are given of 3 types of suburban settlement. These include the settlement of Deusen on the outskirts of the industrial city of Dortmund, the largest such settlement in Germany, those of Gievenbeck and Kappenbergerdamm in the neighborhood of Münster, and those of Senne I and Heepen on the outskirts of Bielefeld.

Gorrie, R. M. The use and misuse of land. 80pp. Oxford, Clarendon
     press, 1935. (Oxford forestry memoirs, no. 19, 1935)   99.9 Ox22 no.19
          Bibliography at end of each chapter.
          "The following report has been prepared from material collected during
     a four months' tour of the United States, which was rendered possible
     through the generosity of the Leverhulme Research Fund. The subject
     for which this research fellowship was awarded was: 'The Correlation of
     Erosion Damage and Grazing in Forest Lands,' but the report now pre-
     sented deals in addition with the somewhat wider implications of the
     misuse and abuse of forest land and the need for a well-considered land
     policy to prevent this. It is felt that if the land as a whole could be
     put to its best uses, and if backward agricultural communities were
     helped towards this aim, the menace of over-grazing would automatically
     disappear. The question of erosion control on farm land has also been
     dealt with as it is felt that recent American developments should be of
     value to workers in this field, particularly in Africa and India where-
     ever 'shifting cultivation' is still practised." - Preface.
          Some of the subjects under which the material in this study is grouped
     are the following: Forestry as a factor in land management; grazing and
     range management, Over-grazing as a primary cause of soil erosion; value
     of vegetational cover in stream-flow control; Forestry as a factor in farm
     and village economy; Farm erosion and its control; Other examples of the
     misuse of land; and Public and private control of land.

Land Use - Ohio

Baker, R. H., Sitterley, J. H. and Falconer, J. I.   Major land-use problem
     areas and land utilization in Ohio, 1935. 98pp., mimeogr. Columbus,
     O., 1935.   282 B17
          "Over a period of years the Department of Rural Economics has been
     collecting material regarding the use of rural lands in Ohio. This
     material was assembled and added to by the State Planning Board, of which
     Dr. J. I. Falconer is a member, and submitted as a part of their report
     to the National Resources Board in August, 1934. Subsequently Mr. R. H.
     Baker, the Ohio land planning consultant for the National Resources Board,
     enlarged upon the material already available and in cooperation with the
     Ohio State Planning Board, the Rural Economics Department and other agen-
     cies outlined the major land use problem areas in Ohio. This material
     was submitted by him to the National Resources Board in September,
     1934.
          "The present report assembles and coordinates the material from these
     various sources. Part I is a presentation and discussion of those areas
     that were considered to present a major land-use problem or problems
     arising out of past and present use of the land. Part II is a presentation
     of some of the significant physical, economic and social factors related
     to land use." - Foreword.

Land Use and Soil Conservation

American bankers association. Agricultural commission. Protecting investment values in land... Conserving soil resources a pressing national
problem. 32pp. [Madison, Wis., The Agricultural commission, American bankers association, 1935] 56.7 Am3

"The degree of intelligence a nation displays in the use of its
land is an index of its civilization. For 150 years America has maintained a reasonably balanced relation between population and land by
'going west' and homesteading new farms. Unfortunately, alarming
acreages have been 'mined' of their fertility and in other ways exploited
and wasted. Losses in productive capacity, largely through mismanagement,
have tended to counteract the wonderful gains made by scientific research.

"Conditions now approach a national emergency. Not desiring conquest
or colonization, America is faced with a serious problem - the handling
of her soil resources for the benefit of both our present and future
generations. This must include the prevention of abuses and exploitation, as well as unwise settlement which frequently involves unwarranted
costs for local government. Factors contributing to soil fertility, land
conservation, and wise farm practices need to be recognized and encouraged
as a matter of service to our national welfare.

"Temporary surpluses of farm products offer no justifiable excuse for
continued mining of soil fertility nor permitting continued wastage of land
through erosion. Fortunately, the public mind is more responsive to a
constructive land use program than heretofore. This makes possible a forward movement to bridge the gap between the laboratory of available facts
and current farm practice." - Introduction

Local Government Reorganization -- New York

New York (State) Commission for the revision of the tax laws. Reorganization
of local government in New York State. Sixth report... submitted February
6, 1935. 695pp. Albany, J. B. Lyon company, printers, 1935.
284.5 N483R 6th

At head of title: Legislative document (1935) no. 63.

"For many years the most crying governmental need in the state of New
York has been for the reorganization of our local governmental machinery
to the end of rendering greater service at less cost...

"Anything fundamental in the way of reorganization of local government
is, of course, unconstitutional at the present time and the Legislature
is helpless in the face of a Constitution which changing conditions have
rendered obsolete. However, if the recommendations of the Commission
for amendment of the state Constitution are carried out, the responsibility
for the condition of local government will be strictly up to the Legislature since it will have the authority to remedy this condition, or at
least to place a remedy at the disposal of the local electorate. In the
accompanying report, this Commission presents, in addition to its description of our present system and its findings in connection therewith,
definite recommendations for constitutional revision and legislation to
carry out an immediate and a long term program of improvement in local
government."

Jerome, Harry. Mechanization in industry. 484pp. New York, National
bureau of economic research, 1934. (National bureau of economic research, inc. Publications no. 27) 380.12 J48
   Bibliography, pp. 463-466.
   Agriculture, pp. 121-130.
   This volume opens with a ten page introduction of great interest by
Dr. Frederick C. Mills. In this, attention is called to Dr. Jerome's
careful technique and the great value of the resulting work. A few
extracts from this introduction are given below:
   "We must note the distinction drawn by Dr. Jerome between 'productivity-
increasing' changes (those which increase the units of output per hour
of labor) and 'labor-displacing' changes (those which reduce the number
of workers required). The two concepts are closely related, of course,
but the distinction refines our tools of analysis in the study of
technological improvement. We do not stop here, however. A given change
in technique may affect the productivity of operating labor (that required directly in a particular process), of auxiliary labor (plant
labor necessitated by the use of a machine, but not engaged directly in
its operation), of embodied labor (labor applied to the production of
the machine itself, or to the production of power oil, or some other
commodity used in its operation), or of indirectly required labor (that
is, all additional labor required, as for transportation, advertising
or merchandising, in putting the given commodity in the hands of the
final consumer ready for use). Furthermore, with reference to labor
displacement, Dr. Jerome insists that we take account of labor requirements in the specific operations directly affected, in the occupation in
question, in the plant, in the industry, and in the economic system as
a whole...
   "But the economic and social consequences of technical innovations
do not depend on the speed of mechanization alone. It is probable that
in post-war years certain other conditions contributed to accentuate the
problems arising out of the widening scope of machine technology. In appraising these conditions we shall do well to recognize the distinction
Dr. Jerome has drawn between changes that increase output and changes
that displace labor. This distinction is highly useful in tracing the incidence of mechanization and in distinguishing different stages of industrial development.
   "One of the major factors determining the economic effects of a given
technical change is the degree of elasticity of demand for the products
of the process affected. With highly elastic demand lower prices stimulate new buying. Under these conditions mechanical improvements leading
to lower per-unit costs and lower selling prices will make possible the
marketing of a much larger volume. Output will be increased, and the
net effect of the innovation may well be a substantial rise in the amount
of labor employed. The growth of the automobile industry is a concrete
manifestation of a series of such improvements in the making of a commodit
for which the demand is elastic. Improvements in industries producing
commodities of inelastic demand, on the other hand, may be expected to
lead to actual displacement of labor or, under certain conditions, to an
uneconomic expansion of output. For such commodities may not be disposed
of in much larger quantities, in a given market, even though costs and
prices are reduced materially by technical changes...

"With the widening, in recent decades, of the area within which mechanical improvements were being applied, it is probable that the proportion of technical changes affecting commodities of inelastic demand was greater than in earlier periods of mechanization. Retail coal handling, street cleaning, train operation, stevedoring provide examples of occupations the products or services of which are not marked by high elasticity of demand. But the outstanding example of such a shift is furnished by agriculture. The mechanization process in this important field lagged for years, and still lags, in comparison with the changes machine technique has brought in manufacturing industries. But recent years have seen a substantial advance in the use of mechanical methods and new sources of power in farming. Tractors, combine harvesters, potato-digging machines, milking machines, the application of gas engines and electric motors to agricultural operations - these are but examples of a process which has been going forward at accelerated speed in the last decade and a half. Dr. Jerome cites figures compiled by the United States Bureau of Labor Statistics indicating that technical improvements in agricultural production were sufficient to have displaced 2,530,000 workers between 1919 and 1927, had volume of output been unchanged. Actually, only some 800,000 workers were displaced, because these improvements, in the main, were used to increase output rather than to reduce the number of workers employed.

"Normally, increased efficiency in the production of goods of inelastic demand would tend to displace labor, rather than to increase output. The great technical advance in agricultural production during the decade in question did not have this result. One reason for this is that agricultural producers are, traditionally, tied to the soil. They do not react to innovation as would a market-conscious manufacturer, with a relatively mobile labor supply at his disposal. The effects of mechanization in this field, therefore, have been quite different from the effects experienced in other industrial areas, at earlier periods. A glutted market, with prices abnormally low even when account is taken of lowered costs of production, has resulted.

"In part, however, mechanization in agricultural industries displaced labor during this period, and probably contributed to the volume of unemployment which characterized the post-War years. Mechanization in other economic areas marked by inelastic demand for commodities produced tended also to displace labor, rather than to increase production, and so to widen the margin of unemployment which has always been a feature of an industrial economy. It is true that the purchasing power released when consumers are able to buy certain commodities at lower prices may be expected, ultimately, to find an outlet in increased demand for other commodities, and so to lead to the absorption elsewhere of the displaced labor. But this may be a very slow process, mitigating but slightly the immediate evils of labor displacement. Some portion of the increased unemployment which characterized the post-War years in the United States may be attributed to the mechanization of industries producing commodities of inelastic demand.

"But other factors, as well, contributed to this widening margin of unemployed men. Among these we must include the pricing policies followed in those industries in which rapid technical improvement occurred in the post-War years. For whether a given technical advance shall be 'labor-displacing' or 'productivity-increasing', in Dr. Jerome's terms,

depends not alone upon the relative elasticity of demand for the commodities effected. With demand elastic the given innovation may still dis-
·lace labor, rather than increase output, if the reduction of costs is
not passed on in the form of correspondingly lowered prices to buyers...

"The process of mechanization described in the following pages is thus
not merely a technical affair, of interest only to production engineers
and factory managers. It needs no argument to establish its relevance to
the major problems of the day, and its bearing on the central processes
of contemporary economic life. When exaggeration and fantasy about the
machine are duly discounted it remains, it is safe to say, the most compelling factor in the changing culture of modern man. It is the story of
the machine, in its recent and mature development, which Dr. Jerome tells
in the pages of this book."

National industrial conference board. Machinery, employment and purchasing
power. 103pp. New York city, National industrial conference board,
inc. [1935] 280.13 N213M
    The foreword reads in part as follows:
    "The available evidence regarding the relation of mechanization to
employment and production shows clearly that during the period of its
most rapid and extensive application there has been no increase in the
proportion of unemployed among the working population, except in periods
of business depression, and that the proportion of the working population
to the whole population has actually grown...

    "While the mechanization of industry has not diminished the need for
human effort and the opportunities for work, it has been accompanied by
great shifts in the occupations of men, women, and children. Such
changes are the price of progress, and willingness to make them is a
responsibility of both workers and employers under an enterprise organization of economic life. They imply adaptation of both capital and
labor to new needs; they entail dissipation of investments, relocation
of industries, increased mobility of enterprise and employment, re-educa-
tion and retraining of labor. Refusal or incapacity to make these in-
cessant adjustments required by progress is the source of most of the
problems and difficulties that the machine superficially appears to have
created. They are not problems of the machine, but problems of men, and
they can best be met, as they have been met, not by government, but by
the ingenuity, industry, enterprise, cooperative effort, and qualities of
character of the men who have made and used the machine so successfully.
    "It is false to the facts and insincere to the spirit of progress to
look back to the prosperity and employment of 1929 - itself an impressive
accomplishment of the machine - as something that cannot be attained or
exceeded by the same means, and to assume that the same powerful agency of
progress dooms a fifth of our working population to unemployment in private
enterprise and support by government in the future. With an increasingly
severe shortage of skilled labor already evident in the early stages of
recovery from business depression, while ten millions of our working population are unemployed, and about twenty millions of our whole population
depending upon government support, wise and sincere statesmen in both industry and public office will rather look forward to the future when,
with a stationary or declining population, we shall have to consider how
the mechanization of industry and trade may be speeded, workers trained
and adapted to new occupations and greater productiveness, and our people

- 26 -

inspired and encouraged to new enterprise in order that the rise in the standard of life may be sustained.

"This study presents the essential available facts regarding the relation of machinery to unemployment, employment, production, and purchasing power of the American working population."

National Country Life Conference

National country life conference. National planning and rural life. Proceedings of the seventeenth American country life conference, Washington, D. C., November 16-19, 1934. 156pp. New York, The University of Chicago press for the American country life association [1935] 281.2 N213 17th, 1934.

Contents: Foreword, by Benson Y. Landis, p. 3; Presidential address, by Nat T. Frame, p. 7; When fortune favored the farmer, by C. J. Galpin, p. 24; Reconstructing our rural policy, by Carl C. Taylor; p. 33; Planning agriculture in relation to industry, by M. L. Wilson, p. 39; The agricultural adjustment program, by John R. Hutcheson, p. 46; Agricultural adjustment and country life, by H. R. Tolley, p. 65; Developments in state planning, by A. R. Mann, p. 72; Educational and cultural changes, by Edmund de S. Brunner, p. 85; International aspects of national planning, by Wallace McClure, p. 96; Population and occupational shifts, by O. E. Baker, p. 108; Is there an American youth movement? by E. L. Kirkpatrick, p. 132; Youth and national planning - Summary of student discussions, p. 143; and Annual report of the executive secretary, By Benson Y. Landis, p. 153.

New Deal

Fairchild, F. R., Furniss, E.S., Buck, N.S., and Whelden, C.H., Jr. A description of the "new deal". Rev. ed. 159pp. New York, The Macmillan company, 1935. 280.12 F162 1935.

"There is observable a present tendency to view the extraordinary events of the last decade as in some way casting suspicion upon the generally accepted principles of economics, with the inference that these principles must now be thrown in the discard and replaced by a 'new economics.' The glorious years of 1922-1929 were regarded by not a few persons as having ushered in a 'new era,' with poverty abolished and the human race lifted to a level of prosperity such as the mind of man had not before conceived. Economic science, casting doubts upon the validity of this roseate dream, was to be cast aside in favor of the 'new economics' of perpetual prosperity. More recently the sad experiences of adversity have brought forth another 'new economics,' which would among other things rationalize the American government's program generally known as the 'New Deal.' It is our belief that a less superficial view would disclose the prevailing body of economic principles as generally competent to explain the economic events of recent years, whether of prosperity or of depression. We are furthermore of the opinion that only in the light of such fundamental economic principles may there be any true analysis and judgment of the 'New Deal.' What is needed is not a new body of principles, but the application of established principles to recent experience and propaganda. The present book essays to present a description and explanation of the principal features of the 'New Deal'

gram... in the experience of another year has induced us to undertake
somewhat more of criticism and judgment than was essayed in the first
edition. It still remains the main purpose of this book to present, not
the verdict, but rather certain facts which will facilitate criticism and
judgment by application of economic principles and the lessons of past
experience." - The Authors in Preface.
Chapter headings follow: Depression and Government Aid Before the
"New Deal". The Banking System; Money, Credit, and the Price Level;
Control of Prices Through the Control of Supply, Public Control of Business Problems of Labor; and The Government Finances.

Planning

American planning and civic annual, a record of recent civic advance including the Proceedings of the Conference on City, regional, state and national planning, held at Cincinnati, Ohio, May 20-22, 1935, and addresses
selected from the National conference on state parks, held at Skyland,
Va., June 18-21, 1935. Edited by Harlean James. 356pp. Washington, D.C.,
American planning and civic association, 1935. 280.9 Am322
Partial contents: Why we need a national planning board, by Harold
L. Ickes, p. 3; National planning in practice, by Charles E. Merriam,
p. 6; Land-use planning, by Hugh R. Pomeroy, p. 10; The place of forestry
in national planning, by F. A. Silcox, p. 42; The forests as playgrounds,
by L. F. Kneipp; p. 45; Land planning and farm adjustment, by Henry A.
Wallace, p. 48; Agriculture's democratic program planning, by H. R.
Tolley, p. 51; Some problems of land policy, by L. C. Gray, p. 55; The
land development program, by Maurice M. Kelso, p. 59; Land settlement -
A permanent policy, by John B. Bennett, p. 61; National significance of
recent trends in farm population, by R. G. Tugwell, p. 65; How population distribution affects agricultural planning, by O. E. Baker, p. 67;
Getting a million families off relief, by J. Phil Campbell, p. 71;
Soil-erosion, by H. H. Bennett, p. 74; Elements in rural land planning,
by Lynn R. Edminster, F. F. Elliott and O. V. Wells, Mordecai Ezekiel,
James G. Maddox, Donald Jackson, C. W. Warburton, p. 76; The rural
housing survey, by Louise Stanley, p. 100; Buildings and utilities for
better farm living, by S. H. McCrory, p. 104; Rural zoning, by C. I.
Hendrickson, p. 204; Population and industrial trends, by L. Segoe and
Robert Whitten, p. 213; Faulty urban land policies, by Philip H. Cornick,
Tracy B. Augur, and Herbert U. Nelson, p. 222; The urban and rural land-
use survey, by A. R. Mann, p. 241; Geography and its function in regional
planning, by G. Donald Hudson, p. 249; Making of the plan, by Russell Van
West Black, p. 254; and Federal Assistance to local planning projects,
by Robert H. Randall, p. 308.

Planning - Regional

Vance, R. B. Regional reconstruction: a way out for the South. Issued in
cooperation with the Institute for research in social science, University
of North Carolina. 31pp. New York, Foreign policy association; Chapel
Hill, University of North Carolina press, 1935. 281.12 V27
"In our own day we have seen social planning by degrees invade the
sanctuary once hallowed by the spirit of social resignation. Social

resignation, whether it be belief in fate, providence, inevitable progress. or laissez faire economics is, I take it, society's method of sitting still and letting something happen to it. Science and the technical arts in the hands of man have pioneered in making things happen rather than waiting for them to happen. No less encouraging in our day has been the rise of national-regional planning and the new regionalism to replace the old fire-eating sectionalism inherent in state's rights.

"Unfortunately we have accepted it as axiomatic that nation cannot plan with nation. Accordingly the first steps toward any program of national planning seem to be for the nation to attempt to restrict its activities to the area it can command. This means economic nationalism; and economic nationalism, as Peter Molyneaux points out, falls with striking incidence on the South. Slightly less than ten per cent of the goods produced in the United States have been uniformly sold abroad. It may be debatable, therefore, as to whether economic nationalism means disaster for our national economy. But the South has regularly sold over 50 per cent of her cotton and over 25 per cent of her tobacco to foreign customers. Here it is evident that economic nationalism if long persisted in, means drastic changes in the Cotton Belt.

"Unjustified as Howard W. Odum shows it to be, this identification of national regional planning with economic nationalism is apt to prove doubly unfortunate for the South. By no means should the confusion of terms be allowed to block the South's consideration of a planned reconstruction of its own economy. Certainly, if either social or regional planning be regarded as a form of economic rehabilitation, it can easily be shown that the South as much as any region stands in need of such a program. Studies of trends show that in practically every per capita count of wealth, welfare, and economic competence the southern states stand at the bottom of the nation's list. The South's deficiencies antedate the present crisis; of most, it can be said, that the depression has but served to reveal them in a more glaring light. After an attempt to characterize the basic regional economy of the South, let us consider the present and probable future trends deriving from the agricultural crisis, the AAA, Federal Relief and Rural Rehabilitation, the breakdown of the tenancy system, and the South's answer to economic nationalism." - Introduction.

Poultry Farming - England

Harper Adams agricultural college, Newport, Eng. Commercial egg farming; an economic study of representative enterprises in the north and west, 1931-1934. Harper Adams agricultural college, Newport [and] Armstrong college, Newcastle-on-Tyne. 44pp. Shrewsbury, Printed by Wilding & son, ltd. [1935?] 281.347 H23
    On cover: Published by the Advisory agricultural economics branches of Armstrong College and Harper Adams Agricultural College.
    "Immediately before the Great War there were less than thirty millions of fowls on agricultural holdings in England and Wales. During the War the numbers fell. By 1924, however, the pre-war position had been fully recovered, and by 1933, only a decade later, the numbers of farm poultry had actually doubled. This remarkable expansion, in the face of a persistently adverse trend of selling prices, and during a period when the field for the investment of capital in productive enterprises was steadily

narrowing. is an outstanding feature of post-war developments in British Agriculture. Unlike other farming enterprises, the poultry industry has grown without the assistance of tariffs, quotas, subsidies or marketing schemes. and its success represents a notable contribution to the general problem of agricultural relief which has commanded so much attention in national affairs." - Introduction.

Price Spreads

Canada. Parliament. House of commons. Royal commission on price spreads. Report of the Royal commission on price spreads. 506pp. Ottawa, J. O. Patenaude, printer to the King's Most Excellent Majesty, 1935. 284.3 C164R

The Royal Commission on Price Spreads was "appointed to inquire into, and investigate the causes of the large spread between the prices received for commodities by the producer thereof, and the price paid by the consumers therefore; and the system of distribution in Canada of farm and other natural products, as well as manufactured products."

The investigation included an examination of conditions in the following industries and trades: Tobacco, meat packing, agricultural implement. canning of fruits and vegetables, rubber footwear and tires, fertilizer, textile manufacturing, milling and baking, and furniture manufacturing.

The scope of the report is described in the introductory chapter as follows.

"Owing to the variety of the subjects investigated and the interests concerned - producer,-manufacturer, distributor, wage-earner, and consumer - it was not easy to compile a report which would be of reasonable length and possess both unity and clarity. At first sight, indeed, it appeared that the separate and distinct problems which emerged in the evidence called for separate treatment and almost separate reports. On closer study, however, it became clear that many of the grievances complained of, and the problems disclosed, were manifestations of one fundamental and far-reaching social change, the concentration of economic power. This idea, therefore, runs through the whole of our report and gives it a certain unity which it might not otherwise possess.

"In the immediately following chapter, we discuss the economic background in an attempt to explain the significance of this concentration, with special reference to the disappearance of what the economists call "simple" competition. This procedure is not only advisable in view of the importance of the subject, but it is also necessary in fairness to the individuals concerned; for it will appear that often the pressure of economic forces, rather than conscious purpose, is the principal cause of the unethical business practices disclosed.

"We follow the discussion of the economic background and the concentration of economic power with an examination of various manifestations of that concentration which came before us in evidence.

"In Chapter III, we refer to the concentration of corporate wealth as a factor in the conditions which bred many of the grievances complained of. In addition to its contribution to the general problem, this chapter deals with corporate practices and abuses during recent years and suggests certain remedies for them.

"In Chapter IV, we discuss the industries investigated, with particular reference to the growth of large productive units and the power of these

units to influence the condition of the wage-earner and the primary
producer.

"Chapter V follows naturally with a discussion of labour and wage
conditions, while Chapter VI deals with the plight of the primary producer.

"In Chapter VII, we discuss the development and effect of concentration
in retail distribution. The growth of the large scale distributor is
described, and particular reference is made to the effects of mass buying.

"Chapter VIII is devoted to the consumer and we submit certain recommendations for his protection.

"Chapter IX deals with the fundamentally important question of state
intervention in business, with particular reference to the nature, methods,
and complexities of such intervention. We outline briefly in this chapter
recent experience with government regulation in various countries, including our own, and conclude with proposals of a general character, which we
hope will be of assistance in solving some, at least, of the problems
which were submitted to us."

The supplementary material includes: Annex VII Summary of legislation of
principal industrial nations relating to trade combinations; Annex VIII
Combines Investigation Act; Annex IX Memorandum on the Use of Taxation
as a Method of Regulation, by H. H. Stevens.

Prices - History

Hamilton, E. J. American treasure and the price revolution in Spain, 1501-
1650. 428pp. Cambridge, Mass., Harvard university press, 1934. (Half-
title: Harvard economic studies. v. XLIII) 284.3 H18
    Bibliography, pp. [xvii]-xxxv.
    The scope of this study is briefly described in the introduction as
follows:

"The sole purpose of the present study, when originally undertaken,
was to ascertain the precise quantities of American gold and silver
imported into Europe through Spain from 1503 to 1660 and to examine the
effects of the treasure upon Spanish prices, wages, and economic welfare.
During the years required to assemble the raw material, however, other
economic questions have forged to the front, and quantitative data,
which, incorporated in monographs, may provide partial answers, have
been sought. It is obvious that no problem simple enough to admit of
definitive solution solely through statistical compilations, however
extensive, could possibly challenge the sustained attention of scholars;
but I believe that the exact measurements rendered possible by satisfactory monetary, price, and wage statistics can illuminate many complex
social phenomena and enhance the significance of other ancillary information. No one can foresee all the scientific ends which the numerical data are likely to serve, and limitations of space preclude an exhaustive list of obvious possibilities." - Introduction.

Public Finance

King, C. L. Public finance. 602pp. New York, The Macmillan company, 1935.
284 K582
    Bibliography at end of each chapter except the last.
    The author writes in the preface:

"The purpose of this book is to bring up to date the recent shifts in public expenditures, in public income, and in public debts. It has been written during the months of increase in public expenditures and in public borrowing of the early years of the Roosevelt Administration. Such changes in public policy have perforce been appraised on their merits. Facts pertaining to these changes are fully presented, for these have been days of great importance to all students of public finance."

It includes chapters on the shifting and incidence of taxation, the property tax, taxation of real estate, improvements, and natural resources; personal income taxes, gasoline and motor vehicle taxes, sales taxes, and other taxes; also on the tariff history of the United States and coordinating federal, state, and local finances.

Public Works as a Stabilizing Influence

Gayer, A. D. Public works in prosperity and depression; prepared for the National planning board, Federal emergency administration of public works. 460pp. New York, National bureau of economic research, 1935. (Half-title: Publications of the National bureau of economic research, inc. no.29) 290 G252

Among the chapters which make up this volume are the following: Planned public works as an agency of economic stabilization: The development of the idea; Public works in the United States, 1919-1934: Their scope, volume, distribution and fluctuation; Total public and private construction in the United States, 1923-1933; Detailed comparisons of different estimates; Federal construction expenditures; The Federal Emergency Program under the PWA; Construction expenditures of state governments; Roadbuilding; Financing public works in prosperity and depression; The National government; The financing of public works; Local governments; The development of a planned public works policy in the light of recent experience; Controlled public works as a stabilizing factor; Some basic problems of theory; Appendix.

U. S. Federal emergency administration of public works. National planning board. Economics of planning public works, by John Maurice Clark. 194pp. Washington, U. S. Govt. print. off., 1935. 173.2 P96E

A study made for the National Planning Board of the Federal Emergency Administration of Public Works.

Contains a short section on land utilization.

Relief - Rural

Beck, P. G., and Forster, M. C. Six rural problem areas. Relief - resources - rehabilitation. An analysis of the human and material resources in six rural areas with high relief rates. 167pp. Washington, D. C., 1935. (U. S. Federal emergency relief administration. Division of research, statistics and finance. Research section. Research monograph 1) 173.2 F27Rm no.1

Bibliography, pp. 165-167.

The regions covered in this report are The Appalachian-Ozark Area, The Lake States Cut-Over Area, The Spring Wheat Area, The Winter Wheat Area, The Western Cotton Area, and The Eastern Cotton Area. For each

of these areas the report considers description of the area, the relief situation, the families receiving relief, the socio-economic resources of these families, and plans and prospects for their rehabilitation.

Relief - Rural - Tennessee

Allred, C. E. Some problems of rural relief in Tennessee. A preliminary
report, by Charles E. Allred...M. Taylor Matthews...Benjamin H.
Luebke. 17pp. mimeogr. [Washington, D.C.] Oct. 1935. (U. S. Federal
Emergency Relief Administration. Report no. 1) 173.2 R27Rep. no.1
Issued in cooperation with Tennessee Emergency Relief Administra-
tion, Tennessee Agricultural Experiment Station.
Based on a survey of seven counties - Cocke, Grainger, Bledsoe,
Overton, Grundy, Williamson and Henderson.

Resettlement Administration

U. S. Resettlement administration. The resettlement administration. 28pp.
Washington, D. C. [U.S. Govt. print. off.] 1935. (U. S. Resettlement
administration. Publication no. 1) 195 P96
The Foreword reads as follows:
"This pamphlet is designed to give a general picture of the problems
with which the Resettlement Administration is called upon to deal, and
to indicate the nature of the program by which it will endeavor to meet
them.
"The fundamental problem is the readjustment of people to the land
resources of the Nation. Land must be adapted to its best economic
use. Our pioneering policies of exploitation and careless use of the
land are no longer possible or feasible and can no longer be continued.
"Millions of American citizens in rural areas require assistance to
enable them to become self-sustaining and to enjoy a decent American
standard of living.
"These problems have been developing over a good many years. It will
take time and patience and the cooperative efforts of the whole country
to solve them."

Rural Housing - Italy

Confederazione fascista dei lavoratori dell' agricoltura. Per le case rurali
(Programma di azione - indagine statistica - progetti di fabbricati
rurali) 177pp. [Rome, Stabilimento tipografico "Arte della stampa"]
1934. 296.2 C76
"After an introduction dealing with the activities of the Fascist Confederation of Agricultural Workers in connection with the building of
houses in rural areas, this report describes the results of the general
enquiry carried out in Italy by the Confederation through its provincial
organisations. This enquiry, which supplements a similar enquiry made
by the Central Statistical Institute, provides much valuable data for
the execution of the Government scheme outlined at the second five-yearly
Assembly of the Fascist regime. The work ends with a number of plans
of model rural dwellings to be built in different agricultural districts
of Italy, varying in design according to the size of the farms." - International Labour Review, v. 31, no. 2, p. 298. Feb. 1935.

American country life association. Student section. A satisfactory life
for rural young people. [Summary of discussion sessions, national conference of the Student section, A.C.L.A., at Columbus, Ohio, September
19-22. 1935] 9pp., mimeogr. [Madison, Wis., 1935] 281.2 Am342S
    "Prepared by E. L. Kirkpatrick and Agnes M. Boynton" - leaf 9.
    The subjects discussed are: Standards of living, Vocations and em-
ployment, spare-time activities, informal or out-of-school education,
community organizations and relations, real values in country life.

Science Advisory Board

Science advisory board. Second report of the Science advisory board, September
1, 1934 to August 31, 1935. 494pp. Washington, D. C., 1935.
330.9 Sci2 1934/35
    Contains a section devoted to the U. S. Dept. of Agriculture and
among the appendices may be found the following: Report to the Secretary
of Agriculture of the Advisory Committee on the Weather Bureau; Memoranda
and report of the committee on the Bureau of Chemistry and Soils [which
includes] Soil erosion in its relation to other soil research and extension projects, by J. G. Lipman; The Administration of Research and
Extension Activities related to soil erosion, by J. G. Lipman;
Report on the relationship of the Bureau of Chemistry and Soils to the
other bureaus of the Department of Agriculture; Report of the committee
on mapping services of the federal government; Report on land-grant
colleges, by Wm. Charles White; Research problems in natural science
bearing on national land planning, by W. L. G. Joerg; Summary of recent
reports on natural resources, by W. L. G. Joerg; The land of your possession, by Isaiah Bowman.

Social Changes

Social changes during depression and recovery (social changes in 1934) Ed. by
William F. Ogburn. pp. 711-828. Chicago, Ill., University of Chicago
press [1935] 252 Sol
    Reprinted from the American Journal of Sociology, vol. XL, no. 6,
May 1935.
    Contents: Movements of population, by Warren S. Thompson; The con-
ditions of rural life, by T. B. Manny; Social adjustments in cities, by
Niles Carpenter; Incidence upon the negroes, by Charles S. Johnson;
The welfare of children, by Katharine F. Lenroot; The relief situation,
by T. C. McCormick and Clark Tibbitts; Economic and political radicalism,
by Maynard C. Krueger; Adaptations of family life, by Ernest R. Groves;
The church and religious activity, by Benson Y. Landis; Community or-
ganization, by Jesse Frederick Steiner; The amount and nature of crime,
by George B. Vold; Causal and selective factors in sickness, by G. St. J.
Perrott, and Edgar Sydenstricker; How education is faring, by Fred J.
Kelly; and Indexes of social trends and their fluctuations, by William
F. Ogburn.

State Grants-in-Aid

Hinckley, R. J. State grants-in-aid. 221pp. Albany, J. B. Lyon company, printers, 1935. (New York (State) State tax commission. Special report no. 9) 284.5 N482 no. 5
Bibliography, pp. 203-215.
The scope of this report is defined by the author as follows:
"This study involves an examination of the bases of distribution of state grants-in-aid and an appraisal of the subvention system in relation to the other methods of rendering financial assistance to local governments. It necessitates consideration of the growing participation of state governments in local affairs - the tendency toward centralization - and the collateral problem of redistribution of functions between state and local governments. The relation of the state to local communities can be determined only by reference to underlying governmental philosophy. Quantitative indexes and statistical studies may serve in determination of costs and needs for particular services and assist in appraisal of the actual operation of subvention systems, but cannot solve the perplexing problem of the extent to which state support should go. The chief intention of this report is to visualize some balance between centralization and local autonomy, and, amid the welter of governmental and financial problems presented, to view the subvention system as a whole, rather than as a mass of separate and unrelated grants-in-aid. Considerable research has been done, particularly in education, with respect to refinements in the measurement of local needs and the bases for distribution of specific grants. This study is aimed at the broad problem of eliminating wastes and leaks in the subvention system and preparing it for future loads. Such an aim brings up the inevitable question of reorganization of local governmental units in such a manner that functions and services for which state aid is granted may be performed as efficiently and as economically as possible." -Preface.

Statistical Analysis

Richardson, C. H. An introduction to statistical analysis. Enlarged edition. 312pp. New York, Harcourt, Brace and company [1935] 251 R39
The enlarged edition contains a chapter on index numbers which did not appear in the first edition. "The opportunity has been taken to recast certain paragraphs, and such errors as were noted have been corrected."

Taxation - Minnesota

Minnesota institute of governmental research. The federal social security act and what it means to Minnesota. 14pp. St. Paul, Minn. [1935] (State governmental research bulletin no. 6, Oct. 1935) 280.9 M664 no.6
"Passage by Congress of the Federal Social Security Act which was signed by the President on August 14, 1935, requires of the legislative bodies of all the states, including Minnesota, some of the most far-reaching governmental decisions in a generation.
"The Social Security Act with its comprehensive proposals to attack the problems of unemployment, old age, poverty, infirmity, and social welfare,

- 35 -

should be thoroughly understood in all its implications and especially
its financial aspects by legislators and public alike.

"The Minnesota Institute, acting in the capacity of research staff for
the Interim Tax Commission of Investigation and Inquiry of the Minnesota
legislature, was requested by the Commission to analyze the act and prepare preliminary estimates of the cost to Minnesota. Inasmuch as this is a
public matter in which there is widespread interest and concerning which
many questions will be asked in coming weeks, the Institute has seen fit
to present this brief summary."

Minnesota institute of governmental research. The property tax problem and
the 1935 legislative session. 39pp. St. Paul, Minn. [1935] (State
governmental research bulletin no. 5, July 1935) 280.9 M664 no.5

"The property tax problem of Minnesota was left unsettled by failure
of any major tax proposals to become law at the recent session of the
Legislature. As a result, the tax problem continues to be a live issue
in Minnesota and will so continue until the tax base has been broadened
to give material relief to the property owner...

"In order to place the tax discussion on a factual basis, this report
has been prepared, covering a brief outline of the legislative history
of the various tax proposals during the recent session of the Legislature; and including charts and graphs, comparing taxes of Minnesota and
other states; as well as an analysis of the provisions and estimates of
revenue of all major tax proposals submitted to the Legislature. The
Institute, as a research organization, has not at any time taken, and is
not taking, a position for or against any of the various tax proposals
discussed herein."

Trade - Foreign - United States

Peek, G. N. The foreign trade problem of the United States. Address... before National industrial conference board, New York city, October 24,
1935. 15pp. [New York? 1935] 286 P34

Mr. Peek traces "the trend and results of our commercial and financial
activities" and urges that a foreign trade board be established.

U. S. Bureau of foreign and domestic commerce. Trade promotion series no.
162. Foreign trade of the United States calendar year 1934, by Grace
A. Witherow. 182pp. Washington, U. S. Govt. print. off., 1935.
157.54 T67 no.162

"This is the thirteenth annual bulletin on United States foreign
trade issued by this Bureau. It is a statistical and analytical summary
for the calendar year 1934 and is intended as a convenient source of information on United States foreign trade for business men, economists,
statisticians, and students. The text deals chiefly with the changes in
trade during 1934 compared with the preceding year, as well as outstanding
trends relative to other recent years. Statistical data recorded in table
and charts cover a number of years.

"The Summary of United States Trade with the World, 1934, issued by this
Bureau in March of this year, showed preliminary data for 1934. This bulletin gives the final figures on the total trade of the United States with
the world for the year 1934 and indicates also principal commodities in th

annual trade of the United States with leading foreign countries. Prior to
the tenth issue of this bulletin the section on principal commodities in
the annual trade with leading foreign countries was included in volume I
of the Commerce Yearbook. Statistics of United States foreign trade in
greater detail than those shown in this report are available in the Monthly
Summary of Foreign Commerce of the United States and the annual issues of
the Foreign Commerce and Navigation of the United States, both issued by
this Bureau.

"The bulletin is arranged in three main sections. The first part covers
total United States exports to and imports from the world; the second part
shows the distribution of exports and imports by economic classes and commodities, while the third part presents the geographic distribution. Supplementary parts of the first section show the relation of exports to domestic production of movable goods, the share of the United States in total
world trade, and the total trade of continental United States with the world,
together with an explanation of the geographic basis of United States foreign trade statistics.

"The reader's attention is directed particularly to the change in the
basis of the commodity statistics from 'General Imports' in 1933 to 'Imports
for Consumption' in 1934. General imports cover merchandise entering into
consumption channels immediately upon arrival in the United States, plus en-
tries into bonded warehouses, while imports for consumption cover merchandise
entering consumption channels immediately upon arrival, plus withdrawals
from bonded warehouses. The change in basis is indicated in headnotes on
the various tables." - Foreword.

Trade - World

League of nations. Economic intelligence service. Review of world trade, 1934.
89pp. Geneva, League of nations, 1935. (Series of League of nations
Publications II. Economic and financial. 1935, II. A.8) 280.9 L47P 1935
II. A.8

"This Review of World Trade contains a general synopsis of world trade
during the year 1934 and a comparison of the figures for that year with
these for the immediately preceding years. Somewhat special attention has
been paid on this occasion to the changes in the direction of trade and to
the effect of the recent tendency of commercial policy to develop reciprocal
trade at the expense of multilateral transactions." - Preface.

Trade Agreements

Asociacion de almacenistas y cosecheros de tabaco de Cuba. El tasajo extranjero
aliado del nacional. Estudio economico sobre las ventajas que ofrece el
proyecto de concertacion de un tratado de comercio entre Cuba y la Republica Oriental del Uruguay. (Presentado a S.E.el sr. secretario de
estado el 21 de febrero de 1935.) 90pp. Habana, Cultural, s.a. [1935]
286 As5

Arguments are presented in favor of a commercial treaty between Cuba
and Uruguay chiefly for the exchange of sugar and tobacco for hung beef.

A number of tables and graphs show mostly production, consumption,
and export and import of livestock and livestock products.

3. Brit. Treaties etc., 1914- (Gr. Brit. V)   Agreement between the government
of the United Kingdom and the Polish government in regard to trade and
commerce <with protocol and notes> London, February 27, 1935 <Ratifica-
tions exchanged at Warsaw, July 24, 1935> 81pp. London, H. M. Stationery
off., 1935.   ([Parliament. Papers by command] Cmd. 4984)   286 G797 Ap
July 24, 1935.
        At head of title: Poland. Treaty series no. 33 (1935)
        English and Polish.

Types of Farming

Whittlesey, D. S.   Types of agricultural occupance of the land. 144pp.,
mimeogr. Cambridge, Mass , Harvard University, 1935.   281 W61
        Discusses livestock ranching, migratory cropping, collecting for
export from the low latitude forests, sedentary non-plow agriculture,
plantation agriculture, intensive subsistence cropping, Mediterranean
agriculture, commercial grain farming, commercial livestock and crop
farming, subsistence crop and livestock farming, commercial dairy farming.

U. S. S. R.

Conolly, Violet.   Soviet trade from the Pacific to the Levant, with an economic
study of the Soviet far eastern region.   238pp. London, Oxford University
press, H. Milford, 1935.   286 C769S
        "The continuation and conclusion of a study of Soviet economic relations
with Eastern countries published in 1933, which dealt with the subject in
so far as Turkey, Persia... are concerned." - p. [v] q.v. 286 C769
        Bibliography, pp. [228]-234.

Leningrad. Akademiia nauk. Institut po izucheniiu narodov. Trud i byt v
kolkhozakh... no.2.   133pp. Leningrad, 1931.   281.179 L54
        Work and life on collective farms.
        Added table of contents in French.

Nikulikhin, IA. P.   Bor'ba za rentabel'nost kolkhozov, pod obshchei redaktsiei
D. P. Davydova. 181pp. Moskva, 1934.   281.179 N58B
        The struggle to make the collective farms profitable.

Tarabukhin, N. M., comp. Garntsevyi sbor (instruktsiia i zakonodatel'stvo po
garntsevomu sboru) 59pp. Moskva, 1935.   284.5 T17
        The milling levy.

U. S. S. R.   Narodnyi komissariat zemledeliia. Sekretariat. O reorganizatsii
tsentral'nogo apparata Narkomzema SSSR, ego khozorganov i organisatsii
pri NKZ SSSR. 116pp. Moskva, 1934.   281.179 Un322
        Reorganization of the central "apparatus" of the People's Commissariat
of agriculture of the USSR.

Vsesoiuznyi s'ezd kolkhoznikov-udarnikov. 2d, Moscow, 1935.   Stenograficheskii
otchet. 302pp. [Moskva] 1935.   281.9 V963 2d
        Stenographic report of the second Congress of the "Shock" or better
farmers - "Udarniki", so-called, Moscow, 1935.

Wool

Dell'Amore, Giordano. La lana; caratteristiche di impresa, della produzione, del consumo e del commercio laniero. 404pp. · Milano, A. Giuffrè, 1934. (Università commerciale L. Bocconi. Istituto di ricerche tecnico-commerciali. Pubblicazioni serie I. no.7)   286.345 D38
    "Abbreviature usate nelle citazioni" pp.xiii-xxiii
    A study of the business of production and manufacture, consumption and marketing of wool, with a chapter on price fluctuations in space and time.

BIBLIOGRAPHIES

Farm tenancy in the United States, 1925-1935. A beginning of a bibliography. Comp. by Louise O. Bercaw and Helen C. Hennefrund, under the direction of Mary G. Lacy, Librarian, Bureau of agricultural economics. 86pp., mimeogr. Nov. 1935. (U. S. Dept. of agriculture. Bureau of agricultural economics. Agricultural economics bibliography no. 59)

Financing American cotton production and marketing in the United States. Comp. by Mildred C. Benton, under the direction of Emily L. Day, Library specialist in cotton marketing, Division of cotton marketing branch library. 45pp., mimeogr. Nov. 1935. (U. S. Dept. of agriculture. Bureau of agricultural economics. Agricultural economics bibliography no. 61)

International institute of agriculture. Library. Liste des periodiques recus couramment par la Bibliothèque de l'Institut international d'agriculture (situation au 1^{er}janvier 1935) Edition provisoire. 133pp., mimeogr. Rome, 1935. 241.9 In822 cop.2
    This is a preliminary list of the periodicals received currently in the library of the International Institute of Agriculture, Rome, Italy. It is arranged alphabetically by title under the names of 65 countries from which periodicals are received. The titles of the periodicals are given in the original language. Place of publication is given and frequency of issue.
    The list is followed by an alphabetical subject index which groups the periodicals according to the character of their contents.

A list of American economic histories, by Everett E. Edwards. 25pp., mimeogr. Nov. 1935. (U. S. Dept. of agriculture. Library, Bibliographical contributions no. 27)

Merrill, Harold. Some recent references (since 1928) on national and state planning in the United States. Comp. by Harold Merrill... James T. Rubey and William H. Heers. 24pp., mimeogr. Washington, D. C., Oct. 1935.   407 G295 no.5
    Also U. S. Geological Survey. Library. Bibliographical list no. 5. Issued by U. S. National Resources Committee.

Processing taxes under the Agricultural adjustment act. A short list of references comp. in the Library, Bureau of agricultural economics, U. S. Dept. of agriculture. 8pp. Sept. 13, 1935.

A selected list of references on the Farm credit administration. Comp.
by Robert Haven Willey of the Library staff under the direct supervision of Mirian C. Vance, librarian. Prepared in the Library of the
Farm credit administration. 56pp., mimeogr. Washington, D. C., Oct.
1935. 166.3 Se4

Selected references on the history of agriculture in the United States, by
Everett E. Edwards. 28pp., mimeogr. Nov. 1935. (U. S. Dept. of agriculture. Library. Bibliographical contributions no. 26)

SELECTED LIST OF RECENT REVIEWS

Compiled by M. I. Herb

American institute of banking. Farm credit administration. [c1934]
    Reviewed by Gabriel Lundy in Jour. Farm Econ. 17 (2): 395-396.
May 1935.

Bergsmark, D. R. Economic geography of Asia. 1935.
    Reviewed by Samuel van Valkenburg in Econ. Geogr. 11 (4): 432.
October 1935.

Black, J. D. The dairy industry and the AAA. 1935. (Half-title: The
Institute of economics of the Brookings institution, Publication no. 64)
    Reviewed in Hoard's Dairyman 80 (23): 559, 577. Dec. 10, 1935.

Burns, A. F. Production trends in the United States since 1870. 1934.
(Half-title: Publications of the National bureau of economic research,
inc., no. 23)
    Reviewed by Lucile Bagwell in Economica (n.s.) 2 (8): 489-491. November
1935.

Chase, Stuart. Government in business. 1935.
    Reviewed by Max Lerner in New York Herald Tribune Books, Sect. VII,
Sept. 22, 1935, p.3.
    Reviewed by Henry Hazlitt in the New York Times Book Rev., Sept. 22,
1935, pp. 3, 18.

Cotta, Freppel. Agricultural co-operation in fascist Italy, with full account
of the general organisation of co-operation, 1935.
    Reviewed by Asher Hobson in Jour. Farm Econ. 17 (3): 605-607.
August 1935.
    Reviewed by R. J. T. in Roy. Statis. Soc. Jour. (n.s.) 98 (2): 407-
408. 1935.

Edwards, E. E. Selected references on the history of English agriculture.
1935. (U. S. Dept. Agriculture, Library, Bibliographical contributions
No. 24)
    Reviewed by G. E. Fussell in Econ. Hist. Rev. 6 (1): 112, October 1935.

Foreign policy association, New York. Commission on Cuban Affairs. Report
of the commission on Cuban affairs. 1935.
    Reviewed by W. S. Robertson in Amer. Econ. Rev. 25 (3): 521, 522.
September 1935.

Great Britain. United Kingdom sugar industry inquiry committee. Report of the
    United Kingdom sugar inquiry committee, 1935.
        Reviewed by J. W. F. Rowe in Econ. Jour. 45 (179): 582-586. September
    1935.

International institute of agriculture, Bureau of economic and social studies.
    The agricultural situation in 1931-32 [and in 1932-33] 1933-34.
        Two publications.
        Reviewed by O. B. Jesness in Jour. Polit. Econ. 43 (3): 425-426.
    June 1935.

International labor office, Geneva. International comparisons of cost of
    living. A study of certain problems connected with the making of index
    numbers of food costs and of rents. 1934. (Studies and reports,
    series N (Statistics) no.20)
        Reviewed by A. L. Bowley in Econ. Jour. 45 (178): 301-303. June 1935.

International labor office, Geneva. Social and economic reconstruction in
    the United States. 1934. (Studies and Reports Series B, (Economic con-
    ditions) no. 20)
        Reviewed by W. A. B. in Roy. Statis. Soc. Jour. (n.s.) 98 (3): 558-
    559. 1935.

League of Nations. Economic intelligence service. World economic survey -
    fourth year 1934-35. 1935. (Series of League of Nations Publications.
    II. Economic and financial. II. A. 14)
        Prepared by J. B. Condliffe.
        Reviewed in Economist (London) 121 (4804): 548, 549. Sept. 21, 1935,
    in an article entitled "Recoveries and Recovery."

League of Nations. Economic intelligence service. World economic survey -
    third year 1933-34. [1934] (Series of League of Nations Publications.
    II. Economic and financial. II. A. 16)
        Prepared by J. B. Condliffe.
        Reviewed by R. B. Lemmon in Econ. Rec. 11 (20): 125-128. June 1935.

Loomis, C. P. The modern settlement movement in Germany. I. Rural. II.
    Suburban. 1935.
        A publication of the U. S. Department of Agriculture, Bureau of Agri-
    cultural Economics, Division of Farm Population and Rural Life.
        Reviewed by J. B. Taylor in Chinese Social and Polit. Sci. Rev. 19
    (3): 459-466. October 1935.

Lyon, L. S., Homan, P. T., and others. The National recovery administra-
    tion: an analysis and appraisal. 1935. (Half-title: The Institute
    of economics of the Brookings institution. Publication no. 60)
        Reviewed by A. R. Burns in Polit. Sci. Quart. 50 (4): 598-602.
    December 1935.

Polin, Raymond, and Charon, J. G. Les cooperatives rurales et l'etat en
    Tchecoslovaquie et en Roumanie. 1934.
        Reviewed by Otakar Machotka in Amer. Jour. Sociol. 41 (3): 403
    November 1935.

<u>U. S. DEPARTMENT OF AGRICULTURE PUBLICATIONS</u>

Economic in Character

Compiled by Katharine Jacobs

<u>Annual Reports of U. S. Department of Agriculture*</u>

Report of the Secretary of agriculture, 1935. 120pp.

Reports of Bureau chiefs and other administrative officers, 1935.
Bureau of agricultural economics. 27pp. - Bureau of agricultural
engineering. 22pp. - Bureau of animal industry. 55PP. - Bureau of
biological survey. 51pp. - Bureau of chemistry and soils. 44pp. -
Bureau of dairy industry. 27pp. - Office of experiment stations.
8pp. - Director of finance. 22pp. - Food and drug administration.
25pp. - The Forester. 55pp. - Grain futures administration. 8pp. -
Bureau of home economics. 13pp. - Director of information. 16pp. -
The Librarian. 12pp. - Division of operations. 7pp., mimeogr. -
Director of personnel and business administration. 6pp. - Bureau of
public roads. 60pp. - Soil conservation. 42pp. - The Solicitor. 28pp. -
The Weather bureau. 13 pp.

<u>Circular*</u>

382. The farm real estate situation, 1934-35. By B. R. Stauber... and
M. M. Regan. 52pp. Dec. 1935.
Bibliography, pp. 51-52.

<u>Farmers' Bulletin*</u>

1441. Rural planning - the village, by W. C. Nason. 41pp. Issued March
1935, slightly rev. August 1935.

<u>Addresses and Radio Talks of Secretary Wallace*</u>

Do consumers protest enough? Remarks... over the National farm and home
hour... Nov. 27, 1935. 4pp.
Farmers and the export market; address... before annual convention of
American farm bureau federation, Chicago... Dec. 10, 1935. 24pp.
How the Canadian trade agreement will affect farmers; remarks... over the
National farm and home hour... Nov. 21, 1935. 5pp.
Payrolls and food prices. Remarks... over the National farm and home
hour, National broadcasting company, December 17, 1935. 4pp. [1935]

---

*Requests for these publications should be addressed to the Office of Informa-
tion, U. S. Department of Agriculture, Washington, D. C.

Publications of the Bureau of Agricultural Economics (Mimeographed)*

Apple summary - 1935. Shenandoah - Cumberland - Potomac district, by R.
Maynard Peterson. 2pp. Dec. 7, 1935.
Directory of teachers giving courses in rural sociology and rural life.
16pp. Oct. 1, 1935.
Estimated colonies and yield of honey by states 1928-1934. 1p. Dec. 2,
1935.
Farm tenancy in the United States, 1925-1935. A beginning of a bibliography.
Comp. by Louise O. Bercaw and Helen C. Hennefrund, under the direction
of Mary G. Lacy, Librarian, Bureau of agricultural economics. 86pp.
November 1935. (U. S. Dept. of agriculture. Bureau of agricultural
economics. Agricultural economics bibliography no. 59)
Financing American cotton production and marketing in the United States.
Comp. by Mildred C. Benton, under the direction of Emily L. Day,
Library specialist in cotton marketing, Division of cotton marketing
branch library. 45pp. November 1935. (U. S. Dept. of agriculture.
Bureau of agricultural economics. Agricultural economics bibliography
no. 61)
Handbook of official United States standards for individual eggs, effective
Feb. 16, 1934. 8pp. June 1935. Printed.
Handbook of official United States standards for soybeans, effective Sept.
3, 1935. 20pp. 1935. Printed. (Form HFS-1663)
Hog outlook charts for use with the agricultural outlook for 1936. 23 charts.
November 1935.
Marketing the southern Illinois peach crop. Brief review of the 1935 season,
by R. E. Keller. 8pp. [1935] (Issued in cooperation with Illinois
Dept. of agriculture, Division of markets)
Memoranda on building and railroad employment and purchases for use in pre-
paring the outlook report on demand for the 1936 agricultural season.
14pp. Oct. 25, 1935.
Milk equivalent of production of manufactured dairy products by states, 1934.
3pp. December 1935.
Poultry and egg outlook charts for use with the agricultural outlook for
1936. 29 charts. November 1935.
Processing taxes under the Agricultural adjustment act. A short list of
references comp. in the Library, Bureau of agricultural economics,
U. S. Dept. of agriculture. 8pp. Sept. 13, 1935.
Prospects for increased foreign cotton production, by P. K. Norris. 13pp.
[1935]
        Address, Farmers' and farm women's short course, Louisiana State
University, Baton Rouge, La., Aug. 13, 1935.
Quality of the 1935 crops. Wheat, barley, oats, rye, and grain sorghums.
Summary report based on inspected receipts at representative markets
first quarter 1935 crop year. 9pp. November 1935.
Report of the Extension conference on barley improvement. University farm,
St. Paul, Minn., June 27, 1935. 26pp. Nov. 15, 1935.
Review of the 1935 California grape season, by A. E. Prugh. 11pp. Nov. 16,
1935. (Issued in cooperation with California. Dept. of agriculture,
Market news service)

*These publications are issued in small editions for immediate use in official
work and are not for general distribution.

Rules and regulations (as amended)of the Secretary of agriculture govern-
    ing the grading and certification of canned fruits and vegetables.
    Under an Act of Congress approved May 17, 1935. (Public no. 62, 74th
    Congress) 12pp. November 1935.
Sheep, lambs, and wool outlook charts for use with the agricultural outlook
    for 1936. 29pp. November 1935.
The status of the dairy industry today. Factors in the dairy outlook, by
    E. E. Vial. 8PP. [1935]
        Presented at the Middle states conference on milk control, Trenton,
    New Jersey, December 9, 1935.
Status of the dairy industry today. Factors in the dairy outlook (charts) by
    E. E. Vial. 10pp. [1935]
        Presented at the Middle states conference on milk control, Trenton,
    New Jersey, December 9-10, 1935.
Survey of protein content and other grading data of the 1935 barley crop of
    the midwestern and Pacific coast states, by D. A. Coleman and Alfred
    Christie... and C. E. Bode. A preliminary report. 39PP. November
    1935.
Tax delinquency of rural real estate in 15 California counties, 1928-32. 11pp.
    Dec. 4, 1935.
        This survey was made under a Civil works project administered by the
    Bureau of Agricultural Economics, assisted by the Agricultural Experiment
    Station of California.
Tax delinquency of rural real estate in 27 Georgia counties, 1928-33. 13pp.
    Nov. 27, 1935.
        This survey was made under a Civil works project administered by
    the Bureau of Agricultural Economics, assisted by the Agricultural Ex-
    periment Station of Georgia.
Tax delinquency of rural real estate in 17 Kansas counties, 1928-33. 14pp.
    Nov. 8, 1935.
        This survey was made under a Civil works project administered by the
    Bureau of Agricultural Economics, assisted by the Agricultural Experiment
    Station of Kansas.
Tax delinquency of rural real estate in 46 Maine towns, 1928-33. 10pp.
    Dec. 11, 1935.
        This survey was made under a Civil works project administered by the
    Bureau of Agricultural Economics, assisted by the Agricultural Experiment
    Station of Maine.
Tax delinquency of rural real estate in 19 Minnesota counties, 1928-33. 14pp.
    Nov. 20, 1935.
        This survey was made under a Civil works project administered by the
    Bureau of Agricultural Economics, assisted by the Agricultural Experiment
    Station of Minnesota.
Tax delinquency of rural real estate in 16 Montana counties, 1928-33. 14pp.
    Nov. 13, 1935.
        This survey was made under a Civil works project administered by the
    Bureau of Agricultural Economics, assisted by the Agricultural Experiment
    Station of Montana.
Tobacco outlook charts for use with the agricultural outlook for 1936. 19
    charts. November 1935.
Wheat and rye outlook charts for use with the agricultural outlook for 1936.
    27 charts. November 1935.

Publications of the Agricultural Adjustment Administration*

Agriculture's share in the national income. October, 1935. 37PP. (G-48)
Balanced production in the corn-hog industry. 6pp. (Commodity information
    series. Corn-hog leaflet no. 2) Issued December 1935.
Louisiana sugarcane administrative rulings (under and pursuant to the 1934-1935
    Louisiana sugarcane production adjustment contract) 2pp. Oct. 25, 1935.
    (Sugar 120-A)
(Paper regulations, Series 1, Supplement 1). Definitions and conversion factor
    with respect to reinforced paper fabric. Reinforced paper fabric regula-
    tions made by the Secretary of agriculture and approved by the President
    under the Agricultural adjustment act. 3PP. Nov. 1, 1935. (P. R. -
    AAA. Series 1, Supplement 1)
The south's choice. By Chester C. Davis... speaking before the Texas agricul-
    tural association in Dallas, Texas... December 3, 1935. 14pp., mimeogr.
    [1935]
Supplement 1 to Wheat adjustment handbook 1936-1939. Part V.- relating to wheat
    administrative rulings. Official instructions relating to administrative
    rulings no. 110, 111, and 113. 16pp. (Wheat 200-A) Issued November 1935.
Tobacco administrative ruling no. 50, amendment no. 2. Disposition of excess to-
    bacco of the 1935 crop. 2pp. November 1935. (Form T-77, Supplement 40)
Tobacco administrative rulings series of 1936-1939 relating to Burley, fire-
    cured and dark air-cured tobacco contracts, 1936-1939. 7pp. October 1935.
    (T-401)

Radio Talks (Mimeographed)**

Adjustment and soil conservation, by J. F. Cox. 2pp. Nov. 29, 1935.
The cost of food; address by Donald E. Montgomery... at the Conference on the
    high cost of living, Hotel Pennsylvania, New York City. 15pp. Dec. 14,
    1935.
The nation plants to prosper; by Chester C. Davis. 2pp. Dec. 11, 1935.
Progress of agricultural adjustment, by William E. Byrd, Jr., 2pp. Nov. 5, 1935.
Progress of agricultural adjustment, by William E. Byrd, Jr. 2pp. Nov. 11, 1935.
Progress of agricultural adjustment, by William E. Byrd, Jr. 2pp. Nov. 18, 1935.
Progress of agricultural adjustment, by William E. Byrd, Jr. 2pp. Dec. 11, 1935.
Progress of agricultural adjustment, by Alfred D. Stedman. 2pp. Nov. 27, 1935.

Group Discussion Material***

Discussion series C. Extracts no. 1. What is the chief cause of the farm de-
    pression? 39PP., mimeogr. [1935]
        The Extension Service and the Agricultural Adjustment Administration,
    cooperating.

---

*Requests for these publications should be addressed to the Agricultural Adjust-
ment Administration, U. S. Departmentof Agriculture, Washington, D. C.
**May be obtained from U. S. Department of Agriculture, Office of Information,
Radio Service.
***May be obtained from the United States Department of Agriculture, Room 202,
Washington, D. C.

Discussion series C. Extracts no. 2. Do farmers want the federal government to help them deal with farm problems? 25pp., mimeogr. [1935]
    The Extension Service and the Agricultural Adjustment Administration, cooperating.
Discussion series C. Forum folder no. 1. The farm depression, explanatory note. 5pp., mimeogr. [1935]
    The Extension Service and the Agricultural Adjustment Administration cooperating.
Do farmers want the federal government to help them deal with farm problems? 4pp. November 1935. (DA-2. Discussion series A, Leaflet no. 2)
    The Extension Service and the Agricultural Adjustment Administration cooperating.
Do farmers want the federal government to help them deal with farm problems? 12pp. [1935] (DB-2. Discussion series B. no. 2)
    The Extension Service and the Agricultural Adjustment Administration cooperating.

Miscellaneous (Mimeographed)*

Agricultural economic extension work in 1934. [Aug. 1935] 15pp. (U. S. Dept. of agriculture. Extension service. Office of cooperative extension work. Extension service circular 221)
Farm family living outlook charts and conference summaries for use with the agricultural outlook for 1936. 43pp. November 1935. (Issued by U. S. Dept. of agriculture. Bureau of home economics)
Farming as a life work [by] O. E. Baker. 12pp. October 1935. (U. S. Dept. of agriculture. Office of cooperative extension work. Extension service circular 224)
A list of American economic histories, by Everett E. Edwards, Associate agricultural economist, Division of statistical and historical research, Bureau of agricultural economics. 25pp. November 1935.
    (U. S. Dept. of agriculture. Library. Bibliographical contributions no. 27)
The outlook for rural youth, by O. E. Baker. [Sept. 1935] 36pp. (U. S. Dept. of agriculture. Extension service. Office of cooperative extension work. Extension service circular 223)
    This circular supersedes E.S.C. 203.
Selected references on the history of agriculture in the United States, by Everett E. Edwards, Associate agricultural economist, Division of statistical and historical research. Bureau of agricultural economics. 28pp. November 1935. (U. S. Dept. of agriculture. Library. Bibliographical contribution no. 26)
Statistical results of cooperative extension work, 1934. [by] M. C. Wilson. 52pp. July 1935. (U. S. Dept. of agriculture. Extension service. Office of cooperative extension work. Extension service circular 217)
What is the opportunity in agriculture for the farm boy? April 1935. 12pp. (U. S. Dept. of agriculture. Extension service. Office of cooperative extension work. Extension service circular 214)

_____

*Requests for these publications should be addressed to the issuing office.

STATE PUBLICATIONS

Compiled by Mary F. Carpenter

California

Shultis, Arthur. A farm enterprise cost accounting system. 13pp., mimeogr. Berkeley. Calif. Univ. Col. Agr. Ext. Serv. 1935,

Colorado

Hunter, Byron, Moorhouse, L. A., Burdick, R. T., and Pingrey, H. B. Type of farming areas in Colorado. Colo. Agr. Expt. Sta. Bull. 418, 135pp. Fort Collins, 1935.
In cooperation with the U. S. Bureau of Agricultural Economics.
Besides the results of the type of farming study, a discussion of the factors in the agricultural development of Colorado is included.
A small type of farming map is given on p. 62.

Georgia

Fullilove, W. T. Tax delinquency of farm real estate in fifty-two Georgia counties, 1928-1933. Ga. Agr. Expt. Sta. Press Bull. 406, 5pp., mimeogr. Experiment. 1935.

Georgia. Agricultural experiment station. Forty-seventh annual report... for the year, 1934/35. 52PP. Experiment. 1935.
Agricultural economics, pp. 6-8.

Idaho

Idaho. University. College of agriculture. 1936 agricultural outlook for Idaho. Idaho Agr. Col. Ext. Serv. Idaho Agr. Situation. Dec. 7, 1935, 20pp., mimeogr. Boise.
In cooperation with the Idaho Dept. of Agriculture and U. S. Dept. of Agriculture.

Illinois

Illinois. Agricultural experiment station. A year's progress in solving farm problems of Illinois. Forty-seventh report for year ended June 30, 1934. 287pp. Urbana. 1935.
Agricultural economics, pp. 163-194.

Lloyd, J. W., and Decker, S. W. Factors influencing the refrigeration of packages of peaches. Ill. Agr. Expt. Sta. Bull. 418, pp. 439-463. Urbana. 1935.
This is the second report of experiments dealing with factors influencing the refrigeration of packages of fruit. The first, dealing with apples, was listed in Agricultural Economics Literature for April, 1935.

Indiana. State bureau of weights and measures. Laws relating to unbonded
agricultural warehouses together with rules and regulations. 12pp.
Indianapolis. 1935.
    Includes text of the state warehouse act, approved February 27, 1935.

Iowa

Iowa State college of agriculture and mechanic arts. Farm handbook ... A
compendium of useful information fully indexed. 5th edition, 1936.
71pp. Ames. 1935.

Kansas

Kansas. State Board of agriculture. Twenty-ninth biennial report... 1933
and 1934. 624pp. Topeka. 1935.
    Similar to previous issues. Includes the following papers. Rural
banks and banking, by W. W. Bowman, pp. 19-30; Marginal and submarginal
lands in Kansas, by W. E. Grimes, pp. 60-67. The section on statistics,
pp. 264-493 includes tables showing population, acreages, and production
of crops and livestock for 1933 and 1934 by counties.

Louisiana

Smith, T. L. The growth of population in Louisiana. 1890-1930. La. Agr. Exp
Sta. Bull. 264, 53pp. State Station, Baton Rouge. 1935.
    First of a series of three reports from a study of the state's popula-
tion.

Maryland

Hunt, W. E. A survey of the sheep industry of Maryland. Md. Agr. Expt. Sta.
Bull. 378, 43pp. College Park. 1935.
    "This bulletin is based upon replies to 206 questions regarding the
breeding, feeding, management, and marketing of sheep, and the production and marketing of wool obtained from about 120 Maryland sheep raisers
located in 15 counties of the State." The survey covers the period 1928 t
1932.

Maryland. University, Extension service. The passing of a decade. A summary
of extension activities in Maryland, 1924-1934. 180pp. College Park. [19
The index may be consulted for activities in economic projects.

Massachusetts

Kroeck, J. Suggestions to retailers on how to comply with the fresh egg law.
4pp. Boston. Mass. Dept. Agr. Div. Markets. 1935.
    Includes copy of the state law relative to the sale and distribution of
eggs, approved June 21, 1935.

Michigan

Motts, G. N.   The production-consumption balance of agricultural products in
      Michigan. Part 1, Fruits and vegetables. Mich. Agr. Expt. Sta. Special
      Bull. 263, 64pp. East Lansing. 1935.
         The first of a series of reports which will include grains and feed-
      stuffs, livestock and meats, dairy and poultry, sugar and other farm
      commodities.

Minnesota

Waite, W. C., and Cox, R. W. A study of the consumption of meats in Minneapolis,
      1934. Minn. Agr. Expt. Sta. Bull. 321. 26pp. University Farm, St. Paul.
      1935.
         "This bulletin first describes the variations found in the rates of con-
      sumption and in the average prices paid by families for meats. Next, it
      outlines the sections of the city having similar rates of consumption,
      similar prices, and similar per capita expenditures. Finally, it pre-
      sents an analysis of the variations in expenditures and the factors in-
      fluencing these variations."

Nebraska

George, A. G. Corn production costs, Nebraska. 1934. Nebr. Agr. Col. Ext.
      Circ. 840, 9pp., mimeogr. Lincoln. 1935.
         Records were obtained from the counties of Cass, Douglas, Saunders,
      Cuming, Fillmore, Phelps and Thurston.

George, A. G. Winter wheat production costs, Nebraska. 1934. Nebr. Agr. Col.
      Ext. Circ. 839, 7 pp., mimeogr. Lincoln. 1934.
         Records were obtained from the counties of Cass, Douglas, Saunders,
      Fillmore, Perkins, and Cheyenne.

Nebraska. Agricultural college, Extension service. Fifth annual farm business
      report, thirty Clay county farms, 1934. Nebr. Agr. Col. Ext. Circ. 850,
      9pp., mimeogr. Lincoln. 1935.

Nebraska. Agricultural college, Extension service. Fifth annual farm business
      report, twenty-four Johnson county farms, 1934. Nebr. Agr. Col. Ext.
      Circ. 852, 9pp., mimeogr. Lincoln. 1935.

Nevada

Buckman, T. E.   The Taylor grazing act in Nevada. Nev. Univ. Agr. Ext. Serv.
      Bull. 76, 75pp. Reno. 1935.
         Includes a record of the proceedings of the Nevada Taylor Grazing Dis-
      trict Hearing held at Reno on January 24, 1935 and the text of the Act
      passed by the 73d Congress, June 28, 1934.

New York. Laws, statutes, etc. Agriculture and markets law, 1935. N. Y.
Dept. Agr. Bull. 296. 329pp. Albany. 1935.
Contains the text of the New York state law (Chapter 48 of the Laws
of 1922) with amendments and rules and regulations, and also the provisions
of the Cooperative Corporations law, (Chapter 231 of the Laws of 1926
as amended)

New York State college of agriculture, Cornell University. The problem of
delinquent taxes in rural New York. 10pp., mimeogr. Ithaca 1935.
"This report summarizes the results of a survey of rural tax delinquency reported more completely in Tax Delinquency in Rural New York
[by T. N. Hurd, O. M. Wiltse and T. Miles]"

Ohio

Ohio. State University. College of agriculture, Extension service. The agricultural outlook for 1936. Ohio Agr. Col. Ext. Serv. Timely Econ. Information for Farmers, no. 95, 32pp. Columbus. Nov. 1935.

Oklahoma

McWhorter. C. C., and Ballinger, R. A. Relative economic advantages of harvesting cotton by picking and snapping in western Oklahoma. Okla. Agr.
Expt. Sta. Bull. 227, 74pp. Stillwater. 1935.
"Particular attention is given to an analysis of differences in prices
paid in the local markets for cotton that was harvested by the two methods
and to differences in the net returns received by farmers for standard
size bales of cotton after cost for harvesting and ginning have been
deducted."

Pennsylvania

Pennsylvania. Agricultural experiment station. Forty-eighth annual report
for the fiscal year ended June 30, 1935. Pa. Agr. Expt. Sta. Bull. 320,
35pp. State College. 1935.
Agricultural economics, pp. 9-10.

Puerto Rico

Puerto Rico. Agricultural experiment station. Annual report of the director,
1933/34. 202pp. San Juan. 1935.
Contains a note of the new Division of Agricultural Economics which
has been organized.

Virginia

Garnett, W. E. A social study of the Blacksburg community. Va. Agr. Expt.
Sta. Bull. 299, 105pp. Blacksburg. 1935.
"In the Blacksburg community most of the families are engaged in agricultural work, in mining, in trade or service occupations or else work
for the Virginia Polytechnic Institute in some capacity... Practically
half of the people of the area are of the marginal to sub-marginal type."

PERIODICAL ARTICLES

Compiled by Louise O. Bercaw and A. M. Hannay

Agricultural Credit - Italy

Pritzkoleit, Kurt. Der italienische agrarkredit. Wirtschaftsdienst (n.F.)
20(40): 1358-1360. Oct. 4, 1935. (Issued by Hamburgisches Welt-Wirtschafts-
Archiv. Published by Hanseatische Verlagsanstalt, A. G., Hamburg 36 ,
Germany.)
A brief historical summary of agricultural credit in Germany is followed by a discussion of the functioning of agricultural credit in the
corporative state, under the headings of mortgage credit and agricultural
credit not secured by mortgage.

Agricultural Indebtedness - India

Banerjea, Benoyendranath. Liquidation of agricultural indebtedness. Bengal
Coop. Jour. 20(4): 202-207. April-June 1935; 21(1): 1-5. July-September
1935. (Published by Bengal Co-operative Organisation Society, Ltd.,
Calcutta. India.)
Summarizes relief of agricultural indebtedness legislation in different
provinces of India.

Agricultural Legislation - Canada

Curtis, C. A. Dominion legislation of 1935. An economist's review. Canad.
Jour. Econ. and Polit. Sci. 1(4): 599-608. November 1935. (Published
by the University of Toronto Press, Toronto, Ontario)
Among the acts discussed which relate to agriculture are the amend-
ments to the Live Stock Act which "made packer stock yards subject to
the same public control and inspection as public stock yards"; The
Canadian Wheat Board Act; amendments to the Farm Loan Act and the Farmers'
Creditors' Arrangement Act; and the Prairie Farm Rehabilitation Act.

McGoun, A. F. Alberta legislation, 1935. Canad. Jour. Econ. and Polit.
Sci. 1(4): 609-611. November 1935. (Published by the University of
Toronto Press, Toronto, Ontario)
Among the acts referred to which relate to agriculture are The Agri-
cultural Industry Stabilization Act, which "exempts from seizure an
unspecified amount in money or marketable produce, sufficient to pro-
vide during the next twelve months all necessary food, clothing, medical
and hospital services, and other necessaries of life", etc.; the United
Irrigation District Relief Act; the Grasshopper Bait Indebtedness Act;
and act with respect to an Agreement for the Provision of a Beet Sugar
Factory in the Lethbridge Northern Irrigation District; the Provincial
Lands Act Amendment Act; and the Rural Mutual Telephone Companies Act.

Agricultural Policy - Great Britain

Pasvolsky, Leo. Britain drops quotas. Country Gent. 105(12): 21, 68, 69,
72. December 1935. (Published at Independence Square, Philadelphia, Pa.)

An account of Great Britain's plans for "revising drastically some of her recently introduced agricultural policies." The most important feature of the plans, says the writer "is a definite trend away from import quotas and other methods of quantitative regulation of international trade in agricultural commodities." The sugar, wheat, hops, potato, milk, pigs and bacon, and beef schemes and their problems are discussed. The new trend is toward increased efficiency in production and marketing and less emphasis is being given to price-raising. It is not planned that the subsidies to be granted in the new program are "to be used for an indefinite expansion of production."

The writer concludes as follows:

"The new plan is far from representing a return to a constructive agricultural policy normal to a country of Great Britain's type, with its dependence upon the exportation of manufactured goods and of capital and its relative paucity of agricultural resources. Apart from everything else, the principle of employing subsidies for the purpose of an artificial expansion of production or the creation of abnormal price differentials is utterly vicious from an economic point of view. But in the present made condition of economic policy generally, the levy-subsidy plan at least involves much less dislocation for world agriculture than would be the case with either high protective tariffs or, especially, with trade-diverting and trade-destroying quotas."

Agricultural Relief - Australia

How countrymen fare under the Federal and State budgets. Land, no.1268,p. 4. Sept. 27, 1935. (Published in Sydney, New South Wales)

"The main provisions of the Federal Budget affecting country people are: Assistance to the citrus industry by means of a bounty of 2/-a case on oranges exported to the United Kingdom; continuance of the subsidy of 15/- a ton on artificial manure used in the production of primary products other than wheat; assistance to Australian tobacco producers by a reduction in excise duties on manufactured tobacco in the production of which all the leaf used is Australian-grown; a slight reduction in the super tax on property income; an extension of thelist of sales tax exemptions and the remission of primage on certain raw materials; and the special provision of £ 100,000 for development of country postal, telegraph, and telephone services."

A reduction of 10 per cent in rail freight on wheat, fruit, and dairy produce is one of the features of the State Budget. So far as wheat is concerned, the rate will "take effect as from November 1 next."

Agricultural Relief - South Africa

Richards, C. S. Subsidies, quotas, tariffs, and the excess cost of agriculture in South Africa. So. African Jour. Econ. 3(3): 365-403. September 1935. (Published by the Economic Society of South Africa, P.O. Box 5316, Johannesburg)

The subject is considered under the following subtopics: The world agricultural position since the war; methods adopted in South Africa for the promotion and assistance of agriculture [includes a complete list of acts passed, from 1911 through 1935, dealing with permanent assistance to the farming community]; special legislative measures; estimate of the excess national costs for 1933; incidence of the excess costs; the results of control; the economics of authoritarian control; the growth of administrative control; the cost of distribution; conclusions and suggestions.

A folded page of schedules is inserted between pages 374 and 375. Schedule I gives an analysis of types of control, and schedule II is a detailed production, price and excess cost schedule of controlled and uncontrolled commodities, 1933.

The writer's conclusions are in part as follows:

"1. The rapid extension of control of agriculture by Government nominated boards or by regulation, has proved nationally excessively costly -- £ 7,470,000 in 1933 alone, and the results obtained are by no means commensurate with the costs incurred;

"2. The new methods are a negation of democratic principles and in the economic world are leading us rapidly and unconsciously to the worst form of inefficient socialism - sectional control;

"3. These methods offer no permanent solution of the agricultural problem - so far from improving the position, they have made it infinitely worse. So far they have been a definite failure, and are highly wasteful of economic resources...

"It is contended that Government, while having a thorough investigation of the whole position, should gradually relinquish its activities in the above directions, and confine itself to its legitimate spheres, namely, research, advice, and suggestion, with regard to the best areas of production, the most payable crops and the most promising lines of future development. It should cease to subsidize inefficiency, and should gradually lower the duties on sugar and wheat, butter and cheese, etc., and the other necessities of life. By these means excess costs would be reduced, and internal consumption (involving further reduction of national losses) increased. The present policy can be summed up only as that of making lower costs illegal. Good farming will be achieved by good farmers and not by perpetual assistance. There is an urgent necessity for an improvement in agricultural technique."

Agricultural Relief - United States

Administration policies flayed by National Grain Association. Grain & Feed Rev. 25(2): 12-17. October 1935. (Published at 408 South 3rd St., Minneapolis, Minn.)

An account of the 39th annual convention of the Grain & Feed Dealers National Association at St. Louis, Sept. 19-20-21. Resolutions adopted are given.

"Administration agricultural relief policies and measures were severely criticized both by speakers and resolutions adopted" at the convention.

Agriculture's large program. Coop. Comment 4(9): 1, 4. November 1935. (Published at the Columbia Bldg., Spokane, Wash.)

"Charles Stewart, representative of Farmers National Grain Corporation, who recently closed a series of meetings with Local Cooperatives, gave a very clear picture of the agricultural program and the part cooperating farmer must take in it."

Mr. Stewart's address is given in part. He expressed the opinion
that agricultural problems will not be solved "until farmers have increased their control over the marketing and distribution of the products
after they are produced. Such control over marketing and distribution
is just as essential to a satisfactory income from the farm as a sane
and sound policy of production control."

Dickinson, L. J.   Agriculture and its future. Vital Speeches of the Day 2(4):
   105-112. Nov. 18, 1935. (Published at 33 W. 42nd St., New York, N. Y.)
      Paper read at the Cornell Forum Conference, College Chapel, Mount
   Vernon, Iowa, November 4, 1935.
      The writer is critical of the whole new deal program for agriculture --
   the A.A.A., resettlement, and export trade.
      He lays down five principles "which must underlie sound program for
   the future." They are:
      "1. To eliminate present contradictions in government policy which
   on the one hand seek to limit crop production, and on the other undermine
   still further the position of agriculture through subsidized competition
   from vast federal irrigation and drainage development projects, which
   under prevailing conditions are neither needed nor economic in character.
      "2. To stabilize present agricultural production through federal
   policies aimed at (a) retirement of marginal land areas from cultivation,
   the substitution of an intelligent land use program, and (b) stimulation
   of diversification for a better balanced production to meet the grave
   social problem of under-consumption and under-nourishment now assuming
   serious proportions throughout the United States.
      "3. Removal of artificial controls and bureaucratic regulations, with
   a return to a policy of federal assistance in development of cooperative
   organizations both for production and marketing, with consequent strengthening of economic self-government among farmers.
      "4. A broad program to restore export markets for American farm
   products through a price-equalizing fee based on tariff duties levied
   on imports, and the application of the principles incorporated and successfully applied by the British Empire in its Ottawa trade agreements,
   in the development of markets for American agricultural commodities
   abroad, encouraged by a stabilized currency and a fixed tariff policy,
   definite in rate and protective of our standard of living.
      "5. Federal cooperation with the states in working out a thorough-
   going revision in methods of taxation which will reduce the ever-growing
   burden placed on farm lands and real property."

Garis, R. L., and Watkins, Lowe. AAA - 1890 style. The People's Money
   1(6): 203-211, 247-248. November 1935. (Published at 280 Broadway,
   New York, N. Y.)
      Discusses government loans to producers, constitutionality of proces-
   sing taxes, the bounty given by the Republicans to domestic sugar producers in the 1830's, the tariff act upheld by the Supreme Court, the
   tariff in politics, test case of the sugar bounty act of Michigan and
   forest bounty acts of Missouri, Kansas, and Nevada, and problems which
   will arise if the processing taxes levied under AAA are declared unconstitutional.

McKelvie, S. R.   After AAA, what? Saturday Evening Post 208(23): 23, 93,
    94, 95, 96, 97, 98. Dec. 7, 1935. (Published at Independence Square,
    Philadelphia, Pa.)
        Following a criticism of the AAA the author presents a substitute
    for "regimentation." The proposed plan would work as follows: "At the
    end of a given production or marketing period, the farmer would be re-
    imbursed by the Government on a percentage of his sales for domestic
    purposes in an amount sufficient to insure him parity as between agri-
    cultural and nonagricultural commodities."
        The beneficial effects of this plan, which "answers at once the
    criticisms to AAA" are enumerated. The writer acknowledges that the
    plan is not simple, that "parity" may present difficulties, and that
    he doesn't know whether it is constitutional, nor how much it will
    cost. It would be administered by regular agencies of the Government
    and the number of "public employees required... would be a fraction of
    those on the pay roll of AAA."
        He concludes as follows:
        "It will be understood by now that the underlying theory of this
    proposal is not an economy of inflation or high prices. It is based on
    the sounder theory of equality among the classes regardless of price
    levels, and a recognition of the futility of trying to hold ourselves
    at arm's length by the seat of the pants. If the plan means anything,
    it is that inducements will have been removed for one class to take
    advantage of another. If industry boosts prices out of reason, it
    will be taken out of them in taxes. The argument of higher living costs
    as a reason for hiking wages will have been removed, except as farm prices
    advance naturally and the farmer is able to pay more for what he buys.
        "The natural checks and balances would become operative again. I
    believe it is sound. Sometimes, it or something like it will be done.
    Or we will bring about equality for agriculture by the other route
    of getting offending classes and groups off the farmers' back. At
    present, the Government is not the least of these groups."

McMillen, Wheeler.   A new plan to create farm wealth. Country Home 59(12):
    9-10, 31. December 1935. (Published at 250 Park Ave., New York, N. Y.)
        The writer proposes and discusses "an entirely new type of farm
    program, for which the following points may be argued: 1. Surpluses
    would be diminished, while new and needed farm crops would be encouraged.
    2. Soil fertility and natural resources would be both conserved and
    improved. 3. Acreage adjustments would involve no regimentation or com-
    pulsion. 4. Home production of commodities for which we are now de-
    pendent upon other countries would be stimulated. 5. Agricultural and
    industrial employment would be increased...
        "The idea may be briefly stated: Instead of paying farmers for not
    growing particular commodities, the government would pay farmers for
    producing commodities which we now import. It would pay farmers for
    growing soil-building crops such as legumes. It would pay farmers for
    efforts devoted to the prevention of erosion and loss of irreplaceable
    soil. It would pay farmers for producing non-food crops for industrial
    uses, in place of the acres now devoted to surplus crops."

[O'Neal, E. A.] Agriculture looks ahead. Bur. Farmer 11(2): 4, 9. November
    1935. (Published at 58 E. Washington St., Chicago, Ill.)
    "A bird's-eye view of trends in farm philosophy and thinking."

Agriculture - China

Agricultural production in Hupeh during 1934. Chinese Econ. Jour. 17(2):
    164-175. August 1935. (Published by Bureau of Foreign Trade, Ministry
    of Industry, 1040 Soochow Road, Shanghai, China.)

Agriculture - Denmark

Hauch, H. The problems of Danish agriculture. Lloyds Bank Ltd. Monthly
    Rev. (n.s.) 6(69): 590-600. November 1935. (Published at 71 Lombard
    St., London, E. C. 3, Eng.)
       Because of the fact that "the economic conditions of Denmark are to
    an exceptional degree determined by her commercial relations with the
    surrounding world" the writer points out that "it was unavoidable that
    the world depression and the consequent policy of trade restrictions
    had a particularly serious effect in Denmark."

Agriculture - Germany

Die Entwicklung der deutschen ernteerträge. Fünfzig jahre deutsche ernte-
    statistik. Wirtschaft und Statistik 15(18): 662-665. September 1935.
    (Issued by [Germany] Statistisches Reichsamt. Published by Verlag für
    Sozialpolitik, Wirtschaft und Statistik, Berlin S.W. 68)
       A statistical and graphic account of agricultural production in
    Germany since 1878. Tables give average yield per hectare of rye, wheat,
    barley, oats, potatoes, hay, and clover from 1878 to 1934 and of sugar
    beets from 1914 to 1934, and consumption of artificial fertilizer from
    1913/14 to 1933/34, with preliminary figures for 1934/35.

Peyret, Henry. L'agriculture allemande sous le IIIe Reich. Revue des
    Agriculteurs de France 67(11): 398-404. November 1935. (Published at
    8, Rue d'Athènes, Paris (9°), France.)
       The author describes the situation of German agriculture at the time
    of Hitler's accession to power, and the measures adopted by the National
    Socialist Government to recreate the peasant class as the backbone of
    the nation, to stabilize agriculture, and to improve the markets and
    raise prices without increasing the cost of living.

Agriculture and Business

Farm pocketbooks and smoking chimneys. Bur. Farmer 11(2): 3, 11. November
    1935. (Published at 58 E. Washington St., Chicago, Ill.)
       General R. E. Wood, President, Sears, Roebuck and Company is quoted
    regarding the direct relationship between farm pocketbooks and smoking
    chimneys, or industrial activity.

"Two factors, in the opinion of General Wood, are responsible for the recovery of American industry and business. One of these is the Administration's monetary policy, which, by revaluing the dollar, has increased prices for more than 30 commodities. The other factor, he adds, is the work of the Agricultural Adjustment Administration."

Agriculture and Directed Economy

L'économie dirigée et l'agriculture. Société d'Encouragement pour l'Industrie Nationale. Bulletin 134(7-9): 417-433. July-September 1935. (Published at 44, Rue de Rennes, Paris (6e), France.)

A series of six lectures on directed economy in agriculture were delivered before the Institut National Agronomique at its meeting in Paris from March 6 to April 10, 1935. The first lecture on the general subject of directed economy, by Gaëtan Pirou is given practically in full. The other five dealing with Great Britain, Italy, the United States, Germany, and the Soviet Union are summarized. They are: L'Économie dirigée et l'agriculture en Grande-Bretagne, by J. B. Verlot; L'Économie dirigée et l'agriculture en Italie, by Roger Grand; L'Économie dirigée et l'agriculture aux États-Unis, by Oualid; L'Économie dirigée et l'agriculture en Allemagne, by Max Hermant; and L'Économie dirigée et l'agriculture en U.R.S.S., by Robert Mossé.

Agriculture and Reconstruction - China

Chen Kung-po. The place of agriculture in national reconstruction. Chinese Econ. Jour. 17(1): 1-9. July 1935. (Published by Bureau of Foreign Trade, Ministry of Industry, 1040 North Soochow Road, Shanghai, China.)

Beef and Veal - Export Bounty - Irish Free State

Irish Free State. Export bounty on beef and veal. Gt. Brit. Bd. Trade Jour. (n.s.) 135(2027): 513. Oct. 10, 1935. (Published by H. M. Stationery Office, London, Eng.)

"A notice issued by the Irish Free State Department of Agriculture... provides for the payment of an export bounty on beef and veal exported from the Irish Free State at the rate of 5s. per cwt. as from September 27, 1935."

Blue Grass Seed - Cooperative Marketing

Royse, M. D. Marketing blue grass seed co-operatively. Bur. Farmer (Ky. Farm Bur. News) 11(2): d. November 1935. (Published at 58 E. Washington St., Chicago, Ill.)

Describes the gains made by growers of blue grass seed by marketing their seed through the Kentucky Blue Grass Seed Growers Cooperative Association, beginning with the 1931 crop, which was unusually large.

Bureaucracy - United States

Clark, B. C. They never die. Country Gent. 105(12): 5-6, 32, 34, 35. December 1935. (Published at Independence Square, Philadelphia, Pa.)

On the growth of, and permanency of, bureaucracy, and the propaganda

used by various government agencies to obtain appropriations. Mention
is made of the conflict between the Bureau of Biological Survey and the
Reclamation Service, the Department of Agriculture and the Department
of the Interior, etc.

Butter As a World Staple

Wright, C. M. Butter as a world staple. Index 10(119): 254-269. November
1935. (Published by Svenska Handelsbanken, Stockholm, Sweden)
Considers price development, government policy, consumption, world
supply, the effects of present government policies, and future butter
policy.

Cartel Legislation

Reichert, J. W. International survey of cartel legislation. Mysore Econ.
Jour. 21(10): 532-534. October 1935. (11): 589-591. November 1935.
(Published in Bangalore City, Mysore, India.)
"The following brief survey of the special laws governing cartels
in the countries chiefly concerned shows the rapid growth of such laws,
both in number and scope, since the American Antitrust Law began the
movement nearly half a century ago, and more particularly in the last
ten or twelve years."

Chicago Board of Trade

Wickham, T. Y. The farmer and his grain. Grain & Feed Rev. 24(9): 12, 13.
May 1935. (Published at 408 South 3rd St., Minneapolis, Minn.)
The writer explains how the Chicago Board of Trade works, and dis-
cusses some of the legislative trade barriers that have been erected.

Coffee

World coffee markets. Empire Producer, no. 229, pp. 195-196. November 1935.
(Published by British Empire Producers' Organisation, 22, Gueen Anne's
Gate, London, S. W. 1, Eng.)
Contains replies to a questionnaire on coffee sent to representatives
of the Department of Overseas Trade and to unofficial correspondents
in Yugoslavia, New Zealand, British Honduras, and the Bahamas.

Colonies

The "necessity" for colonies. Economist 121(4812): 950-951. Nov. 16, 1935.
(Published at 8 Bouverie St., Fleet St., London, E. C. 4, Eng.)
Examines four economic arguments put forward in favor of colonies,
namely: First, "It is necessary to possess colonies in order to ensure
access to essential raw materials, Secondly, colonies are said to
be needed as markets for the industrial output of the mother country; or
thirdly, as fields for the investment of the mother country's surplus
savings. And, fourthly, colonies are demanded as outlets for the
'surplus populations' of the large industrial States."

Control of Production - United States

Controls in major foodstuffs industries. Southwest. Miller 14(38): 21, 22, Nov. 19, 1935. (Published at 306-312 Board of Trade Bldg., Kansas City, Mo.)
Remarks by the managing editor of the The Southwestern Miller in an address, November 19, before students of The School of Business, University of Kansas.
"Current developments in a few branches of the food trade here and in scattered portions of the world furnish an excellent insight into some. of the problems of control in the food industry. Let's examine a few very briefly and endeavor to arrive at conclusions and the offensive and defensive measures which they impose upon us."
Problems of governmental aid for prices, export subsidies or bonuses as control measures are discussed. A national sales tax, to provide benefit payments, instead of the present system of processing taxes, is advocated.

Davis, G. H. Economic aspects of production control. Grain & Feed Rev. 24 (10): 46, 47. June 1935. (Published at 408 South 3rd St., Minneapolis, Minn.)
"Discussion by George H. Davis, President, Davis-Noland-Merrill Grain Co., Kansas City, Mo., at the annual meeting Chamber of Commerce of the United States."

[Sargent, F. W.] Sargent assails crop control program. Grain & Feed Rev. 24(12): 14, 15, 16, 17. August 1935. (Published at 408 South 3rd St., Minneapolis, Minn.)
Address delivered at the banquet of the Milwaukee Grain & Stock Exchange, Milwaukee, July 10, 1935.

Cooperation

Watkins, W. P. Associations of producers; their place in co-operative economy. Coop. Rev. 9(54): 289-293. November 1935. (Published at Holyoake House, Hanover Street, Manchester 4, Eng.)
Contains a summary of the changes in the technique of cultivation and marketing of agricultural products brought about by the efforts of producers' associations in agriculture.

Cooperation - China

Rural co-operative societies in Shantung. Chinese Econ. Jour. 17(2): 176-181. August 1935. (Published by Bureau of Foreign Trade, Ministry of Industry, 1040 Soochow Road, Shanghai, China.)

Cooperation - India

Rao, A. Krishna. Cooperation in Mysore. Mysore Econ. Jour. 21(11): 580-588. November 1935. (Published in Bangalore City, Mysore, India.)

Pritzkoleit, Kurt.   Tendenzen des Weltbaumwollmarktes.   Wirtschaftsdienst
    (n.F.) 20(47): 1593-1595. Nov. 22, 1935. (Published by Hanseatische
    Verlagsanstalt A. G., Hamburg 36, Germany.)
        The author discusses and contrasts the cotton production restruction
    policy of the United States, British India, and Egypt with the policy
    of increased production as exemplified in China, Russia, and South
    America. He believes that the crux of the situation is in the outcome
    of Brazil's cotton crop and the maintenance of North America's cotton
    policy.

Cotton - Brazil

Griffith-Williams, G. G.   Cotton in Brazil. Algodao 2(12): 29-31. October
    1935. (Published in Rio de Janeiro, Brazil)
        A brief history of cotton production and manufacture in Brazil,
    the geographical aspects of the country, the scope of the projected
    State Cotton Service of Pernambuco, and the problems and prospects for
    Brazilian cotton are included.

Cotton - Credit - Argentina

La Junta Nacional del Algodón cooperó con el Banco de la Nación para la
    ayuda a los productores de algodón. Gaceta Algodonera 11(141): 10-11,
    13, 15, Oct. 31, 1935. (Published at Reconquista 331, Buenos Aires,
    Argentina.)
        Gives the terms of an agreement between the National Bank of Argentina
    and the National Cotton Board for the granting of credit to cotton growers
    to cover all necessary operations from the growing of the cotton to its
    sale or export. The conditions of the loans are listed.

Cotton - Export Tolerance Plan

Lamport, S. C.   The cotton tolerance export plan. Textile Bull. 49(8):
    [3], 26. Oct. 24, 1935. (Published at 118 West Fourth St., Charlotte,
    N. C.)
        "Address at Cotton Tolerance Dinner Meeting, October 16th."
        The speaker proposes that the "Administration allot...[to the textile
    industry] 15 million dollars under Section 32 of the AAA Amendments for
    the revival of textile exports."
        Extracts in Amer. Wool & Cotton Reporter 49(44): 16. Oct. 31, 1935.

Moore, Frederick. The proposed export tolerance plan. No time to com-
    promise industry's relation to AAA. Textile Bull. 49(8): 4. Oct. 24,
    1935. (Published at 118 West Fourth St., Charlotte, N. C.)

Cotton - Marketing - South India

Chettiyar, T. A.   Marketing of agricultural produce in South India. Madras
    Jour. Co-op. 26(11): 517-522. May 1935. (Published by Madras Provincial
    Co-operative Union, Royapettah, Madras, India)

Marketing, handling and financing methods for cotton are included in the discussion.

Cotton – North China

Cotton prospects in North China. Internatl. Cotton Bull. 14(53): 26–30. October 1935. (Published at 26 Cross St., Manchester,2, Eng.)
Tables show cotton acreage and production by provinces for 1930 to 1934, and Japanese consumption of Chinese cotton 1930 to 1934.

Cotton – Paraguay

Paraguayan cotton production. Pan Amer. Union. Bull. 69(11): 882. November 1935. (Published in Washington, D. C.)
To promote the cultivation of high-grade cotton the Agricultural Bank of Paraguay has distributed seed and lent money to farmers and agricultural colonies. "Nearly all the cotton produced is exported, because of lack of manufacturing facilities in Paraguay. During the 9-year period 1925–33, the production varied between 4,000,000 and 8,000,000 pounds, but in 1934 it increased to more than 17,500,000 pounds."

Cotton – Price Forecasting

Slater, W. H. Forecasting raw cotton prices. IX. The position of Egyptian cotton. Textile Weekly 16(399): 451. Oct. 25, 1935. (Published at 49, Deansgate, Manchester, 3, Eng.)
The position of Egyptian cotton which has arisen as a result of the Italo-Abysinnian War is discussed.

Cotton – United States

Adams, Clara F. The hierarchy of cotton. Commonweal 22(21): 489–490. Sept. 20, 1935. (Published at 386 Fourth Ave., New York, N. Y.) L.C.
In spite of the changes that impend from acreage reduction, mechanical cotton picker, etc., the ancient hierarchy of cotton still stands. "Its affairs are administered by four successively ranking groups: the planter class who owns the land and pays the taxes, the renter who owns his farming implements and pays money rent for the land he farms, the cropper who owns nothing and works on the shares, and the hired help who works for wages and lives by grace."

Black, A. G. Developments in the American cotton programme. Cotton [Manchester] 41(1985): 25, 27. Oct.. 12, 1935. (Published by the Manchester Cotton Assoc., Ltd., 411 Fourth Floor, Royal Exchange, Manchester, 2, Eng.)
The chief of the Bureau of Agricultural Economics, United States Department of Agriculture, discusses the aims and workings of the various farm relief measures in the United States which led up to the adjustment program and the cotton loan program for 1935–36. Changes in the Universal Standards for American cotton are also mentioned.

[Cassidy, G. A., Jr., and Hurley, C. K.] Federal cotton production control.--
The Bankhead bill. Georgetown Law Jour. 22(4): 821-827. May 1934.
(Published by Georgetown University School of Law, Washington, D. C.)
    Three constitutional questions presented by the act are discussed.

Clayton, W. L.   The Southwest's stake in cotton. Cotton Digest 8(6): 4-6.
Nov. 16. 1935. (Published at 702 Cotton Exchange Bldg., Houston, Tex.)
    The author reviews the present cotton situation with special refer-
ence to government policies.

Cotton in the spotlight. Amer. Bankers Assoc. Agr. Comn. Bull. 9(9): [1-4],
tables, charts. November 1935. (Published by American Bankers Association, 522 First National Bank Bldg., Madison, Wis.)
    American cotton production and textile problems in relation to Govern-
ment policies are discussed.

Cox, A. B.   Approaching a crisis. Cotton Digest 8(2): 5-8. Oct. 19, 1935.
(Published at 702 Cotton Exchange Bldg., Houston, Tex.)
    "The major consideration..is whether cotton in the United States and
cotton goods in general can maintain themselves against foreign cotton
production on the one hand and commodities competing for the consumer's
dollar on the other." The author discusses the value of cotton on a
gold basis and the effect of government policies on production and consumption.

Cox, A. B.   Texas cotton and foreign trade. Tex. Weekly 11(48): 4-7. Nov.
30, 1935. (Published at the Dallas Athletic Club Bldg., Dallas, Texas.)
    "This comprehensive portrayal of cotton in Texas as a factor in
foreign trade was presented by Dr. A. B. Cox, director of the Bureau
of Business Research, University of Texas, on November 20th at Houston
before the convention of the National Foreign Trade Council." --Editor's
note.

Foosne, G. W.   American cotton in 1934-35. Return to freer markets on the
way? Manchester Guardian Com. (World Textiles): 5-7. Oct. 4, 1935.
(Published at the Guardian Bldg., 3 Cross St., Manchester, 2, England)

Molyneaux, P. F.   The cotton crisis. Emory Univ. Bull. 21(7): 35-55. July
1935. (Published at Emory University, Ga.)
    Address at the "Eighth Annual Institute of Citizenship, Emory Univer-
sity, Atlanta, Georgia, February 11th to 15th, 1935," on political and
economic problems of the South.
    The writer's purpose is "to show that cotton-growing in the United
States is facing a crisis, in the most precise sense; that this crisis
has been brought about chiefly by the operation of the commercial
policy of the United States under world conditions which are radically
different from those under which it has operated during most of our
national existence; that the meeting of this crisis in any effective
fashion requires a complete reversal of this commercial policy; that at
present neither the Government of the United States nor the American
people are showing any determined disposition to change this commercial
policy...and finally, that only an awakening of the people, of such a
character as to constitute nothing less than an upheaval, may be expected

to bring about such a change and to effect such an adjustment."

Revere, C. T. Cotton's changing position. Rev. of Reviews 92(4): 49-50, 64.
October 1935. (Published at 233 Fourth Ave., New York, N. Y.)
An analysis of the cotton situation, in which some of the results
of the government cotton program are pointed out. A change for the better
in American cotton from the Government's new loan policy is seen. "And
it is about time, for our high-priced product was losing ground in world
competition with cheaper grades."
A table accompanies the article which shows American cotton production,
exports, and consumption, annually, 1916-1935. (1935 figures preliminary.)

Revere, C. T. The status of American cotton. Policies and their consequences.
Manchester Guardian Com. (World Textiles) Oct. 4, 1935, pp.8-9. (Published at the Guardian bldg., 3 Cross St., Manchester, 2, Eng.)

Cotton Pickers Strike - Alabama

Burke, Thomas. "We told Washington." The cotton pickers visit the government. Nation 141(3674): 649-650. Dec. 4, 1935. (Published in New York,
N. Y.) (Pam. Coll. - Sharecroppers)
This is an account of what a delegation, protesting violence during
the cotton pickers' strike in Alabama, told officials in Washington
about the strike and about conditions among farm hands and sharecroppers, and of the reception the delegation received. The article
was written by a member of the delegation.

Cotton Versus Coffee - Brazil

Keeler, E. P. Cotton versus coffee in Brazil. Foreign Crops and Markets
31(24): 815-836. Dec. 9, 1935. (Published by the Division of Foreign
Agricultural Service, Bureau of Agricultural Economics, U. S. Dept. of
Agriculture.)
Subtopics: Historical background of the cotton industry (early history
of cotton, the American Civil War period, ascendency of rubber and coffee;
the upward trend in cotton production since 1900; depression and post-
depression developments); interrelation of cotton and coffee (economic
importance of coffee, direct effect of coffee situation on cotton
production, indirect effects of coffee on the exchange situation and
cotton production, effect of taxes on returns to coffee and cotton producers, efforts toward crop diversification and effect of cotton);
present world coffee situation and probable influence on Brazilian
cotton production.
Accompanied by charts and tables.

Cottonseed - Uses

Todd, J. A. The uses of cotton seed. Empire Cotton Growing Rev. 12(4); 278-
285, tables. October 1935. (Published by P. S. King & Son, Ltd., 14,
Great Smith St., London, S. W. 1, Eng.)
The processes of manufacture of cottonseed for various products and
uses are briefly described, and the competitive relation of cottonseed
oil to other oils and fats in the market is brought out.

Cottonseed Oil Mills - Texas

Slay, J. W. Texas cottonseed oil mills. Tex. Weekly 11(46): 8-9. Nov.
16, 1935. (Published at the Dallas Athletic Club Bldg., Dallas, Texas.)
"Cotton oil mills have had no small part in raising cottonseed to
its place as the second largest cash crop for Texas farmers."

Credit Unions

Froman, L. A. Credit unions. Jour. Business Univ. Chicago 8(3-4, pt. 1):
284-296, 338-344. July-October 1935. (Published in Chicago, Ill.)
"The purpose of this paper will be to give a limited amount of descriptive material covering the extent, the organization, and the operation of the credit union (Part I), and to appraise its usefulness (Part
II). Some speculation as to the probable position which the credit
union will occupy in the small-loan finance field in the future will
complete the discussion. Very extensive detailed descriptions of the
organization and operation of the credit union have appeared elsewhere.
[See footnote]. Only a brief survey, together with some new developments, will be included here."

Cycles, Trade

Kondratieff, N. D. The long waves in economic life. Rev. Econ. Statis.
17(6): 105-115. November 1935. (Published by the Dept. of Economics,
Harvard University, Cambridge, Mass.)
The following is quoted from the foreword, p. 105:
"The editors of the Review of Economic Statistics are happy to be
able to present in translation the peculiarly important article by
Professor Kondratieff, which, under the title 'Die langen Wellen der
Konjunktur,' appeared in the Archiv für Sozialwissenschaft und Sozialpolitik in 1926 (vol. 56, no. 3, pp. 573-609). The combining circumstances of an increasing interest in 'long waves' and the difficulty
of securing access to the original article would alone justify translation and publication of Kondratieff's contribution to the theory of
the trade cycle. In addition, the editors would take this means of
indicating their intention from time to time of rendering available to
the English-using world outstanding articles in foreign periodicals.
"This translation of Professor Kondratieff's article was made by
Mr. W. F. Stolper of Harvard University. Due to the limitations of
space, the editors have taken the liberty to summarize certain sections
of this translation. With the exception of a ten-page appendix of
tabular material, however, all tables and charts have been included."

Dairy Industry - Canada

Drummond, W. M. Price raising in the dairy industry. Canad. Jour. Econ.
and Polit. Sci. 1(4): 551-567. November 1935. (Published by the University of Toronto Press, Toronto, Ontario)
"For a fuller treatment of these problems see a book on the dairy
industry of Canada by J. A. Ruddick and W. M. Drummond, to be published
shortly by the Ryerson Press, Toronto." -p.551.

Da_iry Industry - South Africa

Alexander, G. D.   The disabilities of the dairy industry in South Africa:
  a criticism. So. African Jour. Econ. 3(3): 354-364. September 1935.
  (Published by the Economic Society of South Africa, P.O. Box 5316,
  Johannesburg)
      In this article the writer takes issue with some of the opinions
  and statements expressed by Mr. J. G. Kneen in an article in the June
  1935 issue of the Journal, entitled "The Dairy Industry in South Africa
  with Special Reference to the Export of Butter."

Kneen, J. G. The present position of the dairy industry in South Africa.
  So. African Jour. Econ. 3(3): 441-447. September 1935. (Published by
  the Economic Society of South Africa, P.O. Box 5316, Johannesburg)

Debts, State and Local

Ratchford, B. U.   Heavy state and local debt cause of curtailment of essential
  services. Annalist 46(1193): 748-749. Nov. 29, 1935. (Published by
  the New York Times Co., New York, N. Y.)
      "This is the second of two articles on State and local debts, the
  accurate measurement thereof, their relation to municipal bond defaults,
  and the causes and results of rising State and municipal indebtedness."

Decentralization of Industry

Baker, O. E.   The decentralization of industry: how far it has progressed;
  future trends. World Today. Encyclopaedia Britannica 3(2): 21-24.
  December 1935. (Published at 342 Madison Ave., New York, N. Y.)

Ferris, J. P.   If we want security. II. Explorations for a new road.
  Survey Graphic 24(12): 612-615, 625, 626, 627. December 1935. (Published at 112 E. 19th St., New York, N. Y.)
      "In his previous article John P. Ferris, industrial engineer, stated
  the case for decentralizing industry and population sufficiently to avoid
  the big swings of the economic pendulum. In this second article he outlines a trend which, with sufficient encouragement, he believes will
  lead in the direction of security." -p. 579.

Economic Developments - Great Britain

Blackett, Sir Basil P.   Economic developments in post-war Britain. Nineteenth
  Century 118(706): 718-737. (Published by Constable & Co., Ltd. Orange
  St., Leicester Square, London, W. C. 2, Eng.)
      This is a summary of the address Sir Basil Blackett was to have de-
  livered in the University of Heidelberg on August 16, 1935.
      Agriculture is considered on pp. 727-728.
      Among other things the writer discusses what form planning will take
  in Britain. He closes with this paragraph: "In his economic aspect the
  individual Briton is ready - indeed eager - to submit to planning for
  the general good. He is ready, if need be, to sacrifice a large part of
  what he has hitherto regarded as his essential economic individuality.
  But the goal in view must be - and he must be fully convinced that this

is indeed the goal - more freedom for the spiritual and intellectual
individuality of all. Planning is valid only if it brings freedom to
that part of man which lives in the realm of mind and spirit."

Economic History Review

Economic History Review, v. 6, no. 1, 142pp. October 1935. (Published for
the Economic History Society, by A. & C. Black Ltd., 4, 5, & 6, Soho
Square, London, T. 1, Eng.)
Partial contents: Assarting and the growth of the open fields, by
T. A. M. Bishop, pp. 13-29; Rural unemployment, 1815-34, by N. Gash,
pp. 90-93.

L'Est Européen Agricole

L'Est Européen Agricole 4. année no. 14, July 1935. (Issued by the Comité
Permanent d'Études Economiques des Etats Agricoles de l'Europe Centrale
et Orientale. Published by Jouve & Cio, 15, Rue Racine, Paris (6e),
France.)
Partial contents: La crise agricole on Europe, by Léon Janta-
Polczynski. -pp. 7-17. (Part of a speech delivered by a former Minister
of Agriculture of Poland at the meeting of the Economic Congress in
Brussels in June 1935, on the agricultural crisis in Europe and the
agrarian bloc of Central and Eastern Europe of which he was one of the
organizers.); L'arrangement polonodantzikois relatif au commerce des
produits agricoles pour 1935-1936, by Stoslaw Zembrzuski.-pp.28-38.
(An account of the Polish-Danzig commercial agreement for 1935/36 relative to agricultural products.); Pologne. Les nouvelles directives
de la politique de la vente des produits agricoles, by Czeslaw Bobrowski.-
pp.39-55. (An account of the Polish Government policy for 1935/36 for
the export of agricultural products.); Pologne. L'industrie laitiere
et son avenir, by Janusz Radnicki.-pp.56-66. (Poland's dairy industry
and the program for its future development are discussed.); Tchécoslovaquie.
L'arboriculture fruitiere, by B. Zezula. -pp. 67-75. (Fruit growing in
Czechoslavakia is described.); Tchécoslovaquie. L'exode rural du point
de vue sociologique, by Karel Galla. -pp.76-79. (The social basis of
the exodus from the country is briefly discussed and the remedy is
indicated.) Prices of agricultural products on various world markets
and export statistics of Hungary are given.

Farming, Mixed

Carter, H. C. Mixed farming, antidote for rural depression. Land, no. 1268,
p. 5. Sept. 27, 1935. (Published in Sydney, New South Wales.)
"This is the fourth, and final, article in Mr. Carter's series on
the need for the greater development of mixed farming... Mr. Carter
advocates greater and systematic attention to the raising of lambs and
pigs, the fattening of vealers and chiller steers, the feeding of dairy
cows, turkey raising, and the production of maize, potatoes, and lucerne
in addition to wheat and wool."

Fats and Oils

Drews, Max. Fettknappheit am weltmarkt? Wirtschaftsdienst (n.F.) 20(42):
1429-1431. Oct. 18, 1935. (Issued by Hamburgisches Welt-Wirtschafts-
Archiv. Published by Hanseatische Verlagsanstalt, A. G., Hamburg 36,
Germany.)
A study of fats and oils on the world market shows that the existing
deficiency is not likely to prove a serious menace for the future.

Fats and Oils - Germany

Heinicke, Günther. Fettmarkt und fetteinfuhr. Wirtschaftsdienst (n.F.)
20(43): 1458-1461. Oct. 25, 1935. (Issued by Hamburgisches Welt-
Wirtschafts-Archiv. Published by Hanseatische Verlagsanstalt, A. G.,
Hamburg 36, Germany.)
An account of Germany's attempt to supply the demand for fats and
oils by means of imports. Tables are given.

Food Consumption and Public Health

Food supplies. Relation of increased consumption to public health. Empire
Producer, no. 229, pp. 181-184. November 1935. (Published by British
Empire Producers' Organisation, 22, Queen Anne's Gate, London, S. W. 1,
Eng.)
Contains a summary of speeches made by Stanley Bruce of Australia
and Earl de la Warr and others at the Assembly of the League of Nations
in September.

Food Habits

The food industries. Changes reflecting shifts in the national diet. Index
15(12): 262-268. December 1935. (Published by the New York Trust Company, 100 Broadway, New York, N. Y.)
"The purpose of the present article is to consider the food manufacturing industries as a whole, with a view of ascertaining such changes
in their relative importance as have taken place during the past quarter
century which may reflect significant changes in our national habits
of food selection."

Food Supply - Germany

Germany. The food shortage and "Manchester liberalism." Economist 121(4810):
852-853. Nov. 2, 1935. (Published at 8 Bouverie St., Fleet St., London,
E. C. 4, Eng.)

Food Supply, Self-Sufficiency In - China

Chen Kung-Po. Self-sufficiency in food supply. Chinese Econ. Jour. 17(2):
97-135. August 1935. (Published by Bureau of Foreign Trade, Ministry
of Industry, 1040 North Soochow Road, Shanghai, China.)
The author outlines a ten-year plan for the improvement of China's
rice crop which has been drawn up for consideration by the government,
and makes a study of China's wheat problem.

Fruit - Great Britain

The Englishman's fruit. Economist 121(4812): 948-949. Nov. 16, 1935.
(Published at 8 Bouverie St., Fleet St., London, E. C. 4, Eng.)
Discusses the consumption, production, imports, and import price of
fruit in Great Britain. Mention is also made of the failure of the fruit
marketing scheme, and the failure of a substantial proportion of home-
produced fruit to reach the market in good condition. The writer concludes that "the grower will best secure a higher return for his produce not by creating scarcity, but by improving his grading, packing and
marketing technique in general."

Fruit and Vegetables - Denmark

Sørensen, Frode. Cultivation and export of fruit and vegetables. Danish
Foreign Office Jour., no. 177, pp. 135-140. October 1935. (Published
in Copenhagen, Denmark.)

Futures Trading

Sturtevant, C. D. The economic value of speculation. Grain & Feed Journals
Consolidated 75(9): 365-366. Nov. 13, 1935. (Published at 332 South
La Salle St., Chicago, Ill.)
From an address before the Nebraska Grain Dealers' Association.
"Trading in futures is not an invention of the Devil, as some of our
antagonists in Congress try to convince the public, but on the contrary,
is a natural outgrowth, conceived and developed by the Yankee traders
who first pioneered the business of distributing the grain crops of the
country through the central markets which they established. The system
was born of economic necessity and is the child of actual experience
and of trial and error, reaching its sturdy maturity by holding fast to
successful improvements and discarding unworkable innovations." The
writer continues by giving a description of the grain marketing system.

Grain Monopoly - Czechoslovakia

Schwarz, Beno. Czechoslovakian evils in controlling crops. Northwest.
Miller 184(7): 588. Nov. 27, 1935. (Published at 118 S. 6th St.,
Minneapolis, Minn.)
"The principle of self-sufficiency and state control has materialized
fully in Czechoslovakia, as is demonstrated by the new decree recently
passed regulating the monopoly management for 1935-36. During the
season 1934-35, only a fraction of the agricultural production was under
the control of the Grain Monopoly Co. Now it will have complete control
of the grain harvested by each farmer, as well as all sales of grain
made by farmers."
After describing in more detail the provisions in the decree, the
author writes in conclusion: "Altogether, the evils inherent in the
monopoly system are so obvious and the experiences of most other
countries who have adopted it so discouraging that its failure in
Czechoslovakia is more than probable."

Grazing - Taylor Act - United States

Gates, P. W. American land policy and the Taylor Grazing Act. Land Policy
    Circ. October 1935, pp. 15-37. (Published by the Resettlement Admin-
    istration, Washington, D. C.)
    The writer's introductory paragraph is as follows:
    "The adoption of the Taylor Grazing Act in 1934 was epochal in the
development of our national program of land utilization. Neither the
most dramatic nor far-reaching of the New Deal measures, its significance
has largely escaped attention outside the areas immediately affected by
it. The explanation of this is simple: the application of the Act is
regional, affecting as it does farming, grazing, and settlement in only
eleven States, all located in the Far West, and comprising an area larger
than all States east of the Mississippi River. This Act, which embodies
the progressive principles of conservation and planned use of land and
its resources is not the first, but rather the last of a series of similar
measures which have completely reversed our traditional land and agricultural policy. Because it marks the culmination of a long process
both of education and agitation on the part of reformers (who sought
to reverse our traditional policies in order to preserve for the future
certain natural resources which were being threatened by wasteful exploitation) it is necessary first to examine the problems created by
such methods of exploitation, and then to trace the movement looking
toward change. The provisions of the Taylor Act, as they affect land
policies, will then be analyzed."

Hurlburt, V. L. The Taylor grazing act amendments. Jour. Land & Pub.
    Utility Econ. 11(4): 410-411. November 1935. (Published by Northwestern
    University, School of Commerce, 337 East Chicago Ave., Chicago, Ill.)
    This is a review of the amendments to the Taylor Grazing Act passed
    by the last Congress and vetoed by President Roosevelt, together with
    the reasons for the veto.

Group Method in Rural Studies

Loomis, C. P. The group method in rural studies. Based on German techniques.
    Sociol. and Social Research 20(2): 126-135. November-December 1935.
    (Published at the University of Southern California, 3551 University
    Ave., Los Angeles, Calif.)

Hawaii

Hawaii. Our most important noncontiguous territory. Index 15(12): 245-251.
    December 1935. (Published by the New York Trust Company, New York, N.Y.)
    For Hawaii's sugar industry and pineapple production see pp. 248-250.

Hogs - Direct Marketing

Carnes, N. K. Direct marketing of hogs. Grain & Feed Rev. 24(9): 38, 39,
    40. May 1935. (Published at 408 South 3rd St., Minneapolis, Minn.)
    A radio talk by the General Manager Central Co-operative Association,
    South St. Paul, Minn., April 9, 1935, critical of a radio talk, made
    by Nils A Olsen on March 27, 1935.

Hogs - Great Britain

Cohen, Ruth, and Barker, J. D.   The pig cycle: a reply. Economica (n.s.)
²(8): 448—452. November 1935. (Published by the London School of
Economics, and Political Science, Houghton, Aldwych, London, Eng.)
    This is a reply to an article by R. H. Coase and R. F. Fowler in the
May 1935 number of Economica, on Bacon Production and the Pig-Cycle in
Great Britain.
    The Pig-Cycle: A Rejoinder, by R. H. Coase and R. F. Fowler, pp.423-
428 of the November issue of Economica, is the authors' rejoinder to
Miss Cohen's and Mr. Barker's criticism of their article. Their introductory paragraph is as follows:
    "The criticisms which Miss Cohen and Mr. Barker make of our paper
relate solely to the theory of the pig-cycle. There is no dispute regarding our criticism of the recommendations of the Reorganisation Commission. In their reply, however, they defend both the methods previously
used in investigating the problem of the pig-cycle, and the conclusion
reached by such investigations that the pig-cycle can be explained by
the 'cobweb theorem.' We believe that the criticisms made by Miss
Cohen and Mr. Barker of our arguments are invalid."

Irrigation - Peru

Klinge, Gerardo.   Política de irrigación. La Vida Agrícola 12(137): 245-253,
255, 257, 259, 261-265, 267-269. April 1935; (138): 319-326. May 1935;
(139): 389-397, 399, 401, 403-405. June 1935; (140): 461, 463, 465,
467, 469-473, July 1935; (141): 607, 609-611, 613-614. August 1935; (142):
705, 707-712. September 1935; (143): 807-820. October 1935; (144): 895,
897-910. November 1935. (Published in Lima, Peru.)
    A summary of irrigation projects carried out in Peru is followed by
a discussion of the necessary conditions for a successful irrigation
policy. Illustrations are taken from irrigation works in other countries
such as the United States and Mexico.

Journal of Farm Economics

Journal of Farm Economics, v. 17, no. 4, pp. 613-793. November 1935. (Published by the American Farm Economic Association, Asher Hobson, Secretary-
Treasurer, University of Wisconsin, Madison, Wisconsin)
    Contents: Farm mortgages and the government, by W. G. Murray, pp. 613-
624; Correct and incorrect methods of determining the effectiveness of
the tariff, by Henry Schultz, pp. 625-641; A reply to Professor Schultz,
by E. R. Rennø, pp. 642-645; The National Institute of Agricultural Economics in Italy, by Arrigo Serpieri, pp. 646-658; The field of agricultural
data, by T. H. Ebling, pp. 659-668; Tax relief through rational expenditure control, by H. L. Lutz, pp. 669-681; Studies of local government as
an approach to the question of farm taxation, by M. P. Catherwood, pp.
682-693; discussion by C. H. Hammar, pp. 693-695; discussion by G. S.
Klemmedson, pp. 695-701; The social effects of land division in relation
to a program of land utilization, by T. L. Smith, pp. 702-709; The subsistence homestead program from the viewpoint of an economist, by W. E.
Zeuch, pp. 710-719; Social and economic significance of the subsistence

homesteads program - from the viewpoint of a sociologist, by Carl C.
Taylor, pp. 720-731.

The following "notes" are given: Problems of creamery operating efficiency in California, by J. M. Tinley, pp. 732-735; Some factors affecting butter consumption, by J. B. Roberts, pp.735-738; The direct
marketing controversy, by F. L. Thomsen, pp. 738-741; Some recent economic
trends of concern to midwest cooperatives, by F. Robotka, pp. 741-748;
Comments on views of the Economic Committee of The League of Nations on
agricultural protectionism, by E. Laur, pp. 748-753; Index to volume
XVII, 1935, pp. 789-793.

Land Settlement - Honduras

Recent agricultural activities. Honduras. Pan Amer. Union. Bull. 69(11):
877. November 1935. (Published in Washington, D. C.)

The Government of Honduras has issued regulations, by Decree no. 866
of July 9, 1935, for the leasing of national lands in the so-called
reserve zones to aid agriculture and to encourage the establishment of
small farms. "Any native born or naturalized citizen of Honduras in
full exercise of his legal rights may apply for a tract measuring up
to 1,235 acres, if the land is to be devoted to agriculture; and up to
1,482 acres if it is for live stock raising. The applicant must show,
however, that he is financially able to develop the property, except
where the grant is for less than 247 acres."

Land Settlement - India

Rahman, Maulvi Mizanur. Co-operative land colonisation. Bengal Co-op.
Jour. 21(1): 14-23. July-September 1935. (Published by the Bengal Co-
operative Organisation Society, Ltd., 3-1, Bankshall Street, Calcutta,
India.)

"The Chittagong Co-operative Land Colonization Movement is a land-
mark and one of the most distinctive features of the Co-operative Movement not only of Chittagong but of Bengal, as a whole, possibly India.
It is designed to provide land-less agriculturists and agricultural
labourers with lands for cultivation and development on cooperative
lines, and to give them local habitations of their own, in the midst
of their economic holdings, on colonization basis." An account of the
origin and development of this colonization scheme is given, and its aims
are enumerated. "Personal cultivation, permanent colonization and
habitation in the colony with family, manual labour in maintaining
embankments and other works of improvements of the colony, compulsory
free primary education of their children, payment of half the produce
of their lands towards repayment of their loans...are the necessary
conditions of membership of the colony...at Badarkhali a forest area
with little amenities near-by, is being developed into a human habitation...
The colony is making steady progress, and promises to be a place of
growing importance."

Land Settlement - Palestine

Lasker, Louis D.   The promised land - 1935.   Survey Graphic 24(12): 602-607,
    607, 608, 629, 630.   December 1935.   (Published at 112 E. 19th St., New
    York, N. Y.)
        Describes the collective and cooperative agricultural colonies of
    Palestine.

Land Settlement — Western Canada

England, Robert.   Land settlement in the northern areas of western Canada
    (1925-35).   Canad. Jour. Econ. and Polit. Sci. 1(4): 578-587.   November
    1935.   (Published by the University of Toronto Press, Toronto, Ontario.)
        The article is divided into three main parts: A, Immigrant settlers
    (1926-31); B, Settlement (1931-35) under which are considered the drought
    area movement and the back-to-the-land movement; C, Ethnic group movement
    and individual settlers.

Land Settlement and Unemployment - England

Land settlement and unemployment.   Country Life 78(2023): 422.   Oct. 26, 1935.
    (Published at 20 Tavistock St., Covent Garden London, W. C. 2, Eng.)
        Editorial regarding land settlement as a possible solution to the
    problem of industrial unemployment in England.   The editor is unfavorable
    to such a plan and does not think that it would work.   The German system
    of selecting, by means of a strict examination, both the prospective
    settler and his wife before settling them on the land is commended.

Land Tenure - Dutch East Indies

Splecatner, F.   Die Dorfwirtschaft Niederländisch - Indiens.   Wirtschaftsdienst
    (n.F.) 20(44): 1494-1496.   Nov. 1, 1935.   (Issued by Hamburgisches
    Welt-Wirtschafts-Archiv.   Published by Hanseatische Verlagsanstalt, A. G.,
    Hamburg 36, Germany.)
        An account of village organization and land tenure in the Dutch East
    Indies and the effect on agriculture.

Meat - Prices

Cabell, R. H.   Who makes the price of meat?   Many factors influence meat
    prices but consumer has the final vote.   National Provisioner 93(23):
    17, 45, 48.   Dec. 7, 1935.   (Published at 407 South Dearborn St.,
    Chicago, Ill.)

Meat Export Board - Australia

Australian Meat Export Board.   Pastoral Rev. 45(10): 1039, 1040.   Oct. 16, 1935.
    (Published at 122-138 King St., Melbourne, Aust.)
        "At the invitation of the Federal Government a conference of repre-
    sentative meat producers and exporters was held at Canberra on 6th October,
    to consider the question of forming an Australian Meat Export Board...

"As a result of their deliberations it was decided that the board should consist of 18 members...As it was felt that a board of 18 would be unwieldy, it was agreed that it should be given power to appoint an executive of five from amongst its members."
The duties of the board are enumerated.

Milk Control - New York

Chase, Allan, and Goldsmith, Alfred. The milk racket. The Nation 141(3669): 501-503. October 30, 1935. (Published at 20 Vesey St., New York, N. Y.)
Critical of the administration of the New York milk control law and of attempts to solve the milk situation. The writers believe that milk should be considered a public utility.

Milling - Annual Review

The Northwestern Miller Production Annual. Northwest. Miller 184(2, Sect.2): 1-80. Oct. 16, 1935. (Published at 118 S. Sixth St., Minneapolis, Minn.)
A technical review of flour, cereal and feed milling.
Partial contents: Operative milling forty years ago, by Thomas Clarke and B. W. Dedrick, pp. 5-7, 74, 75, 79, 80; Co-ordination of mill departments, by E. W. Reed, pp. 9, 72; Baking test as a method of measuring quality in winter wheat, by M. J. Blish, pp. 10-11; The story of a grain of wheat from ripening to bin, by C. O. Swanson, pp. 12-13; Flour storage, by C. H. Briggs, p. 17; Simple lessons in thermohygrics, (Published by special permission, and by the courtesy of Carrier Engineering Corp.), pp. 23, 24, 64; The determination of moisture in wheat and wheat products, by J. E. Anderson, pp. 25, 28; Factors that influence the protein content of wheat, by C. O. Swanson, pp. 26-28; Breeding better quality wheats, by John H. Parker, pp. 30-32; Research on roll speeds, by A. Ougrimoff, pp. 60-62; The 1935 black stem rust epidemic, by E. C. Stakman, p. 62; and Recent developments in mixed feeds, by C. W. Sievert, pp. 71-72.

Money, Public - Constitutional Control

McGuire, O. R. Constitutional control over public moneys. Federal Bar Assoc. Jour. 2(4): 187-191, 200-207, 229. November 1935. (Published in Washington, D. C.)
"An address delivered Wednesday evening, October 9, 1935, in Washington, D. C., before the Inquirendo Club."
"This is but another way of saying that there have been few basic changes since the Subsidy Act of 1624 in the means and methods adopted to insure that the people shall control, through their elected representatives, the raising and spending of public revenues. It is another question whether that system functions today as it should..."

McGuire, O. R. The new deal and the public money. Georgetown Law Jour. 23(2): 155-195. January 1935. (Published by the Georgetown University School of Law, Washington, D. C.)
"It seems abundantly clear that since the Supreme Court of the United States has refused to assume a position of authority over the acts of the people as expressed through their elected representatives

in Congress in the matter of taxing themselves and appropriating the
money as a donation, or subsidy to an individual or group of individuals
or for the construction of roads and railroads or for the dredging of rivers
or building of canals and dams for irrigation or other purposes or for
the support of education in the various states, such Court could not
interfere with the appropriating power in providing public money to
construct dams for the purpose of generating electricity, the purchase of
land and the construction of apartment houses, subsistence homesteads or
for paying bounties, subsidies or benefit payments to farmers in the reduction and control of agricultural products. Regardless of the question
as to the wisdom of such expenditures, with which I am not here concerned,
if the majority of the people see fit through their elected representatives in Congress to tax themselves or others within their taxing power
and distribute the money in the form of appropriations to determine and
limit or expand the functions of government, there is no supervisory
power under our form of government which denies to the law-making power
the right to carry out the will of the people in this respect. It would
seem to be too clear for serious argument that with respect to appropriations, at least, President Roosevelt knew whereof he spoke when he
declared that the Country was progressing towards a new order of things
"'under the framework and in the spirit and intent of the American Constitution.'"

National Economic Council — Germany

Rogers, Lindsay, and Dittmar, W. R. The Reichswirtschaftsrat: de mortuis.
Polit. Sci. Quart. 50(4): 481-501. December 1935. (Published by the
Academy of Political Science, Fayerweather Hall, Columbia University,
New York, N. Y.)
   Discusses the German National Economic Council and its decline.
The Reichswirtschaftsrat was abrogated by the Nazi Cabinet Law of March
25, 1934.

Oil-Seeds - India

Shaw, F. J. F. Indian oil-seeds. Mysore Econ. Jour. 21(10): 539-542.
October 1935; (11): 575-579. November 1935. (Published in Bangalore
City, Mysore, India.)

Packing Industry and Business Situation

German, A. O. Packinghouse policies. This is a good time for packers to
consider what they should be. 1 sheet. Reprint Coll.
   "Reprinted from the National Provisioner of July 29, 1933."
   "This is the introduction to a series of articles analyzing the
business situation as it exists today in relation to the packing industry.
The purpose of this discussion will be to aid packinghouse management
to formulate policies which will be helpful in making packinghouse operations more profitable in the long run."
   Other articles in the series are as follows:
   Packer and Inflation. What it is and how it affects meat packing
activities. Reprinted from the National Provisioner of August 26, 1933. 3pp.

Livestock price control. How supplies and consumer purchasing power
govern prices. Reprinted from the National Provisioner of September 23,
1933. 2pp.
Export and home trade. Importance of agricultural exports in our
domestic economy. Reprinted from the National Provisioner of November
11, 1933. 2pp.
The farm problem. Difficulties encountered in attempting a solution.
Reprinted from National Provisioner of March 3, 1934. 2pp.

Peek, George N., and Agriculture

Kilgore, Bernard. All for agriculture. Today 5(8): 5, 23. Dec. 14, 1935.
(Published at 152 W. 42nd St., New York, N. Y.)
An account of George N. Peek and his fight for agriculture.
"If it takes him the next ten years to put them across, George N. Peek
will go on fighting for his principles in foreign trade and agriculture
which 'can't be compromised.'"

Planning

How much is left for government planning to do? Com. & Financ. Chron. 141:
3589-3591. December 7, 1935. (Published at 25 Spruce St., New York, N.Y.)
Critical of the recent report of the Science Advisory Board, not because
its recommendations are unscientific and not because "its proposals, if
adopted, might rid agriculture of some of the disadvantages under which
it labors", but because "it is precisely such proposals as these, clothed
in the garb of scientific recommendations and free of obvious political
taint, that help to strengthen and extend the Federal regimentation which
New Deal policies have fastened upon the country, and which, as everybody knows, is honeycombed with politics from top to bottom."

Plan Age, v. 1, no. 9, pp. 1-20. November 1935. (Published by National
Economic and Social Planning Association, 726 Jackson Place, Washington, D.C.
Contents: The hiatus in national planning, by D. C. Coyle, pp. 1-5;
Planning the new deal, by R. H. Montgomery, pp. 6-11; Production studies,
an interview with Harold Loob [answers questions on the National Survey
of Potential Product Capacity] pp.12-15; Legislative planning in Colorado,
by A. M. Laird, pp. 16-18; list of planning groups throughout the world,
pp. 19-20.

Planning - Texas

Mooney, Booth. The Texas Planning Board. Tex. Weekly 11(45): 4-5. Nov.
9, 1935. (Published at Dallas Athletic Club Bldg., Dallas, Tex.)
A consideration of the long-range program of the Texas Planning Board.
"In giving consideration to a long-range program for the State, it
is, of course, necessary in the beginning to consider the conditions of
its citizens and the resources of Texas. The condition of the citizens
is naturally dependent upon environment and health; the resources of the
State consist of soil, climate, vegetation, and minerals. And to consider
properly both citizens and resources, the board has evolved the following
nine-point program of activities: Public health, land use and recreation,

water conservation, reforestation, minerals, transportation, industry, education, and government and social aspects."

Planning, Regional - Germany

Hegemann, Werner. Recent trends in German regional planning. Planners' Jour. 1(4): 85-86. November-December 1935. (Published by the American City Planning Institute, Hunt Hall, Cambridge, Mass.)
Discussion of Bruno Wehner's paper in The Planners' Journal for October 1935.

Population

Corey, A. C., and Hartley, R. W. Population planning. Planners' Jour. 1(4): 87-92. November-December 1935. (Published by the American City Planning Institute, Hunt Hall, Cambridge, Mass.)
Concluding discussion of A. C. Comey's paper in the Planners' Journal for July-August 1935.

Thorpson, W. S. Factors conditioning a population policy for the United States. pp. 60-69.
"Reprinted from Publication of the American Sociological Society, vol. XXIX, no. 3, August, 1935."
"To the writer there are three chief purposes to be achieved by a population policy: In the first place, it should aim at securing a population of a size calculated to make a good standard of living possible to all in view of the natural resources available and the techniques of production and distribution in use...Secondly, a population policy should be calculated to produce a healthy population - one in which the standard of physical health is high and in which incompetence resulting from mental defect is reduced to a minimum. In the third place, a population policy should encourage a distribution of people which will make possible as decent a manner of life as is feasible considering the economic means available to the community."

Woofter, T. J., Jr. The natural increase of the rural non-farm population. Milbank Memorial Fund Quart. 13(4): 311-319. October 1935. (Published at 40 Wall St., New York, N. Y.)

Population - France

Boulangé, Joseph. La population agricole du Pas-de-Calais. La Vie Agricole et Rurale 24(44): 279-281. Nov. 3, 1935. (Published by J. B. Baillière & Fils, 19, Rue Hautefeuille, Paris (6e), France.)
An account of the composition of the rural population in the Department of Pas-de-Calais.

Price-fixing and Proration under A.A.A.

Black, P. R. May price fixing and proration devices be utilized by the Secretary of Agriculture appurtenant to the exercise of the license power under the Agricultural Adjustment Act? Georgetown Law Jour. 23(2): 196-217.

January 1935. (Published by the Georgetown University School of Law, Washington, D. C.)

Prices

Fraser, T. H.   Le mécanisme des prix en régime capitaliste et en régime communiste. L'Egypte Contemporaine, no. 155-156, pp. 469-489. March-April 1935. (Issued by the Société Royale d'Économie Politique, de Statistique et de Législation. Published in Cairo, Egypt.)
    A comparative study of the principles that determine prices under the capitalist and the communist régimes.

Thorp, W. L.   The collection and distribution of price information. Dun & Bradstreet Monthly Rev. 43(2092): 2-4. November 1935. (Published at 290 Broadway, New York, N. Y.)
    "As early as 1921, there were about 150 open-price associations that distributed or exchanged price information to members. The difficulties encountered in the attempts to adopt an interchange of such information, the pertinent court decisions, and the proposal submitted to the Federal Trade Commission by the Fertilizer Industry, are explained and summarized.." -p.1.

Prices - Great Britain

The stability of prices in Britain. Westminster Bank Rev. no. 261, pp. 3-6. November 1935. (Published at 41 Lothbury, London, E. C. 2, Eng.)

Primary Industries -- Australia

Gepp, Sir Herbert William.   Australia's primary industries. Their relation to the world's economic position. New South Wales. Agr. Gaz. 46(9): 494-498. September 1935; (10): 559-564. October 1935; (11): 625-627. November 1935. (Published in Sydney, N.S.W. Australia.)
    This address by the Chairman of the Royal Commission on Wheat, Flour and Bread Industries was delivered at the Annual State Conference of the Agricultural Bureau of New South Wales. Some of the reactions of other countries to the economic crisis are sketched, and their effect on conditions in Australia is stressed. The necessity for stabilization of exchange and reduction of tariffs is pointed out, and the appointment of an advisory economic general staff to aid the Government is advocated.

Processing Taxes

Harrower, D. C.   AAA and states' rights. Processing tax challenged as an unconstitutional delegation of legislative power. Involves legality of production control. Legal opinion divided on tax-payment recovery. Barron's 15(47): 10. Nov. 25, 1935. (Published at 44 Broad St., New York, N. Y.)

Processing taxes and the tariff. Northwest. Miller and Amer. Baker 12(11)¦ 358.
Nov. 6, 1935. (Published at 118 S. 6th St., Minneapolis, Minn.)
"By request of a reader, we reprint...a recent argument made public
by Fred J. Lingham, president of the Federal Mill, Inc., Lockport, N. Y.,
and former head of the Millers National Federation."
The principles and effects of both the tariff and the processing taxes
are set forth in this article.

Sloan, G. A. Processing taxes and tariff. Northwest. Miller and Amer. Baker
12(11): 357, 367. Nov. 6, 1935. (Published at 118 S. 6th St., Minneapolis,
Minn.)
From an address before the recent annual convention of the American
Bakers Association.
Regarding the difference between tariff and the processing tax, Mr.
Sloan said in part: "They say the processing tax is the farmers' tariff.
What are the facts?
"The tariff is imposed for revenue of the government. Processing taxes
are imposed for the revenue of a special group in our population. None
of the duties collected on their products are given to manufacturers,
but are used for general expenses and for the general welfare of the entire population. Processing taxes are paid to only about 15% of the
total population; in fact to only a portion of the farm population."
Mr. Sloan outlines some principles, which in his judgment, should be
embodied in a "sound program for co-operation with agriculture." The
following is included: "All processing taxes should be eliminated and
a broader and sounder method for obtaining funds required for the benefit payments to farmers should be adopted."

Raw Materials

Empires and raw materials. Economist 121(4809): 793-795. Oct. 26, 1935.
(Published at 8 Bouverie St., Fleet St., London, E. C. 4, Eng.)

Real Estate Mortgage Loans

Bodfish, Morton. Government and private mortgage loans on real estate.
Jour. Land & Pub. Utility Econ. 11(4): 402-409. November 1935. (Published by Northwestern University, School of Commerce, 337 East Chicago
Ave., Chicago, Ill.)
This is a summary report made by the Brookings Institution on
government and private mortgage loans on real estate. "The report arrived at no important conclusions, but merely summarized the existing
situation. The report has been privately circulated among the institutions at whose instance the survey was undertaken. Because of the
improbability that the report will ever be printed in its entirety,
this summary has been prepared. The data here presented are taken directly
from the original report, except for the addition of certain more recent
figures now available; the descriptive material has been considerably
shortened; and in conclusion some questions as to the implications of
the data for future policy has been raised."
The Farm Credit Administration, Federal Home Loan Bank Board and Home
Owners' Loan Corporation, Reconstruction Finance Corporation, Federal

Housing Administration, Housing Division of Federal Emergency Administration of Public Works, and the Resettlement Administration are the governmental agencies surveyed.

clamation and Land Improvement - Italy

ıgdor, S. Notes et impressions sur la bonification intégrale en Italie. L'Egypte Contemporaine, no. 155-156, pp. 439-467. March-April 1935. (Issued by the Société Royale d'Economie Politique, de Statistique et de Législation. Published in Cairo, Egypt.)

The object of Italy's land reclamation and improvement scheme is defined as being to insure a better utilization of the national agricultural land, to establish new centres of rural life in the vast spaces formerly infested by malaria after they have been made hygienic and habitable, to prevent the decadence of existing systems of production and to improve them with a view to intensive production, to organize new intensive systems and to increase production in proportion to the increase in population and to raise the standard of living of the rural population. The plan includes drainage and irrigation works, river regulation, construction of aqueducts, roads, farms and rural houses, provision of drinking and irrigation water, installation of pertinent industries, and the settlement on the land of a large number of workers and their families. The basic principle on which this whole scheme is founded is the solidarity of all its various parts. Hence there is coordination between the public works undertaken by the State, and the work of land improvement which is the obligation of the landowners aided by subventions and advances from the Government. This tremendous project has been undertaken to make habitable and productive an area of more than four million hectares, or almost double the existing cultivated area of Egypt.

The author makes a rapid survey of the general lines of the physical geography of Italy, the insalubrious regions in 1899, and the causes of the abandonment of lands and rural depopulation. He summarizes the main aims of the Fascist land reclamation scheme, culled from the numerous speeches of Mussolini, its legislative history, the activities planned and carried out, and the results obtained. Tables show the status of the work by provinces on July 1, 1933. Some typical examples of what has been accomplished are given in detail, and a short comparison is made between the work done in Italy and the land improvement work done in Egypt.

Recovery Program

Iooney, Booth. Measures for world recovery. Tex. Weekly 11(47): 6-7. Nov. 23, 1935. (Published at the Dallas Athletic Club Bldg., Dallas, Texas.)
Reviews the discussion at the national convention of the National Foreign Trade Council, held at Houston, Texas, November 18-20.

"On the final day of the meeting the Foreign Trade Council endorsed the 'World Program for World Recovery' which was unanimously adopted by one thousand delegates...at the biennial convention of the International Chamber of Commerce last June...A number of important resolutions are included in those adopted at the convention, of which the most

outstanding are these: Stabilization of exchanges at the earliest date
that can be agreed upon; reduction of trade barriers; final settlement,
on a fair basis to all countries, of all international debts; and the
steady reduction of armaments in order to lessen the heavy weight of
taxation."

Research, Agricultural

[Grommen. H. B.] Promise of farm prosperity seen in research bureau.
Grain & Feed Rev. 24(10): 26-27, 33. June 1935. (Published at 408 South
3rd St., Minneapolis, Minn.)
"The feasibility and necessity of a research bureau for agriculture is
clearly demonstrated in ...[this] address by Homer B. Grommon,...president
of the Illinois Farmers Grain Dealers association. Mr. Grommon, in presenting his thoughts before the agricultural section of the Association
of Commerce at Chicago on May 21, 1935, outlined present agricultural
conditions. He dealt particularly with phases of the Administration's
program which bear on agriculture and expressed little faith in a policy
of production restriction as a permanent means of restoring agricultural
prosperity." - [Editor's note]

Hibbs, Ben. Rim of the future. Country Gent. 105(12): 14-15, 72, 73.
December 1935. (Published at Independence Square, Philadelphia, Pa.)
On the "tangible results of research" in agriculture.

Resettlement Administration

A., R. F. In Washington. Today #5(7): 10, 19. Dec. 7, 1935. (Published at
152 W. 42nd. St., New York, N. Y.)
A statement of the work and program of the Resettlement Administration which consists of rural rehabilitation projects, land utilization,
rural-industrial community projects, and suburban resettlement projects.
Reply is made to the newspaper stories of a "staff of 12,089 to create
5,012 relief jobs," and it is shown that the largest undertaking of the
Administration is the rehabilitation of 354,000 farm families, inherited
from the Rural Rehabilitation Division of the FERA.

Mooney, Booth. Rural Resettlement Administration. Tex. Weekly 11(48): 8-9.
Nov. 30, 1935. (Published at the Dallas Athletic Club Bldg., Dallas, Texas.)
The writer asks and answers the question: "What is rural resettlement?
Just what does it mean, in plain easily understandable language?" He
points out that two phases of the program are peculiarly adapted to the
needs of Texas: resettlement of farm families on relief and land utilization.

Tugwell, R. G. Problems - and goal - of rural relief. The aim, says Tugwell, is soundly to rebuild rural life, the protector of our individualism.
New York Times Mag., Dec. 15, 1935, pp. 3, 22. (Published in New York, N. Y.)
Mainly on the rural rehabilitation work of the Resettlement Administration, although some attention is also paid to the resettlement, land
utilization, and suburban housing work of the Administration.

Rural America

Rural America, v. 13, no. 8, pp. 1-16. November 1935. (Published by the
American Country Life Association, Inc., 105 E. 22nd St., New York, N.Y.)
Partial contents: We need three new R's, by J. H. Kolb, [three new
R's are needed in the repair and rebuilding of rural education, namely
relationships, refinement, and religion] p. 2; Population movements
affecting the welfare of the farm family, by W. S. Thompson, pp. 3-6;
Toward greater security, by W. A. Terpenning [how the Resettlement Administration is undertaking to bring greater security to many families]
pp. 6-8; The development of rural sociological research, by J. T. Jardine
[from a paper before the section on rural sociology of the American
Sociological Society] pp. 8-11.

Rural Rehabilitation and Canning Industry

Campbell, Carlos. Rural rehabilitation and the canning industry. The Canner
821(23): 7-8. Nov. 16, 1935. (Published at 140 N. Dearborn St.,
Chicago, Ill.)
The writer discusses the plans of the Resettlement Administration
to set up canning factories in the community projects for the rehabilitation of distressed farmers. He makes a comparison of five important
economic factors - location, production and sales management, canning
costs, competition - regarding the successful operation of canning factories which "leads to the conclusion that the processing of canning
crops in these resettlement projects would not, in the long run, prove
successful."

Statistics, Economic

Glenday, Roy. The use and misuse of economic statistics. Royal Statis.
Soc. Jour. (n.s.) 98(3): 497-505. 1935. (Published at 9, Adelphi
Terrace, London, W. C. 2, Eng.)
Opening paper in a discussion before the Royal Statistical Society,
April 16, 1935. The rest of the discussion follows on pp. 505-522.
See also pp. 531-535 for the Memorandum by the Manchester Statistical
Society on the Need for Improvement and Extension of Official Statistics.
The Memorandum is signed by Barnard Ellinger, H. Campion, and H. G. Hughes.

Statistics, Retail Trade

Douglas, Iris. Retail trade statistics in different countries. Royal Statis.
Soc. Jour. (r.s.) 98(3): 455-479. 1935. (Published at 9, Adelphi Ter-
race, W. C. 2, Eng.)
Discussion, pp. 479-493.
The operative part of the schedule for the Census of Distribution,
1933, recently taken in the Irish Free State, is given on pp. 493-496.

Subsistence Homestead, Reedsville, W. Va.

Atkeson, Mary M. Too many hopes. Country Gent. 105(12): 12-13, 38, 39.
December 1935. (Published at Independence Square, Philadelphia, Pa.)

An account of the first subsistence homestead project at Reedsville,
West Virginia - its origin, development, mistakes, benefits, attitude of
the local people toward it, etc. The people of Monongahela and Preston
County are all in favor of the project, but they are afraid that "it may
not be properly successful and that West Virginia and the West Virginians
may be unjustly blamed for its lack of success...Much as they believe in
the idea, and hope that Arthurdale will eventually grow up to be a credit
to their community, the wisest of them think that the Experimental Community Project has been founded on too many hopes, too many experts,
and too little of what the local mountaineer calls 'gumption.'"

Sugar - India

Purt, B. C. The Indian sugar industry. Mysore Econ. Jour. 21(8): 416-423.
    August 1935; (9): 472-474. September 1935; (10): 535-538. October 1935.
    (Published in Bangalore City, Mysore, India.)

Sugar - Turkey

Turkey. Sugar taxation. Gt. Brit. Bd. Trade Jour. (n.s.) 135(2027): 518.
    Oct. 10, 1935. (Published by H. M. Stationery Office, London, Eng.)
        By a recent law "the consumption tax on sugar has been reduced from
    12 piastres per kilogramme to 4.10 piastres per kilogramme, and the
    production of the national factories has been limited to a total of
    55,000 kilogrammes. At the same time the import duty on refined and
    semi-refined sugars has been reduced from 27.20 piastres per kilogramme
    to 15 piastres per kilogramme."

Tenancy - Southern States

Nixon, H. C. The historical background of present conditions in the South.
    Emory Univ. Bull. 21(7): 31-34. July 1935. (Published at Emory
    University, Ga.)
        Address at the "Eighth Annual Institute of Citizenship, Emory Uni-
    versity, Atlanta, Georgia, February 11th to 15th, 1935", on political
    and economic problems of the South.
        The author comments on the effect of sharecropping and tenancy on
    conditions in the South.

Tenancy and Relief - Alabama

Hoffsommer, Harold. Landlord-tenant relations and relief in Alabama. U. S.
    Fed. Emergency Relief Admin., Div. Research, Statis., and Finance, Re-
    search Sect., Research Bull., ser. II, no. 9, 33pp., mimeogr. November
    14, 1935. (Published in Washington, D. C.)
        This survey covered 1,022 farm households residing in the open country
    or in places of 1,000 or less population and receiving relief in December
    1933. Many of the households were cropper households. The study is in
    two parts; I, Land-lord tenant relations, in which are considered main-
    tenance of tenants by landlords, indebtedness, relief as a demoralizing
    factor, and landowners attitudes toward tenant relief; and II, The farm
    household receiving relief. In this latter section are considered the
    place of residence, color, nativity and sex of head, size of household,

age and education of head of household, combined families, jobs other
than farm tenure, mobility, the agricultural ladder, contributions of
household members, relief history, and governmental assistance.

Textiles

The new textile. Economist 121(4813): 1002-1003. Nov. 23, 1935. (Published
at 8 Bouverie St.,Fleet St., London, E. C. 4, Eng.)
    On the growth in production and use of a new synthetic textile tech-
nically known as staple fibre and popularized as "fibro." The fibre is
produced from wood pulp and "was first introduced in Germany during the
Great War, but it showed a tendency to crease and to shrink in water.
It is only recently that progress has been made in overcoming these
deficiencies, and bringing large-scale production to the commercial stage.
The strength and resilience of the new fibre have now been increased,
and its scope has been improved by progress in the methods of processing
synthetic textile fibres."

Textile industry reviving. Best production levels of decade with statistical
position strong. Profits, however, handicapped by low margins over costs.
Rayon the phenomenal performer. Barron's 15(46): 15, 18. Nov. 18, 1935.
(Published at 44 Broad St., New York, N. Y.)
    Accompanied by three tables showing equipment, operation and market
data for cotton textiles, annually 1925-1934; wool machinery activity
in the United States, annually 1923-1934; and rayon production, annually,
1920-1935; and a chart showing average prices of textile raw products.
    Tabloid analyses of various textile companies are given on pp. 18 and 20.

Theses - Union of South Africa

List of theses in economics and allied subjects completed or in progress in
universities and university colleges in the Union of South Africa. So.
African Jour. Econ. 3(3): 465-468. September 1935. (Published by the
Economic Society of South Africa, Johannesburg.)

Tobacco - Cooperative Marketing - Philippine Islands

Mabbun, P. N. Cooperative marketing and our tobacco farmers. Philippine Agr.
24(6): 451-463. November 1935. (Published by the College of Agriculture,
University of the Philippines, Laguna, P. I.)
    The author's introductory paragraphs follow:
    "This paper is based on the results of studies on the co-operative
marketing experience of the tobacco growers of Tuguegarao, Cagayan, and
Ilagan, Isabela, and of the tobacco growers in the state of Wisconsin,
United States of America. These studies are supplemented by observations
made by the author of the operations of the 'Land O' Lakes', a large cooperative marketing organization handling butter, in Minneapolis, Minnesota, coupled with information obtained from responsible officials of
the working of the 'California Fruit Growers' Exchange'...
    "The results of these studies and observations suggest three questions:
(1) Can co-operative marketing succeed among our Filipino tobacco growers?

(2) If so, what plan of organization would best fit the level of intelligence, experience, and psychology of these farmers? (3) If cooperative marketing does not succeed would a government sales monopoly
meet the conditions of the tobacco growers of the Islands?"

Tobacco Industry

Tobacco. Agricultural commodity and manufactured product. Index 15(12):
252-253, 258-261. December 1935. (Published by the New York Trust
Company, 100 Broadway, New York, N. Y.)
Discusses the present situation in the tobacco industry, tobacco
growing and the AAA, the effect of the reduction program upon the export
trade, domestic manufacture and taxation. The article is concluded as
follows:
"With tobacco growers threatened with the loss of foreign markets as
exports continue to decline, and manufacaturers of tobacco products forced
to cope with higher production costs and a heavy burden of taxation,
the tobacco industry in this country is not without its serious problems.
Nevertheless, the continued upward trend of domestic consumption, and
the probability that, in some instances, foreign demand - for the superior
American product will again make itself felt as economic recovery increases foreign purchasing power, hold out a promising assurance for the
future of tobacco cultivation. Furthermore, if manufacturers are able
to secure some relief in the matter of taxation, especially in regard to
the processing taxes, the rates of which for certain grades have recently
been adjusted, their present margins of profit should be increased. With
cigarette smoking becoming an even more common practice among the men
and women of the younger generations, there is no reason to believe that
the limits of tobacco consumption have yet been reached."

Trade, Gains of

Coe, W. F. The gains of trade. Canad. Jour. Econ. and Polit. Sci. 1(4):
588-592. November 1935. (Published by the University of Toronto Press,
Toronto, Ontario.)
"This paper was presented at a round table on Economic Theory at the
Annual Meeting of the Canadian Political Science Association, May, 1935."
"By the gains of trade", the author says, "is meant the gains from
free trade between nations or the advantages of free trade as against
no trade or the advantages of more free trade as against less."

Trade Agreement, Reciprocal

Agriculture in the Canadian trade agreement. Foreign Crops and Markets 31(22):
733-739. Nov. 25, 1935. (Published by the Division of Foreign Agricultural
Service, ., Bureau of Agricultural Economics, U. S. Dept. of Agriculture.)

Clarke, J. R. The probable effects of the reciprocal trade agreement with
Canada. Annalist 46(1194): 781-782. Dec. 6, 1935. (Published by the
New York Times Co., New York, N. Y.)

Lawrence, David. The turning point. U. S. News 3(47): 22. Nov. 25, 1935.
(Published at 2201 M St., N. W., Washington, D. C.)
"President Roosevelt has with commendable courage consummated a reciprocity trade agreement with Canada which will give the world an example of how to abandon economic nationalism — a new way to reduce tariffs."

Stahl, G. R. The Hull-King tariff pact. Supersedes Hawley-Smoot and Bennett tariffs. Effects on U. S. minimized by quota provision. Results complicated by non-tariff factors. Barron's 15(49): 9, 10. Dec. 9, 1935.
(Published at 44 Broad St., New York, N. Y.)

Tung Oil — United States

Seybold, G. H. Disappointments in tung oil. Possible American industry of 100 millions scope, in which performance to date falls short of promise. Success waits (preper natural development. Barron's 15(47): 17. Nov. 25, 1935. (Published at 44 Broad St., New York, N. Y.)

Viticulture — France

Control of vine growing. Indus. and Labour Inform. 55(10): 264. Sept. 2, 1935.
(Published by International Labour Office, Geneva, Switzerland. Distributed in U. S. by World Peace Foundation, 8 West 40th Street, New York, N. Y.)
A summary of some of the provisions of a decree relating to viticulture in France, passed on July 31, 1935 and published in the Journal Officiel of the same date. Limitation of sales and compulsory distillation are extended. "If prices on the vine market are obviously below the cost of production, the Government may fix a graduated scale in accordance with which the wine may be released...Vine growers...are exempted from certain charges if they undertake not to replant uprooted vineyards for five years. If they give the same undertaking for 30 years, and provided they do not utilise the lands thus released for the cultivation of tobacco, flax or beet, they are entitled to compensation besides the exemptions referred to. If the areas cleared of vines in France and Algeria do not amount to 150,000 hectares the uprooting of vineyards may be made compulsory."

Wages— China

Tsha, T. Y. A study of wage rates in Shanghai, 1930-34. Nankai Social and Econ. Quart. 8(3): 459-510. October 1935. (Published by Nankai University, Tientsin, China.)

Wealth and Income

Belden, Allen. Income distribution and the relation of population density to income in the United States, 1929. Geogr. Rev. 25(4): 671-674. October 1935. (Published by the American Geographical Society, Broadway at 156th St., New York, N. Y.)

Crum, W. L. Individual shares in the national income. Rev. Econ. Statis. 17(6): 116-130. November 1935. (Published by the Dept. of Economics, Harvard University, Cambridge, Mass.)

Doane, R. R. The geographic distribution of the physical wealth of the United States. Annalist 46(1191): 676-679. Nov. 15, 1935. (Published by the New York Times Co., New York, N. Y.)
"This is the fifth of a series of articles on the nature, distribution and promise of wealth in the United States."
It is accompanied by six tables which show growth and comparative changes of all tangible property values in the various states, 1890-1932; major categories of wealth by states, 1932; percentage distribution of major classes of the total physical wealth among the states, 1932; percentage distribution of major classes of physical wealth within each state, 1932; cumulative percentages, 1932; and subdivision of real property, 1932.
Illustrated also by charts which show cumulative percentage distribution of total physical wealth by states; distribution of the population in relation to physical wealth of the 48 states; relation of productive and consumptive wealth to total wealth of the various states; comparative long-time trends in total wealth, increasing living comforts, current goods on hand and total bank deposits; and changing percentage relationship of total real capital to total consumption goods.

Wealth and its distribution. National City Bank of New York [Monthly letter on] Econ.Conditions, Govt. Finance, U. S. Securities, December.1935, pp. 187-191. (Published in New York, N. Y.)
Subtopics: The need for increasing productive power; the exchange of services; the value of exceptional men; the effects of labor-saving machinery upon the general welfare; the lesson from agriculture; effects of certain changes in industry; the shorter work-week.

Wheat

Gusler, Gilbert. The position of the wheat market. Northwest. Miller 184(5): 433. Nov. 13, 1935. (Published at 118 S. 6th. St., Minneapolis, Minn.)
A summary prepared for the Millers National Federation.

Mayer, R. J. Wheat exports to be resumed? Large American wheat crop and carry-over indicated for 1936. Halt in European acreage expansion. Stage set for resumption of exports. Barron's 15(49): 20. Dec. 9, 1935. (Published at 44 Broad St., New York, N. Y.)

Wheat - Bounty Plan - United States

Davis, G. H. Practical measures for wheat growers. Southwest. Miller 14(37): 21, 43. Nov. 12, 1935. (Published at 306-312 Bd. of Trade Bldg., Kansas City, Mo.)
"That American wheat growers should be paid a bonus on the portion of their annual production consumed in this country to offset tariff advantages enjoyed by the industrial east was urged in Kansas City

Friday by George H. Davis, president of the Davis-Noland-Merrill Grain
Co. Mr. Davis, who spoke before a divisional meeting of the Chamber of
Commerce of the United States, also recommended steps to restore exporting by the wheat industry." His address, dealing with "the outstanding
factors in the Southwestern grain situation" is given.

Wheat - Canada

Evans, W. Sanford. The Canadian wheat situation. Grain & Feed Journals Consolidated 75(10): 409-410, 412. Nov. 27, 1935. (Published at 332 South
La Salle St., Chicago, Ill.)

Wheat - Japan

Alsberg, C. L. Japanese self-sufficiency in wheat. Wheat Studies of the
Food Research Institute 12(3): 57-100. November 1935. (Published at
Stanford University, Calif.)
The following is quoted from pp.59-60:
" A general plan to render Japan more self-sufficient in many directions
seems first to have been made public in 1930 by Jotaro Yamamoto, chairman
of the economic committee of the Seiyukai Party, then in opposition. It
included proposals to make Japan self-sufficient with respect to wheat.
Originally, it was a ten-year plan, but to adapt it to depression conditions it was gradually scaled down until it had become a Five-Year
Plan when the President of the Seiyukai Party, Inukai, formed a new
cabinet of Seiyukai members on December 12, 1931. This ministry began
forthwith to put portions of the Plan into effect, beginning with the
reimposition of the embargo on gold on December 13, 1931. Measures to
stimulate wheat production which were introduced later were merely part
of a general plan for self-sufficiency, exactly as were analagous measures
in Western countries.
"In the first week of April 1932, the Ministry of Agriculture and
Forestry announced its decision to carry out a plan to increase production of wheat at a total cost of about 10 million yen of which 2.04
million yen were to be allocated to the year 1932. At about the same
time, this ministry appointed a commission to work out a practical plan
which was promptly put into effect. Although this entailed a 50 per
cent increase in production, the objective was soon reached, with government measures reinforced by other favorable influences. Following a
marked increase in output in 1933, the crop of 1934 practically equaled
the usual domestic disappearance and that of 1935 exceeded it.
"Five years ago, when we published an analysis of 'Japan as a Producer
and Importer of Wheat,' so large an expansion was not in prospect. Why
the new policy and program were adopted, what steps were taken, what
actually transpired, how non-governmental factors figured in the outcome,
how permanent the change in position and trend are likely to prove,
and what the outlook is in other respects — to some of these questions
this Wheat Study endeavors to give answers."

Wheat - Marketing Regulation - Argentina

The Grain Regulating Board and the wheat market. Argentina. Banco de la
Nación. Econ. Rev. 7(4): 143-148. October - December 1934. (Published
in Buenos Aires, Argentina.)
Contains an analysis of the operations of the Grain Regulating Board
in 1934.

Wheat - Price Stabilization Scheme - Australia

Commonwealth wheat stabilisation scheme. Primary Producer 20(42): 1. Oct. 17,
1935. (Published at 38-40-42-44 Stirling St., Perth, Western Aust.)
Contains the official statement regarding the recent wheat conference
held at Canberra. The conference "urged the temporary reimposition of
the flour tax to enable a home consumption price to be paid. The home
consumption price for wheat recommended by the conference is 4/9 per
bushel fa.q., f.o.r., seaboard."
An outline is given of the Federal scheme as submitted to the conference.

Federal home wheat price plan to operate, despite growers' plea. The Land, no.
1270, p. 4. Oct. 11, 1935. (Published in Sydney, New South Wales.)
"The Federal Government's scheme for the establishment of a home
consumption price and a system of licensing receivers and warehouses ...
will be put into operation for the approaching harvest. If, however,
time proves too limited to enable this to be done, it is probable that
the flour tax will be reimposed to enable a home consumption price to
be paid this season...
"The scheme was accepted after prolonged discussion by last Friday's
wheat industry conference and by the Agricultural Council, which met on
Monday...growers' representatives...strongly opposed the Government's
scheme, pressing for the establishment of a full compulsory pooling
system. They accepted it, as a temporary measure, only when the pool
plans submitted by the Federation and the N. S. W. Government were declared
to be out of order on the score of constitutional difficulties."
The debate at the Wheat Industry Conference is reported on pages 5
and 15, under the caption: Big Wheat Debate at Canberra.

Wheat scheme explained in Federal Parliament. The Land, no. 1273 [1274] p.6.
Nov. 8, 1935. (Published in Sydney, New South Wales.)
A summary of remarks made by Dr. Page, the Minister of Commerce, at
the time he made the motion for the second reading of the Wheat and Wheat
Products Bill, which includes a home consumption price of wheat of 4/9
a bushel. "Action to bring about a home consumption price, he said,
would establish a starting point for comprehensive rural rehabilitation
by supplementing the steps already taken towards adjusting farmers'
liabilities through the grant to the States under the Farmers' Debt
Readjustment Act."

Wheat Pool - Alberta

Purdy, R. D. Alberta gives an answer. United Farmer 15(48): 732. Nov.
29, 1935. (Published in Calgary, Alberta.)

Radio address by the manager of the Alberta Wheat Pool, November 27, 1935.
An enquiry into the affairs of the Alberta Wheat Pool and the progress it is making. The question, "What of the Future?" is discussed.

Wheat Pool - Western Australia

Activities of Wheat Pool of W. A. reviewed. Primary Producer 20(41): 5. Oct. 10, 1935. (Published at 38-40-42-44 Stirling St. Perth, Western Australia.)
Contains the report of the Board of Trustees, reviewing the activities of the Pool for the 1934-35 season.

Wine Industry Regulation - Argentina

Analysis of the wine industry. Argentina. Banco de la Nación. Econ. Rev. 7(4): 148-160. October - December 1934. (Published in Buenos Aires, Argentina.)
A Government plan for the regulation of the wine industry, which has been sanctioned by Congress, "provides for the creation of a Wine Regulating Board, with full powers to spend up to $30,000,000 paper in the purchase of wine and in indemnification for vineyards, with the object of securing a proper balance between production and consumption. A tax of $1,000 paper per hectare is imposed on future plantations, so as to restrict expansion. The scheme will be financed by a surcharge of $0.01 per litre of wine, over and above the unified tax, which surcharge will be in force for 6 years."

Wines and Spirits

Journal of Commerce, [N. Y.] 1936 wines and spirits number. Jour. Com., Nov. 27, 1935, sect. 2, pp. 1-18. (Published in New York, N. Y.)
The third annual review of the wine and spirits industry at home and abroad.

Zoning, County - Wisconsin

Albers, J. M. Recent amendments to the Wisconsin county zoning act. Jour. Land & Pub. Utility Econ. 11(4): 411-413. November 1935. (Published by Northwestern University, School of Commerce, 337 East Chicago Ave., Chicago, Ill.)

NOTES

American cotton manufacturers association. Southern mill rules of 1935 for buying and selling of American cotton. Effective August 1, 1935. Ratified and adopted by the American cotton manufacturers association, The American cotton shippers association. 11pp. Charlotte, N. C. [1935] 304 Am35

Beard, C. A. An economic interpretation of the Constitution of the
United States. With new introduction. 330pp. New York, The Macmillan
company, 1935. 280.12 B38E

Canadian grain trade year book, 1934-35. Full Canadian grain statistics, with
summary tables for principal foreign countries and world's production and
movement, year ending July 31, 1935. Volume XV. 105pp. [Winnipeg]
Sanford Evans statistical service [1935] 286.3599 C16 v.15 1934/35

Civis. Electricity and nationalization; a plea for commonsense. 49pp.
London, E. Benn limited, 1935. 280.171 C49
Reviewed in The Economist (London) May 4, 1935, p. 1014.

Cotton-textile institute, inc. Cotton "farm-to-market" roads. Cotton
fabric used in reinforcing bituminous surface for better, more durable,
low cost secondary roads. 12pp. New York city, The Cotton-textile
institute, inc. [1935] 288 C822

Eaton, Jeanette. Behind the show window. 313pp. New York, Harcourt, Brace
and company [1935] 280 Ea8

Economists' national committee on monetary policy. Statements of the Economists' national committee on monetary policy covering the period
November 24, 1933 - May 23, 1935. 59pp. [Chicago, Printed
at the Lakeside press, R. R. Donnelley & sons company, 1935] 284 Ec72

Evans, W. Sanford, statistical service. Canadian acreage and production
map. Winnipeg, Can., Sanford Evans statistical service, 1935. map.
227 C164C

Evans, W. Sanford, statistical service. United States acreage map by states.
map. Winnipeg, Can., Sanford Evans statistical service, 1935.
252 Ev1 1935

Gt. Brit. Customs and excise dept. Customs regulations and procedure in the
United Kingdom of Great Britain and Northern Ireland. Compiled and published by direction of the commissioners of customs and excise, in accordance with a resolution of the International conference on customs and other
similar formalities, held under the auspices of the League of nations, in
1923. Revised, 1935. 80pp. London, H. M. Stationery off., 1935
285 G794 1935

International institute of agriculture. Annuaire international de législation agricole, v. 24, 1934. 922pp. Rome [Imprimerie de la Chambre
des députés] 1935. 30.5 In82T

Jackman, W. T. Economic principles of transportation. 891pp. Toronto,
The University of Toronto press, 1935. 289.2 J12E
"The present work is based upon a volume issued by the author in
1926 [Economics of transportation] but is largely re-written." - Pref,

League of nations. Annex to the Report on the work of the Council and the
    Secretariat to the sixteenth ordinary session of the Assembly of the
    League of nations. Ratification of agreements and conventions con-
    cluded under the auspices of the League of nations. Sixteenth list.
    122pp. [Geneva, 1935] (Series of League of nations Publications. V.
    Legal. 1935. v.3)   280.9 L47La 1935. v.3
        At head of title: Official no. : A. 6 (a). 1935. V. Annex. Geneva,
    August 28th, 1935.

Lively, C. E.   Social planning for agriculture and its relation to all
    society. 9pp., mimeogr.[Columbus? O., 1935]   281 L74
        Paper read before the annual Conference of Agricultural Extension
    Workers, Ohio State University, October 16-18, 1935.

Milwaukee journal, Research bureau. Consumer analysis and dealer distribu-
    tion check-up of the greater Milwaukee market. 1935. Twelfth edition.
    93pp. Milwaukee [1935] 280.9 M64 12th, 1935
        Among other classes of goods, grocery and tobacco products are in-
    cluded.

Mussolini, Benito. Four speeches on the corporate state, with an appendix
    including the Labour charter, the text of laws on syndical and corpo-
    rate organisations and explanatory notes. 126pp. [Roma] "Laboremus",
    1935.   280.176 M97
        Bibliography, pp. [121]-126.

Oklahoma. Corporation commission. Before the Corporation commission of the
    state of Oklahoma in the matter of determining and prescribing rates,
    charges, practices, and the promulgation of rules and regulations affect-
    ing the operation of cotton gins as a public business within the state of
    Oklahoma for the ginning season 1935-1936... Report of the commission. 7pp.,
    mimeogr. [Oklahoma City, 1935]   281.372 Ok4B

Scotland. Dept. of health. Working-class housing on the continent. Report by
    Mr. John E. Highton, C. B., secretary to the Department of health for Scot-
    land, on a visit to the continent to examine recent developments in
    working-class housing in the cities of Rotterdam, Amsterdam, Hamburg,
    Berlin, Frankfurt, Prague, Vienna and Paris. 44pp. Edinburgh, H. M.
    Stationery off., 1935.   296.2 Sco3W

Soddy, Frederick. The role of money; what it should be, contrasted with what
    it has become. 214pp. New York, Harcourt, Brace and company [1935]
    284 SolR
        Bibliography, pp. 213-214

Thompson, W. S., and Whelpton, P. K.   Estimates of future population of
    states, by urban, rural-nonfarm, and rural-farm areas and by five-year
    age periods and time intervals, 1935 to 1960. 15pp., mimeogr.
    Oxford, O., 1935. 280.12 T37E

Tolley, H. R.   Regional adjustment and democratic planning. Address... be-
    fore the meeting of the Association of land grant colleges, at Washington,
    D. C., November 20, 1935. 26pp., mimeogr. [Washington, D. C., 1935]
    Pam. Coll.

U. S. Bureau of foreign and domestic commerce. Tung oil; The situation
in world markets and economic and commercial factors in the development
of a domestic tung oil industry in the United States. 16pp., mimeogr.
[Washington, D. C., 1935] 157.55 T83
    "Excerpts from recent addresses by C. C. Concannon... at conven-
tions in Beaumont, Texas and Washington, D. C."

U. S. Farm credit administration. Permanent sources of cooperative credit
for agriculture, by W. I. Myers. 20pp. [Washington, U. S. Govt.
print. off., 1935] 166.3 P42
    An address before the annual meeting of the Mortgage Bankers Associa-
tion of America, French Lick, Ind., October 1935."

U. S. National recovery administration. Consumers' division. Retail food
price differences between cities, by Henry B. Arthur. 10pp., mimeogr.
[Washington, D. C.] Aug. 17, 1935. 173.2 N21Ret

U. S. National resources board. Estimates of future population by states.
A series of tables prepared by Warren Thompson and P. K. Whelpton of
the Scripps foundation for research in population problems for the
National resources board, December 1934. 51pp., mimeogr. Washington,
D. C. [1935] 173.2 N214E

Wayne co., Mich. Board of county auditors. County research bureau. The
cost of county government; an analysis of the expenditures of Wayne
county, 1930-1935. Prepared by the County research bureau under the
direction of the Board of Wayne county auditors for submission to the
Board of supervisors. July 15, 1935. 21pp., mimeogr. [Detroit,
Mich.] 1935. 284 W36

Webb, Sir C. M. The money revolution. With an introduction by Frank A.
Vanderlip. 272pp. New York, Economic forum inc., 1935. 284 W38
    Published in Great Britain under the title "Ten years of currency
revolution" - verso of t. p.
    Imprint on cover: Committee for the Nation, 205 East Forty-second
Street, New York.

Weber, Alfred. Alfred Weber's Theory of the location of industries. 256 pp.
Chicago, Ill., The University of Chicago press [1929] (Half-title:
Materials for the study of business) 280 W382
    At head of title: English edition, with introduction and notes by
Carl Joachim Friedrich.

Wishart, John and Sanders, H. G. Principles and practice of field experimentation. 100pp. London, The Empire cotton growing corporation, 1935.
251 W75
    Considered a later edition of Engledow and Yule, The Principles and
Practice of Yield Trials. 1926; Rev. ed., 1930.

AGRICULTU

UNITED STATES DEPARTMENT OF AGRICULTURE RECEIVED
BUREAU OF AGRICULTURAL ECONOMICS

ERVE

1944

Our age has set two mighty purposes before it – the reform of the land and the creation of a new social justice through the transformation of labour from a
marketable commodity to a joyful activity...

L. F. Dvorack

Vol.10   February 1936   No. 2

FEATURES IN THIS ISSUE

SIGNED REVIEWS

U. S. National resources committee. Regional factors in national planning
and development... December 1935. 223pp. Washington, U. S. Govt. print.
off., 1935.   173.2 N214Re

New England regional planning commission. Basic data for a tentative and preliminary plan for New England, designed to stimulate criticism, suggestion,
and eventually action. 117pp., mimeogr. Boston, New England regional
planning commission, National resources ·board, district no. 1... [1935]
280.7 N44B
        Contains a bibliography.

Pacific northwest regional planning commission. Consultant's report on regional planning in the Pacific northwest, January 1934 - January 1935.
Submitted to the Pacific northwest regional planning commission and to
the National resources board, February 1935. 219pp. mimeogr. [Portland,
Ore.] 1935.   280.7 P11C
        On cover: Progress Report... [v.1]

The scope of the report of the National Resources Committee is indicated
by its title, "Regional Factors in National Planning and Development." A
further limitation noted in reading the report is that the national planning and development considered is what is now being referred to as physical planning and development, particularly planning the development and
use of natural resources. "It may be well at this point to speak briefly
of the types of governmental functions related to national development
with which regional considerations are of particular importance on Federal
programs. It is natural that at the beginning of such an inquiry attention
should be centered chiefly on natural resources and environments."[1]
What is often termed social and economic planning and development is
treated only incidentally. The Resources Committee and the Technical Committee were aware, however, of the social and economic problems in national
development. They quoted Dr. Merriam, a member of the Committee: "We
should guard against too narrow a view of the possibilities of natural resources development, attractive as they are. The economic crisis in the
United States was not caused by erosion...; nor is unemployment due chiefly
to lack of adequate flood control..."[2] The emphasis in this report is
laid on the geographical and political aspects of planning and the lack of
agreement between the political boundaries and the geographic areas. This
may be taken as the problem which the report considers. "The qualities,

1. National Resources Committee. Regional factors in national planning and
development. 1935. Page 5.
2. Ibid. Page 5.

resources, and problems of the natural environment occur in particular combinations locally and are distributed unevenly over the earth; and existing areas of government are rarely coterminous with either areas of human or natural resources, or with the 'problem areas' which demand treatment."[3]

The lack of agreement between political boundaries and the geographic distribution of human and natural resources and 'problem areas' as it affects national planning and development was considered by the Committee as involving the following sub-problems: 1. Interstate problems. Those problems of physical development not wholly within one State, yet not national in geographic location; 2. Coordination of planning and development between governmental agencies, between departments of the several governments, and between the several governments: Federal, State, and local. 3. Decentralization of Federal planning and development. 4. Enlistment of regional consciousness in support of national planning and development.

These can be found on page VII under "Findings and Principles." These problems are, of course, not separate and distinct but interrelated.

The Report is divided into five parts: (1) An introductory statement of the problems, (2) evidences of the problem, (3) some attempts at solution of the problem, (4) geographic factors and criteria, and (5) integration of administrative and geographic factors in regional planning.

In Part II the organization of the Tennessee Valley Authority, metropolitan regional planning organizations, the problems the State planning experience has shown to be interstate or "supra-state", the movement towards State cooperation, and the experience of the Federal Government in setting up regional organization for administrative purposes are considered as evidences of the problem of adjusting political boundaries to the natural regions.

In showing the adjustment of governmental machinery to meet the problems which are interstate but not national in area, the Committee considered in Part III: Interstate compacts, Federal departmental regions, Federal regional authorities, the Tennessee Valley Authority, Federal-regional planning organizations - the New England and the Pacific Northwest Planning Commissions. The report is not very hopeful of the compact method. "When an issue involves only two States; when it can be settled once and for all; when continuous planning and administration are not necessary; then the compact method is likely to be a serviceable instrument."[4] A survey of regions now employed by various departments of the Federal Government found "approximately" (?) 74 sets of regions and "approximately" (?) 108 regional schemes. The number of regions per scheme varies from 1 to 30

Under an evaluation of the Tennessee Valley Authority is a discussion of the watershed as a unit for planning and development. "In the case of all questions directly related to water control, no other

3. National Resources Committee. Regional factors in national planning and development. 1935. Page 2
4. Ibid. Page 52.

area is more suitable."[5] But, "... a watershed area is not the 'perfect'
region for all planning and development purposes."[6] Another question
considered was the use of the corporate device for the administration
of a regional development scheme. This is endorsed with less qualification – "It appears to be definitely established that the corporate
principle is a sound one for the conduct of a regional program..."[6]
although suggestions for improvement are made. With respect to the
problem of coordination, the report states: "The TVA has well demonstrated the possibilities of intergovernmental cooperation in the conduct of a regional development program."[7] A previous statement should
probably not be forgotten in connection with this. "It is unquestion-
able that a large measure of the support given the TVA by such agencies (State and local) is due to the money which the authority is able
to spend in the area on programs which the local units have hoped eventually to carry on",[8] and the similar tenor of the quotation from a
governor: "Of course we cooperate with the TVA to the fullest extent...
After all, we have wanted to build dams, attack the erosion problem,
and all these other things. But we have not had the money... When
the TVA's program has been carried out we will be able to take care
of such expenditures ourselves without Federal assistance; we will
then have sufficient taxable value."[8]

Appraising the regional planning commissions the report states:
"These two projects constitute very valuable experiments and demonstrations in the solution of the problems which are raised in this
report."[9] However, "They (the regional planning commissions) possess
little direct authority and their lines of responsibility have been
somewhat indefinite during this formative period."[9] Thirteen findings on such regional planning organizations are set forth.

Part IV entitled "Geographic Factors and Criteria" is the section
devoted to regionalism. There are numerous definitions of "regions"
and "regionalism" in this part. "At the outset, it may be pointed
out that 'regionalism' is a clustering of environmental factors to
such an extent that a distinct consciousness of separate identity
within the whole, a need for autonomous planning" – probably for
purposes of this report –" a manifestation of cultural peculiarities,
and a desire for administrative freedom, are theoretically recognized
and actually put into effect... In one sense and perhaps the best,
regionalism is a way of life..."[10] This is perhaps sufficient to indicate that what is in the minds of the author is regionalism as interpreted by Lewis Mumford and Howard W. Odum. The emphasis is, however

5. National Resources Committee. Regional factors in national planning and
   development. 1935. Page 115.
6. Ibid. Page 113
7. Ibid. Page 115
8. Ibid. Page 107
9. Ibid. Page 134
10.Ibid. Page 138

more on geographic factors. This may be illustrated by the description of the cultural environment. "In every inhabited portion of the earth it may be observed that there is a cultural landscape overlying the natural. This consists of the works and constructions of men and the pattern of human settlement."[11] This appears to be an adequate picture of the cultural landscape but hardly of the cultural environment. If regionalism is to be a way of life, the cultural environment will have to include the things of the mind and spirit and not merely the visible landscape. Ireland and Denmark certainly would rank high on any list as examples of regionalism as a way of life. In both countries, language, literature, and other arts are an essential element of the cultural environment.

Part V and Chapter XV of Part IV bring together and present the conclusions reached by the technical committee from its study. It states: "The foregoing record of the extreme complexity of the problem of relating political boundaries to interstate regional areas, may be a cause of further discouragement to those who hope for solutions in part through the use of government and the public services...

"This discouragement has real dangers. A similar distrust of and sense of frustration at the failure of governmental systems in many parts of the world to function adequately in the face of the problems of recent years has led to revolutionary movements in some States and to a widespread political despair and indifference. There is a feeling that the rearrangement of political boundaries is so difficult of achievement, due to the interests that have grown under their protection and encouragement and the lines of political career and loyalty created by them, that nothing can be accomplished through consent and representative institutions. But this is only part of the difficulty. Even if it were possible to rearrange the boundaries, what should the new boundaries be? How should they be determined? The divergences of view on this point even among those who attempt an objective approach, as revealed in Part IV are very great... It cannot be too often repeated that under any conceivable system of political boundaries this discrepancy between them and some, at least of the problems which require political action... will be present."[12] The Committee, therefore, recommends the division of the country into twelve regions with "moderately elastic" boundaries extensible or retractile for individual planning elements or functions. But it is not altogether discouraged for "From these experiences (interstate and Federal-state cooperation) it is clear that the political inventiveness founded upon experience, observation, and analysis which characterized those who drafted the Constitution has been a resource at later times, as they had hoped, to their successors."[12]

Another note of caution is then injected. "But we must note the dangers inherent in this very response to the recognized need for adjustment. It is a danger present throughout our system and operation of government. The very profusion of government agencies may prevent there being taken at any one point a total view of governmental policies relating to community, State, or group of States; or to an area in which the nature of

11. National Resources Committee. Regional factors in national planning and development. 1935. Page 138
12. Ibid. Page 132

tho major problems is such that they form an organic composite group, to be treated comprehensively, or at least studied in the light of their interdependence, or of the whole of the United States. We are particularly concerned here with this problem as it affects the formulation of the national policies through the instrumentalities of the National Government."[13]

In spite of these difficulties the Committee makes definite recommendations to provide for "the formulation of the national policies" or planning affecting interstate problems, coordinating governmental activities, decentralizing Federal activities, and enlisting regionalism in the support of national policies. It recommends ten to twenty regional planning centers. (See p. 192) In the chapter on "Regions in a Planned National Program", twelve regions and planning centers are determined as the Committee believes they should be - on the basis of "composite problems". (See pp. 165-167) These regions are conceived as having flexible boundaries and varying problems. "A basic principle of the operation is that from any center a whole functional area and not only part of such an area, should be dealt with."[14]

The next question which may arise in the mind of the reader is: What are the problems or types of problems which should be planned from these centers? The Committee takes up this question and answers: "The staff set up at a regional planning center would undertake, by collaboration between State and Federal representatives in the organization, to assist the State and Federal Governments in the formulation of sound policies and programs on regional development matters... There are wide and important functions..."[15] The boundary line between the types of problems which should be planned at the regional center, those which should be planned at the State capitals, and those which should be planned from the National Capital is left even more flexible than the boundaries of the physical regions. It is true that from the stress given to problems which are interstate in character, they should undoubtedly rest with the regional planning center, but what of problems of intrastate or national scope? Every State problem will be within a region, and any national problem will affect the regions. There is no doubt that any regional agency set up will find some line of activity to develop. There would appear to be not only a possibility but a high degree of probability that unless the functions of the regional staff are limited to interstate problems or the coordination of national plans with the State plans a "new level of planning" or "an additional element in the structure of planning" would develop.

The reports of the two existing regional planning commissions, the New England Regional Planning Commission's "Basic Data for a Tentative and Preliminary Plan for New England" and the Pacific Northwest Regional Planning Commission "Progress Report", will give an indication of the answer to what such a planning center might do. The two reports give somewhat different answers to the question regarding the types of problems with which the planning centers might deal. The New England report deals much more with regional problems and less with all planning within the region than does the Pacific Northwest report. The

---

13. National Resources Committee. Regional factors in national planning and development. 1935. Page 183.
14. Ibid. Page 195.
15. Ibid. Page 192

New England report. it is true, gives "basic" data on population, resources. highways, transportation, water resources, conservation, and
recreation. In addition to this material, the Pacific Northwest report
covers land resources, mineral resources, power, industry and commerce,
public works and improvement, public welfare, education, government,
legislation, and State and local planning. Both discuss a regional
plan.

The significant difference in the two attitudes on regional planning
can be brought out by the elements suggested in the two reports as
parts of a regional plan. The New England report states that, when
completed, the regional plan will include: plans for regional highways,
airways, a coordinated transportation system, interstate river valley
conservation and development, better land utilization, a coordinated
program for conservation of forests, streams, and wildlife, and regional recreational facilities, including interstate reservations,
parkways, foot and bridle trails.

The Pacific Northwest report states: "Laterally, in one direction
the plan will consist of the essential elements of the plans of States
and localities..."[16] and probably centrally, "in the other direction
of functional elements as land plans, water plans, etc."[17] The "Framework of Plan" is given on page 201 as land resources, water resources,
mineral resources, transportation, industry and commerce, public works,
education, public welfare, community, city and county planning, and
government. Appropriate subheads are listed under each. The above outline does not include all the elements of a regional plan for the report states: "The foregoing outline includes all of the more important
elements of a regional plan."[18]

In such a wholesale cataloguing of items which might be conceivably
thought of as coming within the field of the commission's activities
there must necessarily be some which are of interest to more than one
State. The problems in which the regional aspects are considered to
some extent are those of water and power. Even here the Fort Peck Dam
is considered in about the same way as the Grand Coulee and the Bonneville
Dams.

No one will deny that any problem affecting any part of the region
affects the region as a whole. But, if this is the field for regional
planning, what is the field for State and for national planning? If
the regional planning commissions are to cover all the fields of planning
in the region then it would appear that there is more than a possibility
that all that is accomplished is that another level of government has
been injected into the system between the States and the Federal Government, which is just what the Resources Committee stated was not the purpose of forming regions for planning. - C. I. Hendrickson, Senior Agricultural Economist, Division of Land Economics.

16. Pacific Northwest Regional Planning commission, Progress report, 1935.
    Page 194.
17. Ibid. 195.
18. Ibid. 203.

len, R. G. D., and Bowley, A. L. Family expenditure; a study of its variation. 145pp. London, P. S. King & son, ltd., 1935. (London school of
economics and political science. Studies in statistics and scientific
method. Edited by Professor A. L. Bowley and Professor A. Wolf. no.2)
284.4 A15

Reviewed in the Economist (London) Nov. 23, 1935, p. 1017

Our understanding of the principles of consumption has increased considerably during the past decade. More and more factual material has become available concerning the amounts of different goods which are consumed and the relationship between rates of consumption, prices, and incomes. The U. S. Department of Labor, together with the National Resources Board, is now engaged in the largest survey of consumption and
expenditure which has ever been undertaken, and the U. S. Bureau of Agricultural Economics has made and is making a number of intensive studies
of the consumption of specific groups of foods, such as dairy products.

But an understanding of the principles underlying consumption requires
more than the gathering and tabulating of statistics. It requires a well-
considered framework of theory which explains why we consume the things
we do and why we make changes in consumption from time to time.

Mathematical analysis is peculiarly well adapted to this branch of
economic theory and the best development of theories of preferences and
of substitution is to be found in such writings as those of Walras, Jevons,
and Pareto. These writings are recalled here because the authors of
"Family Expenditure" have each made notable contributions to the mathematical development of theories of consumption, preferences, and substi-
tutions. Professor Bowley's "Mathematical Groundwork of Economics" is a
very condensed but very useful summary of basic economic principles in
mathematical terms. Mr. Allen is joint author of an important article,
"A Reconsideration of the Theory of Value" which appeared in Economica in
1934. Both authors are well known to mathematical economists and to econ-
ometricians who are interested in theories of utility. Their previous
work in this field, however, has been mainly theoretical and only a few
economists (notably Frisch, Morschak, and Schultz) have previously attempted to apply such theories to the statistical analysis of observed facts.

"Family Expenditure" does not stop with the recording of facts about
consumption by various groups of the population. It attempts an explanation. In the words of the authors, "The purposes of this study are to discover how far the expenditure of individual families, or groups of families,
can be described by rules and formulae, to relate any rules that are found
to the postulates of economic theory and to describe the variations from
the averages that result from the different choices of individual families."

Many "budget" studies have been made for more limited purposes; for example, to determine a satisfactory base for cost of living indexes, or
simply to get a reliable figure on the average per capita consumption of
milk in a particular city at a particular time. Other studies have had
as either a major purpose, or as a kind of by-product, the study of variations in consumption among different groups classified as to income,
nationality, size of family, and other characteristics.

The contribution of Allen and Bowley is that of defining carefully the nature of the relationship between income and consumption. Their researches first confirm what has come to be known as Engel's Law: that as incomes increase the proportions spent for the more urgent needs (such as foods, etc.) decrease while the proportions spent for luxuries and semi-luxuries increase. This law has been confirmed many times and can be considered as universal and lasting. Allen and Bowley are not content, however, with the law in this form and have attempted a quantitative statement based on an empirical formula which appears to fit satisfactorily all available data gathered in a large number of consumption studies in many countries. The formula is simply the straight line: y = ke + c where y is the expenditure for a given commodity; e is the total expenditure for all goods and services; and k and c are constants determined by the data.

Since all the studies refer only to short periods of time and since it is assumed by the authors that prices did not vary, it is apparent that the quantity consumed must be also a linear function of total expenditures. The assumption of a uniform price is open to serious criticism, however, in this study and in practically all studies of consumption. Studies by this Bureau now under way in New York City show wide variations in retail prices in different stores and in different localities. This is true even when differences in quality are small. When quality differences are not eliminated retail prices of foods vary greatly at the same time and place.

Clearly we can not assume that the linear relationship between consumption of a particular commodity and total income holds good throughout the entire income range. The formula is purely empirical and the authors claim only that it does fit most of the observed data fairly well within the observed range. This being true the constant, c, in the formula indicates whether a particular commodity is a necessity or a luxury. If c is positive the proportion of the total income spent for it will decrease with rising income and the commodity may be classified as a necessity. If c is negative the reverse is true and the commodity may be considered a luxury.

For comparing different commodities the value of c divided by the average total expenditure gives a useful measure of the order of urgency of needs. Diagrams X, XI, and XII and the tables on page 49 illustrate the procedure and raise some difficult questions. They are based on a survey of workers in the United Kingdom in 1904, a survey of Liverpool workers in 1929, and a survey of clerks in London and large towns in 1926. The conclusions of most of the studies reported in the book are consistent in their ranking of the main groups, indicating that food is the first necessity, followed by rent, heat and light, furniture, clothing and miscellaneous. When individual foods are studied, however, the results are not so consistent. The three tables summarizing diagrams X, XI, and XII all indicate that cereals and sugar are necessities and that vegetables and meats are luxuries, but dairy products are indicated to be the greatest luxury among the foods in the first diagram and the first necessity in the last diagram.

Part of this difficulty probably is that preferences vary considerably among different groups of people and at different times and therefore that we can not expect consistency in the details of conclusions of different studies. There may be still more difficulty in classifying different foods or other groups of commodities. For example, may not fluid milk be a basic necessity, while the needs for butter, cream, and ice cream represent less and less urgent needs? If so, when we throw all dairy products together we are combining necessities and luxuries.

The article by Mr. Allen in Economica which we have mentioned above discussed in detail the possibility of measuring the degree to which two commodities are substitutes, complements or independents. The authors say on this point, "It would be tempting to explore this question with the aid of the budget data we have available but, in fact, it is easily seen that we can only go so far as to say that the variation of preferences for two items are correlated or not over the groups of families considered. The data do not allow us to distinguish the case where a family, on account of its own special tastes, takes more than the average of butter and less than the average of margarine from the special relation that these are complete substitutes one for the other."

The authors do, however, measure the relationship between consumption of various groups by means of partial correlation, holding constant total expenditures. Table I on page 93 is of particular interest. This shows that the partial correlations between groups are generally negative (tending to indicate substitution in spite of the careful qualifications in the book), but that in Liverpool, at least, the partial correlation between bread consumption and consumption of most other foods is positive (tending to indicate complementary use).

This question of measuring the degree to which two commodities are competing or completing is one of real interest in statistical price analysis and one which needs more thought. Probably competition or completion among commodities could be defined in several useful ways. While Allen has shown clearly that it is not possible to measure from statistics how the marginal utility derived from one commodity varies with the consumption of another it may be questioned whether such a definition is entirely necessary or whether we might for this purpose forget about utility and adopt some simpler definition.

A basic understanding of the principles underlying consumption is possible only by a combination of studies like that of Allen & Bowley which give a cross-section picture of a particular period with time series analysis. The ideal study in this field would be based on a series of detailed expenditure studies which would not only explain the pattern of consumption at a given time but would explain changes in that pattern. Ideally, the study of demand should be made in at least three dimensions representing variations in incomes, in prices, and in consumption. Perhaps the greatest difficulty in demand analysis is our habit of working and thinking in two dimensions.

For the most part Allen & Bowley are considering the two-dimensional relation of consumption to income. Only in the last section of the study do they discuss price elasticities and show that such elasticities can be considered as made up of two parts; the first being due to the change in real income resulting from a price change, and the second being due to substitution. They follow to a conclusion of doubtful validity that, "the elasticity of demand for any item with respect to changes in its price is likely to increase with income. Demands tend to become more elastic as the income level rises."

The reviewer agrees that it is dangerous to assume that as incomes rise the demand curve will be shifted either by the same absolute amounts or by the same relative amounts at all points. Too often the true nature of such shifts is obscured by some kind of mathematical formula which we arbitrarily adopt. But the reviewer believes that as the level of incomes increases the demand for a given commodity is more likely to become more inelastic than it is to become more elastic and this has been confirmed by several unpublished studies. Of course, the demand for margarine might become elastic as incomes rise for the reason stated by the authors that "substitution becomes more easy for most goods as income rises." But for the same reason the demand for butter is likely to become more inelastic. Thus while we agree that the assumptions about shifts in demand made in several statistical studies are of doubtful validity, we believe that the conclusions of Allen and Bowley on this point are of even less validity.

The book represents an important contribution to the subject of consumption and expenditures and will be of interest to most students of demand. — Frederick V. Waugh, in Charge, Division of Marketing Research.

Massmann, Karl. Zur finanzierung der landwirtschaftlichen siedlung. 13 pp. [n.p., 1933?] 282.2 M38

At head of title: Friedrich List-gesellschaft. Zur konferenz von Oeynhausen am 11. bis. 14. februar 1933.

Als manuskript gedruckt (spätere korrekturen vorbehalten)

This paper was presented at a German economic conference in Oeynhausen in February, 1933. It discusses the financing of German agricultural settlement, primarily certain aspects of post-war developments in this field.

For a number of years Massmann was closely connected with German land settlement financing. When he delivered this paper he was chairman of the Executive Board of the German Land Settlement Bank. Being so closely connected with practical operations in this field, he was able to speak with a great amount of authority.

In the years following the World War German land settlement financing passed through very difficult times. The forces of inflation and other unfavorable financial developments dealt heavy blows to the system of both intermediate and long-term credit which had been built up in pre-war days. The task of repairing the damage was not easy. Many obstacles were encountered because of the great scarcity of capital from which Germany has suffered ever since the war; because of rivalries and disputes between the National Government and the Government of the State of Prussia; and because of the special difficulties which arose in connection with the recent economic depression.

Massmann's paper shows how badly land settlement financing was hit in the early post-war period. It also contains an interesting description of the plans developed to rebuild the system and of the amount of progress made in the reconstruction work up to the Spring of 1933.

The paper is divided into ten parts. The first three parts deal with the pre-war period; the period of currency inflation; and the period since

1924, (the year of the stabilization of the German currency). Part 4
describes the participation of the Federal Government in the financing of
land settlement operations since 1926. Parts 5 and 6 deal with more recent
developments in the field of long-term settlement credit, embracing the
creation of the Prussian Land Rent Bank in 1928, and plans of the Federal
Government to establish long-term credit. Part 7 describes the establishment of the German Land Settlement Bank in 1930, which was a measure concerning the supplying of intermediate credit. Part 8 discusses certain
special land credit funds created since 1927. Part 9 refers to the capital
of the land settlement agencies carrying out the practical land settlement
work. Part 10 contains a few remarks on the use of the settlers' own
capital in the financing of land settlement operations.

Massmann points out that the land settlement financing system which the
Prussian Government developed before the World War gave assurance of a
steady supply of land settlement funds at uniform rates and that its long-
term credit was readily available at all times and repayable at low rates.
Due to these accomplishments settlement operations were protected against
unfavorable influences caused by fluctuations in the capital market and
settlers were enabled to repay their debts conveniently over a long period
of time.

During the process of rebuilding capital funds for land settlement in
the post-war period part of the revenue from the Prussian House Rent Tax
was made available for financing the construction of buildings on new
farm holdings. In the opinion of Massmann, agricultural settlement
should have shared in the yield of this tax to a larger extent than it
actually did share. The 117 million marks which it received from 1924
to 1931 represented a very small portion as compared to the 5.4 billion
marks of House Rent Tax money which were made available during the same
time for urban house construction, particularly in large cities. Massmann
calls this distribution of the yield of the Prussian House Rent Tax "a
first rate malinvestment of public funds." He believes that this mal-
distribution contributed to and artificially increased the existing difficulties of unemployment of today. He further thinks that by not appropriating a larger portion of this tax money for agricultural settlement
great opportunities of fostering settlement in the thinly populated German
East were lost.

On various occasions rivalries and disputes between the National and
Prussian Governments have hampered the reconstruction work and caused
unnecessary delays. As Massmann reports, they occurred with reference
to the desire of the National Government in 1926 to participate on a
large scale in financing land settlement operations; in connection with
efforts to rebuild the long-term credit structure; and again when attempts were made to bring about a joint enterprise of the Reich and
Prussian Governments for intermediate credit. There is no doubt that
German agricultural settlement would have progressed much farther in the
post-war period if the National and Prussian Governments could have co-
operated smoothly and effectively in the solution of the financing problems.

Two different plans were developed concerning the reconstruction of
long-term credit. One plan was devised by the Prussian Government at
the time when it attempted to solve the problem alone. The other plan
was developed by the National Government. Massmann gives a good description of the two plans. The Prussian plan provided for the creation of

a new Central Land Rent Bank. It also provided that, in connection with the refinancing of their advances, the settlement agencies were to be paid partly in bonds and partly in cash. It did not include any subventions for the reduction of interest rates. Under this plan the Prussian Government was required to put up a considerable amount of cash money for the purpose of advancing over a long period of time non-interest bearing funds covering about 35 percent of the value of the holdings. On account of this requirement and the banking crisis in the summer of 1931, the activities of the bank temporarily came to a standstill.

The plan of the National Government laid emphasis on the mobilization of non-public capital for the financing of the land settlement operations. It intended to solicit the assistance of the mortgage banks and the so-called "Landschaften". It provided for the payment of subventions to reduce interest rates. In addition it included the granting of loan guarantees to cover the advances of mortgage banks beyond the customary lending limit of 40 percent.

In connection with the plans to establish new funds for long-term land settlement credit it is interesting to note that in the period from 1927 to 1929 efforts were made to obtain foreign capital. These attempts were abandoned due to the problem of reparations and other difficulties.

In the German Land Settlement Bank, established jointly by the National and Prussian Governments in September, 1930, Massmann sees a valuable contribution to the reconstruction of intermediate credit for land settlement. The bank has, as he points out, concentrated all the capital available for intermediate loans in one place, and has done away with the former discrepancies in interest rates. He considers the Bank as an important new agency which will be very useful as soon as internal and world conditions improve and new funds become available.

Since Massmann wrote his paper the National Government has been made solely responsible for land settlement matters in Germany. It, therefore, has also gained complete control over the supply and distribution of funds in this field. This has put an end to the rivalries between the Reich and Prussia with respect to the financing of land settlement. Attempts to bring about a greater participation of the private capital market in the financing of land settlement have continued. But due to the scarcity of capital it is still difficult to sell land rent bonds in the open market. The National Government is making similar efforts in the field of financing supplementary farming homesteads, but also here it probably will take some time before this plan is realized. - Erich Kramer, Associate Agricultural Economist, Land Use Planning Section, Resettlement Administration.

Garland, J. M. Economic aspects of Australian land taxation. 217pp. Melbourne, Melbourne university press in association with Oxford university press, 1934. 284.5 G18
Bibliography, pp. 213-214.

This treatise is written by an Australian, from an Australian viewpoint. To many Americans, perhaps to most, the land tax system discussed will seem strange territory. It has many likenesses to European systems devised largely with the object of breaking up large landed estates.

It is true that in Australia the land taxes bring in considerable revenue, averaging about 20 percent as much as do the income taxes. Yet they are frankly regulatory. Their strangeness consists primarily in their being levied against "unimproved values", and in their rate scale being graded according to the size of the holding (measured in value). Not all parts of the land-tax system have both of these characteristics. Between states and between municipalities there is variation, as there is in the United States, with some municipalities levying no tax on unimproved values as such. The commonwealth tax, however, is levied against unimproved values, and the rate is graded according to the value of holdings.

The description given of the tax structure and its development is both instructive and interesting. The discussion of principles is, from our standpoint, however, academic because the Australia system lies to large extent far from real life as represented by our own property or real estate taxes. It stimulates recollections of text-book economics. But in Australia these text-book problems of incidence, capitalization or "amortization", land value and rent are practical problems current to the thought and action of legislatures, courts, and tax assessors. They are current too in the management of property and business activity.

What is the "unimproved value" of land? Is it "prairie value", which assumes no internal or external improvements, i. e., with no improvements on the land or in its environment; or is it the value of the land itself unimproved but in its actual improved environment? In New Zealand, the original act defines unimproved value essentially as full value less the value of improvements. The Australian act, however, defines unimproved value as the value of the land assuming no improvements. The treatise under review assumes that the Australian concept is impossible to use, and that therefore the New Zealand definition must be employed by the "valuer". One may think of cases where this is a doubtful conclusion.

Further difficulties arise. A swamp is filled, and is licensed by a racing association as a race course. The association then decides to issue no more private licenses. The land changes hands several times, but retains the license with the title. In court the license is held to represent unimproved land value, because it runs with the land. From full value is deducted cost of improvements, but not more than present replacement value. Apparently cost of replacement of the monopolistic license was not admitted. In a later case a liquor license is thus assessed as unimproved value, but the court holds that when the improvements are assumed as non-existent, the license also must be assumed non-existent, because it cannot be obtained without existence of an establishment. Here are two cases establishing leading precedents, in which first appears the New Zealand method, later overthrown by the Australian. Throughout the generation over which such taxes have been utilized many paradoxes have been encountered. It is necessary only to muse over the terms "prairie value" and "bare land value", the two basic definitions of unimproved value, and a land tax at rates progressive with value of holding, to recognize the field as fertile in theoretical difficulties and disagreements.

Effect of the tax in breaking up estates is of interest. In cases where large estates can efficiently be broken up, they have not necessarily suffered decrease in value but have gone into the more intensive use. Farther out on the frontier where small-scale farming is less advantageous the tax apparently has been partially capitalized. The graded rate has in this way accelerated progress toward the original regulatory goal. An exemption of 5000 pounds' value, together with the graded rate, has been fortunate in conjunction with the Australian geographic and climatic features in tending to preserve larger holdings in the areas less well adapted to close settlement.

The political alignments making possible the establishment of the system have been affected by these facts: That the Commonwealth statute exempts estates of less than 5000 pounds' value; that not all types of tenure are included as taxable; that influx of population followed by exhaustion of the richer goldfields brought about a social problem of establishing surplus people; and to some extent that large estates were held by absentees. Making the matter at the start one of Commonwealth interest, rather than state or local, permitted political pressure against the cattle and sheep "barons" by the entire nation instead of by smaller areas which the barons themselves might dominate. In the early days urban sentiment undoubtedly helped to establish the system but in recent years the urban collections have in some states exceeded the rural collections. This possibility often is overlooked until one recalls that size of holding is measured in value.

This urban application also is of more questionable social advantage. Single tax arguments pretty generally assume that urban congestion will be decreased under a system of improvement exemption, but the graded rates and exemption tend to break down urban lots into smaller values, each in distinct ownership. District ownership is necessary because all holdings in one ownership are combined in determining the rates applicable. Furthermore, with undivided interests or other dual or multiple equities the land takes the highest rate applicable to any one of the interests.

One's conclusions in regard to the value of the system as opposed to one of assessing total real-estate values must depend to considerable extent upon social philosophy and leanings. But regardless of this conclusion, in the coordination of federal, state, and local levies, Australia apparently is in much the same position as the United States. States are free to write their own statutes. Municipalities are allowed great leeway under state laws. The result is heterogeneity and a very uneven distribution of burden as between individuals and between areas. Again the variation between classes may be adjudged good or bad, between areas it cannot so readily be adjudged good.

Much political bickering has gone on throughout the development and operation of the system, and one must conclude that again the tax problem is found to be one of perpetual struggle. Not all interests agree; someone's toes are always stepped on; the economic and social position of majorities change; and the changing tax system continues to require important changes. The Australian (and incidentally the New Zealand) Commonwealth is to be admired for the practical and unorthodox manners in which it has developed its tax system, but it has discovered no Mecca.

The book under review does not necessarily force one to the conclusions reached above. It does, however, set forth a good description of the system and an introduction to the economic and social principles involved, which enable the reader to consider the matter with facility and come to his own conclusions. – <u>Donald Jackson, Senior Agricultural Economist, Division of Agricultural Finance.</u>

DESCRIPTIVE NOTES AND ABSTRACTS

Agrarian Reform - Czechoslovakia

Vozenílek, Jan.   Résumé des résultats acquis de la réforme foncière dans les
pays de Bohême et de Moravie-Silésie.   20pp. Praha, Impr. paysanne de
Praha, 1930.   282 V94Re
    Tiré-à-part de la publication parue en tchèque sur les "Résultats
préliminaires de la réforme foncière tchécoslovaque." I. Pays de Bohême
et de Moravie-Silésie.
    A summary with tables, of the results attained by the agrarian reform
in Bohemia and Moravia-Silesia.

Agrarian Reform and Agricultural Credit - Yugoslavia

Nikosavić, Blagoje. Die agrarverfassung und der landwirtschaftliche kredit
Jugoslawiens. 88pp.   Berlin, P. Parey. 1935. ([Germany]. Reichs- und
Pr. Ministerium für Ernährung u. Landwirtschaft, n. f. 112. Sonderheft)
    A study of land tenure as affected by the agrarian reform in Yugoslavia
is followed by an account of agricultural credit conditions and the
indebtedness of the Yugoslav farmer. The author traces the history of
agricultural credit from its beginnings in Serbia in 1930. He discusses
the rôle of private banks and agricultural cooperatives in providing agricultural credit, the part played by agricultural credit cooperatives and
the State in the solution of Yugoslavia's agricultural credit problem, and
the organization and functions of the Privileged Agricultural Bank, established in 1929. The solution of the problem is shown to be to a large
extent dependent on the development of prices of agricultural products and
to be seriously influenced by the depression. The author stresses the
need for an active well-planned agricultural policy in Yugoslavia.

Agricultural Adjustment Act - Supreme Court Decisions

U. S. Supreme Court. United States of America, petitioner,vs. William M.
    Butler, et al., receivers of Hoosac mills corporation. On writ of
    certiorari to the United States Circuit court of appeals for the first
    circuit. January 6, 1936. 28pp. [Washington, U. S. Govt. print. off.,
    1936] 281.12 Un39
        At head of title: Supreme court of the United States. no. 401. -
    October term, 1935.
        Dissenting opinion of Justices Stone, Brandeis and Cardozo: 8 pp.
    at end.

U. S. Supreme court. Lee Moor, petitioner, vs. Texas and New Orleans rail-
    road company. On writ of certiorari to the United States circuit court
    of appeals for the fifth circuit. January 13, 1936. 3pp. [Washington,
    U. S. Govt. print. off., 1936]   281.372 Un35
        At head of title: Supreme court of the United States. No. 49 - October
    term, 1935.

U. S. Supreme court. Rickert rice mills, inc., petitioner, v. Rufus W.
    Fontenot, individually and as acting United States Collector of internal
    revenue for the district of Louisiana. On writ of certiorari to the

United States circuit court of appeals for the fifth circuit. January 1
1936 2pp. [Washington, U. S. Govt. print. off., 1936] 281.359 Un35
  At head of title: Supreme court of the United States. No. 577. –
October term, 1935.

Agricultural Economic Society

Irvine, J. L. Statistical investigations into organized marketing of milk.
  7pp. [Reading? Eng., Agricultural economics society, 1935]
  At head of title: Proof-for private circulation. This proof is
circulated in advance of the Society's meeting at London, 10th and 11th
December, 1935.

Lloyd, E. M. H. Food supplies and consumption at different income levels.
  18pp. [Reading? Eng., Agricultural Economics society, 1935]
  At head of title: Proof-for private circulation. This proof is
circulated in advance of the Society's meeting at London, 10th and 11th
December.

Menzies-Kitchin, A. W. Land settlement and unemployment. 12pp. [Reading?
  Eng., Agricultural economics society, 1935]
  At head of title: Proof-for private circulation. This proof is cir-
culated in advance of the Society's meeting at London, 10th and 11th
December, 1935.

Agricultural Insurance – France

Blanchoin, Albert. L'assurance mutuelle agricole; essai sur l'assurance corporative. Préface de J. M. Gatheron. 450pp. Paris, Librairia technique
et économique, 1935. 284.6 B59
  The theme is mutual agricultural insurance, its origin, history, basi
principles and its relation to the modern idea of collectivization.

Agricultural Policy – Great Britain

Horace Plunkett foundation. Co-operation and the new agricultural policy.
  136pp. London, P. S. King & son, ltd., 1935. 281.171 H78
  "Chronology [of legislation]" pp. 131-132.
  Bibliography, p. 129
  This is an analysis of the British agricultural policy which raises
certain questions as to the place of voluntary cooperation in the new s
tem.
  "In order to answer these questions" the introduction states:
  "It is necessary first to consider the historical and legal backgrou
of the agricultural revolution, to examine closely not only the existing agricultural marketing boards as well as certain of the reorganisation schemes drawn up and not yet adopted, but also the effect of subsidies and import restrictions on branches of agriculture for which no
schemes exist or are likely to exist; for they all form part of a new
system, artificially planned, stimulated, checked and supported, which
is taking the place of the old free scramble. Such an examination can
only be carried out by commodities and will inevitably involve some

repetition and an irreducible minimum of technical minutiae. This section is intended principally for reference purposes. For the convenience of readers, a classified statement covering all schemes has been added on page 81. In the subsequent sections, an attempt is made to assess the effect of planned agriculture, so far as it has yet proceeded, upon different classes of the community: the home farmer, smallholder, labourer and landlord; the agricultural co-operative society; the consumer organised and unorganised; the overseas producer. It is hoped that the conclusions which emerge will themselves supply answers to some of the questions which agricultural reformers of the voluntary school are asking themselves."

Agricultural Problem - United States

Bouvard, Georges. L'agriculture dirigée aux États-Unis; essai critique sur l'économie autoritaire. Preface de m. François Herbette. 296pp. Paris, Librarie technique et économique, 1935. 281.12 B66.
Bibliography, pp. [279]-296.
A study of American agriculture beginning with the middle of the nineteenth century, its typically American problems and its vicissitudes has led the author to the conclusion that the American farmer, unless completely unforeseen circumstances occur, will never regain the wonderful position he occupied at the end of last century, that American agriculture is still suffering from the illusions created by the War, and that the post-war commercial policy of the United States has disregarded certain essential changes and led the nation into a blind alley. He believes that the agricultural problem of the United States can only be solved on an international basis by obliterating or at least attenuating what he calls the tariff paradox.

Agricultural Situation - Portugal

Lisbon. Universidade técnica. Inquérito económico-agrícola promovido pelo senado Universitario: e dirigido pelo professor de economia rural do Instituto superior de agronomia, engenheiro-agrónomo E. A. Lima Basto. v. 2. [Lisboa, Composto e impresso nas oficinas do Instituto superior de ciências económicas e financeiras] 1934. 281.176 L68
Contents. - v. 2. Inquérito à freguesia de Sto. Ildefonso do concelho de Elvas, pelos... D. R. Vitoria Pires e J. J. Paiva Caldeira.
Answers are given to a series of questions on the agricultural economic conditions of a particular parish in Portugal.

Agriculture - Brazil

Pinto, J. J. Política rural (temas agro-zootécnicos) Tomo 1. 229pp. Porto Alegre, Oficinas gráficas da Livraria do globo, 1935. 281 P652
The author discusses and makes suggestions for the improvement of agriculture and livestock raising in Brazil. A chapter deals with the breaking up of latifundia examples of which are given for a number of countries.

Agriculture - Germany

Deutsches forschungsinstitut für agrar- und siedlungswesen, Berlin. Abteilung
Rostock, Erzeugung und absatz landwirtschaftlicher erzeugnisse im nordostdeutschen wirtschaftsraum. III. Teil. Becker K., Magen, H., and
Seeberg, S. Der innere verbrauch. 100pp. Berlin, P. Parey, 1935. ([Ger-
many] Reichs-und Pr. Ministerium für Ernährung u. Landwirtschaft. Bericht
über Landwirtschaft n.F. 110, Sonderheft)
     This third contribution to the study of the production and marketing of
agricultural products in north-eastern Germany contains the following
three articles: Vermögens- und Einkommensschichtung in der Provinz Pommer
by Herbert Magen. - pp. 7-32. (A study of the relation of property and
income to the population of Pomerania); Der Nahrungsmittelverbrauch im
nordostdeutschen Wirtschaftsraum, by Stella Seeberg. - pp. 33-76. (A
study of food consumption in north-eastern Germany); and Naturaler
eigenverbrauch und marktversorgung der landwirtschaftlichen Betriebe, by
Karl Becker. - pp. 77-89. (A discussion of theproportion of agricultural
products reserved for the farmer's own use as compared with the amount
marketed) References to Parts I and II of this study may be found in
Agricultural Economics Literature 8 (3): 170. March, 1934 and 9 (3): 131.
Mar., 1935.

Agriculture and the Depression

Perieteanu, Alexandre. La crise mondiale et le problème agraire. 25pp.
    [Bucuresti, Imprimeria nationala] 1934. 281 P41
        An analysis of the depression and suggestions for its solution.

The "Boerenbond" - Belgium

Varzim, Abel. Le Boerenbond belge; l'oeuvre du relèvement et de la grandeur
de la classe agricole d'un pays. Préface de mgr Luytgaerens. 272pp.
Paris, Desclée de Brouwer et cie, 1934. •280.29 B632
    Bibliography, pp. [251]-259.
        A study of the Belgian,"Boerenbond", or League of Farmers, its origin
constitution, organization, functions and activities. The author stress
the success achieved by this organization, which was founded in 1890 to
promote the religious, intellectual, social, and economic welfare of its
farmer members. It is a corporative organization and it has attained it
ends by such means as educational propaganda, the organization of agricultural credit, low-premium insurance, and purchase and sale in common.

Canada - Agricultural Outlook

Canada. Dept. of agriculture. The agricultural situation and outlook 1936.
58pp. Ottawa [1935] 281.9 C163
        Issued in cooperation with Canada. Dept. of trade and commerce.
        The report summarizes the domestic situation in Canada as follows:
        "The gradual expansion of industrial activity and moderate improvement
in employment, with greater stability in prices of goods for immediate
consumption, indicate that demand in domestic markets is likely to be
well maintained and perhaps increased somewhat during the coming year.
Better prices for most farm products, with the volume of production

about the same as in 1934, implies a moderate increase in income from the 1935 output. This increased income means greater purchasing power in the hands of Canadian farmers at the beginning of 1936."

Carver Essays

Himes, N. E., ed. Economics, sociology & the modern world. Essays in honor of T. N. Carver. 327pp. Cambridge, Harvard university press, 1935. 280 H57

The purpose of this volume is stated by the editor in the preface as follows:

"This volume, consisting of eighteen papers by former students of Professor T. N. Carver, for thirty years (1902-1932) professor of political economy in Harvard University, is published on the occasion of his seventieth birthday (1865-1935). There are ten papers here on economic theory and four each on agricultural economics and sociology, representing, in their weighted order, the academic interests of Professor Carver. While most of the essays are of a research character, a few are argumentative and deal with questions of national, public policy, the importance of dealing with which he always impressed upon his students."

Partial contents: - Agricultural fundamentalism, by Joseph Stancliffe Davis; The Canadian wheat pool in prosperity and depression, by Harold S. Patton; Overhead costs in agriculture: A problem in social control, by Roland S. Vaile; The objectives of economic control, by E. J. Working; Theoretical aspects of the scale of production, by M. M. Bober; Interest in work: some research problems, methods, and results, by Z. Clark Dickinson; The mercantilism of Geronimo de Uztáriz: A re-examination, by Earl J. Hamilton; Pioneer life in western Kansas, by John Ise; On the chemical phase of the industrial revolution, by T. J. Kreps; Some propositions on interest, by R. S. Meriam; Some aspects of the theory of rent: von Thünen vs. Ricardo, by Bertil Ohlin; The nature of our program for national economic recovery, by C. J. Ratzlaff; Business cycles, by John Philip Wernette; The rationalization of production and of reproduction, by A. B. Wolfe; Socialism in theory and in practice, by Frederick A. Bushee; Migration between city and country in the Buffalo Metropolitan area, by Niles Carpenter.

Community Survey - Madison, Wisconsin

Young, Kimball, Gillin, J. L., Dedrick, C. L. The Madison community. 229pp. Madison, 1934. (University of Wisconsin studies in the social sciences and history, no. 21) 280.097 Y8

"This monograph presents a socio-economic analysis of selected aspects of community life in Madison, Wisconsin, especially concerning population, mobility, income, occupation, home ownership, and certain aspects of social pathology. Our frame of reference is the distribution of these characteristics in the city as a whole as compared with certain other cities of like size, and more particularly the distribution of these characteristics in different sections of the city itself." - Introduction and Prospectus.

Appendix A contains Notes on Methodology.

Academy of political science, New York. The Constitution and social progress;
a series of addresses and papers presented at the annual meeting of the
Academy of political science November 14, 1935. Ed. by Parker Thomas Moon.
139pp. [New York] The Academy of political science, Columbia university,
1936. (Proceedings, v. 16, no. 4, Jan. 1936) 280.9 Acl v.16, no. 4.
    Pt. 1. The Supreme Court and the States, contains the following papers:
Introduction, by William L. Ransom; The national powers under the constitution by William Y. Elliott; The States under the Constitution, by John
Dickinson; Constitutional limitations on social legislation, by Orie L.
Phillips; Shall the powers of the Supreme Court be abridged? by John W.
Bricker; Discussion, by Howard Lee McBain.
    Pt. 2. Nation and State in Economic and Social Planning, contains the
following papers: Introductory remarks, by Ogden L. Mills, Agricultural
planning, by Edwin G. Nourse; Industrial planning, by Gilbert H. Montague;
The rights of labor under the constitution, by William Green; The planning
of taxation, currency and finance, by Lewis W. Douglas; Discussion, by
Noel T. Dowling.
    Pt. 3. America Considers its Constitution, contains the following
papers: Introduction, by Wesley C. Mitchell; America considers its
constitution, by Henry A. Wallace; America considers its constitution, by
Joseph Buell Ely; Why the constitution? by Arthur A. Ballantine.

Consumer and the Government

Lamb, B. P. Government and the consumer. 51pp. Washington, D. C., The
    National league of women voters [1935]   280 L16
        Published under the Belle Sherwin fund.
        Bibliography at end of most chapters.
        The author's concluding chapter reads in part as follows:
        "The establishment of informative labeling including grade labeling,
a new food and drug law with funds and efficient personnel for enforcement, the elimination of price fixing by industry, the development of a
coordinated government program of consumer information in regard to both
quality and price, the strengthening of the consumer agencies within the
government, and above all, the provision for real consumer representation
in the administration of government policies toward industry and agriculture - these seem to be among the most important steps that need to be
taken in solving the problem of the consumer.
        "They cannot, however, be achieved over night...
        "What is needed is a change of emphasis in public thought from pro-
duction to consumption, and a new understanding on the part of the public
that, since the purpose of all economic activity is the satisfaction
of human wants, production and distribution must be carried on with the
consumer uppermost in mind.

Control of Production - Italy

Confederazione fascista dei lavoratori dell' agricoltura. Disciplina della
    produzione in agricoltura. 78pp. Roma [Società anonima arte della
    stampa, 1935] 281.176 C762
        "Relazione presentata al Convegno nazionale di Bologna il 14 maggio

dell'anno XIII e redatta dal prof. Aulo Marchi." - p. [1]

The author discusses the regulation of agricultural production under
the Fascist régime, its implications and its aims.

Control of Raw Materials

Holland, W. L. ed. Commodity control in the Pacific area; a symposium on
recent experience. Issued under the auspices of the secretariat of the
Institute of Pacific relations. 452pp. Stanford University, Cal.,
Stanford university press [1935]   280 H71

This book is a compilation of documents dealing with specific schemes
of commodity control which were presented at the Conference of the Institute of Pacific Relations at Banff in August 1933. The book has been
revised and enlarged and seven entirely new essays have been added.
The titles follow: Planned agricultural adjustment in the United States,
by Joseph S. Davis; Stabilization operations of the Federal Farm Board,
by E. S. Haskell; The Canadian wheat pool in prosperity and depression,
by H. S. Patton; The Japanese rice control, by Seiichi Tobata; Silk
control in Japan, by Taikichiro Mori; Control in the Australian sugar
industry, by J. B. Brigden; Co-operation in the Hawaiian Pineapple business, by Royal N. Chapman; Commodity control in Netherlands India, by
Cecile G. H. Rothe; Export control boards in New Zealand, by R. G. Hampton;
Control of primary commodities in Australia, by G. L. Wood; Petroleum
control in the United States, by Barnabas Bryan, Jr.; The international
tin restriction plan, by Oliver Lawrence; The international control of
rubber, by Oliver Lawrence; and International conservation of fisheries
in the north Pacific, by Robert A. Mackay.

Cooperation

Sarandy Raposo, C. A. de. Theoria e pratica da cooperaçao (da cooperaçao em
geral e especialmente no Brasil). Publicado pelo Ministerio da agricultura para distribuiçao gratuita. 3ª. edição. 194pp. Rio de Janeiro,
Directoria de estatistica da producçao (Secção de publicidade) [1935]
280.2 Sa74

A study of the theory and practice of cooperation, with special reference to Brazil.

Cooperation, Consumers

Central co-operative wholesale. Co-operative wholesaling. 16pp. Superior,
Wis., Central-co-operative wholesale, 1935. 280.29 C333C

This is an account of the development of the Central Co-operative
Wholesale which had its origin in a meeting held at Superior, Wisconsin
on July 30 and 31, 1917.

County Consolidation — Kansas

Euler, H. L. County unification in Kansas. 92pp. New York city, Bureau
of publications, Teachers college, Columbia university, 1935. (Teachers
College, Columbia university. Contributions to education, no. 645)
280.029 Eu5

Bibliography, pp. 86-90.

The final chapter reads in part as follows:

"This study endeavors to determine guiding principles for the unification of counties in Kansas through an analysis of an attempted consolidation of three counties, and a comparison of other cases as recorded in the literature in the field... The data were mostly gathered from three hundred and seventeen interviews carried on during a field trip through Kansas, and especially in Marshall, Washington, and Republic Counties...

"Four general conclusions are to be drawn from this study: (1) Owing to modern means of communication, transportation and business administration, local economic and social activities have materially expanded. (2) Because of this expansion, the existing local educational and governmental units have largely outgrown their usefulness and require reorganization and rehabilitation in the face of modern conditions and demands. (3) This needed change is being retarded not so much by economic forces as by concomitant factors which are socio-psychological in nature. (4) Those ideological obstructions can be removed through an efficiently organized and administered program of adult education..."

Dictionary of Agricultural Terms

Bezemer, T. J., comp. Dictionary of terms relating to agriculture, horticulture, forestry, cattle breeding, dairy industry and apiculture in English, French, German and Dutch. 267, 248, 250, 294pp. Baltimore, The Williams & Wilkins company [1935] 209 BMA

Printed in Holland.

Published also in Holland (Arnhem, 1934) with title page in Dutch; published also in Gt. Brit. (London, 1934) with title page in English.

The editor's foreword reads in part as follows:

"As appears from the Publishers' Preface, this work is the first dictionary of its kind in this field, and it is as such that it should be judged by the users. The great number of auxiliary sciences which have to be studied for the practice of agricultural economy rendered it imperative to make a selection of the words to be included in the work. For instance, not all the names of useful and injurious insects have been included, (this subject would require a dictionary of its own), but only those which are most important for agriculture in the widest sense of the term. This work cannot therefore, precisely because it is the first in its field, make a claim to completeness, and the Editor would be grateful if the users would send him any useful suggestions, with regard either to words which have been omitted or to what they consider to be incorrect equivalents...

"Only a few indications need be given as to the arrangement of the dictionary. In the first place it should be pointed out that this is not a descriptive or defining dictionary; it is assumed that the users, each in his own subject, are aware of the meaning of the words. A few indications are given, however, in that we mention the section of agricultural science or practice to which the words refer (sylviculture, etc) unless this is obvious from the word itself."

Dictionary of Statistics

Gleitze, Bruno. Statistisches lexikon. 464pp. Tübingen, J. C. B. Mohr
(P. Siebeck) 1935. 251 G48
   A reference lexicon of German and international statistics in compact
form, arranged alphabetically, based on year books and other official
sources for 1934. Contains comparative tables, brief explanatory notes,
and gives sources so that later figures may be easily found.

Economic Conditions

Unclaimed wealth utilization committee, Geneva. Economic readjustment in
1933; the third series of bulletins issued under the chairmanship of
A. H. Abbati. 102pp. London, P. S. King & son, ltd., 1934.
280 Unl 3d ser.
   Contains bulletins no. 24-29, which deal with reduction of hours of
labor, gold, monetary situation, and the tariff.

Economic Geography

Dubois, Marcel. Geographie économique. Quatrième édition. 962 pp. Paris,
Masson et cie, 1934. 278 D85 Ed. 4
   At head of title: Marcel Dubois et J.-G. Kergomard.
   Earlier editions have title: Précis de geographie économique.
   The fourth edition of this work, prepared entirely by J. G. Kergomard,
appearing as it did twenty years after the exhaustion of the third edition,
is practically a new work. It has in common with the earlier edition only
those sections dealing with general topics or with those countries that
were not excessively affected by the World War. The same plan is followed
for each country, a brief resume of the physical conditions and of the
population and government being followed by an account of economic conditions. Extensive use is made of statistics. The author's expressed
aim has been to produce for the French reader a publication as nearly akin
as possible to the Statesman's Year-Book.

Economic Geography - Southern States

Vance, R. B. Human geography of the South; a study in regional resources
and human adequacy. 2d ed. 596pp. Chapel Hill, The University of
North Carolina press, 1935. [University of North Carolina, Social
study series] 278.002 V26 Ed. 2
   Maps on lining-papers.
   Bibliography, pp. 512-579.
   The preface to the second edition reviews developments in the United
States since the first edition was published in 1932 and points out their
relation to the situation in the Southern States. The author states that
"this opportunity has been taken for making a number of corrections in
the text."

Economic History

Soltau, R. H. An outline of European economic development. 307pp. .
London. New York [etc.] Longmans, Green and co. [1935] 277.17 So4
Bibliography, pp. [301]-303.
The author states his purpose in writing this book as follows:
"This little book is an attempt, by one who is not a specialist in
economic history, to meet a need, hitherto ignored by specialists,
for a short sketch of the economic development of Europe as a whole,
considered, that is, as an area which has experienced a fairly uniform
evolution which has come under the same general influences, and within
which the same processes of production have tended to dominate, while
the same machinery of exchanges has had full sway. Some sections of
economic histories already published have indeed done this for certain
periods, but usually on a scale that makes the work available only to
the advanced student. This book is primarily meant for the Higher
Certificate forms at school, for Intermediate classes at the University
and for members of W.E.A. classes; it is hoped, however, that the general reader who is interested in a simple presentation of the main
problems of economic history will not find this too much of a text-book.
Preface.

Economic Planning

Cole, G. D. H. Economic planning. First American edition. 384pp. New
York, A. A. Knopf, 1935. 280 C67E
London edition (Macmillan and co., limited) has title: Principles
of economic planning. (Some differences in text)
Note including bibliography, p. viii-ix.
Contents: Why do we need a plan?; The resources of production;
Production and distribution in a "free market"; Critique of a planless
economy; Planned capitalism; The planning of capitalist industry and
agriculture; Fascist "planning" – Germany and Italy; American "Planning"
The new deal; Socialist planning in the U.S.S.R.; Principles of Planning – Home production and foreign trade; Capitalist restriction and
state control – planned money under capitalism; Planned distribution
of incomes and production; The machinery of international trade; The
machinery of national planning; Planned economy and workers' control;
A forecast of planned industry; and Conclusion.

Wootton) Mrs. Barbara Frances (Adam) Plan or no plan. 360pp. New York,
Farrar & Rinehart, inc., 1935. 280 W88
Contents: The nature of an unplanned economy; The nature of the
Russian planned economy; The achievements and possibilities of an un-
planned economy; The achievements and possibilities of a planned
economy; What next?; The conditions of successful economic planning.

Economic Problem

Hutton, Graham, ed. The burden of plenty? by the Hon. R. H. Brand, Hugh
Dalton, H. D. Henderson, J. A. Hobson, Graham Hutton, A. R. Orage,
Prof. Lionel Robbins, Sir Arthur Salter, Mrs. Barbara Wootton. Edited

by Graham Hutton. 157pp. London, G. Allen & Unwin ltd. [1935]
280 H97
   Bibliography, pp. 155-[158]
   This book contains eleven of the talks on the economic problem presented by the British Broadcasting Corporation in the fall of 1934 under
the title "Poverty in Plenty". The titles follow: Placing the field,
by Graham Hutton; The slump and the growth in productive power, by H. D.
Henderson; Our present discontents, by Hugh Dalton; Under consumption and
its remedies, by J. A. Hobson; Social credit, by A. R. Orage; A banker's
view of the problem, by R. H. Brand; The breakdown of central organization,
by Graham Hutton; The necessity of planning, by Mrs. Barbara Wootton; The
twofold roots of the great depression: inflationism and intervention;
Planned socialization and world trade, by Sir Arthur Salter; Conclusion,
by Graham Hutton.

Economic Thought

Peck, H. W. Economic thought and its institutional background. 379pp. London,
   G. Allen & Unwin ltd. [1935] 280 P33
   Bibliography, pp. [368]-370.
   Contents: - The factors in economic analysis; The political background
of economic theory; The Canonist doctrine; Mercantilism; Physiocracy; Early
classicism; Later classicism; Marginism and pecuniary analysis; The newer
capitalism; Economic theory and economic history; Welfare economics;
Institutional economics; Collectivism.

Economics

Todd, J. A. The science of prices. A handbook of economics (production,
   consumption and value) Fourth impression - revised. 264pp. London
   [etc.] H. Milford, Oxford university press, 1935. 284.3 T56 4th impression, rev.
   First printed 1925. Reprinted and revised 1927, 1931, 1935. - verso
of title page.
   A note on the fourth impression reads:
   "In reprinting, the opportunity has been taken to bring the statistics
down to date. In some cases the later figures have been obtained from
a different source and are not strictly comparable, but wherever the
difference is material it is specially noted."

Eggs and Poultry Marketing - Great Britain

Gt. Brit. Agricultural marketing reorganisation commission. Eggs and poultry;
   report of Reorganisation commission for Great Britain. 105pp. London,
   H. M. Stationery off., 1935. (Gt. Brit. Ministry of agriculture. Economic
   series, no. 43) 280.9 G792 no.43
   The recommendations of the Commission in respect of import policy "are
intended to assist the industry in carrying out a long-term programme of
development as well as to meet the immediate day-to-day problems of the
proposed marketing schemes." These recommendations include an increase
in the import duties on eggs in shell; an increase in duties on eggs not
in shell "if the home-produced 'seconds' should become seriously affected

by the competition of imported egg products;" the use of a part of the
funds from these revised duties for further development of the industry;
the use of "a formula by which the maximum quantity of eggs allowed to
be imported during any period of storage would be determined"; continuation of the Market Supply Committee and the establishment of a permanent
commission to "keep under review the position in regard to the production,
marketing and consumption of eggs and poultry."

The Commission also recommends the establishment of a permanent Coordinating Committee to provide for close collaboration between the separate marketing authorities of England and Wales, Scotland, and Northern
Ireland.

Estonia

Fullerits, Albert, ed. Estonia: population, cultural and economic life.
235pp. Tallinn [Tallinna eesti kirjastus ühisuse trükikoda] 1935.
280.170 F96E
Bibliography. A list of works on Estonia in foreign languages, pp.[193]-
199.
Sources of economic information, p. [226]
The part devoted to economic life in Estonia contains sections on
Agrarian reform; agricultural production and development; exports of
agricultural products; quality control of agricultural exports such
as butter, cheese, eggs, meat and meat products, potatoes, flax, and
linseed; foreign trade, the cooperative movement, public finance; and
banking.

Exports - France

Association nationale d'expansion économique. Le destin de l'exportation
française (assemblée générale du 8 mai 1935) 51pp. Paris [1935]
286 As72
Some of the problems of French exportation are discussed with illustrative tables. The president of the National Association for Economic
Expansion suggests that the aim of the export of French products is to
maintain the prestige of France abroad, to compensate the purchase of
raw materials and food of which the country has need to facilitate en-
trance of her colonial products into foreign markets, and to contribute
to the equilibrium of the national economy of France. Resolutions are
adopted along those lines.

Farm Tenancy and the New Deal - North Carolina

North Carolina. Agricultural experiment station, Raleigh. The relation of the
Agricultural adjustment program to rural relief needs in North Carolina,
by C. Horace Hamilton, rural sociologist, North Carolina Agricultural
experiment station... A cooperative rural research project, cooperating
agencies: the North Carolina Emergency relief administration, the Federal
Emergency relief administration, the North Carolina Agricultural experiment
station. 9pp., mimeogr. Raleigh, N. C., 1935. 282 N813
At head of title: Preliminary report.
The author summarizes his conclusions as follows:
"The conditions of croppers and renters in North Carolina have been

substantially improved under the New Deal according to a survey of 1703
rural families which was made by the Division of Rural Sociology, North
Carolina Agricultural Experiment Station, with the assistance of the
North Carolina Emergency Relief Administration. The author of this paper
is especially indebted to the Social Service Division of the E. R. A. for
its counsel and cooperation. One of the most significant evidences of
the improvement of renters and croppers is the fact that there has been
a marked and significant shift of such groups up the 'agricultural ladder'.
Renters have been enabled to buy homes; croppers have been enabled to buy
workstock and become renters; and many farm laboring families have become
croppers and renters. On the other hand, the number of farmers who have
lost their tenure status, i.e., those who have dropped down the 'agricultural ladder', has been relatively small during 1934 and 1935. This trend
for the better may be attributed not only to the AAA program but also to
the relief and rehabilitation programs which aided many farm families to
maintain and improve their status.

"This survey covered each and every household in selected townships or
sections of townships in Johnston, Robeson, Richmond, Rutherford, and
Taswell counties of North Carolina. A study of 1200 families in Enfield
Township, Halifax County, North Carolina, made in 1934, substantiates
the findings of this study."

Government, Local - Louisiana

Carleton, R. L. Local government and administration in Louisiana. 333pp.
Baton Rouge, Louisiana state university press, 1935. ([Louisiana state
university studies] no. 17) 280.033 C19
A Diamond jubilee publication.
Bibliography, pp. [325]-330.
"This study has three purposes. The first is to determine the effect
on local institutions of the varied historical background of Louisiana.
In the second place, local government and administration is described
as it exists in Louisiana today. Finally, by means of analyses and
comparisons, local institutional defects and deficiencies are noted, with
suggestions for their improvement. This work is the result of that threefold investigation." - Introduction.

Government Administration - Oklahoma

Institute for government research, Washington, D. C. Report on a survey of
organization and administration of Oklahoma, submitted to Governor E. W.
Marland, by the Institute for government research of the Brookings institution, Washington, D. C. Published by E. W. Marland good government
fund. 483pp. Oklahoma City, Harlow publishing corporation, 1935.
280.069 In7
On cover: Organization and administration of Oklahoma. The Brookings
institution.
Pt. 5. The revenue system, pp. 409-483.
The scope of this report is indicated in the letter of transmittal as
follows:
"The survey began in the latter part of November 1934. Under the

terms of our contract it extended to the major administrative departments and activities of the state and county government. It included
school districts but not cities and villages, and only incidentally
touched upon the legislative and judicial branches of the government.
Special attention was given to the organization and administration
of the following public activities: Administrative organization in general, highways, education, libraries, labor regulation, land office,
conservation of economic resources, law enforcement, public health,
county executive and clerical staff, county finances, county consolidation, public welfare. business regulation, financial administration,
personel administration, purchasing, election administration, and revenue and taxation. On the basis of these studies, suggestions and specific
recommendations have been made. These are designed to point out commendable features, to remedy existing defects, to increase efficiency, and to
reduce expenditures."

Government Control

Lippincott, B. E., ed. Government control of the economic order; a symposium.
119pp. Minneapolis, Minn., The University of Minnesota press, 1935. 280 L66
"The papers in this volume represent the beginning of an inquiry into
the problem of control. They were read or their subject matter was given
orally at the political theory round table of the American Political
Science Association in December, 1933. Mr. Feiler's paper is an exception. having been contributed after the meeting." - Preface
Contents: The distribution of control and responsibility in a modern
economy, by Gardiner C. Means; Economic limitations of government control,
by Gernard Colm; Government control in Russia, by Emil Lederer; Government
and the economic order in Sweden, by Walter Thompson; Cartels and the
state in the light of German experience, by Otto Nathan; Government pro-
prietary corporations in Great Britain, by John Thurston; Public enterprise
in Germany, by Arthur Feiler.

Government Control and Scientific Progress

Hall, Sir A. D. The pace of progress. The Rede lecture delivered before
the University of Cambridge on 4 March 1935. 41pp. Cambridge [Eng.]
The University press, 1935.
The thesis of this lecture is stated in the opening paragraph as follows:
"As I am about to embark upon an intricate argument it will perhaps
make the thread of my discourse more intelligible if I outline my thesis.
The pace of material progress based upon science has become so rapid that
the social structure of the nations cannot adjust itself quickly enough
to assimilate the advances. This is most evident as regards the agriculture of those European states which are based upon a peasant system of
farming. State intervention follows in one form or another with the object of preserving the peasant structure; and it is this State control,
which at once extends to all industry besides agriculture, that will provide the agency effectually to reduce the rate of change."

Canada. Board of grain commissioners. Grain research laboratory. The
fourth protein survey of western Canadian amber durum wheat 1935 crop.
9pp., mimeogr. Winnipeg, Man., 1935. Folio 59.9 C161 Pa

Canada. Board of grain commissioners. Grain research laboratory. The
ninth annual protein survey of western Canadian hard red spring wheat
1935 crop. 46pp., mimeogr. Winnipeg, Man. 1935. 59.9 C161P

Canada. Board of grain commissioners. Grain research laboratory. The
second annual survey of the protein content of western Canadian barley
1935 crop. 14pp., mimeogr. Winnipeg, Man., 1935. Folio 59.9 C161 Pb

Import Quotas - France

Haight, F. A. French import quotas; a new instrument of commercial policy.
131pp. London, P. S. King & son, ltd., 1935. (London school of
economics and political science. Studies in economics and commerce.
no. 6) 286 H12
Bibliography, p. [127]
Reviewed in Economist (London) Aug. 24, 1935, p. 377.

Moroni, Paul. L'agriculture française et le contingentement des importations.
192pp. Paris, Librairie du recueil Sircy [1934] 286 M82
Bibliography, pp. [187]-190.
A study of French agriculture and the import quota; its functions, and
its effect on prices.

International Congress for Scientific Management

International congress for scientific management. 6th, London, 1935.
Sixth International congress for scientific management, London, July
15th to July 20th, 1935. 6 v. London, Published for the Congress
by P. S. King and son limited [1935] 249.09 In8
Articles in English, French, Italian or German; each article has a
summary in French, German and English.
Contents. - Agricultural section; Development section; Distribution
section; Domestic section; Educational and training section; and Manufacturing section.
The Agricultural Section includes the following papers : Le Machinisme
dans l'organisation du travail agricole (the part played by machinery
in farm work) by Georges Bouckaert; Die Maschinen und Geräte in der
Landwirtschaft (The machine and implements in agricultural work), by
K. Dörffel; Die Eingliederung der Maschine in die Arbeitswirtschaft des
Betriebes und die Vorausberechnung ihrer Wirtschaftlichkeit (The use
of machines on German farms and the determination of their efficiency)
by L. W. Ries; Mechanization on the farm, by C. S. Orwin; Agricultural
machines in farm work [in Hungary] by Imre Rothmeyer; Farm management in
Western Canada and the Colonization Finance Corporation of Canada, Lim-
ited, by F. W. Reinoehl; Die Rolle der Buchführung im landwirtschaftlichen
Betrieb (The place of book-keeping on the farm) by H. L. Fensch; The

.ee of accounts in farm management. by R. McG. Carslaw; The importance of
the valuation of assets in agricultural undertakings (Proposes the adoption of uniform rules for the use of different countries in gathering
agricultural statistics) by John Ormandy; La funzione della contabilità
nelle aziende agrarie (The place of accountancy in agriculture) by the
Istituto Nazionale Italiano de Economia Agraria; Die Buchführung als
Mittel der Betriebskontrolle und Wirtschaftsberatung in' der Oster-
reichischen Landwirtschaft (Bookkeeping as a means of controlling work
and giving economic advice in Austrian agriculture) by Wilfried Kahler;
Rôle de la comptabilité agricole (The role of agricultural book-keeping)
by Stefan Moszczenski; Scientific methods in farm management, by Sanford
E. Thompson, and C. Alan Brantingham; Zubereitung des Erzeugnisses für
den Markt (The preparation of produce for market) by Ludwig Herrmann;
The development of standardization as a factor in the preparation of
agricultural produce for market, by A. W. Street; Preparation of produce for market, by J. M. Riemens; La preparazione dei prodotti agricoli
per lo smercio sui mercati (The preparation of agricultural produce for
rapid disposal on the market) by the Istituto Nazionale Italiano per
l'Esportazione; Marketing control in Kenya, by V. Liversage; Spezialisierung
der Landwirtschaft um die Einstellung der nationalen Agrarwirtschaften
für Weltwirtschaft, by José Mallert. (The author demonstrates the
advisability of adapting crop production to the needs of the locality
and the requirements of the market. He would subordinate national
economy to a world agricultural economy if that could be developed);
La normalisation des methodes et des produits de l'arboriculture fruitière
suisse (The standardization of methods and products of the Swiss fruit-
growing industry), by F. E. Tapernoux; Die Vorbereitung landwirtschaftlicher Produkte zum Zwecke des Verkaufes, by Kálmán V. Fellner. (The'
author outlines the method which Hungary has adopted for grading,
standardizing, and inspecting agricultural products and the results
obtained); Rationalisierung der landwirtschaftlichen Betriebsstatistik
(Rationalization of farm management statistics), by Ladislaus Prack;
Four articles on specialized versus mixed farming in Germany, England,
the Netherlands and Italy respectively are Einheits – oder Wechselkultur,
by H. Krohn; Specialized versus mixed farming, by W. Lawson, Specialized
versus mixed farming, by P. A. Van der Ban, and Coltura unica o coltura
differenziata? by Giuseppe Medici and Aldo Pagani; The trend of specialized farming in the United States, by Jacob G. Lipman; A phase of international management. The regulation of production and export of rubber,
by Godfrey E. Coombs; Il catasto agrario nei riflessi della disciplina
delle colture, by the Istituto Centrale di Statistica. (The importance
of Italy's Register of Land Survey is stressed as providing the accurate
knowledge of agricultural conditions and relations necessary for their
regulation); Aspetti dell' organizzazione razionale della produzione,
e vendita dei prodotti agricoli e dell' acquisto e distribuzione delle
materie utili all' agricoltura. (Some aspects of the rational organization of the production and sale of agricultural products and production
goods), by the Confederazione Fascista degli Agricoltori; Illustrazione
dell' indagine sui principali attrezzi a mano adoperati in agricoltura,
by the Confederazione Fascista dei Lavoratori dell' Agricoltura. (An

account of an investigation made by the Fascist Confederation of Agricultural workers of the use of the implements used in agriculture in Italy with a view to possible improvement in their construction and use; and the scientific organization of labour in the live-stock industry, by B. Maymone.

Land - Ireland

O'Neill, Brian. The war for the land in Ireland. With an introduction by Peadar O'Donnell. 201pp. New York, International publishers [1933] 282 On2
A review and analysis of the land problem in Ireland by "a member of the youthful Communist movement in Ireland."

Land - Research - China

China, Commission on land research and planning. The function of the Commission on land research and planning, by Chen Li-Fu, chairman of the Commission on land research and planning. 36pp. Nanking, China, International relations committee [1935?] 282 C44
Translated from the Chinese by Chao Hsi-Lin - p. 1.
The Commission on Land Research and Planning was established in 1934 to investigate and analyze the land problems in the different provinces in China.
This pamphlet contains sections on the following research topics: The value of land; Land ownership; The land tax; The use of land; The Survey and registration of land.

Land of the Free

Agar, Herbert. Land of the free. 305pp. Boston, Houghton Mifflin company, 1935. 280.12 Ag1
If we are to save our historic America from "the tyrant state of fascism or the tyrant state of Marx" we must make a moral issue of it. We have betrayed America for greed. "The men who urged us to the betrayal promised us many pieces of silver... it is worth remembering, and repeating, that we have not been paid the pieces of silver." Those of us who have confidence in America should be "unashamed about making a moral appeal" and should not hesitate to make use of modern propaganda. "The first step in our propaganda, then, is to show Americans the honest choices before them; to make them see that they cannot choose America (as defined, for instance, in that school-children's creed) unless they are willing to save the institution of real private property [meaning by private property "some share in the means of production]; and to present this American choice, not as just another 'economic machine' to be judged solely on the number of goods it promises, but as a chance to make our country what it has never been - a nation with a place in world history because it has something new and significant to add to the long story.
"The second step in our propaganda is to make clear that even at the penalty of going slow, we must carry through our reforms on the basis of what we can afford."

Livestock - Saxony

Bleyl, Walther. Viehwirtschaft und viehstandsbewegung in der landwirtschaft
des Freistaates Sachsen. 80pp. Dresden und Leipzig, T. Steinkopff, 1934.
(Die lage der landwirtschaft im Freistaat Sachsen... hrsg. von... Friedrich
Falke... Ergänzungsheft I)   281.175 F18A no. 1
   "Erscheint zugleich als dissertation in Leipzig" p. [ii]
   Bibliography, p. [81]
   A study of livestock raising, the movement of livestock and its utiliza-
tion in Saxony.

Manchester Merchants and Foreign Trade

Redford, Arthur. Manchester merchants and foreign trade, 1794-1858, by
   students in the Honours school of history in the University of Manchester,
   and Arthur Redford. 251pp. [Manchester] Manchester university press,
   193-. (Publications of the University of Manchester no. 233. Economic
   history series, no. 11)   277.171 R24M
   "This book is based primarily on the manuscript records of the Manchester Commercial Society (1794-1801), the Manchester Commercial Association (1845-58) and the Manchester Chamber of Commerce, which was founded
in 1820. The main part of the volume is concerned with the activities
of the Chamber of Commerce, but no attempt has been made to write an
official history of the Chamber, complete with lists of Presidents and
Directors. The stubborn struggle of the Manchester merchants to surmount
the barriers which obstructed the expansion of their export trade stands
out as the central theme; yet many aspects of Manchester's foreign trade
are described only incidentally, or altogether neglected. Our purpose
has been to analyse the chief problems which confronted Manchester merchants during a most formative period of the city's history, and to
trace the development of local commercial policy, so far as that policy
reflected itself in the proceedings of the merchants' organisations."-
Preface.
   Chapters of special interest are XI which considers free trade and
the corn laws and XVI entitled "The Supply of Raw Cotton."

Marketing Schemes - Canada

Canada. Dominion marketing board. Guide to the preparation of marketing
   schemes under the Natural products marketing act, 1934, and summary of
   schemes approved under the act by the Dominion marketing board to
   September 1, 1935. 16pp. Ottawa, The Dominion marketing board [1935]
   280.3 C155G
   Summaries are given for the following: British Columbia tree fruit
scheme; Fruit export marketing scheme; British Columbia red cedar shingle
scheme; British Columbia dry salt herring and dry salt salmon scheme;
Ontario flue-cured tobacco scheme; Eastern Canada potato marketing scheme;
Milk marketing scheme of the Lower Mainland of British Columbia; Western
Ontario bean marketing scheme; British Columbia (interior) vegetable
marketing scheme; British Columbia coast vegetable marketing scheme;
Canada jam marketing scheme; British Columbia halibut marketing scheme;
B. C. hothouse tomato and cucumber marketing scheme; British Columbia

small fruits and rhubarb marketing scheme; Ontario cheese patrons' marketing scheme; Processed berry marketing scheme; Nova Scotia apple marketing scheme; British Columbia sheep breeders' marketing scheme; Dairy products marketing equalization scheme; Grand Manan smoked herring products scheme; Ontario burley tobacco marketing scheme.

Money

Bernstein, E. M. Money and the economic system. 516pp. Chapel Hill, The University of North Carolina press [1935]   284 B456
    Bibliography, pp.485-495
    Part I, The monetary system; Part II, Prices; Part III, The value of money; Part IV, Monetary problems; Part V, Monetary management.

National Confederation of Fascist Syndicates of Agriculture

Confederazione nazionale dei sindacati fascisti dell' agricoltura. L'azione sindacale del fascismo nell'agricoltura. Atti delle Assemblee nazionali delle federazioni, del Congresso confederale e del Consiglio nazionale. 564pp. Roma, Stabilimento tipografico Società editrice "IL Lavoro fascista", 1933.   281.176 C76A
    This is a report of the addresses, discussions and resolutions that formed the program of the meetings of the various branches of the National Confederation of Fascist syndicates of Agriculture which were held in Rome from May 30 to June 3, 1933. Some of the topics discussed by those National Federations to which they were of particular interest were labor contracts, a number of problems connected with share farming, and questions of interest to the cultivation of special products, such as tobacco, citrus fruits, olives, etc.

Pan American Commercial Conference

Pan American commercial conference, 5th, Buenos Aires, 1935. Acta final de la Conferencia comercial panamericana, reunida en la ciudad de Buenos Aires del 26 de mayo al 19 de junio de 1935. [240pp.] [Buenos Aires? 1935]   286.9 P19F 1935
    Contains Spanish, Portugese, French and English texts, each with separate title page.
    Contains the recommendations of the Fifth Pan American Commercial Conference which met in Buenos Aires from May 26 to June 19, 1935.

Population Changes - Germany

Haufe, Helmut. Deutsches volkstum in der bevölkerungsentwicklung des östlichen mitteleuropa. 62pp. Berlin und Stuttgart, Grenze und Ausland, 1935.
    Schriften zur volkswissenschaft.
    Bibliography, p. 62.
    In this contribution to the literature dealing with the difficult problems which changes in the countries in East Europe have made for Germany, the author presents considerable statistical data which he contends proves the theory of Professor Gunther Ipsen that the population phenomena of Germany and other countries, especially those to the East,

have been greatly conditioned by changes in the traditional agricultural constitution and organization. According to this theory the population in the German East had been automatically restricted since agricultural units held by individual peasants were not to be divided and the whole of society was held by rigid custom. In earlier times increased population pressure expressed itself in migration eastward and elsewhere and not so much in over-population as was the case in some areas. In the typical Slavic agricultural constitution which allowed for division of the land units or in the Russian mir where the size of the land holding of a family came to be in proportion to the number of persons in the families, population increased more rapidly.

With the freeing of the peasants and serfs and the "liberal" reforms which took place from 1811 to 1816, the agricultural constitution of the German East was changed. So called lower classes became laborers and were no longer held so rigidly by the bonds of custom. They lost most of their rights to the land, and began to increase their offspring at a tremendous rate. The peasants also increased their rate of reproduction, although not to the same degree as the laborers. Most of this tremendous increase in the population migrated to the growing industries in the West or overseas. However, the rural population between the years 1818-1867 increased 68 percent in the area affected by the agrarian reforms which freed the peasants.

While in the European countries east of Germany, the proportion of the German population increased during most of the first two-thirds of the nineteenth century, it has decreased since 1870. The introduction into Poland and other eastern countries of land reforms patterned after those which were responsible for this great population increase in East Germany are now having their effect. Germany may witness the transformation of Poland into a world power following the same historical pattern as she herself followed. This development is exceedingly dangerous for Germany because the post-war government allowed the German East to become relatively depopulated at the same time that some other eastern nations were increasing their population. - C. P. Loomis.

Poultry - Germany

Germany. Reichsinteressenvertretung der geflügelwirtschaft. Zur versorgungslage der deutschen bevölkerung mit geflügelerzeugnissen deutscher herkunft.
    t. II. Schlichtgeflugel. 76;p. Berlin, 1933. 281.347 G31
    At head of title: Reichsinteressenvertretung der geflügelwirtschaft (RIG)
    An account of production and consumption of poultry in Germany, including chickens, geese, ducks, and pigeons.

Price Level

Edgeworth, K. E. The price level; a further problem in national planning.
    16;pp. London, G. Allen & Unwin ltd. [1935] 284 Ed3
    "Continues the examination of the monetary system which was commenced in ... The trade balance." - Pref.
    Bibliography, p. [101]
    The author's Preface indicates the scope of this book as follows:
    "This essay continues the examination of the monetary system which

was commenced in the author's earlier essay The Trade Balance.

"In regard to the scope of our inquiry, it may be well to explain that, although a complete programme of national planning must necessarily include the development of an adequate and efficient monetary system, the development of an ideal monetary system will not in itself provide a solution to certain national problems which are also of urgent importance at the present time...

"For the moment we are concerned with monetary problems, and the author's analysis has led to the conclusion that such mechanisms as may have existed during the nineteenth century for controlling the trade balance and the price level have failed to carry out their functions under the more exacting conditions of the present day...

"At the present time there are two fundamental monetary problems to be solved. Firstly, there is the problem of restoring equilibrium between the different national monetary systems, and secondly, there is the problem of devising an international monetary system which will not contain within itself the seeds of its own destruction...

"...It would no doubt be generally agreed that the ideal monetary system should aim at securing the following results:-

"Firstly, the expansion of trade and industry should be facilitated by an ample supply of cheap money, and should be restricted only when there are signs of over-trading and. the development of boom conditions.

"Secondly, violent fluctuations in the activity of trade should be avoided as far as possible.

"Thirdly, there should be adequate control of the trade balance without excessive restriction of international trade.

"Fourthly, the price level should be reasonably stable, particularly over the long period.

"But is it possible to devise a monetary system which will be consistent in itself and which will secure all these perhaps divergent objectives? The author believes that it is, and the purpose of these essays is to indicate the general character of the solution."

Prices and Agricultural Production

Marquardt, Heinrich. Die ausrichtung der landwirtschaftlichen produktion an den preisen; zugleich ein beitrag zur theorie des verbundenen angebots. 138pp. Jena, G. Fischer, 1934. (Probleme der theoretischen national-ökonomie, hrsg. von Walter Eucken, hft. 3)   284.3 M34
A study of the extent to which agricultural production is dependent on prices.

Relief Administration - Arkansas

Arkansas. State emergency relief administration. A review of work relief activities in Arkansas, April 1st, 1934 to July 1st, 1935. 152pp. [Little Rock, Parke-Harper company, 1935]   283 Ar4R
On cover: Arkansas Emergency Relief Administration, April 1, 1934 to April [1] 1935.
Contains a chapter on Colonization Project no. 1, Dyess Colony in Arkansas.

Nevada. Emergency committee on employment. Report of the governor's emergency
committee on employment in Nevada to Richard Kirman, Sr., governor, by
Letson Balliet, industrial-economist, director-chairman. Not relief,
but recovery possibilities in Nevada. 21pp. Carson City, Nov., State
printing office, 1935. 283 N41
    Contains a brief section on the situation among farmers, ranchers,
livestock men and rural workers.

Sugar - Argentina

Centro azucarero nacional. La industria azucarera, editado por el Centro
    azucarero. 222pp. Buenos Aires, 1935. 281.365 C33 1935
    "Preparado por el señor Emilio J. Schleh, gerente-secretario del Centro
azucarero", verso of title page.
    An account of the sugar industry in Argentina under the heading of culti
tion of the cane, acreage prices, labor, consumption and production.
Many tables are given.

Tariff - Puerto Rico

Puerto Ri o. Emergency relief administration. Tariff survey division. The
    tariff problems of Puerto Rico. Report of the Tariff survey division
    of the Puerto Rican Emergency relief administration. 101pp. San Juan,
    P. R., Bureau of supplies, printing, and transportation, 1935. 285 P962
    "The Tariff Survey Bureau was organized as a work project of the
Puerto Rican Emergency Relief Administration in September 1934. Its purpose was to provide a collection of factual material upon which might be
based a determination of whether inclusion within the provision of the
United States' tariff laws was on the whole beneficial or harmful to
the economic welfare of the Island.
    "The material gathered by the survey is presented in the following
pages." - Foreword.

Taxation - Arizona

Roberts, W. A. Arizona tax problems. 29pp. Tucson, Ariz., University of
    Arizona [1935] ([Arizona. University] Social science bulletin no. 8)
    284.4 R54
    University of Arizona bulletin, vol. VI, no. 2.
    Contents: - The present tax burden; Shock absorbers in a revenue
system; Local expenditure control; The administration of the property
tax; The intangibles tax; Recommendations.
    Most of this pamphlet is reprinted from material published in The
Arizona Producer during November, December [1934] and January [1935]

Taxation of Land Values

Muirhead, J. F. Land and unemployment. Edited with an introductory note
    on Henry George, by Garnet Smith... With a foreword by Sir A. T. Wilson,
    M. P. 211pp. London, Oxford university press, H. Milford, 1935.
    282 M93
    A brief review of this book in The Economist (London) for November 30,

1935, p. 1072 reads as follows:

"Dr. Muirhead's posthumous essay - which coincides with quite an outburst of new Henry George literature - will amply repay the reader who studies it with attention. There can be no denial of his request that the proposal to tax land values should be calmly and dispassionately considered by our 'political and philosophical leaders.' While Henry George's analysis of the effect of rent on the other shares in distribution will not find support among economists to-day, his proposal for taxing the public value of land continues to attract the attention and to secure the sympathy of liberal thinkers in many countries. One of the most valuable chapters in Dr. Muirhead's essay is that in which he describes the taxation of land values in different countries.

"It is a pity that the economic as distinguished from the financial advantages of the proposed scheme of taxation are not more fully explained, as the reader is left unconvinced that the introduction of the single tax will in itself increase the incomes of agricultural producers, except, perhaps, indirectly by the remission of other taxes. Nor is it anywhere made clear in what manner the single tax would provide additional employment. One is also puzzled at the title chosen for the volume. The foreword by Sir Arnold Wilson and the introductory note by the editor, Mr. Garnet Smith, will be of interest to students of the life and work of Henry George."

Textile Industry - Catalonia.

Blanco Santamaría, Gregorio, and Ciordia Pérez, Eugenio. La industria textil catalana. Notas acerca del desenvolvimiento del trabajo en este sector industrial. 60pp. Madrid, Imprenta y encuadernación de los sobrinos de la sucesora de M. Minuesa de los Ríos, 1933. (Sociedad para el progreso social. Publicación num. 34) 304 B59
Reviewed in International Labour Review 30 (4): 565. Oct. 1934 as follows:

"Interesting study on the importance and development of the textile industry in Catalonia and on working conditions (wages and hours of work) in that industry. Some of the numerous tables and diagrams show the geographical distribution of spinning mills and weaving factories near the various watercourses. The Spanish textile industry, which is highly mechanised, employs about 180,000 persons, of whom over 86,000 work in weaving factories, and about 53,000 in spinning mills. The authors examine the question of wages fixed by collective agreements, which vary appreciably for the different categories of workers and districts. With regard to hours of work, the statutory 48-hour week is applied in the textile industry; the trade unions urge the introduction of the 40-hour week."

Tropical Agriculture

Greaves, I. C. Modern production among backward peoples. 229pp. London, G. Allen & Unwin ltd. [1935] (London school of economics and political science. Studies in economics and commerce. no. 5) 281 G798
"Based on contemporary agriculture in the tropics." - p.12.
Thesis (Ph.D.) - University of London.
Bibliography, pp. [223]-226
The following extract is taken from a review of this book in the

Economist (London) November 23, 1935, p. 1016:
"The 'backward peoples' studied in this book are those of the tropics, and the main theme is that of peasant versus plantation production in tropical agriculture. Mining and industrial production are excluded from the survey, so that the title of the work is somewhat misleading; within its limits, however, it provides a very clear and systematic account of contemporary economic conditions in tropical lands."

India

Kuczynski, Jurgen. Die entwicklung der lage der arbeiterschaft in Europa und Amerika, 1870-1933. Statistische studien zur entwicklung der reallöhne und relativlohne in England, Deutschland, U S A, Frankreich und Belgien. 7.p. Basel, Philographischer verlag, 1934.   283 K95
    A statistical study of the development of real and social wages in Great Britain, Germany, the United States, and Belgium and their relation to the social status of the worker.

Wheat - France

Waspétiol, Roland, and Demougeot-Perron, G. La crise du blé en France et dans le monde. 135pp. Paris, Éditions A. Pedone, 1935.   281.359 M38
    This book claims to be a popular survey of the wheat problem in the world but more particularly in France, without an impressive array of statistics or a quantity of technical details. The main characteristics of the wheat crisis, the remedies applied in France to date, their efficacy, and the steps that remain to be taken to lessen the difficulties that still exist are discussed.

Women on the Farm - Saxony

Schützhold, Gerhard. Die sächsische landfrau, ihr aufgaben- und pflichtenkreis im bauerlichen landwirtschaftsbetrieb. 78pp. Dresden und Leipzig, T. Steinkopff, 1934. (Die lage der landwirtschaft im Freistaat Sachsen... von. Friedrich Falke... Ergänzungsheft II) 281.175 F18A no.2
    "Erscheint zugleich als dissertation in Leipzig" - verso of title page. Bibliography, p. [79]
    A comprehensive study of the duties of the woman on the farm in Saxony and the time occupied in their discharge, and suggested means for relieving the pressure.

World Production Order

Wibaut, F. M. A world production order. Translated from the Dutch by R. W. Roome, with a foreword by Sidney Webb. 240pp. London, G. Allen & Unwin ltd. [1935] 280 W634
    The foreword reads in part as follows:
    "Dr. Wibaut asks us to consider with him the preponderant direction of the evolution of modern wealth production, which points irresistibly to the necessity of its collective organization on a world scale.
    "Dr. Wibaut sketches for his readers no Utopia. He foresees a very fundamental change in world organization, but he lays stress on the improvements which that organization requires rather than on the exact

shape and nomenclature that it will assume in its perfected form. Nor
does he presume to dogmatize as to the manner, or the stages, by which
the changes that he foresees will actually come about. He demands from
his readers no adhesion to a formal programme, still less to any political
party. He invites adhesion to progressive reforms on large lines, dictated by the necessity for realizing democracy in all quarters of economic
life. But he is most concerned to provoke, in his readers, thought. Perhaps he is right in deeming this to be indispensable to every dynamic!"

BIBLIOGRAPHY

Bibliography of economics 1751-1775. Prepared for the British academy by
Henry Higgs. 742pp. Cambridge, University press, 1935. 241.3 B473
    The general preface outlines the scope and arrangement of this
bibliography as follows:
    "The scope of the bibliography cannot be defined in a few words.
It includes such works, known to exist or to have existed, as are
deemed for one reason or another to be of sufficient economic interest
to justify their inclusion.
    "The entries under each year have been divided into the following
groups: I. General Economics. II. Agriculture, etc., including the
extractive industries generally, Horticulture, Forestry, Agriculture,
Fisheries, Mines, Quarries, etc. III. Shipping, Navigation, etc.
IV. Manufactures. V. Commerce. VI. Colonies, British and Foreign.
VII. Finance - Banking, Money, Taxation, Accountancy, etc. VIII. Transport. IX. Social conditions. X. Topography, of economic interest.
XI. Miscellaneous.
    "The divisions are necessarily somewhat arbitrary as an item may refer
to more than one group and its repetition is unnecessary. The chronological arrangement coupled with the classification, the cross references,
the index of names, and the index of titles will, it is hoped, allow any
entry to be found without difficulty."
    "It is proposed to continue backward and forward "this first section of
the bibliography covering the period 1751-1775, which marks the dawn
of economic science."

U. S. RESETTLEMENT ADMINISTRATION *

Clayton, C. F. The land utilization program of the Resettlement administration, a radio talk... on the Conservation day period of the National farm
and home hour... July 19, 1935. 3pp.; mimeogr. [Washington, D.C., 1935]
1 95 Ad 8[no.1]

Gray, L. C. Can tenancy be made more tolerable? A radio address... August
30, 1935. 3pp., mimeogr. [Washington, D.C., 1935] 1 95 Ad8G [no.2]

---

*Requests for these publications should be addressed to the Resettlement
Administration, Arlington Hotel, Washington, D. C.

Gray, L. C. A national policy for land and water. 19pp., mimeogr. [Washington, D.C., 1935] 1 95 Ad8G [no.4]
A paper read before the National reclamation conference, Salt Lake City, Utah, November 15, 1935."

Gray, L. C. Recent developments in national land policy. 17pp., mimeogr. [Washington, D. C., 1935] 1 95 Ad8G[no.1]
"A paper read at the conference of New York state directors and teachers of agriculture, Geneva, New York, July 1, 1935."

Gray. L. C. Redistribution of population in the United States. 17pp., mimeogr. [Washington, D.C., 1935] 1 95 Ad8G [no.3]
"A paper read to the Pan-American institute of geography and history, October 17, 1935."

Gray, L. C. Urges extension of federal land use policies. 3pp., mimeogr. [Washington, D. C., Dec. 28, 1935] 1 95 Ad8G [no.5]

Manchester, A. W. The problem of land adjustment in the northeastern states. A radio talk... June 7, 1935. 2pp., mimeogr. [Washington, D. C., 1935] 1 95 Ad8M [no. 1]

Nowell, R. I. Land use problems in the lake states and what is being done towards their solution. 36pp., mimeogr. [Washington, D.C., 1935] 1 95 Ad8No [no.2]
"A paper read before the American association for the advancement of science and associated societies, Minneapolis, Minnesota, June 27, 1935."

Nowell. R. I. Resettlement and land use problems in the lake states. A radio address... June 21, 1935. 3pp., mimeogr. [Washington, D. C., 1935] 1 95 Ad8No [no.1]

Reynolds, Lucille. Women and resettlement; a radio talk... delivered in the Department period of the National farm and home hour... September 30 [1935] 3pp., mimeogr. [Washington, D.C., 1935] 1 95 Ad8R [no.1]

Taylor, P. S. The migrants and California's future. The trek to California, and the trek in California. 10pp., mimeogr. [Washington, D.C., 1935] 1 95 Ad8Ta [no.1]
'Delivered before the Commonwealth Club of California, San Francisco, Sept. 13, 1935."

Taylor, C. C. Speech... delivered before Annual conference of Farmers and agricultural extension service, Fayetteville, Arkansas, August 9, 1935. 11pp., mimeogr. [Washington, D. C., 1935] 1 95 Ad8T [no.1]

Taylor, C. C. What kind of rural life can we look forward to in the United States... Presidential address... before the annual meeting of the American country life association, Columbus, Ohio, September 19, 1935. 10pp., mimeog [Washington, D.C., 1935] 1 95 Ad8T [no.2]

Tugwell, R. G. The reason for resettlement... Address... broadcast...
December 2, 1935. 12pp., mimeogr. [Washington, D.C., 1935]
1 95 Ad8Tu [no.2]

SELECTED LIST OF RECENT REVIEWS

Compiled by M. I. Herb

Beard, C. A. The open door at home; a trial philosophy of national interest.
1934.
Reviewed by Kemper Simpson in Bull. of the Taylor Society and of the
Society of Industrial Engineers 1 (7): 241-243. November 1935.

Canada. Parliament. House of Commons, Royal Commission on price spreads.
Report of the Royal Commission on price spreads. 1935.
Reviewed by V. W. Bladen in Econ. Jour. 45 (179): 590-594. September
1935.

Chase, Stuart. Government in business. 1935.
Reviewed in Northwest. Miller 184 (8): 732. Dec. 11, 1935.
Reviewed by C. C. Rohlfing in Amer. Polit. Sci. Rev. 29 (6): 1069-
1070. December 1935.

Davis, J. S. Wheat and the A.A.A. 1935. (Half-title: The Institute of
economics of the Brookings institution. Publication no. 61)
Reviewed by R. B. Bryce in Econ. Jour. 45 (180): 775-777. December
1935.

Dawson, C. A., and Murchie, R. W. The settlement of the Peace river country;
a study of a pioneer area. 1934. (Canadian frontiers of settlement...
v. 6)
Reviewed by Paul Gates in Land Policy Circ. November 1935, pp. 26-31.

Emeny, Brooks. The strategy of raw materials; a study of America in peace
and war. 1934.
Reviewed by B. B. Wallace in Jour. Polit. Econ. 43 (6): 823-825.
December 1935.

Garland, J. M. Economic aspects of Australian land taxation. 1934.
Reviewed by R. L. Hall in Econ. Jour. 45 (178): 353-355. June 1935.
Reviewed by R. C. Mills in Econ. Rec. 11 (20): 100-103. June 1935.

Gayer, A. D. Monetary policy and economic stabilisation; a study of the
gold standard. 1935.
Reviewed by H. W. M. in Roy. Statis. Soc. Jour. (n.s.) 98 (4): 728-731.
1935.

Hamilton, E. J. American treasure and the price revolution in Spain, 1501-
1650. 1934.
Reviewed by Herbert Heaton in Jour. Polit. Econ. 43 (5): 710-711.
October 1935.

Higgs, Henry. Bibliography of economics. 1935.
  Reviewed by Jacob Viner in Jour. Polit. Econ. 43 (6): 817-820. December
  1935.
  Reviewed by J. Bonar in Econ. Jour. 45 (180): 720-723. December 1935.

Holland, W. L., ed. Commodity control in the Pacific area; a symposium on
  recent experience. [1935]
  Reviewed by J. B. Condliffe in Econ. Jour. 45 (180): 762-764.
  December 1935.

International conference of agricultural economists. Proceedings of the
  third international conference... 1935.
  Reviewed by Ruth Cohen in Econ. Jour. 45 (180): 777-779. December 1935.

Kolb, J. H., and Brunner, Edmund de S. A study of rural society; its organization and changes. [1935]
  Reviewed by B. Y. Landis in Information Serv. [Published by Dept. of
  Research and Education, Federal Council of Churches of Christ in America]
  15 (1, pt.1): 4. Jan. 4, 1935.

Layton, Sir Walter T., and Crowther, Geoffrey. An introduction to the study
  of prices. 1935.
  Reviewed by H. W. M. in Roy. Statis. Soc. Jour. (n.s.) 98 (4): 744-
  745. 1935.

Means, Gardiner. Industrial prices and their relative inflexibility. U. S.
  74th Cong., 1st sess. Senate Doc. 13, 1935.
  Reviewed by D. M. Bensusan-Butt in Econ. Jour. 45 (180): 793-797.
  December 1935.

Orwin, C. S., and Darke, W. F. Back to the land. 1935.
  Reviewed in the Economist 121 (4808): 756-757. Oct. 19, 1935 in an
  article entitled "Back to the Land?"

Pigou, A. C. Economics in practice; six lectures on current issues. 1935.
  Reviewed by H. W. M. in Roy. Statis. Soc. Jour. (n.s.) 98 (3): 563-564.
  1935.

Roos, C. F. Dynamic economics; theoretical and statistical studies of demand,
  production, and prices. [1934] (Monograph of the Cowles commission for
  research in economics, no. 1)
  Reviewed by A. L. B. in Roy. Statis. Soc. Jour. (n.s.) 98 (4): 726-728.
  1935.

Social science research council, Advisory committee on social and economic
  research in agriculture. Research in farm real estate values - scope and
  methods... John D. Black editor. 1933. (Bulletin no. 19)
  Reviewed by Homer Hoyt in Jour. Polit. Econ. 43 (6) 850. December 1935.

Willcox, O. W. Nations can live at home. [1935]
  Reviewed in Economist 121 (4817): 1263. Dec. 21, 1935.

U. S. DEPARTMENT OF AGRICULTURE PUBLICATIONS

Economic in Character

Compiled by Katharine Jacobs

Addresses and Radio Talks of the Secretary and Assistant Secretary*

Secretary Wallace

The farm conference, remarks...over National farm and home hour...Jan. 14, 1936. 4pp.

Farm economists and agricultural planning. Address...before the Farm economics association, New York City, December 30, 1935. 14pp.

Farmers and the export market; address...before the annual convention of the American farm bureau federation, Chicago, December 10, 1935. 16pp. (G-51) Issued December 1935 by Agricultural adjustment administration.
    Also issued as mimeographed press release.

Public opinion and the farm fight. Remarks...over the National farm and home hour...December 31, 1935. 4pp.

Remarks [on the economic welfare of agriculture]...at a meeting of farm leaders, Washington, D.C., January 10, 1936. 8pp.

Remarks [on the need for a workable substitute for the Triple A]...over the National farm and home hour, Jan. 21, 1936. 5pp.

The Supreme court decision. Remarks...January 7, 1936. 3pp.
    Radio talk.

Assistant Secretary Wilson

The challenge to agriculture; address...at Des Moines, Iowa, on Jan. 16, 1936...before the annual convention of the Iowa farm bureau federation. 15pp.

Validity of the fundamental assumptions underlying agricultural adjustment. Address...before the American farm economic association, New York City, Dec. 28, 1935. 19pp.

Publications of the Bureau of Agricultural Economics (Mimeographed)**

Amendment no. 2 to Service and regulatory announcements no. 116. Amendment to rules and regulations of the Secretary of agriculture for carrying out the provisions of the Standard container act of 1928. 5pp. [Dec. 14, 1935]

Amendment no. 2 to Service and regulatory announcements no. 143. Amendment to rules and regulations of the Secretary of agriculture for carrying out the provisions of the Export apple and pear act. 2pp., Jan. 1, 1936.

---

*Requests for these publications should be addressed to the Office of Information, U. S. Department of Agriculture, Washington, D. C.
**These publications are issued in small editions for immediate use in official work and are not for general distribution.

Amendment no. 4 to Service and regulatory announcements (B.A.E.) no 124
    [Regulations of the Secretary of agriculture under the United States
    Cotton futures act] 3pp. [Dec. 26, 1935]
Amendment no. 7 to Service and regulatory announcements (B.A.E.) no. 125
    [Regulations of the Secretary of agriculture under the United States
    Cotton futures act] 4pp. [Dec. 26, 1935]
Average prices received by farmers for 1935 crops, with comparisons. 22pp.
    Dec. 20, 1935.
Beef cattle outlook charts for use with the agricultural outlook for 1936.
    27pp. November 1935.
Cotton outlook charts for use with the agricultural outlook for 1936.
    31pp. November 1935.
Cotton production in Mexico, by P. K. Norris. 15pp. December 1935. (F.S.65)
The December pig report, a radio talk by C. L. Harlan. 2pp. Dec. 23, 1935.
Developments in marketing, 1935. By A. G. Black. Address, annual meeting,
    National association of marketing officials, Chicago, December 4, 1935.
    11pp. [1935]
Farm biographies and autobiographies, a radio talk by Caroline B. Sherman.
    2pp. Jan. 6, 1936.
Handbook of official United States standards for beans, rev. effective
    Aug. 1, 1935. 34pp. 1935. (Form HFS-1662) Printed.
The problem of reporting wholesale prices of butter, by L. M. Davis.
    8pp. December 1935.
Review of the 1935 fall bean season. 3pp. Dec. 21, 1935. (Issued in
    cooperation with Florida State marketing bureau)
Rules and regulations (as amended) of the Secretary of agriculture governing
    the grading and certification of canned fruits and vegetables. Under
    an act of Congress approved May 17, 1935. (Public no. 62, 74th
    Congress). 12pp. November 1935.
Rules and regulations of the Secretary of agriculture governing the in-
    spection and certification of hay and straw for class and grade.
    Under an act of Congress approved May 17, 1935 (49 Stat. 247)
    Revised, effective January 2, 1936. 10pp. 1935.
Tax delinquency of rural real estate in six Florida counties, 1928-33.
    11pp. Dec. 24, 1935.
        This survey was made under a Civil works project administered
    by the Bureau of Agricultural Economics, assisted by the Agricultural
    Experiment Station of Florida.
Tax delinquency of rural real estate in nine North Carolina counties,
    1928-33. 12pp. Dec. 18, 1935.
        This survey was made under a Civil works project administered by
    the Bureau of Agricultural Economics, assisted by the Agricultural
    Experiment Station of North Carolina.
Tax delinquency of rural real estate in eight Virginia counties, 1928-33.
    9pp. Jan. 7, 1936.
        This survey was made under a Civil works project administered by
    the Bureau of Agricultural Economics, assisted by the Virginia State
    Department of Taxation and the Agricultural Experiment Station of
    Virginia.
U. S. standards for California and Arizona grapefruit (effective January
    1, 1936). 7pp. [Dec. 14, 1935]

Publications of the Agricultural Adjustment Administration*

The Agricultural adjustment act and national recovery; paper by Chester C.
Davis...for delivery before joint session American farm economic as-
sociation and American statistical association in New York city...
December 27, 1935. 16pp., mimeogr.

Amendment no. 1 to rye administrative rulings, series of 1936-39, relating
to 1936-39 rye adjustment contracts, prescribed by the Secretary of
agriculture. 2pp. (Rye-6-A) Issued December 16, 1935.

(Continental United States beet sugar order no. 7) Readjustment of market-
ing allotments to processors of the quota for the continental United
States beet-sugar producing area for the year 1935. [2] pp. (C.U.S.
B.S.O. no. 7) Issued December 6, 1935.

Corn-hog administrative rulings, series of 1936-37, relating to 1936-37
corn-hog adjustment contracts. (Rulings nos. 201-266, inclusive)
20pp. (C.H.-205) Issued December 6, 1935.

Cotton adjustment under the A.A.A. 8pp. (Commodity information series.
Cotton leaflet no. 7) Issued December 1935.
    Bibliography, p. 8.

Cotton administrative rulings applicable for 1936, relating to 1936-39
cotton adjustment contracts. Rulings nos. 1-25, prescribed by the
Secretary of agriculture. 16pp. (C.A.C.2) Issued December 2, 1935.

Goals in agricultural adjustment [Speech before the County planning project
conference in Washington, D. C., on October 25, 1935] by F. F. Elliott.
21pp., mimeogr.

How much cotton should America produce in 1936? Farmers must decide whether
the A.A.A. program is to continue. 8pp. (Commodity information series.
Cotton leaflet no. 6) Issued December 1935.

Instructions on signatures and authorizations in connection with the execution of rental and benefit contracts and/or related papers. 21pp.
(AAA 331) Issued October 24, 1935.

Instructions pertaining to 1935 cotton price adjustment payments. 19pp.
(Form no. C.A.P.5) Issued December 1935.

Instructions pertaining to potato sales allotments for 1936. 14pp.
(Potato 2) Issued December 1935.

Louisiana sugarcane administrative rulings. (Under and pursuant to the
1934-1935 Louisiana sugarcane production adjustment contract) Prescribed by the Secretary of agriculture. Louisiana sugarcane administrative ruling no. 6. 3pp. (Sugar 120-B) Issued December
3, 1935.

Potato import quota regulations, series 3, no. 1. Potato import quota
regulations made by the Secretary of agriculture under the Potato
act of 1935. 3pp. (Potato reg., series 3, no. 1) 1935.

Procedure for the 1936-37 corn-hog adjustment program and use of related
forms. 30pp. (C.H.-206) Issued December 1935.

Stabilized milk markets, the goal of the dairy industry. 6pp. (G-50)
November 1935.

*Requests for these publications should be addressed to the Agricultural
Adjustment Administration, U. S. Department of Agriculture, Washington, D. C.

Compiled by Mary F. Carpenter

Arkansas

Arkansas. Agricultural experiment station. Forty-seventh annual report,
fiscal year ending June 30, 1935. Ark. Agr. Expt. Sta. Bull. 323,
Supp. Fayetteville, 1935.
Rural economics and sociology, pp. 48-52.

California

California. Department of agriculture, Division of market enforcement.
Official list of commission merchants, dealers, brokers and agents
licensed under the agricultural code of the State of California as
of July 15, 1935. Calif. Dept. Agr. Special Pub. 136, 60pp.
Sacramento. 1935.

California. University. College of agriculture, Agricultural extension
service. The 1936 agricultural outlook for California. Calif.
Agr. Col. Ext. Circ. 94, 74pp. Berkeley. 1935.
Paper no. 58, The Giannini Foundation of Agricultural Economics.

Peterson, G. M. Laissez-faire in theory and practice. [9pp.] mimeogr.
Berkeley, Calif. Agr. Expt. Sta. 1935.
A paper presented at the Annual Meeting of the Western Farm Economics
Association, Corvallis, Oregon, August 12 and 13, 1935.

Connecticut

Connecticut. State college. Agricultural policy conference 1935. Conn.
State Col. Bull. v. 31, no. 2. 24pp. Storrs. August 1935.
Includes two of the papers given at the Conference - Forces and
trends to which farm marketing policies in Connecticut need readjustment, by F. V. Waugh, and Transportation changes in the northeast and
their significance for farm marketing policies in Connecticut, by M. P.
Rasmussen.

Illinois

Illinois. College of agriculture. Agricultural outlook for Illinois. Ill.
Agr. Expt. Sta. Circ. 442, 31pp. Urbana. 1935.

Norton, L. J. and Hedges, T. R. Prices of Illinois farm products, 1931-1934.
Ill. Agr. Expt. Sta. Bull. 422, 73pp. Urbana. 1935.
Partial contents: Trends in prices... 1931-1934; Comparison of prices
of individual products, 1931-1933 and 1934; Prices... compared with
prices of goods bought by farmers, 1931-1933 and 1934; Changes in production on Illinois farms; Changes in exports of important Illinois farm

products in recent years; Reasons for the general price rise, 1933-1934;
Outlook for prices... during next few years.
    An appendix gives tables containing monthly Illinois prices of se-
lected farm products, 1931-1934, and index numbers of prices.

Indiana

Bottum, J. C. How one successful Central Indiana dairy hog farm is operated.
    Ind. Agr. Expt. Sta. Stencil Bull. 9, 6pp., mimeogr. Lafayette. 1935

Iowa

Iowa. Department of agriculture. Thirty-fifth annual Iowa year book of
    agriculture, 1934. 492pp. Des Moines. 1935.
        Partial contents: The agricultural situation in Iowa, pp. 14-22;
    Report of Dairy and Food Division, pp. 35-70. (Includes statistics re-
    lating to creamery and poultry products and a report of the canning in-
    dustry); Report of the Warehouse Division (Corn Loan program) pp.101-115;
    Reports of state agricultural associations, pp. 135-193, 277-292; Report
    of the Iowa Farm Debt Advisory Council, pp. 226-259; Iowa corn-hog pro-
    gram, pp. 260-276; Recovery of Iowa's agriculture and world trade, by
    T. W. Schultz, pp. 293-310; Sixty-eight years of improvement in farm
    machines, by J. B. Davidson and C. H. Chase, pp. 311-336; Report of Iowa
    Weather and Crop Bureau, pp. 377-440 (Includes county data); Statistical
    tables of Iowa's principal farm crops, pp. 441-483. (Gives totals of acre-
    age and production for a series of years and yields of corn, oats and winter
    wheat by counties 1890-1934).

Iowa. State college of agriculture and mechanic arts. The 1936 Iowa farm out-
    look. Iowa Agr. Col. Ext. Circ. 216, 30pp. Ames. 1935.

Kentucky

Oyler, Merton, and Rose, W. W. Part-time farming in four representative areas
    of Kentucky. Ky. Agr. Expt. Sta. Bull. 358, pp. 119-150. Lexington 1935.
        In cooperation with the F. E. R. A. and the Kentucky E. R. A.
        The data upon which this report is based were collected in 1934 from
    part-time farmers in areas near Lexington, Louisville, Richmond and Corbin
    and Barbourville.

Poundstone, Bruce and Roth, W. J. Types of farming in Kentucky. Ky. Agr.
    Expt. Sta. Bull. 357, pp. 19-118. Lexington. 1935.
        In cooperation with the U. S. Bureau of Agricultural Economics.
        The farming of the state has been divided into eight type-of-farming
    areas, and these have been further divided into twenty-three sub-types.

Michigan

Hedrick, W. O. Farm tax delinquency in Michigan from 1928-1932. Mich. Agr.
    Expt. Sta. Special Bull. 264, 62pp. East Lansing. 1935.

Wilyst, L. L., and Hollands, H. F. Creamery business analysis. Minn. Agr.
Expt. Sta. Bull. 322. 48pp. University Farm, St. Paul, 1935.
"The purposes of this bulletin are to indicate the general types
of information that should be included in an annual creamery report,
to show patrons and other persons how to analyze and interpret such
a report and to indicate the general financial condition and the operating efficiency of the cooperative creameries included in the study."

Waite, W. C. Farm income in Minnesota. Minn. Univ. Agr. Ext. Div., Farm
Business Notes, no. 156, pp. 1-3, mimeogr. University Farm, St. Paul.
1935.

Winter, J. D., Alderman, W. H., and Waite, W. C. Packing Minnesota fruits
for market. Minn. Agr. Expt. Sta. Bull. 323. 18pp. University Farm
St. Paul. 1935.
The use of various types of containers for apples, plums, strawberries and raspberries is discussed.

Montana

Renne, R. R. Readjusting Montana's agriculture. I. The need and basis
for readjustment. Mont. Agr. Expt. Sta. Bull. 306, 24pp. Bozeman.
1935.
The first of a series of pamphlets in which the state's agriculture
will be analyzed as an aid for an adjustment program.

Nevada

Nevada. Agricultural experiment station and Nevada Agricultural extension
service. Economic talks with Nevada farmers, v. 1, no. 1, 4pp.
Reno. December 1935.
The first number of this new periodical consists of the 1936 Nevada
farming outlook report.

New Jersey

New Jersey. Department of agriculture. Report of the Governor's emergency
farm mortgage committee for 1934. N. J. Dept. Agr. Circ. 249, 33pp.
Trenton 1935.

New Jersey. Department of agriculture. Upper Freehold township; a survey
of the life, resources and government of a New Jersey rural township
with a program for improvement. 85pp. Trenton, N. J. Dept. Agr. 1935.
In cooperation with the U. S. Bureau of Agricultural Economics, The
Monmouth County Agricultural Extension Service and The Upper Freehold
Better Township Association.

Pitt, D. T. New Jersey prices of hired farm labor, feedstuffs and fertilizer, materials and their index numbers, 1910-1934. N. J. Dept. Agr.
Circ. 252, 15pp. Trenton. 1935.

New York (Cornell) State college of agriculture, Department of agricultural economics and farm management. Farm economics, no. 92, Ithaca. December 1935.

Partial contents: Farm prices, by G. F. Warren and F. A. Pearson, pp. 2230-2231; Value of improved roads to New York farmers, by W. M. Curtiss, pp. 2231, 2237-2239; The value of butter, by E. E. Vial, pp.2239-2241. (A table is included giving the index numbers of the purchasing power of butter in the United States and England, 1782-1934); Rural electrification in nine New York counties, by T. E. La Mont, pp. 2242-2246; Use made of motor trucks by growers and shippers in marketing fruits and vegetables, season 1933-34, by M. P. Rasmussen, pp. 2246-2248; Farm management surveys of grade A dairy farms in the Tully-Homer area of Cortland county, New York, by J. R. Raeburn, pp. 2249-2251; Comparative supplies of fruits and vegetables brought to New York city by railroad, boat, and motor truck, calendar years 1929 and 1934, by M. P. Rasmussen pp. 2251-2252.

White, H. E. Wholesale prices at Cincinnati and New York, N. Y. (Cornell) Agr. Expt. Sta. Memoir 182. 42pp. Ithaca. 1935.

"The purpose of this study is to show the movement of wholesale prices of individual commodities and of groups of commodities at Cincinnati and New York for the 71-year period from 1844 to 1914 inclusive.

"For comparison, monthly wholesale prices of individual commodities and groups of commodities are expressed in terms of index numbers. Prices are missing for the following periods at Cincinnati; nine months January 1844 to September 1844; twenty-two months, November 1846 to August 1848; fifty months, January 1868 to February 1872; one month, May 1883.

"Index numbers were prepared for eight major groups: farm products, foods, hides and leather, textiles, fuel and lighting, metals and metal products, building materials, and miscellaneous products. These groups were used in the calculation of the index numbers of wholesale prices of all commodities. Additional index number of wholesale prices at Cincinnati were prepared for six special groups: livestock, meats and meat products, grains, fruits and vegetables, cotton goods, and furs." The wholesale prices at Cincinnati were taken from the weekly Cincinnati Price Current.

Ohio

Eckert, P. S., and Henning, G. F. The livestock auction in Ohio. Ohio. Agr. Expt. Sta. Bull. 557, 27pp. Wooster. 1935.

Discusses the development of livestock auctions, the handling and selling of livestock through auctions in Ohio and contains a section on the farmers' viewpoint.

Oklahoma

Oklahoma. Agricultural experiment station. Current farm economics. Series 49, v. 8, no. 6. Stillwater. December 1935.

Partial contents: Hogs as a farm enterprise in Oklahoma, by Peter Nelson, pp. 116-118; Cash income to Oklahoma farmers for 1935, by

H. A. Miles, pp. 118-120; The battle against farm tenancy in Oklahoma
has started, by J. T. Sanders, pp. 122-125; Organization of Land Utilization division, Resettlement Administration, Region VIII, by C. P. Blackwell, pp. 125-126; The Rural Resettlement program, by W. J. Green,
pp. 126-129.

Oregon

Oregon. State agricultural college, Extension service. Agricultural situation and outlook, 1935 Circ. 12, pp.1, 3-7. Corvallis. Dec. 17, 1935.
Contains an article on the Farm Business which includes forms for
farm inventory, credit statement and budget plan.

Oregon. State agricultural college, Extension service. The general outlook for farm income and costs in Oregon in 1936. Oreg. Agr. Col. Ext.
Serv. Agr. Situation and Outlook, 1936 Circ. 1, 5PP. Corvallis. 1936.

Pennsylvania

Lininger, F. F., and Cowden, T. K. Preliminary estimates of the production
and utilization of milk in Pennsylvania. 5pp., mimeogr. State College. P
Agr.Expt. Sta. 1935.
Publication authorized as Technical paper no. 680.

Washington

Washington. Laws, statutes, etc. Washington agricultural adjustment act
(Chapter 78, Laws 1935) 11pp. Olympia. Wash. Dept. Agr. 1935.
Approved by the Governor, March 13, 1935.

Wisconsin

Christensen, C. L. Business problems of cooperative marketing associations.
Wis. Agr. Col. Ext. Serv. Stencil Circ. 161. 5pp., mimeogr. Madison.
1935.

Wisconsin. University. College of agriculture, Extension service. A demonstration in public discussion. Report of ... a meeting on "Financing
rural education." Wis. Agr. Col. Ext. Serv. Stencil Circ. 162, mimeogr.
14pp. Madison, 1935.

Mitchell, D. R. How farmers adjust when prices fall. Wis. Agr. Expt. Sta.
Bull. 431, 30pp. Madison. 1935.
An analysis of the results obtained from detailed cost records on
40 farms in La Crosse county for the years 1931 and 1932.

Wyoming

Hepner, F. E. Forty years of weather records. Wyo. Agr. Expt. Sta. Bull. 209,
48pp. Laramie. 1935.
A revision of Bulletin 139, published in 1924 - Data have been compiled to the end of 1930 and apply to the Weather Station at the University
Laramie.

Compiled by Louise O. Bercaw and A. M. Hannay

Agricultural Adjustment Act - Supreme Court Decision

The AAA decision and agriculture. Com. & Financ. Chron. 142: 167-168.
Jan. 11, 1936. (Published at William St., corner Spruce, New
York, N. Y.)
    An editorial devoting its attention "to the fundamental situation
brought into being by this ruling and the problems connected with
agriculture which have long existed but which are now brought again
sharply to the attention of the country." Deplores the fact that
many are insistent on new schemes which are "nearly, if not fully,
as unworthy and as unlikely to accomplish that for which they are
being designed as the one just invalidated by the Supreme Court."
    This is followed by another editorial entitled Farm Programs and
"Planned Economy." The writer finds "the invalidation of the Agricultural Adjustment Act most heartening in that it furnishes additional assurance of a return to sanity in governmental affairs,
but...[he does] not believe that it presents any very serious
general economic situation even for the time being, nor any assurance that perhaps the worst evil of them all - basic inflation -
will be checked."

The AAA decision and its significance. U. S. Law Week 3(19): 361, 400.
Jan. 7, 1936. (Published in Washington, D. C.)
    Text of the majority and minority decisions given on pp. 373-
381 of this issue.

[Constitution does not bar tariff revision] Tex. Weekly 12(2): 1-3.
Jan. 11, 1936. (Published at the Dallas Athletic Club Bldg.,
Dallas, Tex.)
    Editorial discussing the Supreme Court decision invalidating the
AAA and suggesting that there is "a perfectly constitutional way
of dealing with the cotton situation and with our economic situa-
tion generally. The American tariff wall is not sacred under the
Constitution. Congress has complete power to lower it to any
level it chooses or even to demolish it altogether." Secretary
Wallace is quoted on reducing tariffs and on the cotton program.

Farm: Drafting a new crop control program. U. S. News 4(2): 5, 13.
Jan. 13, 1936. (Published at 2201 M St., N. W., Washington, D. C.)
    A discussion of the effect of the AAA decision on the Admin-
istration's farm program.

The Supreme Court again draws the line. Com. & Financ. Chron. 142: 179-
181. Jan. 11, 1936. (Published at William St., corner Spruce,
New York, N. Y.)
    Discusses the AAA decision and thinks that the sensible thing to
do is "frankly to recognize that the 'emergency' is over, demobilze
as rapidly as possible the unconstitutional agencies for which an

emergency has been pleaded as justification, and return to the ways
which the Constitution authorizes."

Agricultural Adjustment Administration

The AAA is here to stay, by the unofficial observer. Today 5(11): 8,
N. Jan. 4. 1936. (Published at 152 W. 42nd St., New York, N. Y.)

Agricultural Credit - British Guiana

Huggins, H. D. Seasonal variation and peasant agricultural credit in
British Guiana. Brit. Guiana. Agr. Jour. 6(2-3): 91-99. June-
September 1935. (Published in Georgetown, British Guiana.)
"In British Guiana provision of credit on an organized basis is
made for small farmers through a chain of district cooperative credit
banks. Although each bank is an independent and self-contained
unit, a coordination of policy is effected by an executive position
being held on the committee of control of each bank by a district
officer of the Agricultural Department.
"The object of this study is to present in an easily available
form data which are intended to be useful to Bank Committees in the
organisation and planning of agricultural credit work. From an
examination of the cash transactions over a series of years it has
been possible to determine the seasons of the year when demands by
borrowers for loans have been greatest and when least, when re-
payments have been highest and when lowest; these facts have been
determined in relation to 10 banks in representative agricultural
districts of the Colony."

Agricultural Credit - Italy

Cotta, Freppel. Agricultural credit in Italy. Indian Co-op. Rev. 1(4):
462-470. October 1935. (Published by V. Ramadas Pantulu, Madras,
India.)
"The Italian Government has...entirely reorganised agricultural
credit, and provided financial facilities:- by means of (1) capital
contributions, (2) interest contributions, (3) short-term loans
and (4) long-term loans." These forms of credit are briefly discussed as well as the organizations that may provide such credit,
of which the chief is the Consorzio Nazionale per il Credito
Agrario di Miglioramento. It is controlled by a Council assisted
by a Technical Office and a Loans Office.

Agricultural Credit - Spain

Los préstamos sobre trigos hechos por la Banca privada. El Progreso
Agrícola y Pecuario 41(1896): 711-712. Nov. 30, 1935. (Published
at Plaza de Oriente, Madrid, Spain.)
Text of a decree of October 22, 1935 which provides for loans
made to small farmers by private banks on the security of their
wheat stocks. The loan is not to exceed 25,000 pesetas, the interest is not to exceed 4 1/2 percent, and the minimum duration of
the loan is set at 6 months.

Agricultural Credit - United States

Eighteen years of financial aid to farmers by the Federal Land Banks.
U. S. News 3(50): 19. Dec. 16, 1935. (Published at 2201 M St., N. W.,
Washington, D. C.)
The first of a series of articles regarding some of the Government
agencies "which are doing some of the biggest jobs in the Government
today. Busy with work of a constructive nature, they seldom make
the headlines... [This] first article deals with an agency that
holds one-third of all the farm mortgages in the United States - the
Federal Land Banks."

Evans, R. T. The where, how and why of intermediate credit for agriculture at cost as low as 2% wholesale. West. States Grower of Agr.
and Livestock 19(10): 14-15. December 1935. (Published at 101 Post
St., San Francisco, Calif.)

Myers, W. I. Farmers do not need interest subsidy, Sphere 17(1): 21-
25. January 1936. (Published in Washington, D. C.)
The writer differentiates between the permanent and the emergency
farm financing work of the Farm Credit Administration, summarizing
the emergency work and giving an indication of the way it is being
liquidated. He believes that subsidized interest rates may be warranted temporarily during a depression, but that "as a permanent
policy, a Government subsidized farm interest rate can play havoc
with an agricultural situation which might otherwise be healthy."

Agricultural Credit and Land Settlement - Argentina

Agricultural credit and land settlement in Argentina. Indus. and Labour
Inform. 56(8): 283-284. Nov. 25, 1935. (Issued by International
Labour Office, Geneva, Switzerland. Distributed in U. S. by World
Peace Foundation, 8 West 40th Street, New York, N. Y.)
"The National Bank of Argentina has recently laid down new regulations for the grant of special loans to agriculturists and agricultural co-operative societies for the acquisition of small farms
and for such sanitary and technical improvements as may be carried
out by the owners. The Bank also published the regulations under
which land belonging to the Bank may be subdivided and conveyed to
settlers. In no case may individual loans to prospective farm-
owners exceed the sum of 30,000 pesos, it being understood that the
total duration of the loan is not to exceed a five-year period,
during which interest will be computed at the rate of 5 per cent.
Ten per cent of the total loan is to be repaid by the end of the
first year, and the remainder of the debt liquidated according to
an ascending scale until the fifth year, during which 30 per cent
of the debt must be refunded. Farmers or cooperative organisations
must themselves work the land ceded to them.., Land conveyed by the
Bank is to be subdivided into farms corresponding to the working
capacity of a family. The ideal settlement will comprise, in addition to arable land, grazing and pasture land, an orchard and
facilities for dairy farming. Under no circumstances may the purchase price exceed 50,000 pesos, or the conveyed area a total surface of 200 hectares."

Agricultural Depression - Japan

Holland, W. L. The plight of Japanese agriculture. Far East. Survey
5(1): 1-8. Jan. 1, 1936. (Published by Fortnightly Research Service,
American Council, Institute of Pacific Relations, 129 E. 52nd St.,
New York, N. Y.)
There is evidence to show that Japanese agriculture has suffered
as severe a depression as American agriculture and "that the present
recovery and boom in Japanese industry and export trade has been
achieved largely at the expense of the rural groups." Causes of the
depression, the almost non-existence of mechanization, the rice problem, the rice control scheme, the Five-Year Wheat Plan, the ineffec-
tiveness of silk price fixing, high interest rates on farm loans,
crushing taxation, and solutions for the problem, are discussed.

Agricultural Indebtedness - Central Europe

Agricultural indebtedness in Central Europe. Indus. and Labour Inform.
56(6): 200-203. Nov. 11, 1935. (Published by International Labour
Office, Geneva, Switzerland. Distributed in U. S. by World Peace
Foundation, 8 West 40th Street, New York, N. Y.)
An account of recent measures taken to relieve agricultural indebt-
edness in Hungary, Poland, and Yugoslavia.

Agricultural Indebtedness - Germany

Agrarian indebtedness decreasing. News in Brief 3(20-21): 16. October-
November 1935. (Published by the Deutscher Akademischer Austauschdienst
e.V., Berlin NW 40, Germany)
The Deutsche Rentenbank-Kreditanstalt recently published statistics
on the agricultural credit situation in Germany in 1933/34. A table
shows the development of indebtedness per hectare in Eastern and
Western Germany from 1928/29 to 1933/34.
"The annual interest service, however, is of greater importance
for agriculture than the absolute indebtedness." A table shows the
interest paid and the sales profits from 1928/29 to 1933/34.
"The ratio of short-term personal debts was considerably diminished in favour of the ratio of long-term real estate debts."

Agricultural Indebtedness - Hungary

Hungary...Agrarian debt relief. Economist 121(4815): 1126. Dec. 7,
1935. (Published at 8 Bouverie St., Fleet St., London, E. C. 4, Eng.)
The Government has issued a decree, approved by the House of
Deputies, "which aims at a final solution for owners of holdings
up to 15 acres, and defines, for another two years, the obligations
of agrarian debtors in general. The decree distinguishes between
two main categories of embarassed debtors: (a) those owning over
1,500 acres and (b) those owning not more than 1,500 acres. The
first category will be considered individually. The second will be
the object of general measures" which are summarized in this item.

Agricultural Indebtedness - India

Narayanaswamy Naidu, B. V.   Relief of rural debt. Indian Co-op. Rev.
    1(4): 471-476. October 1935. (Published by V. Ramadas Pantulu,
    Madras, India.)
        Discusses the necessary provisions of a comprehensive scheme of
    debt relief.

Agricultural Policy - Great Britain

Digby, Margaret.   Co-operation and the new British agricultural policy.
    Indian Co-op. Rev. 1(4): 410-416. October 1935. (Published by V.
    Ramadus Fantulu, Madras, India.)
        The author traces the change in the traditional British agricul-
    tural policy of laissez faire to a planned economy, with Marketing
    Boards with power to compel the minority to market their products
    through the agency of the Boards. The marketing schemes for hops,
    potatoes, bacon, and milk are briefly discussed. The good effects
    of this policy are indicated, but it is pointed out that they have
    been achieved at the expense of the tax-payer and the consumer.

Street, A. G.   The best basis for Great Britain's agricultural policy.
    Land Union Jour. 32(11): 171-172, 179. December 1935. (Published
    at 15 Lower Place, London, S. W. 1, Eng.)
        Paper read at The Farmers' Club on December 9, 1935. A farming
    policy based on livestock raising is recommended. "In addition I
    would suggest... that since the war where our farming policy has
    failed is in that our rulers have consistently refused to consider
    three things: 1. That livestock comprises nearly three-quarters of
    our farming industry. 2. That a prosperous livestock industry re-
    quires the cheapest possible animal feeding stuffs. 3. And that
    the majority of our farmers, including all our market gardeners
    and small-holders, are buyers of grain for more than they are
    sellers, and therefore want to obtain it as cheaply as possible."

Venn, J. A.   The financial and economic results of state control in
    agriculture. Econ. Jour. 45(180): 649-662. December 1935.
    (Published by the Royal Economic Society, 9, Adelphi Terrace,
    London, W. C. 2, Eng.) May be obtained from the Macmillan Co.,
    New York, N. Y.)
        "Extracted from the presidential address to Section M of the
    British Association, 1935."
        The writer enumerates, and assesses the total cost to the state
    of the various reliefs and disbursements of an eleemosynary char-
    acter in post-war Britain and then estimates the results accruing
    from the policy each represents.

Agricultural Policy - Norway

Agricultural programme of the Norwegian Government. Indus. and Labour
    Inform. 56(7): 246-248. Nov. 18, 1935. (Published by International
    Labour Office, Geneva, Switzerland. Distributed in U. S. by World
    Peace Foundation, 8 West 40th Street, New York, N. Y.)

The Norwegian Minister of Agriculture has "outlined the agricultural policy of the Government with special reference to the Social aspects of the agricultural problem in Norway: The Labour Party (he said) seeks a socially planned economy under the management and control of the community." The present position of agriculture and the steps already taken by the Government are indicated. "The grants towards land settlement and the cultivation of waste land have been increased by two million crowns. The rate of the grant for bringing more land under cultivation on older farms has been raised to 25 percent of the cost for the whole of South Norway (30 percent) for North Norway). The demand for subsidies towards the building of dwellings on new farms has been satisfied...A national scheme of land settlement should be prepared. A minimum scheme for the next 10 years would provide for 20,000 new farms and the cultivation of 200,000 hectares of new land. The number of peasant farms, which is at present only about 150,000, would be increased, not only by the new farms, but by at least as many workers' holdings, which by working additional land would become large enough to be classified with the peasant farms...as regards agricultural indebtedness...it is hoped that in about two or three years not only will the heaviest debts have been adjusted, but most of those representing from 75 to 80 percent of the farm value as well." There is need of organization of credit for small farms and agricultural training in schools.

Agricultural Policy - Union of South Africa

Robertson, H. M. Der schutz der landwirtschaft in Südafrika. Welt-wirtschaftliches Archiv 42(3): 504-519. November 1935. (Issued by Kiel University. Institut für Weltwirtschaft. Published by Gustav Fischer, Jena, Germany)

An account of the measures taken for the relief of agriculture by the Union of South Africa.

Agricultural Products on the World Markets

Nogaro, Bertrand. Les grands marchés agricoles et les mouvements generaux des prix dans la crise actuelle. Revue Politique et Parlementaire 42(491): 16-42. Oct. 10, 1935. (Published at 10, Rue Auber, Paris (9e), France)

The author presents a study of sugar, meat, coffee, cotton, rubber, and wood on the world market before and after the World War, and he concludes that over-production is the cause of the depression. And that over-production in the case of meat, sugar, and wood is a direct result of the War which caused acceleration of production in the new world while Europe was fighting, post-war restoration of European production and then its increase far beyond the pre-war level.

The case of cotton and coffee is a little different and yet the increase in their production is also a result of the War inasmuch as their scarcity at the close of hostilities provoked a tremendous price increase which in turn led to excessive production, the accumulation of stocks, and finally to a decrease in prices. The market for agricultural products has been dominated by the law of supply and demand with the supply factor playing the principal rôle.

Agricultural Relief - United States

Livingston, L. F.   The demands of modern agriculture. Vital Speeches of the Day 2(8); 245-247. Jan. 13, 1936. (Published at 33 W. 42nd St., New York, N. Y.)

"Delivered at Washington State College, Pullman, Washington, before a joint meeting of agricultural specialists and students assembled by Washington State College and Idaho State·College, January 7, 1936, and at Oregon State College, Corvallis, Oregon, January 8, 1936."

The writer states that the term "farm problem" is a misnomer and that there are as many farm problems as there are farms in the United States. He believes that a few of the needs of agriculture may be aided by "intelligent legislative control" but that the salvation of the farmer is mainly to be accomplished by the farmer himself on his own farm. The task of the combined agricultural agencies is to help the farmer help himself. The research man and the agricultural engineer should act, rather than the politician. Emphasis should be put on quality and cost rather than price as the major factor governing net income. Production and marketing costs should be lowered. The farmer "needs an engineering diagnosis and treatment for his common engineering difficulties." More good farm cooperatives are needed. The rural press has its part to play. Every farm should have sound business management.

Apiculture - Central America

Sapper, Karl.   Bienenhaltung und Bienenzucht in Mittelamerika und Mexico. Ibero-Amerikanisches Archiv 9(3): 183-198. October 1935. (Issued by Ibero-Amerikanisches Institut, Breite Strasse 37, Berlin C. 2, Germany.)

A study of bee culture in Central America, first of American and then of European species.

Banks, Government

Hansell, N. V.   A survey of government banks. Banking 28(7): 74-84. January 1936. (Published at 22 E. 40th St., New York, N. Y.)

This is a survey in tabular form of the various banking agencies of the government giving information on the date of establishment, authority under which organized, permanency, physical organization, management, lending functions, terms, rates, capital and other funds.

Bread - Consumption

Platt, Washington.   A study of bread consumption. Northwest. Miller and Amer. Baker 13(1): 37, 46-48. Jan. 1, 1936. (Published at 118 S. Sixth St., Minneapolis, Minn.)

The address from which this article has been adapted was delivered on Nov. 12, 1935, before the Association of Agricultural Chemists, at Washington, D. C.; on Dec. 11, before a joint session of the Buffalo and Toronto sections of the American Association of Cereal Chemists at Buffalo; and on Dec. 28 before the New England Chapter of the American Society of Bakery Engineers.

"Much has been said and written on this vital question of flour consumption. Most of the causes...of the decline in volume of use that has characterized the past quarter of a century of breadstuffs history in America have been identified and tagged. The brains of the milling and baking industries have been racked for remedies. All this matter, because of the importance of the subject, bears repetition, and Mr. Platt does an important service through his careful and exhaustive survey, rendered the more significant because of his own suggestions, born of intimate knowledge and experience, as to how the declining use of wheat flour products may be arrested and about-faced."-Editor's note.

A series of charts accompanies the article showing the consumption trends of various foodstuffs.

A bibliography is appended at the end of the article.

Business - Annual Reviews

Annual review and prospect. Barron's 16(1): 1-52. Jan. 6, 1936. (Published at 44 Broad St., New York, N. Y.)
    Partial contents:
    Agriculture on up-grade. Higher farm purchasing power an influence on industrial recovery. Drought deficiencies being caught up. Export markets vital to complete restoration, by David C. Harrower, p.37.
    Balancing abundance. Basically, agricultural and industrial production predicated on needs of population. Balance comes in equitable income distribution between producers and consumers, by Henry A. Wallace, p. 39.
    World wheat crop prospects. Fewer bumper crops in 1935, yet large carryover. Stocks keep wheat prices sluggish. Crop changes affect individual countries, but world supply still adequate, by Alex Feunot and Eric Beresford Townsend, pp. 41, 44.
    Government and business. Further cooperation needed to foster stability. 1935 a recovery year in social as well as economic conditions, by D. C. Reper, p. 42.
    Stability or boom? New deal finance, and its implications. Not too late to set on right road, provided automatic barometer of interest rates is allowed to function, by Sherwin C. Badger, p. 43.

Business Statistics

Copeland, M. A., and Funkhouser, R. L. Current business statistics and economic stabilization. Taylor Soc. and Soc. Indus. Engin. Bull. 1(7): 219-224. November 1935. (Published by Federated Management Societies at Engineering Societies Bldg., 29 W. 39th St., New York, N. Y.)
    The following is quoted in part from the writers' conclusion:

"In the foregoing pages, we have pointed out some of the important
: respects in which our available·current business information needs to
be improved. We have called particular attention to the need for more
adequate current data on construction and real property and also for
better current information in the retail field. We have also pointed
out the need for more complete information on commodity stocks, and
have urged the collection of uniform quarterly financial statements
from leading business corporations. We have also stressed the need
for more complete representation in our current data on employment
and business volume, and for refinements in our wholesale and retail
price information...
    "These types of current economic data are necessary if business
men and public officials are properly to discharge their responsibility
for economic stabilization and for the efficient operation of our
economic system."

McClure, H. H., and Funkhouser, R. L.   The activities of the Division of
    current business statistics of the Central statistical board. Amer.
    . Statis. Assoc. Jour. 30(192): 701-706. December 1935. (Published
    by the Association. Frederick F. Stephan, Secretary-Treasurer, 722
    Woodward Bldg., Washington, D. C.)

Rogers, C. L.   What business indexes mean.   Conf. Bd. Bull. 9(11): 84-88.
    Nov. 10, 1935. (Published by the National Industrial Conference
    Board, Inc., 247 Park Ave., New York, N. Y.)
    Among the various types of indexes which are discussed are the
    Federal Reserve Board index of production, indexes compiled by the
    Annalist, the New York Times, Business Week, the New York Herald-
    Tribune, and the index compiled by Messrs. Carl Snyder and Leroy M.
    Piser of the Federal Reserve Bank of New York.

Canning Trade Statistics

Street, J. P.   The value of statistics. Canning Trade 58(22): 7-8, 10.
    Jan. 6, 1936. (Published at 20 South Gay Street, Baltimore, Md.)
    To be of real value canning trade statistics "should be reliable,
    complete, and issued with reasonable promptness, and the confidence
    of the reporting canners should be rigorously respected." The writer
    sketches briefly the kind of statistics collected in New York State
    and the method of collecting them.

Coffee - Mexico

Mexico's coffee developments and trade. Tea & Coffee Trade Jour. 69(6):
    463-465. December 1935. (Published at 79 Wall Street, New York, N.Y.)
    "Seventh among producing countries with increasing production and
    exports to many consuming countries - United States and Germany are
    her chief customers - Analysis of exports during the past five years."

Coffee and Tea Trade

World-wide coffee-tea trade and trends. Tea & Coffee Trade Jour. 69(6):
471-483. December 1935. (Published at 79 Wall Street, New York, N.Y.)
"A review and analysis of the past year taken from official
government sources, giving comparisons with 1934 and preceding years,
with possibilities of near future - Tables and graphs showing
tendencies of the two commodities."

Coffee Auctions - Kenya

Direct coffee sales. Kenya Coffee Board's initiative. African World 133
(1725): 258. Nov. 30, 1935. (Published at 801, Salisbury House,
London Wall, London, E. C. 2, Eng.)
The Kenya Coffee Board has established a subsidiary body called
Kenya Coffee Auctions to hold auction sales of coffee.

Collective Agreements - Italy

Conditions in Italian agriculture. Indus. and Labour Inform. 56(6): 225.
Nov. 11, 1935. (Published by International Labour Office, Geneva,
Switzerland. Distributed in U. S. by World Peace Foundation, 8 West
40th Street, New York, N. Y.)
"Agreements between the confederations of employers and workers
in Italian agriculture regulating the collective contracts of agricultural workers and the question of sickness funds for such workers
were signed in Rome on 16 October 1935.

Collective Farms - U. S. S. R.

Statistics of collective farms. Indus. and Labour Inform. 56(8): 282.
Nov. 25, 1935. (Issued by International Labour Office, Geneva,
Switzerland. Distributed in U. S. by World Peace Foundation, 8
West 40th Street, New York, N. Y.)
A summary of statistics relating to the condition of collective
farms on January 1, 1935 issued by the Department of Statistics
of the People's Commissariat for Agriculture.

Cooperation

Cavallaro, C. D. 5700 growers can't be wrong. West. States Grower of
Agr. and Livestock 19(7): 5-7. September 1935. (Published at 101
Post St., San Francisco, Calif.)
Presents the advantages of growers' cooperative associations,
using the California Prune and Apricot Growers Association as an
example.

Cooperative Journal, v. 9, no. 6, pp. 177-200. November-December 1935.
(Published by the National Cooperative Council, 1731 I St., N. W.,
Washington, D. C.)
Partial contents: Building membership responsibility, by E. W.
Tiedeman, pp. 177-180; The Senate's one-man investigation of coopera-
tives, by the editor, pp. 181-184; Women's place in a cooperative,

by Vera McCrea, pp. 185-186; Passing of monopoly as an aim of cooperatives, by H. E. Erdman, pp. 187-188; The aims of cooperative
purchasing, by the editor, pp. 190-191, Index to volume IX, pp.
199-200.

Tucker, T. C. Individual freedom through cooperation. Calif. Fruit
    News 92(2469): 4. Nov. 2, 1935. (Published at 405 Montgomery St.,
    San Francisco, Calif.)
        An article in which the writer takes note of the accomplishments
    of cooperation. He says in conclusion: "Of course, cooperation,
    as successful as it has proven in operation, has made only a small
    dent in the problem of preserving our individual freedom but it
    certainly has proven that it works. No other system can work
    without a degree of compulsion which is repugnant to every sense
    of that freedom which is the most precious possession of American
    democracy."

Cooperation - Egypt

Rashad, I. The trend of co-operation in Egypt. Review Internatl. Coop.
    28(12): 466-469. December 1935. (Published at Orchard House, 14,
    Great Smith Street, London, S. W. 1, Eng.)

Cooperation - India

Ata Ullah, Sheikh. The depression and the cooperative movement in the
    Punjab. Indian Co-op. Rev. 1(4): 481-491. October 1935. (Pub-
    lished by V. Ramadas Pantulu, Madras, India)
        "Agricultural Punjab to-day is a vast school in compulsory thrift
    and economy."

Mudaliar, K. D., Dewan Bahadur. Co-operative sale societies in Madras.
    Indian Co-op. Rev. 1(4): 417-428. October 1935. (Published by
    V. Ramadas Pantulu, Madras, India)
        "The financing of agricultural operations may be divided into
    three stages:- Stage 1. Loans for cultivation expenses...Stage 2.
    Loans on standing crops...Stage 3. Loans on the pledge of produce."

Cooperation - Sweden

Lindstedt, H. Agricultural co-operation in Sweden. Monthly Bull. Agr.
    Econ. and Sociol. [reprint from Internatl. Rev. Agr.] 26(9-11):
    330E-339E, 360E-369E, 402E-417E. September-November 1935. (Pub-
    lished by the International Institute of Agriculture, Villa Umberto
    I, Rome, Italy)
        Contents: 1, The legal basis of co-operative organizations;
    2, Co-operative organizations for the purchase of farm requisites
    and for the sale of cereals and seeds; 3, Co-operation and the dairy
    industry (Organization of local dairying association, organization
    of the "Amalgamated Dairies," organization of dairying federations);

4. Co-operation in slaughtering and the sale of slaughter stock;
5. Co-operation in the egg trade; 6, Activity of the agricultural
co-operative banks; 7, Other co-operative organisations (fruit-growing
and other forms of horticulture, grain warehousing associations,
cooperation between forest owners, etc.).

Corn, Canned - Grading

Eickelberg, E. W. Grading canned corn on the cob. Canning Age 16(13):
510-511, 518. December 1935. (Published at 250 W. 57th St., New
York, N. Y.)

Cost of Living

Montgomery, D. E. Future food prices. U. S. News 3(51); 4. Dec. 23,
1935. (Published at 2201 M St., N.W., Washington, D. C.)
Also in Canner 82(3): 9-10,28. Dec. 28, 1935, with title "The
Cost of Food."
"From an address at New York City Conference on the High Cost of
Living, Dec. 14."
"Where food prices would be if there were no AAA programs and if
there had been no drought, we do not know. Meat, poultry and egg
prices are certainly higher than they would be under AAA programs if
there had been no drought. If we had had the drought but no AAA
program, prices of such products would probably be as high as
they are now."

Cost of Living - Southern States

Ogburn. W. F. Does it cost less to live in the South? Social Forces
14(2): 211-214. December 1935. (Published for the University of North
Carolina Press by the Williams & Wilkins Co., Baltimore, Md.)
"In conclusion this investigation does not show that it is cheaper
to live in the South, but rather that the costs are the same in
the South as in the rest of the United States. We infer then that
the popular opinion that it is cheaper to live in the South is
based upon false comparisons or unsatisfactory concepts. If a
laborer spends less in the South than in the North, it is because
he gets less wages and not because it costs less to live there."

Cost of Production Data - Use in Agricultural Price Determination

Booth, J. F. Cost of production records and their use in agricultural
price determinations. Econ. Annalist 5(4): 52-57. December 1935.
(Published by the Agricultural Economics Branch, Department of
Agriculture, Ottawa)
"A summary of an address to the Inter-provincial Conference of
Milk Control Boards, Toronto, November 20, 1935."
Reviews the development of farm cost analysis in the United
States, cost studies in Canada, factors responsible for the interest
in the subject, the accounting, the survey, and experimental farms
method of cost analysis, the use of cost data, and application of
cost data to price determination.

Cotton - Baling

Parham, E. F. Jute vs. cotton bagging. Manfrs. Rec. 104(12): 23, 62.
December 1935. (Published at Commerce and Water Sts., Baltimore, Md.)
"For years efforts have been made to popularize cotton bagging
in place of foreign jute as a means of increasing the use of American
cotton. The latest movement is Representative Fulmer's bill H. R.
8631 before Congress to make it compulsory to sell cotton net weight
instead of gross weight as an inducement to the grower to use the
lighter-weight cotton bagging.
"In the October Manufacturers Record Congressman Fulmer gave his
reasons in favor of cotton bagging.
"In ... [this] article a manufacturer of domestic-made Jute
bagging takes exception to claims that the adoption of cotton fabric
for covering cotton bales would be advantageous to the cotton growers
of the South."

Cotton - Cooperative Marketing - India

Ramakrishnan, K. C. Cotton sale societies in Bombay and Madras. Indian
Co-op. Rev. 1(4): 442-457. October 1935. (Published by V. Ramadas
Pantulu, Madras, India)
"Of all attempts at co-operative marketing that have so far been
made in India the most successful are those of cotton sale societies
in Bombay and Madras, judged by the continuity of service, the
volume of sales, the profits earned for producers, the improvement
of quality of cotton - not to speak of miscellaneous other services
rendered by them." An account is given of the four largest societies
at Hubli, Gadag, Surat and Tiruppur.

Cotton - Nigeria

Browne, G. Cotton-growing in Northern Nigeria. Rapid agricultural expansion envisaged. African World Suppl. 133(1726): vii. Dec. 7,
1935. (Published at 801, Salisbury House, London Wall, London,
E. C., Eng.)
Summary of an account given by the manager of the Northern
Nigerian seed farm of the Empire Cotton-Growing Corporation "of
its work during the past ten years and the future possibilities
of the expansion of cotton-growing in the country as a result of
the adoption of mixed farming by the native cultivators."

Cotton - United States

The Bankhead Act and the AAA decision. Tex. Weekly 12(2): 4-6. Jan.
11, 1936. (Published at the Athletic Club Bldg., Dallas, Tex.)
"The exercise of Federal power under the AAA, which has been
invalidated by the Supreme Court, is much less than that exercised under the Bankhead Act." It is stated that there "is confusion in the public mind with respect to these two laws." Some of
the provisions of the Bankhead law are cited. According to the
writer it is to be regretted that the Supreme Court did not pass

on the constitutionality of the Bankhead Act before invalidating the
AAA. "The AAA decision makes it certain that the Court will in-
validate the Bankhead Act in due course. But if the Bankhead Act
had been passed upon first, and invalidated by unanimous opinion of
the Court, there would have been an interval in which to appraise
the value of what was left in the AAA, without the Bankhead Act,
and a better understanding of just what has been destroyed by the
divided decision handed down last Monday."

The case for and against the cotton control act. Summary of arguments
in briefs of counsel for shipper and government state contentions
to be presented to Supreme Court in Moor case following argument
of Hoosac case. U. S. Law Week 3(15, sect. 1): 243-244, 279.
Dec. 10, 1935. (Published in Washington, D. C.)

Cotton disturbs the peace. By the unofficial observer. Today 5(9): 5,
19, 20. Dec. 21, 1935. (Published at 152 W. 42nd St., New York, N.Y.)
Cotton and the neutrality policy of the United States.

Hazard, J. W. The government and cotton. Disorganized Federal program
of market manipulation and regulation and output control, complicated by political activities of Southern congressmen. Annalist
15(51): 5, 9. Dec. 23, 1935. (Published at 44 Broad St., Now
York, N. Y.)

[South's problem menaces nation] Tex. Weekly 11(50): 1-3. Dec. 14,
1935. (Published at the Dallas Athletic Club Bldg., Dallas, Tex.)
Editorial in which the consumption of American cotton and a
program of restricting cotton acreage are discussed in connection
with the problem of providing employment for a large number of
people formerly engaged in the production of cotton, or lifting
the standard of living for many "living at a level of bare subsistence". The problem is held to be a national one. The way
out is to increase consumption by lowering tariffs.

Wilcox, E. V. Is the king's crown wabbling? Country Gent. 106(1):
19, 64-66. January 1936. (Published at Independence Square,
Philadelphia, Pa.)
The writer's report of a trip through the South to find out how
the Government's cotton policies have affected the cotton industry -
and particularly export trade in cotton.

Dairying - Argentina

Dairying in Argentina. Foreign Crops and Markets 31(27): 935-944.
Dec. 30, 1935. (Published by the Division of Foreign Agricul-
tural Service, Bureau of Agricultural Economics, U. S. Dept. of
Agriculture)
"From a report by P. O. Nyhus, Agricultural Attaché, Buenos
Aires."

Covers such topics as size of dairy farms, cash- and share-rent
dairy farming, dairying practices followed, character and living
conditions of the cash- and share-renters, distribution of fluid
milk, butter and cheese production, trend of butter and cheese production and exports, quality of milk produced, economic conditions
in the dairy industry, etc. Statistical tables show numbers of
milk cows and total cattle, by breeds, 1930; production of butter,
cheese and casein, annually 1924-1934; exports of butter, cheese,
and casein, annually 1914-1934.

Distribution and Distributors

[Deupree, R. R.] Distributer a producer, not a parasite. Who is Who
in Grain and Feed 25(4): 22-24. Dec. 20, 1935. (Published at 413-
414-415 Merchants' Exchange Bldg., St. Louis, Mo.)
Radio address in which the speaker challenges two statements -
that the development of efficiency in distribution lags behind
productive efficiency, and that those engaged in any phase of distributive activity are parasites, living off the labors of producers,
and that whatever is taken as payment for the services of distribution is subtracted from producers.

Economic Adjustment - Canada

Innis, H. A. Notes on problems of adjustment in Canada. Jour. Polit.
Econ. 43(6): 800-807. December 1935. (Published by the University
of Chicago Press, 5750 Ellis Ave., Chicago, Ill.)

Economic Conditions - Manchuria

Hao Wu-Teh. The economic collapse of Manchuria. People's Tribune
(n.s.) 11(4): 261-275. Nov. 16, 1935. (Published at 299 Szechuen
Road, Shanghai, China)

Economic Nationalism and International Trade

Smith, J. G. Economic nationalism and international trade. Econ.
Jour. 45(180): 619-648. December 1935. (Published by the Royal
Economic Society, 9, Adelphi Terrace, London, W. C. 2, Eng. May
be obtained from the Macmillan Company, New York, N. Y.)
"Presidential address before Section F of the British Asso-
ciation, Norwich, 1935."

Economic Policy - Irish Free State

The state of Ireland - II. Economist 121(4815): 1116-1118. Dec. 7,
1935. (Published at 8 Bouverie St., Fleet St., London, E. C. 4, Eng.)
"The rapid change in the national economics of the Irish Free
State, which has been occupying the energies of Mr. De Valera's
Government during the past three years, was made necessary by the
drastic decline in the agricultural export trade since 1929. This
decline has been accelerated, but was not initiated, by the economic

... with Great Britain. The effort of adaptation to these changed external circumstances has had two aspects: the first a negative policy of defense for agriculture, the second a more positive attempt to stimulate industry to take the place of agriculture. The former policy was briefly described in an article in last week's Economist." [Econo.ist 121(4814): 1060-1062. Nov. 30, 1935] The industrial side is discussed in the present article."

Economic Policy - Italy

Salvemini, Gaetano. Can Italy live at home? Foreign Affairs 14(2): 243-258. January 1936. (Published at 45 East 65th St., New York, N. Y.)
  A criticism of Mussolini's economic policy and his attempt to conquer Ethiopia "where he expects to find for his people raw materials to exploit and an abundance of lands to colonize." The writer thinks that the solution of Italy's difficulties lies not in colonial conquest, but in reclamation and land improvement, in domestic economic development, and in emigration.

Economic Reconstruction - China

Chiang Kai-Shek. Economic reconstruction in China. Indus. and Labour Inform. 56(7): 249-250. Nov. 18, 1935. (Published by International Labour Office, Geneva, Switzerland. Distributed in U. S. by World Peace Foundation, 8 West 40th Street, New York, N. Y.)
  A program for the improvement of economic conditions in China, outlined by General Chiang Kai-Shek, includes "compulsory public service, agricultural and industrial development, promotion of reclamation projects, exploitation of mines, regulation of consumption, improvement of communications, and financial readjustment."

Economic Rehabilitation - Puerto Rico

Hill, Harwood. Better times for Puerto Rico. Current Hist. 43(4): 367-372. January 1936. (Published by the New York Times Co., New York, N. Y.)
  An account of the Roosevelt administration's plan for the rehabilitation of Puerto Rico and the movement toward Statehood. Rehabilitation plans include housing and slum clearance, reforestation, forestation and prevention of soil erosion, rural electrification, rural rehabilitation and land utilization, rural resettlement on marginal sugar lands, rural resettlement on good sugar lands, rehabilitation of coffee, tobacco and citrus fruit farms, etc.

Economic Recovery - Germany

Katona, G. M. The "miracle" of German recovery. Foreign Affairs 14(2): 348-350. January 1936. (Published at 45 East 65th St., New York, N. Y.)

Emigration - Great Britain

British emigration schemes, Indus. and Labour Inform. 56(5): 180-182.
Nov. 4, 1935. (Published by International Labour Office, Geneva,
Switzerland. Distributed in U. S. by World Peace Foundation, 8 West
40th Street, New York, N. Y.)
   Reference is made to various proposals for properly supervised
emigration from Great Britain to the Dominions, and a brief account
of the Fairbridge Farm School in Western Australia. A thousand acres
of land have been acquired in British Columbia for a similar scheme
to care for children and train them in farm work and household duties.

L'Est Européen Agricole

L'Est Européen Agricole 4.année, no. 15, October 1935. (Issued by the
Comité Permanent d'Études Économiques des États Agricoles de l'Europe
Centrale et Orientale. Published by Jouve & Cie, 15, Rue Racine
(6e), Paris,France.)
   Partial Contents:- Hongrie, La nouvelle legislation relative
au paiement des dettes des propriétaires fonciers, by Béla de
Perneczky. -pp. 7-24. (A study of Hungarian legislation since 1931
for the relief of agricultural indebtedness.); Pologne. Le systeme
des impôts agricoles et leur réforme, by Michel Wierusz-Kowalski. -
pp. 25-52. (A study of land taxation in Poland, and the land classification on which it is based according to the reform law of 1934;
also suggestions for further reforms.); Les accords agricoles speciaux
polono-dantzikois, by Stoslaw Zombrzuski. -pp.53-74. (An account
of the Polish-Dantzig agricultural agreements, characterized as a
new form of organization of agricultural exchanges.) Roumanie. La
production et le commerce de la laine, by Ion I. Ghelase. -pp.75-
90. (Production of and trade in wool in Rumania.); Tchécoslovaquie.
Les résultats économiques et sociaux de la réforme foncière, by
Antonin Prokeš. -pp.91-99. (Contains an account of the distribution of the land in Czechoslovakia incident to the agrarian reform
of 1919. The establishment of new settlements is noted; also the
fact that the large estates were not suppressed, only diminished
in size. Among the advantageous results of the reform are increased
agricultural production, the capacity of agriculture to provide
for greater numbers of the population, and the provision of plots
of ground in the industrial regions for the benefit of the unemployed workers.); Tchécoslovaquie. La législation des céréales,
by Antonin Prokeš. -pp. 100-106. (A brief discussion of the measures
adopted by the Grain Monopoly Administration of Czechoslovakia to
fix prices and restrict the area of grain.); Tchécoslovaquie.
L'organisation de la vente du bois et la propagande en sa faveur,
by Kokès and Pinc. -pp. 107-115. (Production and sale of wood and
wood products in Czechoslovakia.).
   Among the statistical tables given are those showing prices of
agricultural products in Poland, exports from Bulgaria, and area,
production, and prices of agricultural products in.Czechoslovakia.

Fair Trade Practice Act - California

Carey, C. J. A discussion of the Thorp Fair trade practice act: West.
States Grower of Agr. and Livestock 19(10): 13, 15. December 1935.
(Published at 101 Post St., San Francisco, Calif.)

Farms Apple - Efficiency

Hudson, S. C. A comparison in farm efficiency. Econ. Annalist 5(4):
62-63. December 1935. (Published by the Agricultural Economics
Branch, Dept. of Agriculture, Ottawa.)
    Gives a comparison of the ten most profitable and the ten least
profitable apple farms in Nova Scotia, Quebec and Ontario for the
three year period 1929-1931.

Financial Statements

Chown, W. F. Financial statements. Econ. Annalist 5(4): 58-61. December
1935. (Published by the Agricultural Economics Branch, Dept. of
Agriculture, Ottawa.)
    The following is quoted from the opening paragraphs of this
article:
    "The profit or loss resulting from the operation of a business can
be determined by comparing the Net Worth shown in Statements of
Assets and Liabilities prepared at the beginning and end of the
financial period, subject to adjustment for additions or withdrawals
of capital. To explain how the profit was earned or loss sustained
another form of statement should be prepared which is called variously
Income and Expense, Revenue and Expenditure, Operating, Profit
and Loss. This statement can be constructed in several sections
and in a variety of forms to meet different requirements.
    "The preparation of this statement necessitates a complete set
of double-entry accounts of the completion of single entry records
at the end of the financial period. It is impossible to cover the
subject fully in this article but some discussion of the principles
involved with an illustration of a simple case may be of value."

Forage - Crop Production - Canada

Kirk, L. E. Forage-crop production in dry-land agriculture and on ranges
in Western Canada. Empire Jour. Expt. Agr. 3(12): 320-329.
October 1935. (Published at the Clarendon Press, Oxford, Eng.)
    "In southern Alberta there are several large-scale irrigation
projects not far removed from the ranching areas, and there is a
growing tendency for the irrigation farmer who can grow large quantities
of feed, on the one hand, and the rancher who produces the animals,
on the other, to work out arrangements that are mutually advantageous,
involving the establishment of winter feed-lots close to crop-
production areas."

Foreign Service - United States

Shaw, G. H. The American foreign service. Foreign Affairs 14(2): 323-333.
January 1935. (Published at 45 East 65th St., New York, N. Y.)
"This is one of the winning essays in a competition open to members
of the American Foreign Service for prizes offered by Hon. Robert
Woods Bliss, former ambassador to Argentina. The subject set was
'The Utility of a Trained and Permanent Foreign Service.'" - Editor's
Note.

Forest Situation - Central Pine District, Minnesota

U. S. Department of agriculture, Forest service, Lake States experiment
station. The forest situation in the central pine district,
Minnesota. U. S. Dept. Agr., Forest Serv., Lake States Expt. Sta.,
Econ. Notes no. 3, 19, 3 pp., and 17 tables, maps. University Farm,
St. Paul. October 1935.
Contents: Early development; present conditions in the district
(forest industries, present public forests, Indian forests, state
forests); present forest land ownership; outlook for the future.
Table 4 gives a general classification of land; table 5, area of
forest land by forest cover types and condition classes; table 6,
ownership of forest land by forest cover types and condition
classes; table 7, area of state forests, 1935; table 8, area of
forests under Federal control.

Garden Cities

Macfayden, Dugald. Sociological effects of garden cities. Social
Forces 14(2): 250-256. December 1935. (Published for the University
of North Carolina Press by the Williams & Wilkins Co., Baltimore, Md.)

Germany

Germany. New government regulations. The meat industry. The Statist
126(3017): 873. Dec. 21, 1935. (Published at 51 Cannon St.,
London, E. C. 4, Eng.)
Discusses a new law regulating the industrial consumption of
spinning material passed by the Cabinet on December 6 and the unfavorable condition of the German meat industry.

Grain - Marketing

Horner, H. F. Legal aspects of grain marketing. Grain & Feed Rev. 25
(5): 18. January 1936. (Published at 408 South Third St.,
Minneapolis, Minn.)
Address delivered before Farmers Elevator Association meeting
at Watertown, S. Dak., Dec. 11, 1935.

Activity of the Czechoslovakian Grain Association. Majandusteated.
Inst. Econ. Research, Estonia, Weekly Bull. no. 49, pp. 892-894.
Dec. 10, 1935. (Published in Tallinn, Estonia.)

Grain Trade and Agriculture

Sexauer. E. H. Grain men are friends of agriculture. Who is Who in
Grain and Feed 25(5): 19-24. Jan. 5, 1936. (Published at 413-414-
415 Merchants' Exchange Bldg., St. Louis, Mo.)
Address in full of E. H. Sexauer before the South Dakota Farmers
Elevator Association at Watertown, S. Dak., on December 11, 1935.
In this address Mr. Sexauer "urged a working agreement between
the farmers elevator associations and the independent dealers. This
agreement, he stated, has become necessary because of the presence
of many problems that are common to all distributors of grain. He
pointed out that the independent dealer is a friend of agriculture.
Without his help the products of the farm would have little value
because a market must first be found before these products can be
turned into money. Whether the distribution is made by cooperative
companies or by independent dealers the problems of handling remain,
and these problems can best be solved by some kind of working
agreement between the two."
This address appears also in the Grain & Feed Review 25(5): 16-17.
January 1936, with the title: "The Grain Trade and Agriculture."

Grass Revolution - United States

Davis, C. C. Rise of grass. Country Gent. 106(1): 18, 66, 68, 69.
January 1936. (Published at Independence Square, Philadelphia, Pa.)
The story of the grass revolution that has been taking place
in the United States during the past two or three years.

Income - Taxation

Elbert, R. G. A plan to distribute income. Sphere 17(1): 9-10, 33-34.
January 1936. Published in Washington, D. C.)
"The plan that is presented here requires the division of all
personal income into two parts - one part to be used for investment
or saving; and the other part in living, which means expenditures
for consumable goods or services. The essential idea is to put a
tax so large on the spendable portion of the income - in case it
is not expended in living - that the tax will force that portion
of the income into circulation."

Income, Farm - Method of Estimating

Graves, P. E. A tentative method of estimating net farm incomes. Econ.
Jour. 45(180): 785-789. December 1935. (Published by the Royal
Economic Society, 9 Adelphi Terrace, London, W. C. 2, Eng. May be
obtained from the Macmillan Company, New York, N. Y.)

"An article in a recent issue of the Economic Journal illustrated
that variations in the official price index of agricultural commodities
do not necessarily imply corresponding changes in either the gross
or the net incomes of farmers. The difficulty of establishing an
index for these latter is great, and the result of any tentative com-
putations must be questionable unless there is corroborative evidence
as to their accuracy. But a survey of farming conditions in the
Eastern Counties, undertaken by the Cambridge Department of Agriculture during each of the three years 1931-33, affords certain useful
data, as well as an opportunity for testing methods of estimation.
The purpose of this article is to describe a system of computation
which has apparently given fairly satisfactory results. These surveys covered 1,000 farms of 20 acres or more in each year, and the
sampling was sufficiently representative of the six counties of
Norfolk, Suffolk, Essex, Cambridge (excl. the Isle of Ely), Hertford
and Huntingdon."

Industrial Worker on the Land

Krause, Heinz. Some aspects of the problem of the industrial worker on
the land. Internatl. Labour Rev. 32(6): 780-791. December 1935.
(Published by the International Labour Office, Geneva, Switzerland. Distributed in U.S. by the World Peace Foundation, 8 West 40th St.,
New York, N. Y.)
    The writer considers the problem under three main headings:
Definition of the problem; scope of research; and effects of modern
technical progress. His conclusion is as follows:
    "The problem may thus be approached from two sides: from that of
the worker, and -with more reference to the long-run aspects - from
that of industry. The magnitude of the subject is frequently
recognised, but there is still much uncertainty and groping in the
dark, and rough estimates and hypotheses are often considered sufficient, even where positive knowledge would prevent many mistakes.
To a great extent this deficiency is to be ascribed to the fact
that hitherto there has been no systematic study of the structure
of this interrelationship between agriculture and industry, which
in many cases has existed for several generations. It is very
probable that in the future - within the frame-work of a more system-
atically planned economy - much greater significance will be attached
to this form of relation between industry and agriculture, and therefore also to the rural industrial worker. Research on the lines
indicated above may thus obviously be of great importance in providing facts to serve as a basis for determining future policy.
For in fact there is nothing entirely new in either work on the land
as a subsidiary source of income or industrial decentralisation,
but rather a revival or development of existing forms of economic
organisation."

Inflation - Effect on Commodity Prices

McGowan, J. F. Inflation influences on commodity prices. The Canner
82(2): 7-8, 36. Dec. 21, 1935. (Published at 140 N. Dearborn St.,
Chicago, Ill.)

"An address before the Ohio Canners Association at Cincinnati, Dec. 10, 1935."

Insurance, Hail - France

Arcclec, F. Hail insurance in France. Monthly Bull. Agr. Econ. and Sociol. [reprint from Internatl. Rev. Agr.] 26(10): 369E-385E. October 1935. (Published by the International Institute of Agriculture, Rome, Italy)

Insurance, Social - France

Changes in the French social insurance scheme. Indus. and Labour Inform. 56(8): 295-300. Nov. 25, 1935. (Published by International Labour Office, Geneva, Switzerland. Distributed in U. S. by World Peace Foundation, 8 West 40th St., New York, N. Y.)

In the scheme as applied to agricultural workers a new system of classification has been introduced. There are to be three categories, the first to include children between 13 and 16, the second women, and the third men, irrespective of their earnings.

Interstate Compacts

Clark, Jane P. Little Americas. Innovations in government by interstate compact. Survey Graphic 25(1): 36-38, 60-61. January 1936. (Published at 112 E. 19th St., New York, N. Y.)

A study of the possibilities and shortcomings of interstate compacts.

Pritchett, C. H. Regional authorities through interstate compacts. Social Forces 14(2): 200-210. December 1935. (Published for the University of North Carolina Press by the Williams & Wilkins Co., Baltimore, Md.)

The purpose of this study is "to investigate the possibility of setting up, by compact, interstate authorities with the power and ability to act as true regional planning and developmental agencies."

Labor, Agricultural - Eastern Arable Counties of England

Carslaw, R. McG., and Graves, P. E. The labour bill and output of arable farms. Royal Statis. Soc. Jour. (n.s.) 98(4): 601-622. 1935. (Published at 9 Adelphi Terrace, London, W. C. 2, Eng.)
Discussion, pp. 623-637.

"The purpose of this article is to investigate as closely as possible what may be termed 'the arable farmer's labour bill.' The figures on which it is based were collected in the course of an economic survey of farming in the eastern arable counties of England, in which the organisation of a random sample of 1,000 farms over 20 acres in size was investigated in each of the three consecutive years 1931-33. The number of regular workers connected with those farms is approximately 4,000."

Land Acquisition Program - United States

Gray, L. C. Scope and objectives of public land acquisition explained.
Land Policy Circ. November 1935, pp. 6-11. (Published by the Resettlement Administration, Washington, D. C.)
"From a paper read...before the Association of State Foresters,
Montpelier, Vermont, October 15, 1935."
Discusses the development of the present land acquisition program,
the necessity of coordination among the agencies now active in the
field of land acquisition and administration, and the problems still
to be solved.

Land Settlement - Argentina

Polish settlement in Argentina. Indus. and Labour Inform. 56(5): 182.
Nov. 4, 1935. (Published by International Labour Office, Geneva,
Switzerland. Distributed in U. S. by World Peace Foundation, 8
West 40th St., New York, N. Y.)
"It is announced that a colonisation company under the name of
the Northern Settlement Company has been established in Argentina
with a nominal capital of 700,000 pesos, entirely subscribed from
Polish sources. The company has purchased about 125,000 acres of
land in the north of the Misiones Province and is carrying on
negotiations for the purchase of land in other provinces of Argentina.
The first settlement, which will bear the name of Puerto Wanda,
will be on the banks of the Alto Parana river. Intending colonists
will probably begin to leave for this settlement at the beginning
of 1936. The company, which will collaborate closely with the
Polish authorities, proposes to extend its activities to Brazil
and Paraguay."

Land Settlement - Hungary

Schandl, Charles. La politique foncière de la Hongrie après la réforme
agraire. Société Belge d'Études et d'Expansion. Bulletin Périodique,
no. 99, pp.487-491, December 1935. (Published at Avenue Rogier, 12,
Liège, Belgium.)
Contains a summary of Hungary's proposed post-reform land policy
which stresses land settlement. It involves an attempt to make a
more just division of landed property by taking a certain amount
of land from the still existing latifundia to increase the size of
small farms and to establish new ones. New village colonies will
be created and improvements made to those already in existence.

Land Utilization - Eastern Kentucky

Poundstone, Bruce. Land-use in eastern Kentucky. Mountain Life and
Work 11(3): 11-16. October 1935. (Published at Berea College,
Berea, Ky.) Pam. Coll.
"This paper...was first presented at the 1935 Institute of Public
Affairs, Barbourville, Kentucky."

The writer concludes his article as follows:
"I have endeavored to point out the historical developments of land-use, to characterize its present features, and in some measure to consider its future. The history of land-use in eastern Kentucky parallels that of land-use in much of the United States, showing a tendency to use lands to secure the quickest returns possible. Present policies advocate utilization under regulation for the greatest public benefit. In these policies, and in our willingness to face the problem squarely and to push onward, lies the hope for conserving our natural and social resources."

Maine

Maine State planning board. Progressive development of Maine and its resources. Maine State Planning 1(4): 1-25. February 1935. Mimeogr. (Published in Augusta, Maine)
"The subjects treated in this report reflect the objectives pertaining to the problems, needs, and opportunities in Maine." -p.4.
Land utilization, p. 7; Agriculture (submarginal farms, production and marketing), pp. 8-9; Conservation, pp. 13-15; Recreation, pp. 16-18; Community planning, pp. 22-24.

Meat Imports and Livestock Industry - United Kingdom

Hubback, Caroline, and Montgomery, J. K. Meat imports and the livestock industry in the United Kingdom. Monthly Bull. Agr. Econ. and Sociol. [reprint from Internatl. Rev. Agr.] 26(10-11): 353E-360E, 389E-402E. October-November 1935. (Published by the International Institute of Agriculture, Villa Umberto I, Rome, Italy)

Meat Industry - Kenya

Meat industry of Kenya. Proposed Board of Control. African World 133 (1726): 297. Dec. 7, 1935. (Published at 801, Salisbury House, London Wall, London, E. C., Eng.)
"The Government of Kenya has appointed a committee to make an urgent investigation of the needs of the livestock and meat industry of the colony. The purpose of the committee is to inquire into the possibility of introducing legislation on the South African model for the establishment of a meat industry and livestock control board."

Mechanization of Agriculture and Agricultural and Power Prices

Kappstein, Curt. Studies on the international market for agricultural products. Monthly Bull. Agr. Econ. and Sociol. [reprint from Internatl. Rev. Agr.] 26(8): 298-314. August 1935. (Published by the International Institute of Agriculture, Villa Umberto I, Rome, Italy)
II. Costs and Prices: Some Factors of the Evolution of Mechanical Power in Farming.

"The purpose of this article is to investigate how far the relation between prices of the sources of power utilised in agriculture,
viz., coal, petrol or motor spirit, electric current, etc., on the
one hand, and on the other prices of agricultural products, has
influenced the use of mechanical power in agriculture."
Because the "majority of the countries neither possess nor publish farm returns including utilisation of power machinery in agriculture...this article is confined to the position in four countries
only, viz., Great Britain, Germany, the United States of America and
Italy."

Milk - Import Control - Great Britain and England

Taylor, C. C. The British import control of milk products. Foreign
Crops and Markets 32(1): 10-13. Jan. 6, 1936. (Published by the
Division of Foreign Agricultural Service, Bureau of Agricultural
Economics, U. S. Dept. of Agriculture)
"This is the second of a series of statements by Agricultural
Attache C. C. Taylor covering British agricultural policy."

Milk - Manufacturing and Marketing - England

Bendixen, H. A. An American looks at market milk in England. Food
Industries 7(9): 438. September 1935. (Published at 330 W. 42nd
St., New York, N. Y.)
This is the first of a series of four articles on European dairy
manufacturing and marketing practices.
The second is entitled "An American Looks At Germany's Milk
Problem" and is published in the October 1935(p.491) issue of Food
Industries.

Mortgage Moratoria Laws - California

Sooy, C. H. The helping hand. California's goodwill gesture toward
agriculture; an analysis of the 1935 mortgage and trust deed
moratorium and chattel mortgage moratorium. West. States Grower
of Agr. and Livestock 19(7): 2-4. September 1935. (Published
at 101 Post St., San Francisco, Calif.)
This "digest and outline of procedure under the Mortgage and
Trust Deed Moratorium of 1935 commonly known as the Jones Act
was prepared...for the California Farm Debt Adjustment Committee."

National Resources Committee - United States

Renner, G. T. NRC - the national planning agency. Social Forces 14(2):
300-302. December 1935. (Published for the University of North
Carolina Press by the Williams & Wilkins Co., Baltimore, Md.)
A short article on the origin and scope of activities of the
National Resources Committee.

Neues Bauerntum. Fachwissenschaftliche zeitschrift für das ländliche
Siedlungswesen. Neue Folge des Archivs für Innere Kolonisation,
Bd. 26. April-August 1935. (Published by Deutsche Landbuchhandlung,
Dessauer Strasse, 13, Berlin S W 11, Germany)

April: Gesetz über die Landbeschaffung für Zwecke der Wehrmacht,
by R. Heack. (A section of this law of Mar. 29, 1935 provides for
land for settlement purposes, by expropriation if necessary). -pp.
145-146. The text of the law is given on pp.169-171. Zur Raumfrage
in der deutschen Siedlung, by U. Senf. (The author asserts that
there is enough room left for the establishment on German soil of
strong, healthy, hard-working settlers.) -pp.146-149. Die Bewertung
landwirtschaftlicher Grundstücke und Betriebe, by Eggers. (Not
return is urged as the basis for land valuation in Germany.) -pp.
149-152. Altpreussische Bauern -und Siedlungspolitik, by Ernst
Ferber. (A brief historical survey of the land settlement policy
of Prussia.) -pp.153-155. Das Handwerk in der bäuerlichen Siedlung,
by Schuler. (It is shown to what extent the establishment of new
settlements has contributed to the development of hand work.) -pp.
156-157. Die Leistungsfähigkeit des Siedlerbetriebes im Vergleich
zum Grossbetrieb, by R. Bräuning. (The author replies to criticism
of his publication with the above title made by Dr. v. Rohr.) -pp.
156-160. Bauernsiedlung im Jahre 1934. (Statistics of land settlement in 1934 are reproduced from Wirtschaft und Statistik 15(5):
154-157. March 1935.)-pp.160-165.

May: Auswanderung und innere Kolonisation, by Georg Smolka.
(A brief summary of emigration from Germany and its relation to the
problem of land settlement.) -pp.197-204. Baukredite für die
bäuerliche Siedlung, by Willikens. (Summary of an order of the
Minister of Agriculture of Mar. 27, 1935, providing credit for
new buildings, repairs, and additional farm buildings on settlements.) -pp.204-205. Baukulturelle und bautechnische Gestaltung
und Ausführung der Neubauernhöfe und-dörfer, by R. Walther Darre.
(An order of the Minister of Agriculture of April 9, 1935 concerning
the building and equipment of settlements.)-pp.205-210.

June: Zur Auslegung des Gesetzes zur Ergänzung des Reichs-
siedlungsgesetzes, by H. A. Fiedler. (A discussion of some of the
difficulties that have occurred in the practical interpretation of
certain clauses of the law of January 4, 1935 which supplements the
land settlement law which was discussed in this periodical in January
1935.) -pp.241-244. Gedanken zur West-Ost-Siedlung, by Rudolf
Eggers. (Some of the factors that influenced the migration from
Western to Eastern Germany are pointed out.) -pp.244-247. Richtlinien
für die Neubildung deutschen Bauerntums vom 1. Juni 1935. (An
order of the Minister of Agriculture of June 1, 1935 defines the
aim, scope, and methods of the scheme for the recreation of the German
peasant. Some of the topics touched on are the human element, the
soil, the farm and the village, the basic principles of land settlement, the preliminary operations, financial problems, the obligations of the settler and of the state, and the various types
of land settlement.) -pp.263-273.

July: Die Richtlinien für die Neubildung deutschen Bauerntums vom 1. Juni 1935, by R. Haack. (A discussion of the above.) -pp.297-302. Der "Weg zum Lande" als Problem für Bauerntum und Siedlung, by H. Haefs. (The author discusses and justifies the reasons for the so-called flight from the land and points out the deep national economic and social reasons for the scheme for the reconstruction on a firm basis of the life of the German peasantry.) -pp.304-309. Italiens Siedlungswerk, by Gerhard Schulz-Witthuhn. (An account of Italy's land reclamation and settlement operations.) -pp.309-319. Der Siedlungsgedanke im vormärzlichen Preussen, by Georg Smolka. (A brief account of the beginnings of land settlement in Prussia.) - pp.318-323.

August: Technik in der Siedlung, by Tassilo Tröscher. (A study of the equipment necessary for the settler in order to produce an economic return.) -pp.353-360. Die Siedlung von Zeitpachtdorfern in Schleswig-Holstein, by Christian Rasmussen. (The origin and development of the time lease in Schleswig-Holstein are briefly traced, and its relation to present-day land settlement activity is indicated.) -pp.361-362.

New Zealand

New Zealand. Round Table, no. 101, pp. 196-212. December 1935. (Published by Macmillan and Co., Ltd., London, Eng.)

This article is in five parts as follows: I, The economic situation; II, The meat agreement; III, The election arena; IV, Markets and marketing; V, The budget.

Occupation Statistics - Great Britain

Statistics of occupied population in different countries (Great Britain). Internatl. Labour Rev. 32(6): 851-865. December 1935. (Published by the International Labour Office, Geneva, Switzerland. Distributed in U. S. by the World Peace Foundation, 8 West 40th St., New York, N. Y.)

This article is one of a series of articles on statistics of the occupied population in different countries. Workers in agriculture and fishing are included.

Olive Oil - Mediterranean Basin Countries

Substantial increase in Mediterranean Basin olive-oil production. Foreign Crops and Markets 31(26): 914-919. Dec. 23, 1935. (Published by the Division of Foreign Agricultural Service, Bureau of Agricultural Economics, U. S. Dept. of Agriculture)

"Based on a report from N. I. Nielsen, Agricultural Attaché, Paris, France."

Accompanied by statistical tables which show production of olive oil in Mediterranean Basin countries, average 1928/29 to 1933/34, annually 1932/33-1935/36; trade of these countries, annually 1929-1934; exports of edible olive oil from producing countries and imports into the United States, annually 1929-1934;

imports of edible olive oil into the United States by country of origin, annually 1931-1934, and January-August of 1934 and 1935; estimated average consumption in important producing countries, 1929-1934.

Ozark Mountain Region - Missouri

Cralle, W. O.   Social change and isolation in the Ozark Mountain region of Missouri. Amer. Jour. Sociol. 41(4): 435-446. January 1936. (Published by the University of Chicago Press, Chicago, Ill.)
"Fiction regularly depicts the culture of the Ozarks as strikingly different from that of the rest of the United States, while chamber of commerce literature, seeking to dispel this 'hill-billy' stereotype, presents the picture of a highly developed rural civilization similar to the most favored parts of the United States. The Ozark mountain region of Missouri is an area in transition in which an archaic rural American culture, protected until recently by relative isolation, is rapidly giving ground before the impact of urban civilization introduced by the automobile and improved highway, the newspaper, the radio, and other agencies. The rate of change is closely correlated with accessibility. Agencies of communication and transportation are more important than density of population, wealth, or ethnic stock in influencing the rate of change. "-Abstract, p.435.

Peanuts - Texas

Mooney, Booth. Peanuts in Texas. Texas Weekly 12(2): 8-9. Jan. 11, 1936. (Published at the Dallas Athletic Club Bldg., Dallas, Tex.)
An article regarding the value to Texas farmers of its peanut crop. "In 1935 it was worth more than four million dollars to them."

Pig Breeding and Earning Capacity of Farms

Deslarzes, Joseph.   The importance of pig breeding for the profit capacity of agriculture in certain countries of Europe from 1927-28 to 1931-32. Monthly Bull. Agr. Econ. and Sociol. [reprint from Internatl. Rev. Agr.] 26(8): 285-297. August 1935. (Published by the International Institute of Agriculture, Rome, Italy.)
I. Denmark, Netherlands (Overijssel) Switzerland, Austria, Germany.
"In the present article it is proposed to investigate the development of pig breeding in certain European countries and the effect of the progress of this branch of farming on the returns from agriculture in these countries. The enquiry will be based essentially on the analysis of the farm accountancy results available for these countries. From study of the accountancy data relating to examples of different types of farms representative of the region to which they belong, taken together with other statistical and economic information available in regard to the countries in question, it becomes possible to distinguish certain tendencies which have appeared in the course of the period under review. While avoiding any rash

generalisation, some valuable conclusions may none the less be often reached from such an examination of the material."

This article is continued in the September 1935(pp.317-330) issue of the Monthly Bulletin. The second article is concerned with Norway, Sweden, Finland, Poland, Lithuania, Latvia and Estonia.

Pineapples -- Palembang

Atmodipoerwo, Soenardjo. Ananascultuur en -handel in de residentie Palembang. [Culture and trade of pineapple in Palembang.] Landbouw; Landbouwkundig Tijdschrift voor Nederlandsch-Indië 10(12): 464-483. June 1935. (Published in Buitenzorg, Java)

English summary on p. 483.

Planning, Agricultural

Felcourt, Étienne de. L'économie dirigée et l'agriculture. Revue Économique Internationale, 27. Année, v. 4, no. 2, pp. 231-240. November 1935. (Published by the Institut Économique International, Palais d'Egmont, Brussels, Belgium.)

A summary of a series of conferences held in Paris by the National Institute of Agronomy on directed economy and agriculture in Great Britain, Italy, the United States, the Soviet Union, and Germany. "Viewed from the agricultural angle, directed economy appears more as an attempt to save the social rather than the economic situation."

Planning, Territorial

Tylor, W. R. Socio-economic aspects of territorial planning with special reference to the Mississippi Valley plan. Social Forces 14(2): 193-200. December 1935. (Published for the University of North Carolina Press by the Williams & Wilkins Co., Baltimore, Md.)

The writer considers the farm situation, the distribution of industry, measurement of industrial decentralization, and implications of decentralization. Under the "farm situation" he suggests the undertaking of projects "having to do with the relative socio-economic merits of large-scale versus small- (subsistence) and medium-scale farming," and the securing "from field studies a consensus of representative farming opinion throughout this territory as to the social preferences of farmers as to sizes of farms and the general modus operandi of farming."

The article is concluded as follows:

"Finally, with the toning down of the more radical tendencies in urban thought, and the stimulation to new outlooks of the more conservative elements of the rural community, a newly patterned agrico-industrialized territory should greatly strengthen liberal thoughts and liberal movements, which in turn, representing none of the extremes of either laissez-faire or of dictatorial revolutions, may be viewed as the soundest approach to the socio-economic problems of a planned society."

Karpinos, B. D.   The implications of certain population concepts.   Social
Forces 14(2): 214-226.   December 1935.   (Published for the University
of North Carolina Press by the Williams & Wilkins Co., Baltimore, Md.)
The following is quoted from the author's introductory paragraphs:

"Certain concepts appearing frequently in the literature on population have been so generally misunderstood and misused, even by
some of the outstanding students of population problems, that a special
effort to clarify them and to determine their place in the study of
population seems in order at this time...

"In order to clarify these concepts, it is proposed in this paper
to indicate their meanings and their implications not merely by abstract statement but by demonstration of their proper use through
analysis of specific population data.   After a brief examination of
the simple concepts, birth rate and death rate, which strange as it
may seem, are misunderstood - at least in their implications - not
less than the more complex concepts, attention will be given to the
widely misconceived terms, gross reproduction rate, net reproduction
rate, and true rate of natural increase.   An understanding of these
concepts will then make possible clarification of the concepts,
stabilized population, stationary population, corrected birth rate,
and corrected death rate."

Karpinos, B. D.   The length of time required for the stabilization of
a population.   Amer. Jour. Sociol. 41(4): 504-513.   January 1936.
(Published by the University of Chicago Press, Chicago, Ill.)
"The length of time required for the 'abnormal' age composition
of a population to adjust itself so as to fit its stabilized age
structure is a problem of theoretical and practical significance.
The first attempt in this respect was made by R. K. Kuczynski, who
took as his point of departure a hypothetical stationary population.
A study of four populations, rural farm, rural non-farm, urban,
and total population of the state of Iowa as of 1930 shows great
variance in age structure and reproduction rates.   Nevertheless,
the irregularities of the age factors become adjusted and within
slightly more than two generations the 'true rate of natural increase' becomes the constant rate of growth of the population, as
the 'abnormal' age factors outgrow themselves within the time." -
Abstract, p. 504.

Poultry - Estonia

Paglant, R.   Development and aims of poultry farming in Estonia.
Konjunktuur.   Monthly Rev. Estonian Inst. Econ. Research, no. 12-
13, pp. 788-794.   November-December 1935.   (Published by the
Konjunktuurinstituut, Tallinn, Estonia.)
The export of eggs is subject to Government control and prices
are determined once a week.

Price Psychology

Gabor, Ladislas.   La psychologie des prix. Revue Économique Internationale.
27. année, v. 4, no. 2, pp. 367-370. November 1935. (Published by
the Institut Économique International, Palais d'Egmont, Brussels,
Belgium.)
   A brief discussion of the effect of price inflation on public
psychology and its reaction on national economy.

Prices

Nourse, E. G.   Will prices go boom. It's not impossible, but 1936 conditions are quite unlike those of 1919-1921. Farmers in particular
ought by this time to be boom-proof. Farm Jour. 59(12): 7, 8, 59.
December 1935. (Published at Washington Square, Philadelphia, Pa.)
   Discusses the subject under such topics as: What really happened
in 1919? Were farmers prudent?; farmers wise and otherwise; inflation vs. price advance; debts and taxes; etc.

Processing Taxes

Harrower, D. C. A Judicial pandora's box; a problem in the wake of
death of the AAA - who is to get processing-tax refunds? Barron's
16(2): 28. Jan. 13, 1936. (Published at 44 Broad St., New York, N.Y.)

Rayon and Synthetic Yarn

Rayon and synthetic yarn, a growing and enterprising industry. Index
16(1): 15-20. January 1936. (Published by the New York Trust Co.,
100 Broadway, New York, N. Y.)
   Sketches the early development of the industry, world production
and consumption, the domestic industry, and current conditions.

Real Estate License Laws and U. S. Land Use Program

McEntire, Davis.   Land utilization program and the enforcement of real
estate license laws. Land Policy Circ. November 1935, pp. 13-25.
(Published by the Resettlement Administration, Washington, D. C.)
   "Address...before the National Association of License Law Officials, Atlantic City, New Jersey, October 24, 1935."
   The writer discusses the government land utilization program as
it relates to the problems of real estate promotion and land settlement. He deals with the early land policy of the United States,
recent changes in policy, the need for controlled land settlement,
and possible regulatory programs which include "(1) adequate information and publicity concerning the quality and probable values
of different kinds of land in different parts of the country; and
(2) better regulation and supervision of the activities of real estate dealers and other land selling agencies."
   Close cooperation between State and Federal agencies is essential
to adequate land settlement regulation in the writer's opinion.

Reclamation - San Marino

Land reclamation in San Marino. Indus. and Labour Inform. 56(5): 164-165.
Nov. 4, 1935. (Issued by International Labour Office, Geneva,
Switzerland. Distributed in U. S. by World Peace Foundation, 8 West
40th St., New York, N.Y.)
 A twenty-year land reclamation program has been approved in the
Republic of San Marino, to check erosion, to give work to unemployed
agricultural workers, and to bring back into cultivation land that
may be turned over to those workers.
 "The cost of alteration of water-courses and construction of roads
will be borne by the State...The costs of land reclamation and improvement and of the bringing into cultivation of eroded zones will
be borne by the owners."

Reclamation and Land Improvement - Italy

Ramadoro, Aldo. Il contributo degli agricoltori ai Consorzi di bonifica.
L'Italia Agricola 72(10): 781-796. October 1935. (Published at
Palazzo Margherita, Via Vittorio Veneto, Rome, Italy.)
 An account of the contributions made to the Consorzi for land
reclamation and improvement in Italy. A number of charts show the
contributing areas and the amounts contributed in the various provinces.

Resettlement - Appalachian Mountain Area

Tugwell, R. G. The Resettlement administration and its relation to the
Appalachian Mountains. Mountain Life and Work 11(3): 1-3. October
1935. (Published at Berea College, Berea, Ky.) Pam. Coll.
 Explains the plans of the Resettlement Administration for the
rehabilitation and resettlement of the people of the Applachian
Mountains.

Rubber

Seybold, G. H. Rubber control wabbles. Prices fairly steady, but
fundamental difficulties are more clearly apparent. Dutch native
still crux of problem. Barron's 16(2): 19. Jan. 13, 1936. (Published at 44 Broad St., New York, N. Y.)

Rural America

Rural America, v. 13, no. 9, 16pp. December 1935. (Published by the
American Country Life Association, Inc., 105 E. 22nd St., New York,
N. Y.)
 Partial contents: Local rural social planning, by Bruce L.
Melvin, pp.3-6; Scarcity vs. abundance, by Mordecai Ezekiel, pp.
6-7 [abstract of a talk given before the Alumni Forum of New York
University]; Improving and protecting the farm income, by L. H.
Bean, pp.8-10 [abstract of talk at Forum on country life programs
at Columbus, Ohio, September 20, 1935, American Country Life Asso-
ciation]; President Roosevelt for permanent AAA, text of statement
issued by the President on October 25, 1935]pp.10-11; Report of

Science and Agriculture

Ball, T. W. A suggestion - designed to promote increased use of products
in industry, West. States Grower of Agr. and Livestock 19(7): 19.
September 1935. (Published at 101 Post St., San Francisco, Calif.)
This plan "presents a constructive idea for the development of a
closer alliance between industry and agriculture, wherein science
will work with industry to learn what basic materials for manufacturing use can be obtained from crops grown upon our farms."

Sharecroppers and Relief

Davis, Lillian Perrine. Relief and the sharecropper. Survey Graphic
25(1): 21-22. January 1936. (Published at 112 E. 19th St., New
York, N. Y.)
An FERA administrator in Henderson County, Tennessee, tells what
relief has meant to the Southern sharecropper. "Relief to these
people has meant not a pittance to drag them through till they
might be restored to the normal standards of a few years back, but
a godsend of plenty such as in all their lives for generations
back they have never known before." Relief, she says, has not
harmed the southern sharecropper, "the harm will come later, if we
forget him again and leave him to sink helpless into the suffo-
cating bottom of our economic life."

Sheep Policy - Canada

Tisdale, W. H. J. A national sheep policy. Sci. Agr. 16(2): 57-66.
October 1935. (Published in Ottawa, Canada, Box 625)
Urges the working out of a national sheep policy for Canada,
with special attention to the problems of the small and large sheep
ranchers of Western Canada. Breeding policy, lamb feeding and
marketing, wool marketing, pure-bred flocks, education and publicity, and the appointment of a permanent National Sheep Committee
are topics presented for consideration in this paper which was
read before the annual meeting of the Canadian Society of Animal
Production (Eastern section) at the Ontario Agricultural College,
June 12, 1935.

Sugar - India

Burt, B. C. The Indian sugar industry. Agriculture and Live-stock
in India 5(5): 524-543. September 1935. (Published in Delhi, India)
"Paper read before the Royal Society of Arts...on...May 31st...
Reproduced from the Journal of the Royal Society of Arts."
"Intrinsically the industry is sound, and there is every reason
to believe that the weakness associated with an unexpectedly rapid
development will soon be rectified. This much is certain: during
the present time of agricultural depression, the sugarcane crop has
been the one redeeming feature in thousands of villages in Northern
India."

Carr, R. C.   The British government and sugar control.   Nineteenth
    Century 119(707): 112-122.   January 1936.   (Published by Constable
    & Co., Ltd., Orange St., Leicester Square, London, W. C. 2, Eng.)
        The following extracts are quoted from this article:
        "How is it that a country which produces only 600,000 tons of
    sugar out of a total world production of 27,000,000 tons, and ten
    years ago produced practically no sugar at all, thus dominates the
    future of the sugar-growing populations?   The answer is that the
    problem of restoring equilibrium in the sugar trade and assuring
    a fair price to sugar growers has become insoluble for the sugar-
        "This country holds the key to the situation because it is the
    greatest free market of the world for sugar...
        "The sugar countries are not likely to embark on another re-
    striction scheme without reference to the British Empire.   Moreover,
    Cuba, Java, and certain European countries, such as Poland, have
    conflicting claims to a share in the export market which make any
    new agreement difficult.   These obstacles, however, could probably
    be surmounted by a world plan headed by the British Empire, and
    there is a hope among sugar producers that this country will now
    take the initiative and carry through a plan based on the co-operation
    of the sugar-growing Dominions and Colonies."

Supreme Court - United States

Should the powers of the U. S. Supreme Court be modified?   Cong. Digest
    14(12): 289-320.   December 1935.   (Published at 2131 LeRoy Place,
    Washington, D. C.)
        Partial contents: Introduction to study, by N. T. N. Robinson;
    The trinity of Federal powers created by the U. S. constitution;
    How the constitution provides for the judicial branch; First
    Congress carries our provisions of constitution in judiciary act
    of 1789; The genesis of our Supreme tribunal, by Hon. Charles Evans
    Hughes; Politics involved in early attacks on judicial powers;
    Marshall's famous opinion on powers of Supreme Court, rendered in
    Marbury vs. Madison case, February 24, 1803; Sporadic attacks made
    on Supreme Court since 1803; How the Supreme Court has dealt with
    the "New Deal", by John W. Hester; Pro and con discussion.

Tennessee Valley Authority

Plan Age, v. 1, no. 10, 23pp.   December 1935.   (Published by the National
    Economic and Social Planning Association, 726 Jackson Place,
    Washington D. C.)
        Contents: Planning under the TVA, by Edwin Lemke, pp. 1-5;
    Land planning in the Tennessee Valley, by E. S. Draper, pp. 6-11;
    Productive resources of the Tennessee Valley, by C. W. Farrier,
    pp. 12-15; Elements of cost in the TVA rate structure, by Edward
    Falck, pp. 16-20.

Tobacco - Nyasaland

Arnold, C. W. B. The Nyasaland tobacco industry. Empire Jour. Expt.
Agr. 3(12): 379-383. October 1935. (Published at the Clarendon
Press, Oxford, Eng.)
"Nyasaland was declared a British Protectorate in 1889 and tobacco
first figured among the exports in 1893. Production steadily increased and the progress of the industry [is shown by a] table of
exports of tobacco of all types" from 1911 to 1934. "There has been
a marked reduction of acreage and fall in production in the last
few years.'

Tobacco - Sales by Auction - Rhodesia

Tobacco sales by auction. African World 133(1722): 135. Nov. 9, 1935.
(Published at 801, Salisbury House, London Wall, London, E. C. 2, Eng.)
The tobacco interests of South Rhodesia have agreed to the sale
of tobacco by auction. A marketing board has been formed provisionally
to draw up regulations for the conduct of the auctions.
"The amount of tobacco allowed to be sold for British, Union
and local markets will be controlled by legislation, and all buyers
will have unrestricted opportunities to purchase their requirements."

Tomatoes - Prices - Great Britain

Taylor, H. V. and Johnstone, K. H. A study of tomato prices. Great
Britain. Min. Agr. Jour. 42(7): 667-675. October 1935. (Published
by H. M. Stationery Office, London, Eng.)
"The prices...under review are the weekly figures obtained and
recorded by an English tomato grower from 1908 to 1934. They reveal,
not only the fluctuating fortunes of the grower, but the effects
of changing conditions on the market and the adaptation of production by the grower to meet each new condition."

Tractors - Cost of Operation

Catambay, A. B. and Cuevas, N. L. Comparative cost of operation of
a Fordson tractor using kerosene and alcohol as motor fuels.
Philippine Agr. 24(7): 549-561. December 1935. (Published by the
College of Agriculture, University of the Philippines, Laguna, P.I.)

Trade - U. S. with the U. S. S. R.

Townsend, E. B. What are the Soviets buying? Orders placed with the
U. S. almost doubled since early 1935 at expense of other nations.
A 300% rise in cotton and textile imports. Barron's 15(51): 9.
Dec. 23, 1935. (Published at 44 Broad St., New York, N. Y.)

Trade, Agricultural - U. S. with China

Ladejinsky, W. Tendencies in United States agricultural trade with
China. Foreign Crops and Markets 32(2): 27-56. Jan. 13, 1936.

(Published by the Division of Foreign Agricultural Service, Bureau
of Agricultural Economics, U. S. Dept. of Agriculture)
   "This preliminary report has been prepared by W. Ladejinsky,
Foreign Agricultural Service Division, on the basis of official
reports from Agricultural Commissioner Owen L. Dawson at Shanghai.
The Shanghai office of the Foreign Agricultural Service is making
more detailed studies of the Chinese market situation in relation
to particular American agricultural products. The results of these
studies will be published from time to time in 'Foreign Crops and
Markets.'" - footnote, p. 27.

Trade Agreements and Foreign Trade Policy - United States

Anderson, G. E. America must choose. Banking 28(7): 17-19. January
   1936. (Published at 22 E. 40th St., New York, N. Y.)
   The purpose of this article is to explain the Government's present
foreign trade program" from the standpoint of those who are now
guiding America's foreign trade policy."

Grady, H. F.   The new trade policy of the United States. Foreign
   Affairs 14(2): 283-296. January 1936. (Published at 45 East 65th
   St., New York, N. Y.)

Pasvolsky, Leo. Purposes and machinery of the American trade agreement
   programme. Lloyds Bank Ltd. Monthly Rev. (n.s.) 6(68): 536-548.
   October 1935. (Published at 71 Lombard St., London, E. C. 3, Eng.)

Thomas, E. P.   The reciprocal trade agreement between Brazil and the
   United States. Brazil 7(86): 6-9. December 1935. (Published by
   the American Brazilian Association, Inc., 17 Battery Place, New
   York, N. Y.)

Trade Development

Hantos, Elémer. Les vingt ans de la crise économique mondiale. Revue
   Économique Internationale, 27. année, v. 4, no. 2, pp. 352-367.
   November 1935. (Published by the Institute Économique International,
   Palais d'Egmont, Brussels, Belgium)
   The author traces the post-war structural developments in the
world market. He believes the ideal goal to be a free and powerful
national economy within a free and powerful world economy.

Trade Recovery, Prerequisites of

Fentener van Vlissingen, F. H. Voraussetzungen für eine intensivere
   Weltwirtschaft. Weltwirtschaftliches Archiv 42(3): 347-365.
   November 1935. (Issued by Kiel University. Institut für Weltwirtschaft. Published by Gustav Fischer, Jena, Germany.)
   "The author shows that the decline in world trade is due to the
changes in the international division of labour which functioned
normally before the war and enabled the different national economic

systems to develop along natural lines. It is therefore only natural that world trade, which is the true measure of the international division of labour, should be passing through a crisis. This crisis is the result of organic changes: (a) in industrial and agricultural production, (b) in the balance between the purchasing power of agricultural populations and that of industrial populations, (c) in the structure of the balances of payments of the principal trading nations of the world...The author comes to the conclusion that the prerequisite of international trade recovery lies in the re-establishment of a rational international division of labour. This may be achieved by restoring normal balances of payment, which means that creditor states should agree to having a passive trade balance and thus enable debtor states to discharge their debts in goods and services; this would lead to the progressive reduction of obstacles to international commercial and financial transactions."

Unemployment

Some recent censuses or estimates of unemployment. Internatl. Labour Rev. 32(6): 826-850. December 1935. (Published by the International Labour Office, Geneva, Switzerland. Distributed in the U. S. by the World Peace Foundation, 8 West 40th St., New York, N. Y.)
    "The present article is in continuation of a survey published under the same title in this Review for July 1933. Since then several other estimates have become available, chiefly as a result of publication of reports on the population censuses of 1930 and 1931. This article covers the following nine countries: Germany, Australia, Austria, Belgium, the United States of America, France, Great Britain, Italy, Czechoslovakia.
    "The census results, it should be remembered, are not strictly comparable internationally, since they relate to different dates and the methods and definitions used differ from case to case. They are of value mainly from the following three points of view.
    "First, they give information on the unemployment situation in some countries for which regular data are not available. Secondly, they give a comparatively complete record of unemployment at a certain date...Thirdly, the census returns give the possibility of classifying the unemployed in greater detail than the ordinary statistics. In many cases they give valuable information as to occupation and duration of individual unemployment by age and sex, etc."
    Statistics of unemployed workers in agriculture and forestry are included.

Vegetables - Supplies and Prices - Great Britain

Britain's vegetable supplies. Economist 121(4815): 1115-1116. Dec. 7, 1935. (Published at 8 Bouverie St., Fleet St., London, E. C. 4, Eng.)
    Surveys "the available information relating to supplies and prices of the chief vegetables produced commercially" in Great Britain.

Statistical tables show supplies of tomatoes, potatoes and onions,
1924, 1929-1935; acreage under certain vegetable crops for the same
dates; index-numbers of prices of home-grown produce, 1924, 1929-1934.
  The writer closes, in part, as follows:
  "Despite the irregularities of vegetable prices, it is clear that
the British grower has derived considerable benefit from protection...
Efforts have been made, with some success, to achieve increased
profitability by the extension of the marketing season, the increased
use of glass, the development of special varieties of produce, and
the canning and bottling of home supplies... [The Ministry of Agriculture has suggested as improvements - the standardization of
product, pack and package, and the standardization of trade practices]
The industry cannot expect further favours from the Government, but
it can and should be willing to set its own house in order along the
lines suggested by the Ministry."

Wages - Index Numbers - United Kingdom

Ramsbottom, E. C. The course of wage rates in the United Kingdom, 1921-
  1934. Royal Statis. Soc. Jour. (n.s.) 98(4): 639-673. 1935.
  (Published at 9, Adelphi Terrace, London, W. C.2, Eng.)
    Discussion, pp. 674-694.
    "The object of this paper is to assemble and summarize the avail-
able data for the past fourteen years in the form of a new series of
index numbers which will enable the movements in the average level
of wage rates during that period to be measured with some closer
approach to precision than has previously been attainable; and at
the same time to provide some indication of the extent of the variations, in different industries and groups of industries, which have
been concealed in the general averages represented by the index
numbers hitherto published."
    Ordinary agricultural laborers in England and Wales and married
ploughmen in Scotland are included in the classes of workmen represented in the index numbers.

Wealth

Doane, R. R. Property ownership by states; security holdings, insurance
  equities, &c. Annalist 46(1196): 844-845. Dec. 20, 1935. (Published by the New York Times Co., New York, N. Y.)
    "This is the sixth of a series of articles on the nature, dis-
tribution and promise of wealth in the United States." It is accompanied by three tables which show estimated private property
holdings in millions of current dollars, distributed by states;
percentage distribution of major forms of private property holdings among the states; and percentage distribution of major forms
of property holdings within each state. All data are for 1932.

Wealth and its distribution. National City Bank of New York. [Monthly
  letter on] Econ. Conditions, Govt. Finance, U. S. Securities,
  January 1936, pp. 10-15. (Published in New York, N. Y.)

Wheat

Davis, J. S. The world wheat situation, 1934-35; a review of the crop
    year. Wheat Studies of the Food Research Institute 12(4): 101-182.
    December 1935. (Published at Stanford University, Calif.)
        Contents: Supplies for the year; marketing and visible stocks;
    international trade; disappearance and carryover; prices and price
    spreads; concluding observations; appendix tables and chart.
        "Short crops in most exporting countries, negligible shipments
    from Russia, and liberal use of wheat for feed: these combined to
    reduce world wheat stocks from a record peak in midsummer 1934 at
    least halfway toward normal levels by August 1935. In Canada, as
    an unwelcome result of price-supporting operations, a huge carry-
    over was left in quasi-government hands. Stocks were also heavy
    in numerous importing countries which had big crops in 1933, 1934,
    or both. Such factors, coupled with widespread and effective gov-
    ernment controls, caused international trade in wheat and flour
    to fall to the lowest total in twenty-five years except for the
    war year 1917-18. Wheat prices were extremely divergent in level
    and course. In leading world markets the peak was reached in August
    1934, but subsequent declines held averages for the year little
    above those of 1933-34.
        "Among exporting countries, Argentina took first rank with a
    third of the world's net exports, owing to her large initial stocks,
    a good crop, unrestricted shipments, and Canada's holding policy.
    Despite abundance of exportable supplies, Canada took second place.
    Australia shipped heavily to the Orient. France, subsidizing exports
    of surplus wheat, ranked fourth. The United States took sizable
    amounts of durum and feed wheat from Canada, and was a net importer
    for the first year since 1836-37.
        "Another short world crop in 1935 presages further reduction of
    the 'carryover surplus.' Toward solving the underlying wheat surplus
    problem, however, progress has been slight. Wheat consumption for
    food continues low. Growers are still geared to produce more than
    world markets, hampered by complex restrictions, can absorb at
    prices that producers deem remunerative." -Title page.

Wheat - Canada

Evans, W. Sanford. The Canadian wheat situation. Grain & Feed Rev.
    25(3): 10-14. November 1935. (Published at 408 South 3rd St.,
    Minneapolis, Minn.)
        Address before the annual convention of the Grain & Feed
    Dealers' National Association in St. Louis, September 19-20-21.

Wheat - France

Important changes in French wheat legislation. Foreign Crops and
    Markets 31(25): 861-865. Dec. 16, 1935. (Published by the Division
    of Foreign Agricultural Service, Bureau of Agricultural Economics,
    U. S. Dept. of Agriculture)

"Based on a report by L. D. Mallory, Assistant Agricultural
Attache, Paris."
Discusses some important changes in French wheat legislation as
found in a new decree-law issued on October 31, 1935 and amended
on November 7, 1935. This law includes the following changes:
"1. Abolition of subsidized removal of wheat surplus. 2. Government
confiscation of future wheat surpluses. 3. Abolition of the production
tax. 4. Rigid control of the milling industry."

Wine Industry

Koster, P. C. Problems of the wine industry. Wines and Vines 17(1):
    12. January 1936. (Published at 85 Second St., San Francisco, Calif.)

Pearce, J. C. The current economic wine problem. Wines & Vines 17(1):
    3. January 1936. (Published at 85 Second St., San Francisco, Calif.)
    "The California Wine Industry faces a continued over-supply of
    or pas for several years... The annual production of over 40 million
    gallons of fortified wine and an annual consumption of approximately
    30 million gallons without a determined, planned, and effective
    carry-over for aging will create demoralized fortified wine prices."

                              NOTES

Australia. Laws, statutes, etc. Australian legislative digest. Summary of
    principal bills introduced into, and acts passed by, the parliaments of
    Australia during 1934. Published under the authority of the premier of
    New South Wales. 48pp. Sydney, A. J. Kent, government printer, 1935.
    274 Au7 1934

Bisset, G. B., and Villiers, F. H. Financial results of dairy farming in the
    Blackmore Vale 1934/35. 7pp. [Reading, Eng.] 1935. (Reading, Eng.
    University. Agricultural economics dept. Financial accounts studies - 7,
    Sept. 1935) 281.9 R22 1934/35

Burchfield, Laverne. Student's guide to materials in political science, pre-
    pared... under the direction of the Sub-committee on research of the
    Committee on policy of the American political science association, 426pp
    New York, H. Holt and company [1935] 241.3 B893

Cambridge, Eng. University. Dept. of agriculture. Farm economics branch. In-
    terpretation of farm accounts. 13pp. [Cambridge, Eng., 1935] (Farmers'
    bulletin no. 1, 3d ed., 1935) 281.9 C14F no.1, 3d ed.

Claassen, C. J. Better tenant farming. 46pp. [Omaha] 1935. 281.12 C51B
    E4.4
        On cover: Fourth edition.
        Describes the work of the Farmers National Company.

Dubay, G. H. The power of government. 55pp. Boston, The Christopher
    publishing house [1935] 280.12 D85
        The farming class, pp. 47-48.

                              - 182 -

Evans, W. Sanford, statistical service. Drought areas of the Prairie provinces 1929 to 1934... A survey of the effects upon farm income, and possibilities for 1935. 8pp., multigraphed. Winnipeg, Sanford Evans statistical service [1935] 281.13 Evl

Farmers emergency relief conference. Farmers plan united action... Proceedings of the Farmers emergency relief conference, Sioux Falls, S. D., March, 1935. 64PP. [Philadelphia, Farmers national committee for action, 1935] 281.9 F222

Gammans, L. D. Report on co-operation in India and Europe. 314pp. Singapore, Printed at the Government printing office, by V. C. G. Gatrell, acting government printer, 1933. 280.2 G14

Gt. Brit. Treaties, etc., 1910- (George V) Commercial agreement between His Majesty's government in the United Kingdom and His Majesty's government in the Union of South Africa (dated 30th August, 1935.) 4pp. London, H. M. Stationery off., 1935. ([Parliament. Papers by command] Cmd. 5012) 286 G797Ca

McConnell, Baxter & Eastman limited. The Canadian cupboard; a study of retail distribution and merchandising of food products in the Dominion. (2d ed.; completely revised, June, 1935) 19pp. Montreal [etc.] McConnell, Baxter & Eastman, 1935. 286.2 M13 Ed. 2
    "Originally published during the spring of 1933 as a supplement to three issues of The Trend of Canadian business". p. [3] (not in Agr.)

Millers' national federation. Flour package laws; a summary of federal and state requirements. 19pp. [Chicago] 1935. 280.359 M61 1935

Montserrat. Government marketing depot. Progress report on the operations of the Government marketing depot during the 1935 season, up to July 1935. 4pp. [Antigua, 1935] 280.39 M762 1934/35
    "Supplement to the Leeward Islands gazette of Thursday, the 5th of September, 1935."

Murphy, R. E. The economic geography of York, Pennsylvania, a city of diversified industries. 62pp. State College, Penn., School of mineral industries, 1935. (Pennsylvania State college. Mineral industries experiment station. Bulletin 17) 278.073 M95
    Pennsylvania State College Bulletin v. 29, no. 15.

National conference on social security. Social security in the United States. 1935. A record of the eighth National conference on social security... Apr. 26 and 27, 1935. 239pp. New York, American association for social security, inc., [1935] 284.69 N21

New York state bankers association. Commission for study of the banking structure. Banking developments in New York state, 1923-1934. 157pp. New York, N. Y., Commission for study of the banking structure, New York state bankers association [1935] 284 N487

Royal institute of international affairs. Information dept. The economic
and financial position of Italy. Issued by the Information department,
Royal institute of international affairs. Second revised edition,
September 1935. 59pp. London, Oxford university press, H. Milford,
1935. (Information department papers, no. 15)   280.176 R81 Ed.2

Royal institute of international affairs. Information dept. Sanctions; the
character of international sanctions and their application. September,
1935. 64pp. London, 1935. (Information department papers, no. 17)
280 R81S

Salt Lake tribune- telegram. Market facts about the intermountain empire and
the Salt Lake market. 1935 edition. 48pp. [Salt Lake City, Utah, 1935]
280.32 Sa3

U. S. Farm credit administration. Circular G. Loans for range sheep.
[Washington, D. C., 1935] folder.   166.2 C492 [no.G]

U. S. Farm credit administration. Circular no. 8. Federal farm mortgage corporation bonds. Fully and unconditionally guaranteed by the United States
government. 4pp. [Washington, U. S. Govt. print. off., 1935]

U. S. Farm credit administration. Circular no. 13. Appraising farms for
mortgage loans. 19pp. Washington, U. S. Govt. print. off., 1935.
166.2 C49 no.13

U. S. Federal trade commission. Interim report... on the agricultural income in
quiry. 6pp. [Washington, D. C., 1935] (74th Cong. 2d sess. House. Doc.
no. 380)   173 F32Int
    Signed by Edwin L. Davis, Chairman.

Wisconsin. Tax commission. Assessors' manual.   232pp. Madison, Wis.
1935. 284.5 T195 1935

Wisconsin. University. University extension division. Dept. of debating and
public discussion. County and town government; suggestions for public
discussion and debate. Department of debating and public discussion,
University extension division, the University of Wisconsin and Extension service of the College of agriculture, the University of Wisconsin.
34pp., mimeogr. [Madison] 1935.   280.12 W752
    Bibliography, pp. 19-26.

CORRECTION

   On p. 35 of Agricultural Economics Literature, v.10, no. 1,
January 1936, line 4 should read 284.5 N482 no. 9 instead of 284.5
N482, no. 5.

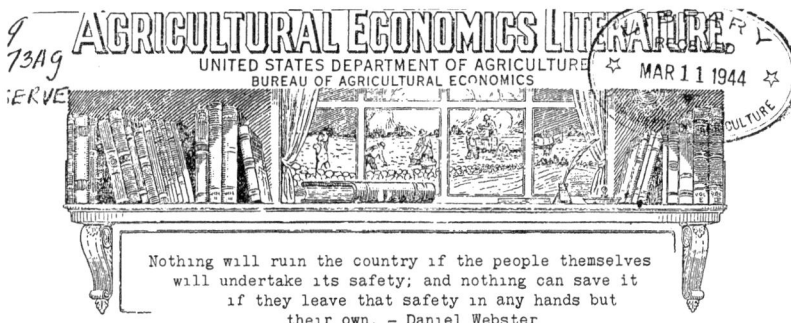

AGRICULTURAL ECONOMICS LITERATURE

UNITED STATES DEPARTMENT OF AGRICULTURE
BUREAU OF AGRICULTURAL ECONOMICS

MAR 11 1944

Nothing will ruin the country if the people themselves
will undertake its safety; and nothing can save it
if they leave that safety in any hands but
their own. - Daniel Webster

| Vol. 10 | March 1936 | No 3 |

FEATURES IN THIS ISSUE

SIGNED REVIEWS

Howard, Lady Louise E. (Matthaei)   Labour in agriculture; an international
survey. 339pp. London, Oxford university press, H. Milford, 1935.
283 H832

Issued under the auspices of the Royal Institute of International Affairs.

This book is a pioneer in that it attempts from as nearly as practicable
a world viewpoint to survey the present agricultural labor situations and
problems of today, to bring out the principles underlying them, and to
draw conclusions. Only one other comparable attempt seems to have been
made. 1/

The author's preface states that her book is based principally on
information dealing with agricultural labor prepared by members of the
Agricultural Service of the International Labor Office and set forth in
official publications of that office. To sum up this work the author
made her presentation of facts as they appeared up to about 1933. She
explicitly concerns herself with the wage paid agricultural laborer whom
she defines as "a person whose time not being occupied, or not wholly
occupied, in cultivating some land of his own, is willing to work on the
land of another for some form of remuneration". Only sufficient attention
is given to other types of farm labor in passing in order to present wage
paid labor in its proper setting.

The book may properly be termed the first comprehensive survey of the
world situation of any type of agricultural labor. However, it has its
limitations. The author states clearly the difficulties of collecting
adequate, accurate and comparable information concerning such labor. The
relatively little popular or official attention given to this subject has
varied greatly in purpose and method. The resulting information and data
have not been comparable to a great extent for these reasons and because
situations vary greatly in the different countries. Agricultural labor
has seldom been investigated on its own account, but usually has been
given consideration secondary to other problems. From many countries
little information is to be had. The author has been handicapped by these
facts and has been unable to include discussion of agricultural labor in
some important countries. Russia, however, was "deliberately" omitted
on the ground that "a great deal of information now exists on the Russian
social experiment." The reviewer wonders if the reason for the omission
may not be that that "deal of information" coming from such wide-spread
varied agricultural regions and peoples now in the throes of a vast experiment, does not really indicate that conditions in this country are
too diverse and unsettled as yet to have the effect of custom, and to
warrant conclusions by outsiders. This complete omission is to be re-

1/ International Labor Office, "Technical Survey of Agricultural Questions".
International Labor Conference, Third Session, Geneva, October 1921, Geneva,
Switzerland. International Labor Office, 1921. This is a compilation of
information concerning topics to be discussed at the International Labor
Conference in October 1921. Existing facts are given with little attempt to
trace historical causes, developments, interrelations or effects.

gretted, but may have been wise. Be that as it may, names of fifty-nine
countries appear in the index of the book.

The work appears fundamentally more European in conception and treatment than was probably intended. This is due, apparently to the resources,
comparatively abundant as they were, which were available to the author.
Only limited references are made to Canadian and American conditions because of relative paucity of information. More attention is given to
those of Australia and New Zealand, with stress upon developments there
in labor organization and collective bargaining. Consideration of
agricultural labor matters in other non-European countries is apt to
be scattering because of scanty stocks of information. While the author
gives no bibliography as such, there are included numerous references to
sources of information.

Lady Howard's volume is easily readable to a student of social and
economic matters. Some terms are technical and almost unknown in the
United States because we have not as yet developed practices or situations giving rise to them; nor have we much knowledge of their existence
abroad. American need of increased knowledge and of better understanding
of foreign agricultural labor practices and conditions is thereby demonstrated. Readers of this book will have made a good beginning toward
such an understanding.

The author is plainly responsive to the social and economic difficulties of the agricultural labor classes, and sympathetic with most
projects for their betterment. She has apparently a sound knowledge
of the economic conditions, possibilities, and limitations of the employing farmers. She seldom, however, lets her feelings sway her in
her able presentation of existing situations, their historic and economic
backgrounds, arguments for and against existing practices, and in drawing rational conclusions.

Lady Howard begins her book with statements of the basic laws governing agricultural production and work.

Part II deals with "The Agricultural Economy". The great variety of
modern agricultural crops and systems and practices is shown to defy
any adjective except kaleidoscopic. The importance of the wage paid
laborer to world agriculture is brought out by estimates. The world
population is stated to be 2,013,000,000, of which nearly two-thirds are
engaged in agriculture, in fractions varying from one-fourth to three-
fourths of the population of individual nations; and from one-tenth to
two-thirds of those so engaged are wage workers.

Part III deals with "Conditions of Work and Life of Agricultural
Laborers." Contracts, or working agreements, laws dealing specifically
with agricultural labor, hours of work, housing, education, rights of
association and combination, collective bargaining, and the agricultural
trade movement are discussed. To present properly the setting of the
agricultural laborer some attention is given also to other elements of
the industrial and agricultural population in this discussion.

Part IV takes up "Economic Conditions." Wages, labor efficiency,
and labor demand and opportunity of employment in agriculture are given
attention.

In Part V, Lady Howard draws conclusions and suggestions. All facts mustered, she concludes, demonstrate the poor position of the wage paid agricultural worker, - his poverty, and lack of social and economic opportunity, despite a measure of improvement since the World War. She notes that part of the situation is due to the not far different plight of the farm operator. She suggests certain measures on behalf of the wage paid laborer, some of them to be carried out by the employers, and many by public resources. The measures include shortening of working hours; protection against occupational hazards of accident, disease, and unemployment; remuneration comparable to that of other industries; rights of organization equal to that of other laborers; measures to eliminate unnecessary fatigue; better educational opportunities; better housing; elimination of systems of indebtedness fostering peonage.

The author's final statement and prophecy make the closing paragraph worth quoting. "Agriculture is a world activity; therefore the treatment of agricultural labor is an international responsibility. The acuteness of agricultural commercial competition is more influential than the diversity of methods of production, for prices are levelling things and prove singularly disregardful of local or regional difficulties. The history of agricultural labor impels us to recognize the great need for protecting the agricultural worker, and not least the wage paid worker, whether from the greed and cupidity of the mere profit-seeking interests or from the inevitable pressure on fair-minded employers of world competition, to which they must submit and in accordance with which they must sell their products. For if agricultural production is a world affair, without a labor policy it is meaningless; human labor is the preponderating instrument in the carrying on of cultivation, and agriculture will stand or fall by the use it makes of its labor."

Appendices deal with the "agricultural ladder", supplemental notes on agricultural labor contracts, agricultural labor in tropical and subtropical countries, hours of work, agricultural laborers' strikes and protest, and nature of wage-paid agricultural workers' income. Conventions, recommendations, and resolutions of the International Labor Office in relation to farm labor are also given.

The author considers that in her book she has "made a fairly thorough survey of the outstanding features of the agricultural labor situation considered as a world problem." And so she has, in that she has treated matters of most interest to Americans at present. As she has pointed out, agricultural labor conditions in certain countries received very little treatment because of lack of information concerning them. American students will regret this because of our increasing desire for well-rounded knowledge of agricultural life and production and conditions in countries competitive with American farmers in foreign markets and even in our domestic markets. These countries include in particular those of South America. Similarly, information concerning agricultural labor of Oriental countries would have been welcome because of our increasing commercial contacts with these countries. It may well be that to properly treat Oriental labor conditions, a separate volume would be required to give Occidentals a better understanding of Oriental practices which in many ways are founded on philosophies entirely different from these of the Occident. - Josiah C. Folsom, Assistant Agricultural Economist, Division of Farm Population and Rural Life.

Locklin, D. P.   Economics of transportation. 788pp.   Chicago, Business
   publications, inc., 1935.   289 L81
   Selected references at end of each chapter.
   In this large volume Professor Locklin ably epitomizes the achievements to date of reflective scholarship in the field of railroad transportation. The economic consequences of improved transportation are reviewed. What is known as the "theory" of freight rates is discussed; the
relationship of freight rates to prices is analyzed in terms of equilibrium economics; and the influence of rates in the location of industries
is explained in general terms, with some apt illustrations from agriculture. Factors which affect or allegedly should affect the "general level
of rates are described; and those which commissions say they consider in
determining rate relationships are reviewed. The history of railroad
legislation is narrated; problems of finance and accounting are noted.
Briefer space is given to other forms of transportation.
   Among the questions which are tied together in the problem of aggregate railway revenues are those of valuation, the rate of return, and the
level of railway costs. The author rightly observes that the act of valuation is not a finding of "fact" in the "objective" sense of physics or
of descriptive and analytic economics; rather, it is a concrete choice
of policy. He inclines, like most students, to the prudent investment
theory. The level of railroad costs he regards as raising no major
questions, arguing that the railroads buy their materials in the markets
and presumably at market prices. This view of the matter overlooks the
fact that the railroads have no competitors for many of the things they
buy: e.g. rails, ties, and locomotives. It also disregards the possibility of associations of interest between railway supply manufacturers
and railway directorates. If railroad costs are taken for granted in fixing railroad rates, the result may be to erect a fortification behind
which the prices of goods and services sold to railroads may be sheltered.
The author mentions in several connections the contention that railroad
rates should move up and down with general prices, but thinks this consideration is outweighed by the advantages of stability in rates to the
business world. What is important to business men, including farmers,
however, is the relationship between prices obtainable and costs. Absolute stability in rates is favorable to the smooth operation of their
plans only when prices are stable. In such cases, the doctrine of simultaneous movement would not recognize changes in rates. Somewhat related
are the problems raised by the author's views on depreciation. He favors
depreciation accounting as compared with retirement accounting, and depreciation on the basis of original prices rather than current prices of
items to be depreciated. Such accounting, however, would tend to keep
"costs" high — and it could be argued, fictitiously high — in a period
of fallen prices and depression and hence to keep rates high. There
would seem to be a lack of harmony between the author's statement of the
place of transportation in the total economy, in one of his earlier
chapters, and his position on flexible rates. In the earlier chapter
he argues, in substance, that transportation adds to economic productivity if it makes the sum of the costs of production and transportation a
minimum, and that this result is worked out through prices. If, however,

- 188 -

this situation prevails initially, but if prices other than those of transportation service decline while the latter do not, there would appear to be a tendency toward uneconomic localization.

In discussing relationships between rates on various commodities, the author states that rates on one commodity are likely to be made by comparison with rates on other commodities, and the more similar the latter are, the better the evidence. This is in fact the administrative practice; rates on commodities having different characteristics are likely to be ruled out as "incomparable". Actually, all commodities are comparable in .that all are called upon to share the burden of total costs; it would seem, therefore, that the comparative propriety of rates on one could be judged as well by making due allowance for differences. The possibilities of cost accounting have significance for questions of rate relationships; and the author seems a little harsh toward these. He says, rightly that attempts to allocate the whole burden of railroad costs give arbitrary and fictitious results. There is room, however, for a more flexible type of cost accounting, which would determine, at least for large blocks of traffic, the minimum amounts which can realistically be charged against them, and the residuum which must necessarily be arbitrarily allocated. In discussing geographical rate relationships, the author repeats the usual argument that authorizing a circuitous line to meet the regular rate over the short route by charging less for the longer haul may actually benefit the shippers for shorter distances by enabling their road to spread its overhead thinner. However, a "line" in this sense should not be confused with a system. Except in the case of badly laid-out systems, gains of traffic because of permitted fourth-section departures will largely be offset by losses of traffic to other systems because of departures permitted the latter in other areas. Meanwhile the total cost of transportation is increased.

The treatment of consolidation is brief and scattered, the subject being discussed chiefly in connection with the problem of equalizing earnings as between roads. The possibilities of economy receive little attention; so, on the other hand, do traffic and financial motives in consolidation.

In discussing other forms of transport, Professor Locklin observes that motor transport is much more a competitive industry, in the theoretical sense of the word, than railroad transportation, and that therefore many of the reasons for regulation of railroads do not exist in the case of truck transportation. This is a point which many advocates of truck regulation overlook. The author is, nevertheless, numbered among them. In some respects he does not carry the application of the point far enough. Thus he thinks that control over abandonments of truck service is desirable. If, however, motor transport springs up readily, and is available on competitive terms, does it seem likely that its abandonment can long persist where it works serious injury? He also accepts the view that "common" carrier motor service is more in the public interest than contract carrier service, but does not indicate his reasons.

In calling his book "Economics" of Transportation, the author suggests a happy emphasis. The study of transportation has been concerned too largely with the texts of laws and commission and court opinions rather than with its broader economic aspects. The book itself, however, suffers considerably from the same limitation. This is not a reflection on the author; in a work covering so large a field he has necessarily been compelled to rely largely on the available material. Indeed, one must admire his enormous and obviously first-hand acquaintance with the literature. A reading of the book nevertheless suggests how much is still to be learned about the economic aspects of transportation. How great, for example, are transportation differentials as compared with other factors in the location of industry? Or consider the traditional doctrine that commodities of great "ability to pay", by paying rates which are relatively high on a cost basis, may be transported at absolutely lower rates than would otherwise be possible, because relatively low rates or other commodities enable the latter to move in large quantities, so that overhead is thinner. This is a quantitative question. Unless the flexibility of demand for transportation of these other goods is great enough, the theory is without foundation. Again, we may note some of the questions raised by the recent amendment of the Transportation Act to make the need of the railroads for credit, together with the free movement of traffic, the final criterion of the "general level" of rates. How much transportation, what kind, and between what places shall the Commission aim at? How much capital expenditure would be economically self-justifying on the basis of operating savings? On what terms are investors currently willing to supply various quantities of funds to railroads? What rate of return is needed to assure this transportation and these improvements? Now that motor transport and perhaps water transport is to be regulated, what is meant by "the field of clear superiority" of each form of transport? How may it be determined in particular cases? Finally, do high freight rates in a price depression actually and materially inhibit the movement of goods? Questions like these call for a far more empirical approach to transportation than has prevailed in the past; for less scrutiny of past decisions of courts and commissions (except for their suggestive value) and more work to create a basis for future decisions. - Thor Hultgren, Agricultural Economist, Division of Statistical and Historical Research

Plummer, Alfred. International combines in modern industry. 191pp.
London, Sir Isaac Pitman & sons, ltd., 1934. 286 P73
    Bibliography, pp.187-188.
    This is a contribution to the growing literature on world economics. It treats of the development and experiences of industrial organization in the sphere of international cooperation and control. It might thus be described as a study of certain aspects of economic planning - a subject which has been receiving increased public attention in recent years. The international aspect of the question attracts not only a great deal of interest but also requires careful examination under the present conditions of tense international politics.
    Dr. Plummer, Vice-Principal of Ruskin College, Oxford university, begins his treatise with a survey of the history of the industrial combination movement and of various types of combines. Under the term "international combines" the author includes "all forms of international combination, whether loosely or closely knit, and whatever their special features or peculiarities." Students of national industrial organization are, of course, quite familiar with such terms as gentlemen's agreements, trusts, cartels, syndicates, holding companies, concerns, conferences, associations, integral

and horizontal combines, etc. To a certain extent, such terms (many of them are, for practical purposes, almost synonymous) are also used in describing types of international industrial organization though such a classification must often appear so abstract that without an examination of the individual concerns themselves the discussion would be rather meaningless. Such analyses are made by the author to a considerable extent and the empiric method of approach provides the basis for most of his comments and conclusions. The texts of several international agreements are also included in an appendix to the book.

The story of these individual international combines reads at times almost like a novel. The growth of certain enterprises into a national combine and then into an international combine (the general form of evolution) is "dynamic economics" par excellence. The movement is largely one of the 20th century and marks the "high spot" of modern capitalism, in the belief of Dr. R. Liefmann, the famous German writer on cartels, and trust, who is frequently quoted by Dr. Plummer. There seems to be little doubt in the author's mind but that the international combine movement will represent, to an increasing extent, the future trend of the world's economic development. (Such a conclusion must naturally be predicated upon the assumption that present political boundaries, especially in Europe, will be maintained) It is noted that the number of international combines had increased rapidly in the few decades just prior to the world war. Something over 100 combines were publicly known at that time. The war disrupted most of these combines, however, as Germany and other beligerent countries were largely involved in them.

After the war the international combine movement received a new impetus for several reasons. (1) new frontiers made international combines out of many previous national combines ("many international agreements would not be international if political frontiers had not been drawn through natural economic units."); (2) the war also increased productive capacity to an enormous extent in the big industrial countries, and in addition it stimulated home industries in many other countries. Then, as market outlets decreased and competition increased, the desire and need of keeping productive plants going and of escaping severe competition and price-cutting as well as the desire to substitute certainty for the uncertainties of business, provided special stimuli for the formation of international combines. Regardless of such needs and desires, however, it is well to note that there are many limits to the extensive formation of international combines.

In discussing the formation of international combines, Dr. Plummer devotes one long chapter to "Aids and Incentives", and another chapter to "Obstacles". Among the aids he notes six rather general ones, namely, (1) the existence of a small number of producing organizations; (2) the natural scarcity of a commodity or the concentration of supplies in a limited number of regions; (3) the existence of national combines having authority to negotiate on behalf of their member-firms or share-holders; (4) the government regarding the formation of an international combine as likely to further the interests of the country; (5) the existence of international financial inter-lacing; (6) the commodity produced being a raw material or in the early stages of manufacture.

If two or more of such combines co-exist, the chances of successful

formation are, of course, enhanced. The absence of any of these circumstances would likewise seem "a priori" to present almost unsurmountable
obstacles. Other obstacles, which the author mentions, that may prevent
a common understanding and successful agreement are (1) the personal
factor - differences in nationality, language and psychology; (2) difference in costs, quality of product, and need of a combine; (3) strong or
potentially strong producers who prefer to remain independent; (4) the
establishment and maintenance of definite production or export quotas,
etc., (5) differences in the legal position in many countries as regards
monopolies or controlled trade; (6) disciplinary methods. This particular
discussion, in the opinion of the reviewer, could have been more effectively
organized and expanded, for the history of international combines to date
has been one of dealing with obstacles and difficulties to a very large extent and there has been a rather high percent of failures.

As regards the effect and prospects of international combines, Dr.
Plummer makes several interesting observations. Some international combines, especially of the trust or individual concern type, establish
branches in many countries and thus overcome national tariffs, etc., to
a significant extent. Such a combine may even then be opposed to a reduction of tariffs and other barriers to international trade. Stability of
prices has nearly always been an objective of international agreements.
"Given a wise price and output policy", says the author, "a combine may
well succeed in imparting greater stability to prices than would otherwise exist, so long as the combine is stable and likely to last." In
respect to dumping, he notes "as the sphere of operations of an international combine widens geographically, dumping disappears, "thus removing many price discrepancies. Though workers and consumers are usually
suspicious of great combines, Dr. Plummer concludes from his study of
them that the large combines "usually pursue a somewhat more enlightened
and generous policy in dealing with the remuneration of labor than the
majority of smaller businesses." Likewise, more stability in employment
can usually be expected.

The problem of the future of international combines, the author notes,
is largely the problem of retaining the advantages while we reduce or limit
the disadvantages. Agriculture, in the opinion of Dr. Plummer, should be
an important field in the future for the development of combines. Two
thirds of the world's population, he points out, are either independent
agriculturists or wage earners directly dependent upon agriculture,
whose purchasing power has been greatly curtailed by unorganized production and marketing measures. Finally he sees international combines as
a factor making for peace because it imparts an increasing awareness of
the disastrous economic consequences of a war. Whether or not these
last two thoughts have been "fathered" by a wish on his part for international economic agreements, it is difficult to say. He does not discuss the role of governments as parties to international agreements, and
it seems not unlikely that most of the progress to be made in developing international agreements or combines that will aid agriculture or promote
peace, will be fundamentally of this type. - Gordon P. Boals, Assistant
Agricultural Attache, Berlin Office, Foreign Agricultural Service
Division.

Agricultural Census - Chile - New Zealand

International institute of agriculture. The first world agricultural census.
Bulletin no. 3. Chile. 15pp. Rome, 1935. 251 In8F

International institute of agriculture. The first world agricultural census.
Bulletin no. 4. New Zealand. 48pp. Rome, 1935. 251 In8F

Agricultural Economics - Wales

Conference on development of agricultural co-operative business, Aberystwyth.
Report of conference... October 18th, 1935. 50pp., mimeogr. Aberystwyth
Department of agricultural economics, University college, 1935. 280.29 C763
Partial contents: Suggestions for marketing potatoes in Wales, by
W. Rees Owen; High-grade basic slag - Price margins, discussion...
[opening with statement] by A. W. Ashby; Review and forecast of trade
in feedstuffs and fertilisers, by W. H. Jones; The needs of the agricul-
tural co-operative movement in Wales, by A. W. Ashby.

Agricultural Labor - Italy

Confederazione fascista dei lavoratori dell' agricoltura. Sei mesi di gestione
commissariale. 159pp. Roma [Stab. tip.s.a. "Arte della stampa"] 1934.
283 C7624
An outline of the aims of the Fascist Confederation of Agricultural
Workers is followed by an account of the activities of six national
federations that form part of it. The organization of the Confederation
and the duties of its various offices are described.

Agricultural Labor - Mexico

Mexico. Secretaría de agricultura y fomento. Dirección de economía rural.
Instituto de investigaciones económicas. Problemas económicos de México.
El salario mínimo en el sector agrícola. 116pp. Tacubaya, Talleres de
la Oficina de publicaciones y propaganda, 1934. 283 M5722
Bibliography, pp. 115-116.
The International Labour Review in its issue for November 1935,
p. 718, reviews this report as follows:
"The Mexican Department of Agriculture has published the first work on
agricultural wages in Mexico. This report summarises the investigations
carried out by the National Committee created in 1934 for the study of
minimum wages. The first chapters are mainly theoretical, while the remainder of the book deals with the concrete question of agricultural wages
in Mexico. Especially important are the statistical data on wages in agriculture, which go back to 1891. This study should be welcomed as fundamental to an understanding of the general social and economic conditions
of Mexican agriculture."

The agricultural dilemma: a report of an enquiry organised by Viscount Astor
and Mr. B. Seebohm Rowntree. 101pp. London, P. S. King & son ltd.,
1935. 281.171 Ag8
    The Economist (London) in its issue for Oct. 19, 1935, (p.756-757)
reviews this volume in part as follows:
    "Lord Astor and Mr. Seebohm Rowntree had each, in earlier independent
inquiries, favoured a rapid extension of smallholding settlement. But
being troubled by doubts they organised a small Committee of Enquiry,
which included, among others, Mr. H. D. Henderson (who has drafted the
Report), Sir Robert Greig and Sir Frederick Keeble. The Report will gain
considerably in weight from the fact that its conclusions are the reverse
of those previously held by its sponsors. The Enquiry sets out to answer two questions: first, whether a large increase in the agricultural
population was practicable; and second, whether smallholdings in particular might be established with advantage on a much larger scale. Both
questions are answered substantially in the negative.
    "The Report ascribes the depression of world agriculture to three
causes - the slowing-down in the increase in population, the rapid advance of agricultural technique, and the agrarian protectionism of Continental Europe. All three are likely to continue. Agriculture, therefore, will be a depressed industry in the world as a whole. To make it
prosperous, nevertheless, in Great Britain would involve either a reduction of imports or an increase in consumption. Both these possibilities
are thoroughly explored. Certain foods - vegetables; fruits, eggs and
poultry - which are particularly suitable for smallholdings in this country
are not vital industries of the countries from which we have bought them
in the past. But imports of these commodities have already been cut down
since 1931 as much as is prudent, without, however, inducing any increase
in the agricultural population. To reduce the imports of staple foodstuffs would still further ruin the export trades; it would be 'to turn
round upon one of the basic principles to which we owe our progress in
the past... It would be in glaring conflict with the main needs of the
economic situation.' It would involve both a higher cost of living and
an aggravation of unemployment. The Enquiry also examines, and rejects,
the argument that a greater production of foodstuffs at home is necessary
for security in time of war. Wheat is the chief case in point, and supplies of wheat could be very much more cheaply assured by storing a year's
supply.
    "The possibilities of increased consumption are more significant. Con-
sumption will naturally increase as the standard of living rises, but it
is likely that agricultural efficiency will increase still faster. A
national Nutrition policy is both desirable and probable, but Budgetary
considerations will probably limit it to the provision of 'protective foodstuffs' for children and for 'persons suffering palpably from malnutrition.'
Even if the consumption of one-fifth of the population were increased by
20 percent., the total consumption of food would increase only by 4 per

cent. The answer given to the first question is, then, the pessimistic one that an increase in the agricultural population would be difficult to secure without a restriction of food imports and would be most uneconomic if it were so secured. This conclusion assumes a more modest margin of potential demand than that which has been accepted by some other recent investigations on this subject.

"But this analysis of consumption and of agricultural technique does not in any case dispose of the argument for small holdings, for there might be a case for increasing the number of small producers, even if the total population engaged in agriculture did not increase. This second question is dealt with at greater length in the book by Mr. Orwin and Mr. Darke, who are more concerned with the technique of agriculture and the place that smallholdings fill in it. They point out that the history of small holdings is one of small results from large hopes. There is an unmistakable tendency for the numbers both of small and of large holdings to fall; the only size which is increasing is that between 50 and 150 acres. There are sound economic reasons for this... If the smallholder is to survive in competition he must accept a lower standard of living.

"Smallholdings are not utterly condemned. They will remain as the bottom rung of the ladder for farm labourers. There is also a very strong case for allotments and even for subsidised subsistence homesteads. But no substantial body of the industrial unemployed can be made to support themselves on the land. Much, however, will be accomplished if the trend to the town is stopped by a wise agricultural policy; for this migration has for long been a cause of urban unemployment. Moreover, the change in the quality and character of our agricultural production will give increased employment in ancillary occupations - canning, transport and the like. All this means 'back to the countryside,' if not 'back to the land.'

"In any case, we may well refuse, with the Astor-Rowntree Committee, to be depressed by the result at which they have arrived. For the troubles of agriculture have their source in the disappearance of those twin nineteenth century bogeys, the law of diminishing returns in agriculture, and the Malthusian law of population. 'We cannot admit that the removal of these age-long obstacles to progress should be greeted with a sour look, merely because it has the incidental result of increasing the difficulty of settling men upon the land'"

Agricultural Policy - Surplus Control

National cooperative council. Special legislative committee. An agricultural policy for the United States. Preliminary report. Special legislative committee, National cooperative council. February 12, 1936. 24pp. [Washington, D. C.] 1936.   281.12 N2142

"At the eighth annual meeting of the National Cooperative Council held in Washington, D. C., January 13 to 15, 1936, the delegates unanimously adopted a resolution setting forth the principles which they believed should underlie a national agricultural policy.

"Under terms of the resolution a special legislative committee consisting of eleven delegates from member organizations was appointed by John

D. Miller, president of the Council. The committee immediately undertook to formulate a plan by which the principles previously adopted might
be put into effect...
    "This booklet is the committee's preliminary report...
    "[It] must not be considered a final word but rather a new beginning
point from which to build an effective policy based on management of potential and actual surpluses." Foreword.

Agriculture - Czechoslovakia

Reich, Eduard. Die tschechoslowakische landwirtschaft; ihre grundlagen u.
    ihre organisation. 312pp. Berlin, P. Parey. 1935. ([Germany] Reichs-
    u. Pr. Ministerium für Ernährung u. Landwirtschaft. Berichte über
    Landwirtschaft, n. F. 108. Sonderheft)
        Bibliography. pp. [305]-312.
        A study of production and marketing conditions and of the organization
    and development of Czechoslovak agriculture and its relation to the
    national economy. The author calls attention to the difference in eco-
    nomic development between the Eastern and the Western provinces and
    makes a number of suggestions for putting them more nearly on a level.
    The book contains a number of tables, maps, and charts.

Cartels

Pribram, Karl. Cartel problems; an analysis of collective monopolies in Europe
    with American application. 287pp. Washington, D. C., The Brookings insti-
    tution, 1935. (Institute of economics of the Brookings institution. Pub-
    lication no. 69)   286 P93
        Dr. E. G. Nourse, Director of the Institute of Economics writes in part
    as follows in the preface:
        "This volume is not a detailed description of cartels in particular in-
    dustries but an analysis of the economic conditions conducive to the forma-
    tion of cartels, the attitudes which dominate cartel policy, the various
    aspects of governmental policy in relation to cartels, and the economic ef-
    fects of these forms of business organization. In the later chapters atten-
    tion is given to the similarities and dissimilarities of business and govern-
    mental relationships in the cartel movement and under the NRA.   Probable
    lines of future development in the United States are suggested.

Cotton

China. National economic council. Cotton industry commission. Central
    cotton improvement institute. Cotton grading office. Report on grad-
    ing cotton in the producing districts, by the Cotton grading office of
    the Central cotton improvement institute, the Cotton industry commission,
    N.E.C. 6pp. [Shanghai? 1935]   280.372 C44

Jacob, Jean. La crise cotonnière. 168pp. Paris, Les Éditions Domat-
Montchrestien, F. Loviton & cie, 1934. 281.372 J15
Bibliography, pp. [163]-165.
A rapid survey of the development of production and consumption
of cotton is followed by a discussion of the causes of the cotton
crisis, its development, and the remedies attempted for its solution.
The author sees no hope in Government intervention, but would prefer
to allow natural laws to have free play.

Joint committee of cotton trade organizations. Economic and statistical
dept. The changing conditions of world trade in cotton and rayon
goods. III. Empire trade in cotton and rayon goods before and after
Ottawa. 18pp. Manchester, Eng. [1935] 304 J662 pt. 3
Have also 15 pp. Statistical appendix with title: Survey of Empire
Trade in Cotton and Rayon goods.
Should be requested from Joint Committee of Cotton Trade Organiza-
tions, Ship Canal House, King St., Manchester, England.

Kühn, Ulrich. Verbände in der baumwollindustrie. 145pp. Bottrop in
Westfalen, Kunstdruckerei W. Postberg, 1934. 304 K95
Bibliography, pp. 142-145.
An account of cotton unions and cartels in Germany and other countries.

Merrill, G. R. Cotton opening and picking. 55pp., multigraphed. [Lowell?
Mass.] 1933. 304 M55C
"Notes... prepared particularly for use in the classes of the Lowell
textile institute." - prelim. leaf 2.
May be purchased from the author at Lowell Textile School, Lowell,
Mass.

Cotton-growing Communities - Arkansas

Landis, B. Y., and Haynes, G. E. Cotton-growing communities. Study no. 2.
Case studies of 10 rural communities and 10 plantations in Arkansas.
47pp. New York, 1935. (Dept. of race relations. Federal council of
churches of Christ in America. Interracial publications no. 28)
281.2 L23
"Ten cotton-growing communities and ten cotton plantations in six
typical counties were surveyed by Dr. Benson Y. Landis and Dr. George
E. Haynes, under the auspices of a state conference of white and Negro
citizens and with the aid of more than twelve staff members of the state
educational and agricultural agencies...
"Recommendations made by the directors of the survey include land purchase and settlement plans by the government for private parties along
such lines that the tenants could begin without capital down payments." -
(Federal Council Bulletin, Vol. XVIII, Nos. 9 & 10, Nov.-Dec.1935, p.13)

Jerkes, John, and Gray, E. M. Wages and labour in the Lancashire cotton
    spinning industry. 322pp. [Manchester] Manchester university press,
    1935. (Publications of the University of Manchester, no. CCXLII)
    283 J54
        Partial contents: The workers and the machines; The income of the
    operative; Wages and cost of production; The mule spinning lists - General;
    The ring spinning list; The piecer problem.

Economic Geography

Jones, C. F. Economic geography. 448pp. New York, H. Holt and company
    [c1935]   278 J71E
        Bibliography, pp. 420-424.
        The arrangement of the material comprising this volume is by indus-
    tries or occupations as follows: Grazing industries, Fisheries of the
    world, Place of farming in human activities, Forest industries, Mining
    industries, Manufacturing and trade. The first three chapters are
    devoted to a discussion of the meaning of economic geography.

Economic Problems

Coni, E. A. Problemas económicos del momento. 208pp.   Buenos Aires, "El
    Ateneo", 1935.   280 C768
        A collection of articles ón economic problems of the day.
        Contents: Una lamentable confusión entre el liberalismo político
    y el económico. (A lamentable confusion between political and economic
    liberalism) - pp. 7-26, Crisis de intercambio (The exchange crisis) -
    pp. 27-40, Economía libre, planeada o dirigida? (Free, planned, or
    directed economy?) - pp. 41-51; Coma más carne! Coma más fruta!
    Coma más! (Eat more meat, Eat more fruit. Eat more.) - pp. 73-91; Super-
    producción y necesidades. (Overproduction and necessities) - pp. 93-106;
    El proceso económico de un pedazo de pan. (The economic progress of a piece
    of bread). - pp. 117-167; La retención postcosecha del trigo. (An argu-
    ment against storing of wheat). - pp. 179-186; La semana de 40 horas. (The
    forty-hour week). - pp. 187-208.

Economics

British science guild. Engineers' study group on economics. First interim
    report on schemes and proposals for economic and social reforms. 44pp.
    London, British science guild [1935]   280 B772
        A review from Labor Management Aug./Sept. 1935, p. 149 was quoted as
    follows in FERA Research library. Relief notices: (Foreign no. 34)
    no. 71, Sept. 30, 1935, pp.4-5.
        "'This is a remarkably interesting report written by a group of technical
    men 'familiar from personal experience with the fact that productive ef-
    ficiency had greatly increased in the last few years; and who were also
    aware that many kinds of production were being throttled down for lack
    of markets, and that strenuous endeavors were being made to maintain or

increase prices, while at the same time poverty was widespread.'

"'These were regarded as symptoms of a disease the nature of which was not apparent, and this group has examined quite without bias the various schemes which have been put forward to deal with the paradox of poverty in plenty. They have examined 24 sets of proposals made by the political parties and other writers and endeavored to assess their value and to place according to their value on the following points which they consider are the main functions of the economic systems: - (1) Abolition of poverty. (2) Lightening of labour. (3) Increase of leisure. (4) Deepening and widening of liberty. (5) Minimizing of friction.

"'Proceeding on these lines, proposals such as Sir Basil Blackett's, the Fascist, Keynes, Harold Macmillan, Douglas Social Credit and other schemes are analyzed impartially so that ground is cleared for correlating results and deciding which scheme or combination of schemes is likely to reach the desired result. This further report has not yet appeared, but meantime it is a service to the community to have a clear analysis of most of the panaceas put forward at this time and presented by men who have no axe to grind.'"

Economics and Politics - Virginia

Sheldon, W. DuB. Populism in the Old Dominion; Virginia farm politics, 1885-
    1900. 182pp. Princeton, Princeton university press, 1935. 277.089 Sh4
    Bibliography, pp.151-161.
    An interesting and informing account of the economic and political
    background of Populism in Virginia and its relation to the Farmers'
    Alliance and other agricultural organizations.

Farm Management - England

Seale-Hayne agricultural college, Newton Abbot, Devon. Dept. of economics.
    Some changes in South Devon farming (a series of articles prepared
    by the Department of economics. Seale-Hayne agricultural college)
    25pp., mimeogr. [Newton Abbot, Devon] Nov. 1935. (Farmers' report
    no. 11)   281.9 Sel
    "In 1928 a farm management survey was conducted in South Devon, and
    usable records were obtained from 205 farmers. These related to the
    year April 1927 to March 1928. In the Spring of the present year another
    survey, less comprehensive in outline, but more detailed in certain as-
    pects, was undertaken. This related to the year January to December 1934.
    "The objects of the first study were to collect data on the financial
    position of farmers in the area surveyed, and to investigate the main
    types of farming. The survey that has recently been concluded was de-
    signed to throw some light on the changes that have occurred in the farm-
    ing of the district during the last 6 or 7 years.
    "The farms included in this study are situated in 18 contiguous per-
    ishes in South Devon." - Introduction.

Albers. Werner. Die stellung der konsumvereine und konsumanstalten in der
fettversorgung des Rheinisch-Westfälischen-industriegebietes. 80pp.
[Bonn] Bonner universitats-buchdr. gebr. Scheur, 1933.   280.2 All
Inaug.-diss. - Landw. hochschule Bonn-Poppelsdorf.
Bibliography, pp. 4-5 .
An account of the marketing and consumption of fats and oils in the
Rhenish Westphalian industrial territory as influenced by the soncumers'
cooperatives and the consumers' establishments.

Governmental Research Organizations - Western States

California. University. Bureau of public administration. Governmental research organizations in the western states; a directory of agencies,
and an index to their studies. 50pp., mimeogr. Berkeley, Aug., 1935.
(Western states research activity series no. 1) 280.9 C125
"In 1934, there was organized by California Economic Research Council a Governmental Research Committee, composed of the heads of principal organizations in this State engaged in that field of work. Thus
there was provided an informal agency, in which various public and private departments might cooperate in the central listing of projects and
data, the exchange of information on current activities, and the practical
coordination of their objectives and projects. Since its formation,
Professor Samuel C. May has served as Chairman of this Committee.
"One of the first activities outlined and initiated was a survey of
the facilities and data available in existing governmental research
agencies in California. This study, extended to include agencies in
other western states, has been carried through to completion by O. W
Campbell of the staff of the Bureau of Public Administration, University
of California. The following Directory and Index is a first result
of the survey.
"This report is primarily intended as a means whereby professional
workers in governmental research may be introduced one to another and
become acquainted with one another's work. Secondarily, it provides
other interested persons with a knowledge of sources, and is impressive
evidence to the public of the extent and intensity of efforts toward
the solution of governmental problems." - Preface.

Japan - Foreign Trade

U. S. Tariff commission. Recent developments in the foreign trade of Japan,
particularly in relation to the trade of the United States. Report under-
the general provisions of Section 332, Part II, Title III, of the Tariff
act of 1930. 207pp. (Report no. 105, second series) 173 T17Rs no.105
"The Tariff Commission published surveys of the foreign trade of Japan
in 1918 and 1922. On account of the important changes that have recently
occurred in Japan's position in world trade and the widespread attention
that some aspects of Japan's trade have attracted, it has been considered
desirable to issue the present report.
"This report is divided into two principal sections. Part I is a gen-

eral study of Japan's foreign trade in recent years, especially of the changes in that trade most directly affecting the industry and trade of the United States. Part II is a detailed analysis of United States imports from Japan in the period 1929 through the first 8 months of 1935"-Introduction.

Labor's Plan for Land Use

Williams, Tom. Labour's way to use the land. 120pp. London, Methuen & co. ltd., 1935. (Labour shows the way) 281.171 W67
  The author's plan provides for the creation of various boards "to control the use of the land, the marketing of agricultural products and the quantity and price of imports." The nationalization of land is considered as absolutely necessary as a preliminary to any effective program. Mr. Elliot's agricultural policy is severely criticized.

Land and Little Waters

U. S. National resources committee. Little waters. A study of headwater streams & other little waters, their use and relations to the land, by H. S. Person, Consulting economist with the cooperation of E. Johnston Coil... Robert T. Beal... for Soil conservation service, Resettlement administration, Rural electrification administration. 82pp. [Washington, U. S. Govt. print. off., 1936] 173.2 N214Lw
  Letter of transmittal dated Dec. 19, 1935 is submitted by National resources committee, Harold L. Ickes, Chairman.
  Secretary Ickes in his letter of transmittal to the President writes in part as follows:
  "This report is noteworthy in that it deals comprehensively with a subject of high importance which has heretofore been neglected. Governments, private enterprises and engineers have been concerned primarily with great waters and with the resulting problems of controlling major floods, developing hydroelectric power, providing for navigation and irrigating arid lands. Yet it is the little waters which form the great waters. We must utilize and control small streams if we are fully to utilize and control great ones.
  "For the first time this problem is here inclusively treated. Scientific data made available by various Federal, State and private agencies have been integrated from the point of view of the long-term public welfare, and the findings and recommendations are here formulated in a simple, clear and convincing statement.
  "A reading of the text suggests the desirability of a comprehensive program of conservation which will enable us to make beneficial use of waters now permitted to go to waste, to save our lands from the disastrous effects of improperly-controlled run-off, and to remedy conditions that have proven socially and economically disastrous in numerous rural communities.
  "It is hoped that such a program may be undertaken without undue delay, and that further studies may be made in the same field. The effective control of little waters would, it is believed, be a lasting contribution to the Nation's prosperity."

Menzies-Kitchin, A. W.   Land settlement; a report prepared for the Carnegie
United Kingdom trustees... With a foreword by the trustees. 175pp.
Edinburgh, Printed by T. and A. Constable ltd., 1935.   282.2 M52
   Bibliography, pp. 169-170.
   "The purpose of the present enquiry... has been to consider in detail the wider political and economic implications and the more particular
issues relating to organisation and size of the agricultural unit, which
must have a bearing on the success of any scheme of Land Settlement, and
to ascertain whether there is in fact a sound economic Land Settlement
policy for this country." - Author's preface.
   It is shown that inasmuch as the small holder must concentrate on
the production of commodities of high cash value, such as milk, eggs,
pigs, poultry, fruit and vegetables, he will be affected by such things
as the future trend of population, the extent to which per capita consumption will be influenced by increased purchasing power, the extent to
which a surplus of commodities is likely to result from land settlement
and by restriction of imports. Information has also been sought with
regard to the financial position of existing producers of the above commodities and the size and type of holding on which they can be most
profitably produced. Chapters II and III contain a general survey of
these problems under the headings of general and economic considerations.
In Chapter IV, Land settlement legislation at home and abroad, the author
discusses briefly land settlement in the nineteenth century in England,
the Small Holdings and Allotments Act, 1908, the Land Settlement (Facilities) Act, 1919, the Small Holdings and Allotments Act, 1926; land settlement in Germany under Frederick the Great and under Bismarck, the Reich
Land Settlement Act, 1919 with its provisions for the acquisition of land,
the protection of agricultural workers affected by settlement schemes
and the settlement of such workers and the financing of land settlement
and its results; land settlement in Denmark in its pre-war and post-war
aspects; and agricultural conditions and the size of holdings in Holland
which, "unlike Germany and Denmark has no land settlement policy."
   In Chapter V the factors that affect certain small holding types, are
enumerated and typical small holdings are described in different countries.
   Chapters VI and VII deal with vegetables and pig and poultry production
because of the author's contention that "it is on the production of these
commodities that any scheme of smallholdings must depend."
   Under the heading, The economics of smallholdings, the author discusses
flexibility of organization to enable them to withstand changes in the
relative price levels of requirements and produce, small holdings versus
large farms, certain factors that influence the success of small holdings,
and the organization of six successful small holdings. In a chapter on
the organization of land settlement the author discusses "(1) the methods
by which maximum efficiency within the productive unit can be obtained;
and (2) the problem of evolving an organisation capable of securing for
these holdings the advantages generally claimed for larger units of production. In this connection the organisation of three types of holding

- 202 -

will be discussed: (a) the 20-50 acre mixed arable holding in which the greater proportion of the gross income is derived from the sale of livestock products, (b) the intensive market garden and/or pig and poultry holding of 3-5 aores, (c) as an alternative to this latter type the 20-50 acre pig or poultry holding on poor land."

The final chapter deals with subsistence holdings in the United States, Germany, and Great Britain. This is followed by a summary of conclusions, fifteen in number. The author finds "that the mixed family farm of 30-50 acres, on account of a flexibility of organisation which enables it to adapt itself to sudden price changes, and of the capacity of the family to live off the holding during a period of low prices, is the most suitable unit of settlement, [and] that in respect of unemployed industrial workers, particularly in rural areas, holdings of the subsistence type of half to one acre in extent, providing poultry, vegetables and eggs for the family as a supplement to unemployment relief, offer considerable opportunity for further expansion, and are highly beneficial in their effect." Six arguments are given in favor of this type of holding which "should be established as rapidly as possible."

In a "Trustees' Foreword", signed by Lord Elgin, approval of or disagreement with the author's conclusions are expressed, and a land settlement policy for the next five-year period is briefly outlined. "With this cumulative evidence before us as to the value of these smallholdings and group-or-subsistence- holding experiments, we have finally decided to make land settlement of these two main types one of our chief activities for the period 1936-40, and to set aside an allocation of £150,000. This allocation will remain in our hands, and applications from the Land Settlement Association and from other sources will be considered on their merits. It must be clearly understood that we regard the scheme frankly as an experiment... We consider also that these settlements may prove of great value in supplying recruits for the larger farming units of 50 acres and over, and in respect of Land Settlement in the Overseas Dominions of the British Empire."

Land Settlement - Canada

Mackintosh, W. A.   Prairie settlement, the geographical setting. 242pp. Toronto, The Macmillan company of Canada limited, 1934. (Canadian frontiers of settlement... v.1)   282.2 M21
    Among the chapter headings in this volume are the following: The land and its climate; Exploring the agricultural possibilities of the west; The prairie plains; The forest areas; and Climatic variability. There is also an appendix on soils.

Land Taxation

Verinder, Frederick. Land and freedom. 199pp. London, Pub. by L. and V. Woolf at the Hogarth press, 1935.   282 V58
    Appendix: Land value taxation in practice, by A. W. Madsen, pp. [175]-192.
    The Economist (London) in its issue for Oct. 12, 1935, p. 708 speaks of this volume as "A restatement of Henry George's land taxation proposals."

Land Use on Peasant Enterprises - Germany

Rolfes, Max. Die bodennutzung in bäuerlichen betrieben. 84PP. Berlin, P.
Parey. 1935. ([Germany] Reichs-und Pr. Ministerium für Ernährung und
Landwirtschaft, n.F., 113. Sonderheft.)
    The author calls attention to the fact that the family farm with its
owner interest in the work of the farm and its results has a special
influence on the use of the land which it comprises. He contributes
a study of the use of the land and its connection with livestock raising
on such farms according to the soil, the climate and the economic conditions determined by the type of farm management in four different sections of the country. He investigates grain production in Eastern
Germany, the three-field system in western Germany, fodder production
on the coast and the cultivation of hoed crops, and their relation to
the operation of the family farm.

Livestock and Dairy Products - Export - East Prussia

Königsberg. Universität. Institut für wirtschaftslenre des landbaus. Die
stellung Ostpreussens in der deutschen ernährungswirtschaft. Erster
teil: Die ausfuhrleistung der ostpreussischen landwirtschaft und die
zusammensetzung ihrer betriebseinnahmen unter besonderer berücksichtigung der rindviehzucht und milchwirtschaft, von dr. Hans Bloech. 80pp.
Berlin, P. Parey, 1935. (Germany. Reichs- und Pr. Ministerium für Ernährung u. Landwirtschaft. Berichte über Landwirtschaft, n. F. 109.
Sonderheft)
    At head of title: Veröffentlichungen aus dem Institute für Wirtschafts-
lehre des Landbaus an der Universität Königsberg. Leiter: Professor
Dr. E. Lang.
    Bibliography, pp. [79]-80.
    A study of Eastern Prussia's export of livestock and dairy products
in 1896 and for the period 1909/1913 and 1925/1930, of the markets
to which they are sent and of the relation of the receipts from the
livestock and dairy industries to the general economy and to economic
results on individual enterprises.

Mail Order Business - Germany

Nieschlag, Robert. Die versandgeschäfte in Deutschland, ihre volkswirtschaft-
lichen funktionen und betriebswirtschaftlichen gestaltungen. 49pp.
Berlin, Hanseatische Verlagsanstalt Hamburg. 1936. (Sonderhefte des
Instituts für Konjunkturforschung, nr. 39)
    A study of the mail order business in Germany, its economic aspects and
business organization. The main agricultural products considered are butter
from Schleswig-Holstein, honey, coffee, tea and cocoa.

Marketing Fruits and Vegetables

Solomon, J. H. Controlled distribution of fruits and vegetables. 73pp.
New York city [Printed by the Craft linotypers, inc.] 1935. 280.3 So4
    "The consignment method of selling, a method which was in favor in
the past, is the best method of all. The writer has attempted to ad-

Just this method to present day conditions. Today, almost everyone
in the fruit and vegetable industry would prefer to do business on a
consignment basis, if he could be assured of proper distribution. The
consignment method of selling, in the long run, is the safest and most
logical way of marketing.

"Common sense dictates the immediate adoption of a plan of controlled
distribution. This plan would not only lead the fruit and vegetable industry out of its labyrinth of difficulties, but would provide the producer with his long sought opportunity for securing returns which would
be both profitable and commensurate with the great service he is rendering in providing the consumer with his daily needs of fruits and
vegetables." - Conclusion.

The Middle Way

Dickinson, John. Hold fast the middle way; an outline of economic challenges
and alternatives. 238pp. Boston, Little, Brown, and company, 1935.
280.12 D56

"This book advocates a middle-of-the-road policy in the sense of a
policy which gives due weight to all, and not merely some, of the factors
and forces which must work together if we are to recover national prosperity. It is written in the conviction that we shall be heading for ruin
if we turn back to an old policy which closed its eyes to all but one group
of interests, or on the other hand turn aside to new policies which utterly
ignore those interests in favor of others equally one-sided.

"There is, of course, no merit in a middle-of-the-road policy merely
as such. It may, for example, mean nothing but compromise with a great
evil, because we are not strong enough or brave enough to combat it. In
that sense a middle-of-the-road policy is a policy of cowardice or resignation.

"But to-day many of our most important national problems are no longer
the simple ones of tilting at devils. The greatest evils from which we
suffer are impersonal evils resulting from maladjustment between forces
and interests which have each a legitimate contribution to make to our
common life and which must all be permitted to make those contributions in
proper proportions if every one of us is not to suffer. Under such circumstances the middle-of-the-road policy which holds open, for each such force
and interest, its proper sphere, and protects it resolutely against en-
croachment from the others, is not merely the best but the only method of
attacking the evils which need to be attacked. A policy which simply backs
one interest against another simply substitutes one evil for another. To
combat evil we need to combat excess.

"The proponents of every interest - be it labor, capital, home trade,
foreign trade, large industry, small industry, borrowers, creditors, government spending, government saving - always tend to push for policies and programs frankly destructive of opposing interests. This is perfectly natural.
And yet in the kind of world we live in to-day all these interests have
their degrees of usefulness which must be fitted together and readjusted
from time to time for the better functioning of our common life. The
program which favors one set of interests exclusively may have the merit
of being logical and forthright, but it will not lead to national well-

being however clean-cut and definite it may look on paper.

"We have passed beyond the time, if ever there was a time, for the simple solution of merely backing one force against another. The danger is that in the clash of contending interests victories will be won by sheer pressure which will leave the victorious force to find that by having destroyed its complementary force it has crippled itself fatally. What we need to-day is a policy which will keep opposite forces at work for their own good as well as for the common good. That kind of policy is what is here advocated as a policy of middle-of-the-road." - Introduction.

Money and Credit

Durbin, E. F. M. The problem of credit policy. 267pp. London, Chapman & Hall ltd. [1935] 284 D93

"This is one of the few books which every serious inquirer into the monetary problem ought to read. Mr. Durbin's first volume, 'Purchasing Power and Trade Depression,' published in 1933, after criticising the views of Major Douglas, Mr. J. A. Hobson and the Austrian school, hinted at a constructive solution. The details of this solution, and the main principles of policy deducible from it, are elaborated in this book.

"It is not an easy book. The more difficult and abstract reasoning comes near the beginning, and the part which will be most intelligible to the non-specialist reader near the end. There are also a rather large number of misprints. Nevertheless, the reader who surmounts these obstacles will be brought close to the heart of the problem. For Mr. Durbin possesses not only a grasp of his subject, which is most uncommon among writers on money, but a levelheadedness which is almost unique. In particular, his new book, like his first, has two shining merits. It recognises, first, that a problem of maintaining the level of general purchasing power exists in the modern economic world; and secondly, that the majority of cost incomes must nowadays be taken as fixed at least in the short period.

"Mr. Durbin first clears the ground by laying down 'three introductory propositions': first, that if all production were conducted by a single trust, total consumers' incomes must be equal to total costs; secondly, that where there is more than one production unit, consumers' incomes can be equal to the cost of final output; and thirdly, that the accumulation of real capital is also compatible with monetary equilibrium in the same sense. It is most useful to have these three axioms clearly established and expressed. Next, Mr. Durbin traces out in detail the process by which an artificially induced credit expansion and credit contraction work themselves out. His analysis goes beyond the orthodox analysis of inflation and deflation in one important respect: it assumes that the various factors of production are not completely mobile, and it attempts to bring their 'velocity' of movement into relation which the velocity of circulation of money. Mr. Durbin concludes, from the first part of this analysis, that the demand for capital depends much less on the rate of interest than on the profitability of production in the consumption trades; and consequently that an increase in consumers' expenditure will normally lead to an increase and not a decrease in the demand for capital...

"Next comes the really controversial part of the argument: the choice of policy. Three suggested policies, in Mr. Durbin's opinion, are worth consideration. First there is Professor Hayek's proposal for a constant effective flow of money. Mr. Durbin has little difficulty in showing that if this is interpreted as meaning a constant flow of money against all goods - consumers', capital and intermediate - then, in the event of new stages being inserted in the production process, a deflationary contraction of consumers' expenditure will result.

"Secondly, there is the proposal to stabilise the price level of final output. Mr. Durbin thinks that this is impossible so long as present banking and financial institutions are preserved. But it is interesting to find that his arguments against price stabilization are different from those made familiar by Professor Robbins and Professor Hayek. They think that the issue of the new producers' credits necessary to stabilise prices must lead to investment in excessive capital which afterwards has to be liquidated. Mr. Durbin argues that the expansion of producers' credits must result in increased profits in the consumption trades, since costs are falling, that this again must increase the demand for producers' credits, that in the end prices must rise, and that if the banks then try to stop them by contracting their new credits, profit expectations will be disappointed and a depression will set in.

"This argument raises many questions. In the first place, it assumes that the rate of monetary expansion in these circumstances must exceed the rate of growth of physical output. This seems at least doubtful. Secondly, it assumes that when business men are expecting rising profits, a mere maintenance of profits will lead to business recession. This also seems arguable. Thirdly, and most important, it assumes that the money incomes of the factors of production cannot be raised so as to offset the fall in costs per unit. Mr. Durbin makes this assumption explicit; and it leads him to consider the possibility of stabilising prices by consumers' credits instead of producers' credits. His investigation into the effects of such a policy is one of the most interesting, illuminating and original parts of the book. It leads him to the striking conclusion that the price level can in fact be stabilised by the issue of free consumers' credits, and in no other way; but that the issue of such credits under our present banking system is impossible.

"Given existing financial institutions, Mr. Durbin's plan is to stabilise 'consumers' income per head.' This at any rate is what he says. It appears at times from the argument, however, and from his elaborate and interesting discussion of the practical execution of his policy, that what he really wants to stabilise is consumers' (including savers') outlay on final output of consumers' and capital goods. Is not this really what advocates of stable prices, neutral money and constant incomes are all getting at? For, given fixed cost incomes, it is surely this which would ensure monetary equilibrium. Whether Mr. Durbin has discovered the ideal way of reaching it, scientifically or practically, economists will not decide in a hurry. But he has certainly done further invaluable service in clearing away some more of the thickets of obscurity that still surround the subject." - The Economist (London) July 27, 1935, pp. 179-180.

Potatoes - England

Makings, S. M. Final report on potato production and marketing in the East
Midlands 1932/4 together with a note on retail distribution and consumption. 124pp. [Nottingham] 1935. (Midland agricultural college, Sutton
Bonington, Loughborough. Survey studies - 3) 281.9 M58
Part I, Costs and returns; Part II, Potato consumption, Part III, Summary and conclusions. Appendices (1) Sunshine and rainfall 1932 and 1933;
(2) Factors used for standard charges; (3) Displacement costs.

Radio and the Farmer

Radio institute of the audible arts. Radio and the farmer, by Edmund deS.
Brunner... and a symposium on the relation of radio to rural life. 65pp.
New York [1935] 335 R112
Bibliography, p. 65.
Contains in addition to the symposium a section giving an abstract
of typical agricultural programs offered by the U. S. Dept. of Agri-
culture, the Land Grant colleges and other educational institutions.

Recovery and Reform

Lippmann, Walter. The new imperative. 52pp. New York, The Macmillan
company, 1935. 280.12 L66
"In their relations to agriculture and to industry there is no sharp
break between the two Administrations, [Hoover and Roosevelt] Both
have recognized that the agricultural staples have unsheltered prices
whereas most manufactured goods have sheltered prices, and that this
produces a disparity which it is a function of government to correct.
The superior position of industry lies in the fact that it can benefit
by the tariff, that much of it is under a centralized control in which
prices can be maintained by regulating the supply through curtailment
of production. The agricultural staples, on the other hand, cannot
without special devices take advantage of tariffs, and the farmers are
the most highly individualistic and competitive of all producers.
President Hoover made many attempts to remedy this disparity. He increased the tariff on farm products. He used government money in an
effort to control the supply offered in the markets. He advised the
farmers to curtail production, and he contemplated the government rental
or purchase of marginal lands in order permanently to reduce production.
The Roosevelt agricultural policy has followed those same principles.
It has used government money to regulate the supply offered for sale.
It has supplemented Mr. Hoover's advice to curtail production by levying a tax to pay farmers who follow the advice, and it is withdrawing
marginal lands permanently. Both Presidents recognized that a satisfactory domestic solution of the farm problem is very unlikely; both
have wanted to see a revival of foreign markets; neither was able or
willing to expand agricultural exports by reducing the tariff on industrial goods...
"In rough fashion, this covers the ground usually marked out as the
recovery program. I do not see how one can fail to conclude that in
all essential matters of policy - dealing with monetary management,

the budget, the agricultural disparity, and industrial 'stabilization' -
there has been no break in principle, and that the Roosevelt measures
are a continuous evolution of the Hoover measures.

"What about the reforms? In one sense the most radical of all the
reforms are these very recovery measures themselves: the acceptance by
the government of responsibility for recovery, and the corollaries of
that - the resort to monetary management, the use of government credit,
the expansion of government enterprise, and the organization of agriculture and of industry under government auspices for the control of production and of supply in the markets. These mark great changes in a
political system which until 1929 was committed to the general doctrine
of laissez faire.

"The measures which are specifically called the 'reforms' are distinguished from the others by the fact that, except as a response to
the challenge of popular discontent, they were not dictated by the
emergency and might have been imposed later and in more leisurely
fashion.

"The reforms extend into new fields the regulation of private enterprises on the one hand, and the expansion of government enterprises on
the other...

"In the present Administration we come soon, however, to regulations
which are novel and radical. In the Securities Act and in the Stock Exchange Act and in certain parts of the Banking Act of 1933, the orbit
of public authority is enlarged. In substance, these reforms lay down
the principle that corporations financed by public subscription are publicly accountable...

"In addition to this extension of the regulatory functions of government, there has been an extension of government enterprise. A part of
it is simply a development of the conservation movement. Reforestation,
measures against soil erosion, the protection of watercourses are not
new in principle: it has long been recognized that there were certain
kinds of capital investment which, because they could not be profitable
to private enterprise, had to be undertaken collectively. Mr. Roosevelt
has, however, made a departure in at least two important directions.
The first is represented by the Tennessee Valley Authority: here collective enterprise has been deliberately undertaken for the purpose of making a competitive demonstration against the electric utility companies.
The second is the social insurance program: here the federal government
enters a field heretofore left to individual or local action.

"It would be an exaggeration to say that either of these Roosevelt
reforms represents a clean break with the past...

"I hold that the transition from automatism to the deliberate government of the main elements of the modern economy is already so far advanced
that it is impossible to retrace our steps. But I hold also that a historic transition of this kind can be effected safely only if those who
have the experience to appreciate its difficulties participate sincerely
in guiding the people...

"If we are not to be swallowed by an emperious state socialism in
some one of its many possible forms, then we have to govern successfully
this capitalist democracy. Ungoverned, it will not drift through stormy

seas into safe harbors. Those who say that it cannot be governed without
sacrificing personal liberties to the authority of the state are in effect
saying that our civilization is doomed. I do not believe them. They
have never given the problem their undivided attention. They cannot see
the way because they have not the will...

"So it is with those who believe in the fatalism of human affairs and
the impossibility of human intervention. It is imperative that we find
a true balance between liberty and authority in the modern state...

"We must answer the question that young men put to us. We must tell
them that they will have to manage the social order. We must call them to
the study, not warn them away from it, of how to achieve the healthy balance of a well ordered commonwealth. We must call them to the task of
preserving the integrity of our civilization as against proletarianism
and plutocracy and the fatal diseases of concentrated power and concentrated wealth. We must call them to the defense of freedom, now imperiled
throughout the world, by showing them not only its value but the method
of its defense. We must dedicate them by rededicating ourselves to the
promise of American life which is that men can govern a state in order
to enlarge and to preserve the rights of men."

Rice - India

Visva-Bharati. Rural studies, nos. 1, 2 and 3.   Three village economic studies on rice. 1. Thirty-eight years of rice yields. 2. Varieties and
yields of rice in Penuria Mauza. 3. The rice industry in lower Birbhum,
by Hashim Amir Ali... assisted by Tara Krishna Basu... and Jitendranath
Talukdar. 45pp. [Calcutta] 1934.   281.29 V82

Rural Economy

Burban, E. Les principes fondamentaux de l'économie rurale familiale.
Édité par l'auteur. 211pp. [Vannes, Imp. Lafolye et J. de Lamarzelle,
1934] 281 B89
A study of rural economy, of the laws that regulate the interrelation
of agricultural activities, and their relation to other activities. The
author draws attention to the differences that exist between rural economy
and the economy of the industrial or commercial enterprise, and points
out that the former cannot be regulated by the theorist or the legislator in
the interest of monetary gain. To him rural economy is a vast field of
special and localized values of infinite diversity. He discusses the
aims of agriculture and the means and methods of achieving them, by
various types of farming, by the use of capital, by material means,
systems of cultivation and the utilization and sale of agricultural products. He discusses briefly agricultural syndicalism, cooperation, insurance, credit, export and the tariff, labor and wages, the return from the
family farm and its taxation, and the choice of a location on which to
establish a family farm.

Rural Life Conference - Kansas

Kansas rural life conference. Proceedings, 1st, 1935. annual conference.
46pp., mimeogr. Manhattan, Kan., 1935. 281.29 K13
Sponsored by the Collegiate 4-H club of Kansas State college.
Partial contents: Social adjustment, by Dr. E. L. Kirkpatrick; Opportunity in agriculture for farm youth, by Eugene Merritt; Adjustments in
agriculture, by L. E. Call; and What Kansas rural youth can contribute
to better rural living, by Dr. E. L. Kirkpatrick.

Social Economics

Essays in social economics in honor of Jessica Blanche Peixotto. 363pp.
Berkeley, Calif., University of California press, 1935. 280 Es7
Foreword by Wesley C. Mitchell.
Partial contents: Jessica Blanche Peixotto, by Henry Rand Hatfield;
Psychiatry and the social sciences: a critical evaluation, by Frederick
H. Allen; A rational old age security program, by Barbara Nachtrieb
Armstrong; The growth of care of the indigent sick and aged as a function of government in California; by Malcolm M. Davisson; A Chinese
green crop society, by Sidney D. Gamble; John Ruskin - John A. Hobson,
by Ewald T. Grether; British health and unemployment insurance and
standards of living, by Emily H. Huntington; The self-help cooperatives
in California, by Clark Kerr and Paul S. Taylor; Industrial change and
unemployment, by Frederick C. Mills; Unemployment relief in California
under the State Emergency Relief Administration, by Sanford A. Mosk;
National planning for recreation in European countries, by Emily Noble
Plehn; The problem of social investigation - the method of Sidney and
Beatrice Webb, by Webster Vennier; Socio-economic conditions in relation
to infant mortality in Berkeley, by Frances M. Welch; and A list of
Professor Peixotto's published writings.

Sugar - Europe

Pennock, J. A. La question du sucre en Europe depuis la guerre mondiale...
254pp. Paris, J.-B. Baillière et fils, 1935. 281.365 P38
Bibliography, pp. 247-250.
This is a detailed study of the development of the sugar industry
in Europe and its relations with the cane sugar industry. After a brief
survey of pre-war conditions including the influence of the Continental
Blockade and the Convention of Brussels in 1902 the author concentrates
his attention on the post-war development of the sugar industry. Decrease in production immediately following the war, the influence of
protection and the tariff policy of the different European countries,
world surplus production and its effects, and the Chadbourne plan are
discussed. Appendices contain the text of the Convention of Brussels
and of the Chadbourne plan.

London. University. School of Slavonic and East European studies. Monograph no.9. The end of rationing and the standard of living in the Soviet Union. 28pp. London, Nov. 1935. 360.9 L8i2 no.9.

Viticulture - Control of Production

Jayat de Wecker, Geneviève. La limitation des plantations de la vigne. Préface de Léon Douarche. 112pp. Paris, Librairie du recueil Sirey, 1934. 261.395 G25
     Bibliography, pp. [141]-142.
     This is a historical survey of control of production of vines and wine with special reference to France. Examples are given from the history of ancient Rome as well as of modern measures adopted in Spain, Greece, Luxembourg, Hungary, Portugal, Rumania, and Tunisia.

Wheat - South Africa

Tomlinson, F. R. Expansion of wheat production in South Africa 1910 to 1934. 32pp. Pretoria, Printed by the Government printer, 1935. (South Africa, Dept. of agriculture. Science bulletin no. 145) 24 So84S no.145
     "South Africa. Dept. of agriculture and forestry. Stellenbosch-Elsenburg series no. 23."
     "Wheat production is one of the oldest agricultural industries in South Africa, and one which has probably received more support from governments than any other agricultural enterprise. Consumers complain that the cost of bread is unduly high because of the high price of wheat, whereas producers complain that prices received for wheat are not high enough to cover cost of production and leave a fair margin of profit.
     "During the past few years the total production of wheat, as well as the area under wheat, has increased rapidly. Whereas formerly the domestic production of wheat supplied a little more than half of the domestic demand, only a small percentage is still imported. At the present rate of increase our normal production will in the near future suffice the domestic needs.
     "The average yield of wheat in South Africa is lower than in any other important wheat-producing country, and because of our variable climatic conditions the fluctuations in the yield per morgen are extremely vigorous. This naturally tends to make wheat farming a very speculative enterprise. Wheat is at present produced and the production is being expanded in some areas which from the production standpoint are much better adapted to other agricultural enterprises.
     "It is the purpose in the present study to present in chart form

the expansion of our wheat industry in the country as a whole as well as in the important areas and districts. The degree of fluctuation in wheat yields will also be determined for various areas.

"Changes in price relationships are the basic factors underlying the great expansion in our wheat industry. An analysis of these is extremely important in view of the probable effects on the wheat industry of any further expansion in wheat production. It seems definite that the present wheat prices paid to producers cannot be maintained should our normal production exceed the domestic requirements. Only by changes in these price relationships will the present upward tendency in our total wheat production be checked." - Introduction.

Woman on the Farm - France

Trouard Riolle, Yvonne. Les activités féminines en agriculture. 267pp. Paris, Éditions Spes [1935] 281.2 T75
    "Quelques indications bibliographiques de technique agricole pour une fermière cultivée", pp. [256]-261.
    The author discusses the rôle of the woman on the farm in connection with the family life, the work in the house and on the farm, and the social life of the community. Part II deals with the relation of French agricultural legislation to the woman, her agricultural training and apprenticeship. And Part III deals with the professional organization of the farm women.

BIBLIOGRAPHIES

Collective farming, 1930-1935; a selected list of references, compiled by Hazel E. Workman. Library, Bureau of agricultural economics, U. S. Department of agriculture. [Washington, D. C.] Jan. 30, 1936. 19pp. Typewritten.
    May be borrowed for copying.

Livestock financing in the United States; selected references to material published 1915-1935, compiled by Katharine Jacobs, under the direction of Mary G. Lacy, librarian, Bureau of agricultural economics. 57pp. December. 1935. (U. S. Dept. of agriculture. Bureau of agricultural economics. Agricultural economics bibliography no. 62. Supersedes bibliography no. 7) mimeogr.

References on the mountaineers of the southern Appalachians, by Everett E. Edwards... Division of statistical and historical research, Bureau of agricultural economics. 148pp. December 1935. (U. S. Dept. of agriculture. Library. Bibliographical contributions no. 28) mimeogr.

Studies of family living in the United States and other countries: an analysis of material and method, by Faith M. Williams... and Carle C. Zimmerman. 617pp. [Washington, U. S. Govt. print. off., 1935] (U. S. Dept. of agriculture. Miscellaneous publication no. 223)
    The U. S. Dept. of Agriculture, Bureau of Home Economics in cooperation with the Social Science Research Council and the Institute of Pacific Relations.
    Bibliography, pp. 68-452.

SELECTED LIST OF RECENT REVIEWS

Compiled by M. I. Herb

Arkin, Herbert, and Colton, R. R. An outline of statistical methods, business, education, social and physical sciences, etc. [c1934] (College
outline series)
Reviewed by Norma L. Goudy in Social Serv. Rev. 9 (3): 588-589.
September 1935.

Astor, Waldorf Astor, 2d viscount. The agricultural dilemma: a report of
a. enquiry organised by Viscount Astor and Mr. B. Seebohm Rowntree.
1935.
Reviewed in Economist 121 (4808): 756-757. Oct. 19, 1935 in an
article entitled "Back to the Land?"
Reviewed in Statist 127 (3020): 46. Jan. 11, 1936 in an article entitled "Land Settlement."

Beard, C. A. An economic interpretation of the Constitution of the United
States. 1935.
Reviewed by L. W. Lancaster in Amer. Acad. Polit. and Social Sci.
Ann. 183: 283-284. January 1936.

Chase, Stuart. Government in business. 1935.
Reviewed by M. J. V. in Sociol. and Social Research 20 (3): 272-274.
January-February 1936.
Reviewed in Economist 122 (4819): 17. Jan. 4, 1936.

Columbia University. Commission on economic reconstruction. Economic reconstruction; report of the Columbia university commission. 1934.
Reviewed by F. A. Knox in Canad. Jour. Econ. and Polit. Sci. 1 (4):
621-625. November 1935.

Cornish, N. H. Marketing of manufactured goods. [1935]
Reviewed by R. F. Breyer in Amer. Acad. Polit. and Social Sci. Ann.
181: 207,208. September 1935.
Reviewed by S. P. Dobbs in Econ. Jour. 45 (179): 565, 566. September
1935.

Converse, P. D. Elements of marketing. Rev. ed. 1935.
Reviewed by W. L. White in Natl. Marketing Rev. 1 (2): 168-169.
Fall 1935.

Duddy, E. A., and Revzan, D. A. The grain supply area of the Chicago market.
[1934] (Chicago. University. School of commerce and administration.
Studies in business administration, v. 4, no. 4)
Reviewed by Frank Robotka in Jour. Farm Econ. 17 (4): 767-770.
November 1935.

Economic essays in honor of Wesley Clair Mitchell. 1935.
    Reviewed by Hans Neisser in Amer. Acad. Polit. and Social Sci. Ann.
    183:279-280. January 1936.

Emeny, Brooks. The strategy of raw materials; a study of America in peace
    and war. 1934.
        Reviewed by W. E. Ekblaw in Econ. Geogr. 12 (1): 106-107. January
    1936.

Great Britain. Unemployment insurance statutory committee. Unemployment in-
    surance act, 1934. Report of the Unemployment insurance statutory com-
    mittee, in accordance with section 20 of the Unemployment Insurance Act,
    1934, on the question of the insurance against unemployment of persons
    engaged in employment in agriculture. 1935. ([Parliament. Papers by
    command] Cmd. 4786)
        Reviewed by W. McM. in Social Serv. Rev. 9 (3): 607-609. September
    1935.

Greaves, I. C. Modern production among backward peoples. [1935] (Half-
    title: London school of economics and political science. Studies in
    economics and commerce, no. 5)
        Reviewed by M. L. Ballinger in South African Jour. Econ. 3(3): 584-
    587. December 1935.

Haight, F. A. French import quotas; a new instrument of commercial policy.
    1935. (Half-title: London school of economics and political science.
    Studies in economics and commerce. no.6)
        Reviewed by E. L. Hargreaves in Econ. Jour. 45 (180): 761-762.
    December 1935.
        Reviewed by H. W. M. in Roy. Statis. Soc. Jour. (n.s.) 98 (4): 740-
    742. 1935.
        Reviewed by M. Pelkowitz in South African Jour. Econ. 3 (3): 593-594.
    December 1935.

Hardy, C. O. The Warren-Pearson price theory. 1935. (The Institute of
    economics of the Brookings institution. Pamphlet no. 17)
        Reviewed by K. B. Walton in Econ. Forum 3 (3): 359-363. winter 1936.

Hawk, E. Q. Economic history of the South. 1934.
        Reviewed by M. B. Scheler in The People's Money 2 (2): 94-95.
    January 1936.

Holtzclaw, H. F. The principles of marketing. [1935]
        Reviewed by R. F. Breyer in Amer. Acad. Polit, and Social Sci. Ann.
    183:278-279. January 1936.
        Reviewed by W. P. Mortenson in Jour. Farm Econ. 17 (4): 770-772.
    November 1935.
        Reviewed by W. L. White in Natl. Marketing Rev. 1 (2): 168-169.
    Fall 1935.

Howard, L. E. Labour in agriculture; an international survey. 1935.
    Reviewed in Economist 121 (4818): 1315. Dec. 28, 1935.

International conference of agricultural economist. Proceedings of the third
    international conference... 1935.
    Reviewed by V. F. in Monthly Bull. Agr. Econ. and Sociol. [reprint
    from Internatl. Rev. Agr.] 26 (12): 448E-453E. December 1935.

Jesness, C. B., and Nowell, R. I., and associates. A program for land use in
    northern Minnesota; a type study in land utilization. 1935.
    Reviewed by E. A. Duddy in Jour. Business Univ. Chicago 8 (4): 403-404.
    October 1935.

Johnson, C. S., Embree, E. R., and Alexander, W. W. The collapse of cotton
    tenancy, a summary of field studies & statistical surveys 1933-35. 1935.
    Reviewed by C. A. M. Ewing in Southwest. Social Sci. Quart. 16 (3):
    87-88. December 1935.
    Reviewed by Cecil Holland in Survey Graphic 24 (12): 622-623. December
    1935.

Jones, C. F. Economic geography. [c1935]
    Reviewed by A. E. Parkins in Econ. Geogr. 11 (3): 324. July 1935.

Kerr, Clark, and Taylor, P. S. The self-help cooperatives in California.
    (Essays in social economics, in honor of Jessica Blanche Peixotto.
    Berkeley, 1935, p. 191-225)
    Reviewed in Monthly Labor Rev. 41 (6): 1504-1509. December 1935.

Knapp, W. H. C. World dislocation and world recovery; agriculture as the
    touchstone of the economic world events. 1935.
    Reviewed by S. D. Neumark in South African Jour. Econ. 3 (3): 596.
    December 1935.

Kolb, J. H., and Brunner, E. de S. A study of rural society; its organization
    and changes. [1935]
    Reviewed by C. C. Zimmerman in Amer. Acad. Polit. and Social Sci. Ann.
    183:301-302. January 1936.

Layton, Sir W. T., and Crowther, Geoffrey. An introduction to the study of
    prices. 1935.
    Reviewed by H. A. Shannon in South African Jour. Econ. 3 (3): 595.
    December 1935.

League of Nations, Economic committee. Considerations of the present evolution
    of agricultural protectionism. [1935] (League of Nations, Publications.
    II. Economic and financial. 1935. II. B. 7)
    Reviewed by S. Neumark in South African Jour. Econ. 3 (3): 422-424.
    September 1935.

Lippincott, B. E., ed. Government control of the economic order; a symposium. 1935.
   Reviewed in FERA Research Library, Relief notices, no. 74, Oct. 21, 1935.

Loeb, Harold, and others. The chart of plenty; a study of America's product capacity based on the findings of the national survey of potential product capacity. 1935.
   Reviewed by Edward Berman in Amer. Acad. Polit, and Social Sci, Ann. 183:. 274-275. January 1936.
   Reviewed by M. J. V. in Sociol. and Social Research 20 (3): 271-272. January-February 1936

Lorimer, Frank, and Osborn, Frederick. Dynamics of population; social and biological significance of changing birth rates in the United States.
   Reviewed by F. H. Hankins in Quart. Jour. Econ. 50 (1): 164-173. November 1935.

Lyon, L. S., Homan, P. T., and others. The National recovery administration: an analysis and appraisal. 1935. (Half-title: The Institute of economics of the Brookings institution. Publication no. 60)
   Reviewed by R. S. Vaile in Jour. Farm Econ. 17 (4): 763-765. November 1935.

Minnesota. Committee on land utilization. Land utilization in Minnesota; a state program for the cut-over lands. Final report... 1934.
   Reviewed by David Weeks in Jour. Land & Pub. Utility Econ. 11 (4): 426. November 1935.

Morgan, O. S., ed. Agricultural systems of Middle Europe; a symposium. 1933.
   Reviewed by E. A. Duddy in Jour. Polit. Econ. 43 (6): 838-840 December 1935.

Moulton, H. G. The formation of capital. 1935, (Half-title: The Institute of economics of the Brookings institution. Publication no. 59)
   Reviewed by A. W. Marget in Jour. Farm Econ. 17 (4): 756-760. November 1935.

Moulton, H. G. Income and economic progress. 1935. (The Institute of economics of the Brookings institution. Publication no. 68)
   Reviewed in Northwest. Miller 184 (8): 728, 730, 732. Dec. 11, 1935.
   Reviewed by A.E.S. in Fed. Counc. Churches of Christ in Amer. Dept. Research and Ed. Inform. Serv. 14 (37): 1-2. Nov. 16, 1935.

Ohlin, Bertil. Interregional and international trade. 1933. (Harvard Economics Studies, no. 39)
   Reviewed by G. R. W. in Roy. Statis. Soc. Jour. (n.s.) 98 (4): 739-740. 1935.

...ord. University. Agricultural economics research institute. The Agricultural register, 1934-35. 1935.
Reviewed in Econon. Jour. 45 (179): 503, 554. September 1935.

Renne, R. R. The tariff on dairy products. 1933. [Tariff research Committee. Agricultural tariff series. no.2]
Reviewed by H. E. Erdman in Jour. Farm Econ. 17 (4): 765-767. November 1935.

Roos, C. F. Dynamic economics; theoretical and statistical studies of demand, production and prices. [1934] (Monograph of the Cowles commission for research in economics, no. 1)
Reviewed by J. P. Dalton in South African Jour. Econ. 3 (3): 404-408. September 1935.

Rorty, M. B. Tobacco under the AAA. 1935. (Half-title: The Institute of Economics of the Brookings institution. Publication no. 62)
Reviewed by C. C. Zimmerman in Amer. Acad. Polit. and Social Sci.Ann. 18 272-273. January 1936.

Schultz, T. W. The tariffs on barley, oats and corn. 1933. [Tariff research committee. Agricultural tariffs series no. 3]
Reviewed by H. E. Erdman in Jour. Farm Econ. 17 (4): 765-767. November 1935.

Taylor, A. E. The new deal and foreign trade. 1935.
Reviewed by E. M. Winslow in Amer. Acad. Polit. and Social Sci. Ann. 183: 272. January 1936.
Reviewed by A. A. Dowell in Jour. Farm Econ. 17 (4): 755-756. November 1935.

Thornthwaite, C. W., and Slentz, Helen I. Internal migration in the United States. 1934. (Half-title: Study of population redistribution. Bull. no. 1. Industrial research department. Wharton school of finance and commerce. University of Pennsylvania)
Reviewed by C. Horace Hamilton in Amer. Statis. Assoc. Jour. 30 (192): 765-766. December 1935.

Willcox, C. W. Nations can live at home. [1935]
Reviewed by L. F. Easterbrook in New Statesman and Nation (n.s.) 11 (255): 56. Jan. 11, 1936.

Williams, Tom. Labour's way to use the land. 1935.
Reviewed by L. F. Easterbrook in New Statesman and Nation (n.s.) 11 (255): 56, 58. Jan. 11, 1936.

Zimmerman, C. C., and Frampton, V. E. Family and society; a study of the sociology of reconstruction. 1935.
Reviewed by G. B. M. in Sociol. and Social Research 20 (3): 275. January-February 1936.

Economic in Character

Compiled by Katharine Jacobs

Statistical Bulletin*

50. Car-lot shipments of fruits and vegetables from stations in the United
     States for the calendar years 1932 and 1933, prepared by the Bureau
     of agricultural economics. 150pp. January 1936.

Technical Bulletin*

497. Utilization and cost of power on Mississippi and Arkansas delta planta-
      tions, by L. A. Reynoldson... W. R. Humphries, S. R. Speelman and
      E. W. McComas... and W. H. Youngman. 46pp. December 1935.
          Issued in cooperation with the Agricultural Experiment Stations of
      Mississippi and Arkansas

Addresses and Radio Talks of the Secretary and Assistant Secretary*

Secretary Wallace

Agriculture: a local activity and a national problem; address... at a meeting
     sponsored by the Indiana farm bureau at Indianapolis, Indiana, February
     12, 1936. 19pp., mimeogr.

Remarks [concerning the decision of the Supreme court in the Hoosac mills
     case] over the National farm and home hour... January 28, 1936. 5pp.,
     mimeogr.

Assistant Secretary Wilson

Another chapter in agriculture; an address... at the observance of Farmers'
     week at the Northwest school of agriculture, Crookston, Minn., on
     February 4, 1936. 27pp., mimeogr.

Publications of the Bureau of Agricultural Economics (Mimeographed)**

Agricultural policy and the economist, by A. G. Black... Address, annual
     meeting, American farm economic association, New York City, N. Y.,
     December 30, 1935. 8pp. [1936?]
Barley handbook. Information on malting barley including official standards
     and a discussion of their use and application, comp. by the Grain
     standards educational committee. 24pp. January 1936.
Cost of production of sweet corn; data from studies in 6 states, selected
     years, 1919-33. Comp. from official sources by H. W. Hawthorne... 13pp.
     January 1936.
          "Sources of data"; p. 13.

*Requests for these publications should be addressed to the Office of Informa-
tion, U. S. Department of Agriculture, Washington, D.C.
**These publications are issued in small editions for immediate use in
official work and are not for general distribution.

-219-

Driven-in receipts of livestock 1935. 28pp. February 1936.

Farm women in fiction: a radio talk by Caroline B. Sherman... delivered in the Home demonstration radio hour, February 5, 1936. 3pp.

Feed crops, corn-oats-barley-hay. Total livestock outlook charts for use with the agricultural outlook for 1936. 31pp. November 1935.

Flax, soybeans, peanuts and cottonseed outlook charts for use with the agricultural outlook for 1936. 20pp. November 1935.

Fruits and vegetables in the program of reciprocal trade agreements, by L. A. Wheeler. 8pp.

 Address, annual business meeting of the American fruit and vegetable snippers association, Chicago, Illinois, January 15, 1936.

Fruits: apples, citrus, peaches, etc. outlook charts for use with the agricultural outlook for 1936. 53pp. November 1935.

Index numbers of prices paid by farmers for commodities bought for family maintenance and for commodities bought to be used in production. 2pp. Jan.29, 1936.

Livestock financing in the United States; selected references to material published 1915 - 1935. Comp. by Katharine Jacobs under the direction of Mary G. Lacy, Librarian, Bureau of agricultural economics. 57pp. Dec., 1935. (Agricultural economics bibliography no. 62. Supersedes Bibliograph no. 7)

The margin between farm prices and retail prices of ten foods, by Frederick V. Waugh. 11pp., tables, charts. March 1935. Data added December 1935.

Marketing Texas vegetables (beans, beets, broccoli, carrots, cucumbers, green corn, peas, spinach, mixed vegetables) Brief review of the 1934-35 season, by W. D. Googe. 26pp. (Issued in cooperation with Texas Department of agriculture, Markets and warehouse division)

A national program of farm management research, by C. L. Holmes... Address, annual meeting, American farm economic association, New York city, N. Y., December 30, 1935. 12pp.

The outlook for potato prices in 1936. 2pp. Feb. 7, 1936.

Potatoes, and truck crops outlook charts for use with the agricultural outlook for 1936. 43pp. November 1935.

Ratio of assessed value to consideration in bona fide transfers of farm real estate. Data for 286 selected counties, 1933 or earlier years. 102pp. January 1936.

Regulations of the Secretary of agriculture governing the inspection and certification of rice. Effective January 15, 1936. 14pp.

A review of the 1935 Arizona fall lettuce season, by A. E. Prugh. 6pp. Jan. 14 1936.

Rice, dry beans, and broomcorn outlook charts for use with the agricultural outlook for 1936. 13pp. November 1935.

Rural zoning: controlling land utilization under the police power, by C. I. Hendrickson... Address, annual meeting, American farm economic association, New York, December 27-30, 1935. 14pp.

Statistics relating to the grapefruit industry 1935, comp. by A. C. Edwards... 25pp. January 1936.   FS CF -85

Studies of terminal marketing problems, by Frederick V. Waugh... Address, annual meeting, National league of wholesale fresh fruit and vegetable distributors, Baltimore, January 8, 1936. 7pp.

A study of ranch organization and operation in North-central Texas. 73pp.
January 1936. (Issued in cooperation with the Bureau of animal industry.)
Tax delinquency of rural real estate in 15 Illinois counties, 1928-33. 10pp.
Jan. 14, 1936.

    This survey was made under a civil works project administered by the
Bureau of Agricultural Economics, assisted by the Agricultural Experiment
Station of Illinois.
Tax delinquency of rural real estate in eight Kentucky counties, 1928 - 33.
10pp. Jan. 16, 1936.

    This survey was made under a civil works project administered by the
Bureau of Agricultural Economics, assisted by the Agricultural Experiment
Station of Kentucky.
Tax delinquency of rural real estate in seven New Jersey counties, 1928-33.
11pp. Jan. 20, 1936.

    This survey was made under a civil works project administered by the
Bureau of Agricultural Economics, assisted by the Agricultural Experiment
Station of New Jersey.
Transfers of farm real estate; number of properties and acreage transferred,
by type of transfer, and average consideration in bona fide sales. Data
for 414 selected counties, for 1933 or earlier years. 115pp. Jan. 1936.
U. S. standards for California and Arizona oranges (effective January 1, 1936)
8pp. Dec. 14, 1935.
Uses and products made of corn; abstracts and references. Supplement 4, comp.
by C. Louise Phillips... and E. G. Boerner. 28pp. October 1935.
(USGSA - GI 31 - Supp. 4)

    Bibliography, pp. 25-28.
Why I want my boy to be a farmer; radio talk by O. E. Baker. 2pp. Feb. 1, 1936.
Why I want my boy to be a farmer (Excerpts from an address by Dr. O. E. Baker...
on the Farm and Home week program at the University of Wisconsin, Feb. 7,
1936) 9pp.
The world cotton situation. Part II. Cotton production in the United States
(preliminary). 67pp., tables. February 1936.

Publications of the Agricultural Adjustment Administration*

(General sugar quota regulations, series 3) Sugar consumption requirements and
quotas for the calendar year 1936. 5pp. Issued Dec. 28, 1935.
(G.S.Q.R., series 3, no. 1)
Order series - order no. 2. Order regulating the handling of oranges and grape-
fruit grown in the states of California and Arizona. Issued by the Secre-
tary of agriculture, January 4, 1936, effective 12:01 a.m., E. S. T.,
January 13, 1936. 16pp. (O-2)
Order series - order no. 3. Order regulating the handling of milk in the St.
Louis, Mo., marketing area. Issued by the Secretary of agriculture
January 30, 1936, effective 12:01 a.m., C. S. T., February 1, 1936. 12pp.
(O - 3)

---

* Requests for these publications should be addressed to the Agricultural
Adjustment Administration, U. S. Department of Agriculture, Washington, D. C.

Miscellaneous (Mimeographed)*

Organization and programs for farm young people. Excerpts from annual reports
of state and county extension agents, 1934. Prepared by... M. C. Wilson.
8pp. 1936. (Issued as U. S. Dept. of agriculture. Extension service.
Division of cooperative extension. Extension service circular 229)
Outlines of marketing agreements and licenses under the supervision of the
General crops section, agricultural adjustment administration, prepared
by William C. Cokey. 108pp. December 1935. (Issued by the Agricultural
economics section, Division of cooperative extension)
References on the mountaineers of the southern Appalachians, by Everett E.
Edwards... Division of statistical and historical research, Bureau of
agricultural economics. 148pp. December 1935. (U. S. Dept. of agriculture, Library. Bibliographical contributions no. 28)
Seasonal tendencies in wheat futures prices, by H. S. Irwin. 27pp. January
1936. (Issued by Grain futures administration)
Size of daily price range of dominant Chicago wheat future in relation to its
price, by Paul Mehl. 11pp. December 1935. (Issued by Grain futures
administration)

Radio Talks**

What kind of an industrial policy is best for agriculture: radio talk, by
Morse Salisbury... Feb. 3, 1936. 3pp., mimeogr.
What kind of foreign trade policies do American farmers want? in peace time? in
war time? A radio discussion by Morse Salisbury and Kenneth M. Gopen.
Jan. 27, 1936. 4pp., mimeogr.

U. S. RESETTLEMENT ADMINISTRATION***

Address by J. S. Lansill, assistant administrator, before Regional planning
commission of Hamilton county, Ohio, Cincinnati... February 3, 1936.
9pp., mimeogr.
    On the objectives of the U. S. Resettlement Administration.
Address of R. G. Tugwell, administrator, at a dinner of the Regional planning
commission of Hamilton county... Cincinnati, Ohio... February 3, 1936.
17pp. 1936. mimeogr.
    An account of the Resettlement Administration's work in Ohio.
Rehabilitation. Address by R. G. Tugwell, administrator, over the network of
the Columbia broadcasting system... February 6, 1936. 7pp. 1936. mimeogr.

---

*Requests for these publications should be addressed to the issuing office.
**Requests for these radio talks should be addressed to the Office of Information
Press Service, U. S. Department of Agriculture.
***Requests for these publications should be addressed to the Resettlement
Administration, Arlington Hotel, Washington, D. C.

Compiled by Mary F. Carpenter

Arizona

Arizona. College of agriculture, Agricultural extension service. Arizona
agricultural situation, 1936. 16pp. Tucson. 1936.

California

Schneider, J. B. The importance of the California truck-crop industry.
2pp 11 tables, mimeogr. Berkeley, Calif. Col. Agr. Ext. Serv. 1935.

Florida

Hawthorne, H. W., and Turlington, J. E. Economic study of absentee ownership
of citrus properties in Florida. Fla. Agr. Expt. Sta. Bull. 287, 32pp.
Gainesville. 1935.
In cooperation with the U. S. Bureau of Agricultural Economics.
Data was obtained relative to costs, returns, and general grove in-
formation from the absentee owners themselves.

Iowa

Iowa. State college of agriculture and mechanic arts, Extension service.
Iowa farm economist, v. 2, no. 1, Ames, January 1936.
Partial contents: They raised their incomes, by J. J. Wallace,
pp. 3-6; Opening foreign markets through trade agreements, by T. W.
Schultz, pp. 6-9; The consumer is the forgotten man, by I. C. Greaves,
pp. 9-11, 16; Higher prices at Kansas City, by R. C. Bentley, p.11.
Analyzing the corn-hog program, by D. A. Fitzgerald, pp. 12-15; Merchan-
dising meat, by E. L. Cady, pp. 15-16.

Mighell, Albert. Changing status of the Iowa dairy industry. Iowa Agr.
Expt. Sta. Bull. 338, pp. 363-416. Ames, 1935.
Discusses the farm dairy plant and the dairy manufacturing and dis-
tributing industries.

Louisiana

Smith, T. L., and Fry, M. R. The population of a selected "Cut-Over" area
in Louisiana. La. Agr. Expt. Sta. Bull. 268, 46pp. Baton-Rouge. 1936.
In cooperation with the F.E.R.A.
The area chosen for this study was Ward 3 in LaSalle parish. The contents of the bulletin include the chief characteristics of the population,
the economic situation, and a discussion of future prospects in the
region.

Maryland

Hurley, Ray, and DeVault, S. H. Production, marketing and consumption of
Maryland tobacco. Md. Agr. Expt. Sta. Bull. 382, 289pp. College Park,
1935.

Includes cost of marketing and production in Maryland and consumption
in foreign countries as well as in the United States.

Walker, W. P., and Hamilton, A. B.   Tax delinquency in Maryland, with special
reference to agriculture. Md. Agr. Expt. Sta. Bull. 381, pp. 155-185.
College Park. 1935.

Massachusetts

Massachusetts. State college, Extension service.   The Massachusetts farm outlook for 1936. Mass. State Col. Ext. Serv. Farm Econ. Facts, v. 9, no.1,
10pp. Amherst. December 1935-January 1936.

Michigan

Michigan. State college of agriculture and applied science. The agricultural
outlook for 1936. Agr. Econ. News for Michigan, no. 8, 14pp. East
Lansing. 1936.

Wright, K. T., and Leonard, A. L.   1935 poultry costs on 76 Michigan farms.
Mich. Agr. Expt. Sta. F. M. 152, 11pp., mimeogr. East Lansing. 1935.

Minnesota

Boss, Andrew.   The farm program for 1936.   Minn. Univ. Agr. Ext. Div. Minn.
Farm Business Notes, no. 157, pp. 1-4, mimeogr. University Farm, St.
Paul. 1936.

Minnesota. Department of agriculture, dairy and food. Minnesota... creameries,
cheese factories, ice cream and milk plants, 1935. 30pp. St. Paul. 1935.
Includes creamery statistics by counties for 1934 and a directory
of creameries, etc. by counties.

Minnesota University. Agricultural extension division. Agricultural outlook
and farm family living outlook in Minnesota for 1936. Minn. Univ. Agr.
Ext. Div. Pamph. 36, 23pp. University Farm, St. Paul. 1935.

Missouri

Etheridge, W. C.   The good use of farm land in Missouri. Mo. Col. Agr. Ext.
Circ. 332, 8pp. Columbia. 1935.
Outlines the State program for better farming practices.

Golden, H. E.   Some economic aspects of the farm poultry enterprise. Mo.
Agr. Expt. Sta. Research Bull. 227. 92pp. Columbia. 1935.
Discusses the history of poultry culture, the poultry industry in
various countries, flock management in the program of American planning,
and costs of operation and income from sales of products for the United
States and Missouri in particular.
A list of references is contained on pp. 75-79 and an appendix gives
statistics compiled from Federal and International Institute of Agriculture sources.

Hammar, C. H.   Factors affecting farm land values in Missouri. (From an appraisal viewpoint) Mo. Agr. Expt. Sta. Research Bull. 229, 62pp.
Columbia. 1935.
    Results of studies on the physical, economic and social factors af-
fecting farm land values. The author says in a foreword that the analysis
is not carried forward to the point of giving exact directions on how to
apply these results in an actual field appraisal. "For this reason the
study is a preliminary and provisional one and is to be so regarded."

Missouri. Agricultural experiment station.   Report... for the year ending
June 30, 1934. Mo. Agr. Expt. Sta. Bull. 358, 123pp. Columbia. 1935.
    Agricultural Economics and Farm Management, pp. 26-31; Rural Sociol-
ogy, pp. 93-95.

Montana

Renne, R. R.   Financing Montana schools. Mont. Agr. Expt. Sta. Bull. 307,
16pp. Bozeman. 1935.
    A summary of a more detailed study which is to be published later.

New Jersey

New Jersey. Department of agriculture.   Twentieth annual report, July 1, 1934-
June 30, 1935. 178pp. 1935. Trenton.
    Partial contents; Effect of AAA policies on New Jersey, pp. 9-11;
Report of the Bureau of Markets, pp. 59-105; Report of the Bureau of
Plant Industry (Statistical and related work; Farm credit and finance)
pp. 106-131.

New York

Drake, L. S.   Some facts concerning profits on celery in Wayne county, 1934.
N. Y.(Cornell) A. E. 103, 13pp., mimeogr. Ithaca. 1935.

Ohio

Morison, F. L.   What are the possibilities of increased crop acreages? Ohio.
Agr. Expt. Sta. Bimonthly Bull. 21 (178): 25-26. January-February, 1936.
Wooster.

Oregon

Scudder, H. D., and Hurd, E. B.   Graphic summary of agriculture and land use
in Oregon. Oreg. Agr. Expt. Sta. Circ. 114, 39pp. Corvallis. 1935.
    Preliminary issue of selected maps and graphs.
    In cooperation with U. S. Bureau of Agricultural Economics.
    "The 1930 census data have been used in preference to 1935 data, where
available, because 1930 conditions are believed to be more nearly normal."

Tolley, H. R.   Philosophy of agricultural adjustment. 14, 14, 12pp., mimeogr.
Corvallis, Oreg. Agr. Col. Ext. Service. 1936.
    Three lectures given at the annual conference of agriculture and home
economics staffs, Oregon State College, Corvallis, Oregon, December 11
and 12, 1935.

South Carolina. Agricultural experiment station. Forty-eighth annual report...
for the year ending June 30, 1935. 162pp. Clemson College. 1935.
Agricultural economics and rural sociology, pp. 6-17.

South Dakota

South Dakota. State college of agriculture and mechanic arts, Extension service.
South Dakota agricultural outlook for 1936. S. Dak. Agr. Col. Ext. Circ.
Letter 126, 24pp. Brookings, 1936.

Texas

Paulson, W. E. Costs, income and financial status of cooperative gins of
Texas, Season of 1933-1934. 33pp., mimeogr. College Station, Texas Agr.
Expt. Sta. Div. Farm and Ranch Economics. 1935.

Virginia

Garnett, W. E. Does Virginia care? Some significant population questions.
Va. Agr. Expt. Sta. Mimeogr. Rept. 3, 16pp. Blacksburg. 1936.

Virginia. Polytechnic institute. Virginia farm economics, no. 34. Blacks-
burg. January 1936.
Partial contents: The outlook [1936], by H. N. Young, pp.507, 510-518;
Cost of producing early potatoes in Virginia in 1935, by W. J. Nuckolls, Jr.,
pp. 518-521; The progress of cooperatives among Virginia farmers, by G. H.
Ward, pp. 521-524; Cost of horse work on Bright tobacco farms, by F. L.
Underwood, pp. 531-534

Washington

Washington. Secretary of state. Washington products, peoples, and resources,
all counties. 109pp. Olympia, Wash., Sec. of State. 1935.
County data are from the Federal Census for 1930.

West Virginia

Herrmann, L. F., Stelzer, R. C., and Bowling, G. A. Milk - production costs in
West Virginia. I. A study of the costs incurred by 51 farms in the Morgantown and Fairmont markets in 1934-1935. W. Va. Agr. Expt. Sta. Bull. 268,
32pp. Morgantown. 1936.

Wisconsin

Hobson, Asher, and Schaars, M. A. Consumer preferences for cheese. Wis.
Agr. Expt. Sta. Research Bull. 128, 48pp. Madison. 1935.
Includes results of studies on cheese consumption, the economic importance of cheese production, and the relationship of cheese quality
to retail prices.

Compiled by Louise O. Bercaw and A. M. Hannay

Agricultural Adjustment Act

The A.A.A. decision. Nat'l. City Bank New York. [Monthly Letter on] Econ.
Conditions, Govt. Finance, U. S. Securities, February 1936, pp.22-26.
(Published in New York, N. Y.)
Discusses the AAA decision, the effect of the AAA on the cotton,
wheat and hog situations, the AAA as a permanent program, the tendency of
AAA to maintain high cost production, the principle of parity, and the
soil improvement proposals.
In conclusion: "In all this discussion there is danger that too little
credit will be given to the ability of American farmers to look out for
themselves, to their advantages in soil, equipment and transportation, and
to the assistance they obtain from the Federal and State Departments of
Agriculture, which have had long and honored records in improving farm practices, supplying information which farmers cannot get for themselves and
fighting their enemies of insects and diseases.
"In last analysis the surplus problem is a problem of inability or un-
willingness to compete in the export markets. Even the cotton program has
been based on the assumption that the living standards of cotton growers
would be intolerable if they sought to hold their accustomed places in the
world cotton markets. But this country is admitted to have the greatest
natural advantages for cotton growing and the best equipment for cotton
marketing in the world, and evidently the living standards of the growers
should be highest in the world. Plainly the way to better living standards
is to utilize their advantages, increase the efficiency of their operations,
and grow more cotton on fewer acres, at lower costs. Of course prices of
things cotton growers buy enter into their costs. This opens up a new
field for comment and we have no space to enter it, except to say that if
these prices are out of line the attack upon them should be direct, instead of attempting to balance them by the wilful creation of a scarcity."

Aftermath. Northwestern Miller 185(2): 171. Jan. 15, 1936. (Published in Minneapolis, Minn.)
A full page editorial discussing the Supreme Court decision invalidating the A.A.A. and the repercussions resulting from the decision. In
conclusion in part:
"The rehabilitation of agriculture, so far as government has to do with
it, lies in recognition that agriculture is not a single industry, but
a great number of human activities akin only in that they produce from
the soil. Because of that, no single formula can be applied to the whole
complex problem. Once that truth is recognized, further steps should be
the undoing of much that government already has done in stimulating expansion of land cultivation and land speculation, in maintaining farmers
on lands incapable of sustaining them, in supporting plausible but im-
practical and ineffective marketing schemes, in placing the blighting
hand of government regulation upon the freedom of markets, in striving
to make farmers wards of government and so subject to the ebb and flow
of politics rather than a great part of self-respecting industry."

Boyle, J. E.   The AAA: an epitaph. Atlantic Monthly 157(2): 217-225. February
1936. (Published at 8, Arlington St., Boston, Mass.)
    This article, written before the Supreme Court Decision, is critical
of the AAA. The results of the AAA's program of "artificial scarcity"
are, according to the author, an unbalanced agriculture, an unbalanced
agriculture as between region, an unbalancing of international agriculture and an increase in unemployment. The author concludes as follows:
"Will high prices and scarcity get us out of the depression? Clearly a
general organization of scarcity, however imposed, will simply make the
depression permanent. Recovery can come only through an expansion of
production."

Death to the New Deal. Economist 123(4820): 57-59; Jan. 11, 1936. (Published at 8 Bouverie St., Fleet St., London, E.C.4, Eng.)
    An article on the situation created in the United States by the
Supreme Court's decision on the AAA, its effect upon economic recovery,
its political effect, and the problem of the Constitution. The embarrass-
ment of both the President and the Republicans is commented upon, also the
"deep-rooted veneration" which Americans have for the Constitution, even
those who benefit from the AAA. The concluding sentences of the article
follow:
    "It is just conceivable that a purely agricultural amendment might
get through the necessary 36 States in two or three years. But any
general amendment to enlarge the Federal Government's powers is quite
out of the question, and any President who campaigned for it would be
riding for a fall.
    "In these circumstances, with the only adequate remedy ruled out, even
the hardiest prophet must admit defeat. It is impossible to foresee the
future of agricultural policy, of the New Deal, of President Roosevelt,
of the existing political parties, or even in the long run, of the Constitution itself."

Lawrence, David. The billion dollar folly. U. S. News 4(3): 20. Jan. 20,
1936. (Published at 2201 M St., N. W., Washington, D. C.)
    An article on the subject of the farm program under the A.A.A. and
the Supreme Court decision invalidating that act.

McBain, H. L.   The issue: Court or Congress? Professor McBain sees basic
questions arising as a consequence of the AAA decision. New York Times
Mag. Jan. 19, 1936, pp.1-2, 22. (Published in New York, N. Y.)
    An extremely critical review of the Supreme Court's decision in the
Hoosac Mills case, which is termed "a shining and warning example of
judicial supremacy at its worst."

Mr. Roosevelt's dilemma. The Statist 127(3020): 45-46. Jan. 11, 1936.
(Published at 51 Cannon St., London, E.C.4, Eng.)
    On the implications of the AAA decision and the resulting political
difficulties. The writer does not "view the collapse of the A.A.A. as a
step forward."

Moley, Raymond. "So may judicial power be abused." Today 5(13): 12-13.
　　Jan. 18, 1936. (Published at 152 W. 42nd St., New York, N. Y.)
　　　Editorial, critical of the majority decision in the Hoosac Mills case.
"It is because I believe so utterly in the preservation of the American
Constitution and in the liberties which it protects that I regret so deeply
the nature and the implications of this unprecedented decision."

Mullen, W. H. The farm market - after AAA. Will buying power hold up, and,
　　if not, to what extent will it change the business picture? Production
　　control and regulation on the docket. Barron's 16(4): 20. Jan. 27, 1936.
　　(Published at 44 Broad St., New York, N. Y.)
　　　The writer's conclusions are as follows:
　　　"With the many confusing - often contradictory - trends which have been
outlined, no exact appraisal can be made of the effect upon the farm market
of the removal of production control. But certain conclusions seem war-
rantable:
　　　"1. With a Presidential election close at hand, it is practically assured that some program of farm relief will be adopted. Present indications
are that the plan will embrace bounties for the raising of crops which
restore soil fertility (such as legumes), or crops adaptable to industrial
uses(such as soy beans, extensively used in the manufacture of paint).
　　　"It seems probable that the days of production restriction are past -
production control and regulation are the new watch words. Under these new
conditions there may even be an expanding market for agricultural machinery.
During 1935, the acreage of important crops declined more than 25 million
acres - 7.3% - below the 1928-32 average. The recultivation of this land
will mean swelling machinery sales.
　　　"2. But even without any plan of governmental relief, prospects for a
maintenance of agricultural buying at the present high levels are bright.
An expansion of domestic demand, a reduction of competitive imports, may
both be counted upon to offset, in part, any expansion in supply. The
marked reduction in the farmer's fixed charges and the improved price relationship now prevailing between agricultural and industrial prices are
added reasons for believing that the present prosperity of the farm market
is more than ephemeral.
　　　"It has taken two years of drought, a dust storm, and $1 billion in
subsidies to put the farm market on its feet. But from every indication,
neither meteorological nor governmental props are needed now to keep it
there."

Nourse, E. G. What next for the farmer? Christian Sci. Monitor, Weekly
　　Mag. Sect., Jan. 29, 1936, pp.1-2, 14. (Published in Boston, Mass.)
　　　A discussion of the Supreme Court's decision in the Hoosac Mills case,
why Federal control of agriculture was considered necessary, the process
by which it came about, and "what results may be expected if now we
follow out long-established tradition and abide by the findings of the
Supreme Court."
　　　The article is concluded with the following paragraph:
　　　"If AAA was a good remedy to use at the time of agriculture's crisis we
may now recognize that something different is called for during the conva-
lescent stage, or, still more so, for the maintenance of health thereafter.

It would be well to take at face value what the act said as to its own
emergency character, though calling into use such of its remaining powers
as will not expose the patient to relapse during the period before he gets
really back on his feet. But we should frankly recognize that production
control is not a type of treatment well suited to an industry in normal
health."

Our plan of Government negatives A.A.A.   Calif. Fruit News 93(2479): 3, 8.
    Jan. 11, 1936. (Published at 105 Montgomery St., San Francisco, Calif.)
    A discussion of both the majority and minority decisions of the
    Supreme Court invalidating the A.A.A.
    "There does not seem to us to be any weakness in the reasoning of the
    majority of the court in this matter and in this we wish also to be under-
    stood, just as the Supreme Court expresses itself, that 'the question is
    not what power the Federal Government ought to have, but what powers in
    fact have been given by the people....
    "As an economic matter the Supreme Court of the United States is not
    called upon to express an opinion. As an economic matter the end sought
    can be argued substantially both ways. But we never have been able to
    see how it could be justified under the present sort of Government we
    have...in this country."

Read, Joan.   Stock prices depend on method of financing farm subsidies.
    Financial Age 73(2): 17, 18. Jan. 11, 1936. (Published at 132 Nassau St.,
    New York, N. Y.)
    A discussion of possible financial consequences in view of the Supreme
    Court decision invalidating the A.A.A.
    "Since the New Deal has pledged itself anew to subsidize the 'under-
    privileged' farmer, the question to be answered by the investor and
    stock trader is how these payments may be financed, and what effect
    such financing may exert on security prices...
    "The logical supposition is that any new method devised to aid the
    farmer...will directly increase the public debt – unless the New Deal
    turns now to where its course must eventually end – at the printing press..
    "Whether the presses turn out currency or bonds, the final and funda-
    mental results will be identical."

Selig, Samson.   What AAA decision discloses about our form of government.
    Will the states forego their rights and permit constitutional changes?
    Mag. Wall St. 57(8): 434-435, 480-481. Feb. 1, 1936. (Published at 90
    Broad St., New York, N. Y.)

Soth, Lauren K.   Weighing the AAA. Facts for fireside arguments as to whether
    the Agricultural Adjustment Administration has been worth its salt.
    Successful Farming 34(2): 16, 30, 31, 32, 33. February 1936. (Published
    in Des Moines, Iowa.)

T., E. X.   AAA decision has broad effect on government, business, industries,
    taxation and agriculture. Mag. Wall St. 57(7): 365, 421, 422. Jan. 18.
    1936. (Published at 90 Broad St., New York, N. Y.)

Travis, Edmunds. Does the Supreme Court rule America? Tex. Weekly 12(3):
5-7. Jan. 18, 1936. (Published at the Dallas Athletic Club Bldg.,
Dallas, Tex.)

"Edmunds Travis points out in this article that the people rule, through
the Constitution they have set up, and that the Court is the people's
servant." -[Editor's note.]

Regarding the decision of the Supreme Court invalidating the AAA the
author writes: "The AAA may have been a great thing for the farmers and
for the country, but the question of its usefulness was not before the
nine distinguished old men at Washington. They were concerned only with
whether it was authorized by the organic law of the nation. They could
only lay the Constitution beside the statute and 'decide whether the
latter squares with the former.' The average unprejudiced layman, attempting the same test, is likely to find himself wondering, not why six members
of the court pronounced the statute in conflict with the Constitution,
but why three members dissented from this finding."

What farm editors think of AAA fall. U. S. News 4(4): 12. Jan. 27, 1936.
(Published at 2201 M St., N. W., Washington, D. C.)

"The first survey made of representative farm publications concerning
the Supreme Court's AAA decision shows that 71 percent of the commenting
papers believe that the action will be detrimental to the farmer unless an
adequate new policy of farm aid is devised. Twenty-nine percent believe
that the elimination of the AAA is beneficial."

Comments from some of the farm papers are quoted.

Where farmers go from here. Business Week no. 333, pp. 27,28. Jan. 18, 1936.
(Published at 330 West 42nd St., New York, N. Y.)

In which the writer attempts to appraise the direct influence of the
AAA on various crops and raises the question " hat next?" In reply to
that question: "The answer comes in two sections. For the immediate future,
no harm to farm income is apparent. There is no division of farm production, hitherto controlled, that can be unleashed over-night to bring about
embarrassing supplies. Cotton is perhaps the greatest problem. It will
be planted in another month and picking will start next August. If some
check is not introduced, it is entirely possible that a heavy acreage
will be planted and a large crop produced. Secretary Wallace speaks of
16 million bales or more...Practically all of the surplus is held by the
government, which is not likely to sell it below 13 1/2¢. Hence the
cotton outlook without an AAA or effective substitute is for sustained
prices through most of this year - afterward weakness."

Agricultural Credit - Cochinchina

Pichot, Olivier. Le crédit agricole mutuel en Cochinchine. L'Économiste
Français 63(49): 712. Dec. 7, 1935; (50): 743-744. Dec. 14, 1935;
(51): 775-776. Dec. 21, 1935; (52): 808-809. Dec. 28, 1935; 64(1):
10-11. Jan. 4, 1936. (Published at Rue Bleue, 9, Paris (9³), France.)

A study of mutual agricultural credit in Cochinchina. The author
recommends its continuation in this form inasmuch as it unites the
interests of the individual, the agricultural groups, and the state.

Agricultural Credit - France

Liesse, André.   Sur le crédit agricole. L'Économiste Français 64(3): 65-67.
    Jan. 18. 1936. (Published at Rue Bleue, 9, Paris (9⁰), France.)
        The author discusses the need for the development of agricultural
    credit in France, and gives a critical account of the report for 1934
    of the operations of the regional banks of mutual agricultural credit.

Agricultural Forecasting

Cromwell, R. O.   Problems in forecasting production of crops. Southwest.
    Miller 14(17): 42. Jan. 21, 1936. (Published at 306-12 Board of Trade
    Bldg., Kansas City, Mo.)
        "Some observations by R. O. Cromwell, Chicago, Crop Statistician of
    Lamson Bros. & Co."

Agricultural Goals - Southwestern States

Tetreau, E. D.   Goals for agriculture in the Southwest. Southwest. Social Sci.
    Quart. 16(3): 45-50. December 1935. (Published by the Southwestern
    Social Science Association, Austin, Tex.)
        Goals for agriculture in the Southwest as seen by the author are as
    follows: A population of superior quality; security for those who live
    on the land; an adequate living for farm people; the discovery and nur-
    ture of unusual personal ability; industrial equality; and beauty of farm
    and countryside. The writer closes the article with an enumeration of
    some of the more important of the means necessary to attain these goals.

Agricultural Policy - Germany

Sohn, F.   Problems of agrarian policy, 1935. News in Brief 3(23-24): 8-10.
    December 1935. (Published by the Deutscher Akademischer Austauschdienst
    e.V., Berlin N W 40, Germany.)
        A brief account of the measures adopted by the Reichsnährstand to count-
    eract the effects of the drought of 1934 on Germany's food supply, of the so
    called production campaign, and of the extension of market regulation.

Agricultural Policy - Irish Free State

Johnston, Joseph.   The Anglo-Irish economic conflict. An Irish view. Nine-
    teenth Century 119(708): 187-200. February 1936. (Published by Constable
    & Co., Ltd., Orange St., Leicester Square, London, W. C. 2, Eng.)
        The writer is critical of the agricultural policy pursued by His
    Majesty's Government of the Irish Free State and His Majesty's Government
    of the United Kingdom. He deplores the attempt to establish small
    holdings and thinks that:
        "On general agricultural grounds it would appear that the farm of 50
    to 100 acres is the most economic unit for the type of agriculture that must
    prevail in this area, on any long-term view provided sane commercial re-
    lations with our neighbours are restored. The increase in the rural
    population of this region that is desirable should take the form of an in-
    crease in the numbers of a well-paid class of agricultural labourers,

as part of a general intensification of the business of live-stock production on a foundation of scientific grass farming."

Agricultural Relief - South Africa

Martin, W. A. Subsidies, quotas, tariffs and the excess cost of agriculture in South Africa. A criticism. South African Jour. 3(4): 559-570. December 1935. (Published by the Economic Society of South Africa, Johannesburg.)

This is a criticism of Mr. Richards' article of the same title in the September number of the South African Journal. Mr. Richards' rejoinder, or "Addendum" to Mr. Martin's criticism is given on pp.571-575.of the December number. The following is quoted from the first paragraph of the "Addendum."

"There is much in Mr. Martin's paper with which I am in entire agreement: notably his criticisms of the present system, the fact that sooner or later it will have to be faced, that it is highly desirable to increase internal consumption, and the impossible position of the sugar industry; the whole of my paper dealt with these points. A careful perusal of Mr. Martin's paper, however, more than ever convinces me that a bounty scheme is emphatically not a suitable alternative and is definitely administratively impossible and impracticable...and the details of how Mr. Martin suggests a bounty scheme should be operated, it seems to me, bring out all the weaknesses inherent in such schemes, and, in addition, appear to show that it would be much more costly even than the present schemes, bad as they are."

"Errata" for the article in the September issue given on pp.607-609 of the December number.

Agricultural Relief - United States

Crutchfield, J. S. Prosperity may loom large for agriculture. Sphere 17(2): 9-10. February 1936. (Published at the Munsey Bldg., Washington, D. C.)

An optimistic view of the outlook for agricultural prosperity. "What American agriculture needs and, I believe, wants is annulment of faulty legislation of the postwar period which resulted in placing an unfair burden on agriculture...In other words, what the American farmer needs during the next ten to twenty years is a square deal and no favors."

Formulating a permanent program for agriculture. Natl. Grange Monthly 33(2): 1, 4, 5. February 1936. (Published in Springfield, Mass.)

"After careful study of the decision of the Supreme Court invalidating the Agricultural Adjustment Act, handed down on January 6, the executive committee of the National Grange formulated a ten-point program to.provide equality for agriculture." The outline of this program is given.

Lowden backs soil conservation plan as permanent policy. Amer. Farm Bur. Fed. Official News Letter 15(3): 1, 4. Feb. 4, 1936. (Published at 58 E. Washington St., Chicago, Ill.)

"This story was written by William J. Conway, Associated Press Staff Writer, as an exclusive interview with Frank O. Lowden...and copyrighted by the Associated Press for January 26 issues..." -Editors' note.

Mayhugh, L. T. Revised farm plan ahead. American farmers are called in conference to start new program. Producer-Consumer 1(7): 1, 20. January
1936. (Published at 517 Fisk Bldg., and 109 Fillmore, Amarillo, Tex.)
Describes briefly the farm conference held on Jan. 10, following the
decision of the Supreme Court invalidating the A.A.A.
"When the seven-point program, preceded by the preamble, was read and
adopted, section by section with such unanimity, one-third of the way had
been covered and the faith of the nation preserved.
"There were few, if any, who desired to amend the Constitution. There
were some who thought that on constitutional rulings seven of the justices
should concur while still others believed that all should agree. However,
no official action was taken for it is believed there is a way out and a
better way will come from this necessity."

New adjustment pattern. Nation's Agr. 11(5): 4-5, 18. February 1936. (Published at 58 East Washington St., Chicago, Ill.)
"A new pattern of agricultural adjustment, designed to bring to the
farmers of the United States a scientifically constructed vehicle by
means of which modern agriculture can continue its march toward permanent
economic equality, is in the offing. As this is being written, details
of this new and all-comprehensive plan are not available, but enough has
been learned about it to warrant the statement that its philosophy and
principles will be most acceptable to American agriculture, north, east,
south, midwest, and west.
"Perhaps, as many observers have pointed out, the action of the Supreme
Court, in declaring the AAA for the most part unconstitutional, is a good
thing, because it did something that never was done before. It united
all of the major farm groups of the nation in a determination to endorse
and support one joint constructive program of legislative aid for agriculture
The new adjustment program is discussed in this article.

Taber, L. J. Ideals for the farmer. That is what the National grange has been
applying to rural problems in the United States since 1867, and although
conditions have changed the fundamentals remain the same. Christian Sci.
Monitor, Weekly Mag. Sect., Dec. 11, 1935, pp. 6, 14. (Published in
Boston, Mass.)
"The solution of the farm problem requires that the interests of all
be considered.
"It is the long-time and permanent program for rural welfare that is of
greatest importance. This program must include the maintenance of a fair
and stable price structure, better marketing methods, a sound land policy,
a fair tariff for agriculture, a sound rural credit system, fair interest
rates, reduced transportation costs, and lightening tax burdens. This
long-time program will fail unless there is maintained an honest dollar,
reasonably constant in purchasing and debt-paying power. The opening of
foreign markets and the utilization of the debenture principle to equalize
tariff inequalities, will also be essential.
"We must develop new industrial uses, also, for farm products...
"The Grange should strike a firm note that the farm problem be not involved in partisan politics. Our problems are economic and not political.
Whenever farm questions become a football of politics, progress stops.

"Any permanent agricultural policy must be built on the foundation of organization, education and teamwork. It will require the assistance of all groups. No one organization, or no one type of farm activity, is sufficient to determine policies fundamental to the open country."

What next in the regulation of agriculture? Com. & Financ. Chron. 142: 352-354. Jan. 18, 1936. (Published at William St. corner Spruce St., New York, N. Y.)

A critical account of some of the farm relief proposals made during the period since the adverse decision of the Supreme Court on the AAA. Plans mentioned are the plan of the Committee of Thirteen of the mass conference of representatives of farm organizations called by the Secretary of Agriculture, the plan for government guarantee of cost of production favored by the Farmers' Union, the plans of the National Cooperative Milk Producers Federation, the National Cooperative Council, and Senator Smith of South Carolina.

[Writing a new farm bill] Tex. Weekly 12(4): 1-3. Jan. 25, 1936. (Published at the Dallas Athletic Club Bldg., Dallas, Tex.)

Editorial pointing out the provisions of the new farm bill which was introduced in both houses of Congress in the form of an amendment to the soil conservation act of 1935, and discussing the question as to whether there was a constitutional way of Federal control of agricultural production by soil conservation and paying a subsidy to farmers in the form of a domestic allotment. "A constitutional way of solving the farmer's problems, without Federal control of agricultural production, in our opinion, can be found. And a proper solution will also solve other problems the country is facing, including the stubborn problem of unemployment....As we see it, there are two problems to be solved. One is the problem of increasing the exchange value of agricultural products in relation to the things the farmer buys, so that the rewards for his labor will be more comparable to the rewards of labor in industry and other fields of economic activity. This, let it be said, is not quite the same thing as 'parity prices'...The other problem to be solved is that of finding markets which are adequate to the capacity of American farmers to produce, so that agriculture may utilize fully and economically the land and labor resources which are available to it in the United States."

Agriculture - Turkey

Ménars, O. La situation agricole en Turquie. L'Économiste Français 64(1): 4-6. Jan. 4, 1936. (Published at Rue Bleue, 9, Paris (9e), France.)

Statistics are given to show Turkey's development as a producer and exporter of agricultural products.

Agrobiology

Willcox, O. W. What is this agrobiology? Econ. Forum 3(3): 302-310. Winter 1936. (Published at 51 Pine St., New York, N. Y.)

This article might be termed a reply to Secretary of Agriculture Wallace's review of Mr. Willcox's book Nations Can Live At Home, published in the October 2, 1935 issue of The New Republic.

Annals of Collective Economy

Annals of Collective Economy, v. 11, no. 1, January-March 1935. (Published
  at 8, Rue Saint-Victor, Geneva, Switzerland.)
    Partial contents: The International Committee for Inter-Co-operative
Relations.-pp. 1-13. (This committee was "constituted on 9 February 1931...
to promote the development of moral and economic relationships between
agricultural co-operative societies and distributive societies and to
act as a liaison body between the co-operative movement as a whole and
international institutions, in particular the Economic Organisation of
the League of Nations, the International Labour Office and the International
Institute of Agriculture." An account is given of its program of work
and its principal activities; The part played by agricultural and distributive co-operative organisations and by their mutual relations in the butter
trade.-pp.22-40; Functions conferred by public authorities on agricultural
and distributive co-operative societies in the organisation and supervision
of the production and marketing of grain.-pp.41-49. (A brief account of
commercial organizations in Bulgaria, Greece, Hungary, and Rumania, and of
compulsory cooperation in different parts of the British Empire and in
Greece.); Wheat-storing Co-operative Societies in France, by Vimeux. -
pp.50-55. ("The legislation and regulations governing the wheat market
in France are decidedly complex, but one dominating principle emerges:
the co-operative movement is recognised as being indispensable as a basis
for all market defence schemes.); The Czechoslovak Grain Company, Prague.
Its functions, its work and the results, by Ferdinand Klindera.-pp.56-63;
Regulation of the marketing of milk products in Czechoslovakia, by F.
Klindera.--pp.64-70; The Czechoslovak Cattle Board, by Emil Lustig.-pp.71-
76. (Outlines the work of the Board which was founded on April 1, 1933.);
The Advisory Board of Consumers' Co-operation in Czechoslovakia, by Emil
Lustig.-pp.77-78; The working of milk marketing schemes in Great Britain, by
Walworth.-pp.79-93; Creation of a joint enterprise between the Distributive
Co-operative Society and the Federation of the Agricultural Co-operative
Dairies in Geneva, by G. Pauquet.-pp.94-99; and A few illustrations of
primary co-operative societies in Yugoslavia.-pp.100-104.

Apple Export Situation

Phillips, R. G. The apple export situation. Amer. Fruit Grower 56(1): 5-7,
  30. January 1936. (Published at 1370 Ontario St., Cleveland, Ohio.)
    "Timely, comprehensive and supported by undisputable facts and figures,
this analysis of the apple export situation should be read by every grower
in the United States, for, no matter where his orchard is located or where
he markets his crop, the problems presented by the export situation as a
new year dawns will, sooner or later, have a bearing, direct or indirect,
upon his business. Mr. Phillips' startling review of the Apple Export
Situation was first presented as an address before the December convention
of the American Pomological Society in Hartford, Conn."-[Editor's note.]

Association of Land-Grant Colleges and Universities

The forty-ninth convention of the Association of Land-grant colleges and
  universities. Expt. Sta. Rec. 74(1): 1-3. January 1936. (Published by

the Office of Experiment Stations; U. S. Dept. of Agriculture)
Editorial summary of the papers given at this meeting.

Bacon Development Scheme - Great Britain

The bacon development scheme. Gt. Brit. Min. Agr. Jour. 42(6): 571-576.
September 1935. (Published by H. M. Stationery Office, London, Eng.)
The Bacon Development Scheme, which was to come into force on September
7, 1935, is "the first scheme of its kind to be brought into operation
under the Agricultural Marketing Act of 1933." The composition and powers
of the Development Board are outlined. The latter include "mandatory powers
to license factories and permissive powers which are concerned mainly with
the exercise of functions delegated to them by the constituent marketing
boards."

Beef - Consumption - Austria

Decline in beef consumption in Austria. Scot. Jour. Agr. 18(4): 378. October
1935. (Published by H. M. Stationery Office, Edinburgh, Scotland)
Reasons are given for the decline of beef consumption in Austria. "Only
1600 to 1800 head of cattle are now required to cover Vienna's weekly requirements, as against 4000 to 5000 before the war."

Berichte über Landwirtschaft

Berichte über Landwirtschaft n.F. Bd. 20, Hefte 1-2, 1935. (Issued by [Germany],
Reichs-und Pr. Ministerium für Ernährung u. Landwirtschaft. Published by
P. Parey, Berlin, Germany)
Partial contents: Erscheinungsformen und Bedeutung der festen Kosten
in der Landwirtschaft, by S. v. Ciriacy-Wantrup.-pp. 1-17. (A study of
fixed costs in connection with land, production, and farm management, and
their relation to the organization and operation of the whole agricultural
enterprise.); Die historischen Voraussetzungen alter Erbhöfe im deutschen
Osten, by Erich Kittel.-pp.18-33. (A historical survey of land tenure and
inheritance in Eastern Germany prior to the passage of the inheritance
law of September 29, 1933.); Der Welthandel mit Butter und Käse und die Lage
der Molkereiproduktion in den wichtigsten Ausfuhrländern, by St. Taussig.
-pp.34-50. (World trade in butter and cheese); Agrarische Grundlage der
Entwicklung der russischen Meteorologie, by W. P. von Poletika.-pp.51-66.
(The author describes the successful development of meteorology in Russia
in spite of the apparent lack of the usual prerequisites); Deutschland.
Allgemeiner Agrarpolitischer Bericht, by F. F. Zimmermann.-pp.67-76.
(A summary of agricultural economic conditions in Germany in 1934/35.
The production campaign, market control and land settlement are briefly
discussed.) Reiswirtschaft in Japan, by H. Krause.-pp.76-86. (An account of rice production, consumption and control in Japan.); Agrarreform
und Agrarverfassung in Albanien, by R. Busch-Zantner.-pp.87-109. (An
account of land distribution and land tenure in Albania, its latifundia and
the need of land improvement in the interest of the masses. The aims and
results of the agrarian reform are discussed.); Vernichtung mecklenburgischen
Bauerntums von 1570-1900, by Wolfram Proposch.-pp.221-242. (A study of
the dispossession of the peasantry by landlordism in Mecklenburg from

1570 to 1900.); Deutschland. Allgemeiner agrarpolitischer Bericht, by
F. F. Zimmermann.-pp.254-288. (Agricultural economic conditions in Germany with special reference to market control, the production campaign,
and the grain, potatoes and meat situation.); Russland. I. Der Anbau von
Flachs und anderen Faserpflanzen in der Sowjetunion; II. Der Stand der
Viehzucht in der Sowjatunion, by O. Schiller.-pp.363-290. (Textile
plant production and the livestock industry in the Soviet Union); Internationale Bibliographie des agrarökonomischen Schrifttums, by S. v. Frauendorfer.-pp.132-180; 310-354.

Bounties - Lithuania

Bounties on agricultural products in Lithuania. Majandusteated. Weekly Bull.
Inst. Econ. Research 2(1): 20. Jan. 8, 1936. (Published in Tallinn,
Estonia.)
    Gives amounts paid annually from 1930 to 1935.

Business - Annual Reviews

Annual review & forecast number. Annalist 47(1200): 67-160. Jan. 17, 1936.
(Published by the New York Times Co., New York, N. Y.)
    Partial contents: Stabilization prospects by activities of anti-
democratic states, by Lionel Robbins, pp.75, 117,118,119,120; Thirty
years of farming; the AAA and the changed outlook for agriculture, by
J. R. Howard, pp.83, 84, 120, 121; World recovery progresses despite
all obstacles; industry up to 1928 level, by Winthrop W. Case, pp.85-87,
139; Farm policies, foreign restrictions, hurt exports; imports rise
further, by Winthrop W. Case, pp.92-93; Canadian business activity re-
covers to highest level in five years, by H. E. Hansen, pp.94-95, 122;
Slower rise in prices: artificial stimuli replaced by "natural" recovery,
by Winthrop W. Case, pp.96, 150; Record consumption of wool and rayon
in generally active textile year, by Winthrop W. Case, p. 100; Livestock
packing industry a focal point of clash over economic controls, by S. L. M.,
pp.104-105; Wheat aided by improved world position, p. 104; AAA invalidation darkens
U. S. future, by Winthrop W. Case, pp.105, 152; World use of American cotton
increases with 10-cent loans and world prices, by Winthrop W. Case, pp.105-
106, 139; Sugar helped by AAA; future clouded, p. 106; Coffee depressed
by Brazilian exchange, pp.106-107; Cocoa bolstered by rising consumption,
p. 107; Rubber troubled by Dutch native problem, pp.107, 123; Silk prices
up, p.123; Hide prices higher, p.123; Wool prices rise, pp.123, 153;
Cottonseed oil in 1935, p.153.

Dun & Bradstreet Monthly Review, v. 44, no. 2094, 56pp. January 1936. (Published at 290 Broadway, New York, N. Y.)
    This is the annual statistical number. Partial contents; 1935, by
Willard L. Thorp, pp.2-4; The California unfair practices act, by Walter
Mitchell, Jr., pp.5-8; Fewest failures since 1920 recorded for 1935, pp.
31-33.

Economist annual review. Economist 95(3, sect. 2), 1-31. Jan. 17, 1936.
(Published in Chicago, Ill.)
Partial contents: Government vies with business to control recovery.
1935 marks further penetration by new deal administration into fields
of private enterprise through increased Federal expenditures, p. 3; 1936
prospects for expansion in mortgage field. Renewed private lending and
government activity provide two principal factors as need looms for
favorable legislation, p. 6.

Financial Age 73(3): 33-56. Jan. 18, 1936. (Published at 132 Nassau St.,
New York, N. Y.)
The annual financial review number. Special features included in this
issue follow: A tabulation of all banks and trust companies in the United
States with deposits over $25,000,000 in numerical order, showing changes
in one and five years; Earnings of New York City banks and trust companies
tabulated for the year 1935; Chronological review of finance, banking and
industry in 1935; and Bond record and market review for 1935.

The Times. Review of the year 1935. xiipp. Jan. 1, 1936. (Published in
London, Eng.)
Partial contents: Trade and industry, p. ix; Agriculture, p. ix.

Business Cycles - Recent Books

Snider, J. L. Recent publications on business cycles. Harvard Business Rev.
14(2): 241-247. winter 1936. (Published for the Graduate School of Business Administration, Harvard University, at 212-220 York St., York, Pa.)
Reviews the following books and pamphlets: Controlling depressions,
by Paul H. Douglas; The British way to recovery, by Herbert Heaton;
Britain in depression, prepared by a research committee of the Economic
Science and Statistics Section of the British Association; Fluctuations
in American business, 1790-1860, by Walter B. Smith and Arthur H. Cole;
Public works in prosperity and depression, by Arthur D. Gayer; The inevitable world recovery, by Harold Fisher; The stagnation of industry;
its cause and cure, by Emil O. Jorgensen; The profit mystery and wealth
illusion, by Clayton D. Browne; The chief cause of this and other depressions, by Leonard P. Ayres; War and depression, by J. B. Condliffe;
The road to recovery, by Sir Henry Strakosch; The building industry and
business cycles, by William H. Newman.

Butter - Export Bounty - France

Export bounty on butter suspended. Gt. Brit. Bd. Trade Jour. (n.s.) 135(2035):
800. Dec. 5, 1935. (Published by H. M. Stationery Office, London, Eng.)
The export bounty of 6 francs per kilo on good quality butter exported
from France has been suspended as from November 22, 1935.

Canada

Economist. Dominion of Canada special review. 68pp. Jan. 18, 1936. (Published at 8, Bouverie St., Fleet St., London, Eng.)
Partial contents: Population and immigration, pp. 8-9; Foreign trade,
pp.15-16; The Ottawa agreements, pp. 16-18; The North American trade

agreement, pp.18, 19, 21; The grain trade of Canada, by H. C. Griffin,
pp.21, 23, 24, 25; Farming in Canada, pp.25, 26, 27; The pulp and paper
industry of Canada. pp.33, 35, 37; Other industries [includes textiles,
flour milling, etc.] pp.37, 38, 39, 41-42; The stabilisation of the
Canadian dollar, by John Percival Day, pp.47-48, 49.

Canal - Florida

Blair, Edson. The prize white elephant. Florida scene of another "White
House pet." despite protest of PWA Ickes. $200 million canal, with
practically no sponsorship, opposed by farmers. Barron's 16(5): 3, 5.
Feb. 3, 1936. (Published at 44 Broad St., New York, N. Y.)

Canned Foods - Labeling

Wernette, Philip. Grade labeling versus descriptive labeling. Natl. Marketing Rev. 1(2): 131-140. fall 1935. (Published by the National Association of Marketing Teachers, 100 Washington Square East, New York, N. Y.)
"Dr. Wernette discusses a timely issue in contrasting the problems and
arguments for grade labeling with those of descriptive labeling. He
presents the viewpoint of the canners, the wholesalers, the chains, and
the can makers, as well as that of the protagonists of the consumer.
In discussing the arguments made by both sides he maintains an objective
position which should be helpful in arriving at a sound solution to
this current marketing problem." -Editor's note.

Canner - Grower Relationships

Urann, M. L. Canner-grower relationship. N.C.A. committeeman discusses one
of chief convention topics describing solution of problem by cranberry
group. Canning Age 17(1): 30-31, 40. January 1936. (Published at 250
W. 57th St., New York, N. Y.)
Solution of canner-grower relationships by Cranberry Canners, Inc.

Canning Industry - Cost Accounting

Campbell, C. E. Cost accounting for canners. Canner 82(7): 13, 28.
Jan. 25, 1936. (Published at 140 N. Dearborn St., Chicago, Ill.)
Address before the National Canners' Association at Chicago, January
21, 1936.

Canning Industry and Supreme Court Decisions

Acheson, T. G. The canning industry and the Federal government. Canner
82(7): 11-12, 24. Jan. 25, 1936. (Published at 140 N. Dearborn St.,
Chicago, Ill.)
What the Supreme Court decisions mean in terms of the relation between
the Federal Government and the canning industry.

Cartel Legislation

Reichert, J. W. International survey of cartel legislation - III. Mysore
Econ. Jour. 22(1): 9-11. January 1936. (Published in Bangalore, Mysore

State, British India.)
Part III of this series of articles deals with post-war legislation in extra-European countries, i.e. in the United States, Canada, Union of South Africa and Japan.

Coffee

World coffee markets. Empire Producer, no. 231, pp.19-20. January 1936.
(Published at 22, Queen Anne's Gate, Westminster, London, S.W. 1, Eng.)
Contains answers to a questionnaire sent to correspondents in Batavia and Germany.

Collective Bargaining by Agricultural Workers

Collective bargaining by agricultural workers in various countries. Monthly Labor Rev. 42(1): 77-79. January 1936. (Published by the Bureau of Labor Statistics, U. S. Dept. of Labor)
"The International Landworkers' Federation recently issued a review of the collective-bargaining practices of those of its affiliated organizations that have definite bargaining machinery and collective agreements, and a summary of minimum-wage legislation where that is the regulatory medium. The data presented herewith are from that review." The review referred to is the Bulletin, issues of September 1935(no.2) and October 1935 (no.3).

Commodity Dollar

Rorty, M. C. The commodity dollar. Harvard Business Rev. 14(2): 133-145. winter 1936. (Published for the Graduate School of Business Administration, Harvard University at 212-220. York St., York, Pa.)
Examines "separately the applications of the commodity dollar to (a) the relief of business depressions, and (b) the prevention of such depressions, with considerations under each heading of its relations to stability in international trade, exchanges, and price levels." The analysis is preceded by a consideration of the "major differences which exist between the proponents and the critics of the commodity dollar."

Cooperation

Review of cooperative movement throughout the world in 1934. Monthly Labor Rev. 42(1): 89-109. January 1936. (Published by the Bureau of Labor Statistics, U. S. Dept. of Labor)
"More than 139 million persons in 43 countries are members of co-operative societies of different types. Data gathered from various sources show that three-fifths of these belonged to consumers' societies and slightly over one-fifth were engaged in agricultural cooperation. The retail consumers' societies had an annual business of more than 12 billion dollars, and the cooperative wholesale societies a combined turnover of over 900 million dollars. In Great Britain the retail societies returned to their members in 1 year (1934) more than 115 million dollars in interest on share capital and rebates on purchases. An added savings of nearly 16 million dollars was made for member retail societies by the three wholesale societies of the country. Comparative figures for all of the countries of the world for which data could be obtained are given...[in this article]." -p.vi.

Cooperation, Consumers'

The church and the consumers' cooperative movement. Inform. Serv. 15(3):
1-[6]. Jan. 18, 1936. (Published by the Dept. of Research and Education,
Federal Council of the Churches of Christ in America, 105 E. 22nd St.,
New York, N. Y.)
        This is "a report of the Seminar on Consumers' Cooperation held under
the auspices of the Federal Council of the Churches of Christ in America
in the First Baptist Church at Indianapolis, December 30, 31, 1935 and
January 1, 1936. The purpose of the Seminar was twofold: (1) to hear
Toyohiko Kagawa, the noted Christian leader of Japan, lecture on the
relation of Christian idealism and the cooperative movement; and (2)
to give an opportunity to study the American cooperative developments."

Sales by consumers' cooperative societies in 1934. Monthly Labor Rev. 41(6):
1310-1311. December 1935. (Published by the Bureau of Labor Statistics,
U. S. Dept. of Labor)

Corn, Canning - Grading - Ohio

Garwood, P. S. Buying sweet corn on grade and results of an inspection ex-
periment conducted at Crampton Canneries, Incorporated, Factory no. 6,
at Plain City, Ohio. Presented by Paul S. Garwood before the Ohio Canners'
Convention, December 11, 1935. And much the same report was made by
E. P. Walls, Tri-state Packers Convention, December 11, 1935. Canning
Trade 58(23): 50-52; (24): 7-8, 10, 28. Jan. 13-20, 1936. (Published in
Baltimore, Md.)
        "Through the cooperation of Mr. W. E. Lewis, Mr. R. L. Spangler, and
Mr. M. Smith of the U. S. Bureau of Agricultural Economics at Washington,
who established the system, Mr. M. W. Baker, Federal Representative and
Marketing Specialist at Columbus, Ohio, who personally supervised the
project, and the corn canners of Ohio who provided funds and facilities,
an experiment was carried on this past season at the Crampton Cannery No.
6 at Plain City, Ohio, on two varieties of sweet corn, Golden Bantam and
Country Gentleman. It is therefore the purpose of this paper to give
a detailed account of the grading system as a whole and present the
material collected as the result of the experiment conducted at this
station."

Cotton - Colombia

Harland, S. C. Some notes on cotton in Colombia. Trop. Agr. 13(2): 31-34.
February 1936. (Published at the Imperial College of Tropical Agriculture, St. Augustine, Trinidad, West Indies)
        "Based on 'Report on a visit to the Cotton Districts of Colombia' made
to the Empire Cotton Growing Corporation."
        The writer visited three representative cotton growing districts of
Colombia during February and March 1935. In two of these districts, cotton
is grown on a commercial scale. In this article the three districts are
described, as are the types of cotton grown. A section of the article is
devoted to the observations made on the insect pests of cotton in these
regions.

Cotton - Futures Trading

Williamson, N. C. Abolish the exchanges? Amer. Cotton Grower 1(3): 11-12.
    Jan. 1, 1936. (Published at 535 Gravier St., New Orleans, La.)
        The author discusses the weaknesses and inequalities involved in the
    present cotton marketing system, especially in futures transactions.

Cotton - Marketing - India

Ajaib Singh, and Partap Singh Bhullar. Some aspects of marketing and cost of
    transportation of cotton. Agr. and Live-stock in India 5(6): 692-702.
    November 1935. (Published for the Imperial Council of Agricultural Re-
    search by Manager of Publications, Delhi, India.)
        An appendix contains tables showing the difference of village and
    market prices of Desi cotton and of American cotton.

Cotton - Punjab

Santokh Singh Jaggi. Causes of fluctuation of area under cotton in the Canal
    Colonies of the Punjab. Agr. and Live-stock in India 5(6): 712-721.
    November 1935. (Published for the Imperial Council of Agricultural Re-
    search by Manager of Publications, Delhi, India.)
        The factors causing fluctuations in area are briefly discussed. They
    are: (1) Market price of cotton during the previous year. (2) Condition of
    previous year's cotton crop or yield per acre in the previous year.
    (3) Area under other competing crops such as sugarcane and maize. (4)
    Supply of canal water at sowing time.

Cotton - United States

Annual textile number - Sections 2, 3 and 4. Jour. Com., Jan. 27, 1936.
    (Published in New York, N. Y.)
        Section two, which is devoted to cotton goods, cotton mills, wool,
    and wool goods contains 22pp; section three has 8pp., and gives a review
    of the rayon industry and of other synthetic fibers; and section four-
    also 8pp., in length, is the Special Cotton Crop and Market Survey - the
    first of the series of special cotton surveys scheduled to appear monthly
    during 1936.

Cohn, D. L. Tariff revision and cotton. Cotton Digest 8(11): 4-6. Dec.
    21, 1935. (Published at 702 Cotton Exchange Bldg., Houston, Tex.)
        "Excerpts from address before Mid-South Farm Forum, Memphis, Tenn.,
    Dec. 11, 1935."
        The author reviews briefly the history of the Government's tariff
    policy since 1861, and its effect on cotton, and points out the need of
    the South and Middle West for tariff revision.

[Cotton and the AAA] Tex. Weekly 12(6): 1-3. Feb. 8, 1936. (Published at
    the Dallas Athletic Club Bldg., Dallas, Tex.)
        Editorial pointing out that while the world used more cotton during
    1935-36 than at any other time, the consumption of American cotton remains
    at a very low level.

Commenting on the repeal of the Bankhead law, the Editor says in part: "The ginning tax was never anything but...a penalty, and it was never intended to be anything but a penalty. It was designed to force into line such farmers as would not agree in consideration of benefit payments to curtail their cotton acreage. And at the time it was offered, the argument was made that unless such a law was enacted, the attempt to control production by means of the AAA program would break down. That was but another way of saying that there is no constitutional way of controlling production, because there never was the slightest doubt about the constitutionality of the Bankhead law...The question naturally arises, it seems to us, that if it was not possible to succeed in controlling acreage under the Agricultural Adjustment Act without a supplementary measure like the Bankhead law, how is it going to be possible to succeed in controlling acreage under a soil conservation law, without some such compulsory measure?"

[Cotton exports declining again] Tex. Weekly 12(5): 1-2. Feb. 1, 1936. (Published at the Dallas Athletic Club Bldg., Dallas, Tex.)
Editorial pointing out the decline in cotton exports since the AAA decision of the Supreme Court. "It is just possible that the cause of this slump in cotton exports is the uncertainty created by the invalidating of the AAA. But there is another possible explanation. It is that the Government has the spot cotton market cornered, and that cotton is not available for shipment abroad at prevailing market prices. If this is not the situation, it will not be long until such a situation exists."
The Editor also draws attention to a news item, stating that Norman S. Pearse, general secretary of the International Federation of Master Cotton Spinners and Manufacturers' Association, passing through New York on his way to Brazil said "I hope as a result [of this visit] to influence cotton planters in Brazil to take even greater care in the preparation of raw cotton." It is also stated that "World spinners... are doing everything possible to encourage the production of cotton outside the United States."

[Cotton consumption] Tex. Weekly 12(3): 1. Jan. 18, 1936. (Published at Dallas Athletic Club Bldg., Dallas, Tex.)
Editorial on the subject of consumption of American cotton and a program of controlled production.

Cox, A. B. Cotton. Tex. Business Rev. 9(10): 4-5. Nov. 30, 1935. (Published by Bureau of Business Research, University of Texas, Austin, Tex.)
The author points out steps taken by the Government to carry out parts of a program proposed by him a year ago.

Cox, A. B. Cotton. Tex. Business Rev. 9(11): 4. Dec. 30, 1935. (Published by Bureau of Business Research, University of Texas, Austin, Tex.)
The author concludes "that the cotton restriction program to raise price has been a disastrous failure, that the advance in the price of American cotton in the United States has been due entirely to the devaluation of the dollar."

Geller, Carl. Has Uncle Sam cornered cotton? Likelihood of squeeze in better
grades - cotton corners of the past. Com. and Finance 25(2): 64-65, 85,
Jan. 25, 1936. (Published at 45 Broad St., New York, N. Y.)

Cotton Spinning Industry Bill - England

Ascoli, W. S. The Lancashire cotton industry; a criticism of the cotton spinning industry bill. Nineteenth Century 119(708): 161-173. February 1936.
(Published by Constable & Co., Ltd., Orange St., Leicester Square, London,
W. C. 2, Eng.)
This is a criticism of the British cotton spinning industry bill which
"aims at creating a shortage of supply to raise prices." The main features
of the bill as summarized by the writer are as follows:
"(a) By removing surplus capacity or creating a shortage of supply, to
stop internal price-cutting. Redundancy of plant is presumed and no
ultimate objective is predicated.
"(b) Provision is made for the removal and destruction of an undefined
quantity of spinning plant (according to the Colwyn Scheme, 10 million
spindles).
"(c) All spinners electing to remain in business must pay for the
plant to be destroyed by means of a levy of one and one-sixth of a penny
per spindle owned, per annum, for a period of fifteen years.
"(d) Absolute power is given, in all matters connected with (1) The
purchase of plant, (2) The enforcement of the levies, (3) Prevention of
extensions to existing plant, (4) Entry of new enterprise into the industry, (5) Entry and inspection of mills and acquisition of statistical
and all other information regarding output, to a Spindles Board of three
members to be appointed by the Board of Trade."

Cotton Textile Industry

Webb, T. H. Cotton textile industry faces better prospects. Manfrs. Rec.
105(1): 22, 66. January 1936. (Published at Commerce and Water Sts.,
Baltimore, Md.)
In which the writer states that "Uncertainty is perhaps the most
disturbing element in industrial life as well as in other forms. That
vague possibility that something may happen, or has happened whose
influences are unpredictable is a baffling hazard that does not permit
the human mind to be able to plan intelligently."

Cottonseed

Rawls, F. H., and Lund, C. E. Cottonseed - a leading cash crop. Survey
of Current Business 15(12): 16-18, tables, charts. December 1935. (Pub-
lished by Bureau of Foreign and Domestic Commerce, U. S. Department of
Commerce)
A survey of the industry.
Also in Cotton and Cotton Oil Press 36(52): 8-9, 13, tables, charts.
Dec. 28, 1935.

Economic Conditions - Germany

Germany's future. Econ. Forum 3(3): 256-272. winter 1936. (Published at
51 Pine St., New York, N. Y.)

An anonymous article by a German business man and student of economic
affairs, in six parts: I, Hitler's original economic program; II, Hitler's
compromises force race issue; III, Practical policy vs. Nazi doctrines;
IV, Germany's financial problems; V, The present racial policy; VI, Conclusions and future outlook.

Economic Geography

Economic Geography, v. 12, no. 1, pp. 1-107. January 1936. (Published by
Clark University, Worcester, Mass.)

Partial contents: The afforestation of Britain, by T. W. Birch, pp. 1-
26; Agricultural regions of Asia. Part IX-Java, by Samuel van Valkenburg,
pp.27-44; A new map of the manufacturing belt of North America, by Richard
Hartshorne, pp. 45-53; New colonies in old Quebec, by Harold S. Kemp
[aided settlement of the unemployed on the land]pp.54-60; Viticulture in
Ohio, by Paul Cross Morrison, pp.71-85; Methods employed by geographers
in regional surveys, by G. Donald Hudson, pp.98-104.

Economic Reconstruction - Recent Books

Wernette, J. P. Capitalism under fire: recent books on economic reconstruction. Harvard Business Rev. 14(2): 248-255. winter 1936. (Published
for the Graduate School of Business Administration, Harvard University,
at 212-220 York St., York, Pa.)

Reviews the following: The liberal tradition, by Lewis W. Douglas;
The great change, by Richard T. Ely and Frank Bohn; A better economic
order, by John A. Ryan; Government in business, by Stuart Chase; Capitalism
and its culture, by Jerome Davis; Socializing our democracy, by Harry
W. Laidler; The nature of capitalist crisis, by John Strachey; The coming
American revolution, by George Soule.

Economic Recovery - Cuba

America's interest in Cuban economic recovery. The AAA decision as it may
affect the Jones-Costigan Sugar Act. Must postpone country's agricultural reorganization. Accomplishments to date threatened. Barron's
16(3): 9. Jan. 20, 1936. (Published at 44 Broad St., New York, N. Y.)

Economic Recovery - Great Britain

Elliston, H. B. How Britain does it. Atlantic Monthly 157(1-2): 20-27,
171-178. January-February 1936. (Published at 8 Arlington St., Boston,
Mass.)

This article is in two parts. The first part is entitled "Readjustment",
the second "Recovery."

"The recovery movement in Great Britain," the writer says, "has been
due to three factors. The first two, an off-gold currency and a protective
tariff, were adjustments arising out of Britain's fundamental crisis; the
third, cheap prices and constructional activity, was recovery from the
depression."

The article is closed with the following paragraph:
"There are many publicists in the United States who base their thinking on the theory that American history repeats European history after
a lag of a generation. Planning has sustained a reverse in popular estimation in the United States. 'Back to normalcy' is once again heard
over the land. 'Normalcy', however, is gone in Britain, along with all
such meaningless shibboleths of the post-war decade. Britain, for good
or ill, appears to be so committed to planning and management by the
state that even a repair of the world system does not seem likely to
mark any retreat to 'letting nature take its course.'"

Estate Management and the Depression - Scotland

Estate management as affected by recent agricultural depression. Scot. Jour.
Agr. 18(4): 309-317. October 1935. (Published by H. M. Stationery Office, Edinburgh, Scotland)
    A brief account of the reaction upon estate management in Scotland
of the agricultural depression. It is found to have varied in degree
and in date.

Factoring

Jones, O. T. Factoring. Harvard Business Rev. 14(2): 186-199. winter 1936.
(Published for the Graduate School of Business Administration, Harvard
University, at 212-220 York St., York, Pa.)
    Subtopics of this article on factoring in the textile and other in-
dustries are: Definition and functions; increased recognition; the factor's
history and evolution (evolution, the factor in law, the leading factors,
developments in the factoring field); the factor's functions and operations (contract, discounting and credit functions, merchandising function,
auxiliary services, compensation); the factor's economic position;
clientele of the factor; the factor's future. A form of factor's contract
is included.

Farm Survey - Belgium

Frateur, J. L., Misner, E. G., Kinget, R., and Jonkmans, V. Étude économique
de quelques exploitations agricoles belges. Louvain. Universite.
Institut des Sciences Économiques. Bulletin 7(1): 37-66. November 1935.
(Published by Institut des Sciences Économiques, Louvain, Belgium.)
    This article gives the results, illustrated by a number of tables, of
an investigation of 34 Belgian farming enterprises made in 1934. The
information was obtained as far as possible from bookkeeping accounts and
available documents and was collected in order to study the factors that
influenced the financial results of the enterprises in question. The
study deals with capital, receipts, expenditure, return from the labor
of the cultivator, return in kind. Under the heading of Analysis of
Results a table lists the factors which have contributed to the analysis
of the 34 enterprises selected. They include revenues from various
sources, extent of the enterprise, rate of production, labor efficiency,
and efficiency in the use of capital.

Walker, L. M., Jr. Increase in farms: 1930-1935. Univ. Va. News Letter,
v. 12, no. 9, Feb. 1, 1936. (Published in University, Va.)
Accompanied by tables showing increase in number of farms in Virginia
and adjoining states and the United States, 1930-1935; and increase in the
number of farms in Virginia counties showing per cent change and rank
in per cent change, 1930-1935.

Flax - France

Le Marché du lin en France. Revue des Agriculteurs de France 68(1): 8-13.
January 1936. (Published at 8, Rue d'Athènes, Paris, France)
A study of flax production and marketing in France and a plea for
state measures to encourage increased production. Tables give area cultivated in 1862, 1882, 1892, 1902, 1912, 1913, 1931-1935, production
for 1913, 1931-1935, and imports and exports for 1933, 1934 and January-
October 1935.

Food Prices and Wages - Germany and Czechoslovakia

Food prices and wages in Germany. Scot. Jour. Agr. 18(4): 376-377. October
1935. (Published by H. M. Stationery Office, Edinburgh, Scotland)
A summary of an article in the Prager Tagblatt in which a comparison
was made of retail prices and workers' wages in Prague and a German
provincial town of about the same size.
A table gives compared prices of food in the two towns.

Food Rationing - U.S.S.R.

Abolition of ration cards and fixing of food prices in the Soviet Union.
Monthly Labor Rev. 42(1): 268-272. January 1936. (Published by the
Bureau of Labor Statistics, U. S. Dept. of Labor)
This article discusses the ration-card system, the decrees abolishing
ration cards and fixing retail prices, and wages. Accompanied by
statistical tables which show retail prices of bread, flour, and other
cereal products in Soviet Government stores, Jan. 1 to Sept. 1, and
since Oct. 1, 1935; retail prices of food products in Soviet Government
stores in force from Oct. 1, 1935; wages of textile workers in Moscow at
the end of 1934.

Food Supply - Germany

Germany's food problem. Economist 122(4822): 173-174. Jan. 25, 1936. (Published at 8 Bouverie St., Fleet St., London, E.C. 4, Eng.)
The following extract has been taken from this article:
"Germany mainly needs foodstuffs of high quality, and the peasants
produce mainly these foodstuffs. But the self-sufficiency in cereals
organised in the interests of the big landowners actually checks the
production of meat, butter and so on. It is precisely this state of
affairs which had declared itself so acutely in the shortage of butter
and pork in Germany this winter. For the development of these commodities

requires cheap fodder, which must be imported. But the German Government, in its zeal to import quite other commodities than foodstuffs,
had ruthlessly cut down imports of fodder and foodstuffs from countries
like Holland, Denmark, Switzerland, etc. Moreover, the Government has
insisted on raising the price of fodder, with the result that all other
prices have risen...
    "In short, the interests of both the peasant and the industrial workers
have been sacrificed to those of the great landed proprietors."

Germany's growing self-sufficiency in food. Scot. Jour. Agr. 18(4): 374-376.
    October 1935. (Published by H. M. Stationery Office, Edinburgh, Scotland)
        "Self-sufficiency in food is the aim of the National Socialist agri-
    cultural policy and the ways and means of attaining the goal are set out
    by the party's Agricultural Group under...ten heads." These are given.
    A table shows the proportion of home production to home consumption of
    foodstuffs and agricultural raw materials.

Government Employees and the Civil Service

Sullivan, Lawrence. Our new spoils system. Atlantic Monthly 157(2): 189-197.
    February 1936. (Published at 8 Arlington St., Boston, Mass.)
        On the growth of the spoils system and the decline of the merit system
    under the present administration.

Weybright, Victor. Our civil servants. Survey Graphic 25(2): 91-95, 116.
    February 1936. (Published at 112 E. 19th St., New York, N. Y.)
        "The best of laws are futile without a trained civil service to carry
    them out. Much of our depression legislation outran our capacity to
    execute. As National Civil Service Week celebrates the 53rd anniversary
    of the merit system Mr. Weybright gives the highlights of patronage,
    pigeonholes and hope for the future in Washington." Mention is made of
    Dr. Stockberger, promotions, and educational activities in the U. S. Dept.
    of Agriculture.

Government Finance

Government finance in the modern economy; edited by Paul Studenski. Amer.
    Acad. Polit. and Social Sci. Ann. 183; 1-243. January 1936. (Published
    at 3457 Walnut St., Philadelphia, Pa.)
        Contents: Theory of public expenditures, by Gerhard Colm; Public ex-
    penditure policies and trends, by Harold W. Guest; Classification and
    measurement of public expenditures, by Wylie Kilpatrick; Modern fiscal
    systems, their characteristics and trends of development, by Paul
    Studenski; Coordination of Federal, state, and local tax systems, by
    Mabel Newcomer; The social aspect of tax exemption, by James W. Martin;
    The use of the taxing power for non-fiscal purposes; by Harvey W. Peck;
    A defense of the single tax principle, by Harry Gunnison Brown; Rates
    and revenues of public enterprises, by John Bauer; The place of personal
    income taxes in a modern fiscal system, by Clarence Heer; The proper sphere
    of death taxes, by Paul Haensel; The taxation of business enterprise - its
    theory and practice, by Alfred G. Buehler; The sales tax, by Carl Shoup;
    Excises in modern times, by Alzada Comstock; Customs duties as a revenue
    resource, by A. M. Fox; The general property tax, the mainstay of local

fiscal autonomy, by Jens P. Jensen; Special assessments and licenses, by
Ernest Herman Hahne; Public credit, its potency and limitations, by Paul
Studenski; The technique of borrowing and repayment, by T. David Zukerman;
A proposal for complete government ownership of currency and credit, by
Irving P. Altman; Financial planning - its political and economic basis,
by A. E. Buck; An inventory of state supervision of local finance, by
Wylie Kilpatrick; Federal tax administration, by Roswell Megill; Administration of state taxes as viewed by an administrator, by Mark Graves;
Administration of the property tax, by J. L. Jacobs; Financing of public
works - an expansionist point of view, by David Cushman Coyle; Financing
social security, by Abraham Epstein; An approach to the problem of war
finance, by John T. Flynn; Soviet government finance and the economic
plan, by Alexander Gourvitch; Notes on books and materials in public
finance, by Mabel L. Walker.
     Pages 241-271 of this issue of the Annals consist of a supplement on
the topic of Rising Prices and the Consumer. It contains the following
papers New deal costs and the high cost of living, by Gilbert H. Montague;
The prospect of rising prices from the monetary angle, by Edwin Walter
Kermerer; The consumer and competition, by Leon Henderson.

Grain - Argentina

Allensworth, A. P.   The Argentine cereal trade.   Northwest. Miller 185(4):
     279, 288, 289. Jan. 29, 1936. (Published at 118 S. 6th St., Minneapolis,
     Minn.)
          "This article by Mr. Allensworth was prepared as one of a series of
     informative lectures on grain and its marketing, under the auspices of the
     Association of Grain Commission Merchants, Chicago." -Editor's Note.

Grain - Canada

Canadian grain situation and outlook.   Modern Miller 63(5): 16, 19. Feb. 1,
     1936. (Published at 175 W. Jackson Blvd., Chicago, Ill.)
          "From a report, 'The Agricultural Situation and Outlook 1936,' issued
     by authority of James G. Gardiner, Minister of Agriculture, and W. D.
     Euler, Minister of Trade and Commerce, Ottawa, Can." The portion
     of the report that is here reprinted covers the Canadian Grain situation.

Grain - Europe

Mayer, Simon.   Grain raising and marketing in Europe.   Modern Miller 63(6):
     17, 29. Feb. 8, 1936. (Published at 175 W. Jackson Blvd., Chicago, Ill.)
          "This is one of a series of informative lectures on Grain and Its
     Marketing sponsored by the Association of Grain Commission Merchants of
     the Chicago Board of Trade." The lecture was delivered on Feb. 6, 1936.
     Also in Southwest. Miller 14(50): 21, 42. Feb. 11, 1936.

Hog Breeding and Earning Capacity of Farms

Leclarzec, Joseph.   Pig breeding as a factor in the earning capacity of
     agriculture in certain European countries from 1927-28 to 1931-32.
     Monthly Bull. Agr. Econ. and Sociol. [reprint from Internatl. Rev. Agr.]

26(12): 421-429. December 1935. (Published by the International Institute of Agriculture, Villa Umberto I(110), Rome, Italy)

This is the concluding article in the series on the extent to which pig-breeding has influenced the earning capacity of farms in certain European countries. Other articles appeared in the May, July, August, and September numbers of the Monthly Bulletin.

Hog Chilling Room - Air Conditioning

Air conditioned hog chilling. One packer's results with new system indicate savings which have been made. Natl. Provisioner 94(3): 9-11, 25, 27. Jan. 18, 1936. (Published at 407 S. Dearborn St., Chicago, Ill.)

"Meat plant air conditioning - what it is, why it is needed, where it should be used - was discussed in detail in the August 10, 1935, issue of The National Provisioner. How may it be used? Its use in the smokehouse was described in the October 5 issue. Its application to the hog chill room was discussed in the November 2 issue. Here the proof of results in one instance is given in detail. Air conditioning in other departments of the meat plant will be described in later articles." - Editor's note.

Hogs - Germany

The pig situation. Scot. Jour. Agr. 19(1): 80. January 1936. (Published by H. M. Stationery Office, Edinburgh, Scotland)

A brief summary of the pig situation in Germany shows that "the pig marketing regulations have been tightened up...A new order prohibits the slaughter of immature beasts."

Housing - England

Housing in Great Britain. Background to the building boom. Index 16(2): 21-26. February 1936. (Published by the New York Trust Company, 100 Broadway, New York, N. Y.)

Shears, R. T. Housing the rural worker: progress of reconditioning in Devon. Gt. Brit. Min. Agr. Jour. 42(6): 542-550. September 1935. (Published by H. M. Stationery Office, London, Eng.)

Under the Housing (Rural Workers) Act, 1926 1,200 dwellings have been reconditioned in Devonshire. "Work is in progress on a further 150, whilst provisional approval has been given in regard to 60 others." The extent and conditions of the grant are explained. The cost of the Devon scheme is estimated, and a number of illustrations show groups of reconditioned cottages.

Income, Agricultural - United States

Purves, C. M. The improvement in agricultural income in 1935. Agr. Situation 20(1): 2-6. January 1936. (Published by the Bureau of Agricultural Economics, U. S. Dept. of Agriculture)

Subtopics: Gross income 12 percent above 1934; cash income 10 percent larger; expenses also increased but not so much; more money chiefly from

grains and livestock; increased income result of higher prices, especially
livestock; larger crops in 1935; less livestock; farmers buying more.
Accompanied by two tables showing gross income from farm production and
rental and benefit payments by groups of commodities, 1932, 1934 and 1935;
index numbers of the volume of agricultural production 1919-1935; and a
chart showing distribution of gross income from farm production, 1924 to
date.

Income, National - United States

Nathan, R. R.   The national income: what the United States produces and earns.
The World Today. Encyclopaedia Britannica 3(3): 10-11.   February 1936.
(Published at 342 Madison Ave., New York, N. Y.)
    Accompanied by three tables which show national income paid out and
produced, annually 1929-1934; national income paid out, by type of payment,
annually 1929-1934; income produced by industrial divisions, for the same
years.

Income and Economic Progress

Moulton, H. G.   The trouble with capitalism is the capitalists. Economic
progress without revolution. 46pp. (Pam. Coll. - Book reviews)
    Reprinted from Fortune, v. 12, no. 5, November 1935, by the Maurice
and Laura Falk Foundation, Farmers Bank Building, Pittsburgh, Pennsylvania.
    Summarizes the study of the distribution of wealth and income in re-
lation to economic progress (4v.) made by the Brookings Institution, but
"lays its emphasis on the conclusions reached in the final volume, Income
and Economic Progress."
    Between pages 4 and 5 are inserted 6 pages of comment on Dr. Moulton's
article by Alfred P. Sloan, Henry A. Wallace, Walter C. Teagle, William
Green, Walter Lippman, Colby M. Chester, and John W. Davis.

Index Numbers

Frisch, Ragnar.   Annual survey of general economic theory: the problem of
index numbers. Econometrica 4(1): 1-38. January 1936. (Published by
the Econometric Society, Mining Exchange Bldg., Colorado Springs, Colo.)

Leontief, Wassily.   Composite commodities and the problem of index numbers.
Econometrica 4(1): 39-59. January 1936. (Published by the Econometric
Society, Mining Exchange Bldg., Colorado Springs, Colo.)

Industrial Utilization of Farm Products

Livingston, L. F.   Chemistry opens new era for agriculture and industry.
The raw materials for the "factory stomach" will come increasingly from
the farm. Mag. Wall St. 57(7): 380-381, 419, 420,421. Jan. 18, 1936.
(Published at 90 Broad St., New York, N. Y.)

Livingston, L. F.   The farm's new day. Nation's Business 24(2): 27-28, 76-77. February 1936. (Published by the Chamber of Commerce of the United States, Washington, D. C.)
     The writer foresees a new day for agriculture in which there will be great industrial utilization of farm products and in which the importance and influence of the agricultural engineer will be greatly increased.

Insurance, Hail - Spain

Arcoleo, F.   Hail insurance in Spain. Monthly Bull. Agr. Econ. and Sociol. [reprint from Internatl. Rev. Agr.] 26(12): 439E-448E. December 1935. (Published by the International Institute of Agriculture, Villa Umberto I(110): Rome, Italy)

Kansas City Board of Trade

Savory, Richard.   Kansas City Board of Trade progress 1856-1936. Modern Miller 63(6): 16. Feb. 8, 1936. (Published at 175 W. Jackson Blvd., Chicago, Ill.)

Labor in Sugar Cultivation under A.A.A.

Ham, W. T.   Regulation of labour conditions in sugar cultivation under the Agricultural Adjustment Act. Internatl. Labour Rev. 33(1): 74-82. January 1936. (Published by the International Labour Office, Geneva, Switzerland. Distributed in the U. S. by the World Peace Foundation, 8 W. 40th St., New York, N. Y.)

Land - Classification

Gooze, Charles.   Progress in rural land classification in the United States. Land Policy Circ. Sup., December 1935. 24pp., mimeogr. (Published by the Resettlement Administration, Washington, D. C.)
     Contents: Classification of land according to use-capabilities; soil surveys (soil productivity ratings, United States soil survey, state productivity ratings); use-capability classification by the U. S. Geological Survey; use-capability classification in Resettlement Administration - region I, New York and Pennsylvania - region II, Alger County, Mich., Minnesota and Wisconsin - region IV, Nicholas and Webster Counties, W. Va. - regions IV, V, and VI, Tennessee Valley - region V, Georgia - region VII, western counties of North Dakota - region IX, California - region X, Montana - region XI, Washington.

Land Improvement - Great Britain

Stapledon, R. G.   The green hills. I. Hill land and high farming. Country Life 79(2033): 22-23. Jan. 4, 1936. (Published at 20, Tavistock St., London, W. C. 2, Eng.)
     "Two-thirds of Great Britain is wasted in hill grazings and rough pastureland - unproductive agriculturally and largely inaccessible. In two articles based on his remarkable book 'The Land Now and Tomorrow,' Professor Stapledon outlines a means of correcting this serious wastage in the national economy. In two sentences, his plan is (i) to double the

agricultural population by reclaiming grass, especially hill, land; (11)
to make these empty spaces available for the health and recreation of the
town population. In...[this] article he speaks with authority as Director
of the Welsh Plant Breeding Station, which has worked a revolution in
grassland farming." -[Editor's note]

Stapledon, R. G.   The improvement of hill land. Scot. Jour. Agr. 19(1): 11-
24. January 1936. (Published by H. M. Stationery Office, Edinburgh,
Scotland)
      "The improvement of hill land must be considered from three points of
view. It is of primary importance to intensify the farming on the intaken
land. The next endeavour should be to increase the acreage of intaken and
formed land. Generally speaking it is only when either or both of these
necessary undertakings have been put in hand that drastic improvements on
the open hill should be contemplated. I will deal with each of these
aspects of the general problem in turn...Land improvement in all its aspects is a long-range undertaking and demands facilities and organisation."

Land Settlement - Colombia

Agricultural colonization in Colombia. Pan Amer. Union Bull. 69(12): 953-954.
December 1935. (Published in Washington, D. C.)
      Contains a description of the advantages of a large territory on which
the Government of Colombia is establishing an agricultural colony at a
place known as Solano Bay. A large area is open to colonization by
settlers who must be between 18 and 50, of good character, healthy, and
with farming experience. "Everyone accepted as a settler has the right
to 75 hectares (approximately 185 acres) of farm land and a plot within
the city limits of the port; he will receive free lodging for himself and
his family for 90 days at the colony dormitory, have work guaranteed
during the first 10 months spent at the colony at a wage of one peso a
day, receive free medicines, seeds, and tools, and a sum of not more than
200 pesos to help him build his house...Ten families...are to go as the
first pioneers...Upon acceptance a settler must promise in writing to
obey the regulations issued by the Ministry; to build his home within
120 days; to cultivate his tract, devoting at least one hectare to truck
farming and six to cattle raising; to work three days a week on community
projects and three on his land receiving the same wage for both types of
labor. Title to the land is given when the settler has half of his
tract under cultivation, has built a home, and has settled his accounts
with the commissary."
      A brief account is given of "the most successful agricultural settle-
ment project recently carried out by the Colombian Government...in the
Department of Tolima, organized in accordance with a decree issued in 1931."

Land Settlement - Matanuska, Alaska

Hynek, F. Former Michiganders in Alaska. Mich. Farmer 186(3): 69, 72.
Feb. 1, 1936. (Published in Detroit, Mich.)
      Discusses the conditions of the colonists in the Alaska settlement.
There is a small inset at the beginning of this article entitled
"High Cost of Pioneering," dealing with the financial cost of the
experiment.

<u>Land Settlement - Scotland</u>

Murray, J. M.   Forest workers' holdings under the Forestry Commission.
    Scot. Jour. Agr. 19(1): 35-40. January 1936. (Published by H. M.
    Stationery Office, Edinburgh, Scotland)
        "While the objectives of the Forestry Commissioners were the establish-
    ment of families on the land for the provision of workers in the forests
    and the development in the people of a 'forest sense,' their scheme was
    no innovation. Indeed it might be considered a modern continuation of the
    pendicle and also a practical means of putting into operation the recom-
    mendations of the Commission of 1892...
        "Holdings of two main types have been formed. Of the agricultural type,
    on which stock might be kept, there have been completed and occupied 151
    holdings; of those designed to carry poultry there are 173. Each holder
    is provided with a dwelling-house and the buildings that may be necessary
    for the management of his holding...The average extents of land included
    in the holdings, are, in the case of the poultry holdings about one acre,
    and in the agricultural holdings five acres. The latter may also have an
    area of outrun...
        "The success of a holding may depend to a very great extent on the
    holder's wife...Generally, men with experience of country life were selected,
    and they usually had a knowledge of farm work. The period of depression
    in arable farming displaced men who found refuge in these holdings.
        "The determination of the proportionate numbers of each kind of holding
    on a scheme has been governed by the needs of the district and the land
    available...The holders are able to live in houses near to their work in
    the forest; they have an interesting spare-time occupation that produces
    enough money to enable them to live in that house without drawing on their
    wages for the rent; and the produce of the holding adds materially to the
    resources of the larder and to the comfort of the holder and his family.
    Perhaps the best indicator of success is the number of applications for
    holdings that come from friends and relatives of holders. The distribu-
    tion of Forest Workers' Holdings is regulated by the extent of land held
    in the various counties...No difficulty has arisen in combining the
    holdings scheme with forestry...the scheme of Forest Workers' Holdings
    has been successful."

<u>Land Utilization</u>

Hall, O. J.   Bases for land utilization programs. Southwest. Social Sci. Quart.
    16(3): 60-67.   December 1935. (Published by the Southwestern Social Science
    Association, Austin, Tex.)
        The writer's conclusions are quoted, in part, as follows:
        "A comparison of the outcome of planning resulting from Federal legisla-
    tion with results of research on physical, economic, and social factors
    shows certain points of common interest. Each basis of planning assumes
    that the profit motive is still the primary force in directing the activities
    of farmers. Each program attempts to improve the income of agriculture.
    At this point, however, different routes are taken.
        "It may be that proponents of each plan are viewing the present Agricul-
    tural Adjustment Administration program as a somewhat temporary measure
    which will be replaced by a program more in keeping with the economic
    principle of comparative advantage. The earlier discussion of Federal

legislation gives some support to this view. Legislation since 1920 has been of a constantly changing nature and appears to have drawn closer and closer to the cause of low prices of farm products in the United States. However, there is still considerable distance to travel to achieve the final results of land planning which are sought at this time.

"At this point it should be indicated that the development of land planning in the United States during the last 12 months has probably exceeded the fondest hopes of land planners...However, an analysis of the 'status quo' of planning leads to the inevitable conclusion that Federal legislation restricting the output of crops does not function in keeping with the economic principle of comparative advantage, which has been the basis of approach by most land planners.

"Crop restriction provisions of the Agricultural Adjustment Administration are possibly a twofold attempt to aid American agriculture. First as an emergency measure, the surpluses of contract crops have been reduced with the strengthening of the price of these crops. The second objective of the Agricultural Adjustment contracts appears to be the establishing of a parity price for farm products. It is doubtful if the same farm contracts can be used to accomplish both these objectives. A revision of Agricultural Adjustment Administration contracts is essential if Federal legislation affecting land use is to operate in keeping with the more natural factors which result in changes in crop acreage on an individual farm or the general location of crop production.

"Two types of Federal legislation are needed. A mandatory provision is needed for the limitation of crop acreage or crop output, such as is now found in the Agricultural Adjustment Administration contracts for use when the price of farm products reaches the low levels of the years of the recent depression. Legislation of this type would be inactive after agriculture recovery had taken place...

"The second type of legislation should be found even after recovery has occurred. This should provide a tariff-like benefit for the amount of agricultural products which are domestically consumed...This plan should not include acreage restriction provisions but should let expansion take place wherever it might under the prevailing prices. Such legislation would result in coordination of results of legislation affecting land planning and the viewpoint that land planning should be based upon the physical, social and economic factors which historically have affected the use to which land would be placed.

"So long as the present restrictions of acreage apply to each farmer, inequities are inevitable and much high cost production will be forthcoming, whereas areas where low cost production would be possible are prohibited from expanding. If or when Federal legislation is amended to make these changes possible harmony will be brought out of the confusion that now results when one considers the bases of land use, from first, the principle of comparative advantage, and second, the effect of legislation on land utilization."

..., B. C. The use and misuse of land. Trop. Agr. 13(1): 1-3. January 1936. (Published by the Imperial College of Tropical Agriculture, St. Augustine, Trinidad, West Indies)

The problem, as the writer sees it, is not so much misuse of land as it is heavy, or over-use of land, in the tropical colonies of the British Empire. He concludes as follows:

"The land then is the peoples', and if owing to conditions which are the result of their contact with civilisation, namely peace for themselves, and freedom from contagious diseases for their flocks and herds, they are now tending to spoil their own property, civilisation must come to their rescue in their own interests, and educate them in better methods. Meanwhile the government must, for the present, exercise control over, not necessarily own, all such common lands in order that their value may be conserved and placed on a steady yield basis."

Land Utilization and Wilderness - Maine

Barnes, C. P. The relation of wilderness to land utilization in northern Maine. Land Policy Circ., pp.15-19. December 1935. (Published by the Resettlement Administration)
    The author points out that northwestern Maine has an expanse of almost unbroken forest land, covering more than 10,000 square miles, and states that "absence of agricultural settlement and continuous forest production, two of the outstanding characteristics of this region, have been mutually dependent to an important degree. Each has tended to promote the other, yet each has also been dependent upon other factors." The ability of private ownership to sustain forest production, the history of our national development, the mixed character of the forest stand, and the moderate tax policy are given as further reasons for the maintenance of these vast forest areas.

Livestock Improvement Scheme - Great Britain

Live-stock improvement scheme: Report for the year 1934-35. I-II. Gt. Brit. Min. Agr. Jour. 42(8): 750-765. November 1935; (9): 871-878. December 1935. (Published by H. M. Stationery Office, London, Eng.)
    Part II contains statistics of milk recording.

Machine Milking - Scotland

McCandlish, A. C., and Struthers, J. P. Milking-machines in Scotland. Scot. Jour. Agr. 18(4): 363-366. October 1935. (Published by H. M. Stationery Office, Edinburgh, Scotland)
    "During the years 1929 to 1934 there has been an increase in the percentage of milk-recorded herds in Scotland, as well as in the absolute number which are machine-milked. The increase may not seem large, but as an additional 1,305 milk-recorded cows are being machine-milked it may be of some significance."

Marketing Research

Taylor, M. D. Progress in marketing research. Natl. Marketing Rev. 1(2): 177-188. fall 1935. (Published by the National Association of Marketing Teachers, 100 Washington Square East, New York, N. Y.)
    This is a review of marketing research in progress in the following universities: Arizona, Boston, Brigham Young, Buffalo, California, Colgate, Columbia, Denver, De Paul, Harvard, Illinois, Indiana, Kentucky, Michigan, New York, North Carolina, Ohio State, Oregon, Pennsylvania, Stanford, Texas, Toledo, Wisconsin and the State College of Washington;

in the Bureau of Agricultural Economics, the Bureau of the Census, Bureau
of Foreign and Domestic Commerce, and the Federal Trade Commission; by
the National Association of Broadcasters; and doctoral dissertations in
marketing.

Marketing Terms

Definitions of marketing terms. Consolidated report of the Committee on definitions [of the National association of marketing teachers] Natl. Marketing Rev. 1(2): 148-166. fall 1935. (Published by the National Association
of Marketing Teachers, 100 Washington Square East, New York, N. Y.)

Meat - Market Regulation - France

Measures to improve French meat market. Scot. Jour. Agr. 18(4): 373-374.
October 1935. (Published by H. M. Stationery Office, Edinburgh, Scotland)
The aim of the French Government's recent decrees dealing with the meat
market is said to have been "to improve the position of the producers and
insure that they get a somewhat larger profit than they have been getting
of late, and to protect consumers by taking meat of bad quality off the market
and bringing about a fall of retail prices."
Prefects of departments are authorized to fix a maximum retail price of
meat, taking into consideration all the elements entering into the cost of
production, particularly the wholesale prices paid by the butchers.

Milk - Control of Production - Netherlands

Restriction of milk production. Scot. Jour. Agr. 19(1): 81-82. January 1936.
(Published by H. M. Stationery Office, Edinburgh, Scotland)
The proposed measure for controlling the production of milk by re-
stricting the subsidy payable to an amount bearing a specified proportion
to the production in the two previous years has been withdrawn by the
Minister of Agriculture and Fisheries.

Milk - Marketing - Great Britain

Committee of investigation. Home Farmer 3(1): 8-16. January 1936. (Published by the Milk Marketing Board, Thames House, Millbank, London, S.W.1,
Eng.)
A summary of the proceedings of the Committee of Investigation, "which
is inquiring into the complaints of the Central Milk Distributive Committee and the Co-operative Congress against the 1935-36 Milk Contract.
In this summary the milk distributors present their case.

Order replaces chaos in British milk marketing. United Farmer 16(2): 1, 3.
Jan. 10, 1936. (Published in Calgary, Alberta)
Contains the "essential details of the marketing system of the Milk
Marketing Board [Great Britain] which has been established...The story
of the development of the Board is the story of the elimination of wasteful cut-throat competition, and the devising of a pooling system which
assures to all producers an equitable distribution of the prices at which
milk in its various forms is sold."

Walworth, George. Distributors and the Committee of Investigation. Producer
20(1): 5-6. January 1936. (Published at 1, Balloon St., Manchester, Eng.)
An article on the present position of the Milk Marketing Scheme for
Great Britain. The following note accompanies the article: "The Committee of Investigation to which the Minister of Agriculture remitted the
complaints of milk distributors regarding the new contract prescribed by
the Milk Marketing Board is still sitting as we go to press. In this
article, Mr. Walworth, who is Secretary of the Co-operative Milk Trade
Association and Agricultural Organiser for the Co-operative Union, briefly
surveys the events which have led up to the present position, and outlines
the recommendations of the co-operative movement."

Money - Devaluation

Weltwirtschaftliches Archiv 43(1): 1-318. January 1936. (Issued by Kiel University. Institut für Weltwirtschaft. Published by Gustav Fischer, Jena,
Germany)
This issue is composed of a number of articles on typical forms of
devaluation. They are: Gründe und Folgen der Abwertung des englischen
Pfundes, by N.F. Hall.-pp.1-28. (A translation of an English manuscript
on the causes and results of the devaluation of the English pound.); Das
Devalvationsproblem in Dänemark, by Carl Iversen.-pp.29-61. (The devaluation problem in Denmark.); Die faktische Schillingkrone Norwegens, by
Wilhelm Keilhau.-pp.62-81. (A summary of Norway's monetary policy since
1914 shows that with the country's abandonment of the gold standard it left
a position already undermined. "After July 1933 the Bank of Norway has,
without any legal obligation, maintained a sterling exchange standard on
the parity £ 1 = Kr. 19.90 which practically gives an equivalence between
the krone and the shilling."); Der Übergang zur Papierwährung in Schweden, by
Erik Lindahl.-pp.82-96. (Sweden's transition to paper money on September
28, 1931, its causes and effects); Die Abwertung des südafrikanischen
Pfundes, by C. G. W. Schumann.-pp.97-131. (The devaluation of the South
African pound, translated from an English manuscript.); Die Devalvation
in Australien und Neuseeland, by J. L. K. Gifford.-pp.132-164. (Translation of an English manuscript on devaluation in Australia and New
Zealand.); Die Abwertung des japanischen Yen, by Koji Matsuoka.-pp.165-187.
("The devaluation of the yen has generally speaking had a favourable effect on business."); Abwertung und Entwertung in Chile, by Hermann Max.-
pp.188-219. (The author distinguishes between currency depreciation and
devaluation, and analyses the monetary policy of Chile during the past ten
years in which he sees four clearly defined periods.); Die Devaluation
der tschechoslowakischen Krone im Jahre 1934, by Oskar Engländer.-pp.220-
252. (An account of the effect of the devaluation of the krone in Czechoslovakia in 1934.); Die Währungsabwertung und die Politik des wirtschaftlichen
Wiederaufbaus in Belgien, by Charles Roger.-pp.255-289. (Translation of
a French manuscript on Belgium's devaluation policy and its results.);
Die Devaluation in den Vereinigten Staaten, by John Donaldson.-pp.290-318.
(Translation of a portion of an English manuscript on the devaluation of
the dollar in the United States.)

Trend, R. H.   Stabilisation. Lloyds Bank Ltd. Monthly Rev. (n.s.) 6(70):
642-652. December 1935. (Published at 71 Lombard St., London, E. C. 3,
Eng.)
     This is the final article in a series of articles on the question of the
stabilisation of the world's leading currencies published in Monthly Review. "It is proposed to reprint all the articles and to issue them in a
pamphlet at an early date."

Money and Economic Problems-- Recent Books

Burnett, Marguerite.   Books of 1935 that have proved useful to us. Special
Libraries 27(2): 38-41. February 1936. (Published at 345 Hudson St.,
New York, N. Y.)
     An interesting article on the books on monetary policy and stabiliza-
tion, gold and silver, international economic problems, banking, etc.,
that have proved useful to the library of the Federal Reserve Bank of
New York. The article covers books and booklets published during 1935,
but some of an earlier date are included.

New Deal - United States

Dougall, H. E.   Third phase of the new deal. Synopsis of legislation enacted
during last year's record-breaking session of Congress. Acts of vital
economic and social importance were passed. Barron's 16(3): 15, 20.
Jan. 20, 1935. (Published at 44 Broad St., New York, N. Y.)
     Acts are summarized under the following headings: money and banking,
finance, agriculture, debt relief, labor and employment, transportation
and communication, public finance and taxation, relief and public works,
liquor, public utilities, and unemployment insurance.

Eisner, L. P.   Constitution vs. New Deal. Rev. of Reviews 93(1): 41-43, 62.
January 1936. (Published at 233 Fourth Ave., New York, N. Y.)
     "The New Deal's fate waits on pending Supreme Court decisions. And
the Court is no free agent but must act within the bounds of the Constitution. Is a liberalizing amendment inevitable?"

Hirst, F. W. Some impressions of America -- the finance of the new deal.
Lloyds Bank Ltd. Monthly Rev. (n.s.) 7(71): 2-10. January 1936. (Published at 71 Lombard St., London E. C. 3, Eng.)

Lock, J. H.   Judicial interpretation of the new deal. Southwest. Social
Sci. Quart. 16(3): 11-19. December 1935. (Published by the Southwestern
Social Science Association, Austin, Tex.)
     "The trends and tentative conclusions which will be stated herein
are based on a consideration of all of the available decisions of the
federal courts -- Supreme, Circuit, District of Columbia, and Claims --
down to approximately April 1."

Macaulay, F. R.   Economic recovery and the new deal.   Econ. Forum 3(3): 245–255. winter 1936. (Published at 51 Pine St., New York, N. Y.)
    Critical of the New Deal.

Macdonald, Stewart.   Intangible costs of recovery.   Though not subject to exact measurement, they undoubtedly outweigh in their effects and permanence fiscal and economic costs. Barron's 16(3): 24. Jan. 20, 1936. (Published at 44 Broad St., New York, N. Y.)

Northwestern Miller Distributors' Yearbook

The Northwestern Miller Distributors' Yearbook.   Northwest. Miller 185 (3, sect. 2): 1–104. Jan. 28, 1936. (Published at 118 S. 6th St., Minneapolis, Minn.)
    "This is the first number of The Distributors.' Yearbook, which The Northwestern Miller proposes hereafter to publish in January of each year as a special service to its regular subscribers and to its friends in the milling industry and the flour distributing trades.
    "Additional to the miscellaneous text and general trade information included, it contains a list of thousands of flour brands regularly in use by millers and of many brands privately used by wholesale flour merchants." -Introduction
    Contents in part are as follows: What the flour distributor ought to know about flour, by Edgar S. Miller, pp.8b-9; Higher tiering lowers cost of warehousing, by C. B. Cook, p. 9a; Stored flour and its enemies, by Charles H. Briggs, pp.9b-10; Credit in food distribution, by Albert N. Merritt, pp.14, 15; The flour distributor and his banker, by Bert H. Lang, p. 15; Flour storage and transportation, by Wayne G. Martin, Jr., p. 27; and Some milling and grain statistics, pp.98-103.

Olive Culture – Italy

L'Italia Agricola 72(12): 919–1066. December 1935. (Published at Plazzo Margherita, Via Vittorio Veneto, Rome, Italy)
    Contains a number of articles on the economic, cultural, and legislative factors connected with the culture of the olive in Italy.

Peanuts and the A.A.A.

Chamberlin, Jo, and Shaw, Harry.   That burrowing bean.   Rev. of Reviews 93(1): 34-36, 62. January 1936. (Published at 233 Fourth Ave., New York, N. Y.)
    "Pertinent facts and figures on the nut [peanut] which is not a nut, and how the AAA is endeavoring to help the peanut industry."

Pecan Industry – Texas

Mooney, Booth.   Pecans from Texas.   Tex. Weekly 12(3): 8-9. Jan. 18, 1936. (Published at the Dallas Athletic Club Bldg., Dallas, Tex.)
    An article pointing out the volume and value of the pecan industry in Texas.

Plan Age, v. 2, no. 1, pp. 1-28. January 1936. (Published by National
Economic and Social Planning Association, 736 Jackson Place, Washington, D.C
     Contents: Planful control [as contrasted with the "panic planning"
of the last few years] by Lewis L. Lorwin, pp.1-2; Social-economic planning
and regimentation, by H. S. Person, pp.6-8; A closer view of the machinery
of control, by Charles E. Merriam, pp.9-16; Planning government for planning, by Phillips Bradley, pp.17-20; Obstacles to central planning, by
M. H. Hedges, pp. 21-26.

Smith, J. G.   The new individualism, the goal of economic planning. Econ.
Forum 3(3): 326-338. winter 1936. (Published at 51 Pine St., New York,
N. Y.)
     The concluding paragraphs of this article follow:
     "We may have economic planning under socialism; we may have economic
planning under fascism, we may have economic planning under capitalism and
democracy. But if we do, it will be essential to remember that the
nature of society, like an organism, is such that it can only perfect itself through the development of the numbers which compose it. And the
members which compose it are individuals whose development is a matter
of self-articulation.
     "Therefore, it is at least conceivable that the primary goal of economic
planning should be the restoration of confidence in the power of individuals
to use their God-given intelligence; to restore the belief in the basically
important ideal of individual responsibility to a self-respecting self,
to family, to society; and strongly suspect that there might be considerable advantage in the restoration of some of the old-fashioned ideas about
accountability to a Divine Creator."

Prices

Prices in 1935. Economist 122(4820): 59-60. Jan. 11, 1936. (Published at 8
Bouverie St., Fleet St., London E.C.4, Eng.)
     "The movements in prices during the year may consequently be accounted
on the whole healthy. The rises have affected most of those commodities
which fell most calamitously in the downswing of the depression; and they
have been preponderantly due to reviving demand rather than artificially
restricted supply. Similarly the few falls recorded during the year have
been due to increased supplies. After the temporary halt of 1934 therefore, the trend in world prices seems now to be unmistakably upwards.
The once of the movement, however, may have been somewhat accelerated in
the later months of last year by 're-stocking,' partly induced by war
fears, and, in the case of certain metals, by rearmament demand."

Processing Taxes

Clifford, J. C.   What nullification of processing taxes means to meat packers.
Earnings of leading companies vary, but prospect brightens for all. Mag.
Wall St. 57(8): 460-461, 486. Feb. 1, 1936. (Published at 90 Broad St.,
New York, N. Y.)

Production and Prices - Italy

Crea, Valentino. Produzioni e prezzi agricoli nel 1935. Cooperazione Rurale
4(12): 14-17. December 1935. (Published by the Federazione Italiana
Consorzi Agrari, Via XXIV Maggio, 43, Rome, Italy)
1935 is shown to have been a favorable year for Italy's agricultural
production.

Prosperity

Jordan, Virgil. Some reflections on prosperity. Econ. Forum 5(3): 311-318.
winter 1936. (Published at 51 Pine St., New York, N. Y.)
This is the last part of an article, the first part of which appeared
in the Summer, 1935, issue of the Economic Forum.
"So, to sum up," says Mr. Jordan, "the prosperity - and security of
prosperity - of a country consist simply in the continuous effective activity of the individuals in it in trying to satisfy their physical needs and
desires themselves; and sound economics and statesmanship are simply the
science and practical art which encourages and enables them to work effectively to this end."

Raw Materials - Prices

Drews, Max. Die weltrohstcffpreise in bewegung. Wirtschaftsdienst (n.F.)
21(1): 14-16. Jan. 3, 1936. (Published by Hanseatische Verlagsanstalt
A.-G., Hamburg 36, Germany)
A discussion of the movement of prices of raw materials on the world
market with special reference to 1935.

Reclamation - Irish Free State

Kelly, John. Land reclamation in the congested districts. Irish Free State.
Dept. Agr. Jour. 33(2): 183-188. 1935. (Published by Stationery Office,
Dublin, Irish Free State)
The Congested Districts area is defined in accordance with the Irish
Land Act of 1909, and the importance of complete and proper utilization
of the land in those districts is stressed. As a result of a survey
it was found that on 151,123 small holdings there were over 300,000
acres of waste land capable of being economically reclaimed. An experimental land reclamation scheme was put into operation in 1931 to
apply to holdings of low valuation and to land capable of being reclaimed.
The area on which a grant may be paid is not less than one statute rood
or more than 2 acres, and all land must be inspected before the work is
authorized. The amount of the grant is to be one-fourth of the total
estimated cost of reclamation, not less than £1 in any case nor more than
£5 per acre. The scheme is said to have been very successful. It has
provided productive employment for needy smallholders and their sons,
relieved the needy, provided small farmers with ready cash when they
needed it most, produced additional crops, and increased the area of
arable land. A table shows the area reclaimed and the grants earned
from 1931/32 to 1934/35.

Resettlement Administration

Resettlement: Its job. Nation's Agr. 11(5): 6-7, 21, 31. February 1936.
(Published at 58 East Washington St., Chicago, Ill.)
"What comprises the work of the Resettlement Administration? What
are its objectives? What part is it playing in the establishment of
new social and economic conditions? These are pertinent questions.
To answer them we asked a competent Washington newspaper man to prepare
this article for you." -[Editor's note.]

Resettlement of Isolated Settlers

Rowlands, W. A. Relocating the isolated settler. Natl. Munic. Rev. 25(1):
21-22. January 1936. (Published by the National Municipal League, 309
E. 34th St., New York, N. Y.)
"Radio address delivered December 17, 1935, in the You and Your
Government series over a nation-wide network of the National Broadcasting
Company, under the auspices of the Committee on Civic Education by Radio
of the National Advisory Council on Radio in Education and the American
Political Science Association, in cooperation with the National Municipal
League."
Points out the need for the relocation of isolated settlers; states
that "the dominating motives behind any well-conceived settler relocation
plans in regions such as the Lake States must be: Government economy in
roads, schools, fire protection, public health, and relief costs; development of forest and recreational resources on land unfit for farming and
desirable for these purposes; elimination of potential forest fire hazards,
reclamation of rural slums, and improved citizenship and morale"; shows
the futility of relocating settlers without zoning of the lands; etc.

Rice - Texas

Looney, Booth. Rice production in Texas. Tex. Weekly 12(4): 8-9. Jan.
25, 1936. (Published at the Dallas Athletic Club Bldg., Dallas, Tex.)

Rural America

Rural America, v. 14, no. 1, 16pp. January 1936. (Published by the American
Country Life Association, Inc., 105 E. 22nd St., New York, N. Y.)
Partial contents: Reorganizing rural health facilities, by Carroll
P. Streeter, pp.3-6 [paper read before the American Country Life Association, Sept. 21, 1935]; World peace and wheat, by Chester C. Davis,
pp.7-8, The improvement of rural government, by Herman G. James, pp.9-11
[an address delivered at the National Forum on Country Life Programs].

Rural Organization - Bulgaria

Organisation of the rural population in Bulgaria. Indus. and Labour Inform.
56(12-13): 443-444. Dec. 23-30, 1935. (Published by International Labour
Office, Geneva, Switzerland. Distributed in U. S. by World Peace Foundation, 8 West 40th Street, New York, N. Y.)

A decree of November 22, 1935 has for its object "to protect the economic interests of the rural population by organising it in economic associations called zadrugas, the zadruga being a sort of rural community of a patriarchal character. The Decree also makes provision for the establishment of mutual insurance and pension funds within the framework of the Federation of Agricultural Economic Associations."

The purpose of the associations, their organization, executive organs and General Assembly, and their resources are briefly discussed.

Seeds Act - Great Britain

The working of the Seeds Act, 1920, in the season, 1934-35. Gt. Brit. Min.
Agr. Jour. 42(9): 920-925. December 1935. (Published by H. M. Stationery Office, London, Eng.)

Soil Surveys - England and Wales

Robinson, G. W. Soil surveys and their applications. Gt. Brit. Min.
Agr. Jour. 42(6): 561-570. September 1935. (Published by H. M. Stationery Office, London, Eng.)

The author calls attention to some of the applications of soil survey work as it is being carried on in England and Wales. Its most immediate practical utility is shown in connection with advisory work, supplemented by field experiments. Detailed surveys are made where intensive utilization of the soil is proposed, and the soil survey is of service in studying the adaptation of soils to particular crops. The survey of rough grazings and waste lands is of importance in schemes of afforestation, and soil surveys are of value in connection with housing schemes. With regard to the future the author says that "some attempt at planning the future of our agriculture, our horticulture, and our forestry, or in other words, how we shall use our soil, seems inevitable...Soil surveys must thus be regarded as long-range research work, which, although it yields immediate results by its assistance to current advisory work, may be expected to perform its greatest service by providing fundamental data for the guidance of planned development in future years."

Soybeans - Manchuria

Manchurian soybean situation. Foreign Crops and Markets 32(3): 80-86. Jan.
20, 1936. (Published by the Division of Foreign Agricultural Service, Bureau of Agricultural Economics, U. S. Dept. of Agriculture)

A review of the situation accompanied by statistical tables showing area and production in Manchuria, annually 1929-1935; production, carry-over from last crop year, total supply, exports, carryover at end of crop year, and home consumption and seed, crop years 1929/30-1935/36; exports of soybeans, and products, crop years 1929/30-1934/35; exports from Manchuria by countries of destination, of soybeans and products, crop years, 1931/32-1934/35; average monthly prices of soybeans and products at Dairen in silver yen and United States currency, October 1932 to November 1935.

State Farms - U.S.S.R.

Agriculture in the Soviet Union. Reorganisation of the Commissariat of State
Farms. Indus. and Labour Inform. 56(12-13): 446. Dec. 23-30, 1935.
(Published by International Labour Office, Geneva, Switzerland. Distributed
in U. S. by World Peace Foundation, 8 West 40th Street, New York, N. Y.)
    Among the objects of an order of November 28, 1935 for the reorganization
of the Commissariat of State Farms are the establishment of closer contact between the Commissariat and the State farms through abolition of
intermediaries, and the extension of the powers of the State farm managers.

Statistical Method

Neyman, J., with co-operation of K. Iwaszkiewicz and St. Kołodziejczyk.
Statistical problems in agricultural experimentation. Roy. Statis. Soc.
Sup. to the Jour. 2(2): 107-154. 1935. (Published at 9 Adelphi Terrace,
London, W. C.2, Eng.)
    Discussion, pp. 154-180.
    Contents: I, Introductory; II, Local experiments (a, The nature of the
experimental error by methods of Randomized Blocks and Latin Square; b,
Randomized Blocks or Latin Square; c, Measures of accuracy; d, Randomized
Blocks or Latin Square? Numerical examples; e, "Second kind errors" in
a comparison of two objects); III, Multiple trials; IV, Appendix: The
variance of error by the methods of Randomized Blocks and the Latin Square.

Yates, F. Complex experiments. Roy. Statis. Soc. Sup. to the Jour. 2(2):
181-223. 1935. (Published at 9 Adelphi Terrace, London, W.C. 2, Eng.)
    Discussion, pp. 223-247.
    The following is quoted from the writer's introductory paragraphs:
    "Several papers have recently been read before this Section or pub-
lished in the Supplement to the Journal which have dealt with one aspect or
another of the randomized block and Latin square methods of carrying out
replicated experiments.
    "These methods were first developed in connection with field trials in
agriculture, but since their inception it has been abundantly clear that
they are of very wide application, and are therefore of interest to experimental workers in almost all branches of science and technology. The
paper I propose to give to-night may be considered as belonging to the
same series. In it I intend to deal with another aspect of the methods
which has not yet been discussed, namely the part which treatments play
in experimental design.
    "Following the previous writers, I shall describe the special technique
which has been developed in agricultural field trials, but it is hoped
that the paper will prove of interest not only to agricultural workers,
but also to workers in many other branches of research."

Subsistence Homesteads - Argentina

Subsistence homesteads in Argentina. Pan Amer. Union, Bull. 69(12): 954-955
December 1935. (Published in Washington, D. C.)
    "A rural settlement plan evolved by the Ministry of Agriculture of the
Argentine Republic, in accordance with a decree issued on August 7, 1935,

seeks to establish villas rurales (farm settlements) for the purpose of
providing permanent homes for peons, laborers and wage earners in general,
who work in the different national Territories, as well as to concentrate
in these villas those squatters who may be found in farming colonies and
who do not have the means for purchasing average-sized parcels of land.
The Villas will be set up in the outskirts of towns or cities or within
the colonies already established in national lands. Lots of nine acres
will be awarded to duly qualified applicants who will be allowed liberal
terms of payment...The settlers will have land on which to build their
homes, and in addition be able to raise crops to meet the immediate needs
of their subsistence."

Sugar - Production Control - Brazil

La convención de la industria azucarera brasileña. Creación de una comisión
de distribución y contralor del azúcar. La limitación de las zafras.
La Industria Azucarera 41(506): 673-675. December 1935. (Published
by the Centro Azucarero, Reconquista 336, Buenos Aires, Argentina.)
    At a convention of the Brazilian sugar industry held in October 1935
in Rio de Janeiro a resolution was accepted suggesting the establishment
of a Commission for the distribution and control of production of sugar
and alcohol. Its functions are outlined.

Sugar and the Jones-Costigan Act

Dalton, J. E. Sugar, a case study of the relationship of government and business.
Harvard Business Rev. 14(2): 172-185. winter 1936. (Published for the
Graduate School of Business Administration, Harvard University at 212-220
York St., York, Pa.)
    The purpose of this paper, written before the Supreme Court decision
in the Hoosac Mills case, is to examine the origin of the Jones-Costigan
Sugar Act, "to consider the attitude of business men towards its creation,
to outline the difficulties which were found in its development, and to
analyze the major economic and political factors which were favorable and
unfavorable to its administration."

Sugar Institute Case

The important features of the Sugar Institute case. U. S. Law Week 3(22):
433, 434. Jan. 28, 1936. (Published in Washington, D. C.)
    The case, which is expected to be argued before the Supreme Court on
February 3 and 4, is considered by some to be more important than the
New Deal cases.
    "The main issue in the case is the legality under the Sherman Act of the
agreement by members of the Institute to sell only at prices and terms
openly announced and after interchange of information with each other in
advance of sale, and to adhere to such prices and terms until advance notice
of a change has been publicly given."

Sugar Policy - Great Britain

Sugar policy: proposals of His Majesty's government. Gt. Brit. Min. Agr.
Jour. 42(6): 533-541. September 1935. (Published by H. M. Stationery
Office, London, Eng.)

Gives the conclusions of the Government with regard to the British Sugar policy adopted after consideration of the reports of the Committee presided over by Mr. Wilfrid Greene. It has been decided that the Government will continue to assist the beet sugar indu.try but that the volume of assisted production will be limited. An independent Sugar Commission will be appointed, and the best sugar factory companies amalgamated under its supervision. The financial arrangements to be submitted to Parliament are outlined as well as the proposed relations between the beet sugar factories and the refineries. An extended program of research and education is proposed. The estimated cost of assistance to the beet sugar industry in 1936 is given.

Tariff and the Farmer

Anderson, B. M., Jr.   The farmer and the tariff. U. S. News 4(6): 12. Feb. 10, 1936. (Published at 2201 M St., N. W., Washington, D. C.)
  From an address before the Indianapolis, (Ind.) Chamber of Commerce, Jan. 30, 1936.
  The solution of the farm problem as seen by the speaker is the "restoration of the export market, the thoroughly Constitutional path of lowering tariffs, letting a wide diversification of foreign manufactures come in to pay for our agricultural exports."

Taxation - Arkansas

Brannen, C. O.   Taxation trends and their relation to agriculture. Southwest. Social Sci. Quart. 16(3): 20-23. December 1935. (Published by the Southwestern Social Science Association, Austin, Tex.)
  State and local taxation trends in Arkansas.

Taxation - Texas

Hughes, Vernon.   Should Texas enact a general sales tax? Southwest. Social Sci. Quart. 16(3): 24-28. December 1935. (Published by the Southwestern Social Science Association, Austin, Tex.)
  The pros and cons of the sales tax are considered.
  "Texas can do much better than to resort to the so-called fiscal panacea of the sales tax."

Tennessee Valley Authority

Morgan, A. E.   Social and economic implications of TVA. pp.[754]-757. (CE-591). Pam. Coll.
  "Reprinted from Civil Engineering for December 1935 [v. 5, no. 12]."
  Social and economic planning in the Tennessee Valley as represented in unified control of the Tennessee River and its tributaries, in forestry work, in soil conservation, in developing a new agricultural policy, and in not working for profits in its electrical business but in working for the public interests.

Tomatoes, Canning - Grading - Ohio

Baker, M. W.   Grading canning tomatoes.   Canning Trade 58(23): 53-54, 56.
    Jan. 13, 1936. (Published in Baltimore, Md.)
        A report on the grading of tomatoes for canning in Ohio, made before
    the Ohio Canners Convention, Cincinnati, December 11, 1935.

Trade, Foreign - United States

Nation must protect its foreign trade. Sphere 17(2): 21-22, 29, 40. February
    1936. (Published at the Munsey Bldg., Washington, D. C.)
        Discusses "a threat of serious proportions to United States foreign
    trade, to the Administration's trade-reciprocity program and to an undeter-
    mined number of United States industries [which] has been created by the
    Supreme Court's decision in the AAA case and by the attitude of Congress
    toward neutrality."

Our export trade still lags. Tex. Weekly 12(4): 4-6. Jan. 25, 1936. (Pub-
    lished at the Dallas Athletic Club Bldg., Dallas, Tex.)
        An article in which it is stated that "We have long been convinced
    that nothing like normal prosperity for the mass of the American people,
    with full and profitable employment in all lines, will be restored until
    American export trade has been restored. And we are likewise convinced
    that there will be no real restoration of our export trade until there
    is a very material revision downward of the American tariff as an essential
    first step toward getting down the trade barriers of the world, coupled
    with stabilization of currencies and international exchange and a drastic
    scaling down and permanent disposal of intergovernmental debts...the
    reciprocal trade agreement policy only scratches the surface of the real
    problem. The real problem is how to restore trade and thus promote domestic
    revival sufficiently to put the unemployed back to work and enable the
    farmers to produce normal crops again profitably."

Peek, G. N.   America's choice. Econ. Forum 3(3): 237-244. winter 1936.
    (Published at 51 Pine St., New York, N. Y.)
        To clarify the question of neutral American trade with belligerent
    nations the writer contrasts the American point of view with the inter-
    nationalist point of view. Extracts from the American policy follow:
    "I. Rigorous tightening of immigration laws...II. Preservation of the
    American market, American price levels and American employment...III.
    Stabilization of American price level - thereafter stabilization by
    agreements with individual countries or blocs where possible (i.e. a
    managed currency based on national bookkeeping). IV. Control of export
    of capital...V. Navy designed to meet American requirements, including
    defense of the Panama Canal and the Pacific Coast. VI. Development of
    American shipping and communications systems. VII. Settlement of dis-
    putes by arbitration confirmed by the Senate. VIII. In case of wars in
    Europe or Asia, strict neutrality and avoidance of 'moral' judgments on
    belligerents. 'Cash and carry' policy for direct or indirect trade with
    belligerents. For the Americas, the Monroe Doctrine plus the Good
    Neighbor Policy."

Peck, G. N.   Let us choose America. Country Home 60(2): 11-12. February
1936. (Published at 250 Park Ave., New York, N. Y.)

"A year ago last March President Roosevelt asked me to make a study
of our foreign trade situation. I went at it the one way I know how, 'the
business way. Foreign trade is a significant part of the business of the
people of the United States. They ought to be shown the books, month by
month. Where do we stand? Which lines are gaining? Which lines are losing?
Are we being paid? If so, How? How can we revise or apply our efforts to
the greatest advantage?"

Following this introductory paragraph, Mr. Peck writes of his findings
in this study of the foreign trade situation. In a brief editorial note
it is stated that Mr. Peck "put dynamite under the current belief that 'we
can export more only if we are to import more.'"

Trade Agreements

Agriculture in the Latin-American trade agreement. Foreign Crops and Markets
32(4): 121-129. Jan. 27, 1936. (Published by the Division of Foreign
Agricultural Service, Bureau of Agricultural Economics, U. S. Dept. of
Agriculture)

Contains "summaries of the agreements with Haiti, Brazil, Colombia, and
Honduras, with details of the tariff concessions granted to the United
States on agricultural products."

Agriculture in the Netherlands trade agreement. Foreign Crops and Markets
32(3): 87-111. Jan. 20, 1936. (Published by the Division of Foreign
Agricultural Service, Bureau of Agricultural Economics, U. S. Dept. of
Agriculture)

Agriculture in the Swiss trade agreement. Foreign Crops and Markets 32(5):
142-151. Feb. 3, 1936. (Published by the Division of Foreign Agricultural Service, Bureau of Agricultural Economics, U. S. Dept. of Agriculture)

Becker, E. L.   America's reciprocal tariff policy. Significance of the trade
agreement between the United States and Canada. World Trade 8(1): 3-5.
January 1936. (Published by the International Chamber of Commerce, 38,
Cours Albert Premier, Paris, France)

Peek, G. N.   Great injustice to farmers are the reciprocal trade agreements.
Natl. Grange Monthly 33(1): 7, 11. January 1936. (Published in Springfield, Mass.)

Radio address on the National Grange hour, in which Mr. Peek discussed
the reciprocal trade agreements program in general, and the Canadian
agreement in particular.

Baikec, C. F. G.   The Holland-American trade treaty, Northwest. Miller 185(4):
230. Jan. 29, 1936. (Published at 118 S. 6th St., Minneapolis, Minn.)
A discussion of some of the provisions in the new trade agreement
between the United States and Holland.

Wallace, H. A.   Trading with our neighbor. Nation's Agr. 11(5): 14-15, 28.
February 1936. (Published at 58 E. Washington St., Chicago, Ill.)
A discussion of the foreign trade situation, including an appraisal
of the Canadian Trade Agreement. Some of the provisions of the agreement
are pointed out.

Unemployment - United States

Carruthers, N. T.   Why "recovery" has not solved unemployment. Mag. Wall
St. 57(7): 375-376, 418. Jan. 18, 1936. (Published at 90 Broad St.,
New York, N. Y.)
"In summary", the writer states, "abnormal unemployment is almost
certainly substantially less than the current estimates of 9,000,000
to 11,000,000 persons. Mechanization has very little to do with the
problem. The percentage of skilled workers unemployed is very small.
The heart of the problem centers in four groups - construction workers,
farm labor, domestic and personal service workers and young people who
have reached working age during the depression.
"It is a social and economic problem of the first rank, but only
partly an industrial problem. Therefore, coercive measures applied to
industry could not possibly attain the objective of normal re-employment
and, if tried further, are foredoomed to failure. The answer is a full
revovery in every branch of an economic organization which always supplied far more work outside of industry than in it."

Nathan, R. R.   Estimates of unemployment in the United States, 1929-1935.
Internatl. Labour Rev. 33(1): 49-73. January 1936. (Published by the
International Labour Office, Geneva, Switzerland. Distributed in the
U. S. by the World Peace Foundation, 8 W. 40th St., New York, N. Y.)
"The United States Security Act of 14 August 1935 provides, inter alia,
for the grant of subsidies to State schemes of unemployment compensation.
As is well known, adequate statistics of unemployment in the United States
have hitherto been woefully lacking. Recognising the need for a sound
statistical basis for their proposals for alleviating unemployment,
the President's Committee on Unemployment Security, which was responsible
for the preparatory work connected with the Act, engaged Mr. Robert E. [?]
Nathan to prepare estimates of unemployment for this purpose. In the
following article Mr. Nathan describes the method adopted in preparing
these estimates, which were used by the Committee in the construction
of the statistical tables upon which its unemployment insurance plan
was based. Tables are annexed [between pp. 80-81] showing the estimates,
both of unemployment and of employment, for a large number of industrial
groups, in each month from January 1929 to October 1935. These tables are
included in the final report of the President's Committee, but have not yet
been published in extenso; they have been brought up to date by the author
for publication in the International Labour Review." -Editorial note.
Number of agricultural workers are included in both tables.

U. S. S. R.

Lorwin, L. L., and Abramson, A.   The present phase of economic and social
development in the U.S.S.R. Internatl. Labour Rev. 33(1): 5-40. January
1936. (Published by the International Labour Office, Geneva, Switzerland.

Distributed in the U. S. by the World Peace Foundation, 8 W. 40th St.,
New York, N. Y.)

This article is an account of some of the information gathered and
of the observations made during a visit to the U.S.S.R. in September
and October 1935. It is "not intended to give a comprehensive view of
conditions in the Soviet Union, but merely an account of some of the
striking changes now taking place."

Conditions in the "Kolkhoz" or collective farm, are described on
pp. 9-12; and the abolition of the ration card system on pp. 12-15.

Wilson, P. W. Soviet and imperial Russia. A comparison. World Today.
Encyclopaedia Britannica 3(3): 24-26. February 1936. (Published at
342 Madison Ave., New York, N. Y.)
Contains a short section on the agricultural revolution, p. 25.

Wealth

Doane, R. R. The division of the national wealth between farm and non-
farm property. Annalist 47(1202): 196-197. Jan. 31, 1936. (Published by the New York Times,Co., New York, N. Y.)
"This is the seventh of a series of articles on the nature, distribution and promise of wealth in the United States." It is accompanied by
five statistical tables and three charts.

Wealth and its distribution. Natl. City Bank of New York. [Monthly letter
on] Econ. Conditions, Govt. Finance, U. S. Securities, February 1936,
pp. 26-31. (Published in New York, N. Y.)
"It is the violent and abnormal disturbances, originating outside of
the economic system and affecting all business, that cause the general
and prolonged depressions. War has been the chief of these causes.
"Agriculture and coal-mining are among the industries that have
suffered most in this depression and in both cases attempts have been
made to provide relief by legislation. The Supreme Court has held
parts of this legislation to be in conflict with the fundamental law
and therefore invalid. The decisions excite much comment. Why is it
that the Constitution adopted by the founders of this Government does
not permit such legislation? Has the country outgrown the Constitution?
Would the legislation have been beneficial or harmful? These questions
are considered in this discussion."

Western States Grower

Western States Grower, v. 19, no. 9, 23pp. November 1935. (Published at
101 Post St., San Francisco, Calif.)
Partial contents: The economic angle of dairy control legislation
and the plan for stabilization and marketing of fluid milk, by H. G.
Claudius, pp. 3-5 [includes a copy of the stabilization and marketing
plan for fluid milk, San Francisco marketing area]; Sales of off grade
quality a source of hidden dangers to the prune industry of California,
by C. D. Cavallaro, pp. 6, 19; Agricultural adjustment and foreign
trade, a statement of AAA foreign trade policy for American growers, by
Brice Mace, Jr., pp. 7-8, 22; Credit for farm production. Here's the

answer to the question of cash for the grower, by T.P. Coats, p. 10;
Permanent co-operative credit for agriculture, by W.I. Myers, pp.12,19;
Agriculture's latest movement - alcohol as a profitable farm product, by
James King Steele, pp.13-14; New marketing agreement for walnuts, by F.
R. Wilcox, p.15.

Western States Grower, v. 19, no. 11, 23pp. January 1936. (Published at 311
California St., San Francisco, Calif.)
Partial contents: How fact-finding econimic research aids California
agriculture. Let us ask "the" foundation. The story of an institution
[Giannini Foundation of Agricultural Economics] founded by a man who
never forgot the soil, as told to James King Steele, pp.3-5; Migratory
farm labor [in northern California] by E. W. Wilson, pp.6, 18; Fidelity
to quality, the acid test of successful co-operative operation, by T. C.
Tucker, p. 18.

Wheat - Australia

Australian wheat industry. Gt. Brit. Min. Agr. Jour. 42(6): 597-601. September
1935. (Published by H. M. Stationery Office, London, Eng.)
Summarizes the "Second and Final Report of the Commonwealth of
Australia Royal commission on the Wheat, Bread and Flour Industries -
issued in February, 1935. It gives a complete economic survey of the industries of growing, handling and marketing wheat and wheat products."

Wheatgrowers' bounty creates disappointment. Primary Producer 20(52): 1.
Dec. 26, 1935. (Published at 38-40-42-44 Stirling St., Perth, West. Aust.)
Contains a statement of J. S. Teasdale, General President of the
Primary Producers' Association regarding the distribution of the wheat
bounty. He said in part; "Definite information has been received by
the Primary Producers' Association that it is the intention of the Federal Government to distribute the wheat bounty on a bushel basis to bring
it into line with the intention of the Federal Wheat Plan to give the
grower a home consumption price. Grants for distressed farmers will be
paid to States for distribution. The distress grant will be distributed
as between States on the basis of relative degree of distress amongst
wheat-growers in various States."
Thes method of distribution is unsatisfactory to Western Australia.

Wheat - Canada

Strang, J. J. "Showing the way!" United Farmer 16 (4): 26. Jan. 24, 1936.
(Published in Calgary, Alberta)
Radio address by the Alberta Wheat Pool Director, 15th January, 1936.
In this address the speaker says: "Summed up the problem of the wheat
grower amounts to this: (1) To continue the production of a high-quality
wheat. (2) To be assured of getting a price for this product that will
support the family in decency and pay interest debts and taxes." He elab-
orates on these two phases of the wheat problem and concludes that the "responsibility rests on the farmers of Western Canada to produce the highest
quality wheat they possibly can, and the Dominion Government must supply
the necessary safeguards through the Wheat Board to keep them in business."

Wheat - International Trade

Reconstruction in international trade. Southwest. Miller 14(46): 21.
Jan. 14, 1936. (Published at 303-12 Board of Trade Bldg. Kansas City, Mo.)
"A Review of Foreign Trade in Wheat and Flour During 1935 by the
English Correspondent of The Southwestern Miller."

Wheat - Market Regulation - France

France: New measures for the regulation of the wheat market. Gt. Brit. Min.
Agr. Jour. 42(9): 938-939. December 1935. (Published by H.M. Stationery
Office, London, Eng.)
   New regulations in connection with wheat production and marketing in
France include the suppression of the tax on production, the limitation of
the working capacity of existing mills and the amount of flour which each
may sell, and provision for fixing import requirements during deficit
years and the quantities to be absorbed from the market in surplus years.
New regulations have also been issued with regard to estimating the crop
and determining the surplus or deficit quantities. They are outlined.

Wheat - Market Regulation - Spain

Martinez de Bujanda, E. The new regulation of the wheat market in Spain.
Monthly Bull. Agr. Econ. and Sociol.[reprint from Internatl. Rev. Agr.]
26(12): 429Z-439E. December 1935. (Published by the International Institute of Agriculture, Villa Umberto I(110) Rome, Italy)

Wheat - Prices and Production - Great Britain

Murray, K. A. H., and Cohen, Ruth L. Wheat prices and the acreage of wheat
in Great Britain. Scot. Jour. Agr. 18(4): 354-363. October 1935.
(Published by H. M. Stationery Office, Edinburgh, Scotland)
   "A study of the relationship between wheat prices and the acreage of
wheat in this country indicates not only that price has played a marked
part in controlling the expansion and reduction of the wheat acreage, but
also that the time - lag in the effect of price on production has been
materially shorter in post-war than in pre-war years." Tables show the
purchasing power and acreage of wheat in Great Britain, 1904-1914 and
1924-1934.

Wheat - Uruguay

Dellazoppa. J. G. El problema triguero del Uruguay.-I. Aspecto Agronomico.
La revista Economica Sudamericana, 2. Epoca, año 37, no. 11, November
1935 (Published in Montevideo, Uruguay)
   A summary of the methods adopted and the results obtained in an attempt to obtain crops best suited to the productive milieu.

Wheat - World Situation and Outlook

Bennett, M. K., Farnsworth, Helen C., and Working, Holbrook, World wheat
survey and outlook, January 1936. Wheat Studies of the Food Research
Institute 12(5): 183-220. January 1936. (Published in Stanford Univer-
city, Calif.)

Contents: Wheat supplies, wheat stocks on January 1, course and level of prices; significant price spreads; the Canadian Wheat Board; imports and exports; outlook for trade; outlook for stocks and consumption; outlook for prices; appendix tables.

Taylor, A. E. Next five years in world wheat. Country Gent. 106(2): 21, 43, 44. February 1936. (Published at Independence Square, Philadelphia, Pa.)

Appraises the world wheat situation in the five-year periods 1915/16-1919/20, 1920/21-1924/25, 1925/26-1929/30 and 1930/31-1934/35, and then considers the prospective position of wheat in 1935/36-1939/40.

"The only method of continuing recovery is to increase consumption." A planned economy for wheat is said to be useless. "The social planners of the world do not know enough to plan an economy for wheat, the governments cannot be made to agree, the wheat growers of the countries will not cooperate, consumers will resist, and in all countries discipline is lacking to enforce agreements governments might make. There will be no adjustments by edict. Adjustment will be secured only through enlargement on the side of consumption."

World wheat prospects. Economist 122(4822): 172-173. Jan. 25, 1936. (Published at 8 Bouverie St., Fleet St., London, E. C. 4, Eng.)

The improvement in the world wheat situation is said to be due, almost entirely, to a sequence of crop failures in some of the large exporting countries.

"The increase in prices during recent months has thus had some economic justification. The present supply-demand position would seem to favour a further advance in prices during the next few months. It would be rash, however, to assume that the wheat problem has been finally solved...The root of the wheat problem will remain so long as importing countries are anxious to increase their exports of manufactured goods without being prepared to provide the agricultural countries which used to import most of their industrial requirements - and are now anxious to do neigher - has been widening ever since the war. It still persists; and little is being done about it."

Wheat and Linseed - Prices - Argentina

New basic prices of wheat and linseed. Rev. of the River Plate 79(2297): 12. Dec. 20, 1935. (Published at Calle Bartolome Mitre, 427, Buenos Aires, Argentina.)

A decree of December 12, 1935 raises the basic price of wheat to ten pesos and of linseed to 14 pesos per hundred kilos. Reasons are given for the reduction in the exportable surplus of those crops.

NOTES

Allred, C. E. Rural relief and rehabilitation possibilities in Houston
county. Tennessee. by Charles E Allred... B. H. Luebke... assisted
by M. Taylor Matthews... Charles A. Tosch. 45pp., mimeog. [Knoxville,
Tenn.] Dec. 1935. (U. S. Federal emergency relief administration.
Report no.3) 173.2 R27Rep no. 3
      Issued in cooperation with Tennessee Agricultural Experiment Station
and Tennessee Welfare Commission.

Allred. C. E. Rural relief in Overton county, Tennessee, by Charles E.
Allred... W. Eugene Collins... M. Taylor Matthews. 33pp. [Knoxville,
Tenn.] Jan. 1936. (U. S. Federal emergency relief administration.
Report no. 4) 173.2 R27Rep no. 4
      Issued in cooperation with Tennessee Agricultural Experiment Station,
Federal Works Progress Administration, Tennessee Welfare Commission.

Andersen, Esther S. The sugar beet industry of Nebraska. 121pp. Lincoln,
Nebr., 1935. (Nebraska. University. Conservation and survey division.
Conservation dept. Bulletin no. 9) 99.47 N27 no. 9
      Bibliography, pp. 118-121.

Banco hipotecario nacional, Buenos Aires. Report on the 49th year 1934.
234pp. Buenos Aires, 1935. 284.9 B2274
      Chapter 4 is largely devoted to rural loans.

The Book of the states, including Handbook of the American legislators'
association, Manual of legislative reference services, The second Interstate assembly, Organization meeting of the Tax revision council, June
meeting of the Council of state governments, vol. 1, 1935. 504pp.
Chicago, Ill., Pub. by the Council of state governments and the American
legislators' association [1935] 280.9 B64 Ed. 3
      Vol. 1 is Ed. 3 and contains "500 pages, the last 200 of which were
not in the second edition." (1st prelim. leaf, v. 1, Ed. 3)

Canada. Board of grain commissioners. Dominion grain research laboratory.
Protein survey map of western Canada, hard red spring wheat... 1935 crop
1 sheet [Ottawa? 1935] 59.9 C161Pr

Central association of agricultural valuers. Twenty-fifth annual report of
the council for the year ended 2nd May, 1935, and statement of account
as presented to the delegates at the twenty-sixth annual meeting held
in London on the 6th June, 1935. 66pp. Leicester, W. H. Lead, printer
[1936?] 10 C332

Cornish, N. H. Marketing of manufactured goods. 282pp. Boston, Mass., The
Stratford company [1935] 280.3 C73M
      Bibliography, pp. 259-266.

Cooperative distributors. A program for the hundred million. Collective
bargaining for consumers.31pp. New York, N. Y., Cooperative distributors 30, Irving Place, N.Y. . 280.2 C784

Crum, W. L.   The distribution of wealth. A factual survey based upon federal
estate-tax returns. 24pp. Boston, Mass. [1935] (Harvard university.
Graduate school of business administration. Bureau of business research.
Division of research. Business research studies no. 13)   280.9 H262 no.13

Davies, C. E.   Agricultural holdings and tenant right, being a treatise on
the law of agricultural holdings... 3d ed. (with chapters on The practice of tenant right valuation) by N. E. Mustoe... and Customs of the
country, by J. E. Tory.   503pp.   London, The Estates gazette, ltd.
[1935] 282 D282 Ed. 3

Dimock, M. E.   Developing America's waterways; administration of the Inland
waterways corporation. 123pp.   Chicago, Ill., The University of
Chicago press [1935] (Studies in public administration. vol. IV)
289.3 D59
   Bibliography, pp. 116-117.

Egypt. Economic mission to Great Britain. Report of the Egyptian economic
mission to Great Britain.   40pp.   Cairo, Government press, 1935.
286 Eg9
   The purpose of this mission was "'to enquire into the position of the
interchange of trade between Egypt and Great Britain, to consider methods
conductive to the increased consumption of Egyptian products in British
markets and to receive such statements and suggestions as may be made
to them with a view to stimulate the demand for British goods in
Egyptian markets.'"

Filipetti, George, and Vaile, R. S.   The economic effects of the NRA; a
regional analysis.   108pp.   Minneapolis, The University of Minnesota
press, 1935.   (Minnesota. University. Studies in economics and business
no. 11)   280.9 M663 no. 11

Gt. Brit. Customs and excise dept.   Customs and excise tariff of the United
Kingdom of Great Britain and Northern Ireland. Part 3 Duties and exemptions from duty under the Import duties act, 1932, consolidated as from
the 1st January, 1936. 68pp.   London, H. M. Stationery. off., 1935.
285.9 G79
   At head of title: Sec. 6737 no. 34 (Sale) Part 3.
                      1935

Hillhouse, A. M.   New sources of municipal revenue. 74pp. Chicago, Ill.,
Municipal finance officers' association of the United States and Canada,
1935. 284.5 H55
   Bibliography, pp. 71-74.

International chamber of commerce. Resolutions adopted by the eighth congress
   of the International chamber of commerce, Paris, June 24th-29th, 1935.
   288pp. Paris, 1935. 287 In8B no. 89
      "Supplement to 'World trade', July 1935."

Interstate commission on conflicting taxation. Report of the Interstate
   commission on conflicting taxation to the second Interstate assembly;
   presented by Senator Seabury C. Mastick, chairman. 20pp., mimeogr.
   Chicago, Ill., American legislators' association, 1935. 284.5 In82

Massachusetts. Dept. of labor and industries. Division of statistics. Report
   on the census of unemployment in Massachusetts as of January 2, 1934...
   Provided for by federal funds granted under CWA and FERA projects.
   Published by Massachusetts Department of labor and industries, Division
   of statistics. 202pp. [Boston, 1935] (Labor bulletin no. 171)
   253 M3823
      At head of title: Public document no. 15. The Commonwealth of Massa-
   chusetts.
      "Part III of the annual report on the statistics of labor for the year
   ending November 30, 1934."

Merriam, C. E. Political power; its composition and incidence. 331pp.
   New York and London, McGraw-Hill book company, inc. [1934] 280 M55P

Michigan municipal league. Michigan city and village debt. 8pp. Ann
   Arbor, Mich., 1935. (Information bulletin no. 24) 284 M584M
      Photo-lithoprint reproduction of author's manuscript -- verso of
   title page.

Myers, W. I. The farmers' own credit system. 22pp. [Washington, U. S.
   Govt. print. off., 1935] (U. S. Farm credit administration. Circular A-4)
   166.2 C492 no. A-4
      "An address at the annual meeting of the Land Grant College Assn.
   Washington, D. C. 1935."

Myres, S. D., Jr. Texas; nationalist or internationalist. 56pp. Dallas, Tex.,
   George F. and Ora Nixon Arnold foundation, Southern Methodist university,
   1935. (Arnold Foundation Studies in public affairs. v. 4, no. 1)
   280.083 M99
      Bibliographical foot-notes.

New York (State) Perishable fruit commission. Report of the Temporary
   state commission to study the grading, packing, sale and distribution
   of perishable fruit in New York state. Submitted March 1, 1935. 17pp.
   Albany, J. B. Lyon company, printers, 1935. (Legislative document (1935)
   no. 66) 280.393 N482

Pound, E. L. Social credit: an impact. 31pp, London, S. Nott [1935]
   (Pamphlets on the new economics. no. 8) 284 P86

Social science research council. Committee on public administration. Administrative redistricting in Germany since 1918. An interview with Wilhelm Cohnstaedt. 18pp., mimeogr. Chicago, Ill. [1935] 280.175 So1
Louis Brownlow, Chairman of the Committee on Public Administration of the Social Science Research Council has written in part as follows in the foreword:
"The subject matter of the interview should be of interest in view of the discussions in this country, of regional planning, the consolidation of governmental units, and allied problems. The interview arose from a chance meeting between the Secretary of the Committee and Mr. Cohnstaedt in Chicago, which led to the thought that it might be profitable to record some of his experiences in dealing with the same problems in Germany."

South Africa. Dept. of agriculture. Statistical wool and mohair bulletin. 98pp. Pretoria, The Government printer, 1935. (South Africa. Dept. of agriculture. Bulletin no. 139) 24 So84P no. 139
"South Africa. Dept. of agriculture. Economic series no. 19"
Text in English and Dutch.

Special libraries association. Statistics of Canadian commodities, comp. by a committee of the Montreal Special libraries association, consisting of Maud E. Martin, chairman...and Mildred I. Turnbull, chart. New York city, Special libraries association, 1935. 241.9 Sp33S

Strachey John. The coming struggle for power. With a new introduction by the author. 412pp. New York, The Modern library [1935] (Modern library of the world's best books) 280 St85
Revised edition.
"A note on American events since the first publication of this book [Feb. 1933]", pp. 396-407.

Trades union congress. General council. Cotton; the T.U.C. plan of socialisation. Foreword by Walter M. Citrine. 32PP. [London] The Trades union congress General council [1935] 304 T67
Caption title: Report on socialisation of the cotton industry.

Unemployment; an international problem. A report by a study group of members of the Royal institute of international affairs. 496pp. London, Oxford university press, H. Milford, 1935. 283 Un2

U. S. Dept. of labor. Bureau of labor statistics. Directory of consumers' cooperative societies. 106 pp., mimeogr. [Washington, D. C. Jan. 1935] 158.61 D62
The names and addresses of the various types of consumers' cooperative societies in the United States, together with a designation of the kind of business done are given.

United States in world affairs; an account of American foreign relations.
1934-1935. Whitney H. Shepardson in collaboration with William O.
Scroggs. Published for the Council on foreign relations. 357pp. New
York and London, Harper & brothers, 1935. 280.8 Un34
   Bibliography, pp. 273-282.

Ware, Edith E., ed. The study of international relations in the United State
survey for 1934. 503pp. New York, Columbia university press [1935]
280 W22
   Published 1934, reprinted 1935.
   Published for the American National Committee on Intellectual Cooperation of the League of Nations.

Washington (State). Emergency relief administration. Report...1933-1934.
37pp. Olympia, 1935. 283.9 W27

[Wybraniec,P. F.] Speratia, by Dr. Raphael W. Leonhart. [pseud.] 271pp.
Boston, Meador publishing company, 1935. 280 L553
' .This book... draws attention to certain errors and defects in the
various fields of economy and politico-social arrangements." -
Foreword.

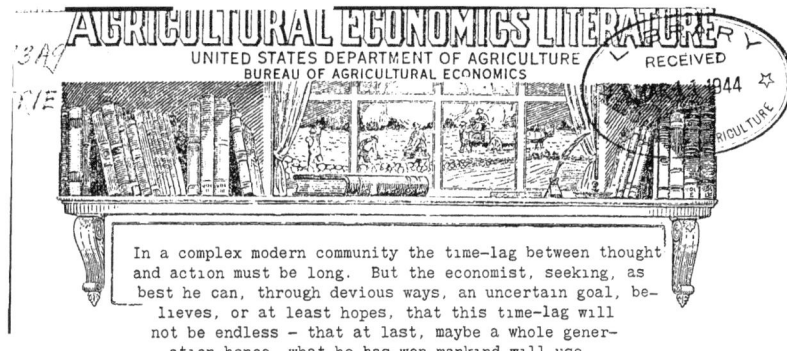

AGRICULTURAL ECONOMICS LITERATURE

UNITED STATES DEPARTMENT OF AGRICULTURE
BUREAU OF AGRICULTURAL ECONOMICS

RECEIVED
1944

> In a complex modern community the time-lag between thought
> and action must be long. But the economist, seeking, as
> best he can, through devious ways, an uncertain goal, be-
> lieves, or at least hopes, that this time-lag will
> not be endless – that at last, maybe a whole gener-
> ation hence, what he has won mankind will use
> That is his act of faith. A. C. Pigou

| Vol. 10 | April 1936 | No. 4 |

FEATURES IN THIS ISSUE

SIGNED REVIEWS

New Jersey. Dept. of agriculture. Upper Freehold Township; a survey of the
life, resources and government of a New Jersey rural township, with a
program for improvement, by the Bureau of agricultural economics, United
States Department of agriculture, the New Jersey Department of agriculture, the Monmouth county agricultural extension service, the Upper
Freehold better township association. 85pp. Trenton, N. J., 1935.
231.2 N46

The uniqueness of this study lies in the fact that it was initiated
by a local organization itself. At a public meeting of the citizens of
Upper Freehold Township, the Upper Freehold Better Township Association
was established. This Association decided that a disinterested investigation of the problems of the township should be made, and Dr. Theodore
B. Manny, then of the Bureau of Agricultural Economics, was asked to
conduct a survey with the aim of making needed recommendations.

The analysis might be described as a case study of a rural township
with special emphasis on local government. The investigation is based
upon data secured by a survey involving house-to-house interviewing of
106 farmers on the 227 farms in the township, and a study of records and
documents. Dr. Manny's survey analysis depicts the organization membership, the mobility, and size of the families, the amount of part time
farming, the extent to which home and farm conveniences are possessed,
the type of farming and marketing facilities, the extent of and remedies
for soil erosion, and, among other things, problems in local government.
Attitudes and opinions of the farmers toward the types of improvement
most needed in individual dwellings and adequacy of the present dwellings, fire protection facilities, roads, police protection, township
governmental organization, taxation, schools, certain organization marketing methods, and other factors were studied. The purpose of the analysis
was to enable the citizens to more intelligently direct their attempts
to improve the township through governmental and other channels.

The improvements most frequently desired by the families were electric
power and better roads. Economy in local government, decrease in taxes
and salaries of local officials were most frequently recommended as proposed changes in government.

In addition to the field survey, Dr. Manny analyzed the local government of the township through a study of the local records. An analysis
of the tax rates for the township indicates that, in spite of the demand
for lower assessments, the rates are relatively lower than those of the
county of which it is a part. Although it was found that certain farmers
who were capable of paying their taxes declined to do so, the township was
in an enviable financial position. A detailed analysis of the expenditures
of the township and recommendations for adjustments were made.

Committees and members of the Upper Freehold Better Township Association prepared sections of the study on the agriculture, electrification,

reads, schools, organizations, and history of the township. The study is a excellent example of cooperation among local, state and national agencies in the interests of fact finding for intelligent guidance of a proposed action program. Chas. P. Loomis, Senior Agricultural Economist, Division of Farm Population and Rural Life.

DESCRIPTIVE NOTES AND ABSTRACTS

Agricultural Depression -- England - 1822

Bramston, T. G. A practical inquiry into the nature and extent of the present agricultural distress, and the means of relieving it. 53pp. London, Printed for J. Hatchard and son, 1822. 281.171 B73

A very interesting discussion of the agricultural distress in England and Wales in the years following the War of 1812 and of the means proposed for its remedy. These include a reduction of taxation and a lowering of the prices of the articles of "primary consumption" followed by a lowering of the prices of articles of "secondary necessity and of more convenience... to the lowest scale of charge which will reasonably compensate for their production." It is also pointed out that "it is a fallacy to suppose that his [the farmer's] situation has been rendered worse in the same proportion as his income has been rendered less; for, on the contrary, the relation between his charges for maintenance, and his means of providing it, has become in a most important degree assimilated."

Agricultural Imports and Prices -- England

Murray, K. A. H. The control of imports and agricultural prices. 6pp. Reading, Greenslade & co. (Reading) ltd. [1936]   Reprint Collection. "Reprinted from the Berkshire farmers' year book, 1936."

"For various reasons, political, social and economic, it has been decided that the agricultural industry should be expanded in this country, and for the last four years various means have been adopted towards this end. There are, however, two considerations which have a very important influence on what, and how much, can be done. Firstly, the urban electorate have accepted this policy on the understanding that it will result in an increased output of food in this country and also in an increase in the numbers of people engaged in farming. Secondly, the mass of the people in this country has long been accustomed to cheap food and is not prepared to pay unlimited amounts for increasing agricultural production. The problem, then is to increase the output of food without a reduction in the labour employed and without too great a rise in the retail prices of food.

"Increased home production can be achieved only if farm returns are increased and there appear to be four distinct ways of doing this: Lower costs of production, lower costs of marketing, subsidies from the Exchequer, or higher retail prices for farm products. The first two of these might make it possible to increase the output without raising the

price to the consumer, and would, of course, be the most satisfactory to
the nation as a whole, in so far as a reduction in production costs were
not obtained by a decline in the use of labour, a development which would
be contrary to the objectives of the policy. The third method, though
unpopular, has the great merit that it increases agricultural returns
without raising the price of food to the consumer, and for many British
farm products, as will be shown later, a rise in their price brings
about a bigger decrease in their consumption, so that there is no net
gain in the return to the farmer.

"It is, however, mainly with the fourth method that this article is
concerned, the control of supplies and, more particularly, of imports.
One of the underlying principles of the Agricultural Marketing Acts is
that it gives organised producers a monopoly of the home output. The
value of this monopoly for price-raising purposes depends on two things:
firstly the proportion which the home output forms of the total
supply, both home-produced and imported, and, secondly, whether the consumer will continue to buy the product if the price is raised. The Agricultural Marketing Act of 1933 was designed to increase the producers'
powers of supply-control by permitting quantitative regulation by the
Government of imports of any commodity for which a marketing scheme was
in force. Though these powers were limited, notably in the case of certain milk products, by certain provisions of existing trade agreements,
the restriction of imports by the Government has been extensive, covering a far greater number of commodities than are covered by marketing
schemes."

Agricultural Marketing Acts - England

Mustoe, N. E. The agricultural marketing acts and schemes, containing the
    texts of the Agricultural marketing acts, 1931-1933, the Wheat act, 1932,
    the Cattle industry (emergency provisions) act, 1934, the Agricultural
    marketing schemes, and the byelaws of the Wheat commission. 440pp. London,
    The Estates gazette, ltd. [1935] 280.3 M97

    "The object of this book is to bring together the statutes, orders,
regulations and cases relating to the marketing of agricultural products,
and to set out the schemes of agricultural marketing which are now in
operation in England.

    "The three Agricultural Marketing Acts are reproduced with notes of
the orders and regulations made under them, and with cross-references as
between the various sections of the Acts and as between the Acts and
the regulations and orders. The schemes which have been made under these
Acts, and which are now in force, are also fully set out, and they have
been annotated and cross-referenced as seemed necessary.

    "The Wheat Act, 1932, has also been supplied with notes, and the Byelaws
of the Wheat Commission are reproduced in full, and have also been annotated.
The orders and regulations made under this Act are given as amended to date.

    "The Cattle Act, 1934, has been similarly treated, and the regulations
made under it are given in full. The Act has been annotated, and references are given both to the regulations and to the Particulars of Arrangements made by the Cattle Committee.

    "The Introduction gives a summary of the economic tendencies in agricul-
tural co-operation and a résumé of the Acts themselves." - Preface

Drescher, Leo.   Landwirtschaftliche planung als merkmal neuer agrarpolitik.pp.33-
    48. [München, Duncker & Humblot, 1936] Reprint Coll.
    "Sonderabzug aus Schmollers jahrbuch für gesetzgebung, verwaltung und
    volkswirtschaft im Deutschen reiche, jahrgang 60, heft 1, 1936."
    An account of the new economic phenomena in agriculture, the agro-
political measures adopted since the depression in Germany, and other
countries leads to a discussion of the genesis and characteristics of
agricultural planning which to be effective should steer a middle course
between the old system of laissez faire and the modern system of the
communist as practised in the U.S.S.R.

Agriculture and Agricultural Statistics - Denmark

Denmark. Landbrugsraadet. Denmark agriculture. 324pp. Copenhagen, The
    Agricultural council, 1935.   33.11 D41D
    Appendice: Statistique agricole: liiipp. at end.
    Partial contents: Denmark's soil and nature, by knud Jessen; Division
of the land and social conditions, by Hans Jensen; The cultivated area
and the yield of the harvest, by H. K. Olsen; The organisation of Danish
agriculture, by A. F. Knudsen; Cooperation in Danish agriculture, by
A. Axelsen Dreyer; Education, general and in rural economy, by N. Bredkjaer;
Reclamation of land, by Niels Basse; Public measures for the furtherance
of plant culture by L.P.M.Larsen; The Danish dairy industry, by L. P.
Frederiksen; Milk recording societies, by H. Wenzel Eskedal; Danish agri-
cultural import and export, by P. A. Moltesen; Agricultural prices, by
Iver Dokken; and The financial results of Danish agriculture, by
O. H. Larsen.

Agriculture and Party Politics - England

National farmers' union. Agriculture, the home market and national security.
    Views of the National farmers' union on current agricultural problems.
    40pp. London, National farmers' union, 1935. (N. F. U. no. 49)
    251.171 N213
    "In the post-war years and prior to the advent of the National Govern-
ment, frequent expression was given in agricultural circles to the desire
that the question of agricultural policy might be taken out of the rut
of Party politics. The handling of the subject by the National Government
represents the nearest approach which we have had to the formulation of
agricultural policy on national rather than Party lines, and this aspect
of the situation is emphasised by the circumstance that the first Agricultural Marketing Act, which has provided a basis for so much of the
activities of the last three or four years, was placed on the Statute Book
by a Labour Government, in which it is worth bearing in mind, the Co-operative Party was represented. For these reasons the Union regards it as
timely to issue for the guidance of members a re-statement of its views
on the main questions which are now before the farming community." -
Introduction.
    The statement of these views constitute this pamphlet. Among the

appendices are the following: Agricultural wages and state assistance, Index numbers illustrating the monthly variations in the prices of agricultural produce; Numbers of agricultural workers; and Operation of the marketing schemes.

Agriculture and the Depression - Argentina

Boglich, Jose. El problema agrario y la crisis actual. 232 pp. Buenos Aires [Ediciones Ares] 1933. 281.161 B63

The author's thesis is that the existing crisis is one of the capitalist régime and its system of production, and his object is to investigate the factors by means of which this crisis of capitalism has affected the agrarian economy of the country more intensely than the other branches of economic production. He gives us a survey of the economic evolution of agricultural exportation under the capitalist régime followed by an account of the economic development of the agricultural classes under the same conditions.

Agriculture and the National Welfare

Baker, O. E.   Better land utilization in the Great Lakes states...   An address delivered at the Extension conference, Michigan state college, Lansing, Michigan, November 7, 1935. 9pp., mimeogr. [Washington? D. C., 1935] Pam. Coll.

"In conclusion, may I again affirm my belief that better land utilization in the Lakes States depends in large measure upon achieving a continuity of family proprietorship in farming. The farmers of 40 centuries in China, the cultivators of the garden-like farms in Japan, the splendid peasant farmers of Germany and Scandinavia and many other parts of Europe, who have cultivated the same land for more than 4,000 years and increased its productivity, all point to the family as the conservator of land as well as of life. We need not imitate the smallness of their farms, for nature has been generous to North America and to the Central West in particular. We need not imitate necessarily their agricultural methods, for conditions are different with us. But we need to consider their philosophy of life, for human nature is much the same everywhere.

"We need to heed the warnings of history as to the fate of those peoples who put the individual above the family, the present above the future, and pleasure before duty. The great need of the Nation, it seems to me, is loyalty to an ideal. May I humbly submit as an ideal the preservation of the family. It is becoming clear that the land is the foundation of the family, and that the family is the foundation of the state."

Baker, O. E. Commercial agriculture and the national welfare . An address... at the Agricultural extension conference, East Lansing, Michigan. November 6, 1935. 12pp., mimeogr. [Washington? D. C. 1935] Pam. Coll.

"The economic argument is not, I believe, the final appeal to farmers, particularly to farm youth. As the population of the Nation, and doubtless the demand for food and fibers becomes stationary, and later declines, as now appears very likely, the highly commercial agriculture on the Corn Belt and Dairy Belt may experience some hard times. If

during these times there is no other appeal to rural youth than that
of a materialistic philosophy, the cities will continue to attract
the best educated and most ambitious youth, as they have in the past,
particularly from the poorer agricultural regions. Education in the
rural regions would tend to be neglected, because of the migration of
wealth and culture to the cities, and the persistent transfer of wealth
to the cities might eventually lead to concentration of land ownership.
    "It is not yet clear how the great national objective of maintaining
a prosperous agriculture, in part to provide intelligent and wise
future leaders of the Nation, can be achieved. But it is clear to me
that a necessary condition is a different philosophy of life, a different set of assumption as to things worth while. I shall try to present
this new philosophy of life, which is also very old, to you tomorrow in
discussing better land utilization in the Lakes States." - Conclusion.

American Sociological Society

American sociological society. Publication, v. 29, no. 3. August 1935. Papers
    presented at the twenty-ninth annual meeting of the society, held at Chicago,
    Ill., December 26-29, 1934. 184pp. Chicago, Ill., Press of the H. G.
    Adair printing company [1935]   280.9 Am37
        Partial contents: Social planning and human nature, by Robert E. Park;
    Planning in a democracy, by Lewis L. Lorwin; Factors conditioning a popula-
    tion policy for the United States, by Warren S. Thompson; Some forerunners
    of regional research, by Shelby M. Harrison; Implications of the concepts
    "Region" and "Regional Planning" by Rupert B. Vance; Sociological phases
    of the proposed southwestern regional survey, by L. L. Bernard; The pros-
    pects of regional research in relation to social planning, by Louis Wirth;
    The role of radio in the new social order, by Malcolm M. Willey; A theory
    for the measurement of social forces, by Stuart C. Dodd; The development
    of research in rural sociology, by T. B. Manny; Appraisal and outlook of
    research in rural sociology at the state agricultural experiment stations,
    by James T. Jardine; Appraisal of and outlook for research in rural sociolo-
    gy under the New Deal, by Mordecai Ezekiel; Social and economic signifi-
    cance of the subsistence homestead program from an Economist's point of
    view, by William Zeuch; Subsistence homestead program from a sociologist's
    point of view, by C. C. Taylor; Relief, rehabilitation and rural youth,
    by E. L. Kirkpatrick; The influence of acreage reduction upon employment
    and mobility of farm labor, by Wilson Gee; The probable social effects of
    purchasing submarginal land in the Great Plains, by Paul H. Landis; The
    A.A.A. and the cropper, by Harold C. Hoffsommer; Status and prospects for
    research in rural life under the New Deal, by Dwight Sanderson; The gen-
    eral development and present status of the F.E.R.A. research program, by
    Howard B. Myers; The contribution of research to rural relief problems,
    by Dwight Sanderson; The functions of social insurance in relation to
    economic security, by R. Clyde White; Trends in cultural participation as
    a background for social planning, by Sanford Winston; Underlying factors
    conditioning competition and social control; The milk industry as a case-
    study, by Carl Hutchinson; Continuity in research and planning, by Neva R.
    Deardorff; and Utilization of census material in social planning, by
    Calvert L. Dedrick.

Cotton

Âbidín, Ihsan. Pamuk, istihsalden istihlâke kadar Turkiye, Misir, Hindistan,
Cin, Amerika, Rusya, Ingiltere Italya ve sair memleketler. Ihsan Âbidin.
371pp. Istanbul, Husnutabiat matbaasi, 1933. 281.372 Ad4
At head of title: Cumnuriyetin onuncu yildonumunde.
Cotton production and consumption in Turkey, America, Russia and other
countries.

Ascoli, W. S. Redundancy or strangulation! The case for the Lancashire
cotton industry against the redundancy scheme. 23pp. [Manchester,
Harlequin press co. ltd., 1935] 204 As2

Economou, G. D. & co. Some information about the Egyptian cotton market.
Futures - spot. 2d ed. (rev. and completed) [Alexandria, 1935] 82pp.
72 Ec7

Gt. Brit. Empire cotton growing corporation. Report of the Administrative
council of the corporation submitted to the fourteenth annual general
meeting on May 28th, 1935. 66pp. London, Waterlow & sons limited,
1935. 72.9 G79

Karachi cotton annual, 1933-34, no. 1. A compendium of all matters relating to
the Karachi cotton trade with particular reference to Sind, the Punjab,
U. P. and Rajputana. Containing statistical tables of crops, exports, prices,
stocks, etc. 27, 35pp. Karachi, The Karachi cotton association, ltd.[1934]
281.3729 K14
Compiled and published by T. B. Dalal, secretary.

Economic History

Economic history; a supplement to the Economic journal, v. 3, no. 11, February
1936. pp. [155]-324. London, Macmillan and co., limited, 1936.
280.8 Ec72E
Partial contents: A college home-farm in the fifteenth century, by
J. Saltmarsh; Statistics of corn yields in mediaeval England, by R. Lennard;
Eighteenth-century traffic in live-stock, by G. E. Fussell and Constance
Goodman; Sir G. Colebrooke's corner in alum 1771-73, by L. Stuart Suther-
land; Excise salaries and a cost of living index (1795-1800), by E. Hughes;
and Bentham and the genesis of neo-malthusianism, by N. E. Himes.

Egg Legislation and Grades

National association of marketing officials. Special committee . Egg legislation and grades in the United States. 253pp., mimeogr. Hartford, Conn.
[1935]   280.347 N2122
Bibliography, p. 244.
Partial contents: State egg and poultry laws (Actual text of the laws
given for each state) Canadian English and German egg laws and grades,
Federal Food and Drug Act decisions pertaining to eggs; Maps showing
trend of laws.

Bridges, Archibald. Scientific progress and agricultural employment. ?2pp.
   [n.p., 1936?] Pamphlet Collection
        At head of title: The Agricultural Economics Society.
        The author in summing up the reasons for the lower labor requirements
   on farms in England and Wales writes in part as follows:
        "Machinery, itself a product, however indirect, of science enabled
   farmers to exploit the virgin soils of oversees countries. This expansion was made possible by plant breeders and other scientists whose work
   greatly increased the potential wheat areas of the world and set the
   stage for production with the aid of labour-saving machinery. The
   economic pressure of this development turned our farmers' attention to
   livestock and grassland farming, a policy which was partly dictated by the
   increasing demand for livestock and livestock products arising from our
   larger population and improved standards of life. This policy has been
   fortified by the work of scientists. Improved standards of rationing
   of stock and improvements in breeding have made it possible to increase
   the yield of livestock products. Progress has been made in securing
   earlier maturing breeds of cattle, sheep and pigs, improvements in the
   quality of both plants and animals have taken place, and losses from
   disease have been reduced. The increased numbers of livestock as a
   whole, and the consolidation of our position as livestock farmers by
   scientific work, was a compensating factor in labour requirements to
   set against the losses involved in the decline of arable farming. But
   with the latter a great change necessarily took place in livestock farming and it is this which has been the principal reason for the reduction
   of people on the land. A great improvement in the output of grass and the
   greater amount of purchased foods available made it possible to dispense
   with the supply of food hitherto obtained from the arable land. No one
   will deny that from the application first of phosphates and later of
   nitrogen, the greater attention which is now being paid to the strains
   of grasses used in temporary leys and to better cultivation we have obtained a very large increase in the productivity of grassland. The extension of grassland and its improvement has been one of the greatest
   labour-saving devices of the present century.
        "The application of power, through the internal combustion engine, has
   not been without its effect on employment on the land...
        "In the last ten years farmers have also been directing attention to
   economising in the dearest item of cost, viz., labour. With the coming
   of mechanical power, operations have been greatly speeded up, and there
   is a tendency to adopt cheaper, if less correct, practices. Many of the
   frills of old-time farming have disappeared.
        "I believe that agriculture has become more efficient in the process and
   labour is now more closely attuned to the needs of production."

Bridges, Archibald. The future of mechanised arable farming. 6pp. Reading,
   Greenslade & Co. (Reading) ltd. [1936] Pam. Coll.
        Reprinted from the Berkshire Farmers' Year Book, 1936.
        "It is a common claim that the mechanisation of farming in this country

has lagged behind that of farming in the newer countries of the world, particularly in such countries as the United States of America, Canada and Australia. In making such a claim, however, critics are apt to forget the great differences in environmental and economic conditions which induce mechanisation there and retard its development here. Favourable climatic conditions, scarcity of labour, the flexibility of sizes of holdings and the comparative simplicity of the farming are factors which make for the fullest development of mechanical aids to production overseas. In this country our mixed systems of arable farming, with their need to provide a variety of foods for livestock, the lack of opportunity to increase the size of holding or the area of farmed land, and our more humid climate are not so favourable for mechanised farming, and modify the form it takes...

"The possibilities of expansion in mechanised arable farming have to be considered in the light of the fact that considerable development has already taken place. It has also to be considered on the basis of the tractor as this is the starting point for mechanised crop growing. The scope for expansion may be dealt with under the following heads:

"(1) - The scope for the introduction of tractors. (2) - The expansion and improvement in the efficiency of tractor work on farms already having tractors. (3) - The introduction of new forms of mechanical appliances, e.g., the combine-harvester and dryer."

Farm Management - Germany

Deutsche rentenbank-kreditanstalt (Landwirtschaftliche zentralbank) Beiträge zur bäuerlichen betriebsforschung: ackernahrung, zinsleistungsfähigkeit, naturalumsatz, mitviehhaltung, schweinezyklus. 38PP. Berlin, R. Hobbing, 1933. 281.175 D483B
    Die Deutsche rentenbank-kreditanstalt hat gemeinsam mit dem Deutschen landwirtschaftsrat die Landwirtschaftliche Betriebsprüfungsstelle g.m.b.h. beauftragt, untersuchungen... durchzuführen... Verfasser der beiden ersten abschnitte... ist dr. H. L. Fensch, der drei übrigen abschnitte dr. K. Padberg." - Vorwort.
    In this second publication of the Landwirtschaftliche Betriebsprüfungsstelle at the instigation of the Deutsche Rentenbank-kreditanstalt on important questions of agricultural economy the author, Dr. H. L. Fensch discusses the fundamental economic problems of farm management and those more particularly connected with grain, potato, and milk production and with livestock raising. The conclusions, as those of the first publication, are based on bookkeeping statistics.

Deutsche rentenbank-kreditanstalt (Landwirtschaftliche zentralbank) Der betriebsgrösseneinfluss in der bauernwirtschaft; beiträge zur bäuerlichen betriebsforschung. 36pp. Berlin, R. Hobbing, 1933. 281.175 D483
    "Die Deutsche rentenbank-kreditanstalt hat gemeinsam mit dem Deutschen landwirtschaftsrat die Landwirtschaftliche betriebsprüfungsstelle g.m.b.h. beauftragt, eine reihe von untersuchungen... zu bearbeiten... Verfasser ist dr. H. L. Fensch." - Vorwort.
    This is a statistically and graphically illustrated discussion of the influence of the size of a farm on its economic status and successful exploitation. The author is Dr. H. L. Fensch who is an authority on the subject.

Food Supply - Germany

Becker. Hans v. d, Deutschlands versorgung mit landwirtschaftlichen
erzeugnissen unter besonderer berücksichtigung der auslandsabhängigkeit.
117 pp Berlin, P. Parey. 1936. ([Germany] Reichs-und Pr. Ministerium
fur Ernahrung u. Landwirtschaft. Berichte über Landwirtschaft n.F.
115. Sonderheft.)
       At head of title: Untersuchungen des Instituts für Konjunkturfor-
schung. Berlin.
       A study of production and consumption of agricultural products
in Germany with a view to discover the possibilities of her being
able to supply her own requirements.

Foreign Trade - U. S.

Sayre. F. B. America must act. 80pp. Boston, New York, World peace foundation, 1936. (World peace foundation. World affairs books no. 13) 286 Sa92
       This small volume provides a useful survey of the trade agreements
policy and disposes of the argument that foreign trade is unimportant
to this country.

Sayre, F. B. The foreign trade of the United States. 9pp. [Washington,
D. C., 1935] Pam. coll.
       Address... at the Chicago world trade conference... Chicago, Illinois,
on October 23, 1935
       Mimeographed press release dated Oct. 19, 1935.
       "Imports are ordinarily a faithful barometer of a nation's consumption.
We have reason to augur from them increasing prosperity. Similar increases
have taken place in the past two years in several other countries, notably
in Great Britain and Sweden; as their domestic situation improved, imports
rapidly increased.
       "It would not be fair to attribute this development to the new trade
agreement program, since during the period covered by the figures only
four trade agreements came into force, and of these one was in force for
eight months, one for four months, one for three and one for only one
month. The movement clearly was initiated by forces outside of the trade
agreement program. It is nevertheless significant that during the limited
time when these four trade agreements have been in force American exports
to each one of the four countries increased substantially while our total
exports declined. Similarly the increase of imports in 1935 over 1934
from the countries with which we have trade agreements exceeded, proportion-
ately, the increase in imports from other countries.
       "The figures for the first six months of 1935 reveal that for the first
time since the war the United States has achieved a position in which its
receipts and payments in respect to commodity and service items are approximately in balance. Had the present approximate balance been achieved sixteen years earlier, many of the difficulties which the United States and
other nations have experienced in recent years might have been avoided.
The staggering decline in our exports, the cruel losses which we have
suffered in our foreign investments, and the constant drain of gold away
from countries where it is sorely needed to prevent further disaster, have
been in large measure the fruits of our failure to bring our international
accounts into proper balance in earlier years."

Fruit Farming - South Africa

Tomlinson, F. R., and W/k, S P. van. An economic study of deciduous fruit
farming in the Western Cape Province, 1933-34. 47pp. Pretoria, Printed
by the Government printer, 1935 (South Africa Dept. of agriculture
Science bulletin no. 144) 24 So84S no.144
"South Africa. Dept. of agriculture and forestry. Stellenbosch-
Elsenburg series no. 22 "
The authors state that:
"The object of this study was to examine the organization of fruit
farming in the Western Cape Province, to analyse the farm businesses,
and to ascertain the main factors influencing the financial returns.
Even at present low prices many fruit farmers still make a financial
success of their farm business. It is our aim to determine the main
reasons for success as well as failure in order to establish some general economic guide to present as well as prospective fruit farmers."

Grants to States - South Australia

Australia. Commonwealth grants commission. Report on the applications made
in 1933 by the states of South Australia, Western Australia, and Tasmania,
for financial assistance from the Commonwealth under section 96 of the
Constitution. 182pp. Canberra, L. F. Johnston, Commonwealth government
printer,[1934?] 284 Au7
This report was reviewed ably and at length by J. B. Brigden of Brisbane
in the Economic record (published by the Melbourne University press) v. 10,
no. 19, Dec. 1934, pp. 230-242.

Hemp - Germany

Der Hanfbau, seine wirtschaftliche bedeutung. Anbau, gewinnung u. verwertung.
47 pp. Berlin, P. Parey, 1936. ([Germany] Reichs-und Pr. Ministerium
für Ernährung u. Landwirtschaft. Berichte über Landwirtschaft n.F.
116. Sonderheft.)
This is a collection of articles on hemp production, utilization and
economic importance in Germany. According to the foreword of Herbert
Backe, State Secretary of Agriculture, Germany in 1935 was in a position
to supply half of the requirements of her linen industry. This has
given a new impetus to hemp production which is as necessary to domestic
industrial requirements as flax. Hemp can be grown on moorland and it
does not enter into serious competition with other important crops. An
increase in hemp production is recommended as necessary and possible.

Land Settlement - Spain

Niemeier, Georg. Siedlungsgeographische untersuchungen in Niederandalusien.
229pp. Hamburg, Friederichsen, De Gruyter & co. m.b.h., 1935.
(Hamburgische universität. Abhandlungen aus dem gebiet der auslandskunde
bd. 42. Reihe B. Völkerkunde, kulturgeschichte und sprachen. bd. 22)
282.2 N55
Bibliography pp. [219]-229.
A study of land settlement in Spain based on the author's personal

.nvestig tions of conditions in Lower Andalusia. An account of the distribution and density of the settlements and their causes is followed by a description of the various types of settlement. Among the subjects discussed are the physical features of the region under consideration, a survey of the number and size of the settlements, the relation of scattered settlements to towns and villages and also to waste land, the relation between movement of population, land reclamation and land settlement, a detailed account of conditions in and types of the so-called "closed" settlements and a description of other types including local types and small settlement.

Land Use - Tennessee

Allred, C. E. Inventory of land use in Tennessee, by Charles E. Allred... Samuel W. Atkins... Walter P. Cotton... John E. Mason. 38PP., mimeogr. [Knoxville, Tenn.] 1936. (U. S. Federal emergency relief administration. Report no. 5) 173.2 R27Rep no.5
Issued in cooperation with Tennessee Agricultural Experiment Station, Federal Works Progress Administration, Tennessee Welfare Commission.

Money

Jerome, E. C. Governments and money, with special reference to financial legislation in the United States, and the establishment of an international standard of trade. 372pp. Boston, Little, Brown, and company, 1935. 284 J48
The nature and legislative history of the dollar are discussed, and "the dollar is also considered as a monetary unit with which a standard of international trade might be established provided the laws to which it owes its existence, and according to which banks must be created and regulated, are correctly revised."

Negro Farmers - Alabama

Otis, J. R. Economic aspects of the farm situation of negro farmers in Macon County, Alabama - 1931. 42pp. [Tuskegee] Tuskegee industrial press, 1933. (Tuskegee normal and industrial institute. [Bulletin] v.1, no.4, Nov.1933) 281.9 T87 v.1, no.4.
At head of title: Division of Agricultural Economics, School of Agriculture.

Otis, J. R. Factors affecting the income of negro farmers in Macon County, Alabama 1931. 23pp. [Tuskegee] Tuskegee institute press, 1933. (Tuskegee normal and industrial institute [Bulletin] v.1, no.3, Nov. 1933) 281.9 T87 v. 1, no.3.
Farmers' edition.

New England Council

New England council. New England today and the New England council; the place and its people, power, transportation, manufacturing, recreation, agriculture, natural resources, banking and trade. 48pp. Boston, Mass., The New England council [1936?] 280.004 N442
An interesting account of ten years of work done by and through the New England Council.

Plan for Leaven Farms - England - 1817

A plan suggested for mature consideration, for superseding the necessity of the
poor rates, by means of cottage acres, and farms, termed leaven farms;
thus denominated from the intended benefits likely to result from its per-
vading the whole mass. Original. pp. [217]-233. [The Pamphleteer. v.9,
no.17, 1817] London, 1817. 282 P692
    This plan proposes the enclosure of open or waste lands into "Leaven
farms" or freeholds to be cultivated for the benefit and support of the
parish poor, who may prefer them to the old mode of parochial relief.
The "Leaven farm" would be divided into one, two or three individual
farms, each to be given to a cultivator in his own parish in need of such
aid. The first or principal "Leaven farm" would supply salaries for judi-
cious and faithful management to the cultivators of all three, to the
apothecary, the miller, the maltster and brewer, expenses of the village
sheep, the House of industry, Sunday schools and an asylum for the aged
and children. The second farm should supply, by the produce raised upon
it, the several establishments noted above, and should advance money for
laborers' wages and other contingent expenses. The third farm should
supply curates, stipends, all other church expenses, taxes, money for
materials to be used in the House of Industry and articles for the village shop - surplus to go into a fund.

Planning

Committee on civic education by radio. You and your government, series XII.
(Planning) lectures no. 1-18 delivered over a nation-wide network of the
National broadcasting company, October 1, 1935 through January 28, 1936.
18 nos. [New York] National municipal league [1935-36] 280.12 N215G
    no. 1. A plan for the nation, by Frederic A. Delano; no. 2. Limita-
tions of planning, by David P. Barrows; no. 3. The best use of the land,
by M. L. Wilson; no.4. The economic value of American scenery, by Horace
M. Albright; no. 5. Head waters and other little waters, by Morris
Llewellyn Cooke; no. 6. A national system of transportation, by Thomas
H. MacDonald; no. 7. Who owns our roadsides, by Harlean James; no. 8.
Regional Planning - The T. V. A. an example, by Arthur E. Morgan;
no. 9. Is local government doomed? by Harold W. Dodds; no. 10 Planning
as a municipal function, by George McAneny; no. 11. Planning as a state
function, by Alfred Bettman; no. 12. Re-locating the isolated settler,
by Walter A. Rowlands; no. 13. Making plans come true, by Chester H.
Rowell; no. 14. The law of the roadside, by Flavel Shurtleff, and Thomas
H. Reed; no. 15. Better housing through better zoning, by Robert D. Kohn;
no. 16. Planning and paying for places for play, by Harold S. Buttenheim;
no. 17. Possibilities in tax title lands, by Frank C. Moore; and no. 18.
From acres to lots, by Gordon Whitnall.

Planning - Regional - South

Odum, H. W. The regional approach to national social planning, with special
reference to a more abundant south and its continuing reintegration in
the national economy. Issued in cooperation with the Institute for research in social science, University of North Carolina. 31pp. New

York, Foreign policy association. Chapel Hill, N. C., University of
North Carolina Press, 1935. 380.002 Od8
"Issued in cooperation with the Institute for Research in Social
Science, University of North Carolina."

The following is quoted from the author's introductory note:
. "The greater part of this paper was presented at the Institute of
Public Affairs, held under the sponsorship of the University of California, at Los Angeles, with the coöperation of the Pacific Southwest
Academy and the Pacific Sociological Society, in the summer of 1934, and
published in Social Forces, October 1934. The general conclusions of
the paper, however, are the outgrowth of the Southern Regional Study
made under the auspices of the Social Science Research Council through
which the Southern Regional Study was begun in 1932. Therefore, for
the purposes of the present bulletin additional material relating to the
southern regions has been added.

"The Southern Regional Committee of the Council was composed at the
time of Benjamin B. Kendrick... Wilson Gee... Walter J. Matherly...
George Fort Milton... Charles W. Pipkin... George W. Stocking... and
Raymond D. Thomas... The objectives of this Southern Regional Study,
featuring inquiry into the South's capacity for development, comprehended
something more than an adequate picture of the southern regions of the
United States in fair perspective to time, quality, geographic factors,
and the cultural equipment and behavior of the people. It was desired
further to present this picture in such ways as to indicate the place of
these regions in the nation and to explain something of the dramatic
struggle of a large and powerful segment of the American people for mastery
over an environment capable of producing a superior civilization, yet so
conditioned by complexity of culture and cumulative handicaps as to make
the nature of future development problematical.

"Over and above any conventional social inventory, it was important
to point toward greater realization of the inherent capacities of the
southern regions; and to indicate ways and means of bridging the chasm
between the superabundance of physical and human resources as potentialities and the actualities of technical deficiencies in their development
and waste in their use. It was equally important to point toward a continuously more effective reintegration of the southern regions in the
national picture and thereby toward a larger regional contribution to
national culture and unity. Furthermore, it was important to make available and to interpret both to special groups and to the people in general
in as many ways as possible the essential facts basic to the understanding
and planning of next steps.

. "To this end it was necessary to approach the problem objectively, on
the one hand, looking at the southern states as a region rather than as
'the South' and in relation to the whole dramatic development of America,
and, on the other, to set up definitive divisions of the southern regions...

"The present study features the eleven Southeastern States corresponding more nearly to the 'Old South,' beginning with Virginia and comprising also the five pairs of states: North and South Carolina, Kentucky and
Tennessee, Georgia and Florida, Alabama and Mississippi, Louisiana and
Arkansas...

"This paper undertakes simply to state the case for regional national

social planning with special reference to the Southeast, emphasizing the
importance of a cooperative and coordinated design of, for, and by all
institutions of all regions as opposed to mere economic planning through
centralized autocracy. A companion brochure by Rupert B. Vance on 'Regional
Reconstruction: A Way Out for the South' adds more facts and findings of
the Southern Regional Study to be presented early in 1935."

Potatoes - Gt. Britain

Gt. Brit. Potato marketing board. Miscellaneous publication no. 1-2. 2 nos.
[London, 1935] 280.3759 G79M
    Contents: no. 1. The potato as an article of diet, by H. K. Archbold.
[1935] 20pp. - no. 2. An experiment in the distribution of potatoes at
Bishop Auckland, February-March, 1935. 32pp.
    .This is the record of a scheme to institute a scale of price differen-
tials for the same produce in accord with the amount of service rendered-
in other words to "divorce the service from the goods."

Gt. Brit. Potato marketing board. Report on the operation of the Potato mar-
keting scheme, year ended 31st August, 1935. 36PP. London, 1935.
(R.P. 28)   280.3759 G79
    Partial contents: Members of the Potato Marketing Board as at 31st
August, 1935; Supply regulation and control; Regulation and control of
foreign imports and of shipments; Marketing regulation and control;
Publicity; and Utilisation of potatoes for industrial purposes.

Price-Spreads - Meat

Tobin, B. F. What becomes of the consumer's meat dollar? With an introduction
and summary by Howard C. Greer. 97pp. Chicago, Ill., The University
of Chicago [1936] (Chicago. University. Bureau of business and economic
research. Studies in the packing industry. [Unnumbered publication])
50.9 C432C
    Also published as part 2 of volume 6 of the Studies in Business Admin-
istration of the University of Chicago.
    "The present study assembles and analyzes certain recent statistical
evidence bearing on prices and their relationships in the production and
marketing of livestock, the processing of edible and inedible products
derived therefrom, and the wholesale and retail distribution of the edible
products... There have been a number of studies, limited in scope and
purpose, of the relationships of individual livestock prices and wholesale
and retail prices of certain meats... there has been lacking a comprehensive picture of the functional distribution of the average price actually
paid at retail for meats.
    "This investigation is an attempt to determine as nearly as possible
the shares in this price accruing to the groups or agencies concerned in
the production of livestock and the marketing thereof, the processing of
meats, and their wholesale and retail distribution." - pp.14-15. The

period covered is 1925 through 1934.

Contents: Introduction and summary; Chapter 1, Scope and objectives –
general findings; II. The choice of a retail price series; III. Construction of retail price composites; IV. Plant values of livestock products;
V. Wholesaling and livestock marketing margins; VI. Unit values per live
cwt. and per pound sold at retail; VII. Division of processing and retail
margins; VIII. Observations of methods and results: Appendix.

Rural Youth

American country life association. Student section. Educating young
people for the rural community. Student section, A.C.L.A. 24pp., mimeogr.
[Madison? Wis.] 1936. 281.2 Am342E
    By Agnes Boynton and E. L. Kirkpatrick. Prepared and published
by the Student section, American Country Life Association, and the Department of rural sociology, University of Wisconsin, cooperating.
    This study outline was prepared for use in group discussions of
young people who plan to serve rural areas and who wish to learn of
the structure and the opportunities for leadership in the typical community. The outline, which is directed toward the National Conference
of the Student Section, American Country Life Association, August 11-14,
1936, "is arranged in four sections. The first, presented primarily
for the purpose of stimulating an interest, describes three typical situations, two of which involve rural neighborhoods centered in or near
open country school districts, and the other a village community. The
second raises questions which apply to the given examples as well as
to most local communities. The third includes vital quotations and
suggestive references and the fourth sketches briefly the framework
around which activities of a typical rural community may be organized
for further study."

Scarcity to Abundance – A Plan

Ezekiel, Mordecai. $2500 a year, from scarcity to abundance. 328pp. New York,
Harcourt, Brace and company [1936] 280.12 Ez3
    Bibliography, pp. 297-298.
    The author proposes a plan which he calls "Industrial Adjustment" which
he thinks would give business men assured markets and larger profits, and
workers assured jobs and higher wages. He writes in part as follows:
    "The Industrial Adjustment proposal depends upon conscious planning
with business, labor, and government cooperating, to coordinate and expand
production, buying power, and consumption. It provides a positive way
to carry these production programs into action, through adjustment contracts with cooperating individual business concerns. The benefit payments to cooperating concerns would insure general cooperation. This
method would not abolish private property or private initiative, but it
would set up, through the planned scheme for expansion, limits on their
action. It would depend upon a decentralized and democratic administration to develop and coordinate the programs, and to see they were carried
into effect. It would make no attempt to break down our big business in-

stitutions, but it would use and coordinate their bigness for full production and consumption.

"Effectively carried out, the Industrial Adjustment method would greatly increase production and incomes. It would assure producers of markets, workers of jobs, and consumers of improved standards of living. It would be a mammoth undertaking to carry through, fraught with difficulties and new problems. Yet it promises a way out of many of our difficulties.

"Industrial Adjustment starts from where we are now. It counts on a continuance of private business and private finance, of labor unions, markets, wages, and prices. But it provides definite mechanisms to bring about more effective coordination of those existing institutions.

"Economically, the Industrial Adjustment program is the most satisfactory of all we have explored. It aims squarely at the prime economic necessity - fuller employment and greater output and consumption. It provides definite mechanisms to keep consumption and production in balance. Administratively, it provides positive means to secure the cooperation of producers, and a flexible decentralized administration to maintain democratic control. Legally, it should rest eventually on the power of the government to provide for the general welfare. Politically, it should appeal to farmers, workers, and consumers, and to those business men who recognize the shortcomings of our present economic system."

Special Areas Report - England

Gt. Brit. Commissioner for the special areas (England and Wales) Second report... presented by the Minister of labour to Parliament by command of His Majesty February 1936 120pp. London, H. M. Stationery off , 1936 ([Gt. Brit. Parliament Papers by command' Cmd 5090) 280.171 G795

Part V of this report is devoted to agriculture - chiefly land settlement. Land drainage, afforestation, subsistence production and the Land Utilization Survey are touched upon.

Statistical Method

Arkin, Herbert. Statistical methods as applied to economics, business, education, social and physical sciences, etc., by Herbert Arkin. . [and] Raymond R. Colton... with a preface by Justin H. Moore. Rev. and enl 228, 47pp. New York, Barnes & Noble, inc. [c1935] 251 Ar4 1935

With this is bound the authors' Tables of Squares, square roots, cubes and cube roots. New York [c1934]

Issued also under title: An Outline of Statistical Methods.

Bibliography at end of each chapter.

"The present volume on statistics does not aim to be a comprehensive treatise on the subject. On the contrary it gives the distilled essence of material which might well require one or more large volumes for a full discussion. For that very reason it ought to be a most useful tool in the hands alike of students and people actually engaged in statistical work, wherever the particular field of activity may happen to lie. The formulas and examples given in it will be ample for the needs of most workers, whether they be concerned with financial, industrial, commercial, recal, or educational statistics." - Preface.

A useful reference tool is supplied in the preliminary pages entitled "Quick reference table to standard textbooks." Eighteen standard texts in the field of statistical methods have been analyzed as to nineteen of the subjects treated and page references are given.

Davis, H .T., and Nelson. W. F. C.   Elements of statistics, with applications to economic data 224pp. Bloomington, Ind., The Principia press, inc. [1935]   251 D29

Bibliography, pp. 364-365

"In 1932 the Social Science Research Council appointed a committee to define the place of collegiate mathematics in the social sciences. This committee was composed of H. R Tolley of the University of California (chairman), P. L. Griffin or Reed College, Holbrook Working of Leland Stanford University, Charles H. Titus of the University of California at Los Angeles and Mordecai Ezekiel of the Federal Farm Board. The report of the committee was read at a joint meeting of the Econometric Society and Sections A and K of the American Association for the Advancement of Science at Syracuse, New York, June 22, 1932, and published in Econometrica, Vol. I. (1933), pages 197-204. The report of this committee urged that students of the social sciences be prepared for the study of statistics by a six to nine semester hour course covering logarithms, graphs, interpolation, equations and forms of important curves, probability, elements of differential and integral calculus, and curve fitting. The report also suggested that 'illustrations from the social sciences should be used freely, and the concepts and processes should be presented in such a manner as to make clear their application in the social sciences.' The committee concluded that statistics courses might thus be utilized to carry the student much farther in the knowledge of statistical methods, and their possibilities and limitations.

"In the development of this book, the authors have had these recommendations in mind, and have prepared a text suitable for a six semester hour course to follow such a course in mathematical analysis as that urged by the committee...

"The illustrative materials and problems have been taken chiefly from data of economic significance. This lends, we believe, an atmosphere of coherence to the development such as is not attained when materials from a variety of disparate and unrelated disciplines are introduced in a capricious succession. The very pronounced drift in our day to a more fully quantitative science of economics would also seem to encourage such a concentration In addition, the authors' connection with the Cowles Commission for Research in Economics afferded opportunity for access to a variety of economic materials and original research.

"It need hardly be remarked, of course, that most of statistical methodology is the same, whether it is being applied to materials from economics or education or physics or astronomy. Thus, even though a student of the present volume should find his major interest in a field other than economics, by a study of this text containing economic applica-

tions he will obtain a training in statistical methodology adequate for
his own field." - Authors' preface and note
    Appendix I Biographical notes on mathematical economists. Includes
Cournot, Jevons, Walras, Pareto and Edgeworth
    Appendix II. Logarithms.
    Appendix III. The use of tables.
    About fifty pages at the end of the volume are devoted to tables includ-
ing among others Five Place Logarithms, Squares, Square Roots, Reciprocals

Taxation

Mustoe, N. E. Income tax on land and buildings, a handbook on the law
    and practice of income tax as it affects real property 144pp
    London, The Estates gazette, ltd., 1932   284 5 M97
    "Income Tax was first imposed in 1799 as a temporary measure for
the purpose of raising a fund to finance the campaign against Napoleon.
After the Peace of Amiens in 1802 the tax was repealed, but on the
renewal of the war in the following year it was revived, and continued to be levied until 1815, when the termination of the war again
removed the reason for its imposition.
    "But in 1842 when the financial position of the country demanded
severe reforms, the income tax was re-introduced at the instance of
Sir Robert Peel, as a transitory means of meeting a specific difficulty; but from that time to this, despite repeated assertions to the
effect that the tax was not intended to be permanent, it has been levied
every year. It is now by far the most productive of the direct taxes.
    "Income Tax is imposed on income from all sources, but this book
deals only with the tax on income derived from the ownership, or the
occupation, or the use of real estate. Income from this source has
the special feature that in general it is not taxed on the actual
amount of income, but on a hypothetical amount, which is ascertained
much in the same way as the rateable value of a hereditament for rating
purposes.
    "This book is, therefore, an attempt to set out the provisions of
the Income Tax Acts as they affect landlords (Schedule A, or landlord's
property tax), farmers and others who occupy land for the purpose of
earning a living therefrom (Schedule B), and traders in land. Chapters
are also included on the payment of mortgage interest, and on the
machinery for the assessment and collection of the tax " - Preface.

National association of real estate boards. National committee on real estate
    taxation. Real estate tax limitation. 46pp. [Chicago, Ill., National
    committee on real estate taxation of the National association of real
    estate boards, 1935]   284.5 N2182
    This pamphlet was prepared by Lawrence G. Holmes, Secretary of the
National Committee on Real Estate Taxation, under the direction of
Herbert U. Nelson, Secretary of the National Association of Real Estate
Boards. The Chairman of the Committee, Paul E. Stark writes in part
as follows in the foreword:
    "The National Association of Real Estate Boards, with the cooperation
of research and educational groups, spent some one hundred thousand

dollars over a period of about ten years studying the taxing systems
of the world, and the corrective measures proposed. Out of this study
the Association evolved six basic proposals for tax action. These, it
was convinced, if put into effect would bring about basic readjustments
essential for a continuation of orderly processes of government.

"During the years from 1929 to 1934 seven states enacted legislation
putting the first one of these six points into operation. This is the principle of an over-all limitation on real estate taxes.

"The purpose of this pamphlet is to review the principle of over-all
limitation and its actual effects on the taxing structures.

Newcomer, M. An index of the taxpaying ability of state and local governments.
65 p New York, Bureau of publications, Teachers college, Columbia
university, 1935. 284.5 N43

A preprint of one phase of the report of the investigation of need and
relative ability of states as they bear on federal aid to education,
now under way under the direction of Paul R. Mort... and under the general supervision of the Columbia university Council on research in the
social sciences ..

The introduction, signed by Professor Mort states:

"The first step in the procedure for the development of measures of
relative ability was the development of a criterion of relative ability
to pay For this purpose it was decided to use the yield of a model tax
system... Dr. Newcomer's report goes in detail into the various issues
involved in developing such a criterion. It should be understood that
this report deals solely with a basis of determining the relative ability
of states to pay taxes. It does not propose a tax system for the use of
states

"The next step, now well under way as this goes to press, is the attempt to develop a usable index for relative ability which would have a
dependable relationship with the criterion and which, at the same time,
would be based on measures of such a nature that they could be specifically
defined in legislation.

"This phase of the investigation is made available at this time because
of the interest it has aroused and its potential value in other investigations now under way."

The following material is appended: Appendix A. Methods of arriving
at estimates of different types of income and wealth; B. Index for the
measurement of the relative taxpaying ability of the different states in
inter-census years; C. Possibilities of the unearned increment tax on
land.

Tenant-right Valuation - Gt. Britain

Adkin, E. W. A handbook of the law relating to landlord & tenant. Eighth
edition revised. 716pp. London, The Estates gazette, ltd., 1932.
282 Ad52 Ed. 8

This publication is authorised by the College of Estate Management
as one of its series of text books

It is a comprehensive outline of the Law of Landlord and Tenant published after the coming into operation of the Law of Property Act, 1925 and the other statistics relating to property which came into force on the first of January 1926 and which, together with the Landlord and Tenant Act, 1927, brought about so great a change in the law of England.

Wood, Leslie S. The principles and practice of farm valuations. Fifth edition, revised by Humfrey Middleton. 336pp. London, The Estates gazette, ltd. [1929] 282 W85 Ed.5
    This publication is authorised by the College of Estate Management as one of its series of text books.
    Appendix contains copies of laws relating to the subject.

Tobacco Monopoly - Poland

Dzierzyński, Józef. Spożycie tytoniu w Polsce. 311pp. Warszawa, Nakladem Dyrekcji polskiego monopolutytoniowego, 1930. 286.369 D99
    Tablice statystyczne, 125 pages at end.
    French summary (Consommation du tabac en Pologne) pp. 113-124 of Tablice statystyczne.
    Bibliography, pp. [185]-186.
    Contains extensive statistical tables and a French summary on the consumption of tobacco in Poland.

U. S. S. R.

Soviet Union, 1935 J. Stalin, V. Molotov, K. Kaganovich, V. Kuibyshev, M. Tukhachevsky, S. Orjonikidze, J. Yakovlev, G. Grinko, A. Rosenholz. 440pp. Moscow-Leningrad, Cooperative publishing society of foreign workers in the U. S. S. R., 1935. 280.179 So8
    "It is the intention of the Publishers to present in this book a vivid and comprehensive picture of the policy and achievements of the Soviet Union in recent years, bringing the picture down to 1935, the third year of the Second Five-Year Plan." - Preface.
    The section devoted to Agriculture (pp. 291-343) was written by J. A. Yakovlev, Chief of the Central Committee of the C.P.S.U., March 1935.

Vanilla - Puerto Rico

Puerto Rico Emergency relief administration. Bureau of agricultural and industrial research. Outlook for vanilla cultivation in Puerto Rico. 34, xxviii pp. San Juan, P. R., 1935. 68.7 P96
    Bibliography, pp. xxvii-xxviii.
    Discusses the sources of vanilla, market trends and potential markets, costs of production, and diseases of the vine.

World Affairs

Institute of world affairs. Proceedings of the Institute of world affairs, twelfth session, Mission Inn, Riverside, California, December 9 to 14, 1934. Edited by Rufus B. von Kleinsmid and Herbert Wynford Hill. v. 12. 241pp. Los Angeles, Calif., Pub. for the Institute of world affairs by the University

of Southern California, 1935, 380.9 In792
    Partial contents: The New Deal and its international implications,
by Charles E. Martin; The New Deal! An appraisal, by William B. Munro;
and The foreign policy of the United States, summary of round table, by
Frank M. Russell.

BIBLIOGRAPHIES

Canadian publications in agricultural economics [compiled by] E. G. Misner,
    Department of agricultural economics and farm management, Cornell
    university. Ithaca, N. Y., 1935. 22pp., mimeogr. 241.3 C81C
        Requests for this publication should be addressed to the Department
    of Agricultural Economics and Farm Management, Cornell university,Ithaca,N.Y.

Government control of cotton production in the United States, 1933-1935; a
    selected list of references, compiled by Emily L. Day... under the direc-
    tion of Mary G. Lacy, librarian, Bureau of agricultural economics. 59pp.,
    mimeogr. January 1936. (U. S. Dept. of agriculture. Bureau of agricultural
    economics. Agricultural economics bibliography no. 63)

Milk; cost of marketing. A selected list of references, compiled by Hazel
    E. Workman, Library, Bureau of agricultural economics, U. S. Department
    of agriculture. 16pp. [Washington, D. C.] Mar. 21, 1936. typewritten.
    May be borrowed for copying.

Publications in agricultural economics, farm management, marketing and other
    economic topics, United Kingdom of Great Britain and Northern Ireland,
    England and Wales, Scotland, Northern Ireland [compiled by] E. G. Misner,
    Department of agricultural economics and farm management, Cornell
    University. 102pp., mimeogr. Ithaca, N. Y. [1935?] 241.3 C81
        Requests for this publication should be addressed to the Department of
    Agricultural Economics and Farm Management, Cornell university, Ithaca,N.Y.

The rubber industry 1935. A bibliography, prepared by P. W. Barker. 20pp.,mim-
    eogr. [Washington, D. C., U. S. Bureau of foreign and domestic commerce]
    157.55 R82
        Requests for this publication should be addressed to the Bureau of
    Foreign and Domestic Commerce, Washington, D. C.

Rural land economics, 1933-1935. Outstanding references relating to rural land
    economics especially to the present national land policy, compiled by
    Orpha Cummings, librarian, Giannini foundation of agricultural economics,
    University of California. 114pp. Berkeley, Calif., Mar. 12, 1936.
    Typewritten.
        Requests for this publication should be addressed to the Giannini founda-
    tion, University of California, Berkeley, Calif.

Textile reading list. A partial bibliography on textile information... Prepared by Harry J. Robinson. 33pp. [Washington, D.C.] 1936. (U. S. Bureau of foreign and domestic commerce. Special bulletin no. 634) 157.54 Sp32 no.634

    Requests for this publication should be addressed to the Bureau of Foreign and Domestic Commerce, Washington, D. C.

The Townsend old-age pension plan: list of references, compiled by Laura A. Thompson, librarian, U. S. Department of labor. 8pp., mimeogr. [Washington, D. C., 1936]

    Requests for this publication should be addressed to the Department of Labor Library, Washington, D. C.

Valuation of real estate, with special reference to farm real estate, compiled by Margaret T. Olcott and Helen E. Hennefrund, under the direction of Mary G. Lacy, librarian, Bureau of agricultural economics. 350pp., mimeogr. December 1935. (U. S. Dept. of agriculture. Bureau of agricultural economics. Agricultural economics bibliography no. 60. (Supersedes no. 29)

SELECTED LIST OF RECENT REVIEWS

Compiled by M. I. Herb

Black, J. D. The dairy industry and the AAA. 1935. (Half-title: The Institute of economics of the Brookings institution. Publication no. 64)

    Reviewed by W. P, Mortenson in Amer. Econ. Rev. 26(1): 106-108. March 1936.

Bohn, Frank and Ely, R. T. The great change; work and wealth in the new age. 1935.

    Reviewed by M.J.V. in Sociol. and Social Research 20(4): 381. March-April 1936.

Brinkmann, Theodore. Economics of the farm business. English edition, with introduction and notes by Elizabeth Tucker Benedict, Heinrich Herman Stippler and Murray Reed Benedict. 1935. (Social science research council. Advisory committee on social and economic research in agriculture. Translation series, no. 2.)

    Reviewed by C. L. Holmes, in Jour. Farm Econ. 18(1): 217-219. February 1936.

Burrows, H. R., and Horsefield, J. K. Economics of planning: principles and practice. 1935. (American academy of political and social science, Philadelphia. Pamphlet series, no. 1)

    Reviewed by Edmund Whittaker in South African Jour. Econ. 3(3): 434-435. September 1935.

Chase, Stuart. Government in business. 1935.

    Reviewed by R. S. Alexander in Polit. Sci. Quart. 51(1): 154-158. March 1936.

Childs, Marquis. Sweden; The middle way. 1936.
    Reviewed by Simeon Strunsky in The New York Times Book Rev.
    February 2, 1936, p.3.

Davis, J. S. Wheat and the AAA. 1935.
    Reviewed by Peter L. Slagsvold in Jour. Farm Econ. 18(1): 200-204.
    February 1936.

Dickinson, John. Hold fast the middle way; an outline of economic
    challenges and alternatives. 1935.
    Reviewed by R. J. Swenson in Amer. Polit. Sci. Rev. 30(1): 178-180.
    February 1936.

Dorfman, Joseph. Thorstein Veblen and his America. 1934; second print-
    ing. 1935.
    Reviewed by A. L. Harris in Jour. Polit. Econ. 44(1): 109-111.
    February 1936.

Douglas, P. H. Controlling depressions. [1935]
    Reviewed by D. T. Jack in Econ. Jour. 46(181): 120-122. March 1936.

Economic essays in honor of Wesley Clair Mitchell. 1935.
    Reviewed by Redvers Opie in Econ. Jour. 46(181): 140-141. March
    1936

Emeny, Brooks. The strategy of raw materials; a study of America in peace
    and war. 1934.
    Reviewed by R. E. Freeman in Amer. Econ. Rev. 26(1): 109-110.
    March 1936.

The Encyclopaedia of the social sciences. 15v. 1930-1935.
    Reviewed by E. A. J. Johnson in Quart. Jour. Econ. 50(2): 355-366.
    February 1936.

Ezekiel, Mordecai. $2500 a year; from scarcity to abundance. [1936]
    Reviewed and discussed in the American Observer v.5, no.27, March
    16, 1936, pp.1,8, in an article entitled "Plans Seek to Raise
    Standards of Living. Economists Grapple with Problem of Using
    Full Productive Capacity of U.S. Distribution is Main Issue.
    Ezekiel Challenges Other Proposals with Plan to Raise Family Income
    to $2500 a Year."
    Reviewed by Mary-Carter Roberts in Washington, D. C. Star,
    Mar. 14, 1936.
    Reviewed briefly in the column entitled "The Book Parade" in
    the Forum 95(4): VI. April 1936.
    Reviewed by V. D. Kazakevich in New York Herald Tribune Books,
    March 22, 1936.
    Reviewed by Robert C. Brooks in the Saturday Review of Literature
    13 (22): 11. Mar. 28, 1936.

Discussed by the conversational method in The American Observer 5(28): 7, March 23, 1936, in the column entitled "Talking Things Over.".

A brief description of Dr. Ezekiel's plan for an annual income for every family of $2500 is given in Manfrs. Rec. 103(3): 58. March 1936, in the column entitled "Financial News."

FitzGerald, D. A. Livestock under the AAA. 1935. (Half-title: The Institute of economics of the Brookings institution. Publication no. 65)

Reviewed by D. G. Card in Jour. Farm Econ. 18(1): 204-208. February 1936.

Gangulee, N. N. The Indian peasant and his environment. 1935.

Reviewed by W. D. Carter in Pacific Affairs 9(1): 149-150. March 1936.

Garside, Alston Hill. Cotton goes to market. 1935.

Reviewed by H. E. Agnew in Natl. Marketing Rev. 1(3): 275-276. Winter 1936.

Ginzburg, Eli. The house of Adam Smith. 1934.

Reviewed by F. B. Garver in Jour. Farm Econ. 18(1): 216-217. February 1936.

Haight, F. A. French import quotas; a new instrument of commercial policy. 1935. (Half-title: London school of economics and political science. Studies in economics and commerce. no. 6) P. S. King & Son, Ltd. 1935.

Reviewed by R. J. Truptil in Economica(n.s.) 3(9): 94-95. February 1936.

Higgs, Henry. Bibliography of economics, 1935.

Reviewed by F. A. von Hayek in Economica (n.s.) 3(9): 98-99. February 1936.

Howard, Lady Louise E. (Matthaei) Labour in agriculture; an international survey. 1935.

"A review of some of the specific data presented in the survey and of the outstanding trends in legislation and collective action which it develops" is given in Monthly Labor Rev. 42(2): 339-346. February 1936.

Reviewed in The Statist 127(3023): 171-172. Feb. 1, 1936, in an article entitled "World Agricultural Labour Problems."

Reviewed in Internatl. Labour Rev. 33(2): 227-231. February 1936.

Reviewed by C. S. Orwin in Econ. Jour. 46(181): 109-111. March 1936.

International institute of agriculture. The world agricultural situation in 1933-34. 1935.

Reviewed by R. J. T. in Royal Statis. Soc. Jour. (n.s.) 98(4): 743-744. 1935.

Jesness, O. B., Nowell, R. I., and associates. A program for land use in northern Minnesota, a type study of land utilization. 1935.
Reviewed by C. S. Ascher in Jour. Land & Pub. Utility Econ. 12(1): 107. February 1936.

Kolb, J. H., and Brunner, Edmund de S. A study of rural society; its organization and changes. [1935]
Reviewed by M.H.N. in Sociol. and Social Research 20(4): 380. March-April 1936.
Reviewed by C. E. Lively in Jour. Farm Econ. 18(1): 214-216. Feb. 1936.

Lippincott, B. E., ed. Government control of the economic order; a symposium. 1935.
Reviewed by Barbara Wootton in Econ. Jour. 46(181): 142-143. March 1936

Menzies-Kitchin, A. W. Land settlement; a report prepared for the Carnegie United Kingdom trustees. 1935.
Reviewed by B. in Scottish Farmer 44(2244): 63-64. Jan. 18, 1936.

Moulton, H. G. Income and economic progress. 1935. (The Institute of economics of the Brookings institution. Publication no. 68)
Reviewed by I. G. Davis in Jour. Farm Econ. 18(1): 208-211. February 1936.
Reviewed by R. S. Vaile in Natl. Marketing Rev. 1(3): 277-278. Winter 1936.

Orwin, C. S., and Drake, W. F. Back to the land. 1935.
Reviewed by W. C. D. Dampier in Econ. Jour. 46(181): 108-109. March 1936

Penrose, E. F. Population theories and their application, with special reference to Japan. [1934] (Food research institute. Leland Stanford junior university. Miscellaneous publication no. 7)
Reviewed by J. B. Condliffe in Geogr. Rev. 26(1): 165-166. January 1936

Taylor, A. E. The New Deal and foreign trade. 1935.
Reviewed by H. W. Macdonald in Pacific Affairs 9(1): 139-141. March 1936.
Reviewed by E. H. Phelps Brown in Econ. Jour. 46(181): 137-138. March 193

United States in world affairs: an account of American foreign relations 1934-1935. v.4. 1935.
Reviewed by B. E. Nelson in the N. Y. Times Book Rev., Jan. 19, 1936, p.10.
Reviewed by R. L. Buell in the N. Y. Herald Tribune Books, Jan. 12, 1936, p.6.

Willcox, O. W. Nations can live at home. [1935]
Reviewed by Wilson Gee in Amer. Econ. Rev. 26(1): 108-109. March 1936.

U. S. DEPARTMENT OF AGRICULTURE PUBLICATIONS

Economic in Character

Compiled by Katharine Jacobs

Miscellaneous Publications*

223. Studies of family living in the United States and other countries; and analysis of material and method, by Faith M. Williams...and Carle C. Zimmerman. 617pp. December 1935.
232. List of bulletins of the agricultural experiment stations for the calendar years 1933 and 1934, by Catherine E. Pennington. 81pp. February 1936.

Service and Regulatory Announcements (Bureau of Agricultural Economics)*

149. Rules and regulations of the Secretary of agriculture under the Tobacco inspection act of August 23, 1935 (49 stat. 731) effective January 2, 1936. 9pp.

Technical Bulletins*

493. Farm prices of cotton related to its grade and staple length in the United States, seasons 1928-29 to 1932-33, by L. D. Howell ... and John S. Burgess. 63pp. January 1936.
505. Refrigeration of oranges in transit from California by C. W. Mann... and William C. Cooper. 88pp. January 1936.
       Bibliography, pp. 86-87.

Radio Talks of Secretary Wallace*

Farm business and science news; a radio talk by Morse Salisbury... delivered during the Department period of the National farm and home hour... March 10, 1936. 4pp.
       Consists of excerpts from Secretary Wallace's statement at the regional meetings "to consider effectuation of the Soil conservation and domestic allotment act."
       The full statement was issued as a 7pp. mimeographed publication by the Agricultural Adjustment Administration.
The new farm legislation remarks ... over the National farm and home hour... March 3, 1936. 4pp.
Region and nation; remarks ... over the National farm and home hour... March 17, 1936. 5pp., mimeogr.
Remarks over the National farm and home hour... March 20, 1936. 3pp.
       Quotes the President's statement made on March 19 at which time he signed the "appropriation bill providing 440 million dollars for the new farm program."
Statement... on possible after-effects of floods on health of cattle, over the National farm and home hour... March 20, 1936. 1p.

---

*Requests for these publications should be addressed to the Office of Information, U. S. Department of Agriculture, Washington, D. C.

Publications of the Bureau of Agricultural Economics (Mimeographed)*

The annual livestock inventory, a radio talk by C. L. Harlan. 2pp. Feb. 14, 1936.

Car-lot shipments of fruits and vegetables, by commodities, states, and months (including boat shipments reduced to car-lot equivalents) calendar year 1935. Preliminary, subject to revision. 25pp. March 1936.

Cost of production of sweet potatoes; data from studies in 10 states selected years, 1914-32, compiled from official sources by H. W. Hawthorne. 16pp. March 1936.
        Sources of data, p. 16.

Dairy and poultry market statistics 1935 annual summary. 39pp. February 1936.

Effect of artificial drying on germination of seed corn, comp. by C. L. Phillips. 2pp. February 1936.

Estimates of livestock on farms January 1, 1930-36 by classes. 28pp. March 9, 1936.

Exporting fresh fruits and vegetables from the United States to Canada, by F. G. Robb. 11pp. [1936]
        Address, Canadian Fruit and Vegetable Jobbers' Association, Toronto, Canada, January 15, 1936."

Extent of protection from fluctuations in spot-cotton prices afforded by future trading, by L. D. Howell... and Leonard J. Watson. A preliminary report. 28pp. March 1936.

Government control of cotton production in the United States 1933-1935; a selected list of references compiled by Emily L. Day... under the direction of Mary G. Lacy, librarian, Bureau of agricultural economics. 59pp. January 1936. (Agricultural economics bibliography no. 63)

List of publications prepared by the Grain division arranged alphabetically by subjects, comp. by C. Louise Phillips. 17pp. February 1936.

Marketing Texas onions; brief review of the 1935 season by W. D. Googe. 17pp. March 1936.
        Issued in cooperation with Texas Department of Agriculture, Markets and Warehouse Division.

Marketing the Michigan grape crop; brief review of the 1935 season, by R. E. Keller. 5pp. [1936?]
        Issued in cooperation with the Michigan Department of Agriculture, Bureau of Foods & Standards.

Marketing the Michigan peach crop; brief review of the 1935 season, by R. E. Keller. 6pp. [1936?]
        Issued in cooperation with Michigan Department of Agriculture, Bureau of Foods and Standards.

Marketing western New York celery; summary of 1935 season, by V. H. Nicholson and A. L. Thomas. 9pp. March 1936.
        Issued in cooperation with New York State Department of Agriculture and Markets.

---

*These publications are issued in small editions for immediate use in official work and are not for general distribution.

Marketing western New York peaches; summary of 1935 season, by V. H.
Nicholson & A. L. Thomas. 8pp. January 1936. (Issued in coopera-
tion with New York State Department of agriculture and markets)
Marketing western New York pears; summary of 1935 season, by V. H. Nicholson
and A. L. Thomas. 8pp. January 1936. (Issued in cooperation with
New York State Dept. of agriculture and markets)
Milk and milk products used in the manufacture of milk chocolate, cocoa
and chocolate coatings. 1p. Feb. 15, 1936.
Mohair production 1933, 1934 and 1935. 1p. March 11, 1936.
Production and carry-over of fruit and vegetable containers for the year
1935, comp. by Lucille Steffel under the direction of L. C. Carey.
8pp. February 1936.
Publications relating to farm population and rural life, issued at the
various state colleges of agriculture. 27pp. January 1936.
Rural poetry; a radio talk by Caroline B. Sherman... National farm and home
hour... March 4, 1936. 2pp.
Seed statistics. 58pp. March 1936.
State agricultural departments and marketing agencies with names of officials.
6pp. March 1936.
Tentative United States standards for split peas. 4pp. April 1, 1936.
(HFS-1750)
Valuation of real estate, with special reference to farm real estate, com-
piled by Margaret T. Olcott and Helen E. Hennefrund, under the direction
of Mary G. Lacy, librarian, Bureau of agricultural economics. 350pp.,
December 1935. (Agricultural economics bibliography no. 60. (Supersedes
no. 29))

Publications of the Agricultural Adjustment Administration*

Income parity for agriculture, by L. H. Bean. 8pp., diagrs. mimeogr. March
1936.
       Pt. 2, is also issued in the Agricultural Situation, v. 20, no. 2
February 1, 1936, pp. 2-8.
Order series - order no. 4. Order regulating the handling of milk in the
greater Boston, Massachusetts, marketing area, issued by the Secretary
of agriculture, February 7, 1936, effective 12:01 a.m., E. S. T.,
February 9, 1936. 16pp. (0-4)
Summary of address by Chester C. Davis... of the Agricultural adjustment
and related acts... Northwestern university, Chicago, Illinois... March
12, 1936. 5pp., mimeogr.

Radio Talk (Mimeographed**)

Can farmers get their foreign markets back? By Chester C. Davis, administrator of the Agricultural adjustment and related acts, broadcast...
March 19, 1936.

---

*Requests for these publications should be addressed to the Agricultural
Adjustment Administration, U. S. Department of Agriculture, Washington, D.C.
**May be obtained from United States Department of Agriculture, Office of
Information.

Compiled by Mary F. Carpenter

California

California. Emergency relief administration. Division of self-help cooperative
service. Annual report, 1934/35. 70, 103pp., mimeogr. San Francisco.
1936.
The appendix includes an article by Clark Kerr and P. S. Taylor, The
self-help cooperatives in California, pp. A2-A21; and a list of references
on the self help cooperative movement, pp. A93-A103.

Wellman, H. R. Some economic aspects of regulating shipments of California
oranges. Calif. Agr. Expt. Sta. Circ. 338. 29pp. Berkeley, 1936.
Paper no. 60, Giannini Foundation of Agricultural Economics.

Connecticut

Connecticut. Department of Agriculture. Bureau of markets. Summary of carlot
unloads, truck receipts and local receipts in Bridgeport, Hartford, New
Haven and Waterbury for the year, 1935. 19pp., mimeogr. Hartford. 1936.
Compiled by D. E. Warner.

Peck, B. T. The Connecticut apple industry. Conn. Dept. Agr. Bull. 37, 10pp.
Hartford. 1935.
A statistical survey of commercial orchards.

Wilkinson, A. E. Grade defects of potatoes. Conn. Agr. Col. Ext. Bull. 222,
19pp. Storrs. 1935.
In cooperation with G. B. Clarke and S. A. Edwards.

Illinois

Illinois. Department of agriculture. Eighteenth annual report... July 1, 1934
to June 30, 1935. 118pp. Springfield. [1936]
Division of Agricultural Statistics, pp. 19-36; Illinois State Grain
Inspection Division, pp. 59-81; Division of Standardization and Markets,
pp. 102-106.

Illinois. University. College of agriculture. Agricultural experiment station
and extension service. Papers presented at the Farm Appraisals Conference,
May 14-16, 1935. 103pp., mimeogr. Urbana. [n.d.]

Lindstrom, D. E., Case, H. C. M. and Leonard, Archie. Farm business survey of
120 farms in southern Illinois. 1934. 15pp., mimeogr. Urbana. 1935.
Data were obtained from farm operators in Union county.

Norton, L. J., and Hedges, T. R. Prices of Illinois farm products, 1931-1934.
Ill. Agr. Expt. Sta. Bull. 422, 73pp. Urbana. 1935.

Indiana

Hinrichs, A. F. An economic analysis of local grain elevators in Indiana.
Ind. Agr. Expt. Sta. Bull. 403, 32pp. Lafayette. 1935.
The analysis includes composition and volume of business, income and
costs.
The duration of this study was for the five crops marketed from 1928
through 1932.

Iowa

Bentley, R. C. Freight costs of moving Iowa feed grains from surplus to
deficit areas. Iowa Agr. Expt. Sta. Bull. 342. pp. 116-148. Ames. 1936.
Includes charts and maps.

Iowa. Agricultural experiment station. Report on agricultural research for
the year ending June 30, 1935. 220pp. Ames. 1935.
Development of a technique for securing farmers' advice, pp. 7-8.
Progress report of Agricultural Economics Section, pp. 16-34.

Iowa. State board of assessment and review. Annual report - Taxable valuation
of property. 294pp. Des Moines, 1935.
Includes number and value of livestock by counties, pp. 28-71.

Nelson, P. M., and others. The food consumption habits of 145 Iowa farm families.
Iowa Agr. Expt. Sta. Bull. 337, pp. 331-359. Ames. 1935.

Thompson, S. H., and Miller, P. L. A method of analyzing the effectiveness of
local livestock cooperatives in selling hogs. Iowa Agr. Expt. Sta. Research
Bull. 193, pp. 36-70. Ames. 1936.
The hog sales of four representative associations were analyzed for 1931.
The effect of the time and place of marketing is discussed and data re-
lating to shipping margins are contained in the appendix.

Wakeley, R. E. Part-time and garden farming in Iowa. Iowa Agr. Expt. Sta.
Bull. 340, pp. 21-63. Ames. 1935.
An analysis of part-time farming in relation to population, home and
community living, occupation and income from employment and agricultural
production and income. It presents also the opinion of operators toward
part-time farming.

Kansas

Green, R. M. Seasonal and short-time fluctuations in wheat prices in relation
to the wheat-price cycle. Kans. Agr. Expt. Sta. Tech. Bull. 39, 52pp.
Manhattan. 1935.

Maryland

Maryland. Agricultural experiment station. Forty-seventh annual report,
1933-1934. XXXIV, 456pp. College Park. [1935]
Agricultural economics, pp. IX-X.
Bulletins 351-363 are contained on pp. 1-456.

Michigan. State College of agriculture. Extension service. Farm management
department. 1934 annual farm business report. 3 nos. mimeographed.
East Lansing.
In cooperation with U. S. Bureau of Agricultural Economics.
Contents: State summary, M-145; Area 5, General summary, M-154; Area 8
Peans. beets and dairying, M-157.

Minnesota

Minnesota. Agricultural experiment station, and Minnesota Department of conserv
tion. Land economic survey of Hubbard county, Minnesota. Minn. Agr.
Expt. Sta. Bull. 317, 264pp. University Farm, St. Paul. 1935.
Report of the Minnesota Land Economic Survey which was undertaken in
response to the direction of the State legislature embodied in Chapter 247
of the session laws of 1929.
A cover type map and a soil map are attached.

Minnesota. Department of agriculture. Minnesota state farm census 1935. Minn.
Dept. Agr. Bull. 21, 9pp. St. Paul. 1936.
In cooperation with U. S. Bureau of Agricultural Economics.
Includes county statistics for land use, number of farm owners and
renters, acreage of crops and number of livestock.

Montana

Lamphere, W. H. Montana agricultural outlook. [1936] Mont. Agr. Col. Ext.
Circ. 75, 7pp. Bozeman, 1936.

Nebraska

Nebraska. State tax commissioner. 15th annual report... 1935. 170pp.
Lincoln, 1935.
Includes number of bushels and valuation of field crops and number
and valuation of livestock by counties.

New Hampshire

New Hampshire. State tax commission. Twenty-fifth annual report... 1935.
191pp. Concord. 1935.
Includes numbers of livestock by counties and towns.

New Jersey

Back, N. A. Survey of mutual fire insurance associations in New Jersey which
insure farm properties. N. J. Dept. Agr. Circ. 253, 15pp. Trenton. 1935

- 312 -

Crisp, G. B. Marketing tomatoes for canning in New Jersey on the basis of
standard grades. Results during the 1935 season. N. J. Dept. Agr. Circ.
254, 8pp. Trenton. 1936.

New Mexico

New Mexico. Agricultural experiment station. Forty-six annual report...
1934-1935. 62pp. State College. 1935.
Agricultural economics, pp. 10-13.

New York

Beers, H. W. Measurements of family relationships in farm families of Central
New York, N. Y. (Cornell) Agr. Expt. Sta. Memoir 183. 38pp. Ithaca. 1935.
"The present study analyzes case material obtained by interviews that
were conducted with an unconcealed research approach. The data provide a
description of selected factors in the homes of normal farm families."

LaMont, T. E., and Tyler, H. S. Land utilization and classification in New
York state. N. Y. (Cornell) Agr. Col. AE 119, 31pp., mimeogr. Ithaca.
1935.

Misner, E. G. Bibliography of Canadian publications in the field of agricultural economics. 22pp., mimeogr. Ithaca. N. Y. Cornell Univ. Dept. Agr.
Econ. and Farm Mangt. 1935.

Misner, E. G. Publications in agricultural economics, farm management, marketing and other economic topics. United Kingdom of Great Britain and Northern
Ireland. 102pp., mimeogr. Ithaca. N. Y. Cornell Univ. Dept. Agr. Econ.
and Farm Mangt. 1935.
Some pages are left blank for the entry of additional publications.

New York (Cornell) State college of agriculture, Department of agricultural
economics and farm management. Farm economics, no. 93. Ithaca.
February, 1936.
Partial contents: Business conditions, pp. 2254-2255, 2262-2268; Causes
of changes in prices of farm products, pp. 2268-2272, by G. F. Warren and
F. A. Pearson; Production of the principal manufactured dairy products in
relation to population and feed production, pp. 2272-2275, by E. E. Vial;
Trends in town taxes in New York, pp. 2275-2277, by M. P. Catherwood;
Rural tax delinquency in New York state, pp. 2277-2278, by G. E. Brandow;
Cycles of the numbers of cattle and of the prices of dairy products,
pp. 2278-2279 by E. G. Misner; Some facts concerning use of motor trucks
by growers in marketing fruits and vegetables, season 1933-34, pp.2279-
2282; Sales outlets used by New York state growers in marketing various
fruits and vegetables, season 1933-1934, pp. 2282-2283, by M. P. Rasmussen;
Survey of land classes I and II in New York state, pp. 2284-2286, by C. N.
Lane and T. E. LaMont; The relation of land class and roads to rural mail
delivery service in Chenango county, pp. 2286-2287, by H. S. Tyler; Returns

for use of capital and for labor of operators and their families on New
York farms, pp. 2287-2291, by E. G. Misner; License cost for farm auto-
-mobiles and trucks in New York, pp. 2291-2292, by W. M. Curtis.

New York (Cornell) State college of agriculture, Extension Service. The New
York State 1936 agricultural outlook. N. Y. Cornell Agr. Col. Ext. Bull.
340, 16pp. Ithaca. 1936.

New York. State college of agriculture, and Cornell agricultural experiment.
station. Forty-eighth annual report 1934/1935. 160pp. Ithaca. 1936.
Extension work in agricultural economics and farm management, pp. 29-
32; in rural social organization, pp. 56-57, Agricultural Experiment
Station report on agricultural economics and farm management, pp. 60-64;
in rural government, pp. 64-65; in rural social organization, pp. 136-137.

Raymond, C. B., and Hurd, T. N. Costs and returns in producing canning factory
sween corn 1935. N. Y. (Cornell) Agr. Col. AE 128, 18pp. Ithaca. 1936.
Summary of 28 enterprise accounts in Madison, Seneca, and Yates counties

Scoville, G. P. Some successful farms in 1935. N. Y.(Cornell) Agr. Col.
AE 126, 26pp., mimeogr. Ithaca. 1936.

North Carolina

Smith, G. R. Cotton marketing practices in North Carolina with special reference to ginner-buyers. N. C. Agr. Expt. Sta. Tech. Bull. 51, 46pp. State
College Station. Raleigh. 1935.
The work was conducted in cooperation with the U. S. Bureau of Agricultural Economics.

Stevens, E.W., and Estabrook, Helen. North Carolina farm housing. N. C. Agr.
Expt. Sta. Bull. 301. 82pp. State College Station, Raleigh. 1935.
Report from the Federal Farm House Survey conducted in January and
February 1935.
The counties surveyed were Avery, Henderson, part of Cleveland, Iredell,
Alamance, Moore, part of Robeson, part of Duplin, Edgecombe, Camden,
Currituck, and part of Pasquoteuk.

North Dakota

North Dakota. Agricultural college, Extension service. Agricultural outlook
and farm family living outlook in North Dakota for 1936. N. Dak. Agr.
Col. Ext. Circ. 139, 29pp. Fargo. 1936.

North Dakota. Emergency relief administration. North Dakota rural survey...
Analysis of the farm relief load, June 1935. 16pp., mimeogr. n.p. 1935.
In cooperation with the Federal Emergency Relief Administration.

Ohio

Lively, C. E. Length of residence of the heads of families in selected rural
areas of Ohio. 5pp., mimeogr. Wooster. Ohio Agr. Expt. Sta. Dept. Rural
Econ. 1935.
A preliminary research bulletin.

- 314 -

Lively, C. E. Origin of the rural population of Ohio. Ohio Agr. Expt. Sta. Bimonthly Bull. 21 (179): 58-59. Wooster. March-April, 1936.

Moore, H. R., and Falconer, J. I. Public revenue in Ohio with especial reference to rural taxation, Ohio Agr. Expt. Sta. Bull. 560, 44pp. Wooster. 1936.

Oregon

Kuhlman, G. W., Flippin, T. J., and Niederfrank, E. J. Part-time farming in Oregon. Oreg. Agr. Expt. Sta. Bull. 340, 49pp. Corvallis. 1935.
Contents include - Part-time farmers and their families; Description of the farms; Financial aspects; Factors affecting success; Industries employing rural labor; Possible expansion of employment, and reactions expressed by part-time farmers. An appendix contains detailed tables.

Rodenwold, B. W., Oliver, A. W., and Potter, E. L. The marketing of country-dressed meat in Portland. Oreg. Agr. Expt. Sta. Bull. 339, 22pp. Corvallis, 1935.
"This study ... was undertaken to determine: (1) the extent to which country-dressed carcasses enter into the meat trade in Portland, (2) the quality of these country-dressed carcasses as compared with meat from other sources, (3) the trade practices of the dealers and agencies handling country-dressed meats, (4) the relative prices received by producers for animals slaughtered on the farm, (5) the economic importance of this trade in farm-slaughtered livestock to producers."

Puerto Rico

Puerto Rico. Emergency relief administration. Outlook for vanilla cultivation in Puerto Rico. 34pp. XXIIIpp. San Juan. 1935.
Includes market trends, cost of production and other economic information.

Rhode Island

Tennant, J. L. Home-grown roughage and milk production costs. R. I. Agr. Expt. Sta. Bull. 254, 28pp. Kingston. 1935.

South Dakota

South Dakota. Department of agriculture. South Dakota agricultural statistics, 1935. [7pp.]- Pierre. [1936]
Includes tables giving numbers of farm owners and tennants, acreage of crops and numbers of livestock by counties for 1935.

South Dakota. State college of agriculture and mechanic arts, Extension service. South Dakota agricultural outlook for 1936. S. Dak. Agr. Col. Ext. Circ. Letter 126, 24pp. Brookings. 1936.

Texas

Texas. Agricultural experiment station. Forty-seventh annual report, 1934. 288pp. College Station. 1935.
Farm and ranch economics, pp. 101-109.

Vermont. University, Extension service. The 1936 agricultural outlook, Vermont. 4pp. Burlington. 1936.

Washington

Tummeier, E. F. Financing cooperative marketing of farm products in Washington. Wash. Agr. Expt. Sta. Bull. 322. 33pp. Pullman. 1935.
"In this bulletin are listed 170 cooperative associations of Washington actively engaged in performing marketing services in 1935."

Washington. Agricultural experiment station. Forty-fifth annual report for the fiscal year ending June 30, 1935. Wash. Agr. Expt. Sta. Bull. 325. 83pp. Pullman. 1935.
Division of Farm Management, pp. 38-42.

Wisconsin

Kirkpatrick, E. L., and Ferguson, Winifred. Survey of relief with reference to rural rehabilitation. 67pp., mimeogr. Madison. Wisc. E.R.A. 1935.
The study was conducted cooperatively by the Rural Division of the Wisconsin Emergency Relief Administration, The Department of Rural Sociology of the Wisconsin Agricultural Experiment Station, and the Division of Research, Statistics and Finance of the Federal Emergency Relief Administration.
"Field work was conducted during the spring and early summer of 1934, in thirteen counties chosen to represent the state from the standpoints of natural resources, type of farming areas, and the extent of relief granted from different sources. The counties included Green, Iowa, and Richland representing the southern areas; Waushara, Clark, Marathon, Oconto, Lincoln, and Rusk representing the central area; and Forent, Iron, Sawyer, and Burnett representing the Northern area."

McNall, P. E., and Roth, W. J. Forces affecting Wisconsin agriculture with resulting types of farming. Wis. Agr. Expt. Sta. Research Bull. 131, 40pp., Madison. 1935.
The state has been divided into five major divisions, which are largely physographic-soil regions, with each sub-divided into type of farming areas.
"Approximately 71% of all farms of Wisconsin are classed as 'dairy' farms."

Price, 7. V. Packaging American cheese. Wis. Agr. Expt. Sta. Research Bull. 130. 32pp. Madison. 1935.
Includes information on freezing cheese.
List of references, pp. 31-32.

Wyoming

Wyoming. College of agriculture, Agricultural extension service. Wyoming agricultural situation for 1936. Wyo. Agr. Col. Ext. Circ. 61, 30pp. Laramie. 1936.

Compiled by Louise O, Bercaw and A. M. Hannay

Agrarian Reform - Spain

Texto refundido de la ley de reforma agraria. El Progreso Agricola y
Pecuario 41(1896): 707-709. Nov, 30, 1935; (1897): 726-728. Dec. 7,
1935; (1898): 743-745. Dec. 15, 1935; (1899): 758-760. Dec. 22, 1935;
(1900): 769-770. Dec. 31, 1935. (Published at Plaza de Oriente,
Madrid, Spain.)
    Official text of the amended law of agrarian reform in Spain,
dated November 9, 1935.

Agrarianism

Cauley, T. J. The integration of agrarian and exchange economics. Amer.
Rev. 5(5): 584-602. October 1935. (Published at 231 W. 58th St.,
New York, N. Y.)
    The author summarizes as follows:
    "With a general redistribution of farm property firmly anchored
to a system of diversified farming, a restoration of the foreign
market for our cotton and tobacco, and the abolition of the great
aggregations of property in our cities, by the methods indicated
above, I think that there is sound reason for a belief in the
workability in the South of an Agrarian economy with its complement
of villages and towns. At least, if there be not such sound reason,
it is not because the Agrarians have overlooked entirely the problem
of the integration of town and country."

Agricultural Adjustment Act

Collier, C. S. Judicial bootstraps and the general welfare clause - the
A.A.A. opinion. Cong. Rec. 80(30): 2005-2010. Feb. 12, 1936. (Published in Washington, D. C.)
    "From the George Washington Law Review, January 1936."
    The writer's introductory paragraph follows:
    "The decision of the United States Supreme Court in United States
v. William M. Butler, et al., Receivers of Hoosac Mills Corporation,
which sets forth a controlling ruling upon the validity of the Agricultural Adjustment Act of 1933, is too recent to permit of a really
adequate discussion of the long-range significance and the permanent
merits of the conclusions reached therein. It is possible, however,
to examine the opinions rendered in the light of other authorities
and establish legal doctrines, and the occasion is one of such great
political and economic importance at the moment that it seems desirable to offer a contemporary and limited discussion of the legal
character and probable effects of the decision."

Ezekiel, Mordecai. Without the AAA. Today 5(20): 17. Mar. 7, 1936. (Published at 152 W. 42nd St., New York, N. Y.)
    Tells what he thinks would happen to farm income, and to the cotton,
wheat, hog, tobacco, dairy and poultry, and beef situations if no

substitute for the AAA were in operation.

"At any rate the AAA has left the farm situation better, because it struck at the root of the trouble and reduced troublesome surpluses. The Farm Board experiment left the farm worse off when it was ended because it encouraged surpluses."

Farm prices minus the AAA. U. S. News 4(8): 13, 17. Feb. 24, 1936. (Published at 2201 M St., N.W., Washington, D. C.)

Three questions are given as "getting official attention as an outgrowth of the AAA control programs in agriculture", etc. The questions are: "What did President Roosevelt, in his famous June 1, 1935, press conference, say would happen to farm prices if the AAA should follow NRA into legal discard?" And, "What did the Bureau of Agricultural Economics find concerning the effect of the cotton control program on southern farming?" The third, "Was there censorship of a BAE report on its findings concerning the effect of the cotton adjustment program?"

Answers to the last two questions, "based upon official reports and upon comments of those involved," are given.

Lawrence, David. In the name of "general welfare". U.S. News 4(7): 18. Feb. 17, 1936. (Published at 2201 M St., N.W., Washington, D. C.)

"An enumeration of possible consequences if the minority opinion in the AAA case had been accepted by the majority of the Supreme Court - national prohibition could then have been revived by act of Congress."

"No argument for handling agriculture as a 'national problem' is today more persuasive than that which was made in behalf of national prohibition."

Shumway, A. R. The Supreme Court decision. Coop. Comment 4(12): 1, 4. February 1936. (Published at the Columbia Bldg., Spokane, Wash.)

A discussion of the Supreme Court decision which declared the A.A.A. unconstitutional.

Agricultural Associations - Iran

Agricultural associations in Iran. Indus. and Labour Inform. 57(8): 197, Feb. 24, 1936. (Issued by International Labour Office, Geneva, Switzerland. Distributed in U.S. by World Peace Foundation, 8 West 40th Street, New York, N. Y.)

"A number of agricultural associations of a co-operative nature have recently been set up in Iran with the assistance of the Agricultural and Industrial Bank. Their purpose is to assist farmers by providing them at low prices with the equipment and seeds they require and with food, clothing, etc., and by giving them a good price for their crops."

Agricultural History - Oregon

Thomas S. Kendall's letter on Oregon agriculture, 1852. Agr. Hist. 9(4): 187-197. October 1935 (Published by the Agricultural History Society, Room 3901 South Bldg., 13th St. and Independence Ave., S.W., Washington, D.C.)

Agricultural Indebtedness – Czechoslovakia

Endettement des cultivateurs en Tchécoslovaquie. Czechoslovakia. Institut
de Comptabilité et d'Économie Rurales. Rapports 6(2–3): 38–39. 1935.
(Published in Prague, Czechoslovakia.)
Charts show the amount of agricultural indebtedness per hectare
of land cultivated on January 1, 1935 expressed as a percentage of
the total number of enterprises; the relative indebtedness as a percentage of the active capital, and the mortgage and non-mortgage
debts per hectare of land cultivated on January 1, 1935 according
to sizes of farms.

Agricultural Periodicals – Ontario

Landon, Fred. The agricultural journals of Upper Canada (Ontario). Agr.
Hist. 9(4): 167–175. October 1935. (Published by the Agricultural
History Society, Room 3901 South Bldg., 13th St,, and Independence
Ave., S. W., Washington, D. C.)
"This article is limited to the farm journals published in the
present Province of Ontario. The Province was known as Upper
Canada from 1791 to 1841, and also as Canada West from 1841 to
1867, and as Ontario since 1867."

Agricultural Policies – Great Britain

Orwin, C. S. Problems of a planned agriculture. Different methods of
stimulating agriculture are still in operation, and, though prosperity still lags, there is more confidence in the future, [6] pp.
Reprint Coll.
"Reprinted from 'The Yorkshire Post' Trade Review, January 9,
1936."
Reviews problems and developments in Britain's planned program
under the Agricultural Marketing Acts and the Import Duties Act.
Wheat, hops, sugar beets, milk, beef, pigs and eggs are the products particularly discussed. Other events of the year – the
weather, wages and employment, the tithe war, and land settlement
are also noted, The future of agricultural policy is briefly discussed.

Agricultural Policies – Japan

Ladejinsky, W. Agricultural policies in Japan. Foreign Crops and Markets 32(9): 255–275. Mar. 2, 1936. (Published by the Division of
Foreign Agricultural Service, Bureau of Agricultural Economics,
U. S. Dept. of Agriculture.)
The writer discusses briefly some of the leading factors contributing to the present agricultural difficulties of Japan – area
of cultivated land, rural population, land distribution and tenancy,
land prices and rents, monoculture, indebtedness and taxation, and
agriculture since 1930 – and then treats in considerable detail the
silk policies of Japan. Subtopics in the main part of the article
are: the early period of silk regulations; the law of 1911; control

of production in 1914; silk prices, 1915-1918; government measures
of regulating silk in 1920; government silk regulations since 1929
(gives outstanding features of the law passed in 1929); the government and cocoon raisers; Silk Manufacturers' Union Law; the license
system (main provisions of the law of Sept. 6, 1932 are given); recent legislation and proposals (chief provisions of the plan for an
Export Raw Silk Sales Control Association are given); conclusion.

Agricultural Protectionism

Pasvolsky, Leo. Back to sanity. Country Gent. 106(3): 21,35,36. January
1936. (Published at Independence Square, Philadelphia, Pa.)
Discusses the disastrous effects of agricultural protectionism,
with emphasis on wheat, which is widely practiced by the food-importing countries of Europe, and the slowly growing tendency to modify
"political agriculture."

Agriculture - China

Agricultural and industrial conditions in Kiangsi. Chinese Econ. Jour.
17(4): 345-359. October 1935. (Published by Bureau of Foreign
Trade, Ministry of Industry, 1040 North Soochow Road, Shanghai,
China.)
"In this article the topic is agriculture and rural conditions.
The principal products are described. An account is given of the
research institutes and experimental farms and of cooperative
societies.

Agriculture - Nigeria

Faulkner, C. T. and Mackie, J. R. The introduction of mixed farming in
Northern Nigeria. Empire Jour. Expt. Agr. 4(13): 89-96, January
1936. (Published at The Clarendon Press, Oxford, Eng.)
"During the last year or two the introduction in Northern Nigeria
of a system of mixed farming cum animal husbandry has progressed at
a rate that is already remarkable, and that continues to increase
every year. This new system represents an improvement of the first
magnitude, and involves a revolutionary change in the farmer's whole
outlook upon his life and business. It may therefore be of interest
to discuss the difficulties we have encountered and the methods by
which we have overcome them."

Agriculture - Situation and Relief - United States

Caserent, D. D. The predicament of agriculture. Rev. of Reviews 92(5):
41-43. November 1935. (Published at 233 Fourth Ave., New York, N.Y.)
The president of the Farmers' Independence Council writes: "Tho-
ever attempts to paint a realistic picture of American agriculture
today must confine himself to dull and sombre colors. Costly efforts
of government to help the farmer have had the inevitable result of
impairing his self-reliance and self-respect, and are robbing him
of his independence.

"Exceptional opportunity for the development of those qualities has always been the one distinctive feature which gave to agriculture certain valuable advantages that are lacking in most other vocations. The Administration now in Washington has persuaded farmers most oppressed by debt or distressed from other causes, along with many in better circumstances, to discard those advantages in exchange for a false promise of limited economic security through higher prices expected for their products and through subsidies paid by government for futile attempts at production control."

Cooke, M. L. An engineer looks at rural America. Jour. Land & Pub. Utility Econ. 12(1): 1-11. February 1936. (Published by Northwestern University, School of Commerce, 337 E. Chicago Ave., Chicago, Ill.)

"The material in this article was originally presented as a lecture in the series in Contemporary Thought, conducted by Professor Baker Brownell, at Northwestern University."

The writer looks at rural America and finds a growing recognition of the interdependence of agriculture and industry, that soil depletion is a national peril and that a new national policy is needed to conserve, control and utilize soil and water, and that effective organization of the farmers and adequate rural education are badly needed. He concludes by discussing the probable contribution of rural electrification to the solution of the problems of rural life.

Livingston, J. A. Who's debt-ridden. Country Home 60(3): 12. March 1936. (Published at 250 Park Ave., New York, N. Y.)

A brief article containing the following statement: "Financially, American agriculture is sound and hearty – in much better shape than the average business. Compared to the utilities, the railroads and urban real estate, the farmer is a pillar of solvency.

"The farmer is in debt, yes. But for that matter, who isn't? And the farmer is not mired in debt. He owns 75 percent of his business, whereas stockholders in the railroads own only 51 percent of theirs; utility shareholders own only 45 percent; and as for urban real estate, owners are in debt for all but 43 percent of their property."

A table showing the property valuation and long-term indebtedness of railroads, urban real estate, public utilities, and farms accompanies the article.

Livingston, L. F. What is ahead for the farmer and the engineer? Agr. Engin. 16(11): 429-430. November 1935. (Published by the American Society of Agricultural Engineers, St. Joseph, Mich.)

Many changes bearing on the future of agriculture – the rise of an organic chemical industry, the increasing interest of big business in the prosperity of agriculture, new pioneers on the land, governmental interest in agriculture as its Problem No. 1 – may mean a different agriculture from the agriculture of the past. The "augumented importance and influence" of the agricultural engineer is commented on.

McMillen, Wheeler. A national agricultural program. Vital Speeches
of the Day 2(12): 352-355. Mar. 9, 1936. (Published at 33 W.
42nd St., New York, N. Y.)
Paper before the Institute of Rural Economics, Rutgers University, New Brunswick, N. J., February 24, 1936.
Outlines and discusses a national agricultural policy which includes the following: "1. American farm producers should be permitted
to enjoy exclusive access to all the American Markets they can equip
themselves to supply. 2. By aggressive measures, every effort should
be put forth to enable American producers to include in their output all products that can be developed profitably on American soil.
3. Through two-way trade agreements, outlets should be made secure
for the spare portions of those crops that ordinarily are required
for foreign consumption. 4. Vigorous measures should be followed
for expanding the proportion of agricultural production which can be
consumed for other than food uses. 5. Conservation and revitalization
of the soil should be fostered. 6. The varied resources of science
should be utilized continuously and to the limit wherever they can
be applied to reduce production costs, improve quality, augment
output, increase consumption, or add new crops. 7. All measures
which tend to conflict with these objectives should be discontinued."
A subsidy plan, offered by the writer last November is also discussed. This plan includes the payment of subsidies to farmers for
growing soil improvement crops, for preventing soil erosion, for
growing products which the U. S. now imports, and for the production
of marketable crops to go into industrial consumption.

Agriculture - Sudan

March, G. F. The development of native agriculture in the Nuba mountains
area of Kordofan Province, Anglo-Egyptian Sudan. Empire Jour. Expt.
Agr. 4(13): 77-80. January 1936. (Published at The Clarendon Press,
Oxford, Eng.)
An account of the Sudan Government's attempts to influence native
agriculture, mainly by the introduction of cotton growing and then
the introduction of a rotation of cotton, grain and legumes. "Up to
the present, agricultural development has not affected the local
native agricultural systems or methods of cultivation to any very
great extent. There is certainly far more land under cultivation
than there used to be, and a valuable cash crop has been successfully introduced."

Agriculture - Uganda

Hansford, C. G. Some effects of the development of the cotton industry
on native agriculture in Uganda. Empire Jour. Expt. Agr. 4(13):
81-82. January 1936. (Published at The Clarendon Press, Oxford,
Eng.)

Agriculture, Industry and Foreign Trade - China

Ho Ping-yin. Development of agriculture and industry and foreign trade.
Chinese Econ. Jour. 17(6): 523-528. December 1935. (Published by

Bureau of Foreign Trade, Ministry of Industry, 1040 North Soochow
Road, Shanghai, China.)
    The author discusses the question of giving preference to agri-
culture or industry in the task of economic reconstruction. "What
we should strive for is the simultaneous development of both. On
the agricultural side, we should aim to attain self-sufficiency in
agricultural products, particularly in rice, wheat, and raw cotton,
and exports of our staple products, such as raw silk, tea, and
wood oil, should be encouraged by all possible means in order to
recover markets that have been lost and secure new ones."

Argentina

The Economist. Republic of Argentina special review. 20pp. Feb. 8, 1936.
    (Published at 8 Bouverie St., London, E.C.4, Eng.)
    Partial contents: Argentina and the crisis, pp. 5-6; Argentina
and world trade, pp. 6-7; Anglo-Argentine trade, pp. 7-9; The "Roca"
agreement, pp. 9-10; Agriculture and stockbreeding, pp. 18-19.

Banks, Government

Government banks; a summary, based on the latest available information
    with reference to the following features of government lending
    agencies: establishment, authority, life, physical organization,
    management, lending functions, terms, rates, capital funds, and
    other funds. Banking 28(9, sect. 2): 1-11. March 1936. (Pub-
    lished by the American Bankers Association at 22 East 40th St.,
    New York, N.Y.)
    "Revising and superseding a preliminary survey on the same sub-
ject in the January issue of Banking."

Bread, Stale

Alsberg, C. L. The stale-bread problem. Wheat Studies of the Food Re-
    search Institute 12(6): 221-247. February 1936. (Published at Stan-
    ford University, Calif.)
    Contents: Economic and social considerations; structure and be-
havior of starch grains; manifestations of staleness; history of
bread-staling theories; critique of competing hypotheses; prolonging the life of bread; food value of fresh and of stale bread.

Business - Annual Reviews

Crum, W. L. Review of the year 1935. Rev. Econ. Statis. 18(1): 42-51.
    January 1936. (Published at the Harvard University Press, Cambridge,
    Mass.)
    Reviews business volumes, commodity prices, money and credit,
public finance and the security markets.

Economist Commercial history of 1935. Economist 122(4825): 1-72. Feb. 15,
    1936. (Published at 8 Bouverie St., London, E.C.4, Eng.)

A commercial history and review of 1935, which is divided into four parts as follows: 1. General; II. Conditions in principal countries. III. Commerce and Trade; and IV. Statistical Appendix.
Section III includes a review of the position of the foodstuffs - wheat, sugar, tea, cocoa, coffee, livestock and meat, dairy products, eggs and poultry, fruits and vegetables and potatoes. Among the industrial raw materials reviewed are coal, oil, rubber, cotton, silk, wool, and other textile fibers.

Business Cycle Theory

Haberler, Gottfried. Some reflections on the present situation of business cycle theory. Rev. Econ. Statis. 18(1): 1-7. February 1936. (Published at the Harvard University Press, Cambridge, Mass.)

Business Depressions and Recoveries

Hubbard, J. B. Business declines and recoveries. Rev. Econ. Statis. 18(1): 16-23. January 1936. (Published at Harvard University Press, Cambridge, Mass.)
"This study covers the years from 1875 to 1935, with the omission of those dominated by the War, 1914-18. The omitted years embrace only one true depression - that which was under way in 1913."

Butter and Cheese - Southern Rhodesia

Levy on butter and cheese. African World 134(1732): 21. Jan. 18, 1936. (Published at 801, Salisbury House, London Wall, London, E.C.2, Eng.)
"The Southern Rhodesia Dairy Control Board has imposed a levy of one penny per pound on all creamery butter manufactured in the Colony, on all butter and cheese imported into the Colony excepting from Northern Rhodesia, the Union of South Africa, Bechuanaland, South-West Africa and Swaziland, and on all farm butter and cheese manufactured in the Colony. The levy took effect from January 1. The levy on farm butter will be collected by means of the franking of butter wrappers at certain prescribed post offices."

Canned Foods - Grades and Sales Contracts

Williams, P. W. Thoughts on canned food grades and sales contracts. Canner 82(13): 9-10,16. Mar. 7, 1936. (Published at 140 N. Dearborn St., Chicago, Ill.)

Canning Trade - Annual Convention

The Canner 82(11, pt.2): 1-130. Feb. 22, 1936. (Published at 140 N. Dearborn St., Chicago, Ill.)
Contains the proceedings of the 29th annual convention of the National Canners Association and meetings of Allied Groups at Chicago, January 18-24, 1936.
Descriptive labeling developments were discussed in the "Pitted Red Cherry Section", and are reported on p. 51.

Canning Age 17(3): 97-150. Feb. 15, 1936. (Published at 250 W. 57th St.,
New York, N. Y.)
The "Convention Digest Number."
The convention features include the "Highlights" of the annual address
of President Orr (p.105), and an article entitled "Corn Maturity Study
Reviewed for Descriptive Labeling" (pp.126-127).
The N.C.A. officers and directors for 1936 are listed on p.145.

The Canning Trade 58(27): 1-122. Feb. 10, 1936. (Published at 20 S. Gay St.,
Baltimore, Md.)
The convention issue of the Canning Trade.

Canning Trade - Statistics

[Campbell, Carlos] Statistics for the canning industry. Canning Trade
58(28): 5-6. Feb. 17, 1936. (Published at 20 Gay St., Baltimore, Md.)
Address before the Indiana Canners' and Growers' School at Purdue
University on February 12.

Church, Rural

The National Conference on the Rural Church. Inform. Serv. 15(9): 1-6.
Feb. 29, 1936. (Published by the Department of Research and Education,
Federal Council of the Churches of Christ in America, 105 E. 22nd St.,
New York, N. Y.)
"The National Conference on the Rural Church was held in Washington,
D. C., January 14-17, 1936, on the general theme of 'The Rural Church
Today and Tomorrow,' under the auspices of the Council of Women for
Home Missions and the Home Missions Council. The substance of the
report of the Findings Committee is published in this issue."

Coffee

World coffee markets. Empire Producer, no. 232, pp. 41-42. February 1936.
(Published at 22, Queen Anne's Gate, Westminster, London, S.W.1, Eng.)
Answers to a questionnaire sent to representatives and correspond-
ents in the Eastern Carribbean Colonies, Jamaica, Nigeria and the
Cameroons (British Mandate).

World coffee markets. Empire Producer, no. 230, pp. 215-216. December 1935.
(Published at 22, Queen Anne's Gate, Westminster, London, S.W.1, Eng.)
Answers to a questionnaire on coffee sent to correspondents in
Kenya and Switzerland.

Coffee - Dutch East Indies

Scheltema, A. M. P. A. The consumption of coffee in the Netherlands Indies.
Netherlands Indies 4(1-2): 1-3. Jan. 16, 1936. (Issued by the Department of Economic Affairs. Published by G. Kolff & Co., Batavia, Java,
N. I.)
"From the statistics available it would appear that the coffee consumption in the Netherlands Indies is around one third of the production.

Colonization - Switzerland

Colonisation by private initiative. Indus. and Labour Inform. 57(7).: 188.
Feb. 1", 1936. (Issued by International Labour Office, Geneva,
Switzerland. Distributed in U. S. by World Peace Foundation, 8 West
40th Street, New York, N. Y.)
Two missions of investigation into possibilities for settlement in
Brazil and in Canada were sent out in 1935 by private organizations
with Federal grants for travelling expenses. "Apparently a first
attempt at colonisation in the State of Parana was not as successful
as had been hoped... Greater success seems to have been achieved in
Canada. The conditions on which Canada will accept Swiss immigrants
are enumerated.

Cooperation

Cooperative Journal, v.10, no.1, 24 pp. January-February, 1936. (Published
at 1731 Eye St., N.W., Washington, D. C.)
Partial contents: Cooperators in council, by Val C. Sherman, pp.
1-3, Is it real cooperation? pp.4-6; Cooperatives pay their share of
taxes, by Gordon H. Ward, pp.7-8; The cooperative gin of Texas, by
W. E. Poulson, pp.9-11; I believe in cooperative marketing, by George
Knorr (prize-winning letter in a contest, Louisville, Ky.), p.15.

Cooperative Journal, v.10, no.1, pt.2, pp.25-48. January-February 1936.
Supplement. (Published at 1731 Eye St., N.W., Washington, D.C.)
This is the 1936 Bluebook of the National Cooperative Council.
Partial contents: Names and addresses of officers, executive
committee, and board of directors for 1936; an explanation of the
purposes and policies of the Council, given under the caption "What
Is The Council?";resolutions of the National Cooperative Council (which
"reflects its current public policies"); Annual report of the Secretary,
The President's message (by John D. Miller); By-laws; and an "Incomplete Roll of Members."

Cost Index - Miscellaneous Farm Expenses - England

Graves, P. E., and Carson, S. H. A cost index for miscellaneous farm
expenses. Gt. Brit. Min. Agr. Jour. 42(8): 745-749. November 1935.
(Published by H. M. Stationery Office, London, Eng.)
"A financial survey of farming in the Eastern Counties during the
years 1931-1933 showed that the annual expenditure on miscellaneous
items averaged in the aggregate, approximately L1 per acre per
annum in this arable area, and represented some 15 per cent of the
gross farm costs... The purpose of this note is to compare the
unit cost of each item in 1934 with the corresponding figure in
1913, and to calculate an index for the total."

Cotton

Bierl, Max. Nord- und Südamerika im kampf um die baumwolle. Wirtschaftsdienst 20(19): 635-638, tables. May 1935. (Published at Poststrasse
13, Hamburg 36, Germany)

North- and South America in the struggle over cotton.
"The influence of the recent crop restriction and control schemes
on the production of cotton in the United States since 1932. The
influence of tariffs and trade agreements is mentioned. Details of
German cotton imports for 1933-35 are given. The figures show a
marked decline in imports of American cotton, some reduction in
imports of Indian and Egyptian cottons, and an increase in imports
from other countries, particularly from Brazil. In 1932/33 Brazil
produced about one million bales of cotton which was used almost
entirely by the home industry but in 1934/35 the crop was practically
doubled and about half became available for export. Further developments are anticipated and the State is supervising seed distribution, standardisation, etc. Other states in South America are
also taking an interest in cotton cultivation.-C." - Textile Inst.
Jour. 26(8): A378. August 1935.

Leake, H. M. Over-production or under-consumption? Empire Cotton Grow-
ing Rev. 13(1): 31-38, January 1936. (Published at 14, Great
Smith St., London, S.W.1, Eng.)
Cotton is considered as an illustration.

Cotton - China

Otte, Friedrich. The story of cotton since 1919. A statistical research
of imports and exports. Chinese Econ. Jour. 17(4): 332-344. October
1935. (Published by Bureau of Foreign Trade, Ministry of Industry,
1040 North Soochow Road, Shanghai, China.)
Contains an account of trends and causes of the expansion of
the cotton industry.

Cotton - China and japan

Biehl, Max. Japans erschliessungspläne. Die chinesische baumwollkultur.
Wirtschaftsdienst 20(28): 961-964, illus., tables. July 12, 1935.
(Published at Poststrasse 19, Hamburg 36, Germany)
Japan's plan for expansion. Chinese cotton cultivation.
"The possibilities of extending cotton growing in China are reviewed, especially in relation to the competition with food crops
and to Japanese influences. Since 1927, the acreage under cotton
in Northern China has doubled, the increase being almost entirely
in American varieties. China produced 3 million bales (500 lbs.)
in 1934, half in the northern provinces. It is thought that by
adjusting the demands of food crops it might be possible to harvest
three crops of cotton in two years and thus add 2-1/2-3 million
more bales to China's yearly output.-C." - Textile Inst. Jour.
26(9): A442. September 1935.

Cotton - Financing

Costanzo, G. The financing of the growing and marketing of cotton.
Monthly Bull. Agr. Econ. and Sociol. [reprint from Internatl. Rev.
Agr.] 27(1): 1E-39E. January 1936. (Published by the International
Institute of Agriculture, Villa Umberto I. Rome, Italy)

"This article is based to a large extent on information obtained
through an enquiry addressed, in a certain number of producing
countries, to banks and to public and private institutions interested in the financing of the cultivation and sale of cotton." -footnote.
..1.
Contents: I. General review of the question; II. Systems of financing (in the United States, India, Egypt U.S.S.R., China, Argentina,
Brazil, Turkey, Uganda, Tanganyika and Kenya, Anglo-Egyptian-Sudan
and the Belgian Congo.]

Cotton - Latin America and West Indies

Keeler E. P. Minor cotton-producing regions of Latin America and the West
Indies. Foreign Crops and Markets 32(7): 197-209. Feb. 17, 1936.
(Published by the Division of Foreign Agricultural Service, Bureau
of Agricultural Economics, U. S. Dept. of Agriculture)
Regions discussed are Paraguay, Colombia, Venezuela, Ecuador,
Bolivia, El Salvador, Guatemala, Nicaragua, Haiti, and the British
West Indies.

Cotton - Prices

Slater, W. H. Forecasting cotton prices. Textile Weekly 16(407): 707-
708, tables. Dec. 20, 1935. (Published at 49, Deansgate, Manchester, 3, Eng.):
"In a lecture to the British Association of Managers of Textile
Works, November 30, 1935."

Cotton - Statistics

Todd, J. A. Cotton statistics. Empire Cotton Growing Rev, 13(1): 39-45,
tables. January 1936. (Published at 14, Great Smith St., London,
S.W.1, Eng.)
The production, consumption and price of cotton of the 1934-35
crop are discussed.

Cotton - Tanganyika Territory

Harrison, E. Cotton in Tanganyika territory. Empire Cotton Growing Rev.
13(1): 1-11. January 1936. (Published at 14, Great Smith St.,
London, S.W.1, Eng.)
"The situation since 1930 is described."

Cotton - United States

Cox, A. B. Restriction program fallacious policy. Cotton Digest 8(16):
5-7. Jan. 25, 1936. (Published at 710 Cotton Exchange Bldg.,
Houston, Tex.)
"Address before American Statistical Association, New York,
December 28, 1935."
Extracts in Cotton Trade Jour. 16(1): 1,3. Jan. 4, 1936.

Parker, Walter. Our crop control policy. Cotton Digest 8(13): 7-8.
Jan. 4, 1936. (Published at 710 Cotton Exchange Bldg., Houston,
Tex.)
The author mentions the results obtained from five years of
crop control and other Government policies, and concludes that
there is "but one remedy for this unsound economic situation, namely,
obedience to the rules applicable to a world creditor nation,"
especially a lower tariff.

Cottonseed Industry

Morgan, J. I. Cottonseed crushing industry. Manfrs. Rec. 105(1): 23,66.
January 1936. (Published at Commerce and Water Sts., Baltimore, Md.)
Factors controlling supply, demand, and price in the cottonseed
industry and the need for government price reports are discussed.

Ward, A. L. One hundred and ten years of usefulness. Cotton and Cotton
Oil Press 37(1): 10-11, illus. Jan. 4, 1936. (Published at 3116-
3118 Commerce St., Dallas, Tex.)
The economic importance of the cottonseed industry and its various
products is discussed.

Dairy Industry - History

Prentice, E. P. A daily milk delivery. Hoard's Dairyman 81(3): 55, 74,
75. Feb. 10, 1936. (Published in Fort Atkinson, Wis.)
The first installment of an article on the beginning of the dairy
industry. "The industry had its beginning almost as soon as man
first began to lift himself above brute creation." Various statements from early writings are quoted which show the importance of
milk as an article of diet.
In the second part of the article, published in the February 1936,
number of Hoard's Dairyman (v.81, no.4, pp.87, 97) the writer describes
the great change that took place in the latter part of the 1600's in
England in farming methods, and quotes from early publications showing the changes in the demand for milk.

Economic Annalist

Economic Annalist, v. 6, no.1, 16pp. February 1936. (Published by the
Agricultural Economics Branch, Dept. of Agriculture, Ottawa, Canada)
Partial contents: Barley and livestock in Canada, by H. R. Hare,
pp.3-5; Some facts concerning life insurance in south-western
Saskatchewan, by W. J. Hansen, pp.6-10; Land utilization in Carleton
and Victoria counties, New Brunswick, by Ian McArthur, pp.11-13;
Terminal markets, by W. C. Hopper, pp.14-16 [to be continued].

Economic Conditions - Dutch East Indies

A short review of the economic condition of the Netherlands Indies.
Netherlands Indies 4(1-2): 4-10. Jan. 16, 1936. (Issued by the
Department of Economic Affairs. Published by G. Kolff & Co.,
Batavia, Java, N. I.)

Vandenbosch, Amry. Special report on economic conditions in Netherlands
India. Far East. Survey 5(4): 36-40. Feb. 12, 1936. (Published by
the Fortnightly Research Service, American Council, Institute of
Pacific Relations, at 129 East 52nd St., New York, N.Y.).

Economic Council - Latvia

A state economic council in Latvia. Indus. and Labour Inform. 57(8): 196-
197. Feb. 24, 1936. (Issued by International Labour Office, Geneva,
Switzerland. Distributed in U. S. by World Peace Foundation, 8 West
40th Street, New York, N. Y.)
 An act of December 30, 1935 provides for the establishment of a
State Economic Council "to bring into harmony all the economic
activities of Latvia and to direct them to a common end by means
of collaboration."

Eggs - Marketing - Rhodesia

Mundy H. G., and Jacklin, E. R. Egg marketing bill. Draft of a bill
having for its purpose the more orderly marketing of eggs. Memorandum
on the draft egg marketing bill. Rhodesia Agr. Jour. 32(9): 630-636.
September 1935. (Published in Salisbury, Rhodesia)
 These comments are followed by the text of the bill to provide
for the compulsory control of the marketing of eggs. -pp,636-645.

Emigration and Settlement - Switzerland

The question of emigration from Switzerland. The Federal Government and
colonisation schemes. Indus. and Labour Inform. 57(7): 185-188.
Feb. 17, 1936. (Issued by International Labour Office, Geneva,
Switzerland. Distributed in U. S. by World Peace Foundation, 8 West
40th Street, New York, N. Y.)
 As a result of an inquiry into the question of emigration as a
means of relieving the domestic labor market, the Swiss Government
is of the opinion that "a remedy for the momentary loss of balance
should first of all be sought in intensive internal colonisation."
Possible schemes of assistance to colonization abroad by buying
land and allotting holdings or by giving financial assistance to
individual settlers are considered and discarded in favor of
supporting the Association for Internal Settlement and Industrial
Workers' Farms as a centre of inquiry concerning settlement in
Europe and giving "material assistance to persons without means
desirous of settling abroad on condition that sums at least as
large are provided by the Cantonal and local authorities or other
interested parties."

Farm Economist

Farm Economist, v. 2, no.1. 20pp. January 1936. (Published by the Agri-
cultural Economics Research Institute, Parks Road, Oxford, Eng.)
 Partial contents: The outlook for milk, by C. S. Orwin, pp.1-2;
Some trends in dairy farming in South Devon, by W. H. Long, pp.5-8;

Changes in milk output on ten West Country grassland dairy farms,
by F. H. Villiers, pp.9-10; Observations on the depreciation of
cows and calving records of a commercial farm, by F. R. G. N Sherrard,
pp.11-13; Fruit consumption - the importance of imports, by J. F.
Cahan, pp.15-17.

Flax

Gibson, W. H. Fibre-flax cultivation in the United Kingdom and the Empire.
Empire Jour. Expt. Agr. 4(13): 36-46. January 1936. (Published at
The Clarendon Press, Oxford, Eng.)

Fodder and Cattle Relationships - Czechoslovakia

Rapport existant entre le récolte des fourrages et la quantité de bovins
d'origine indigène abattus (veaux non compris). Czechoslovakia.
Institut de Comptabilité et d'Économie Rurales. Rapports 6(2-3):
40-48. 1935. (Published in Prague, Czechoslovakia.)
    Tables, charts and graphs are used to determine the effect of the
production of fodder on the number of domestic cattle slaughtered,
not including calves. It is shown that the farmer who desires to
protect himself against serious loss from a poor fodder harvest
followed by a partial loss of his cattle and its sale at subnormal
prices, should provide his supply of fodder in advance, never raise
more cattle than he can feed, and see to it that his fodder harvest
of one year will be sufficient until the next year.

Food Industry

Miller, S. L. Two major conflicting forces likely to determine future
of food industry. Annalist 47(1205): 293-294. Feb. 21, 1936. (Published by the New York Times Co., New York, N. Y.)
    Accompanied by three tables which show: Population trends in the
U. S., 1910, 1920, 1930; changes in per capita food consumption,
about 1899 and 1922-1927; operation results of food companies by
industries, 1927-1935.
    The two conflicting forces discussed are as follows: "There is
the tendency toward expansion evolving out of increasing activity,
especially among the heavy industries, and the concomitant rise
in the number of gainful workers and their earnings. There is
also the tendency toward contraction emanating from Washington
revolving about a substitute farm program."

Government, Local

Reed, T. D., ed. Rural local government. Amer. Polit. Sci. Rev. 30(1):
90-110. February 1936. (Published by the American Political
Science Association, C. L. King, Secretary-Treasurer, 209 South
Hall, University of Wisconsin, Madison, Wis.)
    Consists of the following articles: County government progress
in New York State, by L. R. Chubb, pp.90-96; The progress of county
government reform in Wisconsin, by Lee S. Greene, pp.96-102; Recent

trends in local government in Michigan, by Arthur W. Bromage, pp.102-104. County reorganization in Ohio, by R. C. Atkinson, pp.104-110.

Government Expenditures - United States

Edelberg, Lucy, Horniker, A. L., Kaufmann, Berthold, and Stewart, C. D. Public expenditures and economic structure in the United States. Social Research 3(1): 57-77. February 1936. (Published by the New School for Social Research, 66 W. 12th St., New York, N. Y.)
"This analysis of the public expenditures of the forty-eight states comprising the United States is designed to determine whether any relationship exists between the size of such expenditures and the economic character of the states...
"For comparing the social and economic structure of the states we have utilized four primary indices: density, urbanization, industrialization and per capita income. A statistical study of the states reveals a close relationship between these factors. Highly industrialized states are significant for a high degree of urbanization and consequently of density. Conversely, the non-industrial states are generally rural, with a low density of population. Likewise per capita income is found to rise with higher industrialization.
"Public expenditures of the states have been analyzed primarily with reference to total combined state and municipal expenditures, and with reference to expenditures for education, highways and relief. The years used for comparison have been 1932 and 1929 in most cases. For the statistical comparison of expenditures and economic indices the most simple methods have been applied. Both for analysis and for presentation we have preferred scatter diagrams to the computation of the coefficients of correlation." -pp.57-59.

Kiplinger, W. M. The Federal family budget. Today 5(18); 8-9. Feb. 22, 1936. (Published at 152 W. 42nd St., New York, N. Y.)

Governmental Change and Technology

Ogburn, W. F. Technology and governmental change. Jour. Business Univ. Chicago 9(1, pt.1): 1-13. January 1936. (Published by the University of Chicago Press, Chicago, Ill.)
"This is the first of a series of lectures given in 1935-36 at the University of Chicago under the general title 'The Shifting Borderline between Government and Business.'"

Grain - Spain

La cosecha de trigo y demás cereales en 1935. El Progreso Agrícola y Pecuario 41 (1898); 735-740. Dec. 15, 1935. (Published at Plaza de Oriente, Madrid, Spain.)
Contains tables and charts illustrating the production of wheat, barley, rye, oats, maize and rice in 1935 and in the preceding decade.

Grain - Standards

[Hill, Lew] Grain trade's experience with the revised Federal standards.
Grain & Feed Rev. 25(7): 38-39. March 1936. (Published at 408 South
Third St., Minneapolis, Minn.)
Address before the Illinois Farmers Grain Dealers' convention at
Chicago on Feb. 12.

Grapes - Spain

La cosecha de uva en 1935. El Progreso Agrícola y Pecuario 41(1899):
751-755. Dec. 22, 1935. (Published at Plaza de Oriente, Madrid,
Spain.)
Contains tables and charts showing production of grapes and
must in Spain in 1935 and in the preceding decade.

Hogs - Estonia

Muuga, Aug. Economic results of promotion of pig breeding. Konjunktuur,
no. 15(2): 116-123. Feb. 3, 1936. (Published by Institute of
Economic Research, Tallinn, Estonia.)
Contains paragraphs on bacon prices and conditions of pig breeding before the introduction of guaranteed prices, movement of pigs
1925-1935 with table, bacon exports, 1926-1935 with table, laws
concerning pig breeding and guaranteed bacon prices, turnover of
fund for the promotion of pig breeding and guaranteed bacon prices,
1930-1935, proportion of premiums to prices of bacon pigs, economic
results of guaranteed bacon prices and promotion of pig breeding
and number of bacon pigs exported to England by months, 1929-1933.

Hogs - Prices - Bohemia

Prévision des prix des porcs en Bohême (prix à la ferme). Czechoslovakia.
Institut de Comptabilité et d'Économie Rurales. Rapports 6(2-3):
48-50. 1935. (Published in Prague, Czechoslovakia.)
An analysis of hog prices on the farm in Bohemia showing to
what extent predictions have been verified.

Hop Industry - Great Britain

British hop production and trade. Foreign Crops and Markets 32(6): 231-
235. Feb. 24, 1936. (Published by the Division of Foreign Agri-
cultural Service, Bureau of Agricultural Economics, U.S. Dept. of
Agriculture)
"Based on a report from Agricultural Attaché C. C. Taylor at
London."

Imports and the Depression - Dutch East Indies

Odenkirchen, Th. J. The influence of the depression on the importation
of certain groups of articles in the Netherlands Indies. Netherlands
Indies 4(1-2): 14-25. January 1936. (Issued by the Department of

Economic Affairs. Published by G. Kolff & Co., Batavia, Java, N.I.)

Index Numbers

Further notes on index numbers. Rev. Econ. Studies 3(?): 153-158. February 1936. (Published by London School of Economics, Houghton St., London, W.C.2, Eng.)
This is in three parts. Part I, pp.153-155, is by H. Staehle; Part II, pp.155-157 is by M. F. W. Joseph and is entitled Mr. Lerner's supplementary limits for price index numbers; Part III, pp.157-158 is Mr. A. P. Lerner's reply to Mr. Joseph's article.

Interstate Compacts

Clark, J. P. Interstate compacts and social legislation. II. Interstate compacts after negotiation. Polit. Sc.. Quart. 51(1): 36-60. March 1936. (Published by the Academy of Political Science, Fayerweather Hall, Columbia University, New York, N. Y.)

Journal of Farm Economics

Journal of Farm Economics, v.18, no.1, pp.1-228. February 1936. (Published by the American Farm Economic Association, Asher Hobson, Secretary-Treasurer, University of Wisconsin, Madison, Wis.)
Contents: Farm economists and agricultural planning, by Henry A. Wallace, pp.1-11; Validity of the fundamental assumptions underlying agricultural adjustment, by M. L. Wilson, pp.12-26; Validity of the fundamental assumptions underlying agricultural adjustment, by C. B. Jesness, pp.27-43; discussion of the papers by Wilson and Jesness, by G. F. Warren, J. S. Davis, O. C. Stine, H. E. Erdman, J. D. Black, Don S. Anderson, pp.44-58; Some observations on the agricultural program in Canada, by J. F. Booth, pp.59-63; Progress and problems in agricultural planning in the New England and Middle Atlantic States, by I. G. Davis, pp.64-74; Progress and problems in agricultural planning in the North Central States, by H. C. M. Case, pp.75-85; Progress and problems in agricultural planning in the Southern States, by G. W. Forster, pp.86-94; Progress and problems in regional agricultural planning from the national point of view, by F. F. Elliott, pp.95-105; Some state problems in agricultural statistics, by Walter H. Evling, pp.107-126, discussion by R. L. Gillett, pp.126-130; Some new developments designed to extend the scope and improve the accuracy of agricultural information, by Asher Hobson, pp.131-142. [This paper deals with certain of the recommendations made in a special study. The Division of Crop and Livestock Estimates, the Market News Service of the U.S. Bureau of Agricultural Economics, and statistics of the movement of agricultural products by motor trucks, the prices farmers pay, and farm income are particularly discussed]; The 1935 census - an appraisal from the viewpoint of crop estimates, by Joseph A. Becker, pp.143-150, discussion by Z. R. Pettet, pp.151-152; A National program of farm management research, by C. L. Holmes, pp.153-168; Statistical analysis in farm management research, by Stanley W.

Warren, pp.169-179; Farm management research in relation to agricultural adjustment and rehabilitation, by P. L. Slagsvold, pp.180-
190.

The following "Notes" are also given: What is part-time farming?
by Leonard A. Salter, Jr., pp.191-197; The use of pasture in the
economic production of fluid milk in Delaware, by R. O. Bausman,
pp.197-198.

Land Ownership - Bedfordshire, England

Durant, Henry. The development of landownership, 1873-1925, with special
reference to Bedfordshire. Sociol. Rev. 28(1): 85-99. January 1936.
(Published at LePlay House, Press, 35 Gordon Square, Lond , W.C.1,
Eng.)

The author summarizes as follows:
"It seems that most of the forces we have discussed have been working in one direction: to cause the selling up of the landed estates
and the disappearance to a considerable extent of the landowning class.
Since all the factors have been present it is useless to discuss
whether the same development would have occurred if any one had been
absent. We can note that legislation and taxation have rendered landownership less attractive, but it must also be observed that the selling of land on a large scale already took place before e.g. the Budget
of 1909 and the subsequent campaign against landlordism. The evidence
available suggests that the disadvantages of large-scale ownership is
a contributory motive to selling, but the decisive condition is the
opportunity to realise a favourable price. It is only on this basis
that we can attempt to explain the enormous transfer which took
place in 1919 and the following years."

The probable future trend of ownership of rural land is discussed
on pp.97-99.

Land Planning

Augur, T. B. Land planning for states and regions. Planners' Jour. 2(1):
1-6. January-February 1936. (Published by American City Planning
Institute, Hunt Hall, Cambridge, Mass.)

"Based on a lecture given in a non-technical course on Regional
Planning at the University of Tennessee during the summer of 1935."

In this article the writer defines planning, discusses the two
principle types of planning, defines land planning, shows how land
planning is applied to the land area of a farm, of a village, and to
other areas, discusses what a region is, what regional planning is,
the planning profession, planning terminology, and lastly the meaning of land planning for states and regions.

Land Policies - United States

Tatter, Henry. State and federal land policy during the confederation
period. Agr. Hist. 9(4): 176-186. October 1935. (Published by the
Agricultural History Society, Room 3901, South Bldg. 13th and
Independence Ave., S. W., Washington, D. C.)

The subject of this article is the comparison of State and Federal
policies during the years 1776-1789 with the plans formulated after
1786 by the British Lords of Trade for "the assurance of larger
revenue receipts from the disposal of land in America and for a controlled social order evolved into a drastic modification of the
land system, equalled only by the Homestead Law of 1862 which
reversed the course. The comprehensive plans of the new British
policy called for extensive surveys before sale, progressive sale
of contiguous parcels of land, and sale at auction to the highest
bidder above a defined minimum after due advertisement."

Land Policies and Ownership Trends - Western States

Renne, F. R. Western land policies and recent ownership trends. Jour.
Land & Pub. Utility Econ. 12(1): 33-42. February 1936. (Published
by Northwestern University, School of Commerce, 337 E. Chicago Ave.,
Chicago, Ill.)

The historical background of policies of planless settlement in
the West is first presented, followed by a detailed analysis of the
ownership of Montana lands by public agencies, corporations, and
private individuals. Recent changes in ownership, causes of these
changes, and the future control of the land are then discussed.

Corrections of the maladjustments noted [i.e., overspeculation
in land, overdevelopment of local government, and improper utilization of land] are said to depend "to a large extent upon a grouping
or blocking out of these small tracts into units of economical size
controlled for maximum productivity." This blocking out is being
accomplished by "the consolidation of farms by the more successful
farmers taking over lands abandoned by their less successful neighbors";
by "the voluntary grouping together of ranches to form cooperative
grazing districts and thus acquire effective control of a given area";
by "the establishment of Taylor grazing districts and their administration by the Department of the Interior"; and by "the outright purchase
by the Federal Government of most of the numerous small privately
owned tracts in selected areas." Three projects have been set up
under the submarginal land purchase program.

Illustrated by maps.

Land Reclamation and Improvement - Italy

Sorpieri, Arrigo. La bonifica integrale nell'Italia meridionale.
L'Italia Agricola 72(11): 845-855. November 1935. (Published at
Palazzo Margherita, via Vittorio Veneto, Rome, Italy.)

A historical survey of land reclamation in southern Italy emphasizes
the complexity of the problem as compared with that in the north and
the value of the Fascist schemes for its solution.

Land Settlement - Brazil

Lopes, P. Paula. Land settlement in Brazil. Internatl. Labour Rev. 33(2):
152-184. February 1936. (Published by the International Labour Office,

Geneva, Switzerland. Distributed in the U. S. by the World Peace
Foundation, 8 W. 40th St., New York, N. Y.)

The follo·ing is quoted from the introductory part of the article:

"Of the 4,200,000 immigrants who entered Brazil from 1822 - the
year in which the country obtained its independence - to 1933, a large
number settled on small holdings of which they acquired possession
and which they worked on their own account.

"The purpose of the present article is to explain the factors
which enabled these immigrants to obtain possession of agricultural
holdings. Foremost among these factors was the creation of private
or official settlements, consisting of groups of agricultural holdings, of from 25 to 50 hectares in area and sold for cash, or, more
usually, on credit basis, to Brazilian nationals or immigrants from
abroad. Conditions in some of the Brazilian States, in which land
settlement has already taken place on a considerable scale, have now
advanced beyond the stage of development of others in which there
is scope for future settlement schemes. In view of this fact, it
has been deemed advisable to follow the chronological sequence of
events in certain sections of this article.

"The development of land settlement in Brazil was promoted, in
the first place, by the action of the public authorities...

"The aims of the land settlement·policy adopted in Brazil were ...
to populate the land and ensure its cultivation, while its secondary
objects were to retain the immigrants permanently in the country and
·break up the big estates.

"Although gradual improvements were introduced from the standpoint
both of the country of immigration and of the mass of immigrants,
there has been no appreciable change in the nature of these measures
from 1882 until the present day. They consist mainly in the creation
directly by the authorities of agricultural settlements, and the
conclusion of settlement contracts with undertakings or individuals.
These two groups of measures are described in turn".

Land Settlement - Germany

Riecke. Grenzen der Kleinsiedlung, Germany, Reichsnährstand. National-
sozialistische Landpost, no. 5, Jan. 31, 1936. (Published by
Reichsnährstand, Wedomennstrasse 30, Berlin S.W.11, Germany.)

Inasmuch as there are limits to the possible establishment of
small holdings for German settlers, it is argued that the reconstruction of the German peasantry and the settlement on the land
of agricultural workers are more important for the future of the
country than the creation of small holdings for city workers.
Moreover the necessity of Germany's becoming self sufficient in
the matter of food precludes the establishment of an unlimited
number of small holdings in favor of the use of a more extended
area for increased production of food products.

Land Settlement - Hungary

Apponyi, Georg, Bodenreformpolitik und Siedlungsaktion. Ungarischer
Volkswirt 5(1): 4-6. January 1936. (Published in Budapest, Hungary.
Agent in U. S.,P. Buckwirtz, 2517 Ave. D., Brooklyn, N. Y.)

The author voices the objections of the opposition to the proposed government land reform bill. The time limit of 30 years and
the possibility that landowners might be forced to surrender land
are objected to, and it is pointed out that existing regulations
for expropriation could be extended to agricultural property, especially as there is enough land already available for settlement
purposes.

Land Settlement - New South Wales

Definite closer settlement plan submitted to State Government. Land, no.
1283, p.4, Jan. 17, 1936. (Published in Sydney, New South Wales)
"The State Cabinet Subcommittee on Land Settlement has completed
a preliminary report which has been forwarded to the Premier for
consideration by the Ministry." Some of the conclusions, which it
is understood were reached by the committee, are enumerated and
discussed.

Land Utilization

Waugh, F. A. Reconciliation of land uses. Jour. Land & Pub. Utility
Econ. 12(1): 87-89. February 1936. (Published by Northwestern
University, School of Commerce, 337 E. Chicago Ave., Chicago, Ill.)
Discusses the reconciliation of land uses, particularly in the
national forests. "What the country now mainly needs is a clearer
recognition of the principle of reconciliation and of its primacy
in administrative practice."

Land Utilization - New Zealand

Buzacott, W. J. Land utilization in New Zealand. Queenslander, Jan. 30,
1936, p. 19. (Published in Brisbane, Australia.)
Reviews a study authorized by the Research Committee of the Institute of Pacific Relations, entitled "Agricultural Organisation
in New Zealand."

Legislation, Agricultural - Victoria

Rural legislation. New acts explained. Victoria. Dept. Agr. Jour. 33(12):
577-585. December 1935. (Published in Melbourne, Austr.)
Among the acts discussed are the Marketing of Primary Products Act,
Farmers' Debts Adjustment Act, Milk and Dairy Supervision Act, Dairy
Products Act, Farmers' Advances Act, and Wheat Growers Relief (Com-
monwealth Payment) Act.

Mechanization of Agriculture - Great Britain

M., L. Problems of mechanising mixed farming. Estate Mag. 36(2):
117-121. February 1936. (Published by Country Gentlemen's Association Ltd., Letchworth, Herts, Eng.)

Migration of Laborers and Drought Refugees to California

Taylor, P. S., and Vasey, Tom. Drought refugee and labor migration to
California, June-December 1935. Monthly Labor Rev. 42(2): 312-318.
February 1936. (Published by the Bureau of Labor Statistics, U.S.
Dept. of Labor)
"This study is part of the research initiated under Harry E.
Drobish, director of rural rehabilitation California Emergency
Relief Administration, and continued by the Resettlement Administra-
tion." p.312.
"During the 6 months ending December 15, 1935, 43,180 persons in
need of manual employment entered California in private motor cars,
not including persons arriving by bus or in cars bearing California
licenses. Seventy-five percent of this number came from the drought
States, particularly from Arizona, Arkansas, Missouri, Oklahoma, and
Texas. About 14 percent came from Oregon and Washington, being interstate rural-labor migrants. Practically 90 percent of all the migrants
were white. Mexicans constitute 6.3 percent of the total. These
data are based on a traffic count made at the plant quarantine stations at the State border." -p.v.

Milk - Marketing - Great Britain

Board's case before the Committee of Investigation. Home Farmer 3(2):
5-20,23-27. February 1936. (Published by the Milk Marketing Board,
Thames House, Millbank, London, S.W.1, Eng.)
The case of the Milk Board in reply to the complaints made by the
Central Distributive Committee and the Co-operative Congress against
prices and certain of the conditions in the current milk contract,
was opened before the Committee of Investigation on January 23rd."
A summary of the evidence of witnesses is here presented.

The people's food. New Statesman and Nation n.s.11(261): 253-254. Feb.
22, 1936. (Published at 10 Great Turnstile, High Holborn, London,
W.C.1, Eng.)
Critical of the Marketing Board and its milk policy.

Sorenson, Helen, and Cassels, J. M. The English milk market. Quart. Jour.
Econ. 50(2): 275-296. February 1936. (Published by Harvard University
Press, Randall Hall, Cambridge, Mass.)
"Introduction, 275.- I. Economic and historical background, 276.-
II. Relative effects on producers, consumers and distributors, 280.-
III. Relative gains of different producer groups, 284.- IV. Problems
of production control, 287.- V. Consumption and marketing, 292.-
VI. Comparison with the A.A.A. dairy program, 294."- Summary, p.275.
In conclusion the writers suggest three things "that seem essential
for the success of any permanent program of control; first, a rearrangement of the setups of the existing schemes in such a way as
to give proper representation to all the interests concerned; second,
a broadening of the powers of regulating bodies in such a way as to
include the regulation of the distribution of milk as well as its
production and sale; and third, a definite recognition that the

objective is not to bring special benefits to any one class or group but to require the contribution of the dairy industry to the general welfare of the community."

Money - Devaluation

Hansen, A. H. Devaluation of the dollar in relation to exports and imports. Jour. Polit. Econ. 44(1): 70-83. February 1936. (Published by the University of Chicago Press, Chicago, Ill.).

Money and Credit - German Literature

Neisser, Hans. German literature on money and credit 1933-34. Social Research 3(1): 109-112. February 1936. (Published by the New School of Social Research, 66 W 12th St., New York, N. Y.)
Reviews the following: Geld und Konjunktur, by Otto Donner; Der Kampf um die Gestaltung der englischen Währungsverfassung von der ersten bis zur zweiten Peel's Act, 1819-1844, by L. Liepmann; Die Konjunkturlehren der-Banking- und der Currencyschule, insbesondere von Tooke und Newmarch, by Georg Kepper; Geld-Kredit-Banken, by Georg Halm; Untersuchung des Bankwesens, 1933; Kreditbank und Börse. Die Finanzierungs- und Emissionspolitik der Kreditbanken, by Miodrag Milisewitsch.

Mushrooms- Canton

Benemerito, A. N. Mushroom culture in Canton. Philippine Agr. 24(8): 624-634. January 1936. (Published by the College of Agriculture, University of the Philippines, Laguna, P.I.)
Cost of production is considered on p.632.

National Agricultural Conference, 1936 - United States

Report of the National agricultural conference. Coop. Comment 4(12): 1,4. February 1936. (Published at the Columbia Bldg., Spokane, Wash.)
Report of the National Agricultural Conference, representing the leading farm organizations of America, which met in Washington, D.C., January 16-17, 1936.

Neues Bauerntum

Neues Bauerntum. Fachwissenschaftliche Zeitschrift für das ländliche Siedlungswesen. Neue Folge des Archivs für Innere Kolonisation, Bd. 27, September - December 1935. (Published by Deutsche Landbuchhandlung, Dessauer Stresse, 13, Berlin S.W.11, Germany)
September: Arbeitskräfte für die Landwirtschaft, by Karl Sachse. -pp.394-399. (An account of measures taken by the State to counteract the flight from the land by aiding farmers to obtain needed help from the ranks of the unemployed. The pertinent laws and orders are listed.) Anfänge neuen Bauerntums im Innern des Sollings (Westergland), by Karl Jünemann. -pp.399-403. (An account of the introduction of the glass industry into the forest area of

Sollings, its subsequent failure and the reestablishment of the
people on small farms of their own.)
  October: Neue Waldwirtschaft, by Schieckel. -pp.441-442. (A
brief outline of Germany's new forest policy in the interests of the
State and for the national benefit and also for the development of
the woods on the peasant farms.)
  November: Die Landbeschaffung für Zwecke der Wehrmacht und für
die hiermit zusammenhängende Umsiedlung, by Krug. -pp.481-491. (A
study of the means adopted for procuring land for army purposes
and for the settlement of exservice men and the various legislative
measures connected therewith.) Fahrt in das ostpreussische
Siedlungsgebiet, by R. -pp.491-495. (An account of a journey
through the land settlement region of East Prussia.)
  December: Die bäuerliche Siedlung im Jahre 1934, by Vincke.
-pp.525-532. (Summarizes the report on land settlement for 1934
published in Vierteljahrshefte zur Statistik des Deutschen Reichs
44(3): 30-49. 1935, issued by the Statistisches Reichsamt. q.v.)

Occupation Statistics - Estonia and Hungary

Statistics of occupied population in different countries (Estonia, Hungary).
  Internatl. Labour Rev. 33(2): 263-274. February 1936. (Published by
  the International Labour Office, Geneva, Switzerland. Distributed
  in the U.S. by the World Peace Foundation, 8 W. 40th St., New York,
  N.Y.)

Peasants - U.S.S.R.

Harris, Lement. The new Russian peasant. Current Hist. 43(6): 584-588.
  March 1936. (Published at Times Square, New York, N.Y.)
    "The author of this article is an American who has made first-
  hand studies of farm problems both in the Soviet Union and in this
  country." -[Editor's note]
    The writer describes the change in the life of the Russian
  peasant since 1929. "For ten years after the revolution nothing
  much happened to him, but since 1929 his life has changed completely."

Philippine Islands

Seybold, G. H. Our stake in the Philippines. Philippine commonwealth
  must find new destination for $100 million of exports, and American
  manufacturers for $75 million, in the next ten years. Barron's
  16(7): 3,5. Feb. 17, 1936. (Published at 44 Broad St., New York,
  N.Y.)

Planning, National and International Cooperation

Hodson, H. V. The nemesis of national planning. Pacific Affairs 9(1):
  53-59. March 1936. (Published by the Institute of Pacific Relations, Honolulu, Hawaii, Editorial Office, 129 E. 52nd St.,
  New York, N.Y.)

The concluding paragraphs of this article are in part as follows:
"Hence the world has four main alternatives before it. The first is a return towards greater freedom of trade, internal and external -- a forlorn hope; for the planners have scarcely leapt into the saddle, and the way back is beset with the barriers of vested interests created by protectionism in all its forms. The second possibility is a steady extension of the partitioning of world markets, by means of production control and export quotas, international cartels and industrial agreements, and systems of mutual preference... The third possibility is a general lapse to barter. On a large scale, barter necessitates comprehensive government control of import and export trade. Control of foreign exchange transactions is the first step, but in the absence of acute exchange pressure social-democratic countries, especially those like Great Britain with an intricately ramified system of foreign trade, are unlikely to adopt this ultima ratio of national planning for some time to come.
"A fourth alternative remains. It is that the nations should recognize, while yet there is time, that the present drift toward enforced poverty is also a drift toward world war for secure markets and sources of raw materials, and should express this recognition in a world-wide economic truce. National planning without international cooperation in the essential matters of currencies, tariffs, markets and sources of supply is a movement of mass suicide: but safeguarded by international cooperation it may be the next base for another great advance in the unending war against poverty."

Planning, Regional - Pacific Northwest

Third Pacific northwest regional planning conference. Planning News 4(1-2): 5-8. January-February 1936. (Published by Pacific North West Regional Planning Commission, 220 Federal Court House, Portland, Oreg.)
    Contains summaries of reports of various committees. The report of a program and policies committee recommended, among other things, "the development of a well-defined nation-wide land policy for the beneficial use of land and water resources and including proper recognition of reclamation...
    "The agriculture and land classification sections of the Land Resources division submitted recommendations as to: policies for resettling farmers now on marginal lands, including provisions for advice to settlers; the use and control of marginal and submarginal lands; continuation of cooperation in research on land problems, and land classification and land use planning; the expediting of soil survey work; consideration of recreation in land planning; control of noxious weeds; public information in connection with land planning activities."

Planning, Regional - Southern States

Odum, H. W. Testing grounds for social planning. The promise of the South, a test of American regionalism. Plan Age 2(2): 1-26. February 1936. (Published by National Economic and Social Planning Association, 726 Jackson Place, Washington, D. C.)

Cover title: Planning An American Region.

Advocates the South as a testing ground for regional social planning. The article is evidently based on the Southern Regional Study, a report of which is said to be in press at the present time. Among the topics discussed are farm tenancy, contributions of the South to the national culture in the next period of American development, regionalism vs. sectionalism, social planning;American style, picturization of the South, new approaches to agricultural reconstruction, a cooperative program, modification of political culture, the superabundance of physical and human resources, what the South can do, and a minimum framework for planning.

Population - Estonia

Die Bevölkerung in Estland 1934. Wirtschaft und Statistik 16(2): 81. January 1936. (Issued by Germany. Statistisches Reichsamt. Published by Verlag für Sozialpolitik, Wirtschaft und Statistik, Berlin S.W.68, Germany.)

  The second population census of Estonia was taken on March 1, 1934. Statistics are given and a comparison made with the figures of 1922.

Population - Germany

Die Entwicklung der bevölkerungsdichte im jetzigen Reichsgebiet seit 1816. Wirtschaft und Statistik 16(2): 80-81. January 1936. (Issued by Germany. Statistisches Reichsamt. Published by Verlag für Sozialpolitik, Wirtschaft und Statistik, Berlin S.W.68, Germany.)

  Tables show population by provinces and per sq. kilometre in 1816, 1871 and 1933.

Rayon - Statistics

Annual rayon statistical survey. Rayon Organon 7(1A): 15a-25, tables, charts. Jan. 23, 1936. (Published by Textile Economics Bureau, Inc., 21 East 40th St., New York, N. Y.)

  Certain rayon statistics as far back as 1911 and 1912 to date are given.

Research

Research at the 1935 convention of the Association of land-grant colleges and universities. Expt. Sta. Rec. 74(2): 145-149. February 1936. (Published by the Office of Experiment Stations, U. S. Dept. of Agriculture)

  Editorial review of the papers on research problems at the 1935 convention. Papers by Assistant-Secretary M. L. Wilson, J. G. Lipman, C. T. Dowell, H. R. Tolley, R. E. Buchanan, L. E. Call, W. C. White, and J. T. Jardine are especially noted.

  "Taken as a whole, the convention revealed unmistakably the steady progress which is being made toward the development not only of efficient research units but of a well-organized and effective national system. The will to cooperate, it has often been said, is a fundamental requisite in concerted action. This will was much in evidence at the convention, and with it a distinct consciousness of mutual interdependence and responsibility. This feeling is particularly opportune at the present time, and its growth should be productive of much tangible advancement."

Resettlement Administration

Status of Resettlement Administration construction program at end of 1935. Monthly Labor Rev. 42(2): 358-361. February 1936. (Published by the Bureau of Labor Statistics, U. S. Dept. of Labor)
    Status of rural and suburban resettlement projects.

Rural America

Rural America, v.14, no.2, 43pp. February 1936. (Published by the American Country Life Association, Inc., 105 E. 22nd St., New York, N.Y.)
    "This issue of Rural America is dedicated to the memory of Kenyon L. Butterfield, founder of the American Country Life Association."
    Contents: Kenyon L. Butterfield: an interpretation of his life and work, by Ray Stannard Baker, p.4; Tributes to Kenyon L. Butterfield, pp.5-8, A review of the country life movement in the United States, edited by Charles Josiah Galpin, p.9 (Consists of the following articles: The American Country Life Association, by Benson Y. Landis, p.10; Country life clubs among college students, by E. L. Kirkpatrick and Agnes Boynton, pp.11-12; The Division of Farm Population and Rural Life, U.S. Dept. of Agriculture, by Theodore B. Manny, pp.12-13; The co-operative agricultural extension service, by C. B. Smith, pp.13-14; The farm house and home, by Grace E. Frysinger, pp.15-16; The cultural side of 4-H club work, by Gertrude L. Warren, pp.16-17; Radio and country life, by Morse H. Salisbury, pp.17-18; Social aspects of the farm bureau, by W. H. Stacy, pp.19-20; The rural sociology section of the American Sociological Society, by Fred C. Frey, pp.20-21; Rural sociology in agricultural colleges, by W. A. Anderson, pp.21-22; Rural sociology in non-agricultural colleges and universities, by Wilson Gee, pp.23-24; Textbooks in rural sociology, by Carle C. Zimmerman, pp.24-25; Rural research unit of the Federal Emergency Relief Administration, by E. D. Tetreau, pp.25-26; Books of farm life, by Caroline B. Sherman, pp.26-27; Rural health facilities, by H. S. Cummings, pp.27-28; The farmer's trading facilities, by C. R. Hoffer, pp.28-29; Rural library service, by Julia Wright Merrill, pp.29-30; Consolidation of rural schools, by Ernest Burnham, pp.30-31; Folk schools, by Mrs. John C. Campbell, p.32; Recreation in rural areas, by Ella Gardner, pp.33-34; Boy scout service for rural life, by O. H. Benson, pp.34-35; The Young Men's Christian Association in the town and country fields, by Henry Israel, pp.36-37; The National Catholic Rural Life Conference, by James Byrnes, pp.37-39; National Protestant rural life departments, by Warren H. Wilson, pp.40-41; Rural influence in contemporary American art, by Grant Wood, pp.41-43.

Silk - Japan

Lockwood, W. W. Jr. Japanese silk and the American market. Far East.
Survey 5(4): 31-36. Feb. 12, 1936. (Published by the Fortnightly
Research Service, American Council, Institute of Pacific Relations,
129 East 52nd St., New York, N. Y.)
A discussion of the collapse of the silk market in Japan. The
author writes: "Raw silk had been for decades the mainstay of Japan's
export trade, especially with the United States, and the principal
means of payment for imports. A half century of expanding commerce
had spun a silken web across the Pacific upon which depended the
livelihood of two million Japanese farm families.
"With the onset of the depression this 'life line' sagged alarm-
ingly. For the collapse of silk followed directly upon the collapse
of American prosperity. From June 1929 to June 1931 the price of
silk fell 60%. Three years later it had slumped even lower, its
world price having fallen farther than that of any other leading
staple. The repercussions were far-reaching."
Two tables accompany the article. The first shows cocoon and
silk production in Japan, 1924-1934, and the second one gives figures
of raw silk trade of the United States and Japan, 1924-1935.

Social Insurance - France

Bouffard, Fernand. Le nouveau régime des assurances sociales agricoles.
La Vie Agricole et Rurale 25(1): 7-9. Feb. 5, 1936. (Published by
J. B. Baillière & Fils, 19, Rue Hautefeuille, Paris, France.)
A brief account of some of the changes made in social insurance
legislation with regard to agricultural workers by decree laws of
October 29 and 30, 1935. The changes dealt with affect the workers
entitled to insurance, the dues and their payment, and the adminis-
tration of the insurance.

Soil Conservation and Domestic Allotment Act

Alsop, Joseph, Jr. Agricultural anomaly. Today 5(18): 6,22-23. Feb.
22, 1936. (Published at 152 W. 42nd St., New York, N.Y.)
"The shotgun wedding of crop control and soil erosion presents
a peculiar impasse in which the Administration, to carry out the
mandate of the people, must say one thing and do another."

Case, W. W. The Soil conservation act - a new measure of farm and non-
farm parity. Annalist 47(1207): 366-367,392. Mar. 6, 1936. (Published by the New York Times Co., New York, N. Y.)
Subtopics: The new farm act; measures of farm and non-farm
parity; farm parity in the new act; detailed description of the new
parity index; validity of the new index as a basis for national agricultural policy; aims of new act very loosely defined; carrying out
the act; the farm problem remains.

Murphy, Louis. The new farm relief plan. Vital Speeches of the Day 2(11):
341-344. Feb. 24, 1936. (Published at 33 W. 42nd St., New York, N.Y.)
Radio speech over the National Broadcasting Company, Feb. 10,
1936, on the new soil-conservation bill.

New farm program and the old: An explanation and a contrast. U. S. News 4(8): 8. Feb. 24. 1936. (Published at 2201 M St., N.W., Washington, D. C.)

The writer explains how the new farm program for 1936 and 1937 will work, and points out its cost and purposes. Questions that are raised and considered include the following: "Isn't this the old AAA under a different name?... How effective can a plan of that kind turn out to be in practice?... Is there machinery now available to undertake price 'stabilization' if the new program should not succeed in bolstering farm values?. . But doesn't the soil conservation program result in the same sort of production control [as in the AAA]?"

The new soil conservation act - substitute for A.A.A. Congressional Digest 15(3): 68-96. March 1936. (Published at 2131 LeRoy Place, Washington, D. C.)

Contents: The farm aid fight in Congress, pp.68-69; Steps taken by the New Deal to apply economic planning to the American farmer, p.70; Annual cost of farm aid under the U.S. Department of Agriculture, p.71; How the Farm Credit Administration lends money to the farmer, p.72; The A.A.A. - New Deal instrument for economic planning, p.73, The U.S. Supreme Court declares A.A.A. illegal, p.74, Farm organizations seek legal substitute for A.A.A., pp.75-76; The Administration's viewpoint, by Chester C. Davis, pp.76-78, 96; New Soil conservation act - chosen substitute for A.A.A., p.79; Will the Administration's Soil conservation act prove to be legal - pro and con discussion, pp.81-94; A glossary of terms used in farm aid discussion, pp.95-96.

Spare Time Organizations for Rural Workers - Italy

Dusmet, Giacomo. Spare time organisations for agricultural workers in Italy. Internatl. Labour Rev. 33(2): 231-236. February 1936. (Published by the International Labour Office, Geneva, Switzerland. Distributed in the U. S. by the World Peace Foundation, 8 W. 40th St., New York, N.Y.)

Considers the achievements of the National Workers' Spare Time Organisation (Opera Nazionale del Dopol avoro) in the rural districts of Italy. A few paragraphs are also devoted to rural broadcasting in Italy which is organized by the Rural Broadcasting Institution (Ente Radio Rurale).

States, American - Future

Graves, W. B. The future of the American states. Amer. Polit. Sci. Rev. 30(1): 24-50. February 1936. (Published by the American Political Science Association, C. L. King, Secretary-Treasurer, 209 South Hall, University of Wisconsin, Madison, Wis.)

Contents: I. The states in the depression; II. The federal government and the cities; III. Proposals for regionalism; IV. The progress of regionalism to date; V. The merits of the regional plan; VI. Proposals for city-states; VII. The future of the states.

Sugar - China

Sugar production in Kiangsi. Chinese Econ. Jour. 17(6): 560-582. December 1935. (Published by Bureau of Foreign Trade, Ministry of Industry, 1040 North Soochow Road, Shanghai, China.)

Sugar - Cuba

Cuba commences 1936 campaign. Facts about Sugar 31(2): 47-48. February 1936. (Published at 56 West 45th Street, New York, N.Y. Washington, D.C. Office: 923 - 15th St., N.W.)

"Grinding of the 1936 sugar crop in Cuba commenced January 20, with a production quota of 2,515,000 tons... The new control law effects a complete reorganization of the sugar administration. The Sugar Export Corporation is abolished and administrative powers are given to the Cuban Institute for Sugar Stabilization... The Institute will be charged with the duties of recommending to the President the distribution of quotas for the United States and other countries and for local consumption, and the individual mill quotas. The law is to be in effect for six years, until 1941."

Sugar - Queensland

Queensland sugar industry; its economic and strategic value to the Commonwealth. Empire Producer, no. 232, pp.31-33. February 1936. (Published at 22, Queen Anne's Gate, Westminster, London, S.W.1, Eng.)

Sugar Beet Industry - England

"Sharing the swag." Economist 122(4825): 353. Feb. 15, 1936. (Published at 8 Bouverie St., London, E.C.4, Eng.)

Strong opposition is expressed to the Sugar Industry Reorganisation Bill. It is held that the beet sugar industry is an "uneconomic industry" and as for the "contention that there is no alternative crop for the 40,000 people alleged to be employed in the industry, the same argument would justify the perpetual subvention of a domestic banana or coconut industry."

Supreme Court Decisions

Cushman, R. F. Constitutional law in 1934-35. The constitutional decisions of the Supreme Court of the United States in the October term, 1934. Amer. Polit. Sci. Rev. 30(1): 51-89. February 1936. (Published by the American Political Science Association, C. L. King, Secretary-Treasurer, 209 South Hall, University of Wisconsin, Madison, Wis.)

Tax Laws, Retroactive - Constitutionality

Neuhoff, R. F. Retrospective tax laws. Northwestern Miller 185(6): 489,
491. Feb. 19, 1936. (Published at 118 S. 6th St., Minneapolis,
Minn.)
    An editorial on this article appears on p.483 of this issue of
the Northwestern Miller. According to the editor, this article, which
is a discussion of the constitutionality of retroactive tax laws,
although written "prior to the recent Supreme Court decisions, is
particularly timely because of current consideration by the administration of available constitutional means to recover processing
taxes by retroactive legislation."
    The article was reproduced by permission of Washington University
and through the courtesy of the St. Louis Law Review, in which it
was printed in December 1935.

Tenancy - Southern States

Embree, E. R. Southern farm tenancy, the way out of its evils. Survey
Graphic 25(3): 149-153, 190. March 1936. (Published at 112 E. 19th
St., New York, N. Y.)
    As in the booklet, The Collapse of Cotton Tenancy, the writer
pictures the economic and social condition of the share cropper and
share tenant under the Southern tenant system, shows that the landlord suffers along with the tenant, points out factors that point
to the eventual doom of King Cotton, comments on the effect of the AAA
and its reversal on the Southern tenant, and discusses possible ways
of correcting the evils of cotton tenancy. The way suggested, re-
homesteading of tenants, will not solve all the problems of the
rural South, but is considered "basic to reform in other matters."

Tobacco

The British market for American tobacco. Foreign Crops and Markets 32(8):
220-227. Feb. 24, 1936. (Published by the Division of Foreign
Agricultural Service, Bureau of Agricultural Economics, U. S. Dept.
of Agriculture.)
    "Based on reports from Agricultural Attaché C. C. Taylor at
London."

Trade - Brazil

Biehl, Max. Aussenhandel u. transferabkommen. Brasilbaumwolle als
kampfobjekt der grossmächte. Wirtschaftsdienst 20(29): 992-995,
tables. July 19, 1935. (Published at Poststrasse 19, Hamburg 36,
Germany)
    Foreign trade and transfer agreements. Brazilian cotton as the
object of the struggle of the great powers.
    "The author discusses the economic changes in Brazilian trade
due to the decline of coffee production and the rise of cotton.
Statistics of imports and exports since 1930 are tabulated.-C."
-Textile Inst. Jour. 26(10): A542. October 1935.

Trade, Foreign - United States

Stocking, Collis. United States foreign trade in 1935. Commerce Reports
no. 7, pp.120-131, 135. Feb. 15, 1936. (Published by the Bureau of
Foreign and Domestic Commerce, U. S. Department of Commerce.)
Contains tables showing exports and imports of leading commodities.

Trade, International - Theory

Whale, P. B. The theory of international trade in the absence of an
international standard. Economica n.s. 3(9): 24-38. February 1936.
(Published by the London School of Economics and Political Science,
Houghton St., Aldwych, London, Eng,)
The purpose of this article is "to discuss the maintenance of
international equilibrium when the currencies of the countries concerned are independent and exchange rates are free to vary."

Trade Agreements - Canada

Saunders, W. A. The reciprocity treaty of 1854: a regional study. Canad.
Jour. Econ. and Polit. Sci. 2(1): 41-53. February 1936. (Published
by the University of Toronto Press, Toronto, Canada.)
The concluding paragraph of this article follows:
"The contribution of this study lies not so much in the negative
conclusions as in the positive implications concerning the problem
of regionalism in Canada. Studies of American tariffs, or Canadian
fiscal policy, have neglected the main features of the economic
structure, and have failed to show how they have been modified by,
or have resisted, political changes. The reciprocity agreement of
1935 between Canada and the United States has been consummated since
the completion of this study. Under the Reciprocity Treaty of 1854,
the Maritime Provinces benefited through their ability to purchase
certain commodities more cheaply from the United States rather than
through their ability to dispose of a larger proportion of their
production in the American market; and the terms of the present
agreement justify the speculation that a similar situation will pre-
vail throughout its duration; and, further, that the Maritime
Provinces will profit less than other parts of the Dominion. Regional differences continue, and intensify the difficulties inherent
in tariff bargaining."

Trade Agreements - Great Britain and Argentina

Stewart, R. B. Anglo-Argentine trade agreements. Canad. Jour. Econ. and
Polit. Sci. 2(1): 16-26. February 1936. (Published by the University
of Toronto Press, Toronto, Canada.)

Trade Agreements - United States

Smith, J. G. Development of policy under the trade agreements program.
Quart. Jour. Econ. 50(2): 297-312. February 1936. (Published by

Harvard University Press. Randall Hall, Cambridge, Mass.)

"Origins of the program, 297.- Pitfalls of the policy, 299.- State Department's attempts to avoid them, 300.- Difficulty in application of most-favored-nation principle, 301.- Attempts to meet this, 302.- 'Safeguards,' 303.- Quotas and exchange control, 304.- Prohibitions on sanitary grounds, 305.- Monopolistic practices, 305.- Domestic planning measures, 305.- The problem of monetary instability, 307.- Conflict with bilateral exchange pacts, 309.- Conclusions; no safeguards developed against managed currency and economic planning pitfalls, 311.- Leadership incumbent upon creditor nations, 313." -Summary, p.297.

Wage-earner in the Westward Movement

Goodrich, Carter, and Davison, Sol. The wage-earner in the westward movement. II. Polit. Sci. Quart. 51(1): 61-116. March 1936. (Published by the Academy of Political Science, Fayerweather Hall, Columbia University. New York, N. Y.)

This paper "represents an attempt to discover how much of a migration of wage-earners took place during the half-century or so in which there was at one end of the country a substantial factory population and at the other an actively advancing frontier." The first part of the article appeared in the Political Science Quarterly for June 1935.

The evidence, the author concludes, "points to the conclusion that the movement of eastern wage-earners to the western lands was surprisingly small."

Wages, Agricultural - United States

Black, J. D. Agricultural wage relationships: historical changes. Rev. Econ. Statis. 18(1): 8-15. January 1936. (Published at Harvard University Press, Cambridge, Mass.)

The present article, according to the author's introductory paragraph, "gives a partial report on research into the available data on wages paid farm labor in the United States and certain related factors, to see what such data reveal as to the content and character of the expected relationships. Most of the needed data are available only since 1910. The analysis breaks into three parts: historical changes in farm wage rates, the geographic pattern of farm wage rates, and historical changes in the geographic pattern, in each case with the factors related thereto. This deals only with the first of these."

This particular part of the article deals with the following subtopics: farm wage rates and incomes; farm labor supply and demand; land values and other productive agents.

Wealth

Wealth and its distribution. Natl. City Bank N.Y. [Monthly letter on] Econ. Conditions, Govt. Finance, U. S. Securities, March 1936, pp.42-47. (Published in New York, N.Y.)

This is a "review of progress in the chemical industries, including the manufacture of cement and concrete and the construction of Boulder Dam."

Whitney, S. N. Weakness of data supporting conclusion of increase in diffusion of wealth. Annalist 47(1207): 368-369, 392. Mar. 6, 1936. (Published by the New York Times Co., New York, N. Y.)

This is a reply to a series of articles in The Annalist by Robert Rutherford Doane "showing a steadily increasing diffusion of wealth in the United States since 1880."

Wheat

Taylor, A. E. Wheat outlook of the world. Index 11(122): 23-33. February 1936. (Published by Svenska Handelsbanken, Stockholm, Sweden.)

The article is concluded, in part, as follows:

"To a considerable extent, quite irrespective of price movement, with favourable conditions at the time of seeding, with average yield, and with no unusual succession of crop failures (such as we have witnessed in recent years), the world supply of wheat will tend again relatively to exceed the world demand, in terms of monetary purchasing power.... In the world during the last generation, the various improvements in growing of wheat do not seem to have been reflected in such lowered costs as to have made prices satisfactory to farmers or consumers. The world carryover will tend to rise, just as it rose from 1925 to 1930. This will again provoke political agitation for an International Wheat Conference. -perhaps a revival of the old one or the invention of a new one. A tendency to increase in the carry-over of wheat, with predominance of exporters' surpluses over importers' requirements, is the inevitable expression of the occupational psychology of wheat growers, with the disorganized state of commodity trade and monetary exchanges in the world. It will be relieved only by improvement of the standard of living in the world, with enlargement in the use of wheat. There is no progress in restriction; we must learn to use surpluses. Whatever the difficulties of 'too much', those of 'too little' are worse. Wheat is merely one important material; the problem more or less includes all. The adjustment must come from the side of consumption."

Wool Trade - North China

Rasmussen, A. H. The wool trade of North China. Pacific Affairs 9(1): 60-68. March 1936. (Published by the Institute of Pacific Relations, Honolulu, Hawaii. Editorial Office, 129 E. 52nd St., New York, N.Y.)

Zoning, County - Illinois

Monchow, Helen C. County zoning authorized in Illinois. Jour. Land & Pub. Utility Econ. 12(1): 89-90. February 1936. (Published by Northwestern University, School of Commerce, 337 E. Chicago Ave., Chicago, Ill.)

Critical of the county zoning act of Illinois, approved June 28, 1935. While the act represents a forward step, "as it stands, the

law is little more than a glorified municipal zoning statute,
glorified by being applicable to a wider area than that within the
jurisdiction of a municipality. It applies more or less 'urban'
regulations to the unincorporated areas within county boundaries."

ZONING, Rural

Carrolt, L. J. Rural zoning in suburban metropolitan areas. Planners'
    Jour. 2(1): 7-8. January-February 1936. (Published by American City
    Planning Institute, Hunt Hall, Cambridge, Mass.)

NOTES

American liberty league. National lawyers committee. Report on the consti-
    tutionality of the Potato act of 1935. Issued December 30, 1935. 44pp.
    [Washington?] 1935.   280.375 Am3

Chugai snogyo snimpo-sha Tokyo.   Industrial expansion of Japan and Manchoukuo
    [1936] 106pp. Tokyo, Japan [1935]   Folio 280.9 C47

Ieving, J. E. Post-entry training in the federal service. 73pp. [Chicago?]
    August 1935.   375 D49
        Mimeographed and circulated by courtesy of the Public administration
    fund, University of Chicago.
        Bibliography, p. 72.

Europäische revue. Sonderheft: Sicherheit. [709]-828pp. Stuttgart-Berlin,
    Deutsche verlags-anstalt [1935] 280 Eu7
        Jahrg.11, hft. 11/12, Nov./Dec. 1935.
        This supplement to the Europäische Revue contains a number of articles
    on the general subject of security. They analyze the position of the
    United States and of various European nations on the question of neutrality
    and a hands-off policy with regard to the affairs of other countries
    or a policy of cooperation in the interests of international security.

Gt. Brit. Colonial office. Information as to the conditions and cost of
    living in the colonial empire. (2nd edition - reprinted with amendments,
    July, 1935) 200pp. London, H. M. Stationery off.. 1935. (Colonial
    no.101) 284.4 G793 Ed. 2

Gt. Brit. Commissioner for the special areas in Scotland. Report for the period
    1st July, 1935 to 31st December, 1935. Presented by the Secretary of
    state for Scotland to Parliament by command of His Majesty February 1936.
    32pp. Edinburgh, H. M. Stationery off., 1936. ([Gt. Brit. Parliament.
    Papers by command] Cmd. 5089)   280.171 G796

Gt. Brit. Government actuary's dept. Unemployment insurance (agriculture) bill,
    1935. Report by the government actuary on the financial provisions of the
    bill. 8PP. London, H. M. Stationery off., 1935. ([Parliament. Papers
    by command] Cmd. 5050) 284.6 G792

Gt. Brit. Ministry of agriculture and fisheries. British sugar (subsidy) acts, 1925 and 1934. Statements, in the form of balance sheets, transmitted to the Minister of agriculture and fisheries by companies which manufactured, in Great Britain, in 1934–35, sugar and/or molasses from home-grown beet. Section II. Refineries. 3pp. London, H. M. Stationery off., 1935. 66.9 G792

Gt. Brit. Ministry of agriculture and fisheries. Milk (extension of temporary provisions) Memorandum on financial resolution. Presented to Parliament by the minister of agriculture and fisheries, the secretary of state for Scotland and the secretary of state for the home department by command of His Majesty, February, 1936. 3pp. London, H. M. Stationery off., 1936. ([Parliament. Papers by command] Cmd. 5092) 281.344 G79M Feb. 1936.
    "The financial resolution provides the necessary authority for extending the period of operation of certain provisions of the Milk act, 1934."

Gt. Brit. Ministry of health. Committee on garden cities and satellite towns. Garden cities and satellite towns. Report of Departmental committee. 31pp. London, H. M. Stationery off., 1935. 98.5 G792
    Reviewed briefly in FERA Relief Notices, no. 68, pp.4–5. Aug. 26,1935.

Hentz, Henry & co., New York. The commodity markets [Revised] 158pp. New York, H. Hentz & co., 1935. 286 H36 1935

Honolulu star-bulletin. Merchandising service bureau. General survey, August 1935, on canned food, vegetables - fruits - soups in Honolulu, made by Honolulu star-bulletin, Merchandising service bureau. 23pp., mimeogr. [Honolulu, 1935] 280.32 H75
    On cover: Market study of canned foods in Hawaii.

Manchester guardian commercial. Annual review, January 31, 1936. 100pp. [London, 1936] Folio 286.8 M315A
    Partial contents; Reasons for the rise in commodity prices, by Norman Crump; These agricultural marketing boards, by W. B. Mercer; Economic policy and the cotton trade, by a correspondent; Rayon production passes a milestone, by A. B. Shearer; Wool textiles, by Dudley G. Ackroyd; and Meeting modern requirements, by Horace Spibey.

Missouri. Relief commission. Work relief in Missouri, 1934–35. Compiled by William Gammon, Missouri relief commission. 166pp. Jefferson City, Mo., 1935. 283 M692

Mitchell, G. S. Some problems of the textile industry. 11pp. New York city, The Affiliated schools for workers, inc. [1935] 304 M692
    At head of title: An outline for study and discussion.
    Bibliography, p.11.

Pearson, S. V. The growth and distribution of population. 448pp. New York, J. Wiley & sons, inc., 1935. 280 P312
    Partial contents. - Chapter 4. Developments in agriculture. - Chapter 8. The size of agricultural holdings. - Chapter 13. Rural depopulation. - Chapter 16. The garden city idea. - Chapter 17. Town and country planning.

Peek, G. N. Memorandum on Canadian trade agreement. 7pp., mimeogr. [Washington] 1935. 266 P34m
    Accompanied by statistical tables.

Pennsylvania. Greater Pennsylvania council. Population trends; a study of population facts significant to Pennsylvania's present and future planning. Commonwealth of Pennsylvania, Greater Pennsylvania council. 64pp. [Harrisburg? 1932?] 280.7 P382P

U. S. Bureau of foreign and domestic commerce. Market research series no. 7. Check sheet introduction of new consumer products, by O. C. Holleran. 51pp., mimeogr. [Washington, D.C.] 1935. 157.54 M34 no.7.

Wolfe, E. J. Industrial and agricultural work relief projects in the United States. A report submitted to the Governor's commission on unemployment relief. 68pp., mimeogr. New York [1935] 283 W832
    "Represents one section of a comprehensive report which is being prepared by Mr. Wolfe concerning cooperative and self-help ventures in the United States." - Prefatory note.
    Bibliography pp. 66-68.

AGRICULTURAL ECONOMICS LITERATURE

UNITED STATES DEPARTMENT OF AGRICULTURE
BUREAU OF AGRICULTURAL ECONOMICS

RECEIVED
MAR 1 1 1944

> Governments, like clocks, go from the motion men give
> them and as governments are made and moved by men,
> so by them they are ruined too. Wherefore
> governments rather depend upon men than
> men upon governments. - William Penn

| Vol. 10 | May 1936 | No. 5 |

FEATURES IN THIS ISSUE

SIGNED REVIEW

Iowa. State planning board. Restore the forest cover; a graphic brochure
prepared by the Iowa State planning board. [28]pp. [Des Moines? 1935]
280.7 Io9Re

New Jersey. State planning board. First annual report of progress; a preliminary report upon planning surveys and planning studies for the state
of New Jersey. 147pp. Trenton, 1935   280.7 N46

The little pamphlet issued by the Iowa State Planning Board presents
by means of pictures, a few maps, and a minimum of text the problem of
soil erosion and urges the restoration of forest cover. It is quite evident that this little pamphlet is intended for a wider public than most
of the general and special reports so far issued. It should serve its
purpose very well. The pictures are clear and well chosen, and the few
maps are simple. Planning boards and other agencies interested in popu-
larizing their material could well follow the example of the Iowa State
Planning Board, and prepare more such pamphlets.

The New Jersey report, as its title indicates, is for a more limited
audience. It is a report to the Governor and State Legislature on the
problems with which the Board was concerned.

Part I is an introduction giving the functions and duties of the State
planning board, the planning problems as conceived by the Board and general conclusions and recommendations.

Part II is entitled "State Planning Surveys". This part is quite similar to other State planning reports. Chapter IV is entitled "Physical
conditions and land use". Chapter V, Social and Economic Conditions in
State Growth and Development, includes population, occupational and industrial trends, relief, and political subdivisions. Chapter VI, Improvements and Services, includes transportation, parks and recreation, public
services, meaning evidently State and municipal services, and the housing
problem.

Part III entitled "State Planning Studies" gives the State plan for
the future as visualized at the present time by the Board. Chapter VII
is on the "Future Use of Land". The conclusion is that although New
Jersey is an urban State, urban demand will never exceed fifteen hundred
square miles, leaving six thousand square miles as rural land. This rural
land is divided equally, 3000 square miles of agricultural and 3000 square
miles of non-agricultural land. It is proposed that the non-agricultural
land should be retained or returned to forest for not only forest use but
also recreation, conservation of wild-life, and the protection of water

sources. In line with this, Chapter VIII is entitled "General Park and Forest Requirements". Chapter IX is a discussion of a highway direct onal study. Chapter X is on Land subdivision regulation and control. "The land development problem is acute in New Jersey. Many thousands of acres of land have been plotted prematurely in extended metropolitan areas and in summer resort areas." A study of what might be done in replanning a plotted area is included. - C. I. Hendrickson, Senior Agricultural Economist, Division of Land Econ ics

DESCRIPTIVE NOTES AND ABSTRACTS

Accounting - Cooperative Cotton Gins

Weaver, O. T. Accounting principles for cooperative cotton gin associations. 90pp. Washington, U. S. Govt. print. off., 1936. (U. S. Farm credit administration. Cooperative division. Bulletin no. 2)   166.2 B87 no.2

Agricultural Credit - Italy

Pais, Domenico. Il credito alle opere per la bonifica integrale. Terza edizione. 179pp. Padova, Cedam, Casa editrice dott. Antonio Milani, 1930.   264.2 P16 Ed.3

At head of title: Scuola di scienze politiche e sociali della R. Università di Padova. Corso di preparazione per funzionari amministrativi dei consorzi di bonifica (promosso dal Ministero dei lavori pubblici)

This is a study of the need for and the provision of credit for the carrying out of the Italian program of land reclamation and improvement. These two phases of the program are considered separately. In connection with the agricultural utilization of the land the characteristics of agricultural credit, the institutions to which its dispensation is entrusted and their operation, the assistance of the State in the form of subsidies, prizes, etc., and the functions of the consortia are described.

The book was written as a preparatory study for those preparing to act as administrative officials of the land reclamation consortia.

Agricultural Outlook - Canada

Canada. Dept. of agriculture. Statistical data supplementary to the Agricultural situation and outlook 1936. December 2, 1935. The Dominion Bureau of statistics and the Dominion Department of agriculture co-operating. 110pp., mimeogr. [Ottawa] Pub. by authority of the Hon. W. D. Euler, Minister of trade and commerce and J. G. Gardiner, Minister of agriculture, 1935.   281.9 C163

Ontario. Dept. of agriculture. The Ontario agricultural outlook report 1936. 35pp. [Ottawa?, 1936] 281.9 On8
 Issued in cooperation with the Ontario Agricultural College.
 "An Outlook Report on Agriculture in Ontario has been prepared with the idea of giving assistance in the making of plans for the farm programme of 1936. No attempt has been made to offer specific recommendations. Conditions, circumstances and needs must necessarily govern each individual farmer in making decisions on the various steps of production and marketing. However, in a study of the farm enterprises, the farmer should have all available and helpful information."

Cartel Legislation

Reichert, J. W. Die kartellgesetze der welt; eine deutschsprachige wiedergabe aller kartellgesetze und - verordnungen nebst einer rechtsgeschichtlichen betrachtung. 197pp. Berlin, C. Heymanns verlag, 1935. 286 R272
 In this volume will be found "the original texts of forty cartel laws and administrative orders, covering the following 22 countries: Germany, the U. S. A., Argentine, Australia, Belgium, Bulgaria, Denmark, France (draft law), Great Britain, Netherlands, Italy, Japan, Jugoslavia, Canada, New Zealand, Norway, Poland, Czechoslovakia, Switzerland, Spain, South Africa and Hungary. The text of each law reproduced is preceded by a contents list of the subjects dealt with by the law in question, thus making reference to the text very much easier. In the first part of the book the author deals with the history of cartel legislation, including chapters on pre-war and war legislation in the United States of America, Australia and New Zealand, and post-war legislation in Germany, Canada, South Africa, Argentine, Scandinavia and Switzerland, other countries of the European Continent, Great Britain and the United States of America (the New Deal legislation)." - From World Trade, v. 7, no. 10, Dec. 1935, p. 10.

Commodity Stocks - Cyclical Fluctuations

Blodgett, R. H. Cyclical fluctuations in commodity stocks. 177pp. Philadelphia, University of Pennsylvania press; London, H. Milford, Oxford university press, 1935. 280 B623
 This volume consists of a statistical study made for the purpose of supplying information on the behavior of stocks of goods in prosperity and depression, is the statement of M. A. Brumbaugh of the University of Buffalo, who reviewed it in the Journal of the American Statistical Association for March 1936(pp.238-239)

Consumption

Baars, Ir. A. W. Het verbruik van algemeen benoodigde consumptieartikelen. The consumption of generally used commodities. Een dynamische berekeninge methode van enkele economische structuurwijzigingen. A dynamic method of calculation of changes in economic structure. 105pp. Haarlem, De erven F. Bohn n.v., 1933. (Nederlandsch economisch instituut. Netherlands economic instituut. [Publications] nr.4) 280 B11
 Dutch.

Parker, Florence E. Consumers', credit, and productive cooperation in 1933. 8pp. Washington, U. S. Govt. print. off., 1935. (U. S. Bureau of labor statistics. Bulletin no. 612) 158.6 B87 no. 612

The Commissioner of Labor Statistics states in the Letter of transmittal accompanying this bulletin that "This survey covered the 1933 experience of all types of cooperative associations in this country, except the farmers' marketing associations... This is the fourth study in this field made by the Bureau, the three previous ones having covered the years 1920, 1925 and 1929."

Two chapters are devoted to consumers' organizations, one to credit and banking societies and one to workers productive associations.

Cooperative Marketing - Agriculture

Fetrow, W. W. Cooperative marketing of agricultural products. 106pp. Washington [U. S. Govt print. off.] 1936. (U. S. Farm credit administration. Cooperative division. Bulletin no. 3) 166.2 B87

Selected list of references on cooperative marketing, pp. 104-106.

Partial contents: Cooperative marketing of cotton; Associations marketing dairy products; Cooperatives handling fruits, vegetables, and nuts; Cooperative marketing of grain, Farmers' livestock-marketing organizations; Cooperation among poultry and egg producers; Cooperative marketing of tobacco; Wool and mohair cooperatives; and Cooperative marketing of other farm products.

Cotton

Richards, H. I. Cotton and the AAA. 389pp. Washington, D. C., The Brookings institution, 1936. (Half-title: The Institute of economics of the Brookings institution. Publication no. 66) 281.372 R39

Dr. Edwin G. Nourse, Director of the Institute of Economics of the Brookings Institution writes in part as follows in the preface:

"This is the sixth and last of the commodity studies which constitute the second phase of our concurrent study of the Agricultural Adjustment Act. In drawing this phase of our study to a close, a word of explanation may be in order. We have endeavored to follow inductive methods of study, to approach the agricultural adjustment experiment without bias or preconceived opinions but with receptive attitude. Suspending judgment as to the merits of the plan, we have sought to acquire a thorough understanding of the objectives aimed at in the various phases of the adjustment undertaking, of the actual methods and procedures through which it was sought to attain these ends, of the way in which these devices and efforts have actually worked in practice, and of the reasons for the success or failure so far as available techniques of economic analysis make this possible.

"Owing to the enormous complexity of the undertaking, it has been found necessary to departmentolize our study along commodity lines, each in charge of a man who has specialized in a particular field. We have not sought to secure complete uniformity of view or consistency of analysis throughout the series. For this we must look to the final volume in the series.

"Necessary as the commodity approach was, it inevitably led to a certain sense of incompleteness in each of the separate volumes. In spite of the high degree of commercial specialization to be found in American agriculture, there is a very considerable degree of overlapping and intermingling of the various lines of production, and it is impossible to complete the analysis of the effects of the several programs even upon agriculture in terms merely of single commodities.

"This situation is so marked in the case of corn and hogs that both commodities were treated under a single adjustment program and are covered by a single volume in our study, which includes also a general treatment of the cattle problem. However, corn and hog production is also much involved in the problem of cotton production, dairy production, and the like. It would be desirable in some ways if we could round out this second level of our study with a synthetic analysis of the effect of the adjustment program on agriculture as a whole before proceeding to our final volume of appraisal of the broader effects of the adjustment effort on our economic life as a whole."

It is hoped that a signed review of this volume will appear in Agricultural Economics Literature at a later date

Boy scouts of America. Cotton farming. 57PP. New York city, Boy scouts of America [1931] (Merit badge series)   72 B69
    Bibliography, pp. 55-56
    "This is one of a series of pamphlets published by the Boy Scouts of America in connection with its Merit Badge scheme. This library on Scout activities and vocational guidance has been prepared by experts and is frequently revised and brought up to date." - Introduction.

Cotton - India

Ahmad, Nazir. Technological reports on standard Indian cottons, 1935. 103pp. Bombay, G. Claridge & co., ltd. 1935. (India. Indian central cotton committee, Technological laboratory. Technological bulletin, Series A, no. 28)   72.9 In2332A
    "The term 'Standard Indian Cottons' is applied to certain improved varieties of cotton which are steadily replacing the older varieties in different parts of India and which, at present, cover some 15 per cent. of the total area under cotton cultivation   It is the practice at the Technological Laboratory to subject the standard cottons of each season to a very thorough test for their fibre-properties and yarn characteristics. The Technological Reports included in the present bulletin contain the detailed results of these tests on standard cottons of twelve seasons, viz., 1923-35, together with the Agricultural Details, the Grader's valuation reports, and the Spinning Master's report on each cotton, while the objects and salient features of the various tests are described in the Introduction." - Preface.

India. Indian central cotton committee.   Annual report...for the year
   ending 31st August, 1935.   192pp. Bombay, The Times of India press,
   1936.   72.9 In233A
      This Report covers the work of the Indian Central Cotton Committee
   for the year, the other crop estimates and other statistics, an account
   of the research activities of the Committee which include "the improvement and development of the growing, marketing and manufacture of cotton
   in India," the annual report of the Director of the Technological Laboratory and much other information relating to Indian cotton.

India. Indian central cotton committee.   Summary proceedings of the thirty-
   first meeting of the Indian central cotton committee. 102pp. Bombay,
   held on the 19th and 20th August 1935. [Bombay, G. Claridge & co.,
   ltd., 1935]   72.9 In233Ab

County Finance - Tennessee

Allred. C. E.. Atkins, S. W., Marshall, J. H., Collins, W. E., and Tosch, C. A.
   Comparative ability of Tennessee counties to finance their governmental
   functions. A preliminary report. 44pp. mimeogr. [Washington, D. C.]
   Mar. 20, 1936 (U. S. Federal emergency relief administration. Report
   no 9)   173 2 R27Rep no.9
      Issued in cooperation with Tennessee Agricultural Experiment Station,
   Federal Works Progress Administration, Tennessee Welfare Commission.
      Partial contents: Total fiscal capacity of counties; Per capita fis-
   cal capacity of counties; and Method of procedure in determining total
   fiscal capacity.

Economic Geography - British Empire

Buchanan, R O An economic geography of the British empire. 346pp.
   London, University of London press, ltd., 1935. 278.171 B85
      "My aim has been to write a reasoned account of the Economic
   Geography of the British Empire. No attempt has been made to be
   encyclopaedic. The main economic activities have been picked out
   and emphasised, and treated in relation to the particular geographical
   conditions that have guided the nature and degree of their development."-
   Author's preface.

Economic Nationalism - Canada

Bates, E. S. A planned nationalism: Canada's effort. 171pp.   Toronto, The
   Macmillan company of Canada limited, 1935.   280.13 B31
      This volume is a plea for Canada to return to her old policy of economic
   nationalism and give up her internationalism from which the author thinks
   that she has suffered many ills.

Economic Survey - Colonies - Gt. Britain

Gt. Brit. Colonial office. An economic survey of the colonial empire (1933)
   573pp. London, H. M. Stationery off., 1935. 280.171 G791 1933
      "The present publication, which is a revised version of the first edi-

tion of this work published last year, is an attempt to assemble within
a single volume all the essential facts relating to the economic situation
of the Colonial Empire...

"The work is divided into two Parts.

"The first Part contains a series of memoranda on the economic situation of the individual Dependencies.

"An endeavour has been made to prepare these memoranda on exactly
uniform lines, so that the same essential facts may be given for each
Dependency. Each memorandum is divided into ten Sections.

"The first Section gives the geographical position and area of the
Dependency, the salient facts regarding its climate and a brief account
of the ownership of the land of the Dependency and the uses to which
it is put.

"The second Section gives the total population of the Dependency, the
racial distribution and principal occupations of the inhabitants, so far
as they are known, and the salient facts regarding immigration and emigration, if they are of importance in the economic life of the Dependency

"The third Section relates to finance and is divided into two sub-sec-
tions. The first gives a brief account of the currency system of the Dependency, a list of the banks doing business therein, and an account of
work of a banking nature performed by the Government, if any. The second
sub-section relates to public finance...

"The fourth Section is devoted to trade statistics and gives (a) the total value of the exports from and imports into the Dependency in the years
1913, 1930, 1931, 1932 and 1933, (b) an analysis of the exports and imports
for 1933 according to countries of destination and origin, and (c) a list
of the principal exports and imports with quantities and values and the
values for the principal countries of destination and origin...

"The fifth Section gives an account of the natural resources of the
Dependency divided into six heads: - 1. Agriculture, 2. Forestry, 3. Animal
Husbandry, 4. Minerals, 5. Fisheries, 6. Miscellaneous, and an estimate of
the extent to which the Dependency is self-supporting in foodstuffs.

"The sixth Section gives an account of the industrial activities of the
Dependency, if any.

"The seventh Section gives an estimate of the importance of other economic activities, such as entrepôt trade and tourist traffic, in the economic life of the Dependency." - Preface

Employment and Output

Keynes, J. M. The general theory of employment, interest and money. 403pp.
London, Macmillan and co., limited, 1936. 280 K52G

G. D. H. Cole reviewed this volume at length in The New Statesman and
Nation, Feb. 15, 1936. In this review he characterizes the work as "the
most important theoretical economic writing since Marx's Capital, or, if
only classical economics is to be considered as comparable, since Ricardo's
Principles...

"His book is in form chiefly an attempt to determine the underlying
conditions which, in a capitalistically organised society, determine the
actual volume of unemployment. The classical economists, either explicitly
or more often by implication, have been accustomed to set out from the
assumption of 'full employment' as normal, and to prove their general

theories without regard to the possibility of variations in total employment, treating the actual occurrence of unemployment as a deviation from
the normal, due to some exceptional factor such as monetary mismanagement
or the rigidity of wages...

"Mr. Keynes now sees the factor which determines the total volume of
employment under capitalism as the maintenance of investment at an adequate
level. This seems, at first sight, to put him sharply in opposition to the
'under-consumptionists', but actually it makes him their ally. For the will
to invest depends, in Mr. Keynes's phrase, on the 'marginal efficiency of
capital,' which may be roughly translated as the marginal expectation of
profit from investment over its entire life, as far as this is actually
taken into account by the investor. This expectation, however, depends
absolutely on the demand for consumers' goods; and accordingly the maintenance of investment at a satisfactory level depends on the maintenance of
consumption...

"The book is one which must, sooner or later, cause every orthodox
text-book to be fundamentally re-written. It is true that Mr. Keynes's
conclusion is not that we should destroy the system of 'private enterprise,'
but only that we should drastically re-fashion it. Mr. Keynes rejects
complete Socialism, and looks forward to a society in which private and
collective enterprise will live together, but the rentier class will have
practically disappeared - for the maintenance of full employment with the
aid of industry kept up to the requisite point by State action will, he
thinks, reduce the rate of interest almost to vanishing point. But this
part of his argument is but briefly sketched in his closing chapter and is
not a necessary deduction from his analysis. What he has done, triumphantly
and conclusively, is to demonstrate the falsity, even from a capitalist
standpoint, of the most cherished practical 'morals' of the orthodox economists and to construct an alternative theory of the working of capitalist
enterprise so clearly nearer to the facts that it will be impossible for it
to be ignored or set aside."

The volume is reviewed at length also, by "E.A.G.R." in The Economist
(London) Feb. 29 1936. From this the extract below has been taken:

"Mr. Keynes' new book, like all that he writes or says, will provoke discussion and dispute. The methods of thought that he first developed in his
'Treatise on Money' he has now extended and modified. Where he was concerned before with the problem of prices, implicitly assuming a given level
of output, he is now concerned chiefly with the factors that determine what
that level of output will be.

"At the outset Mr. Keynes claims that the classical and neo-classical
economists have never developed any theory of output as a whole. Ricardo
himself explicitly, and those who have followed in his footsteps sometimes
less consciously, have been concerned with the problem of the pricing system, of the distribution of wealth and of productive resources between alternative uses, on the assumption always that resources devoted to one purpose were withdrawn from another. They assumed, that is, full employment.
The explanations of unemployment were unnecessarily concerned with friction
and rigidities which prevented immediate absorption. The theory of output
as a whole has been neglected, and it has been inferred with altogether too
little consideration that it needed no independent system of thought or
analysis to solve its problems.

"Mr. Keynes argues that this problem requires a technique of its own,
and he has set out to give it to us."

Farm Loan Associations

U. S. Farm credit administration. National farm loan associations A handbook
for officers and directors. 81pp. Washington, U. S. Govt. print. off.,
1935. 166.3 N21
"The important part which the national farm loan associations play
in the successful operation of the Federal farm loan system is becoming
increasingly apparent. The officers of the Federal land banks cannot be
expected to be intimately acquainted either with the farmers applying
for loans or the properties offered as security for such loans. On the
other hand, the officers and directors of a local national farm loan association, organized to operate within a particular community, will ordinarily be familiar with the credit needs of the farmer borrowers of that
community and be in a position to maintain intimate contact with those
farmers.
"By the intimate grouping of borrowers into the local cooperative units
known as national farm loan associations, local interest and farmer participation in the affairs of the association is made possible, thereby
lessening the credit risk and enabling the member borrowers to reach the
money markets of the Nation and secure loans at low rates of interest
suited to the long-time needs of agriculture. Intensive efforts are being
made to strengthen the associations and improve their condition and standing in order to bring them into closer contact and cooperation with the
Federal land banks and the Farm Credit Administration, and generally to
increase their intended usefulness.
"It is the objective of the Farm Credit Administration to assist each
association to become a well-managed, soundly financed, self-sustaining
credit institution owned and controlled by the farmers who use it." -
Introduction.

Farm Management - Bulgaria

Berberoff, Theodor. Untersuchungen über die landwirtschaftlichen betriebs-
systeme Bulgariens. 68pp. Berlin, P. Parey. 1935 ([Germany] Reichs-und
Pr. Ministerium für Ernährung und Landwirtschaft, n. F. 114. Sonderheft)
18 G31A
A historical and critical study of land tenure and farm management in
Bulgaria where the family farm is predominant. The farmer and his family
cultivate the land to supply their own needs and production for the market
is a secondary consideration. As a background the physical factors of
climate and soil and the crops cultivated are described, and an account
is given of the various forms of land tenure and leasing contracts.
Then a systematic attempt is made to present a complete picture of the
economic organization of Bulgarian agriculture and its relation to land
utilization.

Industrialization in the East

Hubbard, G. E., and Baring, Denzil. Eastern industrialization and its effect
on the west, with special reference to Great Britain and Japan, by G. E.
Hubbard assisted by Denzil Baring. With a conclusion by professor T. E.
Gregory. 395pp. London, Oxford university press, H. Milford, 1935.
286 H862
Issued under the auspices of the Royal Institute of International

Bibliography, pp. [372]-377.

The subject of this volume is introduced "by a discussion, supported by statistics, of Japanese competition with the older Western suppliers in world markets. There follows for Japan, China and India in turn a brief history of their industrialisation, a survey of present economic and political conditions and a forecast of the future. The author then turns to a review of the industrial growth of Great Britain and the effect upon her social and industrial structure of changes in the competing international forces of industrialisation; and his study ends with a section on the effects of Eastern industrialisation upon trade relationships in the British Commonwealth.

"This is an ambitious programme. But the attempt is well justified by the result, and although the materials used are not new, the author's treatment of them is excellent...

"Since this book comes from the Royal Institute of International Affairs, the author is prohibited from expressing 'opinions' or grinding axes; but its moral is written on its forehead: 'If a country will not buy, neither shall it sell '" - Economist (London) v. 122, no. 4820, Jan. 11, 1936, p. 74.

Konjunktur-Statistisches Handbuch 1936

Berlin. Institut für konjunkturforschung. Konjunktur-statistiches handbuch 1936. Herausgeber prof. dr. Ernst Wagemann. 349pp. Berlin, Hanseatische verlagsanstalt Hamburg, 1935. 280.9 B45K

This handbook is intended to supply a statistical background for a study of business conditions particularly during the period from 1925 to 1935. Monthly figures are given.

Land Classification

Barnes, C. P. Land classification: Objectives and requirements. 44pp., mimeogr. Washington, D. C., Feb. 1936 (U. S. Resettlement administration. Land utilization division. Land use planning section. Land use planning publication no. 1) 1 95 L23 no.1

Partial contents: Objectives of land classification, Relation of land classification to production control measures, Forms of land classification; Criteria and considerations which may be significant in land classification, Procedure in use-district classification.

Land Planning

Gray, L C. Land planning. 37pp. Chicago, The University of Chicago press [1936] (Public policy pamphlet no. 19) 280.12 P96 no.19
Bibliography, p. 37.

This pamphlet deals largely with the broader aspects of land-use planning, discussing the subject under the following subtopics: Principles of land planning, past land policies, recent activities in land planning, the report of the Land Planning Committee of the National Resources Board, summaries of major factors influencing land requirements as given in the report, recommendations made in the report, and the present land program of the federal government.

U. S. National resources board. Land planning committee   Supplementary report.
    Pts. 1, 4, 9. Washington, U. S. Govt. print. off., 1935-36   173.2 N214Su
        Contents: - Pt. 1. General conditions and tendencies influencing the
    nation's land requirements... prepared by the Division of land economics,
    Bureau of agricultural economics, Department of agriculture; Agricultural-
    industrial relations section, Agricultural adjustment administration,
    Bureau of agricultural engineering, Department of agriculture. 1936.
    47pp. Pt. 4. Land available through reclamation... prepared by the Bureau
    of agricultural engineering, Department of agriculture. 1936. 51pp.
    Pt. 9. Planning for wildlife in the United States... prepared by the
    Bureau of biological survey, Department of agriculture and the Forest
    service, Department of agriculture. 1935. 24pp.

Land Settlement - Palestine

Granovsky, Abraham. Land and the Jewish reconstruction in Palestine. Authorised
    translation. 201pp. Jerusalem, "Palestine and Near East" publications,
    1931. 282.2 G76
        Published also in Hebrew and German.
        This volume contains two essays - Land Settlement and development in
    Palestine, Some critical comments on the Report of Sir John Hope Simpson,
    and The Inalienability of land in Palestine.

Land Use - Saxony

Golf, Ehrhart. Die ernte in Sachsen und ihre verwendung dargestellt auf grund
    von 3903 buchführungsabschlüssen. 96pp. Dresden und Leipzig, T. Stein-
    kopff, 1935. (Die lage der landwirtschaft im freistaat Sachsen, hrsg.
    von Wolfgang Wilmanns... Hermann Isensee... Ergänzungsheft III)
    281.175 F18A no.3
        "Erscheint zugleich als dissertation in Leipzig" - verso of title page.
        Bibliography, p. [97]
        A study of land utilization and crop production according to sizes of
    farms in different sections of Saxony and of the use of the crops for seed,
    for the use of the farmer, for fodder or for sale.

Livestock and Meat - Canada

Canada. Dept. of agriculture. Live stock branch. Market services. Fifteenth
    annual market review 1934. Part 1. The live stock and meat trade.
    Part 2. Output of live stock by counties. 168pp. Ottawa, Pub. by the
    direction of the Honourable Robert Weir, Minister of agriculture, 1935.
    280.39 C16A

Market Research Sources

Bretherton, Rachel. Market research sources. A guide to information on
    domestic marketing. 253pp. Washington, U. S. Govt. print. off., 1936.
    (U. S. Bureau of foreign and domestic commerce. Domestic commerce series-
    55 (1936 ed.))   157.54 D71
        "Market Research Sources contains references to many new research

projects in the field of marketing. From the material which has been reviewed during the compilation of this volume, it is clear not only that, more and more, business and other organizations are engaging in distribution research but that the quality of their labors is constantly improving.

"The preparation of Market Research Sources is an attempt to bring together projects of current value in the field of marketing. Such a compilation serves two purposes – a source book for individuals interested in marketing research and a check upon the plans of others interested in conducting research projects in this broad field. Duplication of effort may thus be avoided." - Foreword.

Marshall, Alfred - Economics

Davenport, H. J. The economics of Alfred Marshall. 481pp. Ithaca, N. Y., Cornell university press; London, H. Milford, Oxford university press, 1935. CSO DC7E

Prepared for publication by a committee of the department of economics of Cornell university consisting of Paul T. Homan and M. Slade Kendrick, in collaboration with Margaret F. Milliken, formerly of the department of economics of Stanford university.

"This work is not only a critical appraisal of Marshall's economics, but it is also an epitome of Davenport's economics. Davenport, throughout his life, used Marshall's Principles as a point of reference in his teaching and thought; and in this book, posthumously published, he brought together the whole body of his criticism and observations upon Marshall."

Partial contents: Demand and supply mechanics; utility, price and measurement; cost of production; Price-determining and price-determined costs· Capital: The tests of land capital; Opportunity costs: Various land costs; quasi-rents: Equipment and effort; Employee and enterpriser labor returns; Normals and representatives; Costs in general; and Laws of return.

Planning - National - Belgium

Belgium. Bureau d'études sociales. L'exécution du plan du travail par le Bureau d'études sociales. 443pp. Anvers, Editions "De Sikkel", 1935. 280.172 B±1 Ed. 2

On cover: Deuxième édition.

This is a discussion of a plan adopted on December 25, 1933 by the Belgian Labor Party, member of the Socialist Labor Internationale to introduce in Belgium a system of planned economy with a view to increasing the purchasing power of the masses and insuring useful and remunerative work for all. It entails nationalization of credit, nationalization of basic industries, organization of transportation, the creation of an Economic Council and parliamentary reform. In other words, it is a plan suggested by the Labor Party for planned economy in Government. It is proposed that it be put into execution by the Bureau d'Etudes Sociales.

Canada. Dominion bureau of statistics. Internal trade branch. Prices and
price indexes, 1913-1934 (Commodities, securities, exchange, services,
import and export valuations) 187pp. Ottawa, J. O. Patenaude, printer
to the King's Excellent Majesty, 1936.   284.39 C15P

U. S. Dept. of labor. Bureau of labor statistics. Division of wholesale
prices. Wholesale prices. Quantity weighting factors used in calculating index numbers 1890 - 1934. 56pp., mimeogr. [Washington, D. C.]
Mar. 1935.   158.61 W62

Prices, Interest and Money

Wicksell, Knut. Interest and prices (Geldzins und güterpreise); a study of
the causes regulating the value of money. Translated from the German
by R. F. Kahn. With an Introduction by Professor Bertil Ohlin. Published on behalf of the Royal economic society. 219pp. London,
Macmillan and co., limited, 1936.   284 W63
    Prof. Bertil Ohlin in his introduction to this volume discusses the
character and importance of Knut Wicksell's monetary doctrines and
does not confine himself to the subject matter of the present volume.
From several of the concluding paragraphs of this introduction the following extracts have been taken:
    "Briefly expressed, Wicksell's doctrine - which on this point coin-
cided on the whole with Cassel's - amounted to this: if more money is
lent to investors, and used by them for real investment, than is saved,
then total purchasing power is increased, and prices rise. But if
equilibrium is maintained between savings and investment, purchasing
power is kept constant and prices cannot rise, at least not more than
in proportion to any reduction in the available volume of commodities.
Discussing the influence of war-time scarcity of commodities, Wicksell
observed that in this kind of reasoning is reflected a 'lack of a clear
conception of the term purchasing power. It is only money purchasing
power which here comes into question. It therefore stands to reason that
a general rise in the market prices of both goods and services itself
creates the purchasing power required for meeting the higher prices.'
In addition is needed only 'an increase in volume of the medium of exchange.
If all payments were made on a cheque basis this increase would, of course,
take place quite automatically.' The velocity of means of payments of
every kind would increase, for most people are more conservative in regard
to their habits of consumption than in regard to their habits of making
payments. Besides, a new demand for credit would arise from people who
wanted to increase their holdings of cash. It cannot be regarded as certain that credit restrictions will keep down such a demand for credit.
'A rise in the rate of interest is certainly an almost infallible means
of restricting the demand for credit on the part of all producers, but
it can hardly have a similar effect on those who merely desire to strengthen
their cash position in view of the increase in the volume of exchange.'
    "These remarks are, in my opinion, worthy of the greatest attention.
The question of the reaction of the monetary mechanism is placed in the
background and the movement of prices is discussed in terms of total in-

comes and the total supply of commodities. It thus becomes evident that,
as in the case discussed by Wicksell, a general rise in prices may well
come about because consumers increase their demand, in terms of money, for
consumption goods. This need not imply any reduction of savings, for it
increases net incomes defined, e.g., as in book-keeping; hence, it may
leave savings - the difference between income earned and income consumed -
unchanged and need not have any thing to do with too large credits to producers. The conclusion to be drawn, although it is not so formulated by
Wicksell, is that, even if there is equilibrium between savings and investment, as commonly understood, incomes and prices may rise or fall ad
libitum. Thus one of the very fundamentals of Wicksell's original theory
would have to be given up.

"Wicksell was, of course, quite right in pointing out that the fundamental concepts, not only of purchasing power or income, but also among
others of savings and investment, had not been defined sufficiently clearly.
When that has been done, it will, in my opinion, be possible to use the
Wicksellian approach to the study of price movements with greater advantage.
Although Wicksell's tools were deficient, his scientific genius led him to
an insight into the character and morphology of the movements of the price
system which will, I think, always be regarded as a great scientific
achievement, even when such concepts as his natural or normal rate of
interest have long since been discarded. Nobody would have rejoiced more
than Wicksell at the present questioning of the very fundamentals of
monetary theory, his own contributions included, had he lived to witness
it."

Among the chapter headings used are the following: Purchasing power of
money and average prices; Relative prices and money prices; The so-called
cost of production theory of money; The quantity theory and its opponents;
The velocity of circulation of money; The rate of interest as regulator of
commodity prices; International price relationships; Actual price movements
in the light of the preceding theory; and Practical proposals for the
stabilisation of the value of money. There is also an Appendix devoted to
a discussion of the monetary problem of the Scandinavian countries.

Recovery

Crowell, C. T. Recovery unlimited; the administration's monetary policy and
the current boom. 64pp. New York, Covici, Friede [1936]   280.12 C882
Partial contents: The monetary policy; A few words about relief;
The Agricultural Adjustment Administration's contribution to recovery;
The coming boom in home-building; Conflicting and overlapping taxation;

Rural Migration - Czechoslovakia

International labor office, Geneva. The rural exodus in Czechoslovakia; re-
sults of investigations made by Dr. H. Böker and F. W. von Bülow. 170pp.,
Geneva, 1935. (Studies and reports (of the I.L.O.) ser. K (Agriculture)
no. 13)   281.177 In8
At head of title: International Labour Office and International In-
stitute of Agriculture.
Studies on movements of agricultural population: II.
Have also copy issued without series title, published in Rome, by
International Institute of Agriculture and International Labour Office.
Partial contents: The Czechoslovak Republic: Economic background; Land
tenure and the agrarian reform; Migration movements of the rural popula-
tion; and Causes of migration movements and measures to restrict them.

Rural Relief & Rehabilitation

Allred, C. E., Luebke, B. H., Sanders, P. C., Matthews, M. T. and Tosch, C. A.
Rural relief and rehabilitation possibilities in Henderson county,
Tennessee. 55pp., mimeogr. [Knoxville, Tenn] March 10, 1936. (U. S.
Federal emergency relief administration. Report no. 7)   173.2 R27Rep no.7
        Issued in cooperation with Tennessee Agricultural Experiment Station,
Federal Works Progress Administration, Tennessee Welfare Commission.
        "This is one of a series of reports on representative counties,
chosen to bring out types of conditions that underlie the need for relief in the economic regions of Tennessee. Henderson County is representative of a predominately rural, cotton growing section of West
Tennessee in which an extensive sub-marginal land purchase area is
proposed.
        "The report is an economic and sociological analysis of all relief
cases in Henderson County. It is based on a schedule for each case,
a blank form of which is shown in the appendix.
        "The purposes of the survey were to secure information on such ques-
tions as: the extent to which certain economic and social factors are
related to the reasons for the opening of relief cases; the length of
time clients were kept on relief; the kind and amount of relief; the
reasons for closing; the possibilities for rehabilitation; and related
problems. The factors chosen for special study may be classified principally under three headings: characteristics of the relief population;
the resources of relief households; and the distribution and trends of
relief." - Introductory statement.

McCormick, T. C. Comparative study of rural relief and non-relief households.
141pp. Washington, D. C., 1935. (U. S. Works progress administration.
Division of social research. Research monograph II)   173.2 W89Re no.2

Rye - World Production & Trade

Mache, Artur. Der roggen in der weltwirtschaft mit besonderer berücksichtigung
Mitteleuropas. 20pp. Wien, 1935.   281.359 M18
        Diss. - Hochschule für welthandel, Wien. Auszug. (cf. slip tipped in
front of publication)
        Bibliography, pp. 19-20.
        This is a summary of the fourth part of the author's work of the same
name which was written as a thesis for the School of World Trade in Vienna.
It deals with world production and trade in rye with special reference to
the Central European countries. It is shown that the production of rye
is less than that of almost all other grains. Tables show to what extent
the importation of rye has increased or decreased in the main European importing countries from the period 1909/13 to 1933. While the importation
of rye into Spain, Portugal and Italy has almost ceased, Denmark has become the largest importer of rye in the world.

Woytinsky, Wladimir. Three sources of unemployment; the combined action of
   population changes, technical progress and economic development. 166pp.
   Geneva. 1935. (International Labour office. Studies and reports. Series
   C (Employment and unemployment) no. 20)   283 W91
   "The development of employment possibilities in the various countries
since the war has not been at all uniform, notwithstanding the fact that
three depressions have shaken the economic life of the world during these
sixteen years and that each of the depressions has been international in
character and spread to a number of countries.
   "The first of these depressions in point of time (1920-1922) was essentially the consequence of demobilisation. It began in the United States
about the middle of 1920 and spread successively to Great Britain, the
Scandinavian countries, Belgium, Italy and a few other countries. France,
Germany, the Danubian States and Japan escaped.
   "When this first wave of depression had passed, there was a spell of
reasonable economic activity in most countries. But it was not long before
a second depression set in (1926-1927) centring this time in Great Britain
and Germany...
   "The period that followed was one of economic recovery, but the boom was
not sufficiently marked to absorb all the existing unemployment.
   "Towards the end of 1929 came the world depression. From the United
States, where it first made itself felt, it spread like wildfire throughout
the world. Unemployment grew beyond all measure, reaching its peak in the
summer of 1932. Since then, employment has improved slightly in most of
the industrial countries; there are only a very few countries in which unemployment has continued to spread.
   "The characteristic feature of the period between the end of the war
and the beginning of the world depression was the fact that in many countries the development of employment failed to keep pace with the growth of
production. This was the case in the United States in the middle of a
period of marked prosperity, as also in Great Britain, with its standing
army of unemployed workers, in Germany during the years of economic
recovery, in Japan, the Scandinavian countries, etc.
   "It was during 1929 that the economic situation of the world was, comparatively speaking, most prosperous. But even at that date there were
more workers unemployed or on short time in many countries than there
usually were during periods of depression before the war. Even before the
world depression, the labour markets of these countries were much over-
crowded, their economic systems could not utilise all the available labour,
and unemployment was gradually spreading. During the war and the period
immediately following the armistice, there was practically no unemployment
in the world; there was enough work for all. But this did not mean that
the supply of and the demand for labour were really in stable equilibrium.
And such a position of equilibrium had first to be found if the economic
and social progress of the world after the war was to be guaranteed. No
such position was found, and in the preceding analysis it has been seen
how the balance was disturbed in various countries by the joint action of
demographic, technical and economic factors.
   "From the demographic point of view, two separate phases can be distinguished in the post-war period: up to 1930, the age groups entering occupational life were well stocked; after that date came the age groups from
the war years, when the birth-rate had been low...

-372-

"In the second phase, which covers the years of world-wide depression, the pressure on the labour market in Germany, Great Britain, France, Italy and some other countries was appreciably relieved by the decline in the influx of new labour. This to some extent mitigated the effects of the decrease in production on employment possibilities.

"The distribution of the population over the various occupational groups may be considered as a demographic problem in the wide sense. The gradual industrialisation of the population was a characteristic feature of the pre-war period: the proportion of the occupied population in industrial occupations rose, and these occupations were able to absorb the surplus supply of labour from rural areas.

"After the war, the industrialisation of the population ceased in many countries. In the United States, Great Britain, Japan and Norway, industrial occupations are so crowded that they have ceased to attract the new elements in the occupied population.

"Everywhere the power of industry to absorb the additions to the occupied population has waned. In every country that has been affected by the latest depression and that has statistics of its labour market it has been found that the seat of the disease of unemployment lies in mining and manufacturing industry (not including building). But this phenomenon is always obscured to some extent by the fact that wage earners in search of employment are gradually forced into other occupational groups...

"Before the depression, then, industrial production in the United States, Great Britain, Japan and Norway was increasing less rapidly than the individual output of the workers employed... The unemployment that had grown up in industrial occupations in the United States, Japan and Norway before the depression may therefore be considered technological unemployment. In the case of Great Britain the situation is rather more complex: the unduly slow growth of production was really the cause of the disproportion in the development of the various factors.

"On the other hand, no evidence of technological unemployment can be found in the case of Germany, France, Italy, Czechoslovakia, Sweden or Denmark. It is true that human labour was displaced by machinery in these countries too, but this was counterbalanced by an increase in production that absorbed the labour thus set free.

"The unemployment that has come into existence since 1929 is due entirely to the decline in industrial production. In every country this unemployment was at first concentrated in the same branch of the economic system — industry. The other groups of occupations were not affected until later, and then much less acutely.

"The amount of work to be performed during the depression kept pace with the falling rate of industrial production, but the undertakings were able, by spreading employment over a larger number of workers, to retain in their service a fraction of those who would otherwise have been dismissed as superfluous. When estimating the extent of unemployment during the depression, therefore, one must add to the official number of registered unemployed persons both those who are on short time and those 'invisible' unemployed persons who did not apply to the exchanges because they did not expect to get any help from them.

-373-

"The tecnological unemployment of 1929 might be thought to be insignif-
icant and harmless when compared with this disastrous unemployment of
economic origin. But nothing could be more mistaken than such a conclusion.
The recent depression might never have reached such alarming preportions if
the economic equilibrium of the world had not first of all been upset by
the growth of unemployment right in the middle of a period of economic
recovery and prosperity." - Conclusions.

Wages - Agriculture - Sweden

Stockholm. Högskolan. Socialvetenskapliga institutet. Wages, cost of living
and national income in Sweden, 1860-1930, by the staff of the Institute
for social sciences, University of Stockholm. v. 2. Wages in Sweden,
1860-1930. Pt. 2. Government and municipal services, agriculture and
forestry, the general movement of wages in Sweden 1860-1930. 393pp.
London, P. S. King & son, ltd. [1935]   280.173 St6
     The Section on agriculture and forestry contains: Working hours in ag-
riculture 1860-1914; Wages in agriculture, 1860-1914; Wages in agriculture,
1911-1928. The Section, The General Movement of Wages in Sweden 1860-
1930, contains a chapter, Industrial Changes and the Trend of Wages in
Agriculture and Forestry.

Western Farm Economics Association

Western farm economics association. Proceedings... 8th annual meeting,
August 12 and 13, 1935. 102pp., mimeogr. Corvallis, Ore., Oregon
state agricultural college [1935]   280.83 W52
     Contents: Laissez Faire in theory and practice, by George M. Peterson;
An evaluation of some phases of the current agricultural program in terms
of the economic theory involved, by M. R. Benedict; The place of agricultural planning in national economy, by J. M. Tinley; Extension work as
related to regional planning, by L. M. Vaughan; Some economic aspects
of marketing agreements for fruits and vegetables, by H. R. Wellman; Some
experiences with marketing agreements in Washington, by E. F. Dummeier;
The organization of land use planning in Oregon, by A. S. Burrier; General
aspects of land use planning, by David Weeks; Aims and objectives of The
Resettlement Administration, by Rex E. Willard; Land use planning, by
H. E. Selby; The rural rehabilitation program, by Leslie S. Sorensen;
Objectives and types of development on submarginal land, by Harry G. Ade,
Production control, by O V. Wells; and Proposed changes in agricultural
adjustment programs, by E. R. Jackman.

Wool Industry - World Situation

Despature, Paul. L'industrie lainière, son organisation corporative, nationale
et internationale. Le Comite central de la laine. La Fédération lainiere
internationale. Préface de m. C.-J. Gignoux. 398pp. Paris, Abbeville,
Impr. F. Paillart, 1935.   286.345 D46
     Bibliography, pp. [381]-389.
     In this monument to the wool industry, as the writer of the introduction
calls it, the importance of the professional organization of all the members of a trade or profession is stressed, especially as a means of economic recovery. That this has been recognized and put into practice by

the wool industry, not only on a national but an international basis, is shown to be an important contribution to world economy.

A rapid survey of the wool situation, its production, marketing, and transformation precedes the study of the corporative organization of the wool industry and of the organization and operation of the Comite Central de la Laine and the International Wool Federation.

BIBLIOGRAPHIES

Gardner, Chastina. Periodicals issued by farmers' marketing and purchasing association. 16pp. Feb. 1936. (U. S. Farm credit administration. Cooperative division, Research, service, and educational series. Miscellaneous report no. 5) 166.3 M68 no.5

George Washington and agriculture. A classified list of annotated references with an introductory note, by Everett E. Edwards. 77pp. Feb. 1936. (U. S. Dept. of agriculture. Library. Bibliographical contributions. no. 22 (Ed.2) Feb. 1936)

McNamara, Katherine, comp. Bibliography of planning, 1928-1935; a supplement to Manual of planning information, 1928, by Theodora Kimball Hubbard and Katherine McNamara. 232pp. Cambridge, Harvard university press, 1936 (Harvard city planning studies X) 98.5 K56 Suppl. 1928-35
   May be purchased from Harvard university press, Cambridge, Mass. $3.50.
   This outstanding bibliography has been published as one of the Harvard City Planning Studies although it includes, in addition to city planning, references to state, regional and national planning in the United States and also a valuable section on planning in other countries. A selected list of periodicals devoting space to planning is included, and also a list of Organizations active in promoting planning in the U. S. A."

Selected list of American agricultural books, compiled in the U. S. Department of agriculture Library. 41pp., mimeogr. Mar. 1936.

U. S. Dept. of the interior. Office of education. Summaries of studies in agricultural education. An annotated bibliography of 373 studies in agricultural education with a classified subject index and a general evaluation. 196pp. Washington, U. S. Govt. print. off., 1935.
   (U. S. Federal board for vocational education. Vocational education bulletin no. 180) 173 V85B no.180
      U. S. Federal Board for Vocational Education. Agricultural series no.47.

SELECTED LIST OF RECENT REVIEWS

Compiled by M. I. Herb

Astor, W. A., 2d viscount. The agricultural dilemma: a report of an enquiry organised by Viscount Astor and Mr. B. Seebohm Rowntree. 1935.
   Reviewed by W. C. D. Dampier in Econ. Jour. 46 (181): 108-109. March 1936.

Baird. Frieda, and Benner, C. L. Ten years of intermediate credits. 1933.
    (Institute of economics of the Brookings institution. Publication no. 48)
        Reviewed by C. J. Bradley in Social Forces 14 (3): 454-455. March
    1936.

Beck, P. G., and Forster, M. C. Six rural problem areas. Relief - resources -
    rehabilitation. 1935. (U. S. Federal emergency relief administration.
    Division of research, statistics and finance. Research section. Research
    monograph 1)
        Reviewed by G. W. Forster in South. Econ. Rev. 2 (3): 78-79. January
    1936.

Fetanson, Anne, Gray, R. D., and Hussey, Miriam. Prices in colonial Pennsyl-
    vania. 1935. (Half-title: Industrial research department, Wharton school
    of finance and commerce. University of Pennsylvania, Philadelphia.
    Research studies XXVI.)
        Reviewed by N.S.B. Gras in Amer. Econ. Rev. 26 (1): 145. March 1936.
        Reviewed by Elizabeth W. Gilboy in Amer. Acad. Polit. and Social Sci.
    Ann. 184: 223-224. March 1936.

Bohn, Frank, and Ely, R. T. The great change; work and wealth in the new age.
    1935.
        Reviewed by W. A. Frost in The People's Money 1 (1): 39. June 1935.

Cauley, T. J. Agrarianism; a program for farmers.   1935.
        Reviewed by S. D. Myers, Jr. in Southwest Rev. 20 (4): 6-12, "books"
    section. Summer 1935.

Cole, G. D. H. Economic planning. 1935.
        Reviewed by J. G. Evans in Amer. Econ. Rev. 26 (1): 160-161. March 1936.
        Reviewed by F. H. Bunting in Works Progress Admin. Research Library
    Abstracts, Foreign. Mar. 18, 1935, pp. 22-24.

Cover J. H. Retail price behavior. [1935] (Half-title: Studies in business
    administration. [The School of business. The University of Chicago] v. 5,
    no.2.
        Reviewed by A. W. Zelomek in Amer. Statis. Assoc. Jour. 31 (193): 239.
    March 1936.

Douglas, P. H. Controlling depressions. [1935]
        Reviewed by Nathaniel Gold in The People's Money 1 (1): 38, 39. June
    1935.

Edgeworth, K. E. The price level; a further problem in national planning.
    [1935]
        Reviewed by Harold Barger in Econ. Jour. 46 (181): 127. March 1936.

Einzig, Paul. World finance since 1914. 1935.
        Reviewed briefly in The People's Money 1 (4): 155, 156. September 1935.

Ezekiel, Mordecai. $2,500 a year; from scarcity to abundance. [1936]
        Reviewed briefly in Fertilizer Review 11 (1): 15. January - February -
    March 1936.

Foreman, Clark, and Ross, Michael. The consumer seeks a way. [1935]
    Reviewed by Maurice William in The People's Money 1 (1): 39, 40.
    June 1935.

Gayer, A. D. Monetary policy and economic stabilization; a study of the gold
    standard. 1935.
        Reviewed by K. J. Binns in Econ. Rec. 11 (21): 304-306. December 1935.

Goodrich, C. L., Allen, B. W., and Hayes, Marion. Migration and planes of
    living, 1920-1934. 1935. (Half-title: Bulletin no. 2. Study of population
    redistribution. Industrial research dept., Wharton school of finance and
    commerce, University of Pennsylvania)
        Reviewed by Eugene Van Cleef in Amer. Econ. Rev. 26 (1): 157-158. March
    1936.

Great Britain. Ministry of health. Committee on garden cities and satellite
    towns. Report of Departmental committee. 1935.
        Reviewed in U. S. Dept. Labor. Bur. Labor Statis. Monthly Labor Rev.
    41 (6): 1521-1523. December 1935.

Great Britain. Ministry of Health. Committee on qualifications, recruitment,
    training and promotion of local government officers. Report to the Min-
    ister of Health... 1934.
        Reviewed by A. W. McM. in Social Serv. Rev. 9 (1): 178-180. March 1935.

Haight, F. A. French import quotas, a new instrument of commercial policy.
    1935. (Half-title: London school of economics and political science.
    Studies in economics and commerce. No. 6)
        Reviewed by Ethel B. Dietrich in Amer. Statis. Assoc. Jour. 31 (193):
    224-225. March 1936.

Holland, W. L., ed. Commodity control in the Pacific area; a symposium on re-
    cent experience. [1935]
        Reviewed by G. L. Wood in Econ. Rec. 11 (21): 300-303. December 1935.

Hunt, R. L. A history of farmer movements in the Southwest, 1873-1925. [1935?]
        Reviewed by W. E. Morgan in Amer. Econ. Rev. 26 (1): 110-111. March 1936.

Johnson, C. S., Embree, E. R., and Alexander, W. W. The collapse of cotton
    tenancy; a summary of field studies and statistical surveys 1933-35. 1935.
        Reviewed by Wilson Gee in South. Econ. Jour. 2 (3): 75-78. January 1936.

Keynes, J. M. The general theory of employment, interest and money. 1936.
        Reviewed by E.A.G.R. in The Economist 122 (4827): 471, 472. Feb. 29, 1936.
        Reviewed by G.D.H. Cole in New Statesman and Nation (n.s.) 11 (260): 220-
    222. Feb. 15, 1936.
        Reviewed in Manchester Guardian Weekly, Feb. 28, 1936. (Clipping)

Kolb, J. H., and Brunner, E. deS. A study of rural society; its organization and
    changes. [1935]
        Reviewed by S. H. Hobbs, Jr. in Social Forces 14 (3): 453-454. March 1936.

Layton. Sir Walter, and Crowther. Geoffrey. An introduction to the study of
    prices. 1935.
        Reviewed by D. B. Copland in Econ. Rec. 11 (21): 311-313. December 1935.

League of nations. Economic intelligence service. World economic survey, fourth
    year, 1934-35. 1935. (Series of League of Nations Publications. II.
    Economic and financial II. A. 14)
        Prepared by J. B. Condliffe.
        Reviewed by D. B. Copland in Econ. Rec. 11 (21): 303-304. December 1935.

Molyneaux, Peter. What economic nationalism means to the South. 1933.
    (World affairs pamphlets no. 4)
        Reviewed by R. B. Vance in South. Econ. Jour. 2 (3): 79-80. January 1936.

Moulton, H. G. The formation of capital. 1935. (Half-title: The Institute
    of economics of the Brookings institution. Publication no. 59)
        Reviewed by H. S. in The People's Money 1 (2): 47. July 1935.
        Reviewed by H. P. Willis in Amer. Statis. Assoc. Jour. 31 (193): 218-220.
    March 1936.

Nash, E. F. Machines and purchasing power. 1935.
        Reviewed by Gilbert Walker in Econ. Jour. 46 (181): 129-130. March 1936.

Passfield, Sidney James Webb, baron, and Webb, Beatrice. Soviet communism: a
    new civilisation. 1936.
        Reviewed by A. C. Pigou in Econ. Jour. 46 (181): 88-97. March 1936 in an
    article entitled "The Webbs on Soviet Communism."
        Reviewed by G. S. Counts in New York Herald Tribune. Books, 12 (27): 1-2.
    Mar. 8, 1936.

Robbins, L. C. The great depression. 1934.
        Reviewed by G. E. McLaughlin in Amer. Statis. Assoc. Jour. 31 (193):
    220-223. March 1936.

Smith, J. G. Economic planning and the tariff. 1934.
        Reviewed briefly in The People's Money 1 (5): 198. October 1935.

Soddy, Frederick. The role of money; what it should be, contrasted with what
    it has become. [1935]
        Reviewed by Herbert Harris in The People's Money 1 (2): 46. July 1935.

Soltau, R. H. An outline of European economic development. [1935]
        Reviewed briefly in The Economist 122 (4830): 648. March 21, 1936.

Taylor, A. E. The new deal and foreign trade. 1935.
        Reviewed by C. E. Griffin in Amer. Statis. Assoc. Jour. 31 (193): 214-
    217. March 1936.
        Reviewed briefly in The People's Money 1 (5): 198. October 1935.

Todd, J. A. The science of prices. A handbook of economics (production, consump
    tion and value) Fourth impression - revised. 1935.
        Reviewed briefly by Harold Barger in Econ. Jour. 46 (181): 127. March
    1936.

Economic in Character

Compiled by Katharine Jacobs

Circular*

383. Market classes and grades of lambs and sheep, by L. B. Burk... C.E.
Gibbons... and M. T. Foster. 35pp. March 1936.

Miscellaneous Publication*

234. Workers in subjects pertaining to agriculture in state agricultural colleges and experiment stations, 1935 - 36, by Mary A. Agnew. 133pp.
March 1936.

Statistical Bulletin*

52. Grade, staple length, and tenderability of cotton in the United States,
1928-29 to 1933-34, prepared in the Division of cotton marketing... in
cooperation with state agricultural agencies. 122pp. March 1936.

Technical Bulletin*

503. Effects of gin-saw speed and seed-roll density on quality of cotton lint
and operation of gin stands, by Charles A. Bennett... and Francis L. Gerdes.
40pp. February 1936.

Radio Talks of Secretary Wallace*

In the wake of the flood, remarks... broadcast during the Department of agricul-
ture period, National farm and home hour, March 24, 1936. 5pp., mimeogr.
Remarks [concerning AAA payments to farmers under past programs] ... over the
National farm and home hour... April 7, 1936. 6pp., mimeogr.
Remarks [on the "back-to-the-land movement"] over the National farm and home
hour... Apr. 14, 1936. 6pp., mimeogr.
Remarks [on the new soil conservation program] over the National farm and home
hour...March 31, 1936. 5PP., mimeogr.

Publications of the Bureau of Agricultural Economics (Mimeographed)**

General review Wisconsin potato season 1935-36. 6pp. [Mar. 26, 1936] (Issued
in cooperation with Wisconsin. Dept. of agriculture and markets)
George Washington and agriculture. A classified list of annotated references
with an introductory note, comp. by Everett E. Edwards. Ed. 2 77pp.,
mimeogr. Washington, D. C., February 1936. (U. S. Dept. of agriculture.
Library. Bibliographical contributions no. 22 Ed. 2)

---

*Requests for these publications should be addressed to the Office of Informa-
tion, U. S. Department of Agriculture, Washington, D. C.
**These publications are issued in small editions for immediate use in official
work and are not for general distribution.

Imports of agricultural products into the United States and estimated acreage
displaced. 13pp. Apr. 7, 1936.
International universal cotton standards conference of 1936, general meetings
of March 9 and 10, 1936. Washington, D. C. 19pp.
Marketing California asparagus; season of 1935, by W. F. Cox [and] W. L. Jackson.
31pp. February 1936. (Issued in cooperation with California. Dept. of
agriculture. Bureau of market news)
Marketing Salinas-Watsonville lettuce, summary of 1935 season, by L. T. Kirby.
6pp. April 1936.
(Issued in cooperation with California Dept. of agriculture, Market
news service)
Marketing Texas tomatoes; brief review of the 1935 season, by W. D. Googe. 17pp.
March 1936. (Issued in cooperation with Texas. Dept. of agriculture.
Markets and warehouse division)
Marketing the Michigan apple crop. Brief review of the 1935 season, by R. E.
Keller. 6pp. Mar. 23, 1936. (Issued in cooperation with Michigan Dept.
of agriculture, Bureau of foods and standards)
Marketing the Michigan pear crop: brief review of the 1935 season, by R. E.
Keller. 6pp. [1936?] (Issued in cooperation with Michigan. Dept. of
agriculture. Bureau of foods and standards)
Marketing western and central New York lettuce; summary of the 1935 season,
by A. L. Thomas. 16pp. March 1936.
Review Idaho potato season 1935-36. 5pp. Apr. 9, 1936.
Summary 1936 strawberry season, by R. Maynard Peterson. 4pp. Apr. 11, 1936.
(Issued in cooperation with Florida State marketing bureau)
Supplement to the Agricultural outlook. 9pp. Mar. 23, 1936.
United States standards for potatoes (effective April 6, 1936) 8pp. [1936]
Wholesale market prices at Los Angeles for certain fruits and vegetables 1935.
16pp. [1936?] (Issued in cooperation with California. Dept. of agricul-
ture. Market news service)

Publications of the Agricultural Adjustment Administration*

Summary of provisions of the Soil conservation and domestic allotment act. 4pp. |
March 1936. (G-52)

Radio Talks (Mimeographed)**

The agricultural conservation program in the northeast, by H. B. Boyd. 3pp.
Apr. 10, 1936.
New plan for marketing loan cotton, by Paul A. Porter. 2pp. Apr. 14, 1936.

Miscellaneous (Mimeographed)***

An appraisal of the programs in recreation, by C. B. Smith. 6pp. (Issued by
Extension service)
Presented at Regional extension conference, Eastern states, Boston, Mass.,
February 19 to 21, 1936.

---

* Requests for this publication should be addressed to the Agricultural Adjust-
ment Administration, U. S. Department of Agriculture, Washington, D. C.
** May be obtained from U. S. Department of Agriculture, Office of Information,
Radio Service.
*** Requests for these publications should be addressed to the issuing office.

The farm family as the unit for extension work, by Grace E. Frysinger. 5pp.
February 1936. (Issued by U. S. Dept. of agriculture. Extension service.
Division of cooperative extension. Extension service circular 236)
The income approach to extension programs, by R. B. Corbett. 6pp. March
1936. (Issued by U. S. Dept. of agriculture. Extension service. Division of cooperative extension. Extension service circular 238)
Quality affecting feeding value of alfalfa hay and suggestions for use in
purchasing alfalfa for dairy feeding, prepared by E. O. Pollock, Hay,
feed and seed division, Bureau of agricultural economics, in collabora-
tion with Bureau of dairy industry, U. S. Department of agriculture. 4pp.
March 5, 1936. (Issued by Extension service)
Selected list of American agricultural books compiled in the U. S. Depart-
ment of agriculture Library. 41pp. Mar. 1936.
Sociological aspects of the new land program, by Jacob G. Lipman, Dean, State
college of agriculture and mechanic arts, New Brunswick, N.J. 4pp.
(Issued by Extension service. Division of cooperative extension)
"Presented at Northeastern states extension conference, held in
Boston, Mass., February 19 to 21, 1936."
What are the aims in rural living, by H. W. Hochbaum. 8pp. March 1936.
(Issued by U. S. Dept. of agriculture. Extension service. Division of
cooperative extension. Extension service circular 237)

U. S. RESETTLEMENT ADMINISTRATION

Better land for better living. 4pp. [1936]
Farm debt adjustment. 4pp. [1936]
Helping the farmer help himself. 4pp. [1936]
"How the Resettlement administration is functioning and should function in
the agricultural program of the south and its relation with the other
state and federal agencies." By L. C. Gray. 15pp. 1936. mimeogr.
A paper read before the conference of Southern agricultural workers,
Jackson, Mississippi, February 6, 1936.
The social and economic implications of the national land program, by L. C.
Gray. 25pp. Dec. 28, 1935. mimeogr.
A paper read before the American sociological society, New York
city, December 28, 1935.
A sound land use policy for the south, by L. C. Gray. 11pp. 1936. mimeogr.
A paper read before the conference of Southern agricultural workers,
Jackson, Mississippi, February 7, 1936.

---

* Requests for these publications should be addressed to the Resettlement
Administration, Arlington Hotel, Washington, D. C.

Compiled by Mary F. Carpenter

California

California. Department of agriculture. Proceedings, sixty-eighth convention
of California fruit growers and farmers. Sacramento, California, December
4, 5, and 6, 1935. Calif. Dept. Agr. Monthly Bull. v. 25, no. 1. 208pp.
Jan.-Mar., 1936. Sacramento. 1936.

California. State relief administration. Division of research and surveys.
Survey of agricultural labor requirements in California, 1935. 253pp.,
mimeogr. Sacramento? 1935.
    A study of the monthly labor requirements of the major agricultural
counties of California.
    Includes a section on individual crop labor requirements.

Schneider, J. B., and Thompson, J. M. Truck crops. Calif. Agr. Col. Timely
Agr. Outlooks, no. 4, 4pp., mimeogr. Berkeley.1936.

Connecticut

Connecticut. Agricultural experiment station, Storrs. Report... for the year
ending June 30, 1935. Conn. Agr. Expt. Sta. Bull. 207, 36PP. Storrs.
1935.
    Agricultural economics, pp. 3-6.

Iowa

Iowa corn research institute. Contributions... v. 1, no. 1. 158pp.
Ames, Iowa Agr. Expt. Sta., January 1935.
    Reprinted from Iowa State College Journal of Science v. IX, no.3,
pp. 409-566. 1935.
    Includes: The future of corn production, by H. D. Hughes, pp. 151-
152; and Six decades of corn improvement and the future outlook by H. A.
Wallace, pp. 153-158.

Kansas

Kansas. State board of agriculture. Beef cattle in Kansas. Kans. State
Bd. Agr. Rept. v. 52, no. 211B. 289pp. September 1934. Topeka. 1935.
    Includes some early history of the state's beef industry and a chapter
on marketing.

Kentucky

Kentucky. State tax commission. Seventeenth annual report, 1934. 135pp.
Frankfort. 1935?
    Includes number and value of livestock and value of other farm
property by counties for 1934.

Michigan

Michigan. Department of agriculture. Crop report for Michigan. [January 1936] Annual crop summary, 1935 and crop statistics, 1925-1935. 43pp. Lansing. 1936.
    In cooperation with U. S. Bureau of Agricultural Economics.

Minnesota

Johnson, E. C. The farm real estate situation in Minnesota. Minn. Univ. Agr. Ext. Div. Minn. Farm Business Notes, no. 159, pp. 1-3, mimeogr. University Farm, St. Paul. 1936.

Montana

Renne, R. R., and Kraenzel, C. F. Readjusting Montana's agriculture. III. Population resources and prospects. Mont. Agr. Expt. Sta. Bull. 309, 19pp. Bozeman, 1936.

Renne, R. R. Readjusting Montana's agriculture. IV. Land ownership and tenure. Mont. Agr. Expt. Sta. Bull. 310, 24pp. Bozeman. 1936.
    Includes several state maps and one of Petroleum county which shows the ownership pattern and "is fairly typical of many areas of Montana, particularly the eastern two-thirds."

Saunderson, M. H. Readjusting Montana's agriculture. V. Economic changes in Montana's range livestock production. Mont. Agr. Expt. Sta. Bull. 311, 30pp. Bozeman. 1936.
    Contains discussion of present situation and some alternatives for adjustment in land charges and land values, land ownership and tenure, relation between livestock numbers and range capacity, ranch organization, and size of ranches.
    Includes maps of Wheatland, Madison, Golden Valley, Blaine, and Custer counties.

Slagsvold, P. L. Readjusting Montana's agriculture. II. Montana farm prices. Mont. Agr. Expt. Sta. Bull. 308, 16pp. Bozeman. 1936.

Nebraska

Nebraska. State board of agriculture. Annual report...for the year 1935. 725pp. Lincoln. 1936.
    Contains proceedings of the annual meeting, January 15-16, 1935 and also those of state agricultural organizations' conventions.

Nevada

Fleming, C. E., and Brennen, C. A. Ranch and range balance. The public lands and ranch stability in Nevada. Nev. Agr. Expt. Sta. Bull. 142, 22pp. Reno. 1936.
    The ranching areas in the Ruby and Santa Rosa divisions of the Humboldt National Forest are compared.

New Jersey. Milk control board. Report... May 24, 1933-June 30, 1935, 5
    Trenton. 1935.

New Mexico

Hollinger, E. C. The effect of population and occupation shifts on rural
    New Mexico. Agr. Col. Ext. Service, E. M. no. 19, 24pp., mimeogr. St
    College. 1935.
        "The facts used in this discussion are mainly selected from data
    by O. E. Baker, U. S. Bureau of Agricultural Economics, and presente
    meetings of the State Club Leaders' Conference at the National 4-H C
    campment at Washington, D.C., last summer."

New York

Efferson, J. N. A preliminary report of a land utilization study in Gene
    county, New York, N. Y. (Cornell) Agr. Col. AE 124, 27pp., mimeogr.
    Ithaca. 1936.

Hudson, S. C. A classification and summary of research projects in dairy
    ing, including a classified list of research projects in the marketi
    dairy products in the United States and Canada. 33PP., mimeogr. It
    N. Y. Cornell Agr. Col. Dept. of Agr. Econ., and Farm Mangt. 1936.

Keepper, W. E. Preliminary report of the land utilization study in Steub
    county, New York. N. Y. (Cornell) Agr. Col. AE 123, 24pp., mimeogr.
    Ithaca. 1936.

New York (Cornell) State college of agriculture, Department of agricultur
    economics and farm management. Farm economics, no. 94. Ithaca. Mar
    1936.
        Partial contents: Livestock on farms, pp. 2294-2295, 2301-2305, b
    G. F. Warren and F. A. Pearson; Pounds of milk required to buy a cow
    New York, pp. 2305-2306, by L. C. Cunningham; Variations in methods
    transporting important fruits and vegetables to market, as reported
    939 New York growers, season, 1933-34, pp.2306-2307, by M. P. Rasmus
    Gross margins taken by retail stores, pp.2308-2309, by O. H. Maughn;
    Farm study courses in agricultural economics and farm management, pp
    2313, by P. J. Findlen; Roads in nine New York counties, pp. 2313-23
    T. E. LaMont; Incomes of dairy farmers in New York. p. 2316, by L. C
    Cunningham.

Scoville, G. P. Apple varieties in New York state. N. Y. (Cornell) Agr.
    AE 120, 19pp., mimeogr. Ithaca. 1936.
        Economic statistical data by varieties.
        Presented at the eighty-first annual meeting New York State Horti
    Society, Rochester, N. Y., January 15, 1936.

- 384 -

Williamson, P. S. Prices and yields of apple varieties. From a study of 47.
    Ulster county farms, Hudson Valley, New York. N. Y. (Cornell) Agr.
    Col. AE 122. 18pp., mimeogr. Ithaca. 1936.

North Carolina

North Carolina. Department of agriculture. Farm forecaster; Crop and livestock
    report for North Carolina, no. 68, 16pp. Raleigh. February 1936.
        In cooperation with the U. S. Bureau of Agricultural Economics.
        Semi-annual issue which includes a 1934-1935 farm census survey by
    counties.

Ohio

Ohio. Agricultural experiment station. Fifty-fourth annual report, 1934-1935.
    Ohio Agr. Expt. Sta. Bull. 501, 133pp. Wooster. 1936.
        Department of Rural Economics, pp. 95-100.

Oklahoma

Oklahoma. Agricultural experiment station. Current farm economics, v. 9, no. 1.
    Stillwater, February. 1936.
        Partial contents: Geographical variability in types of farming in
    Oklahoma, pp. 3-15, by Peter Nelson; An effective homestead exemption
    will reduce farm tenancy, pp. 16-19, by J. T. Sanders; The community
    sale, pp. 19-21, by A. W. Jacob; Response of cotton prices to cotton
    acreage control, dollar devaluation and the 12-cent loan, pp.22-28, by
    T. R. Hedges; Lessons from the old cotton program for the new program,
    pp. 29-36, by J. T. Sanders.

Virginia

Virginia. Polytechnic institute. Virginia farm economics. no. 35. Blacksburg.
    March 1936.
        Partial contents: Cost of producing canning tomatoes in Virginia in
    1935, pp. 536-537, 540-541, by W. J. Nuckolls, Jr., L. B. Dietrick, and
    L. C. Beamer; The cost of terracing farm land cooperatively, pp. 542-549,
    by G. H. Ward; Position of the Virginia poultry industry as indicated by
    the relation of feed costs and egg prices to poultry production per bird,
    pp. 549-550, by J. L. Maxton.

Wisconsin

Ebling, W. H., Gilbert, S. J., and Gustafson, G. T. Wisconsin agriculture.
    Wis. Dept. Agr. and Markets. Bull. 150, 109pp. Madison. 1934.
        Wisconsin Crop and Livestock Reporting Service. In cooperation with U.S.
    Bureau of Agricultural Economics.
        Similar to Bulletin 140 issued in 1932. Contains statistical data
    by counties for 1932 and 1933 and some new material which includes index
    of prices paid by farmers for a series of years, milk prices and other
    data on the dairy industry not in previous bulletins, and in the chapter
    on "Land and its uses" are shown a number of maps and tabulations which
    have not been previously available. (Adapted from the preface.)

Compiled by Louise O. Bercaw and A. M. Hannay

Agrarian Reform - Estonia

Brenkamp. J., La politique agraire en Esthonie. Rev. Écon. Internationale,
28. année, v. 1. pp. 174-182. (Published by the Institut Économique
International, Palais d'Egmont, Brussels, Belgium.)

Land tenure and agrarian reform in Estonia are briefly discussed.
The results of the agrarian reform law of October 25, 1919 are sketched. It is shown that this law has transferred farms belonging to
large landowners to the ownership of 25,000 farmers who had been cultivating them. Five thousand agricultural workers have received
sufficient land to assure them a living without supplementary work.
In this way a means of livelihood has been provided for approximately
100.000 persons, including the farmers and their families.

In addition the number of those who have purchased farms has been
increased to 7,000. The use for this purpose of land hitherto reserved for the State will increase this number to 10,000, including
40,000 persons.

41,000 new properties have been created and 7,000 pieces of
building land have been distributed. The latter which are near
stations and small towns have provided for more than 7,000 families
a permanent home and an opportunity to raise foodstuffs in their
gardens. Almost 10,000 hectares belonging to the State have been
distributed, and it is/calculated that this gift of land has benefited
20,000 families, or 60,000 persons.

The author stresses the advantages that have accrued to the
Estonian people and the country from the operation of the agrarian
reform. A modification of the agrarian law is in preparation with
a view to making it more effective by providing for irrigation, road
building, and land reclamation.

Agricultural Adjustment Program - Virginia

Tate, L. B. The agricultural adjustment program in Virginia. Univ. Va.
News Letter, v. 12, no. 12, March 15, 1936. (Published in University,
Va.)

The writer asks and answers the question, Of what benefit was the
A.A.A. program to the Virginia farmers who participated in its
activities and to the State as a whole?

He concludes as follows: "While it is impossible to say definitely
how much of the increase in farm income is due to the agricultural
adjustment program, it may be said with a fair degree of confidence
that the program, as an emergency measure, was effective in reducing
the supplies of cotton, tobacco, etc., and influential in stimulating
prices; and was at least one of several important factors contributing
to economic recovery."

The article is accompanied by two tables which show AAA expenditures
in Virginia, 1933 through 1935; and AAA rental and benefit payments in
Virginia, by counties, 1933, 1934, 1935, and total for the period.

Agricultural and Industrial Bank - Iraq.

An agricultural and industrial bank in Iraq. Indus. and Labour Inform. 57(2):
28-29. Jan. 13, 1936. (Issued by International Labour Office, Geneva,
Switzerland. Distributed in U. S. by World Peace Foundation, 8 West 40th
Street, New York, N. Y.)
"A Law issued in Iraq on 14 September 1935 provides for the creation
of an agricultural and industrial bank, the measure will come into
force ... not later than 1 April 1936 ... With regard to agriculture,
it will make loans to farmers enabling them to meet the expenses of
cultivation and harvesting, purchase implements and cattle, reclaim or
improve land, plant or improve fruit trees, and market their crops; it
will also sell agricultural requirements on credit, act as agent for
the sale of farm produce, and found and administer establishments for
the cleaning and grading of crops... The Government will aid in the
establishment of the bank by advancing sums not exceeding 150,000 dinars
or by subscribing part of the share capital... Further, the Government
will issue regulations concerning the bank's transactions ... and provide that the maximum period of loans shall not exceed 10 years."

Agricultural Credit - France

Tardy, Louis. Le crédit agricole, le warrantage agricole et les décrets-
lois. La Vie Agricole et Rurale 25(3): 45-48. Feb. 2, 1936. (Published by J. B. Baillière & Fils, 19, Rue Hautefeuille, Paris (6e),
France.)
Two laws of September 28, 1935 refer to the organization and
functioning of agricultural credit and the acceptance of the farmer's
agricultural products as security for loans. The maximum period of
time for which intermediate and long-term loans may be made is extended,
the age limit for repayment is extended, and the rate of interest for
short-term loans, fixed at 4 percent for 1935, will be determined for
the following years by a ministerial order after consultation with the
National Bank of Agricultural Credit. Measures are adopted to increase
the security of the operations of the agricultural credit banks.

Agricultural Credit - Madras

The sixth conference of land mortgage banks in Madras. 23rd November, 1935.
Indian Co-op. Rev. 2(1): 114-120. January 1936. (Published by All-
India Co-operative Institutes' Association, Farhatbagh, Mylapore,
Madras, India.)
Extracts are given from two speeches made at the Conference. While
Madras has taken the "lead in land mortgage banking ... the problem
of long-term credit has just begun to be tackled, and the number of
agriculturists benefitted is an infinitesimal fraction of the number
crying for relief... A plan of productive credit has yet to be drawn
up, which is perhaps difficult in a time of depression."

Agricultural Credit - United States

Myers, W. I. Meeting production credit. Nation's Agr. 11(6): 10, 27. March
1936. (Published at 58 E. Washington St., Chicago, Ill.)

The writer describes the development of production credit associations and the benefits derived from production credit among farmers during the last two years.

Agricultural Indebtedness

Nicotra, Giovanni. Crise agricole et crédit agricole. Rev. Econ. Internationale, 2S. année, v. 1, no. 1, pp. 49-75. January 1936. (Published by the Institut Économique International, Palais d'Egmont, Brussels, Belgium.)

A study of post-war agricultural indebtedness and measures adopted for its relief in Bulgaria, Rumania, Yugoslavia, Poland, Hungary, Czechoslovakia, Germany, the United States, and Italy.

Agricultural Indebtedness - India

Narayana Prasad, P. S. Debt conciliation boards - need for compulsion. Indian Co-op. Rev. 2(1): 31-36. January 1936. (Published by All-India Co-operative Institutes' Association, Farhatbagh, Mylapore, Madras, India.)

Deals with the question of compelling creditors to accept the decisions of the Conciliation Boards.

Soman, V. K. Land mortgage banks and debt conciliation boards. Indian Co-op. Rev. 2(1): 28-30. January 1936. (Published by All-India Co-operative Institutes' Association, Farhatbagh, Mylapore, Madras, India.)

An account of the unsuccessful Government attempt to make the Conciliation Boards and the Land Mortgage Banks work together.

Agricultural Legislation - New Zealand

Morrison, A. E. Agricultural legislation of 1935. New Zeal. Jour. Agr. 52(1): 30-33. Jan. 20, 1936. (Published in Wellington, New Zealand.)

Notes on the provisions of the following laws: Agricultural Regulations Confirmation Act, 1935; Products Export Amendment Act, 1935; Tobacco-growing Industry Act, 1935.

Agricultural Policy - Austria

Austria: agricultural policy. Gt. Brit. Min. Agr. Jour. 42(11): 1147-1148. February 1936. (Published by H. M. Stationery Office, London, Eng.)

"The Minister of Agriculture in a recent speech to representatives of the Tyrol farmers indicated the broad outlines of the Austrian Government's agricultural policy as follows: -(1) The encouragement of exports through 'compensation' agreements... (2) The shortening of the route between the producer and the consumer... (3) Increased consumption of milk at sufficiently low prices for even the poorest sections of the population... (4) The abolition of the fodder import license system and the protection of the livestock industry in the natural producing areas."

New Austrian agricultural policy. Foreign Crops and Markets 32(10): 284-287. Mar. 9, 1936. (Published by the Division of Foreign Agricultural Service, Bureau of Agricultural Economics, U. S. Dept. of Agriculture.)

"Based on a report from Agricultural Attaché L. V. Steere in Berlin."

"Concentration on the production of farm products for which the country is especially fitted by physical and economic conditions has recently been announced as the keynote of a new agricultural policy in Austria. This change from that followed in recent years will involve a change in the foreign trade policy so as to permit closer economic relations with neighboring Danubian countries, particularly those producing animal fats for export.

"The new policy is seen as a means of broadening the export market for Austrian agricultural and industrial products, reducing living costs in Austria, and raising the income of farmers. One of the first steps in the new policy has been to place dairy marketing under close official supervision. It is expected that ways will be found to curtail the present burdensome volume of milk production and to stimulate the production of beef cattle. Relaxation of the efforts to increase domestic pork and lard production also is under consideration. The Austrian regions economically suited to the production of lard are recognized as being too limited to meet national requirements even when imported feeds are used to supplement domestic supplies."

In conclusion the new milk marketing regulations are cited. These regulations are "designed to increase the consumption of milk by reducing retail milk prices but without requiring sacrifices on the part of milk producers."

Agricultural Policy - France

Nogaro, Bertrand. La crise de l'agriculture et la politique agricole en France. Rev. Écon. Internationale, 28. année, v. 1, no. 1, pp. 7-47. January 1936. (Published by the Institut Économique International, Palais d'Egmont, Brussels, Belgium.)

The author sketches the post-war agricultural production in France, the evolution of wholesale agricultural prices, measures taken in the interest of tariff protection and the establishment of quotas, and the organization of the French wheat, wine, meat, and dairy products markets.

Agricultural Policy - Germany

Darré, R. W. Die Erfüllung des Agrarprogramms. Odal 4(5): 348-358. November 1935. (Published at Lutzowstrasse 66, Berlin W35, Germany.) A summary of the accomplishments of the Reichsnährstand and the agricultural and marketing program under the Hitler regime.

Agricultural Relief - United States

Cox, A. B. Effects of agricultural legislation in the Southwest. Grain & Feed Journals Consolidated 76(5): 180, 181. March 11, 1936. (Published at 330 South La Salle St., Chicago, Ill.)

In this discussion of the effects of agricultural legislation in the Southwest, Dr. Cox quotes from the booklet "Economic Bases for the Agricultural Adjustment Act," by Mordecai Ezekiel, and Louis H. Bean, regarding "the administration's philosophy of levying processing taxes to get money to restrict production to bring about parity price as a solution of farm problems." In commenting on this, Dr. Cox says, "This strange philosophy of planned scarcity to secure abundance has apparently grown out of a discovery that short crops in the past have often brought more money than large crops. Evidently it did not and has not occurred to these gentlemen that there may be a great difference between the results of random short crops brought about by unexpected adversities and planned ones, and especially, where an appreciable per cent of the crop is exported, or where the crop or a substitute for it can be grown quite generally...

"As a result largely of the agricultural control policy the Southwest finds itself confronted with a stupendous problem of adult education and reemployment. The problems of relocating and teaching thousands of adults new occupations. Is agriculture resettlement the answer? No. Already the trend of employment in the Southwest was away from agriculture before the beginning of Government control, in spite of the fact that the trend in agricultural production was still sharply up. Under a program of restricted agricultural production of the staple crops of cotton and wheat, the trend away from agriculture will be still greater."

In conclusion the author holds that the "A.A.A. and other agricultural legislation to cut down production and raise prices, and the propaganda that has accompanied the enactment and enforcement of these laws will do more to create chaos and regional strife than all previous agricultural legislation."

Livingston, J. A. Prosperity begins at home. Country Home 60(4): 11-12. April 1936. (Published at 250 Park Ave., New York, N. Y.)

The theme of this article is that we must attempt to fulfill our own economic destiny, and that the answer to the farm problem "is not greater exports, but rather the return to American farmers of that which rightfully belongs to them - the domestic market."

Shaw, Albert. The fall of AAA once more opens up the question of what to do for agriculture. Rev. of Reviews 93(3): 24-26. March 1936. (Published at 233 Fourth Ave., New York, N. Y.)

Included in the items presented in the column entitled "The Progress of the World."

Of the A.A.A. the writer says in part: "The chief fault with the AAA plan of distributing bounties and subsidies... is usually overlooked. That plan diverted attention by pretending to be a policy for farmers whereas in practice it was something largely different. Farming is a mode of life, and the historic basis of our best citizenship. We have many millions of farms and farm families and they must be maintained. The AAA dealt with commercial producers of particular crops. It gave its largest checks to people who were not farmers in the usual sense, but speculators in land and in commodities. It talked about the evils of soil erosion, and then gave subsidies for the encouragement of the devastating methods used by speculators who were squandering the original fertility of new soils, by raising wheat and other single crops on a large-acreage scale, with powerful machinery and with transient or vagrant labor."

Apples - Bonded Label Plan - Michigan

Halliday, Dean. A bonded plan of apple advertising. Amer. Fruit Grower 56(3): 10-11, 36. March 1936. (Published at 1370 Ontario St., Cleveland, Ohio.)

Describes the Michigan Bonded Label plan, which is being inaugurated in Michigan by the State Department of Agriculture, through the Bureau of Foods and Standards "as the first step in the advancement of Michigan Farm Products by distinctive identification." The plan "gives the Commissioner of Agriculture the right to suspend or annual the privilege of using the official label whenever sufficient evidence is discovered that the grower has failed to comply with representations and agreements made with the Department of Agriculture. The grower must also agree to surrender all unused labels should his right to use them be suspended or annulled. The grower also must agree that the Bonded Label will appear on new containers only, to prevent fraud in its reuse."

Barley, Malting

Black, R. H. Malting barley and barley grades. Grain & Feed Rev. 25(8): 10, 11. April 1936. (Published at 408 South Third St., Minneapolis, Minn.)

"Ten points for consideration by barley buyers and barley producers in the growing and handling of that grain were outlined by Robert H. Black, Federal Grain Supervisor at Minneapolis, in his address before the Minnesota Farmers Elevator association at its convention in Minneapolis on February 19." -Editor's note.

Business - Annual Reviews

The Times. Annual financial and commercial review. xxxiv pp. Feb. 11, 1936. (Published in London, Eng.) folio 284.9 T48

Partial contents: Commodity prices. Highest level for five years. Rise more widespread, p. viii; Wheat. Surplus supplies reduced. Improved outlook, p. ix; Egypt. Highest cotton price since 1931, p.xv; Irish Free State. Divergent results of self-sufficiency, p. xv; Germany's shortage of raw materials. Rising unemployment, p.xxiii; The post-war contraction in cotton exports. Plans for reorganization, p.xxxii; Brazil. Large increase in cotton exports, p.xxxiv.

Cacao Production - Trinidad

Shephard, C. Y. Some economic aspects of cacao production in Trinidad with special reference to the Montserrat District. Trop. Agr. 13(4): 85-90. April 1936. (Published in St. Augustine, Trinidad, West Indies.)

"Being the substance of an address delivered to Trinidad planters
at the Imperial College of Tropical Agriculture on 20th February, 1936."

Canning Crops - Grading - Pennsylvania

James. D. M. The grading of canning crops in Pennsylvania. Canner 82(17):
9-10. April 4, 1936. (Published at 140 North Dearborn St., Chicago, Ill.)
  "Pennsylvania growers received the greatest cash income in 1935 they
ever received from the sale of canning crops. These crops had an estimated farm value of approximately twenty million dollars...   :
  "Pennsylvania canned products have gained additional prestige in
the high quality field...
  "In reviewing cannery products grading the steady growth of this
standardization work will be apparent."
  Differences in the price to growers of products of the highest
quality, and of products unfit for "fancy" grades are pointed out.

Canning Industry - Cost Accounting

Campbell, Carlos. Cost accounting. Canning Trade 58(34): 7-8,10. Mar. 30,
1936. (Published at 20 South Gay St., Baltimore, Md.)
  After pointing out briefly the need for keeping accurate and detailed cost accounts, the writer presents a system for uniform cost
accounting for the canning industry, which the National Canners Association began to develop about six months ago.

Coffee

World coffee markets. Empire Producer no. 233, pp. 63-64. March 1936. (Pub-
lished at 22, Queen Anne's Gate, Westminster, London, S.W.1, Eng.)
  Replies to a questionnaire sent to correspondents in Argentina,
Gold Coast, British Solomon Islands and Australia.

Cooperation - China

Chen Kung-Po. The co-operative movement in China. Chinese Econ. Jour.
16(5): 433-439. May 1935. (Published by Bureau of Foreign Trade,
Ministry of Industry, 1040 North Soochow Road, Shanghai, China.)

Cooperation - Denmark

Digby, Margaret. Danish co-operation and the agricultural crisis. Indian
Co-op. Rev. 2(1): 14-19. January 1936. (Published by All-India Cooperative Institutes' Association, Farhatbagh, Mylapore, Madras, India.)

Cooperation - Estonia

Co-operation in Estonia. The new system. Indus. and Labour Inform. 57(11):
286-287. Mar. 16, 1936. (Published by International Labour Office,
Geneva, Switzerland. Distributed in U. S. by World Peace Foundation,
8 West 40th Street, New York, N. Y.)

"An Act of 22 November 1935 establishes a Chamber of Co-operation in Estonia to organise and promote co-operation and to support and represent the interests of the societies." The functions of the Chamber are defined. It is placed under the control of the Minister of Economic Affairs.

Cooperation - Germany

The co-operative movement in Germany. Indus. and Labour Inform. 57(11): 287-288. Mar. 16, 1936. (Published by International Labour Office, Geneva, Switzerland. Distributed in U. S. by World Peace Foundation, 8 West 40th Street, New York, N. Y.)

A table shows the number of societies in the most important groups.

Cooperation - Iraq

Consumers' co-operative societies in Iraq. Indus. and Labour Inform. 57(10): 257-258. Mar. 9, 1936. (Published by International Labour Office, Geneva, Switzerland. Distributed in U. S. by World Peace Foundation, 8 West 40th Street, New York, N. Y.)

"Two consumers' co-operative societies have recently been established in the city of Baghdad. These are the first societies of their kind in Iraq."

Cooperation - Madagascar

The co-operative movement in Madagascar. Indus. and Labour Inform. 57(2): 29-30. Jan. 13, 1936. (Issued by International Labour Office, Geneva, Switzerland. Distributed in U. S. by World Peace Foundation, 8 West 40th Street, New York, N. Y.)

Describes the spread of cooperation in Madagascar since the legislation of 1930 and the types of loans to farmers.

Cooperation - Palestine

Chand, Gyan. Co-operation in Palestine. Indian Co-op. Rev. 2(1): 20-27. January 1936. (Published by All-India Co-operative Institutes' Association, Farhatbagh, Mylapore, Madras, India.)

"The Co-operative Movement in Palestine has some distinctive features of its own which make it different in several respects from similar movements in other countries." It is shown that cooperation is an integral part of the Jewish land settlement movement in Palestine. An account is given of the origin and functions of the Tnuva, the Co-operative Marketing Organisation of Jewish Agricultural Settlements established in 1926.

The co-operative movement in Palestine. Indus. and Labour Inform. 57(3): 65. Jan. 20, 1936. (Issued by International Labour Office, Geneva, Switzerland. Distributed in U. S. by World Peace Foundation, 8 West 40th Street, New York, N. Y.)

A table shows the number and type of cooperative societies registered in Palestine in November 1933 and February 1935.

Cooperation - Yugoslavia

Co-operation and agricultural problems in Yugoslavia. Rev. Internatl.
Coop. 29(3): 106-109. March 1936. (Published at Orchard House, 14,
Great Smith Street, London, S. W. 1, Eng.)
A summary of some Government measures to remedy agricultural con-
ditions and their effect on cooperation.

Cooperation, Consumers

Consumers co-operatives associated. Producer-Consumer 1(9): 3,4. April
1936. (Published at 517 Fisk Bldg., and 109 Filmore, Amarillo, Texas.)
"Consumer's co-operation among farmers is showing gains all over
the territory represented by the stockholders in the Consumers Cooperatives Associated wholesale organization and affairs of this
regional are also in very good shape.
"These facts were brought out at the annual meeting of the stockholders in Amarillo on March 3 at the Herring Hotel where several
hundred gathered for an interesting program.
"The co-operative wholesale, born amid hard times, has steadily
grown in size, usefulness and importance. G. A. Sahli, auditor,
reported that the business is in good condition financially, is
healthy, well-managed and operating satisfactorily."

Jansen, C. H. Watch consumer cooperatives. Nation's Business 24(4): 45,48,51-52.
April 1936. (Published by the Chamber of Commerce of the United
States, Washington, D. C.)
Relates the growth of the new movement toward consumer cooperation
in which government agencies are interested and which is fostered by
various organizations including some churches, and makes suggestions
as to how private enterprise can meet the challenge.

Story of consumers co-operatives. Producer-Consumer 1(9): 4. April 1936.
(Published at 517 Fisk Bldg., and 109 Filmore, Amarillo, Texas.)
A short article in which it is stated that at "Floydada, Plainview,
Lockney,Paducah, Tulia, Hereford, Conway, and all over the plains
farmers organized cooperatives a dozen years ago. They succeeded and
others started. To be able to act together, to get discounts and to
build a real co-operative structure, they organized a wholesale and
Consumers Co-operatives Associated. The C.C.A. - unlike most
wholesale concerns - does not own a lot of retail outlets. A lot of
retail co-operative outlets own it."
The writer continues by describing how the co-operatives operate.

World travelers write of cooperatives. Coop. Comment 5(1): 1,4. March
1936. (Published at the Columbia Bldg., Spokane, Wash.)
The writer reviews briefly several articles dealing with the
subject of cooperatives, including one which appeared in "Harper's
magazine some months ago", entitled "Where Capitalism is Controlled,"
by Mr. Marquis W. Childs. In this article the writer reviews cooperation in the Scandinavian countries, "and speaks of their economic
values."

- 394 -

Cooperation in the United States is reviewed in the concluding part of the article. "Statistics of the number of farm cooperatives in the United States are not available, but there are 10,700 listed by the Farm Credit Administration. They reported a volume of business in 1935 amounting to $1,530,000,000."

Cooperative Farm for Sharecroppers - Mississippi

Self-help for share-croppers. Lit. Digest 121(15): 16. Apr. 11, 1936. Published at 354-360 Fourth Ave., New York, N. Y.)
    Describes the Sherwood Eddy cooperative farm, which is a 2,100-acre cotton cooperative experiment farm for evicted share-croppers near Hillhouse, Mississippi. The farm which is known as the Sherwood Cooperative Farm No. 1, will use the mechanical cotton picker, invented by John D. and Mack D. Rust.
    "Twenty families will take part in the cooperative venture this year. They include nine who were already on the tract. Each family will have its individual home, tho owned in common with all other families. Personal effects will be owned individually. Each house-holder will have his own half-acre garden for raising vegetables."

Corn Yield and Climate - Corn Belt

Rose, J. K. Corn yield and climate in the corn belt. Geogr. Rev. 26(1): 88-102. January 1936. (Published by the American Geographical Society, Broadway at 156th St., New York, N. Y.)
    The following is quoted from p.90:
    "In the present study of the problem the whole Corn Belt has been dealt with on the basis of numerous selected county units. The correlation coefficients calculated for these samples provide a basis for the determination of transitions from areas in which yield is influenced by one factor or set of factors to those in which it is influenced by others. As a result, more detailed and probably more reliable information regarding the correlation of corn yield with climatic factors within, and just beyond the margins of, the Corn Belt is available. Such information, besides bringing an addition to geographical knowledge, may contribute toward better crop-yield forecasting by government and private agencies. It is not too much, perhaps, to expect that, if the present trends toward planned agricultural economy continue, some information so gained may be found useful in modifying or changing present agricultural practices.
    "A second purpose of this study is to illustrate the possibilities of what may be called 'statistical method in geography.' Field methods serve mostly for the collection of data. The problem of analyzing these data is complicated by the fact that the geographer commonly works with many variables, independent and dependent. Hence the method of correlation analysis would seem especially promising tools for geographical investigation."

Cotton

MacLaren, I. R. "Su majestad el algodon." La Hacienda 31(1): 8-11, illus. January 1936. (Published at 20 Vesey St., New York, N. Y.)

Cotton production in Brazil, Egypt, Russia, China, India, Argentina, Mexico, and Peru in relation to the world cotton situation is discussed.

Pritzkoleit, Kurt. Tendenzen des weltbaumwollmarktes. Wirtschaftdienst (neue Folge) 20(47): 1593-1595, tables. Nov. 22, 1935. (Published at Poststrasse 19, Hamburg, 36, Germany.)
Tendencies of the world cotton markets.
The author discusses and contrasts the cotton production restriction policy of the United States, British India, and Egypt with the policy of increased production as exemplified in China, Russia and South America. He believes that the crux of the situation is in the outcome of Brazil's cotton crop and the maintenance of North America's cotton policy.

Cotton - Control of Production

Is cotton cornered? Textile Weekly 17(415): 183,185, charts. Feb. 14, 1936. (Published at 41, Deansgate, Manchester, 3, Eng.)
The similarity of aim of the British Cotton Spinning Industry Bill and the American program to restrict cotton production is commented upon. Discussion of the raw cotton situation is illustrated with charts from the outlook report of the United States Department of Agriculture.

Cotton - Cooperative Marketing

McCullough, W. R. Cooperation defined. Amer. Cotton Grower 1(9): [7]. February 1936. (Published at 535 Gravier St., New Orleans, La.)
The development and advantages of cooperative marketing of cotton are discussed.

Cotton - Cost of Production

Vivet, E. Prix de revient de la culture du cotonnier. Revue Agricole de l'Afrique du Nord 34(859): 33-34. Jan. 17, 1936. (Published at 6, Bd. Carnot, Alger, Algeria.)
Estimation of the net cost of cotton cultivation.

Cotton - Domestic Allotment Plan

Cartwright, H. Y. Domestic allotment plan is entitled to "day in court". Cotton Digest 8(19): 4-5. Feb. 15, 1936. (Published at 710 Cotton Exchange Bldg., Houston, Tex.)
The author comments on the advantages of a domestic allotment plan for the marketing of cotton.

Cotton - Government Loan Policy - United States

Cotton - loss leader. Business Week no. 345, p.11. Apr. 11, 1936. (Published at 330 West 42nd St., New York, N. Y.)
Describes the plan of the Commodity Credit Corporation to dispose of its cotton. "The selling scheme is simple. The corporation

merely announced last week that from here on the cotton growers who
borrowed 12¢ per lb. on their cotton in 1934 and 1935 may have it
back for 1/4¢ less than the average spot price in ten Southern markets
on any day they can sell it to the regular trade provided that the
average market price is not less than 11-1/2¢, which would mean net
of 11-1/4¢ in Washington."

The difference between this plan and Senator Smith's original
cotton disposal bill is pointed out.

In commenting on the plan, the writer says:
"The plan is patently an endeavor to get the government out of a
bag-holding position in the cotton market. As such it is admired
by the cotton trade. But there is no assurance that any substantial
amount of cotton can be disposed of within the time limits, and the
trade is a little worried about this aspect of the plan."

Kerr, T. H. Marketing portion of loan cotton now is proposed. Cotton
Digest 8(17): 3-4. Feb. 1, 1936. (Published at 710 Cotton Exchange Bldg., Houston, Tex.)

The author comments on the Government's cotton loan policy and
suggests renewing "the loan for six months" and liquidating the
remainder of the cotton under loan on July 31 over a period of three
or four years.

Stewart, J. N. Charges on loan cotton should be eliminated. Cotton
Digest 8(19): [3]-4. Feb. 15, 1936. (Published at 710 Cotton Exchange Bldg., Houston, Tex.)

The author discusses the problem of disposal of the 12-cent loan
cotton.

Cotton - Handloom Industry - China

Fong, H. D., and Pi, H. H. The growth and decline of rural industrial
enterprise in North China: a case study of the cotton handloom
weaving industry in Paoti. Nankai Social & Econ. Quart. 8(4):
691-772. January 1936. (Published by Nankai Institute of Economics,
Nankai University, Tientsin, China.)

"This paper furnishes a concrete case study of one of the
principal rural industries in China today. The transition of the
cotton handloom weaving industry in Paoti from the craftsman to the
merchant employer system as described by the authors in detail is
a fact of grave import to the industrial future of China."

Cotton - Mechanical Picker

Carlson, Oliver. The South faces disaster. Amer. Mercury 37(145): 1-8.
January 1936. (Published at 570 Lexington Ave., New York, N. Y.)

"An almost immediate revolution in cotton production is at hand:
the mechanical picker, when introduced in Australia, as well as here,
will destroy the American small producer, wipe out the Southern
tenant farmer, mechanize the entire industry, cut production costs
from fifty to eighty percent, yield enormous profits to its first
users, and throw millions of the South's most helpless population
out of the only employment which they understand."

The author describes the increase in cotton production in foreign
countries, especially Australia.

Cotton - Selling "on Call"

Page, R. Selling Egyptian cotton "on call". Internatl. Cotton Bull. 14(54):
182,185-187. January 1936. (Published at 26, Cross St., Manchester 2,
Eng.)
   Arguments for and against the system are included.

Cotton - Trade and Tariff

Burr, C. H. Lower Tariff would solve farm problem. Cotton Digest 8(19):
8-9. Feb. 15, 1936. (Published at 710 Cotton Exchange Bldg., Houston,
Tex.)
   The author discusses past and present efforts of the Government to
cope with the cotton producers' marketing problems by production control and price fixing.

Caldwell, T. J. Protective tariff blight to farmer.. Cotton Digest 8(17):
5,15. Feb. 1, 1936. (Published at 710 Cotton Exchange Bldg., Houston,
Tex.)
   The author discusses the inequable effects of the protective tariff
on the cotton industry, and the effects of Government policies and
laws intended to relieve agriculture without adjusting the tariff
situation.

[Did the New Deal kill our foreign markets?] Tex. Weekly 12(11): 1-3. Mar.
14, 1936. (Published at the Dallas Athletic Club Bldg., Dallas, Tex.)
   Editorial discussing the visit of Colonel Knox to Texas and pointing out that his statement that the New Deal "has taken your foreign
cotton market away" is not borne out by the facts. Colonel Knox is
reported as saying that he "favors reciprocal trade agreements, but
without the most favored nation clause", which, according to the
Editor, "means that he is not in favor of as much revision of the
Hawley-Smoot rates as the administration is attempting to bring about
under the present reciprocal trade act... Preferential bargaining is
what the policy favored by Colonel Knox is called." The writer continues by quoting Mr. Francis B. Sayre, Assistant Secretary of State
from a recent pamphlet in which he compares this policy with the
policy of "equal treatment." According to Mr. Sayre, "'just as
preferential bargaining leads to economic conflict, so the system
of equal treatment under the most-favored-nation policy makes for
economic peace and stability.' ... In our own view, the reciprocal
trade act is inadequate to meet the situation and is not a satisfactory substitute for unilateral action by the United States to reduce its tariff rates. But it is better than nothing, and in the
long run it may succeed in checking the trend toward extreme economic
nationalism... We believe that sooner or later the necessity of ...
tariff revision will be recognized and the revision will be undertaken. But meantime, it would be a step backward to strike down
the most-favored nation policy."

[We can't escape need of cotton markets] Tex. Weekly 12(13): 1-3. Mar.
28, 1936. (Published at the Dallas Athletic Club Bldg., Dallas, Tex.)
Editorial charging that unjustified optimism tends to obscure the
main issue; that the improvement in cotton exports is not anything to
brag about; that the enthusiasm which some farm leaders of the South
"are displaying for the new soil conservation program of the Government ... is a good thing, but ... does not cancel the absolute
necessity of restoring the world market for American cotton"; and
that the "Chemurgy" movement, which proposes to redeem the Southern
farmer by means of chemistry, transforming new materials into all
kinds of commodities for domestic consumption, is another of the new
enthusiasms which easily undergo transmutation into dangerous optimism."

[Why the world uses less of our cotton] Tex. Weekly 12(12): 1-3. Mar. 21,
1936. (Published at the Dallas Athletic Club Bldg., Dallas, Tex.)
Editorial drawing attention to the fact that the world is consuming
more cotton than ever, but not American grown cotton. The statement
is made that we "can not reduce the production of cotton in this
country to the level of American consumption, not without throwing
hundreds of thousands of people out of employment. So there is no
escaping the necessity of selling our cotton outside the United
States." Secretary Wallace is quoted as saying that "'The increasing
inability of our foreign cotton customers to buy (in the United
States) is the most serious factor....This can be corrected in a
permanent way only by our taking imports in excess of exports, so
as to provide foreigners the dollar exchange to pay the interest owing
us and give them the ability to buy our exports at a fair price. Our
reciprocal tariff-bargaining program is working in this direction
but it is too slow for much effect in 1935. To accelerate the program it would be necessary to bring about modification of our anti-
dumping tariffs, as applied to gold countries, and a general reduction
in tariff rates.' Secretary Wallace made this statement before the
Senate Committee on Agriculture on January 30th, 1935. But no
attention has been paid to this advice since. And the reciprocal
policy has turned out to be too slow for much effect in 1936 as well."

Cotton Industry - Organization

Méeg, Marcel. Les essais d'entente professionnelle dans l'industrie
cotonnière. Soc. d'Encouragement pour l'Industrie Nationale. Bulletin
134(12): 634-644. December 1935. (Published at 44, Rue de Rennes,
Paris (6e), France.)
An account of the effect of the depression on the cotton industry
of France, the formation of syndicates and their attempts to control
prices and production without success. The organization of the
cotton industry in Italy, Germany, the United States, Czechoslovakia,
Austria, Belgium and England is briefly reviewed.

Cotton Pickery - Memphis, Tenn.

Talley, Robert. Making disaster pay dividends. Nation's Business 24(4):
32,34. April 1936. (Published by the Chamber of Commerce of the

United States, Washington, D. C.)

Relates the success of the McCallum & Robinson cotton pickery in
Memphis, Tenn., which is a salvage plant that "reconditions damaged
and irregular cotton and puts it in shape for the market."

Cotton Textile Situation and Southern Agriculture

Windel, Dudley. The farmer must decide. Amer. Cotton Grower 1(11): 8-9.
April 1936. (Published at 535 Gravier St., New Orleans, La.)
A review of the world textile situation by an economist from
Liverpool, England.

A note at the conclusion of the article states that this review
"emphasizes the imperative necessity either for a drastic change
in America's fiscal policy or for a reorganization of Southern agriculture so as to promote more efficient production on fewer acres.
There is no other country in the world possessing the natural and
technical resources of the United States in agricultural production.
It is now the duty of the Southern farmer to take full advantage of
his heritage. Given assistance from Washington in the matter of
bilateral trade agreements, the South can yet retain or even expand its cotton exports by means of intensive cultivation of the
most productive land."

Credit - Rural China

Wu, L. T. K. Merchant capital and usury capital in rural China. Far
East. Survey 5(7): 63-68. Mar. 25, 1936. (Published by Fortnightly
Research Service, American Council, Institute of Pacific Relations,
129 E. 52nd St., New York, N. Y.)
In conclusion the writer gives his conclusions as to the effect
of the system of usury-merchant financing on China's rural economy
and gives the general implications for the whole national economy of
China. A partial quotation of this section follows:
"(1) The operation of the present system of usury-merchant-landlordism must lead to the disintegration of rural China... (2) Under
the present system, the bulk of the peasants are hardly able to
keep body and soul together. It is therefore absolutely impossible
to expect them to make any technical or other scientific advance in
methods of production. In fact an even greater decline in agricultural productivity will probably ensue.
"(3) The pauperization of the peasantry and decline in agricultural productivity means a shrinkage in national purchasing power.
This shrinkage is a fundamental and permanent cause responsible for
the tremendous decline in both domestic and foreign trade during the
past few years. Usury-merchant-landlordism in China is destroying,
instead of creating, markets.
"(4) The extremely high return yielded by the exorbitant interest
charges in the money-lending business and by the high rents is so in
excess of the rate of profit in ordinary fields of production that
it acts to strengthen the strong bonds between the Chinese merchant
class and the rich peasantry with usury capital and landlordism ...

The present study leads the writer to believe that the permanent and indivisible tie-up of merchant capital and rich peasantry with usury capital and landlordism must constitute one of the fundamental causes, if not the only cause, of the protracted stagnation of Chinese social-economy.

"(5) Finally, the general drain on the cash of rural China, caused by the persistent excess of imports from the cities and overseas over the exports of the interior, the exodus of big landlords and rich merchants to the larger cities, the wars and natural calamities, all these factors are resulting in an extremely tight credit situation and at the same time are bringing more and more of the business of money-lending into the hands of the smaller landlords and merchants.

"On the other side of the picture the ever-increasing inability of the peasants to pay their debts is necessitating more and more hesitation on the part of the landlords and merchants who extend loans. Many of the peasants are no longer able to secure credit under any condition and those who still retain any possessions of any kind are forced to pay higher and higher rates and to meet harsher and harsher terms. The fact that the factors mentioned in the preceding paragraph are leading to the concentration of the money-lending business in the hands of smaller landlords and smaller merchants does not mean less hardship for the peasant. On the contrary the former usually demand more usurious terms than the larger merchants or landlords.

"The peasants who constitute the bulk of the 450,000,000 people of China are now undergoing a life and death struggle. The choice for them is either continued collapse of their economy or a complete alteration of the usury-merchant-landlord system."

Debts, Public - Southern States

Ratchford, B. U. Public debts in the South. South. Econ. Jour. 2(3): 13-25. January 1936. (Published by the Southern Economic Association and the University of North Carolina at Chapel Hill, N. C.)
"The purpose of this study is to sketch briefly the course of public indebtedness in the South during the present century, and to give some indication of the debt burden here as compared with the situation in the other 34 states of the Union." By the South, in this study, is meant the states of Alabama, Arkansas, Florida, Georgia, Kentucky, Louisiana, Mississippi, North and South Carolina, Oklahoma, Tennessee, Texas, Virginia and West Virginia.

Economic Depression and Recovery - Argentina

Haring, C. H. Depression and recovery in Argentina. Foreign Affairs 14(3): 506-519. April 1936. (Published at 45 E. 65th St., New York, N. Y.)
A review of the progress of recovery in Argentina. "Three years ago Argentina displayed all the phenomena of the world depression: low commodity prices, unemployment, debtors faced with foreclosure, an unbalanced budget, declining foreign trade. Today she has emerged from the crisis to an extent beyond any other American country."

Economic Geography 12(2): 109-216. April 1936. (Published by Clark University, Worcester, Mass.)
Partial contents: The present situation in the wheat-growing industry in Southeastern Australia, by John Anders, pp.109-135; The olive industry of Spain, by William E. Bull, pp.136-154; Hop industry of the Pacific Coast States, by Otil W. Freeman, pp.155-163; Oregon low-lands suitable for flax, by Charles Sumner Hoffman, Jr., pp.164-166; and The Grain trade of the Port of Vancouver, British Columbia, by Leah Stevens, pp.185-196.

Economic Legislation - Germany

Die Wirtschaftsgesetzgebung seit 1933. Institut für Konjunkturforschung, Wochenbericht, 9. Jahrg. Sondernummer, 28pp. Mar. 21, 1936. (Published in Berlin, Germany.)
A three-year's survey of economic legislation in Germany.

Economic Policy - Czechoslovakia

Economic policy in Czechoslovakia. Indus. and Labour Inform. 57(2): 28. Jan. 13, 1936. (Issued by International Labour Office, Geneva, Switzerland. Distributed in U. S. by World Peace Foundation, 8 West 40th Street, New York, N.Y.)
In a speech delivered in the Chamber of Deputies on December 5, 1935, the Prime Minister of Czechoslovakia, Mr. Hodža, urged the necessity of maintaining a permanent balance between agriculture and industry. He said that "the Government had established a new system of production and marketing of cereals, which safeguarded the agriculturist against speculation and violent price fluctuations, and thereby increased and stabilised his purchasing power."

Economic Policy - Germany

Fischer, C. A. La nouvelle politique économique allemande. Revue Économique Internationale, 28. année, v.1, no.2, pp.237-260. February 1936. (Published by the Institut Économique International, Palais d'Egmont, Brussels, Belgium.)
The new German economic policy is concerned chiefly with the struggle against unemployment and economic recovery.

Economic Program - Iran

Economic expansion in Iran. Indus. and Labour Inform. 57(4): 97-98. Jan. 27, 1936. (Issued by International Labour Office, Geneva, Switzerland. Distributed in U. S. by World Peace Foundation, 8 West 40th St., New York, N. Y.
Iran's economic program includes the establishment of chambers of commerce and of commercial companies, railway and road construction, and town planning.

Economic Program - Japan

Economic recovery in Japan. Indus. and Labour Inform. 57(4): 96-97. Jan.
27, 1936. (Issued by International Labour Office, Geneva, Switzerland.
Distributed in U. S. by World Peace Foundation, 8 West 40th Street,
New York, N. Y.)
    A scheme for Japanese economic recovery includes the population
problem, industrialization of Japan proper and the transfer of agriculture to Korea and Manchuria, the acquisition of new markets, State
control of the money market and of industry, the levelling of incomes and decentralization of industry.

Economics - United States

Clark, J. M. Past accomplishments and present prospects of American
economics. Amer. Econ. Rev. 26(1): 1-11. March 1936. (Published
by the American Economic Association, Northwestern University,
Evanston, Ill.)
    "The present state of American economics gives ground for both
congratulation and humility. A revival occurred after the Civil War,
reoriented by the founders of the American Economic Association.
Though leaning at first toward the historical method, the first great
result was an indigenous growth of systematic economics of marginal
equilibrium. The marginal method, possibly our greatest single tool
of analysis, is not limited to theories of equilibrium, which are
themselves tools of analysis, not finished pictures of the economic
world.
    "The critical movement which followed did not wipe out the marginal
economics, the best test being the continued use and development of
its concepts, though often in modified form, by those now engaged in
positive studies, for example, the theory of imperfect competition
has required a more accurate statement than before of the conditions
necessary to perfect competition, in order to show how different conditions lead to different results.
    "In the present crisis, a few economists have helped shape policy,
many have rendered good service in subordinate positions, but economics
as a whole has not furnished authoritative guidance, owing largely to
the inherent limitations of scientific method in dealing with practical
issues in this field. We are entering a new epoch in the relation of
government to industry, raising the question whether the extension of
control is passing the limits within which gradual change is possible.
The economist will naturally tend to give evolutionary change the
benefit of every doubt, and to hold that it may yet succeed. While
the ultimate answer to this and many other questions rests with
trial-and-error experimentation, economic analysis can still contribute much, and there are many problems which challenge it. The most
important thing is to maintain free scientific inquiry." -p.1.

Ethiopia

Hubbard, W. D. A farmer looks at Ethiopia. Today 5(22): 3-4, 21. Mar.
21, 1936. (Published at 152 West Forty-second St., New York, N.Y.)

Mr. Hubbard, who has recently completed extensive travels in Africa, says, in reply to the question asked by nearly everyone "Why does Mussolini want Ethiopia?" that it is soil. He states "Minerals perhaps. Oil perhaps. But it is the soil that is attracting the Italians for it is a soil which, with the climatic differences, can be made to grow almost any crop under the sun."

Expenditures (Public), Prices and the National Income

Bernstein, E. M. Public expenditure, prices, and the national income. South. Econ. Jour. 2(3): 34-46. January 1936. (Published by the Southern Economic Association and the University of North Carolina at Chapel Hill, N. C.)
    "On the whole, the statistical data seem to confirm the view that a large positive effect on prices, production, and the national income must result from a considerable increase in public expenditure during depression."

Farmers, Stranded - Minnesota

Garey, L. F. Stranded farmers in urban cities. Social Forces 14(3): 388-394. March 1936. (Published for the University of North Carolina Press by the Williams & Wilkins Co., Baltimore, Md.)
    This is a report of a study made in 1934 of stranded farmers in certain cities of Minnesota for "the purpose of finding out why these people left the farm and on what basis a program for returning this kind of city migrant to the farm might be developed."

Field Crops - Cost of Production

Cost of producing field crops, 1934. Crops and Markets 13(2): 74-75. February 1936. (Published by the U. S. Dept. of Agriculture, Washington, D. C.)
    Contains two tables. Table 1 shows, in detail, the estimated cost of production of corn, wheat, and oats by groups of states and for the United States, also net cost per acre and per bushel. Table 2 shows, in detail, the estimated cost of production of cotton by selected states and regions. Net cost of lint per acre and per pound is also given.

Fruits, Dried - Legislation - Australia

Malloch, P. Attack on Australia's dried fruits legislation. Primary Producer 21(9): 1,2. Feb. 27, 1936. (Published at 38-40-42-44 Stirling St., Perth, Western Australia.)
    Reprint of an article which appeared in the "'Australian Dried Fruits News' of January 22. It is of special interest to all producers at the moment, and concisely explains the position relative to the existing dried fruits legislation, the benefits accruing from control, and the probable results of an adverse decision in the appeal case to be heard before the Privy Council." -Editor's note.

Germany

[Germany. Reichsnährstand.] Recht des Reichsnährstandes. Zeitschrift für
Bauern-und Bodenrecht. Im Auftrage des Reichsnährstandes hrsg.
von Dr. Wilhelm Saure. Jahrgang 1, 1933 has title Steuer und Recht
des Landwirts. Mitteilungen des Beirats der Betriebs-und Steuerstelle
des Deutschen Landwirtschaftsrates. Jahrg. 1, 1933- Berlin, 1933.
Published monthly 1933-1934; fortnightly, 1935- L.C. has 1933 to
date.

1933: The volume, Steuer und Recht des Landwirts, contains contributed articles dealing mainly with the various phases and forms
of agricultural taxation and the factors which affect it, summaries
of laws and decrees dealing with taxation and agricultural indebtedness and measures for its relief, and discussions of such measures.
A supplement, Gesetze und Erlasse, contains texts of important
legislation.

Among the articles dealing with land inheritance are the following:
Das bäuerliche Erbhofrecht, by Wöhrmann. -June, 1933, pp.86-88. (An
account of the aims and scope of the Prussian land inheritance law
of May 15, 1933); Das Inkrafttreten des bäuerlichen Erbhofrechts, by
Wöhrmann. -August, 1933, pp.130-132. (An explanation of the putting
into force of the Prussian land inheritance law); Bäuerliches
Erbhofrecht. Die Ausführungsverordnung zum bäuerlichen Erbhofrecht,
by Wöhrmann. -September 1933, pp.150-152. (An account of the regulations for the operation of the inheritance law issued on August 24,
1933); Die nicht eintrangungsfähigen Erbhöfe. (Ein Beitrag zur
Anlegung der Erbhöferolle), by Boehr. -September 1933, p.152.
(Reasons why some land is not affected by the provisions of the land
inheritance law); Bäuerliches Erbhofrecht: Das Reichserbhofgesetz
vom 29. September 1933. (Unter Berücksichtigung der 1. Durchführungs -
verordnung vom 19. Oktober 1933), by Werner Johae. -October 1933,
pp.178-182. (An account of the provisions of the German land inheritance law of September 29, 1933 which according to the author
is the most important agro-political measure which the National
Socialist Government has sponsored or will sponsor); Der Voll-
streckungsschutz des Reichserbhofgesetzes, by Fritz Wenzel. -December
1933, pp.218-219. (The protection against distraint of the peasant
inheritance is discussed); Reichserbhofgesetz und Grunderwerbsteuer,
by Jahn. -December 1933, pp.219-220. (Comments on the clause dealing with inheritance tax exemption.)

1934: No. 1, January 1934 contains a foreword by the editor, Dr.
Wilhelm Saure, in which he outlines the aims of the periodical, Recht
des Reichsnährstandes, which is to take the place of Steuer und
Recht der Landwirts. As a publication of the recently created Reichsnährstand it will cover the entire field of legal problems that
affect the agricultural industry in all its branches and ramifications.
It will deal with the land inheritance law, agricultural indebtedness,
foreclosure, credit, land settlement and tenancy problems, taxation,
cooperation, water, forest, hunting and fishing rights as well as
all economic, insurance and social problems. It claims to be a
scientific publication with preponderantly practical aims. Each
number contains articles by experts in the different fields of interest,

shorter articles on various problems that require comment or discussion, a survey of the agricultural situation of the day, decisions
handed down in the courts, and book reviews. Texts of laws, decrees,
orders, etc. are issued in Gesetzesdienst, as a supplement to Recht
des Reichsnährstandes in 1934 and in a separate publication,
Verkündigungsblatt des Reichsnährstandes beginning with January 1935.

Government and Business

Keister, A. S. Are governments and business separate entities? South. Econ.
Jour. 2(3): 3-12. January 1936. (Published by the Southern Economic
Association and the University of North Carolina at Chapel Hill, N.C.)
Discusses the growing inseparability of government and business and
some of its implications.

Grain - Marketing

Huff, C. E. In the grain pit. Nation's Agr. 11(7): 10,27,31. April 1936.
(Published at 58 E. Washington St., Chicago, Ill.)
"The president of the Farmers National Grain Corporation [as told
to John J. Lacey] describes his start in co-operative marketing, and
gives his views on the evils of speculation in farm products."

Hog Industry - New Zealand

Croucher, W. J. Pig policy for New Zealand. New Zealand Dairy Exporter
11(7): 30-31. Feb. 1, 1936. (Published at P. O. Box 1001, Wellington,
New Zealand.)
In this article the writer "attacks the apathy of the Agricultural
Department so far as the pig industry is concerned, and maintains
that the greatest need today is for a properly directed instructional
service. In other words, he demands that, instead of the pig industry
drifting hither and thither, there should be a definite policy of instruction and expansion." The writer says that in his opinion "the
most essential need in the pig industry is enlightened instruction
in sensible feeding and general management."

Hog Industry - Poland

Reed, H. E. The hog industry in Poland. Foreign Crops and Markets 32(12):
335-359. Mar. 23, 1936. (Published by the Division of Foreign Agricultural Service, Bureau of Agricultural Economics, U. S. Dept. of
Agriculture.)
Subtopics are: Polish agriculture and the place of hogs in Polish
agriculture; Poland as a surplus pork country (hog numbers, trends and
hogfeed relationships; types, breeds and distribution); hog production
practices; marketing; processing (bacon factories, lard production,
veterinary inspection); foreign trade (bacon, ham, lard, other pork,
live hogs); present situation and government policies. Accompanied
by a number of statistical tables, one of which shows production and
per capita consumption of meat, 1934, with comparisons.

- 406 -

Housing - Great Britain

Gardiner, C. H. The rural housing problem; Countryman 13(1): 62-67.
April 1936. (Published at Idbury, Kingham, Oxfordshire, Eng.)
A brief account of the provisions of rural housing legislation.

Income - Southern States

Palmer, E. Z. Sources and distribution of income in the South. South.
Econ. Jour. 2(3): 47-60. January 1936. (Published for the Southern
Economic Association and the University of North Carolina at Chapel
Hill, N. C.)
"The excellent studies of income which have been completed under
the guidance of national research organizations need to be interpreted in terms of particular regions. This paper attempts to apply
some of these figures to the South, to examine some of the difficulties,
and to set forth a few of the results of such a segregation."

Index Numbers - Australia

Phillips, Willmott. Australian export prices, 1880-1935. Econ. Rec.
11(21): 176-186. December 1935. (Published at the Melbourne University Press, Melbourne, N.3, Victoria.)
The Australian export price index was "compiled by the Commonwealth Bank to measure variations in Australia's income from overseas, in so far as they are due to fluctuations in the prices of her
exports." This article gives details of the price quotations and
weights used, and compares this index with the index compiled by the
Commonwealth Statistician.

Polglaze, Jean, and Heath, Eileen. Australian business index. Econ. Rec.
11(21): 280-283. December 1935. (Published at Melbourne University
Press, Melbourne, N.3, Victoria)
An Article in the Economic Record for December, 1933 presented
certain data relating to the Australian business cycle. This article
contains a review of the movements since that date.

Industry and Agriculture

Address of Hudson McCarroll, Chief chemist of Ford Motor Co., at Illinois
Farmers Grain Dealers Convention, Chicago. Farmers' Elevator Guide
31(4): 3-5. Apr. 5, 1936. (Published at 309 South La Salle St.,
Chicago, Ill.)
Mr. McCarroll tells in "as non-technical [a] manner as possible"
something of the efforts of Mr. Henry Ford and the Ford Motor Company
to increase the use of agricultural products in industry. Among the
examples cited is that of the soy bean. Mr. Ford is quoted as saying: "I believe that industry and agriculture are natural partners.
Agriculture suffers from lack of a market for its product. Industry
suffers from a lack of employment for its surplus men. Bringing them
together heals the ailments of both. I see the time coming when the

farmer not only will raise raw materials for industry, but will do
the initial processing on his farm. He will stand on both his
feet - one foot on the soil for his livelihood; the other in industry for the cash he needs. Thus he will have a double security:
That is what I'm working for!"

The farm as a lab. Business Week no. 345, vp.31,32. Apr. 11, 1936. (Pub-
lished at 330 West 42nd St., New York, N. Y.)
     Gives a brief account of a conference sponsored by the Farm
Chemurgic Council and the Chemical Foundation, held recently in
Fresno, Calif., and which was attended by farm leaders of the 11
Mountain and Pacific Coast States.
     F. T. Letchfield, vice-president of the Wells Fargo Bank & Union
Trust Co. of San Francisco, and other speakers advocated this program: "(1) Encouragement of American farmers to raise necessary
commodities now imported. (2) Search for new uses for excess crops
the farmer cannot sell at a profit. (3) Attempt to substitute profitable crops for non-paying crops now being produced by debt-ridden
farmers."
     Some of the "'brilliant advances' recently produced by joint action
of industry, agriculture, and science" were cited by Dr. H. E. Barnard,
research director of the Farm Chemurgic Council. He included the
following: Waste cotton is used experimentally to build superhigh-
ways and airport runways; Tung oil, an Asiatic commodity in paint, is
now produced here; and California and Oregon may be developed as
domestic sources of flax, linseed oil, and linen.

Smith, E. W. Industry's alliance with agriculture. Nation's Agr. 11(4):
15,25. January 1936. (Published at 58 E. Washington St., Chicago,
Ill.)
     "The author of this article is vice-president of the General
Motors Export Company. He writes on a subject of paramount importance
[American exports, including farm exports] and speaks from a life
time of experience." -[Editor's note.]
     Regarding tariffs and imports the author writes in part: "But it
would be far better economics, and far better for all of us, in a
practical dollar-and-cents way, if the farmer were to raise the
volume of crops he is capable of raising, and to sell the surplus
beyond domestic needs in the markets throughout the world that need
this surplus so urgently. He can do this, in the last analysis,
only if his foreign customers can find the means of paying for the
goods they buy, and they can find this means only if imports of
foreign goods into the United States are greatly increased, and such
an increase can only occur, from this point, on, if tariffs are
lowered."

Irrigation - Alberta

Eisenhauer, E. E. Irrigation in Alberta. Sci. Agr. 16(5): 270-274.
January 1936. (Published in Ottawa, Canada.)
     "Paper read before a joint session of the Western Canadian
Society of Agronomy and the Soils Group of the C.S.T.A. at the
University of Alberta, Edmonton, June 27, 1935."

Irrigation - United States

Warne, W. E. The big job of harnessing western waters. Nation's Agr.
11(7): 4-5,28. April 1936. (Published at 58 E. Washington St.,
Chicago, Ill.)
     Describes briefly the first irrigation projects in the United
States, the establishment, development and purpose of the Reclamation
Bureau, and the construction of Boulder Dam. It is stated that
"Boulder Dam marks a new era in western water conservation. It is the
first structure which will control an entire river system for all
types of conservation; flood control, irrigation, domestic water
supply, navigation, hydro-electric power and public parks and fish
and game preserves. It has demonstrated the feasibility of dams of
a size large enough to harness great and erratic rivers. Now, others
of this type are being built by the Bureau of Reclamation."

Jute Industry - Great Britain

Crisis in jute. Economist 122(4831): 694. Mar. 28, 1936. (Published at
8 Bouverie St., London, E.C.4, Eng.)
     "The history of the jute industry in Great Britain has had much in
common with that of the cotton industry. Until the middle of last
century, sacks and packing materials were made largely from flax and
hemp. It was then discovered that jute, which was relatively cheaper,
formed an excellent substitute for the two other textile fibers. A
new branch of the textile industry sprang up and was rapidly developed in this country. British jute manufacturers were first in the
field and for some time succeeded in dominating the industry. The
bulk of the world's jute crop, however, is grown in British India,
and as the manufacture of jute goods is a relatively simple process,
the native factory industry in due course began to compete with the
British industry. By the turn of the last century manufacturers in
Dundee had already lost their dominating position."
     The consumption of jute by Indian mills continued to increase and
by 1894 the consumption was greater than in Dundee. By 1914 manufacturers in Dundee also had to face increasing competition from
countries outside India, and at the time of the Great War consumption
of raw jute in Great Britain"showed an absolute decline." At the
onset of the world depression, the demand for jute began to decline,
and in an effort to improve their position, the Indian manufacturers re-
sorted to a restriction scheme by which "some 15 percent of the
looms in India were sealed up, and working hours were reduced from
54 to 40 per week." This led to the growth of "outside" competition
and to further expansion of total capacity. Appeals to the new mills
to join in the restriction scheme fell on deaf ears, and the Government refused the request of the Indian Jute Mills Association "to
give legislative sanction to the restriction of working hours."
     In conclusion it is stated that although "the demand for jute
goods is on the upgrade, there is little likelihood that the prospective increase in production ... can be sold except at substantially lower prices... There is little likelihood, moreover,

of a sharp decline in the price of raw jute in the near future; for the restriction of the crop, inaugurated last year under Government auspices, is to be continued during the current season. The Indian jute manufacturing industry, therefore, is in a dilemma, from which there seems no escape except through rationalisation and improvement in efficiency, which may involve the writing off of a substantial proportion of the capital invested in the industry." .

Kroger Grocery & Baking Company

Phillips, C. F. A history of the Kroger Grocery & Baking Company. Natl. Marketing Rev. 1(3): 204-215. Winter 1936. (Published for the National Association of Marketing Teachers, by Business Publications, Inc., 332 South Michigan Ave., Chicago, Ill.)

"Dr. Phillips points out that the Kroger Grocery & Baking Company, the second largest grocery chain in the United States, dates from the opening of a small store in Cincinnati in 1882. Steady expansion to 1927 gave this company a system of 3,749 retail units integrated with manufacturing and wholesaling divisions. Early in 1928 a change in management and control led to a change in the method of expansion- the old policy of opening new stores being replaced by one of acquiring other chains. In sixteen months twenty-eight chains operating 1,838 units were acquired. But, in the face of a business recession, the company found the assimilation of these chains a very difficult task. The result: another change in management and the adoption of new operat- ing policies which have made the Kroger Grocery & Baking Company one of the most efficient organizations in the field of distribution." -Editorial note.

Labor - U.S.S.R.

Road work for the agricultural population in the Soviet Union. Indus. and Labour Inform. 57(12): 324. Mar. 23, 1936. (Published by Inter- national Labour Office, Geneva, Switzerland. Distributed in U. S. by World Peace Foundation, 8 West 40th Street, New York, N.Y.)

An order of March 3, 1936 provides that the agricultural popu- lation be called upon twice a year, in spring and autumn, to take part in the building of roads. "The members of collective farms and peasants holding individual farms will be required to perform six days' unpaid work on one occasion each year, and during this time to place their tools and means of transport at the disposal of the authorities. Certain classes of persons, such as peasants pay- ing the agricultural tax on an individual basis, must perform twelve days' labour a year. Road work is exacted from men between the ages of 18 and 45 and women between the ages of 18 and 40."

Labor, Foreign - France

Zuber, H. E. La main-d'oeuvre étrangère en France. L'immigration polonaise. Soc. d'Encouragement pour l'Industrie Nationale. Bulletin 134(12): 645-655. December 1935. (Published at 44, Rue de Rennes, Paris (6e), France.)

In his study of the immigration of foreign labor into France and
the conditions to which it should be made to conform the author
uses Polish immigration as an illustration of the points he wishes
to make. Polish immigration into France is regulated in accordance
with the terms of a Franco-Polish treaty of September 3, 1919,
supplemented by an agreement of October 14, 1920. The terms of the
agreement are summarized, and the advantages and disadvantages of
foreign immigration are outlined. A general policy which would take
into account the vital interests of the country is suggested.

Land Nationalization - Great Britain

Orwin, C. S. What shall we do with the national estate? Countryman
13(1): 33-39. April 1936. (Published at Idbury, Kingham, Oxfordshire, Eng.)
"State ownership is ... a question of social order and good
business. I believe in it solely because I love the land, and
hate to see the way in which it is either exploited or starved
under a system which has outlived its usefulness. There is money
and plenty in the national estate to provide for all the things I
have mentioned - open spaces and national parks for the town dweller,
land for housing and road construction without exploitation of the
public, development of natural resources without prejudice to preservation of amenities, the maintenance of agricultural equipment.
It is only when the land is divided into thousands of small estates
that you have the contrast of unearned increment on the one hand
and inadequate resources on the other."

Land Office - Germany

The functions of the Reich Land Office. News in Brief 4(1-2): 2-3.
January 1936. (Published by Deutscher Akademischer Austauschdienst
e.V. Berlin, Germany.)
"By the provisions of the statute of March 29th, 1935, which deals
with the Government condemnation of land, the Land Office is given
the following Powers: (1) to supervise a complete land survey in
accordance with the needs and best interests of the state and the
nation; (2) to secure the apportioning of government lands according
to a uniform system. According to the terms of the decree issued
by the Führer on June 26th, 1935, the Land Office has been put in
charge of the entire land planning for the Reich area."
A second decree published in the Reichsgesetzblatt for December
23, 1935 "puts the Reich Land Office in charge of land and Reich
planning (Reichs- und Landesplanung). The director of the Land Office
has the power to regulate the organization and administration of all
land development companies or associations. Land development for
specific purposes will remain under the control of the appropriate
government departments, which, however, must submit all land development schemes to the Reich Land Office. Through this second decree
has been warranted a uniform policy of land planning, which is consistent with the Government's policy of distribution of population,

the reorganization of the farmer class, agricultural measures, colonizing, transportation, re-distribution of manufactories... etc... The Land Offices of the various German provinces are now merged in the Land Office of the Reich [Reichsstelle für Raumordnung] and all land development plans will in future become a part of a national cooperative scheme... The actual work of Landesplanung, i.e. the co-ordinating of all local and district planning schemes into a part of the national scheme of Reichsplanung has a distinctly co-operative character and can best be accomplished, as up to now, through the medium of district land offices. As subordinate planning authorities, therefore, the Prussian Provincial Governors (Oberpräsident) and the Federal Governors (Reichsstatthalter) will be appointed district land officers. These District Land Offices will be given a general jurisdiction within which they can carry out their land development policies. The details of executing these policies will remain in the hands of the appropriate expert authorities. The Reich Land Office ... will assume the responsibility of seeing to it that no special form of land development disturbs the general land scheme which Germany has instituted for the benefit of the nation and its people."

Land Purchase Program and Local Government

Hickley, R. J. The problems and local governmental adjustments to the land purchase program. Land Policy Circ. March 1936, pp.13-16. (Published by the Division of Land Utilization, Resettlement Administration)
    The subject is discussed under the following subheads: The effects of Federal purchase, types of governmental adjustment to be made, and state interest in governmental reorganization.

Land Settlement - British Empire

Oversea settlement in the British Empire. Indus. and Labour Inform. 57(12): 321-324. Mar. 23, 1936. (Published by International Labour Office, Geneva, Switzerland. Distributed in U. S. by World Peace Foundation, 8 West 40th Street, New York, N. Y.)
    Comments made in political circles and in the press of Great Britain, Australia and Canada are quoted on the proposed resumption of an active policy of settlement of British migrants in the Dominions.

Land Taxation

Garland, J. M. The incidence of a progressive land tax. Econ. Rec. 11(21): 145-156. December 1935. (Published at the Melbourne University Press, Melbourne, N.3, Victoria)
    Contents: I. The proportional tax; II. The divisibility of land; III. The fall in returns; IV. The losses of transfer; V. The progressive tax.

Land Tenure - Scotland

Harris, Marshall, and Schepmoes, D. F. Scotland's activity in improving
farm tenancy. Land Policy Circ. February 1936. pp.10-33, mimeogr.
(Issued by Division of Land Utilization, Resettlement Administration,
Washington, D. C.)
   A historical sketch of land tenure in Scotland is summarized by
the authors as follows: "The clan system of land tenure in the
Lowlands of Scotland was completely displaced by feudalistic tenure
during the twelfth century. It survived, in the Highlands, in an
attenuated form until the eighteenth century. Both the feudalistic
tenure system and the modified clan system were displaced by an
unregulated, individualistic system of tenancy under which the soil
resources and the rural tenantry were seriously exploited. The
leaders in Parliament and the townspeople soon realized that a
permanently productive agriculture and a virile farm population were
essential to the best interests of the country as a whole, and that
such could not be established and maintained under the existing
system. Therefore, beginning in 1880, a series of Parliamentary acts
designed to correct the many evils which had grown up under the self-
destructive policy of laissez faire were passed."
   The provisions of the following acts are briefly discussed: The
Hypothec Abolition (Scotland) Act, 1880; The Ground Game (Scotland)
Act, 1880; Agricultural Holdings (Scotland) Act, 1883; The Crofters'
Holdings (Scotland) Act, 1886. The Congested Districts (Scotland)
Act, 1897; The Small Landholders' (Scotland) Act, 1911; and Agricultural Holdings (Scotland) Act, 1923. A table gives the number
of farms in Scotland by size and tenure for the years 1912-1914 and
1920-1933.

Land Utilization and Population - Louisiana

Smith, T. L. Population and land utilization. The problem of submarginal
farms in Louisiana. Southwest Rev. 20(4): 392-398. Summer 1935.
(Published by Southern Methodist University and Louisiana State
University, Dallas, Tex.)
   The writer concludes as follows: "All in all, these data and the
analysis of the factors which have contributed to the present problem,
such as the changing means of subsistence, the increasing density of
population, the differential birth rate, and the nature of the process of migration, leave one with little hope that the situation
will work itself out. At the same time, the increasing magnitude and
complexity of the problem speak loudly against delay in coping with
it. The only way out seems to be zoning of agricultural lands and
relocation of part of the population."

Lands, Range - Research - Montana

[Saunderson, M. F.] Basic inventory materials for research in land
economics. Land Policy Circ. January 1936, pp.18-23. (Published
by the Resettlement Administration, Washington, D. C.)

This article is based on "notes" sent by Mr. Saunderson of the
Montana College of Agriculture to the Resettlement Administration.
Outlines the basic inventory materials needed in a research program in the economics of range lands and their problems of adjustment, together with some of the means for their development. The
article refers particularly to research in Montana.

Maple Syrup - Vermont

Packard, A. H. Hot cakes and maple syrup. Nation's Agr. 11(6): 12-13,23.
March 1936. (Published at 58 E. Washington St., Chicago, Ill.)
The president of the Vermont Farm Bureau Federation shows how
Vermonters have made the nation maple syrup conscious. The story
of the beginning of the Vermont Maple Co-operative is also told.

Marketing Agreements and Licenses, A.A.A.

Nourse, E. G. Marketing agreements, licenses and orders. Natl. Marketing Rev. 1(3): 225-231. Winter, 1936. (Published for the National
Association of Marketing Teachers by Business Publications, Inc.,
332 South Michigan Ave., Chicago, Ill.)
"The Agricultural Adjustment Act not only provided for crop control but also included important provisions for marketing agreements
and licenses which are of particular interest to marketing students.
After a brief analysis of the background of these provisions, Dr.
Nourse discusses the marketing agreements and licensing experience
of the past two years. Marketing agreements have been applied to
certain basic crops, to dairy products, and to what are called
'general crops.' These agreements are examined carefully and the
program of agreements and licenses is critically appraised." -Editor s
note.

Marketing Boards - Great Britain

Agricultural marketing boards and producers' prices. Statist 127(3029-
3031): 415-416, 460,462,501,502. Mar. 14,21,28, 1936. (Published
at 51 Cannon St., London, E.C.4, Eng.)
The second and third articles of this series deal with the Pigs
and Bacon Marketing Schemes.

Mechanization - Great Britain

Mechanization in mixed farming: a conference at Oxford. Gt. Brit. Min.
Agr. Jour. 42(11): 1093-1107. February 1936. (Published by H. M.
Stationery Office, London, Eng.)
Summarizes the papers read at a conference on mechanization in
mixed farming held at Oxford on January 7-10, 1936.

Mechanization - Scotland

Traprain, Viscount. My mechanized farming results. Countryman 13(1):
62-74. April 1936. (Published at Idbury, Kingham, Oxfordshire, Eng.)

A statistically illustrated account of four years' mechanized grain growing in East Lothian.

Milk as a Public Utility

Mortenson, W. P. Distribution of milk under public utility regulation. Amer. Econ. Rev. 26(1): 23-40. March 1936. (Published by the American Economic Association, Northwestern University, Evanston, Ill.)

"Why more than half the consumers' milk dollar snould go for the services of processing and distribution is a query which has prompted much discussion, not only among milk producers and consumers, but among those engaged in marketing research as well. If the profits and salaries of milk dealers were reduced to a minimum through public control, the savings would be insufficient to enhance the farm price of milk, or to lower the price to the consumer by an amount sufficient to satisfy either group.

"Of the many perplexing problems which have faced the Agricultural Adjustment Administration, that of the fluid milk industry has been, and still is, among the most baffling. Past experiences in public control of milk, both economic and legal, suggest that, while absolute control will not be welcomed by producers, the untrammeled freedom of action of the past must be curbed to serve the best interests of society. Control likely will become one of degree, added restrictions being incorporated, as they seem to become essential in particular markets or market areas." -p.23.

Several studies of distributors' margins are quoted from in this paper.

Mortgage Credit – Belgium

Husson, F. Le régime hypothécaire en Belgique, après les arrêtés royaux nos. 225 et 226. La Vie Économique et Sociale 13(2): 189-202. Feb. 15, 1936. (Published by l'Institut Supérieur de Commerce Saint Ignace, 13, Rue du Prince, Anvers, Belgium.)

Discusses the importance of mortgage credit in Belgium, its recent organization, and the functions of the Central Office of Mortgage Credit.

Nutrition and Health

Food and health. Statist 127(3031): 503,504. March 28, 1936. (Published at 51 Cannon St., London, E.C.4, Eng.)

The conclusion of an article dealing with food consumption in relation to income.

Food and incomes. Economist 122(4830): 630,631. Mar. 21, 1936. (Published at 8 Bouverie St., London, E.C.4, Eng.)

Reviews a report on a "Survey of Diet in Relation to Income," by John Boyd Orr, entitled "Food, Health and Income."

In one of the concluding paragraphs the author writes in part: "It is clear ... that if a real national food policy is to be under-

taken, and the problems of nutrition and agriculture are to be
simultaneously solved, the buying power of certain classes of the
community must be increased - by economic policies which will affect
both those in work and those out of work. The distribution of the
national income must also to some extent be altered or be changed
by such means as family allowances. But even when this has been done,
there will probably remain a need for the State to make special provision for the supply of free or cheap food to necessitous persons."

Pasvolsky, Leo. Europe sees its errors. Country Gent. 106(4): 21,86,87.
April 1936. (Published at Independence Ave., Philadelphia, Pa.)
    Relates the progress of an idea conceived by Frank L. McDougall,
economic adviser to the Australian High Commissioner in London, of
aiding his country's agricultural condition by increasing the consumption of agricultural food products by that section of the population whose standard of living is far below the level of adequate
nutrition. In addition to British interests, both the International
Labour Office and the Health Organization of the League of Nations
have become interested and are studying the question. Four principal
lines of approach to achieving this proposed "marriage between agriculture and health" have been suggested: 1, educational propaganda;
2, subsidization of consumption; 3, reduction in the cost of retail
distribution; 4, a basic re-orientation of agricultural policies,
especially in the food-importing countries.

Oranges - Demand

Revzen, D. A. The nature of the demand for oranges. News Bull. 2(3):
20-22. Mar. 13, 1936. (Published by the School of Business of the
University of Chicago, Chicago, Ill.)
    Accompanied by a table which shows consumption (total and per
capita) and retail prices of oranges, annually, 1919-1933; and a
chart which shows adjusted total and per capita orange consumption
and retail orange prices for 1919-1933.

Palestine

Melchett, Rt. Hon. Lord. Palestine: A land of hope for Jewish exiles
from other countries. World Today. Encyclopaedia Britannica 3(4):
5-7. April 1936. (Published at 342 Madison Ave., New York, N.Y.)
    An article describing the "striking changes" which, under the
stimulus of Jewish immigration, have recently taken place in
Palestine. "The whole economic structure of the country is in
fact under-going a fundamental transformation. There has been a
rapid expansion of innumerable industrial enterprises, where industry hardly existed. Modern towns have sprung into life where
before were sand-dunes and hillsides, while as far as agriculture
is concerned, there has been a widespread introduction of modern
methods of intensive cultivation, and the phenomenal growth, as a
result of the utilization of hitherto untapped resources of under-
ground water, of the now vitally important citrus industry."

- 416 -

The writer quotes a few "salient" figures which give "some idea
of the development that has taken place, particularly in the last
three or four years." The figures relate chiefly to population and
industry.

Philippine Islands

Farley, M. S. Philippine independence and agricultural readjustment.
Far East. Survey 5(8): 71-77. Apr. 8, 1936. (Published by the American Council. Institute of Pacific Relations, 129 East 52nd St.,
New York, N. Y.)
In the beginning of this article the author writes that the
"stability of the new regime in the Philippines will depend in
large part upon its ability to promote diversification in the economy
of the Islands, unless the terms of independence now contemplated are
greatly modified...
"It is a commonplace that the economic evolution of the Philippines
has been in the direction of specialization in three or four main export crops, relying principally upon free access to the United States
market; that under these conditions there has been little development
of manufacturing industry, the demand for manufactured products having
been supplied mainly by imports, for which, also, the country has depended chiefly upon the United States; and that the entire foundation
of the economy thus developed is threatened by the terms of the
Tydings-McDuffie independence act... There are weighty arguments in
favor of regional specialization; but in the present situation the
Philippines have no choice but to seek greater security by rebuilding
their national economy on a broader base.
"A survey of the possibilities of orderly readjustment is therefore
of the highest importance for an understanding of the Philippine
question. Since the Philippines are overwhelmingly an agrarian
country, and since it is generally conceded that they must remain
so for some time to come, the present survey is confined for the
most part to the agricultural field."

Planning, Regional

Davidson, Donald. The political economy of regionalism. Amer. Rev. 6(4):
410-434. February 1936. (Published at 231 W. 58th St., New York,
N. Y.)

Regional planning technique, by Odum, Becker and others. Plan Age 2(3):
1-21. March 1936. (Published by National Economic and Social Planning
Association, 726 Jackson Place, Washington, D. C.)
Contents: Planning the Southeast; an abstract of the inventory
made by Howard W. Odum for the Southern regional committee of the
Social science research council, by Donald Becker, pp.1-6. Realistic
premises for regional planning objectives, by Howard W. Odum, pp.7-21.
("Coordinated excerpts from Howard W. Odum's 'Southern Regions of
United States' published by the University of North Carolina Press.")

Price Analysis

Stackelberg, Heinrich von. Die grundlegenden Hypothesen der neueren
Preisanalyse. Archiv für Mathematische Wirtschafts- und Sozial-
forschung 1(2): 84-103, 1935. (Published by H. Buske, Leipzig,
Germany.)
The basic hypotheses of the newer methods of price analysis are
discussed, as sponsored by Moore, Schultz, Staehle and Leontief.

Prices, Retail

Retail prices in certain towns in 1935. Internatl. Labour Rev. 33(3):
436-439. March 1936. (Published by the International Labour Office,
Geneva, Switzerland. Distributed in U. S. by the World Peace
Foundation, 8 West 40th St., New York, N.Y.)
Contains a table which gives the retail prices of certain foodstuffs and articles in October 1935, or some neighboring date, in
21 countries, which are "the results of the enquiry carried out by
the International Labour Office into retail prices in different
countries in 1935, in continuation of enquiries on the subject for
previous years, which have been published in the Review under a
similar title."

Prices, Wholesale, and Inflation - France

Wasserman, M. J. The compression of French wholesale prices during inflation, 1919-1926. Amer. Econ. Rev. 26(1): 62-73. March 1936.
(Published by the American Economic Association, Northwestern
University, Evanston, Ill.)
"It has been recognized generally that prices, under inflation,
when measured in terms of the depreciated currency, tend to rise.
However, when measured in terms of gold, inflation may serve to
depress the price level below that which prevails in stable money
countries. This phenomenon characterized the French inflation of
1919-1926. The explanation of the relative compression of the
French price level is to be found in enterpriser price-policy, the
lower costs, the increasing volume of production, and the reduced
purchasing power which characterized the period. According to the
purchasing power parities theory, the rates of exchange should have
equalized French and world prices. Their failure to do so indicates
that this theory presents an oversimplified view of the elements
conditioning price structures." -p.62.

Processing Taxes

Sanders, J. T. The national significance of the Agricultural processing
taxes. Nati. Tax Assoc. Proc.(1935) 28: 163-180.
Dr. Sanders deals with the economic rather than the fiscal aspects
of the question, stating that his purpose is "to deal in particular
with the nature of the agricultural disparity which the tax was
intended to correct, to inquire into the tendency toward a permanent

- 418 -

unbalanced relationship between agricultural and urban industry,
and the necessity for permanent machinery for correcting this lack
of balance between farming and other industry."

Production and Consumption

McCracken, H. L. An appraisal of the possibility of plenty, an article -
review of five books. Soc. Adv. Mangt. Jour. 1(2): 50-59. March
1936. (Published at the Engineering Societies Building, 29 W. 39th
St., New York, N. Y.)
    This is a review of the four books published by the Brookings
    Institution - America's Capacity to Produce, America's Capacity to
    Consume, The Formation of Capital, and Income and Economic Progress;
    and of The Chart of Plenty.

Raw Materials

Colonial raw materials. Round Table, no. 102, pp.306-314. March 1936.
(Published by Macmillan & Co., Ltd., London, Eng. May be obtained
from The Macmillan Co., 60 Fifth Ave., New York, N. Y.)
    In two parts: Part I, Colonial resources and national defense;
    II, The economic complex.

Greaves, H.R.G. Raw materials and war. New Statesman and Nation (n.s.)
11(263): 335-337. Mar. 7, 1936. (Published at 10, Great Turnstile,
London, W.C.1, Eng.)
    A discussion of producers' agreements and of the political con-
    flict that may be a consequence because of the Government's partici-
    pation in the agreement. Special mention is made of the Stevenson
    rubber restriction scheme, The International Tin Committee, The
    International Rubber Regulation Committee, The Chadbourne Sugar
    Agreement, and the Wheat Agreement— one of the "few results" of the
    Economic Conference of 1933.

Relief, Rural, and the Back-to-the-Land Movement

Woofter, T. J., Jr. Rural relief and the back-to-the-farm movement.
Social Forces 14(3): 382-388. March 1936. (Published for the
University of North Carolina Press by the Williams & Wilkins Co.,
Baltimore, Md.)
    The thesis of this paper is that the rural relief situation "in
    part, grew out of a back-to-the-land movement and a cessation of
    the previous movement away from the land." In conclusion the writer
    briefly discusses the question of so reconstructing "agrarian cul-
    ture that it will provide a satisfactory life for a larger number
    of people despite restrictive tendencies in commercial farming and
    increased productivity per man." Among the needs are intensive
    pioneering on the part of some of the newcomers on the land, more
    coordination between the philosophy of the AAA and that of the Re-
    settlement Administration, the adjusting of emergency programs so that
    farmers will not be taken away from the land, and "widespread

dissemination of knowledge as to population trends and agricultural opportunities so that this misdirected back-to-the-poor-land movement may, insofar as possible, be redirected."

Research

Research as visualized in the 1935 report of the Secretary of Agriculture. Expt. Sta. Rec. 74(3): 289-292. March 1936. (Published by the Office of Experiment Stations, U. S. Dept. of Agriculture)
Editorial.

Rural Home-makers' Conference, Columbus, Ohio. 1935.

"Services essential to effective rural living- and how to get them." Presented by rural homemakers at the conference on the rural home held by the American Country Life Association, Columbus, Ohio, September 19, 1935. In cooperation with the Extension Service, United States Department of Agriculture, and the Ohio State University. Rural Amer. 14(3): 3-16. March 1936. (Published by the American Country Life Association, 105 E. 22nd St., New York, N. Y.)
Contains the short papers given by rural homemakers on health, religion, leisure time activities, reading, citizenship, education, housing, electricity, rural credit, taxation, and cooperative endeavors, and a summary of the conference by Theodore B. Manny.

Rural Sociology Research - Relation to Extension Teaching

Melvin, B. L. Extension in relation to research in rural sociology. Social Forces 14(3): 362-367. March 1936. (Published for the University of North Carolina Press, by the Williams & Wilkins Company, Baltimore, Md.)
The following is quoted from the author's introductory paragraphs:
"... the time is ripe for an appraisal of the functions that the extension rural sociologists may perform in the light of the accomplishments of research and in response to the present day needs, opportunities and possibilities for expansion.
"This discussion concerning the relation of extension teaching in rural sociology to research in the same field is incomplete and nonconclusive but it is designed to stimulate coördinated effort in the two aspects of the same field rather than to give any final statements. I am frankly taking two positions which are somewhat opportune: first, that the justification for research in rural sociology today in the state colleges of agriculture is to collect the facts by which rural problems may be solved; and second, that it is the obligation of the extension rural sociologist to assist in the solution of rural social problems by using the accumulated knowledge. An elaboration of this position falls under three topics: (1) the subject matter of rural sociology; (2) the present activities of rural sociological extension; and (3) opportunities for extension based upon present knowledge and possible expansion of both the extension and research activities."

Small Holdings and Handicrafts - Sweden

Smallholdings and handicrafts in Sweden. Indus. and Labour Inform. 57(4):
95-96. Jan. 27, 1936. (Issued by International Labour Office, Geneva,
Switzerland. Distributed in U. S. by World Peace Foundation, 8 West
40th St., New York, N. Y.)
    A commission of enquiry, appointed by the Swedish Government, has
made proposals to provide increased facilities for combining small
holdings with home industries, handicrafts, etc.

Social Legislation - New Zealand

Haslam, E\ P. Social legislation in New Zealand; a comparison. Econ. Rec.
11(21): 214-236. December 1935. (Published at the Melbourne University
Press, Melbourne, N.3, Victoria)
    This article is in three sections. Section I is introductory.
Section II "compares the standards of labour legislation in New
Zealand with the Conventions of the International Labour Conferences,
and is a summary of a more comprehensive study recently made by the
writer. Section III is a brief historical account of the attitude
political circles and the business community have adopted toward
I.L.O. since 1920. The scope of the inquiry is limited to Conventions 1-33."
    Convention 12 of Class I has to do with workers' compensation in
agriculture. Convention 10, Class II is entitled "Minimum Age (Agriculture)"; and Convention 25 of Class III has to do with sickness
insurance among agricultural workers.

Soil Erosion and the Soil Conservation Act

Agriculture is constitutionall, replanted. Sphere 17(4): 21-23. April
1936. (Published at the Munsey Bldg., Washington, D. C.)
    An article in which the new Soil Conservation Act is explained.
Attention is drawn to points in which it differs from the A.A.A., and
to others in which it is similar. The opinion is expressed that the
ultimate program will probably be along lines of milk and other
marketing agreements, with special emphasis on cooperatives.
    A table is given which shows the list of 12 States receiving the
highest farm benefit payments, per capita, for the fiscal year ending June 30, 1935, compared with estimated wealth in the same States.

Bennett, H. H. Menace of soil erosion. Nation's Agr. 11(6): 4-5,18,19.
March 1936. (Published at 58 E. Washington St., Chicago, Ill.)
    The Chief of the Soil Conservation Service, now directing "one of
the nation's most important reconstruction projects" writes of what is
happening to our farm lands through soil erosion and loss of soil
fertility. He also describes briefly the work of the Soil Conservation
Service.

Conservation. Consumers' Guide 3(6): 3-10, 31. Mar. 23, 1936. (Published
by the Consumers' Counsel of the Agricultural Adjustment Administration,

U. S. Dept. of Agriculture!)

An illustrated article in which the writer states that the "major objective of agricultural adjustment was to lift farm prices to 'parity" and that "conserving those gains in income, won under production-control programs which are no longer possible, and conserving and extending those good farm practices started cooperatively under those programs, are the two major objectives of farmers under the Soil Conservation and Domestic Allotment Act." Routes to these objectives are considered, as well as the question as to what the new farm program holds for the consumer.

Fisher, F. A. What America's soil conservation program requires of the engineer. Agr. Engin. 17(2): 45-46, 54. February 1936. (Published at St. Joseph, Mich.)

In conclusion: "The purpose of agricultural engineering work in a soil conservation program is, from the farmer's standpoint, to stabilize and preserve the soil for crop production purposes. The agricultural engineer in soil conservation work must, above everything else, be a man of vision with an open mind who is able and willing to grasp new ideas and apply them in a practical manner to the problems at hand."

The new soil-erosion program: its inducements to the farmer. U. S. News 4(12): 12. Mar. 23, 1936. (Published at 2201 M St., N.W., Washington, D. C.)

O'Neal, E. A. Building better farms. Nation's Agr. 11(6): 7, 21. March 1936. (Published at 58 E. Washington St., Chicago, Ill.)

"The president of the American Farm Bureau Federation describes the underlying philosophy of the proposed farm legislation now before Congress, in the creation of which the Farm Bureau played a significant and leading part. The job of saving our great soil resources, Mr. O'Neal says, out of which to built better farms, is paramount." -[Editor's note]

Taylor, E. H. Who takes the rap? Country Gent. 106(4): 14,91,92. April 1936. (Published at Independence Square, Philadelphia, Pa.)

Critical of the recently enacted soil conservation program because of its "unmistakable marks of political designing" and because of its dangers for the range, dairy and hay interests.

Recommends "an honest and genuine soil-conservation program", free from political auspices, and considering first the man owning or occupying the land, next the interest of the states and local communities, and lastly the national government.

An editorial along the same line, with title, Should We Pay People to Do Right? is printed on p.20.

Tolley, H. R. Conserving our soil resources for future generations. Nation's Agr. 11(7): 16-17, 19. April 1936. (Published at 58 E. Washington St., Chicago, Ill.)

"Because of the lack of a national agricultural policy, it has been impossible for farmers as individuals to live up to a program

which would leave their farms in a higher state of fertility after
they were through farming...

"How to develop a nation-wide cooperation program so that the farmers can work together to limit the effects of competition and prevent
that competition from continuing in the exploitation of soil resources,
is a problem which this country faces. The soil conservation program
represents a starting point toward putting a firmer foundation under
American Civilization."

Wallace, H. A. New vistas for agriculture. Secretary Wallace finds that
the prospects for soil conservation are bright, though much depends
on the attitude of the farmer. New York Times Mag., Mar. 29, 1936,
pp.4-5, 18. Clipping.

Statistics, Agricultural - China

Wishart, John. Statistics in Chinese agricultural research. Amer. Statis.
Assoc. Jour. 31(193): 127-128. March 1936. (Published at 450 Ahnaip
St., Manasha, Wis.)
A brief review of agricultural statistical work in China.

Subsistence Homesteads

Bishop, Warren. A yardstick for housing. Nation's Business 24(4): 29-31,
69, 70-71. April 1936. (Published by the Chamber of Commerce of the
United States, Washington, D. C.)
"'Establishment, maintenance and operation of communities' for low
income families was one of the jobs given to the Resettlement Administration a year ago. Here is a picture of the accomplishments to date
and of the difficulties which unexpectedly multiply the costs of
'planned economy.'"
Communities discussed are the Jersey Homesteads (subsistence homestead) at Hightstown, N. J., and the green belt communities at
Bound Brook, N. J., Milwaukee, Wis., Cincinnati, Ohio, and Berwyn, Md.,
and the proposed green belt community near St. Louis, Mo., which did
not materialize.

The New Deal's housing activities. Cong. Digest 15(4): 103-128. April 1936.
(Published at 2131 LeRoy Place, Washington, D. C.)
The construction activities of the Resettlement Administration in
the fields of subsistence homesteads and rural and suburban resettlement are briefly outlined on p.111.
In the pro and con section of this issue, pp.114-116 there is an
article by Rexford Guy Tugwell which is an extract from an address
before the Hamilton County Regional Planning Commission, Cincinnati,
Ohio, Feb. 3, 1936.
A bibliography on Building, Housing and Construction is given on
pp.127-128. The references were selected from a bibliography prepared
by the Construction and Civic Development Department, Chamber of
Commerce of the U. S., January 1933.

Sugar - Dutch East Indies

The "Sugar Regulations for 1936" in the Volksraad. Netherlands Indies 4(4):
65-70. Feb. 15, 1936. (Issued by Department of Economic Affairs.
Published by G. Kolff & Co., Batavia, Java, N. I.)
   "The measures were finally adopted as proposed by the Government
with the addition of an amendment ... authorizing the Government to
fix a minimum wage for sugar labourers if such were deemed advisable.
The report that follows is not intended to be a complete account of
the proceedings; it is only intended to throw more light on certain
moot points that were discussed during the various debates." It includes reasons for the Government's intervention in the sugar industry,
debate on the interests of the people and the social side of the sugar
problem, the system of distributing the production quota among the
various producers, the regulation of distribution, and the decisions
adopted.

Tergast, G. C. W. C. Proposed sugar regulations for 1936 and subsequent
years. Netherlands Indies 4(3): 51-56. Feb. 1, 1936. (Issued by
Department of Economic Affairs. Published by G. Kolff & Co., Batavia,
Java, N. I.)
   "The Government has recently laid five draft ordinances before the
Volksraad for consideration... This collection of regulations concerning the Java sugar industry was deemed to be necessary in connection with the expiration on April 1, 1936, of the current regulations, and the fact that the situation in which this industry finds
itself is such that continued intervention by the Government must be
considered imperative." The motives leading to further Government
intervention, the subjects to be regulated and the construction of
the draft regulations are discussed and a short summary is given of
the regulations formulated for 1937 to 1940. "The key note of the
whole series of regulations is the prohibition of producing sugar
except when and insofar as it is covered by a production permit."

Sugar - Java

Control scheme for Java ready. Facts about Sugar 31(1): 6. January 1936.
(Published at 36 West 45th St., New York, N. Y.)
   "Regulatory bills now awaiting enactment give Government power to
fix production quotas. Nivas to be continued as sole selling agency."

Supply and Demand - Elasticity

Timpe, Aloys. Elastizität von Angebot und Nachfrage. Archiv für
mathematische Wirtschafts- und Sozialforschung 1(2): 103-114. 1935.
(Published by H. Buske, Leipzig, Germany.)

Tariff and Agriculture

Grady, H. F. Agriculture and the tariff. Nation's Agr. 11(7): 7,30.
April 1936. (Published at 58 E. Washington St., Chicago, Ill.)
   The importance of the change in the position of the United States
from a debtor to a creditor nation following the World War, is

pointed out in the beginning of this article. The farmer, according
to the writer, has been the loser throughout the tariff history of
the United States. "In 1921, when the post-war depression was finally
felt in this country, the first thought of certain of our leaders was
to place a high tariff on foreign merchandise. It was not, however,
a question of retaliation abroad against our high protective tariff
which caused a decrease in our trade. It was, rather, the inability of
our former customers for agricultural products to pay for them."

The Tariff Act of 1930 was "hailed by its sponsors as a measure
to revive industry and agriculture", but in "actual practice, agr-
culture gained very little from the Tariff Act of 1930" because
countries who had been our customers could not sell to us over the
barriers imposed by the Act, and agriculture was the principal
sufferer.

The Trade Agreements Act of June 12, 1934, authorizing the
reciprocal agreements is next discussed. The concessions obtained
for agriculture by these agreements "should be of great assistance
to the American farmer in helping him to recover his foreign markets."

Tithe -- England

Tithe. By the Editor of 'Crockford'. Nineteenth Century and After 119(710):
417-427. April 1936. (Published at Orange St., Leicester Sq.,
London, W.C.2, Eng.)

Regarding the "Report of the Royal Commission [which was]
appointed on August 27, 1934, 'to inquire into and report upon the
whole question of tithe rentcharge in England and Wales'". The report
was published on February 27, 1936.

"The conclusions of the Majority Report, which recommends the
complete abolition of tithe rentcharge, are summarised as follows
on pp. 46-47 [of the Report]:

"The tithepayer will pay in halfyearly instalments at the rate of
L 91 11s. 2d. per annum per L 100 tithe rentcharge (par value) for
a period of forty years. The titheowner will receive a security [in
the form of Government stock bearing interest at 3 per cent,] which
will give him a net income of the highest class equivalent in value
to that which his property, if valued as we propose, would produce.
The State will for forty years contribute an annual sum substantially
less than the amount which under existing legislation it pays in respect of the rates on ecclesiastical tithe rentcharge -- a payment which
under the Tithe Act of 1925 was to continue for a period of eighty-five
years, of which over seventy years still remain unexpired. The State
will, however, support a certain new expense in the collection of the
redemption annuities and in the cost of the Temporary Commission and
may have to consider some concession to certain local authorities in
respect of the loss of rates. [Section 120.]"

The writer explains to those not familiar with the technical-
ities of the subject, "that the rentcharge is the term commonly used
in lieu of tithe since the Act of 1836 substituted a payment in money
based on the average price of corn for the previous seven years for
tithe in kind - i.e., one-tenth of the actual produce of the land."

Tithe. Current Survey Agr. Policy (Digest of Press News) 3(2): 21-23.
Feb. 17 - Mar. 14, 1936, mimeogr. (Published at 3, Magpie Lane,
Oxford, Eng.)

"The Royal Commission on Tithe Rentcharge, appointed in 1934 to
enquire into the whole question of tithe rentcharge in England and
Wales and its incidence, has issued its report. Along with it, the
Government has issued a White Paper of the Government's proposals
based on the report.

"The main conclusions of the Commission are that the existing
system of tithe rentcharge should be extinguished on fair and
equitable terms. The proposal is that the Government should 'buy
out' all tithe owners (ecclesiastical and lay) by means of a new
3% issue of stock. The tithe rentcharge paid by owners of land will
be paid to the Government through the Inland Revenue Department, and
payments will provide for the extinction of the liability in 40 years.

"The Government in the White Paper has accepted these proposals
with the exception that the redemption will be extended to 60 years
instead of 40 years."

Editorials in the London Times and the Manchester Guardian for
February 28 are referred to as approving the scheme on the whole.
Queen Anne's Bounty "commend the main principle of the scheme in the
earnest hope that means may be found for making the terms less severe
on the church."

The Bursar of New College, Oxford (Times, March 3) refers to the
loss of colleges and the council of the National Tithepayers' Association and representatives of titheowners express disapproval.

Tobacco - China

Tobacco production and marketing in China. Chinese Econ. Jour. 16(5): 531-
543. May 1935. (Published by Bureau of Foreign Trade, Ministry of
Industry, 1040 North Soochow Road, Shanghai, China.)

This is the second of two articles, the first having appeared in
the issue for April. Tables show prices, imports and exports.

Trade, International, and Southern Agriculture

Berglund, Abraham. The effect of current international trade conditions
and foreign agricultural developments on Southern agriculture. South.
Econ. Jour. 2(3): 61-68. January 1936. (Published by the Southern
Economic Association and the University of North Carolina at Chapel
Hill, N. C.)

The writer concludes this article by summing up the problem of
adjusting the agriculture of the South to current international trade
conditions as follows:

"1. Southern agriculture still remains in large measure dependent
upon foreign markets... Any adjustment involving a drastic and
permanent curtailment of this export trade in the interest of the
present trend toward a self-contained economy will cause dislocations
in the Southern agriculture which will be peculiarly severe.

"2. The spread of economic nationalism during the post-war years,
and particularly since 1929, is a phenomenon which cannot be ignored

and has for the time being much significance for industries dependent
upon foreign markets. At the same time this development is not unique.
It has taken place before, especially during and following devastating
wars. But it has always, and particularly in recent times, run counter
to economic progress and has sooner or later been modified or destroyed.
Unless the world becomes war-mad – and there are indications that this
is not impossible – this economic nationalism, at least in its present
extreme form, will become a thing of the past. An adjustment, therefore, to a present phase of international trade policy should not leave
out of account its probable temporary duration.

"3. The fact that importing nations often adopt the industrial
technique of the countries from which they derive their foreign wares
and then produce for themselves does necessitate changes in the nature
of the commodities handled. Commerce between such nations, however,
is rarely reduced because of this adoption. In the case of agricultural products with their dependence upon certain climatic and soil conditions foreign adoption of the productive process, particularly with
reference to special grades or varieties, is not so easy. The maintenance of a foreign market for agricultural specialities, once it is
secured, can often continue, when it may be lost in the field of
ordinary manufactures.

"4. The ability to market any domestic product in a foreign land
is profoundly influenced by the general tariff policy of the home
country ... one phase of our Southern agricultural problem is our
country's general tariff policy."

Trade Agreements

The Canadian-American trade agreement. Round Table, no. 102, pp.385-392.
     March 1936. (Published by Macmillan & Co., Ltd., London, Eng. May
     be obtained from the Macmillan Co., 60 Fifth Ave., New York, N. Y.)

Murchison, C. T. The reciprocal trade agreements program and how it is
     working. Natl. Marketing Rev. 1(3): 240-246. Winter 1936. (Published
     for the National Association of Marketing Teachers, by Business Publi-
     cations, Inc., 332 South Michigan Ave., Chicago, Ill.)
          "Dr. Murchison draws a realistic picture of the reciprocal trade
     agreement program and its functioning based upon first-hand contact
     with both. After summarizing briefly the theoretical and practical
     background for the program, he launches into a description of objectives
     of the government, the procedure followed in making trade agreements
     and the results, as far as they can be measured of those agreements
     which were first consummated." –Editor's note.

Reciprocity. Index 16(4): 61-67. April 1936. (Published by the New York
     Trust Co., 100 Broadway, New York, N. Y.)
          A discussion of the ten trade agreements that have been concluded.

Trees and Agriculture -- Prairie Provinces, Canada.

Ross, N. M. The role of trees in modifying the agriculture of the dry
     areas of the Prairie Provinces. Sci. Agr. 16(5): 266-269. January

1936. (Published in Ottawa, Canada.)
"Paper read before a joint session of the Western Canadian Society
of Agronomy and the Soils Group and Engineering Group of the C.S.T.A.
of the University of Alberta, Edmonton, June 26, 1935."

U.S. Dept. of Agriculture

The Department of agriculture ... which kills the farmer's pests, breeds
the farmer's grain, dikes the farmer's soil, calls the farmer's frosts,
finds the farmer's market, and generally justifies the great American
conviction that the farmer is the most independent, self-reliant, and
unregimented of men. Fortune 13(4): 95-103,198,202, illus. April
1936. (Published at 350 East 22nd St., New York, N. Y.)
The following editorial note indicates the tone of the article:
"In March Fortune indicated that the farm problem will be the federal
taxpayer's problem for some time to come. Here Fortune suggests that
the farmer will take very kindly to the federal taxpayer's aid - that
he has, indeed, taken very kindly to federal aid for years past."
The article is mainly concerned with the scientific work of the Department but a little space is devoted to the Crop Reporting Service.
Attention is also called to the efficiency of the Department's
organization and its value to the country as a whole.
"Altogether, one bureau with another, it is extremely doubtful if
there exists even in that Jerusalem of the civil service, London, any
civil-service organization of equal value to society."

Wealth

Doane, R. R. Statistical bases for national wealth estimates. Annalist
47(1210): 478. Mar. 27, 1936. (Published at Times Sq., New York,
N. Y.)
A reply to Mr. Whitney's critical review of a part of Mr. Doane's
study relating to the national wealth in The Annalist of March 6.

Wheat - Canada and Australia

Strange, H.G.L. Wheat in Canada and Australia. Northwest. Miller 185(8):
687,696-697. Mar. 11, 1936. (Published at 118 South 6th St.,
Minneapolis, Minn.)
"This article ... was prepared as one of a series of informative
lectures on grain and its marketing, under the auspices of the Association of Grain Commission Merchants, Chicago." Editor's Note.

Wheat - France

Maspétiol, Poland. Le nouveau statut du blé en France. Revue Économique
Internationale, 28. année, v.1, no.2, pp.279-291. February 1936.
(Published by the Institut Économique International, Palais d'Egmont,
Brussels, Belgium.)
The failure of the attempt at directed economy, the circumstances
that led up to the law of December, 1934, its application, the sub-
sequent development of the market, and the decree-law of October 30,
1935 to consolidate and augment the recent price increase, are discussed

Wheat - Market Stabilization - Canada

Evans, W. Sanford. Canadian wheat stabilization operations, 1929-35. Wheat
Studies of the Food Research Institute 12(7): 249-271. March 1936.
(Published in Stanford University, Calif.)
"In a period dating from the beginning of the crop year 1929-30 in
the United States, and continuing in Canada until the close of the crop
year 1934-35, centralized wheat co-operatives, with the support of
government money and credit, operated in the wheat markets of their
respective countries on a scale never before possible to any regular
market agencies. These co-operatives did not work together and phases
of their activities did not strictly correspond in time, but their
market policies were similar, and a combined influence on world wheat
markets might be expected. A study of this period should yield
important lessons in the principles of marketing.
"It is not yet practicable to bring all relevant facts under review
and some movements initiated in this period are still uncompleted. In
an introductory way the developments in connection with the operations
of the co-operative in the United States are herein sketched; the
developments in Canada are more fully presented, the main elements of
the Canadian situation between August 1931 and July 1935 being assembled
in graphic form.
"Questions are raised as to direct effects produced, and more general
questions as to the extent to which wheat prices can be influenced by
special market operations of this type. In so far as answers seem
clearly indicated by the facts under examination, such answers are
tentatively suggested. Definite conclusions on the broad issues involved are not attempted." -cover page.

Wheat - Prices - Australia

Wheat prices on Sydney market, 1890 to 1935. Agr. Gaz. New South Wales
45(3): 138. March 1936. (Published in Sydney, New South Wales.)
A table shows the average price of wheat for February and March
of each year and also the average annual price from 1890 to 1935.

Wheat - Standards - Australia

Sutton, G. L. The valuation of Australian wheat for commercial purposes.
Econ. Rec. 11(21): 237-248. December 1935. (Published at the
Melbourne University Press, Melbourne, N.3, Victoria)
Contents: I. The necessity for trading standards; II. The adoption
and fixing of the f.a.q. standard; III. The defects of the f.a.q.
standard; IV. Remedies - (a) The use of the pseudo f.a.q. and
arbitrary standards. (b) The proposed modified f.a.q. standard;
V. The advantages of the modified f.a.q. standard.
"The principal standard by which wheat is valued and marketed
throughout Australia is known as the F.A.Q. Under this standard
different parcels of wheat are bulked together, and sold according
to what is regarded as their fair average quality; it is from the
initial letters of the three words in this term that the name of the

standard has been derived. It has become recognized by custom as
the commercial abbreviation for that term. This standard relates to
the crop of a particular season only, and it is, therefore, necessarily
fixed annually."

Wheat - Statistics - France

Proust. Les statistiques officielles et privées du blé en France. Étude
des méthodes et comparaison des résultats. Les méthodes étrangères --
les statistiques mondiales. Societé de Statistique de Paris. Journal
77(1): 4-83. January 1936. (Published by Berger-Levrault, 5, Rue
Auguste-Comte (6°), Paris, France.)

The author makes a rapid survey of the history of agricultural
statistics in France, their evolution and their methods and discusses
the present condition of agricultural statistics and the dependence
to be placed on their conclusions, with a view to determining whether,
from the purely statistical point of view, economy can be directed.

A critical study of consumption-statistics leads to the conclusion
that while such a study is possible for a given period in the past, it
cannot be used as a basis for annual forecasts.

Statistics of production are studied under the following headings:
Before the official investigation of 1840; the investigation of 1840
and the decree of 1852; the investigations conducted in the application
of the provisions of this decree; the present method established by
the decree of 1902.

This historical summary is followed by a critical study of the results obtained from the methods used in the official compilation of
wheat statistics. It is shown that the results obtained by the investigations of the past are not comparable with those of the present
and that all the results are widely divorced from reality. The
estimates of area and production which are basically important are
found to be inaccurate. While the former may be improved it is very
difficult to improve the latter. Hence it is shown that the statistics
of production are only approximations which are entirely insufficient
from the agricultural, commercial, or governmental point of view. Hence
directed economy is a utopian dream with no basis in reality.

The author summarizes briefly the methods adopted in other countries
to compile wheat statistics before and after the establishment of the
International Institute of Agriculture.

A number of appendices contain statistical tables and maps. A
table gives the area, yield per hectare, production, and average price
per quintal yearly from 1815 to 1934, and a chart illustrates the
fluctuations in the price of wheat from 1200 to 1815.

Wine Industry - Germany

The German wine industry in 1935. Foreign Crops and Markets 32(13): 380-385.
Mar. 30, 1936. (Published by the Division of Foreign Agricultural
Service, Bureau of Agricultural Economics, U. S. Dept. of Agriculture.)

"Based on reports from American Consul R. W. Heingartner, Frankfort
on the Main, Germany."

Contains data on German wine acreage, production, yield, consumption,
exports, and imports.

Wool Clip

Gardener, H. J. How to prepare a wool clip for market. Pastoral Rev.
46(1): 31-32; (2): 146-148. Jan. 16, Feb. 15, 1936. (Published
at 122-138 King St., Melbourne)
Characteristics required by manufacturers are considered in this
article.

Wool Futures Market - Antwerp

Wool futures. Pastoral Rev. 46(1): 32,33. Jan. 16, 1936. (Published at
122-138 King St., Melbourne.)
An article on the operation of the Antwerp Wool Futures Market,
an agency for which has been established in Australia.

NOTES

Alsberg, H. G., ed. America fights the depression; a photographic record of
the Civil works administration edited and compiled from photographs
and materials furnished by the Federal emergency relief administration
and the State emergency relief administration... introduction by
H. L. Hopkins. 160pp. New York, Coward-McCann, 1934. 283 A17
Contains a page of text and numerous pictures relating to self-help
cooperatives.

Association of southern agricultural workers. Proceedings of 34th-36th, 1933-
1935 annual conventions. 600 pp. [Atlanta? Ga., 1936?] 4 C82
As the papers read before the Agricultural Economics and Rural Sociology Section of the three conventions noted above were very much
abbreviated for printing in the Proceedings it seems best not to list
them.

Atlanta and West Point rail road company, the Western railway of Alabama,
Georgia railroad. Agricultural dept. Annual report, 1935. 50pp.,
mimeogr. [Atlanta? Ga.] Dec. 31, 1935. 281.9 At6
Among much else gives a survey of agricultural conditions in the
counties served by this railroad in Georgia and Alabama.

Blaisdell, D. C. The farmer's stake in world peace. 16pp. [New York] Oct.
1935. Pam. Coll.
May be obtained from Carnegie Endowment for International Peace,
Division of Intercourse and Education, 405 West 117th Street, New
York, N. Y.

China. Ministry of industries. Bureau of statistics. The Wusih worker's
cost of living and its index-number. 51pp. Nanking, China, Bureau of
statistics, Ministry of industries, 1935. C 284.4 C44
Chinese: added title and table of contents in English.

Cook, J. S. In defence of sugar beet ... With a foreword by Lord Cranworth.
32pp. Ipswich, W. E. Harrison & sons, 1935. 281.365 C77
Bibliography, pp. 31-32
Written in favor of the continuation of the sugar beet subsidy.

Dohr, J. L., Ingham, W. A., and Love, A. L. Cost accounting practice
    problems... 1935 series. 167pp. New York, The Ronald press company
    [1935] (University accounting series, R. B. Kester ... editor)
    325 D58C

Dohr, J. L., Ingham, W. A., and Love, A. L. Cost accounting; principles
    and practice... 2d rev. ed. 631pp. New York, The Ronald press
    company [1935] (University accounting series) 325 D68
        "References" at end of most chapters.

Gt. Brit. Ministry of Agriculture and fisheries. Sugar industry (re-
    organization bill) Explanatory memorandum. 8pp. London, H. M.
    Stationery off., 1936. ([Parliament. Papers by command] Cmd. 5080)
    286.355 G792S

Gt. Brit. Treaties, etc., 1910-1936 (George V) Exchange of notes between
    His Majesty's government in the United Kingdom and the Swedish
    government supplementary to the Commercial agreement of May 15, 1933,
    Stockholm, May 27/June 15, 1935. 3pp. London, H. M. Stationery off.,
    1935. ([Foreign office] Treaty series no. 38 (1935)) 286 G797Ase
        Parliament. Papers by command. Cmd. 5022.

Iversen, Carl. Aspects of the theory of international capital movements.
    536pp. Copenhagen, Levin & Munksgaard; [etc., etc.] 1935. 284 Iv5
        Bibliography, pp. [526] -536.
        A signed review will appear in a later issue.

Julius Rosenwald fund. Hospital facilities in rural areas. 28pp. Chicago,
    Julius Rosenwald fund, 1935. Articles reprinted from The Modern
    Hospital, The Bulletin of the American Medical Association, a statement
    by the Commonwealth fund. 448 J942

Land utilisation survey of Britain. Fifth annual report of the Land
    utilization survey of Britain. February, 1936. 15pp., mimeogr.
    London 1936. 282.9 L222
        At head of title: London School of Economics. L. Dudley Stamp,
    Director.

Lohmann, K. B. A community-planning primer for Illinois. 24pp. Urbana,
    Ill. [1935] (University of Illinois Bulletin v. 32, no. 50, Aug. 13,
    1935) 98.5 L83C
        Bibliography, p.24.

Merchant, C. D. Some "believe-it-or-not's" of the apple industry. 65 pp.,
    mimeogr. Wenatchee, Wash. [1935?] 281.393 M53

Myers, W. I. Building a permanent system of cooperative credit. 17pp.
    [Washington, U. S. Govt. print. off., 1936. (U. S. Farm credit
    administration. Circular A-5)] 166.2 C4922 no.5
        An address at the annual convention of the Maryland Farm Bureau,
    Baltimore, Md.

Philips, Rosa. De invloed van de braziliaansche koffieverdedigings-
politick op de koffie-importen der hoofdconsumptielanden. The
influence of the Brazilian coffee defence policy on the coffee
imports of the principal consuming countries. 131pp. Haarlem,
De erven F. Bohn n.v., 1934. (Nederlandsch economisch institut.
Netherlands economic institute. [Publications] nr.9) 286.368 P53
Dutch.

Robinson & company, inc., Chicago. Concerning joint stock land banks;
containing graphs showing their progress in liquidation under the
Emergency farm mortgage act of 1935. 36pp. Chicago, Robinson &
company, inc. [1936] 284.2 R562

South Africa. Dept. of agriculture and forestry. Fruit production in the
Union (Notes from the Office of the Chief fruit inspector, Capetown).
Report no. 17; The 1933-34 deciduous fruit export season. 74pp.
Pretoria, The Government printer, 1936. (South Africa Dept. of
agriculture and forestry. Bulletin no. 154) 24 So84P no.154.

Tomlinson, F. R. Mechanical and animal draught power on grain farms. 26pp.
Pretoria, the Government printer, 1935. (South Africa. Dept. of
agriculture. Bulletin no. 152) 24 So84P no.152
"South Africa. Dept. of agriculture and forestry. Stellenbosch-
Elsenburg farmers bulletin no. 97."

U. S. Bureau of foreign and domestic commerce. "Devoted to the promotion
of American trade both at home and abroad"... "Over thirty years of
service to American business". 23pp. Washington, U. S. Govt. print.
off., 1935. 157.55 D493
Issued for National Foreign Trade Convention, Houston, Texas,
November 18-20, 1935.

U. S. Congress. House. Committee on interstate and foreign commerce. Farm
agricultural implements and income... Hearing... Seventy-fourth
Congress, second session on H. J. Res. 212 to investigate corporations
engaged in the manufacture, sale, or distribution of agricultural
implements and machinery and H. J. Res. 444 joint resolution to amend
the joint resolution entitled "Joint resolution authorizing the
Federal trade commission to make an investigation with respect to
agricultural income and the financial and economic condition of
agricultural producers generally", approved August 27, 1935. March
10, 25, and 27, 1936. 83pp. Washington, U. S. Govt. Print. off., 1936.

U. S. Congress. Senate. Committee on banking and currency. Reorganization
of farm credit administration. Hearing... Seventy-fourth Congress,
second session on S. 4003; a bill providing for the reorganization
of the Farm credit administration. March 25, 1936. 117pp. Washington,
U. S. Govt. print. off., 1936. 284.2 Un31Rfa

U. S. Farm credit administration. 200,000 farmers use production credit.
    [4]pp. [Washington, U. S. Govt. print. off., 1935]. (U. S. Farm
    credit administration. Circular J) 166.2 C492 no.J

U. S. National emergency council. Report to the President of the United
    States from the acting executive director. 143pp. Washington,
    [U. S. Govt. Print. off.] 1935. 173.2 N212R
        The first section of this report is devoted to agriculture, the
    Agricultural Adjustment Administration, Commodity Credit Corporation,
    Land program, Department of Agriculture, and Farm Credit Administration

UNITED STATES DEPARTMENT OF AGRICULTURE
BUREAU OF AGRICULTURAL ECONOMICS

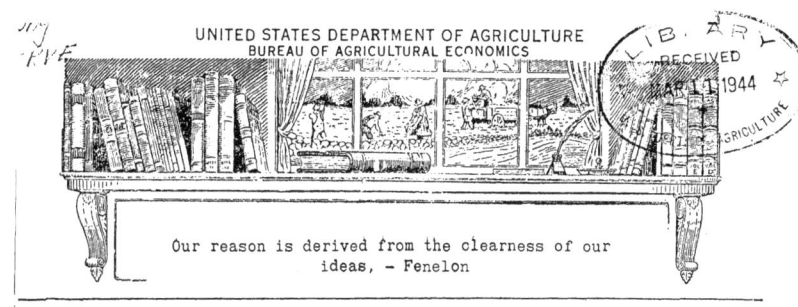

Our reason is derived from the clearness of our
ideas, - Fenelon

Vol. 10   June 1936   No. 6

FEATURES IN THIS ISSUE

AGRICULTURAL ECONOMICS LITERATURE WILL NOT BE
published in July or August   Vol 10, no 7 will
appear in September

SIGNED REVIEWS

Rowe, H. B. Tobacco under the AAA. 317pp. Washington, D. C., The Brookings institution, 1935. (The Institute of economics of the Brookings institution. Publication no. 62) 281.369 R79

"Tobacco Under the AAA" is one of the series of books embodying the results of a "concurrent study of the operation of the Agricultural Adjustment Act" as planned and carried out by Dr. E. G. Nourse of the Brookings Institution and his associates. This study of the operations under the Agricultural Adjustment Act is a unique enterprise in that it attempts to analyze and evaluate concurrently a program that is certain to be of great historical interest. Every analyst who approaches a problem in past relationships wishes for more data and a closer contact with the events and problems of the day. His analysis must be based upon results and the record of concurrent observations. The operator of a program and the current reporter always fail to record some interesting details and fundamental facts that are necessary to a complete understanding and full evaluation of that program. A concurrent study, however, has its disadvantages as well as its advantages. Concurrent evaluation is difficult, even for the analyst. It is difficult for him to see the whole field with its bounds and limitations. It is also difficult to foresee ultimate results and the relative importance of things as they will appear in the fuller perspective of the future. Undoubtedly the analyst can make a real contribution by a concurrent analysis of the program, but however well trained and however free he may be from emotional or political bias, others in the future will find very good reasons for reviewing and re-appraising the Agricultural Adjustment programs.

The author of "Tobacco Under the AAA" presents a very clear description of conditions existing at the time of the inauguration of the program and of its operation through 1934. The author also deals in an admirable manner with many controversial issues as to the intentions of the Act and its actual results.

One of the questions the author undertakes to answer is: Did the original Agricultural Adjustment Act provide only for an emergency program or was it intended to be merely a first step in the development of a long-time program? Mr. Rowe recognizes that there was diversity in the interpretations of the Act and in the intentions of those who were administering it. The legislation and the first formulation of policies and programs were ostensibly for an emergency. Some of those who were responsible for the legislation and for developing policies, however, were from the outset looking forward to a long-time program. Even those who had in view a long-time program considered it politically expedient to take the first step with a program constructed as for an emergency, and to let the permanent program develop from the emergency act and the procedures based upon it.

Another issue at the beginning was, which of two important provisions -- marketing agreements or production control -- would be taken as the major approach to the tobacco situation. The Administrator at the outset was apparently not in favor of production control, but conditions which developed led him to accept it. The choice of production control as the primary means of remedying the tobacco situation was supported by the prospects of a large crop and the very low prices in 1933, the attitude of the buyers, and ultimately by the expression of Congress in the Kerr-Smith Act. Thus contract control became the dominant feature of the tobacco administration. It was supported to some extent by marketing agreements.

The author commends highly the tobacco administration and particularly the flexibility of its programs which were made and carried out always with due regard to diversity of conditions and to the results to be accomplished. He recognizes the importance of very low prices and generally unfavorable conditions in 1933 in securing a high percentage of signers and the cooperation of buyers in a marketing agreement for that year. He also recognizes that improvement in demand was an important factor in making the program generally acceptable. He concludes that the program was a success as an emergency measure, in that it raised prices and increased the incomes to tobacco producers over and above what would have obtained without the program. He also concludes that the gains from the same or a similar program, continued over a series of years, probably would not be as great as in these early years.

The reviewer is somewhat reluctant to present adverse criticisms of a book that is so well done. Perhaps no one would have done better under the circumstances. But it seems worthwhile to indicate some things that are still to be done in appraising the tobacco program.

In considering the suitability of the tobacco program for a long-time measure, it would be necessary to reexamine the achievements under this program to try to determine what they might have been with declining prices and shrinking demand vs. recovering from a depression with prices and incomes of consumers rising. It is recognized that the devaluation of the dollar in 1933 contributed something to the advances in prices, but its significance and the extent of its influence in advancing the prices of tobacco as well as increasing exports has not been adequately treated. The author notes the increase in the consumption of tobacco, but does not develop a reasonably adequate analysis of factors influential in increasing the demand for tobacco. There is also the question as to who paid the processing taxes. The author believes that the processing taxes came out of the processors' margins. This is doubtful. The problem of determining this is complicated by the fact that tobacco is processed over a period of more than one year; and there is not necessarily a close relationship between the current prices paid to farmers for tobacco leaf and the retail prices paid by consumers for tobacco products.

The problems of administration are not adequately treated in this book. We find in it some discussion of the tendency of many farmers to overstate their production, and a description of some of the difficulties of making adjustments in base. When the Domestic Allotment plan was being debated in Congress, many critics said that it would be impossible to administer

436

such an Act. It has been proven possible: But we may properly ask: To what extent were the adjustments in allotments equitable? To what extent can compliance be obtained voluntarily and to what extent must it be forced? Some expected that production control committees would become very influential. Perhaps the emergency required the development of action too fast for the educational development of control committees. What is the evidence that local control might become effective in a long-time program? Part of the plan for the study was to use the services of field observers. These field observers should have been used more extensively upon problems of administration and the reactions of farmers to these problems. We believe that the slight treatment of problems of administration is the most important defect of this survey as a concurrent appraisal of the program.- O. C. Stine, Chief, Division of Statistical and Historical Research

Cohen, Ruth L. The history of milk prices; an analysis of the factors affecting the prices of milk and milk products. 205pp. Oxford, Agricultural economics research institute, 1936. 284.344 C66H
  .This history of milk prices in England covers a period of about 30 years, from 1904 to 1934. The author divides the history into four separate periods which are characterized by decidedly different methods of establishing prices for milk. (1) The pre-war period of individual buying and selling, and little or no difference in price between milk used for fluid consumption and milk used for manufacturing purposes; (2) the World War period with governmental control of prices; (3) the post-war period, 1922 to 1933, with the voluntary price agreements negotiated by the Permanent Joint Milk Committee, representing farmers' and dealers' organizations, and the use of a two price system, one price for milk for fluid use and another price for milk used for manufacturing purposes; and (4) the period since October 1933 when the Milk Marketing Scheme was adopted, which made it illegal to sell milk below minimum prices established by the Marketing Board, and which further developed the classified price system, and established market or area pools which have tended to equalize returns to farmers in various sections of England.
  For each period there is also a discussion in regard to the volume of imports of all dairy products, prices, price differentials between imported and home produced products, and a discussion of developments in the dairy industry in the principal exporting countries. This discussion of imports, production and prices, of butter, cheese, condensed and evaporated milk is necessary because of the relationship of fluid milk prices to prices of manufactured dairy products.
  In reading this history one is impressed with the many similar developments in milk marketing in England and in the United States in regard to bargaining between producers and distributors, price plans, and the general trend toward regulation. In both countries there has been a shift from the flat price system of paying for fluid milk, that was so common prior to the World War, to a classified price system and the development of bases for individual farmers. Many of the experiments that have been tried in this country by State milk control boards as well as the Federal government in controlling prices and price margins and other phenomena in milk distribution have also been tried in England.
  In England as in the United States the distribution of milk has tended to become concentrated in the hands of a relatively few large business organizations. It is stated that the United Dairies Ltd. in 1918 controlled

80 percent of the wholesale and 70 percent of the retail milk trade in London.

There are, however, some striking differences between developments in the two countries. No mention is made of milk strikes in the English history. Neither is any mention made of sanitary regulations or requirements. In several places mention is made of the tendency of producers to shift from butter and cheese production to the shipping of market milk, as though there were no regulations or requirements that would make such a shift at all difficult. In the United States, Board of Health regulations are important factors in milk marketing, and in determining milk prices.

In discussing the effects of the program since 1933 the author concludes as follows: "The introduction of the Milk Marketing Scheme appears to have strengthened the factors tending to increase production, to maintain liquid prices, and to devote a larger and larger proportion of the output to the least remunerative outlets... Had no scheme been formed, and had milk prices in 1933 been left uncontrolled, there is little doubt that the degree of organized bargaining which then existed would have broken down. The low level of manufacturing prices would have forced down liquid milk prices to an equality with them at the edge of the milk-sending areas... Many farmers would have been forced out of the milk business, supplies would have contracted largely, possibly, though by no means certainly, even enough to cause a subsequent milk shortage. Thus some artificial control of prices was probably called for as much in the interest of consumers as of producers."

An interesting statistical study of annual prices of butter and cheese is presented for the period 1923 to 1933. The effect of supply, home production plus imports, on price is shown, and also the effect of "spending power". The index of "spending power" is based on wage rates, employment, and rents. ⊣ Edmund E. Vial, Senior Agricultural Economist, Division of Statistical and Historical Research.

Preisler, Roland. Gedanken zum erbhofrecht, vom werden eines volkstümlichen gesetzes... Mit einem beitrag vom Präsident des Erbhofgerichts, preussischer staatsrat Gustav Wagemann: was man vom bäuerlichen erbhofrecht Preussens wissen muss. 30pp. Berlin, "Zeitgeschichte" [1933] 282 F88

The recent German land legislation, the law creating inherited freeholds, which are inalienable and not to be encumbered with indebtedness, has created new problems in the realm of agricultural credit. The general condition of agriculture as indicated by relative income and indebtedness has greatly improved during the fiscal year 1933-34. A special study was made of from 2,874 to 4,493 agricultural enterprises between the fiscal years from 1927 - 1928 to 1933- 1934 and the debt structure of different types and sizes of enterprises was analyzed for all farming regions. The type of indebtedness was also classified by size, kinds of enterprises, and regions.

General indebtedness of the holdings in Eastern Germany where units are large was greater than that for Western Germany. However, in neither case were the largest units the most encumbered although in general it may be said that the larger units were more encumbered than the small so far as absolute figures are concerned. This is not true when the encumbrance is expressed as percentage of total value of the enterprise. - Charles P. Loomis Senior Agricultural Economist, Division of Farm Population and Rural Life.

lland, Paul. Das Reichserbhofrecht; eine systematische gesetzeserläuterung.
272pp. Berlin, C. Heymanns verlag, 1935, 282 G95
 This is a systematic presentation of the many stipulations and regulations of and relative to the German "Inherited Freehold" law.
 Although rigid specifications concerning the eligibility of a unit to
become an "Inherited freehold" do not exist, the following are their general characteristics; 1. Usually they will range from 18.5 to 308.75 acres
in size. The actual size varies with regions, the acreage necessary to
support a family being the determining factor; 2. The owner must be an
efficient peasant and capable of managing his holding satisfactorily;
3. He must be a citizen and of the "Aryan" race; 4. He must possess only
one unit which is to be an "inherited freehold."
 Land holdings which met these qualifications have arbitrarily been established as "inherited freeholds" according to law. The routine by which
other holdings may become "inherited freeholds" has also been prescribed.
Local courts and a Reich court have been established to administer the
legal aspects of these newly established estates and to enter them in a
"freehold register."
 No "inherited freehold" may be sold or further encumbered without the
consent of an "inherited freehold court" consisting of one judge and two
peasants. Such a holding is no longer an economic good in the classical
sense of the word. It is inalienable. The peasant can borrow money only
on the basis of his own reputation for honesty and capabilities since real
estate and agricultural property cannot be mortgaged. He cannot offer his
property as security. Also an heir may be deprived of the landed estate
if in the judgment of the provincial or Reich's peasant leader his management of the holding is unsatisfactory.
 The "inherited freehold" cannot be divided at or before the death of
the possessor but must pass intact and unmortgaged to certain prescribed
heirs. As was the case in the ancient German kinship groups, at the death
of the possessor, one son or a son's son, inherits the entire estate.
Whether the youngest or oldest child shall inherit depends upon the custom
of the area. Next in line are, first, the father; second, a brother, a
nephew, or a great-nephew; third, a daughter, her son, or his sons; fourth,
a sister, her son, or son's son. The landed estate which passes undivided to
one heir includes all the property on the holding inclusive of buildings,
their furnishings, livestock, machinery, and other equipment used on the
holding whether for the agricultural enterprise or for living. Wives are
not legal heirs to the landed estate. However, heirs other than the one
to whom the landed estate passes have equal right to wealth which does not
belong to the estate. In addition, the heirs who do not inherit the landed
estate have the right to educational preparation to fit them for their
future professions in so far as the income from the estate warrants.
They may return to the "freehold" in cases of emergency and find such refuge
as the income of the estate warrants.
 The teachings of Ernst Moritz Arnt, the poet of the War of Liberation,
as early as 1810 advocated legislation similar to that included in the
New Land Inheritance Laws. He advocated the maintenance of a strong free
peasantry which would own at least one-half of all holdings. The holdings

should be family-sized units which must always remain in the hands of a
single family, be inherited by one person in the family and not dividable.
Also Arnt maintained that no person should possess two such holdings and
that land must not be a free economic good. The peasant should be freed
from the laissez faire economy and Roman land laws.

The author shows that most of the provisions of the law have in the
past been customary. However, he shows that Arnt and the Old Germans
who had obeyed the practices of the time had not been conscious of the
importance of the purity of the race. The work is systematized according to the categories and the various concepts and phases of the "inheritance freehold" itself, the qualifications of the "peasant" (Bauer)
[only the owner of a Freehold can claim this title] and the sequence of
inheritance. The restrictions on sale, debt encumbrances, division,
forced foreclosure and renting of the freehold, and the Freehold register
are discussed and clarified. The succession of heirs of a freehold is
diagrammatically portrayed. - Charles P. Loomis, Senior Agricultural
Economist, Division of Farm Population and Rural Life.

Holt, J. B.   German agricultural policy, 1918-1934; the development of a
national philosophy toward agriculture in postwar Germany. 240pp.
Chapel Hill, The University of North Carolina press, 1936.   281.175 H73
    Bibliography, pp. [225]-232.
    Dr. Holt's description of post-war agricultural policy in Germany will
interest American readers chiefly because it contains the first thorough
exposition in English of the National Socialist agrarian philosophy and
legislation. The author's own particular interest seems to lie, however,
in pointing out the part played by economic necessity and the constant
struggle between the laborite Socialists', the urban liberal industrialists', and the nationalistic farmers' parties over issues of government
food administration, tariffs, prices, subsidies, credit, land settlement,
and labor legislation.

The post-war period in Germany, with its cycle from a Socialist dictatorship immediately following the Revolution through a period of revived liberalism to the National Socialist one-party rule, offers ample
opportunity to observe this interplay of forces in the development of
agricultural policy in a modern industrial nation.

The important subject of the methods used by the Nazis in mitigating
the antagonisms which previously existed between the pressure groups
representing agricultural labor industrial interests by use of race and
nationalistic ideologies is treated.

Readers who are more interested in the actual legislation and governmental machinery established to administer the Inherited Freehold Act,
such as debt liquidation, price control, taxation changes and the establishment of the new department of Agriculture (Reichsnahrstand)
will read the latter part of the book. The work, which was originally
a doctor's dissertation accepted at the University of Heidelberg, is
an excellent treatment of the historical development phases of ideology
and philosophy of those in power in German Nazi State. - Charles P. Loomis,
Senior Agricultural Economist, Division of Farm Population and Rural Life.

Robinson, Solon. Solon Robinson, pioneer and agriculturist. Selected writing, edited by Herbert Anthony Kellar. 582PP. Indianapolis, Indiana historical bureau, 1936. (Indiana historical collections, v. 21) 30.9 R562

"Solon Robinson was a colorful and exceedingly interesting individual. A direct descendant of the famous pastor of the Pilgrims at Leyden, he was left an orphan at the age of ten. After serving as a carpenter's apprentice and a Yankee pedler in rural Connecticut, he migrated to Ohio and later to Indiana where he wrote for the local press, promoted town sites, ran general stores, organized a squatter's union, acted as county clerk, justice of the peace, register of claims, and postmaster, and otherwise dabbled in politics.

Robinson, along with Henry L. Ellsworth and others, worked for the formation of a national agricultural society which they hoped would gain control of the Smithson fund and develop a national agricultural school and journal. The ultimate result of these efforts was the United States Agricultural Society which was a vital factor in the creation of the U. S. Department of Agriculture.

In 1852, Robinson published The Plow in New York City, and the following year he became the agricultural editor of the New York Tribune. His work in the latter connection was largely responsible for the widespread circulation of the weekly edition of the Tribune and its subsequent national influence under the guidance of Horace Greeley.

Having suffered nearly all his life with tubercular tendencies, Robinson was forced to retire to Florida in 1868 where he continued to write novels, short stories, and poetry, and to do editorial work. He died in 1880.

As early as 1837 he began to contribute articles on various aspects of the frontier, including its agricultural possibilities and needs, to the Albany Cultivator and other agricultural periodicals. These essays, written in a simple, homely, and humorous style, reflected his forceful personality and won him a large following. Later he began a series of tours à la Arthur Young and reported his observations, covering practically every settled State in the Union, to the Cultivator, the Prairie Farmer, and the American Agriculturist, from which they were reprinted in the Southern Cultivator and other similar publications.

Herein lies the significance of this volume. Mr. Kellar has selected the more valuable and representative agricultural writings and speeches of Solon Robinson, and the result is a veritable treasure chest of data on American agriculture in the 1840's and 1850's. The editing is everything that even the most critical demand, and the foreword by Dr. Christopher B. Coleman, the preface, the "Content-Calendar", the illustrations, and the thirty-nine page biographical sketch that serves as the introduction are models that other historians may well emulate. In closing, let me repeat ~ together with the second volume that is soon to be issued, Mr. Kellar has provided us with information not only on a colorful and influential personality but also a vast storehouse of information on American agriculture in the middle decades of the nineteenth century. - Everett E. Edwards, Associate Agricultural Economist, Division of Statistical and Historical Research.

Iversen, Carl. Aspects of the theory of international capital movements.
536pp. Copenhagen, Levin & Munksgaard; [etc., etc.] 1935. 284 Iv3
Bibliography, pp. [526]-536.
This work is a rather thorough exposition of the present status of a
major part of international trade theory. It exhibits a strong sense of
the limitations of that theory and a healthy distrust of inductive verifi-
cation. Although the account is somewhat labored and inconclusive, it is
up-to-date; and the recent contributions cited are well correlated with
one another and with the general theory. While not original, the book is,
for the most part, excellently reasoned. Important and often bewildering
changes have characterized international capital movements, and also the
theory of such movements, in recent years. Iversen's book is concerned
with the relation of these changes, of fact as well as of theory, to one
another, to international trade, to the balance of payments, and to the
classical mechanism of international adjustment.

Iversen's discussions of the transfer process are clear without being
oversimplified. He considers, as the first effect of a loan of capital
funds (monetary buying power) in an equilibrium situation, a reverse movement of an equal amount of short-term funds representing the deposit of
the loan to the borrower's credit in a lending-country bank. In the course
of spending these funds, much of the real-capital transfer will at once be
completed by the purchase of lending-country goods and of borrowing-country
goods which would otherwise have been exported. In so far as these two
types of expenditures are made for the same commodities and services which
the funds would have bought in the absence of the loan, no adjustment of
prices or production will be required. In so far as they are made for
different commodities and services, an internal adjustment such as accompanies any shift of demand will have to be made. Before the remainder of the
money can be expended, it must be converted to borrowing-country currency.
This lowers the lending-country exchanges toward the gold(or other commodity) export point. Under ordinary circumstances, however, a "lending
point" is reached first. At this point, there appears a speculative demand for lending-country exchange by holders of borrowing-country exchange.
This is, in effect, an "equalizing" movement of short-term funds as a medium of international exchange replacing the gold flows of classical theory.
With this operation, the monetary transfer is completed. To accomplish the
remainder of the real transfer, an adjustment of prices and production will
be necessary. The extent of the changes required can be measured only with
full knowledge of the various supply and demand schedules involved. Since
the adjustment involves the whole price system (as sometimes expressed in
a series of simultaneous equations), this knowledge can never be available.
However, such knowledge as we have of the general situation leads to the
conclusion that a country's aggregate demand for imports and its aggregate
supply of exports are almost always highly elastic. Hence, the adjustment
of trade to capital transfer is usually accomplished with no changes ••• or
only very slight ones ... in terms of trade. The direction of such changes
as do occur in any particular case is not determinate in advance. Within
the countries where production adjustment must take place, however, changes
will occur in the relative scarcities of the factors of production, and the
prices of domestic goods will be affected considerably at first. By following these relationships clearly, Iversen has forged a valuable tool of analysis with elements from widely scattered sources.

In one respect, however, that weapon remains imperfect. The effect on a general price situation of international flows of money (i.e., short-term capital or effective monetary gold) depends to such a large extent upon the state of business activity in the country in question, that the traditional assumption of an equilibrium situation embarrasses the theorist. Iversen feels this, and it leads him to mention elements which, although assumed to be in (he says, Wicksellian) equilibrium, usually determine the course of the transfer and adjustment mechanism. "It is meaningless," he says at one point, "to discuss the mechanism of international capital movements without reference to some definite monetary policy." Elsewhere, he refers to the "paramount importance" of "the credit policy of the (central) banks" and to the assumption that there had been full utilization of productive resources before the mechanism began to operate. Such references are scattered throughout the book. This is a step in advance of theoretical discussions which ignore the question of the relation of the theory of international trade to the stark fact of business booms and depressions; but it may not prove the most successful approach to the problem. It might be more profitable to consider in detail the differences in the working of the whole mechanism of adjustment at different stages of the cycle and in different types of cycles. At any rate, a systematic theoretical examination of this relationship would be very useful. Attention should be given to the difference in the effects of tariffs imposed or removed at different stages of business activity. It might be found, for example, that certain types of tariffs were highly beneficial if adopted by a nation going into a major depression and threatened with extensive idle resources for a period of years. It might also appear that tariff lowering could be more profitably brought about during industrial recovery -- especially during its advanced stages. Such material would be invaluable in the timing of tariff reform programs, among other things.

As is probably to be expected in a work of its scope, the book has spots which are inconsistent or out of character. One such case, is to be found on p.66 where Iversen goes out of his way to attack the contention, "often asserted in the United States," that increased American tariffs, by preventing imports during the nineteen-twenties, caused an excess of exports, which in turn caused Americans to lend abroad in order to enable foreigners to pay for the goods. The actual relationship, says Iversen, is "much more complicated than this superficial reasoning would suggest." He fears that the layman, "strongly biased as (he) usually is by quasi-mercantilistic ideas," will get a wrong picture. Whether or not anyone in the United States ever made such a grossly oversimplified statement of the relationship, the attack is not justified; for Iversen does not claim to have examined the specific facts and found the analysis erroneous. He does not say openly that it is erroneous; although he fears that it will mislead laymen. He even admits, in his assertion that all balance-of-payment items are mutually interdependent, that the implied direction of causation (from trade balance to capital movement) is theoretically possible. Like Ohlin, however, he finds that the reverse direction of causation usually prevails. The balance of trade (and current transactions) "practically always" adjusts to the balance of capital movements. Iversen does not make the rule absolute;

yet he attacks an analysis which runs contrary to it. Such an apparent abuse of scientific method comes strangely from one who, elsewhere in the book, points out that inductive results in this field are of a relatively negative and inconclusive nature. A further idea of how far out of his way Iversen went to make this special attack may be obtained from the manner in which he brings it in. He cites it as an example of the danger to popular opinion from "calculating the balance of capital transactions as a residue." He may be interested to know that, in the United States statistics upon which the analysis in question is based, capital transactions are not calculated as a residue. They are calculated directly.

Perhaps Iversen makes this attack as a reaction to earlier theories which erred in the opposite direction. It is unfortunate that the rediscovery of the significance of a reverse economic relationship so often leads to the establishment of a group of theorists committed to the new relationship in place of the old one, when the most realistic conception is one of inter-dependence and multiple causation ... i.e. the new relation combined with the old one. Thus, although utility was no new concept, a marginal utility school followed a cost-of-production one before Marshall resolved the apparent inconsistency. Thus, also, as the pegging of money to gold became fairly general, a so-called "commodity" theory "replaced" the quantity theory of money in the United States until American students tired of such profitless hair-splitting. There are other and, doubtless, better examples. It is to be hoped that international trade theory is not now nearing a period during which, as a reaction to previous overemphasis of the effects of trade balances on capital movements, causation will be assumed under all circumstances to run from capital movements to trade balances. Such a development would be undesirable for any reason ... even to avoid confusing the layman.

In discussing the effect of a given economic analysis on "the layman", furthermore, Iversen is on even thinner ice than when ascribing causal quality to a general item of international payment. It may be true that the theory that trade balances cause capital movements has, in the countries with which Iversen is familiar, secured popular support for ill-advised government borrowing. On the other hand, the theory that tariffs unbalance trade and, therefore, make loans necessary if exports are not to decline has probably done a great deal of good in the United States. It has certainly increased the "layman's" understanding of his interest in lower tariffs. It has been an important factor in making possible an administration free to study tariffs scientifically and able in many cases actually to reduce them. It is probably healthy for scientists to interest themselves in the bewildering process by which scientific concepts and analyses filter through the social structure to the springs of political action. However, they are apt to find it more difficult of comprehension than are the principles of their science. They will do better to say whether a given analysis is complete enough to be significant rather than whether it will confuse the layman.

Iversen's book is most distinguished, perhaps, by its appreciation of the limitations of the instrument with whose details it is preoccupied. In the discussion of international demand, Iversen writes, "The system of (simultaneous) equations gives a useful bird's-eye view of the types of relations connecting all economic phenomena, but the equations are too numerous and

444

complex to be much help in the solution of concrete problems." The whole 536-page book concerns the relations on which the system of equations is based. -- R. B. Schwenger, Associate Agricultural Economist, Division of Foreign Agricultural Service.

DESCRIPTIVE NOTES AND ABSTRACTS

Agricultural and Economic Survey – Nova Scotia

Longley, W. V., and Chown, W. F. Antigonish county, Nova Scotia. A study of land utilization, farm production and rural living. 112pp. Halifax, Nova Scotia, Jan. 1936. (Nova Scotia. Dept. of Agriculture. Bulletin no. 118) 7 N85 no. 118
   "The Extension Division, Nova Scotia Department of Agriculture and the Agricultural Economics Branch, Dominion Department of Agriculture cooperating."
   "The field work of the survey was done by John E. C. Smith and W. F. Chown."
   The section entitled "Farm Survey" covers types of farming, land utilization, live stock, farm income and expense, some factors affecting living conditions.
   The section entitled "Population and Production Trends" deals with rural depopulation, trends in agriculture since 1861 by Census periods and by farm enterprises (livestock and field crops).
   The section on Public Services deals with municipal revenue and expenditures, tax delinquency, schools, and communications and services.
   The section on Community Organizations deals with social agencies and co-operative organizations.
   The section on Markets and Marketing contains a brief statement on the major commodities.
   The Appendix contains agricultural and industrial statistics for the county.

Agricultural Credit – India

Ramaiya, A. The Reserve bank and agricultural credits. 55pp. Madura, The Bureau of economic research, 1935. 284.2 R142
   "In this brochure an attempt is made to discuss, in outline, the scope for the Reserve Bank's usefulness to agriculture and make suggestions as to the best way of solving the problem of agricultural credits. It does not, except in a casual way, deal with the general aspects of agricultural indebtedness about which there is already plenty of literature both official and nonofficial, nor does it concern itself with the various measures and schemes proposed and suggested in various Provinces for the reduction of the volume of such indebtedness by such means as Boards of Conciliation between debtors and creditors, agricultural insolvencies and other avenues of relief. The aim of the study is quite different and if I may say so, it breaks new ground. Its purpose is to examine how far the Central Reserve Bank can possibly assist in the affording of agricultural credit facilities and how in the light of the experience of other countries, the special problem of agricultural credit can best be solved."
   – Preface.

Agricultural economics society. Report of conference held... 1935. 2 nos.
   [London, 1935-36] Journal of proceedings, v. 4, no. 1-2, December 1935,
   April 1936. 281.9 Ag8
      v. 4, no. 1. Report of conference held at Downing College, Cambridge,
   28th June to 1st July 1935. 83 pp.
      Partial contents: The expectation of agricultural recovery, by R. R.
   Enfield; Measures taken in France to meet the agricultural depression,
   by M. Augé-Laribé; Scientific progress and agricultural employment, by
   A. Bridges; and The Scottish Crofter, by J. M. Ramsay.
      v. 4, no. 2. Report of conference held in London, 10th and 11th December
   1935, pp. 87-151.
      Partial contents: Food supplies and consumption at different income
   levels, by E.M.H. Lloyd; Statistical investigations into organised marketing
   of milk, by J. L. Davies; and Land settlement and unemployment, by A. W.
   Menzies-Kitchin.

Agricultural Education Association

Agricultural progress; the journal of the Agricultural education association,
   v. 13, 1936. 190pp. Cambridge, W. Heffer & son limited, 1936.
   10 Ag86 v.13, 1936.
      Partial contents: The agriculture of Somerset, by W. D. Hay; The agri-
   culture of Northumberland, by A. R. Wannop; The teart pastures of Somer-
   set, by W. R. Muir; The economic possibilities of rice grass, by J.
   Bryce; Rationing and milk costs, by S. R. Wragg and H. T. Watkins;
   Farm poultry keeping, by H. H. Duckett.

Agricultural Policy - Europe and the United States

Taylor, H. C. Agricultural adjustments in Europe and the farm problem
   in the United States. 9pp., mimeogr. [n.p., 1936] 281 T21Ag
      A paper read before the Economic club of Chicago... February 25,
   1936.
      After making a brief statement regarding the International In-
   stitute of Agriculture, and discussing the question of economic self-
   sufficiency, Dr. Taylor describes the agricultural readjustments of
   Europe, particularly of Italy. He then turns to the situation in the
   United States and concludes with the following:
      "The two elements of a sound national policy should go forward at
   the same time, the restoration of foreign markets, in so far as
   reasonably possible and profitable, and the readjustment of farm
   management along soil conserving lines. If prosecuted with vigor,
   these two lines of action should go far toward restoring the farmer's
   purchasing power.
      "Increase of farmers' purchasing power is essential if country
   life is to be soundly coordinated with our present city and industrial life built upon higher wage scales. Without such coordination
   economic troubles will recur and all classes will suffer from the
   maladjustment, which might be avoided through a sound national agricultural policy."

- 446 -

Agricultural Policy – France

Devinat, P. La politique agricole de la France. Conclusions adoptées par le
Conseil national économique dans sa session du 5 juillet 1935 et rapport
présenté par m. P. Devinat... assisté de m. Garnier... Approuvé par le
Conseil national économique. 56pp. Paris, Imprimerie nationale, 1935.
281.174 D49
     At head of title: Conseil National Économique.
     The National Economic Council of France, in approaching the study of
the future agricultural policy of France formulated certain conclusions
at its session of July 5, 1935. It took cognizance of the lack of equilibrium between production and consumption and its causes, expressed its conviction of the interdependence of all agricultural problems and recognized the necessity of studying production in the colonies as well as at
home, of educating the farmer in improved methods, of production and distribution through the collaboration of the State and the professional
groups formed by the farmers themselves, of decreasing the cost of production, of improved regulation of exports and imports, of the development
of the domestic market and the adoption of measures for the relief of
unemployment.
     The report which follows the adoption of these resolutions contains an
analysis of the problem of overproduction, a discussion of the existing
agricultural policy, and suggested measures for its improvement.

Agricultural Policy – Great Britain

Oxford. University. Agricultural economics research institute. The agricultural
register 1935-6; being a record of legislation, organization, supplies and
prices. 407 pp. Oxford, Agricultural economics research institute, 1936.
281.9 Ox2Ag
     Dr. C. S. Orwin, Director of the Institute writes as follows in his fore-
word:
     "In this, the third issue of The Agricultural Register, it has been
assumed, for the most part, that readers are familiar with the fundamental
legislation which introduced the new agricultural policy. This was fully
described in the first issue, for 1933-4, and it was recapitulated in the
issue for 1934-5. The present volume deals only with the events of the past
year except in so far as reference to earlier years is needed to make them
clear. The plan of the volume has not been altered."
     One section of the volume is devoted to Legislation, another to Marketing
reorganization (schemes in operation and schemes proposed) and still others
to Subsidies and levies, Import regulation, Supplies and prices, Statistics,
and Labour. There is a short section devoted to Land Settlement, and another
to Credit. Among the appendices may be found the following: The Pig Price
Formula under the Pigs Marketing Scheme Contract for 1936; and Rates of
Duties Charged on the Principal Agricultural Products, March 1936.

Agricultural Problem

Sargent, F. W. The importance of agricultural welfare. An address... at meeting
of the Chamber of Commerce of the U.S.A. Washington, D. C. April 30, 1936.
36pp. [New York, 1936] (Chemical foundation. The chemical foundation
no.9) 280 C422 no.9
     This statement of the fundamental importance of the farm problem closes

with a plea for the greater industrial utilization of farm products and
states that there exists an "almost unlimited amount of raw materials that
can be processed from the soils and through the science of chemistry, made
available for industry, not only in experimental fields but in new enterprises and new undertakings, all of which will add to the wealth of the
people and the prosperity of agriculture.

"You have no doubt seen from time to time discussions as to the number
of acres that could be utilized in the production of power alcohol, and
this without injury to the producers of oil - probably to their aid and
advantage; the number of additional acres that could be utilized for paper
and paper stock; vegetable fibers; flaxseed; linseed; cotton, for purposes
to which it is not now devoted in large undertakings; plastics; the innumerable products of the soy bean; tung oil; tanning materials, etc., etc.

"In my opinion, we are moving into a new industrial revolution springing
from the science of chemistry, for we have not yet begun to utilize the unlimited by-products that chemistry can give to us both by the science of
organic and inorganic chemistry. This industry, in its present state of
development, is comparatively new, and I believe it is destined to do as
much for human progress in the second quarter of the present century as did
the electrical and mechanical advances of the first quarter of this century."

Barley - World Trade

Canada. Bureau of statistics. Agricultural branch. World trade in barley,
calendar years 1927-1934. 36PP. mimeogr. Ottawa, 1935. 286.359 C16
   "The first five pages of the report contain figures taken from the annual
reports of the International Institute of Agriculture for the years 1927
to 1933. For the calendar year 1934, the figures were taken from the
'Monthly Crop Report and Agricultural Statistics' issued at Rome, Italy and
are of a preliminary nature. Tables published from page twelve to the end
of this report are based on the Trade Returns of the various countries and
snow slightly different results, but are fairly comparable." - Introduction.

Butter - Standardization - Argentina

Lopez Gonzalez, Antonio. La manteca destinada al consumo de Buenos Aires.
22pp. Buenos Aires [Ferrari hnos impresores] 1935. 307 L88
   An account of the composition of butter and the methods of
classifying it for consumption in Buenos Aires. It is urged that
more butter be consumed.

Canadian Society of Agricultural Economics

Canadian society of agricultural economics. Proceedings of the seventh annual
meeting... held in conjunction with the annual convention of the Canadian
society of technical agriculturists University of Alberta, Edmonton, Alta,
June 25-27, 1935, 102pp., mimeogr. [Winnipeg, 1935] 281.9 C16
   The following papers and discussions are contained in these proceedings:
An agricultural policy, by W. V. Longley; Production trends and policies,
by T. W. Grindley; Land utilization policy with particular reference to
western Canada, by Wm. Allen; Discussion - Land utilization policy, by G. H.
Craig; Farm indebtedness, by E. C. Hope; Farm mortgage situation, land
appraisal aspects, by H. C. Grant and Morgan Brock; Some changes in live
stock marketing, by B. N. Arnason; Milk marketing legislation in Canada, by

C. V. Parker and H. R. Hare; Discussion, by C. A. Lyndon; and An appraisal
of present policies and glimpse of the future, by J. E. Lattimer.

Coffee - World Production and Consumption

Brazil. Directoria de estatistica da produccão. O café na economia mundial.
[Rio de Janeiro?] 1935. 246pp., maps.   286.368 B732
     At head of title: Ministerio da agricultura. Directoria de
estatistica da produccao. 4.ª secçao - Documentaçao e informaçoes.
     "A presente monographia foi executada pelo apurador: Eduardo J.
Gonçalves." - verso of t.-p.
     This statistical compilation covers the most important period in
the economic history of coffee, the years from 1909 to 1934. Its
tables, charts and maps picture the vicissitudes of the production,
distribution and consumption of coffee in the last period of the
laissez faire era, the years of the world war, the period of chaos
which followed, the years of prosperity, and the recent depression.
It is proposed to issue a monograph based on these statistics.

Consumer Cooperation

Fowler, B. B. Consumer cooperation in America; democracy's way out... Introduction by Marquis W. Childs. 305pp. New York, The Vanguard press [1936]
280.2 F82
     The introduction to this volume is signed by Marquis W. Childs who
writes in part as follows:
     "Mr. Fowler shows how in innumerable ways cooperation is taking hold. At
Madison, a group of faculty members of the University of Wisconsin formed
a cooperative for the distribution of oil and gasoline which in three years
has had an extraordinary growth. Negro workers in Gary, Indiana, have
formed a cooperative which has one successful store, with plans for three
more in addition to a cooperative system of milk distribution. Credit
Unions, under the protection of a recently enacted Federal law, are being
organized so rapidly that the total number of such cooperative credit pools
is doubled and tripled within the year. More and more the farmers of America are buying their seed, fertilizer, oil and gasoline through their own
cooperatives. The story is the same throughout the country.
     "As a people we are given to enthusiasms for new causes. And here a
word of caution may not be out of place. Experience in Europe has shown
that successful cooperatives are built not so much by enthusiasm as by
careful, painstaking attention to business details. The cooperative shop
must hold its own at the outset in the sharpest kind of competition. New
members will be attracted to the cooperative society by superior quality
and the prospect of a generous dividend on purchases.
     "One reason, perhaps, why certain earlier cooperatives failed was be-
cause they were built upon a naive faith that still another new way had
been found to transform the world. They attracted earnest individuals who
were eager to discuss the destiny of America in terms of cooperation but
who lacked the business ability required of the average chain store manager.
Because we have been taught to believe that we lived in a society in which
we would all one day become millionaires, it has been difficult for us
to concentrate upon practical economies having to do with the cost of
everyday necessities. It may be that the depression has taught the need

for that concentration. The rise of cooperatives with an intensely practical aim, as described by Mr. Fowler, would indicate that this is true...
"But there is a vast amount of work to be done here at home and now, in
the immediate present. That is what Mr. Fowler's book is about. He gives
practical directions for starting a cooperative society. He traces step
by step the rise of those that have been most successful. He shows the
dangers and pitfalls that threaten the struggling cooperative society.
And he stresses above all the need for detailed study and extensive propaganda such as that which is being done so ardently by the Cooperative League
The consumer, Mr. Fowler makes plain, must understand the functioning of
the economy in which he lives before he can hope to own and direct it."
    There are two appendices - How to Organize a Cooperative, and Statistics
Showing the Growth of Some Consumer Organizations.

Consumer Credit

Massachusetts. Committee on consumer credit. Report of the Committee on con-
    sumer credit, appointed by his excellency the governor of the commonwealth
    of Massachusetts. February 17, 1936. 86pp. [Boston?] 1936.   284 M383
    "The Committee on Consumer Credit [William Trufant Foster, chairman]
    was appointed in April, 1935, by His Excellency, the Governor of Massa-
    chusetts. The first task assigned to the Committee was the study of con-
    sumer credit in connection with instalment selling and financing...
    "Since no provision was made for the wide distribution of the valuable
    report of the Commission, a large part of that report is here reprinted.
    Special attention is called to Appendix C, which summarizes the most ex-
    tensive field study which has ever been made of instalment credit costs."-
    Introductory Statement.

Cooperation

Brown, W. H.   The co-operative way through the economic wilderness.
    48pp. Manchester, National co-operative men's guild [1935]
    280.2 B81
    An interesting and pungent "cooperative pilgrimage" written by
    one who has had 40 years of intimate association with the inner
    councils of cooperation in England, and knows the history of the
    movement. A useful Chronology of cooperation in the twentieth
    century is appended.

Horace Plunkett foundation. Year book of agricultural co-operation 1936.
    623pp. London, P. S. King & son, ltd., 1936.   280.29 H78
    Bibliography, pp. 603-623.
    Partial contents: Agricultural co-operation in 1935; George Russell, by
    H. F. Norman; Agricultural co-operative insurance, by Dr. N. Barou; New
    land settlement enterprise in England, by J. Henderson Stewart; Agricul-
    ture and the state: Ireland, by M. Digby; The position of farming in New
    Zealand [during the crisis], by J. P. Belshaw; The New Zealand Co-operative
    Alliance, by D. von Sturmer; Collectivisation and collective farms in the
    U.S.S.R., by the U.S.S.R. Society for cultural relations with foreign coun-
    tries; The United States of America, by Robin Hood; Agrarian reform in
    Mexico, by Kenneth G. Grubb.

In addition to special articles the progress of cooperation is described by different well known writers in more than thirty countries.

Cooperative Marketing - Cotton

Herrmann, O. W., and Gardner, Chastina. Early developments in cooperative cotton marketing. 46pp. Washington [U.S. Govt. print. off.] 1936. (U. S. Farm credit administration. Circular no. C-101) 166.2 C4923 no.C-101
. Bibliography, pp.45-46.

This interesting and useful bulletin discusses the history of the many efforts made to market cotton cooperatively by various agricultural organizations — the Grange, Farmers Alliance, Farmers Union, Mississippi Valley Cotton Planters Association, Southern Cotton Growers Association, American Cotton Association and many others, which preceded the large-scale state, regional and national cotton marketing associations. A useful short bibliography is appended.

Cooperatives - Self-help

U. S. Federal emergency relief administration. Self-help program of the Federal emergency relief administration. Summary of federal aid to self-help cooperatives in the United States, July 1, 1933 — December 31, 1935. 7pp., mimeogr. [Washington, D. C., 1936?] 173.2 R27Sh
Submitted by the Division of Self-help Cooperatives.

"During the past two and a half years, the Federal Emergency Relief Administration has granted a total of $3,157,613.43 to 27 States and two territories for the development of self-help cooperative activities...

"It is conservatively estimated that about 30,000 needy workers with their dependents, or a total of 100,000 people, have benefited from this program. However, the results of these activities cannot be gauged by criteria usually applied to private business enterprises. In private industry and agriculture, the average capitalization per worker employed is between $1,000 and $1,500. This entire self-help program, on the basis of current membership, has involved a Federal expenditure of only about $200 per worker, and on the basis of the total membership over a two and a half year period only $100. If one considers the actual funds expended rather than the amount of money granted, this average capitalization is still further reduced. In the light of these facts the achievements of these struggling groups of people discarded by industry are nothing short of phenomenal, by and large.

"This program has resulted in the conservation of crops that would otherwise have gone to waste. It has produced new wealth at a minimum of cash cost. It has reduced relief expense and has provided thousands of people with many necessities which they, having no buying power, could never have obtained through the regular channels of trade. It has built up the morale of the participants by showing them a way to employ themselves usefully, productively, and to regain their self-respect. And it has put new hope into the hearts of many technologically displaced and super-annuated workers who had been faced with the ugly prospect of permanent unemployment and permanent dependence on public charity."

Crop Production - Tennessee

Allred, C. E. Regional grouping of crop production in Tennessee. A preliminary
report by Charles E. Allred... William E. Hendrix... Benj. H. Luebke.
38pp., mimeogr. [Knoxville, Tenn.] May 1, 1936. (U. S. Federal works
progress administration. Cooperative plan of rural research. Report no.12)
173.3 W39Co no.12

Issued in cooperation with Tennessee Agricultural Experiment Station and
Tennessee Works Progress Administration.

"This is one of a series of preliminary reports dealing with various aspects of the rural relief problem in Tennessee. Consideration is given in
this report to regional differences in the proportion of land in crops,
pasture and woodland, and to the distribution of the various crops.

"The classification of the regions of the State into Groups I, II, and
III... is based on their relative productivity. This productivity grouping
was derived by generalizations from (1) a weighted crop-yield index of the
counties, adjusted to the percentage of total land area in crops... and
(2) technical descriptions of the soils of the regions... The four urban
counties of Shelby, Knox, Davidson, and Hamilton were eliminated because
of the influence of cities.

"The county selected as representative, in each case, is one in which
the greatest percentage of its area lies within the particular region. The
45 sample counties represent 46.8 per cent of the total area of the State,
and the three groups into which they are classified are of approximately
equal size." - Introduction.

Dairy Industry - France

France. Office national de propagande du lait, beurre et fromages. France, a
milk-producer, edited by the National propagating office for milk, butter
and cheese, in cooperation with the National breeding committee. 221pp.
Paris [Impr. F. Paillart] 1934. 281.344 F84A

Published in behalf of the International Dairy Congress. 10th. Rome,
1934, and of the 16th International Agricultural Congress, Budapest 1934,
in French, German, Italian, Spanish. - p. [224]

Congres international d'agriculture, 16th, Budapest, 1934.

Contains as a preface an interesting historical account of the early
use of dairy products, especially cheese, by Guy Moussu, Archivist Librarian
at the French Ministry of Agriculture. Among the chapter headings are the
following: Species and races grown in France for their milk, French dairy
production and milk (includes the handling, distribution, etc.), Butter
production, Cheese production, Observations on the gastric digestion of
fresh and refined cheeses. Other chapters are devoted to particular cheeses.
The volume contains a directory of the principal officers of various organizations related in some way to the dairy industry in France.

Economic Situat'

Bjürset, Brynjolf. Distribute or destroy! A survey of the world's glut of
goods with a description of various proposals and practical experiments
for its distribution... Translated from the Norwegian by I.R. and E.S.
de Mare. 188pp. London, S. Nott ltd., 1936. 280 B55

Bibliography, pp. 187-188.

The author writes in part as follows in his preface to the English edition:
"The aim of this work is threefold. Firstly to give the reader an impression of the abundance, and especially potential abundance, of goods in the world to-day.

"Secondly, to review the different plans put forward for the better use of existing powers of production. Only a few of the many proposals that have been advanced could be dealt with in this popular work, and it is not claimed that those chosen are the most excellent, but each is well known and typical of its kind. To the Norwegian edition dated April 1934 much has been added, and the whole work has been revised and re-edited to bring the English edition up to date.

"The third specific aim of the book is the drawing of comparisons and a conclusion. The different schemes are compared, and a close study will show important traits common to all of them. I believe it is possible to bridge the gulf between the standpoint of orthodox city finance and that of the so-called 'heretical' pioneers, and that on that bridge we could cross to a saner and happier life. There is need of a greater mutual understanding, and it is hoped that this work will contribute to that end."

Economic Situation - Italy

Università Bocconi di Milano. Prospettive economiche., Quindicesima edizione. I grandi mercati. 492pp. Milano, 1936. 251 Un3
    At head of title: Giorgio Mortara.
    A brief introduction on economic conditions in Italy and the effect of the sanctions is followed by an account of production, marketing, consumption and prices of coal, petroleum, hydroelectric power, iron, copper, cotton, hemp and flax, articial textile fibres, wool, silk, grain, wine and olive oil on the world market and in Italy.

Economics

Goslin, Mrs. Ryllis C. (Alexander) and Goslin, O. P. Rich man, poor man; pictures of a paradox, a publication of the People's league for economic security. Editorial committee; Stuart Chase, Henry Pratt Fairchild, Harry A. Overstreet. 85pp. New York and London, Harper & brothers, 1935. 280.12 G69
    Bibliography, pp. 83-85.
    The Editorial committee responsible for this volume consists of Stuart Chase, Henry Pratt Fairchild and Harry A. Overstreet. The book is the first of a series of publications which the People's League for Economic Security plans to put before the public. It presents the philosophy of the League which it "aims to see realized one day as a practical reality."
    The volume contains many striking graphic charts - such as our production capacity, Consumed energy, Family income 1929, Unemployment, How debts have grown, Ownership of wealth 1929 and 1932, Increases in public service, Technological displacement, etc.

Farm Debt Moratorium Laws - United States

Rood, J. R. An agricultural conciliation commissioner's guide, being a compen-
    dius [!] hand book on the United States farm debt moratorium laws, with
    appropriate forms. 2d ed. 100, 104pp. Detroit, Mich., Detroit law book
    company [1935] 284.2 R67 Ed.2
        A part of the handbook (separately paged, pp. 1-104) contains copies
    of the bankruptcy laws of the United States. Bound with it is a 10-page
    supplement "indicating as to each section whether and if so how far it is
    altered, by the decision of the United States Supreme Court in Louisville
    Joint Stock Land Bank v. Bradford, and by Amendment approved August 28,
    1935."
        The preface states the purpose of this compilation as follows:
        "The special farmer debt moratorium acts are so disconnected and illogi-
    cal in their arrangement, and so dependent on the general law of bankruptcy
    and the U. S. Code; and the commissioners appointed to administer them are
    so often without wide familiarity with the general law, that a compendium
    arranged in some logical order seems almost indispensable to enable them
    to act. That is the excuse for this analysis and accompanying forms, in
    which attempt has been made to get into natural sequence whatever is nec-
    essary to take each step under this law."
        The preface to the second edition adds:
        "Many decisions on these statutes have been rendered since the first
    edition was printed, and with the light they give the text has been largely
    re-written, and all decisions on the statutes to the date of going to press
    cited in the section which they control.
        There is a detailed index to the first part of the handbook, pp. 94-100.

Farm Income - Bulgaria

Mollov, IAn. S., and Kondov, N. K. The incomes of... Bulgarian farms for
    1929/30-1930/31. 2v. Sofia, 1932-34. (Bulletins of the Department
    of agriculture and forestry. University of Sofia. v.5, no. 14; v. 6,
    no. 16) 281.177 M73In
        Text and added title in Bulgarian.
        1929/30 has title: Incomes of 44 Bulgarian farms...; 1930/31, Incomes
    of 73 Bulgarian farms.

Farm Management Survey - England

Cambridge, Eng. University. Dept. of agriculture. Farm economics branch.
    Report no. 22. An economic survey of agriculture in the eastern counties
    of England 1933. 77pp. [Cambridge, 1934] 281.9 C14
        "This Report represents the third of a series covering the results of the
    most extensive Farm Management Survey hitherto undertaken in Great Britain.
    Commencing with the year 1931, financial and economic data relating to the
    organisation of more than 1000 farms in the Eastern Counties of England
    have been secured for each of three successive years. To obtain this in-
    formation approximately 3500 visits have been made to individual farms,
    nearly 80,000 miles have been travelled, and replies have been obtained
    to upwards of one million questions.
        "The results published here and in Reports 19 and 21... cover a wide

variety of information. But the fact that the research organisation has had to work to a definite, and rather crowded, time-table during these three years has precluded the possibility of exploring as exhaustively as is desirable the data secured. Much yet remains to be done in this respect, and it is hoped that from time to time further publications may be issued giving the results of more detailed studies." - Preface.

Cambridge, Eng. University. Dept. of agriculture. Farm economics branch. Report no. 23. Changes in the economic organisation of agriculture. A comparative study of conditions in the eastern counties of England in 1933 and 1935. 36pp. [Cambridge, Eng., 1936] 281.9 C14
   "The field work involved by this investigation was done by S. H. Carson and R. F. Edwards between September and December, 1935. The consequent checking, assembling, and analysis of the data was carried out under the direct charge of P. E. Graves. The general design and control of the enquiry, and the preparation of this report, was undertaken by R. McG. Carslaw."
   "During the three years 1931 to 1933 the Farm Economics Branch of the Cambridge Department of Agriculture carried out an economic survey covering 1,000 farms in the Eastern Counties of England. The results of this large-scale investigation were published in the Branch's Reports 19, 21, and 22, and subsequently a number of articles, referring to special aspects of the data collected, were printed in various scientific journals. Collectively these publications offer a comprehensive body of factual data relating to the economic organisation and financial returns of farming in the Eastern Counties during these three critical and interesting years.
   "The present Report represents the first of a new series of publications, of which the object is to examine changes occurring in farm organisation rather than to present factual data of a representative nature. Here differences between one year and another will be of more significance than the absolute figures for any one year." - Introduction

Farming as a Livelihood

Grosskopf, J. F. W. Farming as a livelihood. 11pp. Pretoria, Printed by the Government printer, 1935. (Pretoria. University. Reprint no. 6) 276.4 T68R no.6
   "Reprinted from 'Farming in South Africa,' Reprint no. 86, 1935."
   "The farmer, and farm life as such, apart from their material and economic importance, are of so much spiritual and social value to the nation, that every effort is justified to ensure their healthy survival. Most decidedly, however, doles and pampering cannot bring this about for thereby the very independence and pride and spirit of enterprise that constitute the true moral work of the farmer, are dulled and poisoned."

Foreign Trade

Gurley, J. M., and Thomas, E. P. Does American prosperity depend on foreign trade? 34pp. New York, American book company [1936] (America's town meeting of the air [no. 24]) 280.12 C92

National foreign trade convention.   Official report of the twenty-second...
convention held at Houston, Texas, November 18, 19, 20, 1935.   558pp.
New York [1936]   286 N46
       At the Agricultural Session, the following papers were read: Cotton in
Texas as a factor in foreign trade, by Dr. A. B. Cox; The value of cotton
exports to the economic life of the United States, by Walter Parker; Some
American tobacco export problems, by Wm. Holmes Davis; and Our trade with
Germany, particularly in relation to cotton, by W. C. Helmbrecht.

U S. Bureau of foreign and domestic commerce.   Summary of United States trade
with world, 1935.   30pp.   Washington, U. S. Govt. print. off., 1936.
(Trade information bulletin no. 831)   157.7 C76 Dt.

Grain - Production and Trade - World

Gt. Brit. Imperial economic committee.   Intelligence branch.   Grain crops.
A summary of figures of production and trade relating to wheat, wheat-
flour, barley, oats, maize & rice.   66pp.   London, H. M. Stationery
off., 1936.   (Gt. Brit. Imperial economic committee. Intelligence
branch. I.E.C./C.3, Mar. 1936)   280.39 G794C no.3
       The introductory statement in this publication reads as follows:
       "A survey of the world cereal situation is limited by the absence
of official information regarding certain countries. The lack of reliable statistics for the vast areas in China and other countries of lesser
importance, such as Iran and Iraq, makes it impossible to estimate the
significance of these countries with any degree of accuracy. The figures
which appear as world totals are therefore exclusive of these countries.
       "This publication deals with the grain crops which are of importance
to British countries, namely, wheat, barley, oats, maize, and rice. No
attempt has been made to deal with other grains, such as the millets produced in various parts of the world, especially in China, India and
Africa. In the aggregate the production of these crops is very large,
but they are mostly consumed in the countries in which they are produced,
the quantity involved in international trade being only a small proportion of the total production. Although the world acreage of rye is
greater than that of barley, the area under rye within the Empire is
negligible in comparison with other cereals. Less than 1 per cent. of the
world's area of rye is found in British countries "
       In addition to the chapters on the various grains there is a chapter on
customs duties and trade restrictions (pp. 12-20).

Graphs

Arkin, Herbert, and Colton, R. R.   Graphs: how to make and use them.   224pp.
New York and London, Harper & brothers publishers, 1936.   251 Ar4G
       The authors write as follows in their preface:
       "Little attempt has been made to standardize practice in the construc-
tion of graphs since the Report of the Joint Committee on Standards for
Graphic Presentation, of the American Statistical Association, in 1915.
The report of the committee largely dealt with the standardization of the
principles involved rather than the form of the graph or the details of
construction.
       "Consequently, authors dealing with the subject have differed sharply.

The present volume points out what the authors believe to be the best
current technique, based on a wide survey of representative experience.
This will perhaps excuse any apparent dogmatism as to the rules laid down
for good procedure."

Land Inheritance Law - Germany and Prussia

Burghoff, Kurt. Die heimatzuflucht nach dem Reichserbhofgesetz. 47pp.
  Hamburg, H. Christians druckerei und verlag, 1934. 282 B91
   Inaug.-diss. - Erlangen.
   Bibliography, pp.5-6.
   "Anerbengesetze", pp.7-8.
   The legal conditions which accompany or simplify land ownership
  under the provisions of the Piussian and the German land inheritance
  laws.

Land Settlement - Hawaii

Keesing, F. M. Hawaiian homesteading on Molokai. 133pp. [Honolulu] 1936.
  (University of Hawaii. Research publications no. 12) 500 H31R
   University of Hawaii publications (formerly quarterly bulletin) v. 1,
  no. 3, January 1936.
   This is a survey of the major homesteads projects - those on Molokai -
  set up under the Hawaiian Homes Commission Act of 1921. It is "designed
  primarily to give a summary of the facts...[and] is the result of observations and enquiries made on the spot during the summer of 1935, together
  with a close study of the documentary records... The aim is to give a clear
  and concise picture of the Hawaiian rehabilitation experiment, as parallel to many others the world over, in which an attempt is being made to
  consciously remould the economic and social life of a human group: in this
  case, first to fit a settlement scheme to the special needs and character
  of the Hawaiian people and second to fit the chosen Hawaiian to the special
  conditions that the island of Molokai provides.
   "The study was undertaken as a result of a request from a hold-over committee of the Territorial legislature to the University of Hawaii for aid in
  analyzing homestead affairs. Travel and other costs were met from a research grant given to the department of anthropology in the University by
  the Rosenwald Fund of Chicago. The University is publishing the study at
  the request of the Legislative Committee." - Introductory.

Land Settlement - Netherlands

Blink, Hendrik. Woeste gronden, ontginning en bebossching in Nederland, voor-
  maals en thans... Uitgegeven door de Nederlandsche vereeniging voor
  economische geographie. 244pp. s'-Gravenhage, N. V. boek- en kunstdrukkerij
  v. h. Mouton & co., 1929. 282.2 B61
   This volume is said by a competent Netherlands economist Dr. A. C. de
  Vooys to give "the best summary on the historical and present situation
  on land settlement in our country." It contains a historical account of the
  clearing, draining, restripping and settlement of land in the Netherlands
  before and after 1800. The aims of the Centrale Commissie voor Riulverka-
  veling are outlined and examples of results accomplished are given such as

the reclamation and settlement of the marsh of Peel in Northern Brabant.
This is followed by a history of forests and afforestation in the Netherlands, with the dividing line also in 1800. A table gives the area of uncultivated land in 1833, 1900, 1920 and 1927 and of forest land in 1833,
1879, 1900, 1920, 1925 and 1927, and shows the increase or decrease of
afforestation by provinces.

Jonge, Anje de. De resultaten onder landarbeiderswet. 164pp. Groningen, 1926.
282 J73
    Proefschrift - Groningen.
    This is a study of the results of the Netherlands Land Workers' Act of
April 20, 1918, based on a questionnaire sent to local authorities and societies, and on a detailed study of the records in certain government departments. The Act provides for the establishment of rural allotments with
a dwellinghouse to be held in ownership and of detached parcels of land to
be held in tenancy. The applicant must be a wage-earning agricultural
worker who will cultivate his allotment in his spare time.

Land Settlement - Western Canada

England, Robert. The colonization of western Canada; a study of contemporary
    land settlement (1896-1934) 341pp. London, P. S. King & son, ltd., 1936.
282.2 En3
    Bibliography, pp. 323-331.
    Partial contents: The physical controls of agricultural settlement:
The settlement of the prairie provinces; Methods and policies of land
settlement and agricultural development; The back-to-land movement in
Western Canada (1930-1934); The structure of the rural population; A
project in the use of group consciousness as a lever in agricultural
development.
    Among the appendices are the following: Racial origin of population
of prairie provinces urban and rural; Summary of methods adopted for
disposal of land in Western Canada; Land Sales (Agricultural): Canadian
Pacific Railway; and Land sales: Canadian National Railways.

Manchester Statistical Society

Manchester statistical society Transactions... session 1934-1935 and index.
    various paging. Manchester, Norbury, Lockwood & co., ltd. [1935?]
251 M31
    Partial contents: Public finance in China, by E. W. Mead; and Housing
the people, by Norman McKellen.

Mechanization of Agriculture

Newman, J. E. Notes on the technique of mechanized farming. 44pp. Oxford,
    Printed at the University press, 1934. 58 N46
    At head of title: Institute for Research in Agricultural Engineering.
University of Oxford.
    The Director of the Institute for Research in Agricultural Engineering,
H. J. Denham, writes in part as follows in the foreword:
    "The Survey of Mechanized Farms was begun in November 1930. Starting

with some seven farms, of which six are still under the same ownership, it now includes a round score, representing a very wide diversity of farming conditions...

"Three important facts have emerged from this survey: the first, that these farms are now directly and indirectly employing more labour than the land carried before its equipment was mechanized; the second, that most of these farms, which started as purely specialized units for the production of one commodity, are now 'diversifying' on an increasing scale; the third, that their yields are as good or better than those of farms run on more traditional lines. Mechanization has been defined in the past as a state of mind rather than a mere matter of machines: it certainly does not depend entirely on tractors, and a very good specimen of the mechanized farm of the past, employing horses, might be claimed in that of Mr. Baylis, on the Berkshire Downs, most admirably described by C. S. Orwin in Progress in English Farming Systems, III, or in that of Mr. Chamberlain at Crowmarsh, of which an account is given by the same author in Progress in English Farming Systems, IV. Mr. Chamberlain now employs tractors, but his methods are the same. Freedom from prejudice, freedom from the burden of obsolete equipment, the capacity to discuss an agricultural problem quite objectively, and a high degree of courage in the face of adverse local comment, are some of the essentials involved in successful new ventures of this type...

"In presenting these notes on the technique of mechanized farming Mr. Newman has drawn almost entirely on the farms included in the Survey, of which, indeed, he was the originator. No man in this country is more competent to describe the present state of this type of agriculture, since as a practical farmer and a practical engineer his knowledge of the problems involved is unequalled; and it was at his suggestion that the first Combine Harvester was introduced to this country in 1928. There were sixty of these machines at work this harvest. On only one point do I disagree with him, when he hints on p. 5 that mechanization makes farming more of an art and less of a science. Farming is an art, in that it includes so many variables that the solution of any of its many problems by sheer reason, without the help of intuition and the other short cuts of the subconscious mind, is impossible. Mechanization reduces the number of variables, and by so doing makes scientific working more possible; but for all that the science of farming still remains an art.

Oxford. University. Agricultural economics research institute.   Studies in power farming.   77pp.   Oxford, Agricultural economics research institute, 1936.   58 Ox22
    Pt. 1-2 in 1 no.
    At head of title: University of Oxford. Agricultural Economics Research Institute.
    Contents. - I. Mechanized corn-growing, by A. Bridges and H. Whitby. - II. The cost of tractor work, by J. R. Lee.

Oxford. University. Institute for research in agricultural engineering. Increased production in agriculture; papers read at the meeting of the British association for the advancement of science at York, 1932, by H. J. Denham... S. J. Wright... A. J. Hosier and D. R. Bomford. With a commentary by C. S. Orwin.   35pp.   Oxford [Hall the printer ltd.] 1932.   58 Ox2In
    Contents. - Some basic problems of mechanised farming, by H. J. Denham;

The role of the tractor in reducing cost of production, by S. J. Wright;
Some problems of extensive farming with mechanised equipment, by A. J.
Hosier; Some problems of intensive farming with mechanised equipment, by
D. R. Bomford; and Commentary, by C. S. Orwin.

Mexico

Martinez de Alva, Ernesto. Vida rural; los campesinos de México. 344pp.
    Mexico, D.F., Talleres gráficos de la nación, 1934. 281.2 M36
    "This volume has been printed by the Mexican Government and dis-
tributed free of cost to the rural population of Mexico by the Ministry
of Public Education. The book is admittedly 'propaganda,' but we must
remember that in Mexico the word 'propaganda' is not used in the same
opprobrious sense that it has in this country. There it is almost
synonymous with 'educacion'.
    "It has always been my opinion that the so-called anti-religious
policy of the Mexican Government was directed against the temporal
and political power of the Roman Catholic Church, and not against religious beliefs either Catholic or Protestant; and that the so-called
'socialistic' policy of education was a part of the effort to build an
economic plan suitable to the needs of the vast Indian and mestizo
population.
    "Señor Martinez's book seems to fully bear out my opinion. It is a
collection of essays, addresses and dialogues touching upon almost
every phase of life that is encountered by those who are participating
in the semi-communal life that grows out of the 'ejidal' system of
land tenure, and is interspersed with a collection of appropriate
proletarian verse." - George Kelly, Tulsa, Oklahoma, in Christian
Science Monitor, Jan. 27, 1936.

Monetary Stabilization and Economic Recovery

Academy of political science, New York. Economic recovery and monetary stabil-
    ization; a series of addresses and papers presented at the semi-annual
    meeting of the Academy of political science, April 2, 1936. Ed. by Parker
    Thomas Moon. 135pp. (Proceedings, v. 17, no. 1, May 1936) 280.9 Ac1
    v.17, no. 1.
    Partial contents: How can credit be controlled? by Emanuel A. Golden-
weiser; The sterling area and the stabilization problem, by Alvin H. Hansen;
The place of gold in the monetary standards of the future, by Frank D.
Graham; Whence and whither in the gold standard? by Adolph C. Miller;
Economic recovery and monetary stabilization, by Leon Fraser; Some essentials of monetary stability, by George L. Harrison; and The prospect of
inflation in the United States, by James Harvey Rogers.

Mortgages

Mortgage bankers association of America. Proceedings of the twenty-second annual
    convention... held October 3 and 4, 1935, French Lick, Indiana. Including
    code of ethics, constitution and by-laws, list of officers and members of
    the association, synopsis of service bulletins issued by the headquarters
    office since last annual meeting. 267pp. [Chicago, Association headquarters
    office, 1935] 284.9 M84

Partial contents: Permanent sources of cooperative credit for agriculture, by W. I. Myers; The enduring value of farm mortgages as security for debt, by Charles Burton Robbins; The building up and functioning of farm sales organizations, by H. A. Merrifield; Perfecting methods of farm supervision, by H. F. Williams. The Code of ethics of the Mortgage Bankers Association of America and its Constitution and by-laws are printed as appendices.

National Bureau of Economic Research

National bureau of economic research, inc. Retrospect and prospect, 1920-1936, by the director of research. 48pp. New York, National bureau of economic research [1936]   280.9 N215Re
    "Publications of the National bureau of economic research", pp.46-48. This very interesting document sets forth with concise competence the purposes, organization, work and plans of the National Bureau of Economic Research. Of especial interest are the Sections devoted to Principles of future policy and Tentative plans of work for 1936.

National Cooperative Milk Producers' Federation

National cooperative milk producers' federation. Educational series, 5-6. 2 nos. Washington, D. C., 1935-1936.   281.3449 N21
    no. 5. The farmer looks at the oleomargarine picture [1935]   105pp.
    no. 6. Present day problems of dairy farmers, by Charles W. Holman; being a discussion of present day problems of dairy farmers arising out of the reciprocal trade policy of our government, the competition of oleomargarine and the expansion of dairying under the new soil conservation program. [1936]   28pp.

Negro Agricultural Worker

Vance, R. B.   The negro agricultural worker under the federal rehabilitation program... prepared by Rupert B. Vance, Ph.D., for the Committee on negroes and economic reconstruction, Edwin R. Embree, W. W. Alexander, Charles S. Johnson. 244pp., mimeogr. [n.p., 1934?]   281.002 V27
    Chapter 1, Dynamics in the Cotton Belt, 1910-1930; Chapter 2, The shifting pattern of tenancy, white and black; Chapter 3, The negro farm operator; Chapter 4, The cotton cropper in depression and readjustment.

Pacific Coast Economic Association

Pacific coast economic association. Papers and proceedings of the fourteenth annual conference... at Mills college, Oakland, California, December, 1935. Ed. by John B. Canning. 80pp. Ann Arbor, Mich., Edwards brothers, inc., 1936. Processed.   280.9 P11
    Partial contents: The new relation of Government to agriculture in the United States, by W. L. Wanlass; Resale price maintenance under the California fair trade law, by E. T. Grether; Some aspects of recent price control experience, by R. B. Heflebower; Changes of emphasis in Government efforts to aid agriculture, by E. F. Dummeier; Economics of production control, by E. L. Potter; and Governmental control of agricultural prices, by Glenn E. Hoover.

461

Górecki, Roman. Poland and her economic development. 124pp. London, G. Allen &
   Unwin ltd. [1935] 280.177 G66P
      A readable account of the economic development of Poland after the restor-
   ation of independence written by the President of the National Economic Bank
   of Warsaw. A few pages are devoted to agriculture.

Prices and Prosperity

Beard, Gilbert. Prices and prosperity. 79pp. Manchester, Kennedy press ltd.
   [1935] 280 B383
      Partial contents: Supply and demand; The consumers' power; Mechanization
   and its contribution to prosperity; Uneconomic production; Economic nationalism; Free versus compulsory co-operation; and Freedom a necessary condition of prosperity.

Rural Life

National Catholic rural life conference. Catholic rural life objectives; a
   series of discussions on some elements of major importance in the philosophy of agrarianism. 56pp.   St. Paul, Minn., National Catholic rural
   life conference [1935?]   281.2 N216
      "The papers in this compilation were prepared for the thirteenth annual
   convention of the National Catholic rural life conference... 1935." -
   Foreword.
      Partial contents: The church and the rural youth, by O. E. Baker; The
   Green revolution, by Michael Williams; The church and rural welfare, by John
   La Farge; The ethical and religious background of cooperation, by Frederick
   P. Kenkel; Agrarianism, the basis of the new order, by W. Howard Bishop.

Sharecroppers

Kester, Howard   Revolt among the sharecroppers. 98pp.   New York, Covici,
   Friede [1936] 282 K48
      Bibliography, pp. 97-98.
      "The purpose of this small volume is three-fold. First, to describe a
   general condition; secondly, to set down the labors of a particular organization working in the midst of these conditions; and thirdly, to suggest a
   way out.
      "The author chose the Southern Tenant Farmers' Union as the vehicle
   through which to express the revolt among the sharecroppers because of
   its extraordinary achievements and his intimate knowledge of its work.
   He is not unmindful of the magnificent contributions which the Sharecroppers' union of Alabama has made toward securing better conditions for
   the cotton field workers, providing them with new incentives and a greater
   hope in the future and in making America conscious of the forgotten men of
   the cotton country. Their achievements are of great significance." - Author's
   preface.

otter, Arundel, and Phelps, T. W.   Your securities under social security; a
   handbook of the labor factor in investments.   153pp. New York, Dow, Jones
   & co., inc. [1936] 284.6 C822
      Based on a series of articles on the Social Security Act and its impact
   on American industry published in the Wall Street Journal early in 1936...
   Since its first publication... all of the material has been revised." -
   Foreword.
      There are four appendices as follows: The Social Security Board Explains
   the act; Germany: Social Security Pioneer; France: The Last to Experiment;
   Britain: Social Security in Full Bloom.

outheastern Planning Conference

outheastern planning conference, Savannah, Ga., 1935.   Proceedings of South-
   eastern planning conference, Savannah, Georgia, December 4-5, 1935.
   Alabama, Georgia, Florida, South Carolina. National resources committee,
   Fourth district.   95pp., mimeogr. Albany, Ga. [1935]   280.7 So829
      H. T. McIntosh, district chairman.
      Partial contents: Organization of city and county planning boards, by
   Robert Randall; State planning, by Morton L. Wallerstein; State planning
   in Florida, by C. B. Treadway; A forestry program, by Joseph C. Kircher;
   The Atlantic and Gulf canal, by Gen. Sumter L. Lowry; Co-operation of
   Federal Agencies National Resources Committee, by Robert H. Randall;
   Federal, state and local co-operation in planning the works program of
   the CWA, FERA and WPA, by Gay Shepperson; Federal, state and local
   co-operation in planning the works program of the CWA, FERA and WPA, by
   Perry A. Fellows; The rural resettlement program, by Philip Weltner;
   Resettlement Administration program of land utilization as it applies to
   planning in the southeast, by W. A. Hartman; Maps and mapping, the
   sine qua non for planning, by Blake R. Van Leer; and Regional planning,
   by E. S. Draper.

State Aid to Local Governments - New York State

New York (State) Commission on state aid to municipal subdivisions. Report of
   the New York state Commission on state aid to municipal subdivisions, submitted February 1, 1936.   357pp.   Albany, J. B. Lyon company, printers,
   1936.
      Legislative document (1936) no. 58. State of New York.   284 N488
      The work of the Commission is briefly described in the introduction as
   follows:
      "This temporary commission was established by an act of the legislature
   approved March 19, 1935 and was appointed by the governor May 25, 1935.
   The statute directs the commission to make a comprehensive study and analysis of state aid to the municipal subdivisions of the state and of the
   laws relating thereto and to collect such facts and make such investigations with respect thereto as will enable it to report thereon and recommend such changes and modifications in the policy of state aid, its nature
   and extent and the formulae and laws governing such state aid, either
   liberalizing, restricting, extending or abolishing the same as, in the
   judgment of the commission, are necessary or appropriate to effectuate

its findings. As required by the statute, a preliminary report of the proceedings of the commission was filed with the governor on December 15,
1935. This document constitutes the final report which the statute directs
shall be placed before the governor and the legislature on or before
February 1, 1936."

A foot-note states that "In this report the term 'state aid' is used
in a broad sense to include not only subventions or grants-in-aid but
also distributions to the municipal subdivisions of state-administered
taxes and, in some instances, even the granting of the right of the localities to tax state-owned property."

The study contains sections on State-collected, locally shared taxes;
State aid for education, highways, social welfare and unemployment relief,
public health, libraries, and general purposes. Memorandum no. 1 gives
the brief history of State aid in New York State. Memorandum no. 2 is
entitled "The Operation of the State-aid System in Seven New York Counties".
Memorandums no. 3 to 9 contain the statements submitted by the various
departments of the State affected by State aid.

Statistical Institute for Economic Research, Sofia

Sofia. Statistical institute for economic research. Publications no. 1-2/3
2v. Sofia, 1935. 280.9 Sol3

The title of the publication is given in both Bulgarian and English.
Articles are in Bulgarian. Most of them have parallel columns in English,
German, or French. Some have only resumes in one of these languages.

The organization and aims of this institute are described in the first
issue. From this account the following excerpts have been taken:

"The idea of establishing an Institute for Economic Research in Bulgaria
seems to have been originated in the Commercial University of Varna in 1924,
when Prof. O Anderson and Prof. N. Dolinsky attempted to organize, in that
direction, the seminar of Economic and Financial Sciences. Due to pecuniary
difficulties and unfavourable conditions, the seminar could not be well
developed. The question was reconsidered and took on a more definite and
concrete form eight years later, in 1932, when Prof. Anderson, in his
personal talk with the directors of The Rockefeller Foundation in Budapest,
succeeded in interesting them in his project and was promised material
support.

"In the beginning it was thought best to establish the Institute in
Varna and use the personnel of the Commercial University, but later, when
it became evident that the stability of the personnel was not guaranteed,
it was decided to establish it in Sofia.

"After a detailed study of the possibilities which Sofia offered, it was
decided to accept the invitation of some professors of the University of
Sofia and to transform into an Institute the seminars of statistics and
economics of the Faculty of Law...

"The interest of the two state banks: The Bulgarian National Bank and the
Bulgarian Agricultural and Cooperative Bank has been aroused and they have
pledged their material support. The final working out of the project was
during the autumn months of 1934 and on 28 of December, 1934 the draft of
the law by decree for the establishment of the Statistical Institute for
Economic Research was passed by the Council of Ministers, later signed by
His Majesty The King and published in the 14th number of the Bulgarian State

Journal (January 21, 1935)

"The main object of the Institute is to undertake special investigations and studies of various questions of economic theory, in as much as they require a statistical elaboration and interpretation of the numerical data. These researches will be done in collaboration with the scholars who are engaged in studies of Bulgarian economy.

"As our Institute is similar to that of Norway and as The Rockefeller Foundation sees no reason to repeat in Sofia the work of Oslo, it was decided in our correspondence in connection with the establishment of the Institute, that unlike Oslo,(where the main work is the study of questions of theoretical-mathematical economy), in Sofia special consideration will be given to the application of the finer mathematical-statistical methods in statistical economic research. Just for that reason the Institute was named as follows: Statistical Institute for Economic Research.

Other articles in no. 1 are: Organisation, Leistungen und weitere Aufgaben der Konjunkturforschung (Organization, accomplishments and further tasks of the investigation of economic cycles) by Oskar Morgenstern; On the scissors of prices in Bulgaria, by Oskar N. Anderson; Resultats preliminaires de l'essai sur la repartition du poids des impôts sur les differents groupes economiques en Bulgarie (Resume) (Preliminary results of the attempt to determine the distribution of the burden of taxation on the different economic groups in Bulgaria) by St. Spassitchev and A. J. Totev; Decret-loi pour la creation de l'Institut Statistique pour Recherches Economiques pres de l'Universite d'Etat de Sofia. (Decree law providing for the creation of a Statistical Institute for Economic Research at the State University of Sofia.)

Contents no. 2/3: - Again on the problem of the scissors of prices in Bulgaria, by O. N. Anderson; Nombres indices pour le volume de la production agricole vegetale en Bulgarie (Index numbers of the volume of production of agricultural crops in Bulgaria) by A. Totev; Resultats preliminaires de l'essai sur la repartition du poids des impôts sur les differents groupes economiques en Bulgarie (Preliminary results of the attempt to determine the distribution of the burden of taxation on the different economic groups in Bulgaria), by St. Spassitchev and V. Parascova; Sur la structure et les ressources de l'economie financiere en Bulgarie (The structure and resources of the Bulgarian financial system), by Ivan Stefanoff; L'industrie du caoutchouc en Bulgarie (The rubber industry in Bulgaria) by D. Mincoff; Ausschaltung der Saisonkomponente nach der methode von Dr. A. Wald. (In this article tables are given which demonstrate the application to three series of prices of Dr. A. Wald's method of computing seasonal variations) by Raschko Zaycoff; Current notes.

Statistics

Wagemann, E. F. Narrenspiegel der statistik; die umrisse eines statistischen weltbildes. 255pp. Hamburg, Hanseatische verlagsanstalt [1935]
251 W12

The author shows how the conception of space and time in cooperation with speech gave birth to the idea of numbers. He admits, however, that this is a hypothesis which is only partially based on etymology, psychology, and ethnology, and partially on deductions which can at best with difficulty be substantiated. He feels under a certain obligation to philosophy inasmuch as he has set himself the task of investigating why and in

rhat sense statistics are the most uncertain and mathematics the most
certain of all sciences. Recognizing that the statistical number is
fundamentally different from the mathematical number, he points out that
many errors and false conclusions have resulted from their interchange
or wrong combination. He shows how the statistical number is closely
connected with the idea of logic, and on this basis he divides his work
into three parts. In the first part we are shown how man counts and mis-
counts, in the second how he makes comparisons that are inexact, and in
the third how he estimates and makes mistakes.

As a statistical conclusion is nothing more than the expression of a
relation between statistical masses it can only be expressed in numbers.
In itself it cannot express any relation of cause or quality. Mass statistics, as an expression of empirical conceptions, represent those conceptions by means of numbers but do not build them up. But that does not
mean that statistics are not an original science, just like mathematics
or philosophy. Statistics have a much smaller field of operation than
logic. Statistics have given the human mind the power to calculate coming
events and so to penetrate the veil that hides the future from the ordinary
view. The statistical and the mathematical view of the world are contrasted.

Tax Delinquency - United States

Dun & Bradstreet, inc. Municipal service dept. The trend of tax delinquency,
1930-1935, cities over 50,000 population, by Frederick L. Bird, director of
municipal research. 26pp., multigr. New York city, Dun & Bradstreet, inc.,
Municipal service department, 1936. 284.5 D91
"This analysis, the fifth of an annual series, presents a six-year record
of municipal experience in collection of the general property tax, beginning
with 1930 as a base and carrying the annual trend to the close of the 1935
fiscal year. The 190 cities (excluding Washington, D. C.) of over 50,000
population are used as a representative cross-section of conditions as they
have existed nationally."

Putney, Bryant. Tax delinquency in the United States. pp. 327-342. Washington, 1935. (Editorial research reports, v.2, 1935, no.15)
280 Ed42 1935, v.2, no.15
The problem of tax delinquency, which "is almost exclusively a
phenomenon of the property tax," is discussed under four main topics
as follows: Growth of the problem; Extent and character of tax
delinquency; Causes of non-payment of property taxes; Methods of
eliminating tax delinquency.

Tax Limitation Amendment - New York

New York state conference of mayors and other municipal officials. Advisory
committee. The way to municipal financial chaos; memorandum prepared
by the Advisory committee of the New York state conference of mayors
and other municipal officials on the proposed constitutional tax
limitation amendment. 32PP. Albany, N. Y., 1935. 284.5 N488
The Introduction to this report reads in part as follows:
"A serious threat to the financial stability and integrity of New
York State municipalities exists. It lies in the proposed amendment
to Article 8 of the Constitution limiting aggregate taxes on real

property in the cities, villages, towns, school districts, special
districts and counties of the state to two per cent of the true value
of real property in money, such limited taxes to cover operating expense as well as interest and principal on indebtedness in these
municipal units...

"This over-all tax limitation is sponsored principally by real
estate groups...

"The Mayors' Conference, alarmed by these efforts to impose upon
municipalities of the state a sweeping tax limitation of a type which
has been generally discredited as to purpose and effect wherever tried,
decided to make a study of the effect of the proposed amendment on
the financial structure of every city and first and second class village
in the state. This study showed clearly that the proposal, if adopted,
would constitute an arbitrary and unreasonable financial limitation
which would impair or destroy entirely essential municipal services.

"In the opinion of the Advisory Committee of the Mayors' Conference, this proposal is fraught with such grave fiscal and social consequences that it is constrained to urge earnestly that the state government and its legislature and every civic group in the state strongly
and actively condemn this unsound and dangerous proposal.

"In support of its viewpoint, the Advisory Committee presents herewith a summary of the study, with attached tables, of the effect of
the proposed over-all tax limitation on the fiscal structure of every
city and first and second class village in the state, including the
procedure followed in making the study and the resulting findings. The
committee concludes its memorandum by listing salient reasons for its
opposition to the proposed limitation."

Taxation - United States

North Carolina. Dept. of revenue. Comparing tax loads, North Carolina and
other states: property, franchise, income. State charters for local
business. A. J. Maxwell, commissioner of revenue. 12pp. [Raleigh?
1936?] 284.5 N815

Putney, Bryant. Reduction of tax burdens on real estate. Washington, 1935
pp. 481-494. (Editorial research reports, v. 2, 1935, no. 23) 280 Ed42
1935, v. 2, no.23

The report points out the defects in existing real estate tax systems
as follows:

"While opposing both tax limitation and homestead exemption, most students
of taxation are firmly convinced that tax burdens on real estate should be
reduced. The existing system of real estate taxation is variously attacked
as a major cause of tax delinquency, as 'a positive factor in aggravating
and prolonging the depression,' and as an important contributory cause of the
trend toward state centralization. Diversification of tax sources is looked
upon as the principal remedy. Tax experts generally are agreed that income,
death, and severance taxes provide the most promising substitutes for real
estate taxation. Business and consumption taxes are also favored by some
students.

"The real estate tax is widely attacked on the ground that it is a fixed charge imposed without reference to current income. Failure of state and local governments to reduce assessments in periods of declining income and declining real estate values serves to increase the proportion of the actual value of real estate represented by the tax. During depression periods, moreover, heavy delinquency compels resort to heavier taxes on surviving taxpayers."

The extent of tax limitation laws is indicated and the opposing views on the desirability of the laws are given.

The movement to exempt property from taxation is also discussed and arguments for and against homestead exemption are quoted.

Trade Agreement - Brazilian American

Foucas, V. F. O tratado de commercio Brasileiro-Norte-Americano. 188pp. Rio de Janeiro, Edição dos Serviços Hollerith, s.a. [1935] 286 B66
"Serie de artigos publicados no.·"Correio da Manhã" do Rio de Janeiro, de 25 de junho a 4 de julho de 1935, pelo sr. Valentim F. Boucas." - Foot-note, p.[3] (see also Foot-note p.55)
Portuguese and English.

Contains a series of articles published in the Correio da Manha in June and July, 1935 protesting against the pessimistic articles signed by "An Industrial observer" which appeared in the daily press, after the signing of the Brazilian American Trade Agreement on February 2, 1935. The present series answers the objections of the industrialists and points out the advantages to Brazil of the treaty. The text of the treaty is given in Portuguese and English.

Trade Agreements and the Farmer

Sayre, F. B. Address... before the Denver chamber of commerce luncheon meeting... May 22, 1936... at Denver, Colorado, The farmers' stake in foreign trade. 11pp., mimeogr. [Washington, D. C., May 18, 1936.] U. S. Dept. of State.

Sayre, F. B. Address... before the Chamber of commerce of Kansas City... May 20, 1936... at Kansas City, Missouri. Trade agreements and the farmer. 13pp., mimeogr. [Washington, D. C., May 18, 1936] U. S. Dept. of State

These two addresses are practically the same and conclude with the following statement:
"To bring continuing prosperity to our farmers and to our country we must look facts boldly in the face. Increased tariffs offer no solution. Economic nationalism is the American farmer's worst enemy. His dire need is increased foreign markets in which to sell his surpluses. Upon this he must insist. And until this is secured to him the fundamental farm problem of America never will be solved."

Trade and Trade Barriers - Pacific Area

Wright, P. G. Trade and trade barriers in the Pacific... with an introduction by W. L. Holland. 530pp. Stanford University, Calif., Stanford university press, 1935. 286 W93
"The problems arising from the commercial relations of the countries

in the Pacific area have long been a subject for study by the Institute
of Pacific Relations. Since about 1927 a number of local and specialized
studies on trade and tariffs have been carried out and published by the
various National Councils. The co-ordination and enlargement of these
reports into a single uniform survey was authorized by the International
Research Committee of the Institute at the Shanghai Conference in November
1931. Such a task was subsequently found to involve such an amount of revision and new investigation as to require practically an entirely new
study. It was entrusted to Mr. Philip G. Wright who had already written
for the American Council of the Institute a valuable report, The American
Tariff and Oriental Trade, presented as a document to the Shanghai Conference. During the next eighteen months Mr. Wright carried out the careful analysis presented in the first seven chapters of this volume, sub-
mitting this report as a document for the Banff Conference of the Institute in August 1933. There it was again considered by the Research Committee, and the Secretariat was instructed to arrange for the final publication of the work after securing more recent statistics together with
a number of new sections in order to make the survey geographically more
comprehensive. Accordingly, since the death of Mr. Wright in 1934, steps
have been taken not only to bring the tables up to date but also to obtain five new chapters, on Manchuria and the countries of south eastern
Asia, specially written by competent authorities. An introduction has
also been prepared by the International Research Secretary of the Institute, giving a brief survey of commercial trends in the Pacific and setting
the book in its relation to the other studies on this subject carried out
by the National Councils." - Preface

Unemployment - Gt. Britain

Gt. Brit. Ministry of labour. Report for the year 1935. Presented by the
Minister of labour to Parliament by command of His Majesty April, 1936.
142pp. London, H. M. Stationery off., 1936. ([Parliament. Papers by
command.] Cmd. 5145) 283.9 G79L
Partial contents: Employment and unemployment; Work of the exchanges
as employment agencies; Provision of training, instruction and welfare
schemes for unemployed men and women; Boys and girls; Unemployment insurance and unemployment assistance legislation.

Wages and Prices

Hotchkiss, W. L. The law of wage action. 238pp. Cleveland, O., Eaton publishing company [1936] 283 H79
The author has made a study of the relationship of wages and prices, resulting in what he calls The law of wage action. Briefly stated, this means
that increased compensation for the production of raw material has little effect upon the price of the finished unit after passing through several merchandising operations and that this increase in wages provides the small
margin which enables salaried workers to buy more goods. To benefit from
this theory, he suggests a national planned economy giving Congress power
over the states in economic affairs. (Publishers Weekly, v. 129, no. 12,
Mar. 21, 1936)

Alberta wheat pool. Annual report, 1934-1935. 88pp. Calgary, Alberta,
    December 1935. 280.39 Al12

Saskatchewan co-operative wheat producers limited. Via Churchill; a shipment
    of Saskatchewan wheat to Europe. 62pp. Regina, Saskatchewan cooperative
    wheat producers limited, 1936. 286.259 Sa7
        "In the following pages an attempt is made to follow, step by step,
    the progress of a shipment of Saskatchewan wheat to Europe by way of Church-
    hill. Thus while the main theme will be the Hudson Bay route, this pam-
    phlet also seeks to present a picture of the transportation overseas of
    Western Canada's most important commodity...
        "The illustrations and the bulk of the material here presented were
    previously published in The Western Producer." - Foreword.

Wool - Consumption

Gt. Brit. Imperial economic committee. Intelligence branch. World consumption
    of wool 1928 - 1935. An analysis of consumption & trade in wool and
    wool products in the empire & in foreign countries. 306pp. London,
    H. M. Stationery off., 1936. (Gt. Brit. Imperial economic committee..
    Intelligence branch. I.E.C./S.4) 280.39 G794
        "A review of the consumption of wool in different countries presents
    peculiar difficulties. Reliable estimates of the actual amount of wool
    consumed in individual countries are almost completely lacking and, further,
    the statistics of trade and production which are available are not uniform.
    The aim of the present volume is, therefore, to assemble as clearly and
    concisely as possible such data as are available, although inevitably
    the information for the different countries must differ both in quantity
    and quality.
        "The plan adopted for each country has been to open with a brief in-
    troductory paragraph followed by a statement of the machine equipment and
    labour supply; then, to estimate from trade and wool production statistics
    the available supplies of raw wool; to summarise the available information
    on production and trade in semi-manufactures, and to conclude with the
    output and trade in finished goods - more particularly clothing tissues.
    The hosiery and carpet industries have been included only where their con-
    sumption of wool is sufficiently high to render them a factor of major
    importance. The highly complicated and technical nature of tariff
    and quota regulations preclude any but the briefest references, as
    an attempt to treat them in detail would involve more space than is
    possible in a volume of this kind.
        "There are very few countries in the world to-day which do not
    consume at least a small quantity of wool. The major consuming
    countries have, of course, been treated in greater detail than those
    with smaller industries. The period covered has for the most part
    been limited to 1928 to 1934, but 1935 figures have been added where
    available for the larger consuming countries. Most 1934 and all
    1935 figures should be regarded as strictly provisional."

World Agricultural Census

International institute of agriculture. The first world agricultural census. Bulletin no. 6, 11. 2 nos. Rome, 1936. 251 In8I

   no. 6. Commonwealth of Australia.
   "In Australia an agricultural Census is taken regularly each year. In 1929-1930, in view of the world agricultural census, certain complementary questions were added to the usual questionnaire.
   "The data published in this bulletin in general refer to the agricultural year 1929-30, those of the territorial area to 31 December 1929 (for New South Wales and Western Australia to 30 June 1929); those for the number and area of private holdings and their distribution according to size to 1928-29 (for New South Wales to 1924-25); those of area manured, quantity of manure used, livestock and slaughtering returns to 1929; those of the number of holdings and number of sheep to 1928.
   "As regards the elaboration of the statistical data the Commonwealth Bureau of Census and Statistics states that uniform principles for measuring the quantity and value of all kinds of production were adopted by the Australian statisticians in conference in 1924 and have been elaborated at successive annual conferences into a definite procedure. It was not, however, possible at the date of the Census to carry this out with complete uniformity for all States, though great progress was made in this direction."
   no. 11. Argentina (census of live stock)
   The Census of the Republic of Argentina was limited to live stock and was taken on July 1930 by means of a Central Commission, Local Commissions and Census officers who attended to the distribution and collection of the questionnaires.
   Animals in towns were enumerated by means of special questionnaires and the numbers were added to those in the country.

U. S. FARM CREDIT ADMINISTRATION

U. S. Farm credit administration. Financing agriculture in 1935. [16] pp. 1936. (Circular A-6)

U. S. Farm credit administration. Interest rates are lowest in history. 4pp. [Washington, U. S. Govt. print. off., 1936?] 166.3 In8

U. S. Farm credit administration. 1936 loan manual of policy and procedure. 15pp. Washington, U. S. Govt. print. off., 1936. 166.3 L782

U. S. Farm credit administration. Revised rules and regulations for production associations organized under the Farm credit act of 1933. 55PP. [Washington, D. C., 1936?] 166.3 R86

U. S. Farm credit administration. Division of finance and research. Some results of a study of the tung-oil industry in the United States. 53pp., mimeogr. WAshington, D. C., May 1935. 166.3 So5

U. S. Farm credit administration. Emergency crop and feed loan section. Manual of central and regional office organization and procedure. Emergency relief appropriation act of 1935, approved April 8, 1935 and executive order no. 7305 dated February 28, 1936. 39PP., mimeogr. [Washington, D. C., 1936] 166.3 M312

BIBLIOGRAPHIES

Agricultural labor in the United States, 1915-1935. A selected list of references, comp. by Esther M. Colvin and Josiah C. Folsom, under the direction
of Mary G. Lacy, Librarian, Bureau of agricultural economics. 493pp.,
mimeogr. Washington, D. C., December 1935. (U. S. Dept. of agriculture.
Bureau of agricultural economics. Agricultural economics bibliography
no. 64) 1.9 Ec73A no.64

Consumers' cooperation. 6PP. (Russell Sage foundation, New York. Library.
Bulletin no. 134. Dec. 1935) 241.3 R91Cc
A selected list of references compiled by Agnes H. Campbell.
May be obtained from Russell Sage Foundation, 130 East 22nd St.,
New York, N. Y. at 20 cents a copy.

A digest of pasture research literature in the continental United States and
Canada, 1885 to 1935. [Comp.] by A. J. Pieters, U. S. Dept. of agricul-
ture. Bureau of plant industry. Division of forage crops and diseases.
130pp., mimeogr. [Washington, D. C.] January 1, 1936. 1.9 P691Di
May be obtained from the office of the compiler, Room 5951 South
Building, United States Department of Agriculture.

A list of recent writings on state government and its reorganization with a
section on interstate compacts, compiled by Anne L. Baden under the direction of Florence S. Hellman, acting chief bibliographer, October 1, 1935.
44pp., mimeogr. [Washington] 1935. 241.3 Un3Li
Issued by Library of Congress. Division of Bibliography.

Preliminary bibliography on youth, prepared by the Research division, the
National education association. 26pp., mimeogr. Washington, D. C.,
May 1935. 241.3 N2132
Address of the National Education Association is 1201 Sixteenth Street,
N. W., Washington, D. C.

State tax surveys: a bibliography. June 1935. 10pp., mimeogr. [Chicago,
1935] 241.3 J66S
Prepared for the Council of State Governments (Drexel Ave. & 58th
St., Chicago, Ill.) by the Joint Reference Library under the general
supervision of Mr. James W. Martin and Mr. Robert M. Paige. The list
contains 143 titles covering 43 states. The material has been selected
on the basis of usefulness to students of state taxation.

NEW PERIODICALS

Rural sociology, devoted to scientific study of rural life, v. 1, no. 1, March
1936. Baton Rouge, La., Rural sociology section, American sociological
society.
Rural Sociology is a new quarterly which "grew out of action taken at
the meeting of the Rural Sociology Section of the American Sociological
Society," in New York in December 1935.
"The purpose of the journal is to afford an additional medium of expres-

sion for scholars in the field of Rural Sociology. The pages will not be confined exclusively to Rural Sociologists as a professional group; articles are invited from workers in related fields of social science, from teachers, and from rural workers who may contribute to the sociology of rural life. Moreover, it will be the policy to solicit manuscripts from workers in foreign countries, although it is intended that all such papers shall deal with some phase of rural social life." It "stands for no special school of social thought; it is rather a forum in which any individual who has a contribution to make can present his findings."

The Managing Editor is T. Lynn Smith of Louisiana State University. The University is not the official publisher of the journal but is the guarantor of the enterprise.

The Board of Editors is composed of Lowry Nelson, Chairman, John H. Kolb, C. E. Lively, Dwight Sanderson, and Carle C. Zimmerman.

The first issue contains the following: National policy and rural public welfare, by E. L. Morgan (pp. 8-19); Size of family in relation to homogeneity of parental traits, by Walter C. McKain, Jr., and N. L. Whetten (pp. 20-27); Localization of dependency in rural areas, by J. O. Babcock (pp. 28-39); Population mobility, by C. E. Lively (pp. 40-53); Littleville: a parasitic community during the depression, by Carle C. Zimmerman, John H. Useem, and Lyman H. Ziegler (pp. 54-72); National policies and rural social organization, by Lowry Nelson (pp. 73-89); County organization for program planning in Virginia, by B. L. Hummel (pp. 90-93); Current bulletins; Book reviews; News notes and announcements.

U. S. Dept. of agriculture. Agricultural adjustment administration. Division of marketing and marketing agreements. Better marketing [semi-monthly] v. 1, no. 1-4 April 4-May 16, 1936. [Washington, D. C., U. S. Govt. print. off.]

Nathan Koenig, editor.

The editorial note states that "Better Marketing is issued as a means of communicating to workers and cooperators of the Division of Marketing and Marketing Agreements information relative to the Division's activities under the Agricultural Adjustment Act and related Acts."

SELECTED LIST OF RECENT REVIEWS

Compiled by M. I. Herb

Astor, Waldorf Astor, 2d Viscount. The agricultural dilemma: a report of an enquiry organised by Viscount Astor and Mr. B. Seebohn Rowntree. 1935.
Reviewed by O. B. Jesness in Jour. Farm Econ. 18(2): 433-434. May 1936.

Black, J. D. The dairy industry and the AAA. 1935. (Half-title: The Institute of economics of the Brookings institution. Pub. no. 64)
Reviewed by Don S. Anderson in Jour. Farm Econ. 18(2): 437-439. May 1936.

Burns, A. F. Production trends in the United States since 1870. 1934.
(Half-title: Publications of the National bureau of economic re-
search, inc., no. 23)
Reviewed by John D. Black in Jour. Polit. Econ. 44(2): 258-262.
April 1936.

Canada. Dominion bureau of statistics, General statistics branch. The
Canada year book, 1934-35. 1935.
Reviewed by G. F. Drummond in Canad. Jour. Econ. and Polit.
Sci. 2(1): 102-105. February 1936.

Canada. Department of trade and commerce. The Dominion Bureau of
statistics; its origin, constitution and organization. [1935]
Reviewed by G. F. Drummond in Canad. Jour. Econ. and Polit.
Sci. 2(1): 97-98. February 1936.

Cauley, T. J. Agrarianism; a program for farmers. 1935.
Reviewed by Malcolm H. Bryan in South. Econ. Jour. 2(4): 86-89.
April 1936.

Childs, M. W. Sweden; the middle way. 1936.
Reviewed by Thurman W. Arnold in Yale Rev. 25(3): 612-615.
Spring 1936.
Reviewed briefly in Barron's 16(8): 28. Feb. 24, 1936.

Comish, N. H. Marketing of manufactured goods. [1935]
Reviewed by Edmund P. Learned in Harvard Business Rev. 14(3):
378. Spring number, 1936, in an article entitled "Recent Books
on Marketing."

Converse, P. D. Elements of marketing. rev. ed. 1935.
Reviewed by Edmund P. Learned in Harvard Business Rev. 14(3):
378. Spring number, 1936, in an article entitled "Recent Books
on Marketing."

Dickinson, John. Hold fast the middle way. An outline of economic
challenges and alternatives. 1935.
Reviewed by Lane W. Lancaster in Amer. Acad. Polit. and Social
Sci. Ann. 185: 212-213. May 1936.

Ezekiel, Mordecai. $2,500 a year; from scarcity to abundance. [1936]
Reviewed briefly in Com. and Finance 25(9): 321. May 2,
1936.
Reviewed by W. E. Grimes in Jour. Farm Econ. 18(2): 432-433.
May 1936.

Garside, A. H. Cotton goes to market. 1935.
Reviewed by Edmund P. Learned in Harvard Business Rev. 14(3):
376,377. Spring number, 1936, in an article entitled "Recent
Books on Marketing."

Goodrich, C. L., Allen, B. W., and Hayes, Marion. Migration and planes
of living, 1920-34. 1935. (Half-title: Bulletin no. 2. Study
of population redistribution. Industrial research dept., Wharton
school of finance and commerce, University of Pennsylvania.)
Reviewed by B. L. in Pacific Affairs 9(2): 309-311. June 1936.

Gray, L. C. Land planning. [1936] (Public policy pamphlet no. 19)
Reviewed by C. L. Stewart in Jour. Farm Econ. 18(2): 441-442.
May 1936.

Haight, F. A. French import quotas; a new instrument of commercial
policy. 1935. (Half-title: London school of economics and
political science. Studies in economics and commerce. no. 6)
Reviewed by K. W. Taylor in Canad. Jour. Econ. and Polit.
Sci. 2(2): 230-251. May 1936.

Hoffer, C. R. Introduction to rural sociology. Rev. ed. 1934.
Reviewed by C. E. Lively in Rural Sociol. 1(1): 107-108.
March 1936.

Holtzclaw, H. F. The principles of marketing. [1935]
Reviewed by Edmund P. Learner in Harvard Business Rev. 14(3):
378, Spring number, 1936, in an article entitled "Recent Books
on Marketing."

Howard, Lady Louise E. (Matthaei). Labour in agriculture; an inter-
national survey. 1935.
Reviewed by Josiah C. Folsom in Jour. Farm Econ. 18(2): 439-441.
May 1936.
Reviewed by Josiah C. Folsom in Amer. Acad. Polit. and Social
Sci. Ann. 185: 237-238. May 1936.

Hunt, R. L. A history of farmer movements in the Southwest, 1873-1925.
[1935?]
Reviewed by Carl C. Taylor in Rural Sociol. 1(1): 109-110.
March 1936.

Johnson, C. S., Embree, E. R., and Alexander, W. W. The collapse of
cotton tenancy; a summary of field studies and statistical surveys
1933-35. 1935.
Reviewed by C. Horace Hamilton in Rural Sociol. 1(1): 110-112.
March 1936.

Jones, J. M., Jr. Tariff retaliation; repercussions of the Hawley-Smoot
bill. 1934.
Reviewed by K. W. Taylor in Canad. Jour. Econ. and Polit.
Sci. 2(2): 251. May 1936.

Keynes, J. M. The general theory of employment, interest, and money.
1936.
Reviewed by A. M. W. in the Christian Science Monitor Weekly
Magazine Section, April 15, 1936, p. 11.

Kolb, J. H., and Brunner, E. de S.   A study of rural society; its
    organizations and changes.
        Reviewed by Otis Durant Duncan in Rural Sociol. 1(1): 103-105.
    March 1936.
        Reviewed by Bruce L. Melvin in Rural Amer. 14(4): 12-13.
    April 1936.

League of nations.   Review of world trade, 1934.   (League of nations.
    Publications. Economic and financial. 1934. II. A. 12)
        Reviewed by Owen Davies in Econ. Rec. 11(21): 291-293.
    December 1935.

Leven, Maurice, Moulton, H. G., and Warburton, Clark.   America's
    capacity to consume.   1934.   (Half-title: The institute of economics
    of the Brookings institution. Pub. no. 56)
        Reviewed by A. E. Grauer in Canad. Jour. Econ. and Polit.
    Sci. 2(2): 246-247. May 1936.

Loeb, Harold, and associates.   The chart of plenty; a study of America's
    product capacity based on the findings of the National survey of
    potential product capacity. 1935.
        Reviewed by E. Johnston Coil in Survey Graphic 25(6): 385.
    June 1936.

McNamara, Katherine.   Bibliography of planning, 1928-1935; A supplement
    to Manual of Planning information, 1928... 1936. (Harvard city
    planning studies, X)
        Reviewed by Elisabeth M. Herlihy in Planners' Jour. 2(2): 52-
    53. March-April 1936.

Menzies-Kitchin, A. W.   Land settlement; a report prepared for the
    Carnegie United Kingdom Trustees. 1935.
        Reviewed by George S. Wehrwein in Jour. Farm Econ. 18(2): 444-
    446. May 1936.

Moulton, H. G.   The formation of capital. 1935. (Half-title: The
    Institute of economics of the Brookings Institution. Pub. no. 59)
        Reviewed by A. E. Grauer in Canad. Jour. Econ. and Polit.
    Sci. 2(2): 247-248. May 1936.
        Reviewed by Walther Lederer in Social Research 3(2): 245-248.
    May 1936.

Moulton, H. G.   Income and economic progress. 1935. (The Institute
    of economics of the Brookings institution. Pub. no. 68)
        Reviewed by A. E. Grauer in Canad. Jour. Econ. and Polit.
    Sci. 2(2): 248-249. May 1936.

Muirhead, J. F.   Land and unemployment.   1935.
        Reviewed by Karl Scholz in Amer. Acad. Polit. and Social Sci.
    Ann. 185: 238-239. May 1936.
        Reviewed by Joseph Dana Miller in Survey Graphic 25(6): 388.
    June 1936.

Nourse, E. G., and associates. America's capacity to produce. 1934. (Half-title: The Institute of economics of the Brookings institution. Pub. no. 55)
    Reviewed by A. E. Grauer in Canad. Jour. Econ. and Polit. Sci. 2(2): 246-247. May 1936.

Nourse, E. G. Marketing agreements under the AAA. 1935. (Half-title: The Institute of economics of the Brookings institution. Pub. no. 63)
    Reviewed by David E. Faville in Natl. Marketing Rev. 1(4): 364-365. Spring 1936.

Odum, Howard W. Southern regions of the United States... for the Southern regional committee of the Social science research council. 1936;
    Reviewed by Wayland J. Haynes in Social Forces 14(4): 606-609. May 1936.

Oppenheimer, Ludwig. Gross- und kleinbetrieb in der siedlung. 1934.
    Reviewed by Marie Jasny-Philippi in Jour. Farm Econ. 18(2): 435-437. May 1936.
    Reviewed by Karl Brandt in Social Research 3(1): 120-123. February 1936.

Pribram, Karl. Cartel problems; an analysis of collective monopolies in Europe with American application. 1935. (Half-title: The institute of economics of the Brookings institution. Publication no. 69)
    Reviewed by E. J. Working in Jour. Farm Econ. 18(2): 442-444. May 1936.

Tugwell, R. G. The battle for democracy. 1935.
    Reviewed by Claude V. Hall in Southwest. Social Sci. Quart. 16(4): 97, 98. March 1936.

.U. S. Federal emergency relief administration of public works. National planning board. Economics of planning public works. 1935.
    Reviewed by W. F. Ferger in South. Econ. Jour. 2(3): 87-88. January 1936.

U. S. National Resources board. A report on national planning and public works in relation to natural resources and including land use and water resources with findings and recommendations. 1934.
    Reviewed by Richard A. Harvill in Jour. Land & Pub. Utility Econ. 12(2): 217-218. May 1936.

Williams, Faith M., and Zimmerman, C. C. Studies of family living in the United States and other countries: an analysis of material and method. U. S. Dept. Agr. Misc. Pub. 223. 1935.
    Reviewed by J. W. Boldyreff in Rural Sociol. 1(1): 105-107. March 1936.

Economic in Character

Compiled by Katharine Jacobs

Circular*

397. Analysis of open commitments in wheat and corn futures on the Chicago board of trade, September 29, 1934, by D. B. Bagnell. 20pp. May 1936. 1 Ag84C no.397

Miscellaneous Publication*

242. Development and use of standards for grade, color, and character of American cotton linters, by Guy S. Meloy. 11pp. May 1936. 1 Ag84M no.242

Service and Regulatory Announcements (Bureau of Agricultural Economics)*

150. Revision of standards for grades of American upland cotton. 10pp. March 1936. 1 M34S no.150

Statistical Bulletin*

53. Carlot shipments and unloads of nineteen important fruits and vegetables for the calendar years 1933 and 1934. 205pp. May 1936. 1 Ag84St no.53

Addresses and Radio Talks of Secretary Wallace*

Farm imports: our favorite personal devil; remarks... over the National farm and home hour... May 12, 1936. 4pp., mimeogr. 1.9 Ag8636 no.119

Flood control at the grass roots; remarks... before the National rivers and harbors congress, Washington, April 27, 1936. 8pp., mimeogr. 1.9 Ag8636 no.116

Greetings to the Associated country women of the world ...at the third triennial conference, Associated country women of the world, Washington, D. C., June 1, 1936. 2pp., mimeogr. 1.9 Ag8636 no.121

How England meets its farm problems; remarks... over the National farm and home hour... May 26, 1936. 4pp., mimeogr. 1.9 Ag8636 no.120

How the water runs off the hills; remarks... over the National farm and home hour... April 21, 1936. 5pp., mimeogr. 1.9 Ag8636 no.115

Making the most of the home market; address... before meeting of farmers at University of Nebraska, Lincoln, Nebraska... May 4 [1936] 24pp., mimeogr. 1.9 Ag8636 no.118.

Issued also as Agricultural Adjustment Administration [publication] G-56. 8pp. June 1936. 1.4 Ad4Ge no.56

_____

Symbol used after each entry is call number assigned to the publication by the Department Library.
*Requests for these publications should be addressed to the Office of Information, U. S. Department of Agriculture, Washington, D. C.

Remarks [on long-range weather forecasts] ... over the National farm and
home hour... April 28, 1936. 4pp., mimeogr. 1.9 Ag8636 no.117

Publications of the Bureau of Agricultural Economics (Mimeographed)*

Agricultural labor in the United States, 1915-1935. A selected list of
references, comp. by Esther M. Colvin and Josiah C. Folsom, under
the direction of Mary G. Lacy, Librarian, Bureau of Agricultural
economics. 493pp., mimeogr. Washington, D. C., December 1935.
(U.S. Dept. of agriculture. Bureau of agricultural economics. Agricultural economics bibliography no. 64) 1.9 Ec73A no.64
Brief review, marketing Louisiana strawberries - 1936 season. 4pp.
May 15, 1936. 1.9 Ec741L
Brief review of the 1936 North Carolina strawberry season. 3pp. May 16,
1936. (Issued in cooperation with North Carolina Dept. of agriculture. Division of markets.) 1.9 Ec741L
Europe as a market for American pecans. 25pp. April 1936. (F.S.-66)
1.9 Ec752 no.66
Farmer bankruptcies decline further in 1935, but are exceeded in number
by debt compositions and extensions. 5pp. May 5, 1936. 1.9 Ec7Fb
Fats and oils, and the excise taxes of 1934. 16pp. May 1936. 1.9 Ec752Fat

Interstate shipments of California deciduous tree fruits 1935, by W. F.
Cox, T. J. Fitzgerald [and] R. M. Bayer. 72pp. April 1936.
(Issued in cooperation with California Dept. of agriculture.
Bureau of market news) 1.9 Ec741L
Interstate shipments of California grapes,1935, by W. F. Cox, T. J.
Fitzgerald and R. M. Bayer. 64pp. April 1936. (Issued in
cooperation with California Dept. of agriculture, Bureau of market
news) 1.9 Ec741L
List of economic reports and services of the Bureau of agricultural
economics. 52pp. May 1936. 1.9 Ec731La
Maine potatoes, 1935-36 season. 14pp. May, 1936. (Issued in cooperation
with Maine State Dept. of agriculture. Division of markets)
1.9 Ec741L
Marketing Arkansas peaches. Brief review of the 1935 season, by W. D.
Googe. 11pp. [April 1936] 1.9 Ec741L
Marketing Colorado peaches. Summary of 1935 season, by Bryce Morris.
9pp. [1936?] 1.9 Ec741L
Marketing Imperial valley cantaloupes. Summary of 1935 season, by A. E.
Prugh and H. A. Anderson. 28pp. April, 1936. (Issued in cooperation with California Dept. of agriculture, Market news service)
1.9 Ec741L
Marketing Michigan onions 1935-36 season. 6pp. April 21, 1936. (Issued
in cooperation with Michigan Dept. of agriculture. Bureau of foods
and standards) 1.9 Ec741L

*These publications are issued in small editions for immediate use in
official work and are not for general distribution.

Marketing Michigan potatoes 1935-36 season. 5pp. April 25, 1936. (Issued in cooperation with Michigan Dept. of agriculture. Bureau of foods and standards.) 1.9 Ec741L

Marketing Northwest fresh cherries 1935, by L. S. Fenn [and] L. B. Gerry. 10pp. [1936?] 1.9 Ec741L

Marketing western and central New York apples. Summary of the 1935-36 season, by H. S. Duncan and A. L. Thomas. 13pp. May 1936. (Issued in cooperation with New York State Dept. of agriculture and markets) 1.9 Ec741L

Marketing western and central New York cabbage. Summary of the 1935-36 season, by A. L. Thomas. 14pp. April, 1936. (Issued in cooperation with New York State Dept. of agriculture and markets) 1.9 Ec741L

Marketing western and central New York onions. Summary of the 1935-36 season, by H. S. Duncan and A. L. Thomas. 11pp. May 1936. (Issued in cooperation with New York State Dept. of agriculture and markets) 1.9 Ec741L

Marketing western New York and Pennsylvania grapes. Summary of 1935 season, by A. L. Thomas and L. D. Spink. 15pp. April, 1936. (Issued in cooperation with New York State Dept. of agriculture and markets) 1.9 Ec741L

Marketing western New York carrots. Summary of 1935-36 season, by H. S. Duncan and A. L. Thomas. 9pp. May 1936 (Issued in cooperation with New York State Dept. of agriculture and markets. Bureau of markets) 1.9 Ec741L

Marketing western New York potatoes. Summary of the 1935-36 season, by H. S. Duncan and A. L. Thomas. 14pp. May 1936. (Issued in cooperation with New York State Dept. of agriculture and markets. Bureau of markets) 1.9 Ec741L

The position of American cotton and the American cotton producer, by Maurice R. Cooper. 13pp. [1936] 1.9 Ec752Pos
      Presented at the ninth annual marketing school and annual meeting of the Arkansas Council for Agriculture, Little Rock, Ark., March 4, 1936.

Quality of 1935 corn crop. 1p. [May 1936] 1.9 Ec72Qu

A review of the 1936 Arizona spring lettuce season, by A. E. Prugh. 7pp. April 18, 1936. (Issued in cooperation with Arizona fruit and vegetable standardization service) 1.9 Ec741L

Revised list of approximate or average weights of various commodities. 4pp. May, 1936. 1.9 Ec752App

Summary 1936 potato season. 6pp. May 14, 1936. (Issued in cooperation with Florida State marketing bureau.) 1.9 Ec741L

Summary of the 1936 celery season. 4pp. [1936] (Issued in cooperation with Florida State marketing bureau.) 1.9 Ec741L

What's happening in farm real estate values, by B. R. Stauber. 2pp. May 21, 1936. 1.9 Ec7Re.
      Radio talk.

Wholesale prices of American-made farm machinery in certain foreign countries and in the United States in 1935, by Charles L. Luedtke. 18pp. April, 1936. 1.9 Ec753Who

Publications of the Agricultural Adjustment Administration*

(Amending Sec. 202 of article II and Secs. 300, 301 and 302 of Article
    III of General Regulations, Series A, No. 1) General regulations
    made by the Secretary of agriculture with the approval of the
    President under the Agricultural adjustment act, May 12, 1933, as
    amended. 3PP. April 10, 1936. (G. R. -A.A.A. Series A, No. 1.
    Amend. No. 1) 1.4 Ad4Ga
(General sugar quota regulations, series 3, Revision 1) Sugar consumption
    requirements and quotas for the calendar year 1936. General sugar
    quota regulations made by the Secretary of Agriculture under the
    Agricultural Adjustment act. 6pp. April 10, 1936. (G.S.Q.R.,
    Series 3, No. 2) 1.4 Su3G
Marketing agreement series - agreement no. 63. Marketing agreement for
    handlers of fresh lettuce, peas, and cauliflower grown in western
    Washington. Issued by the Secretary of agriculture, April 29, 1936.
    Effective 12:01 a.m. E.S.T., May 4, 1936. 17pp. 1936. (A-2)
    1.4 Ad47M no.63
Marketing agreement series - Agreement no. 64. Marketing agreement
    regulating the handling of citrus fruit grown in the state of
    Florida. .13pp. May 4, 1936. (A-3) 1.4 Ad47M no.64
Marketing agreement series - Agreement no. 65. Marketing agreement
    regulating the handling of watermelons grown in Florida, Georgia,
    North Carolina and South Carolina. 14pp. May 8, 1936. (A-4)
    1.4 Ad47M no.65
1936 agricultural conservation program - east central region. Bulletin
    no. 1 - Revised. 13pp. April 15, 1936. (ECR-B-1 Revised)
    1.42 Ea7B
1936 agricultural conservation program, east central region. Bulletin
    no.3. Instructions for preparation of work sheets and listing
    sheets and for establishment of bases, 17pp. May 9, 1936. (ECR-B-3)
    1.42 Ea7B
The 1936 agricultural conservation program for the east central region
    in brief. 4pp. May 1, 1936. (Regional information series.
    E.C.R. Leaflet 2) 1.42 Ea72
The 1936 agricultural conservation program for the north central region.
    19pp. April, 1936. (Regional information series. N.C.R. Leaflet
    1 (Revised)) 1.42 N75N
1936 agricultural conservation program in brief for the southern region.
    4pp. May 1, 1936. (Regional information series. SR Leaflet 2)
    1.42 So8L
1936 agricultural conservation program in brief - north central region.
    4pp. April 23, 1936. (Regional information series. N.C.R.
    Leaflet 2) 1.42 N75N
1936 agricultural conservation program in brief - northeast region
    4pp. April 25, 1936. (Regional information series. NER Leaflet
    2) 1.42 N76N

---

*Requests for these publications should be addressed to the Agri-
cultural Adjustment Administration, U. S. Department of Agriculture,
Washington, D. C.

The 1936 agricultural conservation program in brief - western region.
   4pp. April 20, 1936. (Regional information series. WR Leaflet 1)
   1.42 W5CL
1936 agricultural conservation program. Northeast region. 11pp. April
   15, 1936. (NER-B-1 Revised). 1.42 N76B
1936 agricultural conservation program. Northeast region... Soil-
   building practices - Massachusetts. 3PP. April 23, 1936. (NER-
   B-2-Massachusetts) 1.42 N76B
1936 agricultural conservation program. Northeast region... Soil-building practices - Vermont. 3pp. April 23, 1936. (NER-B-2-Vermont)
   1.42 N76B
1936 agricultural conservation program - southern region. Bulletin no.
   1, revised. 16pp. April 15, 1936. (SR-B-1 Revised) 1.42 So8B
1936 agricultural conservation program - southern region. Bulletin no.
   2. Soil-building practices. 2pp. April 23, 1936. (SR-B-2)
   1.42 So6B
1936 agricultural conservation program - southern region. Bulletin no.3.
   Instructions on establishing bases and filling out work sheets.
   12pp. May 1, 1936. (SR-B-3) 1.42 So8B
1936 agricultural conservation program, western region. Bulletin no. 1,
   rev. 16pp. April 15, 1936. (WR-B-1 Revised) 1.42 W52B
Order series - order no. 5. Order regulating the handling of milk in
   the Fall River, Massachusetts, marketing area. 13pp. (O-5)
   1.4 Ad47C no.5
Order series - order no. 6. Order regulating the handling of fresh
   lettuce, peas, and caul lower grown in western Washington. 16pp.
   April 29, 1936. (O-6) 1.4 Ad470 no.6
Order series - order no. 7. Order regulating the handling of citrus
   fruit grown in the state of Florida. 16pp. May 4, 1936. (O-7)
   1.4 Ad470 no.7
Order series - order no. 8. Order regulating the handling of watermelons grown in Florida, Georgia, North Carolina and South Carolina.
   13pp. May 8, 1936. (O-8) 1.4 Ad470 no.8
Procedure for the north central region, 1936 agricultural conservation
   program, and use of related forms. For use of county and state
   committees. Instructions for checking and listing work-sheet data.
   7pp. April 10, 1936. (NCR-7) 1.42 N75F
Procedure for the north central region, 1936 soil conservation program
   and use of related forms. 11pp. March 1936. (NCR-5) 1.42 N75F
      For use of community, county and state committees.
Puerto Rico sugar order no. 4. Allotment of the quota for Puerto Rico.
   3pp. Mar. 14, 1936. (P.R.S.O.no.4) 1.4 Su3P
Questions and answers. 1936 agricultural conservation program. East
   central region. 11pp. May 1, 1936. (Regional information series.
   ECR Leaflet 1) 1.42 Ea72
Questions and answers - 1936 agricultural conservation program - northeast region. 8pp. May 1, 1936. (Regional information series.
   NER Leaflet 1) 1.42 N76N
Regulations to govern the redemption of taxpayment warrants issued under
   the Kerr tobacco act, as amended. 2pp. May 2, 1936. (KTR no.1)
   1.4 T55K no.1

Saving the soil; what it means to farmers and the nation. 8pp. March,
1936. (G-53) 1.4 Ad4Ge no.53 .
Soil conservation - its place in national agricultural policy. 27pp.
May 1936. (G-54) 1.4 Ad4Ge no.54

Address of Chester C. Davis*

Unshackling our export trade. By Chester C. Davis... at annual dairy day
meeting, University farm, St. Paul, Minnesota... June 5, 1936. 13pp.,
mimeogr. 1.94 Ad4Da

Radio Talks (Mimeographed)**

The agricultural conservation program in the Northeast. By Dr. H. H. Boyd.
April 10, 1936. 3pp. 1.94 Ad4R
Cooperation and conservation - a new two-horse team. By H. R. Tolley...
May 9, 1936. 9pp. 1.94 Ad472T
International trade and the American farm problem. Address of Chester
C. Davis... before meeting of business men and farmers at Des
Moines, Iowa... June 3, 1936. 13pp. 1.94 Ad4Da
Marketing agreements and surpluses. By Jesse W. Tapp, assistant
administrator, AAA... April 20, 1936. 4pp. 1.94 Ad4R
Progress of agricultural adjustment. By A. D. Stedman... May 19, 1936.
3pp. 1.94 Ad4R
Progress of agricultural adjustment. By A. D. Stedman... May 28, 1936.
2pp. 1.94 Ad4R
Progress of the agricultural conservation program. by A. D. Stedman...
May 12, 1936. 2PP. 1.94 Ad4R
Progress of the agricultural conservation program. By A. D. Stedman...
May 26, 1936. 2PP. 1.94 Ad4R
The soil conservation program. By H. R. Tolley... March 23, 1936. 5PP.
1.94 Ad472T
The soil conservation program in the cotton belt. By Cully A. Cobb...
March 25, 1936. 4pp. 1.94 C82R
The soil conservation program in the east central states. By William G.
Finn, acting director of the East central region... April 2, 1936.
4pp. 1.42 Ea7R
The soil conservation program in the north central states. By G. B.
Thorne, director North central division, A.A.A... April 6, 1936.
4pp. 1.42 N75R
The soil conservation program in the western states. By C. C. Conser,
assistant director, Western states division... April 8, 1936.
3pp. 1.42 W52R

---

*May be obtained from U. S. Department of Agriculture, Office of
Information.
**May be obtained from U. S. Department of Agriculture, Office of
Information, Radio Service.

An appraisal of the programs in recreation, by C. B. Smith, 6pp. April,
1936. (Issued by U. S. Dept. of agriculture. Extension service.
Division of cooperative extension. Extension service circular 240)
1.9 Ex892 Esc
A digest of pasture research literature in the continental United States
and Canada, 1865 to 1935. [Comp.] by A. J. Pieters. 130pp., mimeogr.
January 1, 1936. (Issued by Bureau of plant industry. Division of forage
crops and diseases.) 1.9 P691Di
Farm accounting and farm business analysis, by H. M. Dixon. 5pp. 1936.
(Issued by U. S. Dept. of agriculture. Extension service. Division
of cooperative extension) 1.9 Ex892 Fac
    Talk given at ninth Annual cooperative marketing school at
Little Rock, Ark., March 5, 1936.
Impressions concerning country trading in grain futures, with especial
reference to wheat futures, by H. S. Irwin. 29pp. April, 1936.
(Issued by U. S. Dept. of agriculture. Grain futures administration)
1.9 G76Im
Methodology used in compiling a bibliography in the field of agricultural
economics, by Louise O. Bercaw. 6pp. 1936. Supplement to Agricultural library notes, May 1936, vol. 11, no. 5. Published by
U. S. Department of agriculture Library.** 1.9 L61La
    Address, Annual conference of American library association,
Agricultural libraries section, Richmond, Virginia, May 11, 1936.
Situations, problems, and interests of unmarried rural young people
16 - 25 years of age. Survey of five Connecticut townships, 1934.
[by] A. J. Brundage and M. C. Wilson. 47pp. April 1936. (Issued
by U. S. Dept. of agriculture. Extension service, Division of cooperative extension. Extension service circular
239) 1.9 Ex892 Esc
Trading in job lots and round lots in wheat and corn futures at Chicago,
by Paul Mehl... March, 1936. 13pp. (Issued by Grain futures
administration) 1.9 G76Tr

U. S. RESETTLEMENT ADMINISTRATION***

U. S. Resettlement administration. Greenbelt [Md.] folder. [Washington, D.C
1936?]
U. S. Resettlement administration. Interim report... 34pp. Washington,
U. S. Govt.print. off., April 1936. 1 95 In8
U. S. Resettlement administration. One year of resettlement. Address by
R. G. Tugwell... April 30, 1936. 6pp.
[U. S. Resettlement administration. Management division. Education and com-
munity activities section] Private associations with services available
to rural groups. Their organization and function. 16pp., mimeogr.
[Washington, D. C., 1936] 1 95 P93

---

*Requests for these publications should be addressed to the issuing office.
**May be obtained from the Library, Bureau of agricultural economics.
***Requests for these publications should be addressed to the Resettlement
Administration, Arlington Hotel, Washington, D. C.

Compiled by Mary F. Carpenter

Arizona

Arizona. College of agriculture. Agricultural extension service. Twenty-
first annual report for the fiscal year ended June 30, 1935, including a
report on project work to November 30, 1935. Ariz. Agr. Col. Ext. Serv.
Project Circ. 16, 40pp. Tucson. 1936.
Agricultural economics, pp. 36-37.

Arkansas

Heckman, J. H., and White, E. D. The 1936 agricultural outlook for Arkansas.
Ark. Agr. Col. Ext. Circ. 354, 16pp. Little Rock, 1935.

California

Pentzer, W. T., and others. Precooling and shipping California asparagus.
Calif. Agr. Expt. Sta. Bull. 600, 45pp. Berkeley. 1936.
Results of a cooperative investigation conducted by the United States
Bureau of Plant Industry and the California Agricultural Experiment Station

Smythe, D. W. Dry edible beans. Calif. Agr. Col. Timely Agr. Outlooks,no.5,
2pp., mimeogr. Berkeley. 1936.

Stover, H. J. The manufacture and use of California canned orange juice...
A preliminary report. Calif. Agr. Expt. Sta. Giannini Found. Agr. Econ.
Mimeogr. Rept. 45, 27pp. Berkeley, 1936.

Tinley, J. M., Abbott, F. H., Reed, O. M., and Schneider, J. B. Creamery operating efficiency in California. Part III. Relation of creamery capacity
to supply of milk fat in Humboldt county. Giannini Found. Agr. Econ.
Mimeogr. Rept. 44, 75pp. Berkeley. April, 1936.

Colorado

Colorado. Agricultural experiment station. Forty-eighth annual report... for
the fiscal year, 1934-1935. 36pp. Fort Collins. 1935.
Agricultural economics, pp. 15-17.

Connecticut

Connecticut. Department of agriculture. Bureau of markets. Connecticut seed
law, rules and regulations. Conn. Dept. Agr. Bull. 36, 19pp. Hartford.19

Connecticut. Department of agriculture. Bureau of markets. Connecticut vegetable
industry and its outlook for 1936. Conn. Dept. Agr. Bull. 40, 19pp.
Hartford. 1936.

Delaware

Delaware. State board of agriculture. Annual report... 1934-1935. Del. State
Bd. Agr. Quart. Bull. v.25, no.3, 46pp. Dover. 1935.
Report of the Bureau of Markets, pp. 24-30.

Florida

Howard, B. H.   Florida citrus costs and returns. Fla. Agr. Col. Ext.Serv.
Agr. Econ. Dept. Citrus AE 5, 24pp., mimeogr. Gainesville. 1936.
"The second annual summary of costs and returns based upon a crop
year... The costs used in this summary are from September 1, 1933 to
August 31. 1934, and the returns·from the same crop, which was marketed
in the fall of 1934 to the summer of 1935."

Georgia

Fenny, N. M.   Grade and staple length of cotton·produced in Georgia, 1928–35.
Ga. Agr. Expt. Sta. Circ. 107, 8pp.   Experiment. 1936.
Work done in cooperation with U. S. Bureau of Agricultural Economics.

Illinois

Illinois. Agricultural experiment station, Department of agricultural economics,
Illinois farm economics, no.11. Urbana. April, 1936.
Partial contents: More money spent by farm families in 1935, by
Ruth C. Freeman, pp. [49]–50; Farm earnings improved slightly in
1935, by P. E. Johnston, pp. 50–51; Total agricultural production
in Illinois will be changed by the new Soil conservation program,
by J. E. Wills, and H. C. M. Case, pp. 51–52; Land, tenure in
Illinois, by Joseph Ackerman and C. L. Stewart, pp. 52–54; The
relation of seasonal milk production to costs of production and
marketing, by Wayne Caskey, pp. 54–55.

Judson, L. S. A manual of group discussion. Ill. Agr. Expt. Sta. Circ. 446,
184pp. Urbana. 1936?
"Prepared to aid rural groups in organizing and conducting discussion
meetings."

Indiana

Indiana. Agricultural experiment·station. Department of agricultural statistics.
Annual crop summary, 1935. Ind. Crops and Livestock, no.123, 10pp. West
Lafayette. 1935.

Indiana. Agricultural experiment station, Department of agricultural statistics.
Annual livestock summary, 1936. Ind. Crops and Livestock, no. 125, 8pp.
West Lafayette. 1936.

Indiana. Agricultural experiment station, Department of agricultural statistics.
Assessors' enumeration of 1934 crops. Ind. Crops and Livestock, no. 124,
11pp. West Lafayette, 1936.
The three bulletins listed above are in cooperation with U. S. Bureau
of Agricultural Economics, Division of Crop and Livestock Estimates. The
last two contain data by counties.

486

Iowa

Iowa. State college of agriculture and mechanic arts, Extension service. Iowa
farm economist, v. 2, no. 1, Ames. April 1936.
    Partial contents: Iowa taxes, by J. E. Brindley, pp. 3–6; Your own
soil conservation program by W. W. Wilcox, pp. 7–9; Choosing market outlets for livestock, by S. H. Thompson, pp. 9–11; Farm planning, by L. G.
Allbaugh, pp. 11, 16; Sand and man on Muscatine Island, pp. 12–13; Fewer
schools and more education, by Barton Morgan, pp. 14–16.

Kansas

Kansas. State board of agriculture. Report... for the quarter ending December,
1935, v. 54, no. 216–B, 16pp. Topeka. 1935.
    Devoted to Kansas statistics by counties for 1935 and contains data on
population, wheat, corn, oats, grain sorghums, alfalfa hay, livestock, pou
try and dairy products.

Maine

Maine. Agricultural experiment station. Summary report of progress, 1935.
Maine. Agr. Expt. Sta. Bull. 380, pp. 139–258. Orono. 1935.
    For economic studies see table of contents.

Maine. University. Agricultural extension service. Annual report... year ending June 30, 1935, Maine Univ. Agr. Ext. Serv. Bull. 217, 43pp. Orono,
1935.
    Agricultural economics, pp. 8–12.

Maryland

Poffenberger, P. R., DeVault, S. H., and Hamilton, A. B. An economic study
of the broiler industry. Md. Agr. Expt. Sta. Bull. 390, pp. 427–463. College Park. 1936.
    Results of a study made for the year beginning July 1, 1934 and ending
June 30, 1935. Includes data on the costs of production and of marketing.

Massachusetts

Massachusetts. Secretary of the commonwealth. The decennial census, 1935. 30pp.
Boston. 1935.
    Includes population of Massachusetts for 170 years, and of cities, town
and counties as of January 1, 1935 with some comparisons with former years,

Michigan

Aylesworth, P. F. An economic study of the potato enterprise in Michigan. Mich.
Agr. Expt. Sta. Special Bull. 267, 42pp. East Lansing. 1935.
    "This study relates primarily to the determination of the cost and effi-
ciency of production of Michigan potatoes."

Michigan. Laws, statutes, etc. Laws relating to the Department of agriculture 236pp. Lansing. Mich. Dept. Agr. 1935.

Motts, G. N. The production-consumption balance of agricultural products in Michigan. Part II. Livestock and animal products. Mich. Agr. Expt. Sta. Special Bull. 269. 40pp. East Lansing. 1936.

Wright, K. T. 1935 poultry costs in Michigan. Mich. Agr. Expt. Sta. Quart. Bull., v. 18, no. 3, pp. 173-177. East Lansing. February 1936.

Minnesota.

Johnson, E. C., and Warrington, S. T. Cooperative trucking of livestock. Minn. Univ. Agr. Ext. Div., Farm Business Notes, no. 160, pp. 1-3, mimeogr. University Farm, St. Paul. 1936.

Ranney, W. P., and McNulty, J. B. Variations in earnings of twenty selected dairy farmers. Minn. Univ. Agr. Ext. Div. Minn. Farm Business Notes, no. 161, pp. 1-3, mimeogr. University Farm, St. Paul. May 20, 1936.

Missouri

Howell, L. D., Burgess, J. S., Jr.; and Thomsen, F. L. Farm prices and quality of Missouri cotton. Mo. Agr. Expt. Sta. Research Bull. 233, 32pp. Columbi 1936.
> In cooperation with U. S. Bureau of Agricultural Economics.

Montana

Slagsvold, P. L. Readjusting Montana's agriculture. VI. Montana's irrigation r sources. Mont. Agr. Expt. Sta. Bull. 315, 18pp. Bozeman. 1936.

Nebraska

Nebraska. Agricultural experiment station. Forty-ninth annual report... [1935] 43pp. Lincoln. 1936.
> Rural economics, pp. 30-31.

Nevada

Nevada. Agricultural experiment station and Agricultural extension service. Economic talks with Nevada farmers. v. 1, no. 3, 4pp. Reno. April. 1936.
> Partial contents: The 1936 soil conservation program in Nevada, by V. E Scott, p. 1; Payments under the 1936 soil conservation program, by V E. Scott, pp. 1-2; Classification of crops in Nevada, by V. E. Scott, p. 2; County program planning, by Cruz Venstrom, p. 3; Cost of raising hogs in Nevada, by F. B. Headley, p. 4.

New Hampshire

Grinnell, H. C. Rural real estate tax delinquency in New Hampshire. N. H. Agr. Expt. Sta. Bull. 290, 19pp. Durham. 1936.

Rinear, E. H., and Moore, H. C. Maintenance of grade A milk. N.H. Agr. Expt.
    Sta. Bull. 291, 24pp. Durham, 1936.
        "A study of the factors affecting quality, returns and premium losses."

New Jersey

Waller, A. G., and Carncross, J. W. Handbook of economic information. 3 nos.
    mimeogr. New Brunswick, N. J. Agr. Expt. Sta. 1936.
        Contents: Dairy industry, 45pp.; Fruit, 38pp.; Poultry industry, 43pp.

New Mexico

Callaway, R. P., and Cockerill, P. W. Tax delinquency on rural real estate in
    New Mexico. N. Mex. Agr. Expt. Sta. Bull. 234, 28pp. State College. 1935.

Hollinger, E. C. New Mexico agricultural outlook, 1936. N. Mex. Agr. Col.
    Ext. Circ. 135, 24pp. State College. 1935.

New York

LaMont, T. E. An economic study of land utilization in Chemung county, New York
    N. Y. Cornell. Agr. Expt. Sta. Bull, 640, 84pp. Ithaca. 1936.
        The third of a series.

North Carolina

North Carolina. State college of agriculture and Engineering extension service.
    Agricultural program for North Carolina. N. C. Agr. Col. Ext. Circ. 208,
    70pp. Raleigh. 1936.
        A revision of the program adopted in 1929.
        Includes a soil map of the state.

North Dakota

North Dakota. Agricultural experiment station. Experiment station progress for
    the four year period, July 1, 1931 to June 30, 1935. N. Dak. Agr. Expt.
    Sta. Bull. 286, 99pp. Fargo. 1935.
        Agricultural economics, pp. 55-60.

Ohio

Falconer, J. I. Feed sales in Ohio, [1929-1935] Ohio Agr. Expt. Sta.
    Bimonthly Bull. 21(180): 80. Wooster. May-June, 1936.

Hauck, C. W. Fruits and vegetables received in trucks in the Columbus whole-
    sale market, 1929-1935. Ohio State Univ. and Ohio Agr. Expt. Sta. Dept.
    Rural Econ. Mimeogr. Bull. 86, 23pp. Columbus. 1936.
        In cooperation with Ohio State Dept. of Agriculture, Division of Markets.

489

Lively, C. E., and Folse, C. L. Trend of births, deaths, natural increase and migration in the rural population of Ohio. Ohio State Univ. and Ohio Agr. Expt. Sta. Mimeogr. Bull. 87, 10, 20pp. Columbus. 1936.
  In cooperation with the F. E. R. A.

Moore, H. R. Semi-annual index of farm real estate values in Ohio, July 1 to December 31, 1935. Ohio State Univ. and Ohio Agr. Expt. Sta. Dept. Rural Econ., Mimeogr. Bull. 88, 8PP. Columbus. 1936.
  In cooperation with the Farm Lands Division, Ohio Association of Real Estate Boards.

Wallace, B. A. Cooperative marketing: its practical problems. Ohio Agr. Col. Ext. Bull. 170, 20pp. Columbus. 1936.
  The subject is discussed in the field of cooperative buying and selling of commodities through farmer owned organizations.

Oklahoma

Jacob, A. W. Marketing the Oklahoma wool clip. Okla. Agr. Col. Ext. Ci c. 33 15pp. Stillwater. 1936.

Oklahoma. Agricultural experiment station. Current farm economics, v.9, no.2, Stillwater, April 1936.
  Partial contents: Relationship of monetary and credit policies to agriculture, by T. R. Hedges, pp. 42-48; Some things to be considered in a long-time agricultural program, by C. P. Blackwell, pp. 48-52; Soil conservation and domestic allotment act, by E. E. Scholl, pp. 52-54; A marked increase in Oklahoma farm tax delinquency from 1928 to 1932 arose out of a faulty tax machine and severe economic strains on farming, by J. T. Sanders, pp. 54-56; Tenancy and our cotton programs, by J. T. Sanders, pp. 56-58; Oklahoma cooperative vegetable growers' exchange, by A. W. Jacob, pp. 58-61; Agricultural situation, by T. R. Hedges, pp. 61-62.

Oregon

Oregon. Laws, statutes, etc. The laws relating to the manufacture and sale of food products... 1935. 151pp. Salem. Oreg. Dept. Agr. [1935]

South Carolina

Guin, Marvin. An economic study of hog production and marketing in South Carolina. S. C. Agr. Expt. Sta. Bull. 305, 27pp. Clemson. 1936.
  Includes a section on the economic influence of the Agricultural Adjustment Administration's corn-hog production program in South Carolina.
  A list of references is given on p. 26.

Utah

Geddes, J. A. Farm versus village living in Utah. Plain City - Type "A" village. Part III - Use of local community agencies and institutions. Part IV - Use of semi-local community, outside community, and non-community offerings in neighboring towns, cities, and other areas. Utah Agr. Expt. St Bull. 269, 82 pp. Logan. 1936.

The second of a series of bulletins based on a study of Utah village life. Plain City is in Weber County.

Virginia

Maxton, J. L. An economic study of poultry farming in Virginia. Va. Agr. Expt. Sta. Bull. 300, 58pp. Blacksburg. 1936.
Contains data for the years 1931-1932, for egg production costs and labor income.

West Virginia

Cornell, F. D., Jr. A social and economic survey of the Spencer soil-conservation area. W. Va. Agr. Expt. Sta. Bull. 269, 36pp. Morgantown, 1936.
The area comprises parts of Wirt and Roane counties and this report shows conditions prior to the inauguration of the soil-conservation program.

Wisconsin

Bordner, J. S., Aldrich, H. R., Morris, W. W., and Steenis, J. H. Land economic inventory of the state of Wisconsin - Juneau county. Wis. Exec. Off. Div. Land.Econ. Inventory. [Bull.] no. 1, 51pp. Madison. 1934.
25 cover and land use township maps of Juneau county are attached.

Bordner, J. S., Morris, W. W., Steenis, J. H., and Hilburn, E. D. Land economic inventory of the state of Wisconsin. Rusk county. Wis. Exec. Off. Div. Land Econ. Inventory. [Bull.] no. 2, 52pp. Madison. 1935.
26 cover and land use township maps of Rusk county are attached.

Kirkpatrick, E. L., and Boynton, A. M. Interests and needs of rural youth in Wood county, Wisconsin. Wis. Agr. Col. Ext. Serv. Special Circ. 12pp., mimeogr. Madison. January 1936.

Wileden, A. F. What Douglas county young people want and what they are doing about it. Wis. Agr. Col. Ext. Serv. Special Circ. 12pp., mimeogr. Madison. December 1935.

Wyoming

Vass, A. F., and Pearson, Harry. Profitable systems of farm and ranch organizations for certain areas in Wyoming. Wyo. Agr. Col. Ext. Circ. 60, 62pp Laramie. 1935.
Discusses suggested systems of farming for irrigated lnds and of farming and ranching in the plains area.

Wyoming. Agricultural experiment station. Forty-fifth annual report... 1934-1935. 44pp. Laramie. 1936.
Agronomy and Agricultural Economics Department, pp. 4-10.

PERIODICAL ARTICLES

Compiled by Louise O. Bercaw and A. M. Hannay

Accident Compensation - Estonia

Accident compensation in Estonian agriculture. Indus. and Labour Inform. 58(3):
62-63. Apr. 20, 1936. (Published by International Labour Office, Geneva,
Switzerland. Distributed in U. S. by World Peace Foundation, 8 West 40th
Street, New York, N. Y.)
    Outlines the provisions of a Legislative Decree of February 5, 1936
establishing a system of accident compensation for agricultural workers,
effective on May 1, 1936.

Accountancy, Farm - United States

Deslarzes, Joseph. Some observations concerning farm accountancy methods
in the United States. Monthly Bull. Agr. Econ. and Sociol. [reprint from
Internatl. Rev. Agr.] 27(2): 50-60. February 1936. (Published by
the International Institute of Agriculture, Rome, Italy.)
    "It is proposed in this article, to study from the methodological
point of view, the accountancy results of the farms of Illinois, Iowa,
and Indiana in 1932. The method of book-keeping in Michigan is on the
same basis as that in Illinois. The gross return, the farming expenses,
and the final results will be taken in succession."

Agrarian Reform - Spain

Crawford, H. P. Spanish agrarian reform measures. Commerce Repts. no. 18,
p.342. May 2, 1936. (Published by the Bureau of Foreign and Domestic
Commerce, U. S .Dept. of Commerce)
    "Pending the enactment of more extensive legislation, a series of
emergency measures has been decreed for the purpose of permitting
agricultural laborers, in districts where the need is allegedly greatest,
to enter into immediate possession of parcels of land of large estates
which they can cultivate for their own account...
    "For the avowed purpose of solving the problem of better distribution
of lands, the Agrarian Reform Institute, at the proposal of its director and in accordance with article 14 of the law of November 9, 1935,
may declare as of 'public utility' those estates which are located
in a municipal district or those which extend over various municipal
districts and which have (a) concentration of ownership, (b) a high
percentage of agricultural laborers in proportion to the total number
of inhabitants, (c) a limited extension of the municipal district in
comparison with the census of agricultural laborers, and (d) the
predominance of large-scale farming.
    "The law succinctly announces that 'such estates will be expropriated.'
    "And it is further provided that the four characteristics above
enumerated may exist singly or simultaneously, which fact will be established by the technical report of the institute...

"The owners of the land expropriated may appeal from the judgment of 'public utility' and the temporary occupation of their estates as provided in article 5 of the law of November 9, 1935."

A.A.A. Benefit Payments

The bounties of the AAA as paid in various states. U. S. News 4(16): 8. Apr. 20, 1936. (Published at 2201 M St., N. W., Washington, D. C.)
Presents data in tabular form which show the number of farmers in each State, the number of AAA contracts, and the amount of AAA payments made in each State.

Farm bounties: 89% to south and mid-west. U. S. News 4(16): 1. Apr. 20, 1936. (Published at 2201 M St., N. W., Washington, D. C.)
A short article, accompanied by a pictogram, which tell the story of how the AAA money was distributed by sections of the United States.

Agricultural Economic Conditions – China

Wu, Hwa-pao. Agricultural economy of Yung-loh Tien in Shensi Province. Nankai Social & Econ. Quart.9(1): 164-176. April 1936. (Published by Nankai Institute of Economics, Nankai University, Tientsin, China)
"Since China is a country old in agriculture, lands in the warmer, more humid and better situated parts are already under intensive cultivation. Only in such regions as in the Northwestern Section, large areas are still found uncultivated. With a view to facilitating the utilization of the uncultivated land in these areas, a preliminary study of the agricultural economic conditions of Yung-loh Tien...in Shensi Province was made in the summer of 1932, of which the present article represents a summary."
Land values and taxes are briefly discussed. Prices vary on non-irrigated and on irrigated land. Taxes are assessed according to grades of land of which there are seven. Three ways of borrowing money are indicated.
Tables show sizes of farms and of families in 1931; crops planted, production and yield on 21 farms in 1926; cost of production, receipts and profits per mow, and semi-monthly distribution of man and animal labor on 21 farms in 1926.

Agricultural Indebtedness – Australia

The adjustment of farmers' debts. Primary Producer 21(13): 1, 2. Mar. 26, 1936. (Published at 38-40-42-44 Stirling St., Perth, Western Australia)
"In view of the differences of opinion which have been expressed regarding the relative merits of the legislation passed in the various States for the adjustment of farmers' debts, we recently wrote to the authorities in Adelaide, Melbourne and Sydney, asking if they would supply information concerning adjustments made in those States which could be used in the 'Primary Producer' for the benefit of farmers in this State.
"Replies have now come to hand, and information supplied is published herewith."

Agricultural Machinery

Applegate, La Rue. Recovery in farm equipment industry reflects rise in
agricultural income. Annalist 47(1217): 717-718. May 15, 1936. (Published by the New York Times Co., New York, N. Y.)

Davis, H. G. Rubber tires in the furrows. Nation's Agr. 11(8): 6, 15.
May 1936. (Published at 58 E. Washington St., Chicago, Ill.)
    In this article, "the director of the research department of the
Farm Equipment Institute tells of one of the newest developments in
farm machinery."

Agricultural Policy - Germany, Great Britain and the United States

Brandt, Karl. Recent agrarian policies in Germany, Great Britain and the
United States. Social Research 3(2): 167-201. May 1936. (Published
for the New School for Social Research, 66 West 12th St., New York,
N. Y.)
    Contents: I, Germany, heading toward food autarchy, reshapes her
rural sector; II. Great Britain regulates the markets for homegrown
food; III. The United States restores the farmer's income through
output reduction; IV. Common and diverging trends in Germany, Great
Britain and the United States.

Agricultural Policy - Great Britain

Walworth, George. Changes in British agricultural policy. Rev. Internatl.
Coop. 29(4): 127-132. April 1936. (Published at Orchard House, 14,
Great Smith St., London, S. W. 1, Eng.)
    The significant changes in Great Britain's agricultural policy in
her departure from free trade are outlined.

Agricultural Protectionism - Europe

Emanuel, A. Agricultural protectionism and the agricultural situation
1925-1929. Monthly Bull. Agr. Econ. and Sociol. [reprint from Internatl.
Rev. Agr.] 27(3): 75-91. March 1936. (Published by the International
Institute of Agriculture, Rome, Italy.)
    Part I. Origins and evolution of protection 1925-1929.
    Contents: I. Introduction. (Scope and purpose of present series of
articles.) - II. General background of European protectionism 1925-
1929 (A period of re-adjustment. The application of pre-war standards
in the fields of money and trade policy. The importance of stabilisation. Industrial and agricultural protectionism compared.) -III.
Tariff policies of France, Germany and Italy. (Importance of the
trade of these countries in certain agricultural commodities. Extort
of the 'free trade' markets.) -IV. Tariff policy of France (Immediate
post-War period and period 1925-1929. The nature of treaties and
effect on agricultural protection. The lag of tariffs behind prices.
Tariffs and prices in 1928 as compared with before the War) - V.
Tariff policy of Germany. (Conditions determining post-War policy.
Treaty of Versailles. Protection, foundation of agrarian policy.

Development of tariff since 1925, and principle of commercial treaties.
Tariffs and prices in 1928 as compared with before the War.) -VI. Tariff
Policy of Italy. (The tariffs of 1921, Industrial versus Agricultural
protection. Subsequent changes. The Wheat Campaign of 1935. Relation to
monetary circumstances. The growth of the burden of tariffs as prices
fell after 1926.)

Agricultural Relief - United States

The next move in American agriculture. A complete discussion of the farm
problem. Vital Speeches 2(17): 506-518. May 18, 1936. (Published at
33 W. 42nd St., New York, N. Y.)
This consists of two articles. The first is The importance of agricultural welfare, by Fred W. Sargent before the Chamber of Commerce of
the U.S.A., Apr. 30, 1936 (condensed by the author) pp.506-511. The
second is Making the most of the home market (With specific points of
agreement and disagreement with the preceding article) by Henry A.
Wallace, before meeting of farmers at University of Nebraska, May 4,
1936, pp.511-518.

Agricultural Views of 1936 Presidential Candidates

McMillen, Wheeler. They're all for farmers. Country Home 60(5): 11-12.
May 1936. (Published at 250 Park Ave., New York, N. Y.)
In this article the author names the six most conspicuous possibilities for nomination as the Republican candidate for President - Borah,
Dickinson, Hoover, Knox, Landon and Vandenberg - and presents for each
some of their agricultural views. Mr. McMillen says: "To exhibit
agricultural ideas of the various candidates, I have taken sentences
and paragraphs from their public statements without change other
than reducing the length to give the essence of their remarks.
"Virtually all of the candidates agree on the policy of soil conservation. That being hardly an issue, most of the references to
it have been deleted."

American Economic Association

American economic association. Papers and proceedings of the forty-eighth
annual meeting. Amer. Econ. Rev. 26(1): 1-350. March 1936, sup.
(Published by the Association, Northwestern University, Evanston, Ill.)
Partial contents: Some distinguishing characteristics of the current
recovery, by Garfield V. Cox, pp.1-10, discussion, by W. I. King, pp.
11-14; Price theories and market realities, by Willard L. Thorp, pp.15-
22; Notes on inflexible prices, by Gardiner C. Means, pp.23-35; Effect
of the depression upon earnings and prices of regulated and nonregulated
industries, by Ralph C. Epstein and John D. Sumner, pp.36-45; The requi-
sites of free competition, by Henry C. Simons, pp.68-76; Monopolistic
competition and public policy, by Donald H. Wallace, pp.77-87, discussion,
pp.88-94; The trade agreements program and American agriculture, by
Lynn Ramsay Edminster, pp.129-140; The founding and early history of the
American Economic Association, by Richard T. Ely, pp.141-150; Developments

in economic theory, by Emil Lederer, pp.151-160; Relations between
Federal, state, and local finances, by Clarence Heer, pp.174-181;
Equalization of local government resources in Germany and England.
by Mabel Newcomer, pp.182-187, discussion by Carl Shoup and Royal
S. Van de Woestyne, pp.188-195; Institutional economics, by John R.
Commons, pp.237-250, discussion by Willard E. Atkins, and Edward S.
Robinson, pp.250-254; The problem of prices and valuation in the
Soviet system, by Alexander Gourvitch, pp.267-282, discussion by
Calvin B. Hoover, William Orton, and Michael T. Florinsky, pp.283-290.

Barley - Cleaning and Handling

Malloch, J. G. The cleaning and handling of barley. Sci. Agr. 16(6):
289-321. February 1936. (Publisher's address, Box 625, Ottawa, Canada)
"A report prepared for the Sub-Committee on Cleaning and Handling
of the National Barley Committee. Published as Paper No. 91 of the
Associate Committee on Grain Research, National Research Council and
Dominion Department of Agriculture."

Beef - Bounty - Rhodesia

Beef export bounty. Continuity bill introduced. African World 134(1742):
374. Mar. 28, 1936. (Published at 801, Salisbury House, London Wall,
London, E.C. 2.)
"The Southern Rhodesia Government Gazette contains the text of a
Bill, which will be introduced during the present Parliamentary ses-
sion, to continue the operations of the Cattle Levy and Beef Export
Bounty Act of 1935 until the Act is repealed."

Bounties - Venezuela

H., F. J. Venezuela aids agriculture and the unemployed. Pan Amer. Union.
Bull. 70(4): 365-366. April 1936. (Published in Washington, D. C.)
Outlines the provisions of a decree of January 27 authorizing the
payment of export bounties on a number of agricultural products, including coffee, cacao, sugar, livestock, hides, lumber, oil seeds,
fruits and garden products, tobacco and corn, etc.
Prizes are to be awarded for the largest rice crop produced in 1936.

Bureaucracy

Clark, B. C. Billions for bureaus. Country Gent. 106(6): 5-6, 73, 74, 75.
June 1936. (Published at Independence Square, Philadelphia, Pa.)
Critical of the practice of making lump-sum appropriations to be
expended at the will of the executive offices and the President, and
of corporations owned and financed by the Federal Government.

Business Cycle

Armstrong, C. E. The short-term business cycle: its average form and
period as observed in the Axe-Houghton index of business activity.
Rev. Econ. Statis. 18(2): 62-66. May 1936. (Published at the Harvard
University Press, Cambridge, Mass.)

"This paper is a somewhat expanded version of a paper presented at the annual meeting of the American Statistical Association, December 27, 1935."

Hansen, A. H., Boddy, F. M., and Langum, J. K. Recent trends in business-cycle literature. Rev. Econ. Statis. 18(2): 53-61. May 1936. (Published at the Harvard University Press, Cambridge, Mass.)

The authors' introductory paragraph is as follows:

"It is, of course, quite impossible, within the scope of a brief article, to present any adequate analysis of the voluminous literature on business-cycle theory which has appeared during the last two years. No attempt is made here to give any systematic classification of the various contributions, or to appraise the work of individual writers; and certainly no good purpose could be served by a mere summary statement, even if such a project were possible. We shall, however, consider several topics which have played important roles in current discussions."

Subtopics of the article are: the period of investment; neutral money; public works; investment and saving; consumer demand; tools of analysis.

Harrod, R. F. Imperfect competition and the trade cycle. Rev. Econ. Statis. 18(2): 84-88. May 1936. (Published at the Harvard University Press, Cambridge, Mass.)

Cabbage - Grading

Baker, M. W. Grading of cabbage. Canning Trade 58(41): 7-8. May 18, 1936. (Published in Baltimore, Md.)

Address before the Kraut Section of the National Canners Association, Chicago, January 21, 1936.

Canned Foods - Grading

Williams, P. M. Grading canned fruits and vegetables. Canning Trade 58 (37): 14-17. Apr. 20, 1936. (Published in Baltimore, Md.)

Williams, P. M. Progress in canned food grading methods. The Canner 82(20): 13, 14. Apr. 25, 1936. (Published at 140 North Dearborn St., Chicago, Ill.)

From an address before the Spring meeting of the Tri-States Packers Association, at Baltimore, April 8-9, 1936.

Chemistry and Agriculture

Chemistry rather than legislation to help agriculture. Calif. Fruit News 93(2492): 4. Apr. 11, 1936. (Published at 405 Montgomery St., San Francisco, Calif.)

"The several days' meeting at Fresno the latter part of March of the western States, under the auspices of the Farm Chemurgic Council of nationally known agriculturists, industrialists and scientists was filled with more real meat than most gatherings have."

Following this statement some of the objectives of the organization
are reviewed. The program "is diametrically opposed to the present
Federal Government's scarcity policy of reducing agricultural production. Thus, in place of creating higher prices for a little, the Farm
Chemurgic Council program is to produce and sell more of everything,
thereby increasing employment and also living standards through the
opportunity to distribute larger quantities. All this is a much more
practical philosophy than the program of scarcity, of course, and has
a much more hopeful outlook."

Civil Service

Brecht, Arnold. Civil service. Social Research 3(2): 202-221. May 1936.
   (Published for the New School for Social Research, 66 West 12th St.,
   New York, N. Y.)
      Contents: I. Political problems; II. Examination, promotion and
   patronage; III. The wisest form of examination; IV. Training; V. The
   ideal type; VI. Reform; VII. Conclusion.

Coffee

World coffee markets. Empire Producer, no. 234, pp.86-87. April 1936.
   (Published at 22, Queen Anne's Gate, Westminster, London, S.W. 1, Eng.)
      Contains replies to a questionnaire about coffee sent to corre-
   spondents in Hongkong, Japan, Turkey, Shanghai and Brazil.

Constitution - United States

The constitution in the 20th century: edited by Thomas H. Reed. Amer.
   Acad. Polit. and Social Sci. Ann. 185: 1-211. May 1936. (Published
   at 3457 Walnut St., Philadelphia, Pa.)
      Contents: The constitution as an element of stability in American
   life, by David Prescott Barrows, pp.1-10; The spirit of the constitution, by William Hard, pp.11-15; The constitution and the states, by
   Albert C. Ritchie, pp. 16-21; The constitution and social security,
   by John G. Winant, pp.22-28; The living constitution, by Charles A.
   Beard, pp.29-34; The Supreme Court: arbiter and target, by Thomas H.
   Reed, pp.35-44; Curbing the court, by Edward S. Corwin, pp.45-55; The
   constitution and the New Deal, by Donald R. Richberg, pp.56-64; The
   powers of the national government, by Walter F. Dodd, pp.65-72;
   Administrative lawmaking, by O. R. McGuire, pp.73-84; The procedure of
   amendment, by Everett S. Brown, pp.85-91; A socialist looks at the
   constitution, by Norman Thomas, pp.92-101; A unified economy and
   states' rights, by James Hart, pp.102-114; Getting a new constitution,
   by W. Y. Elliott, pp. 115-122; Regional governments for regional
   problems, by William B. Munro, pp.123-132; Property rights as obstacles
   to progress, by Francis W. Coker, pp.133-144; The constitution as the
   guardian of property rights, by William J. Donovan, pp.145-153;
   Personal liberty, by John W. McCormack, pp.154-161; Personal liberty,
   by Roger N. Baldwin, pp.162-169; The rights reserved to the states and
   the people, by William L. Ransom, pp.170-181; The freedom of the press, by
   Chester H. Rowell, pp.182-189; The constitution of the United States -
   a bibliography, by Edward W. Carter and Charles C. Rohlfing, pp.190-200;
   Appendix, The constitution of the United States of America, pp.201-211.

Consumer and the A.A.A.

Hoover, C. B. The status of the consumer during the life of the Agricultural
    Adjustment Act. South. Econ. Jour. 2(4): 12-19. April 1936. (Published
    by The Southern Economic Association and The University of North
    Carolina, Chapel Hill, N. C.)
    "The present article is limited to an analysis of the effect of the
policies carried out under the Agricultural Adjustment Act on the
national food supply, and no attempt is made to extend the analysis
to deal with all consumption goods having their source in agriculture."
The second part of the article discusses the degree of conflict between
the interests of the farmer and the consumer.
    The concluding paragraph follows:
    "If control of agricultural production by the state continues, while
each industrial enterprise is allowed to make its own decisions with
respect to the expansion or limitation of production, then it is probable that the farmer and the consumer will fight and compromise and
again fight over the price at which food is to be sold. If the interests
of farmers and industrialists are to continue to be specifically
represented in the governmental apparatus, then consumers must have
 comparable representation, if we are to have frank and determined, but
orderly, opposition of interests instead of guerilla warfare.".

Cooperation

Cooperative Journal, v. 10, no. 2, pp.49-72. March-April 1936. (Published
    at 1731 Eye St., N. W., Washington, D. C.)
    Partial contents:
    Getting the figures -1, by D. G. White. [This is the first install-
ment of a two-part article, the purpose of which is "to present and
analyze the major items in cooperative financial and operating statements", pp.49-52; Women's curb markets in North Carolina approach big
business class, by Roy H. Park, pp.55-56; New problems confront fruit and
vegetable shippers, by J. D. Horton, pp.57-58; Tariff policy showdown
near at hand? pp.61-62 [extracts from the syndicated column, Washington
Merry-Go-Round, on the dispute between the secretaries of Agriculture
and State over the proposed walnut subsidy].

Paulson, W. E. What is co-operation? Southwest. Social Sci. Quart. 16(4):
    50-58. March 1936. (Published at 3225-29 Swiss Ave., Dallas, Texas)
    In this discussion of the question "What is Co-operation?" the
author writes: "The unique feature about co-operation, and more specifically
agricultural co-operation, is that it represents a type of organized
group action which has been adapted to the problems and needs of the
farmer under his peculiar economic situation. The farmer has products to
sell; or he wishes to buy supplies needed in production; or he requires
certain essential services. The farmer joins a co-operative not with
the idea of establishing a profitable enterprise unrelated to his farming

operations but rather as the means of carrying on his farming operations more profitably. Co-operation places the stress on the members' relation to it as a patron, the one who furnishes the business. The patronage relation between a member and his co-operative stands in sharp contrast to the investor relation of an owner of common stock and his private stock company."

Cooperation - China

M., J. C. Chinese government fosters cooperatives. Far Eastern Survey 5(11): 112-113. May 25, 1936. (Published by Fortnightly Research Service, American Council, Institute of Pacific Relations, 129 E. 52nd St., New York, N. Y.)

A short article on government activities in fostering cooperative societies as a panacea for the "present serious rural problems." Weaknesses in the movement are pointed out.

Cooperation - France

Gaumont, Jean, and Gourdon, A. Co-operative education in France. The history of the central office, 1922-1934. Rev. Internatl. Coop. 29(4): 137-141. April 1936. (Published at Orchard House, 14, Great Smith St., London, S.W. 1, Eng.)

Cooperation - Virginia

Ward, G. H. When Virginia farmers cooperate. Commonwealth 2(12): 13-14, 34. December 1935. (Published by the Virginia State Chamber of Commerce, Central National Bank Bldg., Richmond, Va.)

A description of the development of the cooperative movement in Virginia. In reply to the question: "What manner of institutions are these steadily growing cooperative associations?" the author writes: "They are business institutions owned, controlled, and directed by farmers to serve farmers. They differ from ordinary business corporations in several very important respects. Whereas in the ordinary corporation the stockholder is the basic element in the control of the institution, in a cooperative association the member-patron is the vital element. In a corporation the stockholders each have as many votes as they own shares of capital stock. In a cooperative, however, each member has only one vote regardless of how many shares of capital stock he may own, affording thus, a practical example of economic democracy in actual operation."

A table entitled "Farm Products Sold through Virginia Cooperatives" accompanies the article. It shows the value of numerous farm products sold through cooperatives; the per cent sold through cooperatives; number of cooperatives; and the number of members.

Cooperation, Consumers - Great Britain

Palmer, R. A. Economic significance of British Consumers' coöperation. Natl. Marketing Rev. 1(4): 289-300. Spring 1936. (Published by the National Association of Marketing Teachers, Albert Haring, Secretary-Treasurer, 1621 Millard St., Bethlehem, Pa.)

"Mr. Palmer discusses the subject under five headings, taking up
first the general principles of coöperation and following with the
discussion of coöperative practices, organization of the British
coöperative movement, discussion of supplies and production, and finally,
the relations between the coöperative movement and the state."

Cotton - Egypt

Todd, J. A. The Egyptian cotton crop. I. -Supplies and prices. Gt. Brit.
and the East 45(1284): 829-830, table, charts. Dec. 26, 1935. (Published at 170 Strand, London, W. C. 2, Eng.)
No. II is Consumption and Markets and is published in Gt. Brit. and
the East 46(1285): 29-30. Jan. 2, 1936.

Cotton - Influence of Weather and Prices

Kalamakar, R. J. Influence of weather and prices on the cotton crop of the
Bombay Presidency. Current Sci. 4(7): 484-486, illus. January 1936.
(Published by Indian Institute of Science, Hebbal Post, Bangalore, India)

Cotton - Marketing - India

Duraiswami, S. V. Marketing of cultivators' cotton at Tirupur, Madras
Presidency. Madras Agr. Jour. 24(2): 66-71. February 1936. (Published
by M. A. S. Union, Agricultural College and Research Institute, Coim-
batore, S. India)

Singh, Ajaib, and Singh Bhullar, Partap. Some aspects of marketing and cost
of transportation of cotton. Agr. and Live-stock in India 5(6): 692-
702, tables. November 1935. (Published by Manager of Publications,
Civil Lines, Delhi, India)
"This paper is the outcome of an enquiry conducted to ascertain the
conditions under which kapas (seed-cotton) is transported from villages
to the Lyallpur market for sale. The main object of the enquiry was to
see if there is any difference in the cost of transportation of kapas
on metalled and unmetalled roads." An appendix contains tables showing
the difference of village and market prices of Desi cotton and of
American cotton.

Cotton - Spain

Martinez de Bujanda, E. Cultivation of cotton in Spain. Monthly Bull.
Agr. Econ. and Sociol. [reprint from Internatl. Rev. Agr.] 27(2): 60-66.
February 1936. (Published by the International Institute of Agriculture,
Rome, Italy)
"During the period 1914-19 - that of the Great War - considerable
difficulty was experienced in Spain in obtaining cotton for the textile
industry, since the raw cotton used up to that time was almost entirely
of foreign origin. So great was the scarcity that this industry was to
a large extent paralyzed and the necessity of cultivating cotton in those
parts of Spanish territory most suitable for the purpose was fully realized.

"Apart from industrial considerations there were many reasons for
introducing cotton growing into Spain."
The writer continues by citing these reasons. He also tells of
legislative action taken with a view of promoting the plantation of
cotton and the progressive development of cotton growing in Spain.
"This included the establishment of the State Cotton Commission (Comisaría
Algodonera del Estado), February 1926, which was later dissolved to be
replaced by another institution of wider scope and powers, viz., the one
which now supervises all the services connected with cotton, the Institute for the promotion of cotton growing (Instituto de Fomento del
Cultivo Algodonero). This Institute was established in March 1932, and
now functions in accordance with the terms of the regulations issued
22 March 1934."
Statistical data concerning the cultivation and yield of cotton during the 5 year period from 1930-31 to 1934-35 are included in the article.

Cotton – United States

Cox, A. B.   Cotton. Tex. Business Rev. 10(1): 3-4, Feb. 28, 1936. (Pub-
    lished by Bureau of Business Research, University of Texas, Austin, Tex.)
        The effects of changed Government policies are discussed. The need
    for a sound sales policy for the Producers' Pool and loan cotton is
    mentioned.
        Also in Cotton Trade Jour. 16(10): 1,2. Mar. 7, 1936.

Davezac, G. La politique cotonnière des États-Unis. L'Égypte Contemporaine
    (158-159); 693-721. November-December 1935. (Published by Société
    Royale d'Économie et de Statistique et de Législation, 16, Avenue de
    la Reine Nazli, Cairo, Egypt)
        To be continued.
        The cotton policy of the United States.

Journal of Commerce Sec. 2, 168: 1-A-18-A. May 4, 1936. (Published in
    New York, N. Y.)
        The Southern Cotton Convention Number. Partial contents: Demands
    fair play from government for cotton mills, by Thomas H. Webb, pp.1-A,
    8-A [cites great social accomplishments of industry in South]; Southern
    millmen urge continuance of delivery points, pp.1-A, 11-A (A.C.M.A.
    endorses futures contract, sale of cotton on call); Industry in South
    moves to improve farmers' position, by John W. Murray, pp. 1-A, 14-A
    [Southern cotton mill operators determined to develop closer co-operation
    with agriculturists]; Who will pay the bill? by Edwin Walter Kemmerer,
    p. 2-A; Strengthening of group action essential, by Dr. C. T. Murchison,
    p.3-A [risk of anti-trust battle called alternative to new regulation
    by bureaucrats]; Urges industry to start factories in farm area, by
    J. W. Harrelson, p.5-A [declares solution of unemployment problem rests
    on keeping farm population at home – cites Ford supply factories as
    pointing way for other industries – assorts more research needed];
    McLaurine sees opportunity for helping industry under report of Cabinet
    Committee, by William M. McLaurine, p.6-A [regarding the inquiry by a
    committee of Cabinet members appointed by the President. Excerpts from
    the committee's report are given]; and Farmers and industry have common
    problem, by Donald Comer, p. 7-A.

Newburger, E. K. The 12-cent loan cotton program and outlook for the new
    season. Cotton Digest 8(29): 6, 8-9. Apr. 25, 1936. (Published at
    710 Cotton Exchange Bldg., Houston, Tex.)

Todd, J. A. American cotton legislation. Empire Cotton Growing Rev. 13(2):
    83-91, table. April 1936. (Published by P. S. King & Son, Ltd., 14
    Great Smith St., London, S. W. I., Eng.)
        The author discusses in chronological order American legislation
    and Supreme Court decisions relating to cotton from February 18, 1935
    to February 1936.

Cotton Picker

Rust, J. D. The Rust cotton-picker - Will it solve the labor problem?
    Cotton Digest 8(29): 16-17, illus. Apr. 25, 1936. (Published at 710
    Cotton Exchange Bldg., Houston, Tex.)
        The Rust picker and its operation and use are described.

Cotton Textile Industry - United States

Osborn, Gordon. The development of the cotton textile industry of the
    United States from 1920 to 1930. Textile Inst. Jour. 27(1): P4-P21,
    tables, charts. January 1936. (Published at 16 St. Mary's Parsonage,
    Manchester, 3, Eng.)
        "This study was undertaken as part of the general problem of de-
    termining the nature of the technical and economic forces that led to
    the migration of the cotton textile industry from the New England
    States to the South."

Cottonseed Industry

Allison, J. W. A true story, stranger than fiction. Cotton and Cotton
    Oil Press 37(14): 6-8. Apr. 4, 1936. (Published at 3116-18 Commerce
    St., Dallas, Tex.)
        The development of the cottonseed industry in the United States is
    commented upon. The method of producing cottonseed oil in Asia is
    described.

Cottonseed oil industry is more than 135 years old. Cotton Digest 8(26):
    13-14. Apr. 4, 1936. (Published at 710 Cotton Exchange Bldg., Houston,
    Tex.)
        A brief history of the development of the cottonseed industry is
    given.

Credit Unions

Brenckman, Fred. National Credit Union proves great benefit to the people.
    Natl. Grange Monthly 33(5): 3, 18. May 1936. (Published in Springfield,
    Mass.)
        An article in which the Credit Union movement in the United States
    is described. The writer tells how a farmer can become a member of the
    Credit Union; of its methods of operation; and of its origin in the
    little rural community of Flammersfield, in Western Germany, nearly a
    century ago.

According to this article the "first Credit Union in the United States was set up in 1909... Today there are more than 100 Credit Unions in farming communities in 31 states, and the average amount of savings of each organization is about $5000."

Crop Reporting

Erickson, A. W. Grass Roots crop reporting. Northwest. Miller 186(1): 120. April 8, 1936. (Published at 118 South 6th St., Minneapolis, Minn.)
An article telling why the grain trade pays large sums of money for information from commercial crop reporters when the government services are free. The writer describes the work of a good crop reporter, and points out the value of crop observations to flour millers.

Dairy Farmers

Slawson, H. H. Farmers' folly and the way out. Hoard's Dairyman 81(8): 211, 221. April 25, 1936. (Published in Fort Atkinson, Wis.)
That good prices and large consumption of dairy products depend on payrolls is the theme of this article. The writer explains that milk strikes are futile and quotes from the study of R. W. Bartlett entitled, "Prices and Consumption of Milk in Specific Cities, as Related to Industrial Payrolls and Other Economic Factors" for some of his reasons.

Dairy Products - Guaranteed Prices - New Zealand

Dairy industry changes coming. New Zeal. Dairy Exporter 11(9): 3, 5. Apr. 1, 1936. (Publisher's address, P. O. Box 1001, Wellington, New Zeal.)
"The Government's guaranteed price proposals will shortly be placed before Parliament, and the scheme will become effective on August 1 next. Prior to the proposals going before Parliament, they will be discussed with the Dairy Board and suggestions invited. It is obvious that a comprehensive guaranteed price scheme must involve certain changes." In this article a full outline of Government intentions with regard to guaranteed prices is given by Hon. Walter Nash, Minister of Finance, and Hon. Lee Martin, Minister of Agriculture.

Dairies, Cooperative - Latvia

Kunkis, Voldemārs. The reorganization of dairies in Latvia. Monthly Bull. Agr. Econ. and Sociol. [reprint from Internatl. Rev. Agr.] 27(3): 91-101. March 1936. (Published by the International Institute of Agriculture, Rome, Italy)
Subjects considered are listed at the head of the article as follows: Development of co-operative dairies in Latvia; Mechanisation; Influence of the world crisis; Measures of State aid; Encouragement given to amalgamation of dairies; Measures directed towards increasing supplies of milk to dairies; Scheme for compulsory delivery; Regulation of the market and of exports; Restriction of the establishment of new dairies; Measures directed towards increasing milk consumption; Conclusions.

Drought Stricken States

Cook, L. H. Our greatest honyocker. Country Gent. 106(5): 12–13, 98, 99.
May 1936. (Published at Independence Sq., Philadelphia, Pa.)
"A honyocker, in case you do not know, is a dry farmer. He makes
up the majority of the population in the Dakotas and Northern and
Eastern Montana. He plants wheat every spring, and if there is enough
rain that season, he may raise from twenty to as high as fifty bushels
per acre of the very best milling wheat produced in the United States.
If it doesn't rain he is out of luck and in debt."

Efforts of the Federal Government to remedy many of the ills failed
and "Today he [Uncle Sam] is the greatest honyocker of them all.

"The efforts of the Government to deal with the problems created by
the drought left in their wake a whole train of new problems which vastly
complicated the entire picture." Some of these problems are outlined
in the article. As to the outlook for the future – "Refinancing, if
necessary at considerable loss to the Government, of the farmers who
are in difficulties largely through no fault of their own, resettlement
and rehabilitation of those who have no prospects for the future, and
a permanent policy in the end of compelling the producer to take his
own chances if he cares to battle with Nature for a livelihood, seems
the sensible program."

Hibbs, Ben. Dust bowl. Country Gent. 106(3): 5–6, 83, 84, 85, 86, 87.
March 1936. (Published at Independence Square, Philadelphia, Pa.)

Economic and Social Trends

Ogburn, W. F., and Jaffe, A. J. Indexes of social trends. Amer. Jour.
Sociol. 41(6): 776–782. May 1936. (Published at the University
of Chicago Press, 5750 Ellis Ave., Chicago, Ill.)
"The following charts, forty-three in number, present a quick
view of recent year-by-year changes in many important fields of
economic activity and various social phenomena. They cover from 1920
to 1936, and include two major depressions; and the yearly and monthly
comparisons show the extent and effects of recovery of the great depression of the 1930's." -Abstract, p.776.

Economic Annalist

Economic Annalist, v. 6, no. 2. April 1936. pp.17–32. (Published by the
Agricultural Economics Branch, Department of Agriculture, Ottawa, Canada)
Partial contents: Terminal markets, by W. C. Hopper, pp.19–22 [the
first part of this article was published in the February issue of the
Annalist]; Farm labour in Carleton and Victoria counties, New Brunswick,
by Ian McArthur, pp.22–25; Fifteen years of barley prices, by H. R.
Hare, pp.26–29.

Britnell, G. E. Saskatchewan, 1930-1935. Canad. Jour. Econ. and Polit.
Sci. 2(2): 143-166. May 1936. (Published by the University of Toronto
Press, Toronto, Ontario)
In this article the author presents "in summary form a description
of the impact of drought and depression on Saskatchewan." It is in
four parts as follows: I. Gross farm income; II. Net farm income; III.
Rural relief; IV. Farm debt.

Economic Nationalism

Robbins, Lionel. The consequences of economic nationalism. Lloyds Bank
Ltd. Monthly Rev. (n.s.) 7(75): 226-239. May 1936. (Published at 71,
Lombard St., London, E. C. 3, Eng.)
"Impoverishment, insecurity, war - these, if our argument is correct,
are likely to be the fruits of economic nationalism."

Economic Recovery - Australia

Progress in Australia. Economist 123(4833): 68-70. Apr. 11, 1936. (Published at 8 Bouverie St., London, E. C. 4, Eng.)
The writer describes how Australia dealt with the crisis following
the depression. "One of the first to enter that depression, Australia
was among the first, if not the first, to emerge from it."

Economic Recovery - Great Britain

Hutton, D. G. Mainsprings of British recovery. Causes of the upturn, and
the part played by government. Some dangers in the situation. Three
lessons for the United States. Barron's 16(19): 3, 6. May 11, 1936.
(Published at 44 Broad St., New York, N. Y.)
Factors which were combined to achieve British economic recovery
and which are discussed are: 1, Depreciation of sterling; 2, The new
British tariff; 3, Agricultural protectionism and stabilized markets;
4, Financial policy; 5, The building boom; 6, Re-armament.
"Yet, apart from foreign trade, recovery has been genuine, widespread,
and recognizably general. It has been due to a combination of all the
factors outlined above. But it has been possible only because of three
principal underlying advantages in the British national economy: (1)
a closely integrated and centralized banking system; (2) the 'nursing'
of industry and agriculture by the Government; (3) the maintenance of
consumers' demand by the absence of attacks on wages, by depreciation
of sterling, by the deliberate 'cheap money' boom (e.g., 'forced' investment, building boom), and by the initial 'boom' arising from the
transition from free trade to protectionism."

Electricity in Agriculture - Washington

Marshall, Jim. Flip-a-switch farming. Country Home 60(5): 14-15. May
1936. (Published at 250 Park Ave., New York, N. Y.)
The question as to "what farmers do with cheap power when they get
it" is answered in this article by the citation of savings of individual

farmers in the State of Washington. Equipment used by these farmers includes the following: Electric soil sterilizer, brooders, ultra-violet ray lamps for poultry, water heater for cattle and poultry in winter, milkers, feed hoists, etc.

L'Est Européen Agricole

L'Est Européen Agricole 5. année no. 16. January 1936. (Issued by the Comité Permanent d'Etudes Économiques des États Agricoles de l'Europe Centrale et Orientale. Published by Librairie Jouve & cie., 15, Rue Racine, Paris (6e), France)
    Partial contents: Les transformations de l'exportation agricole hongroise au cours des dernières années, by Arthur Sibelka-Perlenberg, pp.7-29. (A study of Hungary's exportation of agricultural products and of the factors which have influenced it.); Tchecoslovaquie. La seconde annee de fonctionnement du Monopole des cereales, by Vaclav Leština, pp.75-84. (The rights of purchase and sale granted to the grain monopoly are explained.); Statistics of import, export and prices in connection with the various central and eastern European countries are given.

Ever Normal Granary

Erickson, A. W.   The ever normal granary idea in action. Northwest. Miller 186(3): 231, 242. Apr. 22, 1936. (Published at 118 S. Sixth St., Minneapolis, Minn.)
    "By its sponsors this program is frequently called the 'Ever Normal Granary.' In some states the laws governing the 'sealing' of grains have been on the statute books many years and are generally known as farm storage laws. They formed a part of the wheat stabilization operations of the Federal Farm Board and were not annulled when it was abolished. When the Supreme Court invalidated the processing taxes of the Agricultural Adjustment Act many millers and grain men assumed these laws automatically became inoperative. This was not the case. If affected at all by this decision they were strengthened, because they were enacted by the several states in which they operate."
    The writer describes the origin of these laws and explains the original idea of the ever normal granary.

Factoring

First principles of factoring. Factor 4(1): [3-6]   April 1936. (Published at 225 Fourth Ave., New York, N. Y.)
    Definitions of factoring and a factor, and a brief history of the origin and development of factoring are given.

Farm Economist

The Farm Economist, v. 2, no. 2, pp.21-36. April 1936. (Published by the Agricultural Economics Research Institute, Parks Road, Oxford, Eng.)
    Partial contents: Food imports and the Italian sanctions, by C. S. Orwin, pp.21-22; Sugar beet costs and returns, 1932-35, by A. Bridges, pp.22-24; Pig production costs in Denmark, by A. W. Menzies-Kitchin,

pp.25-27: Milk: delivery to the station, by R. N. Dixey, pp.27-28;
Seasonal variation in the output and prices of eggs, by O. J. Beilby,
pp.29-32.

Flour Milling - Minneapolis

Minneapolis, a great milling center. Farmers' Elevator Guide 31(5): 3-7.
May 5, 1936. (Published at 309 S. La Salle St., Chicago, Ill.)
The story of the development of Minneapolis as a milling center.

Flour Production - United States

Working, Holbrook. New data on United States flour production since 1899
by states and by sizes of mills. Wheat Studies of the Food Research
institute 12(8): 273-312. April 1936. (Published in Stanford University, Calif.)
"The present study offers the results of a critical analysis of
census statistics and other data bearing on production of wheat flour
in the United States by mills of different size groups. It presents
revised figures for total flour production, and gives series of estimates
of quantities of flour produced by mills in each of five principal
output groups, by census years since 1899. For the census years 1899,
1919, and 1931 the division of production by output groups is shown
by states. There results a striking picture of the effects of competition in the American milling industry. A main objective of the analysis
has been improvement in the figures for total flour production in the
United States."-p.273.

Food - Consumption

Williams, Faith M. Food consumption at different economic levels.
Monthly Labor Rev. 42(4): 889-894. April 1936. (Published by the
Bureau of Labor Statistics, U. S. Department of Labor)
"The change in food habits as economic level increases is strikingly
shown in a study by the Bureau of Labor Statistics, which compares the
quantities and types of food consumed by families of wage earners at
various economic levels. At the lowest levels the market basket is
heavily weighted with bread, flour and meal, and white and sweet potatoes. At the higher levels, the consumption of cereals is only
slightly larger, but the use of fresh vegetables and fruits doubles
and of meat and eggs increases by more than 50 percent."-p.V.

Fruit and Vegetable Marketing Agreements

Erdman, H. E. Supply and adjustments in fruit and vegetable marketing
agreements. Natl. Marketing Rev. 1(4): 330-338. Spring 1936.
(Published by the National Association of Marketing Teachers, Albert
Haring, Secretary-Treasurer, 1621 Millard St., Bethlehem, Pa.)
"Professor Erdman bases his study of marketing agreements upon
certain fruit and vegetable agreement programs which he has observed
at first hand. He discusses eight major points of conflict which

handicap the success of marketing agreements. The Olive Marketing
Agreement is used to illustrate the problems faced. The administration
of marketing agreements is examined and the major problems of representation, proration, restrictions and divided jurisdiction are analyzed."-p.330.

Government, Local - Japan

Shiomi, Saburo.   The pivot of local finance reform. Kyoto Univ. Econ. Rev.
    10(2): 56-87. December 1935. (Published by The Kyoto Imperial Univer-
    sity, Department of Economics, Kyoto, Japan)
        The author discusses concentration of population and wealth in big
    cities, the loss of balance between urban and rural economic power, the
    unfair incidence of the tax burden, and grants-in-aid as one of the plans
    for the adjustment of local finance in Japan.

Government, Local - Virginia

Fox, E. L.   Economical county government; a study of the comparative costs
    of Virginia's small-county and large-county governments. Commonwealth
    3(2): 11-13, 27. February 1936. (Published by the Virginia State
    Chamber of Commerce, Central National Bank Building, Richmond, Va.)
        The author concludes: "The point we are here concerned with is that
    the large-budget counties, even without economics possible to them
    through one or the other of the new forms of county government, are
    operating much more economically than are the smaller units, which are
    overburdened with officers and under supplied with services."
        Contains tables showing total and per capita cost of operation and
    maintenance for the fiscal year ended June 30, 1934, by counties,
    based on Report of Auditor of Public Accounts of Commonwealth of
    Virginia on comparative costs of local government, 1933/34.

Virginia State chamber of commerce, Committee on taxation and government.
    "Next steps" in state taxation and government in Virginia. Common-
    wealth 3(1): 5-14. January 1936. (Published by the Virginia State
    Chamber of Commerce, Central National Bank Building, Richmond, Va.)
        "In July 1935, the committee [on taxation of the Virginia State
    Chamber of Commerce] was reorganized by consolidation with the State
    Chamber's committee on government, with seven members, under the
    designation, Committee on Taxation and Government. J. Vaughan Gary
    of Richmond...was made chairman...The report presented in this number...
    covers the first of a series of studies on state and local government
    and taxation in Virginia that have been instituted by the committee,
    and deals with questions of state taxation and governmental reorganiza-
    tion." The second discusses local problems and is published in the
    February issue.-pp.5-9.
        Contains recommendations regarding taxation of intangibles; in-
    heritance taxes; business and professional license taxes; and taxation
    of motor vehicle carriers.

Government Spending and Recovery - United States

Colm, Gerhard, and Lehmann, Fritz. Public spending and recovery in the
United States. Social Research 3(2): 129-166. May 1936. (Published
by the New School for Social Research, 66 West 12th St., New York, N. Y.)
In this study the authors "answer the question whether and to what
extent the policy of public spending has helped to bring about recovery
in the United States."

Grain - Grading

Sexauer, E. H. Recommendations of grades committee. Who is Who in Grain
and Feed 25(13): 24-28. May 5, 1936. (Published at 413-414-415 Merchants'
Exchange Bldg., St. Louis, Mo.)
Address given at the thirty-sixth annual convention of the Western
Grain and Feed Dealers Association at Sioux City, Ia., on April 22 and
23. He spoke on the subject of grain grading.

Grain - Truck Marketing

[Scott, W. R.] Truck-peddler competition with established grain merchandising. Grain & Feed Rev. 25(9): 16, 17. May 1936. (Published at 408 S.
Third St., Minneapolis, Minn.)
An address before the Thirty-sixth Annual Convention of the Western
Grain and Feed Dealers' Association at Sioux City, April 22, in which
Mr. Scott tells "of the competition to which grain dealers are subjected by the operation of itinerant trucks and proposes a remedy for
the evil. He tells of the formation of a group embracing nine states
designed primarily to secure relief and curb the truck menace."-Editor's
note

Grain Board - Argentina

Hanson, S. G. The Argentine grain board. Jour. Polit. Econ. 44(2): 240-247.
April 1936. (Published by the University of Chicago Press, Chicago, Ill.)
A discussion of the operations of the Argentine Grain Regulating
Board (Junta Reguladora de Granos), data for which are taken from
press releases of the Ministry of Agriculture. The Board is said to have
been a success in the first year of operation. "However, it should be
noted again that the chief factor in the minimizing of losses was wholly
one of chance - the disastrous weather conditions in North America; without that desgracia con suerte (lucky misfortune) the loss on the wheat
business would probably have touched the original estimate of $50,000,000."

Grain Elevators - Argentina

S., G. A. A national chain of grain elevators in Argentina. Pan Amer.
Union. Bull. 70(4): 354-356. April 1936. (Published in Washington,
D. C.)
"The Government of Argentina is constructing a comprehensive chain
of grain elevators throughout the country, comprising 15 terminal
elevators and 321 field units, to be completed within 4 years at a total

cost of some 105 million paper pesos ($35,000,000). The chain will function under the control of the Government for the benefit of all farmers who want to utilize it, charging moderate rates, but sufficient to cover the cost of construction and maintenance. It will be devoted exclusively to the cleaning, drying, grading and storage of wheat, corn and other cereal crops, trading in grain being specifically forbidden by law... The grain elevator project had its inception in law no. 11742 signed by President Justo on October 7, 1933."

Grain Trade and Agriculture

[Wilder, S. W.] Proper solution of farm problem duty of grain trade, says Wilder. Grain & Feed Rev. 25(9): 18-20. May 1936. (Published at 408 S. Third St., Minneapolis, Minn.)

In addressing the annual convention of the Western Grain and Feed Dealers' Association at Sioux City on April 22, Mr. Wilder "pointed out the close relationship which exists between the grain trade and agriculture. Because of this close union, he said, it is the duty of the trade not only to see that its freedom is unimpaired, but also to see that the farming industry is also accorded an equitable place in the American scheme."-Editor's note.

Income - Index Numbers

Hansen, H. E. Recent economic changes; a new monthly index of non-agricultural income. Annalist 47(1213): 573-574, 606. Apr. 17, 1936. (Published by the New York Times Co., New York, N. Y.)

Income and Economic Progress

Burns, A. F. The Brookings inquiry into income distribution and progress. Quart. Jour. Econ. 50(3): 476-523. May 1936. (Published at Harvard University Press, Randall Hall, Cambridge, Mass.)

This is a review and analysis of the Brookings studies: America's Capacity to Produce; America's Capacity to Consume; Formation of Capital; Income and Economic Progress.

Journal of Farm Economics

Journal of Farm Economics, v. 18, no. 2, pp.229-452. May 1936. (Published by the American Farm Economic Association, Asher Hobson, Secretary-Treasurer, University of Wisconsin, Madison, Wis.)

Contents: The Agricultural Adjustment Act and national recovery, by Chester C. Davis, pp.229-241, Discussion by J. D. Black, pp.241-243; Fundamental significance of the agricultural adjustment concept, by E. G. Nourse, pp.244-255, Discussion by J. I. Falconer, pp.255-256; The social and economic implications of the national land program, by L. C. Gray, pp.257-273, Discussion by Noble Clark, pp.274-280; A future pattern of research in agricultural economics, by Eric Englund, pp. 281-292, Discussion by F. F. Hill, pp.292-295; Research in agricultural economics from the standpoint of the states, by Theodore W. Schultz, pp.296-308, Discussion by F. P. Weaver, pp.308-310; Agricultural policy and the economist, by A. G. Black, pp.311-319; A classification and summary of research projects in dairy marketing, by S. C. Hudson, pp. 320-329; Research in the consumption and demand for milk, by W. C. Waite, pp.330-337; Research in costs of distributing milk, by Leland Spencer, pp.338-351; Transportation of milk in the St. Louis milkshed, by R. W. Bartlett, pp.352-362; Marketing research needs of the dairy industry, by H. A. Ross, pp.363-371; The motor truck in relation to fruit and vegetable marketing, by M. P. Rasmussen, pp.372-384, Discussion by Henry H. Bakken, pp.384-387; New York foods consumption survey, by Alexander Sturges, pp.388-390, Discussion by E. R. French, pp.390-392; Research as a basis for grading fruits and vegetables, by Charles W. Hauck, pp.393-401, Discussion by W. G. Meal, pp.401-404; Urgent needs for research in marketing fruits and vegetables, by Frederick V. Waugh, pp.405-414, Discussion by W. C. Hopper, pp.414-420.

In addition to the papers listed above the following "Notes" are given: California Agricultural Prorate Act constitutional, by E. A. Stokdyk, pp.421-422; Can counties be reorganized - consolidated? by Harrison L. Euler, pp.422-425; Results of the Czechoslovakia land reform, by S. Borodaewsky, pp.425-426; Developments affecting the international trade of the United States in agricultural products, by J. D. Black, pp.427-430

Labor - California

California's farm labor problems. Commonwealth 12(14, pt. 2): 153-196. Apr. 7, 1936. (Transactions of the Commonwealth Club of Calif. v. 30, no. 5) (Published at the Hotel St. Francis, San Francisco, Calif.)
Contents: Section report on migratory farm labor, by E. W. Wilson, pp.155-159; The point of view of the large farmer, by Roy M. Pike, pp. 160-166; The small farmer's viewpoint, by L. K. Marshall, pp.167-170; The migratory laborer's viewpoint, by Jack Neill, pp.171-175; The migratory labor organizer's viewpoint, by Julius B. Nathan, pp.175-181; What I consider the public's viewpoint, by Harry E. Drobish, pp. 182-184; Five-minute discussion from the floor, pp.185-196.

Labor - Southern States

Hood, Robin. Some basic factors affecting southern labor standards. South. Econ. Jour. 2(4): 45-60. April 1936. (Published by The Southern Economic Association and The University of North Carolina, Chapel Hill, N.C.)
"The fact that the South has been traditionally a region of low incomes and wages calls for something more than the usual analysis of labor standards in terms of relative wages, hours, and social legislation. It is not only highly desirable but imperative to go behind these facts and make an examination of the real factors contributing to the region's labor standards; viz., growth and mobility of population, the agricultural situation, and industrial development in relation to available natural and human resources. In addition, the probable repercussions of the policies and plans adopted to solve the present national economic dilemma must be considered."-p.45.

Land Distribution - Estonia

Redistribution of land as a factor of improvement of agrarian conditions.
In Estonian, with English summary. Konjunktuur. Monthly Rev. Estonian
Inst. Econ. Research 17(4): 249-256. April 1936. (Published in
Tallinn, Estonia.)

"The Estonian Republic has inherited from past times several inadequate systems of peasant land ownership which prevent the land from
being properly utilised. One of these is the so-called 'patch' system
under which the arable area of a given peasant holding is parcelled into
a number of scattered pieces. Holdings consisting of more than four
disconnected pieces formerly accounted for over 15% of all holdings.
Steps have been taken towards the remodeling of this impracticable
system. Under the existing scheme distribution of scattered lands in a
given region is undertaken with Government aid the owners concerned
being charged only 1 krone per hectare of the land to be redistributed.

"A second unsatisfactory system is communal land ownership. The
communal lands are the joint property of the village commune as a body
corporate, the individual members of which enjoy the life-long usufruct
of the parcels allotted to them. The available arable soil often was
split up into scores of isolated lots to enable uniform and equitable
distribution, the remaining land being mostly used collectively. At
present the communal and collectively owned landed properties have almost
entirely been rearranged into consistent lots. The latter are registered
in the name of the former users who thus become the legal proprietors
of the land so redistributed "

Land Nationalization - Great Britain

Orwin, C. S. The nation's greatest asset. I-II. New Statesman and Nation
(n.s.) 11(268-269): 558-560, 591-593. Apr. 11-18, 1936. (Published
at 10 Great Turnstile, London, W. C. 1, Eng.)

In part I of this article the writer "outlined some of the more
important disabilities inherent in our present system of land ownership,"
and in this article the question of public ownership of land is considered. Such questions as "how could the transfer of land from private
into public ownership be effected?" and "With the principle of full
compensation established, how is the figure to be arrived at?" are
discussed. The advantages or disadvantages to the landowner, to the
State, and to tenants are pointed out.

Land Ownership and Planning

Coyle, D. C. Land ownership and planning. Planners' Jour. 2(2): 35-37.
March-April 1936. (Published by American City Planning Institute,
Hunt Hall, Cambridge, Mass.)

Address at the annual meeting of the American City Planning Institute,
Washington, D. C., January 18, 1936.

Land Settlement - Australian Tropics

Williams, W. W. The settlement of the Australian tropics. Pacific Affairs
9(2): 231-242. June 1936. (Published by the Institute of Pacific

513

Relations, Honolulu, Hawaii. E. C. Carter, Secretary-Treasurer, 129
E. 52nd St., New York, N. Y.)
The following is quoted from pp.241-242:
"In my opinion the Australian tropics, with the exception of the
narrow east coast strips, will never hold a population of any magnitude
of the Australian or any other people. The only localities capable of
agricultural settlement are shaded on the attached map. Any attempt
to foster agricultural settlement beyond the meteorological limits which
have bounded it hitherto needs to be scrutinized with the gravest
apprehension because, I believe, disaster will follow in its train. It
is full time to recognize that the Australian national destiny does
not lie in the tropics, but in the more temperate coastal regions which
have been partially developed and which are capable of maintaining a
greater population."

Land Settlement - Germany

Kraemer, Erich. Supplementary farming homesteads in recent German land
settlement. Jour. Land & Pub. Utility Econ. 12(2): 177-190. May 1936.
(Published by Northwestern University, School of Commerce, 337 East
Chicago Ave., Chicago, Ill.)
Attention is called to the German movement for the establishment
of what the author calls supplementary farming homesteads (Kleinsied-
lungen). Five characteristics of these homesteads are noted: "(1)
Farming on the holdings is carried out by the homesteaders as a sideline activity for the purpose of supplementing the receipts they draw
from their main occupation or principal source of income. (2) The
agricultural land of the homesteads is not sufficient to sustain a
family. (3) Agricultural production is primarily, if not exclusively,
for home consumption. (4) The holdings are located on the periphery
of large cities and industrial centers, around middle-sized towns, as
well as in the open country. (5) The agricultural land of the homesteads is either directly attached to the dwellings of the homesteads
or located, wholly or in part, nearby."
That this is no new movement is shown by a table giving the number
and percentage of such holdings in Germany in 1933. Their establishment
was encouraged before the World War by Prussia and other States, and by
industrial enterprises and after the War by the National Government,
and other public as well as private agencies. The arguments for the
creation of more such homesteads are briefly discussed as "of biological,
socio-economic, cultural, and national-political character."
Other topics discussed are organization, selection of settlers,
location of holdings and the financing of the work. The results are
summarized and illustrated by means of tables one of which shows the
number of supplementary farming homesteads created with assistance of
public agencies in the four construction periods, 1931-1934.

Land Settlement - Great Britain

Menzies-Kitchin, A. W. The future of land settlement, 23pp. Reprinted
from Garvin's Gazette. [n.p. n.d.]
"Broadly, it would appear that a land settlement policy can be
justified and is likely to succeed only (a) if it provides an income

to settlers comparable to that of an employed agricultural worker; (b) if it provides a 'net' increase, commensurate with cost, to the national employment; (c) if it does not seriously damage the real income of the non-agricultural section of the community; and (d) if conditions are favourable to the survival of these holdings for a considerable period."

In the light of these conditions the author examines the possibilities of land settlement as a cure for unemployment. He concludes that it is "doubtful whether the settlement, even of small family farms, will in the long run succeed. In any case they will require considerable assistance from the state."

Brief paragraphs deal with the use and purpose of part-time farming in the United States and in Germany. In Britain also a limited number of subsistence holdings have provided occupation for the unemployed.

The author concludes that after assessing the relative merits of the full-time and subsistence holdings, "under existing conditions the latter provide a more economic form of settlement and offer considerable scope as a supplement to unemployment relief."

Land Tax and the Fall of Dynasties - China

Tang Yü- ch'üan. The rise of land tax and the fall of dynasties in Chinese history. Pacific Affairs 9(2): 201-220. June 1936. (Published by the Institute of Pacific Relations, Honolulu, Hawaii. E. C. Carter, Secretary-Treasurer, 129 E. 52nd St., New York, N. Y.)

Land Utilization Program - United States

Tugwell, R. G. Our new national domain. Scribner's Mag. 99(3): 164-166. March 1936. (Published at 597 Fifth Ave., New York, N. Y.)
"The states and the nation are now unleashing the greatest broad side attack on land-use problems of our history. The head of the Rural Resettlement Administration outlines the methods of attack and the history of the American attitude on it."

Leaders - Urban Distribution - United States

Smith, Mapheus. The urban distribution of prominent Americans. Southwest. Social Sci. Quart. 16(4): 21-36. March 1936. (Published at 3225-29 Swiss Ave., Dallas, Texas)
A discussion of the place of residence of persons of prominence. The author writes: "It i ...well known that a man's national prominence depends on his urban prominence. Therefore, it is not at all surprising that the cities are predominantly the places of residence of nationally prominent persons, and that this has always been true in historical times...

"Some nationally prominent persons do not reside in cities, to be sure, but all - even agricultural leaders maintain urban affiliations during the time of actual prominence. Rural suburbs claim a considerable number of residents; but only a very small proportion reside in rural communities which are not adjacent to cities."

A table is given which shows the number of notable Americans per ten thousand population, 1930, residing in largest cities and in state university cities.

Market, Farm

Borah, W. E.   The farmer's enemy.   8pp.   Washington, Govt. Print. Off.,
   1936.   Pamph. Coll.
      An article which appeared in Collier's Magazine, issue of Feb. 1,
   1936.   It was printed in the Congressional Record by request of Hon.
   Hamilton Fish, Jr., Feb. 18, 1936.
      The principal theme of this article is that prosperity for agriculture
   depends upon an enlarged market.   "Refinancing of farm indebtedness is,
   of course, important," writes Mr. Borah.   "Reduction of taxes and
   cheaper freight rates are likewise important.   But the fundamental and
   determining factor is that of increased and increasing demands for the
   products of the farm.   Can this demand be created?   Can this market be
   found?   The demand is at hand; that we know.   I feel the market can be
   made available...
      "It appears doubtful whether we shall realize anything like what we
   seem to hope for in the matter of a foreign market.   Everything indicates we are not going to find any considerable demand abroad for our
   agricultural products.   I do not mean to say that we should not by
   all practical and reasonable means seek to enlarge our foreign market.
   And to this end the debenture system will probably be of more service
   than anything which has been suggested.   But at best the foreign market
   will take care of a very small percentage of the products from the
   farm... It would seem that the only market for the American farmer is
   here in the United States, at his very door."

Marketing

Daughters, C. G.   The story of marketing.   Dun & Bradstreet Monthly Rev. 44
   (2097): 2-5, 48.   April 1936.   (Published at 290 Broadway, New York,
   N. Y.)
      "From the first feeble beginning of commercial enterprises down
   through the centuries, the development of transportation facilities,
   population shifts, and revolutionary inventions have been the chief
   factors in providing new fields for the distribution of merchandise.
   The history of such major movements are surveyed"

Marketing Boards - Great Britain

Agricultural marketing boards and producers' prices.   IV-VII. Statist 127
   (3032-3037): 547, 598-600, 645, 646, 679-680, 725, 765.   Apr. 4-May 9,
   1936.   (Published at 51 Cannon St., London, E. C. 4, Eng.)
      Contents: IV. The hops marketing scheme; V. Potato marketing scheme; VI-
   IX. The milk marketing scheme.

Marketing Research

Taylor, ' . D.   Progress in marketing research.   Natl. Marketing Rev. 1(4):
   370-377.   Spring 1936.   (Published by the National Association of
   Marketing Teachers, Albert Haring, Secretary-Treasurer, 1621 Millard
   St., Bethlehem, Pa.)
      Brief accounts of research in progress in the universities of Akron,

Buffalo, Chattanooga, Chicago, Colgate, Colorado, Duke, Harvard, Illinois, Marquette, Minnesota, Missouri, Nebraska, Toledo, and Wisconsin, and in Massachusetts Institute of Technology, the College of the City of New York, Pennsylvania State Credit, the Farm Credit Administration, the Bureau of the Census, the Bureau of Foreign and Domestic Commerce, the National Recovery Administration, and in the Brookings Institution.

Milk - Accredited Scheme - Great Britain

The accredited scheme; its progress and prospects reviewed. Home Farmer 3(4): 7-9. April 1936. (Published by the Milk Marketing Board, Thames House, Millbank, London, S.W.1, Eng.)

"When the [Milk Marketing] Board introduced the Roll of Accredited Producers it was thought that by a sustained effort it might be possible to get a quarter of the milk licensed as Grade 'A' within twelve months. We are now within a few days of the Accredited Scheme's anniversary, and the dairy farmers of this country can take considerable pride in having achieved what they set out to do in the first year."

The writer points out that while the first year's "quota" has been realized there is still much to be done. Some "specimen costings of capital expenditure incurred in Grade 'A' production" are given, but attention is drawn to the "extra penny per gallon which every Accredited producer receives."

Milk - Price Spreads

Spencer, Leland. Spread between farm and retail prices for milk. Hoard's Dairyman 81(5): 114, 134, 135. March 10, 1936. (Published in Fort Atkinson, Wis.)

"This is the first installment of a speech delivered by Professor Spencer of Cornell University before the American Institute of Cooperation." -Editor's note.

Five tables accompany this article, which have the following captions: Table 1 - Ways of measuring the dealers' spread on milk; table 2 - The dealers' spread on retail and wholesale milk in 26 United States' markets; table 3 - Changes in class 1 prices, retail prices and dealers' spread on Grade B milk for New York City, 1922-1935; table 4 - Profits of dairy and other corporations expressed as a percentage of net worth; and table 5 - Profits of New York milk dealers expressed in cents per quart on the milk equivalent of all milk and cream handled.

The second part of this article appeared in Hoard's Dairyman 81(7): 176, 192, 193. Apr. 10, 1936.

National Park - Mexico

New national park in Mexico. Pan Amer. Union. Bull. 70(4): 370. April 1936. (Published in Washington, D. C.)

"The Government of Mexico has declared the two mountains Iztaccihuatl and Popocatepetl and the spur which joins them to be a national park. It is hoped to make of the new part a natural museum of the flora and fauna of the Valley of Mexico."

Planning, National

Plan Age, v. 2, no.4, 26pp. April 1936. (Published by the National
Economic and Social Planning Association, 726 Jackson Place, Washington,D.C.)
Contents: Planning for foreign trade, by John Donaldson, pp.1-4;
United States foreign trade planning, by Robert F. Martin, pp.5-6;
Geography and its function in regional planning, by G. Donald Hudson,
pp.7-11; A question of policy, by John P. Ferris, pp.12-14; USSR document,
pp.15-16[State Planning Board of the Soviet Union as reorganized April
5, 1935]; A note on economic planning, by Albert Baster, pp.17-23.

Robbins, Lionel. The nature of national planning in the sphere of international business. Amsterdamsche Bank n.v. Financial and Economic Review of the Statistical Department no. 47, pp.1-9. April 1936.
(Published in Amsterdam)
The writer's concluding paragraph is as follows:
"Control of trade, control of production, control of the exchanges,
control of the movement of funds and of people - control carried through
by the authorities of national states whose area has been determined by
the accidents of royal marriage, by war and political upheaval, rather
than by economic forces - this is the picture which our study of contemporary tendencies to national planning has revealed. Whether this is
a good thing or a bad thing is a matter which can only be established
after much careful analysis - an analysis which hitherto the advocates
of such measures have been conspicuous in shirking. But one thing is
already certain, if these tendencies go further: the great merchant
centres, the entrepôts of a world organised for relatively free international trade and finance, must expect a still further prolongation of
the grave difficulties with which they are at present confronted."

Planning, Rural - England

Sharp, Thomas, ed. The future of the countryside. I.-The scope of the
inquiry. Country Life 79(2045): 319-320. Mar. 28, 1936. (Published
at 20, Tavistock St., Strand, London, W. C. 2, Eng.)
"Change is inevitable in any living organism, and the countryside -
itself the man-made product of changing history - cannot be exempt.
This generation's task is not to arrest change - that is impossible -
but to divert it into courses producing not ugliness, but a new beauty.
This series of articles is edited by one of the younger generation of
planning architects who, familiar with the realities of industry and
legislation, is yet a champion of England's landscape heritage. Its
purpose is to explain to the laymen the powers that exist for planning
and to examine their working. A concluding article will summarise the
findings of the various contributors to the series, proposing amendments
or adjustments of practice."-p.319.
Other articles are as follows:
II.-The town and the country, by W. Harding Thompson. Apr. 4, 1936,
pp.345-347.
III. -The village, illustrated by the parish of Broadway, by G. A.
Jellicoe. Apr. 11, 1936, pp.374-375.

IV. —Country planning and development, by Patrick Abercrombie, Apr. 18, 1936, pp.397-399.

V. —Agriculture and the countryside, by R. G. Stapledon. Apr. 25, 1936, pp.426-428.

"Agriculture is now only one of the functions of the countryside, and Professor Stapledon considers the industry in relation not only to its own prosperity, but to scenery and recreational facilities. He wants, in place of the Forestry Commission, a 'Rough Land Utilisation Commission' to deal with not only forestry but the reclamation of hill pastures and the recreational aspect of the hills. He also stresses the importance of a soil and vegetation survey as a safeguard against the mis-appropriation of good farming land."

Planning and Zoning – Washington

Blackmore, John.   Planning and zoning in the state of Washington. Jour. Land & Pub. Utility Econ. 12(2): 205-206. May 1936. (Published by Northwestern University. School of Commerce, 337 East Chicago Ave., Chicago, Ill.)

Gives the provisions of a planning and zoning act passed in 1935.

"The law is forward-looking but in places seems inadequate. Specific authority is given for zoning, residential, trade and industrial uses, but no direct mention is made of agriculture, forestry, or recreation. Rather these and other uses of land have been lumped together under 'other purposes,' but it is doubtful if the courts would uphold a specific zoning ordinance based on such generalized phraseology. A broad interpretation of the present law would allow agricultural, forestry, or recreational zoning, but it is not believed likely that any such regulatory measures will be forthcoming until the law is amended to provide specifically for them.

"An act providing for zoning for agricultural, forestry, and recreational uses failed to pass the Legislature at the same time the present law was enacted, primarily because the state program of land classification was in its infancy and the need for such advanced legislation was not apparent to the legislators."

Population – Migration and Redistribution

Goodrich, Carter.   What would Horace Greeley say now? Survey Graphic 25(6): 359-362, 400. June 1936. (Published at 112 E. 19th St., New York, N.Y.)

"Why and how migration can lead to opportunity, not up blind alleys, is the subject of the new Study of Population Redistribution, proposed by the Social Science Research Council, made by a group of scientists under the auspices of the Industrial Research Department of the Wharton School of Finance, and soon to be reported in Migration and Economic Opportunity (University of Chicago Press). Its findings here are summarized by Carter Goodrich, director of the Study and a member of the Faculty of Political Science of Columbia University." –p.355.

519

Is population moving back to the farm? Dun & Bradstreet Monthly Rev. 44(2098): 3-7. May 1936. (Published at 290 Broadway, New York, N.Y.)
"Recent movements of population are depicted graphically in...[this] article abstracted from a report prepared for the National Resources Board by the Division of Land Economics, Bureau of Agricultural Economics of the United States Department of Agriculture."

Price Research

Mills, F. C. Conference on price research. Monthly Labor Rev. 42(3): 836-837. March 1936. (Published by the Bureau of Labor Statistics, U. S. Dept. of Labor)
A statement concerning the Conference on Price Research held at the National Bureau of Economic Research in New York, November 29-30, 1935.
An account of this conference is also given in Amer. Statis. Assoc. Jour. 31(193): 128-130. March 1936.

Price Rigidities and Monopoly Power

Galbraith, J. K. Monopoly power and price rigidities. Quart. Jour. Econ. 50(3): 456-475. May 1936. (Published at Harvard University Press, Randall Hall, Cambridge, Mass.)
Summary, p.456: "I. Some shortcomings of the usual explanations of price rigidities, 456. -The method of attack on the problem, 459. -II. The coexistence of monopoly power and rigid prices, 459. -III. The nature of the monopoly equilibrium and of the movement between positions of monopoly equilibrium as 'causes' of rigidity, 463. -IV. The choice of rigid prices, as such, under conditions of monopoly power: 1. As an aid to oligopoly adjustment, 466; 2. As an aid to resale price maintenance, 468; 3. As result of the use of average costs in pricing, 470; 4. As result of monopoly inertia, 472. -V. Conclusions and bearing on public policy, 473."

Price Spreads

What is the farmers' share? Consumers' Guide 3(7): 8-9, 31. Apr. 6, 1936. (Published by the Consumers' Counsel, Agricultural Adjustment Administration, U. S. Department of Agriculture)
To the Federal Trade Commission Congress assigned the task of looking into the spread between farm and retail prices of six important agricultural commodities [milk, cotton, cattle, and calves; hogs, wheat, and tobacco.] In this article the writer tells how the Commission obtained the necessary information and gives partial answers to some of the questions. The full report of the Commission is to be completed "not later than July 1 of this year."

Prices, Retail

Cover, J. H. Dispersion of retail prices. Natl. Marketing Rev. 1(4): 326-329. Spring 1936. (Published by the National Association of Marketing Teachers, Albert Haring, Secretary-Treasurer, 1621 Millard St., Bethlehem, Pa.)

"In this paper which was read at the joint session of the American Statistical Association and National Association of Marketing Teachers, Professor Cover draws upon his experience in the field of retail price collection. He indicates some of the factors which determine the dispersion and distribution of retail prices and draws upon data collected in Washington, D. C., St. Paul, Manhattan, Minneapolis and Atlanta. Among the factors discussed are the relation of the quality of the commodity to price changes, the geographic location, time, type of outlet and consumer differences. The various points are treated most concisely and indicate many variables which confuse and complicate price analysis."-p.326.

Prices and Economic Planning - United States

Anderson, B. M. Governmental economic planning and prices. Chase Econ. Bull. 16(1): 3-25. April 18, 1936. (Issued by the Chase National Bank of the City of New York)

An address delivered before the Annual Meeting of the Eastern Sociological Conference at New Haven, Conn., April 18, 1936.

"The present paper is primarily concerned with governmental policy regarding market prices in connection with recent governmental efforts at so-called 'economic planning.' In order, however, to set this problem in proper perspective, it is necessary to consider first certain larger questions, and to deal with the general theory of the social control and coordination of the economic activities of men."

Processing Taxes

Kendrick, M. S. The processing tax provisions of the AAA; review of the operation of the taxes in anticipation of their probable revival. Tax Mag. 14(5): 273-278. May 1936. (Published at 205 West Monroe St., Chicago, Ill.)

Purchasing Power, Farm

Mullen, W. H. Tapping farm-market areas. Farmers' cash receipts mount to $8 billion this year, and they are loosening purse strings. The best areas for sales prospects. Barron's 16(20): 15, 18. May 18, 1936. (Published at 44 Broad St., New York, N. Y.)

Farm market indices, by agricultural divisions, in chart and tabular form are presented on p. 18.

Raw Materials - Import - Hamburg

Kölblin. Die Rohstoffeinfuhr über Hamburg. Wirtschaftsdienst (n.F.) 21(17): 582-584. Apr. 24, 1936. (Issued by Hamburgisches Weltwirtschafts Archiv. Published by Hanseatische Verlagsanstalt Aktiengesellschaft, Hamburg 36, Germany)

An account of Hamburg's imports of raw materials in 1932-1935.

Raw Materials - United States

Our natural resources. The Index 16(5): 95-100. May 1936. (Published by
the New York Trust Co., 100 Broadway, New York, N. Y.)
Considers the present and future status of our natural resources.
A table accompanies the article which shows the distribution of the
world's raw material production. The materials listed in the table include various cereals, textiles, rubber, minerals and metals.

Rayon

Miller, S. L. Rayon consumption still expanding; Federal taxes and imports
main worries. Annalist 47(1216): 685-686. May 8, 1936. (Published by
the New York Times Co., New York, N. Y.)

Rayon - Japan

Atsuki, K. The rayon industry in Japan. Soc. Chem. Indus. [Japan] Jour.
(Sup. Binding) 39(2): 43B-44B. February 1936. (Published by the
Society of Chemical Industry, Yuraku Bldg., Marunouti, Tokyo, Japan)
A brief history of the industry.

Reorganization of the Government

Government reorganization. By the unofficial observer. Today 6(1): 10,
20-21. Apr. 25, 1936. (Published at 152 W. 42nd St., New York, N.Y.)
On the present move to investigate the problem of Federal reorganization by a Senate committee, a committee appointed by President
Roosevelt, and a possible House committee.
"The time is coming when the government, being in business, must also
handle itself in a businesslike manner. So far it has poured this new
responsibility into the same old bottles, with results which are now
unsatisfactory. Roosevelt is now preparing to face the problem of reorganization along broader lines than have ever been politically expedient in a system under which mother and father pay all the bills,
while the victors get the spoils."

Research

Cates, J. S. A nation gone to town. Country Gent. 106(5): 21, 41, 43.
May 1936. (Published at Independence Square, Philadelphia, Pa.)
"British agriculture is a relatively small industry, but I am struck
by the fact that it furnishes a background upon which has been hung
a research setup running into pretty large dimensions; and their findings,
as you know, have profoundly influenced us in America...
"In this article I am trying to catch some of the spirit of research
as they attack it in England and to give a picture of the farming
situation in a nation that has gone to town."

Resettlement

Tugwell, R. G. One year of resettlement. U. S. News 4(18): 4. May 4, 1936.
(Published at 2201 M St., N. W., Washington, D. C.)
"From a radio address over an NBC network, April 29."

Retail Trade - Rural and Urban Areas

Mitchell, Walter, Jr.   Is retail trade recovery greatest in the rural
    areas? Dun & Bradstreet Monthly Rev. 44(2097): 9-11. April 1936.
    (Published at 290 Broadway, New York, N. Y.)
        The writer presents figures (from the Dun & Bradstreet Retail Survey
    for 1935) which answer the question as to whether rural purchasing power
    has recovered more rapidly than the purchasing power of city dwellers.
    "In six lines of trade the most rapid improvement was quite clearly in
    the cities. In five lines, best results occurred in the small towns,
    while in the remaining eleven lines there was no clear trend, or the
    comparison was inapplicable."
        A table showing the trend of retail sales 1934-35 by size of city
    or town accompanies the article.

Rice - Burma, Siam and French Indo-China

Robertson, C. J. The rice export from Burma, Siam and French Indo-China.
    Pacific Affairs 9(2): 243-253. June 1936. (Published by the Institute
    of Pacific Relations, Honolulu, Hawaii. E. C. Carter, Secretary-
    Treasurer, 129 E. 52nd St., New York, N. Y.)

Roadside Marketing

Hauck, C. W. Roadside retailing comes of age. Amer. Fruit Grower 56(5):
    12, 20, 26, 28. May 1936. (Published at 1370 Ontario St., Cleveland, O.)
        The transition that is now going on in the roadside produce busi-
    ness is described in this article. The writer states that farmers and
    others who operate retail stands for the sale of agricultural products
    "are gradually awakening to the necessity for something more than a few
    bushels of apples and a prayer if they are to get a fair share of the
    potential business."

Rural America

Rural America, v. 14, no. 4, 16pp. April 1936. (Published by the American
    Country Life Association, Inc., 105 E. 22nd St., New York, N. Y.)
        Partial contents: County achievement contest in Kentucky, by
    Marshall E. Vaughn, pp.3-4; A federated church serving the community
    [North Jackson, Ohio] by James D. Wyer, pp.5-6; Can we build a
    community? by Walter A. Terpenning, pp.6-8; Better organization for
    rural young people, by Charles Gould [Idealia County, Iowa, Junior
    Farm Bureau] pp.9-11.

Rural Discussion Groups

Hendrickson, R. F. A crop of new ideas on the farms. Jour. Adult Ed.
    8(2): 177-180. April 1936. (Published by American Association for
    Adult Education, 1315 Cherry St., Philadelphia, Pa.)
        Describes the rural discussion groups project sponsored by the
    United States Department of Agriculture and a group of agricultural ex-
    periment stations during the year 1935, and draws some conclusions from
    the experiment.

Rural Reconstruction - China

Hsu, L. S. Rural reconstruction in China; a sociological interpretation. Sociol. and Social Research 20: 403-421. May-June 1936. (Published by the University of Southern California Press, 3551 University Ave., Los Angeles, Calif.)
"Rural reconstruction in China, as a social movement, may be regarded as one phase of social planning. It represents a correlated attack of the various technical fields, such as agriculture, industry, co-operation, health, and public administration for the realization of a planned society of China into a modern society. Its methodology is a correlated application of modern sciences to the community life of China, which is 80 per cent rural."

Self-help Cooperatives

Activities of Federally aided self-help cooperatives during 1935. Monthly Labor Rev. 42(3): 609-621. March 1936. (Published by the Bureau of Labor Statistics, U. S. Dept. of Labor.)
"Except where otherwise noted, this article is based upon data furnished by the Division of Self-Help Cooperatives, Federal Emergency Relief Administration."
"The 215 cooperative self-help organizations aided by Federal grant supplied their members with goods and services amounting to $1,216,547 during the first 10 months of 1935. Projects receiving Federal assistance furnished 9,047,923 man-hours' work during the same period. Since August 1933 Federal grants to these organizations have totaled $2,831,413, of which 57.8 percent had been spent or obligated by the end of October 1935. It is calculated that for every $1 of Federal money $2.50 had been obtained in benefits. A considerable number of the members would have had to resort to relief, in the absence of the self-help activities. It is estimated that altogether these organizations have saved the taxpayers $2,278,287."-pp.V-VI.

Rall, Udo. Appraising self-help. Survey 72(5): 134-136. May 1936. (Published at 112 E. 19th St., New York, N. Y.)

Social Science Fellowships

Davis, I. G. The social science fellowships in agricultural economics and rural sociology. Social Forces 14(4): 516-522. May 1936. (Published for the University of North Carolina Press by the Williams & Wilkins Co., Baltimore, Md.)
"This article was the report for a committee which has been discharged for three years."

Soil Conservation and Domestic Allotment Act

Bunn, Charles. The AAA decision and the Soil conservation act. Jour. Land & Pub. Utility Econ. 12(2): 199-200. May 1936. (Published by Northwestern University, School of Commerce, 337 East Chicago Ave., Chicago, Ill.

Harrower, D. C.   Increasing farmers' income. Business not altruistic in
    demanding this. New agricultural law calls for conservation of soil.
    Essential to maintenance of high living standards. Barron's 16(16):
    19. , Apr. 20, 1936. (Published at 44 Broad St., New York, N. Y.)

Save the soil. Rev. of Reviews 93(4): 28-30. April 1936. (Published at 233
    Fourth Ave., New York, N. Y.)
        "Ancient truths are rediscovered - a law is passed [Soil Conservation
    Act] - or is it just election year?" The writer points out that what
    George Washington cared most about, and worked hardest to accomplish,
    was the restoration of the depleted soils of the eastern counties of
    Virginia. Also that "educated and scientific people, in such countries
    as Denmark and the Scandinavian peninsula, Holland, Germany, France,
    Switzerland and Italy have long regarded their soils as a priceless
    heritage and have accordingly maintained and improved them. Owners of
    land in these European countries do not expect government subsidies
    for keeping their soils productive."
        The question is raised just why we should spend so much Federal
    money in 1936 to pay landed proprietors for "ceasing to let their top
    soil clog the creeks and rivers". It is stated that "Our criticism
    of AAA has been due to the fact that the larger subsidy checks, together
    with the benefit of higher prices, went to the enrichment of the very
    people who were breaking down real farming by their commercial production
    of a vast excess tonnage of wheat at low prices... The new law will
    permit the reward of all small farmers who protect their soils for the
    benefit of posterity, and will make possible the elimination of the
    one-crop wheat speculators, all the way from Montana to Texas."

Soybeans

An agricultural crop of tremendous possibilities for industry. Manfrs.
    Rec. 105(4): 30. April 1936. (Published at Commerce and Water Sts.,
    Baltimore, Md.)
        Describes the increase in the production of soybeans during the
    past ten years and gives as a reason for this increase "the growing
    recognition of the value of soybeans for the manufacture of a variety
    of articles used in commerce, as well as the value of the bean and the
    hay for food and cattle feed. Its cultivation is attractive because of
    its immunity to pests, the good prices the crop brings compared with
    other crops, besides its resistance to drought and its large yields."
        Mr. J. I. Morgan, president of the National Cottonseed Products
    Association, Inc., Memphis, Tenn., is quoted as saying that "with very
    minor adjustments, cottonseed crushing equipment can be adapted for
    practically all vegetable oil seeds and nuts."

Speculation and the Carryover

Williams, J. B.   Speculation and the carryover. Quart. Jour. Econ. 50(3):
    436-455. May 1936. (Published at Harvard University Press, Randall
    Hall, Cambridge, Mass.)
        Bibliographical footnotes.
        In this analysis the author shows "how in theory speculators con-
    fronted with questions of probability should act" in order to "throw

fresh light on how in practice they do act."

Summary, p.436: "Speculation upon the supply, and upon the demand, 436. -Definition of the carryover, 436. -The supply curve, 438. -Yields and the weather, 439. -Price of a short crop, 441. -Of a bumper crop, 441. -The carrying charge, 441. -Effect of speculation on consumption, 442. - On production, 442. -Equilibrium in a one year's operation, 443. -In a several-years' operation, 446. -Number of years' holding needed, 447. -Saw-tooth course of prices in years without carryover, 448. -Solution by successive approximation, 449. -Corollaries, 450. -Speculation upon the demand, 450. -Note on probability, 452."

Subsistence Homestead - Reedsville, W. Va.

Rice, M. M. The fuller life at Reedsville. Nation's Business 24(5): 25-28, 86, 87. May 1936. (Published at 1615 H St., N. W., Washington, D. C.)
"This is the story of Arthurdale, officially known as Reedsville (W. Va.) Experimental Community, the national Administration's first adventure in planned economy."
Work on this project was begun in October, 1933, and is still in progress.

Sugar - Brazil

Brazil. Cane purchases by sugar mills regulated. Foreign Legislative News, no. 43, March 1936. Suppl. (Published by Division of Commercial Laws. Bureau of Foreign and Domestic Commerce, U. S. Department of Commerce)
A law of January 9, 1936 regulates "the transactions of purchase and sale of sugar cane between planters and sugar mill owners. A translation of the text of the law, by A. A. Barrington, is given.

Sugar - Chadbourne Plan

Muhle, Hans. Weltzuckerwirtschaft unter dem Chadbourne - Plan. Wirtschaftsdienst (n.F.) 21(16): 549-551. Apr. 17, 1936. (Issued by Hamburgisches Welt-Wirtschafts Archiv. Published by Hanseatische Verlagsanstalt Aktiengesellschaft, Hamburg 36, Germany)
A study of world sugar economy under the operation of the Chadbourne Plan, and the failure of international regulation of sugar production, with statistical illustrations.

Sugar - Control of Production and Export - Cuba

S., G. A. Control of sugar production and export in Cuba. Pan Amer. Union. Bull. 70(4): 364-365. April 1936. (Published in Washington, D.C.)
An account of the provisions of decree-law no. 522, of January 20, 1936 which "authorizes the Cuban Executive to regulate the production and exportation of sugar and the establishment of production quotas among individual sugar mills during the 6-year period beginning January 1, 1936, and ending December 31, 1941... On February 4, 1936, the Government fixed definitely the production of sugar during 1936 at 2,515,000 long tons of 2,240 Spanish pounds net," also the export quota.

Sugar - Turkey

Mikusch, Gustav. Turkey's stabilization program. Facts about Sugar 31(4):
133-134. April 1936. (Published by Palmer Publishing Corp. 56 West
45th St., New York, N. Y.)
An law of June 12, 1936 provided for the reorganization of the Turkish
sugar industry on the basis of "(1) Reduction of the consumption tax
and the customs duty; (2) Adequate reduction of the sugar price; (3)
Amalgamation of the existing sugar companies into one strictly controlled by banks, which on their part are controlled by the government...
The government expects to gain three advantages from the reorganization;
(1) The possibility of a better adjustment of production to requirements...
(2) Considerable savings in the production and administration costs
through the centralization of all activities under a single control. (3)
A material increase of the sugar consumption as an effect of the lower
price, with all the economic benefits of such development."

Sugar Industry

Case, W. W. Outlook for sugar industry improved by quotas and rising consumption. Annalist 47(1218): 757-758. May 22, 1936. (Published by
New York Times Co., New York, N.Y.)
An analysis of the sugar situation. Five statistical tables and chart
accompany the article. Data given include raw sugar supplies and
quotas, world raw sugar production, price received for refined sugar,
and net income of leading sugar companies.

Sugar Institute Case

Murphey, H. K. The Sugar institute case. Conf. Bd. Bull. 10(4): 27-28.
Apr. 10, 1936. (Published by the National Industrial Conference Board,
Inc., 247 Park Ave., New York, N. Y.)

Supreme Court Decisions

Bevis, H. L. The AAA and TVA decisions. Harvard Business Rev. 14(3):
272-278. Spring 1936. (Published at 330 West 42nd St., New York, N.Y.)
Consideration of the question, "What premises do they [the AAA and
TVA decisions] supply for future business reasoning?" The significance
of the two decisions is pointed out, and a summary of the Soil Conservation and Domestic Allotment Act is given in the article.

Mitchell, J. G. Supreme Court decisions in a number of important and far-
reaching cases. Annalist 47(1213): 579. April 17, 1936. (Published
by the New York Times Co., New York, N. Y.)
Among the important cases decided by the Supreme Court, which are
considered in this article, is the Agricultural Adjustment Act.

Surveys

Woodhouse, E. J. City and county surveys. Univ. N. C. News Letter, v. 22,
no. 8, Apr. 8, 1936. (Published by the University of North Carolina
Press, Chapel Hill, N. C.)

This is a survey of various types of surveys - such as the Domesday Book, modern surveys, muck-raker surveys, social welfare surveys, the Cleveland Foundation surveys, and research surveys. The author also discusses action taken following surveys, the scope of the survey, surveys and newspapers, and the general elements of a survey.

Tenancy, Farm

Gee, Wilson. Reversing the tide toward tenancy. South. Econ. Jour. 2(4): 1-11. April 1936. (Published by The Southern Economic Association and The University of North Carolina at Chapel Hill, N. C.)
Discusses the causes of the increase in farm tenancy, evils of tenancy, Communist agitation for state ownership of land, efforts to curb the evils of high tenancy percentages in Ireland, Denmark, and other countries, and the Bankhead "Farmers' Home Act", which the author says "should be enacted into the law of the land, and become translated into the permanent policy of the nation."

Wehrwein, G. S. Changes in farms and farm tenure, 1930-1935. Jour. Land & Pub. Utility Econ. 12(2): 200-205. May 1936. (Published by Northwestern University, School of Commerce, 337 East Chicago Ave., Chicago, Ill.
Contents: Farm population; number of farms and acreage of farm land; changes in land tenure, 1930-1935; changes in tenure in the South.

Tenancy, Farm - Virginia

Walker, L. M., Jr. Increase in farm tenants in Virginia: 1930-1935. Univ. Va. News Letter, v. 12, no. 14, Apr. 15, 1936. (Published in University, Va.
Accompanied by a table which shows farm tenancy in Virginia counties, 1930 and 1935.

Textile Fibers - Value of Consumption

Value of fibers consumed in U. S. Rayon Organon 7(3): 45-47, table, charts. Mar. 10, 1936. (Published by Textile Economics Bureau, Inc., 21 East 40th St., New York, N. Y.)
The values of cotton, wool, silk and rayon consumed in the United States, 1920-1935, are compared.

Timber Market, International

Arcoleo, F. The organisation of the international timber market. Monthly Bull. Agr. Econ. and Sociol. [reprint from Internatl. Rev. Agr.] 27(2): 41-49. February 1936. (Published by the International Institute of Agriculture, Rome, Italy)

Tobacco Trade - Bremen

Bentin, L. Bremen als Tabakmarkt. Wirtschaftsdienst (n.F.) 21(17): 579-582. Apr. 24, 1936. (Issued by Hamburgisches Welt-Wirtschafts Archiv. Published by Hanseatische Verlagsanstalt Aktiengesellschaft, Hamburg 36, Germany)
A historical sketch of Bremen as a tobacco market and an estimate of its importance based on statistical tables.

Trade, Foreign - Germany

Steere, L. V. German imports of agricultural products. Foreign Crops and
    Markets 32(19): 543-563. May 11, 1936. (Published by the Division of
    Foreign Agricultural Service, Bureau of Agricultural Economics, U. S.
    Dept. of Agriculture)
        Accompanied by a number of tables showing imports of agricultural
    products, 1928 to 1935.

Trade, Foreign - United States

Norris, R. T. The physical volume of American foreign trade with leading
    countries, 1920-1932. Rev. Econ. Statis. 18(2): 89-96. May 1936.
    (Published at the Harvard University Press, Randall Hall, Cambridge, Mass.)
    The author's introductory paragraph is as follows:
        "In the study of international trade, it is desirable for many pur-
    poses to possess data upon the quantitative movements of trade between
    regions of countries. For example, in research relative to the gross
    barter terms of trade, the effectiveness of reciprocity treaties, or
    the influence upon living standards of quota and licensing systems, it
    is physical and not value data that are of significance, especially
    physical data as between nations. On the whole, the measure which seems
    most closely to meet the diverse needs of workers in these fields
    appears to be an index of the movement to particular countries of bales,
    bushels, tons, etc., of commodities, each good receiving a weight
    proportionate to its value. Possible methods of approximating such an
    index can be discussed briefly, with special reference to the United
    States."

Tremaine, H. M. Swapping home trade for foreign trade. Mag. Wall St. 58(2):
    79-81, 122. May 9, 1936. (Published at 90 Broad St., New York, N. Y.)

Trade, International, and Devaluation

Cassady, Ralph, Jr., and Upgren, A. R. International trade and the devalua-
    tion of the dollar, 1932-1934. Quart. Jour. Econ. 50(3): 415-435.
    May 1936. (Published at Harvard University Press, Randall Hall, Cam-
    bridge, Mass.)
        "We rarely have in economics one force acting alone and it is dif-
    ficult to disentangle one influence when others are acting also. De-
    preciation of currency tends to alter, other things equal, the prices
    of foreign trade commodities expressed in the depreciated currency.
    The evidence which has been presented does not invalidate this doctrine;
    it has been shown that the currency depreciation does modify demand
    and supply conditions. However, the changes of prices and quantities
    in our international trade from 1932 to 1934 reveal the great importance
    of other influences. They include varying rates of recovery in other
    countries as well as the United States, raw material controls, including
    our own restriction programs, import quotas, and the existence of sub-
    stitutes. These forces to a very considerable extent can be disentangled
    and the effects of each of them upon demand and supply conditions can be

measured with considerable success. It appears that the total effects
of price making forces other than devaluation, in the period considered,
have exceeded the effect on prices arising from dollar devaluation alone.
Clearly they must be considered in an explanation of price behavior even
during a period characterized by very substantial currency depreciation." -
Concluding paragraph.

Trade Agreements

Agriculture in the French trade agreement. Foreign Crops and Markets 32(20):
589-597. May 18, 1936. (Published by the Division of Foreign Agricultural Service, Bureau of Agricultural Economics, U. S. Dept. of Agriculture

Agriculture in the trade agreement with Finland. Foreign Crops and Markets
32(21): 623-632. May 25, 1936. (Published by the Division of Foreign
Agricultural Service, Bureau of Agricultural Economics, U. S. Dept. of
Agriculture)

Doom of 1934 Reciprocal Trade Act is goal of Sioux City conference. Grain &
Feed Rev. 25(9): 22, 23. May 1936. (Published at 408 S. Third St.,
Minneapolis, Minn.)
"More than 500 delegates gathered at Sioux City on April 14 to attend
the eight-state agricultural conference, sponsored by the Sioux City
Chamber of Commerce, went on record as being actively opposed to the
Reciprocal Trade Act of 1934. In a resolution, adopted by the gathering,
the ill effects of the legislation were displayed, its repeal was de-
manded and the utter need for tariff laws designed to protect agriculture
was expressed."
A table is given which shows the increase in imports of 29 specific
items. The data are given for years 1932 and 1935.
Final action of the conference was the adoption of a five-point
program, which is given.

Goldenberg, H. C. The Canada-United States trade agreement, 1935. Canad.
Jour. Econ. and Polit. Sci. 2(2): 209-212. May 1936. (Published by
the University of Toronto Press, Toronto, Ontario)
The article is concluded as follows:
"The Trade Agreement may be subjected to adverse criticism on a
number of grounds. First, while it covers a large number of items, the
tariff reductions are in many cases negligible. Secondly, it intro-
duces the principle of import quotas on Canadian products. Thirdly, it
is subject to termination at the end of three years and may, therefore,
soon upset the newly-created trade channels. But, while these criticisms
are valid they must be considered in the light of all the facts. The
Agreement was negotiated in the face of strong currents of protectionism
in a world of restricted trade. It is essentially a compromise between
conflicting interests in both countries, Nevertheless, it is extensive
and will afford a degree of stability to important industries. Having
regard to all the circumstances it is surprising that so much was
accomplished."

Pasvolsky, Leo. Bilateralism in international commercial relations. Harvard Business Rev. 14(3): 279-289. Spring Number 1936. (Published at 330 West 42nd St., New York, N. Y.)

"The term 'bilateralism' is today frequently employed only with reference to arrangements which affect the balance of trade or of payments —a type of trade compact which represents a distinct departure in the sphere of commercial policy as it has operated in modern times. While there is an advantage in thus reserving this term for a specific type of commercial arrangements, it is more convenient, for the purposes of this discussion, to apply the term 'bilateralism' generally to any trade compact which is bilateral in form, irrespective of whether or not it is also bilateral in substance. The discussion which...[is here given] runs, therefore, in terms of a brief description of the principal types of bilateral commercial arrangements and of some of the implications for international trade of the application of the principle of bilateralism under conditions represented by these various types of trade compacts."

Reciprocal trade agreements and American foreign trade. Conf. Bd. Bull. 10(5): 35-37. May 10, 1936. (Published by the National Industrial Conference Board, 247 Park Ave., New York, N. Y.)

Accompanied by five tables which show index numbers of volume and value of world trade and of the foreign trade of the United States, 1929 to 1935; volume and value of imports, 1929, 1932 and 1934 compared with 1923-25 average; volume and value of imports of leading commodities, 1929 to 1935; value of exports of leading commodities, 1929 to 1935.

Trading Areas, Retail

Converse, P. D. Analysis of retail trading areas - some suggested methods with an example. Natl. Marketing Rev. 1(4): 316-325. Spring 1936. (Published by the National Association of Marketing Teachers, Albert Haring, Secretary-Treasurer, 1621 Millard St., Bethelehem, Pa.)

"Professor Converse sets forth a method for analyzing retail trading areas based upon a combination of official statistics and a supplemental analysis of the trading area of Amboy, Illinois. He indicates the methodology employed and the results secured in measuring this selected local trading area. It is his thesis that there may be a definite relationship between income and retail sales which makes it possible to estimate income from retail sales data. He distinguishes between retail trade areas which do not conform to political boundary lines and the limitations upon the use of census data which are presented for political subdivisions, such as states, counties and cities."-Abstract, p.316.

Wages, Agricultural - United States

Black, J. D. Agricultural wage relationships: geographical differences. Rev. Econ. Statis. 18(2): 67-83. May 1936. (Published at the Harvard University Press, Cambridge, Mass.)

"In the February issue of this Review, farm wage rates were found, when analyzed in terms of their historical changes for the United States

as a whole, to have a consistent pattern of relationships with farm
incomes, farm real-estate values, farm rentals, wages of labor in
industry, supply of farm labor, factory employment, industrial production,
and migration from farms to cities. These rates also were found to dis-
play a rough consistency with changes in the proportion in which other
production agents - land, land improvements, farm buildings,.farm
machinery, horses, and productive livestock - are used with farm labor,
as well as with changes in the values of these other agents, when due
account is taken of the changing conditions of supply of these agents.
The available data did not permit full development of this last stage
in the analysis.
        "In this second installment, farm wage rates are first analyzed in
terms of their geographical differences - states and geographic divisions
being the units employed - to see if any consistent pattern can be
found here also, and if so, the nature of its contours; and secondly,
to the limited extent that the data will permit, in terms of historical
changes by regions."-Opening paragraphs of article.

Walnut Trade - Turkey and Danubian Countries

Recent tendencies in the Danubian and Turkish walnut trade. Foreign Crops
        and Markets 32(17): 494-499. Apr. 27, 1936. (Published by the Division
        of Foreign Agricultural Service, Bureau of Agricultural Economics, U. S.
        Dept. of Agriculture.)
        Information regarding production and trade of walnuts is given for
Rumania, Bulgaria, Yugoslavia, Hungary and Turkey. Tables showing the
exports of walnuts from each of these countries by countries of destination are given. Data in tables are from the Belgrade Office, Foreign
Agricultural Service.

Wealth, Debts and Equities - United States

Doane, R. R. Distribution of corporate, individual and public debts and
        equities, 1932. Annalist 47(1217): 718-719, 725. May 15, 1936.
        (Published by the New York Times Co., New York, N. Y.)
        "This is the eighth of a series of articles on the nature, distri-
bution and promise of wealth in the United States."
        Accompanied by four statistical tables which show: the total esti-
mated national wealth, debts and equities by major categories under
corporate and individual ownership, 1932; national physical wealth under
corporate and individual ownership, 1932; holdings of long-term obligations by major lending groups, 1932; breakdown of total physical wealth
(1932) by evidences of claims and equities and by economic character of
property together with number of owners.

Wheat - Great Britain

Legislation aids wheat producers in the British Isles. Foreign Crops and
        Markets 32(17): 500-507. Apr. 27, 1936. (Published by the Division
        of Foreign Agricultural Service, Bureau of Agricultural Economics, U. S.
        Dept. of Agriculture)
        "Based on a report from Agricultural Attaché C. C. Taylor at London."

"The wheat industry of the British Isles has been materially aided
by the legislative measures enacted during the past few years. This
is evidenced by an expansion in production and an improvement in market
conditions. Although reduced yields in England and Wales lowered the
total wheat outturn for the United Kingdom in 1935, acreage and production have increased substantially since enactment of the Wheat Act
in 1932...

"Since 1931, the Government of the United Kingdom has maintained a
highly protective attitude toward agricultural production. This took
definite shape for wheat growers when a subsidy was instituted under the
Wheat Act of 1932. As a consequence, the wheat acreage of the United
Kingdom increased by 51 percent from 1931 to 1935."

Provisions of the Agricultural Produce Act are also described in this
article, and it is pointed out that since the enactment of the Wheat
Act of 1932, the British Government "has undertaken to guarantee growers
a price of 10 shillings per hundredweight ($1.32 per bushel at current
rate of exchange) for a maximum millable quantity of 27,000,000 hundredweight (50,400,000 bushels). The funds for these deficiency payments
are obtained from a flexible processing tax on wheat and imported flour."

Wheat - Peru

Peru. Wheat regulations. Foreign Legis. News, no. 43, March 1936. Sup.
(Published by Division of Commercial Laws, Bureau of Foreign and Domestic
Commerce, U. S. Dept. of Commerce)

According to a report from A. C. Crilley, "measures were instituted
by the Peruvian Government in 1934...to aid domestic producers. One of
these provided that the minimum selling price of a metric quintal (100
kilos) of natural wheat should be equal to the market value of the flour
produced from it. A new decree was issued on December 31, 1935, to the
effect that the aforementioned price shall be the quotation on wheat
flour milled in the country from foreign wheat at the places where
domestic wheat is being sold." Mills must use a fixed percentage of
national wheat mixed with imported wheat, according to a decree of
August 27, 1934. Monthly reports are required by a decree of January
2, 1936.

Wheat - World Survey and Outlook

Bennett, M. K., Farnsworth, Helen C., and Working, Holbrook. World wheat
survey and outlook, May 1936. Wheat Studies of the Food Research Institute 12(9): 313-338. May 1936. (Published in Stanford University,
Calif.)

Charts accompanying this study are by P. Stanley King and tables are
by Rosamond Peirce.

Wine - Consumption

Caddow, H. A. Better quality and broadened markets increase consumption.
Wines and Vines 17(4): 10. April 1936. (Published at 85 Second St.,
San Francisco, Calif.)

Contains tables showing by states and trade areas - Pacific Coast
trade area, New York trade area, Middle and South Atlantic area, etc. -
the total and per capita consumption of wine during 1935.

NOTES

Allred, C. E., Sanders, P. C., Collins, W. E., Lnebke, B. H., Matthews, M. T., and Tosch, C. A. Rural relief and rehabilitation possibilities in Jefferson county, Tennessee. 47pp. mimeogr. [Knoxville, Tenn.] April 1, 1936. (U. S. Federal works progress administration. Cooperative plan of rural research. Report no. 10) 173.2 W89Co no.10
    Issued in cooperation with Tennessee Agricultural Experiment Station and Tennessee Welfare Commission.

American liberty league. National lawyers committee. The Welfare clause in the light of the AAA decision. 50pp. [New York city] National lawyers committee of the American liberty league [1936] 280.12 Am342

Association of sugar producers of Puerto Rico. The sugar problem of Puerto Rico. 68pp. [San Juan? P.R., 1936] 281.365 As7
    Excerpts from Porto Rico and its problems, ed. by Victor S. Clark and others, for the Brookings institution (280 C552) (see p.2)

Bartels, Alfred. Die fleischversorgung der stadt Magdeburg. 35pp. [Jena? 1935?] 281.350 B28
        Inaug. diss. - Jena, 1934. Teildruck.
        Bibliography, pp. [37-39]
        The general theme is the meat supply of Magdeburg, and the author discusses the meat trade and its agents, livestock slaughter and meat distribution, slaughter cattle insurance, meat consumption, and livestock and meat prices.

Calder, Alexander. The bacon pig. A guide to producers under the pigs marketing scheme. 11pp. [London, Printed by J. Truscott & son, ltd., 1936?] 281.346 C12

Cammell, Dorothy B. Youth. What civic and service clubs can do to help. 29pp., mimeogr. [Washington, D.C., Feb. 1936] (U.S. Dept. of the interior. Office of education. Circular no. 154) 156.3 C4922 no.154
    Prepared by Committee on Youth Problems.

Clay, A. B. The farm problem; a series of papers dealing with the farm problem as it exists today, and proposing a method of relief based upon the methods of the other big businesses of this generation. 63pp., mimeogr. Middle-branch, O. [1932?] 281.12 C572
    American farms incorporated, the plan, pp. 45-63.

Coulter, J. W. A gazeteer of the territory of Hawaii. 241pp. Honolulu, University of Hawaii, 1935. (University of Hawaii. Research publications no. 11) 500 H31R
        Bibliography, pp. 238-239.

Federal reserve bank of St. Louis. The Federal reserve system today. 40pp. [St. Louis?] 1936. 284 F312
        "Prepared under the auspices of the Federal Reserve Agents' Conference" - Foreword.

- 534 -

Finland. Statens smörkontrollanstalt. Regulations relating to the export of Finnish butter, cheese and process cheese. English text published by State butter control. 21pp. Helsinki, 1935. 286.344 F49

Gt. Brit. Ministry of agriculture and fisheries. Sugar industry (reorganization bill. Amalgamation of the beet sugar manufacturing companies. 16pp. London, H. M. Stationery off., 1936. ([Parliament. Papers by command] Cmd. 5139) 281.366 G79S
    Report of the Sugar Tribunal, pp. 4-9.

Gt. Brit. Permanent consultative committee on official statistics. Guide to current official statistics of the United Kingdom, v. 13 (1934). 350pp. London, H. M. Stationery off., 1935. 241.3 G79

Gt. Brit. Scottish office. Arrangements under section II of the Milk act, 1934 (24 & 25 Geo. 5, ch. 51) for increasing the demand for milk by the supply of milk at reduced rates in schools within the area of the Aberdeen and district milk marketing scheme, 1933. 4pp. Edinburgh, H. M. Stationery off., 1936. 280.344 G793

Kansas. Emergency relief committee. A study of public relief cases in Kansas covered by the federal Social security act... The second of a series of studies of social problems in Kansas and their social and economic costs. 13pp. Topeka, Kans., The Kansas Emergency relief committee, 1935. (Bulletin... no. 288) 284.6 K132

Magyar külügyi tarsasag, Budapest. La Hongrie dans les relations internationales. Édition de l'Association hongroise des affaires étrangères et pour la Société des nations. 383PP. Magyar külügyi tarsasag, Budapest [Athenaeum] 1935. (Questions d'actualité. Idoszeru kerdesek. v.7) 280.177 M27
    "Redige par Olivier d'Eöttevényi et Georges Drucker," p. 6
    "Liste des traités, conventions et accords plurilatéraux et bilatéraux inserés aux lois hongroises pendant la période de 1920-1935 [par Thomas de Marffy-Mantuano]", pp. [337]-353.
    Bibliography, pp. [354]-383.
    The international relations of Hungary are discussed in a series of articles by different authors.

Manchuria. Dept. of foreign affairs. General survey of conditions in Manchoukuo, with special emphasis on economic developments, prepared by the Department of foreign affairs, Manchoukuo government. 57pp. Hsinking, 1935. 280.184 M312 1935
    Revised edition.

Pan American commercial conference. 5th, Buenos Aires, 1935. Report of the delegates of the United States of America to the Pan American commercial conference, held at Buenos Aires, Argentine, May 26-June 19, 1935. 164pp. Washington, U. S. Govt. print. off., 1936. ([U. S.] Department of state. Conference series no. 22) 286.9 P19R
    Publication no. 845.

Public affairs pamphlets, no. 1. Income and economic progress. 34PP. [Wash-ington, 1935?] 280.9 P964
Pub. by Public affairs committee, Washington, D. C.
"This pamphlet was prepared by Maxwell S. Stewart on the basis of a four volume study by the Brookings Institution into the effect of income distribution on economic progress."

Royal agricultural society of England. The journal... including the Farmers' guide to agricultural research... v.96. 506pp. London, J. Murray, 1935. 10 R81

Schnurmacher, Leo, inc., Manila. Review of coconut products for 1935. 24PP. Manila [1936] 286.3779 Sch5

U. S. Dept. of the interior. Office of education. Business problems in farming. Suggestions to teachers of vocational agriculture for use in conducting agricultural evening classes. 71pp. Washington, U. S. Govt. print. off., 1936. (U. S. Dept. of the interior. Office of education. Vocational education bulletin no. 183)
U. S. Dept. of the interior. Office of education, Agricultural series no. 48.
Bibliography, p. 71.

U. S. National emergency council. Kansas. Kansas. Report of semi-annual coordination meeting, the National emergency council... Topeka, Kansas, November 25, 1935. Jonas W. Graber, state director, 210 Federal Building, Topeka, Kansas. 80pp. [Topeka, 1935] 280.029 Un3

U. S. National emergency council. Oklahoma. Oklahoma coordination meeting of federal departments and agencies... Oklahoma City, Oklahoma, November 27, 1935. 132pp. [Oklahoma City, Okla., 1935] 280.069 Un3
At head of title: National Emergency Council.
Proceedings of the semi-annual statewide coordination meeting.

U. S. Tennessee valley authority. Report to the Congress on the unified development of the Tennessee River system. Submitted by the Board of directors. 105pp. [Knoxville, Tenn] March 1936. 173.2 T25U

CORRECTION

The second item on page 363 should read: Berberoff, Theodor. Untersuchungen über die landwirtschaftlichen betriebsysteme Bulgariens. 68pp. Berlin, P. Parey, 1935. ([Germany] Reichs-und Pr. Ministeriums für Ernährung und Landwirtschaft. Berichte über Landwirtschaft, n. F. 114. Sonderheft) 18 G31A

AGRICULTURAL ECONOMICS LITERATURE WILL NOT BE PUBLISHED IN JULY OR AUGUST
V. 10. No. 7 WILL APPEAR IN SEPTEMBER

mon resolution to get the work done with the utmost excellence it admits of. — L. P. Jacks

| Vol. 10 | September 1936 | No 7 |

FEATURES IN THIS ISSUE

AGRICULTURAL ECONOMICS LITERATURE was not published in July or August

The Index to Vol 9, 1935 of AGRICULTURAL ECONOMICS LITERATURE has been finished and sent to addresses on the mailing list Copies are still available upon request

AGRICULTURAL ECONOMICS LITERATURE

Vol. 10   September 1936   No. 7

SIGNED REVIEWS

Longobardi, Cesare.   Land-reclamation in Italy; rural revival in the build-
    ing of a nation. Translated from the Italian by Olivia Rossetti Agresti.
    243pp. London: P. S. King & son, ltd., 1936.   54 L86
        The author of this book has been one of the important members of the
    staff of the International Institute of Agriculture ever since the work
    of that institution began. He was present through the early days of
    that institute when David Lubin was patiently and persistently working
    to make a significant International Institution which would enable
    farmers of each part of the world to know what other farmers were doing
    in other parts of the world and to know the facts regarding the inter-
    national exchange of agricultural products.
        The author is an economist, a statistician and a philosopher. That
    he is a philosopher is indicated by the phrase: "Life, thought, material
    facts themselves, contain permanent unchanging elements alongside others
    destined to renew or decay. Progress adds to the permanent and un-
    changing elements, new discoveries, more harmonious adjustment, higher
    ideals."
        Another quotation gives some notion of his idea of the way in which
    progress may be attained: "Religion and science agree in teaching that
    safety, progress, life, strength, are secured at the cost of sacrifice
    and by overcoming difficulties."
        The translator of this work, Mrs. Agresti, also had much to do with
    the formation of the International Institute of Agriculture. From the
    day David Lubin arrived in Rome to interest the King of Italy in taking
    the lead in organizing an International Institute of Agriculture, Mrs.
    Agresti was his competent secretary, interpreter and counselor.
        The American reader may find a number of words somewhat strange to
    him for the reason that the American use of words is sometimes differ-
    ent from that of England and the British Empire, but in all cases the
    text will be easy to follow when the root meanings of the words are
    recognized, e. g., the word "circumscription" is used to describe
    an area of land included in a given reclamation project. We have been
    in the habit of speaking of districts in this same sense, e. g., drain-
    age district, irrigation district, etc. When one is drawn into the in-
    terest of the book these international characteristics are soon for-
    gotten.
        One who is acquainted with Dr. Longobardi and has seen him in action
    will understand why he wrote this book. People are continually writing
    to the International Institute of Agriculture or coming in person to make
    inquiry regarding the new agricultural activities in Italy. Dr. Longobardi,

who speaks English well, is the one person always assigned to give information to the English-speaking visitors. The continuous answering of the
same questions for so many people naturally suggested the writing of a
book for the English readers which would provide those answers.

The table of contents of the book at once indicates the kind of questions that are answered. The major heads are as follows: I. Towards
Higher Standards of Living; II. General Notions on Integral Land-Reclamation; III. Integral Land-Reclamation and the Wheat Campaign; IV. Land-
Reclamation Legislation; V. Integral Land-Reclamation, Executive Organs
and Procedure; VI. Execution and Financing of Land Reclamation Works;
VII. Some Land-Reclamations Described; VIII. Mussolini on Land-Reclamation.

The idealism behind the reclamation projects in Italy is indicated
in the first chapter, which gives the philosophical setting of the whole
undertaking and points toward the improvement of the standard of living
of the people as the major objective. Reclamation is not carried on
for the sake of the land, but for the benefit of the people.

It is the integral character of recent reclamation work in Italy
which distinguishes the present undertaking from those of the past.
By the integral character is meant that all of the phases of work
which are essential to the development of the land of a given area to
the point where it may become the basis of a prosperous community are
undertaken in a coordinated way. Reafforestation, changing the course
of water flow, drainage and irrigation of land, leveling of the land,
construction of roads, putting up of houses and barns, building of
villages with schools, churches, hotels, recreational centers and shops,
putting in of water supplies and electric lines are all carried forward
as a part of one undertaking.

When the foreign visitor drives through an area of the old Pontine
marshes, in the process of being reclaimed, and notes that little tram
lines are being used for hauling the dirt from high places to fill pot-
holes several rods away, he wonders how such great expenditures can be
made to produce farm land. He is soon told that this leveling of the
land is a part of the war against the malaria-producing mosquito and
that this work relates not simply to the value of the particular piece
of land, but to the sanitation of the whole area. The same struggle is
indicated by the presence of screens on all the windows and doors of the
farm houses.

In the last twelve years Italy has put more than a hundred million
days' work into the reclamation of agricultural lands. In the years
1933-4 there were 71,586 workers continuously employed on these projects.
An area of 4,733,982 hectares of land has been or is in the process of
being reclaimed. These projects are scattered widely in the northern,
central, and southern parts of Italy.

Not only have important areas been added to the agricultural land of
Italy, but the productivity of the land formerly in use has been greatly
increased. The best illustration of this comes from the increase in wheat
products. During the past ten years there has been a special campaign to
increase the production of wheat in Italy. Prior to that time Italy was
producing about two-thirds of the wheat required and importing about one-
third. In the past ten years the wheat production has been increased

so that the average for the four years 1932-5 inclusive was approximately 50 per cent greater than the average production for the six years from 1920-5. During this time the area in wheat increased only 7 per cent, showing that the increased production was in a large measure due to the increase in yield. The increase in yield was due to several reasons, the most important of which was the introduction of new varieties of high-yielding, early-ripening wheat suited to the various parts of Italy.

Fortunately, the scientific work essential to the production of new varieties of wheat had been carried on for many years before the wheat campaign began. The bringing of these new varieties of wheat into common use required a thoroughly organized educational campaign in which the agricultural extension service proved invaluable. In addition to the use of better varieties of wheat, better culture added much to the success of the undertaking. The way in which the farmers of Italy cooperated in this undertaking is a matter of great importance. This was stimulated by offering prizes to the farmers to produce high yields of wheat. These prizes stimulated the use of the best seed, more careful cultivation, and increased fertilization of the land as means of increasing the yields.

The book contains the history of land legislation as it relates to reclamation. It describes the way in which the reclamation projects were financed, the extent to which the work has been carried on by public enterprise and the extent to which it has been carried forward by private individuals. It emphasizes particularly the importance of the association of government action and private enterprise such as will insure the productive use and enlargement of the nation's available territory. One point stressed in the book is that for centuries there have been large estates in Italy on which the land has been used very extensively, while at the same time there have been rural people dwelling in poverty on small parcels of land who might have been available for making more intensive use of the land of large estates and in this way have had an opportunity to improve their conditions of living. In the present regime these poor but industrious people are having their opportunity.

In general the spirit of cooperation has prevailed in the conversion of these large estates into intensively cultivated agricultural lands, but where the landlord was indisposed for financial or other reasons to make the necessary improvements in the method of using his land and where the lack of cooperation stood in the way of a district reclamation project, the land was taken over by the semi-public corporation which had the project in hand, was put into condition for more intensive farming, and was disposed of, usually in smaller lots, to those who wished to make use of the land.

Chapter 7 gives a more concrete description of a number of the important reclamation projects and Chapter 8 gives many quotations from Mussolini which go far toward suggesting the spirit in which these courageous undertakings have been carried forward. To the reviewer it seems that the success of these projects has been due quite as much to the cooperation of all the people and the utilization of the best information and the best equipped specialists, as to the large vision and the will-power of The Leader. – H. C. Taylor, director, Farm Foundation, Chicago, Ill.

DESCRIPTIVE NOTES AND ABSTRACTS

Agricultural Atlas - Italy

Marescalchi, Arturo. Atlante agricolo dell'Italia fascista. 92 carte a 16
colori e 145 grafici, con autografo di S. E. il capo del governo. 10pp.
69 maps. Novara, Istituto geografico de Agostini [1933?] 281.176 M33
At head of title: Arturo Marescalchi, Luigi Visintin.
This is a collection of colored maps illustrating the agriculture of
Fascist Italy; Climate, area, population, rural housing and reclamation
are featured as well as the production of the principal crops.

Agricultural Economics Society, England

Cohen, Ruth L. Research and price control. 14pp. [Reading, Eng., 1936]
Proof - for private circulation. This proof is circulated in advance
of the Agricultural Economics Society's meeting at Oxford, 3rd July to
6th July [1936]

Conacher, H. M. The relations of land tenure and agriculture. 19pp.
[Reading, Eng.. 1936]
Proof-for private circulation. This proof is circulated in advance
of the Agricultural Economics Society's meeting at Oxford, 3rd July to
6th July [1936]
Presidential address, 1936.

McDougall, F. L. World agriculture and the problems of nutrition. 11pp.
[Reading, Eng., 1936]
Proof - for private circulation. This proof is circulated in advance
of the Agricultural Economics Society's meeting at Oxford, 3rd July to
6th July [1936]

Agricultural Labor - Italy

Confederazione fascista dei lavoratori dell'agricoltura. L'alimentazione
dei lavoratori agricoli in Italia. 47pp. Roma [Soc. an. "arte della
stampa"] 1936. 283 C7624A
A brief study of the improvement in the diet of rural workers under
the Fascist regime and with special reference to the effect on it of the
collective labor contracts.

Confederazione fascista dei lavoratori dell' agricoltura. Azione, sviluppi
e finalità della Confederazione fascista dei lavoratori dell' agricoltura
(Attività confederale e sindacale 1º gennaio 1934. XII - 10 maggio 1935 -
XIII) 235pp. [Roma, Società anonima arte della stampa, 1935]
283 C7624Az
Relazione presentata dal presidente confederale al Convegno nazionale
di Bologna il 14 maggio dell' anno XIII" - p. [3]
An account of the organization and aims of the Fascist Confederation
of Agricultural Workers.

Confederazione fascista dei lavoratori dell' agricoltura. Il "lavoro" nella
coltura della vite in Italia.   35pp. Roma [Societa anonima arte della
stampa, 1935] 283 C7624La
      Signed: Franco Angelini, presidente della Confederazione fascista dei
lavoratori dell' agricoltura.
      Employment of labor in viticulture in Italy.

Confederazione fascista dei lavoratori dell' agricoltura. Il "lavoro" nella
floro-orto-frutticoltura. 22pp. Roma [Soc. an. "arte della stampa",
1934] 283 C7624L
      Signed: Franco Angelini, presidente della Confederazione fascista dei
lavoratori dell' agricoltura.
      Employment of labor, hours of work, etc. in the cultivation of vegeta-
bles, fruits and flowers.

Agricultural Labor - Scotland

Gt. Brit. Committee on farm workers in Scotland. Report of the Committee on
farm workers in Scotland, 1936. Presented by the secretary of state for
Scotland to Parliament by command of His Majesty. 51pp. Edinburgh, H. M.
Stationery off., 1936.   ([Parliament. Papers by command] Cmd. 5217) 283
G7933
      The terms of reference of this committee follow:
      "'To examine the existing system of employment and remuneration of farm
workers in Scotland; to enquire what changes have taken place in recent
years; and to report whether in their view it is desirable to take any action, and if so what action, for regulating the remuneration or the conditions of employment of these workers.'"

Agriculture - England

Blewitt, Guy. The observations of an owner-occupier. 57pp. Chelmsford
[Eng.] J. H. Clarke & co. [1934] 281.171 B61
      The Journal of the Ministry of Agriculture of Great Britain in its
issue of Nov. 1935, p.843 reviews this publication as follows:
      "In this pamphlet, the author relates an experience of twelve years
as owner-occupier of a mixed farm in Essex. The story originally appeared in serial form in The Essex Farmers' Journal, and is repub-
lished for the benefit of a wider public that will be interested in the
observations of a practical agriculturist. The seven chapters devoted
to management, labour, the balance sheet, buying and selling, rations,
breeding and crops respectively, are followed by tables of dairy and
pig rations, and a specimen quarterly feed sheet.
      "Perhaps not everyone will accept the view that 'from a national
point of view, it is much more important for the farmer to employ
twice the labour at the present wage than the same labour at twice
the wage.' Col. Blewitt defends the existing standard of living of
the agricultural labourer. 'If there is hardship,' he suggests, 'it
is in the legislation which necessitates the payment of ridiculous
wages in the towns... The business of producing food will never allow of extravagant wages or the employment of anyone who is not pulling
full weight.'
      "Possibly the most interesting chapter is that concerned with the

Balance Sheet, which must be ultimately the test of success or failure
in any business. During his twelve years of farming Col. Blewitt has
admittedly lost money, but 'in fairness to agriculture' he suggests
that 'had the money been invested in anything else, the losses might
quite easily have been greater.' There will be differences of opinion
with regard to many of the author's conclusions, but most readers will
agree with Sir Edward Grigg when he says: 'The more men we can attract
to the land with Guy Blewitt's spirit and intelligence the better for
England.'"

Agriculture - Union of South Africa

Leppan, H. D.   The Union's farming resources.   11pp. Pretoria, 1935.
     (Pretoria. University. Series 1, 30)   276.4 T68
          Distributors: J. L. van Schaik, ltd., Pretoria.
          This lecture delivered to the Workers' Educational Association at the
     Witwatersrand University, begins with the following paragraph:
          "The aim of rational production is consumption; obviously, then, any
     appraisal of the resources of a country must involve a consideration not
     only of the dictates of the physical and other controls over production
     but also what the possibilities for the disposal of surpluses are. Con-
     sequently our intention in this survey of the Union's farming resources
     will be: to endeavor to show what can be produced; to give an account
     of what is produced, together with the present local and external consump-
     tion of that production; and, finally, to speculate on the best manner in
     which our rural resources may be reclaimed, conserved and developed."

Agriculture - U. S.

National industrial conference board. American agricultural conditions and
     remedies; preliminary general review. 57pp. New York, National indus-
     trial conference board, inc. [1936] (Studies no. 224)   281.12 N215.
          "This study was made by the following members of the Board's research
     staff: Dr. Robert J. McFall, Dr. John Lee Coulter, Dr. Robert F. Martin,
     Dr. E. G. Montgomery, Mr. O. F. Gardner, and assistants, under the direc-
     tion of Dr. McFall."
          "Ten years have passed since the Conference Board first undertook to
     draw the serious attention of industrial management to the situation of
     American agriculture. Its volume, 'The Agricultural Problem in the United
     States,' published in 1926, was generally regarded as the first important
     indication of the awakened interest of urban business groups in agricultural
     conditions as a factor in national welfare.
          "This study was followed in 1927 by the report of The Business Men's
     Commission on Agriculture, appointed jointly by the Conference Board and
     the United States Chamber of Commerce, with the Honorable Charles Nagel of
     St. Louis as chairman.
          "These books were widely studied and have long since passed out of print
     The problems they considered remain, and the need on the part of industry
     and business for understanding them and assisting in their solution is
     more imperative than ever.
          "The report here presented is a broad review of the results of a new

study which has been in process by the Board's Research Staff since last
year. The statements in it are necessarily general and concise, and omit
supporting detail and qualifying discussion.
"Experienced observers have been in the field for several months studying farm conditions at first hand. They have conferred with farmers, agricultural leaders, educational experts, and business men whose activities
bring them into close touch with farm problems. Others have been engaged
in analyzing statistical and other data bearing upon the subject. In due
course it is intended to follow this general summary with detailed reports
covering the salient features of the agricultural situation, its development
and the effectiveness of the various attempts to deal with the problems of
farming." - Foreword.

Banking

Clark, L. E. Central banking under the federal reserve system; with special
consideration of the Federal reserve bank of New York. 437pp. New
York, The Macmillan company, 1935. 284 C544
Thesis (Ph.D.) - Columbia University.
Bibliography, pp. 413-420.
The author states the purpose of this book in the preface in the following words:
"In this book I have sought to provide an account of the development
of the Federal Reserve system during the twenty years of its existence,
laying particular stress upon its operation in the capacity of a central
banking institution. The development of the system presents certain
features which are common to all the Federal Reserve banks. In order to
gain a clearer understanding, however, of the operation of central banking
under the system, I have given more detailed consideration to the Federal
Reserve Bank of New York because of the relative importance of its size
and power and the special significance which its policies and operations
have held for the people of the whole United States. There are pointed
out the relationships between that Bank and the other Reserve banks and
the Federal Reserve Board, the failures and the achievements of the Federal
Reserve system, and conditions which have been different from those intended in the Federal Reserve Act. The prime purpose of a central banking
institution is public service. I endeavored, therefore, in the analytical
phases of this book, to judge from the point of view of the general welfare.

Census of Agriculture - U. S. - 1935

U. S. Bureau of the census. United States census of agriculture: 1935.
Reports for states with statistics for counties and a summary for the
United States. Farms, farm acreage and value, and selected livestock
and crops. 951pp. Washington, U. S. Govt. print. off., 1936.
157.41 C3322
Contents. - v. 1. Pt. 1. The northern states. Pt. 2. The southern
states. Pt. 3. The western states. 1936.
"The 1935 Census of Agriculture covered as its principal subjects,
general farm data, including the number of farms, farm acreage, uses
of land, value of farm land and buildings, and farm population; the

acreage and production of crops; the number of livestock by principal
classes and age groups; and the production of specified livestock products.

Colonies - Facts and Figures

Clark, Grover.   The balance sheets of imperialism; facts and figures on colonies.   136pp. Processed.   New York, Columbia university press, 1936.
286 C542
   Published for the Carnegie Endowment for International Peace, Division
of Economics and History.
   Bibliography, pp. [128]-136.
   Among the statistical tables in this volume are the following: Territorial holdings; Migration; Trade, foreign and colonial; Trade by commodity classes; Trade, in commodities; World production percentages.
   "This volume covers the principal items for which statistics have
been compiled from the census returns.   For some of the items not shown in
this report the tabulations have not been completed for all States.
Statistics not included in this report will be published as rapidly as
the tabulations are completed."   - Introduction.

The Constitution

Wallace, H. A.   Whose Constitution?   An inquiry into the general welfare.
336pp.   New York, Reynal & Hitchcock [1936]   280.12 W152W
   Part 1, Forces of Change, contains the following chapters: "A more
Perfect Union": 1787; Farmers in the Saddle: 1858; In Gold we Trust:
1896; Down to the Sea in Ships: 1919; Stewing in Our Own Juices: 1932;
1936, Shake Hands with 1787!
   Part 2, The General Welfare Today, contains the following chapters:
"The Blessings of Liberty"; Soil and the General Welfare; Population and
the General Welfare; Foreign Trade and the General Welfare; Machinery
and the General Welfare; Corporations and the General Welfare.
   Part 3, We the People, contains the following chapters: The Wise Young
Men of 1787; The Elder Statesmen; The Court of Last Resort.
   Part 4, Democracy in Action, contains the following chapters: National
Problems Nationally Solved; For the Long Pull; There is an American Way.

Consumer Market Data Handbook - 1936

Dawson, R. W.   Consumer market data handbook 1936.   373pp., mimeogr.
[Washington, D. C.] June 1936.   (U. S. Dept. of commerce. Bureau of
foreign and domestic commerce. Market research series no. 15)
157.54 M34 no. 15
   "This volume should be used in conjunction with related information
available from other sources, such as the 1933 Census of American Business
and the previous volumes in this series of consumer market data handbooks
("Market Data Handbook of the United States", 1929); "General Consumer
Market Statistics", 1932; published by the U. S. Department of Commerce),
as well as in connection with data to be published in the future, such as
that from the comprehensive study of incomes of individuals now being
made by the Bureau of Internal Revenue, and the new 1935 Census of Business.

"This is more than a valuable source book of statistics; it is in effect
a nation-wide survey of the markets for consumer goods. Results of the
original counts of Governmental and private organizations, costing many
millions of dollars, have been combined here, important percentage and per
capita relationships have been worked out, and the whole assembled in a
manner selected by experienced sales and research men as being the easiest
to use in making practical applications of market data." - Foreword.

Consumption

Lough, W. H., and Gainsbrugh, M. R.   High-level consumption: Its behavior;
  its consequences.   345pp.   New York and London, McGraw-Hill book company,
  inc., 1935.   280.12 L92
      The scope of the book is outlined in the preface as follows:
      "This book is addressed, in the first instance, to business men.   It
offers measurements and forecasts of national consumption which should
help us to steer clear of some of the worst blunders of the 1920's...
      "The book is addressed, also, to a wider audience.   Statistical studies
of consumption have been for the most part fragmentary.   Many doubtful assumptions and conclusions have followed.   More important, the changed character of consumption when it advances beyond the subsistence level and the
unsettling effects of high-level consumption have been generally neglected.
      "Those who are interested in economic and social questions will dis-
cover in the following pages considerable fresh material bearing on consumers' savings, family borrowings and spendings, costs of distribution
of consumption goods, American habits of living, validity of cost-of-liv-
ing indexes, main sources of instability of consumption, and the feasibility of achieving a workable balance between consumers' demands and productive capacity.
      "Those who are concerned primarily with national policies will perhaps
see more plainly the unsolved difficulties inherent in attempted control
by government of production and investment, a control which implies either
foreknowledge or regulation of consumers' demands.
      "Consumption is the chief x-factor in many of our vital problems.   Well-
grounded estimates of consumers' outgo, if correctly analyzed and interpreted, have much to contribute, I believe, to a clearer understanding of
depression and recovery.
      "Unfortunately, the estimates here submitted are not at all points well-
grounded, because essential data are lacking.   But they will have to serve
provisionally.   More intensive work in this field by many hands is an urgent
need."
      Appendix G contains notes on the estimates and conclusions in America's
Capacity to Consume which was published by the Brookings Institution in
Washington after the present study was completed in manuscript.

Cooperation

Marriott, V. E., ed. Kagawa and cooperatives. 15pp.   Chicago, Ill., The
  Kingdom of God fellowship, 1936.   280.2 M34
      Bibliography, p. [16]

- 545 -

Warbasse, J. P.   The unending crisis, by Dr. J. P. Warbasse.   Vision and
      loyalty imperative, by L. S. Herron.   Two articles dealing with import-
      ant phases of cooperation.   [8]pp.   Minneapolis, Minn., Northern states
      cooperative league [193-?]   280.2 W19U

Cooperation - Canada

Richards, A. E.   Farmers' business organizations in Canada, 1935.   55pp.
      Ottawa, J. G. Gardiner, 1935.   (Canada. Dept. of agriculture. Publica-
      tions 481. Tecnnical bulletin 3. Oct. 1935)   7 C16T no.3.
         "The contents of this report, which are based on information received
      from farmers' business organizations in Canada in 1933 and 1934, summarize
      the business activities of co-operating associations during the crop years
      1932 and 1933.   The information contained herein supplements and brings up
      to date the results published in Bulletin No. 173, New Series." - Foreword.

Cooperation - United States

Elsworth, R. H.   Statistics of farmers' cooperative business organizations
      1920-1935.   129pp.   Washington [U. S. Govt. print. off.] May 1936.
      (U. S. Farm credit administration. Cooperative division. Bulletin no. 6)
      166.2 E87 no.6
         Contents: Development of cooperative types; Progress of farmer coopera-
      tion; Cotton cooperatives; Associations marketing dairy products; Associa-
      tions handling forage creps; Associations marketing fruits and vegetables;
      Grain-marketing associations; Livestock-marketing associations; Associa-
      tions marketing nuts; Poultry and poultry products; Tobacco-marketing asso-
      ciations; Wool and mohair cooperatives; Cooperative purchasing of farm
      supplies; Associations providing business services.

Cooperation, Consumer

[Chase, Stuart]   The story of Toad lane.   15pp.   [New York city, Consumers'
      cooperative services, inc., 1935.]   280.2 C38
         "In these pages in the story of the twenty-eight weavers of Rochdale
      and how they founded the Cooperative system that went 'round the world."
      Inside cover.

Cowling, Ellis.   A short introduction to consumers' cooperation. 2d ed., re-
      vised.   48pp.   Chicago, Ill., Central states cooperative league, 1935.
      280.2 C832 Ed.2
         This pamphlet "is written primarily for the youth of high school and
      college age and intended principally for use in high schools, colleges,
      church schools and young people's study groups in general.

Negley, Henry.   Principles of consumers cooperation.   [4]pp.   Minneapolis,
      Minn. [1935]   (Pamphlet no. 5. Cooperative educational series. Midland
      cooperative wholesale)   280.2 N312

Northern states co-operative league. Fundamentals of consumer cooperation, by
V. S. Alanne. 120pp. Minneapolis, Minn., Northern states cooperative
league, 1936. 280.2 N815 Ed.4
Bibliography, p. 120.
The chapter headings follow: The Origin of Consumer Cooperation;
The Aims and Purposes of Consumer Cooperation; The Rochdale Principles;
Rochdale Methods and Policies; The Structure and Operation of a Consumer
Cooperative; Organization and Administration of Consumer Cooperatives;
Definitions and Classifications; Various Types of Consumer Cooperatives;
Cooperative Federations; A Consumer Cooperative vs. a Capitalistic Stock
Company; Differences Between Consumer Cooperation and Producer Cooperation;
'Cooperatism' as a Philosophy of Consumer Cooperation; and Miscellany.

Warbasse, J. P. Cooperative democracy through voluntary association of the
people as consumers; a discussion of the cooperative movement, its philosophy, methods, accomplishments, and possibilities, and its relation to the
state, to science, art, and commerce, and to other systems of economic
organization... 3d edition, completely rewritten. 285pp. New York and
London, Harper & brothers, 1936. 280.2 W19C Ed.3
Bibliography, pp.271-273.

Warbasse, J. P. What is consumer's cooperation? A brief answer to a question
of timely interest. 9pp. Minneapolis, Minn. [1935?] (Pamphlet no. 4.
Midland cooperative oil association) 280.2 W19Wh

Webb, Beatrice (Potter) "Mrs. Sidney Webb," The discovery of the consumer.
32pp. New York City [1934] (Cooperative league. Pamphlet no. 353)
280.2 W383
Reprinted by permission of the Cooperative wholesale society, ltd.,
Manchester, England.
The foreword, signed by E. R. Bowen, General Secretary of The Cooperative
League reads as follows:
"The Discovery of the Consumer by Mrs. Sidney Webb is to me the clearest
brief analysis of the fundamentals of a future Consumer-Producer Cooperative
Economic Organization of Society I have ever read.
"It discusses Consumers' Cooperation in its two-fold forms — voluntary
and obligatory — and its relationship to a universal organization of pro-
ducers in vocational groups.
"Before her marriage to Sidney Webb she wrote in 1891, under her maiden
name of Beatrice Potter, the original philosophic analysis of the Consumers' Cooperative Movement in the notable book 'The Cooperative Movement in
Great Britain,' which is still standard to-day. Later, after thirty years
of study in the birthplace of Consumers' Cooperation she and her husband
together wrote in 1921 'The Consumers' Cooperative Movement.'
"Now Mrs. Webb has summed up forty years of research in this pamphlet
which she has entitled by the significant name 'The Discovery of the Consumer.'

"Here in America we have acted largely in the past as producers. We
need to discover that we are also consumers and organize ourselves into
Consumers' Cooperative Purchasing Associations. This pamphlet will help
you to understand the necessity and ways of organizing as a consumer and
induce you to start action in your community."

Cooperation, Consumer - Great Britain

Darling, George. The C W S of today; an illustrated survey of achievements.
32pp., illus., map. Manchester [etc.] Co-operative wholesale society,
limited, Publicity department, Publications and information section [1934
280.29 C785C 1934
    First issued, November 1932... revised and reprinted, June 1933...re-
vised and reprinted July 1934." - p. 2 of cover.

Cotton - Financing

Kennedy, S. J.   Profits and losses in textiles; cotton textile financing
since the war. 257pp. New York and London, Harper &brothers, 1936.
284 K38
    Bibliography, pp. 215-220
    Partial contents: The background of cotton textile financing; Financ-
ing through government agencies; Proposed roads to recovery: increased
consumption; Technological progress in the cotton textile industry; Proposed roads to recovery: increase in consumption through reduction of
price; and Proposed roads to recovery: control of supply.

Cotton - Trade.International

Borroni, Ugo. Il commercio del cotone. I cotoni Americani. 291pp. Milano.
Dott. A. Giuffrè. 1936. (Università Commerciale L. Bocconi. Istituto di
Ricerche Tecnico Commerciali. Pubblicazioni Serie I. n. 9)
    This volume which deals exclusively with the marketing and export of
American cotton, forms the first part of a comprehensive study of the
international cotton trade. A later volume will deal with cotton from
India, Egypt, and other less prominent sources. The book contains three
chapters. In Chapter I we find a description of the physical and economic
characteristics of cotton production in the Cotton Belt, including the
methods of production, the size of the enterprises engaged in cotton production and their administrative methods. Chapter II deals with the many
phases of the marketing of cotton in the United States, from the operations of the local storekeeper to those of the cotton buyer, the scalper,
the fobman and the merchants' take-up man. In Chapter III the author
studies the wholesale trade in and the export of American cotton, the
economic functions and activities of the spot cotton market, the futures
market, the spinners' market, the operations at fixed price or on call
and the factorage system. He concludes with a survey of American cotton
cooperative organizations and its economic activity.

Schriebl, K. G.   Der amerikanische baumwollgürtel mit besonderer berücksichtigung seiner verlagerung. (Teildruck) 44pp. Wien, 1934.
   281.372 Sch72
         Inaug.-diss. - Hochschule für welthandel, Wien.
         Bibliography, pp. 41-44.
         This study undertakes to show the changes in the position of cotton
   in the United States and their causes.

Cotton and Government Activities

Garside, A. H.   Government activities in cotton and their effects on the industry.   11pp. [New York? 1936]   281.372 G19
         An address delivered before the convention of the Atlantic Cotton Asso-
   ciation at Greenville, S. C., April 3, 1936.
         Mr. Garside's conclusions are briefly stated as follows:
         "Now, what are the conclusions to be drawn from all these changes that
   have taken place in the cotton industry and cotton trade, as to the ability of the United States Government to control the world price for cotton,
   and as to the effects of efforts by the Government to that end?
         "First of all, these Government activities have demonstrated that it
   is utterly beyond the power of the United States Government to raise the
   world price of cotton, either by assisting growers in withholding supplies
   from market or by curtailing production of cotton in this country, except
   to the extent of a few cents a pound for a very brief period, pending the
   inevitable increase of foreign acreage and foreign production...
         "Secondly, Government activities in cotton in recent years have shown
   that the only way by which the United States can raise the world price even
   temporarily is by cutting down the American cotton-growing industry and sur-
   rendering a portion of the market for American cotton to foreign producers..
         "Thirdly, the movement of the price of cotton during the last three years,
   while the Government has been bringing about curtailment of production, demonstrates - especially if allowance is made for the effect of devaluation of
   the dollar - that such temporary increase in the price per pound as may be
   brought about by such drastic decrease of production as this country has effected in these years is not enough to increase materially, if at all, the
   growers' net income, since most or all of what the growers gain in added
   price per pound, they lose by reduction of the number of pounds which they
   have for sale...
         "Fourthly, cotton trade developments which have followed lending opera-
   tions by our Government demonstrate that, when a substantial portion of the
   American cotton crop is withheld from market, even for a few months, by such
   methods as Government loans at or near current price levels, a large portion
   of the market for such withheld cotton is lost to foreign growths, and the
   impounded cotton subsequently acts as a depressant to prices. In other words,
   Government loans on the American cotton crop, so near current price levels

that they affect the price, inevitably transfer world consumption from American to foreign cottons, with resultant loss to American cotton growers of a portion of their market. The impounding of cotton under Government loans works this way inevitably, since relative prices of American and foreign cottons always adjust themselves in such a way as to absorb those quantities of each which are offered freely in commercial channels. The belief in some quarters that Government loans to growers are helpful to the producers, by preventing a seasonal decline of cotton prices during the harvesting period, overlooks the fact, readily proven, that cotton prices during the harvesting period average as high as, or higher than, the average of prices during the rest of the season, if allowance is made for carrying charges."

Economic History - China

Chi, Ch'ao-Ting. Key economic areas in Chinese history as revealed in the development of public works for water-control. 168pp. London, G. Allen & Unwin ltd. [1936] 277.184 C43
Issued under the auspices of the American Council Institute of Pacific Relations.
Bibliography, pp. 151-164.
The author states the purpose of his book as follows:
"The present work offers the conception of the dynamics of the Key Economic Area as an aid to the understanding of Chinese economic history. By tracing the development of the Key Economic Area through an historical study of the construction of irrigation and flood-control works and transport canals, it aims to show the function of the Key Economic Area as an instrument of control of subordinate areas and as a weapon of political struggle, to indicate how it shifts, to reveal its dynamic relation to the problem of unity and division in Chinese history, and to give, on the basis of this approach, a concrete and historical-descriptive analysis of one phase of the economic development of China. The book does not purport to give a new interpretation of Chinese history as a whole. However, if the concept of the Key Economic Area proves helpful to the solution of one of the fundamental problems in Chinese history, it cannot but affect the understanding and interpretation of the whole process of Chinese historical development."

Economic History - Europe

Heaton, Herbert. Economic history of Europe. 775pp. New York and London, Harper & brothers, 1936. 277.17 H35 ...
Bibliography at end of most chapters.
The scope of this book is indicated by the author in the preface as follows:
"In the following pages I have attempted to survey the economic life and development of Europe from the emergence of the ancient civilizations in the eastern Mediterranean to the dislocation and perplexities of the nineteen-thirties. Nearly half the space has been allotted to the years since 1700, and as the book has been in preparation since 1930 it could not escape from excessive preoccupation with post-War problems. But I have tried to avoid writing a mere preface to this morning's news, and have given the ancient,

medieval and early modern periods space which they merit because their story
is interesting and their contribution is important. No understanding of
current conditions can be obtained by beginning the study of economic history
at 1760, or 1700 or even at 1492.

"The book is intended for students, especially American students, who have
done no previous work in the subject, apart perhaps from a brief excursion to
a medieval manor or the Industrial Revolution in a general course of European
history. Hence I have omitted discussion of those controversial topics which
belong to the higher altitudes of economic historiography, and have been content to describe and explain conditions and significant developments."

Chapters relating particularly to agriculture are: Rural Change and Expansion (medieval) British Agriculture since 1700; The Agricultural Development
of France and Germany since 1700.

Economic Situation - U. S. - 1934 - 1935

Beard, C. A., ed. Current problems of public policy; a collection of
    materials ... with the collaboration of George H. E. Smith. 527pp.
    New York, The Macmillan company, 1936. 280.12 B38C

The statement which follows has been taken from the preface signed
by Finla G. Crawford, Chairman, Ben A. Arneson, and Charles A. Beard.

"Among the tendencies in American education none is more striking
than the increasing attention given to current social problems in colleges and schools...

"Yet it cannot be said that the materials for instruction in this
field are readily available... Materials pour pell mell from the press,
and may be supplemented, in many cases, by direct observation. On controversial issues it is often impossible to secure effective statements
of all the views in conflict. Even the primary documents cannot always
be obtained for immediate class room use. Nor are teachers always
trained in source methods - the finding and criticism of current materials for balanced and effective presentation.

"Hence it may be said with safety that there is no more pressing
task in contemporary education than that of making available to teachers
authentic and appropriate materials on current social problems. The
task, no doubt, is perplexing and no ready way of disposing of it has been
discovered; but a beginning may be made. It was to make a beginning that
the American Political Science Association, at its meeting in Chicago in
January, 1935, created a sub-committee of its Committee on Policy and
charged that body with surveying the problem of materials and preparing
a volume that might be considered as illustrative, if nothing more.

"This volume is the outcome of the sub-committee's labors. It is
governed by certain limitations adopted at the outset. The field chosen
is that of government. The emphasis is on ideas and functions rather
than the machinery of government. All papers chosen are official in
character. The time covered is, roughly speaking, the federal fiscal
year, 1934-1935. The first Part deals with opinion. It presents the
platforms and declarations of parties and leaders proposing action and
bidding for the support of voters. The second Part contains official
statements of certain leading problems of the period. The nature of

these statements calls for a word of caution. They do not give an all-round view of each issue. They give the official view and are, therefore, merely the starting points of discussion. To present all angles of debate would require a whole volume for each topic. But we have taken the position that both as a matter of training and judicial practice in teaching the beginning should be an authentic statement of the official case. Yet, by no means all the papers included here are ex parte documents. Many of them are fact-statements bearing on contemporary problems. They have been prepared by officials, it is true, but may be taken as reasonably accurate, as far as the facts run. Part III touches only a few striking features of recent administrative development.

"Such is the plan of the book. Overwhelmed by thousands of pages of materials collected at the outset for consideration, the sub-committee simply had to choose some arbitrary principles of limitation. It can only claim that in any broad consideration of contemporary problems of American government the papers here presented deserve to be brought into view."

Chapter 23. Problems of Depression Adjustment in Agriculture, pp. 358-397.

Economic Situation - U. S. and Gt. Britain - 1935

Beveridge, Sir. W. H. Planning under socialism, and other addresses. 142pp. London, New York [etc.] Longmans, Green and co. [1936] 280 B462

The author states in his signed preface that these "talks" all but three of which were broadcast, should be regarded in part as a review of economic events in the year 1935. Some of the titles of the addresses follow: The economic implications of planning under socialism (Herbert Spencer Lecture); Unemployment insurance for agriculture; An American revolution; Unemployment assistance; An economic general staff; Wages and skill; Social investigation and social reform; Leisure as a cure for unemployment; Playing with prices; The paradoxical position of gold; Engineers and economics; Non-economic nationalism; Leisure for men not for machines; Prices and planning; Unemployment and its various causes; and Methods and results in Great Britain and America.

Employment Stabilization Research

Stevenson, R. A., and Vaile, R. S. Balancing the economic controls; a review of the economic studies of the Employment stabilization research institute, University of Minnesota. 96pp. Minneapolis. The University of Minnesota press, 1935. 280 St42

Publications of the Employment Stabilization Research Institute, University of Minnesota, pp. 87-92.

Bureau of Agricultural Economics Market News Service cited on pp. 60-61.

"The Employment Stabilization Research Institute was organized at the University of Minnesota in 1931 for the purpose of making studies of unemployment and conducting certain experiments. Three fairly well-defined types of investigation were involved in the project. The first was primarily a study in economics; the second was in the field of psychology and education; the third was an experiment in the conduct and administration of public employment agencies.

"The Institute conducted its studies over a period of four years and published thirty-six monographs and a number of articles on the several aspects of the problems investigated. It was, of course, necessary to subdivide the field of investigation into many separate projects, each one of which constituted a complete study in itself. With the completion of the work, it seems desirable to bring together the various threads and to review the entire project as a unit. It is for the purpose of giving such an over-all view of the several economic studies that this report has been prepared.

"The report is divided into four parts. In the first there is a general discussion of economic planning. It is the purpose of this section to give a setting and to indicate the broad purposes of a study limited in scope to a regional area.

"The second part is devoted to a series of brief reviews of the several separate studies dealing with economic activities in Minnesota. No attempt has been made to give an inclusive summary of all the findings, since the separate monographs may be had for further inquiry on any of the subjects treated. We have drawn freely from other publications of the Institute without specific citations, since all of the materials are taken from such sources.

"In Part III the problems of balance as between government control and the free working of the price system are once more considered in the light of the conditions described in Part II.

"Finally, in Part IV a program of regional economic planning is suggested. An effort has been made here to consider the problem in its realistic setting and to suggest the immediate steps that might be taken in an effort to introduce a greater degree of stability into the economic system."- Preface.

Experimental Design

Fisher, R. A.   The design of experiments.   252pp.   Edinburgh, London, Oliver and Boyd, 1935.   251 F53D

References and other reading at end of each of the chapters.

"In 1925 the author wrote a book (Statistical Methods for Research Workers) with the object of supplying practical experimenters. and, incidentally, teachers of mathematical statistics, with a connected account of the applications in laboratory work of some of the more recent advances in statistical theory. Some of the new methods, such as the analysis of variance, were found to be so intimately related with problems of experimental design that a considerable part of the eighth Chapter was devoted to the technique of agricultural experimentation, and these Sections have been progressively enlarged with subsequent editions, in response to frequent requests for a fuller treatment of the subject. The design of experiments is, however, too large a subject, and of too great importance to the general body of scientific workers, for any incidental treatment to be adequate. A clear grasp of simple and standardised statistical procedures will, as the reader may satisfy himself, go far to elucidate the principles of experimentation; but these procedures are themselves only the means to a more important end. Their part is to satisfy the requirements of sound and intelligible experimental design, and to supply the machinery for unambiguous interpretation. To attain a clear grasp of these requirements we need to study designs

which have been widely successful in many fields, and to examine their
structure in relation to the requirements of valid inference.
    "The examples chosen in this book are aimed at illustrating the prin-
ciples of successful experimentation; first, in their simplest possible
applications, and later, in regard to the more elaborate structures by
which the different advantages sought may be combined. Statistical discussion has been reduced to a minimum, and all the processes required will
be found more fully exemplified in the previous work. The reader is, however, advised that the detailed working of numerical examples is essential
to a thorough grasp, not only of the technique, but of the principles by
which an experimental procedure may be judged to be satisfactory and effective." - Preface.

Foundations and Trusts

Lindeman, E. C   Wealth & culture... A study of one hundred foundations and
    community trusts and their operations during the decade 1921-1930.   135pp.
    printed and multigraphed.   New York, Harcourt, Brace and company [1936]
    500 L64
        Partial contents: Cultural considerations; The foundation: a symbol
    of surplus wealth; Trends in foundation interests; Notes on a foundation
    bibliography; A list of the foundations and community trusts analysed
    in this study, together with their respective locations and the years of
    organization; and Steps toward a cultural index.

Government Administration

Herring, E. P.   Public administration and the public interest.   416pp.
    New York and London, McGraw-Hill book company, inc., 1936.   280.12 H43
        "This study attempts to analyze the relations between pressure groups
    and officials and to survey various efforts being made to adjust our
    bureaucracy to its heavy responsibilities. In this investigation one is
    tempted to ponder a theory as well as disclose a process. The evidence
    offered in this book suggests the question: what next? Upon what theory
    shall we proceed? What assumptions shall guide governmental action?
        "Economic laissez faire is gone; political laissez faire is passing.
    The government is undertaking the care of groups that are economically
    insecure; it is defending interests that are politically weak. Can a
    democratic government interpret in such positive and specific terms
    the meaning of the general welfare regardless of the strength of the
    underlying interest groups? In theory our government should strike a
    balance among these conflicting forces so as to promote the welfare of
    all. In fact some groups are placed more advantageously than others
    within our governmental structure and under our industrial system. The
    government draws its strength from the very elements it is supposed to
    regulate. Its officials both elective and appointive are subjected to
    constant pressures from these powerful interests. Complete objectivity
    is practically impossible for the elective official. It exposes the
    administrative official to the charge of bureaucratic aloofness. Our
    government must be responsive if democracy is to survive. Yet the cit-

izen in facing public questions seeks to promote his own immediate interests rather than the welfare of all. This attitude becomes the more
dangerous as government extends its activities further into the social
and industrial life of the nation.

"What the final outcome of such tendencies will be no one can say.
The authoritarianism of fascism and the dictatorship of the proletariat
are the two alternatives per istently offered. Before granting the inevi-
tability of either, the possibilities of our present democratic institutions warrant further exploration.

"The administrative experience surveyed in this book gives cause for
hope as well as fear." - Preface.

Among the chapter headings of particular interest are: Political
storms and the Tariff Commission; The place and policy of the Federal
Trade Commission; The Federal Power Commission: The Interstate Commerce
Commission and special interests; Shielding regulatory commissions from
politics; Protecting the consumer; Bringing the consumer interest into
administration; How the Department of Agriculture aids the farmer; Providing services for labor; The Department of Commerce responds to business;
Business support of scientific research.

Grain Trade - Bulgaria

Totev, Anastas IU. The characteristic of the price cathegories [1] and
    their interrelations in the home and export trade of cereals in Bulgaria,
    by Anastas U. Toteff. 48pp. Sofiia, 1933. 284.359 T64
        Text and added title in Bulgarian; summary in English.
        At head of title: Trudove na Institute, po zemledělska ikonomiia pri
    Agronomo-lesovŭdskiia fakultet na Universiteta.
        The English summary states that the aim of this study is to follow
    in both the domestic and the foreign markets, the trade movements and
    prices of the principal grains produced in Bulgaria, namely, wheat,
    maize and barley. Other que.tions relating to the economic policy af-
    fecting their production and trade are considered.

Indian Land Tenure

U. S. National resources board. Lar planning committee. Supplementary re-
    port. Pt. 10. Indian land tenure, economic status, and population trends...
    prepared by the Office of Indian affairs, Department of the interior.
    73pp. Washington, D. C., U. S. Govt.print.off., 1935. 173.2 N214Su
        This report which was prepared under the direction of L. C. Gray and
    John B. Bennett is supplementary to the Report of the Land Planning Com-
    mittee which was issued as part II of the Report on National Planning and
    Public Works in Relation to National Resources and including Land Use and
    Water Resources. 1934.
        This supplementary report is in 4 parts as follows:
        1. Complexities of Indian land tenure arising from the allotment system,
    by Allan G. Harper and Walter V. Woehlke; 2. Social and economic survey of
    selected Indian reservations by Vance Rogers. 3. Agricultural credit
    needs of the Indians, by H. M. Critchfield; 4. The trend of Indian popula-
    tion, by Ray Ovid Hall and Harry I. Nettleton.

International Institute of Agriculture

International institute of agriculture. International yearbook of agricul-
    tural statistics, 1934-35. 896pp. Rome, 1936. 251 In84
    "The present volume does not differ fundamentally from its predecessors
but some additions of detail and some improvements of varying importance
have been made with a view to enhancing the usefulness of the various Tables of the Yearbook...
    "The improvements introduced in the 1934-35 issue of this Yearbook
consist of the additions of some tables to the chapter showing the distribution of crops and production according to country and of a complete
reorganization of the statistical tables relating to vines and viticul-
tural products. The latter innovation is made for the purpose of indicating the relative importance and distribution of the production of table
grapes and grapes for drying.
    "Furthermore, the number of countries included in the section dealing
with trade movements has been considerably increased while special attention has been given to the chapter of index numbers of prices, where certain new series which have recently been compiled have been included. A
beginning has thus been made towards realizing a recommendation to this effect made by the Conference of British Commonwealth Statisticians at Ottawa
in the autumn of 1935." - Letter of transmittal signed by the Secretary -
General of the Institute, Alessandro Brizi.

International Trade

Horn, P. V. International trade, principles and practices. 723pp. New
    York, Prentice-Hall, inc., 1935. 286 H78
    Special references at end of each chapter.
    This volume was reviewed at some length by Gardner Harding in the
New York Times Book Review, Dec. 8, 1935, p. 34. From this, the extract
below has been taken:
    "Professor Horn's work...in comparison with other full-length books
on American aspects of international commerce ...is in reality two excellent books in one. It includes a very comprehensive study of current
foreign-trade problems, including our own reciprocal trade agreement program. It also furnishes the reader with a sound technical digest of exactly what a foreign-trade executive should know, including shipping
documents, credit and sales technique for foreign business, foreign exchange, advertising practice, as well as a competent background in the
status and management of international investments.
    "The book has also a very intelligent innovation, from the teaching
standpoint, in the presentation and arrangement of statistical material
on the share of countries and commodities in modern world commerce. The
tables are supplementary to the text, and spaces are not only left for
figures on subsequent years but for additional developments of vital importance. In consideration of the ever-recurring likelihood of new departures from the gold standard, of sweeping changes for the better in exchange restrictions, and of large-scale changes in the world-trade picture happening beneath our eyes, as in Japan, this is a wise arrangement by which a book with so fine a basic groundwork can be kept for cur-

rent use rather than for increasingly historical reference.

"Beyond a doubt, an international motion of events is returning. Our share in world trade increased last year and probably will be further augmented this year. This is the first really important textbook of the foreign-trade profession which publishers have ventured to put out for several years. Its manifestly increased confidence in the future is a healthy sign that our young men still believe that growth is again possible in American foreign trade and that there should be room for them and for their careers in its renewed expansion."

Land Classification - Tennessee Valley Authority

U. S. Tennessee valley authority. Division of land planning and housing. Land classification section. The rural land classification program, a summary of techniques and uses. 30pp., mimeogr. [Knoxville?, Tenn.] December 1935. 173.2 T25Ru

Partial contents: The nature of the program; The major land classes; The techniques employed; and Possible contributions and applications.

Land Policies - Nebraska

Sheldon, A. E. Land systems and land policies in Nebraska. A history of Nebraska land, public domain and private property, its titles, transfers, ownership, legislation, administration, prices, values, productions, uses, social changes, comparisons from the aboriginal period to 1936. 383pp. Lincoln, Nebr., The Society, 1936. (Nebraska state historical society. Publications, v. 22) 134.9 N27 v.22
Bibliographical footnotes.

The foreword to this volume, signed by Bayard H. Payne of the Nebraska Supreme Court, follows:

"This book deals with the most important subject of interest to the people of Nebraska -land- in its relation to human society.

"It marshals in a masterly way the most important facts connected with the history of land in Nebraska: Indian titles, public domain, homesteading, land grabbing, land frauds, forestry, irrigation, conservation, landlordism, mortgages, rates of interest, moratoriums, land taxation, land riots, land prices, land production and land legislation.

"This book is up to date with presentation of the current problems of social control of crops and land uses now pending before the American public.

"For the citizen of Nebraska the book furnishes indispensable information on the major subject of Nebraska life.

"For scholars and students of all countries the book will be an international authority and reference book in dealing with land questions of every nature.

"It is fortunate indeed that Dr. Sheldon from his wide experience as a homesteader, editor, legislator and scholar has so exhaustively handled this subject of great interest."

Land Use - Gt. Britain

Land utilisation survey of Britain. The land of Britain; tho report of the
Land utilisation survey of Britain, edited by L. Dudley Stamp... Part 78.
Berkshire. by J. Stephenson... with an historical section by W. G. East.
110pp. London, Pub. for the Survey by Geographical publications ltd.,
1936. 282 L223La
Partial contents: Historical introduction; An outline of the geographical background; The land utilisation of Berkshire; The land use regions of Berkshire; and Land utilisation in Berkshire about 1800, by W.
G. East.
The London Daily Mail for March 25, 1936 stated that the material
included in these reports was "arranged as far as possible in such a
manner as to suggest ways in which present land use may be regarded as
indicating potential use, or as a basis for large-scale planning and
development."

Land Use - Planning

U. S. National resources board. Land planning committee. Supplementary report.
pts. 5-6. Washington, U. S. Govt. print. off., 1935. 173.2 N214Su
Contents. - Pt. 5. Soil erosion. A critical problem in American
Agriculture... prepared by the Soil Conservation Service, Department of
Agriculture, Bureau of Agricultural Engineering, Department of Agriculture.
Pt. 6. Maladjustments in land use in the United States... prepared by the
Land Policy Section, Agricultural Adjustment Administration; The Bureau
of Agricultural Economics and the Weather Bureau, Department of Agricul-
ture.

League of Nations Publications

League of nations. Balances of payments 1934. 198pp. Geneva, 1935.
(Series of League of nations Publications. II. Economic and financial.
1935. II. A.20) 280.9 L47P 1935. II. A.20
At head of title: Economic Intelligence Service.

League of nations. Economic intelligence service. Commercial banks, 1929-
1934. 213pp. Geneva, 1935. (Series of League of nations. Publications.
II. Economic and financial. 1935. II. A.2) 280.9 L47P 1935. II. A.2

League of nations. International trade statistics 1934. 364pp. Geneva,
1935. (Série de Publications de la Société des nations. II. Questions
économiques et financières 1935. II. A. 21) 280.9 L47P 1935. II. A.21
At head of title: Service d'études économiques. Statistique du commerce
international 1934.
Text in English and French.
"This volume is intended to be a supplement to Volume II of the 1912-
1926 issue of the Memorandum on International Trade and Balances of Payments (Series of Publications: 1927.II.68/II). It contains statistics
of sixty-five countries, for the years 1932-1934. For information with

regard to the methods employed in different countries in the compilation
of trade statistics and to the definitions of the terms employed, reference should be made to the last-mentioned volume, covering the period
1912-1926.

"The present Volume is bilingual and the countries are given in the
French alphabetical order." - Prefatory Note.

Maps - Gt. Britain

Gt. Brit. Committee on the ordnance survey. Interim report of the departmental
committee on the Ordnance survey. 16pp. London, H. M. Stationery off., 1936.
98.5 G793
    This report contains recommendations for the preparation of a revision
of the Ordnance Survey maps with certain omissions which would make it
possible to complete the maps most needed for town planning purposes. The
Committee considers that this provisional measure "should form a stage in
the subsequent production of revised plans of the normal standard."

Money

Angell, J. W.   The behavior of money; exploratory studies.   207pp. New
York and London, McGraw-Hill book company, inc., 1936.   284 An42
    Prepared under the auspices of the Columbia University Council
for Research in the Social Sciences.
    The author, in his signed preface, writes in part as follows:
"The present volume is an endeavor to increase the supply of facts
about money. It is therefore addressed to all who deal with the fundamental problems of money and banking, whether as bankers, as statesmen,
or as academic students, and to all others who must gauge the significance of current monetary and banking phenomena. It is not a systematic
treatise, and it does not pretend to give complete answers to every question raised. Its several chapters, however, all deal with various aspects of the recent actual behavior of our money supply. They are concerned in part with the internal behavior of the quantity and velocity
of circulation of the money supply itself - with its trends, seasonal
patterns, amplitudes of fluctuation, and the like; and in part with the
relations between the money supply and such things as prices, car load-
ings, industrial production, national income, gold movements, and security transactions. Although the results obtained have been restricted
by the limitations of the materials easily available, and also by the exploratory character of the methods employed, it is hoped that these results will be useful both in the construction of general theoretical analyses and in the formulation of intelligent practical programs for monetary control.

Wicksell, Knut. Lectures on political economy. Edited with an introduction by
Lionel Robbins. v. 2. Money. 238pp. New York, The Macmillan company,
1935.   280 W633L
    Partial contents: The conception and functions of money; Currency; The
velocity of circulation of money. Banking and credit; The exchange value
of money.

National Association of Marketing Officials

National association of marketing officials. Handling of perishable food
products in the terminal market. Proceedings of the seventeenth annual meeting, December 1935, Drake Hotel, Chicago, Illinois. Sidney
A. Edwards, Secretary-Treasurer, Hartford, Connecticut. 64pp.
[n.p., 1936]   280.39 N21SP
    Contents: Greetings by Walter W. McLaughlin; Response, by George
A. Stuart; Developments in marketing, 1935, by A. G. Black; Problems
in packing perishable farm produce, by A. J. Lorion; Report of the
Committee on Standardization of Egg Legislation (Abstract) by James
M. Gwin; Discussion of report, by Charles A. Urner; Interests of Amer-
ican Egg Producers in egg tariffs, by F. A. Donnelly; Perishable transportation developments from the railroad viewpoint, by J. M. Fitzgerald;
Some facts regarding use of the motor truck in marketing perishables,
by M. P. Rasmussen; Transportation problems in terminal produce markets,
by Carl W. Kimball; Mercantile exchanges in terminal markets, by E. H.
Whiting; Functions and operations of the Chicago Poultry Board, by Charles
E. McNeill; Terminal fruit and vegetable auctions in the United States,
by Cutler B. Downer; What title I [National Housing Act] does for you,
by Gael Sullivan; Division of the consumer's meat dollar among distributors, processors, and producers, by Howard C. Greer; Spray residue problems of the Federal Food and Drug Administration, by W. S. Frisbie;
and Administration of the Potato Act of 1935, by A. E. Mercker.

National Resources Committee Report

U. S. National resources committee.   Progress report with statements of
coordinating committees June 15, 1936. Submitted to the President
in accordance with Executive order, no. 7065, June 7, 1935.   61pp.
[Washington, U. S. Govt. print. off., 1936]   173.2 N214P
    List of publications, pp. 53-61
    Part I, Report of Advisory Committee contains sections on Public
Works, Use of land, Production, transportation, consumption, Regional
coordination, State and local planning boards. Part II is Report of
executive officer. Part III contains Report of Land Planning Committee,
Report of Water Resources Committee and Report of the Industrial Committee.

Planning - Regional

U. S. National resources committee. Regional planning. Part 2 - St. Louis
region.   68pp.   Washington, U. S. Govt. print. off., June 1936.
173.2 N214Rp Pt. 2
    "The most significant portion of the report deals with Federal and
interstate problems and includes statements on the variety of interests
which spread beyond the boundaries of any one political unit. The report
stresses the necessity for cooperation to prevent uncoordinated and unrelated development in adjoining areas and to provide a well-rounded and
balanced development of the whole region.
    "The St. Louis Commission recommends the creation of an interstate
authority, with Federal representation, to make an immediate and vigorous

attack on sanitation, highway, transportation, and recreation problems
involving the States of Illinois and Missouri and the interests of the
Federal Government. The Commission believes that only through such a
new agency can an effective attack be made on problems which are now
nobody's business because they are everybody's business.

"The value of a regional authority for planning and later, if conditions warrant an authority to carry through appropriate programs of construction, is already recognized, and the first steps towards the creation
of such an organization will presumably come through the State legislatures
of the States concerned." - Foreword.

Price-fixing

Backman, Jules. Adventures in price fixing. 57pp. New York, Farrar &
   Rinehart, incorporated [c1936] (The Farrar & Rinehart pamphlets. no. 8)
   284.3 B12
      Partial contents: The world experiments with price fixing; The A.A.A.
   and Bankhead Act fiasco; The Stevenson Rubber Plan (1922-1928); The fourth
   coffee valorization; Price fixing in nitrates; Valorization of silk in
   Japan; Fixing wheat prices in France; The Paterson butter plan in Australia;
   The Chadbourne sugar plan; Price fixing for hogs in the Netherlands.

Prices - U. S. - 1790-1860

Smith, W. B., and Cole, A. H.   Fluctuations in American business, 1790-1860.
   195pp. Cambridge, Harvard university press, 1935. (Harvard economic
   studies. v. 50)   284 Sm62
      Bibliographical foot-notes.
      "The book is primarily a presentation of many statistical series, with
   extended comments thereon, measuring changes in commodity prices, stock
   prices, sales of public lands, interest rates, and to a lesser degree -
   because of scarcity of data - the volume of trade. It also presents a
   limited amount of descriptive material on the general economic developments of the period.
      "The student of business cycles will be especially interested in the
   authors' discovery of a sequence in movement of stock prices, commodity
   prices, and interest rates during the years 1790-1860 similar to the sequence previously found by other investigators for later periods." -
   In Harvard Business Review, v. 14, no. 2, Winter 1936, p. 245, Reviewed
   by Joseph L. Snider.

Program for Modern America

Laidler, H. W.   A program for modern America.   517pp. New York, T. Y. Crowell
   company [1936]   280.12 L14P
      Bibliography, pp. 499-502
      "This book is an attempt to outline an American program for the next
   few years which would increase genuine liberty of thought and action, not
   on the part of the 'wolves' of our industrial civilization, but on the
   part of the common man.
      "In a sense, this volume is a political and economic handbook for today,

and a four-year program of social action on many of our most vital problems.

"America is today engaged in a war against unemployment, destitution, bureaucratic and autocratic control of industry and those forces which, if unchecked, may well lead us into another war.

"This struggle is being fought on many fronts. On one are found the advocates of child labor legislation, engaged in an age-long struggle to free the child from the fetters of oppressive toil; on another, are witnessed the leaders of the movement for social insurance, bent on saving the sick, the aged and the involuntarily idle from hunger and privation. In addition to these are the fighters for a shorter work week, for genuine systems of collective bargaining, for scientifically planned public works and low cost housing with a view to reducing the army of the jobless and improving the standards of the nation's workers.

"On still other fronts may be seen those who would redeem from its present low economic state the great industry of agriculture, those who would administer our natural resources, our credit structure, our electrical and transportation industries and our taxation system as instrumentalities devoted solely to the public good; and those who would maintain and extend those civil liberties for which our fathers fought and bled; who would see to it that free speech, free assembly and free press were the possession not of one group, but the heritage of all.

"In other parts of this battle line are men and women who would adjust the Constitution to the lightning changes in our industrial life; who would develop an international program dedicated to world peace; and who would bring reality into our political alignments, building strong and firm a political movement based on the needs and aspirations of the common man.

"I have attempted to describe each of these struggles in some detail in this volume. These individual contests are, in a larger sense, mere skirmishes in the general battle against a system of industry which places profit before human life and for a conception of industry and politics organized with the one aim of utilizing to the full the resources of the nation for the enrichment of the common life." - Preface.

Recovery - Gt. Britain - Australia - Canada

Heaton, Herbert. The British way to recovery; plans and policies in Great Britain, Australia, and Canada. 184pp. Minneapolis, The University of Minnesota press, 1934. 280.171 H35
    Chapter 5. The rediscovery of the farmer: pp. 78-99.
    Joseph L. Snider reviewed this volume at some length in the Harvard Business Review, Winter number 1936 (v. 14, no. 2) in part as follows:
    "By his brief, readable book, The British Way to Recovery, Professor Herbert Heaton of the University of Minnesota has broadened the perspective of the American student of recovery problems, a notable service. The book is a description, rather than an evaluation, of the recovery programs in England, Australia, and Canada.
    "The British problem of recovery was primarily to regain ground lost in her export markets and to replace some of that loss by expanding production for the home market. This problem was, of course, not created in 1929; it was only intensified.
    "The searches for solutions of Britain's recovery problem, made before 1931, were in general of two kinds. The first was directed toward the removal of external obstacles, such as the reparations claims, currency

muddles, interallied debts, and the rush toward economic nationalism. The second was directed toward the 'rationalization of British industry.' This involved a reduction in the number of small units, in the number of middlemen, and in the improvement of equipment and methods of management. The railroads, the coal industry, and the electric power industry were subjected to rationalization. But much of the good done by these measures was undone by the return to the gold standard at pre-war parity in 1925. The author believes there is a good case for declaring that the controllers of Britain's credit sought to maintain or win back the financial supremacy of London at the expense of British industry.

"One of the clearest and most valuable impressions from Professor Heaton's book is that the British government did not let nature take its course in lifting the country out of depression. When the financial crisis of 1931 was over, the government and the banks pursued a policy intended to provide cheap and abundant credit for the state and for private enterprise...

"Many measures were also taken to improve the position of British agriculture - import quotas to prevent the glutting of the market, marketing schemes, subsidies, and better farming methods.

"Turning from Britain to Australia, Professor Heaton records that early in 1931 the banks abandoned their attempts to peg the exchange rate near parity with sterling, which was then still on gold, and real wages were reduced 10% by the Federal Arbitration Court. There followed, shortly an extension of wage cuts to pensioners and public employees and reductions in all possible expenditures. Moreover, a reduction of 15% in interest on internal public debt was carried through. Laws were passed to reduce mortgage rates by 22 1/2%. These attempts to check the drift in public finance restored Australia's credit rating abroad, while the expansion of exports, combined with the decline in imports, restored the country's capacity to meet its external debts. Part of the overseas debt was converted with a substantial saving in interest charges. Australia also followed certain inflationary procedures. In addition to permitting its currency to depreciate in foreign exchange, there was a substantial increase in the floating debt from the sale of treasury bills.

"Canada's depression problems and attempts to cope with them have had no peculiar features. Although the average Canadian may have the impression that the government has done very little to stimulate revival, a great deal has been attempted. The tariff was raised quite early in the depression, taxes have been much increased, a central bank has been established, an agricultural marketing scheme was put into effect, mild inflation of the note issue has come, and elaborate relief plans for debtor farmers have been made."

Rural Library Service

Wilson, L. R., and Wight, E. A.   County library service in the south; a study of the Rosenwald county library demonstration. 259pp.   Chicago, Ill., The University of Chicago press [1935]   (University of Chicago. Studies in library science)   243 W692
    Bibliography, pp. 240-244.
    "Meeting at Signal Mountain, Tennessee, in 1926, librarians of the southeastern states sketched in bold outline a program for the development

- 563 -

of library service for the various publics which were to be found in the
South. This program contemplated: (1) the strengthening of state library
extension agencies; (2) the extension of library service to rural areas
through the development of county libraries; (3) the employment of school
library supervisors by state departments of education; (4) the setting-up
of new standards for libraries of secondary schools and colleges having
membership in the Southern Association of Colleges and Secondary Schools;
(5) the appointment of library field agents or representatives for the South
who would serve as advisers to librarians and foundations interested in
library development within the region; and (6) the establishment of additional library schools for the training of librarians in the southern field.

"In 1929 the officers of the Julius Rosenwald Fund, long interested in
the educational development of the South, decided to undertake the stimulation of library service in the South on a county-wide basis to all residents,
urban and rural, white and black, in school and out. At the same time, they
decided to attempt to stimulate interest in libraries in states without
library extension agencies by providing personnel and other aid essential to
the inauguration of general state-wide library advisory service.

"In carrying this plan into effect, the Fund selected in 1929 and 1930
eleven counties in seven southern states, and appropriated approximately
$500,000 for the aid of libraries which would provide county-wide service
to all the elements of their population. The counties selected and the
amounts appropriated for them were: Mecklenburg, $80,000, and Davidson,
$20,000, in North Carolina; Richland, $75,000, and Charleston, $80,000, in
South Carolina; Knox, $20,000, Hamilton, $80,000, and Shelby, $71,000, in
Tennessee; Walker, $46,666, in Alabama; Coahoma, $17,500, in Mississippi;
Webster Parish, $40,000, in Louisiana; and Jefferson County, $12,500, in
Texas.

"The general financial plan was for the Fund to match local appropriations dollar for dollar the first two years; one dollar for two the second
two years; and one dollar for four the fifth and final year. The demonstrations were to run for five years, the money used in matching the funds supplied by the Fund being 'new' money or amounts in addition to that included
by the counties in their budgets in the year previous to their co-operation
with the Fund; and service was to be provided on a county-wide basis to all
residents, irrespective of color, place of residence in the county or educational status.

"The five-year period of demonstration ended in 1934 and 1935,
though in a number of instances it has been extended on account of
conditions arising during the period which made the modification of
the original plans desirable. Some of the demonstrations did not
start until 1930, and the demonstration in Shelby County did not start
until 1931.

"In order to determine the value of the experiment, the Graduate
Library School of the University of Chicago was asked, at the beginning
of 1934, to review the activities of the libraries, evaluate their
achievements, and offer suggestions which, in the light of the experience gained, might prove of value in plans for future library development in the area. The School assumed responsibility for the study; its
representatives visited all of the libraries, consulted with state

library extension and educational agencies, county departments of education, public health, and agricultural extension, and many individuals, and then visited similar county libraries in California, New
Jersey, and the Middle West, for the sake of comparison. The results
of the study are set forth in the accompanying report." - Preface.

Rural Life

Burnham, Ernest, and Sanders, Lucille E.   Thirtieth anniversary souvenir bulletin
of rural progress day, Western state teachers college, Kalamazoo, Michigan,
March 6, 1936.   An adventure in rural education.   96pp. [Kalamazoo,
Mich., 1935]   (Western state teachers college. Bulletin v. 31, no. 1)
281.2 B93
    On cover: Souvenir thirtieth anniversary rural progress day, March 6,
1936.
    Partial contents: Some experiences in rural education, by C. J. Galpin;
The improvement of democracy, by S. A. Courtis;
Family living in the farm home of tomorrow, by Grace E. Frysinger; The
place of rural life and its problems today and tomorrow, by Charles J.
Galpin; What are the basic elements in rural life, by Ernest Burnham;
The International Institute of Agriculture, by H. C. Taylor; The fact
basis of international planning, by H. C. Taylor; International country
life conferences, by C. J. Galpin; Associated country women of the world,
by Grace E. Frysinger; Rural Asia and Africa, by K. L. Butterfield; Collegiate
country life clubs, by E. L. Kirkpatrick; and What kind of rural life can
we look forward to in the United States, by Carl C. Taylor.

Rural Life and Canadian Wheat Pools

The wheat pools in relation to rural community life in western Canada; an
account of some of the ways in which the wheat pools have endeavored to
assist the prairie community toward a happier and fuller manner of living.
Published by the Canadian wheat pools.   October, 1935.   29pp. [n.p.]
1935.   280.359 W56
    "The services which the Wheat Pools have rendered to the farm famil-
ies of the Western prairies and to all Canada, aside entirely from the
business of actual grain handling, is a story worth telling. It is a
human-interest story; a story of action, perseverance and achievement.
It is a story of how the farmers of Western Canada, acting in unison and
with high determination, have fought vigorously and tenaciously to maintain the standard of living in Canadian prairie homes at a level which
reflects honor and credit upon the nation.
    "In the pages that follow, an effort is made to describe some of the
non-commercial interests and activities of the Wheat Pools. The aim
is to indicate some of the ways in which the Pool movement has endeavored
to smooth out the rough spots of farm life. Because the every-day life
of the Wheat Pools is concerned with the collecting of grain at primary
points and moving it forward into the channels of commerce, it is virtually impossible to discuss the Pool movement without making some reference to this aspect of its activities. It is intended, however, that

these activities shall be regarded as merely the background; as we endeavor to point out the nature of the Pools' other activities, and to
suggest the co-operative and public-spirited attitude which the Pools
have maintained consistently during the past eleven years." - Foreword.

Rural Sociology

Gillette, J. M.   Rural sociology. 3d ed.   778pp.   New York, The Macmillan
company, 1936.   281.2 G41R Ed.3
    References at end of most of the chapters.
    The preface to the third edition reads in part as follows:
    "Presumably every scholar's ideas about his field and subject undergo
a change during a course of years. This has been true certainly in my
own case. When I issued Constructive Rural Sociology over a quarter of a
century ago, the first rural sociology to be published, I attempted two
things: to make a factual study of rural society and to give directions
on how rural society was to be improved or reformed. When this present
volume was first published in 1922, I attempted a more rigid factual
survey and less advice and methodology of rural improvement. In this
present volume I still further minimize the latter and maximize the
former. I regard this course inevitable because information about rural
life has become much more abundant and because advice and directions are
apt to be poorly founded and, anyway, are usually ignored by those who
need them.
    "This volume is almost a new book. First, most of the matter and writ-
ing is new. The following chapters are wholly new: I, V, VI, VIII, XI,
XII, XIII, XIV, XV, XXVII, XXX. The following ones are predominantly new:
IV, IX, X, XVII, XXI, XXII, XXIII, XXIV, XXVIII, XXIX. The following are
considerably new: VII, XVI, XVIII, XIX, XXV, XXVI, XXXI, XXXII, XXXIII,
XXXIV, XXXV. No chapter is without revision. Second, the form of organization of the material has been changed. The present plan of organization is more representative of the matter treated and is consequently
more scientific. It is more comprehensive and also specific. The parts
are designated according to the predominance of the subjects treated, not
because of their exclusiveness, since no exclusive divisions or chapters
are possible. More has been made of the ecological, of the influence of
conditions external to rural society upon it, and this is specifically embodied in Part III, although it is reflected throughout the volume. Third,
this treatise embodies a changed point of view. It is new to the present
author and, so far as I know, is not found as the keynote of any other rural
sociology. I have come to recognize that the major events in rural life,
as in national life, take place and move about the motives and processes
of adjustment of the populations to land. While movements of population are
significant and quite central in our treatment, nevertheless they are results
of the motives and movements by which inhabitants seek to get themselves adjusted to natural resources, immediately or indirectly. Socialization of
rural life both as a process going on and as a desideratum is still regarded
as important. A good deal of Parts IV and V is concerned with it.
    "I have consciously made more of the conceptual and sought to develop a
sociological background for many topics discussed more extensively. This
course I regard as an advantage scientifically and pedagogically. Our

students and readers require an intellectual preparation for viewing and interpreting the mass of facts we heap upon them. Science stands in need of interpretation as well as furnishing a collection and array of facts.

"Much of the material of the book is the product of research work of the author. Chapters IX-X, XI-XIII, XV, and XXVII-XXVIII embody such material, the results of intensive statistical research work, some covering a series of years. This kind of investigative work is not appreciated by many so-called rural researchers and does not get into bibliographies compiled and published by them. To them, because it is the only kind they know, research work is field survey work, very important if well conceived and done, but only one kind of investigation. Chapter XIX embodies an 'intensive case study' of the rural school situation in an agricultural state made under my supervision. It covers nine of the fifty-three counties of the state, a very large sample, and should closely represent the actual school situation in any one section of the nation. Parts of various other chapters are results of concentrated investigation."

Southwest in International Affairs

Institute of public affairs. Southern Methodist university. The Southwest in international affairs; proceedings of the third annual conference... Auspices, Carnegie endowment for international peace, Dallas, Texas, edited by S. D. Myres, Jr. 219pp. [Dallas,] Pub. for the Institute by the Arnold foundation, Southern Methodist university, 1936. 280.9 So85

"On March 10-14, 1936, the Institute of Public Affairs of Southern Methodist University devoted its Third Annual Conference to a study of the question, 'The Southwest in International Affairs.' The meetings were under the auspices of the Carnegie Endowment for International Peace. The Arnold Foundation of Southern Methodist University acted as the organizing agency of the Conference."

Partial contents: Section 1, What world trade means to the southwest, by W. E. Dunn; Cotton in international trade, by Robert Mayer; Problems of rice, sugar, cattle, and sheep, by H. C. Nixon; Measures to restore our foreign trade, by Peter Molyneaux. Section 2 is devoted to Our Relations with Latin America and Section 3, to Broader Phases of our Foreign Policy.

Sugar Consumption

Mosolff, Hans. Der deutsche zuckerverbrauch; seine struktur und elastizität. Ein vergleich des deutschen zuckerverbrauchs mit dem zuckerverbrauch der Vereinigten Staaten von Amerika und anderer länder. 92pp. Berlin [E. Dreyer's buchdruckerei] 1935. 281.365 M85 also in 65.8 D48, v.60

Diese untersuchung erschien zuerst in... [Die Deutsche zuckerindustrie LX. jahrg. (1935) nr. 26, 28 u.29.]

Bibliography, pp. 91-92.

A study of sugar consumption showing the trend of sugar consumption in Germany since 1874, its seasonal fluctuations during the period 1925/33, the elasticity of sugar consumption in the United States and Germany, the general structure of German sugar consumption in 1930 and 1933 as compared with that of the American and Australian sugar markets, household consumption of sugar in the country, in the city and by various organizations in Germany, regional differences in sugar consumption in the United States and Poland, the use of sugar in trade and industry and for sweetening coffee, tea, and cocoa, and sugar substitutes. The author points out that a study of the structure and elasticity of German sugar consumption shows the close interrelation of sugar prices, the people's purchasing power and the consumption of sugar as well as the effect of habits of living, prices of raw materials, propaganda, sugar substitutes, etc. on sugar consumption.

Tariff

Schattschneider, E. E. Politics, pressures and the tariff; a study of free private enterprise in pressure politics, as shown in the 1929-1930 revision of the tariff. 301pp. New York, Prentice-Hall, inc., 1935. (Prentice-Hall political science series) 285 Schl
    Thesis (Ph.D.) - Columbia university (Slip pasted on title page.)
    "Ever since the time of Adam Smith an important body of opinion critical of the protective tariff has flourished among economists. Though the literature produced by these critics has been at once extensive and scholarly, one has only to look about him to see that it has not made a great impression on the course of events... Without the least desire to belittle the labors of scholars who have studied the economic consequences of the protective tariff policy, I make bold to express the opinion that these studies have neglected an important phase of the subject. The tariff is not an economic question exclusively. It is a political problem as well. It is remarkable, therefore, that political scientists have hitherto shown relatively little interest in the tariff. While I should be an innocent optimist to believe that this study furnishes a solution of the problem, I have a clear conviction that an attempt to understand the process of tariff making and the forces behind the policy is a fruitful approach to it." - Preface.

Taxation

Virginia. University. Institute of public affairs. Round table on "Taxation for prosperity". 1935. 16 nos., mimeogr. [Charlottesville, 1935?] Folio 284.5 V815
    Contains papers by Joseph P. Harris, Noel Sargent, Arnold Frye, Henry F. Long, Harold S. Buttenheim, Peter Grimm, Herbert D. Simpson, Jens F. Jensen, R. C. Atkinson, Harry McMullan, Carl Shoup, A. H. Stone, Daniel Bloomfield, Joseph D. McGoldrich, and James W. Martin.

Taxation - Rhode Island

Rhode Island. Commission on ways and means. Report of the Commission on ways and means made to the governor of the state of Rhode Island, November 27, 1935. 132pp. Providence, R. I., W. R. Brown co., 1935. 284.5 R342
    At head of title: State of Rhode Island and Providence plantations.
    Minority report, by Russell H. Handy, pp. [107]-114.
    This report traces the development of the tax system in Rhode Island

and recommends legislation providing for reorganization of the Department of Taxation and Regulation so the Department can provide suitable
assistance to local assessors. The Commission recommends further legislation relating to exemption of property from taxation; extension of
time before taxes become delinquent and of the time property may be re-
deemed; and to sources of revenue.

Tobacco Belt — Kentucky and Tennessee

Miller, J. G. The black patch war. 87pp. Chapel Hill, The University
of North Carolina press, 1936. 277.031 M61
"In compliance with many requests, I record in the following memoir
facts known to me in what may well be called The Black Patch War — an
episode in the history of the Black Tobacco Belt of Kentucky and Tennessee.
"To understand and judge rightly the people engaged in this frenzied
strife, some knowledge of the social and economic history of this particular section of the country, as far back at least as the Civil War, is
necessary. Woodrow Wilson aptly said: 'The history of a nation is only
the history of its villages [communities] written large.'
"The source of the train of tragedies of the Night Rider episode lay
in the fact that the business, social, and cultural life of the community
in the Black Tobacco Belt had long depended almost wholly on the market
price of its tobacco." — Foreword.

Ulster Year Book

The Ulster year book 1935. Published by authority of the Minister of finance.
306pp. Belfast, H. M. Stationery off., 1935. 256.13 U17
This fourth edition of the Ulster Year Book contains a special article
entitled "The Evolution of Agricultural Policy in Northern Ireland."
The volume gives statistics and a brief bibliography of official publications for the following sections: Physiography, including geography,
climate and weather; Population and vital statistics; Land, including
division of land, tenure, and drainage; Production from natural resources
including agriculture and forestry; Industry and trade; Transport and
communication; Education; Labour; State insurance, unemployment assistance,
and pensions; Housing, health and poor relief; Justice and police; Public
finance; Local government finance; Private finance; and government.

Unemployment

Thompson, D. L.   The problem of unemployment. 24pp. [Spokane, Wash.,
Keystone ptg. co.] 1936. 283 T372
On cover-title: Comprising a series of three articles: "Why jobs are
scarce", "The machine theory of unemployment", "The short work day as
a remedy for unemployment."
Our land policy and unemployment, pp. 4–8.

Canada. Dept. of labour. Unemployment relief branch. The relief act, 1935.
Report... March 31, 1936. 36pp. Ottawa, J. O. Patenaude, printer to
the King's Most Excellent Majesty, 1936.
  This Report of the Dominion Commissioner of Unemployment Relief,
Mr. Harry Hereford, sets forth statements of expenditures, guarantees,
and obligations and contains much additional information referring to the
administration of The Relief Act, 1935. It also shows expenditures made
under the relief legislation of 1930, 1931, 1932, 1933 and 1934.

U. S. S. R.

Gabyshev, M. F. Organization of production of hog state farm (sovkhoz) Editor-
in-chief M. F. Gabyshev. 346, [2]pp. Moscow, Lenin academy of agricultural
sciences, 1936. (Vsesoiuznaia akademiia s.-kh-nauk im. V.I.Lenina.
[Doklady] Seriia 19. Ekonomika. no.1) 281.179 G11
  Text and added title page in Russian; summary in English.
  At head of title: All-Union soviet state farm research institute
(Vsesoiuznyĭ nauchnoissledovatel'skiĭ institut)

Veblen, Thorstein

Veblen, Thorstein. What Veblen taught; selected writings of Thorstein Veblen
edited with an introduction by Wesley C. Mitchell. 503pp. New
York, The Viking press, 1936. 280 V49W
  Dated list of Veblen's books, p. 1.
  From Veblen's The Theory of the Leisure Class, the following chapters are
reprinted: Pecuniary Emulation; Conspicuous Leisure; The Higher Learning
as an Expression of the Pecuniary Culture. The selections from The Case of
America are: The Self-made Man; The Independent Farmer; The Country Town.
Other essays reprinted in this volume are: The Place of Science in Modern
Civilization; The Preconceptions of Economic Science; The Limitations of
Marginal Utility; The Savage State of the Industrial Arts; The Cultural
Incidence of the Machine Process; The Captains of Finance and the Engineers;
The Dynastic State; On the State and its Relation to War and Peace.

Vegetables - Italy

Langer, Alfons. Die gemüsewirtschaft italiens; ein beitrag zur wirts-
chaftlichen länderkunde. 68pp. [Klagenfurt, 1934?] 281.391 L26
  Diss. - Hochschule für welthandel, Wien.
  Bibliography, pp. 67-68.
  A statistical study of vegetable production, the preserving of
vegetables and the vegetable trade in Italy.

Wheat Pools - Canada

The Canadian wheat pools on the air; a series of radio messages broadcast by
officials and supporters of the wheat pools of western Canada. Issued
by the wheat pool organizations of Manitoba, Saskatchewan and Alberta.
March 1936. 51pp. [n.p.] 1936. 280.259 C16 2d ser.

Contents: The wheat pools and their objectives, by L. C. Brouillette; The farmer in the modern world, by Dr. H. W. Wood; Another Manitoba milestone, by F. W. Ransom; Alberta gives an answer, by R. D. Purdy; A Saskatchewan survey, by G. W. Robertson; A coast to coast organization, by J. T. Hull; Carrying the farm risk, by George Bennett; The farmer coming into his own, by J. H. Wesson; Showing the way, by J. Jesse Strang; Our successors, by C. H. Burnell; Loyalty to ideals, by Dr. W. C. Murray; The rural co-operative movement, by Dean E. A. Howes, and Farm women's problems, by Mrs. S. V. Haight.

Works Progress Administration

U. S. Works progress administration. Division of research statistics, and records. Report on the works program. 106pp. Washington, U. S. Govt. print. off., March 16, 1936.   173.2 W89Rep
    Accompanied by a pamphlet with title: Interesting facts about the Works Progress Administration.
    Includes sections on the following: Farm-to-market roads; National Youth Administration; and Resettlement Administration.

Works Progress Administration – Tennessee

Allred, C. E., Sanders, P. C., Collins, W. E. Luebke, B. H., Matthews, M. T. and Tosch, C. A. Rural relief and rehabilitation possibilities in Jefferson county, Tennessee. 47pp., mimeogr. [Knoxville, Tenn.] Apr. 1, 1936. (U. S. Federal works progress administration. Cooperative plan of rural research. Report no. 10)   173.2 W89Co no. 10
    Issued in cooperation with Tennessee Agricultural Experiment Station and Tennessee Welfare Commission.

Allred, C. E., Raskopf, B. D., Matthews, M. T., and Tosch, C. A. Rural relief and rehabilitation possibilities in Williamson County, Tennessee. 48 pp., mimeogr. [Knoxville, Tenn.] May 20, 1936. (U. S. Federal works progress administration. Cooperative plan of rural research. Report no. 13)   173.2 W89Co no.13
    Issued in cooperation with Tennessee Agricultural Experiment Station and Tennessee Works Progress Administration.

Allred, C. E., Tosch, C. A., Matthews, M. T., Baker, G. A., Collins, W. E., Sanders, P. C., and Raskopf, B. D.   Grundy County, Tennessee relief in a coal mining community. 51pp., mimeogr. [Knoxville, Tenn.] Apr. 10, 1936.   (U. S. Federal works progress administration. Cooperative plan of rural research, Report no. 11)   173.2 W89Co no.11
    Issued in cooperation with Tennessee Agricultural Experiment Station, Tennessee welfare commission.

Allred, C. E., Luebke, B. H., and Tosch, C. A. Mobility of rural relief families in Tennessee. 35pp., mimeogr. [Knoxville, Tenn.] June 1, 1936.
(U. S. Works progress administration. Cooperative plan of rural research,
Report no. 14)   173.2 W89Co no.14
    Issued in cooperation with Tennessee Agricultural Experiment Station
and Tennessee Works Progress Administration.

Allred, C. E., Hendrix, W. E., and Raskopf, B. D. Regional comparison of
rural standards of living in Tennessee. 36pp., mimeogr. [Knoxville,
Tenn. June 15, 1936] (U. S. Werks progress administration. Cooperative
plan of rural research. Report no. 15) 173.2 W89Co no. 15
    Issued in cooperation with Tennessee Agricultural Experiment Station
and Tennessee Works Progress Administration.

Allred, C. E., Luebke, B. H., and Marshall, J. H.   Trade centers in Tennessee
1900 - 1930.   30pp., mimeogr. Knoxville, Tenn., July 1, 1936.
([U. S. Works progress administration. Cooperative plan of rural re-
search] Report no. 16)   173.2 W89Co no.16
    "Agricultural Economics and Rural Sociology Department, Tennessee
Agricultural Experiment Station, University of Tennessee, Knoxville,
Tennessee."

Works Progress Administration (FERA) - Wisconsin

Kirkpatrick, E. L.   Resettlement and rehabilitation in the central Wisconsin
nesting area. An analysis of data on 461 resident households in Clark,
Eau Claire, Jackson, Juneau, Monroe and Wood counties, Wisconsin, as of
February 1935. [By] E. L. Kirkpatrick, Carl F. Kraenzel and Ruth M. Thomas.
Preliminary report. October 15, 1935.   37PP., mimeogr., maps. [Madison?
Wis.] 1935.   281.2 K63Re
    "Survey... conducted cooperatively by the Rural division of the Wisconsin
Emergency relief administration, Division of research, finance, and statis-
tics of the Federal emergency relief administration, and the Rural sociology
department, Wisconsin Agricultural experiment station." - Footnote, leaf
[1].

BIBLIOGRAPHIES

A bibliographical introduction to nationalism, by Koppel S. Pinson, with a
foreword by Carlton J. H. Hayes.   70pp. New York, Columbia university
press, 1935.   241.3 P65
    Professor Hayes with the financial aid of the Social Science Research
Council and the personal assistance of Dr. Shepard B. Clough had made a
preliminary survey of European and American research in the field of
nationalism.
    "Dr. Koppel S. Pinson, utilizing the materials collected in that
survey and greatly extending and supplementing them from his own research
as well as from his experience as Assistant Editor of the Encyclopaedia
of the Social Sciences, presents the following annotated list of general
treatises and special monographs as an introductory bibliographical guide
to the serious study of nationalism."- Foreword.

Bibliography of works on accounting by American authors, by Harry C. Bentley...
and Ruth S. Leonard. 2v. Boston, Mass., The author, 1934-35. 241.3 B44
Contents: - v. 1. 1796-1900. - v.2. 1901 - 1934.

Consumers' cooperative societies (basic information sources) Comp. by Ruth
C. Leslie of the Marketing research and service division of the Bureau
of foreign and domestic commerce. 26pp., mimeogr. [Washington, D. C.,
Jan. 1936]
"Comp.... in cooperation with the Bureau of Labor Statistics, De-
partment of Labor, and the Cooperative League of the United States of
America... New York."

Cooperation in agriculture. A selected and annotated bibliography with special
reference to marketing, purchasing and credit, compiled by Chastina Gardner.
214pp. Washington [U. S. Govt. print. off.] May 1936. (U. S. Farm credit
administration. Cooperative division. Bulletin no. 4) 166.2 B87 no.4
This bibliography contains 983 references to publications. It is arranged alphabetically, is annotated and contains a brief biographical
sketch following the name of each author. A selected list of periodicals
issued by educational, marketing and purchasing associations is appended
and also an author and subject index.

Reciprocal trade: a current bibliography. Selected list of references. Compiled by the Tariff Commission Library. 89pp., mimeogr. [Washington,
D. C.] May 1936. 173 T17Rec

Rural land economics, 1933-1935. Outstanding references relating to rural
land economics, especially to the present national land policy, comp.
by Orpha Cummings, librarian, Giannini foundation of agricultural
economics... March 12, 1936. 116pp., mimeogr. Berkeley, Calif.,
1936. 241.3 C91 1933-35.
Edition for 1933-1934 has title: Land economics, 1933-1934.
At head of title: University of California. College of agriculture.
Agricultural Experiment Station. Berkeley, California.

SELECTED LIST OF RECENT REVIEWS

Compiled by M. I. Herb

Anderson, William. Local government and finance in Minnesota. [1935.]
Reviewed by H. D. Smith in Amer. Acad. Polit. and Social Sci.
Ann. 183: 223-224. May 1936.
Reviewed by A. W. Bromage in Amer. Polit. Sci. Rev. 30(1): 181-
182. February 1936.
Reviewed by D. C. Horton in Amer. Econ. Rev. 26(1): 151. March 1936.

Arkin, Herbert, and Colton, R. R. Statistical methods as applied to
economics, business, education, social and physical sciences. [1934]
Reviewed by T. C. McCormick in Amer. Jour. Sociol. 42(1): 139-
141. July 1936.

Astor, Waldorf Astor, 2d viscount. The agricultural dilemma: a report of
    an enquiry organised by Viscount Astor and Mr. B. Seebohm Rountree.
    1935.
        Reviewed by R. J. T. in Royal Statis. Soc. Jour. (n.s.) 99(1): 192-
    193. 1936.

Beranson, Anne, Gray, R. D., and Hussey, Miriam. Prices in colonial
    Pennsylvania. 1935. (Half-title: Industrial research department.
    Wharton school of finance and commerce. University of Pennsylvania,
    Philadelphia. Research studies XXVI.)
        Reviewed by R. S. Tucker in Amer. Statis. Assoc. Jour. 31(194):
    430-432. June 1936.

Black, J. D. The dairy industry and the A.A.A. 1935. (Half-title:
    The Institute of economics of the Brookings institution. Publication
    no. 64.)
        Reviewed by A. C. Bunce in Rural Sociol. 1(2): 227-229. June 1936.

Carrión, Pascual. Los latifundios en España. 1932.
        Reviewed by R. E. Crist in Geogr. Rev. 26(2): 327-329. April 1936.

Cassel, Gustav. On quantitative thinking in economics. 1935.
        Reviewed by R. Leslie in South African Jour. Econ. 4(1): 87-88.
    March 1936.

Childs, Marquis. Sweden; the middle way. 1936.
        Reviewed by H. G. Leach in Survey Graphic 25(4): 255. April 1936.
        Reviewed by Lyder L. Unstad in Amer. Econ. Rev. 26(2): 304-305.
    June 1936.
        Reviewed by Carle C. Zimmerman in Amer. Acad. Polit. and Social
    Sci. Ann. 186: 226-227. July 1936.

Cole, G. D. H. Economic planning. 1935.
        Reviewed briefly in People's Money 2(6): 259. July 1936.

Copland, D. B. W. E. Hearn: first Australian economist; the Murtagh
    Macrossan lectures in the University of Queensland, 1935. 1935.
        Reviewed by R. C. Mills in Econ. Rec. 11(21): 297-299. December
    1935.

Douglas, P. H. Controlling depressions. [1935]
        Reviewed by K. J. Binns in Econ. Rec. 12(22): 129-131. June 1936.
        Reviewed by H. L. in Royal Statis. Soc. Jour. (n.s.) 99(1):
    181-182. 1936.

Dummeier, E. F., and Heflebower, R. B. Economics with applications to
    agriculture. 1934.
        Reviewed by R. S. Vaile in Jour. Polit. Econ. 44(3): 423-425.
    June 1936.

Edgeworth, K. E. The price level. A further problem in national
    planning. [1935]
        Reviewed by R. G. H. in Royal Statis. Soc. Jour. (n.s.) 99(1):
    182-184. 1936.

Emeny, Brooks. The strategy of raw materials; a study of America in peace and war. 1934.
Reviewed by W. S. Thatcher in Econ. Jour. 46(182): 338-340. June 1936.

Essays in Social economics in honor of Jessica Blanche Peixotto. 1935.
Reviewed by A. M. Carr-Saunders in Econ. Jour. 46(182): 328. June 1936.

Ezekiel, Mordecai. $2500 a year; from scarcity to abundance. [1936]
Reviewed by W. N. Loucks in Amer. Acad. Polit. and Social Sci. Ann. 186: 231-232. July 1936.

Fowler, B. B. Consumer cooperation in America; democracy's way out. [1936]
Reviewed briefly in American Observer 5(34): 6. May 4, 1936.
Reviewed by R. L. Duffus in New York Times Book Rev., May 17, 1936, p. 6.
Reviewed by Manya Gordon in Saturday Rev. Literature 14(8): 3-4, 14, 15. June 20, 1936.
Reviewed by Alexander Calhoun in Western Farm Leader 1(4): 52. July 3, 1936.

Goslin, R. A., and Goslin, O. P. Rich man, poor man; pictures of a paradox. 1935 (A publication of the People's league for economic security.)
Reviewed by H. R. Mussey in the New York Herald Tribune Books, Jan. 12, 1936, p. 4.

Gülland, Paul. Das Reichserbhofrecht; eine systematische gesetzeserläuterung. 1935.
Reviewed by C. P. Loomis in Rural Sociol. 1(2): 231-232. June 1936.

Himes, Norman E., ed. Economics, sociology and the modern world. Essays in honor of T. N. Carver. 1935.
Reviewed by E. H. Phelps Brown in Econ. Jour. 46(182): 326-328. June 1936.

Holt, J. B. German agricultural policy, 1918-1934; the development of a national philosophy toward agriculture in postwar Germany. 1936.
Reviewed by C. P. Loomis in Rural Sociol. 1(2): 230. June 1936.

Horace Plunkett Foundation. Co-operation and the new agricultural policy. 1935.
Reviewed by K. A. H. Murray in Econ. Jour. 46(182): 344-345. June 1936.

Horn, P. V. International trade principles and practices. 1935.
Reviewed by R. L. Kramer in Natl. Marketing Rev. 1(3): 276-277. Winter 1936.
Reviewed by Gardner Harding in New York Times Book Rev., Dec. 8, 1935, p. 34.

Institute of Pacific relations. Commodity control in the Pacific area.
  A symposium of recent experience, edited by W. L. Holland. [1935]
      Reviewed by H. E. Belshaw in Pacific Affairs 9(2): 304-308.
  June 1936.

International industrial relations institute. Regional study conference,
  New York, 1934. On economic planning. Papers delivered at the
  Regional study conference of the International industrial relations
  institute (IRI), New York, November 23-27, 1934. Edited with an
  introduction by Mary L. Fledderus and Mary van Kleeck. 1935.
      Reviewed by J. G. Smith in Amer. Statis. Assoc. Jour. 31(194):
  427-429. June 1936.

International labour office, Geneva. Social and economic reconstruction
  in the United States. 1934. (Studies and Reports Series B,
  (Economic conditions) no. 20)
      Reviewed by A. R. Burns in Polit. Sci. Quart. 51(2): 290-292.
  June 1936.

Keynes, J. M. The general theory of employment, interest and money.
  1936.
      Reviewed by J. R. Hicks in Econ. Jour. 46(182): 238-253.
  June 1936.
      Reviewed by W. B. Reddaway in Econ. Rec. 12(22): 28-36. June
  1936.
      Reviewed by A. C. Pigou in an article in Economica (n.s.) 3(10):
  115-132. May 1936.

Knapp, W. H. C. World dislocation and world recovery; agriculture as
  the touchstone of the economic world events. 1935.
      Reviewed by J. O. Shearer in Econ. Rec. 12(22): 124-125. June
  1936.

Laidler, H. W. A program for modern America. [1936]
      Reviewed briefly in People's Money 2(6): 260. July 1936.
      Reviewed by E. S. B. in Sociol. and Social Research 20(6): 579-
  580. July-August 1936.

League of Nations, Economic committee. Considerations on the present
  evolution of agricultural protectionism. [1935] (League of Nations,
  Publications. II. Economic and financial, 1935. II. B.7)
      Reviewed by H. W. M. in Royal Statis. Soc. Jour. (n.s.) 99(1):
  195-196. 1936.

League of Nations. Economic intelligence service. World economic sur-
  vey, fourth year, 1934-35. 1935. (Series of League of Nations
  Publications. II. Economic and financial. II. A.14)
      Prepared by J. B. Condliffe.
      Reviewed by Colin Clark in Econ. Jour. 46(182): 314-315.
  June 1936.

Marbut, C. F. Atlas of American agriculture: Part III, Soils of the
    United States. 1936.
        Reviewed by C. F. Shaw in Geogr. Rev. 26(2): 339-341. April 1936.

Maxwell, B. W. The Soviet state; a study of Bolshevik rule. [1934]
        Reviewed by Ryuichi Kaji in Pacific Affairs 9(2): 296-298.
    June 1936.

Moulton, H. G. The formation of capital. 1935. (Half-title: The
    Institute of economics of the Brookings institution. Publication
    no.-59)
        Reviewed by Simon Kuznets in Polit. Sci. Quart. 51(2): 300-306.
    June 1936.

Moulton, H. G. Income and economic progress. 1935. (The Institute
    of economics of the Brookings institution. Publication no. 68)
        Reviewed by H. A. Marquand in Econ. Jour. 46(182): 332-334.
    June 1936.
        Reviewed by Simon Kuznets in Polit. Sci. Quart. 51(2): 300-
    306. June 1936.

Nourse, E. G. Marketing agreements under the A.A.A. 1935. (Half-title:
    The Institute of economics of the Brookings institution. Publica-
    tion no. 63)
        Reviewed by Ruth Cohen in Econ. Jour. 46(182): 343, 344. June
    1936.

Odum, H. W. Southern regions of the United States... for the Southern
    regional committee of the Social science research council. 1936.
        Reviewed by C. McD. Puckette in New York Times Book Rev., June
    28, 1936, p. 3.
        Reviewed by G. T. Renner in Land Policy Circ., May 1935, pp.12-16.
        Reviewed by H. C. Hoffsommor in Rural Sociol. 1(2): 240-242.
    June 1936.

Oxford. University. Agricultural economics research institute. The
    Agricultural register 1935-36. 1936.
        Reviewed briefly in the Statist 127(3042): 1025. June 13, 1936.

Passfield, S. J. W., baron. Soviet communism: a new civilization? 1936.
        Reviewed by H. J. Laski in Saturday Rev. Literature 13(19): 3-4.
    Mar. 7, 1936.
        Reviewed by Kathleen Barnes in Pacific Affairs 9(2): 294-296.
    June 1936.

Peck, H. W. Economic thought and its institutional background. [1935]
        Reviewed by E. W. Goodhue in Amer. Econ. Rev. 26(2): 297-298.
    June 1936.
        Reviewed by T. R. Snavely in Amer. Acad. Polit. and Social Sci.
    Ann. 186: 228-229. July 1936

Pribram, Karl.   Cartel problems; an analysis of collective monopolies
    in Europe with American application. 1935. (Half-title: The in-
    stitute of economics of the Brookings institution. Publication no. 69
        Reviewed by Theodore Bullock in Amer. Econ. Rev. 26(2): 334-335.
    June 1936.
        Reviewed by Wilhelm Cohnstaedt in New York Times Book Rev.,
    June 28, 1936, p. 14.

Rees, C. F.   Dynamic economics; theoretical and statistical studies of
    demand, production, and prices. [1934] (Monograph of the Cowles
    commission for research in economics, No. 1)
        Reviewed by Gerhard Tintner in Jour. Polit. Econ. 44(3): 404-
    409. June 1936.

Shannon, F. A.   Economic history of the people of the United States.
    1934.
        Reviewed briefly by G. S. in Survey Graphic 25(4): 261. April
    1936.

Sims, N. L.   Elements of rural sociology. Rev. ed. [1934]
        Reviewed by E. D. Tetreau in Rural Sociol. 1(2): 233-235.
    June 1935.

Slichter, S.H.   Towards stability; the problem of economic balance.
    [1934]
        Reviewed by Erich Roll in Econ. Jour. 46(182): 325-326. June 1936

Smith, J. G.   Economic planning and the tariff; an essay on social
    philosophy. 1934.
        Reviewed by Abraham Berglund in Amer. Statis. Assoc. Jour. 31
    (194): 429-430. June 1936.

Smith, J. G.   Elementary statistics; an introduction to the principles
    of scientific methods. [1934]
        Reviewed by T. C. McCormick in Amer. Jour. Sociol. 42(1): 139-
    141. July 1936.

Stevenson, R. A., and Vaile, R. S.   Balancing the economic controls.
    A review of the economic studies of the Employment stabilization
    research institute, University of Minnesota. 1935.
        Reviewed briefly in People's Money 2(6): 259. July 1936.

U. S. Department of agriculture.   Economic and social problems and con-
    ditions of the Southern Appalachians. 1935. (U. S. Dept. Agr.
    Misc. Pub. 205)
        Reviewed by William Van Royen and J. H. Reinhardt in Geogr. Rev.
    26(2): 319-320. April 1936.

U. S. National resources committee.   Regional factors in national plan-
    ning and development. 1935.
        Reviewed by E. J. Coil in an article entitled "On the Regional
    Report" in Plan Age 2(5): 18-27. May 1936.

Wallace, H. A.   Whose Constitution? An inquiry into the general
     welfare. [1936]
          Reviewed briefly in The American Observer 5(44): 7. July 13, 1936.
          Reviewed in the Christian Sci. Monitor in an article entitled
     "New Book by Wallace Hints Continuance of Regimentation."
          Reviewed briefly in N. Y. Jour. Com. 169: 2. July 2, 1936 in
     an article entitled "Wallace Advocates Centralization Plan."
          Reviewed in the N. Y. Times, July 1, 1936, in an article entitled
     "Wallace Predicts Liberal Judiciary."
          Reviewed by John Corbin in New York Times Book Rev., July 5,
     1936, p. 3.
          Reviewed in the Washington Post, July 7, 1936 in an article
     entitled "The Conservation Problem."
          Reviewed by Felix Morley in the Washington Post, July 12, 1936.
          Reviewed by David Lawrence in the Washington Star, July 3, 1936.
          Reviewed by Mary Carter Roberts in the Washington Star, July
     4, 1936.

Warbasse, J. P.   Cooperative democracy through voluntary association of
     the people as consumers; a discussion of the cooperative movement,
     its philosophy, methods, accomplishments and possibilities and its
     relation to the state, to science, art, and commerce, and to other
     systems of economic organization. 3d ed. 1936.
          Reviewed by Florence Finch Kelly in the New York Times Book Rev.,
     July 12, 1936, p. 20.

Wicksell, Knut.   Interest and prices; a study of the causes regulating
     the value of money. Trans. from the German by R. F. Kahn. 1936.
          Reviewed briefly in the Economist (London) 123(4834): 130, 131.
     Apr. 18, 1936.
          Reviewed by E. R. Walker in Econ. Rec. 12(22): 134-136. June 1936.
          Reviewed by Brinley Thomas in Econ. Jour. 46(182): 289-293.
     June 1936.

Wicksell, Knut.   Lectures on political economy. Translated from the
     Swedish by E. Classen. v.II. 1935.
          Reviewed briefly in Economist (London) 123(4834): 130, 131.
     Apr. 18, 1936.

Willcox, O. W.   Nations can live at home. [1935]
          Reviewed by H. A. Wallace in the New Repub. 84(1091): 340.
     Oct. 30, 1935.

Wright, P. G.   Trade and trade barriers in the Pacific. 1935.
          Reviewed in Annalist 48(1224): 7. July 3, 1936.

Zimmerman, C. C., and Frampton, M. E.   Family and society; a study of
     the sociology of reconstruction. 1935.
          Reviewed by G. F. Theriault, and E. L. Kirkpatrick in Rural
     Sociol. 1(2): 235-237. June 1936.

U. S. DEPARTMENT OF AGRICULTURE PUBLICATIONS

Economic in Character

Compiled by Katharine Jacobs

Yearbook of agriculture 1936. 1189pp. 1936. 1 Ag84Y
    May be purchased from the Superintendent of Documents, price $1.25 cloth.

Agricultural statistics 1936. 421pp. 1936.
    "This volume presents information formerly published in the statistical section of the Yearbook of agriculture."
    Prepared under the direction of the Yearbook statistical committee: Joseph A. Becker, Paul Froehlich, S. W. Mendum, L. D. Howell, F. J. Hosking, and G. W. Sprague.
    May be purchased from the Superintendent of Documents, price 50 cents, paper covers.

Circular*

393. Care and maintenance of cotton-gin saws and ribs, by Charles A. Bennett and Francis L. Gerdes. 20pp. July 1936. 1 Ag84C no. 393

Miscellaneous Publication*

239. The vertical drier for seed cotton, by Charles A. Bennett and Francis L. Gerdes. 21pp. April 1936. 1 Ag84M no.239

Technical Bulletins*

508. Effect of artificially drying seed cotton before ginning on certain quality elements of the lint and seed and on the operation of the gin stand, by Francis L. Gerdes and Charles A. Bennett. 62pp. May 1936. 1 Ag84Te no. 508
521. Agricultural loans of commercial banks, by Norman J. Wall. 56pp. July 1936. 1 Ag84Te no. 521

Senate Document (Prepared by the Department of Agriculture)**

The significance of agricultural imports. Letter from the Secretary of agriculture to Senator Louis Murphy transmitting a statement prepared by the Department of agriculture with regard to the causes and the significance of the recent increase in agricultural imports into the United States. 27pp. Washington, U. S. Govt. print. off., 1936. (74th Cong., 2d sess. Senate. Doc. no. 263) 1 Ag86Si

---

Symbol used after each entry is call number assigned to the publication by the Department Library.
*Requests for these publications should be addressed to the Office of Information, U. S. Department of Agriculture, Washington, D.C.
**May be obtained from Agricultural Adjustment Administration, U. S. Department of Agriculture, Washington, D. C.

Unnumbered Publications*

Atlas of American agriculture. Physical basis including land relief, climate,
    soils, and natural vegetation of the United States. Prepared under the
    supervision of O. E. Baker, Bureau of agricultural economics. Contribu-
    tions from the Weather bureau... Bureau of chemistry and soils... Bureau
    of plant.industry... Forest service... Bureau of agricultural economics.
    [231]pp. Washington, U. S. Govt. print. off., 1936.   1 Ag864At
        May be purchased from the Superintendent of Documents for $17.00
Laws applicable to the United States Department of agriculture, 1935, em-
    bracing acts and provisions of a permanent character in force September
    6, 1935, compiled by J. P. Wenchel and Morrow H. Moore... 1936.
    750pp.   1 So45L 1935
        May be purchased at Superintendent of Documents for $1.00.Paper.
Science serving agriculture, by Arthur P. Chew. 44pp. 1936. 1 In3S Rev.
        "Prepared in 1933 and slightly revised and reissued for distribu-
    tion at the Texas centennial central exposition, Dallas, Texas, 1936."

Addresses of Secretary Wallace*

Address [concerning the farm problem in various countries.] 4pp., mimeogr.
    [1936] 1.9 Ag8636 no. 122
        Delivered at the Third Triennial Conference of the Associated Country-
    women of the World, Washington, D. C., June 4, 1936.
Agricultural preparedness and the drought; address... before the International
    baby chick association, at Kansas City, Mo. July 22, 1936. 15pp.,
    mimeogr. 1.9 Ag8636 no. 124
Northeast agriculture and the national welfare; address... at Oneida county
    fair at Boonville, New York, Aug. 7, 1936. 18pp.
New England and national agricultural policy; address... June 9, 1936, at the
    ninth annual New England institute of cooperation, meeting at Massachusetts
    State College, Amherst, Mass. 15pp., mimeogr. [1936] 1.9 Ag8636 no. 123

Publications of the Bureau of Agricultural Economics (Mimeographed)**

Amendment no. 1 to Service and regulatory announcements no. 134 (B.A.E.)
    Amendment to the regulations for warehousemen storing cherries in
    sulphur dioxide brine under the United States warehouse act. May 5,
    1936. 1 M34S no. 134. Amend. no. 1
Brief review of the 1936 tomato and celery shipping season. 2pp. May 29,
    1936. (Issued in cooperation with Florida State marketing bureau)
    1.9 Ec741L
Brief review of the 1936 vegetable shipping season. 5pp. June 1, 1936.
    (Issued in cooperation with Florida State marketing bureau) 1.9 Ec741L

---

*Requests for these publications should be addressed to the Office of Informa-
    tion, U. S. Department of Agriculture, Washington, D. C.
**These publications are issued in small editions for immediate use in official
    work and are not for general distribution.

Brief summary, marketing North Carolina potatoes, season of 1936. 4pp. June
29, 1936. (Issued in cooperation with North Carolina Department of agriculture) 1.9 Ec741L
Brief summary, marketing South Carolina potatoes, season of 1936. 3PP. June 4,
1936. (Issued in cooperation with Clemson college. Extension service. Division of markets) 1.9 Ec741L
Carlot unloads of certain fruits and vegetables in 66 cities and imports in 4
cities for Canada calendar year 1935. 73pp. May 1936. 1.9 Ec741U
Construction and use of the official standards for American cotton linters 4pp.
[July 1936] 1.9 Ec7Const.
Cotton fabrics for bituminous-surfaced roads. By R. J. Cheatham and Rodney
Whitaker. 16pp. June 1936. (Issued in cooperation with Textile school
of North Carolina State college of agriculture and engineering. University
of North Carolina). 1.9 Ec733Cfa
Cotton revisions: Acreage, yield and production crop years 1924-1935, by states.
7pp. June 1936. 1.9 Ec71Cot.
Effective precipitation in relation to crop yields. 3pp. May 29, 1936. (CRP-1)
1.9 Ec71Crp
Farm tax data obtained for 45-year period. 4pp. June 27, 1936. 1.9 Ec78Fat
Fats and oils, and the excise taxes of 1936. 17pp. July 1936. 1.9 Ec752Fat
General crop revisions crop years 1924-1935 acreage, yield and production by
states. 103pp. June 1936. 1.9 Ec71Ge
Government grading of canned fruits and vegetables. Questions and answers.
By Paul M. Williams. 16pp. June 1936. 1.9 Ec741Go
Handbook of instructions for the installation and operation of the Tag-Heppen-
stall moisture meter (Revised)...Prepared by D. A. Coleman and H. C.
Fellows. 93pp. July 1936. (USGSA-MB1-1 Revised) 1.9 Ec72Ha 1936.
Livestock, meats, and wool market statistics and related data 1935, comp.
under the direction of Edna M. Jordan. 158pp. June 1936. 1.9 Ec713Ls
1935
Marketing Colorado lettuce, cauliflower, green peas and cabbage. Summary of 1935
season, by Bryce Morris. 23pp. June 1936. 1.9 Ec741L
Marketing Florida citrus. Summary of 1935-36 season, by H. F. Willson. 87pp.
June 20, 1936. 1.9 Ec741L
Marketing northwest lettuce, peas, cauliflower 1935. By L. S. Fenn [and] L. B.
Gerry. 27pp. [1936?] 1.9 Ec741L
Marketing potatoes, Kaw valley, Kansas, Orrik district, Missouri, Arkansas,
Oklahoma. Summary of 1935 season, by R. E. Corbin. 27pp. June 1936.
1.9 Ec741L
Marketing review 1936 Arizona cantaloupe season. 5PP. [1936?] (Issued in co-
operation with Arizona Fruit and vegetable standardization service)1.9 Ec741L
Monthly index of world industrial production 1920-1935. By Norman J. Wall.
22pp. June 1936. 1.9 Ec78Mo
Preliminary review of the 1936 Eastern Shore strawberry season, by A. M.
McDowell. 4pp. June 11, 1936. 1.9 Ec741L
Issued in cooperation with Virginia Department of Agriculture and
Maryland Department of Markets.
Price spreads between the farmer and the consumer, by Richard O. Been, jr. and
Frederick V. Waugh. 73pp. July 1936. 1.9 Ec754P
Quality of cotton linters produced in the United States season 1933-34 and 1934-
35, by Victor R. Fuchs... a preliminary report. 18pp. July 1936.
1.9 Ec733Qcl
Railroad transportation and agriculture during the depression, by Thor Hultgren.
15pp. July 1936. 1.9 Ec752Ra

Review Mississippi tomato season, 1936, by R. G. Risser. 3pp. [1936] 1.9 Ec741L
Review Mississippi vegetable season, 1936, by R. G. Risser. 4pp. June 19,
    1936. 1.9 Ec741L
A review of the 1935 Imperial valley watermelon season, by A. E. Prugh and H.
    A. Anderson. 5pp. June 9, 1936. (Issued in cooperation with California
    Dept. of agriculture. Market news service) 1.9 Ec741L
Review of the 1936 Imperial valley cantaloupe season, by A. E. Prugh and H. A.
    Anderson. 11pp. July 10, 1936. (Issued in cooperation with California
    Department of agriculture, Market news service) 1.9 Ec741L
Review of the 1936 Imperial valley carrot season. By A. E. Prugh and H. A.
    Anderson. 9pp. June 30, 1936. (Issued in cooperation with California
    Department of agriculture. Market news service) 1.9 Ec741L
Review of the 1936 Imperial valley lettuce season. By A. E. Prugh and H. A.
    Anderson. 2pp. June 16, 1936. (Issued in cooperation with California
    Department of agriculture. Market news service) 1.9 Ec741L
Revised estimates of flaxseed production, 1866-1929, and acreage and yield per
    acre, 1889-1929. 18pp. July 1936. 1.9 Ec71Ref
State and federal legislation and decisions relating to oleomargarine. Brief
    summary. Prepared by Anne Dewees, under the direction of O. C. Stine,
    in charge, Division of statistical and historical research. 47pp.
    June 1936. 1.9 Ec752Stf
Suggestions to prospective farmers and sources of information concerning the
    agriculture of a given region. July 1936. 31pp. 1.9 Ec76S
The summer dairy outlook 1936. 16pp. July 29, 1936. 1.9 Ec70d
The summer poultry and egg outlook 1936, 14pp. July 24, 1936. 1.9 Ec70p
Tariff rates on principal agricultural products, by C. F. Wells. 71pp.
    July 1936. 1.9 Ec752T
Tentative U. S. standards and grades for dressed turkeys. 8pp. June 1936.
    1.9 Ec724Tt
Tentative United States standards for grades of canned pears (Effective June
    22, 1936) 11pp. [1936] 1.9 Ec74Pea
U. S. standards for bunched carrots (Effective August 1, 1936) 4pp. July 20,
    1936. 1.9 Ec74Bb
U. S. standards for horseradish roots (Effective July 27, 1936) 6pp. July 20,
    1936. 1.9 Ec74Ho
U. S. standards for onion sets (Effective July 15, 1936) 4pp. July 2, 1936.
    1.9 Ec74Ons
U. S. standards for pears (Effective June 22, 1936) 9pp. June 15, 1936.
    1.9 Ec74Pea
U. S. standards for snap beans (Effective August 1, 1936). 3pp. July 20, 1936.
    1.9 Ec74Bes

Radio Talks and Addresses (Mimeographed)*

Commercial agriculture and the national welfare, by O. E. Baker. 12pp. [1936]
    1.9 Ec76Com
        Address, Agricultural Extension Conference, East Lansing, Michigan,
    November 6, 1935.

---
*Radio talks may be obtained from U. S. Department of Agriculture, Office of In-
formation, Radio Service.

Farm business facts; radio interview between Roy F. Hendrickson and Morse
    Salisbury. June 9, 1936. (5pp.); June 30, 1936 (5pp.); July 8, 1936
    (6pp.); July 21, 1936 (4pp.)   1.9 Ec7Ra
Farm business news; radio interview between Roy F. Hendrickson and Morse
    Salisbury. July 14, 1936 (5pp.); July 28, 1936 (5pp.). 1.9 Ec7Ra
Federal grading of Ohio canned foods, by Paul M. Williams. 7pp. [1936]
    1.9 Ec741Fg
        Address, Canners' Conference and Short Course, Ohio State University,
    Columbus, February 19, 1936.
The long-time significance of a soil conservation program to livestock pro-
    ducers. By A. G. Black. 16pp. 1936. 1.9 Ec7Lon
        For delivery at the annual meeting, American Institute of Cooperation,
    at Urbana, Ill., June 19, 1936.
The 1936 spring pig report, by C. L. Harlan. 2pp. June 29, 1936. 1.9 Ec7Ra
The poultry outlook; radio interview between Dr. A. G. Black and Morse
    Salisbury. July 24, 1936. 3pp. 1.9 Ec7Ra
The relationships of meat distributors' margins to changes in the prices of
    livestock and meats, by C. V. Whalin. 6pp. 4 charts. [1936]
    1.9 Ec713Rel
        Address, annual meeting of the National Livestock and Meat Board,
    Chicago, June 18, 1936.
Summer outlook broadcast on dairying; radio interview between Dr. A. G. Black
    and Morse Salisbury. July 29, 1936. 2pp. 1.9 Ec7Ra

Publications of the Agricultural Adjustment Administration*

Agricultural adjustment 1933 to 1935. A report of administration of the Agri-
    cultural adjustment act May 12, 1933, to December 31, 1935. 322pp.
    1936. (G-55)   1.4 Ad4Ge no.55
General sugar quota regulations, series 3, revision 2. Sugar consumption re-
    quirements and quotas for the calendar year 1936. 5pp. July 2, 1936.
    (G.S.Q R. series 3, no.3)   1.4 Su3G
Marketing agreement series - Agreement no. 66. Marketing agreement regulating
    the shipping of fresh pears, plums, Elberta peaches, apricots, and cherries
    grown in the state of California. Issued by the Secretary of agriculture
    May 23, 1936. Effective 12:01 a.m. E.S.T., May 25, 1936. (A-5)
    1.4 Ad47M no.66
1936 agricultural conservation program, east central region. Bulletin no. 2.
    (As amended by Supplement (a), issued July 7, 1936) Soil-building prac-
    tices and rates of payment. (ECR-B-2 (as amended July 7, 1936)) 1.42 Ea7B
1936 agricultural conservation program. Insular region. Bulletin no. 1. 4pp.
    July 10, 1936. 1.42 In7
1936 agricultural conservation program (northeast region) Bulletin no. 1 -
    Revised, Supplement (b) 2pp. June 19, 1936. (NER-B-1 Revised, Supple-
    ment (b)) 1.42 N76B
1936 agricultural conservation program, northeast region. Bulletin no. 2
    (As amended June 10, 1936) Soil-building practices - New York. 4pp.
    June 10, 1936. (NER-B-2-New York (As amended June 10, 1936))
    1.42 N76B

*Requests for these publications should be addressed to the Agricultural
    Adjustment Administration, U. S. Department of Agriculture, Washington, D. C.

1936 agricultural conservation program, northeast region. Bulletin no. 2
    (as amended June 10, 1936) Soil-building practices - Pennsylvania. 3PP.
    June 10, 1936. (NER-B-2-Pennsylvania (as amended June 10, 1936))
    1.42 N76B
1936 agricultural conservation program. Northeast region... Soil-building
    practices - Connecticut. 3PP. May 25, 1936. (NER-B-2-Connecticut
    (as amended May 25, 1936)) 1.42 N76B
1936 agricultural conservation program. Northeast region... Soil-building
    practices - Maine. 3PP. May 25, 1936. (NER-B-2-Maine (as amended May
    25, 1936)) 1.42 N76B
1936 agricultural conservation program. Northeast region... Soil-building
    practices - New Hampshire. 4pp. May 25, 1936. (NER-B-2-New Hampshire
    (as amended May 25, 1936)) 1.42 N76B
1936 agricultural conservation program (Northeast region)... Soil-building
    practices - New Jersey. 4pp. May 25, 1936. (NER-B-2- New Jersey (as
    amended May 25, 1936)) 1.42 N76B
1936 agricultural conservation program (Northeast region)... Soil-building
    practices - Rhode Island. 4pp. May 25, 1936. (NER-B-2-Rhode Island
    (as amended May 25, 1936)) 1.42 N76B
Order series - order no. 2, amendment no. 1. Order amending the order regulat-
    ing the handling of oranges and grapefruit grown in the states of Cali-
    fornia and Arizona. 2pp. June 9, 1936. (O-2-Amendment 1) 1.4 Ad470
Order series - Order no. 9. Order regulating the shipping of fresh pears, plums,
    and Elberta peaches grown in the state of California. Issued by the Secre-
    tary of agriculture. May 23, 1936. Effective 12:01 a.m., E.S.T., May 25,
    1936. (O-9) 1.4 Ad470
(Puerto Rico Sugar Order No. 4, Revision 1) Allotment of the quota for Puerto
    Rico. 3PP. Issued May 20, 1936. (P.R.S.O. No. 4, Revision 1) 1.4 Su3P
    no. 4, Rev. 1.
Questions and answers concerning the 1936 agricultural conservation program for
    the southern region. 11pp. June 1936. (Regional information series,
    SR leaflet 1 (Revised)) 1.42 So8L
Southern region miscellaneous series - item 1. The South's farm tenancy problem,
    Address by C. A. Cobb... before the Conference of rural ministers, state
    college, Mississippi, June 26, 1936. 6pp. June 30, 1936. (SRM-1)
    1.42 So8M
Unshackling our export trade, adapted in the Division of information from ad-
    dresses by Chester C. Davis... made June 3, 5, and 13, 1936. 8pp.
    July 1936. (G-57) 1.4 Ad4 Ge
        Issued also in mimeographed form (1.94 Ad4Da)

Addresses (Mimeographed)*

The contribution of 1936 to long-time agricultural policy. Address by H. R.
    Tolley... at the American institute of cooperation, University of Illinois,
    Urbana, Ill. ... June 19, 1936. 22pp. mimeogr. 1.94 Ad472T no.11.
Cotton exports and world trade. Address by Chester C.Davis... in Memphis,
    Tenn., under auspices of Memphis Chamber of commerce... June 17, 1936.
    13pp., mimeogr. 1.94 Ad4Da no.62.
_____
* May be obtained from U. S. Department of Agriculture, Office of Information.

European outlets for agricultural products. Excerpt of speech by Chester
C. Davis... before American institute of cooperation, Urbana, Illinois,
June 15, 1936. 9pp., mimeogr. 1.94 Ad4Da no.61
Farm problems and farm policies. Address by H. R. Tolley... before the
Annual farmers' short course at College Station, Texas, July 24, 1936.
12pp., mimeogr. 1.94 Ad472T no.12
The 1935 agricultural conservation program in the north central region, by
G. B. Thorne. 25pp. [1936] 1.42 N76Ag.
     Paper for delivery before the American Institute of Cooperation at
Urbana, Illinois, June 19, 1936.

Radio Talks (Mimeographed)*

Drought situation news. By Nathan Koenig... July 2, 1936. 2pp. 1.94 Ad4R
Meeting the drought emergency. By Jesse W. Tapp... June 30, 1936. 2pp.
1.94 Ad4R
The national program in conservation of rural resources. By C. A. Cobb...
July 4, 1936. 2pp. 1.42 So8Ra
Progress in soil conservation - north central region. By G. B. Thorne...
June 15, 1936. 2pp. 1.42 N75R
Progress of agricultural conservation program. By H. R. Tolley... June 2,
1936. 2pp. 1.94 Ad4R
Progress of the agricultural conservation program. By Alfred D. Stedman...
June 9, 1936. 2pp. 1.94 Ad4R
Progress of the agricultural conservation program; by S. B. Bledsoe...
July 28, 1936. 2pp. 1.94 Ad4R
Progress of the agricultural conservation program in the East central states.
By W. G. Finn. June 19, 1936. 3pp. 1.42 Ea7R
Progress of the agricultural conservation program in the Northeast, by H. B.
Boyd. June 19, 1936. 2pp. 1.42 N75R

Miscellaneous (Mimeographed)**

Digest of Commodity exchange act, by J. M. Mehl. 23pp. June 1936. (Issued
by Grain futures administration) 1.9 G76Dig
Foreign agricultural extension activities. Africa, Australia, British Guiana,
Canada, Ceylon, China, Cyprus, England, Haiti, Holland, Jamaica, Mexico,
Nova Scotia, Scotland. Comp. by Extension studies and teaching section.
26pp. June 1936. (Issued as U. S. Dept. of agriculture. Extension service. Division of cooperative extension. Extension service circular
243) 1.9 Ex892 Esc
Publications of the U. S. Department of agriculture of interest to country
women. 9pp., mimeogr. Washington, D. C., 1936. 1.9 L61P
     "A selected list issued in connection with the Third triennial confer-
ence of the Associated countrywomen of the world, Washington, D. C.,
May 31-June 11, 1936."
     Issued by United States Department of Agriculture Library.
Statistical results of cooperative extension work, 1935 [by] M. C. Wilson.
52pp. June 1936. (Issued as U. S. Dept. of agriculture. Extension service. Division of cooperative extension. Extension service circular 244)
1.9 Ex892 Esc

---

* May be obtained from U. S. Department of Agriculture. Office of Information.
Radio Service.
** Requests for these publications should be addressed to the issuing office.

Compiled by Mary F. Carpenter

Arkansas

Arkansas. Agricultural experiment station. Forty-seventh annual report,
fiscal year ending June 30, 1935. Ark. Agr. Expt. Sta. Bull. 323,
55pp. Fayetteville. 1935.
Rural economics and sociology, pp. 48-52.

Arkansas. University. College of agriculture, Extension service. Annual
report.... 1934/35. Ark. Agr. Col. Ext. Serv. Circ. 355, 67pp.
Little Rock. 1936.
Agricultural economics and marketing, pp. 34-39; Agricultural adjustment activities, pp. 60-63.

Arkansas. University, College of agriculture, Extension service. Types
of farming in Arkansas. Ark. Agr. Col. Ext. Circ. 351, 76pp., map.
Little Rock. June, 1936.

California

Shear, S. W. Apricot market situation, June 17, 1936. 6pp. mimeogr.
Berkeley. Calif. Agr. Expt. Sta. 1936.

Stover, H. J. An analysis of the prices received for canned apricots by
canners in California - seasons, 1924-25 through 1935-36. Calif. Agr.
Expt. Sta. Giannini Found. Agr. Econ. Mimeogr. Rept. 47, 19pp.
Berkeley. June, 1936.

Stover, H. J. An analysis of the prices received for canned Bartlett
pears by canners on the Pacific coast - seasons, 1924-25 through 1935-
36. Calif. Agr. Expt. Sta. Giannini Found. Agr. Econ. Mimeogr. Rept.
49, 19pp. Berkeley. July, 1936.

Stover, H. J. An analysis of the prices received for canned clingstone
peaches by canners in California - seasons, 1924-25 through 1935-36.
Calif. Agr. Expt. Sta. Giannini Found. Agr. Econ. Mimeogr. Rept. 46,
19pp. Berkeley. June, 1936.

Tinley, J. M. Price-factors in the Los Angeles milk market. Calif. Agr.
Expt. Sta. Giannini Found. Agr. Econ. Mimeogr. Rept. 48. 41pp.
Berkeley. July, 1936.

Voorhies, E. C. The dairy industry. Calif. Agr. Col. Timely Agr. Outlooks,
no. 7, 4pp., mimeogr. Berkeley. 1936.

Voorhies, E. C. Eggs and poultry. Calif. Agr. Col. Timely Agr. Outlooks,
no. 6, 4pp., mimeogr. Berkeley. 1936.

Delaware

Daugherty, M. M.   Part-time farming in New Castle county, Delaware.   Del.
Agr. Expt. Sta. Bull. 199, 24pp. Newark. 1936.

Florida

Fifield, W. M.   Potato growing in Florida.   Fla. Agr. Expt. Sta. Bull. 295,
48pp. Gainesville. April, 1936.
Bibliography, pp. 47-48.
Harvesting, pp. 41-43; Grading and packing, pp. 43-45; Marketing,
pp. 45-46.

Florida. Agricultural experiment station.   Annual report for the fiscal
year ending June 30, 1935. 152pp. Gainesville. 1935.
Agricultural economics, pp. 31-35.

Florida. State department of agriculture. Twenty-third biennial report.
1932-34. 63pp.   Tallahassee. 1934.
Partial contents: The State marketing bureau and its work, by
Nathan Mayo, pp. 14-16; Facts about the inspection bureau, by Nathan
Mayo, pp. 20-22; The land division and its functions, pp. 26-28;
Florida's dairy and milk inspection, by Nathan Mayo, pp. 32-34; Florida
crop report for 1934; Increase shown in value of State crops, by H. A.
Maups, pp. 62-64.

Florida. University. Agricultural extension service.   1935 report [of] cooper
ative extension work in agriculture. 98pp. Gainesville. 1936?
Agricultural adjustment program, pp. 28-34; Agricultural economics,
p. 60-64.

Illinois

Johnston, P. E., Andrews, J. B., and Sauer, E. L. Annual farm business report
on eighty-three farms in Jefferson, Edwards, Wabash, Jackson, Marion,
White, Saline, Crawford, Richland, Clay, Washington, Wayne, and Johnson
counties, Illinois, 1934. 17pp., mimeogr. Urbana, Univ. of Ill.,
Col. Agr., Dept. Agr. Econ. and Agr. Ext. Serv. May, 1935.
In cooperation with Farm bureaus in the above counties.

Johnston, P. E., Hodges, T. R., and Ackerman, J.   Annual farm business re-
port on fifty-four farms in Boone, Winnebago, and McHenry counties,
Illinois, 1934. 12pp., mimeogr. Urbana, Univ. of Ill., Col. Agr.,
Dept. Agr. Econ. and Agr. Ext. Serv. May, 1935.
In cooperation with Farm bureaus in above counties.

Johnston, P. E., Sauer, E. L., and Hedges, T. R. Annual farm business report on seventy-three farms in Clinton, Bond, Monroe, and Montgomery
counties, Illinois, 1934. 17pp., mimeogr. Urbana, Univ. of Ill., Col.
Agr., Dept. Agr. Econ. and Agr. Ext. Serv. May, 1935.
In cooperation with Farm bureaus in the above counties.

Indiana

Indiana. Agricultural experiment station. Twenty-first annual report of the Creamery License division for the year ending March 31, 1935. Ind. Agr. Expt. Sta. Circ. 215, 16pp. Lafayette. 1936.
    Includes statistics of the dairy industry and a list of licensed manufacturing plants in Indiana.

Iowa

Reid, M. G. Some factors affecting improvements in Iowa farm family housing. Ia. Agr. Expt. Sta., Bull. 349, pp. 326-361. Ames. 1936.
    In this study the Rural Social Science and Economics section cooperated with the Iowa State Planning Board.

Soth, L. K. Agricultural economic facts basebook of Iowa. Ia. Agr. Expt. Sta. Special Rept. 1, 179pp. Ames. 1936.
    In cooperation with the Extension Service of the Iowa State College.
    Iowa farm income, prices, production, real estate, taxes, types of farming, home conveniences, and population with statistical tables, charts, and an index.

Kansas

Kansas. State board of agriculture. Kansas agricultural convention, 1936, containing the addresses, papers and discussions at the sixty-fifth annual meeting of the Board, January 8-10, 1936. Kans. State Bd. Agr. Rept. for the quarter ending March, 1936, v. 55, no. 217-A, 120pp. Topeka.

Kentucky

Kentucky. Agricultural experiment station. Forty-eighth annual report for the year 1935. Part I, 70pp. Lexington. 1936.
    Economic studies, pp. 8-14.

Kentucky. University. College of agriculture. Extension division. Annual report for the year ended December 31, 1935. Ky. Agr. Col. Ext. Circ. 283, 55PP. Lexington. 1936.
    Farm Economics, pp. 44-48; Markets and Rural Finance, pp. 48-49.

Massachusetts

Moser, R. E. Prices of farm products in Massachusetts, 1910-1935. 21pp., mimeogr. Amherst, Mass. State Col. May, 1935.
    U. S. Department of Agriculture and County extension services in agriculture and home economics cooperating.

Michigan

Gardner, V. R. Factors influencing the yields of Montmorency cherry orchards in Michigan. Mich. Agr. Expt. Sta. Special Bull. 275, 18pp. East Lansing. 1936.

Includes table giving acreage yields in pounds for the years 1925-
1933, p. 6 and cost of production, pp.15-17.

Gross, I. H., and Pond, Julia.   Changes in standards of consumption during
a depression. Mich. Agr. Expt. Sta. Special Bull. 274, 30pp. East
Lansing. 1936.
The study is based upon information collected between October 1932
and May 1933, in seven Townships of Clinton County, Michigan.

Michigan. Agricultural experiment station. Alfalfa in Michigan. Mich. Agr.
Expt. Sta. Circ. Bull. 154, 80pp. East Lansing. January, 1936.
Bibliography, pp. 79-80.
Alfalfa as a cash crop, pp. 26-31; Costs, pp. 58-64.

Michigan. Agricultural experiment station. Quarterly bulletin v. 18, no. 4,
pp. 211-278.   East Lansing. May, 1936.
Partial contents: Costs of producing and marketing sugar beets in
Michigan in 1935, by K. T. Wright, pp. 235-238; 1935 onion costs of production in Michigan, by K. T. Wright, pp. 238-240; Changes in population
of counties in Michigan since 1930, by J. F. Thaden, pp. 242-245; Distribution of red and white wheat in Michigan, by H. C. Rather, pp. 266-268.

Michigan. State department of agriculture. Sixth biennial report for the fiscal
years ending June 30, 1933 and June 30, 1934. 130pp. Lansing. 1934.
Bureau of Agricultural Industry: Division of Agricultural Statistics
(Michigan Co-operative Crop Reporting Service) pp. 19-20; Bureau of Foods
and Standards, pp. 53-66; Bureau of Dairying, pp. 67-83 (Includes statistics of dairy products); Bureau of Animal Industry, pp. 85-112 (Includes
statistics of livestock)

Ulrey, Orion.   Public produce markets of Michigan. Mich. Agr. Expt. Sta.
Special Bull. 268, 87pp. East Lansing. May, 1936.

Wright, K. T.   The economics of bean production in Michigan. Mich. Agr. Expt.
Sta. Special Bull. 270, 46pp. East Lansing. 1936.
Includes general information on beans, costs of production and returns,
labor requirements, and a production program for the future.

Minnesota

Garey, L. F.   A study of the demand for potatoes in the Twin Cities. Minn.
Agr. Expt. Sta. Bull. 324, 24pp. University Farm, St. Paul. October, 1935.

Jesness, O. B.   The new farm program. Minn. Univ. Agr. Ext. Div. Minn. Farm
Business Notes, no. 163, pp. 1-3, mimeogr. University Farm, St. Paul.
July 20, 1936.

Minnesota Agricultural experiment station. Forty-second annual report...
July 1, 1934 to June 30, 1935. 89pp. University Farm, St. Paul. 1935.
Agricultural economics, pp. 51-53; Rural sociology, p.74

Pond, G. A., and Sallee, G. A.   Farmers' earnings in 1935 with comparisons
for previous years. Minn. Univ. Agr. Ext. Div. Minn. Farm Business
Notes, no. 162, pp. 1-3, mimeogr.   University Farm. St. Paul. 1936.

Pond, G. A., and Schwantes, A. J.   Tractor costs and rates of performance. A
preliminary report of data secured in 1935 covering the cost of operation and the rate of performance of farm tractors in Minnesota and summaries for 1933 and 1934. Minn. Univ. Dept. Agr. Econ. Mimeogr. Rept.
74, 9pp. University Farm, St. Paul. 1936.

Ranney, W. P., and Pond, G. A.   Annual report [8th] of the farm management
service for farmers in southeast Minnesota for the year 1935. Minn.
Univ. Dept. Agr. Econ. Mimeogr. Rept. 72, 32pp. University Farm, St.
Paul. 1936.
    In cooperation with the U. S. Bureau of Agricultural Economics and
the Farm Bureaus of Dodge, Freeborn, Goodhue, Le Sueur, Mower, Rice,
Steele, and Waseca counties.

Ranney, W. P., and others.   Fifth annual report of the farm management service for farmers of northern Minnesota for the year 1935 (April 1, 1935
to March 31, 1936). Minn. Univ. Dept. Agr. Econ. Mimeogr. Rept. 77,
19pp. University Farm, St. Paul. 1936.
    In cooperation with the county extension services of Carlton, Itasca,
and St. Louis counties.

Ranney, W. P., Pond, G. A., and Cohee, M. H.   First annual report of the
farm management service for farmers in soil erosion control demonstration areas for the year 1935 (April 1935 to March 1936). Minn. Univ.
Dept. Agr. Econ. Mimeogr. Rept. 78, 21pp. University Farm, St. Paul.
1936.

Sallee, G. A., Pond, G. A., and Loreaux, R. H.   A preliminary report of crop
production costs from data secured in 1935 on the farm accounting route in
Winona county, Minnesota. Minn. Univ. Dept. Agr. Econ. Mimeogr. Rept. 71,
16pp. University Farm, St. Paul. 1936.

Sallee, G. A., and Pond, G. A.   A preliminary report of data secured in 1935
on the farm accounting route in Stevens county, Minnesota. Minn. Univ.
Dept. Agr. Econ. Mimeogr. Rept. 73, 21pp. University Farm, St. Paul. 1936.

Sallee, G. A., Pond, G. A., and Loreaux, R. H.   A preliminary report of data
secured in 1935 on the farm accounting route in Winona County, Minnesota.
Minn. Univ. Dept. Agr. Div. Agr. Econ. Mimeogr. Rept. 76, 29pp. University
Farm, St. Paul. June, 1936.
    U. S. Department of Agriculture, Bureau of Agricultural Economics
cooperating.

Sallee, G. A., Pond, G. A., Loreaux, R. H.   A preliminary report of livestock
costs and returns from data secured in 1935 on the farm accounting route
in Winona county, Minnesota. Minn. Univ. Dept. Agr. Econ. Mimeogr. Rept.
75, 19pp. University Farm, St. Paul. 1936.

Miller, M. P.   Cropping systems in relation to erosion control. Mo. Agr. Expt. Sta. Bull. 366, 36pp. Columbia. 1936.

Missouri. University, College of agriculture, Extension service.   Annual report for 1935. Mo. Agr. Col. Ext. Circ. 344, 59PP. Columbia. 1936.
  Agricultural Adjustment Administration, pp. 7-12; Agricultural economics, pp. 10-14.

Morgan, E. L., and Sneed, M. W.   The libraries of Missouri; a survey of facilities. Mo. Agr. Expt. Sta. Research Bull. 236, 94pp. Columbia. April, 1936.

Montana

Montana. Agricultural experiment station.   Reshaping Montana's agriculture. The forty-first annual report... July 1, 1933 to June 30, 1934. 83pp. Bozeman. [1936]
  Partial contents: Facing new agricultural problems, pp. 5-10. Evolution of an agricultural policy for Montana. (Department of Agricultural Economics), pp. 10-27.

Renne, R. R.   Montana land ownership. An analysis of the ownership pattern and its significance in land use planning. Mont. Agr. Expt. Sta. Bull. 322, 58pp. Bozeman. 1936.
  "A brief summary of some of the more important findings of this study were published in Montana Experiment Station Bulletin 310, 'Readjusting Montana's Agriculture: IV. Land Ownership and Tenure.' This larger bulletin gives the details of the method and the data upon which these findings are based, together with a more complete discussion of their social and economic implications."

Renne, R. R.   Readjusting Montana's agriculture. VIII. Tax delinquency and mortgage foreclosures. Mont. Agr. Expt. Sta. Bull. 319, 27pp. Bozeman. 1936.

Nebraska

Garey, L. F.   Factors determining type-of-farming areas in Nebraska. Nebr. Agr. Expt. Sta. Bull. 299. 32pp. Lincoln. May, 1936.
  Includes description of type-of-farming areas in Nebraska.

Nebraska. Department of agriculture and inspection. Biennial report, 1931-1932 and 1933-1934. 94pp. Lincoln [1936]
  Progress of Nebraska agriculture, 1931-1934, includes statistics of crops and livestock; Division of Agricultural Statistics, pp. 19-21; Division of Weights and Measures, pp. 81-83; Potato inspection, p. 84.

New Hampshire

Grinnell, H. C.   Rural real estate tax delinquency in New Hampshire. N. H.
Agr. Expt. Sta. Bull. 290, 19pp.   Durham. March, 1936.
"During the first three and one-half months of 1934 the Bureau of
Agricultural Economics, Washington, D. C., under a Civil Works project,
in cooperation with the Agricultural Experiment Stations collected data
relative to tax delinquent rural real estate and land values for the six
year period from 1928 through 1933...
"It is the purpose of this bulletin to present a general summary of the
data collected, tabulated and summarized for New Hampshire, which formed
a part of this nation-wide project."

New Hampshire Agricultural experiment station. Agricultural research in New
Hampshire. Annual report of director... for the year 1935. N. H. Agr.
Expt. Sta. Bull. 289, 31pp. Durham. March, 1936.
Agricultural economics, pp.6-10.

New Jersey

Black, L. M., and Taylor, J. C.   Egg production, monthly costs and receipts on
New Jersey poultry farms, November 1934-October, 1935. N. J. Agr. Expt.
Sta. Hints to Poultrymen, v. 23, no. 2, 4pp. New Brunswick. Dec. 1935-
Jan. 1936.

Pitt, D. T.   New Jersey farm prices and their index numbers, 1931-1935. N. J.
Dept. Agr. Circ. 255, 41pp. Trenton. 1936.
A supplement to Circular 221, New Jersey farm prices and their index
numbers, 1910-1930.

New York

Anderson, W. A.   Rural youth: activities, interests, and problems. I. Married
young men and women, 15 to 29 years of age. N. Y. (Cornell) Agr. Expt.
Sta. Bull. 649, 53pp. Ithaca. 1936.

Cunningham, L. C.   Seasonal costs and returns in producing milk in Orange
county, New York. N. Y. (Cornell) Agr. Expt. Sta. Bull. 641, 41pp. Ithaca.
1936.

Knott, J. E.   Quality of lettuce as it affects the New York lettuce industry.
N. Y. (Cornell) Agr. Expt. Sta. Bull. 651, 17pp. Ithaca. 1936.

LaMont, T. E.   An economic study of land utilization in Broome county, New
York. N. Y. (Cornell) Agr. Expt. Sta. Bull. 642, 51pp. Ithaca. 1936.
Includes a folded land classification map of Broome County.

New York (Cornell) State college of agriculture. Department of agricultural
economics and farm management.   Farm economics, no. 95. Ithaca. May, 1936.
Partial contents: Business conditions, by G. F. Warren and F. A. Pearson,
pp. 2317-2319; The use of highways in rural New York, pp. 2319,2325-2327,
by W. M. Curtiss; Factors affecting the operating expenses of feed stores, by
W. Y. Yang, pp. 2327-2329; Relation of number of important business factors

to labor income on market garden farms with greenhouses, by E. G. Misner, pp. 2329-2330; Trends in New York farm prices, 1841-1935, by S. E. Ronk, pp. 2331-2334; Cost of raising heifers, by E. M. Hughes, pp. 2335-2336; Where New York growers disposed of important fruit and vegetable crops season, 1933-34, by M. P. Rasmusson, pp. 2336-2337; Trends of the important costs of producing milk, by L. C. Cunningham, pp. 2338-2339; Prices and yields of apple varieties in the Hudson Valley, by P. S. Williamson, pp. 2339-2340.

New York (Cornell) State college of agriculture. Department of agricultural economics and farm management. Farm economics, no. 96, Ithaca. June, 1936.
    Partial contents: Business conditions, by G. F. Warren and F. A. Pearson, pp. 2341-2342; Cost of operating farm equipment, by J. P. Hertel, pp. 2342-2343, 2349-2350; Labor incomes on Schuyler county vineyard farms, crop year 1935, by E. G. Misner, pp. 2350-2351; Acreage of land classes I and II in the watershed of the Susquehanna river in New York state and its relation to flood control, by T. E. LaMont, pp. 2351-2355.

New York. State department of agriculture and markets. List of milk plants and establishments; also milk dealers in New York State 1935. N. Y. State Dept. Agr. and Markets. Bull. 301, 155pp. Albany. September, 1935.

New York. State department of agriculture and markets. Statistics relative to the dairy industry in New York State, 1934-1935. N. Y. State Dept. Agr. and Markets. Bull. 300, 234pp. Albany. July, 1935.
    In cooperation with U. S. Department of Agriculture, Bureau of Agricultural Economics.

Raeburn, J. R. Economic studies of dairy farming in New York. XII. 150 farms in the Tully-Horner area, crop year, 1931. N. Y. (Cornell) Agr. Expt. Sta. Bull. 644, 53pp. Ithaca. 1936.

Scoville, G. P. Factors affecting the returns from farming, Newfane-Olcott area, Niagara county, New York, 1934-35. N. Y. (Cornell) Agr. Col. AE 139, 16pp., mimeogr. Ithaca. 1936.

Scoville, G. P. Marketing the 1934 apple crop, Newfane-Olcott area, Niagara county, New York. N. Y. (Cornell) Agr. Col. AE 138, 22pp., mimeogr. Ithaca. 1936.

Ohio

Henning, G. F., and Eckert, P. S. Livestock auctions in Ohio. Ohio Agr. Expt. Sta. Bimonthly Bull. 21 (181): 87-104. Wooster. July-August, 1936.

Oklahoma

Oklahoma. Agricultural experiment station. Current farm economics, v. 9, no. 3, Stillwater, June, 1936.

Partial contents: The Oklahoma farm price of cattle as compared with the Kansas City and Chicago price of stockers and feeders, by W. J. Fessler, pp. 65-69; Wheat situation, by T. R. Hedges, pp. 69-71; Quality of the Oklahoma cotton crop for the crop year 1935, by C. B. Barre, pp. 71-74; Some effects of returning classification cards to patrons of gins co-operating with grade and staple statistics section, by C. B Barre, pp. 74-77; Some financial aspects of cooperative ginning of cotton, by A. W. Jacob, pp. 77-78.

South Carolina

Guin, Marvin. An economic study of hog production and marketing in South
  Carolina. S. C. Agr. Expt. Sta. Bull. 305, 27pp. Clemson. April, 1936.
    Bibliography, p. 26.

South Carolina. Department of agriculture, commerce and industries. Yearbook...
  1934-1935. 180pp. Columbia. [1936]
    Includes the annual crop and livestock review, reports on tobacco,
  annual statistical reports of the Warehouse Division, and of the Labor
  Division which contains factory inspection and manufacturing statistics.

Vermont

Norcross, H. C., and Brown, A. A. Prices of farm products in Vermont, 1932-
  1934. Vt. Agr. Col. Ext. Circ. 84, 13pp. Burlington. 1935.

Vermont. University, College of agriculture, Extension service. Farm business
  v. 3, no. 3, 4pp. Burlington, June, 1936.
    Relationship between the price of farm butter and the price of wheat
  bran, by T. M. Adams, p. 1; Farm management survey in Washington County
  completed, by H. C. Norcross, pp. 1-2; Pounds of milk required to buy
  a cow in 'Vermont, by H. R. Varney, p. 3; Maple production low in 1936,
  by H. R. Varney, p. 3.

Virginia

Virginia. Agricultural and mechanical college and polytechnic institute. Extension work... some accomplishments in 1935. Va. Agr. Col. Ext. Bull. 141,
  56pp., Blacksburg. 1936.
    Reports on economic projects may be found under various headings.

West Virginia

Armentrout, W. W., and Stelzer, R. O. Milk-distribution costs in West Virginia.
  II. A study of the costs incurred by 75 producer-distributors in the
  Clarksburg, Fairmont, Morgantown, and Wheeling markets for a twelve-month
  period during 1934-1935. W. Va. Agr. Expt. Sta. Bull. 270, 32pp. Morgantown. June 1936.

Wisconsin

Wisconsin. Department of agriculture and markets. The Wisconsin law governing
  storage of grain. An act to provide for state supervision of licensed
  warehouses, and the issuance of storage certificates on grain stored
  therein. Wis. Dept. Agr. Bull. 169, 12pp. Madison. 1936.

Compiled by Louise O. Bercaw and A. M. Hannay

Agrarian Reform - Honduras

The agrarian law of Honduras. Commerce Reports no. 23, p. 445, June 6,
1936. (Published by the Bureau of Foreign and Domestic Commerce,
U. S. Dept. of Commerce)

"The Republic of Honduras recently passed its new Agrarian law,
clearly defining the rights of the State, the method of acquiring
national lands, the family homestead, commons, and the acquisition
of public lands under lease."

A description of the law is given, including the classification
of salable public lands.

Agrarian Reform - Hungary

Wollner, W. Das Regierungsprojekt einer neuen Bodenreform. Wirtschaftsdienst (n.F.) 21(19): 655-657. May 8, 1936. (Published for
the Hamburgisches Welt-Wirtschafts-Archiv by the Hanseatische
Verlagsanstalt Aktiengesellschaft, Hamburg 36, Germany)

Attention is called to the partial failure of the agrarian reform of 1920. Land was given to many who had neither the necessary
means nor experience to cultivate it. As only a limited amount of
land was available, holdings were in many cases too small to support a family. Hence the farmer had to have another source of income and often hired out to a large landowner. This had a depressing
effect on the agricultural labor market and on wages. Proposals
have been made by succeeding Governments to establish a more economical
ratio between large, small, and medium-sized holdings, and to provide new holdings capable of supporting a family.

Agrarian Reform - Spain

Dobby, E. H. G. Agrarian problems in Spain. Geogr. Rev. 26(2): 177-189.
April 1936 (Published by the American Geographical Society, Broadway
at 156th St., New York, N. Y.)

The writer states that the agrarian problem is not wholly the
breaking down of the large estates, but is "really a series of problems
that differ so sharply from region to region that there seems little
possibility of approaching a general solution through the hands of a
central government in Madrid." He discusses the sizes of agricultural property and the impossibility of making a careful and accurate
analysis of Spanish landholdings, rural social questions, the diverse
systems of land tenure, wheat, uneconomic marginal lands, mechanization, reafforestation, cooperation, agrarian reforms under the Republic,
and irrigation schemes.

Proyecto de ley de bases de la reforma agraria. El Progreso Agricola y
Pecuario 42(1916): 242-244. Apr. 30, 1936. (Published at Plaza de
Oriente, Madrid, Spain)

Text of a bill presented to the Cartes on April 16, 1936 revising the basic principles of agrarian reform in Spain, enumerating the types of land susceptible of expropriation, and determining the eligible recipients.

Agricultural Adjustment Administration

Cox, A. B. The A.A.A., the cotton growers, and the agricultural problem. Amer. Statis. Assoc. Jour. 31(194): 295-305. June 1936. (Published by the Association. Frederick F. Stephan, Sec.-Treasurer, 722 Woodward Bldg., Washington, D. C.)
    Discussion by L. H. Bean, pp.308-314. Rejoinder by Dr. Cox, pp. 314-317.
    The main theses in Dr. Cox's paper as stated by him in his Rejoinder are as follows:
    "(1) That price parity with 1909-1914, which is the main objective of the A.A.A., is unsound and that parity income should be the objective. (2) That the gold price of cotton has not advanced, and that dollar prices advanced almost exactly in proportion to the decline in the gold value of the dollar. (3) That a restriction program to raise price to raise farmers' income will not work in the case of cotton because planned restriction of·production is met by (a) planned restriction of consumption of American cotton, (b) planned expansion of production abroad, and (c) increased competition of substitutes. (4) That cotton production restriction has put hundreds of thousands, even millions, on relief. (5) That specialized cotton production occupies a key position in our system of specialized, large scale, regional production, and that it is of extreme national importance to restore foreign markets for American cotton."

Has the New Deal helped the farmer? A debate on a campaign issue. Forum 95(2): 76-82. February 1936. (Published in New York, N. Y.) (Copy in Pam. Coll.)
    This consists of two articles: I. Farmers still want the AAA, by Chester C. Davis, pp.76-79; II. Crop control brings serfdom, by L. J. Dickinson, pp.79-82.

Agricultural Bookkeeping

Wyllie, James. Farm cost-accounting. Land Union Jour. 33(5): 72-76. May 1936. (Published at 15 Lower Grosvenor Place, Westminster, London, S.W. 1, Eng.)
    "A paper read...at the Farmers' Club meeting on May 4th, 1936.
    The objectives, kinds, uses and advantages of cost-accounting are discussed.
    Digest of paper also in Estate Magazine 36(6): 401-406. June 1936.

Agricultural Indebtedness — Denmark

Denmark. Relief of agriculture. Scot. Jour. Agr. 19(2): 195-196. April 1936. (Published by H. M. Stationery Office, Edinburgh, Scotland.)

Recent legislative proposals would grant relief at the rate of 3 percent for a period of two years to farmers whose indebtedness amounts to at least 85 percent of the mortgage value of their farm, provided that security amounting to between 85 and 110 percent of the mortgage value is available. "The relief will cease in 1937 if by that time prices of butter and pork have risen more than 20 percent above the 1935 level."

Agricultural Indebtedness - Japan

H., W. L.   Farm debts and farm population in Japan.   Far East Survey 5 (12): 126. June 3, 1936. (Published by Fortnightly Research Service, American Council, Institute of Pacific Relations, 129 East 52nd St., New York, N. Y.)

The Trans-Pacific (Tokyo) questioned figures of the farm debt in Japan as discussed in an article entitled "Plight of Japanese Agriculture" (Far Eastern Survey, Jan. 1, 1936, pp. 1-5). This article is in reply to that query.

Agricultural Policy - Manchuria

New agricultural policy. Manchurian Econ. Rev. 3(9): 19. May 1, 1936. (Published by G. Harmsen, Harbin, Manchoukuo.)

Plans have been made to increase the production of soya beans, kaoliang, millet and maize, wheat, cotton, silk, sugar beets, hemp, jute and flax, oil producing products and fruits.

Twelve salient points of the new agricultural policy are listed.

Agricultural Protectionism

Emanuel, A.   Agricultural protectionism and the agricultural situation 1925-29. Part II. Developments in world agriculture in the years preceding the depression. Monthly Bull. Agr. Econ. and Sociol. [Reprint from Internatl. Rev. Agr.] 27(5): 157E-168E. May 1936. (Published by International Institute of Agriculture, Rome, Italy)

"In the first part of our study we have described the attempts which were made during the period 1925-1929 with a view to returning to the so-called 'normal' conditions of before the war...

"In the second part of the present study an attempt was made to analyse the actual changes which either have taken place, or were taking place, in the conditions of agricultural production and trade in the course of the period 1925-29, and which worked at cross purposes with each other, making for conflicts and maladjustment. Our examination of the trends in the production and consumption of agricultural commodities, in monetary conditions and capital movements, in agricultural prices and in the evolution of world trade in agricultural products tend to show that, far from the hoped-for balance being established, the lack of balance in the economic situation of world agriculture was becoming increasingly pronounced.

"As the depression resulting from the accentuation of these maladjustments deepened, the belief in the possibility of economic restoration on the basis of pre-war standards of 'normality' tended to fade and to give place to attempts at intervention and control.

The nature and significance of this change, as well as the evolution
and effects of the various measures of intervention in the domain of
agriculture, will form the subject matter of later studies."

Agricultural Relief - Foreign Countries

Farm aid in foreign countries. Foreign Crops and Markets 32(22): 643-684.
June 1, 1936. (Published by the Division of Foreign Agricultural
Service, Bureau of Agricultural Economics, U. S. Dept. of Agriculture)
Also issued in reprint form.
"The purpose of this article is to present a brief description of
the principal agricultural relief measures adopted in foreign countries.
Emphasis is placed on developments since the beginning of the depres-
sion, but the discussion of each country gives a brief historical back-
ground. No attempt is made...to analyze specifically the results of
the programs in the various countries. Such analyses are reserved for
studies of individual countries now in progress, which will be reached
from time to time by the Foreign Agricultural Service." -Note, p.643.
Countries for which descriptions are given are the United Kingdom,
Canada, Australia, South Africa, New Zealand, Germany, France, Italy,
Sweden, Denmark, the Netherlands, Hungary, Poland, Spain, the Soviet
Union, Argentina, Brazil, Mexico, Japan, and China.

Agricultural Relief - United States

Annual convention devoted to discussion of farm problems. Fertilizer Rev.
11(2): 2-3, 14. April-May-June, 1936. (Published at 616 Investment
Bldg., Washington, D. C.)
Reviews addresses at the twelfth annual convention of the National
Fertilizer Association held at White Sulphur Springs, W. Va., June 8,
9, and 10. The President of the association, Mr. A. D. Strobhar
reviewed briefly the work of the association during the past year;
Governor William I. Myers of the Farm Credit Administration addressed
the convention on "Financing American Agriculture" (he described "in
detail" the Farm Credit structure which has been developed during
the past few years); Dr. H. H. Zimmerley spoke on "New Developments
in Fertilizer Use"; Charles J. Brand discussed "Open Price Fixing";
and Joseph F. Cox described the Soil Conservation Program.

Lord, Russell. The forced march of the farmers. Survey Graphic 25(4):
215-219, 278-281. April 1936. (Published at 112 East 19th St., New
York, N. Y.)
"...the farm march toward a calculated national harvest of essential
foods and fabrics, which started sporadically during the reactionary
post-war administrations, and which in the present administration has
assumed perhaps historic proportions, has been a forced march of departure from instinctive rural principles from the first. Crop control
has gone against Nature. It has gone against the average farmer's
favorite picture of himself as the generous guardian, the bountiful
provider who alone and uniquely feeds and clothes harum-scarum humankind.

Control has gone against the farmer's other most cherished illusion, independence. It has aroused in many farm minds a sense of sin more soundly rooted than shocked disapproval of dancing, cards and liquor. So the marchers, by and large, have advanced one way and gazed another. But they have marched. There seemed no other choice."

Mr. Lord describes various attempts to aid the farming industry and says:

"Looking beyond immediate justification, the late AAA did this: It achieved a mobilization of farmers into planning and bargaining groups, by commodities, building from township committees up through county associations and the state agricultural extension services, to center in Washington, with controls fairly flexible, but strong. Three years ago such an organization of agriculture, with 4600 county production control associations, would have seemed beyond belief."

The author believes that there was "a lack of genuine emotional allegiance to...AAA ...evident in the way farmers took the Supreme Court decision, sitting down..."

Snow, B. W. Agricultural trouble -- cause and cure. Grain and Feed Journals Consolidated 76(10): 403, 405. May 27, 1936. (Published at 332 South La Salle St., Chicago, Ill.)

Address before the Illinois Grain Dealers Association at Peoria, Ill.

In this discussion of the cause and cure of our agricultural trouble the opinion is expressed that high tariffs do not raise wages, and that the protective tariff "actually increases the cost of producing unprotected commodities, by increasing the cost of things needed in their production. It is here that the farmer is hit hard. The artificial price at which the tariff enables the industrialist to sell his goods increases the farmer's cost of producing his crops. This has been happening over a long period of years and gradually has shut our farmer out of foreign markets.

"There is no panacea, no royal road to comfort, nothing but recognition of our mistakes and a retracing of the steps that have led us into this economic morass.

"What I vision is a gradual revision of tariff schedules with a continued moderation of rates permitted, until in the course of time, the injustices shall have been corrected and agriculture and industry shall stand upon the sound basis of tariff equality."

Agriculture -- Santa Clara Valley

Torbert, E. N. The specialized commercial agriculture of the northern Santa Clara Valley. Geogr. Rev. 26(2): 247-263. April 1936. (Published by the American Geographical Society, Broadway at 156th St., New York, N. Y.)

Subtopics: Climate and horticulture; areal specialization; specialization on individual holdings; the labor problem; the water crisis; the approach to complete development.

A map on p. 250 shows land utilization in the Northeastern part of the valley; a soil map of the same area is given on p. 251; a detailed map-diagram of a mile-wide strip extending seven miles northeastward from the southern outskirts of San Jose to the crest of the first range, p.256, also shows land utilization.

Agriculture – Scotland

Cruickshank, James.   Changes in the agricultural industry of Aberdeenshire
   in the last fifty years – I.   Scot. Jour. Agr. 19(2): 130-139.   April
   1936.   (Published by H. M. Stationery Office, Edinburgh, Scotland)
      The author traces the results of the changes in tenure, the breaking-
   up of estates into separate farms, the failure of the owner-occupier
   system and the tendency to have a number of farms with a grieve on
   each.   "It is recorded that in 1875 there were 11,585 holdings in
   Aberdeenshire, 7,331 of which were under 50 acres.   In 1933 there were
   10,181 holdings, only 5,052 of which were under 50 acres."
      Little fundamental change in farm implements is recorded but those
   existing have been improved.   Improvement is noted in tractors and
   threshing machines, in varieties of oats, in the growing of wheat,
   in pastures, and in increased use of artificial fertilizers.

Agriculture and Industry

Lang, A. S.   Agricultural-industrial relationships in a coordinated
   adjustment program.   Southwest. Social Sci. Quart. 17(1): 20-30.   June
   1936.   (Published by the Southwestern Social Science Association,
   Austin, Tex.)
      "This paper is an attempted diagnosis of our unsound agricultural-
   industrial relationships so evident in recent years and a quest for
   means of promoting a sound and durable relationship between agriculture
   and industry."

Apples – Rouville County, Quebec

Gosselin, A.   Economic aspects of apple production in Rouville County,
   Quebec.   Econ. Annalist 6(3): 44-48.   June 1936.   (Issued by the Agricultural Economics Branch, Dept. of Agriculture, Ottawa, Canada.)
      "The purpose of this article is to present a summary of the results
   obtained in a study of the financial returns and the cost of producing
   apples on 30 orchard farms of Rouville County, the oldest district of
   the province of Quebec where apple production is the major farm enterprise."

Bananas – Export Control – Ecuador

Banana export control board of Ecuador.   Pan Amer. Union. Bull. 70(6): 518-
   519.   June 1936.   (Published in Washington, D. C.)
      "The Banana Export Control Board of Ecuador...was established by
   Decree no. 209 of March 31, 1936."   It is to be affiliated with the
   Mortgage Bank of Ecuador and will be financed by a tax of 2 centavos
   per stem on all bananas exported.

Berichte über Landwirtschaft

Berichte über Landwirtschaft n.F. Bd. 20, Heft 3, 1935.   (Issued by [Germany]
   Reichs- und Pr. Ministerium für Ernährung u. Landwirtschaft.   Published
   by P. Parey, Berlin, Germany.)
      Contents: Die Organisation der deutschen landwirtschaftlichen
   Erzeugung und die Marktregelung, by Ludwig Herrmann, pp.357-371.   (The

keys to Germany's agricultural policy are said to be the land inherit-ance law and the Reichsnährstand. The farmer's home and land are protected by the former and his production and the marketing of his produce by the latter. Market regulation is intended to secure profit-able prices for the producer and prices that are not beyond the means of the consumer. The good of the individual must be subordinated to the good of the whole nation. Thus will peace be insured not only within the nation's boundaries but also with other nations.); Die Genossenschaften in der Marktordnung des Schlachtviehverkehrs in Deutschland, by Konrad Langenheim, pp. 372-401. (It is shown that the basic principles of the organization of cooperatives in the field of livestock and livestock products are voluntary mergers and the capaci for economic competition. The importance of marketing and transporta-tion of livestock is stressed, and it is argued that market and price regulation can only be carried out by the Reichsnährstand.); Einzelhof oder Dorf, by C. A. Koefoed, pp.402-425. (The author discusses the advantages and disadvantages of the village settlement as contrasted with the independent farm. Various methods of consolidating scattered parcels of land and their cost are discussed, and the author's con-clusion is that the independent farm is the more economically profitable Bedeutung und Aussichten der Agrarkollektivierung in der Sowjetunion, by O. Schiller, pp. 426-453. (The author discusses the characteristics and probable outcome of collective farming in the Soviet Union, and concludes that the results have to the non-Bolshevist point of view the appearance of the beginning of a national downfall.); Ziele und Erfolge der Organisation der Schlachtviehverwertung in der Schweiz, by O. Howald, pp. 453-464. (A survey of the production and marketing of slaughter cattle in Switzerland and their organization); Lage und Entwicklungstendenzen der Landwirtschaft im Irischen Freistaat, by Mijo Mirković, pp. 464-474. (Agricultural economic conditionsin the Irish Free State.); and the continuation of Dr. S. von Frauendorfer's International Bibliography of Agricultural Economics Literature.

Canning Industry

Campbell, Carlos. The mutual interests of grower and canner. Canning Age 17(7): 276-277, 288. June 1936. (Published at 250 West 57th St., New York, N. Y.)

"The canning industry holds an important place in the food productive system and is correctly classified as a medium of marketing agricultural crops." The writer gives first a brief sketch of the history of the marketing of agricultural products, "in order that one may understand the effect of the relation between the canner and the farmer who grows the canning crops."

Two general systems of marketing that are in operation are outlined: "First, the open market where the various agencies of production have few or no personal contacts. The second system of marketing is that which prevails in the case of canning crops, where there is a closer personal contact between two of the producing agencies, the farmer and the canner, and where production is somewhat more efficiently adjusted by both of these agencies working together."

The relative merits of the two systems are examined.

Chamber of Commerce of the United States

Principles of American enterprise; a supplement carrying a report of the
U. S. Chamber's 24th annual meeting. Nation's Business 24(6): 33-80.
June 1936. (Published by the Chamber of Commerce of the United States,
Washington, D. C.)
The future of agriculture [short report of the round table on Es-
sentials for Agricultural Progress] p.66; The importance of agriculture,
by Fred W. Sargent, pp.67-68.

Coffee

World coffee markets. Empire Producer, no. 236, pp.133-134, 131-132.
June 1936. (Published by British Empire Producers' Organisation, 22,
Queen Anne's Gate, Westminster, London, S.W.1, Eng.)
Reply to a questionnaire sent to representatives and correspondents
in the United States.

Coffee - Dutch East Indies

Netherlands East Indies coffee output. Tea and Coffee Trade Jour. 70(50):
369-371. May 1936. (Published at 79 Wall Street, New York, N. Y.)
"Official report on estates and native production, with areas
under cultivation, kinds grown, exports, and related facts, covering
the five years, 1930-1934 - Estate production is on the increase."

Coffee - Palembang

Rudin, W. F. De bevolkingskoffiecultuur in de marga Ranau (Residentie
Palembang) [The coffee cultivation of the natives in the "marga" Ranau
(Residency of Palembang]. Landbouw; landbouwkundig tijdschrift
voor Nederlandsch-Indië 11(7-8): 266-323. January-February 1936.
(Published in Buitenzorg, Java)
Literatuur, pp.320-323.
English summary, pp.323-325.

Colonization - China and Mongolia

Thorp, James. Colonization possibilities in Northwest China and inner
Mongolia. Pacific Affairs 8(4): 447-453. December 1935. (Published
at 129 East 52nd St., New York, N. Y.)
In conclusion the author writes in part: "When we review the facts
we are forced to the conclusion that China has no great amount of surplus land into which its people may migrate to find new homes and a
larger life. Population has overtaken the food supply and its rapid
increase will either have to stop or the nation will be continually
agonized by famine, war and pestilence in accordance with the Malthusian doctrine. Even migration to the very few foreign countries
where arable land is available would only result in those lands soon
finding themselves in the same plight."

Colonization Scheme - Poland

Polish colonisation scheme. Indus. and Labour Inform. 58(12): 407-408.
June 22, 1936. (Issued by International Labour Office, Geneva,
Switzerland. Distributed in U. S. by World Peace Foundation, 8 West
40th Street, New York, N. Y.)
    Attention is called to the formation in April 1936 of an Inter-
national Colonisation Company by the National Economic Bank of Poland,
the Polish Relief Fund and the State Agrarian Bank, with headquarters
in Warsaw.
    "The aims of the company are to prepare, manage, and organise
colonisation facilities for Polish emigrants. It is authorised to buy,
rent, or sell abroad land suitable for colonisation purposes to set
up colonisation and commercial undertakings, to form emigrants'
associations and unions and to take part in their work, and to subsidise directly or indirectly all institutions, companies, or undertakings likely to aid it in its work."

Commercial Policy and Agriculture - France

Peyret, Henry. La politique commerciale de la France dans ses rapports
avec l'agriculture. Revue des Agriculteurs de France 68(5): 268-271.
May 1936. (Published at 8, Rue d'Athènes, Paris, France.)
    The author traces the vicissitudes of French commercial policy as
it has affected agricultural products since the beginning of the
nineteenth century and its vacillations between protectionism and a
liberal policy. He urges that agriculture and industry be placed on
an equal footing and that their representatives agree as to the measures
necessary to protect French commerce. Agricultural products must be
exported and their quality should be such as to enable them to meet
competition on foreign markets.

Community, Rural - United States

Sanderson, Dwight. The rural community in the United States as an elementary group. Rural Sociol. 1(2): 142-150. June 1936. (Published
by the Rural Sociology Section, American Sociological Society, T. Lynn
Smith, Sec.-Treasurer, Louisiana State University, Baton Rouge, La.)
    "This paper was read at the 12th Congrès de l'Institut International
de Sociologie, Brussels, Aug. 26, 1935."

Consumptive Capacity

Comish, Alison. Capacity to consume. Amer. Econ. Rev. 26(2): 291-295.
June 1936. (Published by the American Economic Association, Northwestern University, Evanston, Ill.)
    "The recent appearance of books concerning American consumption,
particularly its potentialities, has created the concept capacity to
consume. Yet authors of such books have made little attempt to define
the concept or to recognize its major implications. Capacity to
consume can be defined as the power to use goods and services in the
satisfaction of human wants. There are four determining factors of

such capacity: (1) wants; (2) goods and services available; (3) time
and energy; and (4) purchasing power. The importance of purchasing
power usually has been recognized. The Brookings Institution study,
America's Capacity to Consume, strongly emphasizes the income aspect.
But the other three factors are also important in bringing about consumption, especially when viewed as consumption of particular goods
and services. Wants must exist and goods and services must be available. As for time and energy - they are factors resembling purchasing
power since they are needed to make wants effective, that is, to transform wants into demand." -p.290.

Cooperation

Cooperative Journal, v. 10, no. 3, pp. 73-104. May-June 1936. (Published
by the National Cooperative Council, 1731 Eye St., N. W., Washington,
D. C.)
   Partial contents: The relationship of agricultural cooperation to
consumers' cooperation, by Joseph G. Knapp, pp.73-80; Cooperation in
Canada, by A. E. Richards, pp.84-86; May we have up-to-date money? by
Val C. Sherman, pp. 87-88; Getting at the figures, by D. G. White,
pp.89-96 [This is the concluding installment of a two-part article.
The discussion of the principles underlying the construction of a
balance sheet are illustrated by an analysis of the actual balance
sheet of a cooperative creamery].

Cooperation, Consumers - California

Consumers' cooperation in California, 1934-35. Monthly Labor Rev. 42(5):
1216-1225. May 1936. (Published by the Bureau of Labor Statistics,
U. S. Dept. of Labor)
   "The data on which this article is based are from a field study
carried out under the supervision of Clark Kerr, as a research project
of the California Emergency Relief Administration. (California. State
Emergency Relief Administration. Office of Coordinator of Statistical
Projects. Handbook of Consumers' Cooperatives in California. San
Francisco. 1935. (Mimeographed)."

Cooperation in Social Legislation, Federal-State

Clark, Jane P.   Joint activity between federal and state officials. Polit.
Sci. Quart. 51(2): 230-269. June 1936. (Published by the Academy of
Political Science, Fayerweather Hall, Columbia University, New York, N.Y.)
   "This material is part of a study of Federal-State Cooperative
Devices in Social Legislation now in course of preparation under a
grant from the Columbia University Council for Research in the Social
Sciences. In section C, Methods of Joint Activity, pp.248-265, activities
of certain bureaus of the United States Department of Agriculture are
discussed. For the activities of the Bureau of Agricultural Economics
see pp.255-260.

Cost of Living - British Guiana

Huggins, H. D.   Prices, cost of living and wages in British Guiana.   Agr.
Jour. Brit. Guiana 7(1): 27-44.   March 1936.   (Published in Georgetown, British Guiana.)
"In this study...prices from 1911 to 1935 are considered.   The
primary object of the undertaking was to collect, and make available
for reference, prices of the commodities of chief importance in the
economic life of this colony.   The second, but little less important,
object was to compute index numbers of these prices.   Figures for
wages, being so closely inter-related with commodity prices, arc also
presented for the period 1911-35.   In addition the data have been used
as a basis for the calculation of a general price level and a cost of
living index for the period."

Cost of Living - Latin America

Recent family budget enquiries: Recent family budget enquiries in Latin
America.   Internatl. Labour Rev. 33(5): 739-742.   May 1936.   (Published
by the International Labour Office, Geneva, Switzerland.   Distributed
in U. S. by the World Peace Foundation, 8 W. 40th St., New York, N. Y.)
"In a recent issue of this Review, an account was given of a recent
family budget enquiry in Mexico City.   Further details have now become available as to the distribution of expenditure for various
categories of workers and also as to the quantities of foodstuffs consumed; these data are summarised."

Cost of Living - Netherlands

Brouwers, G.   Landbouwprijzen en kosten van levensonderhoud.   Economisch-
Statistische Berichten 21(1054): 178-180.   Mar. 11, 1936.   (Published
by the Nederlandsch Economisch Instituut.   May be obtained from Nijgh
& van Ditmar, Rotterdam, Holland.)
Agricultural prices and the cost of living.

Cotton

Boyle, J. E.   The cotton South and the tariff.   Cotton Digest 8(38-World
ed): 5-6.   June 27, 1936.   (Published at 710 Cotton Exchange Bldg.,
Houston, Tex.)
The author urges a policy of reciprocal trade in order that foreign
trade in cotton may be maintained.

Commerce and Finance, v. 25, no. 11, pp.377-407.   May 30, 1936.   (Published
at 95 Broad St., New York, N. Y.)
This issue has a special section devoted to National Cotton Week.
Among the articles given are the following: Present outlook for cotton
textile industry, by C. T. Murchison, p.390; Cotton week only one
phase of industry's activities to increase cotton uses, by C. K.
Everett, p. 391; Outlook for domestic consumption, by John H. McFadden,
Jr., p.392; Remove artificial obstructions, by Charles E. Fenner, pp.
392, 394; Industrial uses of cotton promising, by W. Ray Bell, p.394;
Use cotton bagging instead of jute, by Donald Comer, pp.395, 406.

Stovall, W. H.   The farm program again.   Staple Cotton Rev. 14(4): 1-12.
      April 1936. (Published by the Staple Cotton Cooperative Association,
      Greenwood, Miss.)
      The author illustrates the new farm program by applying it to a
      1000-acre cotton farm.

Cotton - Argentina

Producción y consumo del algodón y derivados en la Republica Argentina.
      Boletín Oficial de la Bolsa de Comercio 25(582): 1-9. Apr. 15, 1936.
      (Published at Rosario, Argentina.)
      Production and consumption of cotton and its derivatives in Argentina.

Cotton - Prices

Kapadia, D. F.   A statistical study of cotton prices in relation to quality
      and yield. Sankhyā; the Indian Journal of Statistics 2(2): 125-134.
      April 1936. (Published by the Statistical Publishing Society, Calcutta,
      India. Agents: P. S. King & Son Ltd., London, Eng.)
      "The statistical connexions between cotton prices, spinning values
      and fibre-length measurements have been investigated in this paper.
      The coefficients of correlation are sufficiently high (of the order of
      0.7 and higher) to provide a pragmatic test of price judgments in
      respect of quality values of cottons. The existing systems of grading
      and price-fixing and the advantage of introducing objective spinning
      tests for the scientific regulation of prices are discussed in some
      detail. With regard to the supply of larger crops of medium-staple
      varieties it is pointed out that marginal premiums paid in respect to
      quality tenders are more apparent than real, for the yield and ginning
      out-turn of these varieties are so low that they nullify the advantage
      of higher prices per pound. Attention is drawn to the necessity for
      directing agricultural research for developing strains which would
      give high yields of cotton per acre and good ginning out-turn so that
      the larger crops of medium-staple cottons can be harvested from the
      same acreage that is at present under cultivation rather than by an
      extension of the total acreage." - Summary, p.134.
      "A Note on Cotton Prices in Relation to Quality and Yield," by
      P. C. Mahalanobis, follows on pp.135-142.

Cotton - Rhodesia

State aid for cotton growing industry. Important Government bill. African
      World 135(1753): 307. June 13, 1936. (Published at 801, Salisbury
      House, London Wall, London, E. C., Eng.)
      "It is officially announced that the Southern Rhodesian Government
      will introduce a bill in the present session of Parliament setting up
      a Board to supervise research work on cotton and to assist the general
      development of cotton growing in the Colony.
      "The Board will be entitled to make financial provisions for re-
      search and cultivation and to own ginneries, and it would be empowered
      to purchase cotton or make advances on the product. Parliament will be
      asked to make annual grants to the Board which will have the assistance
      of the officials and experts of the Empire Cotton Growing Corporation."

Cotton Picking Machine

Cordell, William, and Cordell, Kathryn. The cotton picker - friend or
Frankenstein? Common Sense 5(6): 18-21. June 1936. (Published at
315 Fifth Ave., New York, N. Y.) L. C.
An article, authorized by the Rust brothers, on the mechanical
cotton picker, its significance, and the efforts of the inventors to
"discover some means of lessening the fearful impact of this machine
upon the tenants." The article includes a description of the machine
(including a sketch of it) and statements as to its low cost of operation and the amount of cotton which the machine can pick in seven and
one-half hours as contrasted with the amount picked by human labor.

The cotton picker. Information Serv. 15(24): [1-2] June 13, 1936.
(Published by the Dept. of Research and Education, Federal Council of
the Churches of Christ in America, 105 E. 22nd St., New York, N. Y.)
This article on the Rust cotton picker and its significance is
based on an article by William and Kathryn Cordell - The Cotton Picker -
Friend or Frankenstein? - in Common Sense for June 1936.

Weybright, Victor. Two men and their machine. Survey Graphic 25(7):
432-433. July 1936. (Published at 112 E. 19th St., New York, N. Y.)
"The Rust Brothers once picked cotton for a living. Now that they
have invented a mechanical picker they seek a way to launch it without bringing catastrophe to the cotton worker."

Cotton Yields and the Weather - India

Ramakrishnan, S. Correlation of weather conditions and yield of cotton
in the 'northerns' and 'westerns' tracts. Sankhyā; the Indian Journal
of Statistics 2(1): 43-54. August 1935. (Published by the Statistical
Publishing Company, Calcutta, India. Agents: P. S. King & Son Ltd.,
London.)
"In this paper an attempt has been made to determine the meteorological factors which give rise to significant variation in yield
per acre of cotton grown in Bellary and Kurnool Districts taking
into account all the area under the crop in these districts. The
method used is in general that adopted by previous workers in the field
of Agricultural Meteorology like H. L. Moore (1917) of the United
States of America and S. M. Jacob (1916) of India. An attempt is
also made to forecast the yield per acre by the help of weather data."

Cottonseed

Meloy, G. S. History of cotton seed and need for established grades.
Cotton Digest 8(38-World ed.): 35-41 table, chart. June 27, 1936.
(Published at 710 Cotton Exchange Bldg., Houston, Tex.)

Crop Forecasting

Yates, F. Crop estimation and forecasting: indications of the sampling
observations on wheat. Gt. Brit. Min. Agr. Jour. 43(2): 156-162.
May 1936. (Published by H. M. Stationery Office, London, Eng.)

An account of a scheme of sampling observations on wheat to determine the yield of the crop.

Deserts, Man-made

Lowdermilk, W. C. Man-made deserts. Pacific Affairs 8(4): 409-419.
December 1935. (Published at 129 East 52nd St., New York, N. Y.)
In the opening paragraph the writer states that the "history of civilization is a record of struggles against the progressive desiccation of civilized lands. The more ancient the civilization, the drier and more wasted, usually, is the supporting country... It becomes important to discover how far human occupation is rendering the earth less inhabitable and at the same time to discover means by which such processes of deterioration may be held in check and productivity sustained. It is possible for man and his animals to render regions uninhabitable, especially in zones of delicate ecological balance between humid and true desert climates. Man-made deserts may extend from semi-arid climates to humid climates, under certain conditions. In the light of this conception, of man-induced desiccation, it is ir place to examine what is now known about the results of human occupation, in the way of increasing aridity due to destruction of vegetative cover, and how these desert conditions are rapidly being brought about in various areas throughout the world."

Economic Conditions -- Great Britain

1936 and after; a survey of British economic prospects. Economist 123
(4842): 600-606. June 13, 1936. (Published at 8 Bouverie St., London, E. C. 4, Eng.)
Contents: Introduction: The structure of unemployment; prospects of the domestic market; the international outlook; and conclusion.
The conclusions are summarized as follows: "(1) So far as a further reduction of cyclical unemployment is concerned, there is comparatively little scope for further progress. Moreover, an analysis of the position in the building industry shows that employment in that industry may be expected to decline, the maximum limit of the decline being as high as 500,000, though the actual figure may be expected to be much lower; (2) There are grounds, however, for hoping that the decline will be neither sudden nor spectacular, and will not initiate a reversal of the general domestic recovery of the last few years. Unemployment caused by a decline in the demand for houses may therefore be offset to some extent by a continuance of expansion elsewhere; (3) Transfer in recent good years from the less prosperous half of the country to the more prosperous areas has found jobs for only 20,000 men a year - apart from transfer between different regions in each area. This movement can be expected to continue. But the expanding industries cannot be expected to find jobs both for the present 'specially' unemployed and also for any men who may be displaced from the building trades; (4) Exports have been expanding for four years, though their improvement appears to have been checked, for the time being, since the beginning of this year. The revival, so far as it has gone, has been mainly due, not to special arrangements such as the Ottawa Agreements, but to recovery in many British and foreign

countries. Accordingly, if the tempo of world-wide recovery increases
the rate of re-employment in the British export industries will also
increase; (5) The materials are to hand for a very extensive rise in
the world price-level. Events in the gold bloc and in the United
States show that the beginning of this rise may not be unconscionably
far distant. A world-wide rising trend of prices would have favourable
effects upon employment everywhere."

Economic Conditions - Uruguay

Charlone, C. The economic and social situation of Uruguay. Internatl.
Labour Rev. 33(5): 607-618; May 1936. (Published by the International
Labour Office, Geneva, Switzerland. Distributed in U. S. by The
World Peace Foundation, 8 W. 40th St., New York, N. Y.)

Economic Depression - France

Coup d'oeil rétrospectif sur l'évolution de la crise économique en France.
L'Observation Économique 7(4): 126-129. April 1936. (Published by
the Société d'Études et d'Informations Économiques, 282, Boulevard
Saint-Germain, Paris, France.)
   A sketch of economic conditions in France during the period of
depression from 1930 to 1936. The movement of prices and of wages,
and the activity of business and finance are outlined.

Economic Forum

Economic Forum, v 3, no. 4, pp.365-468. April-June 1936. (Published at
51 Pine St., New York, N. Y.)
   Partial contents: The church turns economist, by C. M. Adams,
pp.365-377; A diet of debt, by J. S. Crews, pp.378-384; Our economic
thinking, by R. T. Ely, pp.385-394; The new need for conservation,
by John Dreier, pp.395-405; 100% money and the public debt, by
Irving Fisher, pp.406-420; The elements of an American program for
social progress: Introduction, by Virgil Jordan; Government, by Charles
Nagel; Education, by H. W. Chase; Business, by R. E. Flanders; Science,
by K. T. Compton, pp.421-428; The challenge of foreign dumping in the
American market, by W. A. Irvin, pp.437-442; An economic survey of
leading financial opinion on the subject of the long term rate of
interest, its relation to banking and insurance income and costs, and
to the policy of issuing tax exempt government bonds, pp.443-454.

Economic Geography

Economic Geography, v. 12, no. 3, pp.217-324. July 1936. (Published at 10
Ferry St., Concord, N. H.)
   Partial Contents: Amana: A study of occupance, by D. H. Davis,
pp.217-230; Agricultural regions of Asia: Part X. The Philippine
Islands, by Samuel van Valkenburg, pp.231-249; An Algerian oasis
community, by E. A. Ackerman, pp.250-258; Land economy of Amberson
Valley, Pennsylvania, by C. Y. Mason, pp.254-272; English countryside
and population in the eighteenth century, by G. E. Fussell, pp. 294-
310; Economic geography of the port wine region, by E. H. G. Dobby,
pp.311-323.

Economic Policy - Belgium

Braunthal, Alfred. The new economic policy in Belgium. Internatl.
Labour Rev. 33(6): 760-789. June 1936. (Published by the International
Labour Office, Geneva, Switzerland. Distributed in the U. S. by the
World Peace Foundation, 8 W. 40th St., New York, N. Y.)
"Explains the causes, methods, and effects of the new policy."

Economics - Germany

B. German conception of economics. Hamburg World Econ. Archives. Bull.
2(9): 6-8. Mar. 1, 1936; (10): 12-13. Mar. 15, 1936. (Published
at Poststrasse 19, Hamburg 36, Germany.)

Emigration and Immigration - Levant States

Berenstein, M. The Levant states under French mandate and problems of
emigration and immigration. Internatl. Labour Rev. 33(5): 685-720.
May 1936. (Published by the International Labour Office, Geneva,
Switzerland. Distributed in U. S. by World Peace Foundation, 8 W.
40th St., New York, N. Y.)
"In continuation of the series of articles already published in the
Review on questions of internal settlement and immigration considered
from the point of view of the international redistribution of labour
and capital...[this] article indicates the possibilities in this
direction offered by the States of the Levant under French Mandate.
After analysing in detail the social and economic structure of these
States, the author recalls the experiments of immigration on a fairly
large scale that have already been made in Syria and the Lebanon, and
describes the various settlement schemes that have been proposed,
some of them with the assistance of the League of Nations. In conclusion he, expresses the opinion that Syria, with its large stretches
of cultivable but idle land and its limited resources, might find in
immigration the labour and the capital that it lacks at present." -p.685.

Employment, Interest and Money, Mr. Keynes' Theory of

Hicks, J. R. Mr. Keynes' theory of employment. Econ. Jour. 46(182): 238-
253. June 1936. (Published by Royal Economic Society, S. J. Buttress,
Asst. Sec., 6, Humberstone Road, Cambridge, Eng. May be obtained from
The Macmillan Co., New York, N. Y.)
This is a review of J. M. Keynes' The General Theory of Employment,
Interest and Money.

Pigou, A. C. Mr. J. M. Keynes' General theory of employment, interest
and money. Economica (n.s.) 3(10): 115-132. May 1936. (Published
by the London School of Economics and Political Science, Houghton St.,
Aldwych, London, Eng.)
This is a critical and analytical review of J. M. Keynes' General
Theory of Employment, Interest and Money.

Loomis' C. P. The study of the life cycle of families. Rural Sociol.
1(2): 190-199. June 1936. (Published by the Section of Rural
Sociology, American Sociological Society, T. Lynn Smith, Sec.-Treasurer,
Louisiana State University, Baton Rouge.)
    "This article contains the substance of a paper prepared for the
12th Congres de l'Institut International de Sociologie, Brussels,
August 25-29, 1935."

Farm Ownership - Finland

Jutila, K. T. Finland's agricultural activities. Remarkable development
in recent years. Times Trade & Engin. (n.s.) 39(868): viii. June
1936. (Published by the Times Publishing Co., Ltd., London, E. C. 4,
Eng.)
    In the nineteenth century sub-letting of portions of farms became
common in Finland. "Two principal types of rented farms were thus
created: - (1) Real agricultural farms or crofts (torppa), and (2)
dwelling or cottage farms. In addition there were leased or tenant
farms. The crofts and cottage farms were entitled to obtain timber
from the forests and to use the pastureland of the main farm itself,
but while the former had also considerable areas of agricultural land
the latter had much less or none at all. When forests became valuable
and the use of machinery spread the landowners at the beginning of the
twentieth century were no longer ready to renew leases but began to
join the leased areas to the main farm, a procedure similar to the
'enclosures' seen in England in the sixteenth century. In this manner
the so-called croft system began to decline in Finland to a serious
extent and the numbers of those without farms grew to alarming proportions... In 1918 the State began the policy of transferring the
ownership of farms to the tenants, and the result was that 118,000
leased holdings had been made over to them by the end of 1934, 65,000
of them being agricultural...
    "At the end of the nineteenth century attempts were made by the
State to keep farmers without estates on the land by means of settlement schemes and since independence was gained these schemes have
been greatly strengthened. Up to the end of 1934 a total of 31,000
settled estates had been founded and additional land added to 12,500
farms of insufficient size. Some 810,000 hectares (over 2,000,000
acres) of land were used for these purposes."

Farming, Cooperative - Hillhouse, Mississippi

The Delta cooperative farm. Information Serv.15(24): [2]. June 13, 1936.
    (Published by the Dept. of Research and Education, Federal Council of
Churches of Christ in America, 105 East 22nd St., New York, N. Y.)
    This is an account of the Delta Cooperative Farm at Hillhouse,
Bolivar County, Miss., which is being settled by both white and negro
tenant farmers evicted from their homes in Arkansas. Sherwood Eddy
and others are aiding them. "The Rust Brothers, inventors of the

mechanical cotton picker... have formed the Rust Foundation which will
utilize nine-tenths of the profits from the machine to found a series
of cooperative farms, cooperative stores, and educational projects
for white and colored agricultural workers."

"The (cooperative) organization has a vital relation to the
Southern Tenant Farmers' Union. It will seek to encourage the development of a strong union and to train intelligent leaders. It will
stress the need for protection of civil liberties."

Farms, Abandoned - Southern Alberta

Watson, W. N. A study of 126 abandoned farms in the Lomond area of
Southern Alberta. Econ. Annalist 6(3): 38-44. June 1936. (Issued
by the Agricultural Economics Branch, Dept. of Agriculture, Ottawa,
Canada.)

The data contained in this article "were obtained in a study of
land utilization in South Central Alberta begun in 1935. Preliminary
statements, subject to revision and correction."

"This study is a part of the program being carried out under the
Prairie Farm Rehabilitation Act of 1935... A detailed description of
the area, the climate, soils, people, history, etc., will be included
in the major report of the Land Utilization project, and is, therefore,
not presented here. It was impossible to get details of all the abandoned land in the area. However, the 126 abandoned farms concerning
which information was obtained offer a cross-section of abandonment,
and enable one to form a reasonably accurate picture of the nature
of the abandonment which has taken place in the area."

Farms, Earning Capacity - Estonia

Luht, H. Factors determining the earning capacity of farms. Konjunktuur,
no. 19(6): 390-400. June 6, 1936. (Published by Estonian Institute
of Economic Research, Tallinn, Estonia.)

"The fact that self-supporting farms are being found both among the
big and small holdings justifies the conclusion that the differences
in the efficiency of a given farm do not so much depend upon the size
of the establishment as upon factors relating to organisation...
To attain a reasonable rate of profitableness... the writer considers
it essential for a farming establishment to carry on a diversified
programme of work..."

Tables show: Classification of land according to utilisation;
gross returns per ha of farm land in kr.; Production costs per ha
of farm land in krones; and Capital and earnings of farms per ha of
farm land in kr.

Feed Situation - Germany

Boals, G. P. Some aspects of the German feed situation. Foreign Crops
and Markets 32(26): 813-819. June 29, 1936. (Published by the Division of Foreign Agricultural Service, Bureau of Agricultural Economics,
U. S. Dept. of Agriculture.)

The following are discussed: Production limitations and possibilities;
Protein and carbohydrate feed import developments; and The cultivation
of subsidiary or cover crops.

Food Supplies and Defense - Great Britain

Food supplies and defence - IV. The Statist 127(3040): 893, 894. May 30,
1936. (Published at 51 Cannon St., London, E. C. 4.)
    The conclusion of a series of articles on the importance of assuring
adequate supplies of essential foods in any scheme for national defense.
In this article the particulars of imports of different classes of
foodstuffs in 1935, and the principal sources of supplies in each case
are set forth.
    The first three articles appeared in The Statist 127(3036-3038):
72.-721, 763-764, 804-805. May 2-16, 1936.

Forestry - Cuba

Obligatory reforestation in Cuba. Pan Amer. Union. Bull. 70(6): 521-522.
June 1936. (Published in Washington, D. C.)
    "By decree-law no. 681 of March 21, 1936, reforestation was made
obligatory for the Government and private individuals in certain parts
of the Republic, including lands unsuitable for cultivation, 328
feet back from the banks or shores of rivers, brooks, lakes and lagoons,
summits over 200 feet high, the land around springs and sources for
a radius of 650 feet and estate boundaries along highways, railroads,
and public roads. In each Province nurseries are to be established
large enough to provide at least 100,000 fruit and shade trees for
free distribution each year... Each Province will also set aside a
tract of land of at least 3,300 acres, preferably in a mountainous
region, as a park for the conservation and propagation of rare trees
and a bird and animal refuge... For a period of 15 years no wood may
be cut in virgin forests on Cuban mountains without permission from the
Secretary of Agriculture... For cutting wood elsewhere a license must
be obtained."

Fruit - Statistics - California

California Fruit News, v. 93, no. 2501, pp. 1-16. June 13, 1936. (Published
at 405 Montgomery St., San Francisco, Calif.)
    The annual statistical record of California and Pacific Coast
fruits and fruit products of 1935. Tables are given having production
and trade figures.

Grain - Truck Marketing

Scott, J. R. The trucker-peddler. Northwest. Miller and Amer. Baker
13(6): 625, 634. June 3, 1936. (Published at 118 S. 6th St.,
Minneapolis, Minn.)
    An address by the Secretary of the Executive Committee of the As-
sociated Southwest Country Elevators before the Thirty-ninth Annual
Meeting of the Kansas Grain Dealers Association, at Saline, Kansas.
    The problem of the competition of the itinerant trucker in the
grain trade is the theme of this discussion. Attention is called to
the fact that the itinerant trucker, through lack of effective regulation, operates without paying anything like comparable taxes, wages,
interest, and so on, that railroads pay. The need to remedy this
condition is stressed, and various measures are suggested.

Hereditary Farms - Germany

Hereditary farms. News in Brief 4(9-10): 140-141. May 1936. (Published by
the Deutscher Akademischer Austauschdienst, ē. V., Berlin NW 40, Germany)
Last year's registrations of hereditary farms indicate that more
than 80 percent of such farms now in existence have been registered.
It is estimated that the largest number of these farms are in Munich
and that the average area of the hereditary farms is 20 hectares.

Import Control

Easterbrook, L. F. Lessons from food taxes. New Statesman and Nation (n.s.)
11(276): 889-890. June 6, 1936. (Published at 10 Great Turnstile,
High Holborn, London, W. C. 1, Eng.)
The writer concludes in part as follows:
"It seems fair to assume, then, that in time of slump restrictions
can be placed upon imported food without raising prices to any considerable extent; that this may well be worth doing in order to insulate
home agriculture from the worst shocks of international depression
and to maintain rural purchasing power to the benefit of both town and
country; but that we must realise that we may easily be retarding
revival in our export trades by 'making the foreigner pay the duty.'
...It seems broadly true that, in the case of Great Britain - by far
the chief world market for exported foodstuffs - fiscal restrictions
can not only be placed upon imports at a time of slump without raising
prices, but may lower prices through encouraging greater production
at home...or by intensifying the world slump by this further clogging
of the wheels of international trade. But the best may well be the
enemy of the good in this case, and we must judge whether the bad
effects of this clogging are not less in practice than the evils that
arise when desperate producers throw a swelling surplus stock overboard at any price in the rigours of a first-class, world-wide trade
depression. Nor must we forget that the experience in food taxing we
have obtained so far relates only to slump conditions. If world trade
ever booms again, an entirely different set of factors will come into
play that may, and probably will, produce a very different effect.
But that is still in the realm of surmise and theory so far as this
country is concerned."

Income, Farm - European Countries

Deslarzes, Joseph. The social income and family farm earnings of farms
from 1927-28 to 1931-32. [Denmark, Switzerland, Austria, Latvia,
Estonia, Lithuania, Poland, Norway, Finland, Sweden, Germany, Netherlands
(Overijssel), etc.] Monthly Bull. Agr. Econ. and Sociol. [reprint
from Internatl. Rev. Agr. 27(4): 122E-133E. April 1936. (Published
by the International Institute of Agriculture, Rome, Italy)

Ferger, W. F.   Distinctive concepts of price and purchasing-power index
    numbers. Amer. Statis. Assoc. Jour. 31(194): 258-272. June 1936.
    (Published by the Association. Frederick F. Stephan, Sec.-Treasurer,
    722 Woodward Bldg., Washington, D. C.)
        The writer examines "in detail the economic nature of the phenomena
    of prices and money and ...measure[s] these characteristics up against
    the algebraic properties of index number formulas."

Irrigation - Malaya

Moubray, G. A. de C. de.   The Sungei Manik irrigation scheme. Malayan
    Agr. Jour. 24(4): 160-166. April 1936. (Published in Kuala Lumpur,
    Federated Malay States.)
        The Sungei Manik irrigation scheme is called in many respects
    unique. "As a large-scale irrigation scheme it is...unique in that
    it is being carried out in dense virgin jungle... The scheme area
    occupies roughly 30,000 acres, of which probably 23,000 acres net
    will be available for padi fields." A table shows the development
    of the colonization of the area. A Colonization Officer was appointed
    in 1935. Settlers are carefully selected and families are placed on
    the largest area they can take care of efficiently. They are settled
    under a temporary license and the title to the land is only issued when
    they have proved themselves to be desirable colonists. "By March
    1936...colonists have been placed in occupation of just under 2,000
    acres and felling has started."

Labor - Austria

Recruiting of Czechoslovak agricultural workers for Austria. Indus. and
    Labour Inform. 58(5); 127. May 4, 1936. (Issued by Internatl. Labour
    Office, Geneva, Switzerland. Distributed in U. S. by World Peace
    Foundation, 8 West. 40th St., New York, N. Y.)
        An arrangement has been made for the recruiting of 3,500 Czechoslovak
    seasonal workers for agricultural work in Austria and for their
    payment.

Labor - California

Pickett, J. E.   The farm labor problem grows acute. Pacific Rural Press
    131(19): 602, 607. May 9, 1936. (Published at 500 Howard St., San
    Francisco, Calif.)
        Discusses the scarcity of farm labor, especially in California,
    and the apparent unwillingness of WPA workers to work on the farms;
    discusses also labor troubles and discontent.

Labor - Germany

Han, W. I.   The organization of farm laborers in Germany. Jour. Polit.
    Econ. 44(3): 374-397. June 1936. (Published by the University of
    Chicago Press, Chicago, Ill.)
        Discusses the rise of the farm labor problem in East Prussia,
    classes of agricultural workers in Germany, the development of Social

Democratic and Christian organizations for farm laborers, the collective
agreements in German agriculture, and points of comparison with the
situation in the United States.

Labor - Latvia

Polish emigration to Latvia. Indus. and Labour Inform. 58(5): 126-127.
May 4, 1936. (Issued by Internatl. Labour Office, Geneva, Switzerland.
Distributed in U. S. by World Peace Foundation, 8 West 40th St., New
York, N. Y.)
    An arrangement has been made for the recruiting of 12,000 Polish
agricultural workers for Latvia, 80 percent to be women. The amount
of wages to be paid is given.

Labor - Scotland

.Witney, D., and Kay, W. D. Labour on farms in the East and South-East
of Scotland. Scot. Jour. Agr. 19(2): 185-188. April 1936. (Published
by H. M. Stationery Office, Edinburgh, Scotland.)
    "It appears as though in these parts of Scotland falling labour
costs and declining wage rates have been closely associated with the
lean years through which agriculture has recently been passing, and
with the improved economic outlook there will probably be a swing in
the other direction."

Laborers'(Cotton) Strikes - Arkansas

The cotton choppers' strike. Information Serv. 15(26): 1-6. June 27, 1936.
(Published by the Dept. of Research and Education, Federal Council of
the Churches of Christ in America, 105 E. 22nd St., New York, N. Y.)
    This article, descriptive of the cotton choppers' strike in eastern
Arkansas, is based on information obtained by the Rev. James Myers,
industrial field secretary of the Federal Council, while on a field
trip on June 3-9 to Arkansas, and mainly on published studies and newspaper accounts. Subtopics of article: What lies back of labor unrest;
tenancy and sharecropping; the landlord's plight; effect of the agricultural adjustment program; the Southern Tenant Farmers' Union; the
cotton choppers' strike; extent of the strike; the Benson trial;
threats of lynching; Governor Futrell's statement; alleged threats of
violence by strikers; and the Federal investigation.

Land Distribution - Germany

Schaper, Ernst. Das land- und forstwirtschaftliche Grundeigentum im
Deutschen Reich und seine Besitzverhältnisse. Odal 4(10): 806-820.
April 1936. (Published by "Zeitgeschichte" Verlag und Vertriebs-
Gesellschaft m.b. H., Berlin, Germany)
    An account of the distribution of land in Germany among private
owners, states, communities, institutions and various organizations.
A number of tables are given.

<u>Land Inheritance - Germany</u>

Bethge, Werner. Das Reichserbhofgesetz nach praktischen Erfahrungen.
Odal 4(10): 821-824. April 1936. (Published by "Zeitgeschichte"
Verlag und Vertriebs-Gesellschaft m.b.H., Berlin, Germany)
   The author illustrates some of the legal difficulties in the
practical application of the German inheritance law before the mil-
lenium which is expected can be attained.

<u>Land Settlement - Argentina</u>

Nyhus, P. O.   Colonization in the Argentine Chaco. Foreign Crops and
   Markets 32(25): 793-800. June 22, 1936. (Issued by Division of Foreign
   Agricultural Service, Bureau of Agricultural Economics, U. S. Dept.
   of Agriculture.)
      "Colonization work in the Chaco was started only about 10 or 12
   years ago... It is stated that more than half of the cotton crop is
   being produced by... squatters without land contracts or any legal
   status other than the possession of a permit to reside temporarily on
   the land. To become owners of the land it is necessary to enter into
   a land contract which provides for annual payments. So few farmers
   have these 'provisional titles' and payments in the cases of those
   who have are so delinquent that probably 70 percent of the farmers
   in the Chaco have been farming without paying rent, taxes or installments on the land."
      Large tracts of land were acquired by private owners prior to 1903
   and on these colonization has made little progress. In the cereal
   zone during the last 30 years there has been little opportunity for
   settlement by northern Europeans. "To start farming in the cereal
   zone even as a tenant requires $1,500 to $2,000... For a tenant to
   become a landowner is extremely difficult because of high land prices,
   the prevailing large size of holdings, and the infrequent opportunity
   of securing tracts of 100 hectares or less. Some of the most successful farmers in the Chaco at the present time are former tenant
   farmers in the cereal zone who took up land in the Chaco about 1924."
      Families of many nationalities and of little or no farming ex-
   perience have settled in the Chaco.
      Prior to 1903 there were no restrictions on the amount of land that
   could be purchased from the Government. "In 1903 sales to any one
   individual were restricted to 2,500 hectares (6,178 acres). Prior to
   January 15, 1924, when individual purchases of farming land were
   restricted to 100 hectares (247 acres) and of pasture land to 625
   hectares (1,544 acres), about 25 percent of the land in the Chaco
   had been disposed of to large landowners for grazing purposes... The
   passage of the 1924 legislation...also initiated a more active
   colonization policy in respect to subdivision of land and encouragement to colonists." But at the end of 1934 only 10 percent
   of the land was included in agricultural colonies subdivided into
   lots of 100 hectares or less. They are "selected areas of the most
   accessible well-drained tracts." The period of payment has been extended from 6 to 10 years. There are no interest charges. Present
   prices vary from 33 to 61 pesos per hectare. Few farmers have acquired final titles. A survey of land resources and utilization in
   the Chaco has recently been organized by the Governor.

Land Settlement - Estonia

Ant, E. Development of new settlements. Konjunktuur 19(6): 400-408.
June 6, 1936. (Published by Estonian Institute of Economic Research,
Tallinn, Estonia)

"Under the Land Reform Law about 2000 lots of virgin land have so
far been parcelled out in Estonia. The price payable to the State
for a single holding, including the value of the land and timber on
it, is from Ekr. 3,920 to Ekr. 4,000. The average size of a holding
being 17.5 hectares, the per hectare price averages Ekr. 166. Of
this, Ekr. 50 per hectare, on the average, is allowed for ditches
and roads and Ekr. 100 for clearing 2 hectares of land (Ekr. 50 each),
making a total remission of Ekr. 1,000 per holding. There remains
thus an average debt burden of Ekr. 2,900 on the farm payable in 60
annual instalments (at 2% per a.) of Ekr. 95.70 or, in a round figure.
Ekr. 100, i.e. Ekr. 5.5 per hectare. This is less than the average
annual rent charged to leaseholders and is by no means burdensome to
the new settler."

Land Settlement - Germany

Die Bauernsiedlung im Jahre 1935. Vorläufiges Ergebnis der Reichssied-
lungsstatistik. Wirtschaft und Statistik 16(9): 346-349. May 1936.
(Issued by Germany. Statistisches Reichsamt. Published by Verlag
für Sozialpolitik, Wirtschaft und Statistik, Berlin S W 68, Germany)

A preliminary estimate of land settlement activity in Germany
in 1935 shows that at least 120,000 hectares were acquired for settlement purposes. Tables show the area acquired for land settlement
from 1919 to 1935, and such area as distributed among the various
states of Germany and the provinces of Prussia in 1933, 1934, and
1935. In the period from 1919 to 1935 a total area of more than 1,300,000
hectares was acquired for settlement. Tables show the number of new
settlements created since 1919 and their average size, and also the
number and area of the additions to existing farm establishments.

Land Settlement - Mozambique

Mozambique Irrigation Commission. To study settlement and irrigation problems. African World 135(1751): 241. May 30, 1936. (Published at 801,
Salisbury House, London Wall, London, E. C., Eng.)

A decree published in the Mozambique Government Gazette provides
for the creation of a commission of technical experts to study the
problem of the promotion of Portuguese settlement in the colony.
"The specific studies to be made are: -(a) The irrigation and settlement of the Umbelusi Valley; (b) The bridging of the Incomati River
to carry the railway now under construction to the Limpopo Valley, with
a view to the deviation of the waters of the Incomati for the irrigation
of that valley; (c) The economic side of the crops to be grown in
the Limpopo, Umbelusi, and Incomati Valleys; (d) Topographic, agronomic,
and economic conditions in the district of Quelimane and in the areas
served by the Mozambique railway, with a view to the settlement of
Europeans and Natives."

Bernhard, Hans. Aktuelle Kolonisationsprobleme. Schweizerische Landwirtschaftliche Monatshofte 14(2): 33-42. February 1936. (Published
by Benteli A.-G., Bern-Bümpliz, Switzerland.)
After deciding that the furtherance of land settlement at home
is preferable for Switzerland to colonization abroad, the author discusses the problem of land settlement as it has been affected by the
depression. He urges the need for economy in building and in the
preparation of the land. He also discusses the relief of unemployment
by means of part-time farming and the supplying of the needs of settlers
through their own work plants.

Land Settlement - Turkey

Settlement of immigrants in Turkey. Indus. and Labour Inform. 58(7): 195.
May 18, 1936. (Issued by Internatl. Labour Office, Geneva, Switzerland.
Distributed in U. S. by World Peace Foundation, 8 West 40th St.,
New York, N. Y.)
The number of immigrants to Turkey from Rumania and Bulgaria in
1936 has been fixed at 25,000. Land will be given to them with seed
and grain for their personal use.

Land Settlement - Victoria

Taylor, Gordon. The problem of closer settlement in Victoria. Econ. Roc.
12(22): 57-70. June 1936. (Published by Melbourne University Press,
The University, Melbourne, N. 3, Victoria)
In four parts: I. Pre-war closer settlement under the Acts of 1904
and 1909; II. Post-war developments - (a) soldier settlement; (b)
closer settlement; III. Reconstruction - the Act of 1932; IV. Liquidation - the work of the Closer Settlement Commission.

Land Utilization and Planning

Bassett, E. M., Clark, F. P., Hoelscher, L. W., and Augur, T. B. Land
planning for States and regions. Planners' Jour. 2(3): 69-73. May-
June 1936. (Published at Hunt Hall, Cambridge, Mass.)
Concluding discussion. "The original paper, by Tracy B. Augur,
was published in The Planners' Journal, January-February, 1936."
Following are listed subjects which are among those considered:
Land planning for a village; City planning; Methods of accomplishing
land planning for a region; and Land planning is applied geography.

Brown, P. E. Land and land use. Science (n.s.) 83(2154): 337-343. Apr.
10, 1936. (Published by the Science Press, Grand Central Terminal,
New York, N. Y.)
"Address delivered at the Iowa State College, February 20, 1936,
in a series of lectures arranged by the college on national, state,
regional and town planning."
"In conclusion," the author writes, "it would seem most desirable
to emphasize the fact that proper land use requires planning first and
then action. Our plans must be safe and sound, if they are to be put
into effect successfully. We must not plan narrowly, locally or with

too much attention to the immediate present. To be adequate the plans
must take into account many things. First of all, the soil itself,
its characteristics, capabilities and possibilities. Then the proper
use of it in the interests of the future. This involves the elimination
of the uneconomic, submarginal areas and the purchase by the government
of such areas for pastures, forests, parks or recreation or wild-life.
It also involves a planned farm use of the land in accordance with its
abilities to support pastures or cultivated crops... The relation of
industry and close tie-ups to agriculture demands a sound land use
policy. Part-time farming has a direct relationship to industry and
may be important in the future. Subsistence farming may also prove
desirable. Finally, the relation of land use to taxation must be
borne in mind, and the solution of the tax problem must come along to
permit of the utmost success in the adoption of any land use program.
    "The most important thing to remember is that the land is our one
and only real heritage... We must have a land use plan, and then we
must have action."

Ely, R. T. Land underlies all. Christian Sci. Monitor, Weekly Mag. Sec.,
    May 20, 1936, pp.1-2. (Published in Boston, Mass.)
        Discusses the questions involved in the planned utilization of land.
    These questions are local, regional, national and international, and
    involve such things as size of farms, proper utilization of land for
    forests, city planning, harmony of interests, right selection of land,
    proper balance between supply and demand, the need for public regula-
    tion of land use, etc.

Hockley, H. A. State legislation affecting land use enacted since January
    1, 1936. Land Policy Circ. June 1936, pp.14-22. (Published by the
    Land Use Planning Section, Division of Land Utilization, Resettlement
    Administration, Washington, D. C.)

Land-utilization and Water-supply Problems - Palos Verdes Hills, California

Raup, H. F. Land-use and water-supply problems in southern California:
    market gardens of the Palos Verdes hills. Geogr. Rev. 26(2): 264-269.
    April 1936. (Published by the American Geographical Society, Broadway
    at 156th St., New York, N. Y.)
        "The agricultural phase on the Palos Verdes Hills is not likely to
    be of long duration, for the land is already earmarked for urban settle-
    ment. Meanwhile we have here an interesting example of delicately
    balanced agriculture possible only because of careful attention to
    the conservation of the available rainfall. Subnormal precipitation
    or abnormally high temperatures on the Palos Verdes Hills almost im-
    mediately would disturb the balance between the climatic conditions
    and the dry-farmed truck crops." -p.269.
        A land-use map is given on p.265.

Landed Property

Monicault, Pierre de, and others. La propriété rurale. Conférences faites
    à l'Institut national agronomique, Paris, 12 février-11 mars 1936.
    Société d'Encour. pour l'Industrie Nationale. Bull. 135(5): 315-330.
    May 1936. (Published at 44, Rue de Rennes, Paris (6ᵉ), France.)

A series of lectures on landed property were delivered under the auspices of the Association of former pupils of the Institut National Agronomique from February 12 to March 11, 1936. They are summarized prior to their publication in extenso. They are: La propriété rurale. Introduction, by Pierre de Monicault. (A brief survey of the evolution of the idea of property); La propriété rurale en France, by Pierre Caziot. (Discusses land distribution and land values in France); La grande propriété rurale en Europe et son évolution au XXe siècle, by Roger Picard. (Four types of rural property are distinguished: the large estate exploited by the owner or a manager; property exploited by an association; the family farm; and the small uneconomic holding. The causes and results of agrarian reforms in Europe are pointed out.); La propriété rurale en Afrique du Nord, by Pierre Berthault. (The colonization of Algeria, Tunisia, and Morocco by France is briefly outlined.); and La petite propriété rurale en Europe et les reformes agraires, by Fudakowski.

Livestock - Marketing - Wales

Roberts, E. E.   The sales in Wales of fat stock under the grade and dead weight scheme of the Ministry of agriculture. Agr. Business 3(1): 7-9. Spring 1936. (Published by the Welsh Agricultural Organisation Society, Ltd., Aberystwyth, Wales)

Livestock and Meat - Germany

Böker, H.   Development of the production, importation and consumption of meat in Germany. Monthly Bull. Agr. Econ. and Sociol. [Reprint from Internatl. Rev. Agr.] 27(5): 135E-156E. May 1936. (Published by International Institute of Agriculture, Rome, Italy)

Contents: I. The live stock trade; II. Measures of commercial policy taken to protect national production and regulation of the home meat market; III. Development of the importation of live stock and meat; IV. Development of meat consumption according to the different kinds of meat: relative importance of national and foreign supplies.

Statistical tables show numbers of cattle, pigs and sheep in Germany; Duties on live stock and meat by "the Most Favoured Nation" in Germany; Imports into and exports from Germany of cattle, pigs and sheep and of beef, pork and mutton; and Consumption of meat in Germany.

Margarine - Production and Distribution

Monopolistic and state action in the production and distribution of margarine. Rev. Internatl. Coop. 29(5): 161-167. May 1936; (6): 210-218. June 1936. (Published at Orchard House, 14, Great Smith St., London, S. W. 1, Eng.)

A discussion of the importance of margarine in national consumption and in the family budgets is followed by an account of legislative measures affecting the production and distribution of margarine in a number of countries. Certain countries, particularly Denmark, Norway and Holland, found it necessary in the period 1931-1935 to introduce "special protective legislation, the aims of which were -

firstly, to reduce the spread between butter and margarine prices, while, at the same time, maintaining butter prices at as high a level as was practically possible; Secondly, to make compulsory the use of a certain percentage of butter in the production of margarine; and thirdly, to restrict home production and importation of margarine."

Margin of Error in Calculation of Cost of Cultivation

Mahalanobis, P. C. Editorial note on the margin of error in the calculation of the cost of cultivation and profit. Sankhyā; the Indian Journal of Statistics 2(2): 121-124. April 1936. (Published by the Statistical Publishing Society, Calcutta, India. Agents: P. S. King & Son Ltd., London, Eng.)

Tables which precede the "Note" contain the actual data on which the various estimates in the text are based. Paddy is the crop for which the calculations are made.

Meat Policy - Great Britain

Government's meat policy. Statist 128(3046): 49. July 11, 1936. (Published at 51 Cannon St., London, E. C. 4, Eng.)

Comment on the British Government's long-term beef policy, outlined recently by Mr. Elliot.

"Briefly, the Government proposes to continue to subsidise British cattle-raisers up to an amount not exceeding L 5 million a year, and to produce the greater part of the cost of the subsidy out of the proceeds of an import duty on imports of chilled, frozen and other beef from foreign countries, supplies from Empire-sources being duty-free." The home producers are said to be greatly disappointed with the plan.

An article on p. 46, Argentina and the Beef Duty, is concerned with the Argentine situation.

Milk - Consumption - Canada

Boucher, G. P. Some facts concerning milk consumption in Canada. Econ. Annalist 6(3): 35-37. June 1936. (Published by the Agricultural Economics Branch, Dept. of Agriculture, Ottawa, Canada.)

"An analysis of records obtained from 3,213 families in various urban and rural areas during a survey conducted in the summer of 1935 shows a per capita consumption of milk of about .74 pints per day. The survey was undertaken by the Economics Branch and the Dairy Branch of the Dominion Department of Agriculture in cooperation with the Quebec and Alberta Departments of Agriculture. It dealt with the consumption of milk and cheese in relation to locality, income, national type, occupation and various other factors... This article is designed to give only some of the results concerning milk consumption." The statement is preliminary and is subject to revision and correction.

Palmer, J. T. The consumption of fluid milk.. Hoard's Dairyman 81(12):
319, 333. June 25, 1936. (Published at Fort Atkinson, Wis.)
Some effects of maintaining retail prices of whole milk at artificial
levels.

Milk Marketing Scheme - England

The Milk Marketing Board. Statist 127(3042): 1014. June 13, 1936. (Published at 51 Cannon St., E. C. 4, London, Eng.)
A review of the second completed year of the working of the Milk
Marketing Scheme. "The first outstanding fact is the increase of
78 1/2 million gallons in the volume of milk sold and an increase of
4,106 in the number of contracts in operation."

Milk marketing scheme. Statist 127(3042): 988. June 13, 1936. (Published
at 51 Cannon St., E. C. 4, London, Eng.)
Reviews briefly the latest report of the Milk Marketing Board,
which, according to the writer "throws interesting light on the progress
of a great experiment in agricultural marketing reorganisation."

Milk marketing scheme: Report of the committee of investigation. Gt. Brit.
Min. Agr. Jour. 43(3): 219-224. June 1936. (Published by H. M.
Stationery Office, London, Eng.)
Contains a summary of the more important sections of the "Report
of the Committee of Investigation for England on the complaints made
by the Central Milk Distributive Committee and the Parliamentary Committee of the Co-operative Congress as to the prices and certain of
the terms of the 1935-36 contract prescribed by the Milk Marketing
Board for the sale of milk by wholesale."

Milk Marketing Scheme - Wales

Jones, W. H. Butter producers and the milk scheme. Agr. Business 3(1):
3-5.. Spring 1936. (Published by the Welsh Agricultural Organisation
Society, Ltd., Aberystwyth, Wales)
The application of the milk scheme to butter producers in Wales
is described.

Neues Bauerntum

Neues Bauerntum. Fachwissenschaftliche Zeitschrift für das ländliche
Siedlungswesen. Neue Folge des Archivs für Innere Kolonisation, Bd.
28, January-May, 1936. (Published by Deutsche Landbuchhandlung,
Dessauer Strasse, 13, Berlin SW 11, Germany.)
V. 28, 1936
January: Erbhofrecht und Neubildung deutschen Bauerntums, by Hopp.
(The effect of the land inheritance legislation on the establishment
of new settlers on the land is studied from various angles.) –pp.1-9,
Zum preussischen Gesetz zur Beschleunigung der Umlegung vom 3. 12.
1935, by R. Haack. (A digest of the provisions of the Prussian law

of December 3, 1935 to hasten the consolidation of holdings in western
Prussia. The text of the law is given on pp. 17-21.) - pp.10-12.
Heuerlingswesen und sozialer Aufstieg in der Landwirtschaft, by Krug.
(The position of the tenant who works part time for the landowner
is discussed and the advantages of land tenancy by agricultural
workers are pointed out.) - pp.13-17.

    February: Tätigkeitsberichte von Land- und Siedlungsgesellschaften.
(Summaries of the report for 1934 of the Land Company, "Eigene Scholle"
of Frankfurt on the Oder and of the report for 1934/35 of the Company,
"Rheinisches Heim" of Bonn. Land purchases, new settlements, and
building costs are among the subjects covered.) - pp.57-61.

    March: Fragen zum Siedlungsergänzungsgesetz, by Richard Haack.
(Further discussion of some of the questionable provisions of the
supplementary land settlement law of January 4, 1935.) - pp.97-101.
Der landwirtschaftliche Arbeitseinsatz auf weite Sicht ein Bodenproblem,
by W. Barnbeck. (The author argues that the agricultural labor
problem is in the long run a question of land. Give a man a home and
a piece of land that will ensure a living for his family and he will
have a will to work.) - pp. 101-104. Dorf-, Hof- und Hausgestaltung
des Neubauern. (An account of a number of speeches made at a meeting
in Brunswick on January 7 and 8, 1936 on village, farm and home
planning.) - pp. 104-117.

    April: Der Gebäudeaufwand bei der Neuschaffung deutschen Bauerntums.
(A discussion of the economic expenditure for the establishment of a
new farm family.) - pp. 149-151.

    May:Bodentreues Bauerntum, by T. Wutz. (Statistics are given to
show the changes in landownership by the German nobility since the
middle of last century and to emphasize the greater stability and
attachment to the soil of the peasantry.) - pp.193-200. Neubildung
deutschen Bauerntums in Anhalt, Arbeiten und Pläne 1935 und 1936, by
Schmidt. (The progress in land settlement in Anhalt and plans for
1936 are outlined.) - pp. 200-203. Die neuen Bestimmungen des
Reichsarbeitsministers über die Förderung der Kleinsiedlung. (New
regulations issued by the Minister of Labor on April 21, 1936, provide
easier terms for the acquisition of subsistence holdings by industrial
workers.) - pp. 210-211. Ausführung des Gesetzes zur Beschleunigung
der Umlegung. (Regulations of April 16, 1936 for the enforcement of
the law for the consolidation of small holdings.) - pp. 211-218.

New Deal Recovery Measures

Homan, P. T. The pattern of the New Deal. Polit. Sci. Quart. 51(2): 161-
    184. June 1936. (Published by the Academy of Political Science,
    Fayerweather Hall, Columbia University, New York, N. Y.)
    Five groups of New Deal measures are considered. "The first is
government lending; the second, regulation of business and government
enterprise; the third, regulation of money and banking; the fourth,
measures for social amelioration; and the fifth, measures in the interest
of special economic groups. Perhaps in that order the groups represent
increasing degrees of deviation from government practices antedating
the New Deal." The Agricultural Adjustment Administration is discussed on pp. 169-172.

Numbering Farm Homes

Cross, Merton. Putting cash into farmer's pockets. Natl. Grange Monthly
33(6): 10. June 1936. (Published in Springfield, Mass.)
    A system of numbering farm homes, such as has been put into opera-
tion in many counties in the state of Oregon, is described in this
article. Mr. Cross, the writer of this article was the originator
of the plan.
    The object of the plan is two-fold improvement to farm life: "(1)
identical location of the farm; (2) a list of the leading salable
merchandise on each numbered farm, printed in a farm directory issued
annually; the directory to have a wide circulation in each county
where issued."

Occupation Statistics - Austria and France

Statistics of occupied population in different countries (Austria, France).
    Internatl. Labour Rev. 33(6): 873-882. June 1936. (Published by the
    International Labour Office, Geneva, Switzerland. Distributed in
    U. S. by the World Peace Foundation, 8 W. 40th St., New York, N. Y.)
    A continuation of the series of statistics of the occupied population
    in different countries published in the International Labour Review.

Planning, Economic

Batson, Edward. A note on the nature and significance of economic planning.
    South African Jour. Econ. 4(1): 60-74. March 1936. (Publisher's
    address: P. O. Box 5316, Johannesburg, South Africa.)
    "For five years or so, the notion of Economic Planning specifically
    so-called has been fashionable, if ambiguous. It has been advocated,
    debated, repudiated, unlawfully appropriated. It has been deliberately
    and systematically applied in practice, and its name has been carelessly
    misapplied to practices with which it has no other connexion. Now
    that its novelty and its ambiguity have each worn off a little, its
    achievements and promises can be estimated with reasonable accuracy."

Crane, J. L., Jr. Planning organization and the planners. Planners'
    Jour. 2(3): 61-69. May-June 1936. (Published in Hunt Hall, Cambridge,
    Mass.)
    A paper presented at the annual meeting of the American City Planning
    Institute, Washington, D. C., January 19, 1936.
    Discussion by Arthur C. Comey and L. Deming Tilton.
    The following subjects are considered: Personal planning; Government
    agencies plan; Differences between personal and governmental planning;
    and Special planning staffs.

Martin, P. W. The present status of economic planning. I. An international
    survey of governmental economic intervention. Internatl. Labour Rev.
    33(5): 619-645. May 1936. (Published by the International Labour
    Office, Geneva, Switzerland. Distributed in U.S. by The World Peace
    Foundation, 8 W. 40th St., New York, N. Y.)
    "The present article consists of an international survey of the
    various types of State economic intervention actually in operation.

-626-

In an ensuing article some of the main problems arising out of this intervention will be considered." -- p. 619.

Topic headings are: Scope of the survey; Types of state economic intervention; The development of national services; State aid to industry; State interference with management; State adjustment of output; State adjustment of effective demand; State intervention in the conduct of international trade; Conclusion.

Morgan, A. E. The American bent for planning. Survey Graphic 25(4): 236-239, 288. April 1936. (Published at 112 East 19th St., New York, N. Y.)

"Planning is not something new; it is the very stuff of which civilization has been made. Nearly every beginning of civilization was under conditions where individual men could not survive alone, but were compelled to work together and plan together...

"To matter-of-fact people, this process of improving on nature may seem to be nearly finished, but to creative-minded, imaginative, and aspiring men it has just begun. Compared with the Indians we have achieved a stable and economical food supply. Yet agricultural specialists state that if the best of present farming methods were everywhere used, less than one fifth of our present farm land would support our population, and some imaginative minds see that as only the beginning. During the past year certain men with a bent of curiosity have experimented with raising such crops as potatoes and tomatoes entirely without the use of soil. Planted on beds of straw or leaves where their roots can reach through wire netting into shallow troughs containing plant food dissolved in water, tomatoes and potatoes bear twenty or thirty times as much as in a similar area when planted in good soil. At this rate less than two percent of the agricultural area of the United States would produce our food supply. Beyond even this we have the distant prospect of photosynthesis -- the direct manufacture of food products from chemical substances by the sun's energy...

"We shall not learn effective planning all at once. Experience may keep a dear school, but it is the only place for wise men as well as fools to learn... Our prospects will be better if we begin our social and economic planning before disaster has overtaken us. How much better our lot might have been if we had seriously attacked our problems in 1920. How much better to continue to force the issues now than to run away from them at the first sign of returning prosperity."

Plan Age, v. 2, no. 6, pp. 1-32. June-July 1936. (Published by National Economic and Social Planning Association, 726 Jackson Place, Washington, D. C.)

Contents: The Pacific Northwest Regional Planning Commission, by P. Hetherton, pp. 2-5; Social and economic planning in British Columbia, by W. A. Carrothers, pp. 6-8; The beginnings of planning in the State of Washington, by B. H. Kizer, pp. 9-12; Planning in Oregon, by V. B. Stanbery, pp. 13-16; Securing basic data for planning purposes. Some contributions of the Federally supported research program in California, 1933-1936, and the problem of coordination, by J. B. Sharp, pp. 17-20;

Land-use adjustment in California, by David Weeks, pp. 21-25; The Resettlement Administration and migratory agricultural labor in California, by P. S. Taylor, pp. 26-29; State planning in California, by
L. Deming Tilton, pp. 30-32.

Röpke, Wilhelm. Socialism, planning, and the business cycle. Jour.
Polit. Econ. 44(3): 318-338. June 1936. (Published by the University
of Chicago Press, Chicago, Ill.)

Planning, Rural - England

The future of the countryside. VII-IX. Country Life 79(2051-2052): 478-
480, 504-506, 530-532. May 9-May 23, 1936. (Published at 20,
Tavistock St., Strand, London, W. C. 2, Eng.)
    Contents: VII. Roads, by Noel Carrington; VIII. Parks and national
parks, by Clough Williams-Ellis; IX. Conclusion: The need for a planning
commission, by Thomas Sharp.

Platforms, Political, and Agriculture

Farm relief plans and the party platforms. U. S. News 4(24): 5. June 15,
1936. (Published at 2201 M St., N. W., Washington, D. C.)
    An "analysis of the agricultural plank, in relation to past and
prospective performances for the farmers" by both the Republican and
Democratic parties. How the policies of these two major parties clash
on export subsidies, crop control, tariffs and foreign trade is pointed
out.

Political Parties

Starr, J. R. Labor and farmer groups and the three-party system. Southwest.
Social Sci. Quart. 17(1): 7-19. June 1936. (Published by the Southwestern Social Science Association, Austin, Tex.)
    A discussion of the policies of the two major political parties
and of the possibilities of the establishment of a socialistic party
of laborers and farmers.

Population Mobility - Louisiana

Smith, T.L., Byrd, Mary, and Shafer, Karl. Mobility of population in
Assumption and Jefferson Davis Parishes, Louisiana. Southwest. Social
Sci. Quart. 17(1): 31-37. June 1936. (Published by the Southwestern
Social Science Association, Austin, Tex.)
    "This paper deals with social mobility in the State of Louisiana.
Mobility is an extremely broad subject and one which can be attacked
from many angles. Consequently it has been necessary to confine our
remarks to particular phases of the subject, attempting only to cover
as much of the ground as is justified in a short paper, and considering only the aspects of mobility upon which specific information could
be secured. Several considerations...caused us to limit the subject
to an analysis and comparison of territorial and occupational
mobility in the sugar and rice areas of Louisiana."

Potatoes - Marketing - West Wales

Roberts, Cynfab. Potato marketing in West Wales. Agr. Business 3(1):
10-11. Spring 1936. (Published by the Welsh Agricultural Organisation Society, Ltd., Aberystwyth, Wales)
   Potato producers in West Wales had to overcome the handicap of
having too few potatoes to interest the wholesale merchants.
   "To overcome these difficulties the producers in West Wales realised the importance of organisation in potato marketing, and secured
the co-operation of the authorised merchants in the area. Fortunately,
all the Agricultural Cooperative Societies in the area concerned are
Authorised, and are therefore able to give useful service to the producer

Poultry - England

Bridges, A. Flock performance scheme and egg yields in Oxfordshire.
Gt. Brit. Min. Agr. Jour. 43(3): 245-255. June 1936. (Published by
H. M. Stationery Office, London, Eng.)
   Describes the operation of a scheme in Oxfordshire one of the
objects of which was "to stimulate an increase in the production of
eggs on general farms and small holdings where it was believed that
most benefit would accrue from the work. "These brief notes on the
recording and advisory work of the Oxford County Council demonstrate
the usefulness of the scheme as a practical instrument in obtaining
progress in poultry management."

Prices - New Zealand

New Zealand: Labour in office. Round Table, no. 103, pp. 638-654. June
1936. (Published by Macmillan & Co., Ltd., London, Eng.)
   Regulated and guaranteed prices, pp. 643-648.

Production Credit - United States

Galbraith, J. K., and Black, J. D. The production credit system of 1933.
Amer. Econ. Rev. 26(2): 235-247. June 1936. (Published by the American
Economic Association, Northwestern University, Evanston, Ill.)
   "With the establishment of a permanent system of production credits
in 1933, the American farmer was provided with a publicly sponsored
institution to meet each of his credit needs. Although the legislation establishing the earlier agencies was controversial and attracted
general notice, that setting up the production credit system received
comparatively little attention. This paper describes briefly the
structure of the system and outlines the scale of loaning operations
to date. At the end of 1934 it seems probable that the system had
approximately one-tenth as many loans outstanding for agricultural
purposes as did the commercial banks. The competitive position of
the system, particularly in relation to country banks, is discussed
in some detail. Attention is also given to the perplexing problem
which the system faces in its efforts to maintain a uniform loan rate
for all parts of the country." -p.235.

Railroads and Agriculture

Budd, Ralph. Agriculture and the railroads. Nation's Agr. 11(9): 4-5,
    15. June 1936. (Published at 58 E. Washington St., Chicago, Ill.)
        The inter-dependence of the railroad and agriculture upon each
    other is described in this article by the president of the Burlington
    Lines.

Raisins - Australian Competition

Murray, A. T. Some effects of Australian competition in raisins. Foreign
    Crops and Markets 32(24): 745-772. June 15, 1936. (Published by the
    Division of Foreign Agricultural Service, Bureau of Agricultural
    Economics, U. S. Dept. of Agriculture.)
        Subtopics: United States production and exports; The Canadian raisin
    market; The United Kingdom raisin market; British tariff on raisins;
    Price relationships; Marketing seasons; The development of the Austra-
    lian raisin industry; Raisin-grape and currant acreage; Production;
    Australian raisin types; Australian exports of raisins and currants;
    The Australian Dried Fruits Association; The Commonwealth Dried Fruit
    Export Control Board; Method of operation of the Commonwealth Export
    Control Board; Relation of State boards to the board and to each
    other; Financing the control scheme; Export parity price.

Raw Materials - Prices and Trade

Draws, Max. Die Weltrohstoffpreise in Bewegung. Wirtschaftsdienst 21(1):
    14-16. Jan. 3, 1936. (Published at Poststrasse 19, Hamburg 36,
    Germany)
        "The influence of raw materials in World trade is discussed and the
    effects of political questions such as reciprocity are indicated.
    Statistics of German imports of cotton, wool, bast fibres and timber
    are tabulated and it is pointed out that although the average price
    paid to countries without restrictions in foreign trade is higher than
    the average, the tendency is for imports from these countries to in-
    crease at the expense of the 'bound' countries." -Textile Inst. Jour.
    27(4): A195. April 1936.

Recreation and Rural Social Planning

Melvin, B. L. Rural emergency recreation and future rural social planning.
    Rural Sociol. 1(2): 214-220. June 1936. (Published by the Rural Soci-
    ology Section, American Sociological Society, T. Lynn Smith, Sec.-
    Treasurer, Louisiana State University, Baton Rouge, La.)
        The writer's introductory paragraphs follow:
        "Efforts of the Works Progress Administration to carry leisure-
    time programs to rural people have been beset by many disappointments,
    but some accomplishments have actually been realized. Moreover, those
    who have worked to make the programs succeed have felt that they were
    doing much more than merely meeting an emergency. This has definite
    significance for the future.

"This paper is written out of some knowledge of what has been undertaken, if not completely accomplished. It has been prepared with a full appreciation of difficulties involved, and a keen feeling that the work to be of value, must mesh with the permanent programs being fostered in the interests of rural life, especially those carried on by the State colleges of agriculture. The three main headings of this presentation are: (a) program of work, (b) relation to extension, and (c) difficulties and opportunities. The discussion is a synopsis of ideas, rather than a complete presentation of the whole subject of emergency recreation in relation to the extension service."

Rehabilitation Problems and Agricultural Conditions - Hettinger County, N. Dak.

Stewart, H. L.   Natural and economic factors affecting rural rehabilitation problems in southwestern North Dakota (as typified by Hettinger County). U. S. Resettlement Admin. Research Bull., K-4, 39PP., mimeogr. May 1936. (Published in Washington, D. C.)
"The study was initiated by the Division of Farm Management and Costs of the Bureau of Agricultural Economics, United States Department of Agriculture in cooperation with the Division of Research, Statistics and Finance of the Federal Emergency Relief Administration and completed by the Bureau of Agricultural Economics and the Division of Social Research, Works Progress Administration." Research Bulletins K-1 and K-2 were issued by the Works Progress Administration.
Contents: Introduction; Description of Hettinger County and the surrounding area; Organization of farms; Income and Financial progress; Economic status of farmers; Farmers on relief rolls; Rehabilitation prospects.

Rehabilitation Problems and Agricultural Conditions - Hyde County, S. Dak.

Stewart, H. L.   Natural and economic factors affecting rural rehabilitation problems in central South Dakota (as typified by Hyde County, South Dakota). U. S. Works Prog. Admin., Social Research Div., Research Bull. K-2, 41pp., mimeogr. March 1936. (Published in Washington, D. C.)
48 representative farmers in Hyde County, which is considered typical of the entire Missouri Plateau of central South Dakota, were interviewed for this report. The survey was made by the Division of Farm Management and Costs, Bureau of Agricultural Economics, U. S. Dept. of Agriculture in cooperation with the Division of Research, Statistics and Finance of the Federal Emergency Relief Administration, in the spring of 1935.
A description of the topography, soils, and climate, is followed by information on the type of farming in the area, variation in crop yields, organization of farms, farm income, economic status of the farmers, farmers on relief rolls, and rehabilitation prospects.

Rehabilitation Problems and Agricultural Conditions - Perkins County, Nebr.

Pevehouse, H. M.   Conditions in the southwestern wheat area which affect the rehabilitation program (as typified by Perkins County, Nebraska). U. S. Resettlement Admin. Research Bull. K-3. 39PP., mimeogr. May 1936. (Published in Washington, D. C.)

"Permission to publish this bulletin for administrative use was granted by the Works Progress Administration. The material contained herein is the outcome of a survey of the present condition and future prospects of farmers in the drought area of 1934. The study was initiated by the Division of Farm Management and Costs of the Bureau of Agricultural Economics, United States Department of Agriculture, in cooperation with the Division of Research, Statistics and Finance of the Federal Emergency Relief Administration; and was completed by the Bureau of Agricultural Economics and the Division of Social Research, Works Progress Administration." Research Bulletins K-1 and K-2 were published by the Works Progress Administration.

Contents: Summary; Introduction; Type of farming in the area; Description of Perkins County; Variations in crop yields in the area; Organization of farms in the county; Income and financial progress of selected farmers; Economic status in 1935; Farmers on relief rolls in 1935; Rehabilitation prospects.

Rehabilitation Problems and Agricultural Conditions - Sherman County, Nebr.

Kifer, R. S. Farm relief and rehabilitation problems in the Loess Hills of central Nebraska (as typified by Sherman County, Nebraska). U. S. Works Prog. Admin., Social Research Div., Research Bull. K-1, 36PP., mimeogr. March 1936. (Published in Washington, D. C.)

57 representative farmers of Sherman County were interviewed for this study made by the Division of Farm Management and Costs, Bureau of Agricultural Economics, U. S. Dept. of Agriculture, and the Division of Research, Statistics and Finance of the Federal Emergency Relief Administration, in the spring of 1935. A description of the county is followed by information on variations in crop yields, organization of farms, income and financial progress of selected farms, economic status, farmers on relief rolls, and rehabilitation prospects.

Relief, Rural - North Carolina

Blackwell, G. W. Concentration of rural relief in certain localities in North Carolina. Rural Sociol. 1(2): 200-213. June 1936. (Published by the Rural Sociology Section, American Sociological Society, T. Lynn Smith, Sec.-Treasurer, Louisiana State University, Baton Rouge, La.)

Resettlement, Rural - Wisconsin

Rowlands, W. A. Possibilities of rural resettlement in Wisconsin. Agr. Engin. 17(6): 251-253. June 1936. (Published by the American Society of Agricultural Engineers at St. Joseph, Mich.)

Presented before the Soil and Water Conservation Division of the American Society of Agricultural Engineers at Chicago, December 4, 1935.

"A resettlement program is of more than passing interest to the people of Wisconsin. It is a vital part of a comprehensive land program that provides for a more profitable use of our land resources on the one hand; and a new opportunity for isolated, stranded settlers on the other. Such a program will require many years to complete. It will require enlightened leadership and local support.

"Throughout much of northern Wisconsin and also Michigan and Minnesota there are many isolated settlers now chained by the barrenness of their environment to a life of destitution and despair. Located as they are, inside areas of cut-over and non-agricultural lands, they can never hope to have the benefit of neighbors or the conveniences that go with compact agricultural communities...

"The cost of providing these settlers with roads, schools, and public health services is out of all proportion to their contribution in taxes. Under the financial condition of many of our northern counties such services become impossible.

"The chief interest, therefore, of northern Wisconsin people is in a relocation program that gives these settlers an opportunity to trade their isolated holdings for productive land located in established agricultural communities..."

Resettlement, Suburban - United States

Churchill, H. S.   America's town planning begins.   New Repub. 87(1122):
96-98. June 3, 1936. (Published at 40 E. 49th St., New York, N. Y.)
This article on the four new towns being built by the Suburban Resettlement Division of the Resettlement Administration, shows, as commented on by the editor, "the value of these towns as an object lesson in wise community planning." A plan of one unit of the Greenbrook, New Jersey, community is given.

Rice - Marketing - Bolpur (India)

Bose, Santipriya. Marketing of rice at Bolpur. Sankhyā; the Indian
Journal of Statistics 2(2): 105-120. April 1936. (Published by the Statistical Publishing Society, Calcutta, India. Agents: P. S. King & Son Ltd., London, Eng.)
"This paper gives a general description of the marketing of rice at Bolpur. This town is situated at a distance of 99 miles from Howrah on the East Indian Railway (lat. 23° 40′ long. 87° 38′ approximately), and is one of the important towns in Birbhum. Its importance is mainly due to the rice market. In this district there are 72 rice-mills of which 19 are in Bolpur. Unclean rice is obtained from the surrounding area, and even villages as far as 20 to 25 miles send out supplies to this market. Over 8 1/2 lakhs of maunds of clean rice (31,300 tons) were exported from Bolpur station in 1933-34. The various stages of marketing from the cultivator to the consumer will be discussed and an attempt will be made to appraise the services rendered by the various intermediaries and the remuneration received by them." -Introduction.

Rice Policies - Japan

Ladejinsky, W. Agricultural policies in Japan. Foreign Crops and Markets
33(3): 69-96. July 20, 1936. (Published by the Division of Foreign Agricultural Service, U. S. Dept. of Agriculture, Bureau of Agricultural Economics.)

"In the past, Japanese rice has been subjected to violent price fluctuations. These have had a decidedly adverse bearing upon the country's purchasing power. The political repercussions following in the wake of either too high or too low a price were also sufficiently significant to cause concern to the Japanese Government. For these reasons, the Government has made strenuous efforts during the past 15 years to maintain rice prices at levels which would reconcile the divergent interests of the producers and consumers of that product. The methods utilized by the Government to achieve that end and their application and effects upon the country's agricultural economy form the subject matter of this article." -p.69.

Subtopics: Acreage and production; consumption, imports and cost of production; effects of rice price fluctuations; obstacles to government control; regulation before the World War; prices and regulation during the World War; the rice law of 1921; the revisions of 1931 and 1932; the rice monopoly law; the effect of the government policy upon the price of rice; law of March 29, 1933, for the control of rice; the 1933-34 rice crop and measures regulating its price; the effect of the law of 1933; recent developments; conclusions; main provisions of the law for the control of rice, March 29, 1933.

Rural America

Rural America, v. 14, no. 5, pp. 1-16. May 1936. (Published by the American Country Life Association, Inc., 105 E. 22nd St., New York, N.Y.)
Partial contents: Small communities want national news, p. 2 [from an address before the American Newspaper Publishers Association]; Professional leadership in rural education, by Robert D. Baldwin, pp. 3-6; Rural and urban philosophies, by O. E. Baker, pp. 6-8; The best use of the land, by M. L. Wilson, pp. 8-9.

Science and Agriculture

Compton, K. T. Let's go partners. Country Home 60(6): 11-13. June 1936. (Published at 250 Park Ave., New York, N. Y.)
Interviewed by Donald Wilhelm.
Dr. Compton writes that, having tried "nearly everything else in frantic attempts to find means to improve agriculture's prosperity it would seem to be high time that we applied the modern scientific approach. This means finding new crops useful to industry, and much fuller industrial utilization of the products, by-products and wastes of agriculture.
"The supreme problem facing American agriculture is to increase farm income...
"Waste is abhorrent to all human effort and ideals. Science, on the other hand, stands for conservation, seeking the fullest possible utilization of every tree, of every crop. In making these statements, I am not losing sight of the very great importance of a soil conservation program. The national program of soil conservation now being undertaken through Congressional authorization will be a major step forward - if it is administered wisely for the purpose of soil conservation and not merely as an excuse for gaining other ob-

jectives. The argument of the present article merely urges that it be supplemented by equally vigorous and intelligent action in the direction of developing new outlets for agricultural products."

Dr. Compton cites numerous examples of "the kinds of things that science has done or can do for farmers."

Fritsche, C. B. First year's activities of the Farm Chemurgic Council. Utah Farmer 56(22): 3, 6, 8, 14. June 25, 1936. (Published in Salt Lake City, Utah)

"A survey of new chemurgic enterprises launched within the last year since the First Dearborn Conference justifies the estimate that no less than fifty million dollars are being invested in new industries which will use factory crops raised on American farms for raw materials.

"These new industries include American paper mills, power alcohol for motor fuel, vegetable fiber plants, expansion of the plastic industry, new uses for cotton, tung oil extraction plants, starch from Southern sweet potatoes and other miscellaneous new products."

Silk

Dawson, O. L., and Ladejinsky, W. The position of silk in United States-Japanese trade. Foreign Crops and Markets 32(15): 447-457. April 13, 1936. (Issued by the Division of Foreign Agricultural Service, Bureau of Agricultural Economics, U. S. Dept. of Agriculture.)

"This study presents the result of an analysis of factors affecting the price of raw silk in the United States and the significance of the silk-price situation to American-Japanese trade relations."

Tables showing production, consumption, exports, imports of silk are included in the article. A series of charts is given at the conclusion of the article.

Social Changes - Rural Towns of Connecticut

Hypes, J. L. The future of the sparsely populated rural towns of Connecticut. Geogr. Rev. 26(2): 293-298, maps. April 1936. (Published by the American Geographical Society, Broadway at 156th St., New York, N. Y.)

"The purpose of this article is to describe very briefly some of the more recent social changes taking place in the sparsely populated rural towns of Connecticut and the implications of these changes. The number of inhabitants, vocations, national origins, the combination of places of residence and of work (or commuting) and trends toward urbanization are selected for consideration."

More detailed and quantitative accounts of the movements considered in this article may be obtained in Storrs Agricultural Experiment Station Bulletins 161, 182, 194, 196, and 201.

Soil Conservation - United States

Splechtner, F. Vereinigte Staaten. Die "Soil Conservation Act" als Grundlage einer Agrarreform. Wirtschaftsdienst 21(20): 697-698. May 15, 1936. (Published by Hanseatische Verlagsanstalt Aktiengesellschaft, Hamburg 36, Germany)

A discussion of the Soil Conservation Act as the first step in a
possible long-time agrarian policy.

Southern States

Burton, C. S. The South comes back. Still below normal in buying power
but improvement spurs many industries. Mag. Wall St. 58(5): 288-289,
322-323. June 20, 1936. (Published at 90 Broad St., New York, N. Y.)
"The idea seems to gain ground that the Southern cotton farmer lost,
in one way and another, more than he gained by the operations of the
AAA and the benefit checks received.
"Yet taken as a whole it should be realized there has been marked
improvement in the South as elsewhere as compared with 1932-1933
conditions... The South has been buying electrical machinery, refriger-
ators, road building machines, engines and boilers, furniture, cement,
brick, copper and brass goods. All these increased in respectable
percentages as shown by shipments from the North Atlantic Seaboard
and the Chicago district into ten South Atlantic States, There is
prospect that given a fair crop and price relationship such purchases
may increase still further...
"What the Southern cotton planter needs is freedom from interference, an open market, where a bumper crop can be absorbed, at a
price - a world price; and an equally free market for the things he
buys where his dollar has the same purchasing power as the city man's
dollar."

Sugar - Iran

Mikusch, Gustav. Iran becomes a sugar producer. Facts about Sugar 31
(6): 211-213. June 1936. (Published at 153 Waverly Place, New York, N.Y.)
The vicissitudes of beet sugar production in Iran are outlined
with the final successful outcome and a prospect of eight factories
in operation during the coming season.

Sugar - Jamaica

Verity, D. J. Sugar industry of Jamaica. Increasing production in spite
of falling price levels. Empire Producer, no. 236, pp. 120-121. June
1936. (Published by British Empire Producers' Organisation, 22,
Queen Anne's Gate, Westminster, London, S.W. 1, Eng.)
A table gives annual production for 1927/28 to 1935/36, the last
being estimated.

Sugar - Dutch East Indies

F., M. S. Netherlands India prolongs sugar control. Far East. Survey
5(12): 123-125. June 3, 1936. (Published by the Fortnightly Research
Service, American Council, Institute of Pacific Relations, 129 East
52nd St., New York, N. Y.)
"Continuance of government regulation of the Netherlands Indian
sugar industry is assured by the enactment of a new set of sugar

ordinances to replace those expiring on April 1, 1936. The new
measures comprise two Sugar Consolidating Ordinances regulating the
production of estate sugar; one covering a transitional period through
1940, the other, apparently of indefinite duration, covering the period
after 1940; and three measures regulating the distribution of sugar
on the 'single seller' principle: one prolonging and modifying the
Sugar Bond Ordinance of 1931, a new Sugar Exports Ordinance, and a
Sugar Imports Ordinance temporarily continuing the prohibition of
sugar imports."

Sugar - Stabilization Program - Turkey

Mikusch, Gustav. Programa de estabilización de la industria en Turquia.
La Industria Azucarera 42(511): 267-268. May 1936. (Published at
Reconquista 336, Buenos Aires, Argentina.)
It is pointed out that Turkey, after having developed her sugar
industry to the point of being able to supply her own needs, is now
faced with the danger of overproduction. A law of June 12, 1935
provided for the reorganization of the sugar industry on the basis of
reduction of the consumption tax and customs duties, reduction in the
price of sugar, the liquidation of the existing sugar factories and
the establishment of a new company whose shares are held by three
banks which are more or less Government institutions. Three hoped-for
advantages are enumerated. A table gives production and consumption
statistics since 1931-32.

Sugar Agreement - South Africa

The new mutual sugar agreement. South African Sugar Jour. 20(3): 145, 147,
149, 151, 153, 155. March 31, 1936.
"The principal features agreed upon are as follows: Restriction of
production of sugar to 476,488 tons, allocating quotas to all mills.
Establishment of a Central Board of Control with an equalisation fund.
The Industry to be regarded as unified; with no differentiation between producers of cane and sugar. All growers to send cane to the
nearest mill. New cane prices to be based upon a special scale to be
drawn up. Period of agreement five years only."

Sugar Industry Reorganization - Great Britain

Amalgamation of the beet sugar manufacturing companies. Gt. Brit. Min.
Agr. Jour. 43(2): 141-145. May 1936. (Published by H. M. Stationery
Office, London, Eng.)
"A British Sugar Corporation, with limited liability, is to be
formed to acquire and operate the undertakings of the existing com-
panies as from April 1, 1936."

Sugar Institute Decision

Brand, C. J. Legal aspects of statistical activities of trade associations
with special reference to the Sugar Institute decision. Amer.
Statis. Assoc. Jour. 31(194): 367-375. June 1936. (Published by the

Association. Frederick F. Stephan, Sec.-Treasurer, 722 Woodward
Bldg., Washington, D. C.)
   The writer's conclusion is as follows:
   "The legal status of so-called statistical information which a trade
association may collect is one which depends almost entirely upon
whether or not the information so collected in reality constitutes
statistics. The legality of collecting and tabulating facts about
things that have been done or occurrences that have taken place, as
distinguished from information relating to things that have not happened
and may never happen, is scarcely open to challenge.
   "As to the dissemination of statistical information, the opinion
in the Sugar Institute case leaves no doubt that data collected by
an institute or association composed of producers, if it hopes for
legal protection, must be disseminated to the purchasing and distributing public insofar as they have a truly legitimate interest therein.
   "As to both collection and dissemination of information pertaining
to any trade or industry, trade organizations are in no sense curbed
by the Sherman anti-trust law so long as the information pertains to
actual facts and is not gathered or disseminated to foster or promote
any illegal combination in restraint of trade. Within the sphere
thus defined, business organizations seem to be perfectly free to
compile and disseminate any type of statistical data which may be of
interest or benefit to the members of the industry, provided always
that dissemination is not discriminatory. Associations must be careful not to restrict accessibility or release of information collected
in any way that will deprive the purchasing public of benefits obtainable from information in which it has a legitimate interest."

Taxation, Native - South Africa

Trevor, Daphne.   South African native taxation. Rev. Econ. Studies 3(3):
   217-225. June 1936. (Published at the London School of Economics,
   Houghton St., London, W. C. 2, Eng.)
   The article is concluded in part as follows:
   "It is now possible to formulate some conclusions on the native
taxation system as a whole. It is not in itself a fundamental ob-
jection that it taxes the natives and proceeds to appropriate most
of the resulting revenue for purposes which do not benefit them, but
that it is used directly and indirectly to keep them poor, by taxes
on wages and commodities for the benefit of employers, producers and
subsidised white workers. It maintains the supply of cheap labour
to mines and industry, and small as the resulting revenue is, the
whole present structure of South African industry is inconceivable
without it. But it is at the same time a fatal flaw in the national
economy, for it keeps labour far less productive than it might be,
and leaves the large majority of the population an unexploitable
market for agricultural and industrial products. The system of taxation is the State aspect of the exploitation of private enterprise,
which only does not destroy itself because agriculture and industry
can be subsidised as long as gold export supplies its enormous profits
to the mine-owners and the State. The contrast with Russia is
inescapable..."

Tea

Rothe, Cecile. Tea production and tea restriction. Pacific Affairs 8(4):
454-467. December 1935. (Published at 129 East 52nd St., New York, N.Y.)
Contains statistics of the area under tea in the leading tea producing
countries, also of tea exports and imports. Control regulations, agreements and decrees are described, including the Netherlands-Indian
regulations which are described in detail.

Technological Revolution

Polakov, W. N., and Coyle, D. C. Juggernaut - and jobs. Survey Graphic
25(4): 206-209, 282-283. April 1936. (Published at 112 East 19th
St., New York, N. Y.)
"Statistics seem solid but what do they mean? Here, factoring out
the figures which measure horsepower and manpower, two engineers tell
of some of the tides that underlie the charts.
"On the farm the technological revolution is in full career, with
a long clear road ahead. Machines that do the work of many horses,
fertilizers that improve the yield, plants and animals that nature
may have dreamed but never was able to bring to birth until man took
hold of evolution - all these play their part in expanding the productive power of the farmer. In 1800 about 90 percent of our labor
was devoted to supplying farm products for the population. Today
less than 25 percent of the manpower of the country is in agriculture.
Even if we solve the distribution problem and allow all the American
people to get enough to eat, they will do little more than use up
the embarrassing 'export surplus.'...
"The effect of all these developments is to release labor from
employment in the production of necessities - food, raw materials,
and manufactured goods. By the same natural process of evolution
that has transferred most of the 90 percent of farmers of 1800 into
the multitudinous forms of employment of 1936, labor will continue
to shift out of farming and manufacturing. The existing state of
disorganization is partly a phenomenon of social lag. Although there
is a trend toward a natural adjustment, the trend is too slow to
keep up with the effects of technical progress. Another element
of disorganization has been in the tendency to shift too large a
portion of the displaced labor into the capital goods industries."

Tenants and Share Croppers - Southern States

Carr, F. W. Shackled whites of the cotton belt. Marooned where opportuni-
ties for succor are rare, thousands of sharecroppers look toward
Washington for relief said to be on the way. Christian Sci. Monitor,
Weekly Mag. Sec., Apr. 29, 1936, pp.8-9, 14, illus. (Published in
Boston, Mass.)
An account of conditions among the Southern sharecroppers. An
inset on pp.8-9 gives briefly the plan for aiding the sharecropper
and others are embodied in the Farmers' Home Corporation Act, before
Congress at the time the article was writte.

Hamilton, C. H.   The status and future of farm tenantry in the South.
[6]pp. [Atlanta, Ga. 1936]   Reprint Coll.
"Reprint from Commercial Fertilizer 1936 'Yearbook'."
This paper, which was read before the Southern Economic Association, is in six parts. Part I, Introduction; II, Types of farm
tenantry (croppers, renters, part owners, farm laborers); III, Major
factors in farm tenantry (private ownership in land, variation in the
productivity and value of land, variation in human skills and traits,
type of agriculture, population growth and changes, difficulties and
hazards in purchasing land; the business cycle); IV, Present status
of farm tenantry; V, Tenantry under the Agricultural Adjustment program; VI, Future of farm tenantry in the United States, recommends
that the following principles and objectives be kept in mind in
planning for the future of farm tenantry; efficient production, soil
conservation, a fair distribution of farm income, an adequate and
balanced standard of living among all tenure classes, social stability
and security, and efficient rural institutions.

Munro, W. C.   King cotton's stepchildren. Current Hist. 44(3): 66-70.
June 1936. (Published at 63 Park Row, New York, N. Y.)
An article on the Southern sharecroppers - the organization of
the Southern Tenant Farmers' Union, the cooperative farm started for
the benefit of a few evicted families of sharecroppers in Tennessee
by Sam Franklin and Sherwood Eddy, and the Rust cotton picker and
the Rust Foundation organized for "the purpose of utilizing nine
tenths of the inventors' profits for the foundation of cooperative
farms and educational projects for the white and negro." To the
Southern Tenant Farmers' Union John Rust has offered marketing control of the machine.

O'Donnell, G. H.   Looking down the cotton row. Amer. Rev. 7(1): 47-65.
April 1936. (Published at 231 W. 58th St., New York, N. Y.)
A picture of Southern cotton tenant farming and its evils, with
a suggestion for their solution.
"The yeoman farmer is the key to the solution of the main problems in Southern agriculture. And the solution will prove of benefit to the entire nation. A good life is possible in the South -
generally possible, I mean, for in some sections of the South it
is an accomplished fact - if the emphasis is shifted from the plantations working for mass production of cotton to the agrarian plantations and to the small farms operated by yeomen."

Wilson, C. M.   Tenantry comes forward. Country Gent. 106(7): 12-13,
42, 43. July 1936. (Published at Independence Square, Philadelphia, Pa.)
The writer thinks that the advantages of tenancy outweigh the
disadvantages and that the increase in farm tenancy is not something
to be deplored. He tells of three large plantations - the Pfeiffer
plantation in Clay County, Arkansas, Bell Meade Plantation in Mississippi County, and the Sanderlin plantation in southern Alabama -
on all of which the three great faults of tenant farming have been
overcome. These are too much moving, poor soil management, and poor
livestock development.

Tennessee Valley Authority

The Tennessee Valley Authority. Planning, no. 76, pp. 2-16. June 2,
1936. (Published by Political and Economic Planning, 16 Queen
Anne's Gate, London, S. W. 1, Eng.)
   A condensed statement of the activities and problems of the
Tennessee Valley Authority.

Tithe - Great Britain

Tithe. Current survey of agricultural policy 3(5): 11-13. May 11-June 6,
1936. mimeogr. (Issued from 3, Magpie Lane, Oxford, Eng.)
   "The Second Reading of the Tithe Bill was moved in the House of
Commons on May 13 and the debate on the Money Resolution took place
on May 19. The Bill then went into the Committee stage. The second
reading and money resolution were approved by large majorities but
opposition to provisions in the Bill was expressed by members of
all parties."
   The speech of the Minister of Agriculture in the House of Commons
in moving the Second reading of the Tithe Bill is summarized, and
the main points of the discussion are noted. Leaders from the
London Times and the Manchester Guardian are summarized, and opinions
of the clergy, the chartered Surveyors' Institute and other bodies
are indicated. A list of letters to the Times, with dates of publication, is given.

Tobacco - Estonia

Pikner, V. Tobacco imports and changes in consumption. Konjunktuur,
no. 19(6): 414-421. June 6, 1936. (Published by Estonian Institute
of Economic Research, Tallinn, Estonia.)

Tobacco in the French Trade Agreement

American tobacco in the French trade agreement. Foreign Crops and Mar-
kets 32(23): 705-707. June 8, 1936. (Published by the Division of
Foreign Agricultural Service, Bureau of Agricultural Economics,
U. S. Dept. of Agriculture.)

Tobacco Industry - United States

Miller, S. L. Expanding cigarette market chief factor in outlook for
the tobacco industry. Annalist 47(1221): 868, 869. June 12, 1936.
(Published at Times Square, New York, N. Y.)
   The rising trend of cigarette consumption is pointed out in this
discussion of the tobacco industry. In conclusion it is pointed
out that the only "non-economic factor that may in the near future
disturb the orderly rise in the tobacco industry is the possibility
of further taxation by the national and State governments."

Trade - Germany

Germany's trade relations with Southeastern Europe. German Inst.
Business Research. Weekly Rept. 9(23-24): 50-51. June 17, 1936.
Attention is called to the favorable condition for increased
trade between Germany and the Southeastern European countries.
"In 1935 Germany took about half the total exports of Bulgaria,
about a third of the total exports of Greece, a quarter of the
total exports of Hungary, almost a fifth of the total exports of
Yugoslavia and Roumania... Germany took about 50% of the Bulgarian
and over 40% of the Grecian tobacco exports. Moreover, she took
in the case of Hungary 80% of the meat, 56% of the lard, 73% of
the oil seeds and 62% of the fruit exports. Therefore, the increased sales possibilities in Germany have been an important
support for the upswing in the agricultural regions of Southeastern
Europe."
A table gives statistics of the German share in foreign trade of
Southeastern Europe and the share of Southeastern Europe in the
foreign trade of Germany from 1928 to 1935.

Trade, Foreign

The attainment and maintenance of world peace, edited by Ernest Minor
Patterson... Supplement: Economic aspects of neutrality. Foreign
trade. Amer. Acad. Polit. and Social Sci. Ann. v. 186, 251pp.
July 1936. (Published at 3457 Walnut St., Philadelphia, Pa.)
Partial contents: Trade barriers as an obstacle to prosperity,
by W. A. Mackintosh, pp. 1-5; Commercial policy under the trade
agreements program, by Henry L. Deimel, Jr., pp. 16-23; The problem
of international monetary stabilization, by James Harvey Rogers,
pp. 34-40; The question of self-sufficiency, by Francis Bowes
Sayre, pp. 128-134; Foreign trade daydreams, by F. X. A. Eble,
pp. 135-142; Foreign trade and the domestic welfare, by Edgar W.
Smith, pp. 143-150; Economic aspects of United States foreign
trade, by John Lee Coulter, pp. 169-177; Japan's foreign trade, by
Hirosi Saito, pp. 178-182; Commercial relations between Cuba and
the United States, by Guillermo Patterson y de Jauregui, pp. 188-193.

Gilbert, D. W.   Foreign trade and exchange stabilization. Amer. Econ.
Rev. 26(2): 272-279. June 1936. (Published by the American Economic
Association, Northwestern University, Evanston, Ill.)

Peek, G. N.   Farmers' interests suffer from present foreign trade policy.
Natl. Grange Monthly 33(6): 8, 23. June 1936. (Published at Springfield, Mass.)
Radio address on the National Grange program, on the effect
of our foreign trade policy on agriculture. Mr. Peek repeated a
statement he made in a radio address last December when he spoke on
the subject of "'Reciprocal Trade Agreements and Agriculture.'"
He said at that time "that agriculture over wide areas was being

asked to take the rap,... the effect of which will be to depress
farm prices and lessen the ability of the farmer to buy the products
of industry." He also pointed out "that the trade agreements program, as carried out by the Administration, not only ran counter to
President Roosevelt's assurances to agriculture, but through its
threat to farm markets and farm purchasing power, menaced the whole
basis of national recovery and national prosperity."

Unemployment Insurance - Great Britain

Extension of British unemployment-insurance system to agricultural workers.
Monthly Labor Rev. 42(6): 1512-1514. June 1936. (Published by the
Bureau of Labor Statistics, U. S. Dept. of Labor)
A description of the provisions of the act which received the
royal assent April 9, 1936.

Unemployment Insurance (Agriculture) Act, 1936. Estate Mag. 36(6):
440-442. June 1936. (Issued by Country Gentlemen's Association,
Ltd., Letchworth, Herts, Eng.)
"About 750,000 rural workers are now registered under the terms
of the above Act. The scheme embraces almost all those who are
engaged as labourers in agriculture, horticulture (for profit), and
forestry, but domestic workers in country houses and private gardeners
are as yet not included in the scheme." Tables give the weekly
rate of contributions and of agricultural benefit.

Viticulture - France

Roger, Louis. La viticulture et l'etat. Revue des Agriculteurs de
France 68(5): 265-267. May 1936. (Published at 8, Rue d'Athenes,
Paris, France)
The author stresses the failure of government intervention in the
case of viticulture and indeed of directed economy in general.
He believes that the salvation of the wine industry depends on
union within its ranks.

Wheat - Elasticity of Demand - India

Sinha, Amulya Ratan. Elasticity of demand for wheat in India. Sankhya;
the Indian Journal of Statistics 2(1): 55-64. August 1935. (Published by the Statistical Publishing Company, Calcutta, India.
Agents: P. S. King & Son Ltd., London)
"In the present paper an attempt has been made to construct the
statistical demand curve of wheat for India, and to derive from it
the elasticity of demand for the commodity." Accompanied by
statistical tables with the following titles: Consumption and price
of wheat in India [annually 1893-1913]; trend-ratios of unadjusted
and adjusted data; elasticity of demand for wheat; observed and
calculated values of trend-ratios of unadjusted price and consumption;
observed and calculated values of adjusted price and adjusted consumption. Accompanied also by charts illustrating tables 4 and 5.

Wheat - Government Control

Governments and wheat. Statist 127(3042): 981. June 13, 1936. (Published at 51 Cannon St., E. C. 4, London, Eng.)

Reviews articles appearing in Broomhall's Corn Trade Year Book on the subject of Government interference in the grain trade in recent years in Canada, United States, Australia, Argentina and France.

Wheat under the Trade Agreement - Canada

Canada...III. Wheat under the trade agreement. Round Table no. 103, pp. 612-614. June 1936. (Published by Macmillan & co., ltd., London, Eng.)

Wool

Der Weltwollmarkt in Krise und Aufschwung. Institut für Konjunkturforschung 9(24): 95-96. June 17, 1936. (Published in Berlin, Germany)

It is pointed out that, while wool prices on the world market declined appreciably during the depression, production and consumption were relatively unaffected. On the other hand, during the period of recovery wool consumption increased considerably beyond the 1929 mark. Various causes for this are sketched. Tables show world production of wool, without U.S.S.R. from 1928/29 to 1934/35, and consumption by countries from 1929 to 1935.

Youth, Rural

Hamilton, C. H. The annual rate of departure of rural youths from their parental homes. Rural Sociol. 1(2): 164-179. June 1936. (Published by the Rural Sociology Section, American Sociological Society. T. Lynn Smith, Sec.-Treasurer, Louisiana State University, Baton Rouge, La.)

"The purpose of this paper is twofold: (1) to describe and evaluate a method of measuring the exact rate at which young people leave their parental homes, and (2) to present some preliminary results from the application of the method to a study of 1,703 rural families in five North Carolina counties."

Kirkpatrick, E. L., and Boynton, Agnes. Rural young people face their own situation. Rural Sociol. 1(2): 151-163. June 1936. (Published by the Rural Sociology Section, American Sociological Society, T. Lynn Smith, Sec.-Treasurer, Louisiana State University, Baton Rouge, La.)

Relates the results of a survey of rural young people in Waushara County, Wisconsin. Information is given and analyzed on certain of their population characteristics, their economic and occupational status, family living facilities, use of leisure, participation in organizations, and their needs and desires.

"'Something to do' seems to be the greatest need of rural young people according to these findings..."

NOTES

Angas, L. L. B.   The boom begins; a sequel to "The Coming American boom".
        96pp.   New York, Simon and Schuster, inc. [1935]   284 An4

Argentine Republic. Junta nacional del algodón. La industria textil y el
        consumo de algodón en la Argentina en 1935.   10pp., mimeogr. Buenos
        Aires [1936]   304 Ar32
            At head of title: Ministerio de agricultura. Junta nacional del
        algodón.
            The textile industry and the consumption of cotton in Argentina in
        1935.

Bauer, G. N.   Mathematics preparatory to statistics and finance.   337pp. New
        York, The Macmillan company, 1935.   325 B324M

Beesly, Alfred.   Planning potatoes and plundering the public.   16pp.   London,
        The Liberal free trade committee [1936?]   284.375 B39
            At head of title: P.P.P.P.
            A criticism of the Potato Marketing Board of Great Britain.

Bouchard, Georges, ed. La renaissance campagnarde. Préface de G. Bouchard.
        200pp. [Montreal] A. Lévesque [1935] (Albums canadiens) 281.2 B66R
            Radio talks on the renaissance of country life in Canada.

Burns, Mrs. Eveline Mabel.   Toward social security; an explanation of the
        Social security act and a survey of the larger issues.   269pp. New
        York, London, McGraw-Hill book company, inc. [1936]   284.6 B93

Canada. Board of grain commissioners. Dominion grain research laboratory.
        Ninth annual report 1935. 89pp. Ottawa, J. O. Patenaude, printer to the
        King's Most Excellent Majesty, 1936.   59.9 C161R

Canada. Department of agriculture. Fruit branch. Markets and transportation
        division. The apple crop - production and distribution - 1936.   17pp.,
        mimeogr. Ottawa, Canada [May 1936]   280.3939 C16

China.   Cotton industry commission. Central cotton improvement institute.
        Cotton grading office. Reprint no. 2. A proposed plan for the grading
        of seed cotton by the cotton growing and marketing cooperative society.
        3pp. [Nanking?] Jan. 1936.   280.3729 C44

Copland, D. B.   W. E. Hearn: first Australian economist; the Murtagh Macrossan
        lectures in the University of Queensland, 1935.   80pp.   Melbourne,
        London [etc.] Melbourne university press in association with Oxford
        university press, 1935.   120 H35

Dublin, L. I., and Lotka, A. J.   Length of life; a study of the life table.
        400pp. New York, The Ronald press company [1936]   447 D852
            Bibliography, pp. 379-385.

Erdös, J. G.   Die geográphischen grundlagen und standorte der rumänischen
    mühlen- und zuckerindustrie (Teildruck)   64pp. Oradea, 1934.
    281.177 Er2
        Diss. - Hochschule für welthandel, Wien.
        Bibliography, pp. [61]-64.
        Geographic bases and viewpoints of Rumanian milling and sugar industry.

Gt. Brit. Permanent consultative committee on official statistics.   Guide to
    current official statistics of the United Kingdom,   v. 14. 1935.   365pp.
    London, H. M. Stationery off., 1936.   241.3 G79

Gt. Brit. Scottish office.   Arrangements under Section 11 of the Milk act,
    1934 (24 & 25 Geo. 5, Ch.51) for increasing the demand for milk within
    the area of the Aberdeen and the district Milk marketing scheme, 1933,
    by publicity and propaganda.   4pp. Edinburgh, H. M. Stationery off.,
    1936.   280.344 Sco32Arr

Gt. Brit. Scottish office.   Arrangements under section 11 of the Milk act, 1934
    (24 & 25 Geo. 5, Ch.51) for increasing the demand for milk within the area
    of the Scottish milk marketing scheme, 1933, by publicity and propaganda.
    4pp.   Edinburgh, H. M. Stationery off., 1936.   280.344 Sco32Ar

Gt. Brit. Treaties, etc.   List of commercial treaties, etc. with foreign
    powers, January 1, 1936. Foreign office. 52pp. London, H. M. Stationery
    off., 1936.   286 G797L

Hawaii bureau of governmental research.   Some pertinent facts and statistics
    pertaining to the taxation laws and finances of the territory of Hawaii,
    comp. at the request of Lazard frères & company, inc. ... New York city,
    September 10, 1935.   23pp., mimeogr. [Honolulu, T. H.] Hawaii bureau
    of governmental research, 1935.   284.5 H313
        Address of Lazard Frères & Company, Inc. is 15 Nassau Street, New York
    City.

Hulbert, H. H.   Organization and operation of the Illinois livestock market-
    ing association.   140pp. [Washington, U. S. Govt. print. off.] May 1936.
    (U. S. Farm credit administration. Cooperative division. Bulletin no. 5)
    166.2 B87 no. 5

International federation of trade unions.   Economic planning and labour plans.
    81pp. Paris, International federation of trade unions [1935] (Inter-
    national trade union movement v. 15, no. 1/4, Jan./Apr. 1935)   280 In87

Kraemer, Erich. Supplementary farming homesteads in recent German land settle-
    ment.   20pp. mimeogr. Washington, D. C., July 1936. (U. S. Resettlement
    administration. Land utilization division. Land use planning section.
    Land use planning publication no. 3)   1 95 L23 no.3
        "Reprinted with the permission of the editors from the Journal of land
    and public utility economics, XII (2): 177. May 1936." A note on this
    article was given in Agricultural Library Notes for June 1936, p. 514.

Massachusetts. Special commission relative to taxation of tangible and intangible property. Report of the Special commission relative to taxation
of tangible and intangible property and certain related matters. 61pp.
[Boston, 1936] ([General court, 1935] House. [Doc.] no. 143) 284.5 M383
Hon. William A. Davenport, Chairman.

Milhaud, Edgard. A gold truce; a constructive plan for the revival of international trade. 153pp. London, Williams and Norgate ltd., 1933.
284 M59
"Bibliographical note concerning suggestions having the same object in
view as the system here proposed" pp. [152]-153.

Miller, Spencer, ed. What the International labor organization means to
America. With a foreword by John G. Winant. 108pp. New York, Col-
umbia university press, 1936. 283 M61
Addresses at the Institute of Public Affairs, University of Virginia,
1935, on the subject "The significance of American membership in the
International Labor Organization." - cf. p. vi, xiii.

Murray, K. A. H. Second supplement to The planning of Britain's food imports,
containing the revised annual index numbers for 1934, and the monthly and
annual index numbers for 1935. 8pp. Oxford, March 1936. 286 M96
Issued by University of Oxford Agricultural Economics Research Institute.

National industrial conference board. Cost of government in the United
States, 1933-1935. 98pp. New York city, National industrial conference board, inc. [1936] (Its Studies no. 223) 284.5 N212Cos

National industrial conference board. Nineteenth annual report... [1934/35]
75pp. New York, National industrial conference board, inc. 1936?]
280.9 N216

Piccoli, D. S. The youth movement in Italy. 72pp. Roma, Società editrice
di "Novissima" [1936] 280.176 P58

Ronk, S. E. Prices received by producers in New York state, 1841-1933. 2v.
[n.p.] 1934. 284.3 R66
Thesis (Ph.D.) - Cornell University.
Typewritten.

Sharfman, I. L. The Interstate commerce commission; a study in administrative
law and procedure. Part 3, volume B. 833pp. New York, The Commonwealth
fund [etc., etc.] 1936. 286 Sh2

Social science research council. Annual report. 1934-1935. 51pp. New York,
1936. 280.9 So12

Timar, Margarethe. Geographie der landwirtschaftlichen industrien in Australien.
67pp. Wien und Leipzig, 1934. 278.1992 T48
Diss.- Hochschule für welthandel, Wien.
Bibliography, pp. 65-67.
Geography as a determining factor in distribution and development of
agricultural industries in Australia.

Tsuda, Shingo.   Anglo-Japanese rivalry in the cotton industry.   20pp.   [Tokyo]
    The Jiji Shimpo publishing co., 1933.   304 T78

Unclaimed wealth utilization committee, Geneva.   The search for confidence in
    1932; the second series of bulletins issued under the chairmanship of
    A. H. Abbati, with an introduction by Sir Basil P. Blackett.   109pp.
    London, P. S. King & son, ltd., 1933.   280 Unl 2d ser.
        At head of title: Unclaimed wealth utilization committee, Geneva.
        Contains bulletins no. 12-23.

U. S. Bureau of foreign and domestic commerce.   Tung oil.   The situation in
    world markets and economic and commercial factors in the development of a
    domestic tung oil industry in the United States.   16pp., processed.
    [Washington, D. C., 1936]   157.55 T83 1936
        Excerpts from addresses, statements, etc. issued by C.C.Concannon."

U. S. Resettlement administration.   Agricultural landlord-tenant relations
    in England and Wales, by Marshall Harris.   63pp., mimeogr.   Washington,
    D. C., July 1936.   (U. S. Resettlement administration.   Land utilization
    division.   Land-use planning section.   Land-use planning publication no. 4)
    1 95 L23 no.4
        Bibliography, pp. 51-54.

U. S. Resettlement administration.   America's land.   30pp.   Washington [U. S.
    Govt. print. off.]   1936.   1 95 Am3

U. S. Resettlement administration.   The work of Resettlement.   4pp.   Washington,
    U. S. Govt. print. off., [1936?]   1 95 R31W

University college of Wales. Aberystwyth. Agricultural economics dept.
    Report on research and advisory work in agricultural economics, 1934-35.
    19pp.   Aberystwyth, 1935.   281.9 Un32
        "The work of the Department continues to be concentrated in two
    branches, farm organisation and management and marketing, but when
    opportunity occurs there is extension into the broader field of the
    social economics of agriculture.

Uschner, Herbert.   Die mechanisierung der landwirtschaft in Übersee und ihre
    auswirkungen auf die deutsche volkswirtschaft.   92pp.   Berlin, C. Hay-
    manns verlag; [etc., etc.] 1934.   (Volkswirtschaft; eine schriftenreihe...
    hrsg. von... Josef Gruntzel. 9 hft.)   281 Usl
        Bibliography, pp. 89-92.
        The mechanization of agriculture in other countries and its effect
    on German economy.

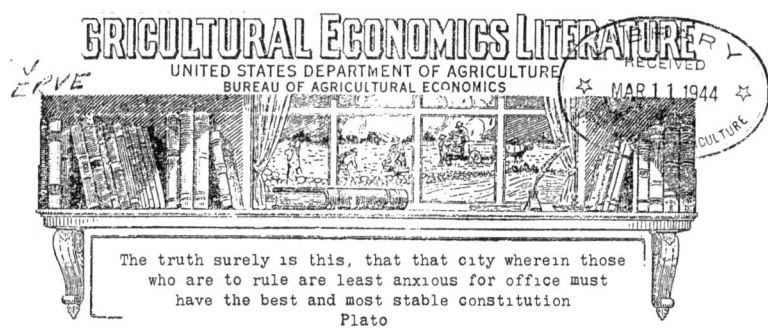

AGRICULTURAL ECONOMICS LITERATURE
UNITED STATES DEPARTMENT OF AGRICULTURE
BUREAU OF AGRICULTURAL ECONOMICS
RECEIVED
MAR 1 1 1944

> The truth surely is this, that that city wherein those
> who are to rule are least anxious for office must
> have the best and most stable constitution
> Plato

| Vol. 10 | October 1936 | No. 8 |

FEATURES IN THIS ISSUE

SIGNED REVIEWS

Anderson, William. Local government and finance in Minnesota. 355pp.
    Minneapolis, Minn., The University of Minnesota press [1935]
    280.043 An2L

Coleman, J. K. State administration in South Carolina. 301pp. New York,
    1935. 280.077 C67
        Thesis (Ph.D.) - Columbia university.
        Issued also as Columbia University. Studies in History, Economics and
    Public Law no. 406.
        Bibliography, pp. 285-292.

Ohio chamber of commerce. The fiscal situation in Ohio, by Arch D. Schultz...
    director of research, Ohio chamber of commerce. 188pp. Columbus, O.,
    Ohio chamber of commerce [1935] 284.5 Oh33F

Van de Woestyne, R. S. State control of local finance in Massachusetts.
    184pp. Cambridge, Harvard university press, 1935. (Harvard economic
    studies. v. 49) 284 V282
        "Originally... submitted as a thesis for the doctorate at Harvard
    University in 1932." - Preface
        Bibliography, pp. [169]-178.

These four books are concerned with the general problem of a more efficient mechanism for carrying on those activities which society carries
on collectively through State and local governments. Anderson and Van de
Woestyne have essentially a historical approach and are concerned primarily with those governmental units subordinate to the State. Coleman
and Schultz, however, deal with the local government units only incidentally.

Anderson divides his discussion of local government in Minnesota into
three parts, (1) the structure of local government, (2) local government
finance, and (3) the functions of local government. The first two parts
consist of the historical background of the town and county governments
and their fiscal affairs. There is nothing particularly new about his
recommendations, unless it is the way in which he treats the problem of
town government. He would retain the town as a nominal unit, but most
of its functions would be transferred to other units better able to perform them efficiently. In connection with this he probably is wise from
a practical point of view, in holding that the replacement of the present
school districts by more populous and wealthier units should be very
gradual.

No special plan is proposed for villages, cities and counties, but
Anderson advocates a simplification of the form of government to remove
difficulties that grow out of the present division of responsibility
among the various elected officers. In general, he would have a clearer
separation between the policy forming and the executive officers in a
particular governmental unit.

He seems to feel that much of the discussion about transferring
functions to States would be avoided if these changes were made in local
governments. His point of view is well summed up in the statement,
"The price to be paid for the restoration of local self-government
is the improvement of the system of local rule."

Van de Woestyne advocates no particular scheme. His analysis of State
control over local finance in Massachusetts is made from what is almost
a purely historical approach. He discusses at some length the various
acts providing for State control over the financial affairs of the
municipalities. By means of specific cases he illustrates the situation that led to the legislation.

It is largely the story of the difficulties faced by local governments in handling their financial affairs as economic, social and
political life became more and more complex. As local officials were
unable to deal with their problems wisely, the central government
stepped in to aid or to restrain them. The measures taken have been
largely concerned with restrictions on borrowing, better accounting
methods and periodic audits, but no control is exercised over expenditures. The question of State control over local expenditures is raised
but not discussed at length, nor is any suggestion offered. Massachusetts was for years an outstanding leader in the field, and Professor
Van de Woestyne's treatment is a good analysis of the development in that
State.

The other two books are concerned primarily with State governments.
The units of government subordinate to the State are considered only
incidentally. Coleman's study of the State government in South Carolina
approaches the problem in a manner similar to Anderson's. He also would
simplify the machinery of government so as to overcome the divided responsibility existing at the present time.

Coleman presents a complete analysis of the present organization of
the State government and then outlines a reorganization plan. Under
his plan the State government would be divided into administrative departments along functional lines. Each department would be headed by
an executive appointed by the Governor. Suggestions are also made for
the organization of each department. The purpose is to make the Governor
the responsible head of the State administration. There would be, of
course, practical difficulties in the way of such a wholesale reorganization involving as it does constitutional changes, but as a goal toward
which to strive there is much of value in the plan.

Schultz does not attempt to analyze the organization of the units of
government in Ohio. He discusses the needs for revenue and the sources
from which it can be obtained. In his discussion of the needs for revenue
he analyzes the financial obligations of the various units of government
in the light of past experiences. The last half of the study is concerned
with the revenue resources of the State. After discussing the revenue

possibilities of the present tax system he takes up the amount of revenue that could be raised by other forms of taxation. The conclusion is that there are no new sources from which large amounts of revenue would be raised. The income tax is passed over because of the heavy expense of administration in relation to the returns. The fact that in recent years operating costs of local governments have been reduced is taken as an indication that these reductions could be made permanent. No reference is made to the possible effect on future budgets of postponed expenditures or to demands for new services when it is concluded that the present sources of taxation are adequate if the revenues are properly distributed among the various functions and jurisdictions.

For those interested in problems of local government, books such as these are useful for purposes of orienting the problems. One looking for help on a particular problem may be disappointed because each of these books deals with a specific situation. The reorganization plan discussed by Coleman probably could be applied to other States, but constitutional provisions would prevent its being put into effect in its entirety even as in South Carolina.

The development of the structure and functions of local government as detailed by Anderson is probably paralleled to a large extent in States contiguous to Minnesota. His solution is more practical than Coleman's in that he differentiates between immediate steps and those to come gradually. Coleman recognizes the exploratory nature of his treatment when in his introduction he expresses the hope that his work will "stimulate research in behalf of better government in South Carolina." This is one of the more important results to hope for from all studies of the sort represented by these four books. The problem must be stated before a solution can be attempted. Here are four writers, each of whom has in his own way, stated some phase of the problem as it relates to his own States. - Gerhard J. Isaac, Assistant Agricultural Economist, Division of Agricultural Finance.

Walker, Helen M., and Durost, W. N. Statistical tables; their structure and use. 76pp. New York, Bureau of publications, Teachers college, Columbia university, 1936. 251 W15S

This small book is one of the most comprehensive guides to the presentation of statistical data in tabular form that is available at present. The treatment of statistical tables in most textbooks on statistics is limited to a brief description of the different kinds of tables and their uses. The details of constructing tables are in most cases neglected and, consequently, there has been a real need for a book such as the present volume. The practical application of the information in Part I of this book, describing the characteristics of good tables, is facilitated by Part II, which presents an analysis and criticism of selected tables. The third and final section gives the steps which must be taken in making a table and preparing it for publication. Without doubt this book will prove of considerable value to the research worker and occasional author confronted with the task of constructing statistical tables. - Gordon E. Ockey, Assistant Agricultural Economist, Division of Statistical and Historical Research.

Odum. H. W. Southern regions of the United States... For the Southern regional
committee of the Social science research council. 664pp., maps. Chapel
Hill. The University of North Carolina press, 1936. 280.002 Od8S
    Bibliography, pp. 605-620.

"The present volume is the formal presentation of the main findings"
of the Southern Regional Study "in eleven chapters of which this summary
and syllabus is one... As a device for presenting a cumulative picture
of many elemental factors, some two hundred and fifty maps have been prepared with a view to giving graphic expression to specific combinations
which may serve as critical analysis. These, together with perhaps as
many statistical tables and charts, each complete in itself, supplement
the text throughout and strive to give vividness and authenticity to conclusions and interpretation." This is Doctor Odum's own description of
the volume.

The Southern Regional Study was made possible by a special grant from
the General Education Board to the Social Science Research Council in
1931. The study was undertaken by Doctor Odum under the sponsorship of
a Southern Regional Committee. The general plan of this Study is given
in Part III of the present volume. A volume, "The South Looks at Its
Past", by Benjamin B. Kendrick and A. M. Arnett and another by Professor
Wilson Gee on "Research Barriers in the South" have been published in connection with the study and other publications are contemplated.

An idea of the contents of this present volume can be secured from
the chapter headings which are: I. The Composite Picture: a Syllabus and
Summary; II. A General Measure of the Southern Regions; III. A New Regional
Analysis: Southern Regions in the National Picture; IV. Regions of Natural
Richness and Abundance; V. Regional Technology, Deficiency, and Waste
VI. An Agrarian Country; VII. Industry and Wealth; VIII. The Southern
People; IX. Institutions and Folkways; X. States and Regions; and XI.
Towards Regional Planning. Chapter I. Makes up Part I of the volume and
Chapters II. to XI. comprise Part II. In addition there is a Part III
giving a bibliography and source materials, acknowledgements and the plan
of study, a list of maps, charts, and tables, a subject index of maps,
charts, and tables, and a general index.

What the author considers the "main" findings of this Study are not
clear to one reader. However "one of the major contributions of the Study,"
no doubt, is "the differentiation between the older Southeast and the emerg-
ing Southwest" and "the definitive six-fold regional divisions of the United
States", the Southeast, the Southwest, the Northeast, the Middle States, the
Northwest, and the Far West. Some may question why this division of the
United States into six regions should be "basic to the study". Given
Doctor Odum's regional philosophy and the distinction he has brought out
between regionalism and sectionalism, it is quite appropriate that the
Southern Regions should be considered as two of the six regions comprising
the nation. The division of the South into the Southwest and the Southeast
as well as the division of the rest of the country into four major regions
was based on a study of several hundred indices of various kinds. In reading this volume one will be impressed by the vast amount of data which has
been assembled not only for the Southern Regions but also for the Nation.

The emphasis is on the Southeast and the relation of the Southeast to the Southwest and the Nation. This was done because the Southwest was considered a special field for further study. It was not only necessary to consider the Southeast in relation to the Nation and the larger regions, but to consider the significance of the States and the subregions within it. The agricultural subregions of the Southeast are shown on the map on page 276, and a map of the Tobacco South is on page 572. The statements are made that "The subregions constitute an unusually promising field for further study and analysis. Although a great deal of valuable material has come from the present study, it must be clear that only a beginning has been made. One of the results of the study has been the clearly defined area of research and planning which subregions afford."

Other "findings" of the study are that the regions have "superabundance of resources alongside of deficiencies in technology, waste in economy, immaturity in culture, and lack of unity in action. It is this measuring and bridging of the chasm between possibilities and actualities which constitutes a definitive quality of this whole southern regional appraisal, which must bring to its task both the sweep of imaginative exploration and the solid base of factual support."

"Some indication of the superabundance in the Southeast of land resources... may be indicated by the fact that this region alone might easily add forty million acres... to its present area;... There is available for replanning and sale no less than 100,000,000 acres within the former area of the South's piney wood alone. Of the Nation's nearly 100,000,000 acres of drainable land suitable for cultivation after reclamation, the Southeast has nearly two-thirds. There is another illustration of a single southern regional land bank, which served three states only, with the prospect of owning and managing 2,000,000 and more acres of farm land whose titles the fortunes of depression had poured into its vaults." Just how significant such "facts" are "to the understanding of the situation and to the planning of the next steps" may be open to question. Especially is this true when other "facts" show the Southeast has approximately 5 percent of the grade 1 land in the United States, 17 percent of grade 2 land, 29 percent of grade 3 land, 21 percent of the total population, 33 percent of the rural population, and 40 percent of the farm population. Or in actual area the Southeast has in round numbers 5 million acres of grade 1 land, 37 million of grade 2, 100 million of grade 3; while the Middle States have 76 million acres of grade 1, the same number of grade 2, and 59 million acres of grade 3; the Northwest, 15 million acres of grade 1, 41 million acres of grade 2, and 68 million acres of grade 3.

An example of the technological deficiency of the region is "pictured in the field of livestock and dairy production, and other aspects of agriculture closely related with the land drainage and technological deficiencies of the Southeast. Suffice it to point out here the consistently uniform deficiencies in number and value of livestock production, and in the consequent low return in money and in man power output and in the similar deficiencies of soil improving crops, and in cooperative activities which result from a reconstructed land use and land conservation." In the chapter, "An Agrarian Country", a new dairy region is proposed "to be projected down from the present designated northern and eastern dairy region to encompass

- 653 -

the Piedmont South, touching also parts of the cotton belt and the
Tennessee Valley." This is made as a part of a study of "possible
procedures for substitute economy which will effectively merge economic
and social diversity with cotton economy." Another was "a special subregional study of nearly a hundred counties in southern Alabama, Georgia,
and Tennessee where actual data are available and where conditions are
representative of subregional analysis. The third (approach to the
study of the possibilities of dairying) is illustrated in the case of
a decade of recent developments in north Mississippi." The following
quotation will illustrate the method used "to discover their present
development (of the subregions) in regard to milk production with a view
to getting at their potentialities. The elementary facts are about as
follows:

"In the Tennessee Valley area of Alabama, cotton and corn together
cover about 75 percent of the crop lands of the region. Hay and forage
production is considerably above state ratios. The average present value
per acre of farm lands is about 50 percent above the state average, while
the per farm value is exceeded only by the Gulf trucking area. The population is approximately three-fourths white, and tenancy exceeds 66 percent. The fertility of the soil as indicated in cotton and corn yields
per acre is consistently high. The index of local contour ranges from
30 to 40, with about 12 percent of the total area ranging around 70."
One further illustration of this study "of the Tennessee subregions,
the Nashville Basin, which is made the criterion of the subregions in
this survey, has an index of contour ranging from 85 to 300 and above.
The valleys are broad and broken by sharp declivities. The soils are
fertile in the valleys, but do not assay out of the class of the better
soils of the other subregions included here. The population has a higher
proportion of Negroes than the other subregions, ranging to a third of the
total in this datum. In the area of relatively retarded development the
proportion of Negroes is considerably lower.

"This subregion is notable for its livestock development. More than 80
percent of all farms reported an average of 3.4 cows milked per farm, with
cows milked totaling 40 percent of all cattle. The growing of potatoes,
vegetables, feed crops and field grains is well advanced. From five to ten
percent of the farms are listed as belonging to the owners or breeders of
thoroughbred Jersey cattle.

"Comparison of the objective conditions of the several subregions, which
has been done above very sketchily, indicates that the Tennessee Valley
dairying region possessed, in the period covered, two definite advantages
over the other subregions here studied - an available and visible market,
and adequate means of transport. Otherwise, in the matter of climate and
weather, soil and topography, there is no effective superiority of the dairying subregion over the subregions where dairying is undeveloped and milk production carried out on a smaller scale. The size and value of farm equipment
in the subregions, varying within the limits of from $1,500 to $3,000 total
per farm, with a high proportion of all farms falling close to the average,
suggests the possibility of a program of stocking the area for increased
milk production on a commercial scale. The local consumption of milk, if
social pressure were applied, could with great benefit be doubled or trebled."

"These studies of new prospects for dairying are fundamental to the whole question of agricultural reconstruction and agrarian life in the South. It is, indeed, through the very realistic, practical, subregion by subregion approach that the picture must be painted or success be attained, rather than through the ideological motivation for an abstract agrarian culture." These rather extensive excerpts on the dairy study have been presented to show what appears to be the method of study and approach to planning which is proposed.

Another emphasis of the study is upon education. This is apparent in the chapter, "Institutions and Folkways", where education, religion, and politics are considered, also in the chapter, "Toward Regional Planning". However, the statement was made that less emphasis on education was given than was planned because of the publication of Doctor Gee's study mentioned above.

This volume will be useful to many people interested in the study of the Southern Regions, especially the Southeast. The methods used may have some application to the social and geographic factors in studies of other regions. But the usefulness of the book to economists will be limited. The first limitation concerns the make-up of the book. The first part which is also the first chapter is entitled "A Syllabus and Summary". This leads to the conclusion that this chapter is intended to give the reader a brief presentation of the outline and main results of the study. It seems doubtful that this has been done when this first chapter covers 205 pages, while the main body of the report covers less than twice that many pages. A table of contents in some detail and a summary of ten pages or possibly twenty would have increased the usefulness of the book and probably eliminated some of the repetition in the main report.

The second is that the volume is compounded largely of sociology and geography with a thread of economics. The economist can, no doubt, profit by a wider acquaintance in the fields of sociology and geography, especially as they affect the regional economy. But his interest will be in the economic relationships among men in the region rather than in their larger social relationships as shown in the religious and political aspects, or in their relationship to the environment. And in the Southeast these economic institutions and relationships are likely to be as important as the broader social and political institutions considered in the study in reducing the gap between actuality and potentiality described there. To be sure there is a discussion of tenancy in a dozen different places, and it is proposed on page 593 that the "experimental approach may center upon the problem rather than the area, such as, for instance, the problem of farm tenancy... Isolated experiments may be made with isolated tenants, in which the special cooperative arrangements with land-owners may be affected, to test proposed plans for reconstruction. Other experiments would focus upon a relatively large group of tenants, experimenting in community arrangements where there is a large measure of homogeneity within specified areas.'

A third point for disagreement, for some at least, will be the emphasis on agrarianism. Although several instances of the author's criticism of an "abstract agrarian culture" could be given, yet as many instances could

be cited showing an indication to favor agrarianism. The question here
may be largely one of definition. "There remain, however, some aspects
of this agrarian ideal which yet retain the motivation of agriculture as
a way of life, to be adapted to a new equilibrium between rural and urban,
between agricultural and industrial life. Here are included the ideals
of those who, as Julia Peterkin points out, yearn for the peace and quiet
of country places with leisure to possess their own souls and with abundance of things for the comfort of minds and bodies. 'To realize the
earth's generosity to those who have joy in sowing and reaping,' so runs
the theme, 'gives a deep sense of security and a faith in the rightness
of things.' For such an ideal the Southeast is peculiarly well equipped
by nature and awaits that new planning which will transvaluate the poverty-
breeding system of tenant and landlord into that abundant life so pictured."

Any disappointment which may be evident in the statements above are
probably due to the fact that so much was expected of this volume. The
volume does not, in its discussion of theory as applied to the actual
regions, come up to Doctor Odum's presentation of regionalism in "Social
Forces" or in the more descriptive phases of Doctor Vance's "Human Geography of the South". That, at least, is the opinion of the reviewer. -
C. I. Hendrickson, Senior Agricultural Economist, Division of Land
Economics.

Argentine Republic. Junta reguladora de granos. Memoria... campaña 1933-1934.
      152pp. Buenos Aires, Guillermo Kraft ltda., 1935. 287 Ar3
      At head of title: República Argentina Ministerio de Agricultura de
la Nacion.
      Toward the end of 1933 the economic condition of the Argentine
grain growers had become a matter of grave concern to the Argentine
Governmental authorities. Prices had declined approximately 33 percent below the level of 1929. Farmers contended that the prices
did not cover the cost of production and in some sections they
resolved not to harvest their crops. Prompt and vigorous action by
the Government was demanded. As the conditions in the world market
offered no prospects of immediate improvement, the Government was
forced to seek a remedy of its own making. There could be no further
delay.

      Accordingly, on November 28, 1933, without any previous announce-
ment, the Government issued an Executive Decree establishing a minimum price for wheat, corn and linseed, and at the same time created a
grain regulating board with authority to purchase grain and linseed
in the open market at the fixed prices whenever the world price, as
reflected in Buenos Aires, should fall below the minimum established
by the Government. The new minima represented an increase of approximately 20 percent over the then ruling market prices. Any losses
sustained by the Government in connection with the sale of grain and
linseed at less than the prices paid for them, as well as the administrative expenses of the Board, were to be defrayed from a fund
derived from the profit on the purchase and sale of foreign exchange bills.

The total purchases of wheat by the Board during the year amounted to some 147,500,000 bushels or about 75 percent of the estimated exportable surplus from the 1933-34 crop. The early period of the Board's operations showed a considerable loss, but with the advance in the world price of wheat, resulting largely from reduced crops in the United States and Canada because of the drought of 1934, the Board was able to dispose of its accumulated stocks at prices well above the minimum and was able, therefore, to reduce its own losses for the entire year to the equivalent of approximately $2,000,000. As the market price for corn and linseed remained well above the fixed price throughout most of this period, the Board's purchases of corn and linseed were relatively negligible.

In addition to the official text of the several decrees issued by the Government in connection with the creation of the Grain Regulating Board and the establishment of the minimum prices and foreign exchange regulations, the report contains a summary statement of the conditions that made these measures necessary and the resulting benefits that have accrued to the Argentine farmer. Part II contains a descriptive and statistical review of the operations of the Board, including the quantities of grain purchased and sold, the average price paid and received, as well as the stocks for given months, etc., together with a financial balance sheet on expenses of operation and losses sustained. There is also an administrative supplement which describes the functions and administrative organization of the Board and the chief features of the regulations governing its operations.

This report covers the operations of the Grain Regulating Board during the first year of its existence, that is, for the crop year 1933-1934. Since then the minimum prices have been further increased but as the world prices have remained above the fixed minima most of the time, the Board has not been compelled to make any further extensive purchases of grain. As a valuable source of reference for information on the historical background and beginnings of the Argentine minimum-price scheme, this report should be of particular interest to those who wish to obtain their facts from original and first-hand sources.—Charles L. Luedtke, Senior Agricultural Economist, Division of Foreign Agricultural Service.

DESCRIPTIVE NOTES AND ABSTRACTS

Agrarian Problem - Chile

McBride, G. McC. Chile: land and society. With a foreword by Don Carlos Davila. 408pp. New York, American geographical society, 1936. (American geographical society. Research series no. 19) 500 Am35R no.19.

Bibliography, pp. [387]-400.

"This work is an attempt to analyze the agrarian problem in Chile. It is based on familiarity with Chilean social institutions gained during a former prolonged residence in that country and during an additional year recently spent there in gathering detailed data by interviews, visiting different kinds of rural properties, and carrying on investigations in libraries, archives, and government offices."

Agricultural Credit

Dobler, August. Bäuerliche schuldenregelung mit beiträgen zur kreditordnung und rechtsbetreuung. 536pp. Stuttgart und Berlin, W. Kohlhammer. 1935. 284.2 D65.
Schrifttum, pp. 445-446.
Have also "Nachtrag [Berichtigungs- und Ergänzun,,sblatt auf Grund der VII. Durchführungsverordnung vom 30. April 1935]"
A study of agricultural indebtedness and measures for its relief and of agricultural credit in Württemberg and in Germany as a whole. Contains text of law of June 1, 1933 and of the regulations from June 15, 1933 to July 7, 1934; also legislation providing against compulsory foreclosure.

Wilden, Hans, and Nonhoff, Fritz. Das landwirtschaftliche schuldenregelungsgesetz vom 1. juni 1933. Eine erläuternde darstellung des gesetzes und der durchführungsverordnungen vom 15 juni, 5. juli, 15. september und 5. oktober 1933 nebst wiedergabe des gesetzes und der verordnungen. Zweite, völlig neubearb. aufl. 112pp. Berlin, P. Parey, 1934. 284.2 W64L Ed2
An account of the provisions of the law of June 1, 1933 for the relief of agricultural indebtedness in Germany and of the enforcement regulations of June 15, July 5, September 15 and October 5, 1933. Text of law and regulations appended.

Agriculture - European - Middle Ages

Neilson, Nellie. Medieval agrarian economy, 106pp. New York, H. Holt and company [1936] (The Berkshire studies in European history. 30.9 N31
Bibliography, pp. 95-96.
"The college teacher of general European history is always confronted with the task of finding adequate reading for his classes which is neither too specialized and technical nor too elementary. For many topics, including several of the greatest importance, no such material is at the moment available. Moreover, in too many instances, good reading which undeniably does exist is in the form of a chapter in a larger work and is therefore too expensive for adoption as required reading under normal conditions.
"The Berkshire Studies in European History have been planned to meet this situation. The topics selected for treatment are those on which there is no easily accessible reading of appropriate length adequate for the needs of a course in general European history. The authors, all experienced teachers, are in nearly every instance actively engaged in the class room and intimately acquainted with its problems. They will avoid a merely elementary presentation of facts, giving instead an interpretive discussion suited to the more mature point of view of college students.
"No pretense is made, of course, that these Studies are contributions

to historical literature in the scholarly sense. Each author, nevertheless, is sufficiently a specialist in the period of which he writes to be familiar with the sources and to have used the latest scholarly contributions to his subject. In order that those who desire to read further on any topic may have some guidance short bibliographies of works in western European languages are given, with particular attention to books of recent date." - Preface.

Consumer - Economics

Henderson, Fred. Capitalism and the consumer. 156pp. London, G. Allen & Unwin ltd. [1936]   280 H382C
"A new definite formulation round a central purpose seems to be beginning in current economic thought and discussion... There has been precious little sense of direction in the economic wisdom served up to us, and very little indication indeed of the centric kind of understanding from which any dependable sense of direction might issue. But now, it seems, a new definition of our problem in terms of central understanding is finding expression; and our current economic thinking tends to move into relation to it with all the appearance of natural gravitation to a real centric concept.
"Mr. Roosevelt has given expression to it in his statement to the American people of the principle of action by which he suggests that any New Deal, if it is to be effective, must be governed. 'We are,' he says, 'at the threshold of a fundamental change in our economic thought; in future we are going to think less about the producer and more about the consumer... The millions who are in want will not stand silently by for ever while the things to satisfy their needs are within easy reach.'
"Consumer-economics: production for use: making the interests of the consumer dominant in economic policy - our current economic thinking, in its direction and outlook, begins everywhere to show this 'fundamental change,' as Mr. Roosevelt very truly describes it. That there should be such a general insurgence of this consumer-motive in our economic thought is not to be wondered at. For, once the thing finds expression, it is like a searchlight on our economic confusions; an illumination in which the present trouble of mankind stands unmistakably defined as the failure of our existing economy to function in the interest of the consumer.
"It is not an isolated local or national trouble. Special national circumstances may modify it in minor details; but in its underlying reality what is happening to the life of the world is the same thing and presents the same problem everywhere. It is just this - that the peoples of the world are being disabled from getting into use and consumption the things they all want and can produce in abundance. Our need for the things is urgent; our power to produce them is ample; but for some reason not yet detected by the governing statesmanship of the world we are having to go without them.
"Whatever difficulty statesmanship may find in detecting the causes of this dislocation in human affairs, at least there can be no mistaking its character. What we are brought up against at every turn in the working of our present economic system is a restrictive veto on consumption;

a veto so peremptory that under its compulsion we have had to labour to
plough back again into the ground the crops we have laboured to produce;
to burn supplies in vast quantities or dump them into the sea while
armies of people are hungering for them...

"This compulsion to go without things is imposed upon us all round;
upon our public life and our social services as well as upon our private
satisfactions. So far, indeed, from detecting and arresting the evil,
the governing statesmanship of the world finds itself not only headed
off at every turn from movement in the consumer direction, but positively driven, in any attempt it makes to cope with it, to do the very
thing it sets out to prevent. The imperative of the system imposes
itself upon the very effort to escape; compelling such effort to take
the form of yet further insistence upon the anti-consumer view of human
affairs; insistence that the world cannot afford to use its own visibly
abundant real resources, and must go on economizing in every direction.
The thing has a grip on the world's life like the ju-jitsu arm-breaking
grip which utilizes the victim's own movement for release as an added
leverage for making the fracture worse. The injunction drastically enforced everywhere - never because of any natural scarcity in our real
resources, but in a world in which everything needful or desirable, everything serviceable for the full satisfactions of human life, can be produced
in greater plenty than any previous generation of men have known or
dreamed of - is that we must cut down to the utmost our consumption of the
things thus lavishly producible, and our carrying-on of the mutual services
by which we might be enriching our common life almost illimitably...

"There is in all this something much more formidable than a chancey
muddle into which incompetence has landed us. There is nothing haphazard
about it. It is the working of a system in whose operations a set direction
is visibly manifest and consistently followed; with a set purpose in it;
a purpose clearly demonstrated, by the test of the results thus eventing
from it in general human experience, to be at war with the consumer needs
of mankind.

"Then, therefore, President Roosevelt, recognizing that making the interest of the consumer the directing purpose in economic procedure must be
the determining policy in any New Deal which is to be effective, describes
such a purpose as 'a fundamental change in economic thought,' he is not
indulging in any rhetorical extravagance. He states a plain fact with
sober precision. It is not merely change, but fundamental change; change
in the very foundations of our economic life; change in the basic purpose
to which economic procedure is directed.

"My aim in this brief study is to set out, as simply as may be, what
seem to me to be the implications in action and procedure of this fundamental change in economic thought and purpose."

Consumer Purchasing

American home economics association. Committee on standardization of
consumers' goods. Scientific consumer purchasing; a study outline on
problems of the consumer in making intelligent selections and recent developments in production and distribution which affect the
consumer's interest... Prepared by the Committee on standardization

- 660 -

of consumers' goods, American home economics association for American
association of university women. 64pp. Washington, [1935]   321 Am 322 1935
    1932 has title: Standardization of Articles for Home Use.
    Copyright, May 1932; revised Sept. 1933, 1934, 1935.
    Bibliography, pp. 63-64.
    "The important economic changes which have accompanied mass pro-
duction in industry have brought about conditions in the retail
trade which the ultimate consumer is poorly prepared to meet. The
constant development of new products for individual and household
use, marketed without any definite information as to quality and
performance, has made wise selection increasingly difficult. This
study outline deals with some present practices in manufacturing
and in retailing which directly affect consumers. It should aid
the individual buyer to determine and define his needs in ways which
will assist manufacturers and retailers to supply the detailed and
accurate information required for intelligent buying."

Cost of Living - U. S.

Beney, M. Ada. Cost of living in the United States, 1914-1936. 99pp. New
    York City, National industrial conference board, inc. [1936] (National
    industrial conference board. Studies no. 228) 284.4 N212Cl 1914-1936.
    Prepared by Miss M. Ada Beney... with the assistance of Miss Edith
Turner and Miss Bertha Jacobson. - p.vi.
    "While problems relating to living costs have occupied the attention
of economists, social investigators, and others for many years, the
question does not generally force itself on public attention until disturbances in price levels bring the matter to the foreground. When
prices rise and the family purse is pinched the question becomes one
of general concern.
    "It was during such times of advancing prices in the war period,
when there was much complaint about the 'high cost of living' but little
accurate knowledge of actual conditions, that the Conference Board first
made an estimate of the changes in living costs since July, 1914. The
estimate for June, 1918, was prepared at the request of the employer
members of the National War Labor Board and to meet the needs of industry in general. In November, 1918, the Conference Board undertook a
more systematic collection of data and, with subsequent improvements in
technique, has continued its investigations of periodic changes in the
cost of living. The Board's studies have become part of the standard
statistical information in this field, and are widely used for many
practical purposes.
    "The measurement of changes in the cost of living from time to time
is only one aspect of the study of living costs. Other aspects relate
to the ways in which families spend their income, to variations in the
family expenditures of different economic groups, and to differences in
living costs in different localities because of variations in prices or
in standards of living, or both.
    "In order to avoid any possible confusion in the use of the results
of studies pertaining to the cost of living, this volume attempts first

to describe briefly the chief types of studies and to set forth some of
the problems encountered in making such studies; second, to describe in
detail the method used by the Conference Board in the construction of its
figures, which are designed to measure changes in the cost of living;
and third, to present the results of the Conference Board's findings in
regard to changes in the cost of living. While the Conference Board has
also studied other aspects of living costs, this volume is confined to the
description of changes in living costs during the course of time. It is
intended to provide a permanent, convenient, and comprehensive record
of the statistical information which the Board has issued on this subject."-
Foreword.

Cotton - Argentina

Argentine Republic. Junta nacional del algodón. Memoria... May/Dec. 1935.
117pp. Buenos Aires, 1936. 281.3729 Ar3M
   At head of title: Republica Argentina. Ministerio de agricultura
de la nación. Junta nacional del algodón.
   Report of the National Cotton Board which was created by decree
of April 27, 1935. Gives account of its experimental work in cotton
culture and the improvement of varieties; of its work in agricultural
colonization, in agricultural credit, with cooperatives; of its work
in cotton grading and gives statistics of the cotton trade in
Argentina.

Cotton and the Gold-price of Silver

Federation of master cotton spinners' associations. Silver in relation to monetary policy and the cotton trade of the world. 35pp. [Manchester, Eng.,
Printed by Taylor Garnett Evans & co. ltd., 1935] 284 F315
   "Paper submitted by the Federation of Master Cotton Spinners' Associations
Limited, Manchester, to the International Cotton Congress, Rome, 1935."
   "Some rather fundamental and intricate problems are tackled in this
short paper - not only the relation between the gold-price of silver and
the cotton industry of the world, and especially of the British Empire,
but also the larger problem of monetary policy and the alleviation of
the world depression." - From review by C. G. W. Schumann in South African
Journal of Economics, v. 3, no. 3, Dec. 1935, pp. 598-600.

Cotton, Tientsin - Marketing

Nankai university. Nankai institute of economics. Terminal marketing of
Tientsin cotton, by H. D. Fong, research director, Nankai institute of
economics, Nankai university. 47pp. Tientsin, China, Printed by the
Chihli press, 1934. 280.372 N15
   A statement of what Tientsin cotton includes is given followed by
statements of the amount of import and export over a period of years,
causes of price fluctuations and suggestions for the development of
the industry.

Dairy Products - Prices - South Australia

South Australia. Royal commission on dairy industry prices. Report of
the Royal commission on dairy industry prices, together with
appendices. (Minutes of evidence not printed.) 56pp. Adelaide,
H. Weir, government printer, 1933. 284.344 So8
     At head of title: No. 63. 1933. South Australia.
     W. J. Dawkins, chairman.
     "The inquiry has as much as possible been confined to matters
relevant under the terms of reference' namely, 'to inquire into and
report upon the disparity between the prices paid by the consumer
for dairy produce, the London parities of dairy produce, and the
prices received by dairymen of South Australia for milk and cream;
the causes of such disparities, and the remedies therefor.' Subsequently to the receipt of these terms of reference, a suggested
Bill for the Control of the Milk Supply of the Metropolitan Area
was also submitted by the Honorable the Chief Secretary for examination
and report."
     The Report is in two parts (1) Whole Milk and (2) Butter.

Denmark - 1935

Economic league (Central council) "Denmark in 1935"; an examination of her
economic position with special relation to agriculture and Anglo-Danish
trade... 5th ed. 63pp. London, Economic league (Central council) [1936]
([Publications] 1936 series; no. 1) 280.173 Ec7
     Foreword signed: J. Baker White, director, the Economic league (Central
council)
     "The chapter on agriculture provides a vivid picture of the chief
features of Danish farming; the scientific methods employed, and the
predominant influence of the co-operative societies, which are now buying
feeding-stuffs, etc., as well as marketing standardised products in the
most economical way." Economist (London) May 2, 1936, p. 249.

Economic Principles and Problems

Spahr, W. E., ed. Economic principles and problems, by Edward Berman,
A. G. Black, J. I. Bogen [and others] Third edition. 2-v.
New York, Farrar & Rinehart, inc., 1936. 280 Sp12E Ed.3
     "Suggested readings" at the end of each chapter.
     Partial contents: Production, by A. G. Black; Population, by
E. E. Muntz; Resources, by J. W. Zimmermann; Land, by H. B. Dorau;
Labor, by C. R. Daugherty; The economics of marketing, by F. E. Clark;
The economics of consumption, by P. H. Nystrom; Markets and prices,
by F. A. Fetter; Cost-prices, product-prices, and profits, by
F. A. Fetter; Business price practices and social price poli-
cies, by F. A. Fetter; Foreign trade and other international eco-
nomic transactions, by E. D. Durand; Tariffs, by F. D. Graham;
Business cycles, by L. H. Haney; Distribution of our national wealth

and income, by S. H. Patterson; Social insurance, by E. E. Muntz;
Agricultural problems, by H. B. Dorau; Public economy and public
expenditures, by Paul Studenski; Government regulation of enterprise,
by W. L. Thorp; Types of economic control, by W. L. Nunn;
Economic planning, by Barbara Wootton; and The evolution of economics,
by L. H. Haney.

Farm Labor - Italy

Confederazione fascista dei lavoratori dell'agricoltura.
    Il lavoro agricolo nelle attività delle corporazioni; relazioni,
proposte e deliberazioni. Pubblicazione edita in occasione dell'Assemblea
nazionale delle Corporazioni del 23 marzo 1936-XIV. 557pp. [Roma, S. A.
arte della stampr, 1936]   281.176 C762L
    At head of title: Confederazione fascista dei lavoratori dell'agricoltura.
    This is a collection of reports and proposals for future activity pre-
sented by the various corporations of the Fascist confederation of agricultural workers to the National Assembly of Corporations on March 23, 1936.

Farm Tenancy - Tennessee

Allred, C. E., Hendrix, W. E., and R skopf, B. D. Farm tenancy in
    Tennessee. 31pp., mimeogr. Knoxville, Tenn., July 15, 1936. ([U. S.
    Works progress administration. Cooperative plan of rural research. Re-
    port no. 17])   173.2 W89Co no. 17
    "Agricultural economics and rural sociology department, Agri-
cultural experiment station, University of Tennessee."
    Chap. I. Characteristics of tenant population which contribute
to the relief population. Chap. II. Distribution of growth of
tenancy in Tennessee.

Federal-State Cooperation

Birdine, J. A. National-state cooperation with special reference to Texas.
    25pp. Dallas, Tex., George F. and Ora Nixon Arnold foundation, Southern
    Methodist university, 1935. (Arnold foundation studies in public af-
    fairs... v.3, no.3)   280.12 B89
    "In the history of American federalism, the constitutional division
of powers between the nation and the states has often proved defective.
Originally established for the needs of a simple agricultural society,
the balance of power has, of necessity, been subject to constant readjustment as great economic and social changes have transformed from
time to time the pattern of American life. These necessary adjustments,
however, have not been effected generally by means of amendments to
the National Constitution, for the rigidity of the amending process and
the general hostility of the states to a constitutional transfer of
power from them to the National Government have prevented any decided
shift in the original distribution of powers...
    "But the inflexible nature of the National Constitution has not
served as a barrier within recent years to a growing influence exerted
by the central government in the actual conduct of state affairs. In

fact, the growth of an extensive system of national-state cooperation in numerous fields of governmental activity forms one of the most interesting chapters in the history of American federalism. To appreciate the real significance of this rather recent development, its background should first be understood."

After this opening statement the author proceeds to a discussion of the specific instances of cooperation between the Federal Government and the State of Texas such as the protection of forest resources, extension work in agriculture and home economics, vocational education, highways. The author then discusses less formal types of cooperation in administration between the federal government and the states such as public health and the conservation and development of the land and water resources of the state. He writes in part as follows:

"The federal subsidy system, however, is not the only means by which the National Government and the states coöperate in various fields of administration. As a matter of fact, there are many other ways, more informal than the procedure just described, in which national authorities aid the states in the performance of numerous functions. As one author points out, there is 'a growing sense of federal leadership in common fields of administration, flowing from the greater prestige of the national government, from the more extensive scope of its operations, from a generally higher standard of technical competence and as a rule from a greater freedom from partisan interference than is characteristic of state and local governments.'

"The inherent value of the research findings of federal agencies, such as the various bureaus of the Department of Agriculture, the Public Health Service, and the Children's Bureau of the Department of Labor, is widely recognized by state legislative and administrative authorities. It is not surprising, then, that through the action of national agencies, sometimes pursuant to provisions of law, an informal leadership of federal officials has developed in many administrative fields...

"The development in the manner described of a broad system of legislative and administrative cooperation between the National Government and the states is the outstanding trend in American federalism at the present time. The practical necessity of such a development under prevailing economic and social conditions can hardly be denied. Avoiding the evils of excessive centralization of authority, such a system also escapes the defects inherent in extreme decentralization. In the field of administration it recognizes local needs and national minimum standards, state control and national leadership. It is essentially a practical method, and its continuance as a permanent feature of American federalism is assured. In fact, a further development of national-state cooperation in legislation and administration may be highly desirable.

"The results of national-state coöperation have been beneficial. State activity has been stimulated in necessary fields, and local standards of administration have been raised. National leadership has been strong, but apparently unreasonable federal interference in state affairs has not resulted. Although there seems to be at the present time a tendency in congressional legislation to make national control in federal-aid fields more rigid, such action may be necessary.

"But even stronger national control, with the assurance of some division of authority between the nation and the states is to be preferred to outright centralization and national standardization. Certain it is that a broader development of national-state coöperation would be a step in the direction of a 'more perfect Union.'"

Fertilizer Industry - Effects of the N.R.A. Code

U. S. National recovery administration. Division of review. Industry studies section. The fertilizer industry study, by Alf O'Donnell. 2 v. in 1. Mimeogr. [Washington, D. C., 1936- (U. S. National recovery administration. Division of review. Industry studies section. Work material no. 63) 173.2 N21Fe

L. C. Marshall, Director of the Division of Review of the National Recovery Administration writes in part as follows in the Foreword: "This study provides a review of the production, distribution and employment conditions in the fertilizer industry. The objectives of the applicable provisions in the code have been indicated and their effectiveness in accomplishing these objectives have been indicated. Where the code fell short of its objectives, the reasons have been analyzed. Where particular types of code provisions worked well in the operation of the fertilizer code, the reasons for such success have been explored...

"The author's position is that the NRA experience with the code for the fertilizer industry indicates that industrial legislation, such as the NIRA is practicable under certain conditions. The fertilizer industry was sufficiently well organized and experienced to know its own problems, and what code provisions would be of service in solving these problems. The National Fertilizer Association had personnel experienced in administering previous codes of fair practice under the Federal Trade Commission so that the administrative work of the fertilizer code was handled with a minimum of NRA assistance. Operating during a period when the demand for fertilizer was much greater than in the immediate precodal period, the fertilizer code contributed to the stabilization of the fertilizer industry, the spread of employment and the increase of wages, and the placing of the industry on a profitable basis with a relatively moderate increase in prices to the consumer."

Food Chain Stores

Schmalz, C. N. Expenses and profits of food chains in 1934. 50pp. Boston, Mass. [1936] (Harvard university. Graduate school of business administration. Bureau of business research. Bulletin no. 99) 280.9 H26 no.99

Publication v.23, no.2, Apr. 1936.

"In 1930 the Bureau of Business Research of the Harvard Business School began a series of studies of the margins, expenses, and profits of chain store companies...

"The current report is the second dealing exclusively with food chains, and it presents figures for the fourth and fifth years for which data regarding the typical operating performance of food chains now are available from the Harvard studies.

"Distribution cost surveys of this type increase in value as the period which they cover grows longer. The Bureau's work in the food chain field was originally financed out of the School's own research funds, but lack of adequate resources made it necessary to interrupt the work in 1930 and to carry forward on a restricted basis for 1931 and 1932. It is gratifying, therefore, that the Food and Grocery Chain Stores of America, Inc., has found it possible to finance the present study, which covers the years 1933 and 1934, through voluntary subscriptions from a number of its members...

"Like most other studies of the Bureau of Business Research, this survey is based upon the actual profit and loss statements and balance sheets of a substantial number of business firms. These underlying data were gathered directly from the individual companies on standard forms which had been prepared by the Bureau out of its experience in earlier studies of food chains and after conferences with food chain executives. The reports as received from the individual chains were examined by the Bureau for arithmetical accuracy and for comparability, adjusted wherever adjustment was necessary to make them comparable, and then classified into significant groups, as will be described in detail later. For each of these various groups average or typical figures were determined; and these figures constitute the data from which the conclusions of the study are drawn."

Foreign Trade

Peek, G. N., and Crowther, Samuel. Why quit our own. 353pp. New York, D. Van Nostrand company, inc., 1936. 280.12 P34

"Published in part in the Saturday Evening Post under the title "In and out" - verso of title page.

The author sets forth with vigor his views in regard to foreign trade and his efforts - first as Administrator of the Agricultural Adjustment Act and later as Special Advisor to the President on Foreign Trade - to have these views adopted as government policies.

Gold

Hardy, C. O. Is there enough gold? 212pp. Washington, D. C., The Brookings institution, 1936. (The Institute of economics of the Brookings institution. Publication no. 70) 284 H22Is (Pt. 2 also 280.9 B79 no.17)

"As part II of this volume there is reprinted, with some revisions, Dr. Hardy's pamphlet entitled The Warren-Pearson price theory, which was published in 1935." -Director's pref.

Contents. - pt. 1. The adequacy of the gold supply. - pt. 2. The Warren-Pearson price theory.

Appendixes: The myth of 1849, by Rufus S. Tucker; Some criticisms of the literature; Estimates of world gold stock of 1913.

Fourin, Joseph. L'évolution économique de la Grande-Bretagne depuis l'abandon
de l'etalon-or, 1931-35. 333pp. Paris, Librairie du Recueil Sirey (société anonyme) 1935. 280.171 F86
Thèse - Univ. de Paris.
Bibliography, pp. [321]-325.
"The author traces the considerable improvement which has taken
place in the British agricultural, industrial, and financial situation
since the departure of the pound from the gold standard. He attributes
the progress in agriculture mainly to the effects of the Agricultural
Marketing Acts; in industry, to the double protection afforded by the
depreciation of the pound and the imposition of tariffs; and in the
financial field to the effect of the balancing of the budget and lowering
of the long-term rate of interest in restoring confidence. He points out
that the recovery has been almost entirely confined to the home market,
and is not likely to spread much further without a revival of international
trade. In spite of certain relative advantages obtained by Great Britain
from her depreciated currency, the author claims that this policy has been
responsible for serious monetary crises elsewhere, and that a return to
stability of exchanges and the gold standard is necessary for the revival
of international trade and world recovery. - International Labour Review,
v. 33, no. 1, p.140. January 1936.

Industrial Uses of Farm Products

Dearborn conference of agriculture, industry and science, Dearborn, Mich.,
1936. Proceedings of the second Dearborn conference of agriculture,
industry and science, Dearborn, Michigan, May 12, 13, 15, 1936.
409pp. [Dearborn, Mich., Farm chemurgic council; New York, The
Chemical foundation, 1936] 281.9 J66 2d, 1936
Running title: Second Dearborn Conference.
"Under the sponsorship of the Farm chemurgic council and the
Chemical foundation, inc."
Partial contents: A chemical engineer looks at the farm problem,
by Dr. A. W. Hixson; Tung oil, by Lamont Rowlands; A domestic sugar
supply, by Dr. H. J. Grant; Perilla and other new oil crops, by
Dr. H. A. Gardner; Cotton roads, by H. E. Coffin; American beverages
and the surplus fruit problem, by J. H. Choate, Jr.; Scientific
method of thought in our National problems, by F. P. Garvan; America's
first power alcohol plant, by W. W. Buffum; Growing artichokes in
America, by Dr. W. L. Burlison; Products of corn, by Morris Sayre;
The Iowa corn research institute, by Dr. R. M. Hixon; Starches and
sugars, by J. F. Walsh; Solvents from the farm, by C. L. Gabriel;
Whole cotton as a source of oil and alpha-cellulose, by Dr. F. K.
Cameron; The industrial utilization of sugar cane fiber, by T. B.
Munroe; The philosophy of Chemurgy, by Wheeler McMillen; The
American farm problem, by Dr. A. E. Taylor; Soy beans as a farm
crop, by E. D. Funk; The processing of soy beans, by Clark Bradley;
The role of soy bean oil in paint formulation, by E. E. Ware; Soy
bean proteins, by W. J. O'Brien; Soy bean chemistry, by Dr. H. R.

Kraybill; Mixing soy bean oil and tung oil, by M. F. Taggart;
Soil decadence, by Dr. J. G. Lipman; Crop protection through industrial and public research, by Dr. W. C. O'Kane; Pyrethrum - A
new crop, by R. E. Culbertson; Profits from wastes, by Dr. Edward
Bartow; The application of physics to agriculture, by Dr. G. R.
Harrison; What agriculture owes to science, by E. A. O'Neal; and The
changing agriculture, by L. J. Taber.

Labor Statistics - 1931-1935

U. S. Dept. of labor. Bureau of labor statistics. Handbook of labor
    statistics 1936 edition. 1151pp. Washington, U. S. Govt. print.
    off., 1936. (U.S. Dept. of labor. Bureau of labor statistics.
    Bulletin no. 616) 158.6 B87 no.616
      "This issue of the Handbook of Labor Statistics, dealing with
the years 1931 to 1935, covers a period of great significance to
American labor. During this period the importance of data dealing
with labor matters was reflected in the vastly increased demand
made upon the Bureau of Labor Statistics and similar agencies for
information on wages, hours of labor, prices, cost of living, industrial relations, and other subjects coming within the field of
the Bureau's activities. This demand has been in large part met by
the various publications of the Bureau, particularly the Monthly
Labor Review, which not only presents the results of the Bureau's
original work but also seeks to follow the more significant studies
made by other authoritative agencies. However, over a period of
years the supply of many of these publications becomes exhausted.
To provide in reference form the basic data accumulated over a
period of time, this series of Handbooks was devised. The present
volume is the fourth of the series. It brings together a digest
of all of the material published by the Bureau since the issue of
the 1931 Handbook insofar as such material seems to be of permanent
value."

The Land - England

Stapledon, R. G. The land, now and to-morrow. 336 pp. 2 folded maps
    in pocket. London, Faber & Faber, limited [1935] 282 St2
      Bibliography, pp. 316-325.
      In the Summary Chapter with which this volume closes the author
writes in part as follows: "He who believes in an ordered evolutionary process ... as opposed to the interaction and intervention of
innumerable and mostly diabolical accidents, has no alternative but
to regard it as the sacred ... duty of man to plan for posterity
which is the care of evolution.
    "The basis of all planning should be experimental and therefore
creative and evolutionary. It should be founded on broad principles
and always with a view rather to the prevention of devastating
errors - for that I believe to be within man's competency - than
with the avowed aim of reaching a goal that has been too narrowly
pre-defined. The greatest dangers to be guarded against are ex-

cessive rigidity and formality in the plans themselves and in the
methods of procedure laid down for carrying them out...

"I have formulated the principle that to allow the whole of Great
Britain to become urbanized would be a criminal error, and that it is
a criminal error to permit nearly 80 per cent. of the population of
the country to be almost completely deruralized. For the rest, and
firstly in so far as agriculture is concerned, I have pinned my faith
firmly to owner-occupation for reasons which I have endeavoured to
explain, and for this very important further reason. The whole tendency
of to-day - an ever-increasing bureaucracy, huge combines, multiple
shops - is towards the creation of salary and wage earners, the vast
majority of whom must obey orders. To plan, moreover, implies not an
inconsiderable measure of standardization, the obeying of orders all
round, and the setting of limits to the independence of individuals.
This carries with it undesirable and unfortunate consequences, the
evils of which must as far as possible be mitigated. A large population of owner-occupiers on the land would make for a great measure
of individual independence and initiative, and this despite the
relentless enforcement of ever more stringent marketing and co-operative
regulations.

"To my mind three corollaries are implicit in a policy based on
owner-occupation. Such a policy is antithetical to the nationalization of the land, and it is for this reason, and this only, that
I must admit to feelings of abhorrence for the very idea of nationalizing the land. Everything that could be achieved by land nationalization can be achieved by other and less irrevocable means. The
concern of the State is to safeguard the uses to which land is put,
and to develop to the maximum the resources of the land... Such
intervention on the part of the State is, however, an entirely
different matter from the wholesale and permanent nationalizing of
the land...

"The second corollary is that owner-occupation on a grand scale
would only be possible if supported by a State scheme of providing
credit facilities for every purposeful activity connected with high
farming, land reclamation and conditioning...

"The third corollary implicit in a policy of owner-occupation is
that we should produce all the food we can within our own shores...

"I need not, I think, summarize the facts that I have brought
forward relative to the present day condition of the land and the
means that I have suggested for re-conditioning and resuscitating the
countryside. To do all this would also be implicit in a policy based
on the furtherance of owner-occupation. I would only emphasize that
I have insisted on various forms of State subsidy to individuals -
subsidy in money and subsidy in kind - and that I want these subsidies
to be so arranged that they react definitely to the good of the land;
in the last resort it is the land and not commodities that should be
subsidized...

"My proposals aim at saving the countryside, at keeping town and
country separate, and at the same time giving the maximum of facilities
to the urban population for enjoying the country and as far as possible
earning a subsidiary income in the country. I attach the greatest

possible importance to the psychological value of a subsidiary income
earned in a creative enterprise...

"I now come to a consideration of administrative ways and means, and
to my final proposal, which calls primarily for the setting up of an
additional State department - a Ministry of Lands. To-day, land
utilization and the land itself are not the supreme care of any one
State department. The Ministry of Agriculture (only mildly interested
in the land itself), the Air Ministry (aerodromes), the Admiralty
(harbours and munition works), the War Office (camps and munition works),
the Ministry of Transport (roads and railways), the Ministry of Health
(houses), and the Board of Trade (trade expansion) are all interested,
and are all rivals for the use of land. There is no Government Department with an overriding authority or with a planning programme for the
better and proper use of the land itself, and yet land is perhaps the
only commodity of which this country has not recourse to an inexhaustible
supply...

"Politically there would be the strongest divergence of opinion as
between a policy of owner-occupation cum land licences cum credit
facilities and the nationalization of the land, and the issue is one
that I should like to see fairly and squarely put before the country,
and debated without the artificial heat engendered by political controversy
and in an atmosphere cleansed of the enervating influences of preconceived notions."

The volume closes with a statement of what the author thinks should
be the duties and responsibilities of a Ministry of Lands, which he
believes might aid in creating "a new and happer England... for deep
in the inner recesses of man's sub-conscious mind lies the indelible
impression of the land - a heritage which, by greatly dreaming and
greatly imagining, could be galvanized into a mighty power, capable of
strengthening the conscious endeavours of mankind and directing them
along paths leading to creative achievement in the spheres of individual
happiness, personal health and social justice."

Land Settlement Technique - Europe

Kraemer, Erich. Land settlement technique abroad. III. Selection of
settlers in agricultural settlement of several European countries.
84pp., mimeogr. Washington, D. C., July 1936. (U. S. Resettlement
administration. Land utilization division. Land use planning
section. Land use planning publication no. 5)   1 95 L23 No.5
"This is the third of a series of reports on the Technique of
Land Settlement Abroad. The first report was undertaken to show
the organization of agricultural settlement in England (and Wales),
Germany, and Italy; the second to describe the financing of this
type of settlement in England (and Wales), Germany, Denmark, Norway,
and Sweden. The present report is designed to discuss the technique
of selecting settlers for new farm holdings in England (and Wales),
Scotland, Northern Ireland, Irish Free State, Germany, Denmark, Norway, and Sweden.

"The countries included in this third report have again been
selected in accordance with the plan of choosing for each topic
a number of nations whose policies and experiences in the field of

land settlement promise to yield a fairly representative picture.
It is planned to supplement this report with a discussion of the
selection of settlers for farm holdings in several other countries,
as well as with a report on the methods of selecting settlers for
part-time or supplementary farming holdings.

"The process of selecting settlers may conveniently be divided
into the following five major parts: (1) setting up of standards
of selection; (2) assigning the selection work to the proper type
of agencies, (3) soliciting settlers; (4) examining applications;
and (5) certifying approved applications and assigning holdings.
Each of these parts is discussed in the report. In addition, in
the Appendix of this publication will be found a number of questionnaires and other forms which have been used in connection with
settler selection in England, Scotland, and Germany."

Land Use Mapping - Methodology

Landernolm, E. F. and Johnson, C. E. Present land-use mapping:
methodology used by high school students state of Washington, 1936.
17pp., mimeogr. Washington, D. C., June 1936. (U. S. Resettlement
administration. Land utilization division. Land use planning
section. Land use planning publication no. 2)   1 95 L23 No. 2
    "Sponsored by the Land-Use Committee of the Washington State
Planning Council and the Lewis County Planning board, present land-
use mapping as a high school project was introduced into Washington
State in 1934 under the direction of Rex. E. Willard, the work being
patterned somewhat after that done in England by Dr. L. Dudley Stamp.
In 1935-36 a revised and refined map was prepared for Lewis County,
and in addition five other counties were mapped by approximately
1,000 students of 27 schools in the six counties who participated
in securing the field data."

Marketing

Pyle, J. F.   Marketing principles, organization and policies. Rev. ed.
783pp. New York and London, McGraw-Hill book company, inc., 1936.
280.3 P99 Rev. ed.
    References at end of each chapter
    "The book presents to the student of marketing (1) a method of anal-
ysis and a body of facts which, it is hoped, will aid in a fuller appreciation of the importance of a thorough knowledge of the marketing
process and a clearer understanding of the problems connected with the
effective buying and selling of tangible goods and of services; (2) a
basis for formulating sound generalization with reference to marketing
functions, organizations, policies, methods, costs, and prices; and (3)
the point of view that the marketing process is in reality an organizing force which coordinates and ties together the work of numberless,
and frequently widely scattered, business and professional specialists."
-Preface.
    Part 3 contains several chapters on the marketing of agricultural
products.

Migration of Workers

International labor office, Geneva. The migration of workers; recruitment, placing and conditions of labour. 205pp. Geneva, 1936.
(Studies and reports. Series O (Migration) no.5)   283 In8mr
    "Migration movements have undergone a profound transformation
during the last decade. So far as total numbers are concerned,
for example, while migration maintained a fairly high level until
1929 and in some countries 1930, with the coming of the depression
it first diminished and then reversed its direction so that the
number of emigrants returning to their countries of origin became
larger than the number of emigrants going out to new countries.
Such a reversal of the stream of emigrants is not without precedent,
as it has occurred in isolated cases in previous depressions, but
never in history has such a reversal been so universal or lasted
for so long a period...
    "It is of interest to note that already by 1932 the return
movement of migrants to their countries of origin showed signs
of diminishing and that, on the other hand, as the depression slowly lifted, the number of outward-bound migrants began to increase.
This tendency is still a very hesitating one. These facts show
once more that migration increases in periods of prosperity and
falls in periods of depression, being influenced more by a demand
for labour in the immigration countries than by the situation in
the emigration countries...
    "The first part of the report is devoted to a statistical review
of the migration of workers throughout the world during the last
few years. Part II consists of an examination of the principles
and methods of recruiting, transporting, placing and repatriating
migrant workers. Part III contains information on the problem
of equality of treatment for immigrant and national workers, on
working and living conditions, and on organisations for the protection of migrants."

Milk Marketing Scheme - England

Gt. Brit. Ministry of agriculture and fisheries. Committee of investigation
for England of any agricultural marketing scheme. Report of the Committee of investigation for England on complaints made by the Central
milk distributive committee and the Parliamentary committee of the Cooperative congress as to the operation of the Milk marketing scheme,
1933. 93pp. London, H. M. Stationery off., 1936.   280.344 G7922
    The complaint considered by this Committee comprised four main heads,
namely: (a) the price to be paid for milk for liquid consumption; (b)
the transit risk charge; (c) the price to be paid for manufacturing
milk; and (d) certain miscellaneous clauses in the contract.
    The committee concludes that "After considering the submissions
made on behalf of the parties and in view of all the evidence put
before us, our recommendations regarding the liquid prices are that
the average wholesale price for the contract period 1935-6 should be
15s. 3d. per 12 gallons, but that the minimum retail prices should
not be increased.

"We desire to say, however, with the utmost emphasis that, for the reasons mentioned above, we do not regard our suggestions as being in any way final and we do not desire to see either the distributive margin or the wholesale price stabilised at these figures. Moreover, we are far from confident that the costs either of production or of distribution are shown sufficiently correctly by the statements before us. In many ways, the hearing of the complaints has taken place too soon. We hope that in a few years time the results of the economists Committee's investigation into costs of production may be available in detail over a longer period, while the results of the Food Council's examination into distributive margins - an examination which may be expected to be much more thorough than has been possible within the scope of our inquiry - will also be known."

"Finally, we desire to express our view that the industry would benefit by a reduction in the retail price of liquid milk. We are sure that the urgency of this need is recognised by both sides of the indust The first aim, in our opinion, should be to reduce the London retail price, for example, to an average of 26s. per 12 gallons, and the ultimate aim, a further reduction by one or two steps to 24s. per 12 gallons Corresponding reductions should be made in the provinces. We do not see much prospect, however, of reductions of this magnitude unless there is an increase in the value of manufacturing milk and at the same time a reduction in distributive costs through the reorganisation of the indust

Negroes - Movable School

Campbell, T. M. The Movable school goes to the Negro farmer. 170pp.
    Tuskegee Institute, Ala., Tuskegee institute press [1936]   275.1 C153
        Dr. Bradford Knapp writes in part as follows in the Introduction:
    "I have known this Movable School work for more than twenty years
    and the author's interesting story of its development is well worth
    preserving as one of the most unique and one of the most successful
    examples of real teaching to be found anywhere in the world. The
    method is being copied in many other countries and is peculiarly
    adapted to work among backward people. The author of this book is
    one of the most outstanding servants of the Negro race in America...
    It must be remembered that the progress of an individual in education
    may be rapid, but the task of training a great mass of people is
    slow and laborious. The finest thing which can be said for the
    Movable School movement is that statistical material now begins to
    show distinct evidences of advancement of Negroes as farmers and as
    a people, which can be traced readily to the work of a number of
    forces among which the Movable School movement from Tuskegee has had
    a most important part."
        The first part of the book is semi-autobiographical and the second
    part describes the work of the school on wheels.

Open Price Systems

Lyon, L. S., and Abramson, Victor. The economics of open price systems.
165pp. Washington, D. C., The Brookings institution, 1936. (The
Institute of economics of the Brookings institution. Publication
no. 71)   284.3 L99
    "From the point of view both of industry and of government, open
price plans as a device in the price-making process are at a particularly important stage. While such plans in one form or another have been
in existence for more than two decades, interest in them, greatly stimulated by the NRA, is at a higher level than has been the case for a long
period. Certain industries are anxious to continue the open price
plans developed under the NRA with such improvements as can be made and
such modifications as the expiration of the Recovery Act may make
necessary. Others are considering the initiation of such plans. An
effort to set forth the general issues of public policy which are involved in the organization of open price plans therefore seems appropriate at this time.
    "The development of open price plans effective in achieving objectives
of public interest requires an analysis of the elements in such plans
and a consideration of each of these elements in terms of the economic
and social issues which it raises. It is with these general questions
and, more specifically, with an attempt to point out certain criteria
to be used in considering the economic effects of open price plans,
that this book is concerned. Emphasis is directed toward the types of
considerations that are important in deciding whether or not an open
price plan is applicable to an industry and the factors that determine
the precise form of the plan that will be most useful socially.
    "No attempt is made to apply the criteria set forth to specific
industry situations. This task would require detailed industry studies,
and the analysis of certain materials concerning American industry not
now generally available.
    "The authors of this volume regard it as a preface to the analysis
of specific cases in which open price plans are being considered and
to further studies of industries and industrial situations, of which
many more must be made before the final word on the economic significance
of open price plans and their relationship to the formulation of sound
public policy in trade regulation can be written."

Pig Industry - Gt. Britain - 1935

Murray, K. A. H. The pig industry in 1935. A survey of pig and feeding-
stuff prices and a review of supplies and marketing schemes. 16pp.
[London, Headley brothers, 1936]
    "Reprinted from the Pig breeders' annual, 1936-37."
    "There were no radical changes in the operation of either the Pigs
Marketing Scheme or the Bacon Marketing Scheme. During 1935, pigs were
received under the third contract and the terms of the fourth contract,
which were more favourable to the producer, were issued in October.
There were no changes in principle except for the re-inclusion of compulsory insurance which had been dropped in the third contract. The

main event in the organization of the industry was undoubtedly the establishment of the Bacon Development Board towards the end of the year.
"On the whole, the year has been more notable for the initiation of
potential future developments, the starting of the Bacon Development
Board and the Government's declaration of a levy-cum-subsidy scheme,
than for actual achievements. Producers generally were disappointed
with the prices obtained under the Marketing Schemes, but if increased
output is accompanied not by higher costs but by lower ones, then even
the stabilization of prices at pre- Scheme levels in the face of a 70
per cent. increase in the home output of bacon may have been of considerable benefit to the industry."

Population

Dublin, L. I.   The population problem and world depression. 32PP. New York,
    Foreign policy association, incorporated, 1936.   (Foreign policy pam-
    phlets. [no.i])   280 F763 no.1.
        "After a general survey of the principal demographic trends throughout
    the world, Mr. Dublin reviews the position of some important countries
    (United States, Great Britain, France, Germany, Italy, U.S.S.R., Japan,
    India). In his conclusions he emphasises the fact that the general out-
    look for the world to-day is under-population rather than over-population,
    and outlines different measures designed to arrest depopulation and
    qualitative deterioration." - From International Labour Review, v. 33,
    no. 5, May 1936, p. 748.

Population Changes - Measurement

Kuczynski, R. R.   The measurement of population growth; methods and results.
    255pp.   London, Sidgwick & Jackson, ltd., 1935.   (Text-books of social
    biology, edited by Lancelot Hogben)   280 K95
        A. M. Carr-Saunders reviews this volume at some length in The New
    Statesman and Nation. (v.10, no.236, p. 285. Aug. 31, 1935)
        From this review the short extract which follows is taken:
        "This book is concerned, not with the causes and consequences, but with
    the measurement of population changes. It is incomparably the best book
    on the subject and is quite indispensable to any serious student of pop-
    ulation problems. If those who do write about the causes and consequences
    could be compelled to read it... we should be spared much literature that
    is worse than useless because the facts of population change are so seldom
    properly understood. It is not too much to ask that they should read it
    because, although the book is devoted to a description of statistical
    methods, it contains no argument or method of importance which cannot be
    understood by anyone whose mathematics extend no further than multiplica-
    tion and division.
        Another review of the volume appeared in the Journal of the Amer.
    Statistical Association for March 1936 (p.228-230)   It was written by
    P. K. Whelpton.

Population, Prehistoric - Britain

Fox, C. F.   The personality of Britain: its influence on inhabitant and in-
    vader in prehistoric and early historic times. 2d ed.   84pp.   Cardiff,
    National museum of Wales and the Press board of the University of Wales,
    1933.   278.171 F83 Ed.2
        At head of title: Amgueddfa genedlaethol cymru. National Museum of
    Wales.
        A reprint of the first edition, the alterations... being few in number
    and relatively unimportant. - Pref. (to the second edition)
        Partial contents: The position and form of Britain, as affecting in-
    habitant and invader; The structure of Britain, affecting inhabitant
    and invader; The climate, flora, and fauna of Britain, as affecting in-
    habitant and invader; The general distribution of population in Britain in
    prehistoric times, and its significance; and Secular changes in the distri-
    bution of population, and their causes.

Primary Industries - Control of Supply

Rowe, J. W. F.   Markets and men: a study of artificial control schemes in
    some primary industries.   259pp.   Cambridge, University press, 1936.
    286 R792.
        The author in his first chapter writes in part as follows: "The
    following chapters attempt to give a general account of the recent
    history of six of the more important primary industries which have
    adopted artificial control schemes, special attention being paid to
    the causes which led to the establishment of these schemes, their
    general character, the changing policies adopted, the nature of the
    results achieved, and the reasons for their success or failure."
    The six commodities studied are coffee, wheat, sugar, American cotton,
    rubber, and tin.

Resale Price Maintenance - Gt. Britain and the U. S.

Grether, E. T.   Resale price maintenance in Great Britain, with an
    application to the problem in the United States. 257-334pp.
    Berkeley, Calif., University of California press, 1935.(University
    of California publications in economics. v.11, no.3) 284.3 G86
        "In the last twenty-five years economic and business literature
    in the United States has carried many discussions of resale price
    maintenance.   The problem has been tinged with sufficient public
    interest to produce a number of governmental hearings and investiga-
    tions.   Much of the argument advanced by the interested parties and
    by economists was weakened because of the lack of evidence concern-
    ing the actual workings of systems of resale price control.   The
    purpose of this monograph is to illuminate the problem by reference
    to conditions and developments in Great Britain, where broad rights
    of resale price fixing have long existed.   Following the review of
    the state of affairs in Great Britain there is a brief appraisal of
    the developments in the United States.

"Resale price maintenance has to do with the vertical relations established between producers and their distributors, particularly the retail dealers. It must be differentiated from horizontal price agreements. The nature of this former type of price fixing limits its application primarily to branded merchandise. Commonly, the problem arises only in connection with the sale of highly advertised and widely known products. Thus, resale price maintenance is merely one aspect of the general problem of price fixing; serious blunders in reasoning may be made when the precise nature of this limitation is overlooked."

Rural Rehabilitation

Pevenouse, H. M.   Conditions in the southwestern wheat area which affect the rehabilitation program (as typified by Perkins county, Nebraska) [by H. M. Pevehouse of the Bureau of agricultural economics.] 39pp., mimeogr. [Washington, D.C.] May 1936. (U. S. Works progress administration. Social research division. Research bulletin K-3)   173.2 W89Rek K-3
    At head of title: Resettlement Administration.

Stewart, H. L. Natural and economic factors affecting rural rehabilitation problems in southwestern North Dakota (as typified by Hettinger county) [by H. L. Stewart of the Bureau of agricultural economics.] 39 pp., mimeogr. [Washington, D. C.] May 1936. (U. S. Works progress administration. Social research division. Research bulletin K-4)   173.2 W89Rek K-4
    At head of title: Resettlement Administration.
    These studies were initiated by the Division of Farm Management and Costs of the Bureau of Agricultural Economics of the U. S. Dept. of Agriculture in cooperation with the Division of Research, Statistics and Finance of the Federal Emergency Relief Administration.

Social Credit - Alberta - Canada

Alberta. Legislature. Agricultural committee. The constitutionality and economic aspects of social credit; evidence of Dean Weir... and Professor Elliott... before the Agricultural committee of the Alberta Legislature, session 1935. Printed by order of the Legislative assembly of Alberta, 1935. 20pp. Edmonton, W. D. McLean, King's printer, 1935.   284 Al12C

Alberta. Legislature. Agricultural committee. The Douglas system of social credit; evidence taken by the Agricultural committee of the Alberta Legislature, session 1934. Printed by order of the Legislative assembly of Alberta. 127pp. Edmonton, W. D. McLean, King's printer, 1934. 284 Al'
    "Evidence was given by the following gentlemen: Mr. William Aberhart... Mr. Herbert Boyd... Professor Elliott... Mr. J. Larkham Collins... Major C. H. Douglas." p. [2]

Douglas, C. H. First interim report on the possibilities of the application
of social credit principles to province of Alberta, submitted to His
Majesty's premier and Legislative council of Alberta, Edmonton, Alberta,
May 23rd, 1935... Together with correspondence which followed the report,
between Premier R. G. Reid and Major Douglas, and between Hon. J. F.
Lymburn, Attorney-general, and Major Douglas. 15pp. Edmonton, W. D.
McLean, King's printer, 1935. 284 D74F

Gibson, A. L. What is this social credit? A verbatim report of a lecture
delivered ... at the Central hall, Westminster, London, on 21st March,
1935. 31pp. London, S. Nott [1935] (Pamphlets on the new economics
no. 17) 284 G352

Sociology

Young, Kimball. Source book for sociology. 639pp. New York, Cincinnati
[etc.] American book company [1935] (American sociology series)
280 Y83
"Suggestions for further reading"; at end of each chapter.
This is a very useful and well arranged collection of readings
on sociology. It contains a group of selections on cooperation, and
another on Social control.

Tax Collecting Procedure

Municipal finance officers' association of the United States and Canada.
Committee on tax collection procedure. Tax collection procedure; preliminary report of the Committee on tax collection procedure to the
1935 conference held at Knoxville, Tennessee, October 21-23, 1935.
4 pp. Chicago, Ill., The Municipal finance officers' association
[1935] 284.5 M92

Young, F. R. Modern tax collecting procedures in Mecklenburg county,
North Carolina. 23 pp. [n.p., 1935] 284.5 Y8

Taxation

Armitage-Smith, George. Principles and methods of taxation. New edition revised by R. G. Hawtrey. 236pp. London, J. Murray [1935] 284.5 Ar5
Ed.11
Bibliography, pp.218-219.
"This is the eleventh edition of Dr. Armitage-Smith's useful little introduction to the study of public finance, published in 1906. It contains
an elementary account of the origin, development and present method of
national and local taxation in this country, supplemented by brief notes
on the system of taxation in France, India and in the United States.
"As a large part of Dr. Armitage-Smith's account was descriptive, its
relevance to current thought and practice diminished as time went on. This
deficiency has now been remedied by Mr. R. G. Hawtrey, who has not only
brought the book up to date, but has almost entirely re-written the section dealing with the incidence of taxation. In this chapter Mr. Hawtrey
traces in some detail the incidence of the various forms of taxation and
he draws attention to the difficulties of satisfying the cannon of equity."
— Economist (London) July 6, 1935, p. 17.

Taxation, Conflicting

Interstate commission on conflicting taxation. Conflicting taxation; the
1935 progress report of the Interstate commission on conflicting taxation, by the Research staff of the Commission. 202pp., multigraphed
Chicago, Ill., The Council of state governments [1936?] 284.5 In82 C
    "Part I of this report constitutes the formal progress report of the
Interstate Commission on Conflicting Taxation. This report was presented in preliminary form to the Second Interstate Assembly in February,
1935. As indicated in the text, the report incorporates a record of
the work done by the Commission and does not formulate a comprehensive
program for legislative and administrative action.
    "Part II brings together in revised form most of the research com-
pleted by the Commission's staff. The first two chapters outline the
problem of conflicting taxation and certain approaches to its solution.
The third chapter includes a brief statistical record of certain conflicting excise taxes which the Commission's staff has not studied
intensively. There is no attempt to develop solutions of the problems
presented by these particular measures, but it has seemed worth while
to incorporate statistical data and brief analyses. The Commission
believed the conflicts involved in these excises sufficiently simple
to justify its offering certain specific recommendations on the basis
of data comparable with facts presented here. Chapters IV to VIII,
inclusive, incorporate the research dealing with particular technical
tax measures subject to important conflicts and analyze the consequences
of one or more specific proposals for solving or alleviating the evils
of these conflicts. In the sense that they do not consider all of the
alternative possibilities for dealing with the types of conflicts involved, these investigations are not comprehensive. Chapter IX presents
the staff point of view respecting the appropriate program of research
in conflicting tax problems."

Taxation - New.York

Tobin, C. J. A model tax and revenue law for the state of New York. Memorandum in support of Senate int. no. 982, print no. 1095. Presented to
the New York State Legislature in February, 1935. 80pp. Albany, N. Y.,
1935. 284.5 T55
    The author states in the foreword that in this memorandum "an attempt
has been made to summarize the substance of the bill, the reason why a
recodification is essential, the basic viewpoint with which it is presented, the manner in which it differs from the present tax law (Chap.60,
Consolidated Laws), and the reasons that underlie its bare provisions."

Taxation - Rural - Ontario

Hudson, S. C. Taxation in rural Ontario... Division of farm management.
Agricultural economics branch. 32PP. Ottawa [1936] (Canada. Dept. of
agriculture. Technical bulletin 4) 7 C16T no.4.
    Canada. Dept. of agriculture. Publication 489.
    "Presented to Cornell University, Ithaca, N. Y. as a thesis in partial

fulfilment of the requirements for the Degree of master of science in agriculture."

"The purpose of this study... is to provide a group of factual data along with contributory factors concerning the rural tax situation in Ontario, thus providing a basis for the better understanding of rural government and consequent improvement of the taxation system."

Tobacco

U. S. National recovery administration. Division of review. Industry studies section. Tobacco unit. The tobacco study. 277 pp., mimeogr. [Wasnington, D. C.] Mar. 1936.   173.2 N21To
    Among the subjects to which chapters of this study are devoted are the following: The economic and social status of labor; Integration with agriculture (includes present methods of selling leaf tobacco and readjustments in demand for various types of tobacco); Foreign trade in leaf tobacco; Distribution of tobacco products; Importance of the tobacco manufacturing industry to the federal government as a source of tax revenue; Possibilities for research in the tobacco industry.

U. S. S. R.

American-Russian chamber of commerce. Handbook of the soviet union. 562pp. New York, The John Day company [1936]   267 Am33H
    "The Handbook of the Soviet Union is the successor of the 'Economic Handbook of the Soviet Union,' published by the American-Russian Chamber of Commerce in 1931, and seeks to present in a concise form, facts and statistics concerning the development of some of the more important phases of the national economy of the Union of Soviet Socialist Republics.
    "The statistics and much of the information contained in this volume were obtained from official Soviet sources... The figures for 1934 are in many cases preliminary and subject to later revision." - Foreword

U. S. S. R. - Geography

Mikhailov, N. Soviet geography: the new industrial and economic distributions of the U.S.S.R., by N. Mikhaylov. With a foreword by the Rt. Hon. Sir Halford J. Mackinder. 232pp. London, Methuen & co., ltd. [1935] 278.179 M58
    H. J. Mackinder writes as follows in the signed foreword:
    "Messrs. Methuen have asked me for a few words of introduction to this book, written for them by a geographer in Russia who has had access to official sources of information which are closed to foreigners. They believe that it presents such a comprehensive account of the economic development of the U.S.S.R. as is at the present time unobtainable elsewhere.
    "Undoubtedly it is a remarkable book, well worthy of the attention of many readers. Not unfairly it may be described as a political pamphlet of the indirect order, a vivid geographical description charged with political electricity. It is written in clear and virile English, oratorical rather than literary, by a born and trained geographer, with

vision and a power of terse imagery. Its short sentences, each with
definite, unqualified meaning, succeed one another like shots from a
machine gun. Altogether it affords a noteworthy insight into the dynamic
mentality of those who, with command of a working population of 160 millions, claim to be re-making the geography, physical as well as human, of
one seventh of the land on this globe.

"That our author does not discriminate nicely between fact and prophecy
was to be expected; to a revolutionary plans may appear more important than
achievement. Geography is a study of the present, but the present is the
past flowing into the future. There is no such thing as a static present;
your description of the present depends on whether your face is turned to
the future or the past. Only the future will tell whether these 'engineers'
both of society and environment have underrated the momentum of human
values from the past. In that difference of outlook is the great rift
between Soviet Russia and the Western democracies.

"Meanwhile we have brought to us in this book, from behind a screen
which is in itself one of the major, although, let us hope, temporary
features of human geography, a first sketch of the new map of Scythia.
Whatever our reserves of scepticism, it will be at our peril that we
neglect to take account of it."

U. S. S. R. - Stakhanov Movement

Molotov, V. M. The Stakhanov movement and the cultural growth of the working
    class. Speech delivered at the first All-union conference of Stakhan-
    ovites, November 15, 1935. 41pp. Moscow, Co-operative publishing so-
    ciety of foreign workers in the USSR, 1935. 280.179 M73St
    "Translated by A. Fineberg" - Verso of title page.

Stalin, Iosif. Speech at the first All-union conference of Stakhanovites,
    delivered November 17, 1935. 26pp. Moscow, Co-operative publishing
    society of foreign workers in the USSR, 1935. 280.179 StlS
    "Translated by A. Fineberg" - Verso of title page.

    These pamphlets undertake to explain the Stakhanov movement which is
    said to be "a movement of working men and women, which makes it its aim
    to surpass the present standards of output, to surpass the existing de-
    signed capacities, to surpass the existing production plans and estimates.
    To surpass them - because these standards have already become antiquated
    for our day, for our new people. This movement is breaking down the old
    views on technique, it is shattering the old standards of output, the old
    designed capacities and the old production plans, and is demanding the
    creation of new and higher standards of output, designed capacities and
    production plans. It is destined to produce a revolution in our industry."

U. S. Dept. of agriculture. Forest service. The western range; letter from
the Secretary of agriculture transmitting in response to Senate resolution no. 289 a report on the western range - a great but neglected
natural resource. 620pp. Washington, U. S. Govt. print. off., 1936.
(74th congress, 2d session, Senate doc. no. 199) 1 F76We
    Bibliography, pp.557-566.
    May be purchased from the Superintendent of Documents Office,
price 60 cents.
    Southern forest ranges, by W. G. Wahlenberg and E. W. Gemmer, pp.
567-578.
    "Additional literature on southern forest ranges" pp.578-580.
    Alaska, by B. F. Heintzleman, pp.581-598.
    The Secretary of Agriculture in his letter of transmittal to the
President emphasizes three of what he considers the most important
phases of the discussion of the Western Range problem, in part as
follows:
    "1. The first of these is the astonishing degree to which the
western range resource has been neglected, despite its magnitude and
importance.
    "One indication of this neglect is the lack of public knowledge.
The general public knows less of the range resource, and as a result
has been and is less concerned about its condition and conservation
than of any other of our important natural resources. This is true
in spite of the fact that the range occupies about two-fifths of the
total land area of the United States and three-fourths of that of the
range country; that the range territory produces about 75 percent of
the national output of wool and mohair, and in pounds about 55 percent of the sheep and lambs, and nearly one-third of the cattle and
calves. In fact, this report represents the first attempt, although
much of the range has been grazed for 50 years at least, to make an
all-inclusive survey of the range resource, its original and present
condition, the causes and effects of changes, the social and economic
function which it does and should render to the West and to the Nation,
and, finally, to outline practical solutions for at least the more
important problems...
    "2. The second phase of the situation to which I wish to call atten-
tion is the fundamental character both of the range resource and of
its use.
    "They have to do with land; with the production on that land of
forage crops, with the utilization of the crops in livestock and, in
a lesser degree, wildlife production; with the management of land and
its forage cover to obtain watershed protection and the services needed primarily by agriculture for irrigation. Effectiveness in all of
these things depends upon the biological and agricultural sciences.
In short, they are a part, and in the West one of the most important
parts, of agriculture...

"3. The third phase of the range situation to which I wish to call attention is a limited number of remedial measures of outstanding importance among the many that are required. The range problem as a whole has been allowed to drift for so long that its difficulties have been accentuated. It has become exceedingly broad and complex, beginning with the basic soil resource at the one extreme, and extending through a wide range of overlapping interrelated problems to human welfare at the other. No single measure offers hope of more than a partial solution...

"The solution of the range problem can be made an important contribution to the conservation of our natural resources. It can be made an important contribution to the rehabilitation of western agriculture. Finally, and most important, it can be made an important contribution to social and economic security and human welfare. Public neglect is partly responsible for the aggravated character of the range problem, and this makes all the more urgent and necessary public action toward its solution."

BIBLIOGRAPHIES

Farm youth in the United States; a selected list of references to literature issued since October 1926. Compiled by Esther M. Colvin, under the direction of Mary G. Lacy, Librarian, Bureau of agricultural economics. 196pp., mimeogr. (U. S. Dept. of agriculture. Bureau of agricultural economics. Agricultural economics bibliography no. 65 (Supplements no. 17)
1.9 Ec73A no.65

An index bibliography of the Tennessee valley authority, compiled by Harry C. Bauer. 60pp., mimeogr. Knoxville, Tenn., July 1, 1936.
173.2 T25B 1936
"This bibliography of periodical articles covers the period January 1933 to June 1936, inclusive. It supersedes 'A bibliography of the Tennessee Valley Authority.'"
Issued by the Tennessee Valley Authority, Information Division, Technical Library. Requests for bibliography should be addressed to Library in Knoxville, Tennessee.

A list of recent references on the reorganization of the executive departments, compiled by Florence S. Hellman,   acting chief bibliographer. 46pp., mimeogr. [Washington, D. C.] April 1936.
Issued by the Library of Congress, Division of Bibliography. Requests for the publication should be addressed there.

List of references on the reorganization of the executive departments, compiled by James W. Sheridan, formerly, researcher; reorganization study of the District of Columbia government (1934) authorized by United States Senate, Committee on the District of Columbia (73-1,

1933) 38pp., mimeogr. Washington, D. C., June 1, 1934.

    Supplementary to the mimeographed lists of November 10, 1925 and February 1, 1932 of the Division of bibliography, Library of Congress.

    Requests for bibliography should be addressed to James W. Sheridan, 2700 Que Street, N.W., Washington, D. C.

Marketing of dairy products in the United States, 1934-1936; a selected list of references which also includes some references to material on related subjects, compiled in the Library, Bureau of agricultural economics. 20pp., typewritten. Washington, D. C. Sept. 1, 1936.

    May be borrowed for copying.

Methodology of social science research: a bibliography [by] Dorothy Campbell Culver. 159pp. Berkeley, Calif., University of California press, 1936. (Publications of the Bureau of public administration, University of California.)   241.3 C89Me

    Classified, with author and subject indexes.

    May be purchased from the University of California. Berkeley, Calif. Samuel C. May, Director, Bureau of Public Administration, University of California writes as follows in the Foreword: "In conducting a research and training program in various fields of public administration, it has been the experience of the staff of the Bureau of Public Administration that it is constantly necessary to determine the relative merits of different approaches to problems under consideration.

    "The recent interest in improving methods of social science research has produced in this field a literature sufficient in size and importance to warrant an orderly listing of published materials so that research students may be guided in using those methods and techniques which seem best adapted to the investigations in which they are engaged.

    "The Bureau of Public Administration of the University of California accordingly presents this bibliography on the methodology of social science research, with the expectation that it will be helpful in encouraging a scientific approach to social science problems."

A selected list of references relating to the marketing of tomatoes with special reference to California, compiled by Orpha Cummings, librarian, Giannini foundation of agricultural economics, University of California, April 6, 1936. 39pp., typewritten. Berkeley, Cal., 1936.   241.3 C91S

    May be borrowed for copying from the Library of the Giannini Foundation of Agricultural Economics, University of California, Berkeley, California.

A selection of books and articles on the purpose, scope, and techniques of
  marketing research, by George W. Kelsey, with the co-operation of Mary
  L. Alexander representing the American marketing society and William F.
  Turnbull representing the A.S.M.E. Management division. 21pp., processe
  New York, N. Y., The American society of mechanical engineers [1935]
  241.3 K29
      May be obtained from The American Society of Mechanical Engineers,
  29 West 39th Street, New York, N. Y.

Social credit; a reading list, comp. by Rollin A. Sawyer. 10pp. New York,
  The New York Public library, 1936. 241.3 Sa9
      Reprinted from the Bulletin of the New York Public Library of May 193
  (243.7 N482)
      May be obtained from the New York Public Library, Economics Division,
  New York, N. Y.

Youth movements here and abroad. 8pp. (Bulletin of the Russell Sage
  foundation Library no. 135, Feb. 1936) 241.3 R91Y
      A selected bibliography with a directory of leading American
  movements, compiled by Marguerita Williams.
      May be obtained from Russell Sage foundation, 130 East 22d
  Street, New York.

SELECTED LIST OF RECENT REVIEWS

Compiled by M. I. Herb

Armitage-Smith, G. Principles and methods of taxation. New edition.
  [11th] revised by R. G. Hawtrey. [1935]
      _ Reviewed by C. O. G. in Royal Statis. Soc. Jour. (n.s.) 98(5):
  742-743. 1935.

Astor, Waldorf Astor, 2d Viscount. The agricultural dilemma; a report of
  an inquiry organised by Viscount Astor and Mr. B. Seebohm Rowntree.
  1935.
      Reviewed by Subhendu Sekhar Bose in Sankhya; the Indian Jour. Statis.
  2(3): 335. July 1936.

Backman, Jules. Adventures in price fixing. [c1936] (On cover: The Farrar
  & Rinehart pamphlets. no. 8)
      Reviewed briefly by Milton Abelson in Com. and Finance 25(12): 441.
  June 13, 1936.

Bernstein, E. M. Money and the economic system. [1935]
      Reviewed by A. W. Marget in Jour. Polit. Econ. 44(4): 565-567.
  August 1936.

Brinkman, Theodor.   Economics of the farm business. English edition,
    with introduction and notes by Elizabeth Tucker Benedict, Heinrich
    Hermann Stippler, and Murray Reed Benedict. 1935. (Social science
    research council. Advisory committee on social and economic research
    in agriculture. Translation series, no. 2)
        Reviewed by G. W. Forster in South. Econ. Jour. 3(1): 76-82.
    July 1936.

British association for the advancement of science. Economic science and
    statistics section. Britain in depression; a record of British
    industries since 1929. Prepared by a research committee of the
    Economic science and statistics section of the British Association.
    1935.
        Reviewed by Austin Robinson in Econ. Jour. 46(181): 148-150.
    March 1936.
        Reviewed by J. S. Robinson in Amer. Econ. Rev. 26(1): 105-106.
    March 1936.

Burn, Bruno.   Codes, cartels, national planning; the road to economic
    stability. 1934.
        Reviewed by M. W. Watkins in Jour. Polit. Econ. 44(4): 563-565.
    August 1936.

Chamberlin, W. H.   The Russian revolution, 1917-1921. 1935.
        Reviewed by W. Ladejinsky in Polit. Sci. Quart. 51(3): 457-460.
    September 1936.

Cohen, Ruth L.   The history of milk prices; an analysis of the factors
    affecting the price of milk and milk products. 1936.
        Reviewed by W. C. Waite in Jour. Farm Econ. 18(3): 628-630.
    August 1936.

Cole, G. D. H.   Economic planning. 1935.
        Reviewed by J. M. Clark in Polit. Sci. Quart. 51(3): 465-467.
    September 1936.

Cole, G. D. H.   Some relations between political and economic theory. 1934.
        Reviewed by G. E. G. Catlin in Polit. Sci. Quart. 51(3): 438-441.
    September 1936.

Comish, N. H.   Marketing of manufactured goods. [1935]
        Reviewed by Melchior Palyi in Jour. Polit. Econ. 44(4): 571-572.
    August 1936.

Creamer, D. B.   Is industry decentralizing? A statistical analysis of
    locational changes in manufacturing employment,1899-1933. 1935.
    (Half-title: Bulletin no. 3. Study of population redistribution.
    Industrial research dept., Wharton school of finance and commerce.
    University of Pennsylvania.)
        Reviewed by Karl Brandt in Social Research 3 (3): 376-379.
    August 1936.

Davis, Jerome.   Capitalism and its culture. [1935]
         Reviewed by Fabian Franklin in the N. Y. Times Book Rev., Aug.
    2, 1936, p. 14.

Douglas, P. H.   Controlling depressions. [1935]
         Reviewed by M. Pelkowitz in South African Jour. Econ. 4(2): 233-
    236. June 1936.

Ezekiel, Mordecai. $2500 a year; from scarcity to abundance. [1936]
         Reviewed by G. M. Janes in Amer. Econ. Rev. 26(3): 529. September
    1936.

Federation of master cotton spinners associations. Silver in relation to
    monetary policy and the cotton trade of the world. [1935]
         Reviewed by C. G. W. Schumann in South African Jour. Econ. 3(3):
    595-600. December 1935.

Forster, G. W.   Farm organization and management. 1935.
         Reviewed by E. C. Young in Jour. Farm Econ. 18(3): 634-635.
    August 1936.

Fowler, B. B.   Consumer cooperation in America; democracy's way out.
    [1936]
         Reviewed by Caroline F. Ware in Survey Graphic 25(9): 536.
    September 1936.

Goodrich, C. L., Allin, B. W., and Hayes, Marion.   Migration and planes of
    living, 1920-1934. 1935. (Half-title: Bulletin no. 2. Study of popula-
    tion redistribution. Industrial research dept., Wharton school of
    finance and commerce, University of Pennsylvania)
         Reviewed by Karl Brandt in Social Research 3(3): 376-379. August 1936.

Górecki, Roman.   Poland and her economic development. [1935]
         Reviewed by Satyabrata Ray in Sankhya; the Indian Jour. Statis. 2(3):
    336. July 1936.

Greaves, H. R. G.   Raw materiels and international control. [1936]
         Reviewed by A. P. Van der Post in South African Jour. Econ. 4(2):
    240-243. June 1936.

Grether, E. T.   Resale price maintenance in Great Britain; with an applica-
    tion to the problem in the United States. 1935. (University of Califor-
    nia publications in economics. v. II, no. 3)
         Reviewed by S. F. Teele in Harvard Business Rev. 14(3): 380, 381.
    Spring number, 1936, in an article entitled "Recent Literature of Re-
    tailing."
         Reviewed by A. M. McIsaac in Amer. Econ. Rev. 26(3): 526-527.
    September 1936.

Haight, F. A.   French import quotas; a new instrument of commercial policy.
    1935. (Half-title: London school of economics and political science.
    Studies in economics and commerce. no. 6)
        Reviewed by Marjorie F. Freeman in Jour. Polit. Econ. 44(4): 573-
    574. August 1936.

Haney, L. H.   History of economic thought; a critical account of the
    origin and development of the economic theories of the leading thinkers
    in the leading nations. 3d and enl. ed. 1936. (Half-title: Social
    science text-books, ed. by R. T. Ely)
        Reviewed by J. M. Ferguson in Amer. Econ. Rev. 26(3): 487-488.
    September 1936.

Harrison, G., and Mitchell, F. C.   The home market; a handbook of statistics.
    [1936]
        Reviewed in the Economist 122(4831): 708,709. March 28, 1936 in an
    article entitled "The British Consumer."
        Reviewed by H. W. McCrosty in Nineteenth Cent. 120(713): 117-119.
    July 1936.

Herring, E. P.   Public administration and the public interest. 1936.
        Reviewed by L. D. White in Amer. Polit. Sci. Rev. 30(3): 567-569.
    June 1936.

Higgs, Henry.   Bibliography of Economics. 1935.
        Reviewed by E. R. A. Seligman in Amer. Econ. Rev. 26(3): 497-498.
    September 1936.

Holt, J. B.   German agricultural policy, 1918-1934; the development of a
    national philosophy toward agriculture in postwar Germany. 1936.
        Reviewed briefly by R. H. Wells in Amer. Polit. Sci. Rev. 30(4):
    798. August 1936.

Jackman, W. T.   Economic principles of transportation. 1935.
        Reviewed in Economist (London) 124(4850): 270. Aug. 8, 1936.

Keynes, J. M.   The general theory of employment, interest, and money.
    1936.
        Reviewed by C. O. Hardy in Amer. Econ. Rev. 26(3): 490-493.
    September 1936.
        Reviewed by A. H. Hansen in Yale Rev. 25(4): 819-821. Summer 1936.

Kuczynski, R. R.   The measurement of population growth; methods and
    results. 1935.
        Reviewed by D. Caradog Jones in Sociol. Rev. 28(1): 100-102.
    January 1936.
        Reviewed by W. F. Willcox in Amer. Econ. Rev. 26(2): 360-362.
    June 1936.
        Reviewed by A. M. Carr-Saunders in New Statesman and Nation (n.s.)
    10(236): 285. Aug. 31, 1935.

Laidler. H. W.   A program for modern America. [1936]
    Reviewed by R. M. Story in Amer. Polit. Sci. Rev. 30(4): 776-777.
August 1936.
    Reviewed by G. P. Scoville in Jour. Farm Econ. 18(3): 631-634.
August 1936.

Lippmann, Walter.   The new imperative. 1935.
    Reviewed by Lindsay Rogers in Yale Rev. 25(4): 854-855. Summer
1936.

Locklin, D. P.   Economics of transportation. 1935.
    Reviewed by H. E. Dougall in Jour. Polit. Econ. 44(4): 569-571.
August 1936.

Lorimer, Frank, and Osborn, Frederick.   Dynamics of population; social
   and biological significance of changing birth rates in the United
   States. 1934.
    Reviewed briefly in Internatl. Labour Rev. 34(1): 147. July 1936.

Lyon, L. S., and Abramson, Victor.   The economics of open price systems.
   1936. (Half-title: The Institute of economics of the Brookings institute. Publication no. 71)
    Reviewed briefly in the N. Y. Herald Tribune Books 12(52): 14.
Aug. 30, 1936.

Nourse, E. G.   Marketing agreements under the AAA. 1935. (Half-title:
   The Institute of economics of the Brookings institution. Publication
   no. 63)
    Reviewed by H. E. Erdman in Jour. Farm Econ. 18(3): 623-624.
August 1936.

Odum, H. W.   Southern regions of the United States...for the Southern
   regional committee of the Social science research council. 1936.
    Reviewed by J. M. Gaus in Survey Graphic 25(9): 535,536. September
1936.
    Reviewed briefly by Warner Moss in Amer. Polit. Sci. Rev. 30(4):
791. August 1936.
    Reviewed by Phoebe O'Neall Faris in Soil Conservation 2(2): 39-40.
August 1936.

Pareto, V. F. D.   The mind and society (Trattato di sociologia generale)
   Edited by Arthur Livingston. Translated by Andrew Bongiorno and Arthur
   Livingston with the advice and active cooperation of James Harvey
   Rogers. 4 v. [1935]
    Reviewed by G. E. G. Catlin in Polit. Sci. Quart. 51(3): 438-441.
September 1936.

Peck, H. W.   Economic thought and its institutional background. [1935]
    Reviewed by Edward Batson in South African Jour. Econ. 4(2): 244.
June 1936.

Pribram, Karl. Cartel problems; an analysis of collective monopolies in Europe with American application. 1935. (Half-title: The institute of economics of the Brookings institution. Publication no. 69)
Reviewed by M. W. Watkins in Jour. Polit. Econ. 44(4): 563-565. August 1936.

Pyle, J. F. Marketing principles; organization and policies. Rev. ed. 1936.
Reviewed by C. W. Barker in Jour. Marketing 1(1): 67. July 1936.

Richards, H. I. Cotton and the AAA. 1936. (Half-title: The Institute of economics of the Brookings institution. Publication no. 66)
Reviewed briefly by H. C. Nixon in Amer. Polit. Sci. Rev. 30(4): 792-793. August 1936.
Reviewed by G. W. Forster in Jour. Farm Econ. 18(3): 635-637. August 1936.

Sayre, F. B. America must act. 1936. (World peace foundation. World affairs books no. 13)
Reviewed by Karl Brandt in Social Research 3(3): 370. August 1936.

Schultz, T. W. Vanishing farm markets and our world trade. 1935. (World affairs pamphlets no. 11)
Reviewed by Karl Brandt in Social Research 3(3): 369. August 1936.

Soddy, Frederick. The rôle of money; what it should be, contrasted with what it has become. [1935]
Reviewed by A. W. Marget in Jour. Polit. Econ. 44(4): 565-567. August 1936.

Stapledon, R. G. The land, now and to-morrow. [1935]
Reviewed by L.F. Easterbrook in New Statesman and Nation (n.s.) 11(255): 56, 58. Jan. 11, 1936.
Reviewed by Edmund Barber in Country Life [London] 78(2026): 518. Nov. 16, 1935.
Reviewed by B. in Scot. Farmer 44(2245): 97-98. Jan. 25, 1936.

Stevenson, R. A., and Vaile, R. S. Balancing the economic controls; a review of the economic studies of the Employment stabilization research institute, University of Minnesota. 1935.
Reviewed by A. R. Burns in Survey 72(8): 254. August 1936.

Thornthwaite, C. W., and Slentz, Helen I. Internal migration in the United States. 1934. (Half-title: Study of population redistribution. Bull. no. 1. Industrial research department. Wharton school of finance and commerce. University of Pennsylvania)
Reviewed by Karl Brandt in Social Research 3(3): 376-379. August 1936.

Thomas, Brinley. Monetary policy and crises: A study of Swedish experience.
Reviewed in Economist (London) 124(4845):17. July 4, 1936 under title "Sweden's Achievement."

Tintner, Gerhard. Prices in the trade cycle. 1935.
        Reviewed by Frederick C. Mills in Amer. Econ. Rev. 26(2): 322-324.
June 1936.
        Reviewed by Simon Kuznets in Amer. Acad. Polit. and Social Science.
Ann. 185: 241-242. May 1936.
        Reviewed by Solomon Fabricant in Amer. Statis. Assoc. Jour. 31(193):
212-214. March 1936.
        Reviewed by M. Tappan Hollond in Econ. Jour. 46(183): 497-499. Septem-
ber 1936.

U. S. Department of agriculture. Yearbook of agriculture. 1936.
        Reviewed by W. E. H. in Lingnan Sci. Jour. 15(3): 502. July 1936.

U. S National resources board. State planning; a review of activities
      and progress. 1935.
        Reviewed by W. H. Blucher in Survey 72(8): 255. August 1936.

U. S. National resources committee. Regional factors in national planning
      and development. 1935.
        Reviewed by S. G. Lowrie in Amer. Polit. Sci. Rev. 30(4): 778-779.
August 1936.

The United States in world affairs; an account of American foreign relations
      1934-1935. v. 4. 1935.
        Reviewed briefly by T. A. Bisson in Amer. Polit. Sci. Rev. 30(2):
408, 409. April 1936.

Van de Woestyne, R. S. State control of local finance in Massachusetts.
      1935. (Half-title: Harvard economic studies. v. 49)
        Reviewed by T. R. Snavely in Amer. Acad. Polit. and Social Sci.
Ann. 186: 225-226. July 1936.

Wallace, H. A. Whose constitution? An inquiry into the general welfare. [1936]
        Reviewed in Barron's 16(30): 10,11. July 27, 1936.
        Reviewed by R. L. Duffus in Survey Graphic 25(8): 483-484. August 1936.
        Reviewed briefly in Review of Reviews 94(2): 8. August 1936.

Warbasse, J. P. Cooperative democracy through voluntary association of the
      people as consumers; a discussion of the cooperative movement, its
      philosophy, methods, accomplishments and possibilities and its relation to
      the state, to science, art, and commerce, and to other systems of economic
      organization. 3d ed. 1936.
        Reviewed by Caroline F. Ware in Survey Graphic 25(9): 536. September
1936.

Williams, Gertrude. The State and the standard of living. 1936.
        Reviewed by H. A. Shannon in South African Jour. Econ. 4(2): 246-248.
June 1936.

Wilmerding, Lucius, Jr. Government by merit; an analysis of the problem of
      government personnel. 1935. (Half-title: Commission of inquiry on public
      service personnel. Monograph 12)
        Reviewed by L. M. Short in Amer. Polit. Sci. Rev. 30(4): 766-768.
August 1936.

Economic in Character

Compiled by Katharine Jacobs

Farmers' Bulletin*

1045. Issued May 1919, revised July 1936. Laying out fields for tractor
plowing, by C. D. Kinsman...and L. A. Reynoldson. 18pp. 1 Ag84F
Revised by A. H. Glaves.

Senate Document (Prepared by Forest Service)**

The western range; letter from the Secretary of agriculture transmitting in
response to Senate resolution no. 289 a report on the western range -
a great but neglected natural resource. 620pp. Washington, U. S. Govt.
print. off., 1936. (74th Congress, 2d session, Senate Doc. no. 199)
1 F76We
    Bibliography, pp.557-566.

Service and Regulatory Announcements (Bureau of Agricultural Economics)*

93, second revision.   Rules and regulations of the Secretary of agriculture
governing the inspection and certification of fruits, vegetables, and
other products. (Revised June 1936) 7pp. August 1936. 1 M34S no. 93,
second revision.
129 revised.   Regulations for warehousemen storing tobacco, approved
August 3, 1935, amended March 26, 1936. Regulations of the Secretary
of agriculture under the United States warehouse act of August 11,
1916 as amended. 22pp. 1936. 1 M34S
151.   United States standards for potatoes. 4pp. September 1936.
1 M34S
152.   Regulations of the Secretary of agriculture under the United States
cotton futures act, Effective August 20, 1936. 22pp. 1936.
1 M34S
153.   Regulations of the Secretary of agriculture under the United States
cotton standards act, effective August 20, 1936. 26pp. August 1936.
1 M34S

Statistical Bulletin*

51.   Stumpage and log prices for the calendar year 1934, compiled by
Henry B. Steer. 61pp. December 1935. 1 Ag84St

Symbol used after each entry is cell number assigned to the publication by
the Department Library.
*Requests for these publications should be addressed to the Office of In-
formation, U. S. Department of Agriculture, Washington, D. C.
**May be purchased from the Superintendent of Documents Office, price 60¢

Common aims in agriculture; address...before a gathering of negro leaders
and farmers at Tuskegee institute, Tuskegee Ala. ... September 10, 1936.
13pp., mimeogr. 1.9 Ag8636 [no. 128]

The impact of technology; remarks...at the Centennial celebration of the
city of Council Bluffs, Iowa, August 11, 1936 13pp., mimeogr.
1.9 Ag9636 [no. 126]

The Joseph idea, the drought, and the American consumer; remarks...at the
Great Lakes exposition, Cleveland, Ohio, August 19, 1936. 15pp.,
mimeogr. 1.9 Ag9636 [no. 127]

Publications of the Bureau of Agricultural Economics (Mimeographed)**

Amendment no. 3 to Service and regulatory announcements no. 143   Amendment
to rules and regulations of the Secretary of agriculture for carrying
out the provisions of the Export apple and pear act. 1 p. July 23,
1936. 1 M34S

Amendment to the standards for brown rice. 1 p. August 19, 1936.
1.9 Ec74Rbr

Amendment to the standards for milled rice. 1 p. [August 1936] 1.9 Ec74Ra

Brief preliminary review, marketing fresh prunes 1936, Pacific northwestern
states. 2pp. August 28, 1936. 1.9 Ec741L

Brief review of the 1936 cantaloupe season. 1 p. July 18, 1936 (Issued in
cooperation with Clemson college, Extension service, Division of
markets) 1.9 Ec741L

Brief review of the 1936 Eastern Shore potato season. 5 pp. July 30, 1936.
(Issued in cooperation with Virginia Dept. of agriculture and Maryland,
Dept. of markets) 1.9 Ec741L

Brief review of the 1936 watermelon season. 2pp. July 28, 1936. (Issued
in cooperation with Clemson college, Extension service, Division of
markets) 1.9 Ec741L

County planning and zoning, lists of enabling acts and commissions, by
C. I. Hendrickson. 30pp. June 1936. 1.9 Ec76Cou

Farm production and income from meat animals, 1924-1935, by states. 135pp.
September 1936. 1.9 Ec71Fp

Farm value, gross income, and cash income from farm production 1934-1935,
by states and commodities. 100pp. August 1936. 1.9 Ec7Fv

Farm youth in the United States. A selected list of references to literature issued since October 1926, comp. by Esther M. Colvin under the
direction of Mary G. Lacy, Librarian, Bureau of agricultural economics.
196pp., mimeogr. Washington, D. C., June 1936. (U. S. Dept. of
agriculture. Bureau of agricultural economics. Agricultural economics
bibliography no. 65. Supplements no. 17) 1.9 Ec73A no. 65

Income from farm production in the United States in 1935. 24pp. September
1936. 1.9 Ec7Ff

Marketing Alabama potatoes, 1936 season. 3pp. August 5, 1936. 1.9 Ec741L

Marketing Arkansas peaches. Brief review of the 1936 season, by W. D.
Googe. 10pp. August 1936. 1.9 Ec741L

---

* Requests for these publications should be addressed to the Office of Information, U. S. Department of Agriculture, Washington, D. C.
**These publications are issued in small editions for immediate use in
official work and are not for general distribution.

Marketing California grapes. Summary of 1935 season, by A. E. Prugh.
25pp. July 1936. (Issued in cooperation with California, Dept. of
agriculture, Market news service) 1.9 Ec741L
Marketing Florida & Georgia watermelons. Summary of 1936 season, by R.
Maynard Peterson. 6pp. August 7, 1936. (Issued in cooperation with
Georgia, State bureau of markets and Florida, State marketing bureau)
1.9 Ec741L
Marketing northwest pears 1935-1936 [by] L. S. Fenn [and] L. B. Gerry.
23pp. August 1936. 1.9 Ec741L
Marketing northwestern fresh prunes. Summary of the 1935 season, by M. M.
Thomas. 15pp. July 1936. 1.9 Ec741L
Marketing northwestern onions (Idaho, Oregon & Washington) summary of the
1935 season, by M. M. Thomas. 16pp. August 1936. 1.9 Ec741L
Marketing Texas cabbage. Brief review of 1935-36 season, by W. D. Googe.
20pp. July 31, 1936. (Issued in cooperation with Texas, Dept. of
agriculture, Markets and warehouse division) 1.9 Ec741L
Marketing Texas citrus, lower Rio Grande valley of Texas; brief review of
the 1935-36 season, by W. D. Googe. 21pp. September 1936. 1.9 Ec741L
Meat grading effective and far-reaching, by B. F. McCarthy. 4pp. [1936]
1.9 Ec713 Meat
    Given "at annual convention of National association of retail meat
dealers at Cleveland, Ohio, August 3, 1936."
Midsummer wheat outlook report. 4pp. August 14, 1936. 1.9 Ec70wsu
Official standard grades for flue-cured tobacco (U. S. types 11, 12, 13, and
14) 11pp. August 1936. 1.9 Ec714Stf
Oleomargarine; statistics of production, materials used in manufacture,
consumption, trade, and prices. Prepared by Anne Dewees, under the
direction of O. C. Stine. 58pp. August 1936. 1.9 Ec7520
Planted acreage, crop years 1929-1935, by states. 8pp. August 1936.
1.9 Ec71Pla
Poultry estimates; chickens on farms, January 1, 1936; chickens produced,
consumed on farms, and sold, 1935; eggs produced, consumed on farms
and sold, 1935; with comparisons. 8PP. August 1936. 1.9 Ec71Pou
Relation of changes in meat production and consumption to changes in farm
income from livestock in the United States, by Preston Richards.
4pp. 1936. 1.9 Ec752Rel
    "Paper for the International conference of agricultural economists
in Scotland, August 30-September 6, 1936."
Review of North Carolina peaches, season of 1936. 4pp. August 13, 1936.
(Issued in cooperation with North Carolina Dept. of agriculture,
Division of markets) 1.9 Ec741L
Review of North Carolina watermelons, season of 1936. 3pp. August 13, 1936.
(Issued in cooperation with North Carolina, Dept. of agriculture,
Division of markets) 1.9 Ec741L
Revised estimates of buckwheat acreage, yield per acre, and production,
1866-1929. 34pp. August 1936. 1.9 Ec7Rebu
Sampling American cotton, prevailing practices and some factors affecting
representativeness of samples, by Sam W. Martin. 37pp. August 1936.
1.9 Ec733Sa

Tobacco revisions, acreage, yield and production, crop years, 1919-1935. By
   states, classes and types. 20pp. June 1936.
U. S. standards for citrus fruits (Effective Sept. 1, 1936) 15pp   August
   3, 1936. 1.9 Ec74Ci
U. S. standards for potatoes (Effective September 15, 1936) 10pp. 1936.
   1.9 Ec74Po
U. S. standards for rough rice, as amended, effective August 1, 1936.
   13pp. [1936] 1.9 Ec74Rr

Radio Talks (Mimeographed)*

Farm business facts. A radio interview between Roy F. Hendrickson...and
   Morse Salisbury...National farm and home hour...August 4, 1936 (4pp.);
   August 11, 1936 (4 pp.); August 25, 1936 (4 pp.); September 1, 1936
   (4 pp.); September 8, 1936 (4 pp.); September 15, 1936 (3 pp.)
   1.9 Ec7Ra
The midsummer outlook for livestock; interview between A. G. Black and Morse
   Salisbury [August 6, 1936] 4pp. 1.9 Ec7Ra
Midsummer wheat outlook broadcast; discussion between Morse Salisbury and
   A. G. Black. August 14, 1936. 3PP. 1.9 Ec7Ra

Publications of the Agricultural Adjustment Administration**

Agricultural imports; their significance to American farmers. 16pp.
   [1936] 1.4 Ad4Ag
Community discussion paper no. 1.-Is soil conservation the answer to the
   farm problem? An outline and selected information. 14pp. August
   1936. (CDP no. 1) 1.4 Ad4Com
Effects of summer soil-conserving crops on yields of other crops; a summary
   of the experimental work done in the southern region and nearby states.
   64pp. (SRAC-1) August 1936. 1.42 So8Sr
       Issued in conjunction with the Cooperative Extension Service of the
   Department of Agriculture and the state agricultural colleges in the
   southern region.
Farm buying and industrial recovery; a survey of shipments of manufactured and
   industrial commodities from manufacturing areas to agricultural areas
   July 1, 1932 to June 30, 1935. Issued August 1936. 22PP. (G-58)
   1.4 Ad4Ge
(General sugar quota regulations, series 3, revision 2, supplement 1)
   Adjustment in quotas for the calendar year 1936. 2pp. July 28, 1936.
   (G.S.Q.R. Series 3, no. 4) 1.4 Su3G
Instructions relative to determining performance under the provisions of the
   1936 agricultural conservation program in the north central region.
   For use of community, county, and state committees. 20pp. August 7,
   1936. (NCR-5a) 1.42 N75F

_____

* Radio talks may be obtained from U. S Department of Agriculture, Office
   of Information, Radio Service.
**Requests for these publications should be addressed to the Agricultural
   Adjustment Administration, U. S. Department of Agriculture, Washington,
   D. C.

Marketing agreement series – agreement no. 67...Marketing agreement for
handlers of fresh peas and cauliflower grown in the counties of Alamosa,
Rio Grande, Conejos, Costilla, Custer and Eagle in the state of Colorado.
14pp. 1936. (A-6) 1.4 Ad47M no. 67
Effective August 9, 1936.
Marketing agreement series – agreement no. 68...Marketing agreement regulating
the handling of milk in the Topeka, Kansas, marketing area. 12pp. (A-7)
1.4 Ad47M no.68
Effective August 16, 1936.
1936 agricultural conservation program – east central region. Bulletin no.
5, parts I, II and III. Instructions for determination of performance,
preparation of report of performance, and related forms. 15pp.
August 1936. (ECR-B-5-Parts I, II, and III) 1.42 Ea7B
1936 agricultural conservation program – insular region. Supplement A to
bulletin no. 1. Diversion of tobacco acreage to protective non-depleting
cover crops. 1 p. July 20, 1936. (IR-B-Supplement A) 1.42 In7
1936 agricultural conservation program – northeast region. 14pp. (NER-B-1
Rev. Sept. 3, 1936) 1.42 N76B
1936 agricultural conservation program – southern region. Bulletin no. 5,
Part 1 (Preliminary) Instructions for filling out report of performance
(form SR-8) 4pp. August 10, 1936. (SR-B-5, Part 1 (Preliminary))
1.42 So8B
1936 agricultural conservation program, western region. Bulletin no. 1,
revised, supplement (b). 3pp. July 31, 1936. (WR-B-1 Revised, Supplement (b)) 1.42 W52B
1936 agricultural conservation program – western region. Bulletin no. 1,
revised, supplement (e) 2pp. August 17, 1936. (WR-B-1 Revised.
Supplement (e)) 1.42 W52B
Order series – order no. 10. Order regulating the handling of fresh peas
and cauliflower grown in the counties of Alamosa, Rio Grande, Conejos,
Costilla, Custer and Eagle, in the state of Colorado. (Issued by the
Secretary of agriculture, August 4, 1936. Effective 12:01 a.m. E.S.T.
August 9, 1936) 14pp. 1936. (O-10) 1.4 Ad47O
(Puerto Rico sugar order no. 4, revision 2) Allotment of the quota for
Puerto Rico. 3pp. August 4, 1936. (P.R.S.O. No. 4, Revision 2)
1.4 Su3P
(Puerto Rico sugar order no. 4, revision 2, supplement 1) Allotment of
additional quota to Puerto Rico. Order made by the Secretary of
agriculture under Public resolution no. 109, and the Agricultural
adjustment act. 3PP. August 20, 1936. 1.4 Su3P
Sources of information on consumer education and organization. 33pp.
1936. (Consumers' counsel series, publication no. 1) 1.4 Ad422
Contains bibliographies.
A survey of milk consumption in 59 cities in the United States. 33pp.
June 1936. (Consumers' counsel series, publication no. 2) 1.4 Ad422

Addresses (Mimeographed)*

The agricultural conservation program. Address by J. B. Hutson...before
the 28th annual convention of the Vegetable growers association of
America, inc., at Cleveland, Ohio, September 10, 1936. 13pp. 1.94 T55H

---

* May be obtained from U. S. Department of Agriculture, Office of Information.

Factors in the dairy situation. Address of Dr. E. W. Gaumnitz. 13pp.
[1936] 1.94 D14Fa
Delivered at the meeting of the Dairymen's Cooperative Creamery of
Boise Valley, Idaho, August 14, 1936.
Farm program essentials. Address of H. R. Tolley...at the West Tennessee
farmers' and home makers institute, Jackson, Tenn., July 29, 1936.
13pp. 1.94 Ad472T [no. 13]
The negro farmer and the A.A.A. Address by C. A. Cobb...at a conference of
negro agricultural leaders and farmers at Prairie View, Texas...August
12. 1936. 13pp. 1.42 So3Ra
Workers' earnings keep pace with food prices...by L. H. Bean. 5pp.
September 4, 1936. 1.94 Ad472W
Press release.

Radio Talks (Mimeographed)*

Agricultural conservation in the Northeast...by H. B. Boyd...July 8, 1936...
2pp. 1.42 N76R
Drought conditions in the corn belt...by Joseph F. Cox...July 14, 1936.
2pp. 1.94 Ad4R
Drought relief ..by J. W. Tapp...July 9, 1936. 2pp. 1.94 Ad4R
The place of soil conservation in national agricultural policy;...by Bushrod
W. Allin...July 27, 1936. 2pp. 1.94 Ad4R
Progress of agricultural conservation program...by S. B. Bledsoe...July
21, 1936. 2pp. 1.94 Ad4R
Progress of the agricultural conservation program;...by A. D. Stedman.
Aug. 11, 1936 (2pp.); Aug. 18, 1936 (2pp.); Aug. 25, 1936 (2pp.);
Sept. 8, 1936 (2pp.) 1.94 Ad4R
Progress of the agricultural conservation program;...by M. L. DuMars...
2pp. Sept. 1, 1936.
The shift to legumes and grasses;...by J. F. Cox...Aug. 12, 1936. 2pp.
1.9 Ad4R
Soil conservation and drought in the western region...by C. C. Conser .
June 25, 1936. 3pp. 1.42 W52R

Miscellaneous (Mimeographed)**

The correlation of soil erosion and tax delinquency in the Piedmont area
of South Carolina, by Brice M. Latham. 22pp. July 1936. (SCS-RB-1)
(Issued by the Soil conservation service) 1.96 P94

---

* May be obtained from U. S. Department of Agriculture, Office of Information, Radio Service.
**Requests for this publication should be addressed to the issuing office.

Compiled by Mary F. Carpenter

California

California. Department of agriculture. Statistical report of California
dairy products, 1935, and list of California dairy products plants.
Calif. Dept. Agr. Special Pub. 142, 74pp. Sacramento. 1936.

California. Department of agriculture, Division of market enforcement.
Official list of commission merchants, dealers, brokers, processors, and
agents licensed under the agricultural code of the State of California
as of May 1, 1936. Calif. Dept. Agr. Special Pub. 140, 102pp.
Sacramento. 1936.

California. Laws, statutes, etc. Extracts from the agricultural code of
California pertaining to general provisions, agricultural commissioners,
plant quarantine, pest control and standardization - with appendix.
Corrected to Sept. 15, 1935. 142pp. Sacramento, Calif. state printing
office. 1935.

Grove, E. W., and Smythe, D. W. Competition between linseed and other
drying oils, with particular reference to California. Calif. Agr.
Expt. Sta. Giannini Found. Agr. Econ. Mimeogr. Rept. 52, 32pp.
Berkeley. 1936.

Tinley, J. M. Supplementary report on the Los Angeles milk market. Calif.
Agr. Expt. Sta. Giannini Found. Agr. Econ. Mimeogr. Rept. 51, 3pp.
Berkeley. August 1936.

Connecticut

Connecticut. Department of agriculture. Connecticut crop and livestock
review, 1935. Conn. Dept. Agr. Bull. 41, 24pp. Hartford. 1936.
In cooperation with the New England Crop Reporting Service.
Includes county statistics.

Delaware

Delaware. University. School of agriculture, Division of agricultural ex-
tension. Annual report...for the year ending November 30, 1935.
Del. Univ. Ext. Serv. Bull. 24, 32pp. Newark. 1936.
County agricultural agent work in agricultural economics, pp. 9-11,13.

Gabriel, H. S. Roadside markets in Delaware. Del. Agr. Expt. Sta. Bull.
201, 25pp. Newark. 1936.

Florida

Florida. Comptroller. Report...for the fiscal year ending June 30, 1935.
127pp. Tallahassee [1936]
County statistics show numbers of livestock by kinds and total real
estate valuations.

Idaho. Agricultural experiment station.   Science aids Idaho farmers.   The
    annual report...for the year ending December 31, 1935. Idaho Agr. Expt.
    Sta Bull. 200, 62pp. Moscow. June 1936.
        Agricultural economics, pp.9-11.

Illinois

Colby, A. S.   Strawberry culture in Illinois.   Ill. Agr. Expt. Sta. Circ.
    453, 53pp. Urbana. May 1936.
        Marketing problems, pp.43-45; Yields, costs, and profits, p.45.

Lindstrom, D. E.   Forces affecting participation of farm people in rural
    organization; a study made in four townships in Illinois. Ill. Agr.
    Expt. Sta. Bull. 423, 127pp. Urbana. May 1936.
        The four townships are Illini and Milam in Macon County and Philo
    and Harwood in Champaign County.

Indiana

Manhart, V. C.   Effect of a milk plant quality program on the price paid to
    producers for milk. Ind. Purdue Agr. Expt. Sta. Bull. 404, 12pp.
    Lafayette. March 1936.

Manhart, V. C., and Moore, A. V.   Milk quality improvement effected at
    the farm by a plant program. Ind. Purdue Agr. Expt. Sta. Bull. 405,
    16pp. Lafayette. March 1936.

Moore, H. E , and Lloyd, O. G.   The back-to-the land movement in Southern
    Indiana. Ind. Purdue Agr. Expt. Sta. Bull. 409, 28pp. Lafayette.
    April 1936.
        The study was made for the period between 1930 and June 1934.

Smith, F. V., and Lloyd, O. G.   Part-time farming in Indiana. Ind.
    Purdue Agr. Expt. Sta. Bull. 410, 28pp. Lafayette. April 1936.
        The income data presented are for the year 1933.

Iowa

Arthur, I. W.   Trends in the hog and pork trade in the United States.
    Iowa Agr. Expt. Sta. Bull. 346, pp.242-278. Ames. 1936.
        Information for the producer.

Iowa. State college of agriculture and mechanic arts, Extension service.
    Iowa farm economist, v. 2, no. 3, Ames. July 1936.
        Partial contents: Iowa farmers "cash in" in 1935, by L. K. Macy,
    pp.3-5; Farm spending increases, pp. 5-6; Iowa land prices rise, by
    R. C. Bentley, pp. 7-8; More grass - less grain, by H. G. Folken and
    R. T. Klemme, pp 9-11; How Iowa egg and poultry prices vary, by A. D.
    Oderkirk, p.12; How Iowa butterfat prices vary, by J. M. Cowden, pp.
    13-14; Better farming on poorer soils, by W. W. Wilcox, pp. 15-16.

Iowa farm debt advisory council.   The Iowa Farm Debt Advisory council,
   organization - activities - results on eight months from May through
   December 1934. Iowa. Dept. Agr. Bull. 67; 54pp. Des Moines. 1935.

Louisiana

Louisiana. State university and agricultural and mechanical college,
   Division of agricultural extension.   Triennial report of agricultural
   extension work in Louisiana, 1932-1934. 190pp. University Station.
   Baton Rouge. 1936?
      A.A.A. activities (including parish cotton, rice, corn-hog, sugar-
   cane and cattle purchase statistics) pp. 12-77; Plan of work for
   Farm Economics, 1934, pp. 112-113; Horticulture (including marketing
   and inspection) pp.115-136; State government officials, pp.146-172;
   List of cotton gins, sugar mills, syrup factories, rice mills,
   creameries, cooling stations, and warehouses by parishes, pp. 173-189.
      A folded soil map of Louisiana is attached.

Maine

Miller, S. R.   Maine agriculture. Maine Agr. Col. Ext. Bull. 224, 24pp.
   Orono. 1936.
      A short description of the principal agricultural industries of
   Maine.

Maryland

Maryland. University, Extension service.   Twenty-first annual report...
   for the year 1935. 80pp. College Park. [1936]
      Agricultural adjustment programs, pp. 4-7; Marketing, pp.54-57;
   Economics and farm management, pp. 75-76.

Meade, DeVoe, and Mead, R. K.   Sale of dairy products at roadside markets
   in Maryland. Md. Agr. Expt. Sta. Bull. 394, pp. 595-626. College
   Park. 1936.
      "The selling of dairy products at roadside markets being a rather
   new adventure in the field of marketing, a survey of these markets
   was made in an attempt to determine the factors responsible for the
   success or the failure of these markets."

Russell, Ralph.   Maryland farm credit handbook. Md. Agr. Expt. Sta. Bull.
   396, pp.635-690. College Park. 1936.
      Part I. The farm credit situation in Maryland; Part II. Credit and
   services available through the Farm Credit Administration.

Massachusetts

Massachusetts State college, Extension service.   Farm economic facts, v. 9,
   no. 7, 4pp. Amherst. July-August 1936.
      Partial contents: Massachusetts farm prices lower, by R. E. Moser;
   Net milk prices in Northampton, by A. A. Brown; Massachusetts deficient
   in turnips, by E. W. Bell; Source of dairy importations, by E. W.
   Bell; Prices for milk are higher, by E. W. Bell.

Michigan. Agricultural experiment station. Quarterly bulletin v. 19, no. 1,
pp. 1-70. East Lansing. August 1936.
Partial contents: 1935 tractor costs in Michigan, by K. T. Wright,
pp. 31-33; Motor truck transportation in relation to cooperative fruit
and vegetable marketing in Michigan, by G. N. Motts, pp. 36-44.

Minnesota

Koller, E. F., and Hollands, H. F.   Butterfat assembly methods used by
Minnesota cooperative creameries. Minn. Univ. Agr. Ext. Div. Minn.
Farm Business Notes, no. 164, pp. 1-3, mimeogr. University Farm,
St. Paul. Aug. 20, 1936.

Missouri

Missouri. State board of equalization. Journal...for the year ending
December 31, 1935. 379pp. [Jefferson City, 1936]
Contains statistics by counties showing valuation of land, live-
stock by kinds, farm machinery and other property.

Montana

Slagsvold, P. L.   An analysis of the present status of agriculture on the
Sun River irrigation project. Mont. Agr. Expt. Sta. Bull. 321, 60pp.
Bozeman. May 1936.

Starch, E. A.   Readjusting Montana's agriculture VII. Montana's dry-land
agriculture. Mont. Agr. Expt. Sta. Bull. 318, 19pp. Bozeman.
April 1936.

New Hampshire

New Hampshire. University, Extension service.   Extension work in New
Hampshire 1935. Annual report. N. H. Univ. Ext. Serv. Ext. Bull.
49, 24pp. Durham. March 1936.
Farm management, pp. 13-14; Marketing, pp. 14-15; Rural recreation,
pp. 20-21.

New Jersey

New Jersey. State Agricultural experiment station.   Fifty-sixth annual
report and the forty-eighth annual report of the New Jersey Agricultural College experiment station for the year ending June 30, 1935.
122pp   New Brunswick. [1936]
Agricultural economics, pp. 7-12.

Oley, W. W.   The fruit and vegetable auction markets of New Jersey.
N. J. Dept. Agr. Circ. 261, 23pp. Trenton. 1936.

New York

Jones, P. B.   An economic study of land utilization in Tioga county, New
York. N. Y. Cornell Agr. Expt. Sta. Bull. 648, 40pp. Ithaca. 1936.
Includes folded land classification map of the county.

New York. Department of agriculture and markets, Division of milk control.
Report...1934. N. Y. Dept. Agr. and Markets. Circ. 511, pp 81-126.
Albany. 1935.
Reprint from the annual report of the Department for the year 1934.

Sharp, P. F., Stewart, G. F., and Huttar, J. C.   Effect of packing materials
on the flavor of storage eggs. N. Y. Cornell Agr. Expt. Sta. Memoir
189, 26pp. Ithaca. 1936.

North Carolina

Greene, R. E. L.   Cost of producing farm products in North Carolina.
N. C. Agr. Expt. Sta. Bull. 305, 127pp. State College Station, Raleigh.
1936.
Data on cotton and tobacco are presented in part II and III, miscellaneous crops in part IV and early Irish potatoes in part V.

Ohio

Dowler, J. F., and Moore, H. R.   Public finance problems in the Zaleski
forest and rehabilitation project of the Resettlement Administration.
Ohio State Univ., Dept. Rural Econ. and Ohio Agr. Expt. Sta., Mimeogr.
Bull. 92, 20pp. Columbus. 1936.

Henning, G. F., and Eckert, P. S.   Analysis of the Dayton livestock price
situation. Ohio State Univ. and Ohio Agr. Expt. Sta. Dept. Rural
Econ. Mimeogr. Bull. 90, 11pp. Columbus. 1936.

Henning, G. F., and Eckert, P. S.   The livestock auction in Ohio from the
farmers' point of view in 1934 and 1935. Ohio State Univ. and Ohio
Agr. Expt. Sta. Dept. Rural Econ. Mimeogr. Bull. 89, 13pp. Columbus. 1936.

Lively, C. E., Smith, R. C., and Fry, Martha.   Some aspects of rural social
organization in Fairfield county, Ohio. Ohio State Univ. and Ohio
Agr. Expt. Sta. Dept. Rural Econ. Mimeogr. Bull. 91, 11pp. Columbus. 1936.

Ohio State university, College of agriculture and domestic science, Department
of rural economics.   AAA and the agricultural situation. Bulletin no. 6.
15pp., mimeogr. [Columbus 1936]

Ohio State university, Department of rural economics.   Current economic topics
for the Ohio farmer. Circulars no. 1-3. Columbus. 1935-1936.
No. 1. The processing tax: the farmer's tariff, by B. A. Wallace; no 2,
The Canadian trade agreement and the American farmer, by V. R. Wertz and
E. P. Heiby; no. 3, Agriculture carried on; industry adjusted, by J. I.
Falconer.

Ohio. State university and Ohio Agricultural experiment station. Preliminary
   research bulletin Sept. 1, Nov. 1, 1935. Columbus. 1935.
      Sept. 1, 1935. Length of residence of the heads of families in se-
   lected rural areas of Ohio, by C. E. Lively; Nov. 1, 1935. The status of
   rural youth, 16-24 years old, in selected rural areas of Ohio, by C. E.
   Lively.

Wallace, B. A.   Where the farmer can borrow. Ohio Agr. Col. Ext. Bull.
   176, 4pp. Columbus. April 1936.
      Long and short time loans are discussed.

Oklahoma

Ballinger, R. A.   Results of the regulation of cotton gins as public
   utilities in Oklahoma. Okla. Agr. Expt. Sta. Bull. 230, 16pp.
   Stillwater. May 1936.

Oklahoma Agricultural experiment station.   Current farm economics, v. 9,
   no. 4. Stillwater. August 1936.
      Partial contents: Social aspects of rural shifts of farm population
   in Oklahoma by O. D. Duncan, pp.88-93; Some factors associated with
   profitableness of northwestern Oklahoma farms during 1935, by E. D.
   Hunter, pp. 94-96; Oklahoma has radically changed its tax machinery
   during the past five years, by J. T. Sanders, pp. 97-99.

Pennsylvania

Cowden, T. K., and Fouse, E. G.   The supply and utilization of milk in
   Pennsylvania. Pa. Agr. Expt. Sta. Bull. 327, 111pp. State College. 1936.
      Besides material on the sources and utilization of milk this report
   includes information concerning cooperatives, health regulations, and
   interstate shipments. Detailed data pertaining to the individual counties
   are presented in the appendix.

McDougall, R. H., and Lininger, F. F.   The Butler egg auction. Pa. Agr.
   Expt. Sta. Bull. 328, 44pp. State College. 1936.
      "A study of egg marketing in Western Pennsylvania showing prefer-
   ences of buyers and factors of production influencing price and quality."

Rhode Island

Rhode Island. Agricultural experiment station.   Forty-eighth annual report...
   1936. 40pp. Kingston. 1936. (R. I. Agr. Expt. Sta. Contr. 483)
      Agricultural economics, pp. 3-6; Rural sociology, pp. 32-35; Land
   utilization, pp. 35-36.

South Carolina

Neely, Juanita.   Economic factors influencing egg marketing in South Carolina.
   Clemson Agr. Col., S. C., Ext. Circ. 149, 8pp. Clemson. 1936.

South Dakota

Johansen, J. P.   Immigrants and their children in South Dakota. S. Dak.
Agr. Expt. Sta. Bull. 302, 47pp. Brookings. 1936.
"The present study deals mainly with numerical aspects of immigration and its effects upon the population of the state. The statistical
comparisons that are made include not only the foreign-born and native
of foreign and mixed parentage, but also the native of native parentage."

Kumlien, W. F.   Public library service in South Dakota. S. Dak. Agr. Expt.
Sta. Bull. 301, 32pp. Brookings. 1936.
"This study was originally made in cooperation with Dr. C. J. Galpin,
Bureau of Agricultural Economics, U. S. D. A."

South Dakota. Agricultural experiment station.   Annual report...for the
fiscal year ending June 30, 1935. 48pp. Brookings [1936]
Agricultural economics, by Gabriel Lundy, pp. 5-8; Rural sociology,
by W. F. Kumlien, pp. 46-47.

Westbrook, R. B., and Strand, N. V.   Inequalities arising from the assessment of farm real estate in South Dakota. S. Dak. Agr. Expt. Sta. Bull.
300, 39pp. Brookings. 1936.

Vermont

Hitchcock, J. A., and Williams, S. W.   Studies in Vermont dairy farming.
IX. The Champlain Valley during a major depression. Vt. Agr. Expt.
Sta. Bull. 405, 24pp. Burlington. 1936.

Vermont. State college of agriculture, Extension service.   Twenty-first
annual report...for the year 1935. Vt. Agr. Col. Ext. Bull. 21, 24pp.
Burlington. 1936.
Farm management, pp. 10-11; Marketing, p. 13.

Virginia

Underwood, F. L.   An analysis of real estate assessments in 28 Virginia
counties, 1930. Va. Agr. Expt. Sta. Bull. 303, 38pp. Blacksburg. 1936.

Vernon, J. J., Dean, T. M., and Hawthorne, H. W.   A study of the organization
and management of farms in Grayson county, Virginia. Va. Agr. Expt.
Sta. Bull. 304, 63pp. Blacksburg. 1936.
The type of farming practiced in this area (in southwestern Virginia)
may be best described as livestock grazing with enough crops grown to
winter the breeding and other livestock.

Virginia. Agricultural and mechanical college and Polytechnic institute,
Extension division.   Annual report of Extension work December 1, 1934
to November 30, 1935. Va. Agr. Col. Ext. Bull. 141, 56pp. Blacksburg.
1936.
Agricultural Adjustment program, pp.5-7; Resettlement program, pp. 12-
15; Farm credit program, pp. 15-17; Agricultural economics, pp. 41-43.

Virginia. Polytechnic institute.   Virginia Farm economics, no. 36.   Blacksburg. August 1936.
   Partial contents: Feed prices in Virginia, by G. H. Ward, pp. 558-567; The effects of soil type and erosion on certain factors affecting costs and returns in producing tobacco in Pittsylvania county, Virginia, 1933, by P. G. Craddock, pp. 567-569.

Washington

Hampson, C. C.   Apple prices received by Washington growers. Wash. Agr. Expt. Sta. Bull. 326, 59PP. Pullman. February 1936.
   "This bulletin furnishes weighted average apple prices for the 12 crop years from 1922 to 1933. Prices are shown separately for the Central Irrigated Region of Washington and for each of the two districts which it comprises - the Wenatchee-Okanogan and the Yakima districts." Includes prices by grades and varieties.

Hampson, C. C.   Indexes of prices received by Washington farmers. Wash. Agr. Expt. Sta. Bull. 328, 29pp. Pullman. July 1936.
   "These indexes represent the general agricultural price level for the state as a whole and for each of the three districts [Western, central, and eastern Washington] from 1910 through 1935."

Johnson, O., and Snyder, J. C.   Peppermint oil production in Washington. Wash. Agr. Col. Ext. Bull. 227, 8pp. Pullman. June 1936.
   Price variations, p. 8.

Turner, R. M., and Carroll, H. B.   Farm trends in Washington counties, 1936. Wash. Agr. Col. Ext. Bull. 228, 23pp. Pullman. May 1936.

Vincent, C. L.   Growing peas for canning in Washington. Wash. Agr. Expt. Sta. Popular Bull. 150, 28pp. Pullman. April 1936.
   Yields, p. 20; Price received, p. 21; Frozen pea industry, pp.21-22.

Washington (State) Secretary of state.   Washington; a workshop and playground for all America. Its products, people and resources...abstracted from various authorities Ed. 2, 199pp. Olympia. 1936.
   Statistics are arranged by counties. Most of the data are from the Federal census.

West Virginia

Cornell, F. D., Jr.   Trends in West Virginia agriculture. W. Va. Agr. Expt. Sta. Bull. 276, 20, 63pp. Morgantown. 1936.
   Includes graphs and historical tables based on Federal sources.

Wisconsin

Wisconsin Agricultural experiment station. Today's science for tomorrow's farming. Annual report of the director 1934-35. Wis. Agr. Expt. Sta. Bull. 435, 158pp. Madison. March 1936.
   Farm income and management, pp. 134-144; Social problems, pp.145-151.

Compiled by Louise O. Bercaw and A. M. Hannay

Agricultural Adjustment Act

Garver, F. B.; and Trelogan, Harry.   The Agricultural adjustment act and
the reports of the Brookings Institution. Quart. Jour. Econ. 50(4):
594-621. August 1936. (Published by the Harvard University Press,
Cambridge, Mass.)
    The reports mentioned are: The Dairy Industry and the AAA, by J. D.
Black; Wheat and the AAA, by J. S. Davis; Livestock under the AAA, by
D. A. FitzGerald; Marketing Agreements under the AAA, by E. G. Nourse;
Cotton and the AAA, by H. I. Richards; and Tobacco under the AAA, by
H. B. Rowe.
    "The unbiased accounts of the performance of the Adjustment Admin-
istration which the Brookings group have published will undoubtedly be
of great service to future students of government control. In all the
books there is some explanation of the economic characteristics of the
production and distribution of the commodities discussed, especially
in the two on dairying and tobacco. The economic effects of the various
activities, being less clearly ascertainable, are not as fully explained.
Hence the readers who are likely to derive most benefit from the reports
are those who may contemplate further improvement of the condition of
agriculture either thru government agencies or thru voluntary marketing
agreements." - Summary and Conclusions.

Agricultural Credit - Portugal

Cotta, Freppel. Agricultural credit in Portugal. Indian Co-op. Rev. 2(2):
164-171. April 1936. (Published at Farhatbagh, Mylapore, Madras,
India)
    An account of the reorganization of agricultural credit in Portugal
by Salazar who became Minister of Finance in 1928 and Prime Minister
in 1932. The sources of agricultural credit were the Caixa Geral de
Credito Agricola, the Bolsa Agricola and the Caixa Geral de Depositos.
The last named was reorganized and renamed Caixa Geral de Depositos,
Credito e Previdencia, and to it were attached two financially autonomous institutions called Caixa Nacional de Credito and Caixa Nacional
de Previdencia, all three having the same Council of Administration.
    The Caixa Nacional de Credito, in addition to making loans "has
the following subsidiary objects: (1) To convert rural mortgages;
(2) To purchase uncultivated lands for colonisation and cultivation
purposes; (3) To distribute those lands on credit, with suitable guarantee, among small farmers and agricultural labourers; (4) To finance
the purchases of land made by small farmers and agricultural labourers
themselves for colonisation and cultivation purposes; (5) To promote
banks of the Luzzatti type; (6) To promote credit societies of the
Raiffeisen type; (7) To promote any other types of credit and providence

institutions of economic and social value."

An account is given of the funds of the institution, the conditions of short-term and long-term credit, the rates of interest, and the composition of the Council of Administration and the Board of Management.

Agricultural Credit and the National Grange - Dakotas

Snell. H. S.   The Grange and the credit problem in Dakota Territory. Agr. Hist. 10(2): 59-83. April 1936. (Published by the Agricultural History Society, Room 3901, South Bldg., 13th St., and Independence Ave., Washington, D. C.)

An historical account of the Grange in the Dakota Territory and the evils of the credit system in force there before the coming of the Grange.

Agricultural Debt Adjustment - Canada

Easterbrook, W. T.   Agricultural debt adjustment. Canad. Jour. Econ. and Polit. Sci. 2(3): 390-403. August 1936. (Published by the University of Toronto Press, Toronto, Ontario)

Discussion, by W. B. H., pp. 402-403.

"This present paper is intended as the background to a more detailed discussion of the facts of agricultural debt adjustment. I propose to discuss briefly the nature and objectives of our machinery of agricultural debt adjustment, the background against which it works, and some of the more important difficulties encountered in practice. The observations are based largely upon experience acquired in the West, although the setting concerns the country as a whole."

Agricultural Indebtedness - Europe

Dzelzitis, H.   L'endettement et le désendettement de l'agriculture, surtout en Lettonie. Bureau International Agraire. Bulletin, no. 3, pp. 125-154. July 1936. (Published in Prague, Czechoslovakia)

A discussion of the causes of the wide-spread agricultural indebtedness of European countries and an account of relief measures adopted, especially in Latvia.

Agricultural Policies and Programs

Feisst Ernest.   Le développement de la politique agraire des différents pays. La Technique Agricole Internationale 6(2): 126-156. April-June. 1936. (Published by the Fédération Internationale des Techniciens Agronomes, 86, Via Regina Elena, Rome, Italy)

A review of the agricultural economic situation in Europe after the war and during the depression, with its trend towards directed economy distinguished by the attempt to harmonize production and distribution while still recognizing the freedom of the individual is followed by a discussion of the agricultural policy of individual nations. The author divides the countries into groups in the first of which he places Italy, Germany and to a certain extent Austria, as those countries which have placed agriculture at the centre of the economic and political life of the State but which have made the economic factor subordinate to the political factor and the prosperity of the individual to the interest of the State. His second group, that of exporting countries, includes Holland and Denmark, his third comprises the Danube countries that export their surplus crops. In a fourth group which he characterizes as importing countries with a democratic or liberal régime he includes Great Britain, France, Belgium, Czechoslovakia, and Switzerland Two countries, Spain and Lithuania, fall outside these groups. He feels that Lithuania has the best prospect of increasing her agricultural production because the Lithuanian farmer has remained a peasant and has not been transformed into a capitalist entrepreneur.

Agricultural Policies and Programs - Australia

Murray, A. T. Australian policies affecting agriculture. Foreign Crops and Markets 33(9): 273-287. Aug. 31, 1936. (Published by the Division of Foreign Agricultural Service, Bureau of Agricultural Economics, U. S. Dept. of Agriculture)

The following are discussed: Australian agricultural settlement and development policy (land settlement, immigration, governmental loans and development projects, settlement and development since the depression, effect of the policy on agriculture); the tariff policy in relation to agriculture; government policy toward major agricultural exports (wheat, dairy products, dried fruits, sugar, cotton, wool, other products).

Agricultural Policies and Programs - France

Fromont, Pierre. Staatliche massnahmen in der französischen landwirtschaft. Weltwirtschaftliches Archiv 44(1): 84-124. July 1936. (Published by Gustav Fischer, Jena, Germany)

The author draws a parallel between the two main attempts to control French agriculture in the wheat and wine legislation. He finds that the wheat policy has been more successful than the wine policy. The latter has led to increased production which contains a serious threat for the future of the industry. But both have had results which "have a suspicious resemblance to destruction of wealth." The author believes that "only very exceptional reasons can possibly justify such measures."

Agricultural Policies and Programs - Manchuria

S., J. R. Two new farm programs for Manchoukuo. Far East. Survey 5(17): 186-187. Aug. 12, 1936. (Published by American Council, Institute of Pacific Relations, 129 E. 52nd St., New York, N. Y.)

The following extracts are taken from this short article:

"In order to strengthen the position of agriculture, the Manchoukuo Government in April 1936 announced a basic policy of farm development. Two main aims are evident in the program. First, it fosters diversification in order to reduce dependence on soya beans. Efforts are to be made to control bean production to bring it in line with domestic and foreign demand, but the methods whereby this is to be accomplished have not been stated. The other crops which are to be stimulated in the place of beans are wheat, cotton, wild silk, sugar beets, hemp, flax, oil seeds, and fruits. Secondly, the program provides for the improvement of farm methods and facilities through farm education, increase in the number of model farms, experiment stations and weather observatories, establishment of cooperatives and the creation of a system of farm warehouses.

"This program will probably be carried into effect in the next fiscal year...

"The South Manchurian Railway Company is also vitally interested in the farm problem...In order to make these lines self-supporting, the Company is planning the development of the regions through which they pass. It has sent experts abroad to study foreign influence in stimulating settlement along new railways, and in addition, is reported to be in the process of establishing the North Manchurian Agricultural Development Company, capitalized at ¥80,000,000. This Company will encourage immigration into North Manchuria, provide credit facilities for farmers, and introduce mechanized agriculture."

Agricultural Policies and Programs - Netherlands

Louwes, S. L. Measures taken by the Dutch government in connection with the agricultural crisis. Amsterdamsche Bank n.v. Financial and Econ. Rev. of the Statis. Dept. no. 48, pp. 1-8. July 1936. (Published in Amsterdam, Netherlands)

The writer points out that there has been much criticism from both non-agricultural and agricultural circles of the measures taken in connection with the agricultural crisis. He then tells briefly "why the measures taken by the Government must be acquiesced in, and why they must be accepted essentially in their present form." The measures for the relief of those products for which Holland is essentially an importing country and those for which she is essentially an exporting country are discussed separately. Under the first is discussed "the wheat regulation scheme as an organization which has proved fully capable of giving farmers, on an otherwise unprotected market, a price fixed beforehand for their produce."

For the second group the measures taken in respect of pigs, dairy products and potatoes are discussed.

Agricultural Policies and Programs - United States

Freund, Rudolf. Agrarpolitik und Krisentheorie in den Vereinigten Staaten von Amerika. Berichte über Landwirtschaft (n.F.) 20(4): 624-654. 1936. (Issued by [Germany] Reichs- und Pr. Ministerium für Ernährung u. Landwirtschaft. Published by P. Parey, Berlin)

This is followed by an English Summary with title: Agrarian Policy and Theory of Depression in the United States.

Tugwell, R. G. Down to earth. Current Hist. 44(4): 33-38. July 1936. (Published at 63 Park Row, New York, N. Y.)

"We seem committed, as the major feature of our agricultural policy in the immediate future, to the objectives of improvement of the land and greater security for those on it. Lacking any good insurance for farm prosperity we can still make advances in these ways. And this is the contribution to be made by such activities as the Grazing Service, the Rural Electrification Administration, the Farm Credit Administration, the Soil Conservation Service and the Resettlement Administration. There are uses for land which do not come in the ordinary classification of agriculture, but which are still much wanted by any developed country. They can and will also support a considerable number of families in pleasant and profitable occupations. One of these is recreation...The National Park Service, The Forest Service, and now the Resettlement Administration are developing these resources as they have never before been developed. With the Resettlement Administration the provision of recreation is not the first objective. The desire is rather to retire unprofitable lands from agricultural uses. But it has been found that much land, particularly in the East, which is hopeless for farming, can be used for these other purposes with greater social values ..

"There is no doubt that if we continue to improve our productivity as we have in the past, fewer farmers will suffice to supply any likely demand. Resettlement, therefore, has a legitimate interest in the development of part-time farms and suburban towns, thus linking up agriculture and industry and providing a more orderly pattern for the inevitable movement from farm to city. It can do only a little in any of these fields, of course, because of the limitation of funds, but it can provide those practical demonstrations which are better than books for argument."

Agricultural Relief - Venezuela

H., F. J.   Credit and financial aid for the Venezuelan farmer. Pan Amer. Union. Bull. 70(7): 594-595. July 1936. (Published in Washington, D.C.)
    Legislation promulgated on March 21, 1936 provides additional funds to be used for short-term loans. "In connection with the original relief measure...the Bank of Venezuela will grant loans to coffee and cacao growers with the crops as security. The bank will advance up to 80 per cent of the value of the crop, including the export bounty granted by law, and will charge interest at the rate of 4 per cent per annum. The crop liens are redeemable within 6 months, as regards the coffee, and within 3 months in the case of cacao. In both cases, the product must be selected and suitable for export. Only recently, the Government extended the scope of the credit provisions to include cotton, the loans in this case being payable within a period of six months."
    Export bounties have been increased. A long-range program for farm relief is being undertaken. It is proposed to stop the "ruthless deforestation which has been going on for years", to set up "a rational farm-credit system" and "to study means for the use of national lands and for the subdivision and distribution of large land holdings, now lying idle, in order to increase the number of small-farm owners."

Agricultural Relief - Victoria

What Victoria's C. P. [Country Party] Govt. is doing. The Land no. 1305, pp. 5,25. June 19, 1936. (Published in Sydney, Australia)
    Contains a review of legislation enacted during the first year of the Country Party Government for the benefit of farmers. Among the bills passed which are listed and briefly explained are the following:

Farmers' Debts Adjustment Act; Marketing of Primary Products Act; The
Auction Sales Act (was amended); Farmers' Advances Act (was liberalized);
and the Seeds Act (amended).

Agriculture - Aberdeenshire, Scotland

Cruickshank, James. Changes in the agricultural industry of Aberdeenshire
in the last fifty years. Scot. Jour. Agr. 19(3): 225-239. July 1936.
(Published by H. M. Stationery Office, Edinburgh, Scotland)
This is the second of two articles on agricultural conditions in
Aberdeenshire. The author decides that "on the whole, the changes
during the past fifty years have undoubtedly been for the better."

Agriculture - Bengal

Chaudhuri, Jatindramohan. The agrarian problems of Bengal. Bengal Co-op.
Jour. 21(4): 174-180. April-June 1936. (Published by Bengal Co-operative
Organisation Society, Ltd., 3-1, Bankshall Street, Calcutta, India)
This is the second of two articles on agricultural conditions in
Bengal. It deals with labor and agricultural indebtedness, with "a
few words about...consolidation of holdings."

Agriculture and Directed Economy

Dietre, C. v. Economie agricole dirigée. Rev. Econ. Internationale, 28.
année, v. 2, no. 3, pp. 489-509. June 1936. (Published by L'Institut
Économique International, Palais d'Egmont, Brussels, Belgium)
A survey of pre-war and post-war measures adopted in various countries
for the regulation of agriculture and an estimate of their results.

Apples - Rouville County, Quebec

Gosselin, A. Economic aspects of apple production in Rouville County,
Quebec. Econ. Annalist 6(4): 60-62. August 1936. (Published by the
Agricultural Economics Branch, Dept. of Agriculture, Ottawa, Canada)
"A summary of the financial returns and the cost of producing apples
on 30 orchard farms of Rouville County was presented in the June issue
of this periodical. This article will deal with the cost of marketing
apples, the price of apples, the cash outlay for operating bearing
orchards and man labour requirements on apple crop."

Appraisal Methods, Rural

Hudson, S. C. Some problems in rural appraisal. Econ. Annalist 6(4):
53-55. August 1936. (Published by the Agricultural Economics Branch,
Dept. of Agriculture, Ottawa, Canada)
"The inadequacy of farm appraisal methods has been forcibly demonstrated by the large number of farm mortgage defaults and debt adjustments which have occurred since 1929..."
The article discusses the basis of appraisal and methods of appraisal
of individual farms.

Argentina

Land settlement in B. A. Province. Rev. River Plate 80(2323): 5. June
    19, 1936. (Published in Buenos Aires, Argentina)
        A Decree issued by the Government of the Province of Buenos Aires
    on June 15, 1936 provides for the creation of a committee of coloniza-
    tion to draw up a preliminary draft of a colonization law. The need
    of a workable plan of settlement is pointed out including subdivision
    of the land and its allotment to farmers who will cultivate it themselves.

Beef Subsidy - Great Britain

Addison, Christopher. The beef subsidy failure. New Statesman and Nation
    (n.s.) 12(284): 153-154. Aug. 1, 1936. (Published at 10 Great Turnstile,
    High Holborn, London, W. C. 1, Eng.)
        Critical of the British beef subsidy schemes, past and proposed.
    The article is concluded as follows:
        "What tens of thousands of people want is more meat, not less; and
    our first duty, plainly, is to have a National Import System, divorced
    from self-interest, which is designed so as to see that they get it.
        "The home-producer, in his turn, is entitled to a price system on
    which he can rely, which will foster good production and carry with it
    the condition of the payment of a vastly improved standard of wages.
    In the case of beef, this can only be achieved through a responsibly
    managed Abattoir system which pays the producer his due and eliminates
    the disgraceful increases of cost that characterise present market
    operations.
        "The needs of the consumer can only be met by arrangements that
    make the most advantageous use of all sources of supply. According
    to the present scheme, both the consumer and the taxpayer are made to
    suffer for the inefficiency of the marketing system. A sensible scheme
    would embody in the prices charged the benefits of the imported supplies.
    Whether for home-produced or imported food the people would be asked to
    pay no more than a reasonably managed marketing system requires."

Budget Equalization Fund - Finland

Suviranta, Br. The budget equalisation fund. Nordiska Föreningsbanken
    Unitas. Quarterly Rev. Illustrating Trade Conditions in Finland, no. 3,
    pp. 65-72. August 1936. (Published in Helsingfors, Finland)
        Contains a translation of a Finnish law of November 30, 1934 pro-
    viding for the establishment of a special "Budget equalisation fund."
    It provides for the transfer of surplus amounts in the finance accounts
    of the State to this fund, and for the investment of the fund and its
    use. The limit of the fund is fixed at 500 million marks.
        "Since 1934 several communes have established special funds for
    equalising taxation, which in their nature closely resemble the State
    budget equalisation fund."

Bartlett, R. W. Consumers' income affects dairymen. Hoard's Dairyman
61(14): 370. July 25, 1936. (Published at Fort Atkinson, Wis.)
A short article drawing attention to the similar "up-and-down"
swings in factory payrolls and butter prices in the United States, since
1919, which, according to the author, indicates "the strong influence
that changes in incomes of consumers have had on butter prices."
Charts accompany the article.

Canning Industry - Grades, Standards and Labels

Standards, grades and labels. Bulletin 116A, June 1936, National canners
association. Canning Trade 58(50): 7-8, 18, 20-21. July 20, 1936.
(Published at 20 South Gay St., Baltimore, Md.)
"In this article the National Canners Association answers many requests for information on standards, grades and labels as related to
the canning industry's products."

Cartels - Germany

Kessler, W. C. German cartel regulation under the decree of 1923. Quart.
Jour. Econ. 50(4): 680-693. August 1936. (Published by the Harvard
University Press, Cambridge, Mass.)
This is mainly a discussion of Article 8 of the decree issued by the
Stresemann cabinet directed against the "misuse of economic power.
It is Article 8 which permits cartel members to denounce and with-
draw from cartel agreements for a 'reason of weight' without the usual
period of prior notice (varying usually from six months to two years,
according to the particular cartel). Such a reason would exist when
the 'economic freedom' of the member is 'unfairly' restricted, especially
with regard to 'production, sales or prices.' The cartel has the right
to challenge the withdrawal within two weeks after it has been announced
by applying to a 'Cartel Court.' a body of five, representative of legal
and economic interests, the general public, and the two sides involved.
Its decisions are binding without appeal."

Civil Service - Canada

Dawson, R. M. The Canadian civil service. Canad. Jour. Econ. and Polit.
Sci. 2(3): 288-300. August 1936. (Published by the University of
Toronto Press, Toronto, Ontario)
The author discusses the civil service of today and the developments
which may be hoped for, or guarded against, to-morrow.

Coffee

Martinez de Bujanda, E. The economic aspects of the world problem of the
production and consumption of coffee. Monthly Bull. Agr. Econ. and
Sociol. [reprint from the Internatl. Rev. Agr.] 27(6-7): 186E-197E,
215E-232E. June-July 1936. (Published by the International Institute
of Agriculture, Rome, Italy)

"Contents: I. Coffee in the World Economy: The place of coffee in the world economy. Competing beverages. Distribution of world coffee production. Consumption of coffee in various countries. - II. The Principal Producing Countries: Brasil; Colombia; Venezuela; Guatemala; Salvador; Haiti; Mexico; Costa Rica; Nicaragua and Ecuador; Colonial Countries; Netherlands Indies; British Possessions and Protectorates; French Possessions; Portuguese Possessions; Belgian Congo; other countries. - III. Conclusions: The present situation and the policy to the [?] followed." - p. 186E

Coffee - Brazil

Brazilian coffee situation. Statist 128(3051): 231-232. Aug. 15, 1936. (Published at 51 Cannon St., London, E. C. 4, Eng.)
"The continued difficulties and complexities of the Brazilian coffee situation were again evidenced this year in the delay which occurred in issuing comprehensive regulations for the disposal of the 1936-37 crops, the season for which commenced on July 1 last...
"The new regulations were actually not signed until July 1 last..."
Provisions of the new regulations are given.

Coffee - Costa Rica

S., E. Costa Rica coffee production and trade. Tea & Coffee Trade Jour. 71(2): 95-96. August 1936. (Published at 79 Wall St., New York, N. Y.)
"Review of introduction and development of the product in the Republic, with growth of exports since 1843." A t le gives coffee production in Costa Rica from 1881/82 to 1935/36.

Collective Farming - U.S.S.R.

Maynard, Sir John. Collective farming in the U.S.S.R. Slavonic and East European Rev. 15(43): 47-69. July 1936. (Published by Eyre and Spottiswoode, Ltd., 6, Great New Street, London, E. C. 4, England, for the School of Slavonic and East European Studies in the University of London)
"More than four-fifths of peasant Russia is now enrolled in collective farms of the type known to Russians by the name of artel. There are minor variations of method, but the tendency is for all of these to conform to the model statute promulgated in 1935...Government is the sole proprietor of land: corporations and families have permanent rights of enjoyment, but no rights of leasing and no rights of alienation...agricultural machinery, with rare exceptions, is the property of the Government, and worked by its paid servants. The less important implements are owned by the collective farms or by particular families for use on the allotment or garden land which is in the permanent enjoyment of those families. Other animals, dairy cattle, sheep, goats, pigs, fowls are either held by what we might call subfarms within the collectives...or by particular families on the allotment of garden land."
The events that led up to the Statute of 1935 and the results of collectivization are discussed. There is also a section on rural taxation.

A new charter for consumer organization. Consumers' Guide 3(12): 317,
June 29, 1936. (Published by The Consumers' Counsel of the Agricultural
Adjustment Administration, U. S. Dept. of Agriculture)
Outlines a new plan of organization for local consumer groups which
has been dia n ue by the Consumers' Project in Wasnington.

Cooperation

Bowen, E. R. Christian idealism and the cooperative movement. Christian
Rural Fellowship Bull. no. 12, pp. [1]-4. May 1936. (Published by The
Christian Rural Fellowship, Room 1201, 156 Fifth Ave., New York, N. Y.)
"Paper presented at the annual meeting of the Christian Rural
Fellowship, December 5, 1935."

Cooperative Journal, v. 10, no. 4, pp. 105-128. July-August 1936. (Published by the National Cooperative Council, 1731 Eye St., N. W., Washington, D. C.)
Partial contents: The human equation in cooperation, by C. C.
Teague, pp. 105-107; The advantages and disadvantages of full supply
milk contracts, by B. B. Derrick, pp. 108-110; Financing the cooperative truck, by A. F. Potter, pp. 111-113; Marketing reforms and the
chains, pp. 114-116; A catechism for directors, by J. W. Jones, pp.
117-119.

Cooperation - Baltic States

Rhyn, A. M. The cooperative systems of the Baltic States. Commerce Repts.
no. 36, pp. 717-719. Sept. 5, 1936. (Published by the Bureau of
Foreign and Domestic Commerce, U. S. Dept. of Commerce)

Cooperation - Canada

Chown, W. F. Farmers' business organizations in Canada, 1934. Econ.
Annalist 6(4): 62-64. August 1936. (Published by the Agricultural
Economics Branch, Dept. of Agriculture, Ottawa, Ca. da)
"Agricultural co-operation in Canada for the year 1934 is summarized
in the accompanying tables. During 1935, the Agricultural Economics
Branch received returns from 697 farmers' business organizations that
were active during 1934. This was an increase of 7 over the previous
year."

Cooperation - Denmark

The Danish cooperative system. Commerce Repts. no. 28, pp. 553-554. July
11, 1936. (Published by the Bureau of Foreign and Domestic Commerce,
U. S. Dept. of Commerce)
"Prepared in the Division of Regional Information from reports re-
ceived from the American consulate and commercial attaché's office in
Copenhagen."

Cooperation - Egypt

Olberg, Paul. Co-operation in the country of the Nile. Rev. Internatl.
    Coop. 29(8): 304-307. August 1936. (Published at Orchard House,
    14, Great Smith Street, London, S. W. 1, Eng.)

Cooperation - Finland

Rhyn, A. M. The Finnish cooperative system. Commerce Repts. no. 29, pp.
    572-573. July 18, 1936. (Published by the Bureau of Foreign and Domestic
    Commerce, U. S. Dept. of Commerce)
        A review, based on authoritative sources, of consumers' cooperatives,
    agricultural production and sales cooperatives, cooperatives in the
    lumber industry, cooperative credit societies, other cooperatives, and
    the Pellervo Society.

Cooperation - Norway

Rhyn, A. M. Norwegian cooperative system. Commerce Repts. no. 30, pp.
    582-583. July 25, 1936. (Published by the Bureau of Foreign and
    Domestic Commerce, U. S. Dept. of Commerce)
        A review of the Norwegian cooperative system, based on authoritative
    sources - consumers' cooperatives, agricultural production and sales
    cooperatives, agricultural purchasing societies, cooperative banking,
    and other cooperatives.

Cooperation - Palestine

Guelfat, Isaac. A survey of the cooperative movement in Palestine. Rev.
    Internatl. Coop. 29(8): 299-303. August 1936. (Published at Orchard
    House, 14, Great Smith Street, London, S.W.1, Eng.)

Cooperation - Sweden

Rhyn, A. M. Swedish agricultural cooperatives. Commerce Repts., no. 33,
    pp.658-659. Aug. 15, 1936. (Published by the Bureau of Foreign and
    Domestic Commerce, U. S. Department of Commerce)
        This article supplements the review of Swedish consumers' coopera-
    tives which appeared in Commerce Reports, June 13, 1936.
        Describes agricultural production and sales cooperatives, agricul-
    tural purchasing societies, other agricultural cooperatives, agri-
    cultural credit   . cooperatives and fishery cooperatives.

Swedish cooperative union. Prepared in the Division of Regional Information
    from reports submitted by Consul General Walter A. Leonard and Trade
    Commissioner Basil D. Dahl. Commerce Repts. no. 24, pp. 472-473.
    June 13, 1936. (Published by the Bureau of Foreign and Domestic Com-
    merce, U. S. Dept. of Commerce)
        Gives information on statistics of consumers' societies of Sweden,
    cooperative purchasing and cooperative production in the Cooperative
    Union of Sweden, banking facilities and disposition of reserve funds
    in the Cooperative Union, the International Coöperative Purchasing
    Society, life and fire insurance companies owned by the Union, coopera-
    tive housing, and the Svenska Hushallsforeningen (The Swedish House-
    hold Society).

Cooperation, Consumers

Fowler, B. B. The coops' challenge to business. Rev. of Reviews 94(1):
44-47. July 1936. (Published at 233 Fourth Ave., New York, N. Y.)
The writer points out that the cooperation of consumers in opening
new channels of distribution, and in the purchasing and manufacturing
of goods, offers a challenge to orthodox business in a dozen basic
fields. He writes in conclusion: "Let no business man delude himself.
The figures of cooperative growth, the appearance of the cooperative
stores, filling stations, farm supply depots, insurance companies, and
buying clubs represent a declaration of economic liberty by consumers.
It is a technique worked out by the people challenging the methods by
which business has been run for years. The only way in which business
men can meet the challenge is by working out better techniques of distribution."

Corporate Bodies Lands Act – Bermuda

Bermuda – Corporate Bodies Lands Act. Commerce Repts. no. 33, p. 647.
Aug. 15, 1936. (Published by the Bureau of Foreign and Domestic Commerce, U. S. Department of Commerce)
"The Corporate Bodies Lands Act, 1936, of Bermuda provides that every
body corporate whether incorporated in the islands or elsewhere, now
seized or possessed, of any land, shall within 6 months after the act
comes into operation, or after the land shall have been acquired, deposit in the registry of the Supreme Court a memorandum in writing
setting forth the situation, area, and boundaries of such land, together with a copy of a section of the ordnance map showing the location
thereof. Every body corporate selling any land in the islands must
within 1 month of the sale, deposit a similar written memorandum."

Cost of Living – Czechoslovakia

La consommation des familles des agriculteurs indépendants en 1934.
Czechoslovakia. Institut de Comptabilité et d'Économie Rurales.
Rapports, Année 7, no. 1. 1936. (Published in Prague, Czechoslovakia)
Tables show the cost of living of farm families in 1934.

Cottage Industries – India

Cottage industries and cooperation. Indian Co-op. Rev. 2(2): 179-242.
April 1936. (Published at Farhatbagh, Mylapore, Madras, India)
A number of articles have been contributed on the general theme of
cottage industries and cooperation. They are: Cottage industries and
co-operation, by K. S. Rao.–pp.179-185; Co-operation and cottage industries in Binar and Orissa, by B. B. Mukherjee. –pp.186-190; Handloom
industry in Madras, by R. Suryanaroyana Rao. – pp.191-197; Cottage
industries and co-operation in the Bombay Presidency, by Vaikunth L.
Mehta. – pp.198-208; Cottage industries in the United Provinces, by
B. Mukherjee. – pp.209-221; An experiment in industrial co-operation in
the United Provinces, by Mohammad Huzur Alain. – pp.222-223; Co-operation

and cottage industries in the Punjab, by Khan Mohammad Bashir Ahmad Khan. - pp.224-238; Co-operation and the Punjab handloom industry, by Khan Nafis-ud-Din Ahmad. - pp.239-242.

Cotton

Agelasto, A. M., and Whitaker, Rodney.   The cotton situation. Agr. Situation 20(7): 4-8. July 1, 1936. (Published by Bureau of Agricultural Economics, U. S. Dept. of Agriculture)
    Production, consumption, stocks, and prices of American and foreign cotton and production of synthetic fibers are discussed.

Geller, Carl. Why cotton has boomed. Increasing speculative interest – prices still moderate –outlook bullish. Com. and Finance 25(15): 535, 548. July 25, 1936. (Published at 95 Broad St., New York, N. Y.)

Mann, A. J. Widespread crop guessing seen as return to 'normalcy' in cotton. Com. and Finance 25(16): 587-588. Aug. 8, 1936. (Published at 95 Broad St., New York, N. Y.)

Vance, R. B.   Changing economy of the southeast. Occupations 14(6): 509-514. March 1936. (Published by National Occupational Conference, 551 Fifth Avenue, New York, N. Y.)
    Address at conference on vocational guidance and education for Negroes at Atlanta University, December 9-14, 1935.
    Effect of the Government's policy of control of cotton production on the population of the Cotton Belt is discussed.

Cotton – British Empire

Currie, Sir James.   Empire cotton production: a review of progress. Empire Cotton Growing Rev. 13(3): 171-177. July 1936. (Published at 14, Great Smith St., London, S. W. 1, Eng.)

Cotton - Italy

Mooney, Booth. [Italy and cotton] Tex. Weekly 12(35): 3. Aug. 29, 1936. (Published at the Dallas Athletic Club Bldg., Dallas, Tex.)
    Editorial, part of which is devoted to the discussion of the efforts of the Italian government to provide its own cotton by cultivating cotton in Ethiopia. The opinion is expressed that Italy found it "extremely difficult" to obtain the means of paying us for cotton, and chiefly because of "trade barriers like our high tariff,...is seeking an area in which it can grow its own cotton."

Cotton Industry – China

Ting, L. G.   Recent developments in China's cotton industry. Nankai Social & Econ. Quart. 9(2): 398-445. July 1936. (Published by Nankai Institute of Economics, Nankai University, Tientsin, China)
    "This paper will be presented at the Sixth Conference of the Institute of Pacific Relations to be held at Yosemite, California, August 15-29, 1936."

The author presents a review of the more important changes that have
taken place in China's cotton industry and deduces therefrom some of
the lines of its probable future development. "The study...will view
the issues primarily from the stand-point of the Chinese-owned section
of the industry, but at pertinent points, comparative data and information about the foreign-owned mills will also be given."

The cotton industry under the depression is studied under the
following topics: The nature and the course of the crisis, and attempts
at reconstruction. This is followed by a discussion of the increase in
China's cotton production, cotton improvement, the movement against
adulteration, and the rôle of the cotton co-operatives. On the industrial side, the author deals with the geographical diffusion of
mills, the tendency toward vertical integration, spinning of finer
counts, and the promotion of mill efficiency.

Cotton Linters

Burrow, A. K. Cotton linters. Bedding Manfr. 32(6): ., 22-24, 26. July
    1936. (Published by the Better Bedding Alliance of America, 608 S.
    Dearborn St., Chicago, Ill.)
    History, production, consumption, uses and grades of linters are
    discussed.

Cotton Picking Machine

Cotton picker portents. Business Week, no. 366, p.15. Sept. 5, 1936.
    (Published at 330 West 42nd St., New York, N. Y.)
    Describes the demonstration of the cotton picker in Mississippi,
    as well as the machine itself. It is held that the "significance of
    the invention ranges from the world-empire of cotton to our domestic
    social set-up."
    According to this article the Rust brothers do not intend to sell
    any of their pickers, except to Russia, which has already taken two
    machines. Markets for the machine are already opening up. "Four
    machines will be used this fall at Clover Hills, a motorized Mississippi
    plantation." The rates at which the pickers will be leased are given.

Dickinson, Roy. Men and machines. The Rust brothers of Memphis propose
    an advertising question that demands an answer. Printers' Ink 174(12):
    17, 20-21. Mar. 19, 1936. (Published at 185 Madison Ave., New York, N.Y.)
    "Undoubtedly in our present problem the answer to unemployment is not
    to smash the machine itself, to refuse to make any new inventions, but
    to have men interested in purchasing power do some intelligent and far-
    reaching research...Certainly men create machines to serve and not to
    enslave them. With better thinking on the part of the owners, machines
    can be made to perform the true function for which they are so eminently
    fitted."

The machine invades the cotton field. U. S. News 4(36): 11. Sept. 7, 1936.
(Published at 2201 M St., N. W., Washington, D. C.)
Describes the cotton picker invented by the Rust Brothers, and its
first public demonstration near Stoneville, Miss., "last week." Comment
of Oscar Johnston on the operation of the machine is given.
John W. Taylor comments on the possibilities of the picker on p. 10,
his remarks appearing under the caption: "South's New Problem. Cotton
Picking Machine: Threat or Promise?"

Straus, R. K. Enter the cotton picker; the story of the Rust brothers'
invention. Harpers' Mag. 173(1036): 386-395. September 1936. (Published
at 49 E. 33rd St., New York, N. Y.)
Sketches the history and background of the Rust brothers' cotton
picker, discussing the Rust brothers' hopes for the machine, cost of
operation, and possible economic and social consequences.

Crop Insurance

Crop insurance: proposed plan to achieve ever-normal granary. U. S. News
4(31): 6. Aug. 3, 1936. (Published at 2201 M St., N. W., Washington, D.C.)
A discussion of a Federal crop insurance plan for achieving the ever-
normal granary goal of Secretary Wallace.

Reaction of press to crop insurance. U. S. News 4(35): 10. Aug. 31, 1936.
(Published at 2201 M St., N. W., Washington, D. C.)
"Proposed plan of crop insurance, by which farmers would pay the
premiums with their surplus, is favorably viewed by 62 percent of commenting newspapers but in the judgment of 38 percent the program would
prove unworkable because of the cost."

Dairy Industry - Insurance - New Zealand

Insurance for dairy industry. New Zeal. Dairy Exporter 11(11): 12, 13, 14, 15.
June 1, 1936. (Published at P. O. Box 1001, Wellington, New Zeal.)
"At the 1935 National Dairy Conference a committee was set up to
go into the question of insurance for the dairy industry, it being considered that great savings in premiums could be effected...Its report
will be placed before Conference this month. This article deals briefly
with the main points of the report and indicates the method proposed
for the development of a mutual insurance scheme for the dairy industry."
An article in the July 1 issue of the Exporter, p. 14, states that
the report was adopted by the Conference.

Dairy Industry - Japan

Dairying industry in Japan. Primary Producer 21(23): 5. June 4, 1936.
(Published at 38-40-42-44 Stirling St., Perth, Western Australia)
Describes the steps taken by the Japanese Government to encourage
the dairy industry, and the results of these efforts. The number of
dairy farmers in Japan "increased from 18,000 in 1927 to 25,000 in 1933,
and the number of dairy cattle from 70,700 to 87,000. During the same

period the output of milk rose from 38,870,000 gallons to 56,229,000 gallons, so that as well as the natural increase in production due to the greater number of cattle, there was also an increase in the yield per cow."

Doctoral Dissertations

Thirty-third list of doctoral dissertations in political economy in progress in American universities and colleges. Amer. Econ. Rev. 26(3): 581-600. September 1936. (Published by the American Economic Association, Northwestern University, Evanston, Ill.)
    Agriculture, mining, forestry, and fisheries, pp. 584-586.

Drought - Southwestern Manitoba

Ellis, J. H., Shafer, W. H., and Caldwell, O. G.   The recent drought situation in southwestern Manitoba. Sci. Agr. 16(9): 478-488.   May 1936. (Publisher's address; Box 625, Ottawa, Canada)
    "In conclusion it may be stated that the drought in Southwestern Manitoba appears to be over for the present. The records of precipitation during the past fifty years, show quite forcibly that drought periods are sure to occur again at irregular intervals. If these drought periods are of short duration, the practices outlined above will enable the farm operator to combat the short drought periods; but, as the drought periods may be of long duration, it is also of first importance that reserves of feed, seed, and money should be carried over from the good years, as an insurance against being compelled to resort to public relief. Finally, the land values should be adjusted and farming operations financed, not on the expectancy of the exceptional good years (that will occur again as in the past), but on the expectancy of the 50-year average which in Southwestern Manitoba is approximately 15.7 bushels of wheat per acre."

Drought - United States

Kincher, J. B. Droughts in the United States. Canning Trade 59(3): 7, 26. Aug. 24, 1936. (Published at 20 South Gay St., Baltimore, Md.)
    A discussion of long-time and transitory droughts, their causes, etc.

Mullen, W. H. The farm market and the drought. High prices offsetting smaller crop yields, giving farmers revenues which compare favorably with returns from larger 1935 harvest. Barron's 16(29): 7. July 20, 1936. (Published at 44 Broad St., New York, N. Y.)

Drought Stricken States

Drummond, W. I.   Dust bowl. Rev. of Reviews 93(6): 37-40. June 1936. (Published at 233 Fourth Ave., New York, N. Y.)
    A description of the short grass country - "where dry years and high winds speed the errant soil, and only Nature can bring relief to stout-hearted Dust Bowl farmers."
    In the concluding part of the article the author discussed control projects. It is conceded that strip farming, cover crops, cross-listing

and rough cultivation will to a large extent prevent soil blowing.
The writer holds, however, that nature can and probably will remedy
the situation if man will give her a chance. "The winds that move
the soil carry with it large quantities of grass seed, and comparatively
little of the heavier weed seeds. This grass seed now is mixed with the
blown soil. It will sprout when it has moisture, and become stablished
when the winds subside, as they do in seasons of more than average
precipitation. Such seasons undoubtedly will recur. This is a natural
and not a new procedure. The grass cover we have seen destroyed was
surely formed in that way. I believe it will be done again."

Economic Conditions - Germany

Zi.   A brief survey of Germany's recent economic development. Hamburg
       World Econ. Archives. Bull. 2(15): 3-6. June 1, 1936. (Published by
       Welt-Wirtschafts-Archiv, Poststrasse 19, Hamburg 36, Germany)
           The author reports on Germany's grain and potato supplies, vege-
       table-growing in Germany, development in the requirements for agricul-
       tural machinery, the German cheese market, the necessary re-distribution
       of land holdings, and wood-cutting in German forests.

Zimmermann,F. F.   Deutschland. Allgemeiner agrarpolitischer bericht.
       Berichte über Landwirtschaft (n.F.) 20(4): 594-605. 1936. (Issued by
       [Germany] Reichs- und Pr. Ministerium für Ernährung u. Landwirtschaft.
       Published by P. Parey. Berlin)
           In a general summary of agricultural economic conditions in Germany
       the author discusses briefly the organization and general situation
       of the Reichsnährstand, the progress of the production campaign, the
       fat situation, market organization, and land settlement.

Economic Council - Rumania

Hibbard, F. P.   Rumania's new superior economic council. Comparative Law
       Series, C. L. No. 586, pp. 13-15. August 1936. (Issued by Division of
       Commercial Laws, Bureau of Foreign and Domestic Commerce, U. S. Dept.
       of Commerce)
           A law, promulgated and published in Rumania's Monitorul Oficial of
       April 29, 1936, provides for the creation of a Superior Economic Coun-
       cil to advise the Government on all projects of law of an economic,
       financial or social nature and to suggest "solutions of problems re-
       garding foreign commerce, the valorization of agricultural products,
       the regulation of labor as well as any other economic, financial or
       social problems...The organization of agriculture will be effected by
       the establishment of (1) communal agricultural committees, (2) Chambers
       of Agriculture and (3) the Union of Chambers of Agriculture."

Employment and Unemployment - Germany

Arbeitslosigkeit und beschäftigung im sommer 1936. Institut für Konjunktur-
       forschung. Wochenbericht 9(33): 129-131. Aug. 19, 1936. (Published by
       Hanseatische Verlagsanstalt, Hamburg 36, Germany)
           A study of employment and unemployment in Germany shows that by the
       end of July 1936 unemployment had decreased by 80,000 since the end of

July 1929, and that there were less than 1 1/2 millions of unemployed. At the same time there is a lack of agricultural workers and skilled workers.

L'Est Européen Agricole

L'Est Européen Agricole, 5. année, no. 17, April 1936. (Issued by the Comité Permanent d'Études Économiques des États Agricoles de l'Europe Centrale et Orientale. Published by Librairie Jouve & Cie. 15, Rue Racine, Paris, France)

Partial contents: La répartition des excédents de céréales en Europe, by L. Feierabend. - pp.7-20. (Urges the need of a permanent regional office for central and eastern Europe for the organization and export of grain.); Le problème du surpeuplement dans l'agriculture polonaise, by J. Poniatowski. - pp.21-60. (An account of the origin and the history of excessive agricultural population of Poland shows that this is a condition to be reckoned with seriously. Overpopulation is more acute in Poland than in any other country of Europe and it has considerable powers of development. The author recommends the adoption of all possible means to alleviate the effects of overpopulation except deliberate limitation of natural growth.); Pologne. L'enseigne-ment agricole, by S. Miklaszewski. - pp. 61-96. (A survey of agricultural instruction in Poland.); L'accord polono-belge et son importance pour les exportations agricoles de la Pologne, by S. Leszczynski. - pp. 97-104. (A discussion of the effect on Poland's export of agricultural products of the Polish-Belgian commercial agreement signed in Brussels on March 2, 1936, to remain in effect until December 31, 1936.); Tchécoslovaquie. La coopération agricole, by A. Hulka. - pp.105-127. (An account of the organization of agricultural cooperation in Czechoslovakia, of the different types of cooperatives, and of efforts made by them to ameliorate conditions due to the depression); Tchécoslovaquie. Réglementation du taux de l'intérêt et facilités accordées aux agriculteurs pour le paiement des créances, by V. Leština. -pp. 128-140. (A discussion of the provisions of two decrees of December 21, 1935, the one fixing a maximum interest rate, and the other providing facilities for the payment of farmers' debts.) Contains also statistical tables showing imports and exports of Latvia, Poland, Hungary, and Czechoslovakia, and prices of agricultural products in Poland and Hungary.

Fairbridge Farm Schools

West, A. G. B. The Fairbridge model. Nineteenth Century and After 120(714): 193-201. August 1936. (Published at Orange St., Leicester Square, London, W. C. 2, Eng.)

A description of the Fairbridge Farm Schools, which were established in Australia some twenty-five years ago. Boys and girls at the ages of ten or eleven are educated here until they reach seventeen. A second school has been founded in Vancouver and preparations for further schools in New South Wales and Queensland are being made. The schools are mainly for children of the unemployed or otherwise underprivileged.

Fats - Sweden

Bonow, Mauritz. Developments in Swedish production of margarine, 1919-1935.
Rev. Internatl. Coop. 29(7):249-255. July 1936. (Published at Orchard
House, 14, Great Smith Street, London, S. W. 1, Eng.)
Tables show production of margarine and average price per kilogram
to producer from 1919 to 1929, production, consumption and retail prices
of butter and margarine, 1925 to 1934, and cost of consumption of cooking
fats from 1925 to 1934.

Fertilizer

Gray, A. N. Fertiliser production and consumption during the world crisis -
1929-1934. La Technique Agricole Internationale 6(2): 81-92. April-
June, 1936. (Published by the Fédération Internationale des Techniciens
Agronomes, 86, Via Regina Elena, Rome, Italy)

Frontier Economy - Southwestern Pennsylvania

Buck, S. J. Frontier economy in southwestern Pennsylvania. Agr. Hist.
10(1): 14-24. January 1936. (Published by the Agricultural History
Society, Room 3901, South Bldg., 13th St., and Independence Ave.,
Washington, D. C.)
"An address read before the joint meeting of the Agricultural History
Society and the American Historical Association at Chattanooga, Tenn.,
on December 27, 1935."

Government, County

Cordell, William, and Cordell, Kathryn. Taxpayer, meet your county. Survey
Graphic 25(8): 463-466, 490. August 1936. (Published at 112 E. 19th
St., New York, N. Y.)
Reviews steps being taken in different parts of the United States in
an attempt to increase efficiency and decrease the cost of county government. One of the steps considered is the adoption of the county manager
form of government. Henrico County, Virginia, is cited as an exhibit of
the success of this form of county government. Another step is county
consolidation which has been undertaken notably in Tennessee and Georgia.
North Carolina and Virginia have sought to reform county government by
giving the state administrative control over certain functions such as
roads and schools.

Government, Rural - Reconstruction - China

Chang, C. M. A new government for rural China: the political aspect of
rural reconstruction. Nankai Social & Econ. Quart. 9(2):239-295.
July 1936. (Published by Nankai Institute of Economics, Nankai University,
Tientsin, China.)
"This paper will be presented at the Sixth Conference of the Institute of Pacific Relations to be held at Yosemite, California, August
15-29, 1936."
"In the following pages we attempt to give a brief survey of the problems confronting the hsien government together with some proposed reforms."

Government Control - Great Britain

Comstock, Alzada. Government control: John Bull's way. Lays heavy hand
  on industry and agriculture, especially textiles and coal. Policy
  of interference has majority of British public support, too. Barron's
  16(29): 9, 10. July 20, 1936. (Published at 44 Broad St., New York, N.Y.)

Holdings - Type-classification of - Scotland

Senior, W. H. Farm economics in Scotland - the value of a type-classification of holdings. Scot. Jour. Agr. 19(3): 258-264. July 1936. (Published by H. M. Stationery Office, Edinburgh, Scotland)
    A brief exposition of the method of obtaining a deta·led statistical
  classification of the different types of farms in Scotland such as has
  been undertaken in the Border country. The value of such an investigation is pointed out.

Income, Farm - Germany

Produktion und verkaufserlöse in der landwirtschaft. Erfolge der erzeugungs-
  schlacht. Institut für Konjunkturforschung. Wochenbericht 9(32): 125-
  128. Aug. 12, 1936. (Published by Hanseatische Verlagsanstalt,
  Hamburg 36, Germany)
    A study of production and sales returns of agricultural products in
  Germany, illustrated by charts and tables. A table shows the annual
  returns from sales of separate products from 1930/31 to 1935/36, showing an increase since 1932/33. The value of agricultural production
  for the years 1928/29 to 1935/36 and index numbers for 1924/25 to 1935/36
  are given.

Income, Farm - Illinois, Iowa and Indiana

Deslarzes, Joseph. Social income of farms in three states of the United
  States of America (Illinois, Iowa, Indiana) in 1932-33. Monthly Bull.
  Agr. Econ. and Sociol. [reprint from Internatl. Rev. Agr. 27(7): 203E-
  216E. July 1936. (Published by the International Institute of Agriculture, Rome, Italy)
    Tables as follows are included: Table I.-- Gross return, farm ex-
  penses, social income in 1932-33 (in gold francs per ha.); Table II. -
  Percentage composition of the social income in 1932-33; Table III. -
  The percentage composition of the social income in 1932-33 in some
  regions of the United States and in Europe.

Income, Farm - Northwestern United States

Northwest farm income over half billion in first six months this year.
  Com. West 72(9): 8. Aug. 29, 1936. (Published at 445 Rand Tower, New
  York, N. Y.)
    Contains a summary of the cash farm income from crops and livestock
  in the six states of the Northwest for the first six months of 1936.
  "The Northwest is coming through this year with one of the largest
  volumes of cash farm income in its history. Between January 1 and June
  30 it was $620,563,000 from crops, livestock, dairying and other live-

stock products alone – at the rate of $3,400,000 a day."

It is also stated that as a whole this area "is far better off... than it was in 1934."

Income, Farm – United States

Case, W. W. Cash farm income by Federal reserve districts: New regional rural indices. Annalist 48(1224): 4-5. July 3, 1936. (Published by the New York Times Co., Times Square, New York, N. Y.)

"This is the fifth of a series of regional studies."

"Cash farm income is a significant indicator of rural prosperity and purchasing power. Hence, the addition of the present group of regional indices of cash farm income to the other regional series previously published by the Annalist is of interest not only to merchandising enterprises, like the mail-order companies that are directly dependent on the farmers' purchases, but to all organizations in any way affected by the condition of the agricultural half of the country."

Income, National – United States

Stern, Laurence. How real is the gain in national income? Fifty three billion for last year represents large gain over former years. Mag. Wall St. 58(8): 458-459. Aug. 1, 1936. (Published at 90 Broad St., New York, N. Y.)

Compares the gain in the national income in the recovery from the depression of 1920-1921 and during the New Deal administration.

Index of Business Activity

The state of trade. The Economist, trade supplement, n.s. no. 158, 12 pp. July 25, 1936. (Published at 8, Bouverie St., London, E. C. 4, Eng.)

"With this issue our Index of Business Activity appears calculated on a new base (1935 – 100). Details will be found in subsequent pages and, in place of our usual monthly graph, readers will find overleaf a chart of the Index from 1924 to date." – Note on p. 1.

Inheritance Tax Returns – Germany

Zawadzki, C. T. German inheritance tax returns. Comparative Law Series, C. L. no. 586, pp. 47-50. August 1936. (Issued by Division of Commercial Laws, Bureau of Foreign and Domestic Commerce, U. S. Dept. of Commerce)

An account of the German inheritance tax returns for 1934 showing the categories of estates taxes, the tax rates, the returns according to values of estates, values of inherited estates and inheritance tax returns according to inheritance tax classes, and inheritance tax returns classified according to values of the inherited estates.

Journal of Farm Economics

Journal of Farm Economics, v. 18, no. 3, pp. 453-644. August 1936. (Published by the American Farm Economic Association, Asher Hobson, Secretary-Treasurer, University of Wisconsin, Madison, Wis.)

Contents: Production and control in agriculture and industry, by
V. R. Benedict, pp. 453-468; Agricultural adjustment and farm tenure,
by D. W. Watkins, pp. 469-476; Rural zoning: Controlling land utilization under the police power, by C. I. Hendrickson, pp. 477-492;
Migration required for best land use, by B. W. Allin, pp. 493-499;
Planning location of hard roads and electric lines, by T. E. LaMont,
pp. 500-507; Enactment and administration of rural county zoning ordinances, by G. S. Wehrwein, pp. 508-522; An approach to the grading of
land for purposes of appraisal, by C. H. Hammar, pp. 523-532; Land
utilization in Nova Scotia, by W. V. Longley, pp. 533-542; Irrigation
policies and programs in the Northern Great Plains region, by S. E.
Johnson, pp. 543-555; Argentine experience with farm relief measures,
by S. G. Hanson, pp. 556-567; Mortgage adjustment and the re-organization
of farm finance in New Zealand, by Horace Belshaw, pp. 568-586; Cotton
gins as public utilities in Oklahoma, by R. A. Ballinger, pp. 587-596;
Covariance used to analyze the relation between corn yield and acreage,
by Gertrude M. Cox, and G. W. Snedecor, pp. 597-607.
    In addition to the papers listed above the following "Notes" are
given: Farm credit research in the FCA, by W. G. Murray, pp. 608-610;
The 1936 agricultural census of the Provinces of Manitoba, Saskatchewan
and Alberta, by O. A. Lemieux, pp. 610-612; Economic status of tenure
groups in Tallapoosa and Chambers counties, Alabama, by B. F. Alvord,
pp. 613-616; A review of the oleomargarine situation, by Harry
Trelogan, pp. 616-621.

Labor - Scotland

Report of the Committee on farm workers in Scotland. Scot. Jour. Agr.
    19(3): 265-267. July 1936. (Published by H. M. Stationery Office,
    Edinburgh, Scotland)
    The main recommendations which have been made by the Committee ap-
pointed in January, 1936 "to examine the existing system of employment
and remuneration of farm workers in Scotland...are outlined. The Committee survey the present position of the farm worker in Scotland,
showing how he is affected by the existing methods of engagement, by
unemployment, by the 'tied' house system and by the lack of machinery
for adjusting wages, hours of labour and other conditions of employment."

Labor, Indian - Ceylon

Indian labour in Ceylon in 1934. Internatl. Labour Rev. 34(1): 93-96.
    July 1936. (Published by the International Labour Office, Geneva, Switzer-
    land. Distributed in U.S. by the World Peace Foundation, 8 West 40th
    St., New York, N. Y.)
    "Indian labour in Ceylon is mainly employed on plantations. Of the
three principal estate crops grown in the Island, tea is worked by
Indian labour almost entirely, and rubber for the greater part. A few
Indians are also employed on cocoanut estates, but the latter mostly
rely on local Sinhalese labour. Indian non-estate labourers are found
particularly in Colombo, where they are employed principally as
stevedore coolies or in the coal yards and marine engineering works.
At the end of 1934, when the estimated total population of Ceylon was
5,637,200, Indians numbered about 800,000, 688,700 of whom were living
on the estates."

Labor and the W.P.A.

Gill, Corrington. WPA replies to farm critics. Says men will be released
     from rolls for seasonal work but not in glut numbers. [New York, 1936]
     Processed. Reprint Coll.
          "Reprinted from the New York Times, Sunday, July 26, 1936."

Labor Unrest - United States

Stark, Louis.   Labor disputes are likely to increase, with important
     political repercussions. Annalist 48(1226): 72-73. July 17, 1936.
     (Published by the New York Times Co., Times Square, New York, N. Y.)
          "There are signs of labor troubles among the migratory workers who
     harvest the crops in the Western States, Among these workers some A.F. of
     L. unions have been formed and there is still a remnant of the I.W.W.
     spirit among them. The usual demands are for higher wages, clean
     living quarters and adequate water."

Land Settlement - Australia

Rural bank chief on closer settlement. The Land, no. 1310 (i.e. 1309), p.8.
     July 17, 1936. (Published in Sydney, Australia)
          Reviews an address "on the possibilities of agricultural expansion
     in relation to closer settlement", by the president of the Rural Bank,
     Mr. C. R. McKerihan, at the 1936 Agricultural Bureau Conference held at
     Richmond.
          Mr. McKerihan is reported as saying that closer settlement "must not
     be taken to mean mere subsistence farming which would support the farmer
     but give him no adequate standard of life. It should enable people to
     produce not merely for their own subsistence but for a market to an ex-
     tent which would allow them to enjoy standards of life similar to those
     enjoyed by other sections of the community."
          Mr. McKerihan also said "that the three problems of marketing,
     migration, and closer settlement were closely related in practice."

Land Settlement - Australia, New Zealand and Canada

Tait, D. C.   Migration and settlement in Australia, New Zealand, and Canada.
     Internatl. Labour Rev. 34(1): 34-65. July 1936. (Published by the
     International Labour Office, Geneva, Switzerland. Distributed in U. S.
     by the World Peace Foundation, 8 West 40th St., New York, N. Y.)
          "The following article is one of a series of articles on migration and
     settlement problems, of which a number have already been published in
     the Review. It deals with the situation in Australia, New Zealand and
     Canada. After showing the numerical importance of the movement of
     migrants and sketching briefly the historical development of migration
     in those Dominions, the author explains how the policy of Empire settle-
     ment agreed upon with the British Government at the Imperial Conference
     of 1921 has worked out, and points out certain lessons to be learnt as to
     the best methods of promoting land settlement and development. Reference
     is also made to the large immigration into Canada from continental Europe.
     In conclusion, the author examines the possibility of migration and settle-
     ment in the future in the light of the present economic situation,

and suggests that less stress should, perhaps, be laid on land settlement and more on migration for industrial employment."

Land Settlement - Buenos Aires

Land settlement in B. A. Province. Rev. River Plate 80(2323): 5. June 19,
1936. (Published in Buenos Aires, Argentina)
    A Decree issued by the Government of the Province of Buenos Aires
on June 15, 1936 provides for the creation of a committee of colonization to draw up a preliminary draft of a colonization law. The need
of a workable plan of settlement is pointed out including subdivision
of the land and its allotment to farmers who will cultivate it themselves.

Land Settlement - Manchuria

Mongols settle. Manchurian Econ. Rev. 3(16): 5-6. Aug. 15, 1936. (Published by G. Harmsen, Harbin, Manchoukuo)
    A brief account of an attempt to settle the nomadic Mongols on the
land which has resulted in the settlement of about 1,000 Mongolians in
East Hsingan Province and the cultivation of 250 ha of land, bringing
the total area under cultivation to 500 ha. It is planned to settle
300 more Mongolians next year.

Land Settlement - Switzerland

The Swiss Government and colonisation schemes. Indus. and Labour Inform.
59(6): 196-197. Aug. 10, 1936. (Published by International Labour
Office, Geneva, Switzerland. Distributed in United States by World
Peace Foundation, 8 West 40th Street, New York, N. Y.)
    An order issued by the Federal Assembly on June 20, 1936 grants
a credit of one million francs to assist qualified Swiss citizens
to emigrate to oversea countries, and a credit of one million francs
for the development of internal settlement and to assist qualified
Swiss citizens to emigrate to European countries.

Land Settlement and Resettlement - United States

Aikman, Duncan. "Tugwelltown" - which, of course, is the story of Greenbelt, the Government's new socialized community - a daring experiment,
impartially described. Current Hist. 44(5): 97-101. August 1936.
(Published at 63 Park Row, New York, N. Y.)
    "The crux of the Resettlement Administration's civic development
project in Greenbelt lies in the fact that the town is being built
as a refuge for modest income groups from high urban rental values.
Greenbelt itself will cost approximately $7,000,000 - a fairly
moderate outlay for a town of 1,000 houses, with adequate shopping
district, civic service, and recreational facilities... each house
will rent for between $20 and $30 monthly...Greenbelt is being built
for District of Columbia families which, if they tried to live in
Washington's congested area, would have to take either a slum tenement
or a one-room-and-kitchenette flat, and which, in the more spacious
residential districts, could find no accommodations at all within
their purse limits."

McNamara, Katherine, and Wehrly, M. S.   A selected list of planned communities in the United States. Planners' Jour. 2(4): 106-112. July-
August 1936. (Published by American City Planning Institute, Hunt Hall,
Cambridge, Mass.)
      "Based on material gathered in the course of a research on Planned
Communities, being conducted by the Harvard School of City Planning for
the National Resources Committee." - footnote.
      These communities "have, in general, incorporated planning principles
in their design, and are representative rather than qualitative in
character. The reference accompanying each development has been confined
to a book or a periodical article, selected on the basis of the information contained therein and the relative ease with which it may be secured."
      Towns and references are grouped under the following headings: Towns
founded by private industry which were forerunners of later pre-planned
communities; Industrial communities developed as town-sites by private
industry; Suburban areas developed by private industry for employees;
Residential communities planned as town-sites by private interests;
Projects developed as town-sites by governmental agencies; Miscellaneous
developments of interest.

Milk toast: With pint bottles, resettled needleworkers drink health of
homesteads. Lit. Digest 122(7): 6-7. Aug. 15, 1936. (Published at
354 Fourth Ave., New York, N. Y.)
      Describes the Jersey Homesteads, near Hightstown, N. J., the Resettle-
ment Administration's first industrial-agricultural cooperative.

Taylor, P. S.   From the ground up. Survey Graphic 25(9): 526-529, 537, 538.
September 1936. (Published at 112 E. 19th St., New York, N. Y.)
      "An informal description of demonstration projects of the Resettlement
Administration on the West Coast."

Wehrwein, G. S., and Baker, J. A.   Relocation of non-conforming land users
of the zoned counties in Wisconsin. Jour. Land & Pub. Utility Econ.
12(3): 248-255. August 1936. (Published by Northwestern University,
School of Commerce, 337 East Chicago Ave., Chicago, Ill.)
      "Relocation of stranded settlers on submarginal land is a worthy
enterprise whether the area is zoned or not zoned. However, it is of
more importance and lasting benefit where zoning has preceded resettlement. In Wisconsin, the purchase of less than 200,000 acres of land now
owned by non-conforming users would remove all agriculture from almost
5,000,000 acres of land. Zoning will insure these restricted districts
against a repetition of the mistakes of the past. If, in addition,
relocation is carried out in some systematic way as suggested above, it
will result in immediate reduction of public costs with the least hardship to the settlers themselves. However, every relocation must be
voluntary; no settler will be coerced into selling his farm. If the
settler representing 'the most extravagant case of governmental expense'
refuses to sell but others who have merely lost their market are willing
to be relocated, the first to be resettled will be sixth in order of
priority as set up by the Land Use Advisory Committee. All this points
to a long-time program administered with tact and an understanding of
the psychology of the people living in 'pioneer fringes.'"

Land Tenure - Southern States

Lewis, E. E.   Some pre-depression land tenure changes in the South and
    their current significance. Amer. Econ. Rev. 26(3): 441-450. September
    1936. (Published by the American Economic Association, Northwestern
    University, Evanston, Ill.)
        "The present paper is based upon a study of certain southern land
    tenure changes, financed by the International Union for the Scientific
    Study of Population Problems."
        "An important feature of the government's cotton program is its effect
    on rural-urban population movement, significant for both the rural and
    the urban economic problem. Recognizing the complexity of the question,
    the present study deals with one aspect: the geographic stability of the
    owner and renter classes in the face of the milder form of economic pres-
    sure characteristic of the pre-depression period from 1925 to 1930.
    It is argued that a study of these groups (most likely to benefit from
    such permanent improvement as the adjustment program may bring) during
    the period preceding five-cent cotton, throws light on possible future
    development, particularly in high-cost areas. The methodology is based
    on a comparison of changes among whites and negroes, the two races ex-
    hibiting significant casual differences. The broad conclusion is that
    in spite of governmental efforts in behalf of cotton growers, the South
    remains a potential source of large additions to our urban labor force,
    and hence a vital factor in the problem of the industrial workers." -p.441.

Land Tenure - Union of South Africa

South African native policy and labour tenants. Indus. and Labour Inform.
    59(4): 125-126. July 27, 1936. (Published by International Labour
    Office, Geneva, Switzerland. Distributed in U. S. by World Peace
    Foundation, 8 West 40th St., New York, N. Y.)
        "On 1 June 1936 the House of Assembly of the Union of South Africa
    passed the Native Trust and Land Bill...to increase the territorial
    segregation between Europeans and Natives by (1) releasing certain areas
    for acquisition by or on behalf of Natives, (2) establishing a South
    African Native Trust to facilitate the acquiring of land, the develop-
    ment of Native-held land and the promotion of native welfare, and (3)
    controlling still further the conditions under which Natives may remain
    on land outside the Native areas and restricting their numbers to the
    actual needs of European farmers.
        Chapter IV of the Bill aims at the elimination of all superfluous
    labour tenants and of all tenants who are paying otherwise than in
    labour."

Land-use Legislation - United States

Hockley, H. A. National cooperation with the states in land-use legisla-
    tion enacted by the 74th Congress, second session (1936). Land Policy
    Circ. August 1936, pp. 19-21. (Published by the Division of Land
    Utilization, Land Use Planning Section, Resettlement Administration)

Land-use Planning - Training for

Suggestions on training for rural land-use planning. Land Policy Circ.
July 1936, pp.6-24. (Published by the Division of Land Utilization,
Land Use Planning Section, Resettlement Administration)
"This statement was prepared at the suggestion of the Social Science
Research Council Committee on Social and Economic Research in Agriculture who felt that suggestions on training for rural land-use planning
would be especially helpful at this time in view of the rapid develop-
ment of public programs of actions in this field. The group which pre-
pared this statement consisted of H.R. Tolley, chairman, and Messrs.
J. D. Black, Jacob Crane, S. T. Dana, J. N. Gaus, L. C. Gray, Carl C.
Taylor, and E. H. Wiecking. The statement is published by the group
on its own responsibility; it is not an official publication either of
the Committee...or of the Social Science Research Council." -footnote,p.6,
The topic is considered under the following headings: The field;
Opportunities in the field; Suggestions for training.

Libraries, Agricultural

Vachon, J. M. Les bibliothèques agricoles. La Technique Agricole Internationale 6(2): 117-125. April-June, 1936. (Published by the Fédération Internationale des Techniciens Agronomes, 86, Via Regina Elena,
Rome, Italy)
Published also in the March-April 1936 issue of the Revue de
l'Institut Agricole d'Oka of Quebec.
The importance of agricultural libraries and the need for their
development are stressed, and a scheme of division and organization is
outlined. The author believes that the country should have a central
agricultural library with a complete collection of the technical literature of the subject published in the country and a selection of foreign
publications; It should publish an agricultural bibliography for the
benefit of other libraries. Among these there should be secondary
school and college libraries and libraries of research institutions,
rural school libraries, public libraries in rural districts, and the
private library of the farmer, and of the technical agriculturist.
He pays a tribute to the work of the library of the International
Institute of Agriculture and regrets that it cannot yet fill a large
rôle as an international agricultural library.

Marketing - United States

Cassels, J. M. The marketing machinery of the United States. Quart. Jour.
Econ. 50(4): 658-679. August 1936. (Published by the Harvard University Press, Cambridge, Mass.)
"An important contribution to our knowledge about the economic machinery for commodity distribution in the United States was made in
1930 when, for the first time in the history of any country, a nation-
wide Census of Distribution was taken. While the material contained in
the voluminous reports that have been published has proved less suitable
for detailed analytical purposes than was originally expected, it has
provided us with the basic data, hitherto entirely lacking, which are

necessary for a general description in quantitative terms of the marketing system as a whole. To most economists the summary figures as presented in the official publications are no doubt familiar; but there remain certain significant comparisons to be more clearly brought out, certain ratios to be computed, and certain adjustments to be made, which may be of assistance even to specialists in this field. On the basis of the Census figures J. K. Galbraith and J. D. Black have already demonstrated that, in terms of income produced and workers employed, marketing ranks in present-day American society as a branch of economic activity which is of coördinate importance with manufacturing and agriculture. In the present paper, which is in a sense a sequel to theirs, attention will be focused on the internal structure and characteristics of this great distributive mechanism."

Marketing, Agricultural - India

Thakore, I. S. Agricultural marketing in Bombay Presidency. Indian Co-op. Rev. 2(2): 172-178. April 1936. (Published at Farhatbagh, Mylapore, Madras, India)
    Describes methods of sale of cotton and shows the inadequacy of the cooperative marketing facilities now in existence.

Master Farmer Movement

Gregory, C. V. The Master Farmer movement. Agr. Hist. 10(2): 47-58. April 1936. (Published by the Agricultural History Society, Room 3901, South Bldg., 13th St. and Independence Ave., Washington, D. C.)
    "A consolidation of the extemporaneous address made by...the retiring president of the Agricultural History Society, at its annual meeting in Washington, D. C., on April 24, 1936."
    Discussion, pp. 55-58.

Meat Stores, Retail - Chicago

Greer, H. C. Business mortality among retail meat stores in Chicago between 1920 and 1933. Jour. Business Univ. Chicago 9(3): 189-209. July 1936. (Published at the University of Chicago Press, 5750 Ellis Ave., Chicago, Ill.)
    This is a report of a study undertaken by the Institute of Meat Packing at the University of Chicago in cooperation with the Social Science Research Council of the University. "The analysis was based on information taken from credit-rating directories published by R. G. Dun and Company (now Dun and Bradstreet, Inc.) and was made possible by the co-operation of that organization."

Mechanization of Agriculture - Great Britain

Wright, S. J. Mechanization in British farming. Empire Jour. Expt. Agr. 4(15): 283-288. July 1936 (Published by the Clarendon Press, Oxford, Eng.)
    The author points out "the rapid evolution in Great Britain of a system which, since it depends very largely on the use of mechanized power, is still called mechanized farming but which...might be described

more accurately as rationalized farming...There is, in fact, no such thing in Great Britain as a typical mechanized farm." Certain general features of so-called mechanized farms are enumerated.

Mechanization of Agriculture - South Africa.

Tomlinson, F. R. Economical use of tractors and mules. South African Jour. Econ. 4(2): 249-255. June 1936. (Publisher's address; P. O. Box 5316, Johannesburg, South Africa)

"South African farming has experienced its share of the general mechanization of agriculture all over the world during the post-war period. The greater use of tractors either as draught power to replace or supplement the draught animal or in stationary beltwork, such as driving a threshing machine, has played an important part in this swing towards greater mechanical farming. It is not here proposed to condemn either mechanical or animal draught power. Each type has its fitting place in our farming organization but it is for each individual farmer to decide upon a line of action which will suit best his individual business."

Milk - Cost of Production

Jolly, A. L. Food costs in relation to milk yield. Wye, Kent. South-Eastern Agr. Col. Jour., no.38, pp. 108-113. July 1936.

Milk - Storage - Germany

German milk-storage invention. Primary Producer 21(28): 4. July 9, 1936. (Published at 38-40-42-44 Stirling St., Perth, Western Australia)

"Details have been published in the German Press recently of an invention which, it is claimed, will revolutionise the dairying industry by enabling milk, cream and other dairy products to be kept quite fresh for long periods by subjecting them to pressure under oxygen at a temperature of six degrees centigrade.

"A Duisberg chemist, Hofius by name, is responsible for the invention, and he has perfected a special vat, known as the Hofius tank."

Milk Distribution Industry - Employment and Earnings

Christenson, C. L. Employment and earnings in commercial milk distribution, 1929-34. Monthly Labor Rev. 43(1): 139-149. July 1936. (Published by Bureau of Labor Statistics, U. S. Dept. of Labor)

"Weekly earnings in March 1934 averaged $24.10 for office employees in the commercial milk-distribution industry, $25.37 for plant employees, and $31.30 for route men. These earnings represented decreases of 17 and 18 percent respectively for office and plant employees as compared with March 1929, but of less than 1 percent for route men. These figures are based on reports from 1,563 milk-distribution plants. The study was an outgrowth of an earlier one made by the Division of Research and Planning of the National Recovery Administration."

National Wheat Office - France

Liesse, André. L'office national du blé. L'Économiste Français 64(31):
129-131. Aug. 1, 1936. (Published at Rue Bleue, 9, Paris, France)
A discussion of the events that led up to and the proposals that
accompanied the passing of the law providing for the establishment in
France of a National Wheat Office. The main function of the office
will be to fix the price of wheat and it will have a monopoly of the
import and export trade in wheat and flour. Consumers as well as producers will be represented on its council.

L'office national interprofessionnel du blé et le sénat. Revue des Agriculteurs de France 68(8): 402-405. August 1936. (Published at 8, Rue
d'Athènes, Paris, France)
An account of some of the views on the proposed National Wheat Office
expressed in the Senate in opposition to the bill.

L'office national professionnel du blé. Revue des Agriculteurs de France
68(7): 355-358. July 1936. (Published at 8, Rue d'Athènes, Paris, France
An account of the organization of the National Wheat Office as proposed by M. Monnet for the French Government, and a discussion of the
aims of the Bill.

Neues Bauerntum

Neues Bauerntum. Fachwissenschaftliche Zeitschrift für das ländliche
Siedlungswesen. Neue Folge des Archivs für Innere Kolonisation. Bd.
28, June-July, 1936. (Published by Deutsche Landbuchhandlung, Dessauer
Strasse, 13, Berlin SW 11, Germany)
June: Neubildung deutschen Bauerntums und landwirtschaftliche
Entschuldung, by K. Ballerstedt (The author discusses the effect of the
measures adopted for the relief of agricultural indebtedness on land
settlement in Germany and the re-creation of German peasantry.)-pp.
241-252; Arbeits- und Lebensgemeinschaft im neuen Dorf, by H. Kugler.
(A picture of cooperative undertakings and community life such as must
inevitably come into being when a new settlement has been created) -
pp. 252-258; Die neue Ausbildungsordnung für den Landarbeiterberuf, by
Karl Sachse. (Attention is called to the new status allocated by the
Reichsnährstand to the agricultural worker. He must pass through an
apprenticeship of two years, and spend other two years as an agricultural aid before he can be a full-fledged or skilled agricultural worker.
Without this training he can only be a temporary or seasonal worker.) -
pp. 258-260; Vorläufige Zahlenübersicht zur Bauernsiedlung im Jahre
1935. (A summary of a preliminary report of the Statistical Office which
appeared in the first May number of Wirtschaft und Statistik on the
status of land settlement in 1935. It covers the acquisition and preparation of the land, the number and area of new settlements and the addition of land to existing small farms.) --pp. 260-264.
July: Zinsloser Beleihungskredit für die ländliche Siedlung. Ein
Vorschlag, by Krug. (A proposal for granting interest-free credit to
settlers on the land.) -pp.297-304; Die Ansiedlung Kriegsfreiwilliger
in Jugoslavien, by Jeftic. (The settlement of war volunteers on the
land in Yugoslavia.)

Part-time Farming

Melvin, B. L. Stake in the land. Rev. of Reviews 94(1): 48-50. July 1936.
(Published at 233 Fourth Ave., New York, N. Y.)
The three main points of this discussion of part-time farming for
industrial workers are: "(1) the recent development of part-time farming
as a pattern of living; (2) the governmental and non-governmental experiments in promoting such homes; and (3) the function of public aid
for those who would choose this way of life."

Planning, Regional - Jackson Hole Country of Wyoming

James, P. E. Regional planning in the Jackson Hole country. Geogr. Rev.
26(3): 439-453. July 1936. (Published by the American Geographical
Society, Broadway at 156th St., New York, N. Y.)
The opening paragraph of this article follows:
"Too many regional plans and too many regional planners have succeeded only in stalling the process of settlement in the Jackson Hole
country of western Wyoming. This situation is the result of the impact
of two opposed projects: one that looks toward the progress of settlement and the shift from cattle ranching to more intensive forms of economy
and another that calls for the removal of the settlement already established, the return of the area to its natural state, and the maintenance
in it of herds of wild game. Thus there has been created an economic and
political situation for which a compromise is difficult to discover."
Subtopics are: The land; the course of settlement; problems and patterns of circulation; wild game; projects for the preservation of the
natural scenery; is Jackson Hole "submarginal"?
Illustrated by maps and photographs.

Planning, Regional - Southeastern States

Vance, R. B. Regional planning with reference to the Southeast. South.
Econ. Jour. 3(1): 55-65. July 1936. (Published at Chapel Hill, N. C.)

Population, Native - Tanganyika Territory

Gillman, Clement. A population map of Tanganyika Territory. Geogr. Rev.
26(3): 353-375. July 1936. (Published by the American Geographical
Society, Broadway at 156th St., New York, N. Y.)
The map given is concerned with the distribution of the native population only, and is a separate, folded map facing p. 374. Contents of
article: Types of land occupation; high rainfall cultivation; alluvial
plains and scarp-foot fans; cultivation steppe; highland-savana settlement; coastal-hinterland settlement; dry-savana and thorn settlement;
nomadic occupation; uninhabited regions; townships; outlook into the
future; method and construction of the map.

Prices

Conacher, H. M. Causes of the fall of agricultural prices between 1875 and
1895. Scot. Jour. Agr. 19(3): 239-247. July 1936. (Published by H. M.
Stationery Office, Edinburgh, Scotland)

Primary Products Marketing Act, 1936 - New Zealand

Morrison, A. E. The primary products marketing act, 1936. New Zeal. Jour.
Agr. 53(1): 45-48. July 1936. (Published in Wellington, New Zealand)
    Contains the provisions of the Primary Products Marketing Act, 1936
which came into force on May 15 "to make better provision for the market
ing of dairy-produce and other primary products so as to ensure for
producers an adequate remuneration for the services rendered by them to
the community. The Act is divided into three parts - viz., Part I,
Administration; Part II, Marketing of Dairy-produce; and Part III, The
New Zealand Dairy Board."

Raw Materials

Deficiency in raw materials. Instances wherein the United States must rely
on imports. Index 16 (7): 135-140. July 1936. (Published by the New
York Trust Co., 100 Broadway, New York, N. Y.)
    "Insofar as tropical food products are concerned, it is true that
neither chemistry nor any other branch of modern science has developed
substitutes for sugar, coffee, tea, cocoa and fruits. Although domestic
beet sugar and cane sugar from our own possessions have modified to a
great extent our dependence on any foreign country, imports of this
product continue important, while coffee imports, in 1934, were valued
at a figure higher than imports of any other commodity. Nevertheless,
such products are not generally actual necessities of life, and, in
any event, can be largely obtained from nearby countries with which our
communications, even in emergency, are not likely to be broken "

De Wilde, J. C. The international distribution of raw materials. Geneva
Special Studies, v. 7, no.5, 20[6]pp. July 1936. (Published by
Geneva Research Center, "Villa Rigot," 14, Avenue de France, Geneva,
Switzerland)
    The following is quoted from the introductory part of the article:
    "Speaking before the League Assembly on September 11, 1935, the
British Secretary for Foreign Affairs, Sir Samuel Hoare, conceded that
as the question of raw materials 'is causing discontent and anxiety,
the wise course is to investigate it, to see what the proposals are for
dealing with it, to see what is the real scope of the trouble and, if
the trouble is substantial, to try and remove it.' Such an inquiry is
the subject of this study. An investigation of this kind must deal not
only with the geographic distribution of raw materials, but with the
factors that prevent or restrict utilization of these products by all
countries. It must explain the paradox that a number of states have
been demanding secure access to raw materials just at a time when supplie
of almost all primary products have been most plentiful and prices have
fallen to exceedingly low levels, Finally, it must devise solutions
enabling all countries to obtain adequate amounts of the raw materials
which they lack and to market on reasonable terms those of which they
have a surplus."
    Tables showing geographic distribution of production of raw materials
for 1930 and 1933 are given on the six unnumbered pages following p. 20.

- 738 -

Rayon Industry

Duncan, Robert. The rise of rayon. Today 6(13): 22, 31. July 18, 1936.
(Published at 152 West 42d. St., New York, N. Y.)

Relief, Rural - Wisconsin

Shafer, Carol L. These country people on relief. Cross section of a Wisconsin
county. Back of rural relief rolls lie debts - owed to grocer, doctor,
tax collector and mortgagee. Can villagers, farmhands and marginal
farmers, with credit exhausted and no industrial job to turn to, get off
relief and catch up with farm recovery. Survey Graphic 25(9): 512-515.
538-539. September 1936. (Published at 112 E. 19th St., New York,N. Y.)
"A study of the farm owners, farm tenants, farmhands and villagers
who have applied for relief in her [the author's] typically rural and
politically insurgent section of the Middlewest."

Resettlement Administration

Schuyler, D. M. Constitutional problems confronting the Resettlement Administration. Jour. Land & Pub. Utility Econ. 12(3): 304-306. August
1936. (Published by Northwestern University, School of Commerce, 337
East Chicago Ave., Chicago, Ill.)

Stevenson, Charles. Dissecting the Tugwell experiment. Is the Resettlement
administration merely an effort to help those who are unable to help
themselves or is it an effort to do away with our present system of
distribution? Nation's Business 24(9): 18- 20, 76, 78-79, 80-81, 82.
September 1936. (Published by the Chamber of Commerce of the United
States, Washington, D. C.)
This article is the result of an investigation of the Resettlement
Administration by a newspaperman. It is critical of Dr. Tugwell's work
and program and the writer states that he learned that "if you probe
deeply enough, you discover Dr. Tugwell engaged in a program which its
sponsors and his advisers openly assert is designed to substitute for
our existing economic-social-political structure, a 'Cooperative Democracy,' devoid of private industry, with a new form of parliament, a new
executive plan, a new set of courts."

Rural Economic Reconstruction - China

Ho, F. L. Rural economic reconstruction in China. Nankai Social & Econ.
Quart. 9(2): 469-535. July 1936. (Published by Nankai Institute of
Economics, Nankai University, Tientsin, China)
"This paper will be presented at the Sixth Conference of the Institute
of Pacific Relations to be held at Yosemite, California, August 15-29,
1936."
Private attempts to bring about rural reconstruction in China were
superseded by the work of Government agencies after the establishment of
the Kuomintang regime in 1927. A series of misfortunes which included
the great Yangtze flood of 1931-32 and the Japanese occupation of
Manchuria in 1931 necessitated "various measures for rural economic

rehabilitation, of which the more important include water conservancy
and afforestation, road construction, agricultural improvement and
extension, cooperative organization, and reform in land tenure and
taxation. In each of these five fields, promising beginning has been
made for future development, but problems are not lacking which require
immediate consideration before the reconstruction work in these fields
can be placed on a sound basis "

Self-help Cooperatives - Utah

Cooperative self-help movement in Utah. Monthly Labor Rev. 43(2): 349-355.
August 1936. (Published by the Bureau of Labor Statistics, U. S. Depart
ment of Labor)
"Utah was the first State to pass legislation setting up machinery
for the encouragement and supervision of self-help cooperatives. A
State board for this purpose was created by an act approved March 25,
1935...
"The act which created the Utah board grew out of a recognition of
the seriousness of the relief situation in that State and the desire to
encourage a movement which, experience had demonstrated, was of value
in assisting the unemployed to become at least partially self-supporting
to retain their industrial skills, and to maintain morale."
These self-help cooperatives are listed and described.

Sheep Rearing - East Prussia

Mickenberger, Konrad. Die schafhaltung im betrieb der ostpreussischen
landwirtschaft. Berichte über Landwirtschaft (n.F.) 20(4): 538-593.
1936. (Issued by [Germany] Reichs- und Pr. Ministerium für Ernährung
u. Landwirtschaft. Published by P. Parey, Berlin)
Sheep rearing in East Prussia is studied under the following topics:
The general importance of sheep rearing for East Prussian agriculture;
its development in East Prussia as compared with Prussia and the Empire;
the natural and economic conditions for sheep rearing in East Prussia;
the special causes of its recent decline, its post-war status; and the
outlook for its future. The present Government is planning a revival
of sheep farming with emphasis on the production of wool.

Soybeans

Slawson, H. H. Agriculture's jack of all trades. Introducing the versatile
soybean nuts which you may either build automobiles or run them and in
which many people see possibilities for farm relief without benefit of
subsidy. Nation's Business 24(9): 21-26, 94. September 1936. (Published by the Chamber of Commerce of the United States, Washington, D. C.

State Economic Control - China

Fong, H. D. Toward economic control in China. Nankai Social & Econ.
Quart. 9(2): 295-357. July 1936. (Published by Nankai Institute of
Economics, Nankai University, Tientsin, China)
"This paper will be presented at the Sixth Conference of the Institute
of Pacific Relations to be held at Yosemite, California, August 15-29, 193

It is pointed out that economic control by the State in China, though it is necessarily limited in scope and effect, has become "an issue of imminent national need." Factors which favor it are briefly reviewed, and the main fields in which it is exercised are described, namely, transport, trade, finance, agriculture, and industry.

Statistics

Coats, R. H. Statistics comes of age. Canad. Jour. Econ. and Polit.
Sci. 2(3): 269-287. August 1936. (Published by the University of
Toronto Press, Toronto, Ontario)
"The Presidential address delivered at a joint meeting of the
Canadian Political Science Association and the Canadian Historical
Association on May 26, 1936."
In this discussion and review of the theory and progress of statistics, Mr. Coats says:
"Agriculture demands a special word. The changed policies of three
countries have narrowed the annual outlet for our wheat by about 100
million bushels; our foreign oat market has likewise shrunk by 100
million bushels per annum; two-thirds of our barley trade has gone;
and the whole of our flax trade. There will be much ploughing of
statistics before this situation can be righted. Again, if Mr. Bruce's
'marriage of health and agriculture' is to be a happy one, better
world statistics of livestock are desirable. The International Institute of Agriculture at Rome was founded a quarter of a century ago
as a statistical clearing house almost pure and simple: it was to keep
us up to the minute about the world's food supply - surely a 'man's
job.' But it has strayed from that great duty. That it be brought
back and rehabilitated, or some substitute found, is of first-rate
international concern at this moment."

Sugar

The world sugar situation. Foreign Crops and Markets 33(7): 201-230.
Aug. 17, 1936. (Published by the Foreign Agricultural Service Division,
Bureau of Agricultural Economics, U. S. Dept. of Agriculture)
Prepared in collaboration with Gustave Burmeister, Division of
Statistical and Historical Research.

Sugar - International Regulation

Arcoleo, F. The internal organisation of the sugar market. Monthly Bull.
Agr. Econ. and Sociol. [reprint from Internatl. Rev. Agr.] 27(6):
171E-186E. June 1936. (Published by the International Institute of
Agriculture, Rome, Italy)
"Contents:- The two periods of the international regulation of the
production and trade of sugar. The Brussels Convention of 1902. The
international sugar market in the post-war period and international
activity aiming at controlling the market up to 1931. The Chadbourne
Agreement. The effects of this agreement during the five years of its
existence. The International Sugar Committee."

Sugar - Rumania

Ioanitziu, Georges, and Calmuschi. L'industrie du sucre en Roumanie.
Rumania. Ministère de l'Industrie et du Commerce. Correspondance
Économique Roumaine 18(2): 1-68. April-June 1936. (Published by
Imprimerie Nationale, Bucarest, Rumania)
   Text in French and English.
   A survey of the origin and development of the sugar industry through-
out the world is followed by an account of its origin and development
in Rumania from the law of 1873 which provided for its introduction
into the country.

Sugar - Union of South Africa

The complete sugar act of 1936. South African Sugar Jour. 20(6): 379,381-
383. June 30, 1936. (Published at 7, St. Andrew's Building, Esplanade,
Durban, Natal)
   "It is to provide for the control of the sugar industry by agreements entered into between growers, millers and refiners of sugar or
by determinations made by the Minister of Commerce and Industries, the
control of the prices at which certain sugars may be sold or disposed
of, and for matters incidental thereto."

Sugar Cane - South China

Rossiter, F J. Sugar cane production in south China. Foreign Crops and
Markets 33(5): 134-139. Aug. 3, 1936. (Published by the Division of
Foreign Agricultural Service, Bureau of Agricultural Economics, U. S.
Dept. of Agriculture)
   "From a report by Assistant Agricultural Commissioner Fred J.
Rossiter."

Taxation

The collection of real property taxes. Law and Contemporary Problems 3(3):
335-463. June 1936. (Published by the Duke University School of Law,
Duke Station, Durham, N. C.)
   Contents; Extent and distribution of urban tax delinquency, by
Frederick L. Bird, pp. 337-346, Tax delinquency of rural real estate,
by Donald Jackson, pp. 347-353; The tax calendar and the use of instalment payments, penalties and discounts, by Jens P. Jensen, pp.
354-361; A new plan for the private financing of delinquent tax payments, by Paul Studenski, pp. 352-370; Recent legislative indulgences
to delinquent taxpayers, by Wade S. Smith, pp. 371-381; Tax receiver-
ships, by Earl H. De Long and Brendan Q. O'Brien, pp. 382-396; Collection of delinquent taxes by recourse to the taxed property, by
H. K. Allen, pp. 397-405; Tax sales and foreclosures under the model
tax collection law [drafted by a special committee of the National
Municipal League] by Henry Brandis, Jr., pp. 406-415; Collection of
delinquent real property taxes by action in personam, by Edward Rubin,
pp. 416-428; The tax lien investor's relation to the collection of

delinquent taxes, by A. U. Rodney, pp. 429-435; An approach to a
system of "perfect" municipal tax collections, by Raymond M. Greer,
pp. 436-444; Impediments to tax collection outside the tax law, by
Philip H. Cornick, pp. 445-452; Utilization of reverted tax delinquent
land in rural area, by Paul W. Wager, pp. 453-460.

Martin, J. W. Trends in federal-state taxation relationships. South.
Econ. Jour. 3(1): 66-72. July 1936. (Published at Chapel Hill, N. C.)
Considers the trends during the past ten years in federal-state
taxation relationships in personal income, corporation income, death,
and selective excises and general sales taxes.

Wehrwein, C. F. Some aspects of the double-taxation problem. Jour.
Polit. Econ. 44(4): 544-553. August 1936. (Published by the University
of Chicago Press, Chicago, Ill.)
"The term 'double taxation' does not accurately reflect the problem
to which it refers. The term 'multiple taxation' should be used instead. It happens often that when the former is used it refers to three
or even more levies upon the same source of revenue, instead of merely
two...
"There are three types of multiple taxation. One is that involved
in the simultaneous levies which a taxpayer is called upon to pay
by the different types of political units of which he is a citizen...
"The other two types of multiple taxation have always been a source
of vexatious problems. One type is that which occurs when the same
source of revenue is, within a year, levied upon by two or more political
units of similar status; e.g., two or more states of the same country
or two or more countries...The last type of multiple taxation is that
involved in two or more simultaneous levies upon the same source of
revenue by the same political unit. This article will deal primarily
with this last type."

Taxation - West Virginia

Booth, Leland. West Virginia slashes taxes. Nation's Agr. 11(11): 5,
13, 14. September 1936. (Published at 58 East Washington St., Chicago,
Ill.)
"How the West Virginia Farm Bureau Federation, after ten years of
unremitting effort, has finally succeeded in lightening the farm tax
burden of the state, is described in the following article by the Secretary of the state organization." -Editor's note

Tea

The tea position. Statist 128(3051): 227-228. Aug. 15, 1936. (Published
at 51 Cannon St., London, E. C. 4, Eng.)
Discusses the tea restriction scheme now in force, the events that
led to such a scheme, and says:
"No one connected with the British controlled tea plantation industry
questions the advisability of continuing regulation. But many contend
that control of output should be of a more fundamental kind than it is
at present and share the opinion of Sir J. P. Hewett that the scheme, as

it now exists. has done nothing permanently to correct the evil of potential overproduction which is the root of most of the troubles of the tea plantation industry. Sir John has gone as far as to suggest that what is needed is a concerted movement to reduce the existing acreage under tea; in other words, a general agreement to uproot a proportion of tea gardens' planted areas."

Ukers, W. H   The world trade in tea. Index 11 (128): 159-173. August 1936. (Published by Svenska Handelsbanken, Stockholm, Sweden)
Following introductory paragraphs on tea cultivation and the history of tea drinking, production, tea restrictions, and consumption are discussed.
Table 1 shows tea exports of producing countries, annually 1926-1934. Table 2 shows consumption and per capita consumption of tea, annually 1925-1934 by principal importing countries. Charts show rise of Netherlands East Indies and decline of China in tea exports, principal tea exporting and importing countries, and per capita consumption of tea by principal importing countries.

Tenancy, Farm

Hays, Brooks. Farm tenancy and the Christian conscience. Christian Rural Fellowship Bull. no. 9, pp. [1]-4. February 1936. (Published by The Christian Rural Fellowship, Room 1201, 156 Fifth Ave., New York, N. Y.)
"This paper is the substance of an address made...at the annual dinner of the Christian Rural Fellowship, December 5, 1935."

Textile Industry - Czechoslovakia

Regulation of textile combines in Czechoslovakia. Indus. and Labour Inform. 59(6): 175-176. Aug. 10, 1936. (Published by International Labour Office, Geneva, Switzerland. Distributed in U. S. by World Peace Foundation, 8 West 40th Street, New York, N. Y.)
A Legislative Decree of July 9, 1936 provides for the establishment of a National Committee of the Textile Industry, composed of representatives of employers and workers, and also for the establishment of branch combines approved and supervised by the Ministries of the Interior and of Commerce in agreement with the Ministry of Social Welfare.

Time Expenditure in Crop Trials

Tinley, F. L. The expenditure of time in the carrying out of agricultural crop trials. Wye, Kent. South-Eastern Agr. Col. Jour. no. 38, pp. 114-116. July 1936.

Tithe - Great Britain

Tithe. Current Survey Agr. Policy 3(7): 18-19. July 6-Aug. 1, 1936. (Issued from 3, Magpie Lane, Oxford, Eng.) mimeogr.
"The Tithe Bill has passed all stages in both Houses, and received the Royal Assent on July 31. It was debated at length on the motion for its second reading in the Lords, and in the Committee Stage (Lords)

several amendments were accepted. These were later agreed to by the
Commons also. Queen Anne's Bounty issued an explanatory memorandum on
the working of the Act...
"The annual report of the Governors of Queen Anne's Bounty has been
published, and we give a Summary of its main points." - Intro.

Trade, Foreign

Wallace, H. A. What about foreign imports? South. Jour. Progress 1(1):
6, 21. June 1936. (Published at the Hurt Bldg., 45 Edgewood, S. E.,
Atlanta, Ga.)

Trade, International, and Population Movements.

Condliffe, J. B. Population movements and international trade. The
breakdown of the trading mechanism. Index 11 (6, whole no. 126): 122-
129. June 1936. (Published by Svenska Handelsbanken, Stockholm, Sweden)
The author discusses the great shrinkage of world trade which is the
outstanding feature and perhaps a lasting consequence of the depression
which is now passing. The beginnings of recovery in world trade are
shown and the spread of scientific knowledge as an economic force which
makes it unlikely that international trade will in the years to come
increase as it did for decades before the war is discussed.
The second part of the article is in July 1936 issue of the Index,
pp. 138-146. The subtitle is The Decline of Fertility in Western Europe.

Trade Agreements

Bidwell, P. W. The Yankee trader in 1936. Yale Rev. 25(4): 702-723.
Summer 1936. (Published by the Yale University Press, 143 Elm St.,
New Haven, Conn.)
This is a discussion of our new tariff policy, the purpose of
which, tariff reduction, "will appear now to Americans and foreigners
alike; the method, tariff bargaining, will be new only to Americans."
Tariff agreements with various countries, thirteen of which have
been concluded, are discussed in detail.

Trade Agreements and the Southern States

Edminster, L. R. The trade agreements program and the South. South.
Jour. Progress 1(1): 12, 21. June 1936. (Published at Hurt Bldg.,
45 Edgewood, S. E., Atlanta, Ga.)

U. S. S. R. and the Business Cycle

Feiler, Arthur. The Soviet Union and the business cycle. Social Research
3(3): 282-303. August 1936. (Published by the New School for Social
Research, 66 West 12th St., New York, N. Y.)
The following is quoted in part from the author's introductory
paragraphs:
"The Soviet Union, in these nineteen years, has gone through
catastrophes, through misfortunes, through bad times and somewhat better

times. But these developments have in no way corresponded to the
cyclical changes in the rest of the world. They have not even been
isolated, domestic cyclical ups and downs. They have been determined
by non-cyclical events; by political decisions, such as the socialization of industry or the collectivization of the peasants, the War
Communism of the first period, the New Economic Policy of 1921 or the
newly accelerated industrialization initiated in 1927 — determined by
these political decisions and by the capacity or incapacity of the land
and the people to live up to them. The problem is whether this absence
of cyclical changes is only transitional or whether it may be regarded
is a permanent new situation, and, in the latter case, what might be the
reasons. An appropriate answer can be found only by applying to this
problem the theory of the business cycle, by examining in the light of
theory cyclical developments in the rest of the world and their absence
in the Soviet Union."

United States and the Far East

Farley, Miriam S. America's stake in the far East. I: Trade. Far East.
Survey 5(16): 161-170. July 29, 1936. (Published by American Council,
Institute of Pacific Relations, 129 E. 52nd St., New York, N. Y.)
    This is the first part of an article in three parts.
    The following is quoted from the introductory part of the first
article:
    "The moment is therefore appropriate for a reexamination of the
economic bases of United States Far Eastern policy. The first step
in such an inquiry must, obviously, be a careful and dispassionate
analysis of the exact nature and extent of that 'economic stake' in
the Orient which is so often alluded to and so seldom defined. Such
is the main purpose of the first and second sections of the present
article, dealing, respectively, with trade and investments. Both will
confine themselves for the most part to the situation as it exists
today, with only enough indication of the historical background and
the possibilities of the future to suggest a perspective. A concluding
section will seek to balance roughly the gains from economic intercourse with the Far East against the costs which it has entailed.
    "To define the American stake in the Orient is comparatively easy;
to evaluate its importance or indispensability to American economic
life is extremely difficult, depending, moreover, in the last analysis
upon the value standards of the individual, his concept of the
dynamics of American society, and his social philosophy. The present
authors have not attempted to enter into these larger and controversial
questions, save for the purpose of defining the issues."
    The subtitle of part II is Investments, by William W. Lockwood, Jr.,
and it is published in the Far East. Survey 5(17): 175-185. Aug. 12,
1936. Part III is The cost, by Frederick V. Field, and it is published
in the Far East. Survey 5(18): 189-193. Aug. 26, 1936.

Unemployment - China

Unemployment in China. Indus. and Labour Inform. 59(5): 163-164. Aug. 3,
1936. (Published by International Labour Office, Geneva, Switzerland.
Distributed in U. S. by World Peace Foundation, 8 West 40th Street,
New York, N. Y.)

"In Kwangtung, measures to relieve unemployment have been decided
upon, such as the encouragement of farming, reclamation projects, construction of roads, and training courses for the unemployed. During
the year 1935 considerable progress was made in the work of water conservation and in the construction of highways and railways. At the
end of October 1935 over 20,000 kilometres of roads had been built,
and in north-west China about 75,000 acres of land were irrigated.
This region is becoming an important cotton-producing centre. Other
projects are now in hand and some nearing completion. Not far from
Hankow 150,000 acres of land were reclaimed, and in the basins of the
Yellow and Yangtze Rivers much work has been done towards flood prevention...the local government of Kiangshan has decided to send 2,000
families (with over 6,000 members) to northern Fukien and eastern Kiangsi
to do reclamation work. Each family will be given a subsidy of $15.00
from the Government."

Wages, Agricultural

Minimum wages in agriculture. Views of International Landworkers' Federation.
Indus. and Labour Inform.59(6): 197. Aug. 10, 1936. (Published by
International Labour Office, Geneva, Switzerland. Distributed in U. S.
by World Peace Foundation, 8 West 40th St., New York, N. Y.)
Lists the resolutions adopted by the Executive committee of the
International Landworkers' Federation, meeting in Stockholm, June 24-25,
1936.

Wattle Industry - South Africa

Coper, Rudolf. Wattle and quebracho. The market and marketing problems of
the South African wattle industry. South African Jour. Econ. 4(2):
182-198. June 1936. (Publisher's address: P. O. Box 5316, Johannesburg, South Africa)
The author goes back to the year 1886 which was the year that the
first exports of wattle products occurred. The total value of the
products for that year amounted to eleven pounds sterling. The highest
export figures since reached were registered in 1927 at £ 1,159,652.

Wealth - United States

Who owns the wealth? Natl. City Bank of New York [Monthly Letter on] Econ.
Conditions, Govt. Finance, U. S. Securities, July 1936, pp. 103-107.
(Published in New York, N. Y.)
Topics discussed include: Two classes of wealth (wealth for production and wealth for consumption), the Federal Trade Commission
survey (1936), land ownership, consumption goods and services, insurance, banking and other services, real distribution of wealth is in
consumption, and distribution of income, 1929-1932.

Wheat

The wheat position. Statist 128(3050): 196-197. Aug. 8, 1936. (Published
at 51, Cannon St., London, E. C. 4, Eng.)
Discusses changes in world demand and supply of wheat and the influence North American conditions have had upon wheat prices.

<u>Wheat - Codification of Laws - France</u>

Codification des textes législatifs concernant l'organisation et la défense
du marche du blé. 12pp. Amiens, Imprimerie Nouvelle. 1936. (Suppl.
à "Les Travaux des Chambres d'Agriculture," June 10, 1936)
   Text of decree of April 24, 1936 by which are codified provisions
of French wheat laws from that of April 1, 1930 to that of December
31, 1935.

<u>Wheat - Government Control - Canada</u>

Howard, Don. Politics and grain marketing. Fallacy of controlling flow to
sustain prices demonstrated in collapse of Canadian wheat pools and
legacy of surplus stocks, Barron's 16(30): 18. July 27, 1936. (Published
at 44 Broad St., New York, N. Y.)

Patton, H. S. Experiments in wheat control: U. S. prices and the Canadian
wheat board. Annalist 48(1228): 148-149. July 31, 1936. (Published
by the New York Times Co., New York, N. Y.)

<u>Wheat - Government Control - Italy</u>

Schnare, L. L. Italian wheat trade under government control. Foreign
Crops and Markets 33(5): 132-133. Aug. 3, 1936. (Published by the
Division of Foreign Agricultural Service, Bureau of Agricultural Economics
U. S. Dept. of Agriculture)
   "Based on a report from Consul Lester L. Schnare at Milan, Italy."
   The first paragraph of this article follows:
   "At a meeting of the Permanent Wheat Committee (Comitato Permanente
del Grano) in Rome on June 15, 1936, a new law was announced under which
complete control of all wheat trade in Italy was assumed by the Italian
Government. This control applies to all wheat produced in Italy or its
colonies or imported from abroad whether for consumption within the
country or for milling and re-export. The Ministry of Agriculture is
to take charge of the new system, working with committees including
representatives of all other Government organizations that are particularly interested in the production and marketing of wheat. The new organization will replace the system of control established last season with
more limited powers and authority. The purpose of this new organization
is to maintain adequate supplies of wheat for the country's requirements and to market them at prices equitable alike to producers and
consumers."

<u>Wheat - Utilization</u>

Bennett, M. K. World wheat utilization since 1885-86. Wheat Studies of the
Food Research Institute 12(10): 339-404. June 1936. (Published in
Stanford University, Calif.)
   The following is quoted from the cover page:
   "This study represents a pioneer attempt to survey developments in
the utilization of wheat, as distinguished from production or supplies of
wheat, in a specially defined 'world' during the past 50 years. The
course of 'world' wheat utilization reflects broadly measurable changes

in population and in per capita utilization. It reflects also developments, sometimes concurrent and sometimes diverse, in wheat utilization in different parts of the 'world'; these regional developments receive emphasis. Over the whole sweep of years, estimates of food-and-feed use are presented for the 'world' and for five large 'regions.' For each of 15 postwar years it is possible to estimate roughly, for most of the 40 countries included, total and per capita amounts of wheat used annually for food, feed, and seed.

"The resulting series of per capita food use of wheat in different countries present important problems of interpretation. In the closing portion of the study, postwar trends and fluctuations of per capita food use of wheat, country by country, are considered with reference to conditioning circumstances. Among the latter are national standards of living, national preferences for wheat as against other cereals on the one hand and non-cereal foods on the other, and the phase of development with reference to a 'normal' course of per capita wheat consumption in which the several countries appear to stand at present. Attention is also given to the relative importance of trend influences, cyclical influences, and accidental influences on the recent course of per capita use of wheat for food throughout the world.

"At many points limitations of data and methods of estimation are responsible for uncertainties There emerges, however, the broad conclusion that the prospects for expansion of world food consumption of wheat are more limited than they have been considered heretofore."

Tables given are by Rosamond Peirce; charts are by P. Stanley King.

Wheat and Cooperation

Digby, Margaret. Co-operation and wheat. Indian Co-op. Rev. 2(2): 155-161. April 1936. (Published at Farhatbagh, Mylapore, Madras, India)
    The development of wheat production and wheat cooperation in Canada is described at some length and outlined in the case of the other large scale producing countries and the so-called peasant countries. It is suggested that international cooperative control of wheat may become necessary, though "no attempt up to the present has achieved any substantial success. It can be said confidently, however, that if the attempt is made not by States but by self-governing co-operative organisations, one great area of difficulty, the political, will be altogether eliminated."

Zoning, Maryland

Johnson, V. W. Notes on Maryland zoning laws. Jour. Land & Pub. Utility Econ. 12(3): 314-315. August 1936. (Published by Northwestern University, School of Commerce, 337 East Chicago Ave., Chicago, Ill.)
    There is no provision in Maryland zoning laws which regulates or restricts agricultural activities.

Whitten, Robert. Rural zoning in New York. Jour. Land & Pub. Utility Econ.
12(3): 313-314. August 1936. (Published by Northwestern University,
School of Commerce, 337 East Chicago Ave., Chicago, Ill.)
    Zoning regulations in New York are under the authority of the city,
village, or town. Counties, while they may establish planning boards,
are not authorized to adopt zoning ordinances. It is believed that
counties should be given broad zoning powers such powers not to conflict with the powers granted to the towns. The author believes that
in large measure, the initiative in strictly rural zoning will have to
be taken by the counties and in some measure by the State.

NOTES

American association of social workers. Directory of members of the
    American association of social workers, 1936. Edited by Jessica H.
    Barr. 241pp. New York, American association of social workers
    [1936] 225 Am344

A directory of organizations in the field of public administration 1936.
    179pp. Chicago, Ill., Public administration clearing house [1936]
    225 P96
        Address of publisher: 850 East Fifty-eighth Street, Chicago.
    Bibliography, 1p. at end.

Purnas, C. C   The next hundred years; the unfinished business of science.
    434pp. Baltimore, The Williams & Wilkins company [1936] 330 F98
    Bibliography, pp. 403-408.
        Part V is devoted to Social consequences of invention, and in
    other parts may be found chapters entitled respectively The Perfect
    Farm, Agriculture Is an Industry, Food Manufacture, and Making the
    Best of Weather.

Gt. Brit. Bacon marketing board. Report of members of the board and in-
    come and expenditure account... 1935 [3d]Balance sheet as at
    31st December, 1935. Bacon indemnity receipts and payments account
    and 1935 pigs delivery bonus fund accounts as at 31st December, 1935.
    12pp. [London, 1936] 280.3509 G79

Gt. Brit. Colonial office. Customs tariffs of the Colonial empire. Part III -
    West Indies. Amending leaflet no. 3. 37pp. London, H. M. Stationery
    off., 1936   (Colonial no. 97-3/3) 285 G793

Gt. Brit. Ministry of agriculture and fisheries. Report of the Standing committee set up by the minister of agriculture and fisheries, the secretary
of state for the Home department and the secretary of state for Scotland
on grapes. 8pp. London, H. M. Stationery off., 1936. ([Parliament.
Papers by command] Cmd. 5147)   280.395 G79
   At head of title: Merchandise marks act, 1926.

Gt. Brit. Pigs marketing board. Pigs marketing scheme, 1933 [Annual
report to registered pig producers... 1935]   4pp. [London] 1936.
280.3469 G79

Gt. Brit. Treaties, etc., 1936-   (Edward VIII) Protocols signed for
the governments of France, United Kingdom, India, the Netherlands
and Siam amending the agreement of May 7, 1934, for the regulation
of the production and export of rubber. London, June 27, 1935, and
May 22, 1936.   4pp. London, H. M. Stationery off., 1936.
([Foreign office] Treaty series 20 (1936))   286.378 G79P
   Parliament. Papers by command. Cmd. 5236.

Holzinger, K. J. Statistical tables for students in education and psychology.
100pp. Chicago, Ill., The University of Chicago press [1934] 251 H74 Ed.,
   Third edition, July 1931... Third impression, November 1934.

Hugh-Jones, E. M., and Radice, E. A. An American experiment.   296pp. London,
Oxford university press, H. Milford, 1936.   280.12 H87
   V. Agriculture and relief, pp. [151]-206.

League of nations. Economic intelligence service. Public finance, 1928-
1935. 15 pts. Geneva, 1936. (Series of League of nations Publications
II. Economic and financial. 1936. II. A. 1) 280.9 L47P 1936. II.A.1
   I. Preface and general explanatory note.- II. Albania.-III.
Austria.- V. United Kingdom of Great Britain and Northern Ireland.-
VI. Bulgaria.- VII. Czechoslovakia.- VIII. Denmark.- IX. Estonia.-
X. Finland.- XIII Greece. XX. Netherlands.-XXII. Poland.- XXIV.
Roumania.- XXVII. Switzerland.- XXX. Yugoslavia.
   Parts covering other countries will follow.

McDonald, A. F. The history of tobacco production in Connecticut. 30pp.
[New Haven] Published for the Tercentenary commission by the Yale
university press, 1936. (Connecticut. Tercentenary commission.
Committee on historical publications. [Publications] 52) 281.369 M14
   Bibliography, p.30.

Manufacturers record. Blue book of southern progress [1936] 81pp.
Baltimore, Md. [1936]   252 M312

Minnesota. Committee on tax delinquency. Tax delinquency; report and
recommendations of a committee appointed by governor Floyd B. Olson.
7pp. [Minneapolis?] 1935.   284.5 M665
   Committee referred to on p. 2, paragraph 1, as Committee on tax
delinquency.

New Hampshire. State tax commission. Report to the governor and council on new sources of revenue. 46 pp. Concord, N. H., State tax commission, 1935. 284.5 N45

New Jersey taxpayers association. Facts about New Jersey and the cost of government, compiled under the direction of A. R. Everson; chief of staff - Jerome M. Ludlow. 95pp. Trenton, N. J., The New Jersey taxpayers association, 1935. 284.5 N463

Ohio. Attorney general. The government of the state of Ohio. An analysis of the various state departments, commissions, bureaus and boards as of January 1, 1935. Prepared by John W. Bricker as Attorney general of Ohio. 113pp. Columbus, O., The F. J. Heer printing co., 1935. 280.067 Oh34

Ohio chamber of commerce. State aids to common schools in Illinois, Indiana, Michigan, Pennsylvania, Wisconsin, and Ohio, by Arch D. Schultz, director of research, Ohio chamber of commerce. 70pp. [Columbus] Ohio chamber of commerce, 1935. 284.5 Oh33St

Tucker, G. M. The path to prosperity. 312pp. New York and London, G. P. Putnam's sons, 1935. 280.12 T79
    This volume was briefly reviewed by George M. Janes in the American Economic Review for June 1936 (p. 368) Mr. Janes writes that:
    "The author endeavors to tell how to get out of the depression and establish society on an enduring economic basis. Nothing new or startl is proposed, but the whole book is pervaded by a sturdy common sense... His main emphasis is on established principles; and, in successive chapters on various economic problems, he endeavors to bring out the lessons of experience. Makeshift legislation he believes does more harm than good."

U. S. National resources committee. Regional planning. Pt. 3. New England. 101pp. Washington, U. S. Govt. print. off., 1936. 173.2 N214Rp Pt.3

Virginia. Commission on county government. A further report on progress in county government and county consolidation. Submitted to the governor and the General assembly, January 1936. 211pp. map Richmond, Division purchase and printing, 1936. 280.089 V81Rf

Worden, R. P. A procedure for market and sales analysis. 85pp.mimeogr. [Boston, Mass.] The Worden corporation [1935?] 280.32 W89

AGRICULTURAL ECONOMICS LITERATURE

UNITED STATES DEPARTMENT OF AGRICULTURE
BUREAU OF AGRICULTURAL ECONOMICS

LIBRARY
RECEIVED
MAR 11 1944

The man who wishes to steer clear of shelves
and rocks must know where they lie.
George Washington

| Vol. 10 | November 1936 | No. 9 |

FEATURES IN THIS ISSUE

SIGNED REVIEWS

Davis, J. S.   Wheat and the A A A. 468pp. Washington, D. C., The Brookings
  Institution, 1935.   (The Institute of economics of the Brookings institution. Publication no. 61)   281.359 D29
    The author of "Wheat and AAA" has a full background of knowledge and
experience for evaluating the wheat program of the Agricultural Adjustment Administration. He describes carefully the program and its operations, and in the last chapter of the book presents "Contributions Toward an Appraisal." His conclusions may be summarized about as follows:
that the wheat administrators have handled a difficult program remarkably well under the circumstances and with fairly good results, but that
neither the results nor prospects justify an indefinite continuation of
the experiment.
    The book is clearly and concisely written. The details with reference
to checking up on the wheat adjustment efforts at times seem a little te-
dious, but these details add a touch of realism to the description, and
suggest many of the practical problems that arise in the administration
of the details of contracting and checking compliance on individual
farms throughout the country. More attention should have been given and
more space devoted to the effect of revaluing the dollar upon wheat prices
and the dollar income from wheat, and the practical problems of farmers
under wheat contracts.
    The first chapter, entitled "The Wheat Background of the Adjustment
Act," presents a clear and concise summary of developments with reference
to wheat supplies and prices, pre- ar and post-war, up to the enactment of
the Adjustment Act. As stated in the final chapter, the author tries to
set forth clearly, objectively, and in perspective the more significant
facts regarding wheat. This first chapter, however, is not a sufficiently
comprehensive statement of the background of the situation to explain
fully the reasons for the adjustment program.
    The explanation as to why farmers and others concerned with the agricul-
tural situation after the war period continued to search for some acceptable scheme for the relief of wheat growers is not to be found alone in the
production and price of wheat. The most significant fact was that the
price of wheat and of other products to which the wheat grower might turn
in the use of his productive resources had fallen sharply and remained at
a relatively low level, whereas the prices that the grower had to pay for
goods and services remained relatively high. This fact and its significance are not adequately presented. In limiting the scope of the first
chapter to a discussion of wheat, the author left out of view many factors that were important in keeping alive the interest in farm relief
measures and in determining the character of those measures.

The first chapter provides the background for a considerable part of the concluding chapter and reflects the attitude of the author on several controversial points relative to the wheat program. Reviewing the pre-war wheat situation, it is concluded that

"Under conditions then prevailing, what are now called 'parity prices' for wheat appear to have stimulated that expansion; and it is impossible to say what further changes would have come if the great War had not radically altered the course of economic history."

Thus he challenges the validity of using the pre-war base in computing parity. A closer analysis of the factors influencing wheat acreage from about 1890 to 1914 might give rise to some doubt as to whether prices prevailing in the period 1909-14 had much, if any, responsibility for acreage expansion in that period. The sharp rise between 1894 and 1909 had provided a stimulus for encouragement, as wheat prices in that period were rising more rapidly than the prices of all other commodities. In the years 1909-14, on the other hand, the price of wheat was declining while the price of all commodities remained fairly stable. The increase of production in this base period was due both to higher yields and some increase in acreage, particularly in the Great Plains area. The expansion in the Great Plains area was due to the opening up of new lands and to improvement in the technique of dry farming. It is possible that had the tendencies of the base period continued for a number of years, the wheat acreage on the Great Plains area would have continued to expand, but not so rapidly, while in the eastern states, it might have declined. The result of these shifts in opposite directions might have been no further significant expansion in the total acreage without the War stimulus. To the extent that this is possible or probable, the pre-war average price of wheat might be considered a reasonable parity base.

Belief that the public had been "mis-educated" and that with proper education production should have been adjusted voluntarily to the market requirements is reflected in his treatment of wheat in the post-war period. Reviewing the post-war wheat developments the author says:

"Looking back, it is easy to see that a vulnerable wheat situation was developing in 1924-29, that false ideas of 'normal' wheat prices were commonly held, and that American wheat growers might well have faced the necessity of adjusting their ideas and their wheat culture to altered economic conditions."

What ideas of normal are here described as false? It is not clear from the text but possibly the author simply means to say that the facts as to the supply and demand situation with respect to wheat were not fully known and not properly evaluated in this period. If this is all that is intended, it may be granted. To sell wheat in competition with the rest of the world and not accumulate stock it would have been necessary to have reduced production or taken lower prices to move the crops. However, some were thinking of "normal" wheat prices in terms of relationship to other prices, and to label such ideas as false would be begging the question.

The part of the above quotation suggesting that wheat growers should have faced the necessity of adjusting their ideas and culture to altered conditions presents an attitude toward the wheat problem not in line with that commonly held by many of the proponents of farm relief. This seems to suggest that if wheat growers had known the facts, they would not have been asking for protection or relief and would have set about doing what they ought to have done. The wheat situation is practically always vulnerable in a depression. If wheat growers knew that a depression was pending and that prices would fall sharply, they might still reasonably protest the assumption that they should meekly submit to the effects of the depression without seeking some protection or aid.

The suggestion of resignation to the depression is expressed later in the same paragraph. After noting that "the rest of the world would not take big exports of American wheat at prices that our growers regarded as remunerative," it is said, "Yet the ideas persisted that the export market was indefinitely elastic; and that wheat prices below average pre-war prices, adjusted for changes in the general price level, were unjustly and uneconomically low." Some, at least, knew that the export market was not indefinitely elastic, and yet they advocated the export debenture or the McNary-Haugen plan. Facts or opinions as to what prices could be obtained in the world markets for wheat under the prevailing conditions simply were not the basis for much of the farm relief argument. The leaders wanted to alter those conditions or to have some compensation for accepting them.

The post-war struggle over farm relief measures was prolonged largely by differences in opinions as to whether or not the government should assume any responsibility for aiding or protecting farmers or let economic forces operate without hindrance or guidance, and by the struggle among those who believed in aid but disagreed as to what was the best measure for relief. Although specific problems arose with reference to each of several important agricultural products, many recognized the fact that all agriculture had to be dealt with directly or indirectly. They believed that farm prices generally must be raised, or the prices of industrial products, taxes, and farm debts had to be scaled down. Some manufacturers and commercial leaders, seeing the effect of depressed agricultural purchasing power upon industry and commerce, joined the agricultural leaders in this view of the situation. The establishment of the Farm Board was a concession to those who urged government aid, without going farther than providing for some aid in the marketing of agricultural products. Under conditions of general economic improvement or stability, the Farm Board might have proven fairly successful in time. It was not designed, however, to lift agricultural prices in general nor to bring down overhead expenses or the high cost of commodities farmers buy. The depression soon demonstrated the inadequacy of the Farm Board to deal with the post-war farm problem. The Agricultural Adjustment Act, together with the provisions for revaluing the dollar and reorganizing the farm credit machinery, represented a full acknowledgement of government responsibility for making radical readjustments in the national economic structure for the relief of agriculture.

The chapters between the first and the last describe the Adjustment Act as it applied to wheat, the wheat programs developed in the first two years under the Act, the results of operations, attitudes toward the program, and elements in the outlook for the wheat program as they appeared early in 1935. The second chapter presents a clear and concise description of the Act and the program. This is followed by descriptions of the operations of the several features of the program and results obtained in 1933 and 1934.

The reader will find interesting the discussion of the reasons for benefit payments and the nature of the services for which farmers were paid. "Not producing" appears to be a unique kind of service. The author points out clearly the conflicting notions of paying for a service and providing an income supplement. He shows also the inconsistency of treating this income supplement as a part of the price or as the farmers' tariff.

The wheat processing tax is described as "regressive" on two accounts: (1) that it bore heavily upon low income groups, and (2) that the funds were used in securing a reduction in supplies with a view to raising wheat prices. The author explains, however, that the tax was justified by its sponsors as a measure of social justice and as such, it was generally accepted without much protest.

The author finds that the wheat program has been administered with remarkable success in maintaining good will. The grain trade and the milling industry were very critical of the program in the beginning and remained so, but found that their worst fears were not justified. Many, though not all, of the wheat growers entered into the program with enthusiasm. Many were disturbed by revisions in estimates, delays in promised payments, and rulings on the contracts, but the additional income largely overcame feelings on these scores. Farmers' organizations were not unanimous in their approval of the program. Some continued to condemn acreage restriction as a policy and advocate other measures for improving the returns to farmers.

In the last chapter entitled "Contributions Toward Appraisal," the author presents a reasonable and fair summary of observations concerning the program and results obtained in the first two years of operation. He says that political and social pressure required the government to do something and among the various proposals that might have been adopted, "the ingenious flexible Adjustment Act had various points of superiority in its application to wheat." He considers that the program worked out for the Act was reasonable and the operations under the Act were highly creditable. He concludes, however, that the "control of wheat production through voluntary contracts... has not yet been a demonstrated success." The accomplishments in reduction are to be accredited mostly to the weather. He believes that there are inherent tendencies which would make trouble for any production control program in normal seasons. He believes that the program has not demonstrated ability to raise farm prices of wheat materially. The advance that has taken place has been due to other factors and he doubts that in the absence of drought and other factors, prices could be raised nearly so far. Although parity prices were not realized, incomes of producers were materially increased. Prices per bushel plus benefit payments practically equaled the computed parity for growers under contract. The income of wheat growers was increased by over $200,000,000 above what they otherwise would have received. This was done at the expense of consumers of wheat. He thinks that "this redistribution of money income somewhat increased the real income of the nation in terms of satisfactions," but he cannot be sure of that. He doubts if it contributed appreciably, if at all, to "promoting general business recovery or to increasing the total national money income."

Notwithstanding the apparent success of the Pacific Northwest export program, he thinks that the AAA should resist the growing pressure for the large-scale subsidizing of wheat exports. He thinks this would be unfair international competition. He recognizes that correction of world wheat maladjustments through international understanding is a worthy objective, but thinks that the experience of the past two years has not demonstrated that international control of wheat production and marketing is practicable.

The ever-normal granary scheme is criticized as being superfluous as a guarantee of food supply. As a measure to protect and strengthen the wheat program, he doubts that the use of public funds can be justified in that it would seem that the public took all the risk and the producer received all the benefits. Furthermore, he believes that the ever-normal granary would develop into a stabilizing measure with all the difficulties realized by the Farm Board. He doubts that the subject has been thoroughly investigated and that workable plans have been developed.

With reference to production control, he poses the following pertinent questions: (1) Was the reduction of wheat production a rational objective? (2) Can the wheat program furnish a desired production control? (3) "Can a government agency bring about better readjustment of wheat production than economic forces will?" He answers those who condemn contraction of food production as wrong and anti-social, by observing that there may be excessive supplies, relatively if not absolutely, of any one product. The public good may be increased by producing less of something and more of something else. He believes that the AAA was right "in its conviction that reduction in our wheat acreage and production was warranted in 1933." He can see "no rational basis for attacking the wheat program because it sought reduction of our wheat production."

His answer to the second question is that the power to control production has not been demonstrated and that certain conditions place important limits upon power to control. In answer to the third question, he says that he sees "justification for attempts to make economic forces serve human ends better," but thinks that "available techniques of social planning, experimentation, and control are ill developed."

The parity price philosophy is dealt with at some length in this last chapter. He recognizes two distinct ideas: (1) parity representing a sort of economic normal price of wheat and (2) a socially just price. He observes that it is difficult to ascertain "what the economic 'normal' price of wheat has been, is, or will be," and then proceeds to indicate his own ideas as to how much the parity price as calculated by the adopted formula overstates what he would consider to be current economic normal prices. By this calculation he reduces the disparity for 1933 to 6.5 cents as compared

with 27.7 cents as computed by the data and method prescribed in the Act.
He arrives at the lower figure not only by scaling down the base period
to a lower level for "normal" but also by modifying the index of prices
farmers pay to allow for improvement in quality of goods purchased.

Skepticism as to the reasonableness of the assumption that the pre-
war price was above normal has been indicated in dealing with the first
chapter. The extent to which the index of prices farmers pay should
be qualified in an expression of exchange values is also questionable.
As indicated by Dr. Davis, his calculations are based upon suppositions
that have not been thoroughly examined, and the index numbers that have
been used were not originally constructed for precise measurements in
dealing with such problems. Judgment on both points can be improved
by some additional painstaking research. Although no specific figure
now available can be taken as a precise determination of disparity,
careful study probably would result in the decision that there was a
significant difference between prices actually obtained for wheat in
the depression and the prices that would be obtained on the average of
normal economic conditions for producing only sufficient for domestic
needs and moderate exports.

An important issue arises out of this discussion of the use of parity
price formulas, that is, what is to be considered as "normal." Dr.
Davis indicates that he considers that the post-war "normal" cannot be
computed from a pre-war "normal" base. Differences in the use of the
word will naturally arise from different ideas as to what is required to
establish a "normal." The price required to obtain a given production
and move it into consumption within a period of one or two years may be
quite different from the price level required to maintain a given production and move it into consumption in a period of five, ten, or twenty-
five years. Apparently Dr. Davis has in mind the idea that the production
and price of wheat should readjust promptly in periods of depression to
changes in economic conditions. To meet his requirements, it would be
necessary to determine the price required to produce the amount of wheat
that could be sold on the domestic and world markets within a very short
time, so that there would be no piling up of carryovers. In contrast,
some who are concerned with the wheat program and agricultural relief
policies are looking to a balancing of conditions for a generation.
Recognizing the inevitable effects of readjustments after the War, they
are looking forward to the position of the wheat grower, together with
the supply and price of wheat when these readjustments are practically
completed. Some, of course, have in mind chiefly an intermediate idea
of adjusting for only the current cyclical depression. Clear thinking
requires clear distinction between policy directed towards clearing
the market in a short period and that towards maintaining the productive
capacity expected to be required at some future date by returning to
the producer what might be necessary or just to him for maintaining
these production services.

Having decided that objectives include maintaining productive capacity
and awarding the producer some return in excess of what the market might
provide in a depression, it becomes necessary to decide upon some measure
or basis for judging what action ought to be taken.

The author has made a significant concession in a footnote in this last chapter in which he says that "as compared with the principal altern-ative 'yardsticks' offered, I consider that 'parity price' was preferable to 'tariff effectiveness' or 'cost of production'." He does not give reasons for preferring parity prices but promises to deal more at length with this subject at a later time. Doubtless many of those who have used the parity price formula would, as a rule, claim for it only prefer-ence as a yardstick and not precision. Although the formula was definitely written into the law, provisions were made for discretion in its use, and the administration exercised discretion.

A vital issue is finding criteria for determining what price is "just or fair." Dr. Davis is disturbed by the fact that the term "just or fair" must necessarily be a matter of judgment. Is it impossible for economists to set up fairly definite concepts of fairness or justice? It has been done in dealing with taxation, tariffs, and monopolies; why not also in dealing with competitive price structures?

Can the government deal successfully with such a problem? Dr. Davis observes that fairness is a matter of opinion and opinions differ. "One Congress may decide what it thinks; but another may decide differ-ently." Furthermore opinions are affected by benefit payments. The dis-tribution of these payments powerfully influences votes. "Thus there is a tendency for the spread of a sinister form of political corruption which even its beneficiaries do not commonly recognize as such, so plausi-ble are the grounds on which it is advocated and its results are accepted." Dr. Davis says that these tendencies are not surprising and that what has been done may be justified as meeting a general emergency but thinks we should avoid accepting it as a continuing policy. Admitting that public opinion may be fickle, it does not follow that public administration should not assume some responsibility for dealing with agricultural price and in-come problems on this account, for it does deal with other problems subject to frequent changes in public opinion and to such subversive influences. Such problems cannot be dodged. The solution for a democracy is to educate the public and improve administration by developing and presenting a clear-cut statement of the problems involved, a careful analysis of facts, and the results of following different policies.

Although Dr. Davis concedes the possibility that the government may con-tribute somewhat to the improvement of economic conditions for the wheat grower, he remains skeptical of what may be accomplished in the future and doubtful of the wisdom of program makers. He stands ready to praise accomplishments but discourages further ventures. His position seems to be clearly indicated in a statement with reference to the international wheat problem as follows:

"For solving a world problem of 'surplus' wheat, I feel certain that freer play of economic forces would accomplish more than the best controls that can be devised; and I believe that efforts to impose in-ternational controls are more likely to hinder than to strengthen ef-forts toward increased freedom."

He would grant the possibility of more effective action by a nation in dealing with the problem within its own borders but doubts the possibility of its being able to carry a program through wisely. His economic philos-ophy with reference to national control is expressed in three sentences quoted as follows:

"Actual changes in prices of wheat and other products constitute economic forces operating to bring about readjustments in and
between agriculture, industry, trade, and services. Mitigation of the
harshness of these forces and acceleration of their speed may well
be sought. But with all that the AAA has done, or shows early promise of doing, no substitute for these forces of readjustment is in
prospect, short of complete socialization."
Thus he states the extremes between allowing economic forces to operate
unmodified, and complete socialization or control. Is there not a reasonably safe course between these extremes? Cannot economic forces be directed so as to greatly improve conditions for a class or for society
as a whole without regimentation and absolute control by a centralized
government? Errors are inevitable, but we are primarily concerned with
making some net gain. Has not some real progress been made in understanding economic laws and in the application of economic principles to political and social problems? Perhaps instead of turning back, we should pro-
ceed with caution, but keep going ahead. - O. C. Stine, Principal Agricultural Economist, Bureau of Agricultural Economics

Pelzer, Louis.   The cattlemen's frontier; a record of the trans-Mississippi
    cattle industry from oxen trains to pooling companies, 1850-1890.   351pp.
    Glendale, Calif., The A. H. Clark company, 1936.   43 P36
        "Cattle brands owned by members of the Wyoming Stock Growers' Associa-
    tion.   Chicago, The J. M. W. Jones Stationery & Printing Co., 1882" re-
    printed as pp.[249-312]
        Bibliography, pp. [313]-323
        The swift spread of the range cattle industry over an area of nearly
    a million and a half square miles of the trans-Mississippi West during
    the quarter-century following the Civil War has received the attention
    of countless popular writers as well as a number of able historians.
    Among the works by the latter group we usually single out Edward Everett
    Dale's Range Cattle Industry (Norman, Okla., 1930), Ernest Staples
    Osgood's Day of the Cattleman (Minneapolis, 1929), and Walter Prescott
    Webb's Great Plains (Boston, 1931) for special mention. To this
    selected list, the volume here reviewed should now be added.
        Comprehending that the "Motives in occupying and stocking the range
    country were fundamentally economic" and that "Profits rather than
    pleasure, wages rather than excitement, interest and dividends rather
    than hardships, and increase of herds more than adventure" were the
    factors in creating the cattle country, Professor Pelzer has made them
    the central theme of his volume. The "more colorful aspects which have
    passed from true narrative to the haze of fiction and legends" are
    subordinated. The scope of the study is indicated by the chapter titles:
    A decade of ox-team freighting on the plains; The Texas cattle trails;
    The shifting cow towns of Kansas; Cattle pools and associations; A
    cattlemen's commonwealth on the western range; The boom in cattle

companies in the eighties; Cattle at $1.80 per hundredweight; Economics
and finances of the cattle ranges; Illegal fencing on the western range;
A decade on the Dakota ranges; and Contemporary portraits of the frontier.
The extensive appendix is devoted to "Cattle Brands Owned by Members
of the Wyoming Stock Growers' Association," a complete reproduction
of a rare 62-page pamphlet published in 1882. The 9-page bibliography
lists the manuscripts and books utilized by Professor Pelzer in the
preparation of his study. - Everett E. Edwards, Agricultural Economist,
Bureau of Agricultural Economics.

DESCRIPTIVE NOTES AND ABSTRACTS

Agrarian Reform - Spain

Kriessmann, Ferdinand. Das spanische agrarproblem und die versuche zu seiner
    lösung; eine studie zur gegenwärtige agrarreform. 118pp. Stuttgart,
    W. Kohlhammer, 1934. (Tübinger wirtschaftswissenschaftliche abhandlungen.
    4 folge... hft. 7)   282 K892
      Bibliography, pp. [117]-118.

      As a background for his study of the agrarian reform of 1932
    the author describes the agrarian conditions which led up to it and
    made it necessary. He outlines the century-long struggle of the
    small farmer and the agricultural worker for his freedom and a right
    to his own economic development. He stresses the inequality of the
    land distribution and its resultant utilization and tells of the
    various attempts at reform which preceded the Act of Sept. 15, 1932
    the provisions of which he discusses.

Agricultural Credit - French Colonies

Tardy, Louis, and Cramois, André.   Le crédit agricole dans nos possessions
    d'outre-mer. 38pp. Paris, Imprimerie nationale [etc.] 1935.   284.2 T17C
      At head of title: Ministère des colonies. Institut national d'agronomie
    de la France d'outre-mer.
      Reprinted from L'Agronomie Coloniale Nov. 1934-Jan. 1935, Mar. 1935
    (20 Ag812)
      Attention is called to the importance of a system of agricultural
    credit in the French Colonies, and in this connection the functions of
    the mutual agricultural credit banks are described which are approximately
    the same in the colonies as in France. An account is given of the organ-
    ization and operation of agricultural credit in Algeria, Tunisia, Morocco,
    La Guadeloupe, La Martinique, Réunion, La Nouvelle Calédonie, French
    West Africa, Madagascar, Indochina, the countries under French mandate
    of Cameroun and Togo, and the New Hebrides (British-French Condominium)

Wilmanns, Wolfgang, und Isensee, Hermann. Die lage der landwirtschaft im
Freistaat Sachsen. Untersuchungen über die rentabilität der sächsischen
landwirtschaft in den erntejahren 1931/32 and 1932/33... hft. 3. 74pp.
Dresden und Leipzig, T. Steinkopf, 1936. 281.175 H18 hft. 3
At head of title: Landesstelle zur erforschung der landwirtschaftlichen
betriebsverhältnisse im Freistaat Sachsen dem Institut für landwirtschaftliche betriebslehre der Universität Leipzig angegliedert begründet
von gen. regierungsrat prof. dr. Friedrich Falke.
A detailed statistical account of agricultural economic conditions
in the Free State of Saxony during the crop years of 1931/32 and 1932/33,
with comparative figures for the years from 1926/27. Expenditures, cost
of production, gross and net return, and income are among the subjects
covered.

Agricultural Economics - Italy

Bologna. Osservatorio di economia agraria per l'Emilia. Annali dell'Osservatorio di economia agraria per l'Emilia. Annesso alla Cattedra di economia agraria della R. Università di Bologna. Volume IV. Direttore Prof.
Giuseppe Tassinari. 439pp. Faenza, Stabilimento grafico F. Lega, 1935.
281.9 B63 v. 4
At head of title: Istituto nazionale di economia agraria.
Contents: Le vicende del reddito dell'agricoltura dal 1925 al 1932, by
Giuseppe Tassinari. - pp. 9-359. (A statistical study of the agricultural
returns on a number of typical agricultural enterprises during the period
from 1925 to 1932) La distribuzione del lavoro manuale in poderi a
mezzadria della Romagna, by Luigi Perdisa. - pp. 360-396. (A study illustrated by tables and graphs of the distribution of labor on 6 small
farms operated on a share farming basis) Imposte, tributi e redditi
dell'agricoltura in provincia di Bologna, by Osvaldo Passerini, - pp. 399-
431. (An account of the effect of taxes on agricultural returns in the
province of Bologna.)

Agriculture - Chile

Matthei, Adolfo. Agrarwirtschaft und agrarpolitik der Republik Chile. 98pp.
Berlin, p. Parey. 1936. ([Germany] Reichs- und Pr. Ministerium für
Ernährung und Landwirtschaft. Berichte über Landwirtschaft. n. F. 119.
Sonderheft)
The author discusses the basic agricultural production of Chile, the
use and distribution of the land, the population and transportation
problems, agricultural credit and measures adopted for the protection
of agriculture. An appendix deals with German settlements in Chile.

Agriculture - England

Rural reconstruction association. The revival of agriculture, a constructive
policy for Britain. Prepared by a committee of the Rural reconstruction
association. With a foreword by Lord O'Hagan and Michael Beaumont.
138pp. London, G. Allen & Unwin ltd. [1936]   281.171 R88R
    Bibliography, pp. 133-134.
    Part I discusses The problem in history, Comments on economics and
the case for rural revival; Part II, A national agricultural policy;
Part III, The national organisation of agriculture.

Agriculture - Germany

Hanefeld, Kurt.   Geschichte des deutschen nährstandes.   514pp.   Leipzig, B.
Franke, 1935.   283 H19
    Bibliography, pp. 482-508.
    " A study of the development of agrarian systems in Germany from the
earliest times down to the present day. The author distinguishes three
principal phases in the history of the German peasant, characterised
respectively by the collective economy of the communes, the feudal system, and the dependence on markets. From January 1933 onwards, a fourth
period opened in the life of the peasants - the period of organic inter-
dependence, characterised by the integral organisation of all agriculturists without distinction of any kind as regards their material or
social position. The Act of 30 January 1933 revived the agricultural
'State' and, according to the author, will have as a consequence the
comprehensive reconstruction of German agriculture and the restoration
of the balance between agriculture and industry, which, during recent
years, has played a predominating part in German national economy. The
work contains many interesting data on the policy of agricultural protectionism in Germany during the great crises of the nineteenth and
twentieth centuries. It also examines the influence of industrialisation on the development of German agriculture." - International Labour
Review, v. 33, no. 4, p. 595, Apr. 1936.

Association of Land-Grant Colleges and Universities - Proceedings

Association of land-grant colleges and universities. Proceedings of the
forty-ninth annual convention... held at Washington, D. C., November
18-20, 1935. Edited by Charles A. McCue for the Executive committee
of the association. 348pp. Wilmington, Del., Cann bros., printers
[1936]   4 As7
    Published August 1936.
    Partial contents: The states, the regions and the nations, by Henry
A. Wallace; The farmer's own credit system, by W. I. Myers; The grass
revolution, by Chester C. Davis; Regional adjustment, by Henry A.
Wallace; Regional adjustments and democratic planning, by H. R. Tolley;
The regional adjustment project - A summary and some suggestions for
further work, by Chris V. Wells; AAA regional adjustment project from

experiment station standpoint, by R. E. Buchanan; Plans, program and
public opinion, by Chester C. Davis, The roles of the United States
Department of Agriculture and the state experiment stations in regional
research programs, by M. L. Wilson; The roles of the United States De-
partment of Agriculture and the state experiment stations in regional
research programs. The experiment stations' viewpoint, by J. G. Lipman;
The roles of the United States Department of Agriculture and the state
experiment stations in regional research programs, by C. T. Powell;
A translation exchange service as an aid to agricultural research;
A research program under the Bankhead-Jones Act, by James T. Jardine;
Relation of extension with Resettlement Administration, by Carl C.
Taylor; Relation of Extension Service with Resettlement Administration,
by W. C. Coffey; Relationship of the Extension Service to the Soil
Conservation Service, by H. H. Bennett; Relationships of Extension with
the Soil Conservation Service, by H. W. Mumford; Rural electrification
and the Extension Service, by W. E. Herring; Relationship of the
Extension Service with Farm Credit Administration, by Dr. W. L. Myers;
The long-time program of AAA, by Chester C. Davis; and The program of the
Farm Chemurgic Council, by Wheeler McMillen.

Chinese Products

Williams, C. A. S.   Manual of Chinese products. 256pp. Peiping, Printed
    at Kwang Yuen press, 1933.   286 W67
    Bibliography, pp. 225-228.
    Sold by Kelly and Walsh, Ltd., Shanghai, China.
    "This publication is the outcome of some years research work on the
various Chinese productions, and is written with the object of providing a number of simple definitions, or short descriptions, of their essential features, for the purpose of ready reference by Customs and
Civil Service employees, merchants, curio dealers, art collectors,
etc., and in order to serve as a basis for lecture material in the various educational establishments, as well as for the general study of the
indigenous fauna, flora and minerology. The classification and numbering of the Customs Export Tariff of the Republic of China (1931) has
been strictly followed."
    Much of the volume is devoted to agricultural products.

Colonies

Clark, Grover. A place in the sun. 235pp. New York, The Macmillan
    company, 1936. 286 C542P
    For "statistical tables and other detailed documentary material which
are the foundation of the statements made" in this vol. see the author's
"The Balance Sheets of Imperialism." (286 C542)
    "This book is the result of an attempt to get, from the actual
records, an answer to the question: Do colonies pay? Most emphatically,
the answer is: No.

"Three principal reasons have been stressed in this past half century, to justify the seizure of colonies: they would provide an outlet for surplus population; the possession of them would give increased trade; and control over them would give access to raw materials not otherwise available and hence bring profits in time of peace and greater security in time of war. These claims have been asserted and re-asserted until they came to be accepted as basic articles of faith by the mass of the people in the countries which were taking new colonies, and even by many of those in positions of responsibility who had the opportunity to learn the facts from the records. Yet a careful analysis of those records shows clearly that these arguments are in large part fallacies - and dangerous fallacies, at that. The records show that:

"First, only a very small number of people, compared either to the population at home or to the whole number of those who emigrated, have gone to the territories over which the colony-holding powers had political control. The emigrants have gone where there was room, opportunity, political or religious freedom. Very clearly, emigration has not followed the flag.

"Second, political control has given only a little trade with the colonial regions which the controlling country could not have secured without that control. Furthermore, the profits on all the trade with all their overseas holdings have not been anything like enough to cover the costs in which possession of the colonies has involved the holding countries. Germany and Italy, in fact, spent more on their colonies than the total value of all their trade with them; Italy, very much more.

"Third, political control has not given nor can it give substantial advantage in access to raw materials in time of peace; in time of war, access to essential materials, whether the sources are located in or out of colonies, depends not at all on political control over territory but on control of lines of communication with those sources." - Preface.

Conservation.

Chase, Stuart.   Rich land, poor land; a study of waste in the natural resources of America. 361pp. New York, London, McGraw-Hill book company, inc. [1936]   279 C38
    Bibliography, pp. 351-352.
    Mr. Chase argues that as "the damage to our natural resources and especially to our land, has been the result of many forces acting together so any program of conservation must be many sided. Only a coordinated plan of regional conservation can hope to succeed."

The Constitution

Patterson, C. P. The Supreme court and the Constitution. 45pp.   Dallas, Tex., Southern Methodist university, 1936. (Arnold foundation studies in public affairs. v. 4, no. 3, winter 1936)   280.12 P27
    "Caleb Perry Patterson is Editor of the Southwestern Social Science Quarterly and Professor of Government in the University of Texas.
    "The first section of his paper traces the history of the principle of judicial review in America before 1787; the second section discusses the doctrine in the Federal Convention of that year; the third section

discusses the role of the Supreme Court in our history down to the time of the New Deal; and the fourth section analyzes the various decisions dealing with the New Deal legislation, including the recent TVA decision.

"It is obvious that Professor Patterson's paper deals with a highly controversial subject. A different approach to the question will be presented in the next number of the Arnold Foundation Studies by James Ernest Pate of the College of William and Mary, who will discuss 'The Decline of States' Rights.'" - Introductory Note.

Consumers' Cooperation

California. State relief administration. Handbook of consumers' cooperatives in California, September, 1935. Submitted to Office of coordinator of statistical projects by SERA research project on consumers' cooperatives in California. 179pp., mimeogr. [San Francisco, 1935?] 280.2 C12
    At head of title: California State Relief Administration.
    Contains bibliographies.
    Partial contents: Brief history of consumers' cooperatives in California, 1867-1935; The contemporary consumers' cooperative movement; Producers' cooperatives in California; Self-help cooperatives in California; Credit unions in California; Cooperative colonies in California, Brief review of agricultural marketing and supply cooperatives; and Pseudo-cooperatives and rackets.

Consumer distribution corporation. The need for consumer cooperation and a plan for its expansion. 20pp. New York city, Consumer distribution corporation [1936?] 280.2 C762
    The statement of the New York Times (June 21, 1936) about this small pamphlet follows:
    "Consumer cooperation offers the 'only constitutional way which has so far been discovered of solving the most menacing of our business problems,' and it is only the 'most superficial observers who see in it any menace to existing business,' according to a study issued yesterday by the Consumer Distribution Corporation, the central wholesale unit of the League of Cooperative Department Stores planned by E. A. Filene.
    "The study, entitled 'The Need for Consumer Cooperation and a Plan for Its Expansion,' outlines the history and growth of the cooperatives abroad and describes the function of the Consumer Distribution Corporation, for which Mr. Filene has furnished a capital of $1,000,000. The assertion is made that 'if consumer cooperation is to succeed here it must attack the problem of large-scale distribution.'
    "It is not necessary, it is stated in the study, 'to duplicate the long experimental processes of the European cooperative systems,' but a new development of consumer organization, typified by the corporation, 'must precede the appearance of the cooperative department store.'"

U. S. Dept. of labor. Consumers' project. Consumers' cooperative statutes in the United States. 186pp., mimeogr. [Washington, D. C.] 1936, 158.241 C76
    "In this country, as elsewhere, cooperatives were begun at first without any realization of the legal pitfalls surrounding an informal

organization. They were organized by neighbors or fellow-workers in the most obvious way possible - in the shape of what the layman calls an association or a society. It soon became clear, however, that such an informal arrangement would involve a constant threat of difficulty in the courts; the inability of the association to appeal as a body to the courts to protect its contracts and the possibility of unlimited liability for each member were the most important considerations.

"Naturally enough, cooperators turned to the corporation for their legal garb. But attempts to organize under the existing corporation laws and to embody in the constitution of the organization the familiar Rochdale principles were in most cases difficult and in some cases impossible. The next step was to seek amendments to the corporation laws which would embody these principles.

"Since that time, development has been largely along two lines: (1) The realization has been growing on the part of cooperators and legislators that the cooperative is or ought to be legally as well as factually, a far different institution from the business corporation. Since the time of the first statutory recognition of cooperatives - it dates back to the middle of the last century in some states - progress has been made towards filling in the outlines of a self-contained code of law for cooperatives, defining their nature by mandatory provisions, permitting them leeway where the business corporation is restricted and restricting them where the business corporation has leeway, and setting out the position of members, patrons and stockholders in explicit language. (2) Along with this development there has been a tendency to differentiate the consumers' cooperative from other forms - the agricultural marketing cooperative or the producers' cooperative, for instance. The first assumption that a cooperative is a cooperative whatever its function has not been borne out; later statutes recognize the important differences between the various types. The statutes which are on the books represent various stages of these two lines of development. They range from the simple provisions of the Ohio law to the elaborate act on the New York books.

"This collection of cooperative statutes includes... the acts of the various legislatures of continental United States... which are intended to facilitate the organization of consumers' cooperatives."

Consumption and Standards of Living

Zimmerman, C. C. Consumption and standards of living. 602pp. New York, D. Van Nostrand company, inc., 1936. 284.4 Z6

The author in his preface writes in part as follows:

"It has been sixteen years since Carl C. Taylor first interested me in writing a Master's Thesis on the standard of living. Since that time, ideas on this subject have been constantly evolving in my mind. In 1924, John D. Black enabled me to start the work which gave me a definite idea of a complete family budget, F. B. Garver led me through the utility analysis, and P. A. Sorokin caused me to inspect Ernst Engel's studies in the original. I was also greatly influenced by a careful study of Frédéric Le Play's work, and by stimulating discussions with Robert E. Park on the psychological phases of consumption. After continued investigations in many parts of America, I was enabled to make studies in Canada in 1930, in Siam in 1930-31, among the Ozark Highlanders in 1932-33, and in Cuba in 1934.

"Frior 1932 to 1936 I was aided in the preparation of this manuscript by funds from the Harvard Committee on Research in the Social Sciences. In 1932, through the interest of Max Handman, I was asked to include some of my materials in an analytical bibliography of existing budget studies to be prepared in cooperation with Faith M. Williams, United States Bureau of Home Economics. (See U. S. D. A., Misc. Pub. No. 233.) By 1935 the rest of my manuscript had become so large that I published the material on Le Play in a separate monograph (Family and Society, D. Van Nostrand Company, 1935). I am now publishing this third volume which I hope, in conjunction with the other two, will be accepted as a definitive analysis of this part of human behavior.

"There are those who say that Social Science is logical, illogical, statistical, non-statistical, purely descriptive, evaluative, and what not. To me, it consists only of a systematic examination of facts and ideas and the relations between these two. In this work I have not only presented a comprehensive study of the pertinent empirical materials but have also ventured to discuss the existing ideas on the subject."

Among the chapter headings are the following: The problem of consumption; Laws of consumption; The rôle of food; The laws of food; The rôle of housing; Laws of housing expense; The rôle of clothing; The laws of clothing expense; Spending or saving; Early studies; Modern studies; The Le Play school; The Russian school; American studies - then and now; Classical economic theory and consumption; Institutional theory and consumption; Austrian hedonism and consumption; Mathematical hedonism and consumption; The nature of a system of living.

Consumption - Dairy Products and Eggs - Tennessee

Allred, C. E., and Powell, J. C.   Consumption of dairy products and eggs in rural Tennessee with regional comparisons. 22pp., mimeogr. Knoxville, Tenn., August 15, 1936. ([U. S. Works progress administration. Cooperative plan of rural research] Report no. 19)   173.2 W89Co no. 19
     "Agricultural Economics and Rural Sociology Department, Agricultural Experiment Station, University of Tennessee, Knoxville, Tennessee."
     Bibliography, pp. 19-21.
     "The principal objectives of this study are to ascertain (1) the per capita consumption of dairy products and eggs among white farm owners in the different regions of Tennessee; (2) the main causes of the regional differences; and (3) the regional variations in amount sold and purchased for home consumption. Data on Tennessee are also compared with similar studies in other states."

Consumption - Evaporated Milk

Milk research council, inc.   The effect of evaporated milk consumption on
fluid milk sales in the United States with special reference to New York
city, by Edward Fisher Brown for the Milk research council, inc. November
15, 1935.   23pp., mimeogr.   New York city [1935]   281.344 M59E
    Supplement to Recent trends in milk consumption in New York as compared
with Boston and Philadelphia (281.344 M59)
    "A survey of the relative situation of evaporated and fluid milk in
the United States reveals these facts: 1. Consumption of evaporated milk
has increased steadily and rapidly in the last twenty years. Between 1920
and 1930 the consumption doubled. Since 1930 the consumption of evaporated
milk has increased by nearly 25 percent. 2. Though the consumption of
fluid milk increased by more than 20 percent from 1920 to 1930, since
that year it has decreased by more than 6 percent. 3. A major cause of
the relative increase in the use of evaporated milk has been the economic
situation - the necessity on the part of many families to seek a low-cost
milk supply. Other causes are: Federal relief buying and distribution of
evaporated milk; State relief purchases and recommendation to relief recipients of evaporated milk; a steady, well-contrived and well-financed propaganda on behalf of evaporated milk, and the relative decrease in the cost
of evaporated milk as compared with fluid milk. 4. The effect of the increase in evaporated milk consumption in the New York City market has been
to decrease the income of the milk producer and adversely affect the fluid
milk distributor." - Summary.

Consumption - Foods - Tennessee

Allred, C. E., and Powell, J. C.   Consumption of vegetative foods in rural
Tennessee, with regional comparisons. 33pp., mimeogr. Knoxville, Tenn.,
September 1, 1936. ([U. S. Works progress administration. Cooperative
plan of rural research] Report no.20)   173.2 W89Co no. 20
    Bibliography, pp. 30-32.
    "Agricultural Economics and rural sociology department, Agricultural
Experiment Station, University of Tennessee, Knoxville."
    "This is the third of a series of studies on food consumption in
Tennessee. The first one dealt with meat consumption, and the second
with dairy products and egg consumption. The objectives of the present
study are to ascertain, and present in a graphic form the regional differences in the per capita consumption of various kinds of vegetative foods
in Tennessee; the causes for these regional differences; how Tennessee
compares with other states; and the amount of vegetative foods that each
family purchases."

Allred, C. E., and Powell, J. C.   Meat consumption in rural Tennessee with
regional comparisons.   26pp., mimeogr.   Knoxville, Tenn., Aug. 1, 1936.
(U. S. Works progress administration. Cooperative plan of rural research]
Report no. 18)   173.2 W89Co no. 18
   "Agricultural Economics and Rural Sociology Department, Agricultural
Experiment Station, University of Tennessee, Knoxville, Tennessee."
   Bibliography, pp. 23-25.
   The objects of this study are to ascertain the per capita meat con-
sumption of Tennessee farm families by regions, and to determine so far
as possible the causes for the regional differences.

Cooperation

Cooperative food distributors of America.   The cooperative challenge to
   American business, by Hector Lazo, executive vice president, Cooperative
   food distributors of America.   31pp.   Washington, D. C., 1936.
   280.2 C785
      Bibliography, p. 31.

Hutchinson, C. R.   Seeking a new world through co-operatives.   63pp.   New
   York, Cincinnati [etc.] The Methodist book concern [1935]   (Everyday adventures in Christian living)   280.2 H97
      References, pp. 38-61.
      Bibliography, p. 6.

Cooperation among the Unemployed - England

Hoyland, J. S.   Digging for a new England, the co-operative farm for unemployed men.   224pp.   London, J. Cape [1936]   283 H85
      This is a vivid account by an eye-witness of and a participant in the
   use of the land for the employment and regeneration of the unemployed.
   It is the story of student work-camps whose members have gone to many
   parts of Great Britain aiding the men on allotments to dig their plots
   of land and plant on them, living with and helping especially those who
   are weak or incapacitated.   The goal is the establishment of cooperative
   farms to which the average man, after his years in industry, may go to
   work as long as his health remains good, and where he will be a part of
   "a hard-working productive and public-spirited yeomanry."   The Hutterian
   communities are instanced as an example of cooperative organization and
   the international significance of the work-camps movement is pointed out.
      The work tends to show that "unemployed, who now seem the waste product
   of a wastefully organized industrialism, are the hope of a new England."

Cotton - Japan

Morse, F. C., firm.   25 years of cotton in Japan.   A compilation showing progress
   made between 1910 and 1935.   51pp.   Kobe, Japan [1936]   304 M832
   A useful compilation of statistical tables and charts.

Economic Changes - New Zealand

Sutch, W. B.   Recent economic changes in New Zealand.   Introduction by Hon.
Walter Nash.   164pp.   [Auckland, Christchurch etc. N.Z.] Institute
of Pacific relations, New Zealand council, 1936.   280.1993 Su8
The Hon. Walter Nash, New Zealand Minister of Finance and Marketing,
writes in part as follows in the introduction:
"I do not think it would be an exaggeration to state that the last
six years have been the most eventful in the economic history of New
Zealand. Not only has the Dominion, in common with the rest of the world,
suffered the devastation of unparalleled depression, but economic changes
of such magnitude have taken place that the very psychological outlook
of the people has changed also. To-day the common conviction in New
Zealand and in other countries too, is that economic forces cannot be
allowed to operate without restraint or regulation. There is a determination that such forces must be rationally controlled as far as it is
humanly possible to control them and that the sole aim and object of
such control should be the provision of the highest possible standard
of living consistent with a country's natural resources and its ability
to utilize them effectively...
"This most informative and valuable publication... constitutes a
record of contemporary economic history, written so to speak as it
unfolds. As such the work is an outstanding contribution to New Zealand's economic literature and one, moreover, which does not cease
with a description and analysis of the facts and phenomena of the contemporary scene, but portrays them in a correct perspective and inter-
prets them against a background which has due regard for human as well
as economic values.
"The background, against which the New Zealand Government is working
at present, has been vividly described by Dr. Sutch in the following
pages. He traces the recent changes in New Zealand's monetary system
and its banking machinery, he describes New Zealand's manufacturing industries and their reaction to the depression, he tells the story of
the dairy industry which shows both the tragedy brought by low prices
and the exhilaration of expanding production, and gives a detailed account of New Zealand's observance of the Ottawa Agreement, particularly
in regard to meat."
The extract which follows is taken from the author's preface:
"The economic adaptations made in New Zealand to meet the depression
are described in the following pages. They are linked up with, and,
to some extent, conditioned by New Zealand's fulfilment of her obligations under the Ottawa Agreement. The adjustments discussed are the
consequences of New Zealand's economic relationships with the outside
world.
"Little reference is made to wool, not because wool prices did not
fall, but because there was comparatively little economic change resulting from these low prices. On the other land considerable space is
given to dairying - New Zealand's sweated primary industry.

"Dairying, still in process of rapid change and development, suffered most in the depression, and is the industry which not only demanded the most definite structural and organizational changes, but is also the first to receive the attention of New Zealand's new Labour Government.

"Nutrition is a fashionable study at the moment, and I hesitated to introduce it into the discussion on the marketing possibilities for dairy produce, especially in view of the underlying economic realities of the market. But while physical needs do not constitute effective economic demand, it appears that popular opinion will soon reach the stage when it will prefer even to alter the mechanics of the economic system rather than to go without essential food.

"However, the competitive price system remains and the process of changing it, even if the will is there, is far from easy.

"As far as New Zealand producers are concerned, a possibility of stable prices is offered by the new Government's guaranteed price procedure. If this is a success, one side of the farmer's problem is solved. The other side - the system of land tenure - is more difficult and fundamental.

"New Zealand combines probably the most efficient land transfer system in the world with a mainly freehold system of land tenure. Leaving aside the recurrent effects of falling prices, the result is, with an active market for farm properties, a tendency for the debts against a farm to be always a little more than the farmer can meet, without lowering his own and his family's living standards.

"If the Government subsidizes the carriage of lime or fertilizer by rail, the subsidy is soon absorbed in the capital value of the farm, if the Government applies a policy of partial derating to rural lands, the concession is capitalized in the value of farm land, if interest rates are lowered, the relief in interest rates is capitalized, if science and invention make farm land more economically productive, the benefits are capitalized, if transport costs are reduced the benefits are capitalized, if the costs of processing farm products decrease, the decrease is capitalized, if wage rates fall, the reduction is capitalized, if wives and children work without a return or with an insufficient return, what is saved is capitalized, if the incoming owner has hopes that he can farm more skilfully, the measures of the hope or the skill is capitalized, if there is an expectation of rising prices - guaranteed or otherwise - the expectation is capitalized.

"Trading in farm lands and cultivating farm lands do not go well together, and while the system of freehold continues to be divorced from the system of usehold, New Zealand's basic farm problem will remain."

Economic Control - Belgium

Roger, Charles. Economic control: the experiment of Belgium. With a preface by Paul van Zeeland, Prime Minister of Belgium and Minister of Foreign Affairs. 80pp. [Oxford, Eng.] The Catholic social guild, 1935. 280.172 R63
    Chapter headings: The Problem and the Moral Principle; Belgium and the Gold Bloc; A "New Deal" for Belgium; Monetary Policy and Bank Control in Belgium, Vocational organization in Belgium, De Man, the Socialist, and Van Zeeland, the Catholic.

Economic History - Canada

Innis, Mary Q. An economic history of Canada. 302pp. Toronto, The Ryerson press [1935] 277.13 In6
 Bibliography, pp. 293-294. "References" and "Readings" at end of each chapter except the last.
 Prof. W. A. Mackintosh of Queens' University reviews this work as follows in the American Economic Review for June 1936, p. 308.
 "Though formal studies of Canadian economic history have been pursued for the past fifty years, no previous author has written a comprehensive economic history of the country. There have been coöperative works such as Canada and Its Provinces and the Canadian volume in the Cambridge History of the British Empire; but in these several authors have collaborated ant there is no single point of view and no unity of interpretation. Further, in such works the economic history is likely to be a mere addendum to general history. Mrs. Innis is to be congratulated on having made a courageous venture, and on having been highly successful in her achievement.

 This volume is much more than a conventional pedestrian chronicle of economic events and policies. It is the result of intensive research, is illuminated by thoughful interpretation, and is an example of scholarly exposition. The approach to the subject is geographical and technological; the geographic formation of the Pre-Cambrian shield which covers a large portion of the Canadian area is basic to an interpretation of economic development. The geographic basis and successive technological changes permitted the development of a series of export staples which with their subordinate industries mark the important periods of Canadian economic history. Since Canada is only emerging into the position of a mature economy, the line of its development to the present is clearly marked for cod, beaver, oak staves, potash, timber, wheat, sawn lumber, gold and silver, pulp and paper, and non-ferrous metals.

 "The book places in its proper perspective the major importance of transportation in the economic life of the country. Its cost is a necessary and heavy overhead whose distribution is at the base of many economy problems and cleavages. Given great length of territory and wide gaps in the traffic areas, the dominant influence of transportation becomes inevitable.

 "It has frequently been said that Canada is a country created in defiance of geography, but Mrs. Innis takes the view that, though divisive in some fields the Pre-Cambrian shield gives the essential unity and character to the country. Its existence may have delayed economic development but it gave to the country its characteristic features. These considerations underlie Mrs. Innis's interpretation of Canadian economic history, but the book is not an essay in interpretation; it is, in addition, a vivid account of the development of economic activities and institutions. There is a sound interpretation of the developing processes through which the present Canadian economy functions.

 "One cannot compare Mrs. Innis's book with others because in its field it is unique. But one can say confidently that it is a good book, well planned, well written, and fully documented."

Economic History - Ohio

Hunter, L. C. Studies in the economic history of the Ohio valley: seasonal
aspects of industry and commerce before the age of big business; the
beginnings of industrial combination. 130pp. Northampton, Mass., The
Department of history of Smith college [1934] (Smith college studies in
history. v. 19, no. 1-2. October, 1933-January, 1934) 277.12 H912
    Reviewed in American Economic Review, June 1936, p. 314.

Economic History - South Africa

Knowles, L C. A. and Knowles, C. M. The economic development of the British
overseas empire... v. 3. The Union of South Africa. 356pp. London, G.
Routledge & sons, ltd., 1936. (Studies in economics and political science,
ed. by the director of the London school of economics and political science
no. 110) 277.171 K76
    Bibliography, pp. 343-346.
    Among the chapters of especial interest to agricultural economists are
the following: The white colonists and the land; The four governments and
their economic rivalries; The farming industry in the primitive and
pastoral stage; Development of commercial farming and growth of the agricultural side; The fight against drought, plagues, and pests; and Farming
as an organized and state-fostered industry.

Economic History - U. S.

Hunter, M. H. Visual outline of economic history of the United States.
130pp. New York, Longmans, Green & co. [1936] (Students outline
series) 277.12 H91
    Bibliography, pp. 129-130

Economic Policy for the Machine Age

McGregor, A. G. The correct economy for the machine age; the economic policy
which must be pursued if prosperity is to be achieved and then maintained.
With a foreword by John A. Hobson. 256pp. London, Sir I. Pitman & sons,
ltd., 1935. 280 M17
    From the foreword signed by J. A. Hobson the extract which follows has
been taken:
    "In closely-reasoned chapters [the author] sets out the root causes of
that lack of balance which is exhibited in every country in the shape of
under-production and under-consumption, and relates this national lack of
balance to the international disturbances which have driven each nation into policies of narrow economic restriction so damaging to free trade intercourse and so wasteful of world resources.
    "The increasing capacity of production, taken in conjunction with the
policies connected with a gold basis of exchange, has given a size, a duration, and special character to our Great Depression. But the whole trouble
is rooted in a mal-distribution of purchasing power, which incites attempts
to over-save, over-invest, and over-produce, and the only sound permanent

remedy is to be found in measures which shall give wage and salary earners a share of the total income adequate to raise their demand for consumption goods so as to correspond with the increasing powers of production.

"This cannot, Mr. McGregor argues, be achieved either by a wasteful struggle between groups of employers and employed in the several trades, or by a general displacement of private initiative and competition under State Socialism. The disappearance of capitalism is neither practicable nor desirable. But, in the process of re-distributing purchasing power so as to restore and maintain the just balance between productive capacity and consumption, the State, as representing the interests of the whole community, must play an important part. Wages and salaries must be raised in the whole industrial system.

"Now this policy, though advantageous to capital as well as labour, cannot be achieved by individual firms or individual trades which stand to lose if they act alone. It can only be achieved by the common simultaneous action of the whole economic community. For only thus can each business and each trade realize that its higher labour costs will be more than compensated by a fuller use of its capital, and a larger, reliable consumer market at a higher price level.

"If every business man knows that all others in his trade and every other trade realized and would act upon this sound economy, State action might not be necessary. But this is an impossible assumption. Hence, Mr. McGregor is driven to a proposal which may shock and disconcert many of his readers until they come to realize its necessity, viz. that the State shall decree a given rise in wages and salaries to take effect on a given date. The delicate task of adjusting the amount of the rise to the condition of the several trades is to be entrusted to a Commission upon whose competence and fairness a great deal must depend. But a higher and a fairer rate of wages is essential, and its achievement cannot safely be left to futile struggles within each trade. Therefore, however difficult this procedure by a national decree may be, the difficulty must be faced.

"Not less radical and important are Mr. McGregor's proposals for dealing with foreign trade and investment. He argues that each nation can and should maintain, by regulated monetary action, a true balance in its import and export trade.

"Under the old order, where the excessive profits from low-paid labour were driven into foreign investments, great trouble arose when payment of interest was required, either in gold, which upset the whole monetary system, or in goods, which reduced home production. Under existing conditions, when this policy of foreign investment is common to many industrial countries and is visibly responsible for unemployment, free individual investment can no longer be tolerated. Control of foreign investment within each nation must be exercised by some central bank, or better still, by an International Clearing House.

"Mr. McGregor's full and close discussion of the operation of such a Clearing House forms one of the ablest and most original parts of his constructive proposals. He does not deny the difficulties attending such a delicate process of international co-operation, holding that the necessary faith will only be achieved by perceiving the greater difficulties attending separate national exchange controls.

"There are three conspicuous merits in Mr. McGregor's economy: First comes his powerful grasp of the conditions essential for a true balance between productivity and consumption. Second, his appeal not to idealism or altruism, but to an intelligent grasp of long-range self-interest among capitalists and employees. Third, his strong realization of the fact that the competitive system of industry is unworkable on pre-war methods of finance. His is an appeal to reason and a belief that as business is normally conducted in its details on reasonable calculations of gain and loss, this process can and must be applicable to the wider, longer scale, and more general conduct which the new industrial and financial inter-dependence in the business world demands."

Economic Terms

Bower, Frank. Dictionary of economic terms. Revised by K.A.H.Egerton, B. A. 159pp. London, G. Routledge & sons, ltd. [1936] 280 B673 Ed.10
"10th new and revised edition", p. [2]
This is a very useful little volume in which "the emphasis has been placed... on terms used in works on economics – both theoretical and practical."

Economics

Ware, Caroline F., and Means, G. C. The modern economy in action. 244pp. New York, Harcourt, Brace and company [1936] 280.12 W22
Bibliography, pp. 233-239.
"This brief volume is designed as an aid to fresh thinking on economic problems... It calls attention to the facts of the present economic situation with which any sound public policy will have to deal. It then poses the problems which must be thought through, indicating how they relate to the factual situation, and some of the possible directions in which solutions to these problems might be sought " - Preface

Economics and Industry – Gt. Britain

British association for the advancement of science. Economic science and statistics section. Britain in depression; a record of British industries since 1929. 473pp. London, Sir I. Pitman & sons, ltd., 1935. 280.171 B77
Bibliography at end of most of the chapters.
Professor J. H. Jones, Chairman of committee.
Partial contents: Agriculture: Introduction; Grain and other crops, by C. S. Orwin; Agriculture: The milk industry, by Professor A. W. Ashby; Agriculture: The livestock and meat industry, by Professor A. W. Ashby; The cotton industry, by Professor G. W. Daniels and H. Campion, The wool textile industry, by A. N. Shimmin; The seed-crushing and oil-milling industry, by Professor G. C. Allen; and Consumers' trades and services, by P. Ford.

Smith, N. S.   An introduction to some Japanese economic writings of the 18th
    century.   72pp. London, P. S. King & son ltd., 1935.   280 Sm62In
        Reprinted from the Transactions of the Asiatic Society of Japan, v. 11,
    second series, 1934.   (513 J27)
        The three chapters which constitute this small volume are the following:
    The monetary proposals of Hakuseki Arai, during a period of inflation;
    The monetary proposals of Sorai Ogiu, during a time of deflation (1. On
    prices. 2. On the contraction in the gold and silver circulation. 3. On
    loans); An elementary theory of value.

Farm Inheritance Act - Germany

Dölle, H. H. L.   Lehrbuch des reichserbhofrechts.   179pp. München und Berlin,
    C. H. Beck'sche verlagsbuchhandlung, 1935.   282 D69
        Contains bibliographies.
    This is a textbook with an index on the German Farm Inheritance Act.

Farm Labor - California

California. State relief administration. Division of special surveys and
    studies. Migratory labor in California. Special surveys and studies.
    224pp., mimeogr. [San Francisco, Calif., 1936]   283 C1262
        A bibliography on migratory labor in California, pp. [217]-224.
        M. H. Lewis, Director of Special Surveys and Studies of the California
    State Relief Administration writes in part as follows in his signed fore-
    word:
        "The study of Migratory Labor in California was prepared under the
    direction and supervision of Alma Holzschuh. The History of Migratory
    Labor was written by Dr. Fred Safier, and the bibliography collected
    by him. The statistical data relating to wages and hours of employment
    of 775 agricultural workers on relief was prepared by Dr. G. Eleanor
    Kimble and Raymond Wilson. They also assisted in preparation of all
    material for mimeographing. Two family histories, 'A Modern Patriarch'
    and 'Stranded' were obtained by Ethel Edwards; 'The Webb Family', by
    Harry White; and 'The Endless Trek', by William J. Plunkert...
        "The first section of this study presents the historical data from the
    gold rush to the present. It traces the agricultural development in
    California, the source of labor supply, the methods employed in keeping
    an available labor supply, the problems resulting and the remedies that
    have been attempted.
        "The second section of the study deals with statistical material re-
    ceived by the State Relief Administration field division from SRA staff
    in ten of the counties. The field division requested all SRA offices
    to supply certain data relating to agricultural workers on relief, but
    due to great pressure of work in counties accumulation of data was not
    mandatory. The ten counties reported 775 California agricultural workers
    who applied for relief during the months of December, 1935, and January,
    1936. From the standpoint of the number of agricultural workers on re-

lief the numerical figure has no value. Important agricultural counties
are not included, nor is it probable that in the rush of work all agricultural workers applying in the ten counties were included. The 775 cases
it is believed, however, represent a large enough group so that certain
conclusions may be drawn from the findings.

"Counties made report on the states in which families had worked
prior to coming to California, the length of time worked in such states,
the age of the family head, the number of members working in the family
group, the sex of members working, the number of children employed,
the wages earned and the number of months worked in agriculture for the
period 1930 to 1935.

"The third section of the study presents three family histories, and
a brief resumé of a fourth, indicating the residence and travels of this
family over a 26 year period. The families were on SRA relief at the
time of study and seemed typical for this relief group. It was felt
that the problem could be portrayed no more vividly than by showing
how it actually affected the lives of those seeking to earn their livelihood in California agriculture."

Farm Youth

Southern woman's educational alliance. [Publications] 17 nos., mimeogr.
Richmond, Va., 1930-36. 281.2 So8
Contains "Growing in the emergency" Bulletin no. 1, 4, 6; Mimeographed
bulletin series 2, no. 3; and 13 separate publications.
These bulletins all relate to rural youth and should be useful in work-
ing out plans to aid the unemployed out-of-school rural youth of the
Southern Highlands. Among the titles of the bulletins are the following:
Breathitt county, Kentucky - Digest of data from the Census, by O. E. Baker;
Interrelations of rural and urban communities in vocational guidance
problems of rural boys and girls, by O. Latham Hatcher; Some suggestions
for a program to promote better opportunities for rural young people
especially in the Southern Highlands, by Arthur E. Morgan.

Food Distribution

Corbaley, G. C. Group selling by 100,000 retailers; the evolution of food
distribution in voluntaries and cooperatives. 196pp. New York city,
American institute of food distribution, inc. 420 Lexington Ave. [1936]
286.2 C81
A Food Institute study from research conducted by Donald E. West
and Ruth P. Delclisur, with editing by Grant P. Gore and Thomas B.
Corbaley.
The author writes in part as follows in his introduction:
"Modern business has become so complex, so sub-divided and so bur-
dened with endless negotiations that the man at the heart of any commercial activity has little opportunity to go to the mountain top and
let his vision sweep understandingly across the entire pattern of the
vast and intricate operations of which he is a part.
"That condition is a rather serious handicap for management. We each
live and work in one little place. We put all the power and force we have

into rather futile efforts to control the course of prices and business methods. The real control is in the forces of the business tide on which we travel.

"This book is a painstaking effort to supply a guide which will enable you to look at these forces, check them against your personal experiences and thus enjoy the privilege of looking at our business from a new and different angle.

"This rather ambitious voyage of discovery was forced on us by a succession of events.

"The Food Institute staff began its regular gathering of thousands of detailed reports to assemble the story of how the methods of the voluntaries and cooperatives were working.

"Tabulating and interpreting these reports seemed to establish the theory that a logical evolution in business methods was well along toward becoming settled in a new and different pattern from 20 years ago.

"We then unearthed the probability that the retail stores of the corporate grocery chains might be transferred to individuals and the corporate chains become voluntaries.

"We learned that a general evolution similar to ours is taking form in other countries. In Sweden and in Holland, voluntaries and retailer-cooperatives are being organized to enable independently owned businesses to work more effectively with each other to meet the competition of consumer-owned cooperatives. The Polish Government is looking at the retailer-cooperative idea to enable independent retailers to compete with the 'capitalistic chains.'

"Through many hours of staff conferences, we traveled back and forth over this larger picture until we located what seems to be the new control point in distribution - the retail store whose activities largely regulate the volume, character and prices for the flow of foods into consumption.

"A technical study into the details of one part of the food business was expanded into a record of how the entire food industry operates, more or less analyzing the human impulses which control each move in that operating.

"Our record starts with a single page on which we diagram the size and importance of the food business. Men seldom think of that. We take our business as a matter of course. We do not realize that our industry is by far the most important single section in the economic organization of the United States - one of the most wonderful mankind has yet devised.

"Six chapters offer our impressions of how the food business is working now - the changes, their relationship to each other and our explanations for these.

"Then eight chapters recite details of evolutionary changes in the operating practices of the voluntaries and cooperatives. One chapter analyzes what the corporate chains have done about becoming voluntaries, with probable effects from the Robinson-Patman law. The concluding chapter carries our picture of this evolution into the future, offers answers to some questions you may have in mind."

Food, Health and Income

Orr, Sir John B.   Food, health and income; report on a survey of adequacy
of diet in relation to income.   72pp.   London, Macmillan and co., 1936.
389.1 Or7JF
   "This investigation was made by the staff of the Rowett Institute in
co-operation with the staff of Market Supply Committee." p. [4]
   Bibliography, pp. 70-72.
   "The state of nutrition of the people of this country is surveyed here
on a broad scale and from a new angle. Instead of discussing minimum requirements, about which there has been so much controversy, this survey
considers optimum requirements. Optimum requirements are based on the
physiological ideal, which we define as 'a state of well-being such that
no improvement can be effected by a change in the diet.' The standard
of adequacy of diet adopted is one which will maintain this standard of
perfect nutrition.
   "The average diet of each of six groups into which the population
has been divided according to income are compared with these requirements
for perfect nutrition. The health of the population is reviewed to see
to what extent inadequacy of diet is reflected in ill-health and poor
physique...
   "The tentative conclusion reached, is that a diet completely adequate
for health, according to modern standards, is reached at an income level
above that of 50 per cent. of the population. This means that 50 per cent.
of the population are living at a level of nutrition so high that, on the
average, no improvement can be effected by increased consumption.
   "The important aspect of the survey, however, is the inadequacy of the
diets of the lower income groups, and the markedly lower standard of
health of the people, and especially of the children in these groups, compared with that of the higher income groups."- Foreword.

Great Plains Drought Area

U. S. Great Plains drought area committee   Report... August 1936.   17pp.,
processed.   [Washington, D. C., 1936]   173.2 G79
   Signed: Hugh G. Bennett... Frederick H. Fowler... Francis C. Harrington...
Harry L. Hopkins... Richard C. Moore... John C. Page... Rexford G. Tugwell...
Henry A. Wallace... Morris L. Cooke, Chairman.
   Have also. Summary of conclusions dated Aug. 27, 1936. (3pp.,mimeogr.)
   "The agricultural economy of the Great Plains will become increasingly
unstable and unsafe, in view of the impossibility of permanent increase
in the amount of rainfall, unless over-cropping, over-grazing and improper
farm methods are prevented. There is no reason to believe that the primary
factors of climate-temperature, precipitation and winds in the Great Plains
region have undergone any fundamental change. The future of the region
must depend, therefore, on the degree to which farming practices conform
to natural conditions. Because the situation has now passed out of the
individual farmer's control, the reorganization of farming practices demands the cooperation of many agencies, including the local, State and
Federal governments.
   "We wish to make it plain that nothing we here propose is expected or

intended to impair the independence of the individual farmer in the Great
Plains area. Our proposals will look toward the greatest possible degree
of stabilization of the region's economy, a higher and more secure income
for each family, the spreading of the shock of inevitable droughts so that
they will not be crusing in their effects, the conservation of land and
water, a steadily diminishing dependence on public grants and subsidies,
the restoration of the credit of individuals and of local and State governments, and a thorough-going consideration of how great a population, and in
what areas, the Great Plains can support.

"These objectives are not now attainable by individual action, but we
believe they will restore an individual independence which has been lost.
Mistaken public policies have been largely responsible for the situation
now existing. That responsibility must be liquidated by new policies.
The Federal Government must do its full share in remedying the damage caused
by a mistaken homesteading policy, by the stimulation of war-time demands
which led to over-cropping and over-grazing, and by encouragement of a system of agriculture which could not be both permanent and prosperous.

"In many measures the Federal Government must take the initiative,
particularly in furnishing leadership and guidance, and in participating
to a substantial extent in the construction or financing of the needed
public works. Through existing agencies it will be able to employ many
of the residents of the region. In other measures the State and local
governments must take the initiative. The emphasis of the program
should be on coordination and cooperation, with each agency and each
group undertaking the functions it is best able to perform. There need
not be, and should not be, conflict of interest or jurisdiction between
State and local agencies on the one hand and Federal agencies on the
other. There need not be, and should not be, impairment of local and
individual initiative.

"There must be, on the other hand, continuous and sustained joint efforts on the part of all agencies concerned. The problem of the Great
Plains is not the product of a single act of nature, of a single year or
even of a series of exceptionally bad years. It has come into being over
a considerable period of time, and time will be required to deal with it.
The steps taken must be continuous, non-intermittent and patiently followed. A reasonably stable agricultural economy must be established,
maintained and handed on to the children of this generation...

"There is no ambiguity as to what is meant by 'the good of all concerned'. As we have gathered the opinions of experts and of the best
thought in the States, the following list of general objectives - some
requiring State, some local and some Federal initiative, and all requiring
cooperation - thus emerge:

"1. Develop and maintain the highest possible income and standard
of living in the region.

"2. Develop a type of economy that will withstand the shocks of recurrent periods of drought.

"3. Make the nature of public grants and subsidies such, and in accordance with a central long-time plan so well conceived, that the
necessity for them will be ultimately eliminated.

"4. Through these and other means restore the solvency of local governments and of the region as a whole.

"5. Stabilize land tenure and occupancy and so reduce the more or less aimless migration out of the region, or from one point to another within the region, which takes place during drought periods.

"6. In carrying out this policy encourage such re-groupings of the population as will permit greatest economy and efficiency in the conduct of schools, courts, policing, sanitation and other public activities. Reduce social isolation.

"7. Modify unsound tax systems in such a way as to proportion taxes to ability to pay, which in turn depends upon the productivity of the land to be taxed. Combine governmental subdivisions too small or too poor to be operated efficiently. By these means reduce the tax burden and that delinquency which is the sure sign of a bankrupt rural economy.

"8. Arrest the wastage of soil by erosion and make efficient use of the water resources of the region."

Graphs are included showing increase of tenancy in 8 Great Plains States, Acreage necessary for a satisfactory family income, Decrease of undersized farms in Montana, Too much cattle in the range portion of 6 Great Plains States.

Housing, Federal Agencies Concerned with

Central housing committee. Activities and organization of federal agencies concerned with housing. 17pp., mimeogr. [Washington, D. C.] Central housing committee, 1936.   296.2 C33
    This pamphlet contains: A. Organization charts of Government housing agencies grouped according to new construction and financing and, according to low-cost housing and other housing activities. B. Summaries showing the purpose, scope, method of operation and accomplishments of the Farm Credit Administration, Federal Home Loan Bank Board, Federal Housing Administration, Public Works Administration (Housing Division), Resettlement Administration. C. Financing policy of the housing agencies noted under "B" and also that of the Reconstruction Finance Corporation.
    The Farm Credit Administration is shown to be concerned with the financing of farm housing, and the Resettlement Administration with the construction of rural housing.

Housing Survey - Scotland

Scotland. Dept. of health. Housing overcrowding survey; summaries of reports and building proposals by local authorities in Scotland, made to the department as at 23rd April 1936, in terms of section I (1) of the Housing (Scotland) act, 1935. 15pp. Edinburgh, H. M. Stationery off., 1936. ([Gt. Brit. Parliament. Papers by command] Cmd. no. 5171)   296.2 Sco38
    Partial contents: Summary of overcrowding reports; Summary of building proposals by local authorities for the relief of overcrowding in the three years 1936-1938; and Summary of principal contents of reports and building proposals received from particular local authorities.

India - Economic Inquiry

India. Punjab. Board of economic inquiry. Publication nos. 29, 41, 43, 45-46.
[Lahore, "Civil and military gazette," ltd.] 1935-36.   281.9 In2
    Contents. - no. 29. Rates of food consumption by 71 families of
tenant-cultivators in the Khanewal Tehsil, Multan district. Inquiry
conducted by Sardari Lal... under the supervision of W. Roberts. 1935. -
no. 41. A cattle survey of the Rohtak district in the Punjab.
Inquiry conducted by Santokh Singh... under the supervision of A. Branford.
1935. - no. 43. An economic survey of Bhadas, a village in the Gurgaon
district of the Punjab. Inquiry conducted under the supervision of F. L.
Brayne... and Shiv Dyal. (Punjab village surveys - 7). 1936. - no. 45.
An economic survey of Bhambu Sandila, a village in the Muzaffargarh district of the Punjab. Inquiry conducted by Ardur Rahim Khan... under the
supervision of K. B. Sheikh Nur Mohammad. (Punjab village surveys -8.)
1935.- no. 46. Farm accounts in the Punjab 1933-1934. Being the tenth
year's accounts of certain farms; with sections on cost of well-irrigation
in the Punjab and cost of irrigation by tube-well, by Sardar Kartar Singh
... and Sardar Arjan Singh. 1936.

Industrial Use of Farm Products

Speece, G. H. After Roosevelt.   289pp.   [New York, The Alliance press,
1936] 280.12 Sp3
    Partial contents; The mechanization of agriculture in the United
States; The annual crops of agriculture as raw materials for industrial
manufacture; The fallacy of foreign trade as a remedy for agriculture;
Economic self-sufficiency the world trend; Population trends in the
United States.

Knowledge, Modern

Rose, William, ed.   An outline of modern knowledge [by] F. Aveling...
    G. D. H. Cole... Maurice Dobb... [and others]   1103pp.   New York,
G. P. Putnam's sons, 1931.   330 R72
    Bibliographical note at end of each article.
    Section B. Economics, devoted to science and history contains the
following: An introduction to economics, by Maurice Dobb; Finance, by
Prof. T. E. Gregory; Modern theories and forms of industrial organisation, by G. D. H. Cole; Theories and forms of political organisation, by
G. D. H. Cole; Modern theories and forms of international organisation,
by C. Delisle Burns; The science of history, by Prof. F. J. C. Hearnshaw;
and Modern geographical ideas, by L. Dudley Stamp.

Land

White, J. D. Nature's budget of land-rent for the people, with improvements
and food and industry tax-free. 159pp.   London, G. Allen & Unwin ltd.
[1936] 284.5 W582
    Partial contents: The earth for all; Land and improvements; National
land-rent; Basis of valuation; Reducing taxation; and Valuations and
values.

Land Ownership - Scandinavia

Führer, Karl. Beiträge zur ältesten agrargeschichte des germanischen nordens. 132pp. Jena, G. Fischer, 1935. 282 W95
    This is a very fully documented account of the agrarian history of the Germanic people of northern Europe from the Stone Age to the early middle ages. It is the story of the settlers in the Danish Islands, Jutland, southern Sweden and the northern coast of Germany. The early settlement of the Germanic people is shown to have been a gradual settlement of individuals or small groups of individuals each of whom had his own piece of ground as a separate entity. There were no closed villages in prehistoric Scandinavia. It was not until about the time of the birth of Christ that irregular, village-like settlements began to appear. Among other causes increase of population gradually led in the first century of the Christian era to subdivision of landed property, to settlement in common, and to the formation of villages. It was not a planned operation but the result of a long development. The so-called hide of land, or holding large enough to support a family, does not date from the time of the earliest settlement in Scandinavia but it is a product of the early middle ages. With increasing population more and more land was cultivated and new settlers established and finally estates increased in size through disputes, inheritance distribution, buying and selling. Finally a community of management but never of ownership was evolved. The development of German agrarian conditions was essentially the same as those of Scandinavia. And in its beginnings, the agriculture of Siberia followed the same general lines. - A. M. Hannay.

Land Policy - U. S.

U. S. National resources committee. Regional planning... Pts. 1-3. Washington, U. S. Govt. print. off., 1936. 173.2 N214Rp
    Contents. - Pt. 1. Pacific northwest. - Pt. 2. St. Louis region. - Pt. 3. New England.

U. S. National resources board. Land planning committee. Supplementary report... Pts. 2-3, 8. Washington, U. S. Govt. print. off., 1935. 173.2 N214Su
    Contents. - Pt. 2. Agricultural exports in relation to land policy. - Pt. 3. Agricultural land requirements and resources. - Pt. 8. Forest land resources, requirements, problems, and policy.

Land Settlement

Bishop, C. D. Land settlement colonisation. 12pp. London, The Distributist league [1936?] 282.2 B54
    A plan to enable workers to raise their own food in their leisure time.

League of Nations

League of nations. Money and banking 1935/36. Series of League of nations Publications. II. Economic and financial. 1936. II A7 I-II. 2v. Geneva, 1936. 280.9 L47P
    v. 1. Monetary review. - v. 2. Commercial banks.

Harrison, G., and Mitchell, F. C. The home market; a handbook of statistics...
    With a foreword by Frank Pick.   149pp. London, G. Allen & Unwin ltd.
    [1936]   280.32 H24
        Partial contents: Regional areas and populations, 1934; The age and
    sex composition of Great Britain's population, 1934; The future popula-
    tion of Great Britain; The changes in regional populations between 1921
    and 1934; The changes in age composition of the population between 1921
    and 1934; The age and sex composition of regional populations in Great
    Britain, 1934; The principal urban centres of Great Britain; The
    rural areas of Great Britain; Regional populations in families, 1934;
    The size of families in Great Britain, 1931; The future number and size
    of families in England and Wales; An analysis of Great Britain's popula-
    tion (1934) into social grades; Two indices of purchasing power; The
    incidence of poor relief in Great Britain; The occupied and unoccupied
    population of Great Britain, 1931; The industries, etc. in which Great
    Britain's working population was found,. 1931; The distribution of in-
    comes and wealth, 1934, An estimate of one year's national expenditure
    (1934); Earnings in some principal industries, 1931; Expenditures of
    sample families; Regional distribution of the daily and Sunday press.
        There are also two appendices - A. Current statistics of commercial in-
    terest and B. Statistical methods employed.

Marketing

Converse, P. D. Essentials of distribution. 588pp.   New York, Prentice-
    Hall, inc., 1936. 280.3 C76Es
        The author writes in part as follows in his signed preface:
        "This volume attempts to condense and simplify the principles of market
    distribution for the use of students beginning the study of distribution
    and of persons engaged in business who want a comprehensive view of the
    field of distribution. It contains a discussion of distribution costs,
    distribution functions, distribution of selected commodities, the opera-
    tions of various types of middlemen, and the principles of merchandising,
    salesmanship, sales management, and advertising. The treatment of so
    many subjects in a volume of this size requires that each be discussed
    briefly."
        Among the chapter headings are the following: Marketing farm products,
    Marketing grain and livestock; Marketing dairy products, Marketing cotton.
    Prices, mark-ups, and margins.

Migration of Population and Economic Opportunity

Goodrich, Carter, Allin, B. W., Thornthwaite, C. W., and others. Migration
    and economic opportunity; the report of the study of population redistri-
    bution.   763pp. Philadelphia. University of Pennsylvania press; London,
    H. Milford, Oxford university press, 1936.   280.12 G62
        "Report of the Study of Population Redistribution which was organized
    in 1934 under the auspices of the Industrial Research Department of the
    Wharton School of Finance and Commerce of the University of Pennsylvania.
    The project was initiated by the Social Science Research Council and

has been supported by a grant from the Rockefeller Foundation. The
Study was asked to consider what movements of population within the
United States might be necessary and desirable, and what part, if any,
the Government should take in encouraging or guiding them. Its commission was thus to make a reconnaissance of the field of internal migration in the hope of discovering bases for the determination of public
policy." - Preface.

Part I is devoted to a consideration of The Need for Migration and
Part II, to The Control of Migration. There is a chapter entitled
"Some Hints from Foreign Experience" in which the practices of Germany,
Russia and Great Britain are considered and still another chapter entitled "A Critique of American Measures" considers land programs, decentralization of industry, part-time farming and the government's communities.

There are also four appendices: A. The analysis of past migration;
B. Wheat production in western Kansas; C. The location of manufactures;
and D. Memorandum on the selection of manufacturing areas for the housing
program.

Steinemann, Eugen. Die volkswirtschaftliche bedeutung der landflucht. 77pp.
   [Aarau] 1934.   281 St36
    Diss.- Bern.
    Bibliography, pp. 75-77.
    Attempts a general economic theory of the exodus from the land. Includes an
investigation of the causes of the exodus, an investigation of its economic
consequences, and a critical consideration of how to combat the movement. -
Preface.

Milk Marketing Scheme - Scotland

Gt. Brit. Scottish office. Committee of investigation for Scotland of any
   agricultural marketing scheme. Report of the Committee of investigation
   for Scotland on complaint made by representatives of milk distributors
   on the Permanent joint committee appointed under the scheme as to the
   operation of the Scottish milk marketing scheme, 1933. 16pp. London,
   H. M. Stationery off., 1936.   280.344 G7932
    Contains also two appendices as follows: Complaint of representatives
of milk distributors on the Permanent Joint Committee appointed under
the Scottish Milk Marketing Scheme, 1933; and Note by consultant appointed
under Section 13 of the Agricultural Marketing Act, 1933.

Money - Sweden

Thomas, Brinley. Monetary policy and crisis; a study of Swedish experience.
   Preface by Hugh Dalton. 247pp. London, G. Routledge and sons, ltd.,
   1936.   334 T363
    Hugh Dalton of the London School of Economics, writes in part as
follows in the signed preface to this volume:
    "Judged by any sensible standard, Sweden is one of the most civilized
countries in the world. And in the field of economics, as in many other
fields, both Swedish theory and Swedish practice are highly distinguished.
Economists in that country are, and have long been, in closer touch with

practical affairs than in some others, with benefit both to themselves
and to public policy. They seem, moreover, as a class, to have a better
public reputation than elsewhere. And individually, to-day not less
than yesterday, they make their mark on the intellectual life, not only
of their own small country, but of the world. Yesterday Wicksell,
Cassel, and Davidson; to-day Myrdal, Lindahl, and Ohlin.

"This book is, in part, an instructive chapter in economic history;
in part, a stimulating chapter in the history of economic thought. But,
best of all, it is a record and an explanation of what must seem, to
dwellers in less happy lands, an economic miracle. In these last years
Swedish Recovery, from trade depression and mass unemployment, has been
sensational. External factors, such as the rise in certain export prices,
have helped a little. But primarily the Recovery is due to internal
action, based largely on the theories of Gunnar Myrdal, and executed
with great political skill and economic insight by Ernst Wigforss, the
brilliant Finance Minister in the Swedish Socialist Government led by
Per Albin Hansson. In this action, monetary and budgetary policy have
been closely linked. And for this purpose it has been of fundamental
importance that in Sweden the Central Bank is publicly owned and under
the direct control of the Government and Parliament. The very rapid
fall in unemployment has resulted from a bold programme of increased
investment, particularly in public enterprises. These play an important role in the Swedish national economy, which is considerably more
socialist than ours. Thus 'public works' is a phrase of much wider
meaning in Sweden than with us, and covers operations of a much more
varied and productive character.

"The budget statement for 1936-7 is a remarkable vindication of
this policy. A substantial surplus is anticipated; a mass of short
term debts is to be paid off; further public investment on a large
scale is provided for, to be financed partly by loan and partly from
revenue; and a reduction of income tax is announced, while the increase
in the death duties, imposed two years ago to cover the service of the
short term debts now to be repaid, is retained. Swedish practice is
in harmony with the more hopeful and constructive economic theories of
the present day. We can learn much from it, through this book."

The Economist (London) in its issue for September 19, 1936, p. 520
makes an interesting comparison of this volume with "Sweden, The Middle
Way" by Marquis W. Childs which it thinks "may be regarded as, in
many ways, a supplement" to Mr. Thomas's book.

National Economic Security

Adams, A. B. National economic security. 328pp. Norman, University of
Oklahoma press, 1936. 280.12 AdlN
"Capitalism is not dead and should not die. The institutions of
private property and of profit-making should be preserved, in my opinion,
and individual initiative should be given ample opportunity to stimulate
desirable productivity of our industrial system. But, under modern industrial and economic conditions, the nation cannot depend on the laissez
faire policy to control the operation of our industrial system to the
best interest of all the people. The so-called natural economic laws,
which heretofore have been depended upon to control the distribution of

the national money income (the net production of industry), have failed
to distribute the national income in such a way that our industries can
be kept operating at full capacity. Neither have the natural economic
laws adjusted the daily and weekly work hours of laborers to the technological progress made in the methods of production in industry in such
a manner as to prevent unemployment. The nation cannot achieve permanent prosperity for all unless our government is able to formulate and
put into operation economic regulatory policies which will remedy these
glaring defects in the operation of our industrial system." - Preface.

Chapter 12 is devoted to Relief for Debtors and for the Agricultural
Industry. In this the author discusses the various acts for the relief
of farm debtors, home owners, the railroads and others. He then proceeds to a consideration of the Agricultural Adjustment Administration
Act and the retirement from cultivation of sub-marginal land. There are
other chapters on other attempts of the present administration to correct the economic difficulties of the country and the book closes with a
chapter on Governmental policies and our economic future from which the
extracts which follow have been taken;

"As a consequence of these analyses of our present national economic
difficulties and of this study of the so-called New Deal legislation,
it is my opinion that the New Deal program should be revamped somewhat
as follows:

"1. Discontinue all governmental efforts to raise the general price
level. Accept the prevailing price level as a basis for recovery and
reconstruction of business and industry. Do not decrease further the
gold content of the dollar or expand the silver purchase policy. Above
all, do not issue Treasury notes or other paper money. Discontinue the
policy of trying artificially to force an expansion of bank credit, but
offer reasonable credit facilities through the banks and the government's
financial agencies.

"2. Continue to encourage the readjustment or refinancing of old
debts of farmers, home-owners, railroads, local governments, and of distressed business enterprises. The principal of these debts in many cases
should be reduced greatly and the interest rates on them should be cut
drastically, so as to reduce materially the annual debt charges on these
debtors. Through the regulation of banks and the control over the government's financial agencies the Administration should keep the current rate
of interest for new loans at a low level.

"3. At the end of the present public works program, the policy of
trying to revive business through a large public works program must be
discontinued; also the policy of attempting to apply artificial stimulation to private construction and to the heavy goods industries should
be stopped. A public works program increases the public debt rapidly
and furnishes to business only a temporary artificial stimulation which
cannot contribute to permanent recovery. Also artificial stimulation
of private construction will further lower the value of existing buildings; such stimulation likely would result in overbuilding many communities, and might result in considerable financial losses to the
government through the guarentee of the mortgages. The heavy goods
industries should be permitted to revive only as there is an actual de-

mand for their goods on the part of solvent expanding business enterprises. It should be remembered that relative to the national money income and to the volume of trade of the consumption goods industries, the so-called heavy goods industries were greatly overexpanded from 1915 to 1929.

"4. Amend the Agricultural Adjustment Act, with its provisions for processing taxes and non-production payments, by giving the government the power to allot to each farmer the maximum quantity of each major agricultural product he may be permitted to produce and sell each year; the act should provide heavy penalties for those who exceed their production allotment. Also continue and enlarge the Administration's program of purchasing submarginal agricultural lands and taking them out of cultivation. The farmers should reduce production in their own interest; in the future they should not be paid to do it, but penalized if they refuse. The submarginal farms should be taken out of cultivation because they are an injury to the agricultural industry as well as a detriment to those who cultivate them.

"5. Prohibit any agreements by industries through trade associations or otherwise in reference to prices or volume of production. Enforce the antitrust acts against monopolistic activities and restraints of trade. In addition to the National Labor Relations Act, the Congress should enact two additional laws to take the place of the National Industrial Recovery Act as follows:

"(a) A Federal trade adjustment act should be enacted to provide for a limited amount of self-regulation of trade practices through codes of fair trade practices...

"(b) A Federal labor adjustment act should be passed to regulate hours and wages of laborers employed in industries engaged in interstate commerce.

"6. The unscientific system of giving direct Federal relief to the unemployed through the FERA should be abolished. Whatever Federal unemployment relief is given should be on a scientific basis. Except through pension systems, no Federal aid should be given to unemployable persons. In so far as practicable, Federal aid to employable jobless persons should be given by furnishing employment; it is much more desirable that this employment be in private industry than in public works projects. When the jobless cannot be given jobs of any kind they should receive adequate unemployment compensation paid for by taxes on industry.

"7. The Securities Act, the Securities Exchange Act, and the Public Utility Act should be supplemented by the passage of a law providing for Federal incorporation of all corporations doing an interstate business. This act should eliminate all unnecessary holding companies in all industries, make impossible the over capitalization of corporations, and effectively prevent inside manipulation of their finances and securities...

"8. The budget should be balanced before many more billions of national debts are accumulated; if it is not soon balanced the government's credit will be injured and it will be difficult to pay the national debt. Balancing the budget will necessitate both decreasing expenditure and increasing revenues."

Belshaw, Horace, Williams. D. O., Stephens. F. B., Fawcett, E. J., and Rodwell,
H. E. Agricultural organization in New Zealand; a survey of land utilization, farm organization, finance and marketing... Published for the New
Zealand Institute of Pacific relations. 818 pp. Melbourne, London [etc.]
Melbourne university press in association with Oxford university press,
1936. (Institute of Pacific relations. International research series)
331.1993 B41

"A bibliography of New Zealand soils". pp. 807-818.

"This book is one of a number of surveys into land utilization in various
Pacific countries authorized by the Research Committee of the Institute of
Pacific Relations. The present project was authorized by the Research
Committee of the Institute at the Kyoto Conference held in October and
November, 1929, the Auckland University College being made Trustee...

"The book is unique for New Zealand in at least two respects. It
represents the first comprehensive survey of Agricultural organization
and land utilization in New Zealand; and it has brought together a larger
number of specialists than have ever before co-operated in one investigation
in this country...

"In planning the book, a broad view of the problem of land utilization
has been adopted. The technique of land utilization is conditioned by a
wide variety of factors such as land tenure, transport, markets, price
movements, organizations, associations and institutions, as well as by
conditions of soil, climate, topography and the stage of development of
the agricultural arts. Because of their bearing on land utilization, the
above and other problems, which may be grouped broadly under the general
heading of organization, have been dealt with as adequately as possible."

Contents: Trends of development, by H. Belshaw; Factors affecting
land utilization in New Zealand, by H. Belshaw; General characteristics
of New Zealand rural economy, by D. O. Williams; The place of primary
industries in the economic life of New Zealand, by D. O. Williams;
Geological structure and topography, by W. N. Benson; Soils of New
Zealand, by B. C. Aston (assisted by R. E. R. Grimmett and F. J. A. Brogan)
and T. Rigg, Climate, by E. Kidson; Land settlement and settlement
finance, by D. O. Williams; The financing of land purchase and of farming operations, by H. Belshaw; Land tenure and land transfer, by D. O.
Williams; Agricultural labour in New Zealand, by H. Belshaw; Taxation,
grants and subsidies in relation to farming, by H. R. Rodwell; Scientific
developments, by F. R. Callaghan and G. S. Peren; Agricultural education,
by J. E. Strachan, Douglas Campbell, and F. W. Hilgendorf; The Department
of Agriculture, by E. J. Fawcett; Farmers' organizations, by F. B. Stephens;
Dairy herd testing in New Zealand, by A. H. Ward; Pastures of New Zealand,
by E. B. Levy; Fertilizers and manures in New Zealand, by A. W. Hudson and
F. L. C. Scrivener; Sheep farming, by E. J. Fawcett; Dairy Farming, by
E. J. Fawcett, The utilization of surplus dairy by-products by pig raising,
by C. P. McMeekan; Beef production, by I. W. Weston; Arable farming, by
I. W. Weston; Fruit, market gardening, tobacco, and tung oil, by J. A.
Campbell; Flax (phormium tenax) or New Zealand hemp, by J. S. Yeates;
Forestry in New Zealand, by E. P. Turner and A. Beasley; General survey of
markets and price movements, by D. O. Williams; Marketing of meat, by F. B.

Stephens and C. R. Barnicoat; The processing and marketing of dairy produce, by F. B. Stephens; Wool markets and marketing, by D. O. Williams;
The marketing of arable products, by I. W. Weston; The marketing of fruit,
by J. A. Campbell; Co-operation in New Zealand, by F. B. Stephens; Control boards, by F. B. Stephens; and Farming industries during the World
crisis.
   Reviewed by J. S. Ballantyne and S. M. Wadham in Economic record,
v.12, no.22, June 1936, pp.37-46.
   Reviewed by W. J. Buzacott in the Queenslander, Jan. 30, 1936, p.19.

New Zealand - Recovery Measures

Belshaw, Horace. Recovery measures in New Zealand; a comparison with the
   new deal in the United States. 61pp. Wellington, New Zealand institute of Pacific relations, 1936. (New Zealand institute of Pacific
   relations. New Zealand papers no. 2) 280.1993 B41
   "Prepared as a data paper for the sixth conference of the Institute
of Pacific relations... Yosemite Park, California, August 15-29, 1936."
   "The purpose of this paper is to describe the recovery programme in
New Zealand and compare it with the New Deal in the United States.
Though the two countries show marked contrasts in size and in economic
and political structure, a comparison between these two programmes is
useful by way of indicating the manner in which such differences lead
to differences in outlook and in economic and political philosophy. It
is interesting in so far as it may reveal similarities in policy which
suggest parallel responses to basically similar historical forces.
   "An understanding of the recovery programme in New Zealand requires
some description of the main economic characteristics of the country.
The New Zealand economy is based mainly on grassland farming. Before
the depression the value of farm production was 54 per cent of the
national income and 65 per cent of the value of all production. Many
nonfarming industries, trades and professions are directly dependent
on agriculture. New Zealand relies to an unusual degree on overseas
trade, which is of a higher per capita value than that of any other
country. In 1928, the value of exports was about 36 per cent of the
national income, nearly 44 per cent of the value of all production, and
about 60 per cent of the value of farm production. Pastoral products
provided 94 per cent of the value of exports. The development of the
country has resulted in heavy private and public indebtedness, and this
makes for rigidity in costs.
   "The world depression was transmitted into New Zealand by the heavy
fall in export prices. This reduced the income of farmers, and the decline in their purchasing power was transmitted to the rest of the community, thus leading to diminished production, trade and employment. Since
a large preportion of public revenue consists of interest and other fixed
obligations which it was difficult to reduce, while revenue, and especially
customs duties, are very susceptible to trade conditions, the depressions
resulted in heavy budget-deficits.
   "Export prices fell by 40 per cent between 1928 and 1931, but internal

prices fell by only about 10 per cent. Since these prices represent
farmers' costs, there was a serious disparity between costs and selling
prices in the export industries. The crux of the problem was to remove
this disparity as a basis for general recovery. Farmers' receipts were
raised by depreciating the New Zealand rate of exchange on London by 25
per cent, and a series of operations was undertaken to reduce costs.
These operations included wage reductions, statutory reductions in mortgage interest and other fixed charges, and reductions in market rate of
interest by agreement with the banks. A mortgage moratorium was enacted
and provision was made for the compulsory writing-down of the excessive
liabilities of farmer mortgagors. The Mortgage Corporation of New Zealand
and the Reserve Bank of New Zealand were established with the intention
of strengthening the financial system; but in addition, they contributed
to the policy of cost reduction. Budget policy was directed towards the
early balancing of the Budget. Expenditure was curtailed and the internal
debt converted. Tax rates were increased and new taxes introduced. The
Budget was balanced in 1934-5 and again in 1935-6.

"Unemployment relief was financed by means of special taxes on wages
and other incomes. The general policy was to provide relief in return
for work done. There was no expansion of public works expenditure to
provide employment. On the contrary, public works expenditure was contracted, largely because it was believed that borrowing for public works
would hinder the government's policy of cost reductions.

"Trade policy was dominated by the Ottawa agreement, by subsequent
negotiations, and by the desire to find new markets. The Executive Commission for Agriculture was established to coordinate the work of the
Produce Control Boards, to develop new markets, and to improve the organization of farming and internal marketing. In the operation of the recovery programmes, there was a noticeable trend toward administrative
devolution.

"During the past two or three years, there has been a marked recovery
in New Zealand, and there is little doubt that the Government's programme
has contributed a great deal toward this.

"The New Zealand recovery programme differs in important respects from
the American New Deal. The banking system was not seriously endangered
by the depression in New Zealand, and a 'banking holiday' was unnecessary.
There is no parallel in New Zealand to the banking reforms enacted in the
United States. The main reform was the establishment of a Reserve Bank.

"The expansion of internal purchasing power was a dominant motive running through most of the New Deal legislation in the United States. The
expansion of public works, large deficits in Federal finances, loans to
agriculture, and to industrial and financial institutions, the extension
of the basis for credit in various ways, and wage policy under the N.R.A.
codes, are all indicative of this intention. Policy in New Zealand was
directed, not to expanding purchasing power (except by the depreciation
of exchange), but to reducing costs. The reasons for this difference are
to be found mainly in the greater importance of export industries in New
Zealand and of domestic demand in the United States.

"The concept of a 'parity price' was basic to the agricultural programme

in both countries, but the concept was differently interpreted. In New
Zealand, there was more direct emphasis on the relationship between costs
and receipts as expressed in export prices and internal prices as a whole.
This was the reason for the depreciation of the exchange and measures
directly designed to reduce costs. While the United States currency was
devalued, less significance seems to have been attached to this than to
exchange depreciation in New Zealand. The emphasis in the United States
was on raising farm income by (a) raising farm prices through restriction
of production (b) rewarding farmers for restriction by benefit payments
financed out of taxes. New Zealand did not adopt a restrictive programme
because its farm prices are determined in overseas markets. Any reduction
in supply would have reacted to the benefit of overseas competitors without
raising domestic prices, and with insufficient effect in overseas prices
to increase the gross return of overseas producers.

"There was nothing in New Zealand comparable with the N.R.A. codes.
Manufacturing industries are of less importance, and 'unfair competition'
was not regarded as being a serious problem. There was little obstacle to
trade union organization so that those aspects of the codes which dealt
with labor organization played no part in the New Zealand programme.

"There was a smaller admixture of social security with recovery legislation in New Zealand, labour laws, although by no means entirely adequate,
were more satisfactory than in the United States, old age andother pension
schemes being already in existence. At the election in November 1935, all
political parties favored an extension of social legislation in the form of
national compulsory superannuation, health insurance and housing.

"Although the different types of economic and political organization in
the two countries led to marked differences in the two programmes, there
was the same underlying trend towards increasing social control of economic
affairs. This is no new thing in either country and seems likely to continue. If such be the case, there are many questions which call for answers. It will be necessary to have an evaluation of economic and social
ends, and to discover the proper means to achieve these ends. Further,
it will be imperative to devise an administrative technique which permits
of resiliency and rapid adjustment to change." - Summary.

Nutrition and Social Policy

International labor office, Geneva. Workers' nutrition and social policy.
    249pp. Geneva, 1936. (International labour office. Studies and re-
    ports. Series B (Social and economic conditions) no. 23)   389.1 In8
    "The Nineteenth Session of the International Labour Conference
adopted a resolution submitted by Sir Frederick Stewart (Government
delegate of Australia), supported by Mr. Verschaffelt and Miss Ada
Paterson (Government delegates of New Zealand), which read as follows:
    "'Seeing that nutrition, adequate both in quantity and in quality,
is essential to the health and well-being of the workers and their
families;
    "And seeing that in various countries evidence has been brought for-
ward to show that large numbers of persons both in town and country are
not sufficiently or suitably nourished;
    "Seeing, moreover, that an increase in the consumption of agricultural
foodstuffs would help to raise standards of life and relieve the existing

depression in agriculture:

"The Conference welcomes the attention drawn by the Director in his Report to the problem of nutrition and requests the Governing Body to instruct the Office to continue its investigation of the problem, particularly in its social aspects, in collaboration with the health and economic organisations of the League of Nations, the International Institute of Agriculture and other bodies capable of contributing to its solution, with a view to presenting a report on the subject to the 1936 Session of the Conference."

The Conference requested the Governing body to instruct the Office to continue its investigation of the problem and to submit a report on the subject to the 1936 Session of the Conference. The Governing Body unanimously decided to give effect to this request, and approved the proposal that a first report by the Office on the problem of workers' nutrition be submitted to the Twentieth Session of the International Labour Conference...

"In accordance with the resolution, the International Labor Office has pursued the study of the nutrition problem since the last Session of the International Labour Conference, in collaboration with the Health and Economic Sections of the League of Nations, and with the International Institute of Agriculture. The International Institute of Agriculture kindly agreed to submit memoranda on the evolution of world production of foodstuffs and on the question of pure food legislation, which have been incorporated in the present Report. The Office takes this opportunity to express again its gratitude to the International Institute of Agriculture for the assistance thus rendered."

Partial contents: Facts on workers' diets; Agricultural production and food consumption; Social-economic aspects of nutrition; Problems of policy; and International statistics of food consumption

Oregon - Laws Relating to Grazing

Oregon. Agricultural college. Extension service. A compilation of recent legislation applicable to lands subject to the Taylor grazing act... April 1, 1935. 10pp., mimeogr. [Corvallis, Ore., 1935?] 275.2 Or3C

At head of title: Oregon State Agricultural College. Extension service.

"The seven acts presented herewith constitute new legislation passed by the thirty-eighth Legislative assembly recently adjourned. These acts appear to be particularly applicable, either fully or in part, to lands which may come under the administration of the Taylor Grazing Act. These new laws together with others already in existence would appear to provide ample legal machinery for full state cooperation in setting up Taylor Grazing Districts in Oregon."

Planning

Rather, A. W. Planning under capitalism; the problem of planning in Great Britain. 199pp. London, P. S. King & Son, Ltd., 1935. 331.171 R18 Bibliography, pp. 195-196.

Part I is devoted to The Economics of Planning and Part II, to Planning in Practice. In the second part are chapters on Agriculture, the Pig and Potato Schemes, the Milk Scheme, and the Critics of the Marketing Schemes.

Planning - World

[Macartney, C. A.] World planning: the I.L.C. and the new economic order.
92pp. [London] League of nations union [1936]   ([Publications]
no. 393)   280 M112
    On cover: Being an account by C. A. Macartney of a conference held
in London by the Industrial Advisory Committee of the League of Nations
Union, February 18-20, 1936.
    This interesting little pamphlet summarizes much of what was said
about international planning by a distinguished group of speakers among
whom were Sir Daniel Hall; Graham Hutton; Dr. Kuczynszl; L. L. Lorwin;
Prof. J. H. Richardson; and Prof. Carr Saunders.

poor Farms - Kansas

Kansas. Emergency relief committee. A study of Kansas poor farms. The third
    of a series of studies of social problems in Kansas and their social and
    economic costs. The Kansas Emergency relief committee. 46pp.
    Topeka, Kan. [1935] (Bulletin KERC no. 307)   280.029 K13 3d
    "This study... was organized in two parts. First, a financial and
    statistical study was made of all poor farms in Kansas followed by an
    intensive study of poorhouses in those counties whose boards of county
    commissioners requested such a study. Financial and statistical data
    pertaining to poor farms was obtained by means of schedules submitted
    to all county poor commissioners. In some counties it was necessary
    to obtain information from very inadequate public records. The survey
    of selected poorhouses included a study of every phase of poor farm ad-
    ministration. A case study of each inmate, made by trained case workers,
    included interviews with the inmate, visits to relatives and friends, con-
    sultation of public records, and mental and physical examinations. Mental
    tests were given by psychologists. Diet studies were made by trained dieti-
    tians and farm management studies by agricultural experts." - Preface.

Population Distribution - South Africa

Hugo, C. F.   A study of the geographical distribution of population within
    the magisterial district of Pretoria and the adjacent portion of the
    District of Brits. 42pp. Pretoria, 1935. (Pretoria. University. Re-
    print no. 8)   276.4 T68R no.8
    "Reprinted from the South African Geographical Journal, vol. XVIII,
    Dec. 1935."
    "Distributors: Messrs. J. L. Van Schaik, ltd., Pretoria."
    "In a national policy of land settlement the potentialities of each
    region should, as far as possible be surveyed and an approximation be
    made as to the optimum distribution and number of inhabitants and the
    trend of population may give an indication in this direction. As C. B.
    Fawcett states: 'The population map has become more important with every
    advance in the study of human geography and its application to problems
    of social organisation and administration. It is also the starting-point
    for any planned organisation of the community.'"

- 795 -

Poultry Industry - New Hampshire

U. S. Federal civil works administration of New Hampshire. Some poultry
problems in New Hampshire; consumer and producer attitudes with regard
to prices, grades and other matters. Report of a Civil works - Emergency
relief administration project, made in cooperation with the New Hampshire
minimum wage office. 66pp., mimeogr. Concord, N. H., 1935. 280.347 Un32
"This study of some of the poultry problems in New Hampshire is one of
several inquiries dealing with spread in prices between producer and consumer conducted by the Minimum Wage Office as part of its Cost of Living
Service.
"A preliminary survey was made in the Spring of 1934 as a Civil Works
Service project. This survey was continued in the Fall of that year on a
somewhat more extensive scale through the cooperation of the Emergency
Relief Administration...
"The report attempts to show the spread in egg and poultry prices, the
attitude of the large consumer, such as hotels and restaurants, with regard to grading and labeling eggs, type of eggs and poultry preferred and
reasons for choice; sources of consumer supply, the markets used by producers and the methods of marketing employed." - Preface.

Price Movements

Nottin, Léopold. Essai de contribution à l'étude du mouvement général des
prix. Recherches sur les variations des prix dans le Gatinais, du
XVIe au XIXe siècle. 130pp. Paris, Les Éditions Domat-Montchres-
tien, F. Loviton et cie, 1935. 284.3 N84
Bibliography, pp. [iii]-xv.
Price movements in France (Le Gatinais) from the 17th to the 19th
centuries.
Reviewed in Bulletin de la Société d'Encouragement pour l'Industrie
Nationale, no. 4, p. 257, Apr. 1936.

Prices, Agricultural

Nogaro, Bertrand. Les prix agricoles mondiaux et la crise. 167pp. Paris,
Librairie générale de droit & de jurisprudence, 1936. 284.3 N68
"The principal point that Professor Nogaro here makes is that the
part played by monetary influences in the recent fall of agricultural
prices has been exaggerated. The true explanation of the price movements which have taken place must be sought, he suggests, in the conditions of demand and supply; and, since demand is relatively stable and
inelastic, it is the variations in supply that are really significant.
An examination of the history of the market conditions of the most important agricultural products leads to the conclusion that there has
been an abnormal increase of output and an accumulation of stocks, which
have caused the fall in the agricultural price-level.
"The reasons for these developments, the author thinks, are to be
found in the expansion of overseas production during the war and the post-
war restoration of production in Europe; and the downward tendency in the
price-level has been aggravated by many of the ill-judged protectionist
devices adopted by governments with the object of saving farmers from

the consequences of the depression. Professor Nogaro is sympathetic to schemes for the restriction of output, but is sceptical of their successful operation in a world where international co-operation is so difficult to secure, and he urges that the best way to end the agricultural depression is to restore freedom of trade in the widest possible market, when, in his opinion, the appropriate adjustments in production would take place under the influence of the laws of demand and supply. It is doubtful whether Professor Nogaro gives sufficient weight to the influence of monetary factors in determining the effective demand for food." - The Economist (London) v. 122, no. 4831, p. 709, Mar. 28, 1936.

Prices and the Business Cycle

Tintner, Gerhard. Prices in the trade cycle. Foreword by Oskar Morgenstern. 204pp. Vienna, J. Springer, 1935. (Austrian institute for trade cycle research, in cooperation with the London school of economics and political science) 284 T49
 French and German summaries.
 Tables in English, French and German.
 Two envelopes containing cellophane graphs in pocket at end of book.
 Oskar Morgenstern, Director of the Austrian Institute for Trade Cycle Research writes as follows in the signed foreword:
 "The study of prices is the main concern of economics and, therefore, an investigation like the present one will be welcomed, we hope, by anyone seriously interested in economic problems, no matter from what specific angle this interest may arise. The book in which Dr. Tintner has collected the results of a long and elaborate study, carried out at the Austrian Institute for Trade Cycle Research, certainly deserves the attention of the pure theorist as well as of the economic statistician. Although in itself not precisely intended as a contribution to the theory of prices it touches upon many aspects of price theory that the results shown will undoubtedly put the theorist on his guard against that type of rash generalisation which emerges when theory is formulated at too great a distance from the facts. The theory of prices is based - or at least is supposed to have been based -- on observation of the actual behaviour of prices. These observations relate to a given time and space. Thus they are subject to all the elements that act upon them such as casual happenings, seasonal variations and the special point in the trade cycle -- provided there is one - which coincides with the time of observation. Everyone of those elements is liable - if no further analysis is applied to the material - to become a source of error. Therefore, even the purest of theorists cannot object to the empirical conclusions being subjected to the kind of treatment which is outlined, developed and applied in detail and with the greatest care in this book. Moreover, some of these methods are either novel or have, at least, so far never been applied on any large scale. They are used by a scholar who is well aware of the many traps which unfortunately enough make the progress of economic statistics so difficult. It is not certain whether the scientific world will agree that all of them have been avoided, but there is little doubt that few statistics of prices have been presented in such close connection with the findings of economics as in this book. It is evident that the sep-

aration, either in principle or in fact, between statistics and economics
is the reason why so little use has been made of the price material
lately in the hands of the economists.

"It seems hardly necessary to explain why the period covered was
chosen so as to end with the beginning of the Great War. It has in recent years become more and more evident that the disturbance caused by
the war has been so great and so lasting that one may question altogether
the fact of a regular cycle after 1914. In the light of these developments Dr. Tintner's conclusion that for the quiet times prior to 1914
his statistics prove the cycle to be a far more complicated process
than hitherto generally supposed, seems to me of particular importance.
If this book puts the workers in this field of research on their guard
to a far greater extent than is common to-day, it will have rendered no
small service. This is particularly the case when one considers the
current dilettantic and oversimplifying ideas of crisis-policy which
have really been formed on the basis of certain erroneously simplified
views about the explanation of the crisis.

"Such a book as the present one could only have been prepared with
the aid of a great many helpful institutions, scholars and men of affairs in a number of countries. It is a pleasant duty of mine duly to
thank every one of them, particularly, however, the London School of
Economics and Political Science which has given so much assistance
that the book now appears as a publication of the Austrian Institute
for Trade Cycle Research in cooperation with this institution."

Prices - Robinson-Patman Act

Institute of distribution, inc. [Booklets on the Robinson-Patman act. 7 nos.
New York, Institute of distribution, inc., 1936] 286.2 In7
    All numbers, except those which are texts of laws, signed by Nathan
    Isaacs.
    Contents. - What the national distributor should know about the new
Robinson-Patman act; What manufacturers should know about the new Robinson-
Patman act; Important constructions of the wording of the new Robinson-
Patman act; Present text of the Clayton act; Text of the Robinson-Patman
act; Federal Trade Commission act and the Sherman act; and The Robinson-
Patman act, what is important to know about it.

Prices - Spain - 1351-1500

Hamilton, E. J   Money, prices, and wages in Valencia, Aragon, and Navarre,
    1351-1500. 310pp. Cambridge, Mass., Harvard university press, 1936.
    (Harvard economic studies. v. 51) 284 H18
    Bibliography, pp. [xix]-xxviii
    "This is the second of three studies of money, prices, and wages in
Spain covering four and a half centuries. The first, American Treasure
and the Price Revolution in Spain, 1501-1650, appeared in 1934, as Volume
43 of the Harvard Economic Studies; and the concluding volume, treating
the period 1651-1800, will probably go to press next year. In the final
study attention will be devoted to secular price and wage movements over
the entire period 1351-1800; and a consideration of cyclical fluctuations

has been reserved for that volume, when all of the material will be available.

"As in the previous book, all the quantitative data relating to money, prices, and wages have been taken from contemporaneous documents in the private, ecclesiastic, and public archives of Spain." - Preface.

Public Affairs Pamphlets

Public affairs pamphlets, no. 2-4.   3 nos. [Washington, 1936]   280.9 P964
    No. 2. Labor and the new deal. 34pp. [1936?]
    No. 3. Our government for spoils or service? 31pp. 1936.
    No. 4. Security or the dole? 32pp. 1936.
       Bibliography, p. 32

Public Policy Pamphlets

Public policy pamphlets no. 16-18, 20. Harry D. Gideonse, editor.   4 nos.
    Chicago, University of Chicago press [1935-36]   280.12 P96
    no.16. Banking and the new deal, by Charles R. Whittlesey.   24pp.
    [1935]
       "Significant progress in the American banking system has come only as the result of a serious crisis. In the history of banking in this country there have been three great stages of reform. The first, which gave us the national banking system, was a product of the Civil War. The second, which gave us the Federal Reserve system, was directly caused by the crisis of 1907 and indirectly by earlier crises. The third, which constitutes the subject of this paper and bids fair to equal if not surpass either of the other two periods in scope and significance of the changes introduced, is an outcome of the present depression. In each case, the outstanding weaknesses of the existing system had been glaringly evident for years. The crises did not disclose the need for reform; they merely made reform politically feasible.
       No. 17. The United States and neutrality, by Quincy Wright.   29pp.
    [1935]
       No. 18. Foreign investment and war, by Eugene Staley.   23pp.   [1935]

Puerto Rico - Reconstruction

Puerto Rico. Reconstruction administration. The need for federal aid in
    Puerto Rico. The purposes of the Puerto Rico reconstruction administration. 6pp. Washington, U. S. Govt. print. off., 1936. 173.2 P962

Puerto Rico. Reconstruction administration. Planning division. The agricultural problems of Puerto Rico, by Rafael Pico. 35pp., mimeogr. [San Juan] May 18, 1936. 173.2 P962A
       Partial contents: Relation of population to land; Physical factors influencing land utilization; Land utilization in Puerto Rico; Land tenure and ownership; Facilities needed for the better planning of our agricultural resources.

Puerto Rico. Reconstruction administration. Planning division. Interim report on the organization and activities of the Planning division... [by]
Earl Hanson, Planning consultant, National resources committee, Secretary
Planning committee, Puerto Rico Reconstruction administration. 56pp.,
mimeogr. San Juan, May 28, 1936.   173.2 P963I
    The aims of the Planning Division of the Puerto Rican Reconstruction
Administration are summarized as follows:
    "1. To develop a general 'Puerto Rico Plan', based on thorough analy-
ses of the Island's present condition, to be used in part as a goal
for social-economic reconstruction, and in part for information to the Federal Government and other agencies concerned with Puerto Rico.
    "2. To coordinate the work of the PRRA into one central functional pro-
gram.
    "3. To extend the present program of the PRRA into the future through
appropriate research and recommendations for future action, and to keep
up to date the general 'Puerto Rico Plan.'
    "4. To coordinate the work of the PRRA with that of other local agen-
cies, such as the local branch of the FERA, the University of Puerto Rico,
and the various Departments of the Insular Government.
    "5. To bring about a maximum amount of coordination between the work
of the PRRA and that of other Federal agencies.
    "6. To develop and define a Puerto Rican policy, founded on Puerto
Rican needs, for recommendation to the Federal Government."

Puerto Rico. Reconstruction administration. Planning problems and activities
in Puerto Rico; preliminary report to the Puerto Rico Reconstruction administration and the National resources committee, by Earl Hanson, Planning consultant   34pp. San Juan, November 23, 1935.   173.2 P962P
    Amended as of February 17, 1936.
    Partial contents: I. The problem, including Standards of living,
Population and employment, The economic structure, The planning problem.
II. The Federal Emergency Relief Administration and the Puerto Rico
Reconstruction Administration, including Rural rehabilitation,Forestry
program, Slum clearance project, Hydroelectric project, The University
of Puerto Rico Program. III. Planning work and organization.

Purchasing Power

Simpson, H. D. Purchasing power and prosperity; an essay in the economics
of recovery. 149pp.   Chicago, The Foundation press, inc. [1936]
334 S152
    Among the chapter headings may be found the following: The nature
of purchasing power; Our first experiment; Our second experiment;
Keynes' theory of public expenditure; Obstacles to the flow of purchasing power; The nature of frozen assets; How purchasing relationships have been reestablished in past depressions; Why purchasing relationships have been so slowly reestablished in the present depression;
Types of governmental policy which would release the flow of purchasing power.

Raw Materials and Colonies

Royal institute of international affairs. Information dept. Raw materials
    and colonies. 68pp. London, Royal Institute of International Affairs.
    (Its Papers, no 18) 286 R812
        This memorandum concentrates its attention upon the "raw materials"
    issue in the problem of expansion, and sets out the facts without which
    it is impossible to assess the value of any changes contemplated.
        "Though primarily concerned with 'colonial raw materials' the memorandum
    cannot be confined to them for no important raw materials, except rubber,
    are even preponderantly produced in colonial territories. It therefore
    covers the production of the more important raw materials in all parts of
    the world.
        "Part I deals with production in general and shows what part the exist-
    ing colonial areas play in providing the world's supplies. It is intended
    to enable the reader to judge whether purely colonial adjustments could
    open up resources adequate for the needs of the dissatisfied Powers, or
    whether the gesture would prove to be merely of psychological value.
        "Part II describes the present and potential barriers to access. Some
    of these are directly due to the policy of the colonial Powers, notably
    discriminatory export duties, discrimination in the granting of conces-
    sions, and producers' restriction schemes; others are indirect, in particu-
    lar the stagnation of international trade which has led to the shortage of
    foreign exchange. A comparison of the relative importance of the direct
    and indirect barriers shows how far a change in present colonial policies
    could allay the prevailing dissatisfaction.
        "In the interests of compactness, the writers took an original decision
    to exclude foodstuffs and tobacco."

Raw Materials and International Control

Greaves, H. R. G. Raw materials and international control. 166pp. London,
    Methuen & co. ltd. [1936] 286 G7993
        "The subject matter of this study is constantly changing; conditions
    in the case of no raw material or service are static. At the same time,
    writing it has taken considerable time, the more so in that it has had to
    be undertaken parenthetically to my other work and without the research
    assistance such a vast field requires. I must emphasize therefore that
    it is not completely up to date. But I do not believe that to be of much
    importance, for my aim has not been to present the economist with a descrip-
    tion that a statistician might better supply to him, but to trace certain
    tendencies of development in government policy, and to indicate the growth
    of governmental or semi-governmental machinery of an international kind,
    that aims at regulating the production and distribution of raw materials,
    foodstuffs and services. In doing so I have had in mind the student of
    politics and of international institutions, for it is he primarily who is
    interested in the purposive direction of economic as well as political change."
        There are chapters devoted to Wheat, Timber, Sugar, Cotton and other
    non-agricultural commodities and one, also, on General Economic Planning
    Organization.

Benefer, S. C.   A plan for regional administrative districts in the state of
Washington: an ecological study. pp.29-80. Seattle, Wash., 1935.
(University of Washington publications in the social sciences v. 8, no.2,
pp.29-80.)   280.091 W52

Bibliography, p. 80.

"Until comparatively recently, the community has been stressed as the
basic unit of social organization... In recent years, however, a trend
toward larger units of social control has gradually become apparent...

"At the same time, the economic crisis has brought to the forefront
another unit of social organization, the region, which may be defined as
a constellation of communities with similar activities and resources.
The most striking development of regionalism is to be seen in the Tennessee
Valley Authority, which involves a regional drainage basin extending into
seven states. Electric power, flood and erosion control, and industrial
development are the material objects, and broader and happier lives for
the inhabitants of the region the non-material objects of this project.
These objectives somehow refuse to be halted by the arbitrary boundaries,
so a new form of organization arises...

"The application of the concept of regionalism is not merely the result of the depression, however...

"On the national scene, some fifty-three treaties between two or more
states have been ratified by Congress. Many of these have been regional
in character...

"The concept of regionalism has been advancing, both in theory and in
practice. But as yet little comprehensive work has been done to delimit
smaller units than natural regions, such as the local administrative districts suggested. Nor is much help to be derived from work done on the
basis of natural regions...

"Regions form the logical basis for political administration. Large
natural regions are important, but some functions of government need to be
administered on a smaller basis. This study is an attempt to extend the
regional concept to smaller local areas. The administrative districts
described in this monograph are not natural regions in the full sense,
but rather an approximation of local regions or sub-regions."

Resettlement Administration

U. S. Resettlement administration. Resettlement administration program.
Letter... transmitting in response to Senate resolution no. 295, a
report on the objectives, accomplishments and effects of the Resettlement
administration program. 70pp., maps, charts. Washington, U. S. Govt.
print. off., 1936. (74th Congress, 2d sess. Senate. Doc. no. 213)
135 R31R

This report presents the information requested as follows:

"(1) The nature and extent of all expenditures made or proposed to
be made by such administration (this subject is treated in part I and
part III of this report.) (2) The nature and extent of projects undertaken by it, and the advisability of undertaking future projects (this
subject is treated in part I and part III of this report). (3) The
effect of each such project on State and local taxation and on local

real estate values (this subject is treated in part II of this report).
(4) The extent to which such projects have benefited and will benefit
labor (this subject is treated in part II of this report). (5) The
circumstances relating to the securing of persons as tenants or purchasers in connection with such projects, and the effect on such persons of becoming such tenants or purchasers (this subject is treated
in part II of this report).

   "Additional material, historical, statistical, and graphic, on the
program of the Resettlement Administration, is presented in part I,
part III, and part IV, of this report." - Foreword.

Social Codes - Pre-Greek

Hertzler, J. O. The social thought of the ancient civilizations.
   403pp. New York and London, McGraw-Hill book company, inc. 1936.
   (McGraw- Hill publications in sociology) 280 H44
      Bibliography, pp. 389-395
      "This book is a scientific examination - the first of its kind -
into the social codes, ideas and general principles of the pre-Greek
civilizations. As the author points out in his preface, our knowledge
of these ancient cultures is much more extensive and intimate now than
it was even a few decades ago; and we understand better, too, not only
the diffusion but the continuity of culture itself. 'The careful
student is struck by the frequent applicability of much of the thought
of the ancients to present-day conditions,' ...
      "Throughout his book [the author] has worked strictly as a social
scientist, separating the precepts which had to do with men's group
life as completely as possible from their religious significance, and
avoiding any literary consideration of his sources.
      "They were very practical, these pre-Greek 'social thinkers.' The
individual was almost always the center of the picture, and the 'social situation was viewed as it affected the individual rather than
the group.' Social thought was 'prescientific' and immature. But
in all these ancient civilizations, the study of man's relationship to
man was a matter of keen importance; they worried about bad social conditions; their moral codes and expressions of social obligations were
extremely strict; the Golden Rule is a precept laid down 'among almost
all these ancient pre-Greek thinkers'; and what Dr. Hertzler sums up
as 'the amazing and unexpected social erudition of these ancients'
must impress itself strongly on the readers of this book.
      "It is a book not only scholarly and important in its special field,
but exceedingly interesting. (New York Times Book Review, July 26,
1936, p. 10)

Social Security

Dobbins, J. L. Dividends for citizenship... Preface by Dr. Paul F. Cadman.
   216pp. Los Angeles, San Francisco [etc.] Suttonhouse, ltd , 1936.
   280.12 D65
      The author in his introduction writes in part as follows:
      "In venturing to offer any new contribution to the discussion of

Social Security in any of its many phases, it is the desire of the author
to propose for consideration the introduction of an entirely new element
in the relationship which exists between citizen and government, which
may make it quite impossible in the future for the individual citizen
to exist in abject poverty at a time when the commercial activities of
the nation as a whole are prospering, - an element which will give new
and realistic emphasis to the belief that in a truly democratic government
the nation exists for the people, not the people for the nation...

"In presenting this proposal for the introduction of certain new and
unusual elements in government procedure, it is the intent of the author
to adopt a somewhat unusual procedure himself; and to present as a first
chapter an outline summary of causes and of desired objectives and a
definite statement of the method proposed for their accomplishment together with a summary of anticipated results.

"The reader may thus be able to visualize the controlling purposes
as he follows in succeeding chapters:

"1. The analyses of certain underlying economic trends which have
led up to conditions of today;

"2. The analysis of the mathematics of maintaining a balanced budget
in the operation of the proposed system, and the details of its proposed
administration;

"3. The effects which it will produce upon family incomes and family
habits of spending in the different economic groups of Americans;

"4. And finally, the justice of the philosophy which calls for greater
recognition of the individual citizen per se as one of the unit measures
for distribution of income, quite separate and apart from his possession
of wealth or ability to produce."

Social Security Act

Douglas, P. H. Social security in the United States; an analysis and appraisal
    of the federal Social security act. 384pp. New York, London, McGraw-
    Hill book company, inc. [1936] 284.6 D74
        The text of the Federal Social Security Act, pp. 327-376.
        Bibliography, pp. 325-326.
        The author states in his preface that he has "tried not only to explain
    what the Federal Social Security Act provides, but also to trace the steps
    by which it came into being and to outline some of the problems in the
    field of social security which lie ahead."

Tixier, P. A., and Davison, R. C. Suggestions on the administration of the
    Social security act and state unemployment compensation laws. 35pp.,
    mimeogr. [Washington? D. C., 1936?] 284.6 T54
        Partial contents: Administration of Federal old age retirement benefits;
    Coordination of the administration of The Social Security Act and state
    unemployment compensation laws; and Notes on the administration of un-
    employment compensation laws.

Southern Policy Papers

Hood, Robin. Industrial social security in the south. With a preface by
    Mercer G. Evans. 22pp. Chapel Hill, The University of North Carolina
    press, 1936. (Southern policy committee. Southern policy papers no. 5)
    280.9 So86 no.5
        Bibliography, on back of cover.
        "It seems... that the South must turn to rehabilitation of agricul-
    ture as the most obvious way of relieving this pressure upon industrial
    standards and security. This approach to the problem transcends the
    powers of the individual states and even regional action. Therefore,
    the attempts made by the Federal government to deal with the agricultural
    situation are most encouraging signs. Not all of these experiments
    have been productive of fruitful results, it is true. Subsistence home-
    stead and farming developments proved impractical. The Agricultural Ad-
    justment Act, before its effects could be fully evaluated, was declared
    unconstitutional.
        "Other plans, however, if continued, give more promise of success.
    The Resettlement Administration with plans for land retirement, coöpera-
    tive agricultural communities, and the location of farm families on their
    own full time, full sized farms may break the chains of tenancy and of
    the one-crop system."

Howard, T. L. The T V A and economic security in the south. 11pp. Chapel
    Hill, The University of North Carolina press, 1936. (Southern policy
    committee. Southern policy papers no. 7) 280.9 So86 no.7
        Bibliography, on back of cover.
        "The immediate program of the Tennessee Valley Authority does not in
    itself insure economic security to the South. It does, however, provide
    an instrument which may be used for raising the economic level of the
    area in which it operates by introducing elements of order, design, and
    forethought. The introduction of these elements will make it possible
    for the region to support its population in comfort. It will remove the
    necessity for economic insecurity, if in fact such necessity ever existed.
        "On the other hand, certain parts of the program of the Tennessee Val-
    ley Authority must be accomplished, either by it or by some other agency,
    if there is not to be an alarming increase in economic insecurity in the
    South. The control and proper use of water resources, the conservation and
    preservation of land resources, and a more widespread use of electrical
    energy are all conservation and utilization programs upon which the well-
    being of the entire country depends. Their relationship to economic se-
    curity must be apparent to every student of southern problems." - Conclusion.

Miller, F. P., ed. The southern press considers the constitution. 28pp.
    Chapel Hill, The University of North Carolina press, 1936. (Southern
    policy committee. Southern policy papers no. 6) 280.9 So86 no.6
        Bibliography, on back of cover.
        This pamphlet consists of reprints of editorials from Southern papers
    at the time of the Supreme Court's decision against the Agricultural
    Adjustment Act in the Hoosac Mills Case.

Woofter, T. J. Southern population and social planning. 10pp. Chapel
Hill, The University of North Carolina press, 1936. (Southern policy
committee. Southern policy papers no. 1) 280.9 So86 no. 1
Issued in cooperation with the Institute for Research in Social
Science, University of North Carolina.
Bibliography, on back of cover.
The author concludes this pamphlet as follows:
"This paper has probably gone far enough to indicate some of the in-
adequacies of present plans to meet the situation in the rural South
and to enable us to draw together a general basis for planning which
will start with the South as it is. Some of the salient points are:
(1) an expanding population; (2) limitation of the past opportunities
for employment in cities; (3) much unused land and much land which,
through a ruinous system of culture, is eroding and becoming unusable;
(4) backward techniques of utilization of natural resources and lack of
cultural institutions for the conservation of human resources: (5) necessity for radical reorganization of the system of land use - a shift from
production of the overproduced money crops and a shift to the production
of other crops of which there is a great deficiency in the South, such
as livestock products and foodstuffs necessary for an adequate diet.
"In short, the program should be the reconstruction of an agrarian
culture of expanding numbers, the rehabilitation of rural institutions
and rural families, and the integration of this development with that
of the other major regions of the nation.
"Some observers conclude from the fact that the South ranks low in
almost every index of wealth and culture that there are too many people
in the area. As the economy of the region is at present organized, this
is true, but this condition does not necessarily have to continue. More
rational land use, more diversification of production and, above all, an
increase in the standard of living of the people through the use of more
home-produced goods can provide for an increased Southern rural population at a higher level of living.
"What happened in depressions of the past was that the displaced excess population moved westward and took up new lands. They had to live
according to pioneer standards until they accumulated goods and increased
the value of their holdings, but here in the South there is unused land
much better than that taken up west of the Great Plains. The climate
and rainfall are the most favorable to agriculture of any section. This
means that the section is amply able to take care of a new crop of pioneers
"But whether you and I feel that the rural population of the South is
too large or not, whether you and I feel that planning can cope with the
situation or not, the concrete fact remains that the next mature generation has already been born and is now living on southern farms. They will
mature in the next twenty years and, in the absence of a revival of rapid
migration to cities, they must be fitted into an expanding agrarian culture or sink to an almost unendurable poverty."

Standard Grading - Wheat - Barley - Peas - Australia

Standards association of Australia. Report to the Council for scientific and
industrial research on standardised grading of primary products. 39pp.,mimeogr.
[Sydney, A. J. Kent, govt. printer, 1936]   280.3 St2
    At head of title: Standards association of Australia; at head of cover-
title: Publication no...
    "Results of investigations... With particular reference to wheat, malting
barley and peas, and the allied subject of standardisation of equipment for
bulk elevators for grain." - leaf [2]

Standard of Living and the State

Williams, Mrs. Gertrude (Rosenblum)   The state and the standard of living.
354pp.   London, P. S. King & son, ltd., 1936.   284.6 W67
    This volume is reviewed at some length in The Economist (London)
for May 23, 1936, page 426. From this the extracts below have been
taken:
    "Fifty years ago liberty was still regarded as the main goal of polit-
ical and social activity. Since then ideas have so changed that in the
twentieth century security has come to be emphasised more strongly even
than liberty. This book is an admirable description of the main causes
of this change. The author takes as her starting point the social ideas
of the 'eighties and 'nineties, when the seeds of the early twentieth
century social legislation were being sown. The origins of the various
reform movements are well summarised in the first chapter...
    "The history of unemployment legislation is told very fully by the
author, and this part of the book will be especially valuable. The
conclusions are moderate and well-balanced; and full weight is given
to the feelings and emotions of the workers themselves, which are so
often neglected in the findings of Royal Commissions. Thus one of the
reasons given for the opposition to the Means Test is that the poor are
not regarded as equals by members of public assistance committees. So
long as this feeling remains, the fear of the stigma of pauperism is
likely to continue.
    "In the last chapter some tentative estimates are given of the addi-
tion to wages made by the social services."

Statistical Analysis

Goulden, C. H. Methods of statistical analysis.   165pp., mimeogr.   Minneapolis, Minn., Burgess publishing company, 1936.   251 G73
    "The application of statistical methods to research problems is gaining
rapidly in momentum, but there are still many workers who have not obtained a sufficiently firm grasp of the principles involved to make correct
applications, or to realize fully the degree to which those methods can
extend the scope of experimental science. Since most of these workers
are not mathematicians and perhaps not even mathematically inclined,
they are loath to step into a field that to them is entirely new and
strange and seems to abound with snares and pitfalls to catch the unwary.
It is primarily for such workers, and especially those who are accustomed

to thinking in terms of practical units of measurement rather than in algebraic formulae, that this book has been designed...

"Another and perhaps more important reason for the publication of this book is to fill a growing need for the presentation under one cover of a series of examples of the application of the methods recently developed by Dr. R. A. Fisher and his associates. These methods have been responsible for an intense stimulation of interest in statistical procedures." - Preface.

Statistics

Rodríguez, Jorge. Lecciones de estadística (segunda edición) 286pp.
Medellín, Imprenta oficial, 1935. 251 R61 Ed.2
    Bibliography, p. [11]
    A text book of statistics written by the author for his students and used as lectures in the faculty of law and political science of the University of Antioquia in Colombia.

Sugar - Control of Production

Gutierrez, Viriato. The world sugar problem, 1926-1935. 188pp. London, N. Rodger, 1935. 286.365 G98
    "In view of the prevailing passion for restrictionism, great interest attaches to this informative survey of recent attempts to restrict the whole world production of raw sugar. The author - an eminent Cuban who has been intimately connected with these attempts - states that his main object is to assemble the relevant data, so that others may study them and draw their own conclusions.

    "The expansion of world productive capacity and the consequent decline in prices were responsible for the first attempts at restriction in Cuba - the world's largest producer - in 1925. Realisation of the futility of unilateral action, however, soon inspired the Cuban producers to sponsor an international scheme. A nebulous agreement was reached in Paris in November, 1927, and the question of international action was also considered by the Economic Section of the League of Nations in the following May; but with negative results.

    "Undaunted, the Cubans made new proposals, in consequence of which the 'Chadbourne Agreement' was eventually signed in Brussels in May, 1931. This agreement, which is reproduced as an Appendix to Dr. Gutierrez's book, terminated last year. It aimed at the limitation of exports from the principal producing areas, but, for reasons discussed by the author, it proved ineffectual. It was considered at the World Economic Conference in 1933 and at a special conference in London in March, 1934, but the signatory countries were unable to agree upon its continuance.

    "A consideration of this record of failures leads Dr. Gutierrez to suggest that the solution of the sugar problem should be left to the natural working of economic laws. 'In a world with excess productive capacity,' he concludes, 'it is not possible to go on believing that all the wealth invested in creating that excess capacity can be saved.' We commend the results of this study to all those who see in restriction schemes the panacea for the ills which afflict the producers of primary products at the present time." - Economist (London) v. 122, no. 4826, Feb. 22, 1936, p. 414.

<u>Syndicalism, Agricultural - France</u>

Congrès national des syndicats agricoles de France. 17th, Versailles, 1935.
  Le XVIIe Congrès national des syndicats agricoles, Versailles, 31 mai,
  1er et 2 juin 1935. 191pp. Paris [Impr. d'Art F.-R.] 1935.   280.29 C7627
  At head of title: Union Nationale des Syndicats Agricole.

Union nationale des syndicats agricoles, Paris.   Vers la corporation agricole;
  cinquantenaire du syndicalisme, 1884-1934. 158pp. Paris, Union nationale
  des syndicats agricoles, 1934.   280.174 Un3
       Contains proceedings of Congrès du Cinquantenaire du Syndicalisme
  Agricole, Paris, 1934.
       An account of the proceedings of a conference held in Paris on May
  29, 1934 to celebrate the fiftieth anniversary of the birth of agricultural syndicalism in France. Reports presented are: L'organisation de
  l'agriculture française avant le syndicalisme, by Roger Grand. - pp. 37-
  44. (A brief sketch of agricultural history in France provides the background and shows the need for internal organization); La loi du 21 mars
  1884 sur les syndicats professionels et ses premières applications dans
  l'agriculture, by H. de Gailhard-Bancel. - pp. 45-50. (Report by one of
  the first founders of an agricultural syndicate after the passing of the
  law of 1884 which granted to the French people the right to form associations. Some of the difficulties encountered in the early days are noted);
  Le droit syndical, by Adrien Toussaint. - pp. 51-65. (A summary of the
  legislative history of the movement from the law of March 21, 1884 to
  that of February, 1927 which codifies the earlier laws.); Le Syndicat,
  cellule-mere de l'organisation professionnelle, by P. de Monicault. - pp. 66 -
  73. (Shows to what extent individual members of the organization have abandoned its original principles); L'activité et le rôle economique du syndicalisme agricole, by Joseph Artigala. - pp. 74-80. (The economic rôle of
  agricultural syndicalism is outlined); L'activité sociale du syndicalisme
  agricole, by F. M. Jacq. - pp. 81-88. (A brief study of the extent to which
  the original principles of agricultural syndicalism have been realised, and
  the outlook for the future); Le syndicalisme et l'activité professionnelle
  d'apres guerre, by S. de Lestapis. - pp. 89-98. (The author shows how
  agricultural syndicalism has prepared the way for and aided in the development of professional organization of agriculture); Le rôle du syndicat
  agricole dans l'organisation corporative, by Ambroise Rendu. - pp. 99-105.
  (The author examines the rôle that agricultural syndicalism ought to play
  in a corporative state); La place du syndicalisme agricole dans l'ensemble
  du syndicalisme professionnel français, by Le Roy Ladurie. - pp. 106-123.
  (The place of agricultural syndicalism with regard to French professional
  syndicalism as a whole); L'evolution du syndicalisme et l'integration de
  la profession dans l'État, by Louis Salleron. - pp. 124-147. (A survey
  of the development of syndicalism as a professional organization and its
  place in the State); L'Union nationale des syndicats agricoles et sa mission
  devant les problèmes actuels, by H. de Guébriant. - pp. 148-158. (A brief
  account of the history and duties of the National Union of Agricultural
  Syndicates. - A. M. Hannay

Taxation

Committee on civic education by radio. You and your government, series XI
    (Taxation for prosperity) Delivered June 18-September 24, 1935, over
    a nation-wide network of the National broadcasting company.   15 nos. in
    1 v.   New York city, National municipal league [1935] 280.12 N215G ser.11.
    Paged continuously.
        Presented by the Committee on Civic Education by Radio of the National
    Advisory Council on Radio in Education and the American Political Science
    Association, in cooperation with the National Municipal League.
        Brief list of references on taxation, by Mabel L. Walker at the end
    of each radio talk.
        Contents. - no. 1. Just taxes [by] F. A. Vanderlip and T. H. Reed. -
    no. 2. Paying for social security [by] E. E. Witte. - no. 3. The tariff
    and business recovery [by] F. B. Sayre. - no. 4. How much should the drinker
    pay? [by] C. H. Morrissett. - no. 5. Missing the intangibles [by] W. B.
    Munro. - no. 6. Does real estate pay too much? [by] J. D. McGoldrick. -
    no. 7. Tax exemptions [by] Lawson Purdy. - no. 8. Tax dodging by con-
    stitutional amendment [by] E. A. Cottrell. - no. 9. Single tax vs. triple
    tax [by] Walter Fairchild and H. S. Buttenheim. - no. 10. Who gets the
    tax money? [by] J. N. Edy. - no. 11. Processing tax [by] William Hard. -
    no. 12. Sales tax - pro and con [by] H. F. Long and Daniel Bloomfield. -
    no. 13. Federal taxation and business recovery [by] F. R. Kent. - no. 14.
    Coordinated tax administration [by] J. G. Winant. - no. 15. Harmonizing
    the tax system, by F. R. Fairchild.

Seligman, Eustace, Gerstenberg, C. W., Montgomery, R. H., Knollenberg, Bernhard;
    Montague, G. H., and Wickersham, C. W.   Taxation today.   24pp.
    New York, American management association, 1935. (American management
    association. Financial management series. F. M. 48)   280.9 Am38F no. 48
        Partial contents: An appraisal of the orthodox principles of taxation
    and recent variations therefrom, by Charles W. Gerstenberg; Some legal
    and practical phases of the federal tax act of 1935, by Bernhard
    Knollenberg; and Some legal aspects of processing taxes which are im-
    portant to business men, by Gilbert H. Montague.

Taxation of Agricultural Profits - France

Garnier, Paul.   L'impôt sur les bénéfices de l'exploitation agricole. 54pp.
    Paris, Editions du Tableau fiscal et juridique [1936?] 284.5 G182
        This is a study of the taxation of agricultural profits first pro-
    vided for by a law of July 31, 1917. It describes the taxable profits,
    the persons eligible to pay the tax, the place where it may be levied,
    the calculation of the tax and the information to be supplied by the
    farmer. Tables give the tax rates from 1918 to 1935 and the dates of
    the laws establishing them, and the number of taxpayers and the amount
    collected annually from 1918 to 1932.

<u>Tobacco Regulation - Colonial Maryland</u>

Wyckoff, V. J.   Tobacco regulation in colonial Maryland. 228pp.   Baltimore,
    The Johns Hopkins press, 1936. (Johns Hopkins university studies in
    historical and political science. Extra volumes. New series, no. 22)
    281.369 W97
        Bibliography, pp. 217-226.
        Partial contents: American tobacco before 1634; Early tobacco regula-
    tions; The economic crisis of 1663-1666; The bulk tobacco controversy;
    Miscellaneous tobacco legislation 1700-1725, Marketing troubles and re-
    occurring depressions; The tobacco inspection law of 1747; and Improve-
    ment in the tobacco trade.

<u>Trade Agreements - Gt. Britain</u>

Dorman-Smith, R. H.   Trade agreements and the farmer; notes for a statement
    submitted... to the conservative Parliamentary Agricultural committee on
    25th February, 1936. 30pp. London, National farmers' union, 1936.
    (N.F.U. no.50)   285 D73
        This pamphlet undertakes to indicate "the effects of the trade agree-
    ments on imports of butter, beef, mutton and lamb, apples and tomatoes.
    This list of commodities is by no means exhaustive, but it is signifi-
    cant to note that the value of the output of the livestock, milk and
    dairy produce, fruit and vegetables (including glasshouse produce)
    branches of farming constitute nearly 85 per cent. of the value of the
    total agricultural production in England and Wales."
        The matter is summed up as follows:
        "If the Government are to implement their promise to restore agricul-
    tural prosperity, it is clear that either there must be drastic revision
    of the policy as exemplified in these trade agreements or adequate com-
    pensating measures, covering all agricultural commodities affected, must
    be enacted speedily. The matter is one which concerns vitally not only
    agriculture but the whole nation. Apart from the value of a prosperous
    agriculture as a matter of social welfare or in emergencies such as war
    or economic and financial crises, it is to-day, more than ever before,
    an essential home market for other industries. Even now, in a time of
    depression in the industry, the value of produce sold off farms in the
    United Kingdom, which represents the purchasing power of agriculture
    alone, is at least £250 million per annum and, if to this there were
    added the purchasing power of allied industries, market towns and the
    countryside generally, whose prosperity is bound up with agriculture, it
    will be realised that this is a market which other industries cannot af-
    ford to see neglected. Further, it is a market within our boundaries
    from which we cannot be excluded by prohibitions and tariffs imposed by
    other governments and is one capable of very considerable expansion if
    the Ottawa principle of giving first place to home agriculture in our
    home market is to be accepted in practice as well as in theory.
        "Farming opinion to-day definitely favours - (a) the prompt termination
    of all existing trade agreements; (b) the negotiation of new agreements
    on a basis which will specifically give effect to the right of the home
    agricultural producer to priority in his home market; (c) modification of
    the 'Most-Favoured-Nation' clause in our commercial treaties, and (d) con-

sultation with the responsible representatives of home producers' interests during the progress of trade agreement negotiations in the same way
as Overseas Government Delegations consult with their producers' representatives."

Truck Transportation - Fruits and Vegetables - Maryland

Russell, Ralph. Truck transportation of fruits and vegetables in western
Maryland. 15pp. [College Park? Md., 1935] Reprint collection.
"Reprinted from the 1935 annual report of the Maryland Agricultural
Society - The Maryland Farm Bureau Federation."
This is a presentation of some of the findings for Maryland resulting
from the study of motor truck marketing of fruits and vegetables in nine
northeastern states, initiated by the Farm Credit Administration. It is
based on reports for 189 farms in 1933-34, located in the areas around
Baltimore and the District of Columbia and in Washington County. It is
shown that farmers in the more remote area depend to a much greater extent
on sales at the farm, a short truck haul to a railroad loading point, or
hired trucks than do farmers in the areas near the city markets, who
mostly truck their produce themselves. The amount of time consumed per
trip to and from market is analyzed. A strikingly large percentage is
found to be spent in waiting for the market to open, making sales, and
waiting to unload sold produce, as compared with the amount spent in
actual road movement. The average annual cost of operating a farm truck
is found to have been $295. No allowance for driving labor is included.
The outstanding items are gasoline, depreciation, and repairs. An average annual cost assignable to marketing fruits and vegetables, including
an allowance for driving time, is also computed. This is found to be
$219. Transportation costs are compared with other items of marketing
cost incurred by farmers. For these short hauls containers are found to
be a larger item than transportation. Trucking costs per ton mile are
shown to vary inversely with size of load and length of haul.

U. S. S. R.

Associations ouvrières de production. Chambre consultative. La production
coopérative en U.R.S.S. Compte rendu du voyage d'études et de documentation, organisé par la Chambre consultative, 16 juin - 3 juillet 1935.
171pp. Paris, 1935. 280.2 As7
"An account of cooperative production in the Soviet Union, as revealed
in the course of a sightseeing trip through that country, arranged by
the Central organization of workers' cooperative production associations
of France." - U. S. Dept. of Labor. Bur. of Labor Statis. Monthly Labor
Review, v.42, no.4, p.1170. Apr. 1936.

Stalin, Iosif. Marxism and the national and colonial question... A collection
of articles and speeches. 304pp. Moscow, [etc.] Co-operative publishing society of foreign workers in the U.S.S.R., 1935. (Marxist-Leninist
library) 280.179 StlM
"Edited by A. Fineberg. Translated from the Russian edition published
by Partizdat, Moscow, 1934." - Verso of title page.
The period covered by these articles and speeches is 1917-1934.

Committee on government statistics and information services. Wholesale price
    work of the Bureau of labor statistics [by] Henry B. Arthur. 51pp.,
    mimeogr. Washington, D. C., Committee on government statistics and
    information services [1935]   284.3 C732
      At head of title: Memorandum.
        Contains recommendations on publication of wholesale price material
    and much else of interest.

World Economic Review

U. S. Dept. of commerce. Bureau of foreign and domestic commerce. World eco-
    nomic review 1935. 421pp. Washington, U. S. Govt. print. off., 1936.
    157.54 W892 1935
      "This, the third edition of the World Economic Review, presents a
    concise summary of major economic developments throughout the world in
    1935.
        "For convenience the report is divided into two parts. Part I,
    which deals with the United States, presents the changes which have
    taken place in our domestic economy during the past year. Part II
    deals with the principal foreign countries and presents major economic
    changes for the year; in selecting the material relating to these coun-
    tries both its general importance and its bearing on the economic in-
    terests of the United States have been taken into consideration. The
    appendixes contain a chronology of major economic events in the United
    States, a digest of the more important laws pertaining to economic af-
    fairs enacted by Congress during 1935, and statistical tables showing
    the trend of major economic indicators, statistics of world trade, and
    production of important commodities." - Foreword.

BIBLIOGRAPHIES

Bibliography of social studies; a list of books for schools and adults, com-
    piled by the Association for education in citizenship. 111pp. London,
    Oxford university press, H. Milford, 1936.   241.3 As72

Cottonseed marketing. Selected references, 1926-1936. Comp. in the Division
    of cotton marketing branch library, Bureau of agricultural economics,
    U. S. Department of Agriculture. 9pp., Typewritten. Oct. 7, 1936.
        May be borrowed for copying.

Guide to the official publications of the new deal administrations (mimeo-
    graphed and printed) Supplement April 15, 1934-December 1, 1935. Comp. by
    Jerome K. Wilcox, chief Acquisitions division, Duke university Library.
    184pp., mimeogr. Chicago, American library association 1936.   242.1
    W64G Suppl.
        May be purchased from the American Library Association, 520 North
    Michigan Avenue, Chicago, Illinois.

Measures of major importance enacted by the 74th Congress, January 3 to August
26, 1935 and January 3 to June 20, 1936, comp. by Vajen H. Fischer under
the direction of Mary G. Lacy, Librarian, Bureau of agricultural economics.
209pp. July 1936. (U. S. Dept. of agriculture. Bureau of agricultural
economics. Agricultural economics bibliography no. 66)   1.9 Ec73A no.66.

SELECTED LIST OF RECENT REVIEWS

Compiled by M. I. Herb

Adams, A. B.   National economic security.   1936.
 Reviewed by John J. Corson, 3d, in South. Econ. Jour. 3(1): 92-93.
July 1936.
 Reviewed by W. M. Leiserson in Amer. Acad. Polit. and Social Sci. Ann.
187: 213. September 1936.
 Reviewed by John J. Corson in Amer. Econ. Rev. 26(2): 363-364.
June 1936.
 Reviewed in Annalist 48(1224): 7. July 3, 1936.

Bates, E. S.   A planned nationalism; Canada's effort. 1935.
 Reviewed by H. S. Patton in Pacific Affairs 9(3): 454-457.   September 1936.

Burns, Mrs. Eveline M. Toward social security; an explanation of the Social
 security act and a survey of the larger issues. [1936]
  Reviewed by C. A. Kulp in Amer. Acad. Polit. and Social Sci. Ann. 187:
210-212. September 1936.

Chase, Stuart. Rich land, poor land; a study of waste in the natural re-
 sources in America. [1936]
  Reviewed in Lit. Digest 122(14): 27, 28. Oct. 3, 1936.
  Reviewed in the Washington Evening Star. Sept. 26, 1936.
  Reviewed by Francis Brown in the New York Times Book Rev., Sept.
13, 1936, p. 1.

Childs, M. W. Sweden; the middle way. 1936.
 Reviewed in The Economist (London) 124(4856): 520. Sept. 19, 1936,
in an article entitled "Social-Democracy in Sweden."

Cohen, Ruth L. The history of milk prices; an analysis of the factors af-
 fecting the price of milk and milk products. 1936.
  Reviewed by R. McG. Carslaw in Econ. Jour. 46(183): 521-523.
September 1936.

Douglas, P. H. Social security in the United States; an analysis and appraisal
 of the federal Social security act. [1936]
  Reviewed by W. M. Leiserson in Amer. Acad. Polit. and Social Sci. Ann.
187: 212. September 1936.
  Reviewed by Honor Croome in New Statesman and Nation 11(279, n.s.):
1037-1038. June 27, 1936.

Fowler, B. B. Consumer cooperation in America; democracy's way out. [1936]
 Reviewed in The People's Money 3(1): 29. August 1936.

Gayer, A. D. Public works in prosperity and depression; prepared for the
 National planning board, Federal emergency administration of public works.
 1935. (Half-title: Publications of the National bureau of economic
 research, inc. no. 29)
  Reviewed by R. F. Kahn in Econ. Jour. 46(183): 491-493. September 1936.

Great Britain, Colonial office. An economic survey of the colonial empire
 (1933). Rev. ed. 1935.
  Reviewed by Pardee Lowe in Pacific Affairs 9(3): 468-470. September 1936.

Great Britain. Ministry of agriculture and fisheries. Committee of investigation
 for England of any agricultural marketing scheme. Report of the Committee
 of investigation for England on complaints made by the Central milk distributive committee and the Parliamentary committee of the Co-operative
 congress as to the operation of the Milk marketing scheme, 1933. 1936.
  Reviewed by R. F. Kahn in Econ. Jour. 46(183): 554-559. September 1936.

Haney, L. H. History of economic thought; a critical account of the origin
 and development of the economic theories of the leading thinkers in the
 leading nations. 3d and enl. ed. 1936. (Half-title: Social science textbooks, ed. by R. T. Ely)
  Reviewed briefly in Econ. Jour. 46(183): 582. September 1936.

Hubbard, G. E. Eastern industrialization and its effect on the west, with
 special reference to Great Britain and Japan. 1935.
  Reviewed in Annalist 48(1224): 7. July 3, 1936.
  Reviewed by P. D. Phillips in Econ. Rec. 12(22): 140-143. June 1936.

Hugh-Jones, E. M., and Radice, E. A. An American experiment. 1936.
  Reviewed by Honor Croome in New Statesman and Nation 11(279, n.s.):
 1037-1038. June 27, 1936.

Institute of public affairs. Southern Methodist University. Proceedings of
 the second annual conference. The cotton crisis. Edited by S. D.
 Myres, Jr. 1935.
  Reviewed by W. E. Paulson in Jour. Farm Econ. 18(3): 624-625. August 1936.

Knowles, L. C. A., and Knowles, C. M. The economic development of the British
 Overseas Empire. v. 3. The Union of South Africa. 1936.
  Reviewed by S. Herbert Frankel in South African Jour. Econ. 4(1):
 104-106. March 1936.

Laidler, H. W. A program for modern America. [1936]
  Reviewed by W. N. Loucks in Amer. Acad. Polit. and Social Sci. Ann.
 187: 219. September 1936.

Longobardi, Cesare. Land-reclamation in Italy; rural revival in the building of a nation. Translated from the Italian by Olivia Rossetti Agresti. 1936.
　　Reviewed by G. C. in Monthly Bull. Agr. Econ. and Sociol. [reprint from Internatl. Rev. Agr.] 27(6): 198E. June 1936.
　　Reviewed by David Weeks in Jour. Farm Econ. 18(3): 625-626. August 1936.

Lough, W. H., and Gainsbrugh, M. R. High-level consumption: its behavior; its consequences. 1935.
　　Reviewed by J. Marschak in Econ. Jour. 46(183): 489-491. September 1936.

McBride, G. McC. Chile: land and society. 1936.
　　Reviewed by N. L. Whetten in Rural Sociol. 1(3): 389-390. September 1936.

Menefec, S. C. A plan for regional administrative districts in the state of Washington; an ecological study. 1935.
　　Reviewed by George H. Hansen in Rural Sociol. 1(2): 239-240. June 1936.

Menzies-Kitchin, A. W. Land settlement; a report prepared for the Carnegie United Kingdom Trustees. 1935.
　　Reviewed by O. S. Orwin in Econ. Jour. 46(183): 532-534. September 1936.

Moulton, H. G. Income and economic progress. 1935. (The Institute of economics of the Brookings institution. Publ. no. 68)
　　Reviewed by R. W. in People's Money 3(2): 62. September 1936.
　　Reviewed by Emil Lederer in Amer. Statis. Assoc. Jour. 31(195): 629-631. September 1936.

National industrial conference board. American agricultural conditions and remedies; preliminary general review. [1936] (Studies no. 224)
　　Reviewed by A. B. Cox in Amer. Statis. Assoc. Jour. 31(195): 638-640. September 1936.

National industrial conference board, inc. Cost of government in the United States, 1933-1935. [1936] (Its studies no. 223)
　　Reviewed by Paul Studenski in Amer. Acad. Polit. and Social Sci. Ann. 187: 229. September 1936.

National survey of potential product capacity. Report of the National survey of potential product capacity; prepared under the sponsorship of the New York city housing authority and Works division of the Emergency relief bureau, City of New York. 1935.
　　Reviewed by Walter N. Polakov in the Society for the Advancement of Management Journal 1(3): 90-92. May 1936.

Nogaro, Bertrand. Les prix agricoles mondiaux et la crise. 1936.
　　Reviewed by V. P. Timoshenko in Amer. Acad. Polit. and Social Sci. Ann. 186: 236-237. July 1936.
　　Reviewed by Robert B. Schwenger in Amer. Statis. Assoc. Jour. 31(195): 637-638. September 1936.
　　Reviewed briefly in Economist (London) 122(4831): 709. March 28, 1936.

Peek, G. N., and Crowther, Samuel. Why quit our own. 1936.
    Reviewed briefly in Fertilizer Rev. 11(3): 12. July-August 1936.

Public administration clearing house. A directory of organizations in the
    field of public administration. 1936.
        Reviewed in People's Money 3(2): 63. September 1936.

Rather, A. W. Planning under capitalism; the problem of planning in Great
    Britain. 1935.
        Reviewed briefly in Annalist 47(1221): 870. June 12, 1936.
        Reviewed by Edward Batson in South African Jour. Econ. 4(2): 245.
    June 1936.

Richards, H. I. Cotton and the A.A.A. 1936. (Half-title: The Institute
    of economics of the Brookings institution. Publ. no. 66)
        Reviewed by Carle C. Zimmerman in Rural Sociol. 1(3): 386-389.
    September 1936.
        Reviewed in The People's Money 3(1): 29. August 1936.

Rowe, J. W. F. Markets and men: A study of artificial control schemes in
    some primary industries. 1936.
        Reviewed by G. D. H. Cole in New Statesman and Nation (n.s.) 11(269):
    606, 607. Apr. 18, 1936.
        Reviewed by Vesta Godsell in Econ. Rec. 12(22): 136-138. June 1936.
        Reviewed by H. Belshaw in Pacific Affairs 9(3): 496-498. September 1936.
        Reviewed by Louis Rich in New York Times Book Rev., June 21, 1936, p. 11.
        Reviewed in The Producer (Manchester, Eng.) June 1936, pp. 184, 195.

Sharfman, I. L. The Interstate commerce commission; a study in administrative
    law and procedure. Part III, Vol. B. 1936.
        Reviewed by Leslie Craven in Jour. Land & Pub. Utility Econ. 12(3): 329.
    August 1936.

Smith, N. S. An introduction to some Japanese economic writings of the
    eighteenth century. (Reprinted from the Transactions of the Asiatic
    Society of Japan, vol. xi, 2nd ser., 1934) 1935.
        Reviewed briefly by R. S. Howey in Amer. Econ. Rev. 26(3): 502-503.
    September 1936.

Williams, Faith M., and Zimmerman, C. C. Studies of family living in the
    United States and other countries; an analysis of material and method.
    1935. (U. S. Dept. Agr. Misc. Pub. 223)
        Reviewed by Warren C. Waite in Amer. Statis. Assoc. Jour. 31(195):
    617-618. September 1936.

Wilson, L. R., and Wight, E. A. County library service in the South; a
    study of the Rosenwald county library demonstration. [1935] (Half-
    title: The University of Chicago. Studies in library sciences)
        Reviewed by Caroline B. Sherman in Rural Sociol. 1(3): 382-383.
    September 1936.

U. S. DEPARTMENT OF AGRICULTURE PUBLICATIONS

Economic in Character

Compiled by Katharine Jacobs

Circulars*

413. An improved method for converting an observed skein strength of cotton
    yarn to the strength of a specified yarn count, by Malcolm E. Campbell.
    18pp. October 1936.   1 Ag84C
        The Bureau of Agricultural Economics in cooperation with Clemson
    Agricultural College.
417. The farm real estate situation, 1935-36, by B. R. Stauber... and M. M.
    Regan. 40pp. October 1936.   1 Ag84C

Farmers' Bulletin*

1558. Preparation of eastern grapes for market, by B. E. Shaffer.   18pp.
    Issued March 1928, revised July 1936.   1 Ag84F

Service and Regulatory Announcement (Bureau of Agricultural Economics)*

104, revised. Rules and regulations of the Secretary of agriculture under
    the United States standard container act of August 31, 1916 (39 Stat. 673)
    as amended June 11, 1934 (48 Stat. 930) effective September 1, 1936.   4pp.
    1936.   1 M34S.

Technical Bulletin*

535. Wheat requirements in Europe (especially pertaining to quality and type,
    and to milling and baking practices) by J. H. Shollenberger.   190pp.
    September 1936.   1 Ag84Te

Unnumbered Publications**

Soil and water conservation in the Pacific northwest. 5pp. 1936. (Issued
    by the U. S. Dept. of Agriculture, Soil conservation service, Region 11.
    Spokane, Wash.)   1.6 So39S

Address of Secretary Wallace*

The farmer and the general welfare; remarks... at the Sixth annual forum on cur-
    rent problems, under the auspices of the New York Herald-Tribune, New York
    city, September 23, 1936. 7pp., mimeogr. 1.9 Ag8636 [no. 129]

Symbol used after each entry is call number assigned to the publication by
    the Department Library.
*Requests for these publications should be addressed to the Office of Informa-
    tion, U. S. Department of Agriculture, Washington, D. C.
**Request for this publication should be addressed to the issuing office.

Publications of the Bureau of Agricultural Economics (Mimeographed)*

Amendment no. 4 to Service and regulatory announcement no. 126. Amendment
    to regulations for warehousemen storing cotton under the United States
    warehouse act. Effective October 7, 1936. 1p. 1936. 1 M34S
Brief preliminary review; marketing Idaho fresh prunes 1936. 2pp. September
    17, 1936. (Issued in cooperation with Idaho, Dept. of agriculture and
    Idaho shippers traffic association) 1.9 Ec741L
Crop insurance, selections and excerpts. 26pp. October 1936. 1.9 Ec7Cro
        Contents; Crop insurance; risks, losses, and principles of protection,
    by V. N. Valgren. - Insurance and farm hazards, by V. N. Valgren. -
    Excerpts from address of Henry A. Wallace on agricultural preparedness
    and the drought, July 22, 1936. - Letter from the President of the United
    States to the Secretary of agriculture appointing Crop insurance committee.
    Dated September 19, 1936. - Crop insurance problems, address of Roy M.
    Green before the national convention of the Association of mutual in-
    surance companies, Philadelphia, October 13, 1936.
Dairy products manufactured, 1935, by states. 5pp. September 22, 1936.
    1.9 Ec724Apr
Hay seed revisions, acreage, yield and production crop years 1919-1935, by
    states. 13pp. September 1936.
Marketing Georgia peaches 1936 season. 7pp. September 26, 1936. (Issued
    in cooperation with Georgia Dept. of agriculture, Bureau of markets)
    1.9 Ec741L
Marketing northwestern potatoes (Idaho, Oregon and Washington) Summary of
    the 1935 season, by M. M. Thomas. 25pp. August 1936. 1.9 Ec741L
Marketing Texas spinach; brief review of 1935-36 season, by L. G. Hooks.
    14pp. September 1936. (Issued in cooperation with Texas Dept. of ag-
    riculture, Markets and warehouse division) 1.9 Ec741L
Marketing the lower Rio Grande valley Texas potato crop; brief review of
    the 1936 season, by W. D. Googe. 11pp. September 1936. (Issued in
    cooperation with Texas Dept. of agriculture, markets and warehouse di-
    vision) 1.9 Ec741L
Measures of major importance enacted by the 74th Congress, January 3 to
    August 26, 1935 and January 3 to June 20, 1936, comp. by Vajen H.
    Fischer under the direction of Mary G. Lacy, Librarian, Bureau of ag-
    ricultural economics. 209pp. July 1936. (U. S. Dept. of agriculture.
    Bureau of agricultural economics. Agricultural economics bibliography
    no. 66) 1.9 Ec73A no.66.
Official standard grades for fire-cured tobacco. (U. S. types 21, 22, 23,
    and 24)... Prepared under authority of the Tobacco inspection act (49
    Stat., 731) 9PP. September 1936. 1.9 Ec792Tfc
Preparation of burley tobacco for market, by Hugh W. Taylor. 7pp. September
    1936. 1.9 Ec714 1936
Tentative United States standards for grades of canned lima beans (Effective
    September 1, 1936) 8pp. 1936. 1.9 Ec792Lb

---

*These publications are issued in small editions for immediate use in official
  work and are not for general distribution.

Radio Talks (Mimeographed)*

Farm business facts. A radio interview between Roy F. Hendrickson... and Morse
Salisbury... National farm and home hour... September 22, 1936 (4pp.);
September 29, 1936 (6pp.); October 6, 1936 (5pp.)   1.9 Ec7RA

Farm business news. A radio interview between Roy F. Hendrickson... and Joseph
A. Becker... October 13, 1936. 6pp. 1.9 Ec7Ra

Publications of the Agricultural Adjustment Administration**

Effects of winter soil-conserving crops; a compilation of experimental work on
winter soil-conserving crops in the southern region and nearby states.
54pp. September 1936. (SRAC-2) 1.42 So8Sr no.2
  Issued in conjunction with the Cooperative Extension Service of the
  Department of Agriculture and the state agricultural colleges in the
  southern region.

Farm imports and national prosperity. 11pp. September 1936. (G-59)
  1.4 Ad4Ge

(General sirup quota regulations, series 1, no. 1) 1936 quotas for sirups and
  sugar mixtures. 2pp. September 3, 1936. (G. Sirup Q.R. Series 1, No. 1)
  1.4 Su3Ges

Instructions on signatures and authorizations in connection with the execution
  of applications for payment or related papers under the agricultural conservation program. 10pp. October 1, 1936. (ACP-16)   1.42 Ad4F

Marketing agreement series - agreement no. 62, amendment no. 1... Amendment of
  marketing agreement regulating the handling of walnuts grown in California,
  Oregon and Washington. 9pp. 1936. (A-1-Amendment 1) 1.4 Ad47M
    Effective September 27, 1936.

1936 agricultural conservation program, east central region. Bulletin no. 1-
  revised (as of September 22, 1936) 18pp. 1936. (ECR-B-1 Revised As
  of September 22, 1936) 1.42 Ea7B

1936 agricultural conservation program, east central region. Bulletin no. 5.
  Instructions for determination of performance, preparation of report of
  performance, application for payment and related forms. 24pp. September
  1936. (ECR-B-5) 1.42 Ea7B

1936 agricultural conservation program - north central region. Bulletin no. 1,
  revised, as of September 17, 1936. 29pp. (NCR-B-1 (Rev.) Sept. 17, 1936)
  1.42 N75B

1936 agricultural conservation program - north central region. Bulletin no. 2,
  revised, as of September 9, 1936. Soil-building practices. 11pp.
  (NCR-B-2 (Rev.) Sept. 9, 1936) 1.42 N75B

1936 agricultural conservation program, southern region. Bulletin no. 1, revised as of September 1, 1936. 21pp. September 1, 1936. (SR-B-1 revised) 1.42 So8B

1936 agricultural conservation program, southern region. Bulletin no. 5. Instructions for filling out report of performance and application for payment. 13pp. September 26, 1936. (SR-B-5) 1.42 So8B

---

* Radio talks may be obtained from U. S. Department of Agriculture, Office
  of information, Radio Service.
**Requests for these publications should be addressed to the Agricultural Ad-
  justment Administration, U. S. Department of Agriculture, Washington, D. C.

1936 agricultural conservation program – western region. Bulletin no. 1, revised, supplement (c) 1p. September 14, 1936. (WBR-B-1 Revised, Supplement (c)) 1.42 W52B
1936 agricultural conservation program, western region. Bulletin no. 1, revised,
supplement (f) 5pp. October 7, 1936. (WR-B-1 Revised Supplement (f))
1.42 W52B
1936 agricultural conservation program – western region. Bulletin no. 1 revised, supplement (g). Range land. 3pp. September 26, 1936. (WR-B-1
Revised, Supplement (g)) 1.42 W52B
Order series – order no. 1, amendment no. 1. Amendment of order regulating
the handling of walnuts grown in California, Oregon, and Washington.
(Issued by the Acting secretary of agriculture Sept. 23, 1936. Effective
12:01 a.m., E.S.T., Sept. 27, 1936) 10pp. 1936. (O-1-Amendment 1)
1.4 Ad470
Order series – order no. 11. Order regulating the handling of milk in the
District of Columbia marketing area. (Issued by the Secretary of agri-
culture Sept. 17, 1936) Effective 12:01 a.m., E.S.T., Sept. 21, 1936)
11pp. 1936. (O-11) 1.4 Ad470
Order series – order no. 12. Order regulating the handling of milk in the
Dubuque, Iowa, marketing area. (Issued by the Secretary of agriculture
Sept. 17, 1936) (Effective 12:01 a.m., C.S.T. Oct. 1, 1936) 9pp. 1936
(O-12) 1.4 Ad470
Planning the 1937 farm program. 8pp. September 25, 1936. (G-60) 1.4 Ad4Ge

Addresses (Mimeographed)*

County agricultural adjustment planning. By Bushrod W. Allin. 7pp. 1936.
1.94 Ad472A1 [no.1]
A paper presented at the Conference on Planning, Richmond, Virginia,
May 5, 1936.
Is planning compatible with democracy? By Bushrod W. Allin. 10pp. 1936.
1.94 Ad472A1 [no.2]
A paper presented before the Annual Institute of the Society for Social
Research at the University of Chicago, Chicago, Illinois, August 22, 1936.
Soil conservation and production control in the South. Address... by C. A.
Cobb... at Signal Mountain, Tennessee... August 25, 1936. 10pp.
1.42 So8Cc [no.2]
Wisconsin's part in the nation's agriculture. Address by H. R. Tolley... at
the Wisconsin farmers get-together conference sponsored by the Wisconsin
council of agriculture, at Eau Claire, Wisconsin... October 21, 1936.
8pp. 1.9 Ad472T

Radio Talks (Mimeographed)**

Economic democracy in the agricultural conservation program... by H. R. Tolley...
September 29, 1936. 2pp. 1.94 Ad4R
Planning ahead for agricultural conservation... by Gerald B. Thorne... October
1, 1936. 2PP. 1.94 Ad4R
Progress of the agricultural conservation program... by Alfred D. Stedman...
September 15, 1936 (2pp.); September 22, 1936 (2pp.) 1.94 Ad4R

*May be obtained from U. S. Department of Agriculture, Office of Information.
**May be obtained from U. S. Department of Agriculture, Office of Information,
Radio Service.

Compiled by Mary F. Carpenter

Arkansas

Arkansas. State plant board. Arkansas crops. Annual crop summary, 1935
and crop statistics, 1924-1935. 39PP. Little Rock. 1936.
    In cooperation with U. S. Bureau of Agricultural Economics.
Includes county figures for corn, rice, and cotton.

California

Adams, R. L. Seasonal labor needs for California crops. Calif. Agr.
Expt. Sta. Giannini Found. Agr-Econ. Mimeogr. Rept. 53. Berkeley. 1936.
    Preliminary reports are being issued by counties. The library has
received the following: Alameda county, Progress report, no. 1, 16pp.;
Contra Costa county, Progress report no. 7, 18pp.; Imperial county,
Progress report, no. 13, 21pp.; Los Angeles county, Progress report,
no. 19, 37pp.; Monterey county, Progress report, no. 27, 28pp.; Orange
county, Progress report, no. 30, 25pp.; Santa Barbara county, Progress
report, no. 42, 20pp.; Riverside county, Progress report, no. 33, 40pp.

California. Department of agriculture. Bulletin... v.25, no. 3, Sacramento.
July - September, 1936.
    Partial contents: Recent developments in organized marketing, by
Theodore Macklin, pp. 289-294; Regulating the marketing of farm prod-
ucts by state authority, by Theodore Macklin, W. J. Kuhrt, and E. L.
Vehlow, pp. 295-340.

California. Department of agriculture. Sixteenth annual report... for the
period ending December 31, 1935. Calif. Dept. Agr. Monthly Bull. 24
(4): 555-549. Sacramento. October - December 1935.
    Includes reports of Bureau of Field Crops; Bureau of Fruit and Vege-
table Standardization; Division of Market Enforcement; Market News Service; Division of Markets; Bureau of Shipping Point Inspection.

Stover, H. J. Annual index numbers of farm prices, farm crop production,
farm wages, estimated value per acre of farm real estate and farm real
estate taxes, California, 1910-1935. Calif. Agr. Expt. Sta. Giannini
Found. Agr. Econ. Mimeogr. Rept. 60, 47pp. Berkeley. 1936.

Tinley, J. M. Price factors in the San Diego milk market. Calif. Agr.
Expt. Sta. Giannini Found. Agr. Econ. Mimeogr. Rept. 54, 25pp.
Berkeley. [1936]

Connecticut

Connecticut. Department of agriculture. Bureau of markets. Statistical
information pertaining to the marketing of agricultural products in
Connecticut, 1935. 62PP., mimeogr. Hartford. 1936.
    Compiled by D. W. Jope and E. B. Hook.

ollins, H. A., and Peck, B. T.   Connecticut apples from tree to consumer.
Conn. Agr. Col. Ext. Serv. Bull. 232. 11pp. Storrs. 1936.
Information on handling in picking and in storage. A table showing
the marketing season of apple varieties is shown on p. 5.

Idaho

e, P. A., and Benson, E. T.   The sources and uses of state and county revenue
in Idaho. Idaho. Agr. Expt. Sta. Mimeogr. no. 1, 15pp. Moscow. March,
1936.

Idaho. University. College of agriculture, Agricultural extension service.
Midsummer livestock outlook, 1936. 12pp., mimeogr. Boise. 1936.

Illinois

Mumford, H. W.   It still pays to farm well. Ill. Agr. Expt. Sta. Circ. 458.
31pp. Urbana. 1936.
An address delivered at Farm and Home Week, Universities of Kentucky,
Missouri, Illinois, and Wisconsin, 1935 and 1936.

Iowa

Morgan, Burton, and Lancelot, W. H.   A possible intermediate step in the
reorganization of rural elementary education in Iowa. Iowa Agr. Expt.
Sta. Research Bull. 200, pp. 281-330. Ames. 1936.

Kansas

Kansas. State college of agriculture and applied science. The Kansas agricultural outlook for 1936-37. Kans. Agr. Col. Ext. Circ. 126. 8pp.
Manhattan. 1936.

Maine

Merchant, C. H.   Maine agriculture in 1935. A statistical presentation.
Maine Agr. Expt. Sta. Bull. 382. pp. 147-295. Orono. 1936.
Includes material by towns taken by Federal census enumerators but
tabulated and published in this bulletin at the joint expense of the
Maine Department of Agriculture and the Maine Agricultural Experiment
Station. A map of the state is attached.

Minnesota

Murchie, R. W., and Jarchow, M. E.   Population trends in Minnesota. Minn.
Agr. Expt. Sta. Bull. 327, 99pp. University Farm, St. Paul, 1936.
"Practically all of the material has been secured from the Federal
Census reports."

Silcox, W. B.   Some aspects of the cheese industry in Minnesota. Minn. Univ.
    Agr. Ext. Div. Minn. Farm Business Notes, no. 165, pp. 1-3, mimeogr.
    University Farm, St. Paul. September 20, 1936.

Warrington, S. T., Dvoracek, D. C., and Johnson, E. C.   Community livestock
    auctions. Minn. Univ. Agr. Ext. Div. Minn. Farm Business Notes, no. 166,
    pp. 1-3, mimeogr. University Farm, St. Paul. October 20, 1936.

Mississippi

Mississippi. State college, Extension department. Annual report... 1935, 44pp.
    A. & M. College. 1936.
        Agricultural Economics, pp. 1-5, AAA, pp. 5-7.

Montana

Saunderson, M. H., and Monte, N. W.   Grazing districts in Montana; their pur-
    pose and organization procedure. Mont. Agr. Expt. Sta. Bull. 326, 39pp.
    Bozeman. 1936.
        An appendix contains legislation and administrative rules and proce-
    dure relating to grazing districts in Montana.

Nevada

Headley, F. B.   Determining the tonnage of hay in long stacks and round stacks.
    Nev. Agr. Expt. Sta. Bull. 143, 14pp. Reno. 1936.

New Jersey

Pitt, D. T.   The canning industry in New Jersey, 1924-1935. N. J. Dept. Agr.
    Circ. 264, 23pp. Trenton. 1936.

New Mexico

Cockerill, P. W., and Callaway, R. P.   Economics of the production and marketin
    of apples in New Mexico. N Mex. Agr. Expt. Sta. Bull. 242, 74pp. State
    College. 1936.

New York

Catherwood, M. P. Receipts and expenditures of 876 New York towns in 1934.
    N. Y. Cornell Agr. Expt. Sta. Bull. 659, 50pp. Ithaca. 1936.

Catherwood, M. P.   Variations in town taxes in New York. N. Y. Cornell Agr.
    Expt. Sta. Bull. 658, 43pp. Ithaca, 1936.
        Includes an analysis of the trend in town and special district taxes
    from 1900 to 1934.

Curtiss, W. M.   Use and value of highways in rural New York. N. Y. Cornell
    Agr. Expt. Sta. Bull. 656, 30pp. Ithaca. 1936.

New York

Hood, Kenneth. An economic study of part-time farming in the Elmira and
Albany areas of New York, 1932 and 1933. N. Y. Cornell. Agr. Expt.
Sta. Bull. 647, 139pp. Ithaca. 1936.

Hurd, T. N. Local government in Tompkins county, New York. N. Y. Cornell
Agr. Expt. Sta. Bull. 657, 44pp. Ithaca. 1936.

New York (State) Perishable fruit commission. Report of the Temporary state
commission to study the grading, packing, sale and distribution of
perishable fruit in New York state submitted February 24, 1936. 24pp.
Albany. 1936.
    At head of title Legislative document (1936) no. 77, State of New
York.

Ronk, S. E. Prices of farm products in New York State, 1841 to 1935. N. Y.
Cornell Agr. Expt. Sta. Bull. 643, 76pp. Ithaca. 1936.
    "More detailed and complete data by price, districts and by individual
commodities, of the study on which this bulletin is based, are to be found
in the thesis presented to the Faculty of the Graduate School of Cornell
University, July, 1934." Noted on p. 647, of Agricultural Economics
Literature, September, 1936.

Ohio

Comin, Donald. The common storage, its construction and management. Ohio.
Agr. Expt. Sta. Bull. 573, 49pp. Wooster. 1936.
    Storages for apples on the farm.

Henning, G. F., and Eckert, P. S. Farmers' attitudes toward livestock auctions. Ohio Agr. Expt. Sta. Bimonthly Bull., v. 21, no. 182, pp. 118-121.
Wooster. September – October 1936.

Moore, H. R. Semi-annual index of farm real estate values in Ohio, January 1
to June 30, 1936. Ohio State Univ. and Ohio Agr. Expt. Sta. Dept. Rural
Econ. Mimeogr. Bull. 94, 4pp. Columbus. October, 1936.
    In cooperation with the Ohio Association of Real Estate Boards.

Ohio. Department of agriculture, Division of markets. Statistical review of
the Columbus, Cleveland, Cincinnati, New York, Chicago, Pittsburgh,
Philadelphia egg markets. 12pp. mimeogr. Columbus [1936]
    Daily prices for 1935.

Wallrabenstein, P. P., and Falconer, J. I. The estimated cash income from
the sale of agricultural products from Ohio farms by counties – 1933,
1934 and 1935. Ohio State Univ. and Ohio Agr. Expt. Sta., Mimeogr.
Bull. 93, 26pp. Columbus. 1936.

Oregon. State agricultural college, Extension service. A compilation of recent legislation applicable to lands subject to the Taylor grazing act. 10pp., mimeogr. Corvallis. April 1, 1935.
"The seven acts presented herewith constitute new legislation passed by the Thirty-eighth Legislative Assembly."

Tennessee

Tennessee. Agricultural experiment station. Forty-eighth annual report, 1935. 51pp. Knoxville, Tenn. Agr. Expt. Sta. 1936.
Economics and sociology, pp. 30-32.

Washington

Landis, P. H., Pritchard, Mae, and Brooks, Melvin. Rural emergency relief in Washington with attention to characteristics of rural relief households. Wash. Agr. Expt. Sta. Bull. 334, 39pp. Pullman. 1936.
Rural Sociology Series in Rural Relief, no. 3.

Landis, P. H. Rural population trends in Washington. Wash. Agr. Expt. Sta. Bull. 333, 64pp. Pullman. 1936.
Rural Sociology Series in Population, no. 1.

Wisconsin

Christensen, C. L. Wisconsin — then and now, 1836-1936. Its contribution to the nation's agriculture. Wis. Agr. Col. Ext. Serv. Stencil Circ. 180, 3pp., mimeogr. Madison. 1936.

Rowlands, W. A., and Trenk, F. B. Rural zoning ordinances in Wisconsin. Wis. Agr. Col. Ext. Serv. Circ. 281, 40pp. Madison. 1936.
Includes the text of the state county zoning law, the zoning ordinance for Florence county and a selected list of articles on land planning and land zoning in Wisconsin.

Wisconsin. College of agriculture, Extension service. Security and permanence for the farm home. Annual report... 1935. Wis. Agr. Col. Ext. Circ. 279, 48pp. Madison. 1936.
[Agricultural Economics], pp. 32-36.

Wisconsin. Department of agriculture and markets. Laws of Wisconsin covering activities of the Department of agriculture and markets. Wis. Dept. Agr. and Markets Bull. 171, pp. 1257-1369. Madison. March 1936.

Wisconsin. Department of agriculture and markets. Wisconsin crop and livestock reporter, v. 15, no. 9, September 1936. Madison.
Dairy manufactures in Wisconsin by counties, 1935, p. 59.

PERIODICAL ARTICLES

Compiled by Louise O. Bercaw and A. M. Hannay

Agricultural Credit - Hungary

Reményi-Schneller, Ludwig.   Die neue Agrar-Grossbank Ungarns.   Ungarischer
Volkswirt 5(7): 3-5.   July 1936.   (Published in Budapest, Hungary)
In place of the three institutions which hitherto had provided agricultural credit in Hungary, namely, the Landes-Bodenkredit-Institut für
Kleingrundbesitzer, the Landesverband der Ungarischen Bodenkreditinstitute
and das Ungarische Bodenkreditinstitut, one central institution, the
Landes-Bodenkreditanstalt was constituted on June 23, 1936.   It is charged
with the financial arrangements connected with the new land settlement
law and the law for the reform of the system of entail.   It is a cooperative institution with a capital of 20 million pengö of which 13.5 million
have been contributed by the State.

Agricultural Indebtedness - Hungary

Reményi-Schneller, Ludwig.   Die endgültige Regelung der Landwirteschulden
in Ungarn.   Ungarischer Volkswirt 4(10): 2-3.   October 1935.   (Published
in Budapest, Hungary)
A decree of the Gömbös government provides for the settlement of the
debts of 80,000 farmers who have enjoyed a partial moratorium.   The
interest rate is reduced to 4 1/2 percent per annum.   Provision is made
for the conversion into a long-term obligation of debts not exceeding
40 times the net cadastral income of the land in the case of property
not exceeding 10 cadastral yokes.

Agricultural Marketing Bill, 1936 - Union of South Africa

Union of South Africa: Agricultural Marketing Bill, 1936.   Gt. Brit. Min. Agr.
Jour. 43(5): 474-475.   August 1936.   (Published by H. M. Stationery Office,
London, England)
Summarizes the main features of the bill which provides "for the
regulation of the production and sale of agricultural products through
the establishment of commodity marketing boards."

Agricultural Outlook and Situation - United States

Burton, C. S.   Crop outlook points to better business.   Mag. Wall St.
58(8): 460-462, 496, 498.   Aug. 1, 1936.   (Published at 90 Broad St.,
New York, N. Y.)
Discusses the outlook for wheat, corn, cotton and says that business
and agriculture "only need to be let alone."

Editor and Publisher, v. 69, no. 34, section 2, XXXIIpp.   Aug. 22, 1936.
(Published at Suite 1700, Times Bldg., New York, N. Y.)
Partial contents: Seven and one-half billion farm income for 1936
aids national recovery, by H. R. Tolley, pp. II, XXI; Wide variations

in effect of drouth, but cash income of farmers will be higher than a
year ago due to increased prices - principal crops 15.5% below normal,
by Joseph A. Becker, p. III; Farm income expected to exceed '35.
Research expert shows how higher prices will offset decreased production -
reveals drouth areas not as hard hit as in 1934, by Harry G. Davis, p. IV.

Farm: Drought and machinery present two great problems. U. S. News 4(35):
3. Aug. 31, 1936. (Published at 2201 M St., N. W., Washington, D. C.)
    A discussion of two great problems in agriculture - the drought and
machinery, including the new cotton-picker which was invented by John
and Max Rust. Both Mordecai Ezekiel and Secretary Wallace are quoted
on the problem of technology. It is held that "Technology, in farming as
in industry, is found by the Government's experts to be creating basic
problems that cut more deeply into the life of the country than do the
surface and temporary problems of drought."

[Prosperous agriculture]   Com. and Financ. Chron. 143(3718): 1924-1926.
Sept. 26, 1936. (Published at William & Spruce Sts., New York, N. Y.)
    Editorial - given under the heading: The Financial Situation - critical
of the "two leading candidates for the Presidency" for vieing with one
another for the support of the farmer by "promising him continuous and
wholly undeserved subsidies, and at the same time undertaking to lead
the rest of us to believe that in some mysterious way the welfare of the
country depends upon a 'prosperous' agriculture made so by bounties
furnished by those who do business with the farmer...
    "What is there about agriculture that demands that we keep it in a
'prosperous' condition by taxing ourselves to the limit to provide
subsidies for the purpose?... Certainly history has repeatedly shown
that under such influences industries and other branches of business,
although stimulated by such treatment, do not attain the solidity and
vigor which is essential to real well-being. Agriculture itself has,
indeed, demonstrably suffered from rather than been helped by the relatively limited treatment of this sort that has been accorded it in this
country during the past two decades."

The situation in agriculture. Natl. City Bank N. Y. [Monthly Letter on]
Econ. Conditions, U. S. Securities, Govt. Finance. August 1936,
pp. 112-113. (Published at 55 Wall St., New York, N. Y.)
    Discusses the bullish situation of the world wheat crop, the higher
costs of feeding crops, and the outlook for farm income.

Stanford, J. E.   A new and greater farming era.   South. Agr. 66(10): 5.
October 1936. (Published in Nashville, Tenn.)
    "All indications point to the next ten or fifteen years as being the
most amazing and revolutionary in farming practices, in new uses of agricultural production and in rural living conditions, that agriculture has
experienced in all its long and interesting history."
    Some of these changes are pointed out. Soybean oil may soon replace
linseed oil; dams promise farmers cheap power and soil and water conservation, and in the future plants may be produced to order by scientific
methods.

Agricultural Policy - Lesser Antilles

Agricultural policy in the Lesser Antilles. Trop. Agr. 13(9): 225-227.
September 1936. (Published by the Imperial College of Tropical Agriculture, Trinidad, B. W. I.)
"In these days of low prices, it is generally realized that the effort
to establish agriculture on a basis as near permanently profitable as
possible must be governed by two cardinal points of agricultural policy.
Firstly, the crop must be of very high quality, and must be produced as
economically as is practicable, and secondly, it should be bulked and
graded by some responsible organization to ensure uniformity of material
for the buyer. Both points have been commonplace for so long now that
it might seem fatuous to mention them. Yet a survey of the methods of
production of the chief tropical crops, both in the West Indies and elsewhere, reveals the fact that, although these considerations are accepted
as belonging to the fundamentals of planting, the lacuna between what is
possible in this direction and what is actually done is still unnecessarily great."
The article discusses the handicaps and how they might be overcome.

Agricultural Relief - China

Chen Han-seng. The good earth of China's Model Province. Pacific Affairs
9(3): 370-380. September 1936. (Published by the Institute of Pacific
Relations, Honolulu, Hawaii. Editorial Office, 129 East 52nd St., New
York, N. Y.)
"The solution of the agrarian problem in China has been attempted both
in revolutionary and in reformist ways: the redistribution of land in
Kiangsi Province by the Chinese Soviets, and the reduction of rent in
Chekiang Province by the Kuomintang Government. More recently a new
reformist program has been advocated in Shansi, once known as the 'Model
Province,' by General Yen Hsi-shan, who wishes to establish a system of
'public ownership of land by the village' together with a government
monopoly of agricultural marketing."
Some observations are made on the "general agrarian situation and on
the rapid falling off of Shansi's usury and trade capital," and the
most "salient" points of the reformist policy are given.

Leong Yew-Koh. China's half-filled rice-bowl. People's Trib. (n.s.)
14(4): 235-245. Aug. 16, (1936). (Published at 299 Szechuen Road
and 103 Kiukiang Rd., Shanghai, China)
A discussion of the problem of bringing back to the land two million
farming families who left their holdings during recent years "to seek
elsewhere, not fortune, but a bare livelihood." The writer states
that China has the extraordinary situation of "importing large quantities
of foodstuffs to feed her people, while Chinese farmers are drifting
from the land into the cities because they cannot make a living by growing
the very grain that is bought annually, not only from near-by countries
but from the very ends of the earth, North America and Australia."
The writer reviews what has been accomplished in Russia "in the handling
of a very similar problem to that which faces China," and concludes that

the need for agriculture in China is large co-operative farms "on which it
will be possible to apply, to the best advantage, modern methods of drainage, irrigation, fertilizing, and all the operations connected with primary
industry...

"Instead of large families on small farms, China needs smaller groups
on much larger holdings... Instead of struggling for existence from the
cradle to the grave... they should have an opportunity to enjoy a much
higher standard of living, and if cooperative methods have brought about
such a change in the rural economy of Russia, why should they not produce
the same results in China?"

Agricultural Relief - Europe and the United States

Hibbs, Ben.   Smarter than history   Country Gent. 106(10): 5-6, 67-71.
     October 1936. (Published at Independence Square, Philadelphia, Pa.)
     Reviews briefly the modern history of political agriculture in Europe
as written for the Country Gentleman by Leo Pasvolsky of the Brookings
Institution.
     "Read in sequence, his articles present a devastating picture. The
one lesson which stands out above all the others is that every system of
subsidies and controls yet tried has set up an endless and vicious chain
of consequences which is felt in every walk of life.
     "A secondary lesson is that once a nation embarks upon a program of
political agriculture, it cannot easily extricate itself...
     "The third lesson - and the truth of this eventually will have to be
recognized by farmers everywhere - is that subsidies inevitably are coupled
with, or eventually lead to, strict crop controls. When bounties are paid,
it is axiomatic that something is expected in return. Regimentation - we
haven't even begun to taste the full flavor of the word in this country -
deepens until the farmer is told what he can and cannot do with each half
acre.   :
     "All these things have happened in Europe."
     A discussion of recent developments in political agriculture in the
United States follows.

Agricultural Relief - United States

Howe, E. J.   The mortgage is due. Calif. Cult. 83(20): 685, 705. Sept. 26,
     1936. (Published at 317 Central Ave., Los Angeles, Calif.)
     The writer explains that by the quick transfer of land from public to
private hands, beginning in 1850, we adopted a program as a national policy
"which was sure to result in land speculation of the wildest sort." It was
at the time when cheap land was to be had for the asking, and when industrial New England went abroad for labor to replace that which had gone to
new land in the west that "we mortgaged our greatest natural resources, our
agricultural lands."
     With a historical background which looks to land as a means of specula-
tion and profit, difficulties are anticipated in a program of soil conservation by legislative means. A remedy is suggested in conclusion: "It is
simply the reorganization of farm production from a specialty crop basis to
a diversified basis. If each farm family would set as its goal the production of enough food of various sorts to supply all the normal needs of

the family; if also they would produce and learn to process at least a part of the material for their own clothing, they will inaugurate farming practices which will not only conserve the present resources of their land but they will be taking a definite step in the restoration of its original productive capacity. That starts payment on the mortgage."

Agriculture - England

Farming in the Eastern Counties. Estate Mag. 36(8): 602-603. August 1936. (Published by Country Gentleman's Association, Ltd., Letchworth, Herts, Eng.)
Summarizes briefly "the main changes in the economic organisation of agriculture as recorded in some exhaustive observations taken from more than two hundred farms in the Eastern Counties during the two years 1933 and 1935 in a report published by the Farm Economics Branch of the University of Cambridge Department of Agriculture."

Business Conditions

Weld, L. D. H. New barometers for measuring trade by regions. Dun & Bradstreet Monthly Rev. 44(2102): 2-5. September 1936. (Published at 290 Broadway, New York, N. Y.)
This article by the "Director of Research, McCann-Erickson, Inc., is in reality the announcement of a new service to be performed regularly by the Dun & Bradstreet Monthly Review. Each month, trade barometers will be published for twenty-nine regions, accompanied by comments on local conditions prepared by the District Offices of Dun & Bradstreet. The method whereby these barometers are constructed is here described in detail by Mr. Weld."-p.1.

Business Conditions - Index Numbers

Case, W. W. On the world economic front: revised world output index highest since 1929. Annalist 48(1235): 384-385, 389-390. Sept. 18, 1936. (Published by the New York Times Co., New York, N. Y.)
Includes a table showing index numbers for world commerce and industry and industrial production in leading countries, monthly January 1929-December 1935 and annual averages.

Cajuput Oil - Dutch East Indies

Cajuput oil. Netherlands Indies 4(13): 253-255. July 1, 1936. (Published in Batavia, Java, N. I.)
An account of the production, properties, preparation, and prices of cajuput or "white wood oil", produced exclusively in the Netherlands Indies.

Canning, Cooperative

Rohse, Grace. Portrait of a growing cooperative project. Canner 83(12): 7-8. Aug. 29, 1936. (Published at 140 North Dearborn St., Chicago, Ill.)
This is a description of the progress of the Washington Canners' Cooperative, which was organized in 1928.

Canning Industry

Cameron, E. J. Development of the canning industry. Canning Trade 59(4):
    7-8, 26. Aug. 31, 1936. (Published at 20 South Gay St., Baltimore, Md.)
        "It seems appropriate to forget for the time all about such things as
    can making and mechanization and center attention on canning as a method
    of food preservation. In so doing, we must treat the subject in two
    phases - canning as an art and canning as an established branch of applied
    science. · Canning is no longer a matter of practical skill, or individual
    facility, or knack. It is now coordinated knowledge arranged and systema-
    tized with reference to general laws..."

Canning Industry - California

[Kempton, Sylvia] Growth and development of canning industry in California.
    Calif. Fruit News 94(2513): 5, 9, 10. Sept. 5, 1936. (Published at 405
    Montgomery St., San Francisco, Calif.)
        "Radio Broadcast Prepared by Miss Sylvia Kempton, Assistant Secretary
    of the Canners League of California."
        A discussion of the general growth and development of the canning in-
    dustry as a whole, and of the industry as applied to California.

Cattle and Sheep - England

Roberts, C. W. Cattle and sheep fattening on a Leicestershire grazing farm.
    Gt. Brit. Min. Agr. Jour. 43(5): 428-439. August 1936. (Published by
    H. M. Stationery Office, London, England)
        Statistics are given which show that on this farm... fattening cattle
    have produced gross profits which have exceeded the cost of purchased foods
    and hired keep by about 3s. 2d. per live cwt. sold during 8 years. As
    their share of all the other expenses of the farm have amounted to about
    5s. 2d. per cwt., they have left net losses of about 2s. per cwt... On
    the other hand, sheep have, despite losses in 1931 and 1932, provided an
    average net profit of about 12s. per head of non-breeding sheep sold."

Cheese, Canned

Cahalin, V. The canning of cheddar cheese. Cheese in hermetically sealed
    cans offers important advantages that may raise the per capita consumption
    of this food. Canner 83(14): 10-11. Sept. 12, 1936. (Published at 140
    North Dearborn St., Chicago, Ill.)

Citrus Fruits - Cost of Production

Rutherford, D. M. Five years of citrus costs. Pacific Rural Press 132(5): 110.
    Aug. 1, 1936. (Published in San Francisco, Calif.)
        Includes a table entitled "Comparison of Navel, Valencia and Lemon
    Orchards Over Five Years - Los Angeles County." This table gives numerous
    data relating to costs.

Coffee - Dutch East Indies

A., M. Netherlands East Indies coffee output. Tea & Coffee Trade Jour. 71(3):
    181-182. September 1936. (Published at 79 Wall Street, New York, N. Y.)

"Estimate for present year and figures covering 1935, with distribution and ownership of plantations, varieties raised during past sixteen years, area under production and facts concerning trading."

Commodity Exchange Act

Bryant, G. B., Jr. Commodity exchange act of 1936. Major changes in trading practices seen under new rules. Market operations subject to close Federal scrutiny. Some salutary bans. Barron's 16(31): 3, 12. Aug. 3, 1936. (Published at 44 Broad St., New York, N. Y.)

"Another of the reform measures placed on the statute books by Congress at the insistence of the New Deal Administration - The Commodity Exchange Act of 1936 - will become operative on September 13.

"In addition to bringing futures trading in leading commodities under new and increased regulation from Washington, this law will force major departures from trading practices which have been developed over a period of nearly four score years and more than that, will place at the finger tips of the ever-expanding federal bureaucracy a mass of information which heretofore has been considered the private affairs of the trade.

"Cotton, rice, mill feeds, butter, eggs, and Irish potatoes are the commodities which are about to experience their first contact with federal regulation. ."

The article explains the objectives of the law.

Sturtevant, C. D., and Wade, J. F. The Commodity Exchange Act. Who is Who in Grain and Feed 25(18): 27-30. July 20, 1936. (Published at 413-414-415 Merchants' Exchange Bldg., St. Louis, Mo.)

An analysis of the new provisions in the Commodity Exchange Act, approved June 15, 1936. This act - "takes the place of the short title 'The Grain Futures Act' as prescribed in the Act of Congress approved September 21, 1922. The new act is an amendment to the original Grain Futures Act."

The Constitution of the United States

Maxey, G. W. Whose constitution? The people's or the President's. Vital Speeches of the Day 2(23): 702-707. Aug. 15, 1936. (Published at 33 W. 42nd. St., New York, N. Y.)

Address made at New York City, July 23, 1936, under the auspices of various Republican Clubs.

Mr. Maxey, Justice of the Supreme Court of Pennsylvania, in discussing Secretary Wallace's book "Whose Constitution?" says:

"...Reviewers of this book think they have found in it by clear implication the author's answer, and that it is: 'The Constitution is the President's and it is the duty of the Supreme Court so to interpret it as to make it yield to the presidential program.'"

Mr. Maxey evidently agrees with these reviewers and cites history in taking issue with the Secretary's views.

Mullen, W. H.   Future trends in consumer demand. Barron's 16(36): 3, 18.
    Sept. 7, 1936. (Published at 44 Broad St., New York, N. Y.)
        The author thinks that a less stable economy is almost sure to result
    from a period of advancing prosperity, of greatly elevated living standards
    for the nation as a whole.
        "More and more of the nation's future productive capacity will be con-
    centrated in industries where demand is highly elastic. More and more
    merchandise units of high unit-price will be produced where purchases are
    infrequent rather than regular. Greater numbers of people will be em-
    ployed in furnishing luxury services which can be easily discontinued in
    times of depression...
        "Progressively higher living standards will almost inevitably result,
    therefore, in a more erratic economy - an economy characterized by in-
    creasingly severe depressions, by cumulatively spectacular booms. This is
    a high price to pay for two cars in every garage. But very probably it
    is an unavoidable price."

Reddaway, W. B.   Irrationality in consumers' demand. Econ. Jour. 46(183):
    419-423. September 1936. (Published by Royal Economic Society,
    4 Portugal St., London, W. C., 2, Eng. May be obtained from The Macmillan
    Co., New York, N. Y.)
        The object of this article, as described by the author, is not "to
    attempt a complete or systematic analysis of the motives which determine
    consumers' preferences," but "to examine a very common case, where
    decisions are taken on the basis of reasoning which is clearly faulty.
    In itself it is perhaps of only academic interest, leading to a slight
    loss of welfare through misdirected spending of income; but it has reper-
    cussions which may be of considerable importance."

Consumer's Dollar

Where your food money goes. A new study of 58 foods shows how much of your
    money finds its way back to the farmers who produced the raw materials for
    your food. Consumers' Guide 3(15): 12-15, 19. Aug. 24, 1936. (Published
    by the Consumers' Counsel, Agricultural Adjustment Administration, U. S.
    Dept. of Agriculture)
        "Dollars you pay the retailer for food go into the cash register but not
    for long. Last year 42 cents of the average food dollar spent by a typical
    workingman's family went back to farmers. The remaining 58 cents went to
    distributors and processors."

White, W. L.   The consumer's dollar, where does it go? The Canner 83(17):
    9-12, 16. Oct. 3, 1936. (Published at 140 North Dearborn St., Chicago, Ill.)
        From a talk before the Eighth Boston Conference on Distribution at
    Boston, Mass., September 29, 1936. Both family income and expenditures are
    considered in this discussion. A table is given which shows the estimated
    national income paid out in the United States for years 1929-1936 annually
    (1936 figure is preliminary). Estimates are given of the way wage earners
    and salaried workers spend their income, but in answer to the question
    "Where does the consumer's dollar go?" Mr. White says: "We do not know.

Possibly 5 or 10 years from now we may be able to point with pride to a finished statistical report which will contain all the implied answers to this question. Today we have surprisingly few data of any wide application. The subject has been neglected. Many necessary figures have been considered confidential."

Control of Production

O'Neal, E. A. Why we need production control. Nation's Agr. 11(12): 7-8, 12, 13. October 1936. (Published at 58 E. Washington St., Chicago, Ill.)
"This article, based on a radio talk by Mr. O'Neal, explains just why the American Farm Bureau Federation has spent 12 years in fighting for the principle of production control... Mr. O'Neal contends that so long as industry is subsidized by tariff and other devices, the farmer must be given equivalent advantages in order that the country may develop as it should." - [Editor's note]

Cooperation

Gallacher, W. Co-ops and big business. Coop. Comment 5(7): 1. September 1936. (Published in Spokane, Wash.)
Reprinted from The Scottish Cooperator by the Director of Scottish Cooperative Wholesale Society. The writer states: "It is absurd to suggest that cooperators regard large-scale business as harmful to the general interest. Our own vast wholesale organizations are proof to the contrary. What we do object to is the creation of monopolies and the exploitation of the public by big business."

Heckman, J. H. Successful co-operation in Arkansas. Farm and Ranch 55(17): 16. Sept. 1, 1936. (Published in Dallas, Tex.)
"The South Arkansas Truck Growers' Association, known over a wide trade area by its 'Pine Cone Brand' products, has developed in four years to a $125,000 business. The increase in the income of truck growers in that section of the State which can be traced to the activities of the association is actually more than twice this amount."
The organization, objectives, and development of this association are described.

Hill, F. F. The farmer's part in financing his co-op. News for Farmer Cooperatives 3(5): 7, 10-11. August 1936. (Published by the Farm Credit Administration)
Mr. Hill thinks it is essential that the farmer have a stake in the cooperative – an investment in it. He should realize the risks as well as the profits involved.

Wolf, George. Goodlettsville, coops' birthplace. Amer. Cotton Grower 2(3): 8. Aug. 1, 1936. (Published at 713 Glenn St., Atlanta, Ga.)
"In the town of Goodlettsville, in Tennessee, there was last year erected a tablet...
"The tablet reads: 'Home of the Goodlettsville Lamb Club, Organized May, 1877. Birthplace of the Farmers' Cooperative Marketing Movement in the United States'." This club is alive today and is prospering.

Cooperation - California

Davidson. Bob.   Cooperation in California. Amer. Cotton Grower 2(4): 8-9.
    Sept. 1, 1936. (Published at 535 Gravier St., New Orleans, La.)
        The cooperative movement in California has made great progress.
    "Twenty-eight Cooperatives are now represented on the Agricultural
    Council of California with a total membership of 70,000 farmers handling
    everything from A (avocados) to Z (zinfandels)"

Cooperation - China

F., M. S.   China's cooperative movement beset by obstacles. Far East Survey
    5(19): 205-206. Sept. 9, 1936. (Published by the American Council, In-
    stitute of Pacific Relations, 129 East 52nd St., New York, N. Y.)
        Summarizes a report on Chinese cooperatives, prepared by C. F. Strick-
    land for the Universities China Committee in London.

Cooperation, Consumers

Consumer 'co-ops': can they cure economic ills? U. S. News 4(34): 3, 15.
    Aug. 24, 1936. (Published at 2201 M St., N. W., Washington, D. C.)
        The question is raised as to what will follow the report of the com-
    mittee sent to Europe to make a study of the cooperative movement there.
    The writer asks: "Will the country witness new efforts by the Federal
    Government to encourage the development of cooperatives and if so, with
    what expected results?" It is held that the experience of this and other
    countries "with movements designed to take private profit out of the system
    of distribution can provide the clue to an answer." The example of Sweden
    is first cited, and then the experience with cooperatives in the United
    States is described.

Knapp, J. G.   Cooperative purchasing comes of age. News for Farmer Cooperatives
    3(4): 8-10. July 1936. (Published by the Farm Credit Administration,
    Washington, D. C.)
        Figures (from the Bureau of the Census) are presented to show the growth
    of cooperative purchasing during the past ten years. In view of the growth
    in cooperative purchasing, "an attempt is here made to give a bird's-eye
    view of some of the outstanding trends during this period."

Miller, S. L.   Total sales volume of consumers' cooperatives small despite
    recent expansion. Annalist 48(1233): 316-318, 326. Sept. 4, 1936.
    (Published by the New York Times Company, Times Square, New York, N. Y.)
        The author discusses the evolution of consumers' cooperatives, the
    methods taken by business men to discourage them, and says:
        "The American cooperative movement, despite its rapid growth during
    the last two years, is still an infant. The total business of all retail
    and wholesale cooperatives in 1935 was less than one-half of 1 per cent
    of the total volume of retail and wholesale trade in the country. The
    efficiency of American commerce and industry should easily be able to keep
    this movement an infant. The task is simple and requires just a little
    vision. The most efficacious weapon with which industry can smite the David

of cooperation is lower or low prices. Certainly with prices low there is no motivating force impelling the consumer to organize. One lesson American men of business can learn, and that is not to tamper with the cooperatives' source of materials. These two swords can easily hold the cooperative movement in the United States at bay if not slay it altogether."

Cooperation, Consumers - New Zealand

Fay, C. R. Co-operative trading in New Zealand. Producer, September 1936, pp.264-266. (Published at 1 Balloon St., Manchester, Eng.)

"The contacts between the agricultural co-operative movement, which is mainly a movement of producers, and the industrial co-operative movement, which is mainly a movement of consumers, have been frequently stated from a theoretical standpoint, and have been the subject of more than one formal scheme of cooperation integrale. But the aggregate of business conducted between the two is only a small part of the aggregate business either of agricultural producers' societies or of industrial consumers' societies. Moreover, the contact may be real and important, yet unorganised, as when the Danish farmers sell butter through their co-operative organisations to the English and Scottish Co-operative Wholesale Societies, which are among the largest buyers of Danish dairy produce. This article is neither theoretical nor schematic, but is confined to an account of the deliberate efforts which the consumers' movement of Great Britain has made to develop organic reciprocal relations with the co-operative movement of New Zealand; and I add, by way of an appendix, an account of the Municipal Milk Scheme of Wellington, New Zealand, because of its intimate bearing on the future of consumers' co-operation in the Antipodes."

Cooperation, International

Lawrence, David. In the name of "peace." U. S. News 4(39): 16. Sept. 28, 1936. (Published at 2201 M St., N. W., Washington, D. C.)

"The Administration's policy of nationalistic isolation in relation to problems of world peace and economic stability" is discussed in this article. Mr. Lawrence sees an opportunity for America to save the world by a sane policy of whole-hearted international cooperation.

Cooperation and the National Grange

Elsworth, Merle M. Buying together. Natl. Grange Monthly 33(8): 4. August 1936. (Published in Springfield, Mass.)

This article is preceded by an editorial account of Miss Elsworth and plans for articles on cooperation to be published in the National Grange Monthly.

- "In her interesting article on 'Buying Together' Miss Elsworth not only gives valuable historical data concerning early Grange adherence to the principle of economic cooperation, but she cites numerous present instances denoting Grange leadership in this important work."

The cost of living. The Index 16(10): 180-191, 194-197. October 1936.
(Published by the New York Trust Co., 100 Broadway, New York, N. Y.)
Sub-heading: Factors controlling more abundant existence.

Cost of Living - England

Gilboy, Elizabeth W.   The cost of living and real wages in eighteenth century
England.   Rev. Econ. Statis. 18(3): 134-143.   August 1936. (Published by
the Harvard University Press, Cambridge, Mass.)
Statistical appendix, pp. 142-143.
"Crude as our index is, it is based on the most complete, continuous,
and homogeneous series now available. It affords a better basis for
estimating the condition of the working classes in eighteenth-century
England than the grain prices used earlier. It is necessary to modify
somewhat the conclusion there expressed concerning the trend of the
standard of living of the London laborer. The present index shows a much
more certain decline in real wages for London in the last half of the
century. Real wages in the North, however, rose consistently during the
entire hundred years, as indicated by the earlier investigation...Regional
differences in the course of real wages in eighteenth-century England are very
evident."

Cotton

Commerce and Finance 25(19): 666-707. Sept. 19, 1936. (Published at 95
Broad St., New York, N. Y.)
The Annual Cotton Crop Number. Partial contents: American cotton in
1935-36, by Carl Geller, pp. 672, 691; Annual cotton crop estimate of
Commerce and Finance, p. 673; Trade outlook warrants optimism, by John
C. Botts, p. 674; Textile Industry prospects bright, by Dr. Claudius T.
Murchison, pp. 674, 692; Agricultural prosperity the keynote, by Donald
Comer, p. 692; World developments affect American cotton trade outlook,
by Alston H. Garside, p. 693; Supply and demand again govern prices, by
Frank I. Neild, p. 693; Larger production of foreign cotton an unfavorable
factor, by Andrew Stewart, III, p. 694; Scarcity of desirable cotton
possible, by T. M. Fewell, p. 694; Active consumer demand high light of
cotton goods situation, by Floyd W. Jefferson, p. 695; Long term cotton
outlook promising, by Wm. R. Meadows, p. 696; Cottonseed oil outlook
bullish, by John McD. Murray, pp. 697, 698; Government estimate whirls
cotton upward, pp. 699, 700, 701; Large spot cotton turnover cheers New
Orleans market, by A. J. Mann, pp. 701, 702; Irregularity marks Liverpool
trading, p. 702; and Cotton goods sales climb, p. 703.

Cotton movement and crop of 1935-36. Com. & Finance. Chron. 143(3718): 1940-
1956. Sept. 26, 1936. (Published at William and Spruce Sts., New York, N.Y.
Contains the statement of the Commercial & Financial Chronicle of the
commercial cotton crop of the United States for the year ended July 31, 1936.
Tables, together "with suggestions and explanations as the peculiar features
of the year appear to require", present the whole movement of cotton for
the year. Data of production, exports, consumption, etc., are given.

- 838 -

Fate of American cotton. Living Age 349(4432): 460-461, table. January 1936.
(Published at 10 Ferry St., Concord, N. H.)
An article from Neue Freie Presse of Vienna "on the results of the
Roosevelt program for controlling the production of cotton."

Journal of Commerce and Commercial. Special cotton exchange edition. 1936.
Survey no. 8, 16pp. Aug. 5, 1936. (Published in New York, N. Y.)
Partial contents: Cotton exchange history reveals a notable record,
by Clement Moore.- Clayton sees trade reviving as the government with-
draws, by W. L. Clayton.- Clearing house guarantor of cotton futures con-
tract.- American shippers largest handlers of U. S. farm crops, by J. H.
McFadden, Jr.- New U. S. policies more in interest of cotton grower, by
J. C. Botts.- Supply and demand in cotton approach balanced position by
A. H. Garside.

Cotton - Germany

New restrictions on use of cotton. Times Trade & Engineering (n.s.) 39(871):
20. September 1936. (Published by The Times Publishing Company, Ltd.,
London, E. C. 4, England)
"By a decree issued by the German Government on July 31 all cotton
knitted underwear...for the home market must contain, by weight, a 16
percent percentage of 'Zellwolle'- i.e. spun rayon or rayon, from
November 1, 1936, onwards. This does not mean that the yarn from which
the articles are made must contain this percentage, but that the manufacturer must arrange that the articles mentioned are made in such a way
that the decree is complied with. It does not apply to goods for export
or to material needed for the making of fabric gloves. These may still
contain 100 per cent cotton yarn for both the home and export trade."

Cotton Ginning, Cooperative

Herrmann, O. W. Co-op gins point way. Amer. Cotton Grower 2(1): 6-7.
June 1936. (Published at 535 Gravier St., New Orleans, La.)
The first of a series of articles on cooperative ginning.
Mr. Herrmann points out that there are now "over 260 cooperative cotton
gin associations operating in the South, principally in Texas and Oklahoma...
"Records show that farmers attempted in an organized way to gin cotton
cooperatively as early as 1887, although the actual date is probably before that time. The coming of custom ginning had a definite influence
on farmers' interest in cooperative cotton ginning. During the past 75
years several changes have occurred in the cotton ginning industry which
have contributed materially to the development of commercial or custom
ginning. Principal among the reasons for these changes was the development
by the cottonseed crushing industry of lines of gins owned and operated for
the purpose of controlling the supply of seed. No less important a factor
was the breaking up of the plantation system in many parts of the old South
and the opening up of the newer cotton producing area in the Southwest."
The writer continues by describing how dissatisfaction among cotton
farmers with the evils in custom ginning brought about attempts of farmers
to operate their own gin plants.

Herrman, O. W.   Cooperative ginning takes last hold.   Confined at present
chiefly to Texas and Oklahoma, the movement has possibilities of wide
and important developments.   News for Farmer, Cooperatives 3(5): 8-9, 11.
August 1936.   (Published by the Farm Credit Administration)

Cotton Industry - Index Numbers

Elsas, M. J. and Ellinger, Barnard.   Cotton-indices.   Econ. Jour. 46(183):
431-442.   September 1936.   (Published by the Royal Economic Society, 4
Portugal St., London, W. C. 2, Eng.   May be obtained from The Macmillan Co.,
New York, N. Y.)
    Attention is called to the various criteria that have been employed as a
measure of the activity and prosperity of the cotton industry - the amount
of raw cotton consumed; the value of the exports of cotton goods; the unemployment figure; etc.   For the most part these measures have been
unsatisfactory.
    "In order to supply a more accurate measure of the activity and pros-
perity of the industry, index-numbers have been constructed, in the compilation of which several suitable homogeneous criteria have been employed,
and the object of this study is to explain the method which has been
adopted in compiling two indices, one of Cotton Grade Activity and one of
Cotton Trade Prosperity, in order that comparisons may be made between one
period and another."

Cotton Picker

Butler, Eugene.   Cotton picker - saint or devil?   Prog. Farmer (Texas ed.) 51
(9): 3, 47.   September 1936.   (Published in Birmingham, Ala.)
    Discusses the many changes which the Rust cotton picker and other labor
saving machinery may make in the agriculture of the South.
    "After considering the advantages and disadvantages and striking a
balance, it seems to the writer that even though the coming of mechanical
choppers and pickers may displace labor temporarily and threaten us with
over production, it is likely to benefit Southern agriculture in the
long run."

Stanford, J. E.   The mechanical cotton picker.   South. Agr.   66(10):
11.   October 1936.   (Published at Nashville, Tenn.)
    Describes the Rust Brothers cotton picker, tells what it can do, and
lists the major criticisms expressed by observers at the demonstration
held at Stoneville, Miss., August 31, 1936.

Wolf, George, Jr.   The Rust cotton picker still a question.   Amer. Cotton
Grower 11(5): 8-9, 12.   October 1, 1936.   (Published at 535 Gravier St.,
New Orleans, La.)
    Describes the three general classes of automatic cotton picking machines
that have been invented since the Civil War - seven hundred and fifty
patents have been issued since that time - none of which have proved themselves in field tests.   Contains also a description of the Rust cotton
picker, and lists valid objections to the work of the picker.

Dairy Products - Export Control - New Zealand

New Zealand...II. Marketing by the state. Round Table, no. 104, pp. 856-871.
    September 1936. (Published by Macmillan & Co., Ltd., London, Eng.)
        "When Parliament reassembled after Easter it was presented with another
    major Bill providing for the marketing of New Zealand produce by the State
    and the payment of a guaranteed price to producers. Mr. Nash explained
    that the measure was designed to protect the producer against market
    fluctuations. The method was that the Crown should purchase the produce
    at prices to be fixed from time to time and sell it overseas. As for
    produce intended for consumption in New Zealand, the Government could
    either purchase outright or merely control the sale and distribution.
    For the present, dairy produce only is to be purchased, but the shipping of
    all produce will be under state control."

New Zealand Government controls dairy exports. Foreign Crops and Markets 33
    (12): 348-350. Sept. 21, 1936. (Issued by the Division of Foreign
    Agricultural Service, Bureau of Agricultural Economics, U. S. Dept. of
    Agriculture)
        "Effective August 1, 1936, the New Zealand government assumed complete
    control of butter and cheese exports from that country... On the basis of
    a scale of fixed prices to producers...all butter and cheese entering
    export trade becomes the property of the government when placed on board
    export vessels. Since exports account for the bulk of production in New
    Zealand, this action represents practical control of the New Zealand dairy
    industry as far as sales are concerned."

Drought and Food Prices

Bean, L. H.   The drought and prices of food. Canner 83(14): 7-8. Sept. 12,
    1936. (Published at 140 North Dearborn St., Chicago, Ill.)
        "Employed consumers can still buy more food with their present earnings
    than they were able to buy in 1928 or 1929, in spite of the record droughts
    of 1934 and 1936."

Drought-Stricken States

Dailey, J. L.   Is the west drying up? Nation's Agr. 11(11): 2-3, 10.
    September 1936. (Published at 58 East Washington St., Chicago, Ill.)
        "Is the West drying up? Are deserts on the march, driving man out of the
    Great Plains?
        "Weather experts assure us that there is no reason for holding such a
    pessimistic view. This 'family' of droughts which has afflicted agriculture
    during the past seven years is something temporary and will make no dif-
    ference to the sum total of weather when we balance wet seasons and dry
    seasons for a generation or more.
        "Series of droughts are bound to occur in the West. They are not caused
    by the cultivation of the Plains and cannot be prevented by the building of
    ponds and lakes."
        The writer continues by discussing the cause of rain, the farmer's
    prospects and the relief program.

The future of the Great Plains: grasslands or waste lands? U. S. News 4(35):
  6. Aug. 31, 1936. (Published at 2201 M St., N. W., washington, D. C.)
     An article in which the causes are given of the agricultural problem
  in the Great Plains; and the result of the early homestead policy. How
  the government experts propose to deal with the problem is described.

Equality of Opportunity for the Farm

Samuelson, Agnes. The objective of equality of opportunity. Rural Amer. 14
  (6): 7-10. September 1936. (Published by the American Country Life
  Association, Inc., 105 East 22nd St., New York, N. Y.)
     An address at the National Rural Forum, 1936.
     A section of this address is devoted to a discussion of the subject,
  "The Farmer's Contribution to Human Advancement." The writer holds that,
  not only "in the material sense is the farm the main source of national
  wealth, but inasmuch as the farm is the chief source for the production
  of future population, it is the chief means of creating wealth through
  human resources." Some of the major problems and conditions facing farmers
  are next considered while in conclusion reasons are given why the "march
  of equalization" is delayed. It is urged that stops be taken to remedy
  the situation that results in unequal advantages in physical, educational,
  economic or social conditions for children in the rural areas.

Farm Economist

Farm Economist, v. 2, no. 3. July 1936. (Published by the Agricultural
  Economics Research Institute, Parks Road, Oxford, Eng.)
     Partial contents: Tenancy changes on small holdings [in six South-
  Midland counties] by J. F. Darke, p. 37; Giving the consumer the manufacturing milk, by S. M. Makings, pp. 41-44; The trend of milk prices in the
  eastern counties, by P. E. Graves, pp. 44-46; Changes in market receipts
  of fat cattle since the introduction of the subsidy, by R. P. Askew, pp.46-48.

Fertilizers - Cooperative Marketing

Yagi, Yoshinosuke. On the co-operative distribution of fertilizers in Japan.
  Econ. Rev. 11(1): 52-74. July 1936. (Published by the Kyoto Imperial
  University, Tokyo, Japan)
     A discussion of the merits of co-operative purchasing societies for
  farmers in Japan. Differences between farmers' co-operative purchasing
  societies and the consumers' co-operative societies are pointed out after
  which the importance of marketed fertilizers is considered. Ten statistical tables accompany the article which have the following data: Consumption of marketed fertilizers, years 1913-1934; Tendency in the consumption
  [by kind] of marketed fertilizers; Comparison between the price of sulphate
  of ammonia and that of rice in recent years; The amount of fertilizer distributed by the co-operative purchasing societies, years 1924-1934; The
  rate of the utilization of the societies by their members in the purchase of
  fertilizers; and The state of exclusive transactions between co-operative
  societies and their federations in the distribution of fertilizers.

Flax - Philippine Islands

Garrido, T. G., and Torres, J. P.   Flax in the Philippines. Philippine Jour. Agr. 7(2): 229-241. Second Quarter, 1936. (Published by the Bureau of Plant Industry, Department of Agriculture and Commerce, Manila, Philippines)
  A discussion of the statistics pertaining to flax and of the methods of culture. The results of some preliminary tests, "including the methods involved in the manufacture of crude fiber" are presented. The hope is expressed that this crop will find a place in the program of crop diversification and so increase the list of possible home industries for the islands.

Food - United States

Outhwaite, Leonard.   Clean food - an American habit. Today 6(21): 10-11, 24, 25. Sept. 12, 1936. (Published at 152 West Forty-second St., New York, N. Y.)
  According to the author of this article clean food is an American habit, and American food is either "better or cleaner" than European food. Reference is made to the safeguards and conventions with regards to fruits, milk, eggs and water in America, and then facts that account for the "prevailing cleanliness and convenience" of the American food system are enumerated and discussed.

Food Policies

World food policies. Statist 128(3049): 158-160. Aug. 1, 1936. (Published at 51 Cannon St., London, E. C. 4, Eng.)
  Based on the interim report of the "Mixed Committee" on the relationship between nutrition and health. This Mixed Committee on the Problem of Nutrition was set up by the council of the League of Nations under the chairmanship of Lord Astor.

Fruit - China

Fruit cultivation in Kuangtung. Chinese Econ. Jour. and Bull. 18(5): 716-725. May 1936. (Published by Bureau of Foreign Trade, Ministry of Industry, Shanghai, China)
  Tables give imports and exports.

Government, Local - Europe

European local government number; edited by International Union of local authorities and International institute of administrative science. Natl. Munic. Rev., 25(9): 478-534. September 1936. (Published by the National Municipal League, 309 E. 34th St., New York, N. Y.)
  Contents: Planning and cooperation among international organizations, by Louis Brownlow, pp.480-482; The International union of local authorities, by Emile Vinck, pp.483-486, 500; The International Institute of Administrative Sciences, by Edmond Lesoir, pp. 487-489, 494; Mainly about words, by Jules Lespes ["A definition of the terms frequently used in discussions of local government"], pp.490-494; Recent developments in English local government, by Herman Finer, pp.495-500; The outlook for local government in France, by Henri Sellier, pp. 501-503, 519; The changing state-local financial

picture in France, by Walter R. Sharp, pp. 501-510; The new local government of Germany. The local government act, by Fritz Morstein Marx, pp. 511-51; Municipal economy, by Roger H. Wells, pp. 511-516; Home rule - old and new, by Gottnilf Pronisch, pp. 516-519; The Italian law on communal and provincial government, by H. Arthur Steiner, pp. 520-527; Local government in Scandinavia, by Roy V. Pool, pp.528-534.

Grain Elevators, Cooperative

Green, R. M. Yardsticks of success in co-op elevators. News for Farmer Co-operatives 3(5): 3, 10. August 1936. (Published by the Farm Credit Administration)

"In the experience of farmers' elevators in Kansas are found certain standards that, when conformed with, favor successful operation."

Grain Industry Power Costs

Van Ornum, H. H.   Controllable factors of power costs in the grain industry. I-II. Grain & Feed Journals Consolidated 77(4-5): 153, 165, 193, 199. Aug. 26-Sept. 19, 1936. (Published at 332 South La Salle St., Chicago, Ill.)

Address before the Society of Grain Elevator Superintendents of North America.

"To be concluded in the next number."

Groceries - Chain and Cooperative Marketing - Chicago

Read, E. Van Wert.   Voluntary chains and cooperative groups in the marketing of groceries in Chicago. News Bull. 2(4): 25, 32. Aug. 12, 1936. (Published by the School of Business of the University of Chicago, Chicago, Ill.)

"During the past five years voluntary chains and cooperative groups have approximately doubled in importance in the marketing of groceries in Chicago. In 1935 more than one-third of all grocery and combination grocery-and-meat stores in the city were members of a voluntary or cooperative group. It is estimated that stores thus affiliated accounted for nearly one-third of the total sales volume."

Handicrafts - Tunisia

Plissard, Roger.   Handicrafts in Tunisia: I. Internatl. Labour Rev. 34(1): 66-83. July 1936. (Published by International Labour Office, Geneva, Switzerland; Distributed in U. S. by World Peace Foundation, 8 West 40th St., New York, N. Y.)

The development of handicrafts "is of particular importance in essentially agricultural countries, such as those of Africa and the East. There handicrafts, of both old and new types, are often the principal form of industrial activity; for the indigenous populations, who are chiefly occupied in cultivation and stock raising, they supplement the operations of the small farm or holding and constitute the traditional occupation of the women and girls, who weave and embroider at home or in workshops.

"In many of these countries the authorities, backed by a growing body of public opinion, have already taken steps to safeguard certain industrial arts

with vitality and intrinsic worth against what they regard as excessive
industrial and commercial competition. They have also begun to modernise
the equipment of handicraftsmen in regions with an old civilisation of
their own, where 'utility' crafts can easily and cheaply be adapted to the
needs of a family economy, and of native communities often differing in
type and stage of development. Among the methods used for this purpose
is the organisation of vocational training and of credit facilities.
"Tunisia is a remarkable instance of this process."
Part II is in the Review 36(2): 198-219. August 1936.

Homestead Act

Gates, P. W.   The homestead law is an incongruous land system. pp.652-681.
"Reprinted from the American Historical Review, vol. XLI, no. 4, July
1936."
Bibliographical footnotes.
The purpose of this article is stated by the writer as follows:
"It is the purpose of this paper to show that the Homestead Law did not
completely change our land system, that its adoption merely superimposed
upon the old land system a principle out of harmony with it, and that until
1890 the old and the new constantly clashed. In presenting this view it
will appear that the Homestead Law did not end the auction system or cash
sales, as is generally assumed, that speculation and land monopolization continued after its adoption as widely perhaps as before, and within as well
as without the law, that actual homesteading was generally confined to the
less desirable lands distant from railroad lines, and that farm tenancy
developed in frontier communities in many instances as a result of the
monopolization of the land. The efforts to abolish cash sales will also be
outlined briefly."

Homestead Act and the Labor Surplus

Shannon, F. A.   The Homestead Act and the labor surplus. pp.637-651.
"Reprinted from the American Historical Review, vol. XLI, no. 4, July
1936."
Bibliographical footnotes.
"This paper was first read at a meeting of the Mississippi Valley Historical Association at Cincinnati, on Apr. 26, 1935."
The author's concluding paragraph follows:
"But, whatever the basis of calculation, it cannot be denied that unemployment was a major economic ailment in every decade from 1865 to the close
of the century, and it is equally certain that free land did not solve the
problem. No doubt there was once a time in American history when underpaid,
unemployed, or dissatisfied laborers could take their choice between continuing as intermittent wage employees or becoming freehold farmers; that
wages of industrial labor were higher for that undefined period than they
otherwise would have been; and that industrial strife, in consequence, was
kept at a minimum. A more certain fact is that such conditions have not
existed since the coming of the factory system. In other words, the much
vaunted cheap or free public lands of the country, whatever may have been
their effect in other regards, since the rise of a class-conscious labor
group have not been of measurable consequences as an alleviator of labor
conditions."

Wood, Sir Kingsley. Rural housing. Estate Mag. 36(8): 561-565. August 1936.
(Published by Country Gentlemen's Association, Ltd., Letchworth, Herts, Eng.)
The importance of rural housing is stressed, and the work being done in
connection with rural slum clearance and the town and country planning
movement is indicated.

Income

Crum, W. L. Regional diversity of income distribution. Amer. Jour. Sociol.
42(2): 215-225. September 1936. (Published by the University of Chicago
Press, Chicago, Ill.)
"A survey of pertinent statistics compiled from federal income-tax returns
indicates that although differences in sex and family status of the taxpayers,
reflecting industrial and occupational differences among the states, may partly
account for the regional diversity of income distribution, and although such
factors as climate and race undoubtedly have influence, a dominant factor is
the regional dissimilarity in the structure or source of the income. States
having economic and social structures founded largely upon agriculture, mining,
or other basic industries show generally low concentration and small inequality
while those states, mainly east of the Mississippi and north of the Potomac,
in which income from ownership of and dealings in property is most important,
show sharp inequality of distribution and large concentration in high income."

The Washington statistical society. Amer. Statis. Assoc. Jour. 31(195): 572-577.
September 1936. (Published by the Association. Frederick F. Stephan,
Secretary-Treasurer, 722 Woodward Bldg., Washington, D. C.)
This is a report of the annual meeting of this society held at the Cosmos
Club on May 30, 1936. The subject of the meeting was "The National Income
and What We Know About It." The principal speakers were O. C. Stine, Clark
Warburton, and R. R. Nathan. A digest of their papers and of Mr. L. H.
Bean's discussion of them is given.

Insurance, Crop

Crop insurance implies production control. Sphere 18(3): 22. September 1936.
(Published by the Whaley-Eaton Publishing Corporation, Munsey Bldg.,
Washington, D. C.)
"The ravages of the 1936 drought, and the contemplation that 1930 and 1934
were years of national crop disaster, induce a new thought in farm thinking
that may give the New Deal a political club for November perhaps strong enough
to revive waning farm support. It is crop insurance. The promise of it may
be effective enough to overcome the conviction, rooted by Republicans and
other critics, that agriculture planning under the New Deal has been positively
detrimental, at least to certain farm groups."
The plan which Secretary Wallace proposes in connection with his "ever-
normal granary" proposal, "would insure 75 per cent of the yield on farms by
collecting a percentage of surplus production as insurance premium, and distributing insurance payments in kind.
"By bringing crop insurance about, the New Deal would secure what it believes is sufficient power to effect stabilization in prices and assurity of

income. This implies continuance of other powers to (1) regulate production,
(2) control exchanges, (3) remove temporary surpluses through Relief distribution, and (4) encourage cooperative marketing."

Hazard, J. W. Implications of crop insurance. Barron's 16(39): 3, 8. Sept.
28, 1936. (Published at 44 Broad St., New York, N. Y.)
        Contains an outline of the crop-insurance history in the United States
to date, and describes how the proposed Roosevelt-Wallace crop-insurance
plan will work if put into effect. The difference between this plan and some
of the older plans is pointed out. The burdens to be imposed on Federal
finances are considered also.

Kilgore, Bernard. Crops - an unpredictable risk. Today 6(22): 18-19. Sept.
19, 1936. (Published at 152 West 42nd St., New York, N. Y.)
        "Superficially, at least, the very phrase 'crop insurance' has a re-
assuring sound. It connotes certainty in the midst of uncertainty, stability in the midst of instability. The average substantial citizen, who
insures his house, his automobile, his furniture, his jewelry and silver-
ware, his health and his life, is predisposed to accept the theory that
similar protection can be made available to the farmer.
        "Perhaps, some day, somehow, it can. But it is important, I think, to
understand that there are certain serious difficulties in the way. It is
the purpose of this article to discuss a few - certainly not all - of those
difficulties. The fact that nearly everyone agrees that crop insurance
would be a good thing if it will actually work justifies, I believe, by stress
on objections rather than objectives."
        Some of the difficulties listed are: That of estimating the risk and
equitably distributing them; the tremendous task of setting up and administering a crop-insurance program; the fact that government participation will lead
to a new crop-benefit system instead of insurance, etc.
        Mentions Mr. Wallace's plan which he says is sometimes known as the
'Joseph plan.' The biggest difficulty with this plan, he thinks, is that
"we do not know exactly when a crop represents 'surplus' and when it does not."

Teuton, F. L. Crop insurance guarantees a farm income. South. Agr.
66(10): 13, 23. October 1936. (Published at Nashville, Tenn.)
        After answering the question "What is Crop Insurance?" the writer con-
siders briefly our past experience with crop insurance and then discusses
possible plans for a crop insurance program.

Insurance, Fire

Valgren, V. N. Current trends in farm mutual insurance. News for Farmer
Cooperatives 3(4): 7, 13-14. July 1936. (Published by the Farm Credit
Administration, Washington, D. C.)
        In conclusion: "A number of other current trends among the farmers'
mutual fire insurance companies could be pointed out, if space permitted.
Those already indicated - namely, standardization of insurance forms, shift
toward advance assessment and the building up of reasonable reserves or
safety funds, and use of re-insurance to avoid unduly heavy losses in relation to the volume of risks in force - all point toward increased importance
and usefulness of these farmer-owned insurance mutuals."

Insurance, Hail - Italy

Arcoleo, F. Hail insurance in Italy. Monthly Bull. Agr. Econ. and Sociol.
[Reprint from the Internatl. Rev. Agr.] 27(8): 256-270. August 1936.
(Published by the International Institute of Agriculture, Rome, Italy)
   Contents: "Societies or companies dealing with this branch of insurance
in 1935. Agreements between these societies - The insurance contract -
Regulation of insurance societies - Non-compensation for losses under a
certain limit. - Resolution taken in 1935 by the Corporation of Insurance
and Credit... - The meteorological problem - Statistics on the activity of
these societies."

Investment - United States

Keynes, J. M. Fluctuations in net investment in the United States. Econ. Jour.
46(183): 540-546. September 1936. (Published by the Royal Economic Society,
4 Portugal St., London, W. C. 2, Eng. May be obtained from The Macmillan Co.,
New York, N. Y.)
   Mr. Keynes writes as follows in part: "In my General Theory of Employment,
Interest and Money, Chap. VIII, pp. 98-104, I made a brief attempt to illustrate the wide range of fluctuations in new investment, basing myself on
certain calculations by Mr. Colin Clark for Great Britain and by Mr. Kuznets
for the United States [Published in Bulletin 52, Nov. 15th, 1934, of the
National Bureau of Economic Research (New York)].
   "In the case of Mr. Kuznets' figures I pointed out (p. 103) that his allowances for depreciation, etc., included 'no deduction at all in respect of
houses and other durable commodities in the hands of individuals.' But the
table which immediately followed this did not make it sufficiently clear to the
reader that the first line relating to 'gross capital formation' comprised
much wider categories of capital goods than the second line relating to
'entrepreneurs' depreciation, etc.'; and I was myself misled on the next page,
where I expressed doubts as to the sufficiency of the latter item in relation
to the former (forgetting that the latter related only to a part of the former)
The result was that the table as printed considerably under-stated the force
of the phenomenon which I was concerned to describe, since a complete calculation in respect of depreciation, etc., covering all the items in the first
line of the table, would lead to much larger figures than those given in the
second line. Some correspondence with Mr. Kuznets now enables me to explain
these important figures more fully and clearly, and in the light of later
information."

Labor - France

Working conditions in French agriculture. Indus. and Labour Inform. 59(10):
309-310. Sept. 7, 1936. (Issued by International Labour Office, Geneva,
Switzerland. Distributed in U. S. by World Peace Foundation, 8 West 40th
Street, New York, N. Y.)
   An account of proposed measures to extend the social policy of the French
Government to agriculture, and of the progress of collective agreements in
French agriculture.

Clark, N. M.   The closing door. Country Gent. 106(9): 12-13, 76-77.
September 1936. (Published at Independence Square, Philadelphia, Pa.)
The author says that "political efforts to mitigate unemployment have had
one curious effect: They have helped to close the door, perhaps permanently,
on a large number of jobs."
The article discusses the question of the displacement of farm labor
through various causes - mechanization, higher wages paid for WPA work, etc.

Noel, L. R.   The farm labor problem. South. Agr. 66(10): 8. October 1936.
(Published in Nashville, Tenn.)
The following conclusions are reached in this article on farm labor:
Too much cheap labor on the farm has been a curse rather than a blessing in
the South; and that better equipment and methods must replace antiquated ones
while quality of labor must be greatly improved.
"There is a horde of labor that is dear at almost any price and this is
one of our problems that has to be dealt with. At the same time every effort
must be made to improve living conditions for all farm people, owner and
tenant or laborer, and to increase greatly the hourly wage."

Land

Henderson, H. C.   Uncle Sam, landlord. Today 6(21): 12-13, 22, 29. Sept. 12,
1936. (Published at 152 West Forty-second St., New York, N. Y.)
Two letters are quoted at the beginning of this article. One was written
in 1900 and the other in 1936. The first tells how farmers and ranchmen
helped themselves following a season of dry weather, and the other how they
waited to be helped. The story is next told of the acquisition of Uncle
Sam's land and then of its disposition. It is stated that in 160 years
"Uncle Sam has disposed of 1,019 million acres", and has in his possession
in one way or another "approximately 350 million acres." In the rest of
the article the writer discusses the "business ramifications" which inevitably
follow soil acquisition.
In conclusion Mr. Henderson says: "Uncle Sam is a titanic landlord today.
He has extended his benefits, services and superintendence over so much territory that if he keeps up at the rate he's going, in 50 years there will be
mighty few Americans who won't be his tenants."

Land Reclamation - Italy

Alfani, Augusto. Aspects of land reclamation in Italy. Agr. Engin. 17(7):
296, 320. July 1936. (Published by the American Society of Agricultural
Engineers, St. Joseph, Mich.)
"There is a difference between what is understood by land reclamation in
United States and what the term has come to mean in Italy. In the United
States 'reclamation' means essentially the improvement of land and control
of water courses, the end in view being economic profit, sanitary advantages,
or the conservation of natural resources. In Italy the purposes of land
reclamation is different in many ways and is suggested by the qualification
'integral.'"

The main aspects of the physical problem of reclamation are considered, but the writer states that the case involving only one problem has been rare. Generally the problems dovetailed and interlocked; their solution created new and more complex but unsuspected problems.

"Once the reclamation of a district has been decided upon, it has been undertaken and carried out thoroughly and comprehensively, leaving no gaps which might jeopardize the fullest agricultural use of the district reclaimed. If often the solution of the problems presented by the physical aspect of the project has been difficult, equally difficult has been the solution of those arising from the most disparate rights and privileges, vested and consolidated through centuries of history. Therefore, in this field, it was necessary also to discard decrepit, unwieldy, and sluggish tenures and privileges and create new ones, consistent with rejuvenated lands and enlightened agricultural economy."

Land Settlement – Australia

Critical of land settlement delay. The Land, no. 1314, pp. 7, 8. Aug. 14, 1936. (Published in Sydney, New South Wales)
"The discussion on closer settlement was a feature of the deliberations of the Annual Conference of the Farmers and Settlers' Association," which convened in Sydney.
"Delegates were unanimously of the opinion that the introduction of a closer settlement scheme should be regarded as a matter of extreme urgency, and several criticized the Government for its delay in issuing a pronouncement of policy on the subject.
"A number of practical suggestions recommended by a special sub-committee of the Association were agreed to, and these will be submitted to the Government for its consideration."
The recommendations made by the sub-committee are listed on page 8 of the article. Features of the recommendations include the raising of a special land settlement loan, and the provision of a wide variety of tenures.

"Most fruitful period in Land Settlement." The Land, no. 1313, pp. 4, 29. Aug. 7, 1936. (Published in Sydney, New South Wales)
Quotes a statement by the Acting-Premier, Col. M. F. Bruxner in which he reviews the work done by the government in land settlement since 1932.

Land Settlement – England

Back to the land. Country Life 80(2070): 312, 313. Sept. 19, 1936. (Published at 20 Tavistock St., Covent Garden, London, W. C. 2, Eng.)
Describes the work of the Land Settlement Association which "was formed by the Minister of Agriculture just two years ago 'to carry out an experimental scheme for the provision of small holdings for unemployed persons, with financial assistance from the Government.'"
According to the writer, twenty-four properties for settlement have been acquired, the nature of the estates varying greatly, and consequently "their methods of management have to be designed to fit them individually." Examples are given of the variety of problems to be overcome. How some of the problems have been met is also told.

Land Settlement - Estonia

Sinberg, T. Developments of new settlements in Estonia, 1929-35. Konjunktuur
Monthly Rev. of the Estonian Institute of Econ. Res. nr. 21/22(8/9): 510-
521. Sept. 7, 1936.
Text in Estonian.
Tables show the numbers of settlement farms established from 1929 to
1935 according to size, and the income and expenditure of the settlement fund.

Land Settlement - Manchuria

Grandiose farm planned by the Firm of Totaku in the vicinity of Peiancheng.
Readjustment of land lease rights. Manchurian Econ. Rev. 3(8): 25. Sept.
15, 1936. (Published by G. Harmsen, Harbin, Manchoukuo)
A plan is proposed to settle 2,000 families, or 10,000 persons on a plot
of 90,000 hectares of land. A law for the conversion of lease rights in
Manchoukuo held by Japanese subjects into land ownership has been passed by
the State Council.

Japanese emigration to Manchuria. Indus. and Labour Inform. 59(11): 348. Sept.
14, 1936. (Published by International Labour Office, Geneva, Switzerland.
Distributed in U. S. by World Peace Foundation, 8 West 40th Street, New
York, N. Y.)
Attention is called to the Japanese Government's plans for sending between
1,000,000 and 5,000,000 emigrants to Manchuria over a period of twenty years,
beginning in 1937. "These will consist of agricultural groups, independent
agricultural workers and persons engaged in other occupations. It is hoped
that 10,000 families, or 50,000 persons, can be sent during the first year,
and 8,000,000 yen have been included in the budget for travelling and other
expenses. One thousand yen will be allotted to each family in the collective
groups; independent agricultural emigrants will be given 500 yen per family
for expenses, and those in other occupations 200 yen per family. The land
to be occupied is owned by the Manchuria Development Company, which will cooperate with the Manchuria Emigration Association in carrying out the
programme."

Land Utilization Program - United States

Gray, L. C. Crop reduction and the land-use program. Agr. Situation 20(7):
11-13. July 1936. (Published by the Bureau of Agricultural Economics,
U. S. Dept. of Agriculture)

Gray, L. C. The resettlement land program. Amer. Forests 42(8): 347-349, 389.
August 1936. (Published by the American Forestry Association, 919, 17th St.,
Washington, D. C.)
Describes the land use program of the Resettlement Administration, whose
function, "as distinct from that of any other branch of the Federal Government, is to convert misused and unproductive land now largely in farms, to
conservational uses as a means of improving the local economy and living
standards in rural communities, while retiring from cultivation lands poorly
adapted to arable farming." The Beltrami Island Project in northern
Minnesota and a southwestern Kansas project are called attention to as being
projects typical of other projects in the cut-over region of the Great Lakes
States, and of projects where the advisability of restoring arid farmlands to
grass is being demonstrated, respectively.

Legislation - Alberta

Brownlee, J. E. Alberta legislation and the Alberta farmer. Western Farm
Leader 1(5): 6C. Aug. 7, 1936. (Published in Calgary, Alberta)
The sixth of a series of articles. This article deals with drought and
debt legislation. The following acts are briefly described: The Farmers'
Creditors Arrangement Act; The Debt Adjustment Act; and The Crop Payment Act.
An explanation of the Crop Payment Act is given in the fifth article of
the series in West. Farm Leader 1(5): 66. July 17, 1936.

Brownlee, J. E. Far-reaching legislation of session reviewed. West. Farm
Leader 1(8): 1, 9. Sept. 4, 1936. (Published in Calgary, Alberta)
"The session of the Alberta Legislature just closed only lasted one
week, but during that time legislation of far reaching effect and importance
was passed...
"Three acts stand out of particular importance and an effort will be made
to give an intelligent summary."
The three acts are: 1. The Reduction and Settlement of Debts Act; 2. Consolidation Debt Adjustment Act; and 3. Alberta Credit House Act.

Brownlee, J. E. Farmers' position under Debt Reduction Act. West Farm Leader
1(9): 13C. Sept. 18, 1936. (Published in Calgary, Alberta)
A further examination of the Debt Reduction Act passed at the recent
Special Session of the Provincial Legislature.

Livestock - Cooperation

Mann, L. B. Co-ops that pioneered the Range Country. News for Farmer Cooperatives 3(5): 6, 12-14. August 1936. (published by the Farm Credit Administration)
In 1919, cooperative livestock marketing got a foothold in the range country with the establishment of the Farmers Union Livestock Commission of
Denver. In 1935, cooperative associations were in operation on 37 of the
principal markets of the United States and served all major livestock section
of the United States except parts of Oregon and Washington.

Livestock Policy - Great Britain

Elliot, Rt. Hon. Walter. Livestock policy; statement made...on Monday, July 6,
1936 in reply to a question in the House of Commons. Gt. Brit. Min. Agr.
Jour. 43(5): 425-427. August 1936. (Published by H. M. Stationery Office,
London, Eng.)
The Minister of Agriculture and Fisheries outlines the Government's
proposed livestock policy which aims at "a regulated market with the maximum
supplies for the consumer consistent with a reasonable level of remuneration
for the producer."

Marketing - Legislation - California

Corey, C. J. Review of the new marketing laws. Calif. Cult. 83(17): 589, 592,
593. Aug. 15, 1936. (Published in Los Angeles, Calif.)

Marketing of Eggs Act, 1936 - Northern Ireland

Northern Ireland: Marketing of Eggs Act, 1936. Gt. Brit. Min. Agr. Jour.
43(5): 475-476. August 1936. (Published by H. M. Stationery Office,
London, Eng.)
Brief summary of provisions.

Markets, Farm

Schultz, T. W.   Sell abroad, shift, or shrink. It is extremely important that
we decide which way we want to adjust agriculture. Successful Farming
34(8): 10, 11, 18. August 1936. (Published in Des Moines, Ia.)
"There are a number of reasons why agriculture finds itself with a
weak outlook. Only one of these will be considered here - our vanishing
farm markets abroad, a subject of much serious argument."

Meat - France

De Viguerie, P.   Production and consumption of and external trade in meat in
France. Monthly Bull. Agr. Econ. and Sociol. [Reprint from the Internatl.
Rev. Agr.] 27(8): 235-256. August 1936. (Published by the International
Institute of Agriculture, Rome, Italy)
In two parts: I.-Live stock numbers and production of meat; fluctuations
before and after the war; II.-Variations in meat consumption. The following
sub-headings appear in part I: General development during the pre-war period;
Reconstitution of live stock and direction given to breeding in the post-war
years; Recent period, from 1929 to 1934; and Situation in 1935.

Migrants to Iowa Industries - Farm Background

Zorbaugh, Grace S. M.   Farm background of country migrants to Iowa industries.
Iowa Jour. Hist. and Politics 34(3): 312-318. July 1936. (Published by the
State Historical Society of Iowa, Iowa City, Iowa)
This partial account of country migrants to Iowa industries is "based
on interviews by the writer, in the spring of 1927, with some 1200 persons
in twenty-one industrial establishments located in six representative communities. The men and women interviewed were practically all wage earners;
few employers and executives were included.
"The answers to six questions were sought in each plant: 1. What proportion of the personnel had come from farms. 2. What was the status and
tenure of the migrants' farm homes. 3. How far the migrants had come.
4. How long it was since they had come. 5. Their reasons for leaving the
farm. 6. Whether they expected to return.
"Information was also sought as to what, if any, relationship existed
between the town occupations of farm-bred men and women and their previous
experience, and as to their approximate annual earnings in town."

Milk - Consumption - Canada

Boucher, G. P.   More facts concerning milk consumption in Canada. Econ.
Annalist 6(4): 56-59. August 1936. (Published by the Agricultural Economics
Branch, Dept. of Agriculture, Ottawa, Canada)

Tables show relation between family income and non-consumption of milk; also between family income and beverages other than milk by children of various age groups in the cities of Oshawa, Quebec and Calgary and in the provinces of Quebec, Ontario, and Alberta.

Negro As a Factor in Labor Force

Edwards, Alba M. The negro as a factor in the nation's labor force. Amer. Statis. Assoc. Jour. 31(195): 520-540. September 1936. (Published by the Association. Secretary-Treasurer, Frederick F. Stephan, 722 Woodward Bldg., Washington, D. C.)

Overproduction

Patterson, E. M.. The over-production myth. Canner 83(16): 10. Sept. 26, 1936. (Published at 140 North Dearborn St., Chicago, Ill.)
    The writer disagrees with the common thought that we have passed from a period of scarcity into one of surplus. He says: "First we should get it firmly fixed in our minds that we do not have too much production...
    "Second, we must realize that our troubles are due to our failure to prevent those ups and downs known as business cycles...
    "Third to be remembered is that the basic causes are not in our monetary system. It has its weaknesses and it is to be hoped that we can correct them. Crude tinkering with money, however, of the sort that we have been carrying on and that many want us to continue, only serves to make matters worse. The basic troubles are not with money but with a large number of other matters...
    "There is no single remedy. Most emphatically it is not to be found in merely pushing up the level of prices. That will give relief to none except a few limited groups and will instead create new difficulties for almost all of us."

Part-time Farming - Alabama, Georgia, and South Carolina

U. S. Works Progress Administration. Research bulletin, J-1, J-2, J-3. mimeogr. (Published in Washington, D. C.)
    These bulletins present the results of a study of combined farming-industrial employment in Alabama, Georgia and South Carolina. They are not for general distribution. However, the material contained in them is to be published by the WPA sometime before the close of 1936 in a bulletin, "Part-time Farming in the Eastern Cotton Belt."
    Contents: J-1: Combined farming-industrial employment in the cotton textile subregion of Alabama, Georgia and South Carolina. Preliminary report, by W. W. Troxell, L. S. Cottrell, Jr., A. D. Edwards, and R. H. Allen. 67 pp. illus. (Chapter titles: The cotton textile subregion; The counties covered in the field survey: Greenville County, S. C., and Carroll County, Ga.; Farming activities of part-time farmers; Employment and earnings in industry; Conditions of living and organized social life; Comparisons in economic status between part-time farmers and full-time farmers; Case studies of part-time farmers; Appraisal of combined farming-industrial employment,Possibilitie for further development of combined farming-industrial employment).
    J-2: Employment in the cotton textile industry in Alabama, Georgia, and South Carolina. Preliminary report, by W. W. Troxell, 31pp., illus.

February 1936. (In two parts. Part I "seeks to answer the question: Will employment in the cotton mills of Georgia, Alabama, South Carolina tend to be greater or less in the future than in recent years? An examination of the trends and problems of the industry is undertaken to point the answer. Part II discusses those features of the industry which must be considered in any combination of farming with cotton mill employment."

J-3: Combined farming-industrial employment in Charleston County, South Carolina. Preliminary report, by W. W. Troxell, L. S. Cottrell, Jr., A. D. Edwards, and R. H. Allen. 66pp., illus. June 1936. (Chapter titled: Charleston County; White part-time farmers (farming activities, employment and earnings in industry, living conditions and organized social life), Negro part-time farmers (same sub-topics as previous chapter); Appraisal of combined farming-industrial employment.)

Plantation Life - Southern States

Ravenel, H. W. Recollections of southern plantation life. Yale Rev. 25(4): 748-777. Summer 1936. (Published by the Yale University Press, 143 Elm St., New Haven, Conn.)

"These recollections go back to the childhood and youth of the author, Henry W. Ravenel of South Carolina (1814-1887), planter, botanist, and writer. They were set down in February, 1876, to describe a portion of the old life that was patently gone - the life of the Negro slaves. Pooshee, the ancestral Ravenel plantation, lay in the section known as St. John's Berkeley, about forty miles northwest of Charleston...

"The life of the Negroes - their customs, habits, and superstitions - is here presented with the acuteness of observation which made Henry W. Ravenel the leading American mycologist of his day. The manuscript is a part of the collection of materials for a history of natural science in the South which Professor W. C. Coker of the University of North Carolina has been making for some time past; he has kindly given permission for its publication."

Pork - Czechoslovakia

L'evolution des quantités de viande provenant de l'abatage des porcs d'origine indigene par rapport au prix des porcs et de la quantité de viande de boeuf. Czechoslovakia. Institut de comptabilité et d'Economie Rurales. Rapports 7(2): 28-34. 1936. (Published in Prague, Czechoslovakia)

Analyzes the evolution of the pork obtained from the slaughter of domestic hogs from January 1923 to May 1936 by means of a table and graphs.

Price Discrimination Legislation

Michener, D. W. The origins and some of the economic ramifications of Robinson-Patman Act. Annalist 48(1230): 213-214. Aug. 14, 1936. (Published by the New York Times Co., Times Square, New York, N. Y.)

National Industrial Conference Board, Inc. The Robinson-Patman Act. Natl. Indus. Conf. Bd., Inc., Conf. Bd. Inform. Serv., Domestic Affairs Series, Memorandum no. 51, 8pp. Sept. 16, 1936. (Published in New York, N. Y.)

An analysis of the Robinson-Patman Act, approved June 19, 1936. The contents as listed in the sutdy follow: Provisions of the Act; Persons and

Transactions Subject to the Act; Prohibited Practices; Permitted Price
Differentials; Selection of Customers; Economic Effects; Unfavorable Effects;
Feasible Benefits, and Steps for Self-Protection.

Ralph, H. D. Business ponders the Patman law. Out-lawing of all forms of price
discrimination may have broad effect on profits in many industries. Mag.
Wall St. 58(9) 520-521, 554-556. Aug. 15, 1936. (Published at 90 Broad
St., New York, N. Y.)

Sales policies affected by recent legislation. Natl. Provisioner 95(8): 21.
Aug. 22, 1936. (Published at 407 South Dearborn St., Chicago, Ill.)
    Sales policies affected by the Robinson-Patman Act are discussed.

Thorp, W. L., and George, E. B. Check list of possible effects of the Robinson-Patman act. Dun & Bradstreet Monthly Rev. 44(2101): 2-17. August
1936. (Published at 290 Broadway, New York, N. Y.)
    "Enough is now known of the Robinson-Patman Act to make generally clear
(1) that many aggravating uncertainties lurk in its language which only the
courts can resolve, and (2) that these uncertainties are quite secondary to
the fact that a new working principle has been injected into business life
which promises definitely to alter existing practices and trade relationships."

Uncertainties and dangers of the Robinson-Patman Act. Com. and Financ. Chron.
143(3714): 1293-1294. Aug. 29, 1936. (Published at 25 Spruce St., New
York, N. Y.)

Price Fixing – Haiti

Price fixing in Haiti. Pan Amer. Union. Bull. 70(8): 674-675. August 1936.
(Published in Washington, D. C.)
    "A law signed by President Sténio Vincent on April 11, 1936, provides
that: 'Any unjustified increase in the price of commodities imported into
or produced in Haiti, or any decrease in the price of export products not
justified by the quotations prevalent in world markets, taking into consideration the usual expenses and profits will be considered an offense'
punishable by imprisonment for not less than six months or more than a year,
or by a fine of not less than $1,000 or more than $5,000, or both in case of
a second offense. A price commission (Comité des Prix) has been established
which is empowered, when the President of the Republic so orders, to fix
the minimum purchase price of export commodities in accordance with world
prices for similar foreign products so as to assure a just remuneration
to the producer and to fix the maximum selling price of commodities imported
into or produced in Haiti in such a way as to protect the consumer."

Price Forecasting

Pette, E. W. Short-term price forecasting, 1920-29. II. Jour. Business
Univ. Chicago 9(3): 280-300. July 1936. (Published at the University of
Chicago Press, 5750 Ellis Ave., Chicago, Ill.)
    "This is the second of three articles on price forecasting. As explained
in the first instalment appearing in the April, 1936, (pp.95-113) issue of
this Journal, the present article attempts to set down some of the main con-

clusions suggested by a detailed analysis of some one hundred and fifty
different price forecasts. In the original study each appraisal was
explained individually and supported by the appropriate quotations, but
space limitations here permit only a suggestion of the nature of the
various forecasts and of the reasons for the ratings assigned. The particular services included in the study are the ones whose forecasting
letters happened to be available at the time of the investigation. Most
of the statistical data incidental to the main study were taken from the
Standard Statistical Bulletin: Base Book Issue, 1931-32."

Prices

Corey, Herbert. Prices are wiser than men... an interview with Benjamin M.
Anderson, Jr., who explains the action of prices. Nation's Business
24(8): 27, 70, 72-73. August 1936. (Published by the Chamber of Commerce of the United States, Washington, D. C.)

Primary Products Marketing Act - New Zealand

New Zealand: Primary Products Marketing Act. Gt. Brit. Min. Agr. Jour. 43(5):
472-474. August 1936. (Published by H. M. Stationery Office, London,
Eng.)
Summary of the provisions of this Act which was passed in May, 1936,
its main object being to protect producers from price fluctuations by
granting power to the state to acquire control of the sale and export
of primary products at prices to be fixed from time to time. A new
State Department, to be known as the Primary Products Marketing Department will replace the Executive Commission of Agriculture.

Purchasing Power - United States

Sales management, inc. Survey of spending power. Total spendable money
income in 1935 from all sources, for counties and cities; urban family
median incomes; passenger car sales and registrations, and other data on
wealth, incomes and standards of living. Sales Management 38(8): 491-604.
Apr. 10, 1936. (Published at 420 Lexington Ave., New York, N. Y.)
An explanation of the data given, sources of the data and suggestions
on uses are given on pp. 491-500. Data are given for each state and county
on population, bank deposits, rent and ownership, factory wages, income
tax, telephones, passenger car registrations, new car sales, and spendable
money income.
Library has also the survey for 1932 published in Sales Management,
v. 32, no. 8, Apr. 10, 1933.

Rayon

F., M. S. Control measures for Japan's rayon industry. Far East Survey 5(18):
194-195. Aug. 26, 1936. (Published by American Council, Institute of
Pacific Relations, 129 East 52nd St., New York, N. Y.)
Regulations for the control of production and export of rayon in Japan
are discussed.

Self, S. B.   Rayon's next move. With costs steadying at one-third former
  prices, industry can compete with other textile products. Boon to chemical
  companies. Barron's 16(37): 13, 18. Sept. 14, 1936. (Published at 44
  Broad St., New York, N. Y.)

Resettlement - United States

Tugwell, R. G.   Changing acres. The Resettlement Administrator meets his
  critics and acknowledges the obstacles before his program. Then he gives
  his reasons. Current Hist. 44(6): 57-63. September 1936. (Published
  at 33 Park Row, New York, N. Y.)
    "The real hazards of resettlement have little to do with the unwilling-
  ness of anyone to cooperate in a plan. There are hazards, nevertheless,
  for in this phase of work the Government comes hard up against intangible
  aspects of human psychology. Frankly, there was no example of governmental land settlement completely successful in every way in the United
  States before 1933, and the projects launched in that year have not yet
  proved their worth one way or the other. But there have been tremendously
  successful land settlement programs in other lands. The Irish Free State
  convertedits farm population from one of tenants to one of landowners by
  a system of governmental resettlement...
    "The Resettlement Administration has proceeded with the utmost caution
  in launching its resettlement projects. Each one has been carefully planned
  and all factors checked, from the quality of its soil to the types of buildings. Moreover, each family is investigated to determine its abilities,
  and its evidences of being able to make a success out of its new opportunity
  The RA is now initiating rural resettlement projects which involve new
  homes for 3,000 families, throughout the United States. It is a small
  program in relation to the national need, but its success will be measured
  in larger terms, for it will lay the basis for possible future action on
  a broader scale."

Social Security - Colombia

M., B.   Compulsory savings for social security in Colombia. Pan Amer. Union.
  Bull. 70(8): 672-673. August 1936. (Published in Washington, D. C.)
    "Law no. 66 of March 31, 1936, made savings accounts obligatory for
  wage-earners and salaried employees in Colombia, and created, as a part
  of the Savings Bank of Colombia, the Savings and Social Security Division
  (Sección de Ahorro y Prevision Social), to be established with funds
  provided by the Government...The law will go into effect on January 1,
  1937, and from that date 3 percent of all wages, salaries, commissions, or
  other form of remuneration will be deducted at the source and 2 percent of
  the payroll added thereto for deposit at stated intervals in a bank to be
  designated by subsequent regulations. The sums credited to any employee
  or worker are nontransferable and nontaxable." The functions of the
  Savings and Social Security Division of the Bank of Colombia are listed.

Social Security - Ecuador

Cuban and ecuadorean social welfare organizations. Pan Amer. Union. Bull.
  70(8): 673. August 1936. (Published in Washington, D. C.)

Attention is called to the inauguration at Quito on May 1, 1936 of the National Social Welfare Institute of Ecuador, created by law to establish a system of compulsory social insurance in the country.

Soil Conservation - United States

Wallace, H. A.   A communication to state legislators and state officials. State and federal coöperation in the agricultural conservation program. State Govt. 9(5): 99-103. May 1936. (Published by the Council of State Governments, Drexel Ave. and 58th St., Chicago, Ill.)

Southern States

Edmonds, J. E.   The paradox of cottonland. Country Gent. 106(9): 8-9, 73-74. September 1936. (Published at Independence Square, Philadelphia, Pa.)
    The author's trip over the Southern States, talking with all sorts of people - WPA, CCC, Rural Resettlement workers, sharecroppers, farm laborers, landowners, bankers, etc. - brought out the following trends:
    "First - The countryside is moving to soil saving by better tillage and land use, and to folk assurance by a more skilled approach to self-sufficiency in food and feedstuffs; though a long road remains for each movement.
    "Second - White people are going from towns and cities to the farms, and Negroes are leaving the farms for the towns and cities; with a net rural gain.
    "Third - Landownership is increasing and share croppers are stepping up to the higher social and economic rank of tenants; but the change is slow and a multitude will remain, for generations or forever, working on the soil by the will and order of someone else. A realist must know it is inevitable."

Edmonds, J. E.   Six ways in cottonland. Country Gent. 106(10): 14-15, 84, 86-87. October 1936. (Published at Independence Square, Philadelphia, Pa.)
    Describes the plight of the cotton South; cites views of cotton merchants, farmers and others as to the situation and its remedy and describes some of the attempts to alleviate the trouble.

Soybeans

Barnard, H. E.   Soy beans and products...Their uses in commercial feeding. Grain & Feed Rev. 25(12): 18-21. August 1936. (Published at 408 South Third St., Minneapolis, Minn.)
    Address of the Director of Research for the Farm Chemurgic Council, before the Forty-eighth Annual Convention of the American Feed Manufacturers' Association at White Sulphur Springs, West Virginia, on June 13.

Burton, C. S.   Industrial magic in beans. Mag. Wall St. 58(12): 702-703, 737. Sept. 26, 1936. (Published at 90 Broad St., New York, N. Y.)
    A discussion of the many new uses of the soy bean and of the industries it affects. The concluding paragraph states: "This is a more or less complicated story in that we have the soy bean dividing into food use, farm feed use and industrial use. Industrially, it divides into crude oil and oil cake, the oil cake into proteins and soy bean meal. Refining processes are of great variety and the uses multiply. The position of the

- 859 -

chemists, that a great new industry beckons and promises to join agriculture
and industry to the profit of both, seems justified."

File, Howard. We can make almost anything from soy beans. Farmers' Elevator
Guide 31(9): 3-4. Sept. 5, 1936. (Published at 300 South La Salle St.,
Chicago, Ill.)
"An Illuminating Article Published in Staley Journal."
Describes the activities of the A. E. Staley Manufacturing Company with
soy beans, including their efforts to merchandise an edible grade of soy
flour in 1926. A section of the article is devoted to the discussion of the
industrial possibilities of this crop.
A table on page 20, entitled "Growth of Soy Beans in Illinois" has
figures of total acres, and total bushels threshed of soy beans in Illinois
from 1919 to 1936 inclusive.

Hayward, J. W. Utilization of soybeans. Grain & Feed Rev. 26(1): 12, 13, 14-17.
September 1936. (Published at 408 South Third St., Minneapolis, Minn.)
"This paper was prepared by Dr. J. W. Hayward for delivery on Tuesday,
June 23, before the Fifty-Seventh Annual Convention of the Ohio Grain,
Mill and Feed Dealers Association...Sandusky, Ohio."

Sugar - China

Sugar Association in China. Facts about Sugar 31(9): 332. September 1936.
(Published by Palmer Publishing Corp., 56 West 45th St., New York, N. Y.)
A National Sugar Production and Distribution Association was organized
at Shanghai on July 27, according to a report from U. S. Commercial attache,
Julean Arnold. Its purposes are: "The certification of origin of Chinese
domestic sugar products; facilitation of transportation and distribution;
improvement and encouragement of production; financial aid to sugar cane
growers, and cooperation with government authorities in suppressing the
smuggling of sugar. Expenses of the association are to be met in part by a
subsidy from the Finance Ministry.

Sugar - Cuba

News of the Cuban sugar industry. Facts about Sugar 31(9): 329-330. September
1936. (Published by Palmer Publishing Corp., 56 West 45th Street, New
York, N. Y.)
"Cane develops remarkably as rains continue - Question of molasses
quota renewed - Labor laws raise complaint of discrimination."

Sugar - India

Srivastava, R. C. Review of the sugar industry of India during the official
year 1933-34. Agriculture and Live-stock in India 6(4): 451-487. July
1936. (Published in Delhi, India)
Contains 17 tables.

<u>Sugar - Java</u>

Java sees trade still falling away. Facts about Sugar 31(9); 331-332. September
1936. (Published by Palmer Publishing Corp., 56 West 45th Street, New
York, N. Y.)
"Increased sales to Japan regarded as only temporary. Better world market
or new crop restrictions seen as alternatives."

<u>Tenancy, Farm</u>

Ostrolenk, Bernhard. New system of long tenure would cure problem of farm
tenancy in Corn Belt. Annalist 48(1236): 422. Sept. 25, 1936. (Published
by the N. Y. Times Co., Times Square, New York, N. Y.)
According to the writer, farm tenancy has taken the "foreground as the
leading problem in the Corn Belt. For the last few months virtually every
newspaper in Iowa and other Corn Belt States has been forced to take cognizance of the growing hostility to absentee land ownership; of the growing
movement to form tenant unions; of the widespread proposals for severely
radical legislation to curb corporation ownership of land and to tax absentee owners; of the radical discussion which includes such terms as
'exploitation of land workers' and 'collective bargaining.'"
The farm tenancy increase in the United States and reasons for it are next
described, and the difference between tenancy in Europe and in the United
States is pointed out. In conclusion it is stated: "Tenancy cannot be
abolished. But its evils are not inherent. It is possible to assign a
more wholesome role to the tenant, protect the interests of the landlord and
conserve the fertility of land. European systems of long tenure, and reward
to tenant for improvements and for farming that will maintain soil fertility
would make for a tenancy that is not incompatible with social and agricultural objectives."

<u>Tobacco - Europe</u>

Minneman, P. G. The European tobacco situation. Foreign Crops and Markets
33(14): 401-412. Oct. 5, 1936. (Issued by the U. S. Bureau of Agricultural
Economics, Washington, D. C.)
The tobacco situation is reviewed for the various countries of Europe
with the exception of the Balkan States. In these States - Bulgaria, Yugoslavia, Rumania and Greece - monopolies in 1934 ordered plantings to be
reduced "so that burdensome accumulations of stocks might be reduced.
In 1935, when stocks had been adjusted, plantings were again permitted at or
near the former level," etc. A table shows the acreage in these countries
in tobacco in 1929-1933 (average), 1934, and 1935.

<u>Tobacco - Manchuria</u>

Tobacco cultivation. Manchurian Econ. Rev. 3(18): 16-17. Sept. 15, 1936.
(Published by G. Harmsen, Harbin, Manchoukuo)
"The Government of Manchoukuo [has] a 20 year plan of leaf tobacco cul-
tivation to produce eventually 10,000,000 kan in a normal year."
The Fengtien Provincial Government is planning to invite 4,400 Japanese
families to settle on the land and cultivate "yellow" leaf tobacco. Certain

areas will be set aside for this settlement plan which will cover a period
of ten years. Immigrants must be experienced in agriculture, especially in
the cultivation of yellow leaf tobacco and must have more than 500 yen in
cash. Each family must consist of more than three persons engaged in farming.
Subsidies and loans will be made to settlers to cover certain expenses.
Each household is to have 5.7 cho of arable land, 1.5 cho for tobacco and
1 cho for rice.

Tobacco - Sumatra

Wautner, W.   Sumatra tobacco in the world markets.   Netherlands Indies 4(13):
    256-261. July 1, 1936. (Published in Batavia, Java, N. I.)
        Tables show the destination of the Sumatra tobacco crop in 1934 and 1935;
    production, price and total value of the crop at five-year intervals from
    1864 to 1905, and annually from 1910 to 1935; prices and yields of the crops
    of 1932, 1933 and 1934 which have been offered for sale in 1933 to 1935; and
    financial results of the four principal Sumatra tobacco concerns from
    1913 to 1935.

Trade, Foreign

Harding, Gardner.   Renaissance in our foreign trade. New commitments, new
    customers, new credit arrangements bring results. Economic nationalism
    abroad calls for shift by U. S. farmers. Barron's 16(31): 11,12,
    Aug. 3, 1936. (Published at 44 Broad St., New York, N. Y.)
        "This is the first of two articles dealing with foreign trade and America's
    interest in the alignment of importing and exporting countries."

Peek, G. N.   Farming and foreign trade. [A non-partisan view] Vital Speeches
    of the Day 2(24): 737-740. Sept. 1, 1936. (Published at 33 W. 42nd St.,
    New York, N. Y.)
        Radio talk over N.B.C., auspices of the National Grange, August 15, 1936.
    An indictment of the administration's farm and foreign trade policies.

Trade, Foreign - Germany

German trade policy. Statist 128(3056): 375, 376. Sept. 19, 1936. (Published
    at 51 Cannon St., E. C. 4, London, Eng.)
        A discussion of some of the consequences resulting from the New Plan
    in effect in Germany. The writer says it "is important to remember that
    German foreign trade has become a kind of State monopoly, and the State has
    a decisive influence on its geographical direction as well as on the method
    of competition employed...
        "An investigation into the geographical distribution of German foreign
    trade reveals important changes in the sources from which raw materials are
    bought. This is specially striking in the case of cotton," as a table which
    is given shows.

Trade, Foreign - Great Britain

Trade recovery and cheap money. Statist 128(3051): 3, 5-6. Aug. 15, 1936.
    (Published at 51 Cannon St., E. C. 4, London, Eng.)

"The economic situation in this country has in recent months entered upon a new and most interesting stage. Every index in the economic prospect is still favourable. Much to the surprise of those who even two years ago were beginning to prophesy that the limits of a purely isolated and domestic recovery were being reached, the present gathering of momentum in industrial and commercial activity in this country is taking place at the very time when export trade has begun to show definite signs of hesitancy. The inability of our external trade to keep pace with the improvement in domestic trade is not a matter for congratulation, but it places greater emphasis upon the undoubted acceleration which is taking place to-day in the growth of economic activity in this country."

Trade, Foreign - Japan

Taniguchi, Kichihiko.   The concentration and dispersion of Japan's foreign trade. Kyoto Univ. Econ. Rev. 11(1): 32-51. July 1936. (Published by the Kyoto Imperial University, Tokyo, Japan)

In conclusion in part: "Changes in the constitution of the foreign trade of a nation are important both on their own account and as phenomena which reflect the internal structure of the national economy of the nation. The question of trade constitution also may take various forms. For instance, the concentration and dispersion of trade discussed in this article may also be regarded as a matter of trade constitution in its broad sense.

"I have shown that both the concentration and the dispersion of trade have manifold aspects and have pointed out that concentration or dispersion may be taken in terms of international factors, time, industrial relations and commodity classification, in each of which it constitutes a special question. Considering the significance, in particular, of trade concentration or dispersion in terms of the commodities involved, both from theory and from economic policy, I have restricted my task to a statistical analysis of the leading trade commodities of Japan. I have arrived at the following conclusions from this investigation.

"(1) In our export trade, silk and cotton fabrics constitute 49.5%, ten leading commodities constitute 64.2% and twenty commodities, 74.2%. Thus, our export trade has been quite concentrative, although in recent years a tendency towards dispersion has been manifested. On the other hand, in our import trade, cotton and wool constitute 34.5%, ten principal commodities, 61.1% and twenty commodities, 73.1%. Thus, our import trade has been somewhat dispersive as compared with our export trade, but during the last ten years it has been also quite concentrative in its tendency."

Trade, Foreign - United States with Canada

Progress of agricultural trade with Canada. Foreign Crops and Markets 33(12): 351-362. Sept. 21, 1936. (Issued by the U. S. Bureau of Agricultural Economics, Washington, D. C.)

A change of procedure by Foreign Crops and Markets in presenting information relative to trade with Canada under the United States Canadian Reciprocal Trade Agreement is explained in the footnote to this article as follows: "Heretofore, the record of the trade with Canada under the agreement has been treated in two separate issues each month. The first article commented upon the volume of trade in certain outstanding agricultural products. The second article summarized the value of all trade with Canada, with special emphasis on concession and non-concession agricultural items. This issue is the first to carry an article combining the two formerly published independently. The tabulations will continue to include all of the concession items carried in earlier articles. Beginning with the present issue, these statements on trade with Canada will be available in separate form."

Trade, Import

Bean, L. H.   Recovery and imports of farm products. Agr. Situation 20(7):
14-17. July 1936. (Published by the Bureau of Agricultural Economics,
U. S. Dept. of Agriculture)

Trade Agreements

Draper, E. G.   Surmounting trade barriers: our reciprocity program. U. S. News
4(39): 4. Sept. 28, 1936. (Published at 2201 M St., N. W., Washington, D.C.)
"From an address at a Schenectady, N. Y., business men's luncheon,
Sept. 23."

Harding, Gardner.   Our new foreign trade policies. Barron's 16(40): 7. Oct.
5, 1936. (Published at 44 Broad St., New York, N. Y.)
"Former secretary of the National Foreign Trade Council and more
recently chief of public relations of the Export-Import Bank of Washington,
Mr. Harding views reciprocal-trade agreements from a background of knowledge
and experience by no means limited to his service under the Roosevelt Administration. He concludes that bargains already made seem to justify
going on with the program." - Editor's note.
Mr. Harding writes in the concluding paragraph in part: "Agriculture has
not been 'sold down the river' nor have either our exports or our imports
primarily derived their boom from the trade agreements. Rather a symptom
than a cause of reviving world trade, they are neither so dreadful as their
foes imagine nor so potent as their friends fondly hope. They are a very
intelligent experiment in decency in tariff-making, with due regard to the
interests of the man who consumes our goods in return...If they are the
principal cause of our present very small income surplus, it is a development for which they should be applauded. For we cannot continue to participate substantially in foreign trade, nor can our debts and investments be
unfrozen abroad, unless we permit the world to pay us at least a reasonable
proportion of this income in terms of goods."

Vegetables - Quick Freezing

Lacey, J. J.   A cold proposition. Nation's Agriculture 11(10): 5, 15. July-
August 1936. (Published at 58 East Washington St., Chicago, Ill.)
In this article the writer tells of a new method of distributing vegetables "that promises to revolutionize the market gardening industry."
He explains that the "new method of marketing involves the quick-freezing
of the vegetables within a few hours after harvesting, and holding them in
cold storage until sold to the grocer. It was in 1931 that they installed
the first freezers. Frozen goods sold readily from the start. Demand grew
by leaps and bounds until this year they will freeze vegetables from 12,000
acres of land."

Vernalization

Caffrey, M., and Carroll, P. T.   Vernalization, its principles and practice.
   Irish Free State. Dept. Agr. Jour, 34(1): 53-62. June 1936. (Published
   by the Stationery Office, Dublin, Irish Free State)
      Describes experiments on the vernalization of winter wheat, barley, maize
   and soya beans and their results.

Wages - Estonia

Wages of agricultural day-labourers. Majandusteated. Weekly Bull. Inst. Econ.
   Res. 2(37): 667. September 1936.
      A table gives wages of agricultural day labourers, by districts, in the
   summer of 1935 and 1936 in krones per day, plus board for men and women,
   grown-up and under age.

Wheat

Hansen, Axel.   What's ahead for wheat? U. S. crop may not be much over 600
   million bushels - carryover small - world stocks low - Canada's outturn
   important. Com. and Finance 25(15): 528-529. July 25, 1936. (Published
   at 95 Broad St., New York, N. Y.)

Mayer, R. J.   Sellers' market in wheat. Round of harvest disappointments in
   prospect as U. S. and Canada fail world. Half-billion-bushel drop in
   surplus stocks likely. Barron's 16(31): 9, 14. Aug. 3, 1936. (Published
   at 44 Broad St., New York, N. Y.)

Rose, M. A.   The wheat rolls in. Today 6(13): 5-7, 28-29. July 18, 1936.
   (Published at 152 West 42nd St., New York, N. Y.)
      "It is apparent already that drought has cut the spring-wheat crop again
   this year. It will be the fifth short crop in as many years. Our cupboard
   has been swept almost bare, for the 125,000,000 bushels or so that we have
   are hardly fit for milling.
      "We have been using about 625,000,000 bushels a year and experts estimated
   we would increase consumption to 650,000,000 bushels this year. A winter
   wheat crop which turned out to be 500,000,000 bushels, as expected, plus
   150,000,000 bushels of spring wheat would just do the trick. Early guesses
   on the spring-wheat crop were 260,000,000 bushels - but how the guesses have
   shrunk! Drought already has wreaked havoc and these are still critical
   weeks for the Northern belt. Shall we grow our own bread this year, or
   must we import wheat? What will prices do? Welfare of millions of men is
   at stake. How many thousands of them must sit idly under a brazen sky and
   see a year's work scorched away by a merciless sun? This is the great drama
   that is being played out on the plains these midsummer days...
      "Be it remembered that while a short crop, boosting prices, may be good
   for the farmer who escaped the drought, everyone else along the line - the
   railroads, the shipping fleets, the inspectors and the dealers - thrive on
   quantity. Price means little to them; they live on the handling of bulk.
   The 'economics of scarcity' makes no appeal to them. Nor, to tell the truth,
   to Ole Svenson, back on the farm."

Wheat - Australia

Australia does not need wheat grading system. Primary Producer 21(32): 12.
Aug. 6, 1936. (Published at 38-40-42-44 Stirling St., Perth, Western
Australia)
"That the present f.a.q. system, with some slight modification to take
hard wheats away from it, is the best for Australia and the most economical,
and that this country does not at present need a grading system in the
marketing of wheat, is the opinion expressed by Mr. L. S. Harrison (assistant
manager of the Government grain elevators of New South Wales)." Reasons for
this opinion are stated.

Wheat - Canada

Boyle, J. E.   Wheat out of politics. Barron's 16(38): 5, 8. Sept. 21, 1936.
(Published at 44 Broad St., New York, N. Y.)
"When news went out from Winnipeg a few weeks ago that the Government
Wheat Board had disposed of the last of its holdings of cash wheat, finis
was written to 12 years of costly experimentation in wheat-marketing.
These 12 years include the seven years of bungling by the Central Pool,
which set the stage for the five years of worse bungling by the Bennett
Government. Well, now that the agony is over, two lessons, at least stand
out: The nonsense of selling wheat by that statistical formula known as
'orderly marketing'; the greater nonsense of mixing economics and politics
in marketing the farmers' crops. In Canada, as in the United States, hard
times always bring many weird and novel proposals for political solution
of the farmers' problems. A little further examination of Canada's recent
experiences may prove helpful to ourselves."

Wheat - France

Déclarations de récolte, taxe à la production et redevances et cotisations
prévues par la loi du 15 août 1936 instituant l'Office National Interprofessionnel du Blé. France. Jour. Officiel 68(211): 9634-9636. Sept.
9, 1936. (Published at Quai Voltaire, no. 31, Paris 7e., France)
Text of decree of Sept. 8, 1936 providing for the terms of the declaration of the total wheat crop to be made each year by the farmers before
September 30, the bases of calculation of the production tax for 1936/37
provided for by the law of August 15, 1936, and the collection of the 15
centimes per quintal of wheat sold due the National Wheat Office and
other dues.

Liesse, André.   L'Office du Blé. L'Economiste Français, 64. année, no. 37,
pp. 281-283. Sept. 12, 1936; no. 38, pp. 305-307. Sept. 19, 1936. (Published at Rue Bleue, 9, Paris (9e), France)
The Wheat Office Law is said to be an outstanding example of directed
economy, definitely socialist in character, and the first step on the
way towards collective or communist property. The author discusses the
provisions of the law in support of his thesis.

Loi tendant à l'institution d'un Office National Interprofessionnel du Blé.
Travaux des Chambres d'Agriculture. Aug. 10, 1936. Suppl. (Published by
Imprimerie Nouvelle, Amiens, France)
Text of law of August 15, 1936 establishing the National Wheat Office.

Wheat - Hungary

Friedländer, Emil.   Unsere Weizenernte, Export- und Verwertungsprobleme.
Ungarischer Volkswirt 5(8): 7-9. August 1936. (Published in Budapest,
Hungary)
The quality of this year's wheat is reported as being very satisfactory.
The quantity has been officially estimated at 24 million metric quintals,
the exportable surplus being about 8 million metric quintals of which from
7 to 7.5 million metric quintals have been sold in advance by the Government. Minimum prices, which are at the same time maximum prices, have
been fixed.

Wool - China

China's raw wool trade.   Chinese Econ. Jour. and Bull. 18(6): 863-877. June
1936. (Published by Bureau of Foreign Trade, Ministry of Industry,
Shanghai, China)
Contains tables.

NOTES

Agar, Herbert, and Tate, Allen, ed.   Who owns America? A New declaration of
indpendence. 342PP. Boston, New York, Houghton Mifflin company,
1936. 280.12 Ag1W
Agriculture and the property state, by John C. Rawe, pp. 36-51;
Looking down the cotton row, by G. M. O'Donnell, pp. 161-177; The
small farm secures the state, by A. Lytle, pp. 237-250.

Ayres, L. P.   Inflation.   36pp.   [Cleveland] The Cleveland trust company
[1936] 284 Ay7In

Bahia, Brazil (State). Cooperativa instituto de pecuaria. Estatutos da Cooperativa
instituto de pecuaria da Bahia. 22pp. Bahia, Imprensa official do estado,
1936. 280.2409 B14
Cooperative livestock institute regulations.
Bureau of Agricultural Economics has an English translation in Foreign
Files.

Black, H. L., and Hart, M. K.   Has the new deal promoted or retarded business
recovery? 32pp. New York, N. Y., American book company [1935]
(America's town meeting of the air [no.6])   280.12 B563

Bopp, K. R.   The agencies of federal reserve policy. 83pp. Columbia, Mo.,
1935. (The University of Missouri studies... v. 10, no. 4) 284 B642
also 470 M69 v. 10, no. 4
Bibliography, pp. 81-83

Borak, A. M., and Blakey, Gladys C.   Fees and other non-tax revenues of
   Minnesota local units... [Prepared] under the direction of Roy G.
   Blakey. 144pp. Minneapolis, The University of Minnesota press, Oct.
   1935. (University of Minnesota studies in economics and business,
   no. 13, October 1935)   280.9 M663 no.13
      Bibliography, pp. 143-144.

China. Government testing bureau of Shanghai. The organization and activities
   of the Government testing bureau of Shanghai. 52pp. [Shanghai] Government testing bureau of Shanghai, Ministry of industry, 1935.   286 C442

China. Government testing bureau of Shanghai. Special report no. 1. [22pp.]
   [Shanghai] 1935. 280.3729 C443
      Chinese, with English summaries.

Dawson, C. A.   Group settlement; ethnic communities in western Canada. 395pp.
   Toronto, The Macmillan company of Canada limited, 1936.   (Canadian frontiers of settlement, edited by W. A. Mackintosh and W.L.G. Joerg. v.7)
   282.2 M21 v.7

Douglass, B. W.   The new deal comes to Brown county. 86pp. Garden City,
   N. Y., Doubleday, Doran and company, inc., 1936.   281.025 D 74

Farm chemurgic council.   A plan coordinating agriculture, industry and science.
   40pp., mimeogr. [Dearborn, Mich., 1935]   309 F 22
      "A survey of research on the industrial utilization of farm products." -
   p. 2

The Farmer's wife. The rich country home supplies and equipment market. The
   Farmer's wife magazine. 62pp. [St. Paul, Minn., Webb publishing company,
   1935] 280.32 F223

Gannett, F. E., Butler, Tait, and Bosch, John.   The farm problem and prosperity.
   33pp. New York, N. Y., American book company [1935]   (America's town
   meeting of the air. [no.2])   281.12 G15

Gt. Brit. Board of trade. Safeguarding of industries act, 1921 (part 1)
   Finance act, 1926 (section 10) Report of a committee appointed by the
   Board of trade. 18pp. London, H. M. Stationery off., 1936.
   ([Parliament. Papers by command] Cmd. 5157)   285 G795

Gt. Brit. Customs and excise dept.   Customs and excise tariff of the United
   Kingdom of Great Britain and Northern Ireland in operation on the 1st
   August 1936. 332pp. London, H. M. Stationery off., 1936.   285.9 G79

Gt. Brit. Hops marketing board. English hop season 1936. 3pp. London, 1936.
   280.3709 G79
      May be obtained from the Hops Marketing Board 30/33 Central Buildings,
   Southwark St., London, S. E. 1, England.

Gt. Brit. Ministry of agriculture and fisheries. Arrangements under the Milk
    acts, 1934 and 1936 for increasing the demand for milk within the area of
    the Milk marketing board for England and Wales by publicity and propaganda.
    2pp. London, H. M. Stationery off., 1936.   280.344 G792Ar 1936.

Gt. Brit. Sugar beet marketing board. Scheme under the Agricultural market-
    ing acts, 1931 & 1933 regulating the marketing of sugar beet. 26pp.
    London, Sugar beet marketing board [1936]   280.366 G79

Handbook to British Malaya, 1935. Pub. by authority and compiled by R. L.
    German. 233pp. [London, 1935?]   280.186 H19
        Obtainable at the Malayan Information Agency, Malaya House, 57, Charing
    Cross, S. W. 1 London.

Haney, L. H.   History of economic thought; a critical account of the origin
    and development of the economic theories of the leading thinkers in
    the leading nations., 3d and enl. ed. 827pp. New York, The Macmillan
    company, 1936. (Social science text-books, ed. by R. T. Ely) 280 H19 Ed.3
        "Chief works of American economists active between 1850 and 1915,"
    pp. 789-802; Bibliography, pp. 803-809.

International institute of agriculture. Protocol between the United States
    of America and other powers amending the international convention of
    June 7, 1905. Signed at Rome, April 21, 1936... Proclaimed by the
    President of the United States, January 24, 1936. 7pp. Washington, U. S.
    Govt. print. off., 1936.   ([U. S. Dept. of state] Treaty series no. 903)
    28 In8P

Kansas. Emergency relief committee. A study made of 719 rural rehabilitation
    families relative to their standard of living. 20pp., mimeogr. Topeka,
    Kan., The Kansas Emergency relief committee [1935]   284.4 K132
        "Study was made by Miss Conie Foote... of the Kansas Emergency Relief
    Committee." - p. 1.

Kansas. Emergency relief committee. A study of social problems. One of a
    series of studies of social problems in Kansas and their social and eco-
    nomic costs. The Kansas Emergency relief committee. 16pp. Topeka,
    Kan. [1935] (bulletin K.E.R.C. no. 167)   280.029 K13[1st]

Land settlement association, ltd., London. Land settlement; the official
    journal... no. 3-5; Jan. 1936 - July 1936. 3 nos. London, 1936.
    282.29 L23
        No. 4, March, 1936 is the first annual report.

Lind, C. The provision trade. 52pp. [Copenhagen] Gyldendalske boghandel,
    nordisk forlag, 1935. (Statistical investigations into the economy of
    retailing. Bulletin no. 2. Institute of economics and history, Copenhagen)
    286.2 L64

Manchester, Eng., Markets dept. Markets committee.   Report... for the year
    ending 31st March 1936. 24pp. Manchester, H. Blacklock & co. limited,
    printers [1936]   280.39 M312
        Relates to public and private slaughter-houses and the prevention of
    exposure for sale of unwholesome and unseasonable food.

Matolcsy, Mátyás, and Varga, István.   Magyarország nemzeti jövedelme 1924/25-
    1934/35, irták dr Matolcsy Matyás es dr. Varga István.   144pp. Budapest,
    A Magyar gazdasagkutatóintezet, 1936. (Budapest. Magyar gazdasagkutató
    intezet. Szamu különkiadványa. 11)   280.9 B85S
        The Hungarian national income 1924/25 - 1934/35.

Minnesota. University.   The day and hour series. 2 nos. Minneapolis, The
    University of Minnesota press, 1936.   280.9 M663D
        no. 12. Income distribution under capitalism; a challenge to American
    business men, by H. G. Moulton. 27pp.
        no. 14. Old age security, by Emerson P. Schmidt. 32pp.
        Bibliography, p. 32.

Morgan, A. E., and Hooker, E. H.   Is government competition retarding busi-
    ness recovery? 29PP. New York, N. Y., American book company [1936]
    (America's town meeting of the air [no.10])   280.12 M82

National live stock marketing association, Chicago.   Cattle handbook for the
    grower and feeder, by H. M. Conway, director of research. 64pp. Chicago,
    Ill., National live stock marketing association [1935]   43 N21

New Zealand. Ministry of finance.   Budget 1936. 41pp. Wellington, by authority:
    G. H. Loney, Government printer, 1936.   284.9 N484

Oregon. State planning board.   Final report on the state capitol building
    program submitted to the Honorable Charles H. Martin, governor of
    Oregon, and the Legislative assembly of the state of Oregon by the
    State planning board. 32pp. [Salem? 1935]   280.7 Or33

Reine und angewandte soziologie; eine festgabe für Ferdinand Tönnies zu
    seinem achtzigsten geburtstage am 26. juli 1935, dargebracht von Al-
    brecht, Boas, Bohnstedt... [u.a.] 403pp. Leipzig, H. Buske, 1936. 280 R27
        "Redaktion: Ernst Jurkat". - p. [ii]
        "Schriften von Ferdinand Tönnies aus den jahren 1875-1935, chrono-
    logisch zusammengestellt von Else Brenke": pp. [383]-403.
        These essays in the field of sociology were collected and published
    in honor of Ferdinand Tönnies on the occasion of his 80th birthday.

Riggleman, J. R.   Graphic methods for presenting business statistics... Intro-
    duction by M. C. Forty... 2d ed.   259pp. New York and London, McGraw-
    Hill book company, inc., 1936.   325 R44 Ed.2

Rood, J. R.   This way out: ration the consumer's dollar to increase the profits
    of business and industry.   80pp. Detroit, Mich., Detroit law book company
    [1935] 280.12 R672

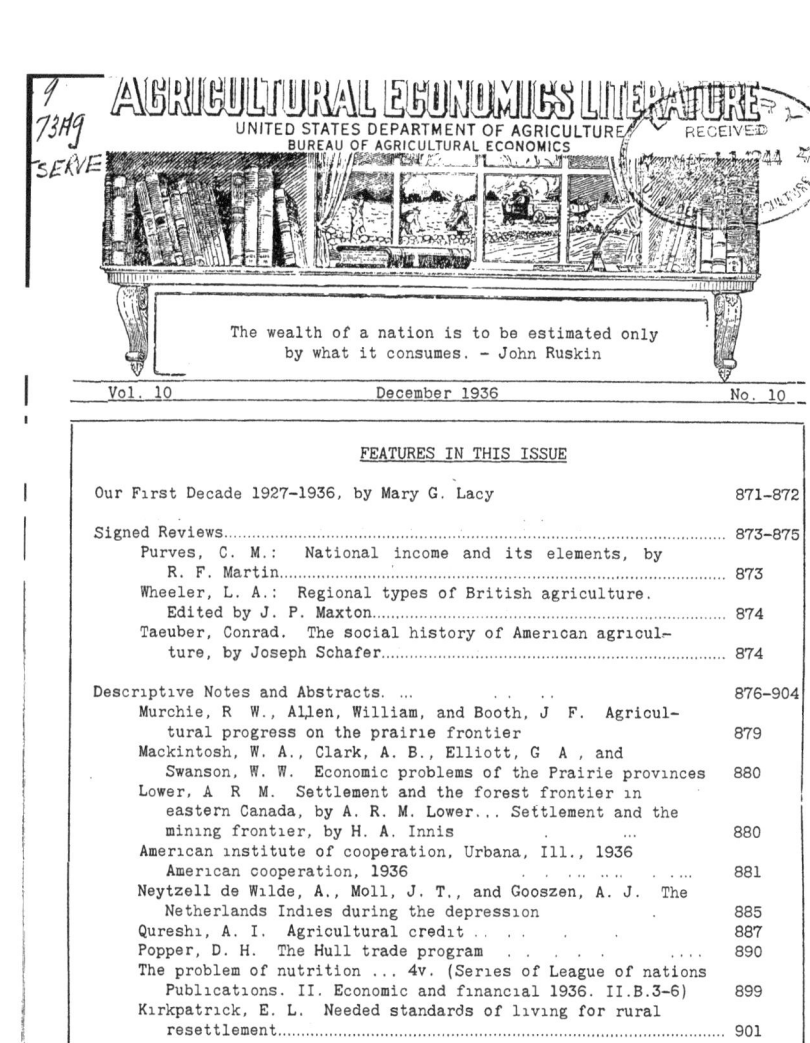

AGRICULTURAL ECONOMICS LITERATURE

UNITED STATES DEPARTMENT OF AGRICULTURE
BUREAU OF AGRICULTURAL ECONOMICS

RECEIVED

The wealth of a nation is to be estimated only
by what it consumes. — John Ruskin

| Vol. 10 | December 1936 | No. 10 |

FEATURES IN THIS ISSUE

AGRICULTURAL ECONOMICS LITERATURE

Vol. 10   December 1936   No. 10

OUR FIRST DECADE 1927-1936

Agricultural Economics Literature completes its first decade of life
with this issue, for volume 1, no. 1 was dated January, 1927.

To contribute to the organization of the printed records of economic
data or knowledge relating to agriculture, so that it is available to the
thinkers of our time who are struggling with problems of prime importance
to the welfare of our people is no mean responsibility and we feel that the
compiling and publishing of Agricultural Economics Literature is a means to
this end. We believe that through the study of the printed records in the
field of agricultural economics, "understanding may be distilled from the
past and insight provided for the future", at least in part.

In view of the fact that our mailing list is constantly changing and
growing we think that this may be a good opportunity to set forth again just
what it is that we are undertaking to do each month, and what means we use
to accomplish our purpose.

In each issue of Agricultural Economics Literature we publish a few reviews of books that have been received during the previous month. These reviews are made by specialists in the Bureau or elsewhere whose training and
experience seem to fit them best to review the book.

The section entitled Descriptive Notes and Abstracts consists, as the
title indicates, of descriptive notes and abstracts of the most important
books and pamphlets received in the Bureau library during the previous month.

In the section entitled Bibliography we note bibliographies compiled in
the Bureau library and also those received from other sources which are of interest to agricultural economists.

The Selected List of Recent Reviews includes only reviews of books which
are economic in character and which are filed in the Library of the Bureau of
Agricultural Economics. These reviews are obtained in connection with the
current reading of periodicals referred to elsewhere.

In the list entitled U. S. Department of Agriculture Publications Economic
in Character, we note, each month, all of the Circulars, Farmers Bulletins,
Miscellaneous Publications, Service and Regulatory Announcements, Technical
Bulletins, Radio Talks, and miscellaneous items, including the mimeographed
publications of the Bureau of Agricultural Economics and the other agencies
of the Department which are economic in character. A systematic use of this
list should enable an economist to know just what the Department has issued
during the previous month which would be of use in the field of agricultural
economics.

In order to compile the list entitled, State Publications we examine
carefully each month the publications issued by all of the experiment stations
in the United States, all of the extension divisions of the State Agricultural
Colleges, and the publications of the State Departments of Agriculture, Bureaus

of Marketing, etc. From these we select the publications which are economic in character. This list should therefore be of great use in keeping economists informed for the work being done in the States.

In order to compile the list entitled, Periodical Articles the Bureau library staff reads, each month, 398 domestic and foreign periodicals and selects those articles which seem to be the most important and useful in the field of agricultural economics. Short abstracts or descriptive notes are given in each case in order to enable an economist to decide whether he needs actually to read the article. An occasional feature in connection with periodicals is the inclusion of descriptive notes for New Periodicals which deal with some part of the subject matter of agricultural economics.

The Section headed Notes consists of items which are of related interest only, second or later editions of books which have previously been noted in Agricultural Economics Literature, and annual reports or other publications whose titles are such that no description of contents seems necessary.

In the January 1936 issue there appeared a survey of American Rural Fiction for the year 1935 by Caroline B. Sherman. It is hoped that this survey will continue as an annual feature. It is particularly useful as no attempt is made to list rural fiction currently in Agricultural Economics Literature no matter how well it depicts the life of a locality or the farm conditions under which a specific agricultural commodity is produced.

Perhaps attention should be called also to the detailed author and subject Index which is designed to provide an annual ready reference index to the literature of agricultural economics both domestic and foreign in so far as it has been received in the Library of the U. S. Department of Agriculture.

In looking over the early issues the editor is surprised to find how little change there has been in either format or character of contents. In the first issue there were three signed reviews - Dr. John D. Black's Production Economics was reviewed by Dr. W. J. Spillman, Dr. Carl C. Taylor's Rural Sociology, by Dr. E. L. Kirkpatrick, and Dr. Kurt Ritter's Der Getreideverkehr der Welt, by Mrs. A. M. Hannay. There was a group of Descriptive notes and comments on new publications, as now, and lists of State Publications, and Periodical articles of interest. Not until the fifth issue of the first year did the list of Publications of the U. S. Dept. of Agriculture, Economic in Character make its appearance. The Selected List of Recent Reviews became a regular feature upon the request of a reader with the second issue of the fourth volume, February, 1930. From this point on the regular features of Agricultural Economics Literature have remained approximately the same.

The chief change in the publication has been the increase in its size. The first issue of volume 1 consisted of 23 pages. The first issue of volume 10 consisted of 92 pages. This increase in the size of each of the 10 monthly issues which constitute a volume reflects directly, we believe, the increase in the volume of publications on the economics of agriculture in the last 10 years. There has also been a broadening, we believe, of the boundaries of agricultural economics.

Mary G. Lacey

Martin, R. F. National income & its elements. 134pp. New York city,
National industrial conference board, inc. [1936] (National industrial
conference board. [Studies no. 227]) 284 M353

In National Income and Its Elements, Mr. Martin has added two more
concepts of National Income to the many that were already in existence.
One of these is called "realized production income" which includes salaries and wages, incomes of individuals engaged in business, such as
farmers, retail merchants, doctors, lawyers, etc., dividends, business
interest, net rent on business properties, and the international balance
of dividends and interest. In other words, it is the receipts by individuals of goods and services from the national economy viewed as a
single business enterprise. Mr. Martin's second definition of National
Income is called "accountable realized income". This includes all of
the items under "realized production income" and in addition all other
items for which reasonable estimates can be made, including net rent on
rented homes, interest on mortgages on owned homes, pensions, compensa-
tions for injuries, relief payments and rental and benefit payments.
Estimates of National Income under these two definitions have been prepared for the period 1929-34.

The discussion accompanying the income estimates contains a description of the various sources of income included, a discourse on the problems involved in measuring national income, and an appraisal of the accuracy of the various statistical series used.

One of the important contributions of the study is a distribution of
the National Income by states for the years 1929 and 1933. The State
estimates of income are given both in totals for the State and in income
per capita for each State. The estimates for 1929 are also broken down
to show income by industries and by States for these years.

Another worthwhile contribution is the comparison of the items included
in the various National Income estimates now commonly used. This is presented in tabular form in auditing note No. 1. This table clearly brings
out the similarity between Mr. Martin's estimates of "accountable realized
income" and the Department of Commerce estimate of "national income paid
out." Mr. Martin has included relief payments, public and private, and
rental and benefit payments in his estimates of National Income whereas
the Department of Commerce has not. On the other hand, the Department of
Commerce includes royalty payments while Mr. Martin has not included these
in his National Income estimates. Because of these differences and slightly different methods used in estimating the various components which are
included in both series, Mr. Martin's estimate of "accountable realized
income" for 1929 was $80,029,000,000 and for 1934 was $50,889,000,000,
whereas the estimates of "income paid out" by the Department of Commerce
for the same years were $78,632,000,000 and $50,174,000,000 respectively. -
C. M. Purves, Senior Agricultural Economist, Bureau of Agricultural
Economics.

Maxton, J. P., ed. Regional types of British agriculture, by fifteen
authors. 318pp. London, G. Allen & Unwin ltd. [1936]   281.171 M45
    This book brings together for the first time detailed information
in regard to the various types of farming carried on in Great Britain.
It consists of fourteen essays on separate farming regions preceded by
a chapter entitled "General Features of Farming in Great Britain."
American readers will undoubtedly find this general chapter of particular interest, giving as it does and in a very brief space a comprehensive picture of such fundamental conditions as topography, climate,
soils, and distribution of population. It also includes information as
to the location of the production of all of the more important crops
and livestock. Each of the individual essays covers one of the "advisory
provinces" - eleven in England and Wales and three in Scotland - established under an advisory and research scheme financed by the British
Ministry of Agriculture and the Department of Agriculture for Scotland.
Each essay is contributed by an agricultural economist who has been directly associated with economic research in the province of which
he writes. The book as a whole represents an important contribution
in the field of agricultural economics literature. - L. A. Wheeler,
Principal Agricultural Economist, Bureau of Agricultural Economics.

Schafer, Joseph. The social history of American agriculture. 302pp. New
York, The Macmillan company, 1936. 277.12 Schl
    "Written orginally as successive offerings in a lecture course of
University college, University of London." - Preface
    The various chapters of Dr. Schafer's volume represent successive
offerings in a lecture course at University College, University of
London. It was not intended to be an exhaustive treatise but rather
to stimulate the reader to further study of the subject. After a discussion of the efforts to provide land for farmers, the author traces
the development from the primitive subsistence farming characteristic
of colonial and early pioneer agriculture to big business, improved,
and professional farming. There follow chapters on social and political
trends in rural life, and a concluding chapter on the outlook for farmers.
For the author the most important phase of this social history of American
agriculture is the development of the typical free democratic American
farmer under the influence of the ever-changing frontier and the changing requirements of farm life. This typical American farmer has tended
to be an individualist, aggressively resisting attempts to invade his
personal liberty as well as the forces which tended to reduce his economic status. He has frequently taken an active part in political movements to achieve his ends, though Southern and Western farmers have not
always been united.
    Considerable attention is devoted to the role of the speculator in
the transfer of apparently limitless acreages from government to private
ownership and to the varied role of the railroads in promoting settlement; less to the origins of settlers on the different frontiers or to
the effects of some of the land policies which are described. Especial
attention is given to the role of machines, improved methods of breeding

and cultivation, and the scientific laboratory in the rapid transformation of the primitive subsistence farmer, following European and Indian traditions, into the modern agricultural entrepreneur. Good roads were not the least important factor in this development.

In passing, attention is given to an infrequently discussed phase of the relations of mechanical inventions and the farm family. The development of the small combine is traced to the demand of the operators of "family size" wheat farms. In this case mechanization has tended to strengthen the family farm.

Members of the Staff of the U. S. Department of Agriculture may be particularly interested in the resume of the development of federal and state research and promotion agencies, from the Congressional grant in 1839 to the Patent Office for "the collection of agricultural statistics, investigations for promoting agriculture and rural economy", through the Morrill and Hatch acts, the early work in agricultural research at Harvard and Yale, and the work of Norton, Turner, Babcock, Ruffin and others.

Both the presence of the frontier and the growth of scientific agriculture contributed to the development of a farmer type quite different from the original peasant and other settler stock. Cotton and tobacco and later cattle raising, types of agriculture which required a large and stable labor supply, led to the development of landed aristocracies. The wheat farmers, who came into their own through the use of machines, were migrants, and in many ses speculators, and did not develop an aristocracy. The fact that on the frontier a man's accomplishments were largely due to his own efforts and that among the settlers there was no room for the person unwilling to work, became an important factor in the development of the modern American farmer. The agricultural frontier, as developed under our land policies, had an important influence in the melting pot process, for it discouraged settlement in compact nationality groups and placed the settlers of whatever origin on an equal footing. The frontier-developed farmer has always played a large political role. The administrations of Jefferson and Jackson, the protracted controversies over the tariff, the Civil War when northern agriculture was arrayed against the southern planters, the Populist movement, and the more recent attempts to secure relief from oppressive conditions through political measures as well as the sporadic instances of direct action are instances of the faith in political remedies for economic and financial difficulties.

For Dr. Schafer, the development of the American farmer and the family farm is an important contribution to the development of this country, and the preservation of many of the values of frontier rural America.

"An opposed to the great city's mad pursuit of wealth and the things an excess of wealth has made fasionable, the small city, town, village, and the countryside, dominated up to now by a rural psychology, still retain the old primal American virtues; a sense of human values, neighborliness, morality, and religion. The country people are not yet generally blase, but reflect that buoyant spirit which comports with genuine independence, creative activity, and self-respecting industry. The farmers, from this point of view, are the hope of the nation's future as they have been the chief dynamic force of our country's past." - Conrad Taeuber. Agricultural Economist, Bureau of Agricultural Economics.

DESCRIPTIVE NOTES AND ABSTRACTS

Agriculture - Bulgaria

Sofia. Institut po zemledelska ikonomiia. Reorganizing plan of a farm near
the village of Marashki Trustenik, Pleven County, by Professor Jan. S.
Molloff and At. I. Quzounoff. 117pp. Sofiia, Pechatnitsa "Radikal",
1933. 281.177 So2R
    Text and added title in Bulgarian; summary in English.
    At head of title: Trudove na Instituta po zemledelska ikonomiia pri
Agronomo-lesovudskiia fakultet na Universiteta.
    Bibliography, pp. [116]-117.
    The income from the capital invested in this farm was increased
from 4.73% to 11.39% by the reorganization.

Sofia. Institut po zemledelska ikonomiia, Economic evaluation of some farm
crop rotations in the County of Sofia, by Professor Jan. S. Molloff
and G. D. Kalapchieff. 85pp. Sofiia, Pechatnitsa na Armeiskiia
Voenno-izdatelski fond [1935] 281.177 So2E
    Text and added title in Bulgarian, summary in English.
    At head of title: Trudove na Instituta po zemledelska ikonomiia
pri Agronomo-lesovudskiia fakultet na Universiteta.
    Bibliography, pp. [84]-85.
    "With this work we have as an aim to examine from an economic point
of view the results obtained from different crop rotations by the
Sofia Agricultural Experiment Station during the period 1919-1929 giving an opportunity to determine which one of the experimental crop rotations gives the highest net income, having in mind the natural and
economic conditions of the Sofia region." - Summary.

Agriculture, Native - Population and Public Health

Hall, Sir A. D. The improvement of native agriculture in relation to population and public health. 104pp. London, H. Milford, Oxford university
press, 1936. (University of London. Heath Clark lectures, 1935) 281.19 H1
    Delivered at the London School of Hygiene and Tropical Medicine.
    References at the end of each chapter.
    The author writes in part as follows in his preface:
    "When the University of London did me the honour of inviting me to
deliver the Heath Clark lectures and I began to consider in what way the
conditions laid down in the Trust Deed could be met, it seemed that I
might be able to serve a useful purpose by bringing together in brief
compass a large volume of work of which the essential unity was perhaps
unappreciated because it was scattered among so many and diverse reports
and publications. As Chairman of the Kenya Agricultural Commission in
1929 I had been seized of the necessity of reforming the native methods
of agriculture if the tribes were to be saved from reducing their reserves
to a state of desert. Since that time Sir Albert Howard's farseeing work
at Indore had offered a solution to the prime problem of maintaining the
fertility of the soil under tropical and semi-tropical conditions. The
growth of our knowledge of food accessories had indicated the causes of

some of the defects of nutrition which do much to maint~in m~ny primitive
peoples at so low a level of physique and health that they cannot take their
due place alongside the white man's civilization, and Sir John Orr's pioneer
work had showed how large was this factor of malnutrition among the African
natives. I have therefore endeavoured, however summarily, to outline on a
fundamental scientific basis the means by which the African tribes can be
given a higher standard of living and be relieved of the pressure of over-
population, of the incidence of much preventable disease, and of the imminent menace of the destruction of their land. It is always before my mind
that this is very much a British responsibility, for we have definitely declared ourselves trustees for the natives of so large a portion of Africa.
We are there neither to displace the natives nor to exploit them; actually
we have to save them from themselves, for the intrusion of our Western
civilization has a destructive effect upon the tribal cultures, whether we
rate them high or low. There is room for the white man in Africa, he has
much to gain there, provided he does his duty by its inhabitants."

Agriculture - Scotland

Scotland. Dept. of agriculture. Sixth report on the profitableness of farming
    in Scotland 1933-4. The financial results obtained on certain groups of
    farms in Scotland in 1933-4. 63pp. Edinburgh, H. M. Stationery off., 1936.
    281.9 Sco3
        Title page printed, text mimeographed.
        "This Report is the sixth in the series dealing with the economic position
    of the agricultural industry in Scotland. It deals with an analysis of 239
    farm accounts and relates to the year 1933-4." - Prefatory note.

Balkan States - Economic Conditions

Royal institute of international affairs. Information dept. The Balkan states.
    I. Economic. A review of the economic and financial development of Albania,
    Bulgaria, Greece, Roumania and Yugoslavia since 1919. Specially prepared
    for, and with the assistance of, the Information department of the Royal
    institute of international affairs. 154pp. London, Oxford university
    press, H. Milford, 1936. 280.17 R81
        "The object of this work is to provide a review, concise but within
    its limits comprehensive, of the economic structure and development of
    the five States which with certain exceptions once formed part of the
    Ottoman Empire - that is to say Albania, Bulgaria, Greece, Roumania, and
    Yugoslavia. The grouping is admittedly an artificial one, for the five
    States in no sense form an economic unit. In many ways Roumania and
    Yugoslavia belong to the Danubian and Central European region, while
    Albania by force of circumstance belongs to the Italian sphere, and the
    economic structure of Greece differs radically from that of the other coun-
    tries. The five States, nevertheless, share certain characteristics, and
    an examination under one cover of their essential structure and development,
    and their commercial and financial relations with other States will, it is

hoped, prove useful, especially in view of the dearth of such assembled material.

"As in the case of China and the States of South America, the Balkan States should provide scope for development as soon as favourable circumstances are present. The development of these countries is considerably behind that of Central Europe, and their lack of capital has been a serious obstacle to progress...

"Given a period of stability in the future in which confidence can be restored, their natural resources may be developed and their potentialities once more attract attention. With a population which is rapidly expanding, an increase in purchasing power would create new markets... Unable to export sufficient goods to purchase the industrial goods they require, and harassed by exchange difficulties, they tend more and more to regard industrialization as a possible solution to some of their economic difficulties. Though still on a comparatively small scale this movement is progressing rapidly and may have far-reaching effects on foreign trade relationships.

"But if this process is to be carried out on a large scale, capital is required, and it remains to be seen from where it is to be obtained. The experience of foreign creditors, faced with moratoria and defaults, has been unhappy, nor has the record of the Governments or their financial administration always been above criticism. In the circumstances the resumption of foreign lending, if indeed it is resumed, is likely to be delayed.

"It is in this connection that the progress of the German policy of clearing and compensation agreements at present in process of evolution has a marked significance. During the past two years Germany has succeeded not only in taking payment in primary products for the merchandize debts owed to her, but also in running up large bills for very considerable amounts in Bulgaria, Roumania, Yugoslavia, and Greece. As under the clearing agreements these accounts can be settled only in goods, the creditors are forced to choose between foregoing payment indefinitely with the risk of the value of the Reichsmark being changed to their disadvantage, and increasing their imports from Germany. In their present financial difficulties they appear to have no choice but to adopt the latter alternative. As the goods taken in settlement are largely capital goods the process of industrialization is thus being carried a stage farther. France, Italy, the United States, and particularly Great Britain have considerable investments in the countries concerned, the future of which may well be affected by these new economic developments.

"The present review, which aims at furnishing the essential background to these developments, is divided into two main parts, the first dealing with the structure and development of the various States up to the incidence of the crisis in 1931, the second describing the effects of that crisis upon their economy and their attempt to combat its repercussions. As far as possible the examination has been taken down to the end of 1935, subject to one important qualification. The imposition of sanctions upon Italy in October and November 1935 introduced a new factor the ultimate effects of which cannot yet be fully estimated. This must be borne in mind in forming any judgment based on the facts and figures set out in the following pages." - Preface.

Murchie, R. W., Allen, William, and Booth, J. F. Agricultural progress on the
     prairie frontier. 344PP. Toronto, The Macmillan company of Canada
     limited, 1936. (Canadian frontiers of settlement, ed. by W. A. Mackintosh
     and W. L. G. Joerg. v.5)   282.2 M21 v.5
     "Since the inception of this study of the development of the pioneer
regions of the world in 1927, many important changes have taken place in
the economic world. In so far as these changes have affected the agricultural industry they bear witness to the prophetic insight of the
sponsors of the project, chief among whom was Dr. Isaiah Bowman...
     "Dr. Bowman's proposal called for the development of a 'science of
settlement' by an examination of the 'pioneering process' in the regions
of recent or progressive settlement.
     "The idea of directing or controlling settlement in new areas had
few friends but scientific planning of land utilization in older areas
had already been experimented with, and governments were beginning to
question the wisdom of subsidized immigration. By the close of 1933,
planning of agricultural development and control of agricultural production had many friends, and numerous schemes had been proposed ranging from 'national quotas' to 'district allotments'.
     "The need of a science of settlement no longer requires argument but
there remain the questions 'How much control?' and 'On what principles?'
     "The series of which this volume is the fifth is an attempt to pro-
vide partial answers to such questions. The physical and the economic
factors, the social and historical aspects are reviewed in the attempt to
analyse the successes and the failures of schemes and policies both public
and private.
     "The present volume must therefore be more limited in scope than its
title would suggest for only brief reference need be made to phases of
the study which have been fully dealt with in other volumes. It deals
not with all the factors in agricultural development but only with a few
of the more technical phases. It presents a rapid summary of the development of western agriculture leading up to the present utilization of agricultural land. It deals with the changes, which have been taking place in
the capitalization of the industry, in order to show the difference between
pioneering of the past and pioneering of the present. It attempts to show
the import of the changes taking place in land tenure, and the economic
and social aspects of the trend from farm operation by land owners to tenant operation. It deals with some of the changes in the techniques of
production and especially with the development of mechanized farming. It
presents a series of 'snap-shot' pictures of the financial condition of
several hundred farmers in various areas of the Prairie Provinces."
     Appendix A. Trends in farm power and their influence on agricultural
development; and Appendix B. Efficiency of power units under actual farm
conditions.

Canada - Economic Problems of the Prairie Provinces

Mackintosh, W. A. Clark, A. R., Elliott, G. A., and Swanson, W. W. Economic
problems of the Prairie provinces. 308pp. Toronto, The Macmillan
company of Canada limited, 1935. (Canadian frontiers of settlement, ed.
by W. A. Mackintosh and W. L. G. Joerg. vol. 4) 282.2 M21 v.4
"Though attention has necessarily been given to the immediate problems
of the present (1934) depression, the chief concern has been with problems
which at all times are inherent in the pioneer economy." - Preface.
The chapter headings follow: Economic trends; Economic fluctuations:
Acquiring a transportation system; Problems of marketing; Provincial
finances, with special reference to Alberta; The distribution of financial burdens and services in Alberta; Rural local government and taxation
in Saskatchewan; Local taxation and expenditure in Saskatchewan; Taxation in representative rural municipalities of Saskatchewan; Financial
problems of the depression in rural Saskatchewan; The weight of rural
taxation in Saskatchewan; and Farm credit.
Appendix A. Statistics relating to the Prairie Provinces. Appendix B.
Problems of a retrograde area in Alberta. Appendix C. Taxation in pioneer
areas of Manitoba.

Canada - Land Settlement in Eastern Provinces

Lower, A. R. M. Settlement and the forest frontier in eastern Canada, by
A. R. M. Lower... Settlement and the mining frontier, by Harold A. Innis.
424pp. Toronto, The Macmillan company of Canada limited, 1936. (Canadian
frontiers of settlement, ed. by W. A. Mackintosh and W. L. G. Joerg. v.9)
282.2 M21 v.9
"The studies on which this series, Canadian Frontiers of Settlement,
is based, have been directed almost entirely toward settlement in the
prairie region. Those studies would, however, be incomplete, were no
attention given to the sharply contrasting problems of settlement in the
forest and mining regions. Such settlement is likely to be temporary
and leave in its wake those serious social and economic problems associated
with shrinking incomes, declining population, and abandoned homes, unless
during the period of exploitation there have been built up subsidiary industries, capable ultimately of independent existence. The exploiting industries build up subsidiary developments not only in their immediate
neighbourhood but also throughout the whole country. The interrelations
of mining and lumbering, on the one hand, and agricultural, manufacturing,
transportation, and power industries, on the other, are many and important.
"In the two studies contained in this volume Professors Lower and Innis
analyse the historical developments of the forest and mining industries and
in particular their relations to other industries. No attempt is made to
tell the full story of mining and lumbering in Canada, but the significant
problems of settlement as they have emerged in 'leading cases' on the forest and mining frontiers are analysed. Among Canadian frontiers of settlement those of the mines and the forests have, in the past decade, been
among the most important and they are likely to be equally important in the
future." - Foreword.

China - Trade and Commerce

Watson, Ernest. The principal articles of Chinese commerce (import and
    export); with a description of the origin, appearance, characteristics,
    and general properties of each commodity; an account of the methods
    of preparation or manufacture; together with various tests, etc.,
    by means of which the different products may be readily identified.
    2d ed. 630pp. Shanghai, Statistical department of the Inspectorate
    general of customs, 1930. (China. Inspectorate general of customs.
    The maritime customs. II. - Special series: no. 38) 286 W33 Ed.2
        Bibliography, pp. viii-ix.
        Contains sections devoted to Fibers; Oils, fats and waxes; Gums and
    resins; Dyes, colors, pigments, paints and tans.

Consumer Primer

Landis, B. Y. A primer for consumers. 2d ed. 32PP. New York, Associa-
    tion press, 1936. 280.2 L23P Ed.2
        Bibliography, pp. 29-32.
        A popular primer for the consumer telling what has been done to pro-
    tect and guide him, what Federal government agencies do, what consumers'
    cooperatives offer him, and what political action is needed if his in-
    terests are to be advanced, and giving a list of organizations that help
    consumers and a list of pamphlets and periodicals providing information
    of interest to the consumer.

Cooperation

American institute of cooperation, Urbana, Ill., 1936. American cooperation,
    1936; a collection of papers and discussions comprising the twelfth sum-
    mer session of the American institute of cooperation at the University
    of Illinois, June 15-19, 1936. 750pp. Washington, D. C., American in-
    stitute of cooperation [1936] 280.29 Am3A
        Partial contents: The philosophy of cooperation, by J. R. Barton;
    Cooperative marketing of cotton, by N. C. Williamson; Producer-consumer
    cooperative relationships, by Murray D. Lincoln, M. J. Briggs, Quentin
    Reynolds; Legally accepted principles of cooperation, by Donald Kirk-
    patrick; Legal fundamentals of cooperation, by Karl D. Loos; Essentials
    of management and control, by C. C. Teague; Preventive medicine for
    cooperatives, by F. W. Peck; The cooperative as a farm implement, by
    Ralph Allen; Developments and problems in the cooperative marketing of
    dairy products, by Charles W. Holman; Changes in city market outlets for
    fluid milk, by R. W. Bartlett, Changes in procurement from the local
    creameries, by W. A. Gordon; Extent to which cooperative creameries are
    truly cooperative, by T. G. Stitts; Economic location of creameries, by
    F. A. Gougler; Competition among cooperative creameries, by Frank Robotka;
    Finding manufacturing outlets for the fluid milk market, by H. R. Leonard;
    Finding manufacturing outlets for fluid milk markets, by A. H. Heggen;
    Producer competition in the same milk shed, by John P. Case; Solving pro-
    ducer competition in the same milk shed, by Wesley H. Bronson; Standardiz-

ing and grading for more efficient merchandizing, by Roy C. Potts; Cooperation between creamery cooperatives, by Oscar A. Swank; The operations of
Iowa state brand creameries, by R. O. Storvick; Classified price plans with
and without base set-ups, by Walter Hunnicut; Market, association, and individual dealer pools, by Jesse M. Huston; Advantages and disadvantages
of full supply contracts with distributors, by B. B. Derrick; Services
rendered local member creameries by Illinois producers creameries, by J. B.
Countiss; The history and present program of the Wisconsin Cheese Fedora-
tion, by F. W. Huntzicker; Building better membership understanding, by
H. W. Mainland; Milk marketing from a bargaining association viewpoint, by
F. T. Flynn; Building better membership understanding, by E. W. Tiedeman;
Developments and problems in livestock marketing, by Charles A. Ewing;
Membership and personnel problems of livestock cooperatives, by J. W. Jones;
Field service for cooperatives, by Ray E. Miller; County committees and
their relation to marketing agencies, by Roy Burrus; Membership relations
in livestock cooperatives, by V. Vaniman; Operation and financing of motor
trucks by cooperatives, by A. F. Potter; Transportation problems in relation to livestock, by L. J. Quasey; Factors affecting livestock price levels, by J. S. Campbell; Relations of meat prices to livestock prices from
farm to market, by D. L. Swanson; The basic problems affecting livestock
prices, by R. C. Ashby; The composite factors in supply and demand, by
C. R. Henderson; The variable influences affecting price levels, by John E.
Brown; Centralized marketing of livestock, by D. O. Gettinger; Cooperative
purchasing of feeder cattle and lambs, by C. B. Denman; Purchasing of feeder
cattle and lambs, by H. P. Rusk; Financing feeder purchases, by Scott Meiks;
Contract feeding of lambs and cattle, by C. G. Randell; Direct movement of
feeder livestock through cooperatives, by I. H. Jacob; Holding temperatures
and interior egg quality, by E. M. Funk; Egg auctions - A demonstration of
auction selling, by R. B. Treat; Chain store buying of eggs, by D. W.
Ferneau; Recent development in broiler production, by L. C. Todd, C. P.
Rudd; Buying live poultry by grade, by J. W. Evans; Problems in marketing
dressed poultry, by W. T. S. White; Developments and problems in grain
marketing, by M. W. Thatcher; Commodities adapted to elevator distribution, by V. M. Rucker; Establishing a supply service for farmer elevators,
by Harold Hedges; Transportation problems relating to grain, by Clyde M.
Reed; Long-time effects of trucking on farmers' elevators, by M. R.
Miller; Adjustments in terminal operations, by H. E. Witham; Financing
and auditing service, by D. M. Hardy; Standards for successful elevator
operations, by Roy M. Green; Reorganizing the local farmer-elevator,
by Harrison Fahrnkopf; The Canadian and world wheat situations, by C. W.
Peterson; Developments and problems in the marketing of fruits and vegetables, by N. L. Allen; Membership cooperation in marketing fresh fruits,
by Cornelius Bus; Transportation problems in relation to fruits and vegetables, by M. P. Rasmussen; Motor truck transportation, by Charles W.
Hauck; Motor truck transportation in relation to Michigan cooperatives,
by G. N. Motts; Grading and packing of fruits and vegetables, by Frederick
V. Waugh; The relation of the spray residue problem to cooperative marketing, by J. W. Lloyd; Financing a cooperative apple washing and packing
unit, by J. E. Hayes; Relation of the spray residue problem to cooperative marketing, by W. A. Ruth; Competition between cooperatives - due
to overlapping of service in territory, by M. J. Briggs; Yardsticks of

efficiency for cooperative purchasing associations, by Joseph G. Knapp;
Methods of measuring success of cooperative business organizations, by
Ralph Ingerson; Financing cooperative purchasing associations, by S. D.
Sanders; Responsibilities and duties of directors and managers of cooperatives, by F. W. Peck; Effective financing of cooperatives, by S. D.
Sanders; Cooperative production credit, by S. M. Garwood; Cooperative
credit responsibility, by Albert S. Goss; The first twenty years of
cooperative farm mortgage credit, by Ernest Rice; Development of coopera-
tive features in the strengthening of the land bank system, by O. J. Lloyd;
Responsibilities of boards of directors of production credit associations,
by W. P. Oliver; European outlets for agricultural products, by Chester
C. Davis; Major economic trends in world agriculture, by C. W. Peterson;
The future of transportation in the United States, by J. B. Eastman;
Future of agricultural freight rates in the United States, by Donald Conn;
Motor truck legislation, by G. W. Baxter; The growing importance of in-
land waterways, by J. O. McClintock; The trade policy of the United States,
by L. R. Edminster; How the foreign trade agreements affect dairy farmers,
by Charles W. Holman; International trade policies and the farmer, by
Charles A. Ewing; Foreign trade policies in their relation to cotton, by
N. C. Williamson; Agriculture and industry in foreign trade relations,
by C. E. Huff; The contribution of the 1936 AAA programs to future
national farm policy, by H. R. Tolley; The 1936 agricultural conservation
program in the north central region, by G. B. Thorne; The long-time significance of a soil conservation program to livestock producers, by A. G.
Black; Illinois production trends in relation to the soil conservation
program, by H. C. M. Case; Agricultural adjustment in relation to grain
and dairy production, by O. B. Jesness; Training of personnel for the cooperative field, by L. J. Norton; and Needed research in cooperation, by
O. B. Jesness.

Cooperation, Agricultural - Wales

Conference on development of agricultural co-operative business, Aberystwyth,
    1936.   Report... June 19th, 1936.   35pp., mimeogr. Aberystwyth,
    Department of agricultural economics, University college, 1936.
    280.29 C763
        Partial contents: The present position of the agricultural co-operative
    movement in Wales, by H. E. Roberts, Welsh Agricultural Organization
    Society; The condition of the livestock industry in Wales and considera-
    tion of remedies by A. W. Ashby, Chief, Department of Agricultural Eco-
    nomics, University College of Wales.

Cooperation - Sweden

Kooperativa förbundet.   Swedish cooperative wholesale society's architects'
    office, 1925-1935.   148pp. [Stockholm, Kooperativa förbundets bokförlag,
    1935]   280.29 K83S
        Contains a good concise statement about cooperation in Sweden, with
    some statistics showing among other items the percentage distribution of
    the "numbers" among different trades and occupations in the year 1934.   It

is interesting to note that 14.8% were farmers and 4.3% farm laborers. The volume is well illustrated - showing both interior and exterior of various types of shops, eating places, dwelling houses, apartments, factories, furniture, etc.

Sweden. Socialstyrelsen. Kooperativ verksamhet i Sverige... 1933. 57pp. Stockholm, 1935. (Sveriges officiella statistik. Socialstatistik) 280.29 S73
    Table of contents and resumé also in French.

Cotton

Joint committee of cotton trade organisations. Economic and statistical dept. The changing conditions of world trade in cotton and rayon goods. IV. Collective regulation in the world's cotton industries. 32pp. Manchester, Economic and statistical department, Joint committee of cotton trade organisations [1936]   304 J662
    "The cotton industries of the world, taken together, suffered less from the depression of 1929-32 than most manufacturing industries. The world's consumption of raw cotton, and therefore the production of cotton yarn, declined between the years 1928-29 - immediately before the depression - and 1931-32 - the worst season of the slump - by little more than 11 per cent... though the League of Nations index of world manufacturing activity was 30 per cent less in 1932 than in 1929. With the general revival of economic activity which began towards the end of 1932, cotton consumption increased again, and by 1934-35 had almost returned to the level of 1928-29. During the first half of the season 1935-36 (the six months ending January 31, 1936) world cotton consumption was not only about 5 per cent above the corresponding period of 1928-29, but was greater than in any previous half-year. These figures suggest that the demand for cotton goods in the world as a whole has now regained its normal level. At the same time the capacity of the world's cotton industries, measured by the number of spindles in place, has continuously declined. During the depression, between 1929 and 1932, the estimated total number of spindles in the world fell from 165 millions to 162 millions. During the recovery period between 1932 and 1936, the rate of decline was even greater, and in January, 1936, the estimated world total was 153 million spindles.
    "It is, of course, recognised that the capacity to produce cotton yarn is governed not only by the number of spindles in existence but also by the type of spindles used, by their technical efficiency, by the efficiency of the workers engaged, by the number of hours in the working week, and by the quality of yarn to be spun, among many other factors. But even when all these have been taken into account, there is reason to believe that the world's productive capacity is now more nearly adjusted to the demand for cotton goods at present prices than before the depression.
    "These world totals, however, conceal the great changes that have taken place in the fortunes of individual industries."

- 884 -

Depressions and Deficits

Smith, D. T. Deficits and depressions. 264pp. New York, J. Wiley & sons,
    inc.; London, Chapman & Hall, limited, 1936. 284 Sm52
        Bibliography, pp. 255-259.
        "The purpose of this book is to investigate the relations between
Treasury financing and the economic system, with particular reference to
the condition of the national budget. We have all heard, with increasing
frequency, that the monetary system is, at least in part, responsible
for the disruptions that occur in our economic structure, and that a proper
control of money and of credit would do much to prevent our recurring
booms and depressions. Some maintain that all difficulties are to be
traced to the inflation or deflation of bank credit, or to hoarding, or
to changes in the customary uses of all kinds of money. Whether such
factors are the only disturbing elements to be found is a matter of current dispute among economists - a dispute which may continue for some time
into the future. But we can agree that monetary maladjustments may at least
be a contributing factor in accentuating movements that have started for
other reasons. And perhaps many economic disturbances may be accounted
for in the first instance by credit creation and contraction, and time-lags
in spending, which throw out of balance the production of goods and their
absorption by purchase. This book is intended to provide a survey of the
government's financial activities as a part of this broader problem, to
determine wherein the Treasury's operations may themselves be a cause of
disturbance in the economic system, and in what respects they may be designed to offset or alleviate disturbances which arise outside the sphere
of the Treasury's own transactions." - Introductory.

Economic Foreign Policy - Dutch East Indies

Neytzell de Vilde, A., Moll, J. T., and Gooszen, A. J. The Netherlands
    Indies during the depression; a brief economic survey... National
    council for the Netherlands and the Netherlands Indies of the Insti-
    tute of Pacific relations. 94pp. Amsterdam, J. M. Meulenhoff, 1936.
    280.1994 N49
        "The facts of the situation are such that, for any rise of the pop-
ulation above the level of a simple, self-contained agricultural community, the Netherlands Indies can procure the means only by selling
its products to the outside world, and is, therefore, to a very great
extent dependent upon the willingness and capacity of the world at
large to buy and pay for these products.
        "There is no running away from these facts; they must be coped with.
Moreover, we must accept the hard truth that the majority of recent
phenomena tend to prove that their character is not that of a 'crisis',
from which a quick recovery seems always possible; many of the changes
wrought by the depression have come to stay and must be dealt with accordingly, which is an entirely different proposition." - Introduction.
        "When in 1932 the Government introduced its first attempt at an
'Economic Plan', it was severely criticized in the 'Volksraad' or
People's Council - which is the Netherlands Indies' legislature - for
not doing more in the way of direct protection of those economic in-

terests which had received the first blows in the depression contest.
Many members desired the Government to give its economic policy a wider
basis. When, however, the Government continued to develop the new ideas,
observing on the whole the principles indicated in the beginning, and
when to this end one bill after another was introduced during the following years in order to obtain the necessary powers of enforcement, the
legislature began to voice more and more its concern at the prospect of
so much Government interference in spheres where the country was not accustomed to official activity. This concern is reflected in the rigid
time limits which were fixed to the powers conferred upon the Government
for the application of these enactments. The system requires, naturally,
a certain degree of unity and coherence in order to make it 'hole proof'.
Both the Government and the 'Volksraad' are conscientiously treating each
separate item in the economic structure which is deemed to require regulation in such a way as to leave no doubt whatever concerning their determination to see the country through. But all the same, time limits
are strictly adhered to and private initiative is given the greatest
scope which is considered compatible with the nearest objective that
must be gained.

"No better proof than this could be given of the reluctance with which
the country as a whole deviated from its time-honoured policy of free trade,
and of its sincere and general hope that the present forced suspension of
this policy may eventually prove to have been of a temporary character.

"For the Netherlands Indies, as a country, this is more than a hope.
It is an expectation which is based on the general conviction rooted and
alive in all the thinking sections of the community there and in the
mother country, that the structure of the country is fundamentally
sound. It is a productive territory. Its equipment from the point of
view of both government and economy is adequate, not to say excellent.
It produces goods which, in the long run, the outside world cannot
dispense with. The difficulties which at present a world wide depression has forced upon the Netherlands Indies and, consequently, on the
mother country, require a great deal of adaptation. This adaptation
is painful because it tends towards a lower level of prosperity than
what the country has been accustomed to in the preceding period of its
history. But all levels of prosperity are relative, fundamentally;
and both Holland and the Netherlands Indies are strongly convinced
that the level which the rising generation has in front of it for its
future, shall not lie 'below par'. Like in any community, it is the
process of adaptation that tells on the present generation. Once finished, the policy of adaptation which at the present moment appears to
require the concentrated energy of every section of the community,
will have mobilized all mental and material powers of resistance in
the country. The progress of this policy augurs well for the possibilities of recovery which, however, remain dependent on the developments in the outside world, generally, and in the Pacific, specially."-
Conclusion.

Economic Foreign Policy - Gt. Britain

Richardson, J. H. British economic foreign policy. 250pp. London, G. Allen
& Unwin ltd. [1936]   280.171 R39
   One chapter is devoted to Agricultural policy. Other chapters discuss
monetary, financial, commercial, trade and labor policies.

Economic Organization - Syria

Himadeh, Sa'id Beymed, ed.   Economic organization of Syria. 466pp. Beirut,
   Printed at the American press, 1936. (American university of Beirut. Pub-
   lications of arts and sciences. Social science series no. 10) 280.185 H57
   Bibliography, pp. 439-445.
   Chapter III. Land Tenure, by Albert Khuri, pp. 51-69; Chapter IV. Ag-
riculture, by Albert Khuri, pp. 73-115
   Review in American Economic Review v. 26, no. 3, pp. 510-511.
Sept. 1936.

Economics

Brown, E. H. P. The framework of the pricing system. 221pp. London, Chapman
& Hall, ltd. [1936]   280 B813
   "The intention of this work... is to take the barest framework of the
pricing system, and to expound it so that the student may take hold of
propositions stated in the exactness of abstraction, may see the place of
pure theory in the whole of economic study, and may be guided in the paths
of quantitative thought." - Introduction.

Farm Credit

Qureshi, A. I. Agricultural credit, being a study of recent developments
   in agricultural credit administration in the United States of America...
   With an introduction by Joseph Johnston.   190pp.   London, Sir I. Pitman
   & sons, ltd., 1936.   284.2 Q6A
   Bibliography, pp. 181-184.
   Joseph Johnston, Fellow and Tutor of Trinity College, Dublin has
written the introduction to this volume. From it the extracts which
follow have been taken:
   "At first sight it might appear that this book is of interest to
only a limited number of specialists, that is, to the class of prac-
tising agricultural economists and administrators... As a class the
latter may be said to have learnt all they can from the pundits of
economic theory, and it has not helped them very much in their daily
tasks...
   "The reader, who is looking for light from the West on the problems
of European agriculture, will need to be on his guard against too ready
an application of American ideas and institutions to the conditions of
his own country. The institutional problem of agricultural credit in the
U. S. A. is largely governed by the fact that the ordinary commercial
banks, though numerous, do not reach down and give adequate banking service to outlying rural communities in that vast country. So far as
short-term credit is concerned the National State found it necessary

to supply the deficiencies, as well as remedy the faults, of ordinary
commercial banking enterprise. In a country like Great Britain and
Ireland, where a few powerful banks are widely represented by branches
in rural as well as urban areas, the institutional setting of the problem
is entirely different.

"On the other hand, where long-term credit is concerned, it is possible
that American enterprise and achievements may be more fruitfully studied.
Nearly 75 per cent. of the indebtedness of American farmers is long-term
indebtedness. In any progressive country, as agricultural production
becomes more mechanized, more intensive, and more continuous, the need
for the command of capital for long-term periods must become proportion-
ately greater. The legal ownership of farms by individual farmers imposes a heavy handicap on those who seek to enter on an agricultural
career. The old landlord-tenant system of Ireland was open to many
objections, but at all events it provided a ladder by which the landless
man might ascend to large-scale agricultural enterprise, with the minimum of capital commitment at each stage of his ascent. One unsatisfactory consequence of the land legislation, by which the Irish tenant
farmer is in process of becoming an occupying owner, is that it tends
to fix a great gulf between landless men and landowners. On the other
hand, the gulf existed in some degree before, because Irish landlords,
as a class, did not provide the fixed assets of agriculture, and equity
required that the 'Ulster tenant right custom' should be recognized by
law, and the outgoing tenant be allowed freely to sell his interest
in his holding. The English landlord-tenant system went a long way towards the solution of the long-term credit problem in English agriculture,
but its efficiency in this respect has been undermined in consequence
of the high level of post-war taxation on agricultural real estate values.
Such a system cannot be extemporized in countries where it does not
exist. The more recent experience of the federal land banks in the
United States would suggest that in one way or another the State must
cushion the shocks occasioned by the recent collapse of agricultural
real estate values, and that, in America and elsewhere, the State may
find itself creating institutions the object of which is to fulfil some
of the functions of the English landlord class.

"Certain general questions suggest themselves to a thoughtful reader
who is interested in the phenomena of the business cycle. Does the no-
toriously weak credit and capital position of the farming industry in
most countries favour weak selling, more so in certain phases of the
cycle than in others? Does this tend to produce disordered relations
between agricultural and non-agricultural prices, and is this a major
cause of business depression? If the answer to all these questions is
in the affirmative, then the well-known tendency of credit and capital
to flow more readily into commerce and industry than into agriculture
is a permanent cause of instability in the business economy, and students of agricultural credit problems are in fact seeking a remedy for
a disorder which economists in general cannot afford to ignore.

"The hire-purchase credit afforded by producers of agricultural machines, who were concerned only to sell the largest possible number, was
an important factor in the expansion of certain types of agricultural

production in the post-War years in many overseas countries. Whatever view may be taken of the part played by 'unbalanced' agricultural production in the great depression, it cannot be denied that such hire-purchase credit is an anarchical element in the credit structure as a whole, which may defeat an otherwise well-conceived national credit policy, and that agriculture may suffer from excess as well as deficiency of credit.

"It also seems clear that credit policy for agriculture cannot safely be divorced from national commercial policy, or the latter from national financial policies which effect international relations. The fundamental defect of American agricultural credit policy in the post-War years was that it was an effort to finance the continued production of a volume of agricultural goods which, owing to various causes, could not possibly achieve complete consumption in markets at home and abroad. If America had pursued a commercial policy less exclusive of European industrial products in the years following 1928, it is possible that we should have heard less of the 'uneconomic surpluses' of American wheat and cotton in the years following 1930.

"This raises an interesting question of pure economic theory. What is the ultimate real, as distinct from the temporary financial, basis of credit, anyhow, for agricultural or any other kind of economic production? One might summarize part of the answer by saying that the ultimate real basis of credit is the belief that what one proposes to produce will ultimately be bought and paid for out of money income by consumers at a price which covers all the intermediate costs that have meanwhile been hopefully incurred. Thus production credit in the long run depends on economic consumption at home or abroad, and can have no other foundation. If that be so, to cut the arteries of international commerce is to destroy the basis of credit for export industries. Thus the real foundation of agricultural credit in the U.S.A., or any other agricultural surplus exporting country, is provided by domestic consumers of foreign imported goods. Thus, too, the destroyers of agricultural credit in America and elsewhere are the industrial interests which exclude foreign imported goods.

"These are the major impressions derived by the present writer from excursions with Dr. Qureshi into the jungle of American agricultural credit problems and institutions. The jungle is now becoming a well-kept public park under the fostering management of President Roosevelt's recently established Farm Credit Administration. Dr. Qureshi has hacked clear paths through the historical background of this Administration. Thanks to him it is now more accessible than before, but in the nature of the case it must always remain something of a jungle. There are complexities of human affairs whose essential obscurity can be illuminated only by the light that makes darkness visible.

"Now that the institutional machinery of agricultural credit has attained a well-balanced completeness in the U. S. A. there still remain certain fundamental problems which are problems not only for the men who operate the machine. Again I ask, what is the ultimate real basis of agricultural credit anyhow? The pioneers of agricultural credit in America and elsewhere can hardly be blamed for giving a wrong answer to this question, and for building their agricultural credit policies on the shifting sands of incompatible national commercial policies. It is a question primarily for the financial expert or the economic theorist. Unfortunately, the men of theory are by no means agreed about the answer to it, and in the meanwhile the men of action must be excused if they ignore the welfare of the schools, and approach their tasks in the light of common sense. Perhaps the theoretical question will eventually achieve solution by the method of solviture ambulando. The foregoing hint about the possible reactions of national commercial and financial policies on the basis of agricultural credit is all that an academic economist may dare to suggest to the men of action in this field of economic statesmanship."

Fibers, Industrial

Gt. Brit. Imperial economic committee. Intelligence branch. Industrial fibres. A summary of figures of production, trade and consumption relating to cotton, wool, silk, flex, jute, hemp and rayon. 112pp. London, H. M. Stationery off., 1936. (Gt. Brit. Imperial economic committee. Intelligence branch [I.E.C./C. 4]) 280.39 G794C no.4.
     The fibers studied are cotton, wool, silk, flax, jute, hemp, and rayon. The appendix discusses certain measures regulating production, distribution and consumption of fibers in the U. S., U. S. S. R., Brazil, Baltic States, Japan, Germany, France, and Italy.

Foreign Trade Agreements

Popper, D. H. The Hull trade program... pp. [190]-200. New York, 1936. (Foreign policy association. Foreign policy reports, v. 12, no. 15, October 15, 1936) 280.9 F76R v.12, no. 15
     After presenting a statistical table entitled "Effects of Reciprocal Trade Agreements, January - June 1936" the author writes in part as follows:
     "If any conclusion may be drawn from the table, it is that trade agreements appear to be accomplishing their purpose: the lowering of carriers so as to permit freer response to the normal economic forces which give rise to commerce. Because of the exigencies of the United States' domestic and international economic position, greater pressures have been set up for an increase in imports than for higher exports. Trade with the agreement countries as a whole has increased in both directions. Imports from these states, however, have shown far greater relative response to current conditions than imports from all our suppliers taken as a unit. Should the general trend of American foreign trade be reversed, a corresponding spurt in exports to agreement countries might be anticipated. In any event the increase in total trade with the agreement countries is the important factor...
     "It is hardly necessary to state that the trade agreements program has not yet brought about profound economic changes in American life. By its very nature tariff bargaining must be a slow, gradual process, especially in a democratic state. Yet accomplishments under the program have not been inconsiderable. It is estimated that the United States has given assurances that it will retain on the free list roughly one-

quarter of its non-dutiable imports, while it has reduced rates on one-fifth or more of its dutiable imports. Approximately one-sixth of all American exports have received concessions. For the present, therefore, a term has been put to the steady whittling down of the free list and the general upward trend of duties in American post-war tariff and revenue acts.

"Concessions and assurances gained for American enterprise extend over the whole broad range of our typical exports. A start has obviously been made in breaching barriers raised against American agricultural products. The outlook for shipment of fruits and vegetables abroad would appear to be better than that for basic foods such as grain, home production of which is deemed essential for self-sufficiency in Europe. While a careful balance between gains to American agriculture and industry has apparently been sought, a survey of the agreements indicates that it will probably be easier to secure additional foreign markets for finished articles such as machinery and automobiles than for most farm products.

"Reductions and assurances with regard to American imports also cover a large number of commodities. Nevertheless, changes in tariffs have been made with such caution and technical skill that it appears no efficient industry has been substantially injured. The Administration, limited by law to a 50 percent cut, has in many instances left sizeable protective margins...

"The conclusion is inescapable that the effect of the Hull program on consumers and efficient producers is salutary. The former benefit by lower prices and a higher standard of life; the latter gain expanded markets. The process of readjustment, to be sure, is only beginning. Nevertheless the gradual removal of tariff barriers, often a cloak for monopoly, cannot logically be resisted by those who decry government intervention in business."

Foreign Trade - Clearing Agreements

League of nations. Enquiry into clearing agreements. 154pp. Geneva, 1935.
(Series of League of nations. Publications. II. Economic and financial.
1935. II. B.6)   280.9 L47P 1935. II. B.6
    "C. 153. M. 83. 1935. II. B."
    "(a) In conclusion, while it recognises that the clearing system may, in certain cases, have helped to prevent a still more serious collapse of trade that might otherwise have occurred as the result of the general introduction of control of foreign exchange transactions, the Committee recommends that the clearing system should not be extended.
    "(b) It further considers, like most of the Governments consulted, that this system can only be regarded as an expedient or makeshift involving a number of drawbacks, and that it should therefore be abolished as soon as possible.
    "(c) The best, though not the only, solution would be the complete abolition of exchange control facilitated by measures designed at once to promote permanent arrangements in regard to financial debts and a less restrictive commercial policy which would afford minimum guarantees for export. Should such complete abolition be impossible, commercial transactions should at any rate be freed from the obstacles placed in

their way by exchange control.

"(d) Pending these measures of recovery, the Committee considers that all proposals and all action designed to counteract, directly or indirectly, the grave drawbacks to international commercial relations resulting from the application of an artificial exchange rate in order to relieve the situation of the debtor country should be encouraged.

"(e) All measures reducing import restrictions and opening the way to the export of increasing quantities of goods from debtor States should also be encouraged - even in the interest of creditor countries with a sound currency - first in order to ensure the payment for their exports and secondly in order to promote general recovery.

"(f) Measures designed to leave the conditions - including exchange conditions - under which imports and exports are effected to the initiative of the parties concerned should also be encouraged.

"(g) The more definite this tendency towards a return to normality becomes, the nearer we shall get to a situation in which it will be possible to replace clearing agreements by less vexatious arrangements, such as transfer and payment agreements, and finally to abolish them."

Annex I. Structure, operation and effects of clearing agreements; Annex II. Replies of governments to the questionnaire on clearing agreements; Annex III. Countries with clearing agreements.

Geography - Man and His Environment

White, C. L., and Renner, G. T.   Geography; an introduction to human ecology. 790pp. New York, London, D. Appleton-Century company, incorporated [1936] (Century earth science series. K. F. Mather, ed.)   278 W582

Dr. Kirtley F. Mather, general editor of The Century Earth Science series to which this volume belongs, writes in part as follows in the preface:

"It is increasingly recognized that the problems which press so relentlessly upon mankind to-day are fundamentally a result of the necessity for making satisfactory adjustment between human behavior and the conditions imposed by the environment within which man must live. There is of course the age-old paradox of the individual in society - a paradox which becomes ever more poignant as the number of individuals increases toward the maximum which can be supported by the limited resources of the earth and as the social unit expands until it includes all men everywhere. But even that paradox is a phase of adjustment between the creature, man, and the environment, the earth. No wonder that the science of geography is acquiring new vitality and that upon it the modern educator is looking with increased interest and great concern.

"When geography is considered as the study of the relationships between man and his natural environment, the character of the science is completely changed. No longer is it a static, lifeless form; now it may function as a dynamic and constructive power. It opens many a door for analysis, the essential note in scientific research; it provides many a platform for synthesis, a necessary element in modern education. To gain accurate concepts and valid generalizations concerning the significant relationships between man and environment is above all to fit oneself for a place of leadership in the intellectual world. Without such understanding one is doomed to drift like a rudderless boat in a storm-tossed sea." -

<u>Grain Trade - Canada</u>

Canada. Dominion bureau of statistics. Agricultural branch. Report on the
grain trade of Canada for the crop year ended July 31 and to the close
of navigation, 1935. 202pp. Ottawa, J. O. Patenaude, printer to the
King's Most Excellent Majesty, 1936. 59.9 C164
"Statistics are presented showing in detail the various channels
and markets through which the grain passes from the farm to its final
destination. Comparative data are included for countries other than
Canada bringing the grain and cereal resources and trade of the world
into review.
"The first part of the report deals with the domestic movement of
grain - the production, inspection and handlings at country, interior
terminal, public, semi-public and private terminals, also mill elevators
in the Western Inspection division (comprising Fort William and Port
Arthur and all territory west thereof) and at Eastern elevators. Handlings of United States grain and foreign grain in the Eastern elevators
and of Canadian grain in the United States are covered. Records of
prices at representative markets and insurance charges are also included."-
Introductory Statement.

<u>International Trade</u>

Haberler, Gottfried von. The theory of international trade with its applications to commercial policy... Translated from the German by Alfred Stonier
and Frederic Benham. 408pp. London, Edinburgh [etc.] W. Hodge & company,
limited, 1936. 286 H112
"In his preface to the English edition the author states that he is
very conscious of the various shortcomings of this book as published in
German two years ago. Nevertheless, he has agreed to the publication of
an English translation without substantial changes from the German original,
in the hope that even in the present form it will be of some use.
"Apart from improvements in detail and statistical researches with a
view to verifying and applying to concrete cases the general theoretical
statements, it seems to the author that the theory of international trade,
as outlined in this volume, requires further development in two main directions. The theory of imperfect competition and the theory of short-run
oscillation (business cycle theory) must be applied to the problems of
international trade. It will soon be possible to do this in a systematic
way, since much progress has been made in both fields in recent years.
"With regard to the first of these questions, states the author, there
is the literature which centres around the two outstanding books, Monopolistic Competition, by Professor E. Chamberlin, and Imperfect Competition,
by Mrs. Joan Robinson. In the second field where further development is
required, it is not so easy to refer to a body of accepted theory. But
it seems that a certain measure of agreement as to the nature of the cumulative processes of general economic expansion and contraction is gradually
beginning to emerge. By starting or reversing, accelerating or retarding
these cumulative processes, changes in the international economic relations
of a country may give an unexpected and perplexing turn to events, not
predictable on the basis of a more rigidly static analysis. There is certainly a wide field of international economic problems which promises a rich

- 893 -

crop if tilled with the aid of imperfect competition and business cycle
theory. The theory of commercial policy, in particular, will profit therefrom.

"During the last two years great progress has been made in the technique
of Protection. Not only have tariffs been piled on tariffs and quotas on
quotas: not only have the old methods been used much more boldly and unhes-
itatingly than before, but new devices have been invented: clearing and
compensation agreements, export and import monopolies, discriminating exchange rates, methods of controlling tourist traffic and expenditure, standstill agreements and so on, with an infinite number of variations in detail.
Many interventionist measures, which seemed two years ago either technically
impossible or so manifestly undesirable as to be quite out of the question,
are to-day adopted without reluctance. In the present book the discussion
of the new commercial policy is confined for the most part to fundamentals.
After all, the general principles and the technique of analysis have remained unaltered and are just as applicable to the new as to the old methods.
If one has a firm grasp of these principles, it is comparatively easy to
apply them to the new techniques of Protection." - Quoted from The Board of
Trade Journal May 7, 1936.

Japan - Economic Conditions

Mitsubishi economic research bureau, Tokyo. Japanese trade and industry,
    present and future. 603pp. London, Macmillan and co., limited, 1936.
    280.183 M69
        Bibliography, pp. 641-645.
        "The Mitsubishi Economic Research Bureau was founded in April, 1932
by Baron Koyata Iwasaki, President of the Mitsubishi Goshi Kaisha, as
an independent institution, succeeding to the Economic Research Department of the said company. The Bureau is conducted on strictly scientific
lines, with the main object of investigating and interpreting economic
problems in Japan and foreign countries. The results of its investigations are compiled in a number of periodical as well as special publications.
        "The following analysis of the expansion of Japanese trade and in-
dustry is a translation of a Japanese edition which appeared last December.
The publication of the English version in May, 1936 has permitted the
insertion of the newest statistical data which cover in most instances
the whole of the year 1935." - Preface.
        There are chapters devoted to Agriculture, The cotton industry, The
silk industry, Foodstuffs and provisions manufacturing industries, and
Warehousing. From the chapter devoted to "Conclusions" the extract
which follows has been taken:
        "Of the total national production, agriculture now accounts for only
about one-fourth, but affords employment for about 47% of the population. The density ratio of the population to cultivated land in Japan
is the highest in the world, and agricultural production capacity has
almost reached the maximum; therefore it is evident that agriculture cannot be depended upon to absorb the expanding population and to support
a future advance in the standard of living. On the contrary, owing to

the distress prevailing in the agricultural areas, which unhappily continues, there has been for many years a steady exodus of people to the
cities. The degree of self-sufficiency in agricultural products is
steadily declining due to the advance of industrialization, and about
one-fourth of the country's requirements has to be imported. In staple
foodstuffs, Japan has managed so far to be self-supporting, but it is
probable that increased importation will be necessary in order to support the growing population. In the face of this situation, it is apparent that the promotion of agriculture, and if possible, the augmenta-
tion of agricultural products should be one of the first considerations
in the formulation of a national policy...

"The establishment of a concrete policy relating to overseas trade
will also require attention. There has been a tendency in some quarters
to consider the attainment of an excess of exports as the principal object of foreign trade. It would be more correct to formulate foreign
trade policy as an adjunct to the development of national industries,
and such a policy would inevitably serve to expand exports...

"Textile manufacturers constitute at present the greatest part of the
Japanese export trade. The future expansion of this trade, which is
indispensable to the Japanese national economy, will depend to a large
extent on the ability of Japanese industry to compete in other finished
products, particularly machinery and chemical manufacturers. Even more
than in the past, the direction of Japanese trade expansion is bound to
be towards East and South Asia, as these regions are important sources
of raw materials and offer the best prospects for reciprocal trade."

Land Economics - Bengal

Sen, Sachin.   Studies in the land economics of Bengal... With a foreword
by the Hon'ble Sir B. P. Singh Roy.   402pp. Calcutta, The Book Company
ltd., 1935. , 282 Se52
       "The land system of Bengal touches the life of nearly 48 million of the
inhabitants of this Province out of fifty... The system has brought into
existence different grades of interest beginning from proprietorship of
land to annual tenancy of the under-ryot, enjoying the right of cultivation of the holding and appropriation of a share of the produce... It
is by no means correct to suggest that the Zemindary system is an introduction of the British. The Permanent Settlement of Lord Cornwallis
did no doubt effect a change in the status of the Zemindars by elevating
them to the position of owners of land from farmers of revenue. But
this change had a far-reaching effect in creating a large number of ten-
ureholders, under-tenureholders, ryots and under ryots, all of whom except the few at the bottom of the hierarchy secured permanent or semi-
permanent interests in land... Mr. Sachin Sen... has tried to trace the
origin and development of the present system and its evolution through
the different stages." - Foreword.
       Chapter headings are: Introduction; Land revenue administration up
to 1789; Decennial and permanent settlements; Taxation of land; Agricultural rent; the Zemindar; and The ryot.

Land - Hawaii

Hobbs, Jean. Hawaii, a pageant of the soil... With a foreword by Felix M. Keesing. 165pp. Stanford University, Calif., Stanford university press; London, H. Milford, Oxford university press [1935] J82 H68
Bibliography, pp. 133-141.
Partial contents: Land customs in early Hawaii; Revolutionizing the land system, Aftermath of the mahele; Lands acquired by westerners; Land in the modern economic setting.

Land Ownership - Germany

Rohr, H. O. von, ed. Grossgrundbesitz im umbruch der zeit. Unter mitarbeit von dr. W. Biereye, E. F. Gordon, kammerdirektor a.d. dr. O. W. Hager... [u.a.] Dritte, verbesserte auflage. 159pp. Berlin, G. Stilke, 1935. 282 R63 E4.3
This book contains a number of articles on the general subject of large landed property. The question, as posed by the editor, is whether a Prussian Socialist State needs as a political organ large landed estates held in the bounds of tradition.
Contents: Bauerntum, by C. G. von Platen, pp. 11-30. (It is shown that peasantry and nobility sprang from the same roots, and that the nobleman is essentially only a higher type of peasant who has consciously or unconsciously reached a special plane of achievement. The history of these two parts of a whole is traced from the time of the early Germanic settlers, with special reference to their relation to land ownership and tenure.); Kolanistion, by Wilhelm Biereye, pp. 31-43. (A survey of the part played by the nobility in the work of colonization in the middle ages in opening the door into a new land in which the peasant could settle and perform outstanding service.); Staatsdienst, by von Rohr-Haus Demmin, pp. 44-63. (A survey of the services rendered to the State by the large landed proprietors since the time of Frederick the Great.); Siedlung, pp. 64-81. (The story of the need for and the development of land settlement in Germany, especially in its post-war stages. Tables show the distribution of settlements in 1919/33, and 1923-1933 and statistics are given showing the origin of the land used for settlement, the cost of land settlement and the possibilities of future land settlement.), Landarbeiter, by Gustav Mörke, pp. 82-87. (Attention is called to the fact that it is on the large estates that the agricultural worker finds work and a home.); Grundbesitzverteilung, by O. W. Hager pp. 88-110. (The five classes into which the agricultural land of Germany is divided according to sizes of farms are enumerated and attention is called to the changes in their distribution according to the agricultural censuses of 1882, 1895, 1907, 1925 and 1933. Extensive tables are given showing the land distribution according to the census of 1933. It is shown that in 1933 88.7 percent of the agricultural land was owned by farmers while 10.7 percent was leased land. A table shows the number and area of the inherited freeholds.); Volkswirtschaft, by E. F. Gordon, pp. 111-123. (A study of the importance of the different sizes of agricultural enterprise for the provisioning of the German people.); Volkszahl, by Peter Cramte, pp. 124-137. (The author refutes the charges made against large estates to the effect that they cause a rural exodus, that they keep the land depopulated, and that they are the cause of an unsound social position

of the rural population.); Rasse, by Frederich Wilhelm, Prinz zur Lippe, pp. 138-146. (The landed proprietor, not because of his ownership of land, but because of his race, can again be roused to great accomplishments as an example to the German peasant.); Kultur, by Börries, Fr. von München-hausen, pp. 147-153. (The author enumerates the contributions of the noble landowners to the culture of the nation.); Politische Aufgabe, by H. O. von Rohr, pp. 154-160. (And so the decision is that the large landed property has a task to perform as an organ of the State) - A. M. Hannay.

League of Nations - Statistical Yearbook

League of nations. Economic intelligence service. Statistical year-book... 1935/36. 339pp. Geneva, 1936. (League of Nations Publications. II. Economic and financial. 1936. II. A.8) 280.9 L47P
"The object of this Year-Book is to give an international synopsis of available statistics relating to the most important demographic, economic, financial and social phenomena. As many countries as possible are included in each table and the figures are rendered as comparable as the phenomena which they measure or the methods by which they have been compiled permit.
"The scope and nature of the data and the limits of their comparability are indicated briefly in the notes.
"A number of tables have been recast or modified and, it is hoped, improved. The most important changes have been made in the tables on population movements, production of a number of commodities, the exchange rates, bond yields, budgetary accounts and capital issues." - Preface.

League of Nations - World Economic Survey

League of nations. Economic intelligence service. World economic survey. Fifth year, 1935/36. 338pp. Geneva, 1936. (Series of League of nations Publications, II. Economic and financial. 1936. II. A.15) 280.9 L47P
"The present Survey has been prepared by Mr. J. B. Condliffe, of the Economic Intelligence Service of the League of Nations. It is the fifth of an annual series undertaken in consequence of resolutions passed by the Assembly of the League in 1930 and 1931." - Preface.
Partial contents: The progress of recovery; Increased production and national self-sufficiency; Rising prices and profits; The trend of consumption; Recovery and the wage-earner; The lag in world trade; The evolution of autarchy; Some problems of public finance; Money and banking; The situation in July 1936; and Chronological list of economic events.

Milk-Consumption Trends

Milk research council, inc. Current trends in milk consumption in the New York metropolitan market, by Edward F. Brown for the Milk research council, inc. 7pp., mimeogr. [New York, 1935] 281.344 M59 2d
"Second of a series of interpretative memoranda on recent trends in milk consumption."

Milk research council, inc.   Current trends in milk consumption; perform-
ance of the milk market in New York, Boston and Philadelphia... by
Edward Lisner Brown for milk research council, inc. 2d-3d ser., mimeogr.
New York, 1936.   281.344 M590
     2d covers 1935, 3d, Jan.-Apr.1936.
     "It is interesting to compare the trends of milk consumption in
New York, Boston and Philadelphia over the full period for which
there are comparable figures - namely, the period in which the United
States Department of Agriculture has been gathering statistics regularly in these markets...
     "It will be seen that New York experienced a steady rise in total
consumption until 1930. There is evidence that this represented a
net gain in per capita consumption also. From the peak year, 1930,
consumption dropped off rapidly to 1932, then more rapidly still to
1934, at which time a comparatively slight gain commenced.
     "Boston, on the other hand, experienced increased milk consumption
until 1931, and even in 1932 had a greater consumption than in 1930.
After 1933 the consumption plummeted, reaching a low in 1933, showing
a slight gain in 1934, then sinking again. Comparatively, Boston's
consumption is still considerably above New York's.
     "The trend in Philadelphia followed a middle course. Remaining
level from 1929 to 1930, it sagged slightly in 1931, rapidly in 1932,
then began to gain. Philadelphia is now appreciably ahead of both
Boston and New York on the path back to normal milk consumption."

Milk - Cost of Production - England

Dawe, C. V., and Blundell, J. E.   The financial aspect of milk production.
17pp. mimeogr. [Bristol, Eng., 1936?] (Bristol. University. Dept. of
agriculture and horticulture. Bulletin no. 15)   10 B775 no.15
     "In the summer of 1934 the Milk Marketing Board approached the Ad-
visory Economists through the Ministry of Agriculture with a view to
instituting an inquiry into the cost of milk production, and as a result
a national investigation into this question was commenced in October and
November of that year.
     "In the following pages a summary is given of that part of the inquiry
for which Bristol University was responsible, but this report is purposely
confined to the financial aspects; other problems being left to be dealt
with in further bulletins. It is also pointed out that since this report
deals only with the results of the first year i.e. from 1st October 1934
to 30th September 1935, it should be read with due reservation and with
the knowledge that (a) the results of a second year will undoubtedly differ from the first on account of changes in climatic conditions etc.
and (b) the results of the national inquiry of which this forms only a
part may also differ for obvious reasons." - Introduction.

New Deal and Supreme Court

Coudert, F. R.   The new deal and the United States Supreme court; a lecture
   delivered before the University of Oxford.   57pp.   Oxford, Clarendon
   press, 1936.   280.12 C83
      The author of this useful resumé is American Legal Adviser to the
   British Embassy at Washington.

Nutrition

The problem of nutrition... 4v.   Geneva, 1936.   (Series of League of nations
   Publications II. Economic and financial 1936.   II. B.3-6)   280.9 L47P
      v. 1.   Interim report of the mixed Committee on the problem of nutri-
   tion.   98pp.
         Partial contents: General survey of the nutrition problem; Nutrition
            and health; Nutrition and labour; Some considerations on the eco-
            nomic aspects of the nutrition problem; and Nutrition and agri-
            culture.
      v.2.   Report on the physiological bases of nutrition drawn up by the
   Technical Commission of the Health Committee at the meeting held in
   London (November 25th-29th, 1935), revised and amplified at the meeting
   held at Geneva (June 4-8th, 1936)   27pp.
         Pt. I, Energy, protein and fat requirements. Pt. II, mineral and
            vitamin requirements.
      v.3.   Nutrition in various countries.   271pp.
         Contains a survey of the measures taken in certain countries by
            governments, public authorities and national organisations to
            bring about an improvement in the nutrition in various sections
            of the population.
      v.4.   Statistics of food production, consumption and prices, documenta-
   tion prepared by the International Institute of Agriculture presented to
   the Mixed Committee on the Problem of Nutrition at its second session,
   June 4th, 1936.   110pp.
         Partial contents: Production, consumption and prices of the protec-
            tive and other foodstuffs; Wholesale and retail prices of pro-
            tective and other food stuffs; Measures of financial assistance
            to agriculture;
         Appendices: General tables of production; General tables of con-
            sumption; Sources and methods of compilation of the estimates
            of production and consumption in each country considered; Index
            numbers of wholesale prices; and Index numbers of retail prices.

Population

Glass, D. V.   The struggle for population... With an introduction by A. M.
   Carr-Saunders.   148pp. Oxford, The Clarendon press, 1936.   280 G462
      Partial contents: The population position in England and Wales;
   Population and policy in Germany; Italian attempts to encourage popula-
   tion growth; Family allowances; Family allowances and the birth-rate in
   France and Belgium.

Population - World

Carr-Saunders, A. M.   World population; past growth and present trends.   xv,
366pp. Oxford, The Clarendon press, 1936. 360 C232W
    "Published under the auspices of the Royal Institute of International
Affairs." - verso of title page.
    Bibliography, pp. [xiv]-xv.
    The author states in his preface that this "book was designed to fill
a gap in population literature. Many valuable studies of population problems have recently appeared, but there is no general survey of the world
situation. Such a survey might take the form of an abstract of the position in the various continents and countries, or it might treat the different problems of population one by one. But the danger of surveys
planned in such ways is that the trees might hide the wood. In order to
avoid this danger and to give the study conerence, an historical approach to the problems of the day has been made in this book. Beginning
with such knowledge as we have of world population three hundred years
ago, the book attempts to discuss the causes and consequences of the im-
mense expansion in numbers which has taken place since that time and to
indicate the problems which arise from the position as it is now. It
hardly needs to be said that only the most important matters can be mentioned in a work of this length. The book is merely a brief introduction
to a subject of enormous scope and complexity."

Prices

Zuckerkandl, Robert.   Zur theorie des preises, mit besonderer berücksichti-
    gung der geschichtlichen entwicklung der lehre.   Zweite unveränderte
    auflage.   384pp. Leipzig, J. Stein & Co., 1936.   28-.3 Z8 Ed.2
        Originally issued 1889.
    In discussing the theory of values and prices the author stresses the
    historical development of the subject and then discusses the most recent
    solutions of his time.

Rural Rehabilitation - Drought Areas

U. S. Works progress administration, Division of social research.   Research
    bulletin, K-5, K-6, K-7, K-8, K-9. Mimeogr. [Washington, D. C.] 1936.
    178.2 W89Rek
        At head of title: Resettlement Administration.
    The material contained in these bulletins is the "outcome of a survey
    of the present condition and future prospects of farmers in the drought
    area of 1934. The study was initiated by the Division of Farm Management
    and Costs of the Bureau of Agricultural Economics, United States Depart-
    ment of Agriculture in cooperation with the Division of Research, Statis-
    tics and Finance of the Federal Emergency Relief Administration and com-
    pleted by the Bureau of Agricultural Economics and the Division of Social
    Research, Works Progress Administration."
    In addition to a description of the county and the area represented most
    of the reports contain information on variation in crop yields, organiza-
    tion of farms, income and financial progress, economic status of farmers,

farmers on relief rolls, and rehabilitation prospects.

Contents:

K-5. Natural and economic factors which affect rural rehabilitation on the north plains of Texas (as typified by Dallam County, Texas), by H. M. Pevehouse. 44pp. July 1936.

K-6. Natural and economic factors which affect rural rehabilitation in the high plains area of eastern Colorado (as typified by Cheyenne County, Colorado), by H. M. Pevehouse. 38PP. July 1936.

K-7. Natural and economic factors affecting rural rehabilitation problems in northwestern North Dakota and northeastern Montana (as typified by Divide County, North Dakota) by H. L. Stewart. 42pp. August 1936.

K-8. Natural and economic factors affecting rural rehabilitation in central North Dakota (as typified by Sheridan County, North Dakota) by H. L. Stewart. 38PP. August 1936.

K-9. Natural and economic factors affecting the possibility of closer settlement in the Red River Valley of eastern North Dakota (as typified by Traill County, North Dakota) by H. L. Stewart. 30pp. September 1936.

Rural Standards of Living

Kirkpatrick, E. L. Needed standards of living for rural resettlement. 62pp. Madison, Wis., Wisconsin Rural rehabilitation division, Resettlement administration, 1936. 284.4 K63N

"Conducted [cooperatively] between the Department of Rural Sociology, Wisconsin Agricultural Experiment Station; Division of Research, Finance and Statistics, Federal Emergency Relief Administration; and Rural (rehabilitation) Division, Wisconsin Emergency Relief Administration. With transferral to the Resettlement Administration in July 1935, the Wisconsin Rural Rehabilitation Division assumed responsibility for completion of the study." - Foot-note, leaf [1]

"The study points to the need of attention to minimum standards below which the families should not be allowed to go in the resettlement program in order to prevent planned developments from becoming set at too low levels for community, state and national well-being. With individual families, and in all communities, standards must be kept up by means of educational programs to direct the desires along the lines of greatest needs. With the objective for satisfactory standards uppermost, emphasis on farm management aspects and supplemental opportunities for earning will be most effective in rehabilitating these as well as all rural families in enlivened American communities."

South Africa - Economic Development

Kock, M. H. de. The economic development of South Africa. 131pp. London, P. S. King & son, ltd., 1936. 277.193 K81E

Bibliography, pp. 127-128.

Chapter five is entitled, The first two decades of union: slackening of progress in the mining industry and great expansion of farming and manufacturing operations.

Taxation - Michigan

Michigan. University. Bureau of government. New series bulletin no. 4, 6,
June, Aug. 1936. 2 nos., lithoprinted. Ann Arbor, 1936. 284.39 M3822
    no. 4. Recent developments in the Michigan tax situation, by A. S.
Ford. June 1936. 26pp.
    no. 6. The retail sales tax in Michigan, by R. S. Ford... and Sidney
Orkin. August, 1936. 24pp.

Taxation - New Hampshire

Grinnell, H. C.   Rural real estate tax delinquency in New Hampshire.   19pp.
    Durham, N. H. [1936]   (University of New Hampshire.   Bulletin 290)
284.5 G68
    The purpose of this bulletin is "to present a general summary of the
data collected, tabulated and summarized for New Hampshire" which was
a part of the nation-wide Civil works project undertaken in 1934 by the
Bureau of Agricultural Economics of the U. S. Dept. of Agriculture in
cooperation with the Agricultural Experiment Stations.
    The author points out the need for further study of local procedure
in the collection of taxes and in the advertisement of delinquent propertie
for sale in order "to recommend a corrective procedure with respect to a
more uniform tax system."
    He also suggests that there are potential dangers to the welfare of
rural communities in "the continuance of a property tax so burdensome on
farm real estate and so inelastic to this class of tax payers."

Trade

Angell, Sir Norman.   Raw materials, population pressure and war.   46pp.
    Boston, New York, World peace foundation, 1936.   (World affairs books
no. 14)   280.8 W89 no.14
    "Once we recognize that the essence of the difficulties in the matter
of raw materials or population is markets, and that better markets mean
merely an increase in the exchange of goods or services to mutual advantage, certain clear lines of policy are indicated.
    "We must face the fact that a nation's tariff, monetary policy, ex-
change restrictions, have ceased to be purely its own affair. After
all, if a tariff which we make will have the effect of doing great
damage to a neighbor, ruin possibly some hundreds of thousands of his
people, we cannot say that he is not concerned. It is surely therefore
part of neighborliness, of decent behavior, to consult with him about
it; to try to discover whether the protection of our interests cannot
be achieved in such a way as to do as little damage as possible to his.
This does not mean immediate world wide free trade, which would be disastrous even if it could be achieved. But it does mean that consultation with those affected by any change we contemplate should be recognised as a basic principle of international good behavior. These con-
sultations should aim at a measure of stability in tariffs (constantly
changing tariffs are even more destructive of international trade than

high tariffs) as well as at their reduction.

"But tariffs are not to-day the main obstacle to the restoration and development of international trade. The main obstacle is monetary instability, the wide fluctuations in the values of the national currencies and the restrictions by which attempts are made to meet the difficulty. Here again, individual action by each nation separately has unusually the effect, ultimately, of worsening the conditions which it purports to remedy. Not only must there be concerted action towards monetary stability, but it is in the long run impossible to separate the tariff from the monetary question, for it is precisely the refusal of creditor states to accept payment in goods which is the main cause of the exchange dislocations.

"It is easy enough to suggest World Economic Conferences to deal with these problems. We have had such conferences and they have failed, failed precisely because governments dare not stand for policies which run counter to prevailing ideas of national interest, however fallacious those ideas may happen to be. Furthermore World Conferences are not the only form, nor perhaps the best form of machinery for this purpose. Policy may move in the right direction in very many different ways: through the International Labor Office, through working agreements between Central Banks, through Bi-Lateral Commercial Treaties. But steady movement in the right direction will be impossible if public opinion, expressing itself in pressure upon politicians and governments, continues to be dominated by certain misconceptions which have hampered sound policy in the past.

"The purpose of these pages has been to help clear away at least one group of those misconceptions."

U. S. S. R.

Malevskii-Malevich, Petr N., ed. The Soviet union today; being a supplement to "Russia - U.S.S.R." and containing a complete index to both volumes. Edited by P. Malevsky-Malevich... With a critical review by V. F. Calverton. 102pp. [New York] The Paisley press, 1936. 280.179 M29

U. S. S. R. Narodnyi komissariat zemledeliia. Sel'skoe khoziaistvo SSSR Ezhegodnik, 1935. 1465pp. Moskva, 1936. 287 N165
  Agricultural economy in USSR. Year book.

Unemployment - Massachusetts

Davenport, D. H., and Croston, J. J. Unemployment and prospects for reemployment in Massachusetts with particular reference to manufacturing industries. 73pp. Boston, Mass. [1936] (Harvard university. Graduate school of business administration. Bureau of business research. Division of research. Business research studies no. 15) 280.9 H262 no. 15
  "Publication of the Graduate School of Business Administration, George F. Baker Foundation - Harvard University, volume XXIII, number 5, August,1936."
  Pt. I. Background of the unemployment problem in Massachusetts; Certain aspects of unemployment in 1930 and 1934; Incidence of unemployment upon

different classes of occupations.

Pt. II. Incidence of unemployment and prospects for reemployment in the different manufacturing industries.

Pt. III. Conclusions - Prospects for reemployment in Massachusetts.

Wealth

Beard, William.   Create the wealth. 314pp. New York, W. W. Norton & company, inc., [1936]   280.12 B383
Contents: The nature of a technological society fosters abundance as a national goal; The efficiency movement lights the way especially when studies are made of national efficiency; The studies show higher living standards are technically possible unless foreign trade influences living standards adversely; The profit system and production for use combined in an experimental program for creating wealth.

World Production and Prices

League of nations. Economic intelligence service.   World production and prices, 1935/36. 156pp. Geneva, 1936. (Series of League of nations. Publications. II. Economic and financial. 1936. II. A. 16)   230.9 L47P
"This tenth survey of world production and prices contains a revised world index of primary production as well as a new world index of industrial activity. The first section of Chapter I is concerned with the production and stocks of primary products, the second with industrial activity in general, the third with the activity of individual industries and the production of raw materials of those industries considered severally. While the statistical tables in this chapter cover the period 1925-1935 (1925/26-1935/36), the observations in the text refer mainly to 1935 and the early part of 1936." - Preface.

BIBLIOGRAPHIES

Crop and livestock insurance; a selected list of references to literature issued since 1898, compiled by Esther M. Colvin and Margaret T. Olcott, under the direction of Mary G. Lacy, librarian, Bureau of agricultural economics. 264pp. Washington, D. C., Nov. 1936. (U. S. Dept. of agriculture. Bureau of agricultural economics. Agricultural economics bibliography no. 67)   mimeogr.

National and farm income. A selected bibliography of studies and discussions, comp. by Orpha Cummings, Librarian, Giannini foundation of agricultural economics, University of California. 15pp., typewritten. Berkeley, Calif., Oct. 15, 1936.
May be borrowed for copying from Orpha Cummings, Librarian, Giannini Foundation of Agricultural Economics, University of California, Berkeley, Calif.

References on the Great Lakes-Saint Lawrence waterway project. By Everett E.
Edwards... and Edith J. Lowe. 184pp. October 1936. (U. S. Dept. of ag-
riculture. Library. Bibliographical contributions no. 30)   1.9 L61B1 no.30
"Anne C. Chew assisted with the editing."

Some references on state and federal activities in marketing with particular
reference to California, comp. by Orpha Cummings, Librarian, Giannini
foundation of agricultural economics, University of California. 29pp.,
typewritten. [Berkeley, Calif., Sept. 1936]
May be borrowed for copying from Orpha Cummings, Librarian, Giannini
Foundation of Agricultural Economics, University of California, Berkeley,
Calif.

NEW PERIODICALS

Nanking. University, College of agriculture and forestry. Dept. of agricultural
economics. Economic facts, no. 1, September, 1936.   Nanking, China.
The announcement accompanying the first issue states:
"Economic Facts will be published about once a month... It will include
articles on money and prices, supply and other factors affecting prices,
prices and economic conditions, agricultural marketing, farm management,
land utilization, rural social economics, and related subjects.
"All of the articles will be based upon research work being conducted
by the Department and will be written by the persons who are doing the work.
"Only articles of interest to the public will be published. Relationships will be shown by graphs, some of them printed in color, and by statistical tables.
"For the convenience of readers of different nationalities, the Chinese
and English texts will be printed in parallel columns. The style, both in
English and Chinese, will be as simple and clear as possible."
The first issue contains the following: Changes in currency and prices
in China, by A. B. Lewis, and Lien Wang, pp. 1-22; Silver export fees, and
the devaluation of the paper Yuan in foreign exchange, by A. B. Lewis and
Lien Wang, pp. 22-28; Changes in the value of Chinese currency, and changes
in wholesale commodity prices in Shanghai, by A. B. Lewis and Lien Wang,
pp. 28-46; Currency changes in Canton, by A. B. Lewis and Lien Wang, pp. 46-
65; Birth and death rates in Kiangyin registration area, by Tsai-Djang Chen
and Chi-Ming Chiao, pp. 66-71.

National association of manufacturers. Committee on agricultural cooperation.
Bulletins nos. 1-22, March 1936 - Oct. 24, 1936. New York.
Issued weekly since no. 6, July 4. No. 2 was issued April 24, no. 3
May 13, no. 4 June 6, and no. 5 June 27.
The address of the National Association of Manufacturers is 11 West
42nd Street, New York.
The Committee on Agricultural Cooperation was organized as a result of a
resolution passed at the meeting of the National Association of Manufac-
turers in December 1935. The purpose of the Committee is stated by the
chairman, Lewis H. Brown in the first issue of the Bulletin as follows:
"The object of the Committee then, is to make a study of the farm
problem. Agriculture and industry are the two biggest productive and

creative units in the economic system – the farm needs the city market and the city needs the farm market. An ability to exchange products is absolutely essential to a continued and permanent prosperity.

"The Committee will attempt to take the long-range view so unpopular at present, yet so vitally important to the achievement of a lasting prosperity based on firm, economic foundations.

"It is, in short, an attempt at self-education. But to avoid the pitfalls of generalities and inexperience, the Committee has secured the co-operation of the National Industrial Conference Board and through them, of Dr. John Lee Coulter, eminent in the field of agricultural economics.

"It is sheer nonsense to attempt to separate these two groups that produce the entire wealth of the country, because the future welfare of the American people depends so definitely on the prosperity of both. It is to the end of keeping these two great groups prosperous that we are trying to educate ourselves on the farmer's problems. We believe that the farmer, in turn, will cultivate an understanding of our problems."

Contents: no. 1. Better grasp of farm situation by industry is object of plan outlined by N. A. M. Committee, by Lewis H. Brown; 2. Understanding the relationship between industry and agriculture; 3. The size, trend and character of the agricultural industry; 4. Acreage trends in agriculture and the "back to farm" movement; 5. Relationship between farm commodity prices and market value of farm real estate; 6. The commodity price structure, farm products vs. non-farm products, farm purchasing power; 7. Farm power – horses vs. power machinery, has mechanization hurt the farmer? 8. Production control and feed grains; 9. The development and present status of the dairy industry; 10. Meats: production, consumption and foreign trade, 11. Wheat and progress; 12. Cotton in America; 13. "The little crops", vegetables, fruits and nuts; 14. Special farm crops, sugar, tobacco, flax, peas, beans, etc.; 15. Our foreign trade and the agricultural situation; 16. The farmer's income; 17. Reserving the American market for the American farmer; 18. Restoration of the foreign farm market; 19. Unemployment and the farm market; 20. New fields for the farmer; 21. The American farmer's net real income; 22. The typical American farm.

Many of the Bulletins carry the following notice: "This bulletin is one of a series prepared by this committee for the information of industrialists. The facts it contains are part of the general study and should not be used as a basis for conclusions until the entire study is completed."

SELECTED LIST OF RECENT REVIEWS

Compiled by M. I. Herb

Angell, Sir Norman. Raw materials, population pressure and war. 1936. (World affairs books no. 14)
    Reviewed by J. E. Pomfret in Amer. Acad. Polit. and Social Sci. Ann. 186: 192-199. July 1936.
    Reviewed by Arthur Feiler in Social Research 3 (3): 367-369. August 1936.

Beard, William. Create the wealth. [1936]
    Reviewed briefly by C. L. King in Amer. Polit. Sci. Rev. 30 (4): 807-808. August 1936.

Belshaw, Horace, and others. Agricultural organization in New Zealand; a survey of land utilization, farm organization, finance and marketing. 1936. (Institute of Pacific relations. International research series)
    Reviewed by J. S. Ballantyne and S. M. Wadham in Econ. Rec. 12 (22): 37-46 June 1936, in an article entitled "The Organization of Rural New Zealand as Seen from the Australian Standpoint."
    Reviewed by W. J. Buzacott in The Queenslander, Jan. 30, 1936, p. 19.

Beney, M. Ada. Cost of living in the United States, 1914-1936. [1936] (National industrial conference board. Studies no. 228)
    Reviewed in Com. and Financ. Chron. 143 (3722): 2584. Oct. 24, 1936.
    Reviewed briefly in The Annalist 48 (1237): 455. Oct. 2, 1936.
    Reviewed in Barron's 16 (39): 12. Sept. 28, 1936.

Black, J. D. The dairy industry and the AAA. 1935. (Half-title: The Institute of economics of the Brookings institution. Publication no. 64)
    Reviewed by Leland Spencer in Jour. Polit. Econ. 44 (5): 710-712. October 1936.

Brinkmann, Theodore. Economics of the farm business. English edition, with introduction and notes by Elizabeth Tucker Benedict, Heinrich Hermann Stippler and Murray Reed Benedict. 1935. (Social science research council. Advisory committee on social and economic research in agriculture. Translation series, no. 2)
    Reviewed by Rainer Schickele in Jour. Farm Econ. 44 (5): 713-714. October 1936.

Brown, E. H. P. The framework of the pricing system. [1936]
    Reviewed in New Statesman and Nation (n.s.) 12 (295): 604. Oct. 17, 1936.

Burns, Eveline M. Toward social security; an explanation of the Social security act and a survey of the larger issues. [1936]
    Reviewed by John J. Corson, 3rd in South. Econ. Jour. 3 (2): 208-211. October 1936.

Carr-Saunders, A. M. World population; past growth and present trends. 1936.
    Reviewed in Economist (London) 124 (4852): 353. Aug. 22, 1936.
    Reviewed by Arthur L. Bowley in New Statesman and Nation (n.s.) 12 (287): 261, 262. Aug. 22, 1936.

Cassel, Gustav. The downfall of the gold standard. 1936.
    Reviewed in Economist (London) 123 (4842): 611. June 13, 1936.

Childs, M. W. Sweden; the middle way. 1936.
    Reviewed by Bruce L. Melvin in Rural Sociol. 1 (3): 384-386. September 1936.
    Reviewed by Brinley Thomas in New Statesman and Nation (n.s.) 12 (296): 642, 644. Oct. 24, 1936.
    Reviewed in the Economist (London) 124 (4856): 520. Sept. 19, 1936 in an article entitled "Social-democracy in Sweden."

Douglas, P. H. Social security in the United States; an analysis and appraisal of the federal Social security act. [1936]
     Reviewed by John J. Corson, 3rd in South. Econ. Jour. 3 (2): 208-211. October 1936.

Durbin, E. F. M. The problem of credit policy. [1935]
     Reviewed by W.A.E. in Jour. Roy. Statis. Soc. (n.s.) 99, Part II, 1936, pp. 391-393.

Fowler, Bertram. Consumer cooperation in America; democracy's way out. [1936]
     Reviewed by Roy A. Ballinger in Rural Sociol. 1 (3): 390-391. September 1936.

Glass, D. V. The struggle for population. 1936.
     Reviewed by William Shands Meacham in the New York Times Book Rev., Oct. 11, 1936, p. 18.

Heaton, Herbert. Economic history of Europe. 1936.
     Reviewed by M. M. Knight in Jour. Polit. Econ. 44 (5): 699-704. October 1936.

Keynes J. M. The general theory of unemployment, interest, and money. 1936.
     Reviewed by Alvin H. Hansen in an article entitled "Mr. Keynes on Underemployment Equilibrium" in Jour. Polit. Econ. 44 (5): 667-686. October 1936
     Reviewed by A.W.F. in Jour. Royal Statis. Soc. (n.s.) 99, Pt. II. 1936. pp 383-388.

Lyon, L. S., and Abramson, Victor. The economics of open price system. 1936.
     (Half-title: The Institute of economics of the Brookings institution. Publication no. 71)
     Reviewed in Jour. Marketing 1 (2): 169. October 1936.

Maxton, J. P. ed. Regional types of British agriculture, by fifteen authors. [1936]
     Reviewed in The Economist (London) 125 (4861): 166, 167. Oct. 24, 1936.

Mitchell, W. C., ed. What Veblen taught; selected writings of Thorstein Veblen. 1936.
     Reviewed by Tipton R. Snavely in South. Econ. Jour. 3 (2): 216-218. October 1936.

Murchie, R. W. Agricultural progress on the prairie frontier. 1936. (Canadian frontiers of settlement, ed. by W. A. Mackintosh and W. L. G. Joerg. v. 5)
     Reviewed by G. L. Wood in Econ. Rec. 12 (22): 143-146. June 1936.
     Reviewed by G. E. Britnell in Amer. Econ. Rev. 26 (3): 516-517. September 1936.
     Reviewed by J. E. Lattimer in Jour. Land & Pub. Utility Econ. 12 (3): 322-323. August 1936.
     Reviewed by G. L. Wood in Econ. Rec. 12 (22): 143-146. June 1936.
     Reviewed by R. O. B. in Geogr. Jour. 88 (4): 366-367. October 1936.

Odum, H. W.   Southern regions of the United States . for the Southern regional
    committee of the Social science research council. 1936.
        Reviewed by Wallace W. Atwood in South. Econ. Jour. 3 (2): 211-212.
    October 1936.

Peek, G. N., and Crowther, Samuel.   Why quit our own. 1936.
        Reviewed by P. T. Hitchens in the New York Times Book Rev. Oct. 18,
    1936, p. 16.

Rowe, J. W. F   Markets and men; a study of artificial control schemes in some
    primary industries. 1936.
        Reviewed by Erich W. Zimmermann in South. Econ. Jour. 3 (2): 213-216.
    October 1936.

Royal institute of international affairs.   Information department.   Raw materials
    and colonies. 1936. (Its Papers, no. 18)
        Reviewed by Amry Vandenbosch in Amer. Polit. Sci. Rev. 30 (5): 997-998.
    October 1936.

Sharfman, I. L.   The Interstate commerce commission; A study in administrative
    law and procedure. Part III, Vol. B. 1936.
        Reviewed by C. K. Brown in South. Econ. Jour. 3 (2): 220-222.
    October 1936.

Smith, D. T.   Deficits and depressions. Chapman & Hall, limited. 1936.
        Reviewed in Economist [London] 124 (4848): 169. July 25, 1936.
        Reviewed by E. A. Gilmore, Jr., in Amer. Econ. Rev. 26 (3): 553-554.
    September 1936.
        Reviewed briefly in People's Money 2 (6): 260. July 1936.
        Reviewed by E. M. Bernstein in South. Econ. Jour. 3 (2): 227-228.
    October 1936.

Wallace, H. A.   Whose constitution? An inquiry into the general welfare.
    [1936]
        Reviewed by Edward S. Corwin in Amer. Polit. Sci. Rev. 30 (5): 981-933.
    October 1936.

Warbasse, J. P.   Cooperative democracy through voluntary association of
    the people as consumers; a discussion of the cooperative movement, its
    philosophy, methods, accomplishments and possibilities and its relation
    to the state, to science, art, and commerce, and to other systems of
    economic organization. 3d ed. 1936.
        Reviewed briefly by Arthur E. Albrecht in Jour. Marketing 1 (2): 169.
    October 1936.

Wilson, L. R., and Wight, E. A.   County library service in the South; a
    study of the Rosenwald county library demonstration. [1935] (Half-
    title: The University of Chicago Studies in library science)
        Reviewed by Robert B. Downs in Social Forces 15 (1): 123-127.
    October 1936.

Economic in Character

Compiled by Katharine Jacobs

Circular*

414. Farmer bankruptcies, 1898-1935, by David L. Wickens. 32pp. September
      1936. 1 Ag84C

Farmers' Bulletin*

1560, revised. Preparing strawberries for market, by R. G. Hill. 22pp.
      Rev. July 1936. 1 Ag84F

Leaflet*

67. Beef grading and stamping service, by W. C. Davis. 8pp. Revised 1936.
     1 Ag54L

Miscellaneous Publication*

255. The farm outlook for 1937. 48pp.

Technical Bulletin*

539. Federal seed-loan financing and its relation to agricultural rehabil-
      itation and land use, by Norman J. Wall. 60pp. October 1936. 1 Ag84Te

Group Discussion Material issued by the Extension Service and Agricultural Adjustment Administration Cooperating**

Discussion: a brief guide to methods (Revised 1936) 11pp. 1936 (D-1 Revised)
      1 Ag86D1   Bibliography, pp. 9-11.
Exports and imports. How do they affect the farmer? 14pp. December 1936.
      (DS-4) 1 Ag86Ds   Bibliography, p. 14.
How do farm people live in comparison with city people? 14pp. December 1936.
      (DS-2) 1 Ag86Ds   Bibliography, p. 14.
How to organize and conduct county forums (Revised 1936) 6pp. 1936. (D-2
      Revised) 1 Ag86D1   Bibliography, pp. 4-6.
Is increased efficiency in farming always a good thing? 14pp. December 1936.
      (DS-5) 1 Ag86Ds   Bibliography, p. 14.

Symbol used after each entry is call number assigned to the publication by
   the Department Library.
*Requests for these publications should be addressed to the Office of Informa-
   tion, U. S. Department of Agriculture, Washington, D. C.
**May be obtained from United States Department of Agriculture, Extension Ser-
   vice. See also Section "Group Discussion Material" under Publications of
   the Agricultural Adjustment Administration.

Should farm ownership be a goal of agricultural policy? 14pp. December 1936.
(DS-3)   1 Ag86Ds   Bibliography, p. 14.
What kind of agricultural policy is necessary to save our soil? 14pp. December 1936. (DS-7)   1 Ag86Ds   Bibliography, p. 14.
What part should farmers in your county take in making national agricultural policy? 14pp. December 1936. (DS-8)   1 Ag86Ds   Bibliography, p. 14.
What should be the farmers' share in the national income? 14pp. December 1936. (DS-1)   1 Ag86Ds   Bibliography, p. 14.
What should farmers aim to accomplish through organization? 14pp. December 1936. (DS-6)   1 Ag86Ds   Bibliography, p. 14.

Address of Secretary Wallace*

Responding to change in agriculture; an address... at the annual meeting of the Land grant college association at Houston, Texas, on November 16, 1936. 11pp., mimeogr.   1.9 Ag8636 no. 130.

Publications of the Bureau of Agricultural Economics (Mimeographed)**

Agricultural outlook charts 1937. Cotton. 27pp. November 1936. 1.9 Ec70c
Agricultural outlook charts 1937. Dairy products. 13pp. November 1936.
   1.9 Ec70dc
Agricultural outlook charts 1937. Demand, credit, prices. 53pp. November 1936. 1.9 Ec70de
Agricultural outlook charts 1937. Farm family living and summaries. 27pp.
   November 1936. (In cooperation with the Bureau of home economics)
   1.9 Ec70fs
Agricultural outlook charts 1937. Fruits: apples, citrus, peaches, etc. 44pp.
   November 1936. 1.9 Ec70fr
Agricultural outlook charts 1937. Hog. 15pp. November 1936. 1.9 Ec70hc
Agricultural outlook charts 1937. Poultry and eggs. 53pp. November 1936.
   1.9 Ec70pc   1937.
Amendment no. 1 to Service and regulatory announcements no. 121, revised.
   Amendment to rules and regulations of the Secretary of agriculture for
   carrying out the provisions of the Perishable agricultural commodities
   act, 1930 (46 Stat. 531), as amended April 13, 1934 (48 Stat. 584) and
   June 19, 1936 (49 Stat. 1533) 1p. 1936. 1 M34S
Butter: Supply, distribution, and per capita consumption in continental United
   States. 1p. October 31, 1936. 1.9 Ec724Bd
Cheese: Supply, distribution and per capita consumption in continental United
   States. 1p. October 31, 1936. 1.9 Ec724Che
Condensed & evaporated whole milk: Supply, distribution, and per capita consump-
   tion in continental United States. 1p. October 31, 1936. 1.9 Ec724Ce
Cotton loan policies and the method of weighting monthly cotton prices 1933-34
   and 1934-35. 7pp. October 1936. (CRP-2) 1.9 Ec71Crp no.2
      Prepared by Roger F. Hale and Robert N. Walsh.

*Request for this publication should be addressed to the Office of Information,
   U. S. Department of Agriculture, Washington, D. C.
**These publications are issued in small editions for immediate use in official
   work and are not for general distribution.

Crop and livestock insurance; a selected list of references to literature issued since 1898, compiled by Esther M. Colvin and Margaret T. Olcott
under the direction of Mary G. Lacy, Librarian. 264pp. November 1936.
(U S. Dept. of agriculture. Bureau of agricultural economics. Agricultural economics bibliography no. 67)   1.9 Ec73A no.67
Economic objectives; the place of the Department in the American economic system and the ideals toward which it is working, by A. G. Black. 9pp. 1936.
1.9 Ag81 Edo [no.1]
     Address, Department of agriculture auditorium, October 23, 1936. One
of a special series of lectures on Department objectives presented under
the auspices of the Graduate School.
Farm population estimates, January 1, 1936. 12pp. October 27, 1936.
1.9 Ec763Fap 1936.
Farm returns 1935, with comparisons Summary of reports of farm owner operators
for the calendar year. 6pp. November 1936. 1.9 Ec7Far
Index numbers of prices paid by farmers for commodities bought for family mainte
nance and for commodities bought to be used in production 1910-1914 = 100
1p. October 30, 1936. 1.9 Ec752In
List of manufacturers of fruit and vegetable hampers and baskets including manufacturers' identification numbers (revised to October 1936) 20pp. Novembe
1936. 1.9 Ec741C
List of rice grading apparatus and firms from whom same can be purchased. 5pp.
November 1936. 1.9 Ec72Lg
Milk equivalent of production of manufactured dairy products by states, 1935.
2pp. October 1936. 1.9 EcMil
Rice production and marketing in California Prepared by R. M. Mehl... Bureau
of agricultural economics, and Loren L. Davis... Bureau of plant industry.
4pp. October 1936. (Issued in cooperation with Bureau of plant industry.)
1.9 Ec72Ric
Tables of refrigerated space as of October 1, 1935 with comparisons. 13pp.
September 1936. 1.9 Ec7Tab
What should be included in economic research programs, by A. G. Black. 4pp.
1936. 1.9 Ec7Wae
     Address annual meeting, Association of Land Grant Colleges, Houston,
Texas, November 16, 1936.

Radio Talks*

Farm business facts. An interview between Roy F. Hendrickson and Dr. C. C.
Taylor. . and Morse Salisbury. October 27, 1936. 5pp. 1.9 Ec7Ra
Farm business facts. An interview between Roy F. Hendrickson... and Morse
Salisbury. November 3, 1936. 5pp. 1.9 Ec7Ra
Farm credit outlook... by R. M. Green. November 6, 1936. 2PP. 1.9 Ec7Ra
The fruit outlook, 1937, by Sterling R. Nowell. 2pp. November 16, 1936.
1.9 Ec7Ra
The hog outlook... by C. A. Burmeister. November 11, 1936. 2pp. 1.9 Ec7Ra
The 1937 beef cattle outlook... by C. V. Whalin. November 12, 1936. 2pp.
1.9 Ec7Ra

---

* Radio talks may be obtained from U. S. Department of Agriculture, Office
of Information, Radio Service.

The 1937 cotton outlook... by C. H. Robinson. November 11, 1936. 2pp.
1.9 Ec7Ra

The 1937 dairy outlook. . by L. M. Davis. November 11, 1936. 2pp. 1.9 Ec7Ra

The 1937 outlook for miscellaneous crops. A radio interview between M. R.
Cooper... and Morse Salisbury. November 12, 1936. 2pp. 1.9 Ec7Ra

The 1937 tobacco outlook, by C. E. Gage. 2pp. November 16, 1936. 1.9 Ec7Ra

The 1937 truck crop outlook... by Gustav Burmeister. November 12, 1936. 2pp.
1.9 Ec7Ra

The 1937 wheat outlook... by R. E. Post. November 11, 1936. 2pp. 1.9 Ec7Ra

The poultry, egg and turkey outlook 1937... by G. W. Sprague. November 12,
1936. 2pp. 1.9 Ec7Ra

Prospective demand for farm products, 1937..., by Dr. F. L. Thomsen. November
6, 1936. 2pp. 1.9 Ec7Ra

Sheep, lambs, wool, mohair outlook, 1937... by Morse Salisbury, Radio service.
2pp. November 16, 1936. 1.9 In3Ra

Publications of the Agricultural Adjustment Administration*

An economic survey of the commercial broiler industry, by W. D. Termohlen,
J. W. Kinghorne, E. L. Warren and J. H. Radabaugh. 54PP. 1936 (G-61)
1.4 Ad4Ge

*The farmer, the college, the Department of agriculture – their changing re-
lationships. Address of H. R. Tolley... before the general session of
the fiftieth annual convention of the Association of land grant colleges
and universities, at Houston, Texas, November 18, 1936. 13pp., mimeogr.
1.94 Ad472T [no.15]

Marketing agreement series – agreement no. 64, amendment no. 1. Amendment
of marketing agreement regulating the handling of citrus fruit grown
in the state of Florida. (Issued by the Secretary of agriculture
October 24, 1936. Effective 12:01 a.m., E.S.T., October 28, 1936) 2pp.
(A-3-Amendment 1) 1.4 Ad47M

1936 agricultural conservation program, northeast region. Bulletin no.5.
Instructions for determination of performance, preparation of report of
performance, application for payment and related forms. 19pp. September
30, 1936. (NER-B-5) 1.42 N76B

Order series – order no. 7, amendment no. 1. Order amending the order regulating the handling of citrus fruit grown in the state of Florida. (Issued
by the Secretary of agriculture October 24, 1936. Effective 12:01 a.m.
E.S.T., October 28, 1936) 2pp. (O-7-Amend 1) 1.4 Ad470

Order series – order no. 13. Order regulating the handling of milk in the
Kansas City, Missouri, marketing area. (Issued by the Secretary of agriculture, November 3, 1936. Effective 12:01 a.m., C.S.T., December 1,
1936) 12pp. (O-13) 1.4 Ad470

---

* Requests for these publications should be addressed to the Agricultural
Adjustment Administration, U. S. Department of Agriculture, Washington,
D. C.

**May be obtained from U. S. Department of Agriculture, Press Service.

Group Discussion Material (Mimeographed)*

4-H club discussion paper. Do we want to be farmers? 19pp., mimeogr.
October 1936. 1.94 Ad45F
    This publication, prepared especially for the use of 4-H club leaders
and members, is intended to assist in discussion of the future of farming, especially as this future may be affected by the agricultural conservation program.
Young farmer discussion paper. Do we want to be farmers? 19pp., mimeogr.
November 1936. 1.94 Ad45Y
    This publication, prepared especially for the use of vocational teachers
is intended to assist in discussion of the future of farming, especially
as this future may be affected by the agricultural conservation program.

Miscellaneous (Mimeographed)**

References on the Great Lakes-Saint Lawrence waterway project, by Everett
E. Edwards... and Edith J. Lowe. 185pp., mimeogr. October 1936. (U.S.
Dept. of agriculture. Library. Bibliographical contributions no. 30)
1.9 L61B1
    "Anne C. Chew assisted with the editing."
U. S. Department of agriculture. List of references on its history and objec-
tives. 7pp. 1936. 1.9 L61Un
    Prepared in the Library of the Department.

U. S. RESETTLEMENT ADMINISTRATION ***

Ahrens, T. P. The utilization of aerial photographs in mapping and studying land features. 27pp., processed. Washington, D. C., Oct. 1936.
(U. S. Resettlement administration. Land utilization division. Land
use planning section. Land use planning publication no. 6) 1 95 L23 no.6

Plath, C. H. Present land use in Morton county, North Dakota: a comparison
of mapping methods. 5pp., processed. Washington, D. C., Nov. 1936.
(U. S. Resettlement administration. Land utilization division. Land-use
planning section. Land-use planning publication no. 7) 1 95 L23 no.7

---

  * Requests for these publications should be addressed to the Agricultural
    Adjustment Administration, U. S. Department of Agriculture, Washington,
    D. C.
 ** Requests for these publications should be addressed to the issuing office.
*** Requests for these publications should be addressed to the Resettlement
    Administration, Arlington Hotel, Washington, D. C.

STATE PUBLICATIONS

Compiled by Mary F. Carpenter

California

Peterson, G. M.   Agriculture's share of the national income. Calif. Agr.
    Expt. Sta. 6pp., mimeogr. Berkeley. 1936.
        A paper presented at the Annual meeting of the Western Farm Economics
    Association, Laramie, Wyoming, July 31, 1936.

Wellman, H. R., and Street, M D.   The pooling of lemons with special refer-
    ence to the Santa Paula Citrus Fruit Association. A progress report.
    Calif. Agr. Expt. Sta. Giannini Found. Agr. Econ. Mimeogr. Rept. 55, 67pp.
    Berkeley. 1936.

Connecticut

Connecticut. Department of agriculture, Bureau of markets.   Official list
    live poultry dealers and carriers licensed to operate in the state as
    of October 1, 1936. Conn. Dept. Agr. Bull. 42, 19pp. Hartford. 1936.

Hawaii

Hawaii. University. Agricultural extension service.   Census of truck crops
    produced in Hawaii, January-May, 1936. 24pp., mimeogr. Honolulu. 1936.
        Includes acreage and production of truck crops, fruits and nuts for
    each of the five principal islands with maps.

Illinois

Illinois. Department of agriculture.   Nineteenth annual report... July 1, 1935
    to June 30, 1936. 117pp. Springfield. 1936.
        Division of Agricultural Statistics, pp. 29-41; Chicago Grain Inspec-
    tion Division, pp. 64-79; East St. Louis Grain Inspection, pp. 80-81;
    Division of Markets, pp. 102-107.

Illinois. University. Extension service in agriculture and home economics.
    Illinois farm economics, no. 16-17, September - October 1936.
        Partial contents: Costs of harvesting with combines, by R. C. Ross
    and B. R. Hurt, pp. 79-80; Shifting real estate values in Illinois, by
    C. L. Stewart and W. J. Wills, pp. 80-81; Corn prices in years of short
    crops, by E. J. Working, pp. 81-83.

Iowa

Iowa. State college of agriculture and mechanic arts. Extension service.
    Iowa farm economist, v. 2, no. 4, Ames, October 1936.
        Partial contents: Looking at the new farm program, by O. B. Jesness,
    pp. 3-4; Income goes up when costs come down, by P. E. Quintus, pp. 5-7;

County zoning in Wisconsin, by G. S. Wehrwein, pp. 8-10; Toward better farm housing, by M. G. Reid, pp. 10-12; Land, landlord and tenant, by Rainer Schickele, pp. 12-15.

Schultz, T. W. Economic conditions in Iowa, 1935. Iowa Dept. Agr. Bull. 79, 39pp. Des Moines. 1936.

Louisiana

Louisiana. State university and Agricultural and mechanical college. Circular 16, 7pp. Baton Rouge. 1936.
Part 1, Report on gins in Louisiana and the proper ginning of cotton, by G. A. Gerdis. Part II, Introduction and summary of U. S. Department of Agriculture Technical bulletin no. 503 entitled, "Effects of Gin-Saw Speed and Seed-Roll Density on Quality of Cotton Lint and Operation of Gin Stands."

Massachusetts

Stevens, C. D., Franklin, H. J., Gunness, C. I., and Peterson, V. C. The cranberry industry in Massachusetts. Mass. Agr. Expt. Sta. Bull. 332, 36pp. Amherst. 1936.
"This study brings together both the historical and the latest available statistical information regarding the development of this important industry."

Michigan

Michigan. State college of agriculture and applied science. Agricultural economic news for Michigan, no. 11, October, 1936.
Partial contents: Crop review - October 1, by V. H. Church, pp. 6-10; Michigan farm incomes continue to increase, by C. O. May, pp. 10-11.

Minnesota

Waite, W. C., and Garver, W. B. Variation in agricultural prices among different sections of Minnesota. Minn. Univ. Agr. Ext. Div. Minn. Farm Business Notes, no. 167, pp. 1-3, mimeogr. University Farm, St. Paul. November 20, 1936.

Missouri

Missouri. State department of agriculture. Missouri farm census by counties, 1935. Mo. Dept. Agr. Bull. v. 34, no. 5. 20pp. Jefferson City. September 1936.
Figures are for one year later than the "Federal Census of 1935."

Montana

Cushman, H. E., and Slagsvold, P. L. Marketing Montana's turkey crop. Mont. Agr. Col. Ext. Serv. Bull. 150, 19pp. Bozeman. 1936.

Renne, R. R. Organization and costs of Montana schools. An analysis of the
system of financing elementary and secondary education with suggested
changes. Mont. Agr. Expt. Sta. Bull. 325, 104pp. Bozeman. 1936.

Nebraska

George, A. G. Certified potato production costs (Growing and harvesting costs
only) Nebraska, 1935. Nebr. Agr. Col. Ext. Circ. 865 (1935), 7pp.,
mimeogr. Lincoln. 1936.

George, A. G. Corn production costs, Nebraska, 1935. Nebr. Agr. Col. Ext.
Circ. 840 (1935), 17pp., mimeogr. Lincoln. 1936.

George, A. G. Winter wheat production costs, Nebraska, 1935. Nebr. Agr.
Col. Ext. Circ. 839 (1935), 20pp., mimeogr. Lincoln. 1935.

Nevada

Nevada. Agricultural experiment station and agricultural extension service.
Economic talks with Nevada farmers. v. 1, no. 5, 4pp. Reno. August 1936.
Contents: Living expense of farmers in Nevada, by V. E. Scott, pp. 2-3;
Farm incomes in depression and prosperity, by Mabel Connor, pp. 3-4; Re-
lation of size and investment to net farm incomes, by Mabel Connor, p. 4.

Nevada. Agricultural experiment station and agricultural extension service.
Summary of family classification, farm privilege and cash cost of living.
Nev. Agr. Expt. Sta. News Bull., v. 10, no. 1, 8pp., mimeogr. Reno. 1936.

New Hampshire

New Hampshire. University. Extension service. The marketing programs on fruits
and vegetables in areas close to the market with reference to questions
of grading, standardization, and type of market (called by the Fruit and
Vegetable and Marketing Committees of the New England Research Council)
Amherst, Massachusetts, June 9, 1936. 6PP., mimeogr. Durham, N. H. Univ.
Ext. Service. 1936.

New York

Maughan, O. H. The cost of store credit. N. Y. (Cornell) Agr. Col. Ext.
Bull. 349, 26pp. Ithaca. 1936.

New York (Cornell) State college of agriculture, Extension service. The potato
situation and the status of potato research in New York. N. Y. Cornell
Agr. Col. Ext. Bull. 352, 60pp. Ithaca. 1936.
By various authors. Economic facts and factors concerning the potato
situation, pp. 5-15, is by M. P. Rasmussen.

North Carolina

Smith, G. R. Gin damage of cotton in relation to rainfall. N. C. Agr. Expt.
Sta. Bull. 306, 26pp. State College, Raleigh. 1936.
This investigation was conducted in cooperation with the Division of
Cotton Marketing, U. S. Bureau of Agricultural Economics.

Moore, H. R.   The farm foreclosure situation. Ohio Agr. Expt. Sta. Bimonthly
    Bull., v. 21, no. 183, pp. 140-141. Wooster. November - December 1936.

Sherman, R. W.   A study of cooperative milk marketing associations in four
    Ohio markets. Ohio Agr. Expt. Sta. Bull. 574, 61pp. Wooster. 1936.
        This study was a joint project with the Cooperative Division, Farm
    Credit Administration.
        The Akron, Dayton, Portsmouth, and Columbus markets were chosen as
    representative markets of the State.
        An appendix contains a list of cooperative milk marketing associations
    in Ohio formed before July 1, 1933.

Oklahoma

Oklahoma. Agricultural experiment station. Current farm economics, v. 9, no. 5.
    Stillwater. October 1936.
        Partial contents: Effect of 1936 drouth on Oklahoma farmers, by H. A.
    Miles, pp. 107-109; The Oklahoma farm price of cotton is closely related
    to the price of futures at New York, by T. R. Hedges, pp. 109-112; Seasonal
    aspects of Oklahoma hog prices and marketing, by A. W. Jacob, pp. 120-122.

Washington

Orr, A. Z., and others.   Trends and desirable adjustments in Washington agricul-
    ture. Wash. Agr. Expt. Sta. Bull. 335, 45pp. Pullman. 1936.
        Includes map of the wheat land of the Big Bend area, classified by
    yields, 1929-1932. Data from AAA allotment records.

West Virginia

Henderson, H. O., Bowling, G. A., and Herrmann, L. F.   Amounts of feed and
    labor used in raising dairy heifers. W. Va. Agr. Expt. Sta. Bull. 277,
    27pp. Morgantown. 1936.
        Data was obtained from Experiment Station herd records and from a
    survey of practices on 122 farms in different parts of the state in
    which material was collected by Dr. P. A. Eke during the summer of 1926.

West Virginia crop and livestock reporting service. West Virginia agricul-
    tural statistics, 1934-1935 (with historic data) W. Va. Dept. Agr.
    Bull. (N.S.) 1, 41pp. Charleston. 1936.
        In cooperation with United States Bureau of Agricultural Economics.
    Contains statistics by counties.

Wisconsin

Delwiche, E. J.   Succulent feed crops. Cost of producing in Northern Wis-
    consin. Wis. Agr. Expt. Sta. Bull. 436, 16pp. Madison. 1936.
        Results of experiments with corn silage, rutabagas, and sunflower
    silage.

Compiled by Louise O. Bercaw and A. M. Hannay

Agricultural Crisis - China

Wu, L.T.K. Rural bankruptcy in China. Far East. Survey 5(20):209-216. Oct. 8,
1936. (Published by the American Council, Institute of Pacific Relations, 129 East 52nd St., New York, N.Y.)
"If any one problem can be said to overshadow all other internal economic questions facing harassed China today, it is the rural crisis.
Over three fourths of the Chinese population are peasants and no less than
four fifths of the national income is derived from agriculture. Nearly
all nations are today attempting to remedy the lot of those whose lives
are spent tilling the soil. But in few areas are conditions more desperate and the scope of the problem as great as in China.
"The present state of rural China may be summarized in one word -
bankruptcy. This word flows freely from the pen of any army of writers.
But what do they mean by rural bankruptcy? In the account... [here given]
we will try to answer this question from two angles: through a brief survey of the manifestations of the rural crisis, and through an examination
of the structural causes inherent in China's present economy which are
primarily responsible for the bankruptcy."

Agricultural Policy - Great Britain

Taylor, C.C. Trends in British agricultural policy. Foreign Crops and Markets
33(16):459-465. Oct. 19, 1936. (Published by the Division of Foreign
Agricultural Service, Bureau of Agricultural Economics, U.S. Dept. of
Agriculture)
"Prepared by Agricultural Attaché C.C. Taylor at London."
Includes a discussion of the Market Control Schemes, which in spite of
criticisms are in no "real danger of failure because of lack of producer
support", except possibly that for bacon hogs.
"Schemes have been proposed for a few additional commodities, and
some consideration is being given to the extension of the present benefits.
The principal discussion, however, now centers around a plan to impose
higher import duties and to pay more and higher subsidies to producers.
The wheat plan, whereby a fixed price for a given output is guaranteed, is
being vigorously pressed by several active organizations; but the united
appeal of most farm groups is for higher tariffs, even at the expense of
Empire countries."

Agricultural Relief - United States

Henderson, H.G. The farmer on the dole. Today 6(26):6-7, 24, 25. Oct. 17,
1936. (Published at 152 West Forty-second St., New York, N.Y.)
Federal farm relief programs and relief to farmers in the drought areas
are the subjects considered in this article. Several examples are cited
of farmers in the drought area - which are not special cases - going on
the relief list - looking to the Government before they looked to themselves. The opinion is expressed that the present measures which are being
applied by our current relief agencies "are the worst remedies of all."

Heywood, H.B.   Our present agricultural imbroglio - is there a solution?.
Will consumer acquiescence continue to submit to political exploitation?
- An analysis and some suggestions. Modern Miller 63(44):16-17. October 1936 (Published at 175 W. Jackson Blvd., Chicago, Ill.)
      An article expressing strong opposition to agricultural relief
measures of the Roosevelt Administration.

Agriculture - Future

Davis, A.C. The future farm picture as a farm leader sees it. Missouri
Farmer 28(20): 307, 310. Oct. 15, 1936. (Published in Columbia, Mo.)
      Address delivered by A.C. Davis, former National Secretary of the
Farmers Union at the recent M.F.A. Annual Convention.
      "Summing up, the picture of future farming I would leave with you is
a solidly organized industry, class conscious if you please, engaged in:
      "(a) Closely cooperating community groups protecting farm life and the
farm home as a way of life rather than as a cold blooded factory. Studying the hundred and one economic problems facing the nation and the
world, all of which have a bearing upon agriculture and its adaptation
to changing needs.
      "(b) Ever widening the field of co-operative business activity in the
markets of the world.
      "(c) Since legislation is tending more and more to become specific
rather than general, seeking fairly to represent agriculture in the legislative halls."

Apples - Pacific Northwest

Hudson, George. "Doc Apple" goes to town. Coop. Jour. 10(5):129-132. September-
October 1936. (Published at 1731 Eye St., N.W., Washington, D.C.)
      The Pacific Northwest fruits, comprised of four fruit associations has
developed a grower and industry program. Reference is made in this article
to eight "significant points" in the program. Mr. Hudson writes in conclusion: "The entire fruit industry has become aroused to a realization of
the importance of a united approach to its problems. The program of
Pacific Northwest Fruits is designed to meet the major problems in the industry, and its first year's operations will be watched with great interest by growers throughout the fruit-growing districts. If the program
accomplishes what its participants expect of it, it will not only attract
the support of large numbers of fruit growers not now in the program, but
will establish itself as a pattern for growers in many other fruit and
vegetable producing areas to follow."

Banking and Agriculture

Otis, D.H. The farmer's banker. Banking 29(3):12-13. September 1936. (Published by the American Bankers Association, New York, N.Y.)
      Advocates a farm inventory as a basis for a credit statement, since the
banker who is responsible for the depositors' funds, must base his judgment upon facts. Thinks that a soil reserve should be created.

Beet Sugar Industry

Farnham, John. Beet sugar industry's future. Barron's 16(43):11. Oct. 26,
1936. (Published at 44 Broad St., New York, N.Y.)
An appraisal of factors affecting the present revival of the beet
sugar industry.
Under the Jones-Costigan Act, signed by President Roosevelt on May 9,
1934, both the sugar-beet farmers and processors have prospered, but
"nevertheless, not all parties serving the American market are satisfied
with the quota system. Revisions are certain to be sought when the
measure expires by limitation next year."
Three possible plans are suggested as follows:
"1-A continuance of the present Jones-Costigan Act, approximately as
it is.
"2-A return to the old system of the protective tariff.
"3-An amplification of the Jones-Costigan principle to allow the
beet-sugar and insular cane-sugar growers (including in the latter group
the amount of duty-free imports given the Philippines under the legislation providing for independence) to supply as much of the American market as they can, the deficiency between this domestic-insular production
to be made up by Cuban imports."
Advantages and disadvantages of the three propositions are discussed.

Business Conditions

The Annalist. Fourth quarter review and forecast number. Annalist 48(1239):
515-560. Oct. 16, 1936. (Published by the New York Times Co., New
York, N.Y.)
Partial contents: Canadian business activity slightly higher; heavy
loss in farm production, by H. E. Hansen, p.525; On the world economic
front: French devaluation a prelude to stability? by Winthrop W. Case, pp.
528-529,550; Tobacco manufacturers profiting from record demand and AAA
tax removal, by La Rue Applegate, p.531; Curtailed world output and
prospective increase in European needs buoy wheat, pp.531-533; Cotton
market: drought and heavy world consumption offset by new crop hedging,
pp.533,539; Other commodities in the third quarter: new high for cocoa;
cottonseed also up, pp.539,552.

Business Cycles

Mitchell, W. C., and Burns, A. F. Production during the American business
cycle of 1927-1933. Natl. Bur. Econ. Research. Bull.61, 20pp.
November 9, 1936. (Published at 1819 Broadway, New York, N.Y.)
"This bulletin presents a part of the results that the National Bureau
is obtaining by making systematic measurements of business cycles. Our
chief aim here is to describe the behavior of American production during
the cycle of 1927-33 and to compare that behavior with its analogues
during preceding cycles." - p.2.

Cacao Industry - Trinidad

Shephard, C.Y. The cacao industry of Trinidad. Some economic aspects.
Series II. A financial survey of estates during the seven years 1923-4
to 1929-30. Trop. Agr. 13(11):285-291. November 1936. (Published at the
Imperial College of Tropical Agriculture, St. Augustine, W.I.)
The following is quoted from the introduction, p.285:
"The aim of the present investigation is to discover means of improving the efficiency of Trinidad cacao estates. In the first series
of articles the history of the industry was traced from its origin to
1932. In this, the second series, the records of a large number of estates are examined with the object of ascertaining those factors associated
with the profitable and unprofitable estates which appear worthy of more
detailed investigation. For purposes of convenience the analyses of estate records are presented in five parts:-
"I. A detailed account of the average expenditure, yields, cost of production, profits and losses, &c, of all the estates visited, pp.285-291.
"II. A comparison and contrast of the records of the 'best' and 'worst'
estates.
"III. A brief examination of the records of different years.
"IV. A comparison and contrast of the more important cacao growing districts.
"V. An examination of estates grouped according to (a) yields per
1,000 pockets. (b) area under cacao cultivation. (c) expenditure per acre
on cultivation. (d) age of cultivation."

Canned Foods - Consumption - Milwaukee Market

The consumer and canned foods. I-III. The Canner 83(2):7-8; (3):10-11,24;
(5):18. June 20-27, July 11, 1936. (Published at 140 N. Dearborn St.,
Chicago, Ill.)
An analysis of the consumption and distribution of canned foods in the
Greater Milwaukee market. Among the statistics given are average monthly
consumption by families using products of canned soups, pork and beans,
canned salmon, canned peaches, canned pineapples, tomato juice, grapefruit
juice, pineapple juice, strained vegetables, canned spaghetti, and
bottled catsup. Statistics are given for the year ending Jan. 15, 1936,
and for some earlier years.

Cold Storage Locker Plants

Henry, John. Community ice box. Rural Progress 100(10): 3, 12. October 1936.
(Published at 22 West Monroe St., Chicago, Ill.)
"Some six years ago a group of Oregon farmers discussed the constantly
widening spread between what they received for their farm products and
what they had to pay for the goods they bought. They were tired of doing
without fresh meat all summer, and very, very tired of canned beef, larded
sausage, and salt pork."
These farmers organized the first cold storage plant for the sole purpose of renting storage space to consumers. While this plant was "extremely crude" it answered the need of the farmers. Today modern cold
storage locker plants are not only suitable for meats, but for perishable
fruits and vegetables as well. The writer tells of several modern plants

and how farmers have been benefited by them.

Collective Farming - U.S.S.R.

The collective market-farms. Russian Econ. Notes, no.326, pp.1-3. Aug. 30, 1936. (Published by Division of Regional Information, Bureau of Foreign and Domestic Commerce, U S. Dept. of Commerce)
Summarized from the The Plan, no.12, 1936.
"During the past year the collective farms made great progress in stock-raising, and the State plan for all forms of stock, except colts, was overfulfilled. This result was largely the consequence of the re-organization of the collective farm into market-farms, i.e., farms producing primarily for sale. This form of organization was recognized by the Government in June 1934, as the basic one for collective cattle-raising, and farm managers were urged to strive to create a market section in every collective farm. This agency is considered a counter-part of the machine-tractor stations, representing as it does a higher level of technical attainment than the collective with a herd of com-munally-owned cattle "

Cooperation

Collins, E. H. The growth of cooperatives. Banking, 24(4 sec.I): 29, 30, 31. October 1936. (Published at 22 East 40th St., New York, N.Y.)
In this discussion of the growth of the cooperative movement, the move-ment in Denmark is first briefly described, since it is believed that that country is one of the best examples today. The movement in Denmark extends into practically every field of the country's economic life, ac-cording to the writer. That the movement has lagged in the United States has been due to "lack of leadership such as was to be found in Europe," and the nature of economy and our economic philosophy. It is pointed out that cooperatives are organized not only on a national basis today, but on an international basis as well.
Conclusion in part: "The question that one is immediately inclined to ask, once he grasps the size and scope of the cooperative movement, is: What does it mean to the future of the profit system? Is it a threat to that system, or merely a challenge? That is a subject all by itself. This much may be said, however. If some of those in the movement have their way it will be no more than a challenge - a challenge for business to put its house in order and to demonstrate that the profit system is able to hold its own in the face of any competition. If others in the movement have their way it will be a real threat. For it is no secret that the 'left' element in the movement regards it as a means of under-mining private enterprise."

Hood, Robin. Lessons we have learned. Coop. Jour. 10(5):137-142. September-October 1936. (Published at 1731 Eye St., N.W., Washington, D.C.)
"These remarks were made by Mr Hood at the biennial convention of con-sumer cooperatives at Columbus, October 9."

Mr. Hood said in part: "At the risk of wasting time harrowing soil
which has already been extensively cultivated, I should like to address
myself chiefly to an exposition of agricultural co-operation - indicating
some of the problems and difficulties encountered in its steady development through a century, the attitude which farmers hold toward their
cooperatives, and the reasons why they think as they do. Such a discussion, I believe, will prove a more adequate treatment of the relations of agricultural and consumer cooperatives than a mere statement
of my personal opinions. I may at least be able to suggest some avenues
of thought which can be constructively explored."

Howe, E. J. The job of a cooperative. Calif. Cult. 83(21):717, 733. Oct. 10,
1936. (Published at 317 Central Ave., Los Angeles, Calif.)
     Consideration of the question as to what the task of the cooperative
is. After discussing the two distinct views held - that the "sole job
of cooperative action as producers, is to see to it that certain
economies are enjoyed in the assembling, processing and preparation for
market" or that the most valuable work which can be accomplished under
the banner of cooperative organization is that of distribution - the
writer concludes that it is "quite impossible to indicate where the true
path of producer cooperative success should lead. It is certain only
that this is no time to rest on the laurels of past performance, but that
it is the time to reconsider the possible functions of joint effort in
the marketing of our farm products and set our course, not for a year,
but if possible for 10 or 15 years in the future.
     "That future must take into consideration the welfare of the consumer,
and those who serve to get the product from here to there and its price
back to us with the least cost. It must also take into consideration the
fact that farming must continue to be a prosperous and happy life for
increasingly large numbers of individual, independent families. Any other
aim means failure in the end."

Knapp, J. G. Agricultural cooperation in a changing world. Coop. Jour. 10(5):
143-144 Sept.-Oct. 1936. (Published at 1731 Eye St., N.W., Washington,
D C.)
     Reviews the 1936 Year Book of Agricultural Cooperation, published by
the Horace Plunkett Foundation. It is apparent, according to information
from the Year Book that "cooperative marketing organizations in many
countries have been going through a process of adaptation to national
agricultural programs ..
     "The term, 'agricultural cooperation' as this Year Book well shows,
covers, in addition to cooperative marketing, all joint activities of
farmers in improving their economic and social condition. For example,
cooperative purchasing, cooperative credit, cooperative insurance, cooperative electrification, cooperative irrigation, cooperative processing, are
all important segments of agricultural cooperation."

Ritchie, R W. Two splendid illustrations of farmer owned cooperatives. Natl.
Grange Monthly 34(10):3, 12. October 1936. (Published at Springfield,
Mass.)

"In New England and the East Central states are two purchasing cooperatives that have signally distinguished themselves for the past 16 to 18
years by their successful operations over wide territories. These are
the Eastern States Farmers' Exchange, numbering 62,000 members, and the
Grange League Federation Exchange., with a membership of around 110,000."
The first of these cooperatives is operating from a central office located at Springfield, Mass., and the second at Ithaca, N.Y. How each
of these cooperatives has approached the problem of distribution is told
by the writer.

Cooperation, Consumers.

Chase, Stuart. Consumers' cooperation in America: Early failure, present day
    success of the movement World Today Encyclopaedia Britannica 4(1): 3,4.
    September 1936 (Editorial office: 342 Madison Ave., New York, N.Y.)

Emery, F.A. Consumer'co-ops' in American scene. U.S. News 4 (42): 19. Oct. 19,
    1936. (Published at 2201 M. St., N.W., Washington, D C)
       In the column entitled "Uncle Sam's News Reel" the writer tells how
    the cooperative associations operate and what they sell.

Granducci, O.S. The co-op - a new bogeyman. Today 7(2):6-7, 28-29,31. Oct.
    31, 1936. (Published at 152 W. 42nd St., New York, N.Y.)
       The story of the presidential commission sent to Europe to study con-
    sumer cooperation and reasons why businessmen need not fear consumer
    cooperation.

Gunnarson, A.B. Consumers' co-ops on main street. Nation's Business 24(11):
    34,36,38,100-101. November 1936. (Published by the Chamber of Com-
    merce of the United States, Washington, D.C)
       An account of the Cloquet Cooperative Society's stores in Cloquet,
    Minn.

Kelly, F.C. The Swedish road to socialism? Barron's 16(43): 3. Oct. 26, 1936.
    (Published at 44 Broad St., New York, N.Y.)
       "Membership of 'consumer societies' equals about a third of the popu-
    lation of Sweden, making co-operatives a major factor in the economic life
    of the nation.
       "In this article, the author... relates the interesting, and timely, story
    of their growth, from a background of first-hand information gathered
    during a summer in Europe." - [Editor's note.]
       In reply to the question "Just how far will the cooperative movement
    go, and what is the goal?" the author writes in part: "There is a differ-
    ence of opinion about that, even among enthusiastic members of the co-
    operatives. I was told more than once:
       "'The idea is to have just enough co-operative competition to keep
    private enterprise within reasonable bounds. Private business, properly
    controlled, is a highly desirable defense against too much bureaucracy.'
       "But, especially among the younger administrators in the consumer-owned
    enterprises, I found a strong feeling that co-operatives will encroach
    more and more on private business.

"'That's to stop it?' they ask. 'It stands to reason that business not
run for profit, - maintaining only enough reserves for emergency and gradual
expansion, - can undersell a business operated for the purpose of making
money. Then the co-operatives do most of the business of the country,
the situation will be about the same as if the enterprises they carry on
were socialized by the State.'

"'Then why,' I asked, 'don't you just socialize everything and be done
with it?'

"'Ah,' I was told, 'that would alarm the opposition if we tried to do it
all at once.'"

Ralpn, H.D. Consumer co-operatives are growing. Mag. Wall St. 58(13):758-
   759,796,797,798. Oct. 10, 1936. (Published at 90 Broad St., New
   York, N.Y.)
      A discussion of the co-operative movement and of the question, how
   much of a threat are consumer co-operatives to retail trade or to the
   American profit system?
      In conclusion: "We have consumer co-operatives in this country. We
   always have had some, always will. Other countries likewise. They may
   grow, perhaps rapidly, and the government may aid somewhat. They may
   cause some changes in business methods, prodding private business to try
   to give the consumer more for his dollar than the co-op offers. But the
   co-op is not much of an immediate threat to most lines of private enterprise."

Van Boskirk, R.L. Uncle Sam flirts with the co-ops. Nation's Business 24(10)
   17-19,119,120,121. October 1936. (Published by the Chamber of Commerce
   of the United States, Washington, D.C.)
      Two questions are discussed in this article: How far has the Govern-
   ment gone in sponsoring consumer cooperatives - and can this form of
   distribution thrive in America?

Cotton

Burton, C.S. Cotton must go up. Surplus stocks have been greatly reduced,
   our crop is short and consumption is rising. Mag. Wall St. 59(1):36-37,
   61. Oct. 24, 1936. (Published at 90 Broad St., New York, N.Y.)

Commercial and Financial Chronicle. Cotton movement and crop of 1935-36.
   Com. & Financ. Chron. 143(3718);1940-1956. Sept. 26, 1936. (Published
   at 25 Spruce St., New York, N.Y.)
      Annual review of world cotton production, consumption and trade, in-
   cluding a discussion of the activities of the United States Government
   and its agencies.

Cotton - China

C., H-S. Cotton production in China doubled. Far East Survey 5(21):229,
   230. Oct. 21, 1936. (Published by the American Council, Institute of
   Pacific Relations, 129 East 52nd St., New York, N.Y.)
      "Behind this relatively phenomenal stimulation of cotton production

in China can be discerned several factors. There is of course the
general rise in price. But equally, if not more, important are the
governmental decrees of compulsory cultivation, such as has been recently promulgated in Shansi, the promotion of the cooperative movement
by the provincial governments and many of the big banks, and the actual
Japanese propaganda for more extensive cultivation."

Cotton - Cooperative Marketing

Hermann, O. W. Moving cotton to market cooperatively. News for Farmer Cooperatives 3(6):8-10. September 1936. (Issued by the Farm Credit Administration, Washington, D.C.)
    The writer tells of the amount and value of cotton that has been
marketed cooperatively since the first association was organized in
1921, and of the assistance rendered in bringing about widespread improvements in cotton marketing.

Cotton Picker

Barnwell, M.G. Rust cotton picker means gradual motorization, but not violent
economic upheaval. Textile World 86(10):1806-1808,1878, illus. September
1936. (Published at 330 West 42d St., New York, N.Y.)

Talley, Robert. Cotton's new social problem Nation's Business 24(11):29-
31,91. November 1936. (Published by the Chamber of Commerce of the
United States, Washington, D.C)
    On the Rust cotton picker.

Westbrook, E.C. Cotton picker - friend or foe? Prog. Farmer (Ga.-Ala.-Fla.
ed.) 51(10):12. October 1936. (Published at 821 North Nineteenth St.,
Birmingham, Ala.)
    A discussion of the question "What will be effect [of the Rust Cotton
picker] on South's agriculture?" The author writes in part: "In my
opinion, if the Southeastern States continue to work toward one-variety
cotton communities in the production of quality cotton, the Southeastern
cotton will sell for enough above the machine-picked Western cotton to
enable it to compete successfully."

Credit, Cooperative - France

Lyons, C.E. French Government assists cooperative credit organizations. Com.
Repts. 40: 79?, 304. Oct. 3, 1936. (Issued by the Bureau of Foreign and
Domestic Commerce, U.S. Dept. of Commerce)
    "The wide variety of economic measures passed by the French Parliament
in June, when the present Government began, at once gave rise to a very
general expectation that prices would rise sharply. This expectation was
based particularly on the laws calling for increased wages and for pay
during workers' holidays...
    "In order to control the situation, the French Government at once set
up a rather elaborate scheme to keep check on prices current, with authority to penalize those who raised their prices too high. A month or two

-927-

subsequently (Aug. 26, 1936) another law was passed, to authorize agricultural cooperative societies and consumer cooperatives to group themselves into unions, 'with the object of reducing the cost of living.' The national agricultural credit bank will continue to make long-term loans to cooperative unions."

A section of the article is devoted to the discussion of the spread of Cooperative Credit Societies, and another section tells of the various types of Credit Cooperatives. Efforts to encourage Consumers' Cooperatives are also considered.

Crop Insurance

Rogers, C L Crop insurance Conf. Bd. Bull. 10(11):81-88. Oct. 20, 1936. (Published by the National Industrial Conference Board, Inc., 247 Park Ave., New York, N.Y)

In this discussion of crop insurance and its problems the writer includes a review of early attempts to write all-risk insurance in America - the first in Minneapolis in 1899, the next in 1917, and others in the post-war period He also reviews and gives information from a preliminary report made by the Committee on Crop Insurance and released by the Department of Agriculture at Regina, Saskatchewan, regarding premium rates on wheat in Saskatchewan, 1936, in nine municipalities. The present proposals for crop insurance in the United States are discussed. The major difficulties to be overcome are listed. In the conclusion it is stated:

"From the foregoing it will be seen that the feasibility of a public plan of all-risk insurance is by no means assured. The dangers that the entire plan may come under political control and be used in a general scheme of government control of all individual farm operations are very great.

"On the other hand, there unquestionably is some justification in attempting to provide the farmer with a measure of insurance against crop failures so serious as to make it impossible for him to continue operating his farm."

At the conclusion of the article a selected bibliography on crop insurance is given.

Crop Reporting, U S. Dept. of Agriculture

Fox, Derek. Prediction plus - in crop reporting. U.S. News 4(41):13. Oct. 12, 1936. (Published at 2201 M St., N.W., Washington, D.C.)

Describes the care with which the Crop Reporting Board works when issuing one of its periodic forecasts of food supplies to insure secrecy until time for the report to be released.

Dairy Products - Guaranteed Prices - New Zealand

The industry's viewpoint. New Zeal. Dairy Exporter 12(2):3-4, 33. Sept. 1, 1936. (Publisher's address , P.O. Box 1001, Wellington, New Zealand.)

"This article seeks to give impartially, and without any comment by ourselves, views of various sections of the dairy industry [on guaranteed

prices] as expressed, firstly by certain people prominently connected
with the co-operative side of the industry, and secondly at the annual
meetings of factories, many of which have been held during recent weeks."

Debt Legislation - Canada

Brownlee, J.D. Further comments on debt reduction. West. Farm Leader 1(10):
141 Oct 2, 1936 (Published in Calgary, Alberta.)
   One of a series of articles on debt legislation. In this article Mr.
Brownlee describes the attitude of the Board of Review under the Farmers' Creditors Arrangement Act, and states farmers affected by the debt
legislation should be encouraged to make applications under the Farmers'
Creditors Arrangement Act.

Demand Curves

Shepherd, Geoffrey. Vertical and horizontal shifts in demand curves. Econometrica 4(4):361-367. October 1936 (Published by the Econometric
Society, Mining Exchange Bldg., Colorado Springs, Colo.)

Democracy and Education

Wilson, M.L. Education for democracy. Rural Amer. 14(6):3-6 September
1936. (Published by the American Country Life Association, Inc., 105
East 22nd St., New York, N.Y.)
   Address before the American Country Life Association, 1936, in which
the problems of democracy and the relationship between democracy and
education are discussed. Mr. Wilson suggests a national program of
group discussion and in conclusion presents five points in connection
with such a program. He makes brief suggestions in reference to each of
these points.

Drought - Alberta

Drought problem is concern of all Alberta people. West. Farm Leader 1(7):
1,5. Aug. 21, 1936. (Published in Calgary, Alberta)
   One of a series by articles by "the Editor" on the need for speedy
action looking to the rehabilitation of the drought areas in Alberta.
   A few of the features of a "comprehensive report on the rehabilitation
of the dry areas based on information accumulated and compiled by Donald
Cameron for Mr. Longman's committee" are touched upon in this article.
"It is hoped that this will give an understanding of the grounds on which
the committee's recommendations are based."

Drought - United States

From abundance to scarcity: a new farm threat. U.S. News 4(27): 3, 18. July
6, 1936. (Published at 22 O.N.Y. st., N.W., Washington, D C.)
   Describes the extent of the damage already done by the drought and
the measures the Government is taking to relieve the stricken areas.

[Shaw, T.R] The story of the extraordinary drouth. Southwest. Miller 15
(35): 20, 40, 41. Oct. 27, 1936. (Published at 860-869 Board of Trade
Bldg., Kansas City, Mo.)
    The story of the drouth as outlined by T.R Shaw, editor of Cargill
Crop Bulletin, before the Grain and Feed Dealers' National Association.
    The story includes a discussion of the numerous reasons assigned for
drouths; the suffering in ancient times due to drouths; the far-
reaching effects of this disaster; how fall rains affect succeeding
crops; the almost unbelievable toll of crops; and the prospects for
1937
    Also printed in Grain & Feed Journals Consolidated 77(8):345, 346.
Oct. 28, 1936; and Grain & Feed Rev 26(3):32-34. November 1936.

Economic Annalist

Economic Annalist, v.6, no.5, pp.65-80   October 1936. (Published by the
Agricultural Economics Branch, Department of Agriculture, Ottawa,
Canada)
    Partial contents: Privy Council finds Australia's Dried Fruits Act
unconstitutional, pp.67-68; Marketing legislation in New Zealand, by
C V. Parker, pp.69-70; Objectives in the Alberta land utilization survey,
by G.M. Craig, pp.70-71; Some data on the consumption of maple products,
by G P Boucher, pp.72-73. Assistance to farmers in dried-out areas of
prairie provinces, summarized by R S. Hamer, p.73; Survey relating to
the consumption of meats in Canadian cities, p.74; Cost of milk production study, pp.74-75, Life insurance carried by farmers in the Lomond
and Vulcan districts, Alberta, by W.J. Hansen, pp.76-79.

Economic Conditions - Scottish Highlands

The state of the Highlands. Planning, no.81, pp.2-15. Sept 8, 1936. (Published by PEP, 16, Queen Anne's Gate, London, S W.1, Eng.)
    A review of economic conditions in the Scottish Highlands and of the
need for special treatment of the problem. Paragraph topics are: The
Highland tragedy; a disappearing people; villages on the dole; how the
crofter exists; when the fishing boat is given up; little employment and
low pay; fewer children and more old people; surprising mobility of the
Highlander; can Highland industries be developed; the Highlands must earn
money from outside; what the Highlands have given the Empire; obstacles
to increased tourist traffic; tourism as a base for other industries;
development of natural resources; Highland conditions make orthodox
methods inapplicable; etc.

Economic Geography

Economic Geography, v.12, no.4, pp.325-432. October 1936. (Published by Clark
University, Worcester, Mass.)
    Contents: Northern Nigeria - a study in political geography, by John
B. Appleton and Tilma Belden, pp.325-339; Mining patterns of occupance in
five South American districts, by Robert S. Platt, pp.340-350; Fairs and
markets in the Department of Gers, France, by Henry Madison Kendall,

pp.351-358; Swine production in the corn belt of the United States, by
Earl Shaw, pp.359-372; Sugar plantations of the Irish Bend District,
Louisiana, by Edwin J. Foscue and Elizabeth Troth, pp.373-380; Dis-
sected drift plain of southeastern Nebraska, by Walter Hansen, pp.381-
391, Regionalism; its cultural significance, by Helen M Strong, pp.392-
410, English countryside and population in the eighteenth century (concluded - second instalment) by G E. Fussell, pp.411-430 (bibliography,
pp.427-430)

Economic Policy - France

French economic legislation. Fed. Reserve Bull. 22(10):782-788. October 1936.
(Issued by the Board of Governors of the Federal Reserve System, Washington, D C.)
   Translations of two measures enacted during the first session of the
new French Parliament, which ended August 14, 1936, are given. "The
first is a decree of August 13 issued in accordance with the law revising
the Bank of France statutes, fixing August 17, 1936, as the date of
application of the law, and setting forth the procedure governing the
conduct of the General Meeting of shareholders and other administrative
details   The second measure, passed August 13, further amends the Code
of Direct Taxes by requiring financial and business interests to furnish
the Minister of Finance with copies of documents relative to international transactions effected for the account of any natural or legal
person."
   Summaries of some of the more important social and economic measures
enacted are given. This includes the law creating an Interprofessional
National Wheat Board.

Economic Policy - United States

Hyde, D.C. National economic policy: the American tradition. South. Econ.
Jour. 3(2):148-160. October 1936. (Published at Chapel Hill, N.C.)
   "An article written in connection with a project of the Institute for
Research in the Social Sciences, University of Virginia."
   "The American tradition in national economic policy must be considered
with reference to the political and economic conditions under which it
grew and flourished. The first century of American independence presented the spectacle of an essentially agricultural people expanding the
area of settlement from the Atlantic coastal plain to the Pacific. Free
land and seemingly inexhaustible natural resources formed the basis of
an economic life marked by ample opportunity and promise of success. As
individual initiative was necessary to the conquest of the wilderness,
the country produced a type of man fully capable of taking care of his
own economic welfare. Bearing in mind the contemporary popularity of the
liberal individualistic philosophy that dominated the economic thought of
the day, we are prepared to find that the national economic policy of
the first years of the Republic was marked by absence of government interference with the economic life of the citizen. Stalwart individualism, neither needing nor desiring the aid and protection of the state,

was long considered to be the source of American power and prosperity."
The writer continues by tracing the development of national economic
policy from the e liest days of the Republic.

Egg Auctions

Treat, E B. Operating an egg auction News for Farmer Cooperatives 3(6):
7, 12, 13. September 1936. (Published by the Farm Credit Administration,
Washington, D.C.)
"The auction system of marketing eggs at country points originated
in New Jersey in 1930 and spread quite rapidly into surrounding States.
At the present time there are more than 20 producer-owned auction
associations located in New Jersey, Pennsylvania, Connecticut, New York,
Massachusetts, New Hampshire, and Ohio. This method of egg marketing
has been constantly expanding, and there is no apparent reason why it
should not expand further "
How these auctions operate is described in the article.

Elevators, Cooperative

Rucker, V. M. Profits for cooperative elevators. Coop. Jour. 10(5):135-136.
September-October 1936. (Published at 1731 Eye St , N.W., Washington,
D.C)
"The definite relationship which exists between sideline operations
and profits for cooperative elevators indicates that this business, if
it is to succeed, is going to take on more and more sidelines."
Among the commodities named which have been carried as sidelines with
some elevators are: poultry, eggs, and cream; gas and oil; livestock
shipping; and lumber. It is believed that the day is passed when everything from a "needle to a threshing machine" can be handled, but there are
"without question, sidelines which lend themselves very well to cooperative associations with which the managers are familiar."

Employment, Interest and Money

Hansen, A H. Mr. Keynes on underemployment equilibrium. Jour. Polit. Econ.
44(5):667-636. October 1936. (Published by the University of Chicago
Press, 5750 Ellis Ave., Chicago, Ill.)
A review of J.M. Keynes' book, The General Theory of Employment, Interest and Money

Farm Economist

Farm Economist, v.2, no.4, pp.53-72. October 1936. (Published by the Agricultural Economics Research Institute, Parks Road, Oxford, Eng.)
Contents: Combine-harvesting costs in 1935, by R.P. Askew, pp.53-57;
Machine versus hand-milking, by A L. Jolly, pp.57-59; The relationship
between the prices and costs of pork and bacon pigs, by J.R. Lee, pp.59-
60; Causes of the recent rise in egg prices [in Great Britain] by O.J.
Beilby, pp.61-63; The effect of recent currecy depreciation on British
agriculture, by Ruth Cohen, pp.63-67; Milk in schools, by K.A.H. Murray,
pp.67-68.

Feed - Drought Area

Pollock, E. O. "Headlights of the feed situation in the drought area" Grain
& Feed Rev. 26(3): 54, 55. November 1936   (Published at 408 South
Third St., Minneapolis, Minn.)
"An address made by E. O. Pollock, In Charge, Federal Livestock Feed
Agency, at the convention of the Grain and Feed Dealers National Associa-
tion, at Milwaukee, Wisconsin, on October 12."

Food Supply - United States

Harrower, D. C   "Our daily bread". Barron's 16(41): 23. Oct. 12, 1936.
(Published at 44 Broad St., New York, N.Y.)
"Important not only to the individual or the family group but to
every employer of labor, as well as to lawmakers and merchandisers of
every other item competing for the consumer's dollar are the nation's
food supply and its probable cost.
"Mr. Harrower not only analyzes the present situation in major foods
but also sizes up the outlook six months ahead." - [Editor's note.]
A table compiled by the Bureau of Agricultural Economics is given.
It shows the per-capita food supplies available for domestic consumption,
1936-37.

Fruit - Precooling

Hienton, T.E., and Fawcett, K.I. The precooling of fresh fruit. Agr. Engin.
17(9):377-378, 382. September 1936. (Published by the American Society
of Agricultural Engineers, St. Joseph, Mich.)
"Presented before the Power and Machinery Division at the annual
meeting of the American Society of Agricultural Engineers, at Estes Park,
Colorado, June 1936."

Future Trading

Lovatelli, James. Commodity--vs. security--trading. Com. and Finance 25(18):
641-653. Sept. 5, 1936. (Published at 95 Broad St., New York, N.Y.)
Advantages to the investor of trading in commodities are described.

Mehl, J.M. The Commodity Exchange Act as it affects the grain trade. Grain
& Feed Journals Consolidated 77(8):344. Oct. 28, 1936. (Published at
332 South La Salle St., Chicago, Ill.)
An address before the Grain and Feed Dealers National Association, at
Milwaukee
This address is also given in The Grain & Feed Review 26(3):36,67,68.
November 1936.

White, G. R. Some statistical aspects of future trading on a commodity exchange. Roy. Statis Soc. Jour. 99(2):297-329, 1936. (Published at 4,
Portugal St., London, W.C.2, Eng.)

Paper read before the Royal Statistical Society, February 18, 1936.
"The primary object of this paper... was to investigate whether the
adoption of future trading in a particular commodity - hides - has been
of real benefit to the trade concerned. The two principal claims made
on behalf of future trading are (a) it tends to reduce major price
fluctuations, and (b) it offers a means of price insurance by the
facilities afforded for hedging. The analysis has shown: (a) there is
no evidence that the introduction of future trading in America has had
any damping effect on hide-price fluctuations, in fact, the evidence
tends to point in the opposite direction, and (b) hedging has only provided imperfect price insurance, in some cases the operator making unexpected profits and in others heavy losses. Investigation of an
alternative method of price insurance suggests that this might be worthy
of more attention than has been given to it in the past."
Discussion on Mr. White's paper is given on pages 329-342.

Grapes, Wine - Harvesting and Transportation

Winkler, A J. Harvesting and transportation of wine grapes. Wines and Vines
17(10):22, 23, October, 1936. (Published at 85 Second St., San Francisco,
Calif.)

Greenbelt Communities - Constitutionality

Abbott, Grace and Breckinridge, S.P. New chapters in the history of the courts
and social legislation Social Serv. Rev. 10(3):483-499. September 1936.
(Published by the University of Chicago Press, 5750 Ellis Ave., Chicago,
Ill.)
Delegation of powers: Resettlement under the Emergency Relief Act unconstitutional, pp.489-491. Relates to the Bound Brook, N.Y. greenbelt community.

Hogs - Rail Grading - Canada

Rail grading of hogs is growing in Canada. Natl. Provisioner 95(15): 13,14.
Oct. 10, 1936. (Published at 407 So. Dearborn St., Chicago, Ill.)
"Buying hogs on basis of grade is important to packer and producer in
Canada, where Wiltshire sides for export is an important phase of meat
packing operation.
"Grading hogs on a live basis was not found entirely satisfactory,
and grading of carcasses on the rail has been developed. Both kinds of
grading are still used, but the rail grading method is growing in favor.
"Standards for live hog grading were established in Canada in October,
1922. These were designed to provide a system whereby farmers producing
better hogs would receive better returns than farmers marketing poorer
animals. Nine grades were prescribed."
The writer explains how the hogs are graded and how the price is determined and then considers rail grading and its problems. "Rail grading
of hogs was started at one Canadian plant in 1934. Today every packing
plant in Canada is either buying a considerable number of hogs on the

rail basis, or has completed its preparations and assembled sufficient
test data to enable it to do rail buying in the very near future "

Hog and Pork Outlook - Europe

Reed, H E. European hog and pork outlook Foreign Crops and Markets 33(15):
435-439. Oct. 12, 1936. (Published by the Division of Foreign Agricultural Service, Bureau of Agricultural Economics, U S. Dept of
Agriculture.)

"Under present conditions in Europe, supply and demand alone no longer
determine the movement of hogs and pork products from surplus to deficit
areas   Instead, the movement of hogs to Great Britain is determined
by the British import quota and the movement of hogs and pork products
to deficit countries on the Continent is determined by the ability of
the exporting country to absorb the industrial and other goods with
which deficit hog countries pay for imports   During the past year the
movement of continental pork to Great Britain has been reduced as
British and Empire production expanded, but the movement from surplus
and deficit areas on the Continent has increased under barter and
similar agreements.

"There are two great uncertainties in the trade in hog products and
its effect on European hog production during the coming year. British
plans for placing the hog and pork industry in Great Britain on a sound
basis, and the ability of surplus hog-producing countries on the Continent to absorb the goods of the deficit countries   The only really
important outlet in Europe remaining free from quantitative and other
restrictions is the British lard market."

Income, Farm - United States

Income from farm production in the United States, 1935. Crops and Markets
13(9):328-331. September 1936. (Published by the U S. Dept. of Agriculture).

Consists of eight statistical tables   A footnote on p 328 states that
"A discussion of this subject, with definition of terms, and additional
statistics are contained in 2 mimeographed reports, copies of which may
be had upon application to the Bureau of Agricultural Economics, Washington, D C. One report, entitled 'Income from Farm Production in the
United States in 1935,' discusses farm income and analyzes total expenses of farm production; the other report, entitled 'Farm Value,
Gross Income and Cash Income from Farm Production, 1934-35, contains
estimates of farm values of 78 crops and 13 livestock items, and the
gross and cash income received by farmers therefrom, by commodities and
by States."

Income, Farm - Virginia

Koiner, G. W. Farm income for 1936. Commonwealth. 3(10):15. October 1936.
(Published at Central National Bank Bldg., Richmond, Va.)
The Commissioner of Agriculture of Virginia writes of the farm income

from the leading crops grown in his state during 1936 He holds that
while most Virginia farmers "will receive more money for their products
this year, a large number will receive smaller net returns because of
drought conditions Yet it would appear that, of two evils attending
agriculture, drought is less devastating than price depression."

Income from Manufacturing - United States

Slaughter, Jack Income in the various states, from manufacturing, 1929-
1935. Conf.Bd.Bull.10(12):89-104. Nov. 2, 1936. (Published by the
National Industrial Conference Board, Inc., 247 Park Ave., New York,
N Y.)
"This article is part of a comprehensive study of incomes in the
various states that is being made by the Conference Board." It is accompanied by charts, tables and a map

Institute of American Meat Packers

National Provisioner v 95, no. 16, pp.1-222. Oct. 17, 1936. (Published at
407 S Dearborn St., Chicago, Ill.)
Convention number Contains proceedings of the 31st annual convention
of the Institute of American Meat Packers, held in Chicago, Ill., Oct.
9-13, 1936 Besides the address of Chairman Frank A Hunter, who
sounded the "key-note" of the convention, the following addresses are
also noted: The outlook for supplies of livestock, by C.L Harlan,
pp.80-86; The outlook for meat packing, by W. W. Shoemaker, pp.86-90;
Our cooperative commonwealth, by Colby M Chester, pp.90-93; New legislation affecting the packing industry, by Charles Aaron, pp.93-102;
The status of trade practices in our industry, by Paul S. Willis, pp.
102-109; Practical methods of improving hog production, by J R. Wiley,
pp.109-113; Trends in merchandising meat at retail, by A.J. Kaiser,
pp.113-114; 13C; What the meat consumer wants, by Mrs. Wilbur E.
Fribley, pp.136, 138, 139; The cattle producer and his problems, by
Albert K. Mitchell, pp.141, 142, 144; The view ahead, by William Whit-
field Woods, pp.144-150; and The European situation, by Sir Willmott
Lewis, pp.151, 152-156

Journal of Marketing

Journal of Marketing, v.1, no.2, pp.75-174. October 1936. (Published by
the American Marketing Society and the National Association of Marketing
Teachers, 383 Madison Ave , New York, N.Y.)
Partial contents: Implications of the Robinson-Patman Act for marketing by N.H. Engle, pp.75-81; Comparison of chain and independent grocery
stores in the San Francisco area, by David E. Faville, pp.87-90; The
public warehouse an essential tool in wholesale distribution, by Albert
Haring, pp.106-114; Economic provisions of marketing agreements for
general crops, by Budd A. Holt, pp.115-126; Comments on "Economic Provisions of marketing agreements for general crops," by James E. Boyle,
pp.127-128; The significance of early economic thought on marketing, by

J. M Cassels, pp.129-133; Retail stores in the United States, 1800-1860, by Fred Mitchell Jones, pp.134-142; Seasonal storage in China, by W. Mackenzie Stevens, pp.143-149 (gains or losses from seasonal storage of wheat in China); Legislative trends of interest to students of marketing, pp.154-155; Progress in marketing research, Malcolm D. Taylor, editor, pp.156-168.

Labor - California

[Taylor, H.] Farm labor organization case. Calif. Fruit News 94 (2519): 3,4. Oct. 17, 1936. (Published at 405 Montgomery St., San Francisco, Calif.)
"Ralph H. Taylor, executive secretary of the Agricultural Council of California, has just written three articles for the bulletin he issues entitled 'The Farmer's Corner' for the past three weeks, on the California farm labor problems. These deal with the present effort at unionizing farm workers, the preferential hiring hall and the farmer's responsibility for eliminating causes of unrest... [This article] is a composition of the three articles in their order, with elimination of some of the less essential parts to bring the whole within reasonable length for one story."

Land - Legislation - United States

Hockley, H.A. Digest of state legislation affecting agriculture and land from June 1, 1936 to August 1, 1936. Land Policy Circ. pp.13-16. September 1936. (Published by the Land Use Planning Section, Division of Land Utilization, U. S. Resettlement Administration.

Land Policy - Southern States

Blackwell, C.P. What kind of land policy shall we have in the South? Com. Fert. 53(3):24,26,27. September 1936. (Published at 223 Courtland St., N. E., Atlanta, Ga.)
"An address before the Agronomy Section of the Association of Southern Agricultural Workers at Jackson, Miss."
The writer summarizes as follows: "It seems desirable to work out a land policy for the South which would protect against erosion, provide for the maintenance and improvement of fertility, which would encourage home ownership on a selective basis, and which would help to hold down the price level of land to the point where the revenues from the land might, in a reasonable period of years, pay out the indebtedness."

Land Program, Effect on Local Government - Great Plains

Renne, R.R. Probable effects of Federal land purchase on local government. Natl. Munic. Rev. 25(7):401-406, 411. July 1936. (Published by the National Municipal League, 309 East 34th St., New York, N.Y.)
"Contribution from Montana State College, Agricultural Experiment Station Paper No.68, Journal Series."

Analyzes the effects of land purchase and resettlement on local
government in the Great Plains area where maladjustments in the use of
land seem to be particularly acute. The writer concludes that the program will do much to correct "present fundamental maladjustments in the
Great Plains area by blocking out the scattered tracts into economical
units" and that it will be beneficial to local governments in the area.
Several factors have kept the program from going forward rapidly and
smoothly - insufficient funds, misunderstandings, and charges of too
much government in business and government "red tape."

Land Settlement - Chile

Land settlement in Chile. Internatl. Labour Rev. 34(3):361-369. September
1936. (Published by International Labour Office, Geneva, Switzerland.
Distributed in U.S. by World Peace Foundation, 8 West 40th Street, New
York, N.Y.)
    By an act of December 10, 1928 a "Public Land Settlement Fund" was
created, an autonomous institution to found and administer agricultural
settlements and to promote the breaking up of agricultural estates. It
has the power to request the President to expropriate any land it may
need over and above that which can be purchased in the open market.
"The widow and children of a deceased settler may retain joint possession
of the holding, subject to agreement among themselves."
    Three types of settlement are organized. The first type, intended
primarily to encourage the systematic development of production, recruits settlers with special qualifications for a particular kind of
farming. They pay a minimum deposit of 5 or 10 percent, the remainder
being payable in 33 annual installments, beginning 2 or 4 years after
they take possession of the holding. The main object of the second type
is to facilitate the breaking up of large estates. The settlers pay a
minimum deposit of 10 or 20 percent and usually have a small working
capital.
    The "training settlements" are for Chilean workers. There they may be
trained before being placed on the land. An example of this type is the
settlement of El Sauce near Los Andes. The activity of the Settlement
Fund from 1929 to 1934, its reorganization in 1935, and the settlement
of Penaflor are described.

Land Settlement - Great Britain

Yates, P.L. The land and the unemployed industrial worker in Great Britain.
Internatl. Labour Rev. 34(3):339-360. September 1936. (Published by
International Labour Office, Geneva, Switzerland. Distributed in U.S.
by World Peace Foundation, 8 West 40th Street, New York, N.Y.)
    "In the following article the author describes the various types of
land settlement that have been tried, indicating for each type its advantages and disadvantages and the factors tending to success or failure."
    A distinction is made between "allotment" and subsistence holdings
and small holdings or small family farms, the former being defined as
including "all holdings larger than an allotment (in practice from ¼
acre upwards) from which the cultivator is not expected to earn the

-938-

major portion of his livelihood", and the latter as "holdings of 5 acres and upwards from which the occupier should be able to sell enough to be independent and maintain a proper standard of living."

Land Tenure - Mexico

Adams, Huntington. The agrarian system of Mexico. Amer. Rev. 7(4): 409-421. September 1936. (Published at 231 W. 58th St., New York, N.Y.)

The author stresses the fact that there has always been a deficiency of tillable land in Mexico in proportion to the population - a contrast to conditions in the United States. "At the time of the Spanish Conquest... the basis of land tenure was communal ownership by towns and villages. The tillable land was distributed among the heads of families, and, if continuously cultivated, remained indefinitely in the family and passed by inheritance from one generation to another. In addition to the individual holdings of tillable plots, the village holdings included areas cultivated for the Emperor or King and for district chieftains, as well as common lands, such as forests, etc. for general communal use of the village.

"In addition... there had developed a system of large estates owned by the nobility and worked by people attached to the land like serfs. They worked as share-croppers, and paid no taxes or tribute as did the freemen...

"During the Spanish Colonial régime of nearly 300 years, the lands of the free villages were in general respected, although gradually encroached upon; but the large estates of the Aztec nobles were taken over by the Spaniards and formed the basis for the system of vast estates which continued to grow in size and number... down to the time of the Revolution of 1910."

An account is given of the provisions of the Agrarian Code of 1934 which codified previous land laws passed since 1915. "The system adopted is not only interesting but unique in that it is not based on the experience of our civilization derived from Europe, nor upon new theory as in Russia, but on the system used in the Aztec Empire before the coming of the European.

"Any village or legally registered nucleus of 20 families or more, whose members lack land on which to support themselves, may apply for land, or, if they lack sufficient land, may apply for an extension of it...

"The land required is taken from the lands of all large landholdings within a radius of 7 kilometers... of the village, in proportion to the total areas of these properties " This becomes an ejido which is the property of the village and is divided into plots assigned by lot to heads of families for their support. The plot is inherited by the heir of the head of the family and is inalienable. But it may be taken from the owner if he fails to cultivate it for two succeeding years. The qualifications of an ejidatario, provisions that protect landowners who might be affected, the financing of the scheme and its results to date are described.

"In addition to the Ejido system the laws provide for colonization projects for new centers of population as small landowners, in such a form as to encourage the large landholders to organize them for their own account and thus avoid condemnation of their land for Ejidos."

Land Utilization Units

Andrews, H.E. Land utilization units Land Policy Circ. September 1936, pp.
9-12. (Published by the Land Use Planning Section, Division of Land
Utilization, U.S. Resettlement Administration)
    Presents his concept of the land utilization unit, compares this
concept with the concept of land-use districts as described in Resettlement Administration's Field Instruction LU-32 and Land-Use Planning
Publication No. 1 and discusses three methods of facilitating the development of land utilization units.

Livestock - Cooperative Marketing - Oklahoma

Roberts, Clarence. Livestock co-op leads the yards. Farmer-Stockman 49(20):
    507, 513 Oct. 15, 1936. (Published in Oklahoma City, Okla.)
    A story of cooperative effort. The writer tells of the organization of
the Oklahoma Livestock Marketing Association; how they signed "a contract
to run for five years to purchase the National Commission company"; the
difficulties involved in raising the necessary funds for loans; and the
benefits reaped by this co-operative effort.

Marketing Schemes - Great Britain

Agricultural marketing schemes. Statist 128(3061): 539-540. Oct. 24, 1936.
    (Published at 51 Cannon St., London, E.C.4, Eng.)

What has been done - 3 Planning no.74, pp.1-14. May 5, 1936. (Published by
    PEP, 16, Queen Anne's Gate, London, S.W 1, Eng.)
    "As it is so difficult to keep abreast of the new organisations which
are constantly being set up, and of the adjustments taking place in the
national structure, it seems worth issuing at intervals broadsheets aiming
to give a bird's-eye view of recent progress. The present number of
Planning is a sequel to Nos. 12 and 45, in which similar reviews were
undertaken, and read aide by side with them it will give an up-to-date
brief account of many of the recent developments in agricultural marketing, in the evolution of public concerns, in the machinery of government,
and so forth." - p.1.
    See pp.5-8 for the Scottish Raspberry Marketing Scheme, the Potato
Board, Pigs and Bacon Marketing Boards, the Milk Boards, and new sugar
scheme.

Meat - France

Viguerie, P. de Production and consumption of and external trade in meat in
    France. Monthly Bull. Agr. Econ. and Sociol. [reprint from Internatl.
    Rev. Agr.] 27(9): 275-293. September 1936. (Published by the International
    Institute of Agriculture, Rome, Italy)
    Contains Parts III and IV, which concludes the article. Part III deals
with the course of foreign trade, exports and imports, while part IV is
entitled: "The Crisis in Meat Production and the Measures Taken with a
view to Overcoming it."

Mechanization of Agriculture - Great Britain

Agricultural tractors. Economist 124(4856):506,507. Sept. 19, 1936. (Published at 8 Bouverie St., London E C.4, Eng.)

"One of the most striking results of the measures taken during the past few years to stabilise the position of British agriculture has been a rapid increase in mechanisation following directly from the improved purchasing power of the agricultural community. This process has been noticeably accelerated during the past year. It is opening up an unexpectedly large market for agricultural tractors, the production and sale of which is shared between makers of commercial road vehicles and agricultural machinery manufacturers."

An estimate of the number of tractors actually in use is given as well as a description of the kind most commonly used.

Mechanization of Agriculture - Latvia

Kunkis, Voldemar. The mechanisation of agriculture in Latvia. Monthly Bull. Agr. Econ. and Sociol. [reprint from Internatl. Rev. Agr.] 27(9):293-306. September 1936. (Published by the International Institute of Agriculture, Rome, Italy)

In two parts. Part I: Mechanisation as one of the Fundamental Problems of Agriculture in Latvia and Part II: Measures Taken by the Government to Encourage the Mechanisation of Agriculture.

Mechanization of Agriculture - United States

Mauldin, W. P. Trends in farm mechanization. Univ. Va. News Letter, v.13, no.3, Nov. 1, 1936. (Published in University, Va.)

This article is based on census statistics. Tables show mechanical devices on farms in the United States, in principal geographic divisions, and in Virginia, 1920 and 1930; and number of horses and mules in the United States, in principal geographic divisions, and in Virginia, 1900, 1910, 1920 and 1930.

Milk - Price Control - New York

Eastman, E. R. Some conclusions about milk. Amer. Agr. 133(20):551,565. Sept. 26, 1936. (Published at the Savings Bank Bldg., Ithaca, N.Y.)

A review of the facts that led up to the present "seething" milk situation in New York State.

Fixing prices of milk by the State must be discontinued, in the opinion of the writer. "No better proof of this is needed than the utter failure of the Milk Board to meet the present situation. Nearly all of the present disturbance could have been avoided if the Milk Board had promptly granted dairymen a reasonable raise as soon as milk costs began to go up. This meant taking the responsibility, also, of raising the price to consumers. Had the Milk Board done this, backed by the authority of the State, there would have been no consumer strike in New York City. As it is, it will take months before consumers get the idea out of their heads again that they are paying too much for milk."

Wagenen, Jared Van, Jr. The ripe fruit of emergency milk control. Amer.
Agr. 133(20):559. Sept. 26, 1936. (Published at the Savings Bank Bldg.,
Ithaca, N.Y.)

An account of the hearing called by Governor Lehman for September 12
to consider the questions arising out of State Milk Control.

The writer concludes, in part, as follows: "I have the warmest ad-
miration for our Governor [Lehman], and I have every confidence in the
integrity and high-minded devotion of the men charged with the administration of the Milk Control Act. None-the-less they are charged with an
impossible task. I even subscribe to the statement that during the
earlier years of the Act, price control by Legislative fiat gave to the
dairymen of the state millions of dollars more than they would have
otherwise received. But the sweeping tide of economic forces cannot be
dammed back for long. From the day that the idea was broached, I have
believed that in the long run it was impossible to legislate value into
a product. The difficulties multiply with the passing months.

I have yet to meet a thoughtful man in responsible position who was
ready to avow that price control of any agricultural product ought to be
made a part of the permanent State policy... It seems a foregone conclusion that some day the State must step from under the price of milk.
I am wondering if there will ever be a better time than in the coming
autumn months when there will be no large surplus to vex the markets."

Milk - Vacuum Packing

Greene, H. T. Milk kept fresh 42 days by vacuum packing. Food Industries
8(7):328-329. July 1936. (Published at 330 W. 42nd St., New York, N.Y.)

Describes the method of "vacuum sealing of raw or pasteurized milk in
a bottle by the vapor system developed by the White Cap Co., Chicago."
The Brook Hill Farms has undertaken commercial introduction of milk thus
packed to the Milwaukee market "with promising results."

National Economic and Planning Association

ESPA - next steps, by the board of trustees. Plan Age 2(8):[1]-5. November
1936. (Published by National Economic and Social Planning Association,
1721 Eye St., N.W., Washington, D.C.)

"To sum up, the program of ESPA, in its long range as well as in its
short run aspects, is both critical and constructive. It has to be
critical in the sense of analyzing what work is being done in the field
of consistent planning of policy from the point of view of the objectives
set by the Association. To the extent to which local, state and the federal
Government may continue to develop activities which may be classified as
planning, there is need for analysis and stimulation by outside voluntary
and non-partisan organizations such as the ESPA. In so far as the work
of the Government may be limited both in scope and in character, there is
an opportunity for filling in gaps, for suggesting new lines of development and for helping to extend and elucidate such policies."

National Grain Trade Council

Lathrop, W. B. The National Grain Trade Council. Grain & Feed Journals Con-
    solidated 77(7):311. Oct. 14, 1936. (Published at 332 South LaSalle St.,
    Chicago, Ill.)
        Address by the Chairman of the National Grain Trade Council, before
    the Grain & Feed Dealers National Association, Oct. 12, 1936, at Milwaukee,
    Wis. The functions of the council are outlined in this address.
        Also printed in Grain & Feed Rev. 26(3):34, 35. November 1936; and
    Northwest. Miller 188(1):111. Oct. 14, 1936.

New Deal

The Economist. The New Deal; an analysis and appraisal. 24pp. [Supplement to
    the] Economist, v.25, no.4858, Oct. 3, 1936. (Published at 8 Bouverie
    St., Fleet St., London, E.C. 4, Eng.)
        The following is quoted, in part, from the Introduction:
        "The [political] campaign [of 1936 in the United States] has been
    vigorous and the contest is expected to be close. All sorts of issues
    have played their part in the speeches of candidates and partisans, but
    the dominant ones are economic and social. Has the policy pursued by the
    President succeeded in its dual aim of restoring the activity of the
    economic system and of correcting some of its abuses? Has there been
    enough Recovery? Has there been enough (or perhaps too much) Reform?
    Beneath the glossy surface of the slogans and platitudes, these are ques-
    tions that electors will have to answer next month.
        "No one can anticipate the answer they will give. But it may be of
    assistance, especially to observers who have watched the New Deal from
    afar, to summarise what has been done and to point the morals which appear
    to emerge from the record. This is what has been attempted in the follow-
    ing pages. In each chapter an attempt is made to sketch the situation at
    the pit of the depression; to outline the remedy adopted; to record the
    results, in so far as they emerge in a form susceptible of record; and to
    suggest a conclusion on the merits of the experiment.
        "This attempt has been subject to two difficulties in particular. The
    first is space... The second difficulty is subjective. Only to a very
    limited extent is it possible to judge the actions of a whole nation by
    any absolute criterion. For the rest, he who expresses a judgment merely
    exposes his own preconceptions. This risk has been recognized and faced.
    Judgments will be found in the succeeding pages, and in a leading article
    in the accompanying issue of the Economist [pp.6-7], which should be read
    as a synthesis of the whole survey. An effort has been made to make these
    judgments consistent with each other. Beyond that they claim no absolute
    authority."
        Phases of the New Deal which are considered are unemployment and relief,
    public works, housing, industry and labour, agriculture (pp.10-12), banks
    and bankers, the budget, the dollars, foreign trade, security markets, and
    the power controversy.
        The following is a brief extract from the synthesis of the survey, as
    given in the regular issue of the Economist for October 3:

"If the criterion be Utopian, the achievements of the New Deal appear to be small...

"If the New Deal be compared, not with the absolute standards of Utopia, but with the achievements of other Governments, the former adverse judgment must be modified. If it be compared with either the performance or the promise of its rivals, it comes out well. If its achievements be compared with the situation which confronted it in March, 1933, it is a striking success. Mr. Roosevelt may have given the wrong answers to many of his problems. But he is at least the first President of modern America who has asked the right questions."

Nutrition and Social Policy

Claeys, R. Workers' nutrition and social policy. Amsterdamsche Bank n.v., Finan. and Econ. Rev. of the Statis. Dept. no.49, pp.4-12. (Published in Amsterdam)

A review and discussion of the report, "Workers' Nutrition and Social Policy", issued by the International Labour Office.

Planning - Columbia River Region

Glover, Katherine. Planning for power. Survey Graphic 25(10):568-572, 582, 583. October 1936. (Published at 112 East 19th St., New York, N.Y.)

An account "of the synthesis of power and people, forestry, agriculture, transportation and industry, which the development of the Columbia River [Grand Coulee Dam] region promises to exhibit."

In conclusion the author writes: "If we could find a less controversial word than planning, we should have a clearer idea of what is happening in this Pacific Northwest experiment. It is really an attempt to substitute cooperative exploration for individualistic exploitation. Here are people re-examining their natural resources of water, soil and forest, acknowledging the mistakes they have made in the past, trying to go forward on a sounder basis."

Planning, Economic

Landauer, Carl. Essentials of economic planning; an outline for study. Plan Age 2(7):12-22. October 1936. (Published by National Economic and Social Planning Association, 1721 Eye St., N.W., Washington, D.C.)

The following is quoted in part from the editorial note, on p.12:
"The following outline has been prepared by Professor Carl Landauer of the University of California and is used by him as the basis of one of the courses in current economic problems which he offers. We have made a few minor changes in the outline as originally submitted.

"An examination of the outline shows that it proceeds from the assumption that a study of economic planning must begin with a thorough analysis of the market mechanism of the present industrial capitalistic order. This is essential since all proposals for social change must start from a criticism of the existing system. The outline gives especial attention to those features of the present industrial system which have elicited the greatest objections, namely, the phenomena of monopoly and of the business cycle.

- 944 -

"The outline offered here distinguishes between two basic concepts of planning: partial planning and central planning by a national body on a national scope. The central interest of the outline is in the problems raised by a completely planned economy."

Planning, Economic - Bibliography

Landauer, Carl. Essentials of economic planning - bibliography. Plan Age 2 (8): 14-18. November 1936. (Published by National Economic and Social Planning Association, 1721 Eye St., N. W., Washington, D. C.)
    "The titles have been selected largely on the basis of the educational value of the books, or more accurately of their class-room value. Only writings in the English language are recommended In compiling this list the assumption has been made that it should support a lecture course in the upper division of an economic department of a university " - The editors.

Planning, Rural

Wager, P. W. Design for rural living. Natl. Munic. Rev. 25 (10): 604-608. October 1936. (Published by the National Municipal League, 309 E. 34th St., New York, N. Y.)
    "County planning boards, planned land use and rural zoning may be the instrumentalities which will not only give new vitality to county government, but which will remake the face of rural America."

Population - Great Plains

Taeuber, Conrad. The farm population of the great plains. Agr. Situation 20 (9): 13-17 September 1936. (Published by the Bureau of Agricultural Economics, U. S. Dept. of Agriculture)

Price Discrimination Act

Daughters, C. G. Lawful discrimination under the Robinson-Patman act. Dun & Bradstreet Monthly Rev. 44(2103): 7-8, 40. October 1936. (Published at 290 Broadway, New York, N. Y.)

[Thorp, W. L.] Outline of new price law to bakers. Southwest. Miller 15 (32): 40, 41. Oct. 6, 1936. (Published at 860-869 Board of Trade Bldg., Kansas City, Mo.)
    The full text of an address before the Bakers' Conference at Atlantic City by Willard L. Thorp, director of economic research of Dun & Bradstreet, Inc., in which he discussed the Robinson-Patman price law. The subject of his address as given in the Editor's note at the head of the article is: "Trends in Our Economic Development."

Price Fixing

Backman, Jules. Direct price fixing. South. Econ. Jour. 3 (3): 189-207.
October 1936. (Published at Chapel Hill, N. C.)
"The methods by which prices can be fixed are many and varied. Perhaps
the broadest and most logical classification is direct and indirect price
fixing. These two broad types are not mutually exclusive and many attempts
at price fixing have been a combination of the two. In this article the
writer will be concerned only with an analysis of the methods and consequences of direct price fixing."

Price Spreads

Work, Paul. Price spreads between farmer and consumer. Market Growers Jour.
59 (8): 411. Oct. 15, 1936. (Published in Louisville, Ky.)
Comments briefly on the mimeographed report by the Bureau of Agricultural
Economics, on Price Spreads between Farmer and Consumer, by R. O. Been
and F. V. Waugh. The value of such studies is conceded. Limitations in
them are pointed out.
A table entitled Farm-to-Retail Price Margins - Average for 1935 accompanies the article.

Prices and Price Research

Mills, F. C. Price data and problems of price research. Econometrica 4 (4):
289-309. October 1936. (Published by the Econometric Society, Mining
Exchange Bldg., Colorado Springs, Colo.)
Bibliographical footnotes.
"In the present survey, some recent accessions of historical data are
described and existing materials are briefly reviewed with reference to some
of the specific problems with which students of price are concerned. Indeed, such problems are as broad as economic science." - p. 289.
The article is in seven parts: I. Historical studies of prices movements;
II. The construction of price index numbers; III. Price-quantity relations
for individual commodities; IV. The component elements of selling prices; margins and costs; V. The structure of prices; VI. The deflation of cost, price
and value series, VII Summary: some limitations of the statistical record.

Reclamation - Western States

Warden, O. S. Reclamation is cornerstone of our agriculture. Mont. Farmer
24 (3): 6, 27. Oct. 1, 1936. (Published in Great Falls, Mont.)
Address delivered by Mr. Warden, president, National Reclamation Association at the meeting of the Pacific Northwest Business conference at
Boise, Ida.
In this defense of reclamation it is stated that "If we can store and
use the water of the west - all of it - the relief problem will be solved.
There will be regional self-support. The experience on reclamation projects for 30 years, and the lessons of the depression, complete the proof
that this is so."

Velmonte, J. E. Palay and rice prices. Philippine Agr. 25 (5): 382-410.
October 1936. (Published by the College of Agriculture, University of
the Philippines, Laguna, P. I.)
    The following extracts have been quoted from the writer's summary,
pp. 402-404:
    "1. An attempt has been made to discuss the principal forces that de-
termine palay [palay is rice with the hulls] and rice prices based on
conditions prevailing in Nueva Ecija which is the premier rice producing
province.
    "2. The discussion centers in the relation between the prices of palay
received by farmers of Nueva Ecija and the wholesale prices of rice in
the Manila market. It is shown that market quotations for palay in
Cabanatuan are not the real buying prices of millers who control the trade.
A discounted price, known as liquidacion price, is actually the buying price
of palay in Nueva Ecija...
    "3. The facts about the marketing of palay and rice in so far as they
relate to prices are exceedingly complex. It is shown in this paper that
forces of monopoly appear to be at work in determining prices of palay
and rice. On the other hand, there are certain facts which show that competition doubtless plays also its part...
    "4. Government intervention in the rice industry by means of the or-
ganization of a Rice and Corn Corporation involves a number of problems.
The analysis of the proposed activities of this corporation is based on
the report of the Government Rice Commission. While in theory stabilization operations as are being contemplated appear simple and essentially
sound, in practice, these operations are fraught with difficult problems...
    "8. The field of government activities in solving the rice problems
needs not, however, center unduly in stabilization operations. It would
seem that the same objectives may be accomplished with less financial
risk and along more conservative lines. A simple solution may be found in
making the rice tariff flexible so as to make the available rice supply more
responsive to changing demand. Also, importation of rice by the government
may be undertaken to meet an emergency but, unlike the practice last year,
the distribution of this rice should be improved so that it may enter into
competition with rice handled by merchants through the regular trade
channels.
    "9. This study does not presume to fully cover the field of palay and
rice prices. The statistical material covers a relatively short period
[1930-1934, and also 1935]"

Rural America

Rural America, v. 14, no. 7, October 1936. (Published by the American Country
Life Association, Inc., 105 East 22nd St., New York, N. Y.)
    Partial contents: A cooperative Czechoslovak village, by C. J.Galpin,
p. 2; The improvement of rural education, by W. R. Ogg, pp. 3,4; The
financing of rural education, by Julian E. Butterworth, pp. 4-6; In aid
of youth, by John J. Corson, pp. 7,8; The situation faced by younger
adults, by Bruce L. Melvin, pp.9-12; How to obtain rural library service,
by Julia Wright Merrill, pp. 13-14.

Rural Sociology, v. 1, no.3, pp. 259-396. September 1936. (Published by the
Rural Sociology Section, American Sociological Society. T. Lynn Smith,
Managing Editor, Louisiana State University, Baton Rouge)
Partial contents: Historical back ground of California farm labor, by
Paul S. Taylor and Tom Vasey, pp. 281-295, Social attitudes of the Czechoslovakian peasant towards the other occupational groups, by Antonin Obrdlik,
pp. 296-305 ("This study is a part of numerous concrete investigations organized by the sociology department of the Masaryk University... The author
summarizes here a section of the 'Questionnaire'submitted to the various
groups of Czech people for the purpose of ascertaining the attitudes of
the public opinion with regard to the concept of general welfare"); Rural
educational institutions and social lag, by Roland R. Renne, pp. 306-321;
Some characteristics of rural families on relief in New York State, by
W. A. Anderson, pp. 322-331; Some observations on Oklahoma population movements since 1930, by Robert T. McMillan, pp. 332-343.

Security in Agriculture

Nelson, Lowry. Social security in agriculture. Utah Farmer 57 (4): 3, 6, 8.
Sept. 25, 1936 (Published at 45 7. South Temple St., Salt Lake City, Utah)
A discussion of security and an examination of the sources of insecurity
which are peculiar to agriculture. Among the factors named as creating insecurity in the country are the following: Shifting markets; the tenure
risk; taxation; improper land use; and weather crisis. In the discussion
of ways to secure greater security the writer says: "Before great social
objectives in agriculture can be attained, it is going to be necessary to
change the outlook, the psychology, of our people. They must come to a
realization that the outlook possible to their grandfathers is no longer
possible to people living today. The frontier period, the exploitation
period, is at an end. The attitudes toward the natural resources, which
are based upon the assumption that those resources were unlimited, must be
supplanted by attitudes more in line with present realities.
"Furthermore, we have not yet learned an adequate technique of co-operation by which we can achieve, as a group, the fullest measure of economic
and social satisfaction. 'We lay waste our powers' in futile conflict,
when intelligent group action would reward us richly."

Silk - Brazil

Brazil as a silk producer. Brazil 8 (27): 10-11. January 1936. (Published
by the American Brazilian Association, Inc., 17 Battery Place, New York,
N. Y.)
"From the Bureau of Ind. Statistics, Rio Translated by S. Pierini."

Social Forces

Social Forces, v. 15, no. 1, pp. 1-146. October 1936. (Published for the
University of North Carolina Press by the Williams & Wilkins Co.,
Baltimore, Md.)
Partial contents: Regions, by William F. Ogburn, pp. 6-11; Standardiza-

tion of Federal administrative regions, by James W. Fesler, pp. 12-21;
The southern crisis and social control, by Wayland J. Hayes, pp. 21-29
("it is the problem of this paper to present whatever theoretical framework we have for interpreting mass processes and social movements; and
especially to apply this framework to the past and current developments
in the southern regions of the United States."); The social scientist
in the Tennessee Valley Authority program, by T. Levron Howard, pp. 29-
34; The university and social planning. I. Beginnings at the University
of Illinois, by Rexford Newcomb; II. Cooperative research in territorial
planning: the Kaskaskia River Valley study in Illinois, by W. Russell
Tylor, pp. 34-46; Scope of the research on rural youth needed today, by
Bruce L. Melvin, pp. 55-58; Family-capitalism in a community of rural
Louisiana; by Harlan W. Gilmore, pp. 71-75; The Civil War agricultural
new deal, by Earle D. Ross, pp. 97-104; Economic control by interstate
compact, by Edwin M. Duerbeck, pp. 104-111; Political regionalism in
the United States - fact or myth, by Walter Kollmorgen, pp. 111-122.

Source Materials for Quantitative Production Studies

Brown, E. H. P.   First [-third] reports of the Econometrica committee on source
materials for quantitative production studies.   Econometrica 4 (2-4): 123-
137, 242-263, 310-323. April-October 1936. (Published by the Econometric
Society, Mining Exchange Bldg., Colorado Springs, Colo.)
    Bibliographical footnotes.
    "The Econometrica Committee on Source Materials for Quantitative Pro-
duction Studies was set up during the Paris meeting of the Econometric
Society in 1932 on the initiative of the Editor of Econometrica.   The
Committee decided first to concentrate on collecting and presenting some
samples of statistical and other numerical data that illustrate how the
principles involved in the theory of production work in practice." -
p. 133.
    The first report is entitled, The Marginal Efficacy of a Productive
Factor; second report, Cost Categories and the Total Cost-Function; third
report, the Profit-Experience of Producers and their Response to Price.

Soybean Industry - Manchuria

Stewart, J. R.   The soya bean and Manchuria. Far East. Survey 5 (21): 221-
226. Oct. 21, 1936. (Issued by the American Council, Institute of
Pacific Relations, 129 East 52nd St., New York, N. Y.)
    An examination of Manchuria's soya bean industry and its present prob-
lems. It is pointed out that heretofore Manchuria has had a dominating
position in both the production and export of soya beans. "From the purely
domestic side, Manchuria's concentration on soya bean production has made
her an excellent example of agricultural specialization. Soya beans are
not only the principal crop; but beans, together with bean cake and oil,
also regularly supply over half of the nation's total exports. Moreover,
bean oil refining is the principal industry. The economic life of Manchuria is so closely tied to the state of the bean trade that in the past
bean prices have been one of the most reliable guides to the state of the

- 949 -

na'ion's prosperity   It is in this light that Manchuria's soya bean industry and its present problems will be examined."
    Tables showing Manchurian export of soya beans and bean products; crop
area and production, world production of soya beans; and world trade in soya
beans are given.

Statistical Methods - United States

Apchie, Magdelaine.   Les méthodes statistiques dans les études d'économie rurale
    aux Etats-Unis. Revue d'Économie Politique, no.4, pp. 1331-1337. 1936.
    (Published by Librairie du Recueil Sirey, Paris, France) Photostat copy
    in Library.
    Bound with the photostat is a two-page typewritten translation of
    pp. 1335-1337, Conclusion: Quelques Resultats.

Tariff and Agriculture

Potts, C. S.   Farm relief not found in tariff. Texas Weekly 12 (44): 4-6.
    Oct. 31, 1936. (Published at the Dallas Athletic Club Bldg., Dallas, Tex.)
    It is the opinion of the writer that the "great majority of farmers
    are not benefited but are actually injured by the tariff when levied on
    an article produced in this country in quantities far short of our domes-
    tic consumption."
    Practical examples are cited to show that the tariff "is a deceptive
    means of farm relief."

Taxation, Agricultural - U. S. S. R.

Decree modifying agricultural tax. Russian Econ. Notes 328: 3,4, Sept. 30,
    1936. (Published by the Division of Regional Information, Bureau of
    Foreign and Domestic Commerce, U. S. Dept. of Commerce)
    From Economic Life, July 21, 1936.
    "A decree of the Central Executive Committee and the Council of People's
    Commissars of the USSR dated July 20, 1936, modifies the agricultural
    tax collected from collective farms, substituting an income tax paid in
    money for the present money payment system...
    "This decree ... abolishes the old money tax on collective farms be-
    ginning with the present year, and imposes for collection in 1937 and
    thereafter of an income tax based on the gross income of a collective
    for the previous year, including all money income, and also receipts in
    kind from farm production, calculated according to the prices paid by
    the Government-collecting agencies. The rate of tax shall be 3 percent
    for agricultural artels and communes, and 4 percent for associations for
    joint use of land   Payment of tax shall be in installments, from March
    1 to December 1 of each year."

Trade, Foreign - United States

Agricultural exports of the United States, 1935-36. Foreign Crops and Markets
    33 (17): 485-502. Oct. 26, 1936. (Published by the Division of Foreign
    Agricultural Service, Bureau of Agricultural Economics, U. S. Dept. of
    Agriculture)
    The quantity and value of agricultural and forest products exported
    during 1934-35 and 1935-36 (preliminary) are presented in tabular form.

Glover, L. B. What should our foreign trade policy be? The People's Money
3 (1): 18-23. August 1936. (Published at 381 Fourth Ave., New York, N.Y.)
Since our foreign trade is "so closely connected with our domestic
business that it is impossible to separate the two,".the writer begins
by examining the present condition of domestic business. He next presents
and discusses two platforms concerning our foreign trade policy, suggested
by George N. Peek, and published in the New York Times for November 19,
1935. A return to the gold standard "at present or in the predictable
future, is out of the question. It simply would not work...
"What are the problems that must be considered? We have seen that to
increase production without making certain that consumption will keep
pace, results in surpluses. We have also seen the result of attempting
to finance the exportation of these surpluses. None of the previous
methods of handling the problem of surpluses have been successful. On
the other hand, imports must be prevented from ruining our domestic industries. Since these problems have not been solved by private enterprises left to themselves, it is obvious that some sort of planning and
control of domestic and foreign trade is necessary. The difficulty lies
in determining how the planning and control can best be put into operation.
One fact is becoming more obvious every day, namely, that the development
of monopolies and international combines has made the theory of free trade
obsolete. Unless we take steps to protect ourselves from this competition,
by using the same or similar weapons, we will lose out in the race for international trade."

Peek, G. N. World market - closed. Today 7 (1): 6-7, 22. Oct. 24, 1936.
(Published at 152 West Forty-second St., New York, N. Y.)
"Most of the farmer's problems fall into two general classes: Those
arising from the hazards of nature and those arising from the hazards
of markets." After discussing some of these hazards, Mr. Peek presents
the "background for the farm movement of the 1920's that sought its expression in the McNary-Haugen legislation. Most of the leaders in that drive
were western men. These men knew the farm problem at first hand. They
regarded 'production control' as too fantastic to consider; they regarded
the farm problem involved in the production of surpluses primarily as one
of marketing and of marketing assistance and credit. They knew and were
agreed as to the principles upon which its solution must rest. These
principles were:
"1. Protection of the American market for the American farmer.
"2. Government assistance in the removal of surpluses.
"3. Government assistance in securing a fair return for the farmer
on export crops, the price of which was set in the world markets, without permitting the export price to determine the price of the whole crop.
"In short, they asked for an extension of the American protective system to include agriculture... These principles were sound at the time,
and they are just as sound today."
Mr. Peek lists some of the pledges made to agriculture by Mr. Roosevelt
in 1932, and then describes the policy carried out by the President and
Secretary Wallace, and enumerates instances when these policies prevented
sales of farm products to foreign nations.

Trade Agreements - United States

Edminster, L. P.   Trade treaty procedure: An answer to critics. U. S.
    News 4 (41): 4. Oct. 12, 1936. (Published at 2201 M St., N. W., Wash-
    ington, D. C.)
        "From a recent address at the annual international dinner of Southern
    Maryland Rotary Clubs, at College Park, Md."

Trade Policy - Sweden

Sehlberg, Nils Guiding principles in Sweden's trade policy. Index 11 (130):
    206-213. October 1936 (Published by Svenska Handelsbanken, Stockholm,
    Sweden)

Vegetables - Quick Freezing

App, Frank. Quick freezing the fourth milestone in vegetable distribution.
    Market Growers Jour. 59 (7): 396, 397, 398, 399. Oct. 1, 1936. (Pub-
    lished in Louisville, Ky.)
        "Quick freezing is the fourth milestone in the distribution of vegeta-
    bles. Freezing will not make poor quality vegetables good. But quick
    frozen vegetables are delivered to the consumer with the quality harveste
    and frozen.
        "Approximately one-third of our vegetables in the future will be
    processed in cans, one-third shipped as fresh to market, and one-third
    quick frozen. This last third will represent expansion in the vegetable
    industry instead of substitution and will tend to stabilize the fresh
    vegetable market by taking the peak loads and competing for acreage in
    the fresh vegetable districts.
        "The above assertion will appear optimistic in the minds of some.
    I wish to show not only the importance of quick freezing, but also its
    relationship with the fresh vegetable industry and the canning industry."

Wheat

The wheat position. Economist 125 (4859): 53, 54. Oct. 10, 1936. (Pub-
    lished at 8 Bouverie St., London, E. C. 4, Eng.)
        An analysis of the wheat situation. The main features of the re-
    cent history of the wheat markets are summarized in a table which accom-
    panies the article. The table shows by seasons, beginning with 1926-27
    through 1935-36 (1936 figures are provisional) world production, trade,
    stocks and prices of wheat.

Working, Holbrook. How far will history repeat in wheat? Span of four
    decades offers interesting parallels in light of present recovery fol-
    lowing long depression. Barron's 16 (44): 11. Nov. 2, 1936. (Pub-
    lished at 44 Broad St., New York, N. Y.)
        Compares the present international wheat situation with that of
    the late summer of 1897.

Wheat - France

The French National wheat board. Foreign Crops and Markets 33 (18): 513-520
Nov. 2, 1936. (Published by the Division of Foreign Agricultural Service, Bureau of Agricultural Economics, U. S. Dept. of Agriculture)
"Based on a report by L. D. Mallory, Assistant Agricultural Attache,
Paris."
This is a consideration of the details of the law and of such action
as has already resulted from it. Subtopics of the article are: Administration of the National Wheat Board; price fixing; control of production
and trade; the role of wheat cooperatives; wheat dealers, financing the
wheat program.

Wheat - World Survey and Outlook

Farnsworth, Helen C., and Working, Holbrook. World wheat survey and outlook
September 1936   Wheat Studies of the Food Research Institute 13 (1):
1-31. September 1936. (Published in Stanford University, Calif.)
Contents: Crops of 1936; Prices and spreads; International trade;
Year-end stocks; Summary of supplies for 1936-37; Outlook for trade;
Outlook for carryover in 1937; Outlook for prices; and Appendix
tables.

Windfall Tax

Dudley, C. W. The windfall tax. Northwest. Miller and Amer. Baker 13 (10):
37, 58, 59. Oct. 7, 1936   (Published at 118 S. Sixth St., Minneapolis,
Minn.)
An address delivered by Claude W. Dudley, Attorney and Counselor at
Law, Washington, D. C., at a meeting held under the joint auspices of
the Millers National Federation and the Spring Wheat Millers Club at
Minneapolis, Minn.

Wool Textile Industry - Great Britain

Wool textile prospects. Economist 124 (4857): 552, 553. Sept. 26, 1936.
(Published at 8 Bouverie St., E. C. 4, London, Eng.)
The writer takes stock of the position of the wool textile industry,
considering especially the position held by Great Britain. A table
showing the available supplies of raw wool in principal manufacturing
countries, 1929-1935 accompanies the article.

Zoning, Rural - Wisconsin

Trackett, Mary C. Rural zoning in Wisconsin. Natl. Munic. Rev. 25 (10):
609-612. October 1936. (Published by the National Municipal League,
309 E. 34th St., New York, N. Y.)
"Surveys, maps and public discussion precede the passage of zoning
ordinances which raise problems of constitutionality and of administrative organization."

NOTES

American institute of food distribution, inc   An index to the voluntaries
and cooperatives, a directory for rating the buying and selling methods
used by 809 groups with 110,010 retail food stores, July, 1936. 113pp.
New York, 1936.   286.3 Am32
    Loose leaf binder; kept up to date by correction slips.

Australia Tariff board. Annual report for the year ended 30th June,
1935. 20pp. Canberra, L. F. Johnston, Commonwealth government
printer [1935]   285.9 Au7

Canadian grain trade year book, 1935-36. Full Canadian grain statistics, with
summary tables for principal foreign countries and world's production and
movement, year ending July 31, 1936, volume XVI... 105pp. [Winnipeg]
Sanford Evans statistical service [1936] 286.3599 C16

Cassel, Gustav. The downfall of the gold standard. 262pp. Oxford, The
Clarendon press, 1936.   284 C27D
    Reviewed in Economist (London) June 13, 1936.

Conférence agricole paneuropéenne. 1st, Vienna, 1936. Résultats de la le
Conférence agricole paneuropéenne, Vienne, du 9 au 12 septembre 1936.
14pp. Vienne - Zurich, Editions paneuropéennes [1936] 281.9 C764
    Summary of the Proceedings of the First Pan-European Agricultural
Conference, held in Vienna, September 9-12, 1936.

Covenanter, pseud. Labour and war resistance. 40pp. London, V. Gollancz l
[1936] [New Fabian research bureau. Publication. no. 29] 280.171 C83

Gillanders, James, ltd., London. Half-yearly egg review, Jan./June 1936, no.
6pp. London, James Gillanders ltd. [1936]   286.3479 G41

League of nations. Double taxation and fiscal evasion. Collection of international agreements and internal legal provisions for the prevention of
double taxation and fiscal evasion. Volume VI. 119pp. Geneva, 1936.
(Series of League of nations Publications. II. Economic and financial.
1936. II. A.10)   280.9 L47P
    "Official no. C.118.M.57. 1936. II. A."

Minnesota. Tax commission. Assessors' manual including assessment laws,
with questions and answers relating thereto. 138pp. [St. Paul, Minn.]
1936. 284.5 M66 1936

Oregon. State relief committee. A history of the work program of the state
and county relief committees of Oregon. 82pp. [Salem? 1935] 283 Or32
    On cover: 20,000 manpower plus.

Pennsylvania state chamber of commerce. Facts and problems of Pennsylvania
state finance, prepared by Leonard P. Fox... manager, Research &
information bureau. 63pp. [Harrisburg] 1936. 284.5 P382F

Prentice, E. P. Farming for famine. 146pp. Garden City, N. Y., Doubleday,
Doran and company, inc., 1936. 281.12 P91

St. Louis. First national bank. Soil products dept. Crop statistics, 1935.
Production, exports, imports, values. 32PP. St. Louis, 1935. 251 Sa2

Schmeckebier, L. F. Government publications and their use. 446pp. Washington, D C., The Brookings institution, 1936. (The Institute for
government research of the Brookings institution. Studies in administration no. 33) 242.1 Sch4

Sofia. Institut po zemledelska ikonomiia. Prices of the agricultural
products in Bulgaria during the last 54 years, 1881-1934 years,
by Professor Jan. S. Molloff and A. U. Toteff. 2pts. Sofia, Pechat-
vitsa na Armeiskiia Voennoizdatelski fond [1935] 284.3 So2
Text and added title in Bulgarian; summary in English.
At head of title: Trudove na Instituta po zemedelska ikonomiia
pri Agronomo-lesovudskiia fakultet na Universiteta.

Southern tenant farmers' union. Convention proceedings. Official report of
second annual convention, Jan. 3,4,5, 1936. 34pp., mimeogr. Little
Rock, Ark., 1936. 282.9 So8

Tax policy league. The home owner and the sales tax. 14pp. New York,
N. Y., Tax policy league, 1935. 284.5 T194H
By Mabel L. Walker.

Thompson, J. Walter, company. Brookings primer of progress illustrated.
23pp. [New York? J. Walter Thompson company, 1936] 280.12 T372
"A popular interpretation made by the J. Walter Thompson Company,
of the Brookings institution's studies of income distribution in relation to economic progress... [i.e.] America's capacity to produce,
by E. G. Nourse...; America's capacity to consume, by Maurice Leven
[and others]; The formation of capital, by H. G. Moulton; Income and
economic progress, by H. G. Moulton."

U. S. Farm credit administration. Circular no. 5, revised September 1936.
Agricultural financing through the Farm credit administration. 32PP.
[Washington, D. C., U. S. Govt. print. off.] 1936. 166.2 C49

U.S. National emergency council. Florida. Report of the proceedings of the
statewide coordination meeting of federal agencies operating in Florida,
held at Mayflower hotel, Jacksonville, Florida, April 6, 1936. [106]pp.,
mimeogr. Jacksonville, Fla., The National emergency council, [1936]
280.017 Un3

U. S. National resources committee. Research committee on urbanism. Interim
report to the National resources committee. 189pp., mimeogr. [Washington,
D. C.] July 1936. 173.2 N214In

U. S. War industries board. Price fixing committee. Munitions industry.
Minutes of the Price fixing committee of the War industries board,
from March 14 to December 30, 1918... Printed for the use of the
Special committee investigating the munitions industry. 4v. Washington, U. S. Govt. print. off., 1936 (74th Cong., 2d sess. Senate
committee print no. 3) 284.3 Un39?
    Printed from certified copies of the original... minutes. – Ex-
planatory note.

Von Liedtke, R. H. A brief of the agricultural plan. 67pp., mimeogr.
    [n.p., 1936] 281.12 V39

Wisconsin. Laws, statutes, etc. The banking law and other laws relating
    to and governing the organization of banks and conduct of the banking
    business: revised to close of General session 1935. Prepared under the
    direction of Banking commission. various paging. [Madison? 1935?]
    284 W75

Wye, Kent. South-eastern agricultural college. Dept. of economics. Report
    no. 23. Investigation into farming costs of production and financial
    results. XVII. Financial problems in pig keeping, by James Wyllie.
    pp. [217]-254. [Wye, Kent, 1936] 280.9 W97 no. 23

Lightning Source UK Ltd.
Milton Keynes UK
UKHW041818250219
337978UK00011B/750/P